T0135181

Lecture Notes in Computer Science 13684

Shai Avidan · Gabriel Brostow ·
Moustapha Cissé · Giovanni Maria Farinella ·
Tal Hassner (Eds.)

Computer Vision – ECCV 2022

17th European Conference
Tel Aviv, Israel, October 23–27, 2022
Proceedings, Part XXIV

 Springer

Editors
Shai Avidan
Tel Aviv University
Tel Aviv, Israel

Gabriel Brostow 🔟
University College London
London, UK

Moustapha Cissé
Google AI
Accra, Ghana

Giovanni Maria Farinella 🔟
University of Catania
Catania, Italy

Tal Hassner 🔟
Facebook (United States)
Menlo Park, CA, USA

ISSN 0302-9743 ISSN 1611-3349 (electronic)
Lecture Notes in Computer Science
ISBN 978-3-031-20052-6 ISBN 978-3-031-20053-3 (eBook)
https://doi.org/10.1007/978-3-031-20053-3

This Springer imprint is published by the registered company Springer Nature Switzerland AG
The registered company address is: Gewerbestrasse 11, 6330 Cham, Switzerland

Foreword

Organizing the European Conference on Computer Vision (ECCV 2022) in Tel-Aviv during a global pandemic was no easy feat. The uncertainty level was extremely high, and decisions had to be postponed to the last minute. Still, we managed to plan things just in time for ECCV 2022 to be held in person. Participation in physical events is crucial to stimulating collaborations and nurturing the culture of the Computer Vision community.

There were many people who worked hard to ensure attendees enjoyed the best science at the 16th edition of ECCV. We are grateful to the Program Chairs Gabriel Brostow and Tal Hassner, who went above and beyond to ensure the ECCV reviewing process ran smoothly. The scientific program includes dozens of workshops and tutorials in addition to the main conference and we would like to thank Leonid Karlinsky and Tomer Michaeli for their hard work. Finally, special thanks to the web chairs Lorenzo Baraldi and Kosta Derpanis, who put in extra hours to transfer information fast and efficiently to the ECCV community.

We would like to express gratitude to our generous sponsors and the Industry Chairs, Dimosthenis Karatzas and Chen Sagiv, who oversaw industry relations and proposed new ways for academia-industry collaboration and technology transfer. It's great to see so much industrial interest in what we're doing!

Authors' draft versions of the papers appeared online with open access on both the Computer Vision Foundation (CVF) and the European Computer Vision Association (ECVA) websites as with previous ECCVs. Springer, the publisher of the proceedings, has arranged for archival publication. The final version of the papers is hosted by SpringerLink, with active references and supplementary materials. It benefits all potential readers that we offer both a free and citeable version for all researchers, as well as an authoritative, citeable version for SpringerLink readers. Our thanks go to Ronan Nugent from Springer, who helped us negotiate this agreement. Last but not least, we wish to thank Eric Mortensen, our publication chair, whose expertise made the process smooth.

October 2022

Rita Cucchiara
Jiří Matas
Amnon Shashua
Lihi Zelnik-Manor

Preface

Welcome to the proceedings of the European Conference on Computer Vision (ECCV 2022). This was a hybrid edition of ECCV as we made our way out of the COVID-19 pandemic. The conference received 5804 valid paper submissions, compared to 5150 submissions to ECCV 2020 (a 12.7% increase) and 2439 in ECCV 2018. 1645 submissions were accepted for publication (28%) and, of those, 157 (2.7% overall) as orals.

846 of the submissions were desk-rejected for various reasons. Many of them because they revealed author identity, thus violating the double-blind policy. This violation came in many forms: some had author names with the title, others added acknowledgments to specific grants, yet others had links to their github account where their name was visible. Tampering with the LaTeX template was another reason for automatic desk rejection.

ECCV 2022 used the traditional CMT system to manage the entire double-blind reviewing process. Authors did not know the names of the reviewers and vice versa. Each paper received at least 3 reviews (except 6 papers that received only 2 reviews), totalling more than 15,000 reviews.

Handling the review process at this scale was a significant challenge. To ensure that each submission received as fair and high-quality reviews as possible, we recruited more than 4719 reviewers (in the end, 4719 reviewers did at least one review). Similarly we recruited more than 276 area chairs (eventually, only 276 area chairs handled a batch of papers). The area chairs were selected based on their technical expertise and reputation, largely among people who served as area chairs in previous top computer vision and machine learning conferences (ECCV, ICCV, CVPR, NeurIPS, etc.).

Reviewers were similarly invited from previous conferences, and also from the pool of authors. We also encouraged experienced area chairs to suggest additional chairs and reviewers in the initial phase of recruiting. The median reviewer load was five papers per reviewer, while the average load was about four papers, because of the emergency reviewers. The area chair load was 35 papers, on average.

Conflicts of interest between authors, area chairs, and reviewers were handled largely automatically by the CMT platform, with some manual help from the Program Chairs. Reviewers were allowed to describe themselves as senior reviewer (load of 8 papers to review) or junior reviewers (load of 4 papers). Papers were matched to area chairs based on a subject-area affinity score computed in CMT and an affinity score computed by the Toronto Paper Matching System (TPMS). TPMS is based on the paper's full text. An area chair handling each submission would bid for preferred expert reviewers, and we balanced load and prevented conflicts.

The assignment of submissions to area chairs was relatively smooth, as was the assignment of submissions to reviewers. A small percentage of reviewers were not happy with their assignments in terms of subjects and self-reported expertise. This is an area for improvement, although it's interesting that many of these cases were reviewers hand-picked by AC's. We made a later round of reviewer recruiting, targeted at the list of authors of papers submitted to the conference, and had an excellent response which helped provide enough emergency reviewers. In the end, all but six papers received at least 3 reviews.

The challenges of the reviewing process are in line with past experiences at ECCV 2020. As the community grows, and the number of submissions increases, it becomes ever more challenging to recruit enough reviewers and ensure a high enough quality of reviews. Enlisting authors by default as reviewers might be one step to address this challenge.

Authors were given a week to rebut the initial reviews, and address reviewers' concerns. Each rebuttal was limited to a single pdf page with a fixed template.

The Area Chairs then led discussions with the reviewers on the merits of each submission. The goal was to reach consensus, but, ultimately, it was up to the Area Chair to make a decision. The decision was then discussed with a buddy Area Chair to make sure decisions were fair and informative. The entire process was conducted virtually with no in-person meetings taking place.

The Program Chairs were informed in cases where the Area Chairs overturned a decisive consensus reached by the reviewers, and pushed for the meta-reviews to contain details that explained the reasoning for such decisions. Obviously these were the most contentious cases, where reviewer inexperience was the most common reported factor.

Once the list of accepted papers was finalized and released, we went through the laborious process of plagiarism (including self-plagiarism) detection. A total of 4 accepted papers were rejected because of that.

Finally, we would like to thank our Technical Program Chair, Pavel Lifshits, who did tremendous work behind the scenes, and we thank the tireless CMT team.

October 2022

Gabriel Brostow
Giovanni Maria Farinella
Moustapha Cissé
Shai Avidan
Tal Hassner

Organization

General Chairs

Rita Cucchiara   University of Modena and Reggio Emilia, Italy
Jiří Matas   Czech Technical University in Prague, Czech Republic
Amnon Shashua   Hebrew University of Jerusalem, Israel
Lihi Zelnik-Manor   Technion – Israel Institute of Technology, Israel

Program Chairs

Shai Avidan   Tel-Aviv University, Israel
Gabriel Brostow   University College London, UK
Moustapha Cissé   Google AI, Ghana
Giovanni Maria Farinella   University of Catania, Italy
Tal Hassner   Facebook AI, USA

Program Technical Chair

Pavel Lifshits   Technion – Israel Institute of Technology, Israel

Workshops Chairs

Leonid Karlinsky   IBM Research, Israel
Tomer Michaeli   Technion – Israel Institute of Technology, Israel
Ko Nishino   Kyoto University, Japan

Tutorial Chairs

Thomas Pock   Graz University of Technology, Austria
Natalia Neverova   Facebook AI Research, UK

Demo Chair

Bohyung Han   Seoul National University, Korea

Social and Student Activities Chairs

Tatiana Tommasi   Italian Institute of Technology, Italy
Sagie Benaim   University of Copenhagen, Denmark

Diversity and Inclusion Chairs

Xi Yin   Facebook AI Research, USA
Bryan Russell   Adobe, USA

Communications Chairs

Lorenzo Baraldi   University of Modena and Reggio Emilia, Italy
Kosta Derpanis   York University & Samsung AI Centre Toronto,
                         Canada

Industrial Liaison Chairs

Dimosthenis Karatzas   Universitat Autònoma de Barcelona, Spain
Chen Sagiv   SagivTech, Israel

Finance Chair

Gerard Medioni   University of Southern California & Amazon,
                         USA

Publication Chair

Eric Mortensen   MiCROTEC, USA

Area Chairs

Lourdes Agapito   University College London, UK
Zeynep Akata   University of Tübingen, Germany
Naveed Akhtar   University of Western Australia, Australia
Karteek Alahari   Inria Grenoble Rhône-Alpes, France
Alexandre Alahi   École polytechnique fédérale de Lausanne,
                         Switzerland
Pablo Arbelaez   Universidad de Los Andes, Columbia
Antonis A. Argyros   University of Crete & Foundation for Research
                         and Technology-Hellas, Crete
Yuki M. Asano   University of Amsterdam, The Netherlands
Kalle Åström   Lund University, Sweden
Hadar Averbuch-Elor   Cornell University, USA

Matthijs Douze   Facebook AI Research, USA
Mohamed Elhoseiny   King Abdullah University of Science and
                                    Technology, Saudi Arabia
Sergio Escalera   University of Barcelona, Spain
Yi Fang   New York University, USA
Ryan Farrell   Brigham Young University, USA
Alireza Fathi   Google, USA
Christoph Feichtenhofer   Facebook AI Research, USA
Basura Fernando   Agency for Science, Technology and Research
                                    (A*STAR), Singapore
Vittorio Ferrari   Google Research, Switzerland
Andrew W. Fitzgibbon   Graphcore, UK
David J. Fleet   University of Toronto, Canada
David Forsyth   University of Illinois at Urbana-Champaign, USA
David Fouhey   University of Michigan, USA
Katerina Fragkiadaki   Carnegie Mellon University, USA
Friedrich Fraundorfer   Graz University of Technology, Austria
Oren Freifeld   Ben-Gurion University, Israel
Thomas Funkhouser   Google Research & Princeton University, USA
Yasutaka Furukawa   Simon Fraser University, Canada
Fabio Galasso   Sapienza University of Rome, Italy
Jürgen Gall   University of Bonn, Germany
Chuang Gan   Massachusetts Institute of Technology, USA
Zhe Gan   Microsoft, USA
Animesh Garg   University of Toronto, Vector Institute, Nvidia,
                                    Canada
Efstratios Gavves   University of Amsterdam, The Netherlands
Peter Gehler   Amazon, Germany
Theo Gevers   University of Amsterdam, The Netherlands
Bernard Ghanem   King Abdullah University of Science and
                                    Technology, Saudi Arabia
Ross B. Girshick   Facebook AI Research, USA
Georgia Gkioxari   Facebook AI Research, USA
Albert Gordo   Facebook, USA
Stephen Gould   Australian National University, Australia
Venu Madhav Govindu   Indian Institute of Science, India
Kristen Grauman   Facebook AI Research & UT Austin, USA
Abhinav Gupta   Carnegie Mellon University & Facebook AI
                                    Research, USA
Mohit Gupta   University of Wisconsin-Madison, USA
Hu Han   Institute of Computing Technology, Chinese
                                    Academy of Sciences, China

Bohyung Han	Seoul National University, Korea
Tian Han	Stevens Institute of Technology, USA
Emily Hand	University of Nevada, Reno, USA
Bharath Hariharan	Cornell University, USA
Ran He	Institute of Automation, Chinese Academy of Sciences, China
Otmar Hilliges	ETH Zurich, Switzerland
Adrian Hilton	University of Surrey, UK
Minh Hoai	Stony Brook University, USA
Yedid Hoshen	Hebrew University of Jerusalem, Israel
Timothy Hospedales	University of Edinburgh, UK
Gang Hua	Wormpex AI Research, USA
Di Huang	Beihang University, China
Jing Huang	Facebook, USA
Jia-Bin Huang	Facebook, USA
Nathan Jacobs	Washington University in St. Louis, USA
C. V. Jawahar	International Institute of Information Technology, Hyderabad, India
Herve Jegou	Facebook AI Research, France
Neel Joshi	Microsoft Research, USA
Armand Joulin	Facebook AI Research, France
Frederic Jurie	University of Caen Normandie, France
Fredrik Kahl	Chalmers University of Technology, Sweden
Yannis Kalantidis	NAVER LABS Europe, France
Evangelos Kalogerakis	University of Massachusetts, Amherst, USA
Sing Bing Kang	Zillow Group, USA
Yosi Keller	Bar Ilan University, Israel
Margret Keuper	University of Mannheim, Germany
Tae-Kyun Kim	Imperial College London, UK
Benjamin Kimia	Brown University, USA
Alexander Kirillov	Facebook AI Research, USA
Kris Kitani	Carnegie Mellon University, USA
Iasonas Kokkinos	Snap Inc. & University College London, UK
Vladlen Koltun	Apple, USA
Nikos Komodakis	University of Crete, Crete
Piotr Koniusz	Australian National University, Australia
Philipp Kraehenbuehl	University of Texas at Austin, USA
Dilip Krishnan	Google, USA
Ajay Kumar	Hong Kong Polytechnic University, Hong Kong, China
Junseok Kwon	Chung-Ang University, Korea
Jean-Francois Lalonde	Université Laval, Canada

Vittorio Murino	Istituto Italiano di Tecnologia, Italy
P. J. Narayanan	International Institute of Information Technology, Hyderabad, India
Ram Nevatia	University of Southern California, USA
Natalia Neverova	Facebook AI Research, UK
Richard Newcombe	Facebook, USA
Cuong V. Nguyen	Florida International University, USA
Bingbing Ni	Shanghai Jiao Tong University, China
Juan Carlos Niebles	Salesforce & Stanford University, USA
Ko Nishino	Kyoto University, Japan
Jean-Marc Odobez	Idiap Research Institute, École polytechnique fédérale de Lausanne, Switzerland
Francesca Odone	University of Genova, Italy
Takayuki Okatani	Tohoku University & RIKEN Center for Advanced Intelligence Project, Japan
Manohar Paluri	Facebook, USA
Guan Pang	Facebook, USA
Maja Pantic	Imperial College London, UK
Sylvain Paris	Adobe Research, USA
Jaesik Park	Pohang University of Science and Technology, Korea
Hyun Soo Park	The University of Minnesota, USA
Omkar M. Parkhi	Facebook, USA
Deepak Pathak	Carnegie Mellon University, USA
Georgios Pavlakos	University of California, Berkeley, USA
Marcello Pelillo	University of Venice, Italy
Marc Pollefeys	ETH Zurich & Microsoft, Switzerland
Jean Ponce	Inria, France
Gerard Pons-Moll	University of Tübingen, Germany
Fatih Porikli	Qualcomm, USA
Victor Adrian Prisacariu	University of Oxford, UK
Petia Radeva	University of Barcelona, Spain
Ravi Ramamoorthi	University of California, San Diego, USA
Deva Ramanan	Carnegie Mellon University, USA
Vignesh Ramanathan	Facebook, USA
Nalini Ratha	State University of New York at Buffalo, USA
Tammy Riklin Raviv	Ben-Gurion University, Israel
Tobias Ritschel	University College London, UK
Emanuele Rodola	Sapienza University of Rome, Italy
Amit K. Roy-Chowdhury	University of California, Riverside, USA
Michael Rubinstein	Google, USA
Olga Russakovsky	Princeton University, USA

Mathieu Salzmann	École polytechnique fédérale de Lausanne, Switzerland
Dimitris Samaras	Stony Brook University, USA
Aswin Sankaranarayanan	Carnegie Mellon University, USA
Imari Sato	National Institute of Informatics, Japan
Yoichi Sato	University of Tokyo, Japan
Shin'ichi Satoh	National Institute of Informatics, Japan
Walter Scheirer	University of Notre Dame, USA
Bernt Schiele	Max Planck Institute for Informatics, Germany
Konrad Schindler	ETH Zurich, Switzerland
Cordelia Schmid	Inria & Google, France
Alexander Schwing	University of Illinois at Urbana-Champaign, USA
Nicu Sebe	University of Trento, Italy
Greg Shakhnarovich	Toyota Technological Institute at Chicago, USA
Eli Shechtman	Adobe Research, USA
Humphrey Shi	University of Oregon & University of Illinois at Urbana-Champaign & Picsart AI Research, USA
Jianbo Shi	University of Pennsylvania, USA
Roy Shilkrot	Massachusetts Institute of Technology, USA
Mike Zheng Shou	National University of Singapore, Singapore
Kaleem Siddiqi	McGill University, Canada
Richa Singh	Indian Institute of Technology Jodhpur, India
Greg Slabaugh	Queen Mary University of London, UK
Cees Snoek	University of Amsterdam, The Netherlands
Yale Song	Facebook AI Research, USA
Yi-Zhe Song	University of Surrey, UK
Bjorn Stenger	Rakuten Institute of Technology
Abby Stylianou	Saint Louis University, USA
Akihiro Sugimoto	National Institute of Informatics, Japan
Chen Sun	Brown University, USA
Deqing Sun	Google, USA
Kalyan Sunkavalli	Adobe Research, USA
Ying Tai	Tencent YouTu Lab, China
Ayellet Tal	Technion – Israel Institute of Technology, Israel
Ping Tan	Simon Fraser University, Canada
Siyu Tang	ETH Zurich, Switzerland
Chi-Keung Tang	Hong Kong University of Science and Technology, Hong Kong, China
Radu Timofte	University of Würzburg, Germany & ETH Zurich, Switzerland
Federico Tombari	Google, Switzerland & Technical University of Munich, Germany

James Tompkin	Brown University, USA
Lorenzo Torresani	Dartmouth College, USA
Alexander Toshev	Apple, USA
Du Tran	Facebook AI Research, USA
Anh T. Tran	VinAI, Vietnam
Zhuowen Tu	University of California, San Diego, USA
Georgios Tzimiropoulos	Queen Mary University of London, UK
Jasper Uijlings	Google Research, Switzerland
Jan C. van Gemert	Delft University of Technology, The Netherlands
Gul Varol	Ecole des Ponts ParisTech, France
Nuno Vasconcelos	University of California, San Diego, USA
Mayank Vatsa	Indian Institute of Technology Jodhpur, India
Ashok Veeraraghavan	Rice University, USA
Jakob Verbeek	Facebook AI Research, France
Carl Vondrick	Columbia University, USA
Ruiping Wang	Institute of Computing Technology, Chinese Academy of Sciences, China
Xinchao Wang	National University of Singapore, Singapore
Liwei Wang	The Chinese University of Hong Kong, Hong Kong, China
Chaohui Wang	Université Paris-Est, France
Xiaolong Wang	University of California, San Diego, USA
Christian Wolf	NAVER LABS Europe, France
Tao Xiang	University of Surrey, UK
Saining Xie	Facebook AI Research, USA
Cihang Xie	University of California, Santa Cruz, USA
Zeki Yalniz	Facebook, USA
Ming-Hsuan Yang	University of California, Merced, USA
Angela Yao	National University of Singapore, Singapore
Shaodi You	University of Amsterdam, The Netherlands
Stella X. Yu	University of California, Berkeley, USA
Junsong Yuan	State University of New York at Buffalo, USA
Stefanos Zafeiriou	Imperial College London, UK
Amir Zamir	École polytechnique fédérale de Lausanne, Switzerland
Lei Zhang	Alibaba & Hong Kong Polytechnic University, Hong Kong, China
Lei Zhang	International Digital Economy Academy (IDEA), China
Pengchuan Zhang	Meta AI, USA
Bolei Zhou	University of California, Los Angeles, USA
Yuke Zhu	University of Texas at Austin, USA

Todd Zickler   Harvard University, USA
Wangmeng Zuo   Harbin Institute of Technology, China

Technical Program Committee

Davide Abati
Soroush Abbasi
   Koohpayegani
Amos L. Abbott
Rameen Abdal
Rabab Abdelfattah
Sahar Abdelnabi
Hassan Abu Alhaija
Abulikemu Abuduweili
Ron Abutbul
Hanno Ackermann
Aikaterini Adam
Kamil Adamczewski
Ehsan Adeli
Vida Adeli
Donald Adjeroh
Arman Afrasiyabi
Akshay Agarwal
Sameer Agarwal
Abhinav Agarwalla
Vaibhav Aggarwal
Sara Aghajanzadeh
Susmit Agrawal
Antonio Agudo
Touqeer Ahmad
Sk Miraj Ahmed
Chaitanya Ahuja
Nilesh A. Ahuja
Abhishek Aich
Shubhra Aich
Noam Aigerman
Arash Akbarinia
Peri Akiva
Derya Akkaynak
Emre Aksan
Arjun R. Akula
Yuval Alaluf
Stephan Alaniz
Paul Albert
Cenek Albl

Filippo Aleotti
Konstantinos P.
   Alexandridis
Motasem Alfarra
Mohsen Ali
Thiemo Alldieck
Hadi Alzayer
Liang An
Shan An
Yi An
Zhulin An
Dongsheng An
Jie An
Xiang An
Saket Anand
Cosmin Ancuti
Juan Andrade-Cetto
Alexander Andreopoulos
Bjoern Andres
Jerone T. A. Andrews
Shivangi Aneja
Anelia Angelova
Dragomir Anguelov
Rushil Anirudh
Oron Anschel
Rao Muhammad Anwer
Djamila Aouada
Evlampios Apostolidis
Srikar Appalaraju
Nikita Araslanov
Andre Araujo
Eric Arazo
Dawit Mureja Argaw
Anurag Arnab
Aditya Arora
Chetan Arora
Sunpreet S. Arora
Alexey Artemov
Muhammad Asad
Kumar Ashutosh

Sinem Aslan
Vishal Asnani
Mahmoud Assran
Amir Atapour-Abarghouei
Nikos Athanasiou
Ali Athar
ShahRukh Athar
Sara Atito
Souhaib Attaiki
Matan Atzmon
Mathieu Aubry
Nicolas Audebert
Tristan T.
   Aumentado-Armstrong
Melinos Averkiou
Yannis Avrithis
Stephane Ayache
Mehmet Aygün
Seyed Mehdi
   Ayyoubzadeh
Hossein Azizpour
George Azzopardi
Mallikarjun B. R.
Yunhao Ba
Abhishek Badki
Seung-Hwan Bae
Seung-Hwan Baek
Seungryul Baek
Piyush Nitin Bagad
Shai Bagon
Gaetan Bahl
Shikhar Bahl
Sherwin Bahmani
Haoran Bai
Lei Bai
Jiawang Bai
Haoyue Bai
Jinbin Bai
Xiang Bai
Xuyang Bai

Yang Bai
Yuanchao Bai
Ziqian Bai
Sungyong Baik
Kevin Bailly
Max Bain
Federico Baldassarre
Wele Gedara Chaminda
    Bandara
Biplab Banerjee
Pratyay Banerjee
Sandipan Banerjee
Jihwan Bang
Antyanta Bangunharcana
Aayush Bansal
Ankan Bansal
Siddhant Bansal
Wentao Bao
Zhipeng Bao
Amir Bar
Manel Baradad Jurjo
Lorenzo Baraldi
Danny Barash
Daniel Barath
Connelly Barnes
Ioan Andrei Bârsan
Steven Basart
Dina Bashkirova
Chaim Baskin
Peyman Bateni
Anil Batra
Sebastiano Battiato
Ardhendu Behera
Harkirat Behl
Jens Behley
Vasileios Belagiannis
Boulbaba Ben Amor
Emanuel Ben Baruch
Abdessamad Ben Hamza
Gil Ben-Artzi
Assia Benbihi
Fabian Benitez-Quiroz
Guy Ben-Yosef
Philipp Benz
Alexander W. Bergman

Urs Bergmann
Jesus Bermudez-Cameo
Stefano Berretti
Gedas Bertasius
Zachary Bessinger
Petra Bevandić
Matthew Beveridge
Lucas Beyer
Yash Bhalgat
Suvaansh Bhambri
Samarth Bharadwaj
Gaurav Bharaj
Aparna Bharati
Bharat Lal Bhatnagar
Uttaran Bhattacharya
Apratim Bhattacharyya
Brojeshwar Bhowmick
Ankan Kumar Bhunia
Ayan Kumar Bhunia
Qi Bi
Sai Bi
Michael Bi Mi
Gui-Bin Bian
Jia-Wang Bian
Shaojun Bian
Pia Bideau
Mario Bijelic
Hakan Bilen
Guillaume-Alexandre
    Bilodeau
Alexander Binder
Tolga Birdal
Vighnesh N. Birodkar
Sandika Biswas
Andreas Blattmann
Janusz Bobulski
Giuseppe Boccignone
Vishnu Boddeti
Navaneeth Bodla
Moritz Böhle
Aleksei Bokhovkin
Sam Bond-Taylor
Vivek Boominathan
Shubhankar Borse
Mark Boss

Andrea Bottino
Adnane Boukhayma
Fadi Boutros
Nicolas C. Boutry
Richard S. Bowen
Ivaylo Boyadzhiev
Aidan Boyd
Yuri Boykov
Aljaz Bozic
Behzad Bozorgtabar
Eric Brachmann
Samarth Brahmbhatt
Gustav Bredell
Francois Bremond
Joel Brogan
Andrew Brown
Thomas Brox
Marcus A. Brubaker
Robert-Jan Bruintjes
Yuqi Bu
Anders G. Buch
Himanshu Buckchash
Mateusz Buda
Ignas Budvytis
José M. Buenaposada
Marcel C. Bühler
Tu Bui
Adrian Bulat
Hannah Bull
Evgeny Burnaev
Andrei Bursuc
Benjamin Busam
Sergey N. Buzykanov
Wonmin Byeon
Fabian Caba
Martin Cadik
Guanyu Cai
Minjie Cai
Qing Cai
Zhongang Cai
Qi Cai
Yancheng Cai
Shen Cai
Han Cai
Jiarui Cai

Bowen Cai
Mu Cai
Qin Cai
Ruojin Cai
Weidong Cai
Weiwei Cai
Yi Cai
Yujun Cai
Zhiping Cai
Akin Caliskan
Lilian Calvet
Baris Can Cam
Necati Cihan Camgoz
Tommaso Campari
Dylan Campbell
Ziang Cao
Ang Cao
Xu Cao
Zhiwen Cao
Shengcao Cao
Song Cao
Weipeng Cao
Xiangyong Cao
Xiaochun Cao
Yue Cao
Yunhao Cao
Zhangjie Cao
Jiale Cao
Yang Cao
Jiajiong Cao
Jie Cao
Jinkun Cao
Lele Cao
Yulong Cao
Zhiguo Cao
Chen Cao
Razvan Caramalau
Marlène Careil
Gustavo Carneiro
Joao Carreira
Dan Casas
Paola Cascante-Bonilla
Angela Castillo
Francisco M. Castro
Pedro Castro

Luca Cavalli
George J. Cazenavette
Oya Celiktutan
Hakan Cevikalp
Sri Harsha C. H.
Sungmin Cha
Geonho Cha
Menglei Chai
Lucy Chai
Yuning Chai
Zenghao Chai
Anirban Chakraborty
Deep Chakraborty
Rudrasis Chakraborty
Souradeep Chakraborty
Kelvin C. K. Chan
Chee Seng Chan
Paramanand Chandramouli
Arjun Chandrasekaran
Kenneth Chaney
Dongliang Chang
Huiwen Chang
Peng Chang
Xiaojun Chang
Jia-Ren Chang
Hyung Jin Chang
Hyun Sung Chang
Ju Yong Chang
Li-Jen Chang
Qi Chang
Wei-Yi Chang
Yi Chang
Nadine Chang
Hanqing Chao
Pradyumna Chari
Dibyadip Chatterjee
Chiranjoy Chattopadhyay
Siddhartha Chaudhuri
Zhengping Che
Gal Chechik
Lianggangxu Chen
Qi Alfred Chen
Brian Chen
Bor-Chun Chen
Bo-Hao Chen

Bohong Chen
Bin Chen
Ziliang Chen
Cheng Chen
Chen Chen
Chaofeng Chen
Xi Chen
Haoyu Chen
Xuanhong Chen
Wei Chen
Qiang Chen
Shi Chen
Xianyu Chen
Chang Chen
Changhuai Chen
Hao Chen
Jie Chen
Jianbo Chen
Jingjing Chen
Jun Chen
Kejiang Chen
Mingcai Chen
Nenglun Chen
Qifeng Chen
Ruoyu Chen
Shu-Yu Chen
Weidong Chen
Weijie Chen
Weikai Chen
Xiang Chen
Xiuyi Chen
Xingyu Chen
Yaofo Chen
Yueting Chen
Yu Chen
Yunjin Chen
Yuntao Chen
Yun Chen
Zhenfang Chen
Zhuangzhuang Chen
Chu-Song Chen
Xiangyu Chen
Zhuo Chen
Chaoqi Chen
Shizhe Chen

Xiaotong Chen
Xiaozhi Chen
Dian Chen
Defang Chen
Dingfan Chen
Ding-Jie Chen
Ee Heng Chen
Tao Chen
Yixin Chen
Wei-Ting Chen
Lin Chen
Guang Chen
Guangyi Chen
Guanying Chen
Guangyao Chen
Hwann-Tzong Chen
Junwen Chen
Jiacheng Chen
Jianxu Chen
Hui Chen
Kai Chen
Kan Chen
Kevin Chen
Kuan-Wen Chen
Weihua Chen
Zhang Chen
Liang-Chieh Chen
Lele Chen
Liang Chen
Fanglin Chen
Zehui Chen
Minghui Chen
Minghao Chen
Xiaokang Chen
Qian Chen
Jun-Cheng Chen
Qi Chen
Qingcai Chen
Richard J. Chen
Runnan Chen
Rui Chen
Shuo Chen
Sentao Chen
Shaoyu Chen
Shixing Chen

Shuai Chen
Shuya Chen
Sizhe Chen
Simin Chen
Shaoxiang Chen
Zitian Chen
Tianlong Chen
Tianshui Chen
Min-Hung Chen
Xiangning Chen
Xin Chen
Xinghao Chen
Xuejin Chen
Xu Chen
Xuxi Chen
Yunlu Chen
Yanbei Chen
Yuxiao Chen
Yun-Chun Chen
Yi-Ting Chen
Yi-Wen Chen
Yinbo Chen
Yiran Chen
Yuanhong Chen
Yubei Chen
Yuefeng Chen
Yuhua Chen
Yukang Chen
Zerui Chen
Zhaoyu Chen
Zhen Chen
Zhenyu Chen
Zhi Chen
Zhiwei Chen
Zhixiang Chen
Long Chen
Bowen Cheng
Jun Cheng
Yi Cheng
Jingchun Cheng
Lechao Cheng
Xi Cheng
Yuan Cheng
Ho Kei Cheng
Kevin Ho Man Cheng

Jiacheng Cheng
Kelvin B. Cheng
Li Cheng
Mengjun Cheng
Zhen Cheng
Qingrong Cheng
Tianheng Cheng
Harry Cheng
Yihua Cheng
Yu Cheng
Ziheng Cheng
Soon Yau Cheong
Anoop Cherian
Manuela Chessa
Zhixiang Chi
Naoki Chiba
Julian Chibane
Kashyap Chitta
Tai-Yin Chiu
Hsu-kuang Chiu
Wei-Chen Chiu
Sungmin Cho
Donghyeon Cho
Hyeon Cho
Yooshin Cho
Gyusang Cho
Jang Hyun Cho
Seungju Cho
Nam Ik Cho
Sunghyun Cho
Hanbyel Cho
Jaesung Choe
Jooyoung Choi
Chiho Choi
Changwoon Choi
Jongwon Choi
Myungsub Choi
Dooseop Choi
Jonghyun Choi
Jinwoo Choi
Jun Won Choi
Min-Kook Choi
Hongsuk Choi
Janghoon Choi
Yoon-Ho Choi

Yukyung Choi
Jaegul Choo
Ayush Chopra
Siddharth Choudhary
Subhabrata Choudhury
Vasileios Choutas
Ka-Ho Chow
Pinaki Nath Chowdhury
Sammy Christen
Anders Christensen
Grigorios Chrysos
Hang Chu
Wen-Hsuan Chu
Peng Chu
Qi Chu
Ruihang Chu
Wei-Ta Chu
Yung-Yu Chuang
Sanghyuk Chun
Se Young Chun
Antonio Cinà
Ramazan Gokberk Cinbis
Javier Civera
Albert Clapés
Ronald Clark
Brian S. Clipp
Felipe Codevilla
Daniel Coelho de Castro
Niv Cohen
Forrester Cole
Maxwell D. Collins
Robert T. Collins
Marc Comino Trinidad
Runmin Cong
Wenyan Cong
Maxime Cordy
Marcella Cornia
Enric Corona
Huseyin Coskun
Luca Cosmo
Dragos Costea
Davide Cozzolino
Arun C. S. Kumar
Aiyu Cui
Qiongjie Cui

Quan Cui
Shuhao Cui
Yiming Cui
Ying Cui
Zijun Cui
Jiali Cui
Jiequan Cui
Yawen Cui
Zhen Cui
Zhaopeng Cui
Jack Culpepper
Xiaodong Cun
Ross Cutler
Adam Czajka
Ali Dabouei
Konstantinos M. Dafnis
Manuel Dahnert
Tao Dai
Yuchao Dai
Bo Dai
Mengyu Dai
Hang Dai
Haixing Dai
Peng Dai
Pingyang Dai
Qi Dai
Qiyu Dai
Yutong Dai
Naser Damer
Zhiyuan Dang
Mohamed Daoudi
Ayan Das
Abir Das
Debasmit Das
Deepayan Das
Partha Das
Sagnik Das
Soumi Das
Srijan Das
Swagatam Das
Avijit Dasgupta
Jim Davis
Adrian K. Davison
Homa Davoudi
Laura Daza

Matthias De Lange
Shalini De Mello
Marco De Nadai
Christophe De
    Vleeschouwer
Alp Dener
Boyang Deng
Congyue Deng
Bailin Deng
Yong Deng
Ye Deng
Zhuo Deng
Zhijie Deng
Xiaoming Deng
Jiankang Deng
Jinhong Deng
Jingjing Deng
Liang-Jian Deng
Siqi Deng
Xiang Deng
Xueqing Deng
Zhongying Deng
Karan Desai
Jean-Emmanuel Deschaud
Aniket Anand Deshmukh
Neel Dey
Helisa Dhamo
Prithviraj Dhar
Amaya Dharmasiri
Yan Di
Xing Di
Ousmane A. Dia
Haiwen Diao
Xiaolei Diao
Gonçalo José Dias Pais
Abdallah Dib
Anastasios Dimou
Changxing Ding
Henghui Ding
Guodong Ding
Yaqing Ding
Shuangrui Ding
Yuhang Ding
Yikang Ding
Shouhong Ding

Haisong Ding
Hui Ding
Jiahao Ding
Jian Ding
Jian-Jiun Ding
Shuxiao Ding
Tianyu Ding
Wenhao Ding
Yuqi Ding
Yi Ding
Yuzhen Ding
Zhengming Ding
Tan Minh Dinh
Vu Dinh
Christos Diou
Mandar Dixit
Bao Gia Doan
Khoa D. Doan
Dzung Anh Doan
Debi Prosad Dogra
Nehal Doiphode
Chengdong Dong
Bowen Dong
Zhenxing Dong
Hang Dong
Xiaoyi Dong
Haoye Dong
Jiangxin Dong
Shichao Dong
Xuan Dong
Zhen Dong
Shuting Dong
Jing Dong
Li Dong
Ming Dong
Nanqing Dong
Qiulei Dong
Runpei Dong
Siyan Dong
Tian Dong
Wei Dong
Xiaomeng Dong
Xin Dong
Xingbo Dong
Yuan Dong

Samuel Dooley
Gianfranco Doretto
Michael Dorkenwald
Keval Doshi
Zhaopeng Dou
Xiaotian Dou
Hazel Doughty
Ahmad Droby
Iddo Drori
Jie Du
Yong Du
Dawei Du
Dong Du
Ruoyi Du
Yuntao Du
Xuefeng Du
Yilun Du
Yuming Du
Radhika Dua
Haodong Duan
Jiafei Duan
Kaiwen Duan
Peiqi Duan
Ye Duan
Haoran Duan
Jiali Duan
Amanda Duarte
Abhimanyu Dubey
Shiv Ram Dubey
Florian Dubost
Lukasz Dudziak
Shivam Duggal
Justin M. Dulay
Matteo Dunnhofer
Chi Nhan Duong
Thibaut Durand
Mihai Dusmanu
Ujjal Kr Dutta
Debidatta Dwibedi
Isht Dwivedi
Sai Kumar Dwivedi
Takeharu Eda
Mark Edmonds
Alexei A. Efros
Thibaud Ehret

Max Ehrlich
Mahsa Ehsanpour
Iván Eichhardt
Farshad Einabadi
Marvin Eisenberger
Hazim Kemal Ekenel
Mohamed El Banani
Ismail Elezi
Moshe Eliasof
Alaa El-Nouby
Ian Endres
Francis Engelmann
Deniz Engin
Chanho Eom
Dave Epstein
Maria C. Escobar
Victor A. Escorcia
Carlos Esteves
Sungmin Eum
Bernard J. E. Evans
Ivan Evtimov
Fevziye Irem Eyiokur
    Yaman
Matteo Fabbri
Sébastien Fabbro
Gabriele Facciolo
Masud Fahim
Bin Fan
Hehe Fan
Deng-Ping Fan
Aoxiang Fan
Chen-Chen Fan
Qi Fan
Zhaoxin Fan
Haoqi Fan
Heng Fan
Hongyi Fan
Linxi Fan
Baojie Fan
Jiayuan Fan
Lei Fan
Quanfu Fan
Yonghui Fan
Yingruo Fan
Zhiwen Fan

Zicong Fan
Sean Fanello
Jiansheng Fang
Chaowei Fang
Yuming Fang
Jianwu Fang
Jin Fang
Qi Fang
Shancheng Fang
Tian Fang
Xianyong Fang
Gongfan Fang
Zhen Fang
Hui Fang
Jiemin Fang
Le Fang
Pengfei Fang
Xiaolin Fang
Yuxin Fang
Zhaoyuan Fang
Ammarah Farooq
Azade Farshad
Zhengcong Fei
Michael Felsberg
Wei Feng
Chen Feng
Fan Feng
Andrew Feng
Xin Feng
Zheyun Feng
Ruicheng Feng
Mingtao Feng
Qianyu Feng
Shangbin Feng
Chun-Mei Feng
Zunlei Feng
Zhiyong Feng
Martin Fergie
Mustansar Fiaz
Marco Fiorucci
Michael Firman
Hamed Firooz
Volker Fischer
Corneliu O. Florea
Georgios Floros

Wolfgang Foerstner
Gianni Franchi
Jean-Sebastien Franco
Simone Frintrop
Anna Fruehstueck
Changhong Fu
Chaoyou Fu
Cheng-Yang Fu
Chi-Wing Fu
Deqing Fu
Huan Fu
Jun Fu
Kexue Fu
Ying Fu
Jianlong Fu
Jingjing Fu
Qichen Fu
Tsu-Jui Fu
Xueyang Fu
Yang Fu
Yanwei Fu
Yonggan Fu
Wolfgang Fuhl
Yasuhisa Fujii
Kent Fujiwara
Marco Fumero
Takuya Funatomi
Isabel Funke
Dario Fuoli
Antonino Furnari
Matheus A. Gadelha
Akshay Gadi Patil
Adrian Galdran
Guillermo Gallego
Silvano Galliani
Orazio Gallo
Leonardo Galteri
Matteo Gamba
Yiming Gan
Sujoy Ganguly
Harald Ganster
Boyan Gao
Changxin Gao
Daiheng Gao
Difei Gao

Chen Gao
Fei Gao
Lin Gao
Wei Gao
Yiming Gao
Junyu Gao
Guangyu Ryan Gao
Haichang Gao
Hongchang Gao
Jialin Gao
Jin Gao
Jun Gao
Katelyn Gao
Mingchen Gao
Mingfei Gao
Pan Gao
Shangqian Gao
Shanghua Gao
Xitong Gao
Yunhe Gao
Zhanning Gao
Elena Garces
Nuno Cruz Garcia
Noa Garcia
Guillermo
    Garcia-Hernando
Isha Garg
Rahul Garg
Sourav Garg
Quentin Garrido
Stefano Gasperini
Kent Gauen
Chandan Gautam
Shivam Gautam
Paul Gay
Chunjiang Ge
Shiming Ge
Wenhang Ge
Yanhao Ge
Zheng Ge
Songwei Ge
Weifeng Ge
Yixiao Ge
Yuying Ge
Shijie Geng

Zhengyang Geng
Kyle A. Genova
Georgios Georgakis
Markos Georgopoulos
Marcel Geppert
Shabnam Ghadar
Mina Ghadimi Atigh
Deepti Ghadiyaram
Maani Ghaffari Jadidi
Sedigh Ghamari
Zahra Gharaee
Michaël Gharbi
Golnaz Ghiasi
Reza Ghoddoosian
Soumya Suvra Ghosal
Adhiraj Ghosh
Arthita Ghosh
Pallabi Ghosh
Soumyadeep Ghosh
Andrew Gilbert
Igor Gilitschenski
Jhony H. Giraldo
Andreu Girbau Xalabarder
Rohit Girdhar
Sharath Girish
Xavier Giro-i-Nieto
Raja Giryes
Thomas Gittings
Nikolaos Gkanatsios
Ioannis Gkioulekas
Abhiram
  Gnanasambandam
Aurele T. Gnanha
Clement L. J. C. Godard
Arushi Goel
Vidit Goel
Shubham Goel
Zan Gojcic
Aaron K. Gokaslan
Tejas Gokhale
S. Alireza Golestaneh
Thiago L. Gomes
Nuno Goncalves
Boqing Gong
Chen Gong

Yuanhao Gong
Guoqiang Gong
Jingyu Gong
Rui Gong
Yu Gong
Mingming Gong
Neil Zhenqiang Gong
Xun Gong
Yunye Gong
Yihong Gong
Cristina I. González
Nithin Gopalakrishnan
  Nair
Gaurav Goswami
Jianping Gou
Shreyank N. Gowda
Ankit Goyal
Helmut Grabner
Patrick L. Grady
Ben Graham
Eric Granger
Douglas R. Gray
Matej Grcić
David Griffiths
Jinjin Gu
Yun Gu
Shuyang Gu
Jianyang Gu
Fuqiang Gu
Jiatao Gu
Jindong Gu
Jiaqi Gu
Jinwei Gu
Jiaxin Gu
Geonmo Gu
Xiao Gu
Xinqian Gu
Xiuye Gu
Yuming Gu
Zhangxuan Gu
Dayan Guan
Junfeng Guan
Qingji Guan
Tianrui Guan
Shanyan Guan

Denis A. Gudovskiy
Ricardo Guerrero
Pierre-Louis Guhur
Jie Gui
Liangyan Gui
Liangke Gui
Benoit Guillard
Erhan Gundogdu
Manuel Günther
Jingcai Guo
Yuanfang Guo
Junfeng Guo
Chenqi Guo
Dan Guo
Hongji Guo
Jia Guo
Jie Guo
Minghao Guo
Shi Guo
Yanhui Guo
Yangyang Guo
Yuan-Chen Guo
Yilu Guo
Yiluan Guo
Yong Guo
Guangyu Guo
Haiyun Guo
Jinyang Guo
Jianyuan Guo
Pengsheng Guo
Pengfei Guo
Shuxuan Guo
Song Guo
Tianyu Guo
Qing Guo
Qiushan Guo
Wen Guo
Xiefan Guo
Xiaohu Guo
Xiaoqing Guo
Yufei Guo
Yuhui Guo
Yuliang Guo
Yunhui Guo
Yanwen Guo

Akshita Gupta
Ankush Gupta
Kamal Gupta
Kartik Gupta
Ritwik Gupta
Rohit Gupta
Siddharth Gururani
Fredrik K. Gustafsson
Abner Guzman Rivera
Vladimir Guzov
Matthew A. Gwilliam
Jung-Woo Ha
Marc Habermann
Isma Hadji
Christian Haene
Martin Hahner
Levente Hajder
Alexandros Haliassos
Emanuela Haller
Bumsub Ham
Abdullah J. Hamdi
Shreyas Hampali
Dongyoon Han
Chunrui Han
Dong-Jun Han
Dong-Sig Han
Guangxing Han
Zhizhong Han
Ruize Han
Jiaming Han
Jin Han
Ligong Han
Xian-Hua Han
Xiaoguang Han
Yizeng Han
Zhi Han
Zhenjun Han
Zhongyi Han
Jungong Han
Junlin Han
Kai Han
Kun Han
Sungwon Han
Songfang Han
Wei Han

Xiao Han
Xintong Han
Xinzhe Han
Yahong Han
Yan Han
Zongbo Han
Nicolai Hani
Rana Hanocka
Niklas Hanselmann
Nicklas A. Hansen
Hong Hanyu
Fusheng Hao
Yanbin Hao
Shijie Hao
Udith Haputhanthri
Mehrtash Harandi
Josh Harguess
Adam Harley
David M. Hart
Atsushi Hashimoto
Ali Hassani
Mohammed Hassanin
Yana Hasson
Joakim Bruslund Haurum
Bo He
Kun He
Chen He
Xin He
Fazhi He
Gaoqi He
Hao He
Haoyu He
Jiangpeng He
Hongliang He
Qian He
Xiangteng He
Xuming He
Yannan He
Yuhang He
Yang He
Xiangyu He
Nanjun He
Pan He
Sen He
Shengfeng He

Songtao He
Tao He
Tong He
Wei He
Xuehai He
Xiaoxiao He
Ying He
Yisheng He
Ziwen He
Peter Hedman
Felix Heide
Yacov Hel-Or
Paul Henderson
Philipp Henzler
Byeongho Heo
Jae-Pil Heo
Miran Heo
Sachini A. Herath
Stephane Herbin
Pedro Hermosilla Casajus
Monica Hernandez
Charles Herrmann
Roei Herzig
Mauricio Hess-Flores
Carlos Hinojosa
Tobias Hinz
Tsubasa Hirakawa
Chih-Hui Ho
Lam Si Tung Ho
Jennifer Hobbs
Derek Hoiem
Yannick Hold-Geoffroy
Aleksander Holynski
Cheeun Hong
Fa-Ting Hong
Hanbin Hong
Guan Zhe Hong
Danfeng Hong
Lanqing Hong
Xiaopeng Hong
Xin Hong
Jie Hong
Seungbum Hong
Cheng-Yao Hong
Seunghoon Hong

Yi Hong
Yuan Hong
Yuchen Hong
Anthony Hoogs
Maxwell C. Horton
Kazuhiro Hotta
Qibin Hou
Tingbo Hou
Junhui Hou
Ji Hou
Qiqi Hou
Rui Hou
Ruibing Hou
Zhi Hou
Henry Howard-Jenkins
Lukas Hoyer
Wei-Lin Hsiao
Chiou-Ting Hsu
Anthony Hu
Brian Hu
Yusong Hu
Hexiang Hu
Haoji Hu
Di Hu
Hengtong Hu
Haigen Hu
Lianyu Hu
Hanzhe Hu
Jie Hu
Junlin Hu
Shizhe Hu
Jian Hu
Zhiming Hu
Juhua Hu
Peng Hu
Ping Hu
Ronghang Hu
MengShun Hu
Tao Hu
Vincent Tao Hu
Xiaoling Hu
Xinting Hu
Xiaolin Hu
Xuefeng Hu
Xiaowei Hu

Yang Hu
Yueyu Hu
Zeyu Hu
Zhongyun Hu
Binh-Son Hua
Guoliang Hua
Yi Hua
Linzhi Huang
Qiusheng Huang
Bo Huang
Chen Huang
Hsin-Ping Huang
Ye Huang
Shuangping Huang
Zeng Huang
Buzhen Huang
Cong Huang
Heng Huang
Hao Huang
Qidong Huang
Huaibo Huang
Chaoqin Huang
Feihu Huang
Jiahui Huang
Jingjia Huang
Kun Huang
Lei Huang
Sheng Huang
Shuaiyi Huang
Siyu Huang
Xiaoshui Huang
Xiaoyang Huang
Yan Huang
Yihao Huang
Ying Huang
Ziling Huang
Xiaoke Huang
Yifei Huang
Haiyang Huang
Zhewei Huang
Jin Huang
Haibin Huang
Jiaxing Huang
Junjie Huang
Keli Huang

Lang Huang
Lin Huang
Luojie Huang
Mingzhen Huang
Shijia Huang
Shengyu Huang
Siyuan Huang
He Huang
Xiuyu Huang
Lianghua Huang
Yue Huang
Yaping Huang
Yuge Huang
Zehao Huang
Zeyi Huang
Zhiqi Huang
Zhongzhan Huang
Zilong Huang
Ziyuan Huang
Tianrui Hui
Zhuo Hui
Le Hui
Jing Huo
Junhwa Hur
Shehzeen S. Hussain
Chuong Minh Huynh
Seunghyun Hwang
Jaehui Hwang
Jyh-Jing Hwang
Sukjun Hwang
Soonmin Hwang
Wonjun Hwang
Rakib Hyder
Sangeek Hyun
Sarah Ibrahimi
Tomoki Ichikawa
Yerlan Idelbayev
A. S. M. Iftekhar
Masaaki Iiyama
Satoshi Ikehata
Sunghoon Im
Atul N. Ingle
Eldar Insafutdinov
Yani A. Ioannou
Radu Tudor Ionescu

Umar Iqbal
Go Irie
Muhammad Zubair Irshad
Ahmet Iscen
Berivan Isik
Ashraful Islam
Md Amirul Islam
Syed Islam
Mariko Isogawa
Vamsi Krishna K. Ithapu
Boris Ivanovic
Darshan Iyer
Sarah Jabbour
Ayush Jain
Nishant Jain
Samyak Jain
Vidit Jain
Vineet Jain
Priyank Jaini
Tomas Jakab
Mohammad A. A. K.
   Jalwana
Muhammad Abdullah
   Jamal
Hadi Jamali-Rad
Stuart James
Varun Jampani
Young Kyun Jang
YeongJun Jang
Yunseok Jang
Ronnachai Jaroensri
Bhavan Jasani
Krishna Murthy
   Jatavallabhula
Mojan Javaheripi
Syed A. Javed
Guillaume Jeanneret
Pranav Jeevan
Herve Jegou
Rohit Jena
Tomas Jenicek
Porter Jenkins
Simon Jenni
Hae-Gon Jeon
Sangryul Jeon

Boseung Jeong
Yoonwoo Jeong
Seong-Gyun Jeong
Jisoo Jeong
Allan D. Jepson
Ankit Jha
Sumit K. Jha
I-Hong Jhuo
Ge-Peng Ji
Chaonan Ji
Deyi Ji
Jingwei Ji
Wei Ji
Zhong Ji
Jiayi Ji
Pengliang Ji
Hui Ji
Mingi Ji
Xiaopeng Ji
Yuzhu Ji
Baoxiong Jia
Songhao Jia
Dan Jia
Shan Jia
Xiaojun Jia
Xiuyi Jia
Xu Jia
Menglin Jia
Wenqi Jia
Boyuan Jiang
Wenhao Jiang
Huaizu Jiang
Hanwen Jiang
Haiyong Jiang
Hao Jiang
Huajie Jiang
Huiqin Jiang
Haojun Jiang
Haobo Jiang
Junjun Jiang
Xingyu Jiang
Yangbangyan Jiang
Yu Jiang
Jianmin Jiang
Jiaxi Jiang

Jing Jiang
Kui Jiang
Li Jiang
Liming Jiang
Chiyu Jiang
Meirui Jiang
Chen Jiang
Peng Jiang
Tai-Xiang Jiang
Wen Jiang
Xinyang Jiang
Yifan Jiang
Yuming Jiang
Yingying Jiang
Zeren Jiang
ZhengKai Jiang
Zhenyu Jiang
Shuming Jiao
Jianbo Jiao
Licheng Jiao
Dongkwon Jin
Yeying Jin
Cheng Jin
Linyi Jin
Qing Jin
Taisong Jin
Xiao Jin
Xin Jin
Sheng Jin
Kyong Hwan Jin
Ruibing Jin
SouYoung Jin
Yueming Jin
Chenchen Jing
Longlong Jing
Taotao Jing
Yongcheng Jing
Younghyun Jo
Joakim Johnander
Jeff Johnson
Michael J. Jones
R. Kenny Jones
Rico Jonschkowski
Ameya Joshi
Sunghun Joung

Felix Juefei-Xu
Claudio R. Jung
Steffen Jung
Hari Chandana K.
Rahul Vigneswaran K.
Prajwal K. R.
Abhishek Kadian
Jhony Kaesemodel Pontes
Kumara Kahatapitiya
Anmol Kalia
Sinan Kalkan
Tarun Kalluri
Jaewon Kam
Sandesh Kamath
Meina Kan
Menelaos Kanakis
Takuhiro Kaneko
Di Kang
Guoliang Kang
Hao Kang
Jaeyeon Kang
Kyoungkook Kang
Li-Wei Kang
MinGuk Kang
Suk-Ju Kang
Zhao Kang
Yash Mukund Kant
Yueying Kao
Aupendu Kar
Konstantinos Karantzalos
Sezer Karaoglu
Navid Kardan
Sanjay Kariyappa
Leonid Karlinsky
Animesh Karnewar
Shyamgopal Karthik
Hirak J. Kashyap
Marc A. Kastner
Hirokatsu Kataoka
Angelos Katharopoulos
Hiroharu Kato
Kai Katsumata
Manuel Kaufmann
Chaitanya Kaul
Prakhar Kaushik

Yuki Kawana
Lei Ke
Lipeng Ke
Tsung-Wei Ke
Wei Ke
Petr Kellnhofer
Aniruddha Kembhavi
John Kender
Corentin Kervadec
Leonid Keselman
Daniel Keysers
Nima Khademi Kalantari
Taras Khakhulin
Samir Khaki
Muhammad Haris Khan
Qadeer Khan
Salman Khan
Subash Khanal
Vaishnavi M. Khindkar
Rawal Khirodkar
Saeed Khorram
Pirazh Khorramshahi
Kourosh Khoshelham
Ansh Khurana
Benjamin Kiefer
Jae Myung Kim
Junho Kim
Boah Kim
Hyeonseong Kim
Dong-Jin Kim
Dongwan Kim
Donghyun Kim
Doyeon Kim
Yonghyun Kim
Hyung-Il Kim
Hyunwoo Kim
Hyeongwoo Kim
Hyo Jin Kim
Hyunwoo J. Kim
Taehoon Kim
Jaeha Kim
Jiwon Kim
Jung Uk Kim
Kangyeol Kim
Eunji Kim

Daeha Kim
Dongwon Kim
Kunhee Kim
Kyungmin Kim
Junsik Kim
Min H. Kim
Namil Kim
Kookhoi Kim
Sanghyun Kim
Seongyeop Kim
Seungryong Kim
Saehoon Kim
Euyoung Kim
Guisik Kim
Sungyeon Kim
Sunnie S. Y. Kim
Taehun Kim
Tae Oh Kim
Won Hwa Kim
Seungwook Kim
YoungBin Kim
Youngeun Kim
Akisato Kimura
Furkan Osman Kınlı
Zsolt Kira
Hedvig Kjellström
Florian Kleber
Jan P. Klopp
Florian Kluger
Laurent Kneip
Byungsoo Ko
Muhammed Kocabas
A. Sophia Koepke
Kevin Koeser
Nick Kolkin
Nikos Kolotouros
Wai-Kin Adams Kong
Deying Kong
Caihua Kong
Youyong Kong
Shuyu Kong
Shu Kong
Tao Kong
Yajing Kong
Yu Kong

Zishang Kong
Theodora Kontogianni
Anton S. Konushin
Julian F. P. Kooij
Bruno Korbar
Giorgos Kordopatis-Zilos
Jari Korhonen
Adam Kortylewski
Denis Korzhenkov
Divya Kothandaraman
Suraj Kothawade
Iuliia Kotseruba
Satwik Kottur
Shashank Kotyan
Alexandros Kouris
Petros Koutras
Anna Kreshuk
Ranjay Krishna
Dilip Krishnan
Andrey Kuehlkamp
Hilde Kuehne
Jason Kuen
David Kügler
Arjan Kuijper
Anna Kukleva
Sumith Kulal
Viveka Kulharia
Akshay R. Kulkarni
Nilesh Kulkarni
Dominik Kulon
Abhinav Kumar
Akash Kumar
Suryansh Kumar
B. V. K. Vijaya Kumar
Pulkit Kumar
Ratnesh Kumar
Sateesh Kumar
Satish Kumar
Vijay Kumar B. G.
Nupur Kumari
Sudhakar Kumawat
Jogendra Nath Kundu
Hsien-Kai Kuo
Meng-Yu Jennifer Kuo
Vinod Kumar Kurmi

Yusuke Kurose
Keerthy Kusumam
Alina Kuznetsova
Henry Kvinge
Ho Man Kwan
Hyeokjun Kweon
Heeseung Kwon
Gihyun Kwon
Myung-Joon Kwon
Taesung Kwon
YoungJoong Kwon
Christos Kyrkou
Jorma Laaksonen
Yann Labbe
Zorah Laehner
Florent Lafarge
Hamid Laga
Manuel Lagunas
Shenqi Lai
Jian-Huang Lai
Zihang Lai
Mohamed I. Lakhal
Mohit Lamba
Meng Lan
Loic Landrieu
Zhiqiang Lang
Natalie Lang
Dong Lao
Yizhen Lao
Yingjie Lao
Issam Hadj Laradji
Gustav Larsson
Viktor Larsson
Zakaria Laskar
Stéphane Lathuilière
Chun Pong Lau
Rynson W. H. Lau
Hei Law
Justin Lazarow
Verica Lazova
Eric-Tuan Le
Hieu Le
Trung-Nghia Le
Mathias Lechner
Byeong-Uk Lee

Chen-Yu Lee
Che-Rung Lee
Chul Lee
Hong Joo Lee
Dongsoo Lee
Jiyoung Lee
Eugene Eu Tzuan Lee
Daeun Lee
Saehyung Lee
Jewook Lee
Hyungtae Lee
Hyunmin Lee
Jungbeom Lee
Joon-Young Lee
Jong-Seok Lee
Joonseok Lee
Junha Lee
Kibok Lee
Byung-Kwan Lee
Jangwon Lee
Jinho Lee
Jongmin Lee
Seunghyun Lee
Sohyun Lee
Minsik Lee
Dogyoon Lee
Seungmin Lee
Min Jun Lee
Sangho Lee
Sangmin Lee
Seungeun Lee
Seon-Ho Lee
Sungmin Lee
Sungho Lee
Sangyoun Lee
Vincent C. S. S. Lee
Jaeseong Lee
Yong Jae Lee
Chenyang Lei
Chenyi Lei
Jiahui Lei
Xinyu Lei
Yinjie Lei
Jiaxu Leng
Luziwei Leng

Jan E. Lenssen
Vincent Lepetit
Thomas Leung
María Leyva-Vallina
Xin Li
Yikang Li
Baoxin Li
Bin Li
Bing Li
Bowen Li
Changlin Li
Chao Li
Chongyi Li
Guanyue Li
Shuai Li
Jin Li
Dingquan Li
Dongxu Li
Yiting Li
Gang Li
Dian Li
Guohao Li
Haoang Li
Haoliang Li
Haoran Li
Hengduo Li
Huafeng Li
Xiaoming Li
Hanao Li
Hongwei Li
Ziqiang Li
Jisheng Li
Jiacheng Li
Jia Li
Jiachen Li
Jiahao Li
Jianwei Li
Jiazhi Li
Jie Li
Jing Li
Jingjing Li
Jingtao Li
Jun Li
Junxuan Li
Kai Li

Kailin Li
Kenneth Li
Kun Li
Kunpeng Li
Aoxue Li
Chenglong Li
Chenglin Li
Changsheng Li
Zhichao Li
Qiang Li
Yanyu Li
Zuoyue Li
Xiang Li
Xuelong Li
Fangda Li
Ailin Li
Liang Li
Chun-Guang Li
Daiqing Li
Dong Li
Guanbin Li
Guorong Li
Haifeng Li
Jianan Li
Jianing Li
Jiaxin Li
Ke Li
Lei Li
Lincheng Li
Liulei Li
Lujun Li
Linjie Li
Lin Li
Pengyu Li
Ping Li
Qiufu Li
Qingyong Li
Rui Li
Siyuan Li
Wei Li
Wenbin Li
Xiangyang Li
Xinyu Li
Xiujun Li
Xiu Li

Xu Li
Ya-Li Li
Yao Li
Yongjie Li
Yijun Li
Yiming Li
Yuezun Li
Yu Li
Yunheng Li
Yuqi Li
Zhe Li
Zeming Li
Zhen Li
Zhengqin Li
Zhimin Li
Jiefeng Li
Jinpeng Li
Chengze Li
Jianwu Li
Lerenhan Li
Shan Li
Suichan Li
Xiangtai Li
Yanjie Li
Yandong Li
Zhuoling Li
Zhenqiang Li
Manyi Li
Maosen Li
Ji Li
Minjun Li
Mingrui Li
Mengtian Li
Junyi Li
Nianyi Li
Bo Li
Xiao Li
Peihua Li
Peike Li
Peizhao Li
Peiliang Li
Qi Li
Ren Li
Runze Li
Shile Li

Sheng Li
Shigang Li
Shiyu Li
Shuang Li
Shasha Li
Shichao Li
Tianye Li
Yuexiang Li
Wei-Hong Li
Wanhua Li
Weihao Li
Weiming Li
Weixin Li
Wenbo Li
Wenshuo Li
Weijian Li
Yunan Li
Xirong Li
Xianhang Li
Xiaoyu Li
Xueqian Li
Xuanlin Li
Xianzhi Li
Yunqiang Li
Yanjing Li
Yansheng Li
Yawei Li
Yi Li
Yong Li
Yong-Lu Li
Yuhang Li
Yu-Jhe Li
Yuxi Li
Yunsheng Li
Yanwei Li
Zechao Li
Zejian Li
Zeju Li
Zekun Li
Zhaowen Li
Zheng Li
Zhenyu Li
Zhiheng Li
Zhi Li
Zhong Li

Zhuowei Li
Zhuowan Li
Zhuohang Li
Zizhang Li
Chen Li
Yuan-Fang Li
Dongze Lian
Xiaochen Lian
Zhouhui Lian
Long Lian
Qing Lian
Jin Lianbao
Jinxiu S. Liang
Dingkang Liang
Jiahao Liang
Jianming Liang
Jingyun Liang
Kevin J. Liang
Kaizhao Liang
Chen Liang
Jie Liang
Senwei Liang
Ding Liang
Jiajun Liang
Jian Liang
Kongming Liang
Siyuan Liang
Yuanzhi Liang
Zhengfa Liang
Mingfu Liang
Xiaodan Liang
Xuefeng Liang
Yuxuan Liang
Kang Liao
Liang Liao
Hong-Yuan Mark Liao
Wentong Liao
Haofu Liao
Yue Liao
Minghui Liao
Shengcai Liao
Ting-Hsuan Liao
Xin Liao
Yinghong Liao
Teck Yian Lim

Che-Tsung Lin
Chung-Ching Lin
Chen-Hsuan Lin
Cheng Lin
Chuming Lin
Chunyu Lin
Dahua Lin
Wei Lin
Zheng Lin
Huaijia Lin
Jason Lin
Jierui Lin
Jiaying Lin
Jie Lin
Kai-En Lin
Kevin Lin
Guangfeng Lin
Jiehong Lin
Feng Lin
Hang Lin
Kwan-Yee Lin
Ke Lin
Luojun Lin
Qinghong Lin
Xiangbo Lin
Yi Lin
Zudi Lin
Shijie Lin
Yiqun Lin
Tzu-Heng Lin
Ming Lin
Shaohui Lin
SongNan Lin
Ji Lin
Tsung-Yu Lin
Xudong Lin
Yancong Lin
Yen-Chen Lin
Yiming Lin
Yuewei Lin
Zhiqiu Lin
Zinan Lin
Zhe Lin
David B. Lindell
Zhixin Ling

Zhan Ling
Alexander Liniger
Venice Erin B. Liong
Joey Litalien
Or Litany
Roee Litman
Ron Litman
Jim Little
Dor Litvak
Shaoteng Liu
Shuaicheng Liu
Andrew Liu
Xian Liu
Shaohui Liu
Bei Liu
Bo Liu
Yong Liu
Ming Liu
Yanbin Liu
Chenxi Liu
Daqi Liu
Di Liu
Difan Liu
Dong Liu
Dongfang Liu
Daizong Liu
Xiao Liu
Fangyi Liu
Fengbei Liu
Fenglin Liu
Bin Liu
Yuang Liu
Ao Liu
Hong Liu
Hongfu Liu
Huidong Liu
Ziyi Liu
Feng Liu
Hao Liu
Jie Liu
Jialun Liu
Jiang Liu
Jing Liu
Jingya Liu
Jiaming Liu

Jun Liu
Juncheng Liu
Jiawei Liu
Hongyu Liu
Chuanbin Liu
Haotian Liu
Lingqiao Liu
Chang Liu
Han Liu
Liu Liu
Min Liu
Yingqi Liu
Aishan Liu
Bingyu Liu
Benlin Liu
Boxiao Liu
Chenchen Liu
Chuanjian Liu
Daqing Liu
Huan Liu
Haozhe Liu
Jiaheng Liu
Wei Liu
Jingzhou Liu
Jiyuan Liu
Lingbo Liu
Nian Liu
Peiye Liu
Qiankun Liu
Shenglan Liu
Shilong Liu
Wen Liu
Wenyu Liu
Weifeng Liu
Wu Liu
Xiaolong Liu
Yang Liu
Yanwei Liu
Yingcheng Liu
Yongfei Liu
Yihao Liu
Yu Liu
Yunze Liu
Ze Liu
Zhenhua Liu

Zhenguang Liu
Lin Liu
Lihao Liu
Pengju Liu
Xinhai Liu
Yunfei Liu
Meng Liu
Minghua Liu
Mingyuan Liu
Miao Liu
Peirong Liu
Ping Liu
Qingjie Liu
Ruoshi Liu
Risheng Liu
Songtao Liu
Xing Liu
Shikun Liu
Shuming Liu
Sheng Liu
Songhua Liu
Tongliang Liu
Weibo Liu
Weide Liu
Weizhe Liu
Wenxi Liu
Weiyang Liu
Xin Liu
Xiaobin Liu
Xudong Liu
Xiaoyi Liu
Xihui Liu
Xinchen Liu
Xingtong Liu
Xinpeng Liu
Xinyu Liu
Xianpeng Liu
Xu Liu
Xingyu Liu
Yongtuo Liu
Yahui Liu
Yangxin Liu
Yaoyao Liu
Yaojie Liu
Yuliang Liu

Yongcheng Liu
Yuan Liu
Yufan Liu
Yu-Lun Liu
Yun Liu
Yunfan Liu
Yuanzhong Liu
Zhuoran Liu
Zhen Liu
Zheng Liu
Zhijian Liu
Zhisong Liu
Ziquan Liu
Ziyu Liu
Zhihua Liu
Zechun Liu
Zhaoyang Liu
Zhengzhe Liu
Stephan Liwicki
Shao-Yuan Lo
Sylvain Lobry
Suhas Lohit
Vishnu Suresh Lokhande
Vincenzo Lomonaco
Chengjiang Long
Guodong Long
Fuchen Long
Shangbang Long
Yang Long
Zijun Long
Vasco Lopes
Antonio M. Lopez
Roberto Javier
    Lopez-Sastre
Tobias Lorenz
Javier Lorenzo-Navarro
Yujing Lou
Qian Lou
Xiankai Lu
Changsheng Lu
Huimin Lu
Yongxi Lu
Hao Lu
Hong Lu
Jiasen Lu

Juwei Lu
Fan Lu
Guangming Lu
Jiwen Lu
Shun Lu
Tao Lu
Xiaonan Lu
Yang Lu
Yao Lu
Yongchun Lu
Zhiwu Lu
Cheng Lu
Liying Lu
Guo Lu
Xuequan Lu
Yanye Lu
Yantao Lu
Yuhang Lu
Fujun Luan
Jonathon Luiten
Jovita Lukasik
Alan Lukezic
Jonathan Samuel Lumentut
Mayank Lunayach
Ao Luo
Canjie Luo
Chong Luo
Xu Luo
Grace Luo
Jun Luo
Katie Z. Luo
Tao Luo
Cheng Luo
Fangzhou Luo
Gen Luo
Lei Luo
Sihui Luo
Weixin Luo
Yan Luo
Xiaoyan Luo
Yong Luo
Yadan Luo
Hao Luo
Ruotian Luo
Mi Luo

Tiange Luo
Wenjie Luo
Wenhan Luo
Xiao Luo
Zhiming Luo
Zhipeng Luo
Zhengyi Luo
Diogo C. Luvizon
Zhaoyang Lv
Gengyu Lyu
Lingjuan Lyu
Jun Lyu
Yuanyuan Lyu
Youwei Lyu
Yueming Lyu
Bingpeng Ma
Chao Ma
Chongyang Ma
Congbo Ma
Chih-Yao Ma
Fan Ma
Lin Ma
Haoyu Ma
Hengbo Ma
Jianqi Ma
Jiawei Ma
Jiayi Ma
Kede Ma
Kai Ma
Lingni Ma
Lei Ma
Xu Ma
Ning Ma
Benteng Ma
Cheng Ma
Andy J. Ma
Long Ma
Zhanyu Ma
Zhiheng Ma
Qianli Ma
Shiqiang Ma
Sizhuo Ma
Shiqing Ma
Xiaolong Ma
Xinzhu Ma

Gautam B. Machiraju
Spandan Madan
Mathew Magimai-Doss
Luca Magri
Behrooz Mahasseni
Upal Mahbub
Siddharth Mahendran
Paridhi Maheshwari
Rishabh Maheshwary
Mohammed Mahmoud
Shishira R. R. Maiya
Sylwia Majchrowska
Arjun Majumdar
Puspita Majumdar
Orchid Majumder
Sagnik Majumder
Ilya Makarov
Farkhod F.
   Makhmudkhujaev
Yasushi Makihara
Ankur Mali
Mateusz Malinowski
Utkarsh Mall
Srikanth Malla
Clement Mallet
Dimitrios Mallis
Yunze Man
Dipu Manandhar
Massimiliano Mancini
Murari Mandal
Raunak Manekar
Karttikeya Mangalam
Puneet Mangla
Fabian Manhardt
Sivabalan Manivasagam
Fahim Mannan
Chengzhi Mao
Hanzi Mao
Jiayuan Mao
Junhua Mao
Zhiyuan Mao
Jiageng Mao
Yunyao Mao
Zhendong Mao
Alberto Marchisio

Diego Marcos
Riccardo Marin
Aram Markosyan
Renaud Marlet
Ricardo Marques
Miquel Martí i Rabadán
Diego Martin Arroyo
Niki Martinel
Brais Martinez
Julieta Martinez
Marc Masana
Tomohiro Mashita
Timothée Masquelier
Minesh Mathew
Tetsu Matsukawa
Marwan Mattar
Bruce A. Maxwell
Christoph Mayer
Mantas Mazeika
Pratik Mazumder
Scott McCloskey
Steven McDonagh
Ishit Mehta
Jie Mei
Kangfu Mei
Jieru Mei
Xiaoguang Mei
Givi Meishvili
Luke Melas-Kyriazi
Iaroslav Melekhov
Andres Mendez-Vazquez
Heydi Mendez-Vazquez
Matias Mendieta
Ricardo A. Mendoza-León
Chenlin Meng
Depu Meng
Rang Meng
Zibo Meng
Qingjie Meng
Qier Meng
Yanda Meng
Zihang Meng
Thomas Mensink
Fabian Mentzer
Christopher Metzler

Gregory P. Meyer
Vasileios Mezaris
Liang Mi
Lu Mi
Bo Miao
Changtao Miao
Zichen Miao
Qiguang Miao
Xin Miao
Zhongqi Miao
Frank Michel
Simone Milani
Ben Mildenhall
Roy V. Miles
Juhong Min
Kyle Min
Hyun-Seok Min
Weiqing Min
Yuecong Min
Zhixiang Min
Qi Ming
David Minnen
Aymen Mir
Deepak Mishra
Anand Mishra
Shlok K. Mishra
Niluthpol Mithun
Gaurav Mittal
Trisha Mittal
Daisuke Miyazaki
Kaichun Mo
Hong Mo
Zhipeng Mo
Davide Modolo
Abduallah A. Mohamed
Mohamed Afham
   Mohamed Aflal
Ron Mokady
Pavlo Molchanov
Davide Moltisanti
Liliane Momeni
Gianluca Monaci
Pascal Monasse
Ajoy Mondal
Tom Monnier

Aron Monszpart
Gyeongsik Moon
Suhong Moon
Taesup Moon
Sean Moran
Daniel Moreira
Pietro Morerio
Alexandre Morgand
Lia Morra
Ali Mosleh
Inbar Mosseri
Sayed Mohammad
    Mostafavi Isfahani
Saman Motamed
Ramy A. Mounir
Fangzhou Mu
Jiteng Mu
Norman Mu
Yasuhiro Mukaigawa
Ryan Mukherjee
Tanmoy Mukherjee
Yusuke Mukuta
Ravi Teja Mullapudi
Lea Müller
Matthias Müller
Martin Mundt
Nils Murrugarra-Llerena
Damien Muselet
Armin Mustafa
Muhammad Ferjad Naeem
Sauradip Nag
Hajime Nagahara
Pravin Nagar
Rajendra Nagar
Naveen Shankar Nagaraja
Varun Nagaraja
Tushar Nagarajan
Seungjun Nah
Gaku Nakano
Yuta Nakashima
Giljoo Nam
Seonghyeon Nam
Liangliang Nan
Yuesong Nan
Yeshwanth Napolean

Dinesh Reddy
    Narapureddy
Medhini Narasimhan
Supreeth
    Narasimhaswamy
Sriram Narayanan
Erickson R. Nascimento
Varun Nasery
K. L. Navaneet
Pablo Navarrete Michelini
Shant Navasardyan
Shah Nawaz
Nihal Nayak
Farhood Negin
Lukáš Neumann
Alejandro Newell
Evonne Ng
Kam Woh Ng
Tony Ng
Anh Nguyen
Tuan Anh Nguyen
Cuong Cao Nguyen
Ngoc Cuong Nguyen
Thanh Nguyen
Khoi Nguyen
Phi Le Nguyen
Phong Ha Nguyen
Tam Nguyen
Truong Nguyen
Anh Tuan Nguyen
Rang Nguyen
Thao Thi Phuong Nguyen
Van Nguyen Nguyen
Zhen-Liang Ni
Yao Ni
Shijie Nie
Xuecheng Nie
Yongwei Nie
Weizhi Nie
Ying Nie
Yinyu Nie
Kshitij N. Nikhal
Simon Niklaus
Xuefei Ning
Jifeng Ning

Yotam Nitzan
Di Niu
Shuaicheng Niu
Li Niu
Wei Niu
Yulei Niu
Zhenxing Niu
Albert No
Shohei Nobuhara
Nicoletta Noceti
Junhyug Noh
Sotiris Nousias
Slawomir Nowaczyk
Ewa M. Nowara
Valsamis Ntouskos
Gilberto Ochoa-Ruiz
Ferda Ofli
Jihyong Oh
Sangyun Oh
Youngtaek Oh
Hiroki Ohashi
Takahiro Okabe
Kemal Oksuz
Fumio Okura
Daniel Olmeda Reino
Matthew Olson
Carl Olsson
Roy Or-El
Alessandro Ortis
Guillermo Ortiz-Jimenez
Magnus Oskarsson
Ahmed A. A. Osman
Martin R. Oswald
Mayu Otani
Naima Otberdout
Cheng Ouyang
Jiahong Ouyang
Wanli Ouyang
Andrew Owens
Poojan B. Oza
Mete Ozay
A. Cengiz Oztireli
Gautam Pai
Tomas Pajdla
Umapada Pal

Simone Palazzo
Luca Palmieri
Bowen Pan
Hao Pan
Lili Pan
Tai-Yu Pan
Liang Pan
Chengwei Pan
Yingwei Pan
Xuran Pan
Jinshan Pan
Xinyu Pan
Liyuan Pan
Xingang Pan
Xingjia Pan
Zhihong Pan
Zizheng Pan
Priyadarshini Panda
Rameswar Panda
Rohit Pandey
Kaiyue Pang
Bo Pang
Guansong Pang
Jiangmiao Pang
Meng Pang
Tianyu Pang
Ziqi Pang
Omiros Pantazis
Andreas Panteli
Maja Pantic
Marina Paolanti
Joao P. Papa
Samuele Papa
Mike Papadakis
Dim P. Papadopoulos
George Papandreou
Constantin Pape
Toufiq Parag
Chethan Parameshwara
Shaifali Parashar
Alejandro Pardo
Rishubh Parihar
Sarah Parisot
JaeYoo Park
Gyeong-Moon Park

Hyojin Park
Hyoungseob Park
Jongchan Park
Jae Sung Park
Kiru Park
Chunghyun Park
Kwanyong Park
Sunghyun Park
Sungrae Park
Seongsik Park
Sanghyun Park
Sungjune Park
Taesung Park
Gaurav Parmar
Paritosh Parmar
Alvaro Parra
Despoina Paschalidou
Or Patashnik
Shivansh Patel
Pushpak Pati
Prashant W. Patil
Vaishakh Patil
Suvam Patra
Jay Patravali
Badri Narayana Patro
Angshuman Paul
Sudipta Paul
Rémi Pautrat
Nick E. Pears
Adithya Pediredla
Wenjie Pei
Shmuel Peleg
Latha Pemula
Bo Peng
Houwen Peng
Yue Peng
Liangzu Peng
Baoyun Peng
Jun Peng
Pai Peng
Sida Peng
Xi Peng
Yuxin Peng
Songyou Peng
Wei Peng

Weiqi Peng
Wen-Hsiao Peng
Pramuditha Perera
Juan C. Perez
Eduardo Pérez Pellitero
Juan-Manuel Perez-Rua
Federico Pernici
Marco Pesavento
Stavros Petridis
Ilya A. Petrov
Vladan Petrovic
Mathis Petrovich
Suzanne Petryk
Hieu Pham
Quang Pham
Khoi Pham
Tung Pham
Huy Phan
Stephen Phillips
Cheng Perng Phoo
David Picard
Marco Piccirilli
Georg Pichler
A. J. Piergiovanni
Vipin Pillai
Silvia L. Pintea
Giovanni Pintore
Robinson Piramuthu
Fiora Pirri
Theodoros Pissas
Fabio Pizzati
Benjamin Planche
Bryan Plummer
Matteo Poggi
Ashwini Pokle
Georgy E. Ponimatkin
Adrian Popescu
Stefan Popov
Nikola Popović
Ronald Poppe
Angelo Porrello
Michael Potter
Charalambos Poullis
Hadi Pouransari
Omid Poursaeed

Shraman Pramanick
Mantini Pranav
Dilip K. Prasad
Meghshyam Prasad
B. H. Pawan Prasad
Shitala Prasad
Prateek Prasanna
Ekta Prashnani
Derek S. Prijatelj
Luke Y. Prince
Véronique Prinet
Victor Adrian Prisacariu
James Pritts
Thomas Probst
Sergey Prokudin
Rita Pucci
Chi-Man Pun
Matthew Purri
Haozhi Qi
Lu Qi
Lei Qi
Xianbiao Qi
Yonggang Qi
Yuankai Qi
Siyuan Qi
Guocheng Qian
Hangwei Qian
Qi Qian
Deheng Qian
Shengsheng Qian
Wen Qian
Rui Qian
Yiming Qian
Shengju Qian
Shengyi Qian
Xuelin Qian
Zhenxing Qian
Nan Qiao
Xiaotian Qiao
Jing Qin
Can Qin
Siyang Qin
Hongwei Qin
Jie Qin
Minghai Qin

Yipeng Qin
Yongqiang Qin
Wenda Qin
Xuebin Qin
Yuzhe Qin
Yao Qin
Zhenyue Qin
Zhiwu Qing
Heqian Qiu
Jiayan Qiu
Jielin Qiu
Yue Qiu
Jiaxiong Qiu
Zhongxi Qiu
Shi Qiu
Zhaofan Qiu
Zhongnan Qu
Yanyun Qu
Kha Gia Quach
Yuhui Quan
Ruijie Quan
Mike Rabbat
Rahul Shekhar Rade
Filip Radenovic
Gorjan Radevski
Bogdan Raducanu
Francesco Ragusa
Shafin Rahman
Md Mahfuzur Rahman
    Siddiquee
Hossein Rahmani
Kiran Raja
Sivaramakrishnan
    Rajaraman
Jathushan Rajasegaran
Adnan Siraj Rakin
Michaël Ramamonjisoa
Chirag A. Raman
Shanmuganathan Raman
Vignesh Ramanathan
Vasili Ramanishka
Vikram V. Ramaswamy
Merey Ramazanova
Jason Rambach
Sai Saketh Rambhatla

Clément Rambour
Ashwin Ramesh Babu
Adín Ramírez Rivera
Arianna Rampini
Haoxi Ran
Aakanksha Rana
Aayush Jung Bahadur
    Rana
Kanchana N. Ranasinghe
Aneesh Rangnekar
Samrudhdhi B. Rangrej
Harsh Rangwani
Viresh Ranjan
Anyi Rao
Yongming Rao
Carolina Raposo
Michalis Raptis
Amir Rasouli
Vivek Rathod
Adepu Ravi Sankar
Avinash Ravichandran
Bharadwaj Ravichandran
Dripta S. Raychaudhuri
Adria Recasens
Simon Reiß
Davis Rempe
Daxuan Ren
Jiawei Ren
Jimmy Ren
Sucheng Ren
Dayong Ren
Zhile Ren
Dongwei Ren
Qibing Ren
Pengfei Ren
Zhenwen Ren
Xuqian Ren
Yixuan Ren
Zhongzheng Ren
Ambareesh Revanur
Hamed Rezazadegan
    Tavakoli
Rafael S. Rezende
Wonjong Rhee
Alexander Richard

Christian Richardt
Stephan R. Richter
Benjamin Riggan
Dominik Rivoir
Mamshad Nayeem Rizve
Joshua D. Robinson
Joseph Robinson
Chris Rockwell
Ranga Rodrigo
Andres C. Rodriguez
Carlos Rodriguez-Pardo
Marcus Rohrbach
Gemma Roig
Yu Rong
David A. Ross
Mohammad Rostami
Edward Rosten
Karsten Roth
Anirban Roy
Debaditya Roy
Shuvendu Roy
Ahana Roy Choudhury
Aruni Roy Chowdhury
Denys Rozumnyi
Shulan Ruan
Wenjie Ruan
Patrick Ruhkamp
Danila Rukhovich
Anian Ruoss
Chris Russell
Dan Ruta
Dawid Damian Rymarczyk
DongHun Ryu
Hyeonggon Ryu
Kwonyoung Ryu
Balasubramanian S.
Alexandre Sablayrolles
Mohammad Sabokrou
Arka Sadhu
Aniruddha Saha
Oindrila Saha
Pritish Sahu
Aneeshan Sain
Nirat Saini
Saurabh Saini

Takeshi Saitoh
Christos Sakaridis
Fumihiko Sakaue
Dimitrios Sakkos
Ken Sakurada
Parikshit V. Sakurikar
Rohit Saluja
Nermin Samet
Leo Sampaio Ferraz
    Ribeiro
Jorge Sanchez
Enrique Sanchez
Shengtian Sang
Anush Sankaran
Soubhik Sanyal
Nikolaos Sarafianos
Vishwanath Saragadam
István Sárándi
Saquib Sarfraz
Mert Bulent Sariyildiz
Anindya Sarkar
Pritam Sarkar
Paul-Edouard Sarlin
Hiroshi Sasaki
Takami Sato
Torsten Sattler
Ravi Kumar Satzoda
Axel Sauer
Stefano Savian
Artem Savkin
Manolis Savva
Gerald Schaefer
Simone Schaub-Meyer
Yoni Schirris
Samuel Schulter
Katja Schwarz
Jesse Scott
Sinisa Segvic
Constantin Marc Seibold
Lorenzo Seidenari
Matan Sela
Fadime Sener
Paul Hongsuck Seo
Kwanggyoon Seo
Hongje Seong

Dario Serez
Francesco Setti
Bryan Seybold
Mohamad Shahbazi
Shima Shahfar
Xinxin Shan
Caifeng Shan
Dandan Shan
Shawn Shan
Wei Shang
Jinghuan Shang
Jiaxiang Shang
Lei Shang
Sukrit Shankar
Ken Shao
Rui Shao
Jie Shao
Mingwen Shao
Aashish Sharma
Gaurav Sharma
Vivek Sharma
Abhishek Sharma
Yoli Shavit
Shashank Shekhar
Sumit Shekhar
Zhijie Shen
Fengyi Shen
Furao Shen
Jialie Shen
Jingjing Shen
Ziyi Shen
Linlin Shen
Guangyu Shen
Biluo Shen
Falong Shen
Jiajun Shen
Qiu Shen
Qiuhong Shen
Shuai Shen
Wang Shen
Yiqing Shen
Yunhang Shen
Siqi Shen
Bin Shen
Tianwei Shen

Xi Shen
Yilin Shen
Yuming Shen
Yucong Shen
Zhiqiang Shen
Lu Sheng
Yichen Sheng
Shivanand Venkanna
    Sheshappanavar
Shelly Sheynin
Baifeng Shi
Ruoxi Shi
Botian Shi
Hailin Shi
Jia Shi
Jing Shi
Shaoshuai Shi
Baoguang Shi
Boxin Shi
Hengcan Shi
Tianyang Shi
Xiaodan Shi
Yongjie Shi
Zhensheng Shi
Yinghuan Shi
Weiqi Shi
Wu Shi
Xuepeng Shi
Xiaoshuang Shi
Yujiao Shi
Zenglin Shi
Zhenmei Shi
Takashi Shibata
Meng-Li Shih
Yichang Shih
Hyunjung Shim
Dongseok Shim
Soshi Shimada
Inkyu Shin
Jinwoo Shin
Seungjoo Shin
Seungjae Shin
Koichi Shinoda
Suprosanna Shit

Palaiahnakote
    Shivakumara
Eli Shlizerman
Gaurav Shrivastava
Xiao Shu
Xiangbo Shu
Xiujun Shu
Yang Shu
Tianmin Shu
Jun Shu
Zhixin Shu
Bing Shuai
Maria Shugrina
Ivan Shugurov
Satya Narayan Shukla
Pranjay Shyam
Jianlou Si
Yawar Siddiqui
Alberto Signoroni
Pedro Silva
Jae-Young Sim
Oriane Siméoni
Martin Simon
Andrea Simonelli
Abhishek Singh
Ashish Singh
Dinesh Singh
Gurkirt Singh
Krishna Kumar Singh
Mannat Singh
Pravendra Singh
Rajat Vikram Singh
Utkarsh Singhal
Dipika Singhania
Vasu Singla
Harsh Sinha
Sudipta Sinha
Josef Sivic
Elena Sizikova
Geri Skenderi
Ivan Skorokhodov
Dmitriy Smirnov
Cameron Y. Smith
James S. Smith
Patrick Snape

Mattia Soldan
Hyeongseok Son
Sanghyun Son
Chuanbiao Song
Chen Song
Chunfeng Song
Dan Song
Dongjin Song
Hwanjun Song
Guoxian Song
Jiaming Song
Jie Song
Liangchen Song
Ran Song
Luchuan Song
Xibin Song
Li Song
Fenglong Song
Guoli Song
Guanglu Song
Zhenbo Song
Lin Song
Xinhang Song
Yang Song
Yibing Song
Rajiv Soundararajan
Hossein Souri
Cristovao Sousa
Riccardo Spezialetti
Leonidas Spinoulas
Michael W. Spratling
Deepak Sridhar
Srinath Sridhar
Gaurang Sriramanan
Vinkle Kumar Srivastav
Themos Stafylakis
Serban Stan
Anastasis Stathopoulos
Markus Steinberger
Jan Steinbrener
Sinisa Stekovic
Alexandros Stergiou
Gleb Sterkin
Rainer Stiefelhagen
Pierre Stock

Ombretta Strafforello
Julian Straub
Yannick Strümpler
Joerg Stueckler
Hang Su
Weijie Su
Jong-Chyi Su
Bing Su
Haisheng Su
Jinming Su
Yiyang Su
Yukun Su
Yuxin Su
Zhuo Su
Zhaoqi Su
Xiu Su
Yu-Chuan Su
Zhixun Su
Arulkumar Subramaniam
Akshayvarun Subramanya
A. Subramanyam
Swathikiran Sudhakaran
Yusuke Sugano
Masanori Suganuma
Yumin Suh
Yang Sui
Baochen Sun
Cheng Sun
Long Sun
Guolei Sun
Haoliang Sun
Haomiao Sun
He Sun
Hanqing Sun
Hao Sun
Lichao Sun
Jiachen Sun
Jiaming Sun
Jian Sun
Jin Sun
Jennifer J. Sun
Tiancheng Sun
Libo Sun
Peize Sun
Qianru Sun

Shanlin Sun
Yu Sun
Zhun Sun
Che Sun
Lin Sun
Tao Sun
Yiyou Sun
Chunyi Sun
Chong Sun
Weiwei Sun
Weixuan Sun
Xiuyu Sun
Yanan Sun
Zeren Sun
Zhaodong Sun
Zhiqing Sun
Minhyuk Sung
Jinli Suo
Simon Suo
Abhijit Suprem
Anshuman Suri
Saksham Suri
Joshua M. Susskind
Roman Suvorov
Gurumurthy Swaminathan
Robin Swanson
Paul Swoboda
Tabish A. Syed
Richard Szeliski
Fariborz Taherkhani
Yu-Wing Tai
Keita Takahashi
Walter Talbott
Gary Tam
Masato Tamura
Feitong Tan
Fuwen Tan
Shuhan Tan
Andong Tan
Bin Tan
Cheng Tan
Jianchao Tan
Lei Tan
Mingxing Tan
Xin Tan

Zichang Tan
Zhentao Tan
Kenichiro Tanaka
Masayuki Tanaka
Yushun Tang
Hao Tang
Jingqun Tang
Jinhui Tang
Kaihua Tang
Luming Tang
Lv Tang
Sheyang Tang
Shitao Tang
Siliang Tang
Shixiang Tang
Yansong Tang
Keke Tang
Chang Tang
Chenwei Tang
Jie Tang
Junshu Tang
Ming Tang
Peng Tang
Xu Tang
Yao Tang
Chen Tang
Fan Tang
Haoran Tang
Shengeng Tang
Yehui Tang
Zhipeng Tang
Ugo Tanielian
Chaofan Tao
Jiale Tao
Junli Tao
Renshuai Tao
An Tao
Guanhong Tao
Zhiqiang Tao
Makarand Tapaswi
Jean-Philippe G. Tarel
Juan J. Tarrio
Enzo Tartaglione
Keisuke Tateno
Zachary Teed

Ajinkya B. Tejankar
Bugra Tekin
Purva Tendulkar
Damien Teney
Minggui Teng
Chris Tensmeyer
Andrew Beng Jin Teoh
Philipp Terhörst
Kartik Thakral
Nupur Thakur
Kevin Thandiackal
Spyridon Thermos
Diego Thomas
William Thong
Yuesong Tian
Guanzhong Tian
Lin Tian
Shiqi Tian
Kai Tian
Meng Tian
Tai-Peng Tian
Zhuotao Tian
Shangxuan Tian
Tian Tian
Yapeng Tian
Yu Tian
Yuxin Tian
Leslie Ching Ow Tiong
Praveen Tirupattur
Garvita Tiwari
George Toderici
Antoine Toisoul
Aysim Toker
Tatiana Tommasi
Zhan Tong
Alessio Tonioni
Alessandro Torcinovich
Fabio Tosi
Matteo Toso
Hugo Touvron
Quan Hung Tran
Son Tran
Hung Tran
Ngoc-Trung Tran
Vinh Tran

Phong Tran
Giovanni Trappolini
Edith Tretschk
Subarna Tripathi
Shubhendu Trivedi
Eduard Trulls
Prune Truong
Thanh-Dat Truong
Tomasz Trzcinski
Sam Tsai
Yi-Hsuan Tsai
Ethan Tseng
Yu-Chee Tseng
Shahar Tsiper
Stavros Tsogkas
Shikui Tu
Zhigang Tu
Zhengzhong Tu
Richard Tucker
Sergey Tulyakov
Cigdem Turan
Daniyar Turmukhambetov
Victor G. Turrisi da Costa
Bartlomiej Twardowski
Christopher D. Twigg
Radim Tylecek
Mostofa Rafid Uddin
Md. Zasim Uddin
Kohei Uehara
Nicolas Ugrinovic
Youngjung Uh
Norimichi Ukita
Anwaar Ulhaq
Devesh Upadhyay
Paul Upchurch
Yoshitaka Ushiku
Yuzuko Utsumi
Mikaela Angelina Uy
Mohit Vaishnav
Pratik Vaishnavi
Jeya Maria Jose Valanarasu
Matias A. Valdenegro Toro
Diego Valsesia
Wouter Van Gansbeke
Nanne van Noord

Simon Vandenhende
Farshid Varno
Cristina Vasconcelos
Francisco Vasconcelos
Alex Vasilescu
Subeesh Vasu
Arun Balajee Vasudevan
Kanav Vats
Vaibhav S. Vavilala
Sagar Vaze
Javier Vazquez-Corral
Andrea Vedaldi
Olga Veksler
Andreas Velten
Sai H. Vemprala
Raviteja Vemulapalli
Shashanka
    Venkataramanan
Dor Verbin
Luisa Verdoliva
Manisha Verma
Yashaswi Verma
Constantin Vertan
Eli Verwimp
Deepak Vijaykeerthy
Pablo Villanueva
Ruben Villegas
Markus Vincze
Vibhav Vineet
Minh P. Vo
Huy V. Vo
Duc Minh Vo
Tomas Vojir
Igor Vozniak
Nicholas Vretos
Vibashan VS
Tuan-Anh Vu
Thang Vu
Mårten Wadenbäck
Neal Wadhwa
Aaron T. Walsman
Steven Walton
Jin Wan
Alvin Wan
Jia Wan

Jun Wan
Xiaoyue Wan
Fang Wan
Guowei Wan
Renjie Wan
Zhiqiang Wan
Ziyu Wan
Bastian Wandt
Dongdong Wang
Limin Wang
Haiyang Wang
Xiaobing Wang
Angtian Wang
Angelina Wang
Bing Wang
Bo Wang
Boyu Wang
Binghui Wang
Chen Wang
Chien-Yi Wang
Congli Wang
Qi Wang
Chengrui Wang
Rui Wang
Yiqun Wang
Cong Wang
Wenjing Wang
Dongkai Wang
Di Wang
Xiaogang Wang
Kai Wang
Zhizhong Wang
Fangjinhua Wang
Feng Wang
Hang Wang
Gaoang Wang
Guoqing Wang
Guangcong Wang
Guangzhi Wang
Hanqing Wang
Hao Wang
Haohan Wang
Haoran Wang
Hong Wang
Haotao Wang

Hu Wang
Huan Wang
Hua Wang
Hui-Po Wang
Hengli Wang
Hanyu Wang
Hongxing Wang
Jingwen Wang
Jialiang Wang
Jian Wang
Jianyi Wang
Jiashun Wang
Jiahao Wang
Tsun-Hsuan Wang
Xiaoqian Wang
Jinqiao Wang
Jun Wang
Jianzong Wang
Kaihong Wang
Ke Wang
Lei Wang
Lingjing Wang
Linnan Wang
Lin Wang
Liansheng Wang
Mengjiao Wang
Manning Wang
Nannan Wang
Peihao Wang
Jiayun Wang
Pu Wang
Qiang Wang
Qiufeng Wang
Qilong Wang
Qiangchang Wang
Qin Wang
Qing Wang
Ruocheng Wang
Ruibin Wang
Ruisheng Wang
Ruizhe Wang
Runqi Wang
Runzhong Wang
Wenxuan Wang
Sen Wang

Shangfei Wang
Shaofei Wang
Shijie Wang
Shiqi Wang
Zhibo Wang
Song Wang
Xinjiang Wang
Tai Wang
Tao Wang
Teng Wang
Xiang Wang
Tianren Wang
Tiantian Wang
Tianyi Wang
Fengjiao Wang
Wei Wang
Miaohui Wang
Suchen Wang
Siyue Wang
Yaoming Wang
Xiao Wang
Ze Wang
Biao Wang
Chaofei Wang
Dong Wang
Gu Wang
Guangrun Wang
Guangming Wang
Guo-Hua Wang
Haoqing Wang
Hesheng Wang
Huafeng Wang
Jinghua Wang
Jingdong Wang
Jingjing Wang
Jingya Wang
Jingkang Wang
Jiakai Wang
Junke Wang
Kuo Wang
Lichen Wang
Lizhi Wang
Longguang Wang
Mang Wang
Mei Wang

Min Wang
Peng-Shuai Wang
Run Wang
Shaoru Wang
Shuhui Wang
Tan Wang
Tiancai Wang
Tianqi Wang
Wenhai Wang
Wenzhe Wang
Xiaobo Wang
Xiudong Wang
Xu Wang
Yajie Wang
Yan Wang
Yuan-Gen Wang
Yingqian Wang
Yizhi Wang
Yulin Wang
Yu Wang
Yujie Wang
Yunhe Wang
Yuxi Wang
Yaowei Wang
Yiwei Wang
Zezheng Wang
Hongzhi Wang
Zhiqiang Wang
Ziteng Wang
Ziwei Wang
Zheng Wang
Zhenyu Wang
Binglu Wang
Zhongdao Wang
Ce Wang
Weining Wang
Weiyao Wang
Wenbin Wang
Wenguan Wang
Guangting Wang
Haolin Wang
Haiyan Wang
Huiyu Wang
Naiyan Wang
Jingbo Wang

Jinpeng Wang
Jiaqi Wang
Liyuan Wang
Lizhen Wang
Ning Wang
Wenqian Wang
Sheng-Yu Wang
Weimin Wang
Xiaohan Wang
Yifan Wang
Yi Wang
Yongtao Wang
Yizhou Wang
Zhuo Wang
Zhe Wang
Xudong Wang
Xiaofang Wang
Xinggang Wang
Xiaosen Wang
Xiaosong Wang
Xiaoyang Wang
Lijun Wang
Xinlong Wang
Xuan Wang
Xue Wang
Yangang Wang
Yaohui Wang
Yu-Chiang Frank Wang
Yida Wang
Yilin Wang
Yi Ru Wang
Yali Wang
Yinglong Wang
Yufu Wang
Yujiang Wang
Yuwang Wang
Yuting Wang
Yang Wang
Yu-Xiong Wang
Yixu Wang
Ziqi Wang
Zhicheng Wang
Zeyu Wang
Zhaowen Wang
Zhenyi Wang

Zhenzhi Wang
Zhijie Wang
Zhiyong Wang
Zhongling Wang
Zhuowei Wang
Zian Wang
Zifu Wang
Zihao Wang
Zirui Wang
Ziyan Wang
Wenxiao Wang
Zhen Wang
Zhepeng Wang
Zi Wang
Zihao W. Wang
Steven L. Waslander
Olivia Watkins
Daniel Watson
Silvan Weder
Dongyoon Wee
Dongming Wei
Tianyi Wei
Jia Wei
Dong Wei
Fangyun Wei
Longhui Wei
Mingqiang Wei
Xinyue Wei
Chen Wei
Donglai Wei
Pengxu Wei
Xing Wei
Xiu-Shen Wei
Wenqi Wei
Guoqiang Wei
Wei Wei
XingKui Wei
Xian Wei
Xingxing Wei
Yake Wei
Yuxiang Wei
Yi Wei
Luca Weihs
Michael Weinmann
Martin Weinmann

Congcong Wen
Chuan Wen
Jie Wen
Sijia Wen
Song Wen
Chao Wen
Xiang Wen
Zeyi Wen
Xin Wen
Yilin Wen
Yijia Weng
Shuchen Weng
Junwu Weng
Wenming Weng
Renliang Weng
Zhenyu Weng
Xinshuo Weng
Nicholas J. Westlake
Gordon Wetzstein
Lena M. Widin Klasén
Rick Wildes
Bryan M. Williams
Williem Williem
Ole Winther
Scott Wisdom
Alex Wong
Chau-Wai Wong
Kwan-Yee K. Wong
Yongkang Wong
Scott Workman
Marcel Worring
Michael Wray
Safwan Wshah
Xiang Wu
Aming Wu
Chongruo Wu
Cho-Ying Wu
Chunpeng Wu
Chenyan Wu
Ziyi Wu
Fuxiang Wu
Gang Wu
Haiping Wu
Huisi Wu
Jane Wu

Jialian Wu
Jing Wu
Jinjian Wu
Jianlong Wu
Xian Wu
Lifang Wu
Lifan Wu
Minye Wu
Qianyi Wu
Rongliang Wu
Rui Wu
Shiqian Wu
Shuzhe Wu
Shangzhe Wu
Tsung-Han Wu
Tz-Ying Wu
Ting-Wei Wu
Jiannan Wu
Zhiliang Wu
Yu Wu
Chenyun Wu
Dayan Wu
Dongxian Wu
Fei Wu
Hefeng Wu
Jianxin Wu
Weibin Wu
Wenxuan Wu
Wenhao Wu
Xiao Wu
Yicheng Wu
Yuanwei Wu
Yu-Huan Wu
Zhenxin Wu
Zhenyu Wu
Wei Wu
Peng Wu
Xiaohe Wu
Xindi Wu
Xinxing Wu
Xinyi Wu
Xingjiao Wu
Xiongwei Wu
Yangzheng Wu
Yanzhao Wu

Yawen Wu
Yong Wu
Yi Wu
Ying Nian Wu
Zhenyao Wu
Zhonghua Wu
Zongze Wu
Zuxuan Wu
Stefanie Wuhrer
Teng Xi
Jianing Xi
Fei Xia
Haifeng Xia
Menghan Xia
Yuanqing Xia
Zhihua Xia
Xiaobo Xia
Weihao Xia
Shihong Xia
Yan Xia
Yong Xia
Zhaoyang Xia
Zhihao Xia
Chuhua Xian
Yongqin Xian
Wangmeng Xiang
Fanbo Xiang
Tiange Xiang
Tao Xiang
Liuyu Xiang
Xiaoyu Xiang
Zhiyu Xiang
Aoran Xiao
Chunxia Xiao
Fanyi Xiao
Jimin Xiao
Jun Xiao
Taihong Xiao
Anqi Xiao
Junfei Xiao
Jing Xiao
Liang Xiao
Yang Xiao
Yuting Xiao
Yijun Xiao

Yao Xiao
Zeyu Xiao
Zhisheng Xiao
Zihao Xiao
Binhui Xie
Christopher Xie
Haozhe Xie
Jin Xie
Guo-Sen Xie
Hongtao Xie
Ming-Kun Xie
Tingting Xie
Chaohao Xie
Weicheng Xie
Xudong Xie
Jiyang Xie
Xiaohua Xie
Yuan Xie
Zhenyu Xie
Ning Xie
Xianghui Xie
Xiufeng Xie
You Xie
Yutong Xie
Fuyong Xing
Yifan Xing
Zhen Xing
Yuanjun Xiong
Jinhui Xiong
Weihua Xiong
Hongkai Xiong
Zhitong Xiong
Yuanhao Xiong
Yunyang Xiong
Yuwen Xiong
Zhiwei Xiong
Yuliang Xiu
An Xu
Chang Xu
Chenliang Xu
Chengming Xu
Chenshu Xu
Xiang Xu
Huijuan Xu
Zhe Xu

Jie Xu
Jingyi Xu
Jiarui Xu
Yinghao Xu
Kele Xu
Ke Xu
Li Xu
Linchuan Xu
Linning Xu
Mengde Xu
Mengmeng Frost Xu
Min Xu
Mingye Xu
Jun Xu
Ning Xu
Peng Xu
Runsheng Xu
Sheng Xu
Wenqiang Xu
Xiaogang Xu
Renzhe Xu
Kaidi Xu
Yi Xu
Chi Xu
Qiuling Xu
Baobei Xu
Feng Xu
Haohang Xu
Haofei Xu
Lan Xu
Mingze Xu
Songcen Xu
Weipeng Xu
Wenjia Xu
Wenju Xu
Xiangyu Xu
Xin Xu
Yinshuang Xu
Yixing Xu
Yuting Xu
Yanyu Xu
Zhenbo Xu
Zhiliang Xu
Zhiyuan Xu
Xiaohao Xu

Yanwu Xu
Yan Xu
Yiran Xu
Yifan Xu
Yufei Xu
Yong Xu
Zichuan Xu
Zenglin Xu
Zexiang Xu
Zhan Xu
Zheng Xu
Zhiwei Xu
Ziyue Xu
Shiyu Xuan
Hanyu Xuan
Fei Xue
Jianru Xue
Mingfu Xue
Qinghan Xue
Tianfan Xue
Chao Xue
Chuhui Xue
Nan Xue
Zhou Xue
Xiangyang Xue
Yuan Xue
Abhay Yadav
Ravindra Yadav
Kota Yamaguchi
Toshihiko Yamasaki
Kohei Yamashita
Chaochao Yan
Feng Yan
Kun Yan
Qingsen Yan
Qixin Yan
Rui Yan
Siming Yan
Xinchen Yan
Yaping Yan
Bin Yan
Qingan Yan
Shen Yan
Shipeng Yan
Xu Yan

Yan Yan
Yichao Yan
Zhaoyi Yan
Zike Yan
Zhiqiang Yan
Hongliang Yan
Zizheng Yan
Jiewen Yang
Anqi Joyce Yang
Shan Yang
Anqi Yang
Antoine Yang
Bo Yang
Baoyao Yang
Chenhongyi Yang
Dingkang Yang
De-Nian Yang
Dong Yang
David Yang
Fan Yang
Fengyu Yang
Fengting Yang
Fei Yang
Gengshan Yang
Heng Yang
Han Yang
Huan Yang
Yibo Yang
Jiancheng Yang
Jihan Yang
Jiawei Yang
Jiayu Yang
Jie Yang
Jinfa Yang
Jingkang Yang
Jinyu Yang
Cheng-Fu Yang
Ji Yang
Jianyu Yang
Kailun Yang
Tian Yang
Luyu Yang
Liang Yang
Li Yang
Michael Ying Yang

Yang Yang
Muli Yang
Le Yang
Qiushi Yang
Ren Yang
Ruihan Yang
Shuang Yang
Siyuan Yang
Su Yang
Shiqi Yang
Taojiannan Yang
Tianyu Yang
Lei Yang
Wanzhao Yang
Shuai Yang
William Yang
Wei Yang
Xiaofeng Yang
Xiaoshan Yang
Xin Yang
Xuan Yang
Xu Yang
Xingyi Yang
Xitong Yang
Jing Yang
Yanchao Yang
Wenming Yang
Yujiu Yang
Herb Yang
Jianfei Yang
Jinhui Yang
Chuanguang Yang
Guanglei Yang
Haitao Yang
Kewei Yang
Linlin Yang
Lijin Yang
Longrong Yang
Meng Yang
MingKun Yang
Sibei Yang
Shicai Yang
Tong Yang
Wen Yang
Xi Yang

Xiaolong Yang
Xue Yang
Yubin Yang
Ze Yang
Ziyi Yang
Yi Yang
Linjie Yang
Yuzhe Yang
Yiding Yang
Zhenpei Yang
Zhaohui Yang
Zhengyuan Yang
Zhibo Yang
Zongxin Yang
Hantao Yao
Mingde Yao
Rui Yao
Taiping Yao
Ting Yao
Cong Yao
Qingsong Yao
Quanming Yao
Xu Yao
Yuan Yao
Yao Yao
Yazhou Yao
Jiawen Yao
Shunyu Yao
Pew-Thian Yap
Sudhir Yarram
Rajeev Yasarla
Peng Ye
Botao Ye
Mao Ye
Fei Ye
Hanrong Ye
Jingwen Ye
Jinwei Ye
Jiarong Ye
Mang Ye
Meng Ye
Qi Ye
Qian Ye
Qixiang Ye
Junjie Ye

Sheng Ye
Nanyang Ye
Yufei Ye
Xiaoqing Ye
Ruolin Ye
Yousef Yeganeh
Chun-Hsiao Yeh
Raymond A. Yeh
Yu-Ying Yeh
Kai Yi
Chang Yi
Renjiao Yi
Xinping Yi
Peng Yi
Alper Yilmaz
Junho Yim
Hui Yin
Bangjie Yin
Jia-Li Yin
Miao Yin
Wenzhe Yin
Xuwang Yin
Ming Yin
Yu Yin
Aoxiong Yin
Kangxue Yin
Tianwei Yin
Wei Yin
Xianghua Ying
Rio Yokota
Tatsuya Yokota
Naoto Yokoya
Ryo Yonetani
Ki Yoon Yoo
Jinsu Yoo
Sunjae Yoon
Jae Shin Yoon
Jihun Yoon
Sung-Hoon Yoon
Ryota Yoshihashi
Yusuke Yoshiyasu
Chenyu You
Haoran You
Haoxuan You
Yang You

Quanzeng You
Tackgeun You
Kaichao You
Shan You
Xinge You
Yurong You
Baosheng Yu
Bei Yu
Haichao Yu
Hao Yu
Chaohui Yu
Fisher Yu
Jin-Gang Yu
Jiyang Yu
Jason J. Yu
Jiashuo Yu
Hong-Xing Yu
Lei Yu
Mulin Yu
Ning Yu
Peilin Yu
Qi Yu
Qian Yu
Rui Yu
Shuzhi Yu
Gang Yu
Tan Yu
Weijiang Yu
Xin Yu
Bingyao Yu
Ye Yu
Hanchao Yu
Yingchen Yu
Tao Yu
Xiaotian Yu
Qing Yu
Houjian Yu
Changqian Yu
Jing Yu
Jun Yu
Shujian Yu
Xiang Yu
Zhaofei Yu
Zhenbo Yu
Yinfeng Yu

Zhuoran Yu
Zitong Yu
Bo Yuan
Jiangbo Yuan
Liangzhe Yuan
Weihao Yuan
Jianbo Yuan
Xiaoyun Yuan
Ye Yuan
Li Yuan
Geng Yuan
Jialin Yuan
Maoxun Yuan
Peng Yuan
Xin Yuan
Yuan Yuan
Yuhui Yuan
Yixuan Yuan
Zheng Yuan
Mehmet Kerim Yücel
Kaiyu Yue
Haixiao Yue
Heeseung Yun
Sangdoo Yun
Tian Yun
Mahmut Yurt
Ekim Yurtsever
Ahmet Yüzügüler
Edouard Yvinec
Eloi Zablocki
Christopher Zach
Muhammad Zaigham
  Zaheer
Pierluigi Zama Ramirez
Yuhang Zang
Pietro Zanuttigh
Alexey Zaytsev
Bernhard Zeisl
Haitian Zeng
Pengpeng Zeng
Jiabei Zeng
Runhao Zeng
Wei Zeng
Yawen Zeng
Yi Zeng

Yiming Zeng
Tieyong Zeng
Huanqiang Zeng
Dan Zeng
Yu Zeng
Wei Zhai
Yuanhao Zhai
Fangneng Zhan
Kun Zhan
Xiong Zhang
Jingdong Zhang
Jiangning Zhang
Zhilu Zhang
Gengwei Zhang
Dongsu Zhang
Hui Zhang
Binjie Zhang
Bo Zhang
Tianhao Zhang
Cecilia Zhang
Jing Zhang
Chaoning Zhang
Chenxu Zhang
Chi Zhang
Chris Zhang
Yabin Zhang
Zhao Zhang
Rufeng Zhang
Chaoyi Zhang
Zheng Zhang
Da Zhang
Yi Zhang
Edward Zhang
Xin Zhang
Feifei Zhang
Feilong Zhang
Yuqi Zhang
GuiXuan Zhang
Hanlin Zhang
Hanwang Zhang
Hanzhen Zhang
Haotian Zhang
He Zhang
Haokui Zhang
Hongyuan Zhang

Hengrui Zhang
Hongming Zhang
Mingfang Zhang
Jianpeng Zhang
Jiaming Zhang
Jichao Zhang
Jie Zhang
Jingfeng Zhang
Jingyi Zhang
Jinnian Zhang
David Junhao Zhang
Junjie Zhang
Junzhe Zhang
Jiawan Zhang
Jingyang Zhang
Kai Zhang
Lei Zhang
Lihua Zhang
Lu Zhang
Miao Zhang
Minjia Zhang
Mingjin Zhang
Qi Zhang
Qian Zhang
Qilong Zhang
Qiming Zhang
Qiang Zhang
Richard Zhang
Ruimao Zhang
Ruisi Zhang
Ruixin Zhang
Runze Zhang
Qilin Zhang
Shan Zhang
Shanshan Zhang
Xi Sheryl Zhang
Song-Hai Zhang
Chongyang Zhang
Kaihao Zhang
Songyang Zhang
Shu Zhang
Siwei Zhang
Shujian Zhang
Tianyun Zhang
Tong Zhang

Tao Zhang
Wenwei Zhang
Wenqiang Zhang
Wen Zhang
Xiaolin Zhang
Xingchen Zhang
Xingxuan Zhang
Xiuming Zhang
Xiaoshuai Zhang
Xuanmeng Zhang
Xuanyang Zhang
Xucong Zhang
Xingxing Zhang
Xikun Zhang
Xiaohan Zhang
Yahui Zhang
Yunhua Zhang
Yan Zhang
Yanghao Zhang
Yifei Zhang
Yifan Zhang
Yi-Fan Zhang
Yihao Zhang
Yingliang Zhang
Youshan Zhang
Yulun Zhang
Yushu Zhang
Yixiao Zhang
Yide Zhang
Zhongwen Zhang
Bowen Zhang
Chen-Lin Zhang
Zehua Zhang
Zekun Zhang
Zeyu Zhang
Xiaowei Zhang
Yifeng Zhang
Cheng Zhang
Hongguang Zhang
Yuexi Zhang
Fa Zhang
Guofeng Zhang
Hao Zhang
Haofeng Zhang
Hongwen Zhang

Hua Zhang
Jiaxin Zhang
Zhenyu Zhang
Jian Zhang
Jianfeng Zhang
Jiao Zhang
Jiakai Zhang
Lefei Zhang
Le Zhang
Mi Zhang
Min Zhang
Ning Zhang
Pan Zhang
Pu Zhang
Qing Zhang
Renrui Zhang
Shifeng Zhang
Shuo Zhang
Shaoxiong Zhang
Weizhong Zhang
Xi Zhang
Xiaomei Zhang
Xinyu Zhang
Yin Zhang
Zicheng Zhang
Zihao Zhang
Ziqi Zhang
Zhaoxiang Zhang
Zhen Zhang
Zhipeng Zhang
Zhixing Zhang
Zhizheng Zhang
Jiawei Zhang
Zhong Zhang
Pingping Zhang
Yixin Zhang
Kui Zhang
Lingzhi Zhang
Huaiwen Zhang
Quanshi Zhang
Zhoutong Zhang
Yuhang Zhang
Yuting Zhang
Zhang Zhang
Ziming Zhang

Zhizhong Zhang
Qilong Zhangli
Bingyin Zhao
Bin Zhao
Chenglong Zhao
Lei Zhao
Feng Zhao
Gangming Zhao
Haiyan Zhao
Hao Zhao
Handong Zhao
Hengshuang Zhao
Yinan Zhao
Jiaojiao Zhao
Jiaqi Zhao
Jing Zhao
Kaili Zhao
Haojie Zhao
Yucheng Zhao
Longjiao Zhao
Long Zhao
Qingsong Zhao
Qingyu Zhao
Rui Zhao
Rui-Wei Zhao
Sicheng Zhao
Shuang Zhao
Siyan Zhao
Zelin Zhao
Shiyu Zhao
Wang Zhao
Tiesong Zhao
Qian Zhao
Wangbo Zhao
Xi-Le Zhao
Xu Zhao
Yajie Zhao
Yang Zhao
Ying Zhao
Yin Zhao
Yizhou Zhao
Yunhan Zhao
Yuyang Zhao
Yue Zhao
Yuzhi Zhao

Bowen Zhao
Pu Zhao
Bingchen Zhao
Borui Zhao
Fuqiang Zhao
Hanbin Zhao
Jian Zhao
Mingyang Zhao
Na Zhao
Rongchang Zhao
Ruiqi Zhao
Shuai Zhao
Wenda Zhao
Wenliang Zhao
Xiangyun Zhao
Yifan Zhao
Yaping Zhao
Zhou Zhao
He Zhao
Jie Zhao
Xibin Zhao
Xiaoqi Zhao
Zhengyu Zhao
Jin Zhe
Chuanxia Zheng
Huan Zheng
Hao Zheng
Jia Zheng
Jian-Qing Zheng
Shuai Zheng
Meng Zheng
Mingkai Zheng
Qian Zheng
Qi Zheng
Wu Zheng
Yinqiang Zheng
Yufeng Zheng
Yutong Zheng
Yalin Zheng
Yu Zheng
Feng Zheng
Zhaoheng Zheng
Haitian Zheng
Kang Zheng
Bolun Zheng

Haiyong Zheng
Mingwu Zheng
Sipeng Zheng
Tu Zheng
Wenzhao Zheng
Xiawu Zheng
Yinglin Zheng
Zhuo Zheng
Zilong Zheng
Kecheng Zheng
Zerong Zheng
Shuaifeng Zhi
Tiancheng Zhi
Jia-Xing Zhong
Yiwu Zhong
Fangwei Zhong
Zhihang Zhong
Yaoyao Zhong
Yiran Zhong
Zhun Zhong
Zichun Zhong
Bo Zhou
Boyao Zhou
Brady Zhou
Mo Zhou
Chunluan Zhou
Dingfu Zhou
Fan Zhou
Jingkai Zhou
Honglu Zhou
Jiaming Zhou
Jiahuan Zhou
Jun Zhou
Kaiyang Zhou
Keyang Zhou
Kuangqi Zhou
Lei Zhou
Lihua Zhou
Man Zhou
Mingyi Zhou
Mingyuan Zhou
Ning Zhou
Peng Zhou
Penghao Zhou
Qianyi Zhou

Shuigeng Zhou
Shangchen Zhou
Huayi Zhou
Zhize Zhou
Sanping Zhou
Qin Zhou
Tao Zhou
Wenbo Zhou
Xiangdong Zhou
Xiao-Yun Zhou
Xiao Zhou
Yang Zhou
Yipin Zhou
Zhenyu Zhou
Hao Zhou
Chu Zhou
Daquan Zhou
Da-Wei Zhou
Hang Zhou
Kang Zhou
Qianyu Zhou
Sheng Zhou
Wenhui Zhou
Xingyi Zhou
Yan-Jie Zhou
Yiyi Zhou
Yu Zhou
Yuan Zhou
Yuqian Zhou
Yuxuan Zhou
Zixiang Zhou
Wengang Zhou
Shuchang Zhou
Tianfei Zhou
Yichao Zhou
Alex Zhu
Chenchen Zhu
Deyao Zhu
Xiatian Zhu
Guibo Zhu
Haidong Zhu
Hao Zhu
Hongzi Zhu
Rui Zhu
Jing Zhu

Jianke Zhu
Junchen Zhu
Lei Zhu
Lingyu Zhu
Luyang Zhu
Menglong Zhu
Peihao Zhu
Hui Zhu
Xiaofeng Zhu
Tyler (Lixuan) Zhu
Wentao Zhu
Xiangyu Zhu
Xinqi Zhu
Xinxin Zhu
Xinliang Zhu
Yangguang Zhu
Yichen Zhu
Yixin Zhu
Yanjun Zhu
Yousong Zhu
Yuhao Zhu
Ye Zhu
Feng Zhu
Zhen Zhu
Fangrui Zhu
Jinjing Zhu
Linchao Zhu
Pengfei Zhu
Sijie Zhu
Xiaobin Zhu
Xiaoguang Zhu
Zezhou Zhu
Zhenyao Zhu
Kai Zhu
Pengkai Zhu
Bingbing Zhuang
Chengyuan Zhuang
Liansheng Zhuang
Peiye Zhuang
Yixin Zhuang
Yihong Zhuang
Junbao Zhuo
Andrea Ziani
Bartosz Zieliński
Primo Zingaretti

Nikolaos Zioulis
Andrew Zisserman
Yael Ziv
Liu Ziyin
Xingxing Zou
Danping Zou
Qi Zou

Shihao Zou
Xueyan Zou
Yang Zou
Yuliang Zou
Zihang Zou
Chuhang Zou
Dongqing Zou

Xu Zou
Zhiming Zou
Maria A. Zuluaga
Xinxin Zuo
Zhiwen Zuo
Reyer Zwiggelaar

Contents – Part XXIV

Improving Vision Transformers by Revisiting High-Frequency Components

Jiawang Bai[1], Li Yuan[2,5(✉)], Shu-Tao Xia[1,5(✉)], Shuicheng Yan[4],
Zhifeng Li[3(✉)], and Wei Liu[3(✉)]

[1] Tsinghua Shenzhen International Graduate School,
Tsinghua University, Shenzhen, China
bjw19@mails.tsinghua.edu.cn, xiast@sz.tsinghua.edu.cn
[2] School of ECE at Peking University, Beijing, China
yuanli-ece@pku.edu.cn
[3] Data Platform, Tencent, Shenzhen, China
michaelzfli@tencent.com, wl2223@columbia.edu
[4] Sea AI Lab, Singapore, Singapore
yansc@sea.com
[5] Peng Cheng Laboratory, Shenzhen, China

Abstract. The transformer models have shown promising effectiveness in dealing with various vision tasks. However, compared with training Convolutional Neural Network (CNN) models, training Vision Transformer (ViT) models is more difficult and relies on the large-scale training set. To explain this observation we make a hypothesis that *ViT models are less effective in capturing the high-frequency components of images than CNN models*, and verify it by a frequency analysis. Inspired by this finding, we first investigate the effects of existing techniques for improving ViT models from a new frequency perspective, and find that the success of some techniques (*e.g.*, RandAugment) can be attributed to the better usage of the high-frequency components. Then, to compensate for this insufficient ability of ViT models, we propose HAT, which directly augments high-frequency components of images via adversarial training. We show that HAT can consistently boost the performance of various ViT models (*e.g.*, +1.2% for ViT-B, +0.5% for Swin-B), and especially enhance the advanced model VOLO-D5 to 87.3% that only uses ImageNet-1K data, and the superiority can also be maintained on out-of-distribution data and transferred to downstream tasks. The code is available at: https://github.com/jiawangbai/HAT.

1 Introduction

Recently, transformer models have shown high effectiveness in various vision tasks and attracted growing attention. The pioneering work is Vision Transformer (ViT) [20], which is a full-transformer architecture directly inherited

Supplementary Information The online version contains supplementary material available at https://doi.org/10.1007/978-3-031-20053-3_1.

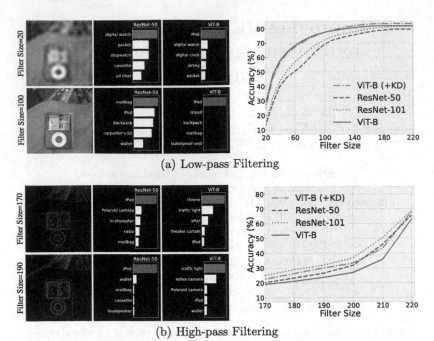

Fig. 1. Comparison of ViT-B, ResNet-50, ResNet-101, and ViT-B(+KD) on low- and high-pass filtered validation set with different filter sizes. ViT-B is the base ViT model taking as input a sequence of 16 × 16 patches.KD denotes knowledge distillation, where the teacher model is a RegNetY-16GF [46] following [54]. The top-1 accuracy of ViT-B, ResNet-101, ResNet-50, and ViT-B (+KD) on the ImageNet validation set is 82.0%, 79.8%, , 81.6%, and 83.6%, respectively.

from natural language processing [55] but taking raw image patches as input. After that, many ViT variants [13,21,32,40,59,60,69] have been proposed and achieved competitive performance with Convolutional Neural Network (CNN) models.Though promising in vision tasks, ViT models suffer training difficulty and require significantly more training samples [20] compared with CNN models.

One reason for this difficulty may be that ViT models can not effectively exploit the local structures as they split an image to a sequence of patches and model their dependencies with the self-attention mechanism [44,68]. In contrast, CNN models can effectively extract local features within the receptive fields [3,23] with convolution operation. From some previous studies [6,17,53], the local structures (*e.g.*, edges and lines) are more related to the high-frequency components of the images. We then naturally make such a hypothesis: *ViT models are less effective in capturing the high-frequency components of images than CNN models.*

To verify our hypothesis, we use the discrete Fourier transform (DFT) to decompose the original images into the low- and high-frequency components and evaluate the model performance on them respectively [57,67]. Figure 1 shows a comparison between ViT-B [20] and ResNet-50 [28], where a larger filter size for the low- and high-pass filtering means more low- and high-frequency components, respectively. In our experiments, ViT-B has a higher top-1 accuracy on the original ImageNet validation set (82.0% vs. 79.8%) and a larger model size (86.6M vs. 25.6M). We can see that ViT-B performs better than ResNet-50 on the low-frequency components (Fig. 1(a)), but worse than ResNet-50 on the high-frequency components (Fig. 1(b)), which supports our hypothesis.

Motivated by the above observation, we study existing techniques for ViT models from a frequency perspective, including knowledge distillation [37,54], architecture design [13,21,40], and data augmentations [44,54], and provide some useful insights which are beneficial to improving performance of ViT models. Through extensive experiments, we find that *i*) knowledge distillation is helpful to a ViT model using a CNN teacher in capturing high-frequency components of the images; *ii*) compared to the original ViT [20], some advanced architectures utilizing convolutional-like operation [21] or multi-scale feature maps [13,40] can more effectively exploit high-frequency components of the images; *iii*) RandAugment [14] is more helpful for catching high-frequency components of the images than CutMix [70] and Mixup [73].

Furthermore, we propose to compensate for the insufficient capacity of ViT models in capturing the high-frequency components of the images by directly augmenting the high-frequency components via adversarial training [43,72]. Specifically, we craft adversarial examples by altering clean images with high-frequency perturbations, and jointly train ViT models over clean images and adversarial examples. Our results indicate that this training strategy improves the performance of the ViT model by compensating for its ability to capture the high-frequency components of the images. Moreover, since adversarial perturbations can naturally influence the high-frequency components in our case, we directly use adversarial perturbations without high-frequency limitation, resulting in a simple but effective method, named HAT, standing for improving ViT models on the high-frequency components via adversarial training. Note that HAT does not bring extra complexity during the inference stage or alter the model architecture.

Our main contributions are summarized as follows:

- Based on our frequency analysis, we validate that compared to CNN models, ViT models are less effective in capturing the high-frequency components of images, which may lead to the difficulty of training ViT models.
- We analyze the effects of existing techniques for improving the performance of ViT models from a frequency perspective.
- We propose HAT, which improves the performance of ViT models by influencing the high-frequency components of images directly.
- Our results on ImageNet classification and out-of-distribution data demonstrate the superiority of HAT. We also find that pre-trained models with HAT are beneficial to downstream tasks.

2   Related Work

Transformer Models in Vision Tasks. Transformer models [55] entirely rely on the self-attention mechanism to build long-distance dependencies, which have achieved great success in almost all natural language processing tasks [4,19,39]. Vision Transformer (ViT) [20] is one of the earlier attempts to introduce transformer models into vision tasks, which applies a pure transformer architecture on non-overlapping image patches for image classification and has achieved state-of-the-art accuracy. Since ViT models excel at capturing spatial information, they have also been extended to more challenging tasks, including object detection [7,15,77], segmentation [50,52], image enhancement [9,66], and video processing [61,71,75]. Besides, many efforts have been devoted to designing new ViT architectures [13,21,32,40,59,60,69]. For example, Liu *et al.* [40] presented a hierarchical architecture with shifted window based attention that can efficiently extract multi-scale features; Yuan *et al.* [69] introduced outlook attention to efficiently encode finer-level features and contexts into tokens.

Training Strategies for ViT Models. It is shown that training ViT models is more challenging than training CNN models, and requires large-scale datasets (*e.g.*, ImageNet-22K [18] and JFT-300M [51]) to perform pre-training [20]. To enable ViT to be effective on the smaller ImageNet-1K dataset [18], many training strategies have been explored. In [49,54], applying strong data augmentation and model regularization makes a quick solution to this problem. Among them, CutMix [70], Mixup [73], and RandAugment [14] are proven to be particularly helpful [54]. Besides, some customized augmentations for training ViT models are presented [10,59]. Utilizing a trained CNN teacher, knowledge distillation (KD) [37,54] can significantly boost the performance of ViT models. There are also some works solving this problem by using a better optimization strategy, such as promoting patch diversification [24] and sharpness-aware minimizer [11]. Unlike these works, we focus on directly compensating for the ability of ViT models in capturing the high-frequency components for better performance.

3   Revisiting ViT Models from a Frequency Perspective

To investigate ViT models from a frequency perspective, we use the discrete Fourier transform (DFT) to evaluate the model performance on certain frequency components of test samples [67]. Let $x \in \mathbb{R}^{H \times W}$ (omitting the dimension of image channels) and $y \in \mathbb{R}^C$ represent an image in the spatial domain and its label vector, where C is the number of classes. We transform x to the frequency spectrum by the DFT $\mathcal{F} : \mathbb{R}^{H \times W} \to \mathbb{C}^{H \times W}$ and transform signals of the image from frequency back to the spatial domain by the inverse DFT $\mathcal{F}^{-1} : \mathbb{C}^{H \times W} \to \mathbb{R}^{H \times W}$. In this work, the low-frequency components are shifted to the center of the frequency spectrum.

For a mask $m \in \{0,1\}^{H \times W}$, the low-pass filtering $\mathcal{M}_l^S$ and high-pass filtering $\mathcal{M}_h^S$ with the filter size S are formally defined as:

$$\mathcal{M}_l^S(x) = \mathcal{F}^{-1}(m \odot \mathcal{F}(x)), \text{ where } m_{i,j} = \begin{cases} 1, & \text{if } \min(|i - \frac{H}{2}|, |j - \frac{W}{2}|) \leqslant \frac{S}{2} \\ 0, & \text{otherwise} \end{cases}, \quad (1)$$

$$\mathcal{M}_h^S(x) = \mathcal{F}^{-1}(m \odot \mathcal{F}(x)), \text{ where } m_{i,j} = \begin{cases} 0, & \text{if } \min(|i - \frac{H}{2}|, |j - \frac{W}{2}|) \leqslant \frac{\min(H,W)-S}{2} \\ 1, & \text{otherwise} \end{cases}, \quad (2)$$

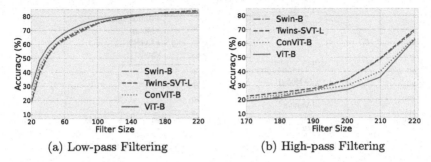

(a) Low-pass Filtering   (b) High-pass Filtering

Fig. 2. Comparison of ViT-B, ConViT-B, Twins-SVT-L, and Swin-B on low- and high-pass filtered validation set with different filter sizes. The top-1 accuracy of ViT-B, ConViT-B, Twins-SVT-L, and Swin-B on the ImageNet validation set is 82.0%, 82.3%, 83.7%, and 83.5%, respectively.

where $\odot$ is element-wise multiplication and $m_{i,j}$ denotes the value of m at position (i, j). For images containing multiple color channels, the filtering operates on each channel independently. To make a comprehensive analysis, we evaluate various ViT architectures and training strategies with different filter sizes based on the ImageNet validation set. We provide the visualized examples in Fig. 1.

Comparison of ViT and CNN Models. Firstly, we compare the performance of ViT-B with ResNet-50 and ResNet-101, which are trained with the same data augmentations. The plots in Fig. 1(a) show that ViT-B surpasses ResNet on the low-frequency components of images. However, although ViT-B achieves a higher accuracy (82.0%) than ResNet-50 (79.8%) and ResNet-101 (81.6%) on the original ImageNet validation set, its performance is lower than CNN models on the high-frequency components of images, as shown in Fig. 1(b). This observation indicates that ViT models can capture the global contexts effectively, but fails to well leverage local details compared to CNN models. It may be because cascading self-attention blocks in ViT models is equivalent to repeatedly applying a low-pass filter, corresponding to the theoretical justification in [58], while CNN models utilizing convolution operations behave like a series of high-pass filters [44] to catch more high-frequency components [57].

We further study the distillation method introduced in [54], i.e., transferring the learned knowledge in a ViT model using a CNN teacher. We use a RegNetY-16GF model [46] as a teacher with the hard-label distillation, and adopt all settings in [54]. The results in Fig. 1 show that the improvement of KD (from 82.0% to 83.6%) is primarily attributed to the stronger ability to exploit the high-frequency components of images. It also confirms that there is a gap between the abilities of ViT and CNN models in capturing the high-frequency components.

Various ViT Architectures. Recently, various ViT architectures are proposed and show excellent results [13,21,40]. We compare ViT-B with three advanced architectures, including ConViT-B [21], Twins-SVT-L [40], and Swin-B [13], with a similar model size, and present a reason for the success of these architectures from the frequency perspective. As shown in Fig. 2, all architectures perform

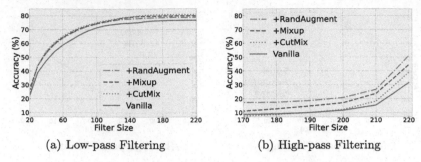

(a) Low-pass Filtering   (b) High-pass Filtering

Fig. 3. Comparison of vanilla training and three data augmentations on low- and high-pass filtered validation set with different filter sizes. The top-1 accuracy of Vanilla, +CutMix, +Mixup, and +RandAugment on the ImageNet validation set is 76.7%, 80.8%, 79.9%, and 78.8%, respectively.

similarly on the low-frequency components, while three advanced architectures achieve higher accuracy than ViT-B on the high-frequency components. Our results also provide evidence for the effects of the proposed components of these recent architectures. Specifically, the convolutional-like operation in ConViT and multi-scale feature maps in Swin Transformer and Twins-SVT can help the vision transformer capture the high-frequency components.

Data Augmentations. As demonstrated in recent works [44,54], training ViT models relies heavily on strong data augmentation. Compared to the vanilla training, the improvements of the commonly used augmentations are significant, including CutMix [70] (+4.1%), Mixup [73] (+3.2%), and RandAugment [14] (+2.1%). We make a comparison between the effects of these three augmentations from the frequency perspective. The results are shown in Fig. 3. We can see that the ranking of these three augmentations *w.r.t.* improvements they bring is CutMix > Mixup > RandAugment on the low-frequency components. However, on the high-frequency components, the case is opposite: RandAugment > Mixup > CutMix. Our observation reveals that CutMix can help ViT models leverage the global context information of an image by removing a random region and replacing it with a patch from another image. Moreover, it also indicates that the transformations used in RandAugment can force the trained model to pay more attention to high-frequency information.

4   The Proposed Method

In this section, we firstly describe the proposed HAT, and then demonstrate its effects on ViT models via a case study.

4.1   Adversarial Training with High-Frequency Perturbations

As demonstrated by the analysis in Sect. 3, the ability of ViT models to capture the high-frequency components is limited, and compensating for this limitation is a key to boosting their performance. Therefore, different from previous data augmentation methods, we propose to directly augment the high-frequency components during the training stage. We alter the high-frequency components of training images by adding adversarial perturbations and training ViT models on these altered images. It corresponds to adversarial training [43,72] with high-frequency perturbations and is stated formally below.

Given a ViT model f with the weights $\boldsymbol{\theta}$, $f_{\boldsymbol{\theta}}(\boldsymbol{x})$ denotes its softmax output of the input sample $\boldsymbol{x}$. Inspired by the min-max formulation of adversarial training [43], the objective function of adversarial training with high-frequency perturbations is as follows:

$$\mathbb{E}_{(\boldsymbol{x},\boldsymbol{y})\sim\mathcal{D}}\left[L(\boldsymbol{\theta},\boldsymbol{x},\boldsymbol{y}) + \max_{||\boldsymbol{\delta}||_{\infty}\leqslant\epsilon}\left(\alpha L(\boldsymbol{\theta},\boldsymbol{x}+\mathcal{M}_h^S(\boldsymbol{\delta}),\boldsymbol{y}) + \beta L_{kl}(\boldsymbol{\theta},\boldsymbol{x}+\mathcal{M}_h^S(\boldsymbol{\delta}),\boldsymbol{x})\right)\right],$$
(3)

where ϵ denotes the maximum perturbation strength. $L(\boldsymbol{\theta},\boldsymbol{x},\boldsymbol{y}) = \mathrm{CE}(f_{\boldsymbol{\theta}}(\boldsymbol{x}),\boldsymbol{y})$ and $L_{kl}(\boldsymbol{\theta},\boldsymbol{x}_1,\boldsymbol{x}_2) = \frac{1}{2}[\mathrm{KL}(f_{\boldsymbol{\theta}}(\boldsymbol{x}_1),f_{\boldsymbol{\theta}}(\boldsymbol{x}_2)) + \mathrm{KL}(f_{\boldsymbol{\theta}}(\boldsymbol{x}_2),f_{\boldsymbol{\theta}}(\boldsymbol{x}_1))]$, where $\mathrm{CE}(\cdot)$ and $\mathrm{KL}(\cdot)$ calculate the cross-entropy and the Kullback-Leibler divergence, respectively. α and β are two hyper-parameters. We use the high-pass filtering $\mathcal{M}_h^S$ with a given filter size to limit the perturbations in the high-frequency domain. Our experiments in Sect. 4.2 demonstrate that optimizing Eq. (3) can compensate for the ability of the ViT model to capture the high-frequency components of images and thus improve its performance.

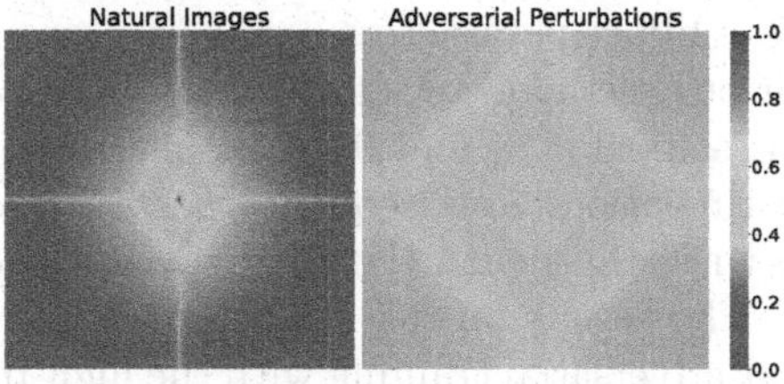

Fig. 4. Heat maps of Fourier spectrum for natural images and adversarial perturbations. They are obtained by averaging over a batch of data.

Then, we notice that adversarial perturbations are naturally imposed on the high-frequency components in our case [16,41]. It is validated in Fig. 4 that compared to natural images, adversarial perturbations show higher concentrations in the high-frequency domain. Therefore, we directly use full-frequency adversarial perturbations in our HAT with the below objective:

$$\mathbb{E}_{(\boldsymbol{x},\boldsymbol{y})\sim\mathcal{D}}\left[L(\boldsymbol{\theta},\boldsymbol{x},\boldsymbol{y}) + \max_{||\boldsymbol{\delta}||_{\infty}\leqslant\epsilon}\left(\alpha L(\boldsymbol{\theta},\boldsymbol{x}+\boldsymbol{\delta},\boldsymbol{y}) + \beta L_{kl}(\boldsymbol{\theta},\boldsymbol{x}+\boldsymbol{\delta},\boldsymbol{x})\right)\right].$$
(4)

The inner maximization in Eq. (4) can be solved by project gradient descent (PGD) for K steps [43]. Different from the standard PGD, following [22,76], we accumulate the gradients of the model weights in each PGD step, and update the parameters at once with the accumulated gradients. In this way, the perturbations in each PGD step can be used for training. This procedure is detailed in Algorithm 1 in Appendix C. Besides, to address the mismatched distribution between clean images and adversarial examples [65], we perform adversarial training in some initial epochs (200 epochs in our setting) and train normally in the rest epochs.

Table 1. Comparison of the baseline and adversarial training (AT) with three types of perturbations, where the case of using the full-frequency perturbations corresponds to the proposed HAT.

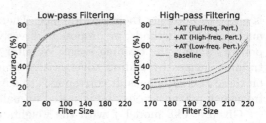

Training strategy	Top-1 ACC (%)
Baseline	82.0
+AT (Low-freq. Pert.)	81.9
+AT (High-freq. Pert.)	83.0
+AT (Full-freq. Pert.)	**83.2**

Fig. 5. Comparison of the baseline and adversarial training (AT) with three types of perturbations on low- and high-pass filtered validation set with different filter sizes.

4.2   A Case Study Using ViT-B

To illustrate how the proposed method influences the ViT models, we conduct a case study using ViT-B on ImageNet. For training ViT-B, we adopt the hyper-parameters in [25] in all cases. Without considering our adversarial training, these hyper-parameters result in a strong baseline with a 82.0% top-1 accuracy. For our method, we set $\epsilon = 2/255$, $K = 3$, and $\eta = 1/255$. The parameters α and β are fixed at 3 and 0.01, respectively. We compare three types of adversarial perturbations: low-frequency perturbations with the filter size 10, high-frequency perturbations with the filter size 10, and full-frequency perturbations.

The results on the ImageNet validation set are shown in Table 1. We can see that adversarial training with the high-frequency perturbations brings 1.0% gains over the baseline. Figure 5 reveals the reason for that: the ability of ViT-B to capture the high-frequency components of images is stronger than the baseline, which exactly confirms our expectation. In contrast, there is no improvement for the case of using low-frequency perturbations. For adversarial training with the full-frequency perturbations, without the high-filter operation and setting the filter size, it is more simple, but can also improve the performance of ViT-B. This case study illustrates that using the full-frequency perturbations is a reasonable choice for our HAT, which will be further verified in our below experiments.

5   Experiments

5.1   Experimental Setup

We evaluate the proposed method on ImageNet [18]. Our code is implemented based on PyTorch [45] and the timm library [62]. We conduct experiments on various model architectures: three variants of ViT [20] (ViT-T, ViT-S, and ViT-B with 16×16 input patch size) following [54], three variants of Swin Transformer [40] (Swin-T, Swin-S, and Swin-B), and two variants of VOLO [69] (VOLO-D1 and VOLO-D5). "T", "S", and "B" denote tiny, small, and base model sizes, respectively. Following the standard training schedule, we train all models on the ImageNet-1K training set for 300 epochs with strong data augmentation

Table 2. Performance of various ViT architectures trained without and with the proposed HAT on the ImageNet, ImageNet-Real, and ImageNet-V2 validation set.

Model	Params	FLOPs	Test size	Top-1	Real Top-1	V2 Top-1
ViT-T	5.7M	1.6G	224	72.2	80.0	60.1
+HAT				**73.3**	**81.1**	**61.0**
ViT-S	22.1M	4.7G	224	80.1	85.7	68.2
+HAT				**80.9**	**86.6**	**70.0**
ViT-B	86.6M	17.6G	224	82.0	87.1	71.0
+HAT				**83.2**	**87.9**	**72.6**
Swin-T	28.3M	4.5G	224	81.2	86.8	70.5
+HAT				**82.0**	**87.3**	**71.5**
Swin-S	49.6M	8.7G	224	83.0	87.8	72.4
+HAT				**83.3**	87.7	**72.8**
Swin-B	87.8M	15.4G	224	83.5	87.9	72.9
+HAT				**84.0**	**88.2**	**73.8**
VOLO-D1	26.6M	6.8G	224	84.2	89.0	74.0
+HAT				**84.5**	**89.2**	**74.9**
VOLO-D1	26.6M	22.8G	384	85.2	89.6	75.6
+HAT				**85.5**	**89.8**	**76.6**
VOLO-D5	295.5M	69.0G	224	86.1	89.9	76.3
+HAT				**86.3**	**90.2**	**76.8**
VOLO-D5	295.5M	304G	448	87.0	90.6	77.8
+HAT				**87.2**	90.6	**78.6**
VOLO-D5	295.5M	412G	512	87.1	90.6	78.0
+HAT				**87.3**	**90.7**	**78.7**

(*e.g.*, CutMix [70], Mixup [73], and RandAugment [14]) and model regularization (*e.g.*, stochastic depth [35] and weight decay [42]). Specifically, we use the hyper-parameters in [25] for training ViT-B, and train ViT-T and ViT-S with the same hyper-parameters except for throwing away EMA, resulting in strong baselines. For training variants of Swin Transformer and VOLO, we follow the training setup of the original paper [40, 69] (including token labeling [37] for VOLO). The default image resolution for these models is 224×224. We also finetune variants of VOLO on larger image resolutions (384×384, 448×448, and 512×512).

For the proposed HAT, in all cases, the PGD learning rate η is $1/255$, and the parameters α and β are set to 3 and 0.01, respectively. We set the maximum perturbation strength ϵ as $2/255$ and the number of PGD steps K as 3 by default. For VOLO-D5, the largest model in our experiments, we set $K = 2$ with $\epsilon = 1/255$ to reduce the training time. For all ViT models, we adopt the training strategy in Algorithm 1 in the first 200 epochs and perform normal training in the rest 100 epochs. In our HAT, each PGD step requires one forward and backward pass. Accordingly, for the whole training, HAT leads to about $1.7\times$ and $2.3\times$ computation cost for $K = 1$ and $K = 2$, respectively.

5.2   Results on ImageNet Classification

Results of Various ViT Architectures. We present the results of variants of ViT, Swin Transformer, and VOLO trained without and with our HAT in Table 2.

"Top-1", "Real Top-1", and "V2 Top-1" refer to the top-1 accuracy evaluated on the ImageNet [18], ImageNet-Real [2], and ImageNet-V2 [48] validation set, respectively, where ImageNet-Real is built by relabeling the validation set of the original ImageNet for correcting labeling errors and ImageNet-V2 is a newly collected version of the ImageNet validation set.

Table 3. Comparison of HAT with other training strategies. All results are based on the ImageNet-1K training set and ViT-B. Results of other methods are drawn from original papers. The methods with blue color mean self-supervised learning.

Note that these models in Table 2 are with different architectures and sizes, and the baselines are all carefully tuned with various data augmentation and model regularization techniques. As can be seen, HAT can steadily improve the performance of all models. To be specific, we boost top-1 accuracy on the ImageNet validation set by 1.1%, 0.8%, and 1.2% for ViT-T, ViT-S, and ViT-B, respectively. Even for Swin Transformer and VOLO, more advanced architectures, we can still consistently improve the performance of their

Method	Top-1	Real Top-1	V2 Top-1
Vallina	76.7	82.3	64.1
DeiT [54]	81.8	86.7	71.5
DeiT(+KD) [54]	83.4	88.3	73.2
PyramidAT [33]	81.7	86.8	70.8
TransMix [10]	82.4	–	–
SAM [11]	79.9	85.2	67.5
DINO [8]	82.8	–	–
MoCo v3 [12]	83.2	–	–
BEiT [1]	83.2	–	–
MAE [25]	83.6	–	–
HAT(ours)	83.2	87.9	72.6
HAT(+KD)	**84.3**	**88.8**	**73.9**

variants. The performance gains of our method are preserved through finetuning at higher resolutions. In particular, when the image resolution is 512×512, VOLO-D5 with our HAT reaches a top-1 accuracy of 87.3% on the ImageNet validation set.

Comparison to Other Methods with ViT-B. We compare our proposed HAT with other state-of-the-art training strategies in Table 3. We conduct these experiments using ViT-B. Compared to DeiT [54] and TransMix [10], which utilize data augmentations to empower ViT models, we achieve a significantly higher top-1 accuracy. Most closely related to our work is pyramid adversarial training (PyramidAT) [33], which leverages structured adversarial perturbations. However, due to a bigger number of PGD steps, its training cost is twice as high as ours, but resulting in a lower top-1 accuracy than our HAT. Besides the supervised training methods, we also compare with the methods that pre-train on the ImageNet-1K training set in a self-supervised manner and then perform supervised finetuning, including DINO [8], MoCo v3 [12], BEiT [1], and MAE [25]. Our HAT shows very competitive performance with them. Furthermore, combining the proposed HAT with knowledge distillation [54], we obtain the performance of 84.3%, which is the highest top-1 accuracy among these methods.

Table 4. Performance of various ViT architectures trained without and with the proposed HAT on five out-of distribution datasets. Note that for mean Corruption Error (mCE), lower is better. The test resolution of all below models is 224 × 224.

Model	ImageNet-A		ImageNet-C		Sketch		Rendition		Stylized	
	Top-1	+HAT Top-1	mCE↓	+HAT mCE↓	Top-1	+HAT Top-1	Top-1	+HAT Top-1	Top-1	+HAT Top-1
ViT-T	7.7	7.3	70.0	**66.8**	19.8	**22.9**	31.9	**35.8**	9.5	**12.5**
ViT-S	18.5	**23.1**	53.3	**49.7**	29.3	**32.3**	41.6	**45.1**	15.8	**18.1**
ViT-B	25.3	**30.6**	46.4	**42.2**	36.1	**38.5**	49.6	**51.3**	21.8	**24.7**
Swin-T	22.1	**25.7**	58.0	**53.9**	28.5	**31.0**	41.4	**43.8**	13.1	**13.8**
Swin-S	32.7	**34.6**	51.8	**48.6**	32.7	**33.9**	45.2	**46.5**	14.2	**15.1**
Swin-B	35.8	**40.0**	51.7	**46.9**	32.2	**36.4**	45.8	**49.0**	15.7	**16.4**
VOLO-D1	39.0	**42.9**	46.8	**43.7**	38.5	**39.5**	50.3	**51.9**	19.2	**21.2**
VOLO-D5	50.9	**54.5**	41.8	**38.4**	44.3	**45.7**	57.9	**59.7**	24.6	**25.9**

5.3 Results on Out-of-distribution Data

We evaluate the proposed HAT on five out-of-distribution datasets: ImageNet-A which contains 7,500 examples that are harder and may cause mistakes across various models [31]; ImageNet-C [30] which applies a set of common visual corruptions to the ImageNet validation set; ImageNet-Sketch [56] which contains sketch-like images and matches the ImageNet validation set in categories and scale; ImageNet-Rendition [29], a 30,000 image test set containing various renditions (*e.g.*, paintings, embroidery); Stylized ImageNet [23] which is a stylized version of ImageNet created by applying AdaIN style transfer [36] to ImageNet images. We report the top-1 accuracy on all datasets, except ImageNet-C where we report the normalized mean Corruption Error (mCE) (lower is better) following the original paper [30].

The results are shown in Table 4. Note that all models are trained on the ImageNet-1K training set and tested on these five out-of-distribution datasets. As can be seen, our method can bring performance gains for all architectures, demonstrating that HAT can enhance the robustness of ViT models to out-of-distribution data. Accordingly, HAT breaks the trade-off between in-distribution and out-of-distribution generalization [47,72], or in other words, it can achieve better performance in these two cases simultaneously.

5.4 Transfer Learning to Downstream Tasks

ImageNet pre-training is widely used in various vision tasks [26]. For the downstream tasks, the backbones can be initialized by the model weights pre-trained on ImageNet. In this section, we demonstrate that the advantages of HAT can be transferred to the downstream tasks, including object detection, instance segmentation, and semantic segmentation. More implementation details can be found in Appendix D.

Object Detection and Instance Segmentation. We take three variants of Swin Transformer trained without and with our HAT as pre-trained models to

Table 5. Object detection and instance segmentation performance of the models pre-trained without and with HAT on COCO *val* 2017. We adopt the Cascade Mask R-CNN object detection framework. AP^{box} and AP^{mask} are box average precision and mask average precision, respectively.

Backbone	Params	FLOPs	AP^{box}	AP^{box}_{50}	AP^{box}_{75}	AP^{mask}	AP^{mask}_{50}	AP^{mask}_{75}
Swin-T	86M	745G	50.5	69.3	54.9	43.7	66.6	47.1
+HAT			**50.9**	**69.4**	**55.6**	**43.9**	**66.8**	**47.3**
Swin-S	107M	838G	51.8	70.4	56.3	44.7	67.9	48.5
+HAT			**52.5**	**71.2**	**57.1**	**45.4**	**68.8**	**49.4**
Swin-B	145M	982G	51.9	70.9	56.5	45.0	68.4	48.7
+HAT			**52.8**	**71.5**	**57.5**	**45.6**	**69.1**	**49.6**

Table 6. Semantic segmentation performance of the models pre-trained without and with HAT on the ADE20K validation set. We adopt the UperNet segmentation framework. MS denotes testing with variable input size.

Backbone	Params	FLOPs	mIoU	mIoU (MS)	mAcc
Swin-T	60M	945G	44.5	46.1	55.6
+HAT			45.6	46.7	57.4
Swin-S	81M	1038G	47.6	49.5	58.8
+HAT			48.1	49.7	59.5
Swin-B	121G	1088G	48.1	49.7	59.1
+HAT			48.9	50.3	60.2

Table 7. Performance of ViT-B trained with the proposed HAT under different maximum perturbation strength ϵ.

ϵ	Top-1	Real Top-1	V2 Top-1
1/255	83.1	87.8	72.4
2/255	**83.2**	87.9	**72.6**
3/255	83.1	**88.0**	72.5
4/255	83.1	87.9	72.5
5/255	83.0	87.9	72.3

evaluate the performance in object detection and instance segmentation. The experiments are conducted on COCO 2017 [38] with the Cascade Mask R-CNN object detection framework [5,27]. We present the results in Table 5. As can be seen, HAT helps three variants of Swin Transformer achieve higher detection performance. These results show that the superiority of HAT can be transferred to downstream tasks. Moreover, we would like to emphasize that HAT does not introduce extra parameters or computation cost in inference.

Semantic Segmentation. We also use Swin Transformer to evaluate the performance in semantic segmentation. We report results on the widely-used segmentation benchmark ADE20K [74] with the UperNet [64] segmentation framework. The results are shown in Table 6. We can see that HAT brings significant gains for these three variants. Especially for Swin-T and Swin-S, the improvements of HAT are more than 1.0% mIOU. These results further show the benefits of our proposed HAT to downstream tasks.

5.5   Ablation Studies

Ablation on Maximum Perturbation Strength. We ablate the effects of the maximum perturbation strength ϵ, where a larger ϵ indicates stronger adver-

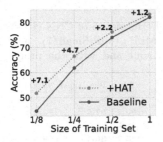

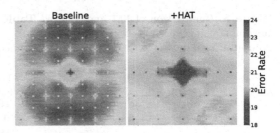

Fig. 6. Performance of ViT-B trained without and with the proposed HAT on various sizes of training sets.

Fig. 7. Fourier heat maps of ViT-B trained without and with HAT. The Fourier heat map reflects the sensitivity of a model to high- and low-frequency corruptions. Error rates are averaged over the entire ImageNet validation set.

sarial examples for the adversarial training. We test HAT with $\epsilon \in \{1/255, 2/255, 3/255, 4/255, 5/255\}$. Correspondingly, we set the number of PGD steps as $K \in \{2, 3, 4, 5, 6\}$. The PGD learning rate η is fixed at $1/255$. The results are shown in Table 7. We can see that HAT can achieve superior performance when ϵ is set as $2/255$ or $3/255$. It demonstrates that medium strength adversarial examples are more helpful for training ViT models than weaker or stronger adversarial examples. This ablation study and other experiments in this paper verify that $\epsilon = 2/255$ and $K = 3$ are reasonable choices in most cases.

Scaling the Training Set Size. HAT In this part, we investigate the effects of with various training set sizes. Specifically, we experiment on training sets with different sizes by randomly sampling $1/8$, $1/4$, and $1/2$ images from the original ImageNet-1K training set, resulting in training sets with 16K, 32K, and 64K samples. Then, we train ViT-B on these datasets without and with the proposed HAT and evaluate on the original ImageNet validation set. The comparison is presented in Fig. 6. It is shown that HAT can improve the performance of ViT-B under all sizes of the training set. Especially for the small-scale training set, HAT brings more gains, *e.g.*, +7.1 for the smallest training set. It may be because the insufficient ability of ViT models to capture high-frequency components is amplified on the small-scale dataset and the effectiveness of HAT on compensating for this ability is more significant in this case. In short, our results illustrate that HAT enables ViT models to handle the small-scale training set better.

5.6 Discussions

Fourier Heat Maps of ViT Models. We investigate the effects of HAT on the model sensitivity to low- and high-frequency corruptions. We adopt the Fourier heat map [67], which visualizes the error rates of a model tested on perturbed images with additive Fourier basis noise. We fix ℓ_2-norm of the additive noise as 15.7 and average the error rates over the entire ImageNet validation set.

Table 8. Comparison of HAT and longer normal training with ViT-B under various computational costs.

Cost	Normal training		+HAT	
	Setting	Top-1	Setting	Top-1
1×	300 epochs	82.0	–	–
1.7×	500 epochs	82.5	$K = 2$	**83.1**
2.3×	690 epochs	82.4	$K = 3$	**83.2**

Table 9. Performance of CNN (ResNet-50) and MLP (ViP-Small/7) models trained without and with the proposed HAT.

Model	Top-1	Real Top-1	V2 Top-1
ResNet-50	79.8	86.9	70.7
+HAT	**80.2**	**87.2**	**71.3**
ViP-Small/7	81.6	85.5	67.8
+HAT	**82.2**	**86.1**	**69.6**

Following [67], we present the 63×63 square centered at the lowest frequency in the Fourier domain. The Fourier heat maps of ViT-B trained without and with HAT are shown in Fig. 7. As we can see, the baseline model is highly sensitive to additive noise in the high-frequency. In contrast, the model trained with HAT is more robust to the noise, especially in the high-frequency.

Longer Normal Training. To further verify the effectiveness of HAT, we increase the number of epochs of normal training to match the computational cost of HAT. The results are presented in Table 8. We can see that 500 epochs are enough for the normal training to converge, and HAT surpasses normal training under 1.7× and 2.3× cost.

Beyond ViT Models. We explore the performance of HAT on the CNN and MLP models. We conduct experiments on ResNet-50 [28] and ViP-Small-7 [34]. We train ResNet-50 for 800 epochs following the setup in [63] and ViP-Small-7 for 300 epochs following the setup in [34]. For our HAT, we perform adversarial training in the first 600 epochs for ResNet-50 and in the first 200 epochs for ViP-Small-7, and keep other settings unchanged. The results in Table 9 show that HAT brings improvements of 0.4% and 0.6% for ResNet-50 and ViP-Small-7, respectively. Therefore, the proposed training strategy is promising to be extended to other models.

6   Conclusions and Future Work

In this paper, we study ViT models from a frequency perspective. We find that compared to CNN models, ViT models can not well exploit the high-frequency components of images. We also present a new frequency analysis of existing techniques for improving the performance of ViT models. To compensate for this insufficient ability of ViT models, we propose HAT, a simple but effective training strategy based on adversarial training. Extensive experiments verify its effectiveness on diverse benchmarks.

Despite achieving higher performance, HAT has an increased training time compared to the normal training. Therefore, a future study is to improve the efficiency of the proposed HAT. Also, the insights provided in this paper further prompt us to explore other techniques to compensate for the ability of ViT models to capture the high-frequency components of images.

Acknowledgments. This work is supported in part by the National Natural Science Foundation of China under Grant 62171248, and the PCNL KEY project (PCL2021A07). Li Yuan was supported in part by PKU-Shenzhen Start-Up Research Fund (1270110283) and PengCheng Laboratory.

References

1. Bao, H., Dong, L., Wei, F.: BEiT: BERT pre-training of image transformers. arXiv preprint arXiv:2106.08254 (2021)
2. Beyer, L., Hénaff, O.J., Kolesnikov, A., Zhai, X., Oord, A.V.D.: Are we done with imagenet? arXiv preprint arXiv:2006.07159 (2020)
3. Brendel, W., Bethge, M.: Approximating CNNs with bag-of-local-features models works surprisingly well on ImageNet. In: ICLR (2019)
4. Brown, T., et al.: Language models are few-shot learners. In: NeurIPS (2020)
5. Cai, Z., Vasconcelos, N.: Cascade R-CNN: delving into high quality object detection. In: CVPR (2018)
6. Campbell, F.W., Robson, J.G.: Application of Fourier analysis to the visibility of gratings. J. Physiol. **197**(3), 551 (1968)
7. Carion, N., Massa, F., Synnaeve, G., Usunier, N., Kirillov, A., Zagoruyko, S.: End-to-end object detection with transformers. In: Vedaldi, A., Bischof, H., Brox, T., Frahm, J.-M. (eds.) ECCV 2020. LNCS, vol. 12346, pp. 213–229. Springer, Cham (2020). https://doi.org/10.1007/978-3-030-58452-8_13
8. Caron, M., et al.: Emerging properties in self-supervised vision transformers. In: ICCV (2021)
9. Chen, H., et al.: Pre-trained image processing transformer. In: CVPR (2021)
10. Chen, J.N., Sun, S., He, J., Torr, P., Yuille, A., Bai, S.: TransMix: attend to mix for vision transformers. arXiv preprint arXiv:2111.09833 (2021)
11. Chen, X., Hsieh, C.J., Gong, B.: When vision transformers outperform ResNets without pre-training or strong data augmentations. In: ICLR (2022)
12. Chen, X., Xie, S., He, K.: An empirical study of training self-supervised vision transformers. In: ICCV (2021)
13. Chu, X., et al.: Twins: revisiting the design of spatial attention in vision transformers. In: NeurIPS (2021)
14. Cubuk, E.D., Zoph, B., Shlens, J., Le, Q.V.: RandAugment: practical automated data augmentation with a reduced search space. In: CVPR Workshops (2020)
15. Dai, Z., Cai, B., Lin, Y., Chen, J.: UP-DETR: unsupervised pre-training for object detection with transformers. In: CVPR (2021)
16. Das, N., et al.: Shield: fast, practical defense and vaccination for deep learning using JPEG compression. In: ACM SIGKDD (2018)
17. De Valois, R.L., De Valois, K.K.: Spatial vision. Annu. Rev. Psychol. **31**(1), 309–341 (1980)
18. Deng, J., Dong, W., Socher, R., Li, L.J., Li, K., Fei-Fei, L.: ImageNet: a large-scale hierarchical image database. In: CVPR (2009)
19. Devlin, J., Chang, M.W., Lee, K., Toutanova, K.: BERT: pre-training of deep bidirectional transformers for language understanding. In: NAACL (2019)

20. Dosovitskiy, A., et al.: An image is worth 16×16 words: transformers for image recognition at scale. In: ICLR (2020)
21. d'Ascoli, S., Touvron, H., Leavitt, M.L., Morcos, A.S., Biroli, G., Sagun, L.: ConViT: improving vision transformers with soft convolutional inductive biases. In: ICML (2021)
22. Gan, Z., Chen, Y.C., Li, L., Zhu, C., Cheng, Y., Liu, J.: Large-scale adversarial training for vision-and-language representation learning. In: NeurIPS (2020)
23. Geirhos, R., Rubisch, P., Michaelis, C., Bethge, M., Wichmann, F.A., Brendel, W.: ImageNet-trained CNNs are biased towards texture; increasing shape bias improves accuracy and robustness. In: ICLR (2018)
24. Gong, C., Wang, D., Li, M., Chandra, V., Liu, Q.: Vision transformers with patch diversification. arXiv preprint arXiv:2104.12753 (2021)
25. He, K., Chen, X., Xie, S., Li, Y., Dollár, P., Girshick, R.: Masked autoencoders are scalable vision learners. arXiv preprint arXiv:2111.06377 (2021)
26. He, K., Girshick, R., Dollár, P.: Rethinking ImageNet pre-training. In: CVPR (2019)
27. He, K., Gkioxari, G., Dollár, P., Girshick, R.: Mask R-CNN. In: ICCV (2017)
28. He, K., Zhang, X., Ren, S., Sun, J.: Deep residual learning for image recognition. In: CVPR (2016)
29. Hendrycks, D., et al.: The many faces of robustness: a critical analysis of out-of-distribution generalization. In: ICCV (2021)
30. Hendrycks, D., Dietterich, T.: Benchmarking neural network robustness to common corruptions and perturbations. In: ICLR (2018)
31. Hendrycks, D., Zhao, K., Basart, S., Steinhardt, J., Song, D.: Natural adversarial examples. In: CVPR (2021)
32. Heo, B., Yun, S., Han, D., Chun, S., Choe, J., Oh, S.J.: Rethinking spatial dimensions of vision transformers. In: ICCV (2021)
33. Herrmann, C., et al.: Pyramid adversarial training improves ViT performance. arXiv preprint arXiv:2111.15121 (2021)
34. Hou, Q., Jiang, Z., Yuan, L., Cheng, M.M., Yan, S., Feng, J.: Vision permutator: a permutable MLP-like architecture for visual recognition. IEEE Trans. Pattern Anal. Mach. Intell. (2022)
35. Huang, G., Sun, Y., Liu, Z., Sedra, D., Weinberger, K.Q.: Deep networks with stochastic depth. In: Leibe, B., Matas, J., Sebe, N., Welling, M. (eds.) ECCV 2016. LNCS, vol. 9908, pp. 646–661. Springer, Cham (2016). https://doi.org/10.1007/978-3-319-46493-0_39
36. Huang, X., Belongie, S.: Arbitrary style transfer in real-time with adaptive instance normalization. In: ICCV (2017)
37. Jiang, Z.H., et al.: All tokens matter: token labeling for training better vision transformers. In: NeurIPS (2021)
38. Lin, T.Y., et al.: Microsoft COCO: common objects in context. In: Fleet, D., Pajdla, T., Schiele, B., Tuytelaars, T. (eds.) ECCV 2014. LNCS, vol. 8693, pp. 740–755. Springer, Cham (2014). https://doi.org/10.1007/978-3-319-10602-1_48
39. Liu, Y., et al.: RoBERTa: a robustly optimized BERT pretraining approach. arXiv preprint arXiv:1907.11692 (2019)
40. Liu, Z., et al.: Swin transformer: hierarchical vision transformer using shifted windows. In: CVPR (2021)
41. Liu, Z., et al.: Feature distillation: DNN-oriented JPEG compression against adversarial examples. In: CVPR (2019)
42. Loshchilov, I., Hutter, F.: Decoupled weight decay regularization. In: ICLR (2018)

43. Madry, A., Makelov, A., Schmidt, L., Tsipras, D., Vladu, A.: Towards deep learning models resistant to adversarial attacks. In: ICLR (2018)
44. Park, N., Kim, S.: How do vision transformers work? In: ICLR (2022)
45. Paszke, A., et al.: PyTorch: an imperative style, high-performance deep learning library. In: NeurIPS (2019)
46. Radosavovic, I., Kosaraju, R.P., Girshick, R., He, K., Dollár, P.: Designing network design spaces. In: CVPR (2020)
47. Raghunathan, A., Xie, S.M., Yang, F., Duchi, J., Liang, P.: Understanding and mitigating the tradeoff between robustness and accuracy. In: ICML (2020)
48. Recht, B., Roelofs, R., Schmidt, L., Shankar, V.: Do ImageNet classifiers generalize to ImageNet? In: ICML (2019)
49. Steiner, A., Kolesnikov, A., Zhai, X., Wightman, R., Uszkoreit, J., Beyer, L.: How to train your ViT? Data, augmentation, and regularization in vision transformers. arXiv preprint arXiv:2106.10270 (2021)
50. Strudel, R., Garcia, R., Laptev, I., Schmid, C.: Segmenter: transformer for semantic segmentation. In: ICCV (2021)
51. Sun, C., Shrivastava, A., Singh, S., Gupta, A.: Revisiting unreasonable effectiveness of data in deep learning era. In: ICCV (2017)
52. Sun, Z., Cao, S., Yang, Y., Kitani, K.M.: Rethinking transformer-based set prediction for object detection. In: ICCV (2021)
53. Sweldens, W.: The lifting scheme: a construction of second generation wavelets. SIAM J. Math. Anal. **29**(2), 511–546 (1998)
54. Touvron, H., Cord, M., Douze, M., Massa, F., Sablayrolles, A., Jégou, H.: Training data-efficient image transformers & distillation through attention. In: ICML (2021)
55. Vaswani, A., et al.: Attention is all you need. In: NeurIPS (2017)
56. Wang, H., Ge, S., Lipton, Z.C., Xing, E.P.: Learning robust global representations by penalizing local predictive power. In: NeurIPS (2019)
57. Wang, H., Wu, X., Huang, Z., Xing, E.P.: High-frequency component helps explain the generalization of convolutional neural networks. In: CVPR (2020)
58. Wang, P., Zheng, W., Chen, T., Wang, Z.: Anti-oversmoothing in deep vision transformers via the Fourier domain analysis: from theory to practice. In: ICLR (2022)
59. Wang, W., et al.: Pyramid vision transformer: a versatile backbone for dense prediction without convolutions. In: ICCV (2021)
60. Wang, W., et al.: CrossFormer: a versatile vision transformer hinging on cross-scale attention. In: ICLR (2022)
61. Wang, Y., et al.: End-to-end video instance segmentation with transformers. In: CVPR (2021)
62. Wightman, R.: PyTorch image models (2019). https://github.com/rwightman/pytorch-image-models. https://doi.org/10.5281/zenodo.4414861
63. Wightman, R., Touvron, H., Jégou, H.: ResNet strikes back: an improved training procedure in TIMM. arXiv preprint arXiv:2110.00476 (2021)
64. Xiao, T., Liu, Y., Zhou, B., Jiang, Y., Sun, J.: Unified perceptual parsing for scene understanding. In: Ferrari, V., Hebert, M., Sminchisescu, C., Weiss, Y. (eds.) ECCV 2018. LNCS, vol. 11209, pp. 418–434. Springer, Cham (2018). https://doi.org/10.1007/978-3-030-01228-1_26
65. Xie, C., Tan, M., Gong, B., Wang, J., Yuille, A.L., Le, Q.V.: Adversarial examples improve image recognition. In: CVPR (2020)
66. Yang, F., Yang, H., Fu, J., Lu, H., Guo, B.: Learning texture transformer network for image super-resolution. In: CVPR (2020)

67. Yin, D., Gontijo Lopes, R., Shlens, J., Cubuk, E.D., Gilmer, J.: A Fourier perspective on model robustness in computer vision. In: NeurIPS (2019)
68. Yuan, L., et al.: Tokens-to-token ViT: training vision transformers from scratch on ImageNet. In: ICCV (2021)
69. Yuan, L., Hou, Q., Jiang, Z., Feng, J., Yan, S.: VOLO: vision outlooker for visual recognition. arXiv preprint arXiv:2106.13112 (2021)
70. Yun, S., Han, D., Oh, S.J., Chun, S., Choe, J., Yoo, Y.: CutMix: regularization strategy to train strong classifiers with localizable features. In: ICCV (2019)
71. Zeng, Y., Fu, J., Chao, H.: Learning joint spatial-temporal transformations for video inpainting. In: Vedaldi, A., Bischof, H., Brox, T., Frahm, J.-M. (eds.) ECCV 2020. LNCS, vol. 12361, pp. 528–543. Springer, Cham (2020). https://doi.org/10.1007/978-3-030-58517-4_31
72. Zhang, H., Yu, Y., Jiao, J., Xing, E., El Ghaoui, L., Jordan, M.: Theoretically principled trade-off between robustness and accuracy. In: ICML (2019)
73. Zhang, H., Cisse, M., Dauphin, Y.N., Lopez-Paz, D.: mixup: beyond empirical risk minimization. In: ICLR (2018)
74. Zhou, B., et al.: Semantic understanding of scenes through the ade20k dataset. Int. J. Comput. Vision 127(3), 302–321 (2019). https://doi.org/10.1007/s11263-018-1140-0
75. Zhou, L., Zhou, Y., Corso, J.J., Socher, R., Xiong, C.: End-to-end dense video captioning with masked transformer. In: CVPR (2018)
76. Zhu, C., Cheng, Y., Gan, Z., Sun, S., Goldstein, T., Liu, J.: FreeLB: enhanced adversarial training for natural language understanding. In: ICLR (2020)
77. Zhu, X., Su, W., Lu, L., Li, B., Wang, X., Dai, J.: Deformable DETR: deformable transformers for end-to-end object detection. In: ICLR (2020)

Recurrent Bilinear Optimization
for Binary Neural Networks

Sheng Xu[1], Yanjing Li[1], Tiancheng Wang[1], Teli Ma[2], Baochang Zhang[1,3(✉)],
Peng Gao[2], Yu Qiao[2], Jinhu Lü[1,3], and Guodong Guo[4,5]

[1] Beihang University, Beijing, China
{shengxu,yanjingli,bczhang}@buaa.edu.cn
[2] Shanghai Artificial Intelligence Laboratory, Shanghai, China
[3] Zhongguancun Laboratory, Beijing, China
[4] Institute of Deep Learning, Baidu Research, Beijing, China
[5] National Engineering Laboratory for Deep Learning Technology and Application,
Beijing, China

Abstract. Binary Neural Networks (BNNs) show great promise for real-world embedded devices. As one of the critical steps to achieve a powerful BNN, the scale factor calculation plays an essential role in reducing the performance gap to their real-valued counterparts. However, existing BNNs neglect the intrinsic bilinear relationship of real-valued weights and scale factors, resulting in a sub-optimal model caused by an insufficient training process. To address this issue, *Recurrent Bilinear Optimization* is proposed to improve the learning process of *BNNs* (RBONNs) by associating the intrinsic bilinear variables in the back propagation process. Our work is the first attempt to optimize BNNs from the bilinear perspective. Specifically, we employ a recurrent optimization and Density-ReLU to sequentially backtrack the sparse real-valued weight filters, which will be sufficiently trained and reach their performance limits based on a controllable learning process. We obtain robust RBONNs, which show impressive performance over state-of-the-art BNNs on various models and datasets. Particularly, on the task of object detection, RBONNs have great generalization performance. Our code is open-sourced on https://github.com/SteveTsui/RBONN.

Keywords: Binary neural network · Bilinear optimization · Image classification · Object detection

1 Introduction

Computer vision has been rapidly promoted, with the widespread application of convolutional neural networks (CNNs) in image classification [8,37], semantic segmentation [9], and object detection [6,22]. It does, however, come with a huge demand for memory and computing resources. These computation and

---

S. Xu, Y. Li—Equal Contribution.

S. Avidan et al. (Eds.): ECCV 2022, LNCS 13684, pp. 19–35, 2022.
https://doi.org/10.1007/978-3-031-20053-3_2

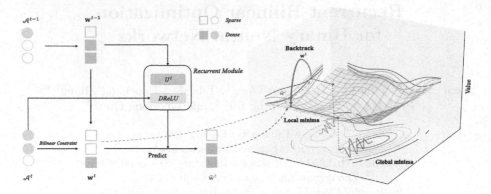

Fig. 1. An illustration of the RBONN framework. Conventional gradient-based algorithms assume that the hidden variables in bilinear models are independent, which causes an insufficient training of **w** due to neglecting the relationship with $\mathcal{A}$ as shown in the loss surface (right part). Our RBONN can help **w** escape from local minima (green dotted line) and achieve a better solution (red dotted line). (Color figure online)

memory costs are incompatible with the computing capabilities of devices, particularly those with low resources, *e.g.*, mobile phones and embedded devices. As a result, substantial research has been invested to reduce storage and computation cost. To accomplish this, a number of compression methods for efficient inference have been proposed, including network pruning [13,15,16], low-rank decomposition [5,20], network quantization [18,29,34], and knowledge distillation [36]. Network quantization, for example, is particularly well suited for using on embedded devices since it decreases the bit-width of network weights and activations. Binarization, a particularly aggressive kind of quantization, reduces CNN parameters and activations into 1 bit, reducing memory usage by 32× and calculation costs by 58× [34]. Binarized neural networks (BNNs) are employed for a wide range of applications, such as image classification [28,29,34], object detection [41,43] and point cloud recognition [42]. With high energy-efficiency, they are potent to be directly applied on AI chips. However, due to the limited representation capabilities, BNNs' performance remains considerably inferior to that of their real-valued counterparts.

Previous methods [10,24] compute scale factors by approximating the real-valued weight filter **w** such that $\mathbf{w} \approx \alpha \circ \mathbf{b}^{\mathbf{w}}$, where $\alpha \in \mathbb{R}_+$ is the scale factor (vector) and $\mathbf{b}^{\mathbf{w}} = \text{sign}(\mathbf{w})$ to enhance the representation capability of BNNs. In essence, the approximation can be considered as a bilinear optimization problem with the objective function as

$$\underset{\mathbf{w},\alpha}{\arg\min}\, G(\mathbf{w}, \alpha) = \|\mathbf{w} - \alpha \circ \mathbf{b}^{\mathbf{w}}\|_2^2 + R(\mathbf{w}),$$

or

$$\underset{\mathbf{w},\mathcal{A}}{\arg\min}\, G(\mathbf{w}, \mathcal{A}) = \|\mathbf{b}^{\mathbf{w}} - \mathcal{A}\mathbf{w}\|_2^2 + R(\mathbf{w}), \tag{1}$$

where $\mathcal{A} = diag(\frac{1}{\alpha_1}, \cdots, \frac{1}{\alpha_N})$, N is the number of elements in α. $\circ$ denotes the channel-wise multiplication, and $R(\cdot)$ represents the regularization, typically the ℓ_1 or ℓ_2 norm. $G(\mathbf{w}, \mathcal{A})$ includes a bilinear form of $\mathcal{A}\mathbf{w}$ widely used in the field of computer vision [4,14,30]. Note that the bilinear function is $\mathcal{A}\mathbf{w}$ rather than $G(\mathbf{w}, \mathcal{A})$ in Eq. 1. Equation 1 is rational for BNNs with $\mathcal{A}$ and $\mathbf{w}$ as bilinear coupled variables, since $\mathbf{w}$ is the variable and $\mathbf{b}^{\mathbf{w}}$ is just the sign of $\mathbf{w}$. However, such bilinear constraints will lead to an asynchronous convergence problem and directly affect the learning process of $\mathcal{A}$ and $\mathbf{w}$. We can know that the variable with a slower convergence speed (usually $\mathbf{w}$) is **not as sufficiently** trained as another faster one. Moreover, BNNs are based on non-convex optimization, and will suffer more from local minima problem due to such an asynchronous convergence. A powerful instance is that $\mathbf{w}$ will tendentiously fall into the local optimum with low magnitude when the magnitude of $\mathcal{A}$ is much larger than 0 (due to $\mathbf{b}^{\mathbf{w}} \in \{-1, +1\}$). On the contrary, $\mathbf{w}$ will have a large magnitude and thus slowly converge when elements of $\mathcal{A}$ are close to 0.

In this paper, we introduce a recurrent bilinear optimization for binary neural networks (RBONNs) by learning the coupled scale factor and real-valued weight end-to-end. More specifically, recurrent optimization can efficiently backtrack the weights, which will be more sufficiently trained than conventional methods. To this end, a Density-ReLU (DReLU) is introduced to activate the optimization process based on the density of the variable $\mathcal{A}$. In this way, we achieve a controlled learning process with a backtracking mechanism by considering the interaction of variables, thus avoiding the local minima and reaching the performance limit of BNNs, as shown in Fig. 1. Our contributions can be summarized as

- We are the first attempt to address BNNs as a bilinear optimization problem. A recurrent bilinear optimization is introduced for BNNs (RBONNs), which can more sufficiently train BNNs and approach its performance limit.
- A Density-ReLU (DReLU) is introduced to activate the optimization process based on the interaction of BNN variables, which can efficiently improve the training process of BNNs.
- Extensive experiments show that the proposed RBONN outperforms state-of-the-art BNNs on a variety of tasks, including image classification and object detection. For instance, on ImageNet, the 1-bit ResNet-18 achieved by RBONN obtains 66.7% Top-1 accuracy, outperforming all prior BNNs and achieving a new state-of-the-art.

2   Related Work

Bilinear Models in Deep Learning. Under certain circumstances, bilinear models can be used in CNNs. One important application, network pruning, is among the hottest topics in the deep learning community [21,30]. The vital feature maps and related channels are pruned using bilinear models [30]. Iterative methods, *e.g.*, the Fast Iterative Shrinkage-Thresholding Algorithm (FISTA) [21] and the Accelerated Proximal Gradient (APG) [14] can be used to prune bilinear-based networks. Many deep learning applications, such as fine-grained categorization [17,23], visual question answering (VQA) [46], and person re-identification [39], are promoted by embedding bilinear models into CNNs, which model pairwise feature interactions and fuse multiple features with attention.

Binary Neural Network. Based on BinaryConnect, BinaryNet [3] trains CNNs with binary parameters. By binarizing the weights and inputs of the convolution layer, the XNOR-Net [34] improves the efficiency of CNNs. Based on a discrete backpropagation process, a binarization approach is proposed in [10] to learn improved BNNs.

ReActNet [28] substitutes the traditiona sign function and PReLU [11] with RSign and RPReLU based on learnable thresholds, resulting in improved BNN performance. RBNN [19] rotates the real-valued weights for fruitful information, thus improving the feature representation of BNNs. SLB [45] introduces the NAS [26] into the binarization of weights.

Unlike prior work, our work is the first attempt to solve BNNs as a bilinear optimization problem. We achieve training BNNs sufficiently to bridge the performance gap between them and their real-valued equivalents.

3 Methodology

In this section, we describes RBONN in detail. We first describe the bilinear model of BNNs, then introduce a recurrent bilinear optimization method to calculate BNNs, followed by a summary of the whole training process. For a better presentation of our approach, we first briefly describe the preliminaries.

3.1 Preliminaries

In a specific convolution layer, $\mathbf{w} \in \mathbb{R}^{C_{out} \times C_{in} \times K \times K}$, $\mathbf{a}_{in} \in \mathbb{R}^{C_{in} \times W_{in} \times H_{in}}$, and $\mathbf{a}_{out} \in \mathbb{R}^{C_{out} \times W_{out} \times H_{out}}$ represent its weights and feature maps, where C_{in} and C_{out} represents the number of channels. (H, W) are the height and width of the feature maps, and K denotes the kernel size. We then have

$$\mathbf{a}_{out} = \mathbf{a}_{in} \otimes \mathbf{w}, \tag{2}$$

where $\otimes$ is the convolution operation. We omit the batch normalization (BN) and activation layers for simplicity. The 1-bit model aims to quantize $\mathbf{w}$ and $\mathbf{a}_{in}$ into $\mathbf{b}^{\mathbf{w}} \in \{-1, +1\}^{C_{out} \times C_{in} \times K \times K}$ and $\mathbf{b}^{\mathbf{a}_{in}} \in \{-1, +1\}^{C_{in} \times W_{in} \times H_{in}}$ using the efficient XNOR and Bit-count operations to replace real-valued operations. Following [34], the forward process of the BNN is

$$\mathbf{a}_{out} = \mathbf{b}^{\mathbf{a}_{in}} \odot (\mathcal{A}^{-1} \mathbf{b}^{\mathbf{w}}), \tag{3}$$

where $\odot$ denotes the efficient XNOR and Bit-count operations. We divide the data flow in BNNs into units for detailed discussions. In BNNs, the original output $\mathbf{a}_{out}$ is first scaled by a channel-wise scale factor (matrix) $\mathcal{A} =$

$diag(\frac{1}{\alpha_1}, \cdots, \frac{1}{\alpha_{C_{out}}}) \in \mathbb{R}_+^{C_{out} \times C_{out}}$ to modulate the amplitude of full-precision counterparts. It then enters several non-linear layers, *e.g.*, BN layer, non-linear activation layer, and max-pooling layer. We omit these for simplification. And then, the output is $\mathbf{a}_{out}$ via the sign function. Then, $\mathbf{b^{a_{out}}}$ can be utilized for the efficient operations of the next layer.

3.2   Bilinear Model of BNNs

We formulate the optimization of BNNs as

$$\underset{\mathbf{w}, \mathcal{A}}{\arg \min} \, L_S(\mathbf{w}, \mathcal{A}) + \lambda G(\mathbf{w}, \mathcal{A}), \tag{4}$$

where λ is the hyper-parameter. G contains the bilinear part as mentioned in Eq. 1. $\mathbf{w}$ and $\mathcal{A}$ formulate a pair of coupled variables. Thus, the conventional gradient descent method can be used to solve the bilinear optimization problem as

$$\mathcal{A}^{t+1} = |\mathcal{A}^t - \eta_1 \frac{\partial L}{\partial \mathcal{A}^t}|, \tag{5}$$

$$
\begin{aligned}
(\frac{\partial L}{\partial \mathcal{A}^t})^T &= (\frac{\partial L_S}{\partial \mathcal{A}^t})^T + \lambda (\frac{\partial G}{\partial \mathcal{A}^t})^T, \\
&= (\frac{\partial L_S}{\partial \mathbf{a}_{out}^t} \frac{\partial \mathbf{a}_{out}^t}{\partial \mathcal{A}^t})^T + \lambda \mathbf{w}^t (\mathcal{A}^t \mathbf{w}^t - \mathbf{b}^{\mathbf{w}^t})^T, \\
&= (\frac{\partial L_S}{\partial \mathbf{a}_{out}^t})^T (\mathbf{b}^{\mathbf{a}_{in}^t} \odot \mathbf{b}^{\mathbf{w}^t})(\mathcal{A}^t)^{-2} + \lambda \mathbf{w}^t \hat{G}(\mathbf{w}^t, \mathcal{A}^t),
\end{aligned}
\tag{6}
$$

where η_1 is the learning rate, $\hat{G}(\mathbf{w}^t, \mathcal{A}^t) = (\mathcal{A}^t \mathbf{w}^t - \mathbf{b}^{\mathbf{w}^t})^T$. Conventional gradient descent algorithm for bilinear models iteratively optimizes one variable while keeping the other fixed. This is actually a sub-optimal solution due to ignoring the relationship of the two hidden variables in optimization. For example, when $\mathbf{w}$ approaches zero due to the sparsity regularization term $R(\mathbf{w})$, $\mathcal{A}$ will have a larger magnitude due to G (Eq. 1). Consequently, both the first and second values of Eq. 6 will be suppressed dramatically, causing the gradient vanishing problem for $\mathcal{A}$. Contrarily, if $\mathcal{A}$ changes little during optimization, $\mathbf{w}$ will also suffer from the vanished gradient problem due to the supervision of G, causing a local minima. Due to the coupling relationship of $\mathbf{w}$ and $\mathcal{A}$, the gradient calculation for $\mathbf{w}$ is challenging.

3.3   Recurrent Bilinear Optimization

We solve the problem in Eq. 1 from a new perspective that $\mathbf{w}$ and $\mathcal{A}$ are coupled. We aim to prevent $\mathcal{A}$ from going denser and $\mathbf{w}$ from going sparser, as analyzed above. Firstly, based on the chain rule and its notations in [32], we have the scalar form of the update rule for $\widehat{w}_{i,j}$ as

$$
\begin{aligned}
\widehat{\mathbf{w}}_{i,j}^{t+1} &= \mathbf{w}_{i,j}^t - \eta_2 \frac{\partial L_S}{\partial \mathbf{w}_{i,j}^t} - \eta_2 \lambda (\frac{\partial G}{\partial \mathbf{w}_{i,j}^t} + Tr((\frac{\partial G}{\partial \mathcal{A}^t})^T \frac{\partial \mathcal{A}^t}{\partial \mathbf{w}_{i,j}^t})), \\
&= \mathbf{w}_{i,j}^{t+1} - \eta_2 \lambda Tr(\mathbf{w}^t \hat{G}(\mathbf{w}^t, \mathcal{A}^t) \frac{\partial \mathcal{A}^t}{\partial \mathbf{w}_{i,j}^t}),
\end{aligned}
\tag{7}
$$

which is based on $w_{i,j}^{t+1} = w_{i,j}^t - \eta_2 \frac{\partial L}{\partial w_{i,j}^t}$. $\hat{\mathbf{w}}^{t+1}$ denotes $\mathbf{w}$ at the $t+1$-th iteration when considering the coupling of $\mathbf{w}$ and $\mathcal{A}$. When computing the gradient of the coupled variable $\mathbf{w}$, the gradient of its coupled variable $\mathcal{A}$ should also be considered using the chain rule. Vanilla $\mathbf{w}^{t+1}$ denotes the computed $\mathbf{w}$ at $t + 1$-th iteration without considering the coupling relationship. Here we denote $I = C_{out}$ and $J = C_{in} \times K \times K$ for simplicity. With writing $\mathbf{w}$ into a row vector $[\mathbf{w}_1, \cdots, \mathbf{w}_I]^T$ and writing $\hat{G}$ into a column vector $[\hat{g}_1, \cdots, \hat{g}_I]$ and using $i = 1, \cdots, I$ and $j = 1, \cdots, J$, we can see that $\mathcal{A}_{i,i}$ and w_{nj} are independent when $\forall n \neq j$. Omitting superscript $\cdot^t$, we have the i-th component of $\frac{\partial \mathcal{A}}{\partial \mathbf{w}}$ as

$$
(\frac{\partial \mathcal{A}}{\partial \mathbf{w}})_i = \begin{bmatrix} 0 & \cdots & \cdot & \cdots & 0 \\ \cdot & & \cdot & & \cdot \\ \frac{\partial \mathcal{A}_{i,i}}{\partial w_{i,1}} & \cdots & \frac{\partial \mathcal{A}_{i,i}}{\partial w_{i,j}} & \cdots & \frac{\partial \mathcal{A}_{i,i}}{\partial w_{i,J}} \\ \cdot & & \cdot & & \cdot \\ 0 & \cdots & \cdot & \cdots & 0 \end{bmatrix}, \tag{8}
$$

we can derive

$$
\mathbf{w}\hat{G}(\mathbf{w}, \mathcal{A}) = \begin{bmatrix} \mathbf{w}_1\hat{g}_1 & \cdots & \mathbf{w}_1\hat{g}_i & \cdots & \mathbf{w}_1\hat{g}_I \\ \cdot & & \cdot & & \cdot \\ \cdot & & \cdot & & \cdot \\ \cdot & & \cdot & & \cdot \\ \mathbf{w}_I\hat{g}_1 & \cdots & \mathbf{w}_I\hat{g}_i & \cdots & \mathbf{w}_I\hat{g}_I \end{bmatrix}. \tag{9}
$$

Combine Eq. 8 and Eq. 9, we get

$$
\mathbf{w}\hat{G}(\mathbf{w}, \mathcal{A})(\frac{\partial \mathcal{A}}{\partial \mathbf{w}})_i = \begin{bmatrix} \mathbf{w}_1\hat{g}_i\frac{\partial \mathcal{A}_{i,i}}{\partial w_{i,1}} & \cdots & \cdots & \mathbf{w}_1\hat{g}_i\frac{\partial \mathcal{A}_{i,i}}{\partial w_{i,j}} \\ \cdot & & \cdot & & \cdot \\ \mathbf{w}_i\hat{g}_i\frac{\partial \mathcal{A}_{i,i}}{\partial w_{i,1}} & \cdots & \cdots & \mathbf{w}_i\hat{g}_i\frac{\partial \mathcal{A}_{i,i}}{\partial w_{i,J}} \\ \cdot & & \cdot & & \cdot \\ \mathbf{w}_I\hat{g}_i\frac{\partial \mathcal{A}_{i,i}}{\partial w_{i,1}} & \cdots & \cdots & \mathbf{w}_I\hat{g}_i\frac{\partial \mathcal{A}_{i,i}}{\partial w_{iJ}} \end{bmatrix}. \tag{10}
$$

After that, the i-th component of the trace item in Eq. 7 is then calculated by:

$$
Tr[\mathbf{w}\hat{G}(\frac{\partial \mathcal{A}}{\partial \mathbf{w}})_i] = \mathbf{w}_i\hat{g}_i \sum_{j=1}^{J} \frac{\partial \mathcal{A}_{i,i}}{\partial w_{i,j}} \tag{11}
$$

Combining Eq. 7 and Eq. 11, we can get

$$
\hat{\mathbf{w}}^{t+1} = \mathbf{w}^{t+1} - \eta_2\lambda \begin{bmatrix} \hat{g}_1^t \sum_{j=1}^{J} \frac{\partial \mathcal{A}_{1,1}^t}{\partial w_{1,j}^t} \\ \cdot \\ \cdot \\ \cdot \\ \hat{g}_I^t \sum_{j=1}^{J} \frac{\partial \mathcal{A}_{I,I}^t}{\partial w_{I,j}^t} \end{bmatrix} \circledast \begin{bmatrix} \mathbf{w}_1^t \\ \cdot \\ \cdot \\ \cdot \\ \mathbf{w}_I^t \end{bmatrix} \tag{12}
$$

$$
= \mathbf{w}^{t+1} + \eta_2\lambda \boldsymbol{d}^t \circledast \mathbf{w}^t,
$$

where η_2 is the learning rate of real-valued weight filters $\mathbf{w}_i$, $\circledast$ denotes the Hadamard product. We take $\boldsymbol{d}^t = -[\hat{g}_1^t \sum_{j=1}^J \frac{\partial \mathcal{A}_{1,1}^t}{\partial \mathbf{w}_{1,j}^t}, \cdots, \hat{g}_I^t \sum_{j=1}^J \frac{\partial \mathcal{A}_{I,i}^t}{\partial \mathbf{w}_{I,j}^t}]^T$, which is unsolvable and undefined in the back propagation of BNNs. To address this issue, we employ a recurrent model to approximate d^t and have

$$\hat{\mathbf{w}}^{t+1} = \mathbf{w}^{t+1} + U^t \circ DReLU(\mathbf{w}^t, \mathcal{A}^t), \tag{13}$$

and

$$\mathbf{w}^{t+1} \leftarrow \hat{\mathbf{w}}^{t+1}, \tag{14}$$

where we introduce a hidden layer with channel-wise learnable weights $U \in \mathbb{R}_+^{C_{out}}$ to recurrently backtrack the $\mathbf{w}$. To realize a controllable recurrent optimization, we present $DReLU$ to supervise such an optimization process. We channel-wise implement $DReLU$ as

$$DReLU(\mathbf{w}_i, \mathcal{A}_i) = \begin{cases} \mathbf{w}_i & if \ (\neg D(\mathbf{w}_i')) \wedge D(\mathcal{A}_i) = 1, \\ 0 & otherwise, \end{cases} \tag{15}$$

where $\mathbf{w}' = diag(\|\mathbf{w}_1\|_1, \cdots, \|\mathbf{w}_{C_{out}}\|_1)$. And we judge when an asynchronous convergence happens in the optimization based on $(\neg D(\mathbf{w}_i')) \wedge D(\mathcal{A}_i) = 1$, where the density function is defined as

$$D(\boldsymbol{x}_i) = \begin{cases} 1 & if \ ranking(\sigma(\boldsymbol{x})_i) > \mathcal{T}, \\ 0 & otherwise, \end{cases} \tag{16}$$

where $\mathcal{T}$ is defined by $\mathcal{T} = int(C_{out} \times \tau)$. τ is the hyper-parameter denoting the threshold. $\sigma(\boldsymbol{x})_i$ denotes the i-th eigenvalue of diagonal matrix $\boldsymbol{x}$, and $\boldsymbol{x}_i$ denotes the i-th row of matrix $\boldsymbol{x}$. Finally, we define the optimization of U and as

$$U^{t+1} = |U^t - \eta_3 \frac{\partial L}{\partial U^t}|, \tag{17}$$

$$\frac{\partial L}{\partial U^t} = \frac{\partial L_S}{\partial \mathbf{w}^t} \circ DReLU(\mathbf{w}^{t-1}, \mathcal{A}^t), \tag{18}$$

where η_3 is the learning rate of U. We elaborate on the training process of RBONN outlined in Algorithm 1.

3.4   Discussion

In this section, we first review the related methods on "gradient approximation" of BNNs, and then further discuss the difference of RBONN with the related methods and analyze the effectiveness of the proposed RBONN.

In particular, BNN [3] directly unitize the Straight-Through-Estimator in training stage to calculate the gradient of weights and activations as

$$\frac{\partial \mathbf{b}^{\mathbf{w}_{i,j}}}{\partial \mathbf{w}_{i,j}} = 1_{|\mathbf{w}_{i,j}|<1}, \quad \frac{\partial \mathbf{b}^{\mathbf{a}_{i,j}}}{\partial \mathbf{a}_{i,j}} = 1_{|\mathbf{a}_{i,j}|<1} \tag{19}$$

Algorithm 1. RBONN training.

Input: a minibatch of inputs and their labels, real-valued weights $\mathbf{w}$, recurrent model weights U, scale factor matrix $\mathcal{A}$, learning rates η_1, η_2 and η_3.

Output: updated real-valued weights $\mathbf{w}^{t+1}$, updated scale factor matrix $\mathcal{A}^{t+1}$, and updated recurrent model weights U^{t+1}.

1: **while** Forward propagation **do**
2:     $\mathbf{b}^{\mathbf{w}^t} \leftarrow \text{sign}(\mathbf{w}^t)$.
3:     $\mathbf{b}^{\mathbf{a}^t_{in}} \leftarrow \text{sign}(\mathbf{a}^t_{in})$.
4:     Features calculation using Eq. 3
5:     Loss calculation using Eq. 4
6: **end while**
7: **while** Backward propagation **do**
8:     Computing $\frac{\partial L}{\partial \mathcal{A}^t}$, $\frac{\partial L}{\partial \mathbf{w}^t}$, and $\frac{\partial L}{\partial U^t}$ using Eq. 6, 7 and 18.
9:     Update $\mathcal{A}^{t+1}$, $\mathbf{w}^{t+1}$, and U^{t+1} according to Eqs. 5, 13, and 17, respectively.
10: **end while**

---

which suffers from an obvious gradient mismatch between the gradient of the binarization function. Intuitively, Bi-Real Net [29] designs an approximate binarization function can help to relieve the gradient mismatch in the backward propagation as

$$\frac{\partial \mathbf{b}^{\mathbf{a}_{i,j}}}{\partial \mathbf{a}_{i,j}} = \begin{cases} 2 + 2\mathbf{a}_{i,j}, & -1 \leq \mathbf{a}_{i,j} < 0, \\ 2 - 2\mathbf{a}_{i,j}, & 0 \leq \mathbf{a}_{i,j} < 1, \\ 0, & otherwise, \end{cases} \tag{20}$$

which is termed as ApproxSign function and used for back-propagation gradient calculation of the activation. Compared to the traditional STE, ApproxSign has a close shape to that of the original binarization function sign, and thus the activation gradient error can be controlled to some extent. Likewise, CBCN [25] applies an approximate function to address the gradient mismatch from the sign function. MetaQuant [1] introduces Metalearning to learning the gradient error of weights by a neural network. The IR-Net [33] includes a self-adaptive Error Decay Estimator (EDE) to reduce the gradient error in training, which considers different requirements on different stages of the training process and balances the update ability of parameters and reduction of gradient error. RBNN [19] proposes a training-aware approximation of the sign function for gradient backpropagation.

In summary, prior arts focus on approximating the gradient derived from $\frac{\partial \mathbf{b}^{\mathbf{a}}}{\partial \mathbf{a}_{i,j}}$ or $\frac{\partial \mathbf{b}^{\mathbf{w}}}{\partial \mathbf{w}_{i,j}}$. Differently, our approach focuses on a different perspective of gradient approximation, *i.e.*, gradient from $\frac{\partial G}{\partial \mathbf{w}_{i,j}}$. Our goal is to decouple $\mathcal{A}$ and $\mathbf{w}$ to improve the gradient calculation of $\mathbf{w}$. RBONN manipulates $\mathbf{w}$'s gradient from its bilinear coupling variable $\mathcal{A}$ $\left(\frac{\partial G(\mathcal{A})}{\partial \mathbf{w}_{i,j}}\right)$. More specifically, our RBONN can be combined with prior arts, by comprehensively considering $\frac{\partial L_s}{\partial \mathbf{a}_{i,j}}$, $\frac{\partial L_s}{\partial \mathbf{w}_{i,j}}$ and $\frac{\partial G}{\partial \mathbf{w}_{i,j}}$ in the back propagation process.

4   Experiments

Our RBONNs are evaluated first on image classification and then on object detection tasks. First, we introduce the implementation details of RBONNs. Then we validate the effectiveness of components in the ablation study. Finally, we illustrate the superiority of RBONNs by comparing our method with state-of-the-art BNNs on various tasks.

4.1   Datasets and Implementation Details

Datasets. For its huge scope and diversity, the ImageNet object classification dataset [37] is more demanding, which has 1000 classes, 1.2 million training photos, and 50k validation images.

Natural images from 20 different classes are included in the VOC datasets. We use the VOC `trainval2007` and VOC `trainval2012` sets to train our model, which contains around 16k images, and the VOC `test2007` set to evaluate our IDa-Det, which contains 4952 images. We utilize the mean average precision (mAP) as the evaluation matrices, as suggested by [6].

The COCO dataset includes images from 80 different categories. All of our COCO dataset experiments are performed on the object detection track of the COCO `trainval35k` training dataset, which consists of 80k images from the COCO `train2014` dataset and 35k images sampled from the COCO `val2014` dataset. We report the average precision (AP) for IoUs $\in [0.5 : 0.05 : 0.95]$, designated as mAP@[.5, .95], using COCO's standard evaluation metric. For further analyzing our method, we also report AP_{50}, AP_{75}, AP_s, AP_m, and AP_l.

Implementation Details. PyTorch [31] is used to implement RBONN. We run the experiments on 4 NVIDIA GTX 2080Ti GPUs with 11 GB memory. Following [29], we retain the first layer, shortcut, and last layer in the networks as real-valued. We modify the architecture of the BNNs with extra shortcuts, and PReLU [11] following [29] and [10], respectively.

For the image classification task, ResNets [12] and ReActNets [28] are employed as the backbone networks to build our RBONNs. We offer two implementation setups for fair comparison. First, we use **one-stage training** on ResNets, using Adam as the optimization algorithm, and a weight decay of $1e-5$. η_1 and η_2 are both set to $1e-3$. η_3 is set as $1e-4$. The learning rates are optimized by the annealing cosine learning rate schedule. The number of epochs is set as 200. Then, we employ **two-stage training** on ReActNets following [28]. Each stage counts 256 epochs. Thus the number of epochs is set as 512. In this implementation, Adam is selected as the optimizer. And the network is supervised by real-valued ResNet-34 teacher. The weight decay is set following [28]. The learning rates $\{\eta_1, \eta_2, \eta_3\}$ are set as $\{1e-3, 1e-4, 1e-4\}$ respectively and annealed to 0 by linear descent.

We use the Faster-RCNN [35] and SSD [27] detection frameworks, which are based on ResNet-18 [12] and VGG-16 [38] backbone, respectively, to train our

RBONN for the object detection task. We pre-train the backbone for image classification using ImageNet ILSVRC12 [37] and fine-tune the detector on the dataset for object detection. For SSD and Faster-RCNN, the batch size is set to 16 and 8, respectively, with applying SGD optimizer. Both η_1 and η_2 are equal to 0.008. The value of η_3 is set to 0.001. We use the same structure and training settings as BiDet [41] on the SSD framework.

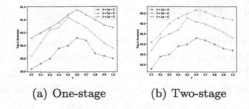

(a) One-stage   (b) Two-stage

Fig. 2. Effect of hyper-parameters λ and τ on one-stage and two-stage training using 1-bit ResNet-18.

4.2 Ablation Study

Hyper-Parameter λ and τ. The most important hyper-parameter of RBONN are λ and τ, which control the proportion of L_R and the threshold of backtracking in recurrent bilinear optimization. On ImageNet for 1-bit ResNet-18, the effect of hyper-parameters λ and τ is evaluated under both one-stage and two-stage training. RBONN's performance is demonstrated in Fig. 2, where λ is varied from $1e-3$ to $1e-5$ and τ is varied from 1 to 0.1. As can be observed, with λ reducing, performance improves at first before plummeting. When we increase τ in both implementations, the same trend emerges. As demonstrated in Fig. 2, when λ is set to $1e-4$ and τ is set to 0.6, 1-bit ResNet-18 generated by our RBONN gets the best performance. As a result, we apply this set of hyper-parameters to the remaining experiments in this paper. Note that the recurrent model does not effect when τ is set as 1.

Weight and Scale Factor Distribution. We first analyze the weight distribution of training ReActNet [28] and RBONN for comparison to analyze the sparsity of **w**. For a 1-bit ResNet-18, we analyze the 1-st and 6-th 1-bit convolution layer of ResNet-18. The distribution of weights (before binarization) for ReActNet and our RBONN is shown in the left section of Fig. 3. The weight values for ReActNet can be seen to be closely mixed up around the zero centers, and the value magnitude remains sparse. Thus the binarization results are far less robust to any possible disturbance. In contrast, our RBONN gains weight forming a bi-modal distribution, which achieves its robustness against disturbances. Moreover, we plot the distribution of non-zero elements in scale matrix $\mathcal{A}$ in the right part of Fig. 3. The scale values of our RBONN is less dense compared with ReActNet. Thus, the result demonstrates that our RBONN prevents $\mathcal{A}$ from going denser and **w** from going sparser, which validates our motivation.

4.3 Image Classification

We first show the experimental results on ImageNet with ResNet-18 [12] backbone in Table 1. We compare RBONN with BNN [2], XNOR-Net [34], Bi-Real

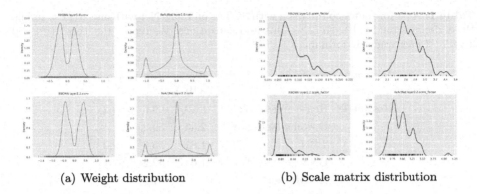

(a) Weight distribution   (b) Scale matrix distribution

Fig. 3. Weight (red) and scale matrix (blue) distribution of the RBONN and ReActNet in 1-bit ResNet-18 with two-stage training. (Color figure online)

Net [29], IR-Net [33], BONN [47], RBCN [24], and RBNN [19]. We also report mult-bit DoReFa-Net [48], and TBN [40] for further reference. RBONN outperforms all of the evaluated binary models in both Top-1 and Top-5 accuracy, as shown in Table 1. RBONN achieves 61.4% and 83.4% in Top-1 and Top-5 accuracy using ResNet-18, respectively, with 1.8% and 1.9% increases over state-of-the-art RBNN. In this paper, we use memory usage and OPs following [29] in comparison to other tasks for further reference. We also analyze the inference speed on hardware in Sect. 4.5.

Furthermore, we compare with ReActNet [28] using the same architecture. It uses full-precision parameters, data augmentation, knowledge distillation, and a computationally intensive two-step training setting with 512 epochs in total. We use the same implementation as [28] to evaluate our RBONN to ReActNet. As shown in Table 2, our method still achieves an impressive 0.8% Top-1 accuracy improvement on the same ResNet-18 backbone, which verifies the effectiveness of our method. Also, our method outperforms state-of-the-are ReCU [44] by 0.3% Top-1 accuracy. Moreover, we evaluate the performance of our RBONN on another strong backbone, *i.e.,*, ReActNet-A. Our strategy improves Top-1 accuracy by 1.2% on ReActNet-A, which is substantial on the ImageNet dataset classification challenge.

In a word, when compared to several BNN methods, our RBONN achieves the best performance on the large-scale ImageNet dataset, proving that our method achieves a new state-of-the-art on image classification tasks.

4.4 Object Detection

PASCAL VOC. On the PASCAL VOC datasets, we compare the proposed RBONN against existing state-of-the-art BNNs, such as XNOR-Net [34], Bi-Real-Net [29], and BiDet [41], on the same framework for object detection. The detection result of multi-bit quantized networks DoReFa-Net [48] is also reported. In Table 3, we show the results for 1-bit Faster-RCNN [35] on VOC

Table 1. A performance comparison with SOTAs on ImageNet with one-stage training. W/A denotes the bit length of weights and activations. We report the Top-1 (%) and Top-5 (%) accuracy performances.

Network	Method	W/A	OPs ($\times 10^8$)	Top-1	Top-5
ResNet-18	Real-valued	32/32	18.19	69.6	89.2
	DoReFa-Net	1/4	2.44	59.2	81.5
	TBN	1/2	1.81	55.6	79.0
	BNN	1/1	1.63	42.2	67.1
	XNOR-Net			51.2	73.2
	Bi-Real Net			56.4	79.5
	IR-Net			58.1	80.0
	BONN			59.3	81.6
	RBCN			59.5	81.6
	RBNN			59.6	81.6
	RBONN			**61.4**	**83.5**

Table 2. A performance comparison with ReActNet [28] on ImageNet using two-stage training. W/A denotes the bit length of weights and activations. We report the Top-1 (%) and Top-5 (%) accuracy performances.

Network	Method	W/A	OPs ($\times 10^8$)	Top-1	Top-5
ResNet-18	Real-valued	32/32	18.19	69.6	89.2
	ReActNet	1/1	1.63	65.9	–
	ReCU			66.4	86.5
	RBONN			**66.7**	**87.0**
ReActNet-A	Real-valued	32/32	48.32	72.4	–
	ReActNet	1/1	0.87	69.4	–
	RBONN			**70.6**	**89.0**

test2007 from lines 2 to 7. With 50.63× and 19.87× rate, our RBONN greatly accelerates and compresses the Faster-RCNN with ResNet-18 backbone. We see significant improvements with our RBONN over other methods as compared to 1-bit approaches. With the same memory utilization and FLOPs, our RBONN outperforms XNOR-Net, Bi-Real-Net, and BiDet by 17.0%, 7.2%, and 5.9% mAP, which is substantial on the object detection task.

For the SSD [27] with VGG-16 backbone, The bottom section in Table 3 shows that our RBONN can save the computation and storage by 14.76× and 4.81×, as compared to real-valued alternatives. The difference in performance is rather slight (69.4% *vs.* 74.3%). Moreover, compared with other 1-bit SOTAs, our

Table 3. Comparison of memory usage, OPs, and mAP (%) with state-of-the-art BNNs in SOTA binarized detection frameworks on VOC `test2007`.

Framework	Input resolution	Backbone	Method	W/A	Memory usage (MB)	OPs ($\times 10^9$)	mAP
Faster-RCNN	1000 × 600	ResNet-18	Real-valued	32/32	47.48	434.39	74.6
			DoReFa-Net	4/4	6.73	55.90	71.0
			XNOR-Net	1/1	2.39	8.58	48.4
			Bi-Real Net				58.2
			BiDet				59.5
			RBONN				**65.4**
SSD	300 × 300	VGG-16	Real-valued	32/32	105.16	31.44	74.3
			DoReFa-Net	4/4	29.58	6.67	69.2
			XNOR-Net	1/1	21.88	2.13	50.2
			Bi-Real Net				58.2
			BiDet				66.0
			RBONN				**69.4**

Table 4. Comparison of mAP@[.5, .95] (%), AP (%) with different IoU threshold and AP for objects in various sizes with SOTA 1-bit detectors on COCO `minival`.

Framework	Input resolution	Backbone	Method	mAP @[.5, .95]	AP_{50}	AP_{75}	AP_s	AP_m	AP_1
Faster R-CNN	1000 × 600	ResNet-18	Real-valued	26.0	44.8	27.2	10.0	28.9	39.7
			DoReFa-Net	22.9	38.6	23.7	8.0	24.9	36.3
			Xnor-Net	10.4	21.6	8.8	2.7	11.8	15.9
			Bi-Real Net	14.4	29.0	13.4	3.7	15.4	24.1
			BiDet	15.7	31.0	14.4	4.9	16.7	25.4
			RBONN	**20.6**	**37.3**	**19.9**	**7.4**	**21.3**	**32.8**
SSD	300 × 300	VGG-16	Real-valued	23.2	41.2	23.4	5.3	23.2	39.6
			DoReFa-Net	19.5	35.0	19.6	5.1	20.5	32.8
			XNOR-Net	8.1	19.5	5.6	2.6	8.3	13.3
			Bi-Real Net	11.2	26.0	8.3	3.1	12.0	18.3
			BiDet	13.2	28.3	10.5	5.1	14.3	20.5
			RBONN	**17.4**	**33.2**	**16.4**	**5.3**	**17.1**	**26.7**

RBONN's performance stands out by a sizeable margin. For example, RBONN surpasses BiDet by 3.4% with the same structure and compression.

COCO. Because of its size and diversity, the COCO dataset presents a greater challenge than PASCAL VOC. On COCO, our RBONN is compared against state-of-the-art BNNs such as XNOR-Net [34], Bi-Real Net [29], and BiDet [41]. We present the performance of the 4-bit DoReFa-Net [48] for comparison. Table 4 does not indicate memory use or FLOPs due to page width constraints. With just different fully-connected layers, the COCO dataset's practical memory utilization and FLOPs are similar to those on VOC.

Compared to state-of-the-art XNOR-Net, Bi-Real Net, and BiDet, our method enhances the mAP@[.5, .95] by 10.2%, 6.2%, and 4.9% using the Faster-RCNN framework with the ResNet-18 backbone. Moreover, our RBONN clearly outperforms competitors on other APs with various IoU thresholds. Our RBONN

Table 5. Comparing RBONN with real-valued models on hardware (single thread).

Network	Method	W/A	Size (MB)	Memory Saving	Latency (ms)	Acceleration
ResNet-18	Real-valued	32/32	46.8	–	1060.2	–
	RBONN	1/1	4.2	11.1×	67.1	15.8×
SSD-VGG16	Real-valued	32/32	105.16	–	2788.7	–
	RBONN	1/1	21.88	4.8×	200.5	13.9×

achieves only 2.3% lower mAP than DoReFa-Net, a quantized neural network with 4-bit weights and activations. Our method yields a 1-bit detector with a performance of only 5.4% mAP lower than the best-performing real-valued counterpart (20.6% *vs.* 26.0%). Similarly, using the SSD300 framework with the VGG-16 backbone, our method achieves 17.4% mAP@[.5, .95], outperforming XNOR-Net, Bi-Real Net, and BiDet by 9.3%, 6.2%, and 4.2% mAP, respectively.

In conclusion, our method outperforms previous BNN algorithms in the AP with various IoU thresholds and AP for objects of various sizes on COCO, demonstrating the method's superiority and applicability in a wide range of applications settings.

4.5   Deployment Efficiency

We implement the 1-bit models achieved by our RBONN on ODROID C4, which has a 2.016 GHz 64-bit quad-core ARM Cortex-A55. With evaluating its real speed in practice, the efficiency of our RBONN is proved when deployed into real-world mobile devices. We leverage the SIMD instruction SSHL on ARM NEON to make the inference framework BOLT [7] compatible with RBONN. We compare RBONN to the real-valued backbones in Table 5. We can see that RBONN's inference speed is substantially faster with the highly efficient BOLT framework. For example, the acceleration rate achieves about 15.8× on ResNet-18, which is slightly lower than the theoretical acceleration rate discussed in Sect. 4.3. Furthermore, RBONN achieves 13.9× acceleration with SSD. All deployment results are significant for the computer vision on real-world edge devices.

5   Conclusion

This paper proposed a new learning algorithm, termed recurrent bilinear optimization, to efficiently calculate BNNs, which is the first attempt to optimize BNNs from the bilinear perspective. Our method specifically introduces recurrent optimization to sequentially backtrack the sparse real-valued weight filters, which can be sufficiently trained and reach their performance limit based on a controllable learning process. RBONNs show strong generalization to gain impressive performance on both image classification and object detection tasks, demonstrating the superiority of the proposed method over state-of-the-art BNNs.

Acknowledgement. This work was supported in part by the National Natural Science Foundation of China under Grant 62076016, 92067204, 62141604 and the Shanghai Committee of Science and Technology under Grant No. 21DZ1100100.

References

1. Chen, S., Wang, W., Pan, S.J.: MetaQuant: learning to quantize by learning to penetrate non-differentiable quantization. In: Procedings of the NeurIPS, vol. **32**, pp. 3916–3926 (2019)
2. Courbariaux, M., Bengio, Y., David, J.P.: BinaryConnect: training deep neural networks with binary weights during propagations. In: Proceedings of the NeurIPS, pp. 3123–3131 (2015)
3. Courbariaux, M., Hubara, I., Soudry, D., El-Yaniv, R., Bengio, Y.: Binarized neural networks: training deep neural networks with weights and activations constrained to+ 1 or-1. In: Proceedings of the NeurIPS, pp. 1–9 (2016)
4. Del Bue, A., Xavier, J., Agapito, L., Paladini, M.: Bilinear modeling via augmented lagrange multipliers (balm). IEEE Trans. Pattern Anal. Mach. Intell. **34**(8), 1496–1508 (2011)
5. Denil, M., Shakibi, B., Dinh, L., Ranzato, M., De Freitas, N.: Predicting parameters in deep learning. In: Proceedings of the NeurIPS, pp. 2148–2156 (2013)
6. Everingham, M., Van Gool, L., Williams, C.K., Winn, J., Zisserman, A.: The pascal visual object classes (VOC) challenge. Int. J. Comput. Vision **88**(2), 303–338 (2010). https://doi.org/10.1007/s11263-009-0275-4
7. Feng, J.: Bolt (2021). https://github.com/huawei-noah/bolt
8. Gao, P., Ma, T., Li, H., Dai, J., Qiao, Y.: ConvMAE: masked convolution meets masked autoencoders. arXiv preprint arXiv:2205.03892 (2022)
9. Girshick, R., Donahue, J., Darrell, T., Malik, J.: Rich feature hierarchies for accurate object detection and semantic segmentation. In: Proceedings of the CVPR, pp. 580–587 (2014)
10. Gu, J., et al.: Projection convolutional neural networks for 1-bit CNNs via discrete back propagation. In: Proceedings of the AAAI, pp. 8344–8351 (2019)
11. He, K., Zhang, X., Ren, S., Sun, J.: Delving deep into rectifiers: surpassing human-level performance on imageNet classification. In: Proceedings of the ICCV, pp. 1026–1034 (2015)
12. He, K., Zhang, X., Ren, S., Sun, J.: Deep residual learning for image recognition. In: Proceedings of the CVPR, pp. 770–778 (2016)
13. He, Y., Kang, G., Dong, X., Fu, Y., Yang, Y.: Soft filter pruning for accelerating deep convolutional neural networks. In: Proceedings of the IJCAI, pp. 2234–2240 (2018)
14. Huang, Z., Wang, N.: Data-driven sparse structure selection for deep neural networks. In: Proceedings of ECCV, pp. 304–320 (2018)
15. LeCun, Y., Denker, J.S., Solla, S.A.: Optimal brain damage. In: Proceedings of the NeurIPS, pp. 598–605 (1990)
16. Li, H., Kadav, A., Durdanovic, I., Samet, H., Graf, H.P.: Pruning filters for efficient convnets. In: Proceedings of the ICLR, pp. 1–13 (2016)

17. Li, Y., Wang, N., Liu, J., Hou, X.: Factorized bilinear models for image recognition. In: Proceedings of the ICCV, pp. 2079–2087 (2017)
18. Lin, M., et al.: SiMaN: sign-to-magnitude network binarization. arXiv preprint arXiv:2102.07981 (2021)
19. Lin, M., et al.: Rotated binary neural network. In: Proceedings of the NeurIPS, pp. 1–9 (2020)
20. Lin, S., Ji, R., Chen, C., Huang, F.: ESPACE: accelerating convolutional neural networks via eliminating spatial and channel redundancy. In: Proceedings of the AAAI, pp. 1424–1430 (2017)
21. Lin, S., et al.: Towards optimal structured CNN pruning via generative adversarial learning. In: Proceedings of the CVPR, pp. 2790–2799 (2019)
22. Lin, T.-Y., et al.: Microsoft COCO: common objects in context. In: Fleet, D., Pajdla, T., Schiele, B., Tuytelaars, T. (eds.) ECCV 2014. LNCS, vol. 8693, pp. 740–755. Springer, Cham (2014). https://doi.org/10.1007/978-3-319-10602-1_48
23. Lin, T.Y., RoyChowdhury, A., Maji, S.: Bilinear CNN models for fine-grained visual recognition. In: Proceedings of the ICCV, pp. 1449–1457 (2015)
24. Liu, C., et al.: RBCN: rectified binary convolutional networks for enhancing the performance of 1-bit DCNNs. In: Proceedings of the IJCAI, pp. 854–860 (2019)
25. Liu, C., et al.: Circulant binary convolutional networks: enhancing the performance of 1-bit DCNNs with circulant back propagation. In: Proceedings of the CVPR, pp. 2691–2699 (2019)
26. Liu, H., Simonyan, K., Yang, Y.: DARTS: differentiable architecture search. In: Proceedings of the ICLR (2019)
27. Liu, W., et al.: SSD: single shot MultiBox detector. In: Leibe, B., Matas, J., Sebe, N., Welling, M. (eds.) ECCV 2016. LNCS, vol. 9905, pp. 21–37. Springer, Cham (2016). https://doi.org/10.1007/978-3-319-46448-0_2
28. Liu, Z., Shen, Z., Savvides, M., Cheng, K.-T.: ReActNet: towards precise binary neural network with generalized activation functions. In: Vedaldi, A., Bischof, H., Brox, T., Frahm, J.-M. (eds.) ECCV 2020. LNCS, vol. 12359, pp. 143–159. Springer, Cham (2020). https://doi.org/10.1007/978-3-030-58568-6_9
29. Liu, Z., Wu, B., Luo, W., Yang, X., Liu, W., Cheng, K.-T.: Bi-Real Net: enhancing the performance of 1-Bit CNNs with improved representational capability and advanced training algorithm. In: Ferrari, V., Hebert, M., Sminchisescu, C., Weiss, Y. (eds.) ECCV 2018. LNCS, vol. 11219, pp. 747–763. Springer, Cham (2018). https://doi.org/10.1007/978-3-030-01267-0_44
30. Liu, Z., Li, J., Shen, Z., Huang, G., Yan, S., Zhang, C.: Learning efficient convolutional networks through network slimming. In: Proceedings of the ICCV, pp. 2736–2744 (2017)
31. Paszke, A., et al.: Automatic differentiation in PyTorch. In: NeurIPS Workshops (2017)
32. Petersen, K., et al.: The matrix cookbook. Technical University of Denmark 15 (2008)
33. Qin, H., et al.: Forward and backward information retention for accurate binary neural networks. In: Proceedings of the CVPR, pp. 2250–2259 (2020)
34. Rastegari, M., Ordonez, V., Redmon, J., Farhadi, A.: XNOR-Net: ImageNet classification using binary convolutional neural networks. In: Leibe, B., Matas, J., Sebe, N., Welling, M. (eds.) ECCV 2016. LNCS, vol. 9908, pp. 525–542. Springer, Cham (2016). https://doi.org/10.1007/978-3-319-46493-0_32
35. Ren, S., He, K., Girshick, R., Sun, J.: Faster R-CNN: towards real-time object detection with region proposal networks. IEEE Trans. Pattern Anal. Mach. Intell. **39**(6), 1137–1149 (2016)

36. Romero, A., Ballas, N., Kahou, S.E., Chassang, A., Gatta, C., Bengio, Y.: FitNets: hints for thin deep nets. In: Proceedings of the ICLR, pp. 1–13 (2015)
37. Russakovsky, O., et al.: ImageNet large scale visual recognition challenge. Int. J. Comput. Vision **115**(3), 211–252 (2015). https://doi.org/10.1007/s11263-015-0816-y
38. Simonyan, K., Zisserman, A.: Very deep convolutional networks for large-scale image recognition. In: Proceedings of the ICLR, pp. 1–13 (2015)
39. Suh, Y., Wang, J., Tang, S., Mei, T., Mu Lee, K.: Part-aligned bilinear representations for person re-identification. In: Proceedings of the ECCV, pp. 1449–1457 (2018)
40. Wan, D., et al.: TBN: Convolutional neural network with ternary inputs and binary weights. In: Proceedings of the ECCV, pp. 315–332 (2018)
41. Wang, Z., Wu, Z., Lu, J., Zhou, J.: Bidet: An efficient binarized object detector. In: Proceedings of the CVPR, pp. 2049–2058 (2020)
42. Xu, S., Li, Y., Zhao, J., Zhang, B., Guo, G.: POEM: 1-bit point-wise operations based on expectation-maximization for efficient point cloud processing. In: Proceedings of the BMVC, pp. 1–10 (2021)
43. Xu, S., Zhao, J., Lu, J., Zhang, B., Han, S., Doermann, D.: Layer-wise searching for 1-bit detectors. In: Proceedings of the CVPR, pp. 5682–5691 (2021)
44. Xu, Z., et al.: ReCU: reviving the dead weights in binary neural networks. In: Proceedings of the ICCV, pp. 5198–5208 (2021)
45. Yang, Z., et al.: Searching for low-bit weights in quantized neural networks. In: Proceedings of the NeurIPS, pp. 1–11 (2020)
46. Yu, Z., Yu, J., Fan, J., Tao, D.: Multi-modal factorized bilinear pooling with co-attention learning for visual question answering. In: Proceedings of the ICCV, pp. 1821–1830 (2017)
47. Zhao, J., Xu, S., Zhang, B., Gu, J., Doermann, D., Guo, G.: Towards compact 1-bit CNNs via Bayesian learning. Int. J. Comput. Vision **130**(2), 201–225 (2022)
48. Zhou, S., Wu, Y., Ni, Z., Zhou, X., Wen, H., Zou, Y.: DoReFa-Net: training low bitwidth convolutional neural networks with low bitwidth gradients. arXiv preprint arXiv:1606.06160 (2016)

Neural Architecture Search for Spiking Neural Networks

Youngeun Kim$^{(\boxtimes)}$, Yuhang Li , Hyoungseob Park ,
Yeshwanth Venkatesha, and Priyadarshini Panda

Department of Electrical Engineering, Yale University, New Haven, CT, USA
{youngeun.kim,yuhang.li,hyoungseob.park,
yeshwanth.venkatesha,priya.panda}@yale.edu

Abstract. Spiking Neural Networks (SNNs) have gained huge attention
as a potential energy-efficient alternative to conventional Artificial Neural Networks (ANNs) due to their inherent high-sparsity activation. However, most prior SNN methods use ANN-like architectures (*e.g.*, VGG-
Net or ResNet), which could provide sub-optimal performance for temporal sequence processing of binary information in SNNs. To address this,
in this paper, we introduce a novel Neural Architecture Search (NAS)
approach for finding better SNN architectures. Inspired by recent NAS
approaches that find the optimal architecture from activation patterns at
initialization, we select the architecture that can represent diverse spike
activation patterns across different data samples without training. Moreover, to further leverage the temporal information among the spikes, we
search for feed-forward connections as well as backward connections (*i.e.*,
temporal feedback connections) between layers. Interestingly, SNASNet
found by our search algorithm achieves higher performance with backward connections, demonstrating the importance of designing SNN architecture for suitably using temporal information. We conduct extensive
experiments on three image recognition benchmarks where we show that
SNASNet achieves state-of-the-art performance with significantly lower
timesteps (5 timesteps). Code is available on Github.

Keywords: Spiking Neural Networks · Neural architecture search ·
Neuromorphic computing

1 Introduction

Spiking Neural Networks (SNNs) [12,23,45,71,84,85] have gained increasing
attention as a promising paradigm for low-power intelligence. Inspired by biological neuronal functionality, SNNs process visual information with binary spikes
over multiple timesteps. So far, the majority of works on SNNs have focused

---

Supplementary Information The online version contains supplementary material
available at https://doi.org/10.1007/978-3-031-20053-3_3.

S. Avidan et al. (Eds.): ECCV 2022, LNCS 13684, pp. 36–56, 2022.
https://doi.org/10.1007/978-3-031-20053-3_3

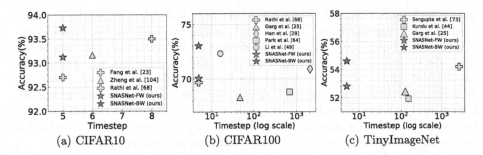

Fig. 1. Accuracy and timesteps for different SNN models on (a) CIFAR10, (b) CIFAR100, and (c) TinyImageNet dataset. While showing comparable accuracy with state-of-the-art networks, SNASNet achieves significantly lower latency. Also, SNASNet-Bw where we search both forward and backward connections provides better performance than the SNASNet-Fw with only forward connections.

on image classification problem [71] to develop an energy-efficient alternative to Artificial Neural Networks (ANNs). To this end, recent SNN works utilize ANN architectures (*e.g.*, VGG-Net [77] or ResNet [33]) designed by human experts. While SNNs show an impressive advantage on energy-efficiency, they still lag behind ANNs in terms of accuracy.

In this paper, we argue that the inherent structural/functional difference between ANNs and SNNs induces an unignorable architectural gap, resulting in a sub-optimal solution when we naively deploy ANN architectures on SNNs. Specifically, different from ANNs with ReLU neurons, SNNs consist of Leaky Integrate-and-Fire (LIF) neurons which store and transmit temporal information. However, manually searching for SNN-friendly architectures is laborious. Therefore, we use Neural Architecture Search (NAS) [6,34,75,102,106,107], which can automatically discover the optimal SNN architecture. Although NAS has become a prevalent technique in various ANN tasks [9,11,26,101], NAS for designing SNNs has not been investigated. In this work, we ask two questions:

Q1. Which NAS algorithm is suitable for SNNs?
Q2. Which SNN architecture provides better performance on an image recognition task?

For the first question, we highlight that the mainstream NAS algorithms either require multiple training stages [2,78,105–107] or require training a supernet once with all architecture candidates [6,28,54,86] which takes longer training time to converge than standard training. As SNNs have a significantly slower training process compared to ANNs (*e.g.*, training SNN with timestep 10 on MNIST with NVIDIA V100 GPU takes 11.43× more latency compared to the same ANN architecture [52]), the above NAS approaches are difficult to be applied on SNNs. On the other hand, recent works [10,57,88] have proposed efficient NAS approaches that search the best neuron cell from initialized networks without any training. Specifically, [57] shows that the network architecture with a high representation power at initialization is likely to achieve higher post-training accuracy. Motivated by this, without the training process, we select the SNN architecture that can represent diverse spike activation patterns across different data samples. To quantify the diversity of networks, we measure the distance of temporal activation patterns between different mini-batch samples. However, SNNs show high sparsity variation on the temporal patterns across different mini-batches, resulting in inaccurate distance measures. To address this, we normalize the distance measure based on the sparsity of given activation patterns, that we term as Sparsity-Aware Hamming Distance (SAHD).

To answer the second question, we search the optimal architecture block for SNNs. Here, we find the connection topology as well as the corresponding operation for each connection following previous works [20, 95]. Different from ANNs, SNNs can leverage backward connections as they convey information through time. The backward connections in SNNs can compute more efficiently because each neuron can participate several times in a network computation [3], and they are likely to capture the temporal correlation of the given input. A line of work has studied backward connections in SNNs with various architectures and training methods [3, 14, 37, 62, 63, 98]. Therefore, we search backward connections as well as forward connections through our NAS algorithm. Surprisingly, SNNs with backward connections yield improved accuracy by up to 3% across various benchmark datasets compared to SNNs with forward connections only. Also, as shown in Fig. 1, *SNASNet* founded by our NAS algorithm achieves state-of-the-art performance with a significantly small number of timesteps.

In summary, our key contributions are as follows: (1) So far, most SNN literature deploys architectures from ANN models which can yield sub-optimal performance for SNNs. For the first time, we showcase a NAS technique for finding better SNN architecture on the image recognition task. (2) Motivated by the prior work [10, 57, 88], we find an SNN-friendly architecture by comparing temporal activation without any training process. Eliminating the training cost to find the optimal architecture brings a huge advantage for SNNs that require significantly longer training time compared to ANNs. (3) We also propose Sparsity-Aware Hamming Distance (SAHD) for addressing sparsity variation of LIF neurons. (4) Furthermore, we search backward connections for leveraging temporal information in spiking inputs, which has not been explored before in NAS approaches for ANN architecture.

2   Related Work

2.1   Spiking Neural Networks

Spiking Neural Networks (SNNs) have gained great attention as an energy-efficient alternative over standard Artificial Neural Networks (ANNs) [7, 13, 17–19, 29, 38–42, 45, 49–51, 59, 62, 71–73, 79, 94, 96]. SNNs process temporal information through weight connections and a Leak-Integrate-and-Fire (LIF) neuron [36] which works as a non-linear activation in SNNs. The LIF neuron has its own memory called membrane potential that can store the temporal spike dynamics by accumulating incoming spike signals. If the membrane potential exceeds a firing threshold, the neuron generates a post-synaptic spike. The integrate-and-fire behavior of neurons induces non-differentiable transfer function. As a result, standard backpropagation is difficult to be applied during the training phase [61].

To address this, various methods have been proposed to circumvent the non-differentiable backpropagation problem. Among them, surrogate gradient learning approaches have become popular [27,47,48,61,74,84] due to their higher performance and smaller number of timesteps compared to other training techniques. They define a surrogate function for LIF neurons when calculating backward gradients. Wu *et al.* [85] represent the LIF model in a discrete-time domain and enable SNN training with a Pytorch platform. The authors of [81] propose a training algorithm that calculates backward gradients of the accumulated input and output spikes over the time window. Tandem learning [82,83] utilizes an auxiliary ANN that facilitates stable error back-propagation for SNN training. A line of work [24,68] train membrane decay or firing threshold in an LIF neuron, which improves the representation power of SNNs. Also, Batch Norm (BN) [35] has been applied to accelerate the training process of SNNs [39,46,104]. In spite of the recent developments in SNN training techniques, all of the prior methods leverage ANN architecture, such as, VGG and ResNet families. We assert that these architectures may provide sub-optimal solution for SNNs. Different from previous methods, we search better SNN architectures for the image recognition task which has not been explored so far. We notify that the concurrent work [60] also aims to find SNN-friendly architecture using evolutionary algorithm, whereas our work is based on NAS without training technique. We also have different search spaces from [60] where we more focus on searching backward connections.

2.2 Neural Architecture Search

Neural Architecture Search (NAS) has been proposed to discover high-performing networks [6,34,75,102,106,107]. The early stage of NAS algorithm uses reinforcement learning [2,78,105–107] or evolutionary algorithm [70]. However, such methods require training the searched architecture from scratch for each search step, which is extremely computationally expensive. To address this, weight-sharing approaches have been proposed [4–6,8,28,54,66,80,86,92,100]. They train the supernet once which includes all architecture candidates. For instance, Darts [54] jointly optimizes the network parameters and the importance of each architecture candidate. Also, SPOS [28] trains the weight parameters with uniform forward path sampling and finds the optimal architecture via evolutionary strategy. The weight-sharing methods do not require training the architecture from scratch at each search step, resulting in better efficiency compared to previous NAS algorithms. In very recent works, the key focus has been the efficiency of the NAS technique [1,90,91,93,103] owing to the growing size of dataset and architecture. Interestingly, a line of work suggests the concept of NAS without training where the networks do not require training during the search stage [10,57,88]. This can significantly reduce the computational cost for searching optimal architecture. At the same time, several benchmarks [20,21,76,95] have been proposed in order to remove the burden of training time. Following the success of NAS on image classification domain, NAS has been deployed on various tasks such as object detection [11], segmentation [53,101], GAN [26], transformer [9], and human pose estimation [89,97]. Despite the huge progress of NAS algorithm in ANN domain, NAS for SNNs has not been developed yet. In this work, we aim to build better SNN architecture by leveraging NAS. Different from the previous methods that search only forward connections of the networks, we search for backward connections in addition to forward, which furthers leverage the temporal information of spikes.

3   Preliminaries

3.1   Leaky Integrate-and-Fire Neuron

Leaky Integrate-and-Fire (LIF) neuron is widely used for constructing SNNs [24,71,85]. A neuron has a membrane potential that stores the temporal spike information. We convert the above continuous differential equation into a discrete version as in previous works [24,85]:

$$u_i^t = (1 - \frac{1}{\tau_m})u_i^{t-1} + \frac{1}{\tau_m}\sum_j w_{ij}o_j^t, \qquad (1)$$

where, u_i^t represents the membrane potential of a neuron i at timestep t, τ_m is a time constant for decaying the membrane potential. Also, w_{ij} stands for weight connections between neuron j and neuron i. The neuron i accumulates membrane potential and generates a spike output o_i^t whenever membrane potential exceeds the threshold. After firing, the membrane potential is reset to zero.

3.2   NAS Without Training

Compared to standard ANNs, SNNs require significantly higher computational cost for training due to multiple feedforward steps [52]. This makes it difficult to search for an optimal SNN architecture with NAS techniques that train the architecture candidate multiple times [2,78,105–107] or train a complex supernet [6,28,54,86]. To minimize the training budget, our work is motivated by the previous works [10,57,88] which demonstrate that the optimal architecture can be founded without any training process. Specifically, Mellor et al. [57] provide the interesting observation that the architecture having distinctive representations across different data samples is likely to achieve higher post-training performance. To measure the discriminative power of initialized networks, they utilize the activation pattern of ReLU neurons as a binary indicator. If the ReLU neuron generates a positive value (i.e., input > 0), the neuron is mapped to 1; otherwise 0. As a result, ReLU neurons in one layer can be encoded to binary vector **c**.

Given N samples in a mini-batch, they construct a kernel matrix by computing Hamming distance $d_H(\mathbf{c}_i, \mathbf{c}_j)$ between different samples i and j, which can be formulated as follows:

$$\mathbf{K}_H = \begin{pmatrix} N_A - d_H(\mathbf{c}_1, \mathbf{c}_1) & \cdots & N_A - d_H(\mathbf{c}_1, \mathbf{c}_N) \\ \vdots & \ddots & \vdots \\ N_A - d_H(\mathbf{c}_N, \mathbf{c}_1) & \cdots & N_A - d_H(\mathbf{c}_N, \mathbf{c}_N) \end{pmatrix} \tag{2}$$

Here, N_A stands for the number of ReLU neurons in the given layer. The final score of the architecture candidate is obtained by:

$$s = \log(\det |\sum_l \mathbf{K}_H^l|), \tag{3}$$

where, $\mathbf{K}_H^l$ is the kernel matrix at layer l. A high score implies low off-diagonal elements of kernel matrix $\mathbf{K}_H$, which means that the activation patterns from different samples are not similar. Finally, the highest-scored architecture among the candidates is selected for training.

4   Methodology

In this section, we first introduce a temporal binary indicator of an LIF neuron based on the concept of linear region in neural networks. After that, we present sparsity-aware hamming distance that accounts for the sparsity variation of an LIF neuron. Finally, we provide the search space for our NAS algorithm where we find both forward and backward connections.

4.1   Linear Regions from LIF Neurons

NAS without training approaches in ANN domain [10,57] are based on the theoretical concept of linear region in neural networks [30,31,58,67,87]. That is, each piecewise linear function (such as, ReLU) divides the input space into multiple linear regions. The composition of multiple piecewise linear functions brings multiple linear regions on the input space. Such a pattern of linear regions is used for measuring the representation power of initialized networks by comparing the patterns between different samples. Here, based on previous work, we introduce the definition of neuron transition (*i.e.*, the boundary of linear region) in a piecewise linear function.

Definition 1 (Raghu *et al.* [67]). *For fixed W, we say a neuron with piecewise linear region transitions between inputs x, x+δ if its activation function switches linear region between x and x + δ.*

For instance, ReLU and Hard Tanh have neuron transition at 0 and $\{-1, 1\}$, respectively [67]. Figure 2(a) also shows the simple example with three ReLU neurons. The input space is divided into two regions by a single ReLU neuron.

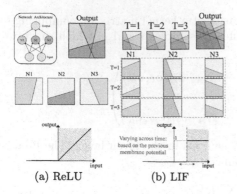

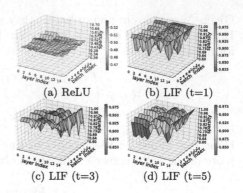

Fig. 2. Illustration of the concept of linear regions from ReLU and LIF neurons. Each ReLU (or LIF neuron) divides the two-dimension input space into active and inactive regions.

Fig. 3. Sparsity variance of activation pattern across different layers and different samples in a mini-batch. LIF neuron shows higher variance of activation pattern compared to ReLU neuron.

By composing ReLU neurons, the input space is partitioned into multiple regions where each region represents a different linear function.

According to Definition 1, a LIF neuron can be regarded as a piecewise linear function. For each timestep, the LIF neuron transfers 0 if the membrane potential is lower than a firing threshold, otherwise it generates 1 (*i.e.*, spike). Thus, neuron transition occurs when a given input generates an output spike. We illustrate the transfer function of an LIF neuron in Fig. 2(b). Different from ReLU neuron, the output of LIF neuron is not solely dependent on the input. As we shown in Eq. 1, the output of LIF neuron is based on the current input as well as the previous membrane potential. Therefore, the neuron transition point can be changing across time. For example, suppose that the firing threshold is 1 and the membrane potential from the previous timestep is 0.3. In this case, neuron transition happens at $input = 0.7$. After the neuron fires, the membrane potential is reset to 0, where, the neuron transition point becomes 1. With this time-varying transfer function, the linear region of SNNs becomes more diverse.

4.2 Sparsity-Aware Hamming Distance

In NASWOT [57], Hamming Distance (HD) is a key metric to compare the binary activation pattern $\mathbf{c}_i, \mathbf{c}_j$ between two different mini-batch samples i, j. However, standard HD gives inaccurate distance measurement for SNNs due to the large sparsity variance of binary activation pattern $\mathbf{c}$ of LIF. Here, the term "sparsity" denotes the percentage of 0 in binary activation pattern $\mathbf{c}$ from one layer at a given timestep t. Note, the definition of "sparsity" here is slightly different from the previous works which defines "sparsity" from the activation across all timesteps.

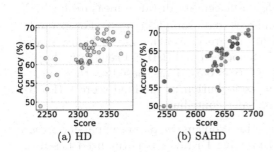

(a) HD   (b) SAHD

Fig. 4. Accuracy with respect to architecture score. We randomly select 50 architectures from search space. We show Kendall's τ correlation for quantitative comparison (HD: $\tau = 0.519$, SAHD: $\tau = 0.646$).

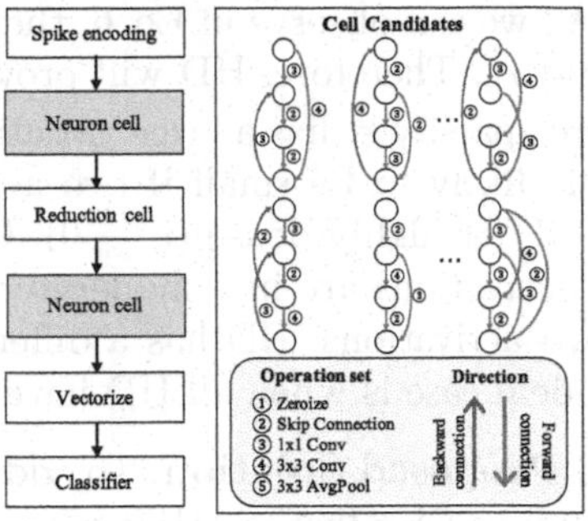

Fig. 5. Illustration of cell-based neural architecture search.

Observation on the Sparsity of Activation Pattern. A ReLU neuron provides a binary activation pattern with about 50% sparsity from Gaussian/Uniform weight initialization [32], which is similar across all data samples. On the other hand, a LIF neuron shows a large variation of sparsity across different data samples since the activation pattern is based on the previous membrane potential which is different in each sample. In Fig. 3, we visualize the sparsity of binary activation pattern with 16 mini-batch samples. The results demonstrate that LIF neuron causes a large sparsity variation across different samples.

A Problem due to Large Sparsity Variation. This large sparsity variation induces different scales of HD. To explain this, for the data sample i, we model the distribution of LIF neuron output (at each timestep) as i.i.d. Bernoulli distribution where the probability of observing 1 is $1 - r_i^l$:

$$o_i^l \sim \text{Bern}(1 - r_i^l). \tag{4}$$

Here, r_i^l is sparsity of binary activation pattern at layer l. Then, the probability of an activation difference (at the same neuron position) between two data samples i, j can be represented as:

$$Pr(|o_i^l - o_j^l| = 1) = \text{Bern}(r_i^l(1 - r_j^l) + (1 - r_i^l)r_j^l). \tag{5}$$

Considering that each element of binary activation patterns $\mathbf{c}^l \in \mathbb{R}^{N_A^l}$ is sampled from Bernoulli distribution (Eq. 4), where N_A^l denotes the number of neurons at layer l. Then, the expectation of HD (*i.e.*, $d_H(\mathbf{c}_i^l, \mathbf{c}_j^l)$) can be formulated as:

$$\mathbb{E}[d_H(\mathbf{c}_i^l, \mathbf{c}_j^l)] = N_A^l \mathbb{E}[Pr(|o_i^l - o_j^l| = 1)] = N_A^l \{r_i^l(1 - r_j^l) + (1 - r_i^l)r_j^l\}, \tag{6}$$

Note, all quantities in Eq. 4, Eq. 5, and Eq. 6 are evaluated per timestep, and we average them across timesteps.

As we can observe in Eq. 6, the expectation of HD is the function of sparsity r_i^l and r_j^l. Therefore, HD will provide an inaccurate distance measure for SNN where sparsity r^l has a large variation across data samples (Fig. 3). For example, HD is likely to be small if two activations are in extreme cases, highly-sparse $(r \to 1)$ or highly-dense $(r \to 0)$. On the other hand, HD is likely to be high if two activations are in a moderate range $(r \approx 0.5)$. Thus, based on the sparsity of two activations, HD has a different contribution to the final score s (Eq. 3); the ideal case is when all HD have the same contribution.

The Proposed Solution. To address this problem, we propose Sparsity-Aware Hamming Distance (SAHD) where Hamming Distance is normalized based on the sparsity of two binary activation patterns. This can be simply done by normalizing the expectation of HD value to a constant α:

$$d_{SAH}(\mathbf{c}_i^l, \mathbf{c}_j^l) = \frac{\alpha}{N_A^l \{r_i^l(1 - r_j^l) + (1 - r_i^l)r_j^l\}} d_H(\mathbf{c}_i^l, \mathbf{c}_j^l). \tag{7}$$

We compute the global SAHD score by accumulating layer-wise SAHD across all layers, $i.e.$, $d_{SAH}(\mathbf{c}_i, \mathbf{c}_j) = \sum_l d_{SAH}(\mathbf{c}_i^l, \mathbf{c}_j^l)$. Instead of HD, we use SAHD for computing the kernel matrix (Eq. 2) at each timestep. After that, we sum all kernel matrices to compute the final score using Eq. 3. In Fig. 4, we compare the correlation between architecture score and post-training accuracy for HD and SAHD. The results demonstrate that the proposed SAHD has a higher Kendall's τ value which implies it is a more accurate metric for architecture selection.

4.3   Searching Forward and Backward Connections

Cell-based approach [54,66,70,75,86,107] is widely used in NAS research. These methods usually search for the connection topology as well as the corresponding operation for each connection. Then, multiple generated cell architectures construct the whole network. In our search algorithm, we also investigate cell-based architectures. Figure 5 shows the macro skeleton of our SNN architecture. The first block is the spike encoding layer which directly converts a float value image into spikes like previous works [85,99,104]. The main body of the skeleton consists of two searched neuron cells and one reduction cell. The reduction cell includes one convolution layer and 2-by-2 Average pooling with stride 2. Finally, a linear classifier is used for prediction.

Cell Search Strategy. Our cell search space is identical to NAS-Bench-201 [20] (except for backward connections) where each cell includes $V = 4$ nodes with multiple connections sampled from operation set $O = \{zeroize, skip connection, 1\text{-}by\text{-}1 convolution, 3\text{-}by\text{-}3 convolution, 3\text{-}by\text{-}3 average pooling\}$ (see Fig. 5). Each node contains the sum of all incoming feature maps from edge operation. However, different from [20], we search backward connections in addition to forward connections. In backward operation, we add transformed node feature of l-th layer at timestep $t - 1$ to the node of l'-th $(l' < l)$ layer at timestep t. The backward connections also have the same operation set search space O as forward

Table 1. Classification Accuracy (%) on CIFAR10, CIFAR100, and TinyImageNet.

	Dataset	Training method	Architecture	Timesteps	Accuracy (%)
Wu *et al.* [85]	CIFAR10	Surrogate Gradient	5Conv, 2Linear	12	90.53
Wu *et al.* [82]	CIFAR10	Tandem Learning	5Conv, 2Linear	8	89.04
Rathi *et al.* [69]	CIFAR10	Hybrid	VGG9	100	90.50
Han *et al.* [29]	CIFAR10	ANN-SNN Conversion	VGG16	2048	93.63
Kundu *et al.* [44]	CIFAR10	Hybrid	VGG16	100	91.29
Zheng *et al.* [104]	CIFAR10	Surrogate Gradient	ResNet19	6	93.16
Deng *et al.* [16]	CIFAR10	ANN-SNN Conversion	ResNet20	16	92.42
Li *et al.* [49]	CIFAR10	ANN-SNN Conversion	VGG16	32	93.00
Fang *et al.* [24]	CIFAR10	Surrogate Gradient	6Conv, 2Linear	8	93.50
Rathi *et al.* [68]	CIFAR10	Hybrid	VGG16	5	92.70
SNASNet-Fw (ours)	CIFAR10	Surrogate Gradient	Searched Architecture	5	93.12 ± 0.42
SNASNet-Fw (ours)	CIFAR10	Surrogate Gradient	Searched Architecture	8	93.64 ± 0.35
SNASNet-Bw (ours)	CIFAR10	Surrogate Gradient	Searched Architecture	5	93.73 ± 0.32
SNASNet-Bw (ours)	CIFAR10	Surrogate Gradient	Searched Architecture	8	94.12 ± 0.25
Lu and Sengupta [56]	CIFAR100	ANN-SNN Conversion	VGG15	62	63.20
Park *et al.* [64]	CIFAR100	TTFS	VGG15	680	68.80
Rathi *et al.* [69]	CIFAR100	Hybrid	VGG16	125	67.80
Han *et al.* [29]	CIFAR100	ANN-SNN Conversion	VGG16	2048	70.90
Garg *et al.* [25]	CIFAR100	DCT	VGG9	48	68.30
Kundu *et al.* [44]	CIFAR100	Hybrid	VGG11	120	64.98
Deng *et al.* [16]	CIFAR100	ANN-SNN Conversion	ResNet20	32	68.40
Li *et al.* [49]	CIFAR100	ANN-SNN Conversion	ResNet20	16	72.33
Rathi *et al.* [68]	CIFAR100	Hybrid	VGG16	5	69.67
SNASNet-Fw (ours)	CIFAR100	Surrogate Gradient	Searched Architecture	5	70.06 ± 0.45
SNASNet-Bw (ours)	CIFAR100	Surrogate Gradient	Searched Architecture	5	73.04 ± 0.36
Sengupta *et al.* [73]	TinyImageNet	ANN-SNN Conversion	VGG11	2500	54.20
Kundu *et al.* [44]	TinyImageNet	Hybrid	VGG16	150	51.92
Garg *et al.* [25]	TinyImageNet	DCT	VGG13	125	52.43
SNASNet-Fw (ours)	TinyImageNet	Surrogate Gradient	Searched Architecture	5	52.81 ± 0.56
SNASNet-Bw (ours)	TinyImageNet	Surrogate Gradient	Searched Architecture	5	54.60 ± 0.48

connections. In Fig. 5, we show examples of cell candidates. In the predefined search space, we select the optimal spiking neuron cell. Reduction cell downsamples the spatial size of the feature map. We do not illustrate Zeroize operation for simplicity. The forward connections and backward connections can be combined seamlessly. Surprisingly, adding backward connections improves the accuracy of SNNs especially on complex datasets such as CIFAR100 and Tiny-ImageNet. To train the searched SNNs, we use surrogate gradient training [61,84,85] (see Supplementary C for details).

5   Experiments

5.1   Implementation Details

Dataset. We evaluate our method on CIFAR10 [43], CIFAR100 [43], TinyImageNet [15]. The details of datasets can be found in Supplementary.

Hyperparameters. Our implementation is based on PyTorch [65]. We train the networks with standard SGD with momentum 0.9, weight decay 0.0005 and also apply random crop and horizontal flip to input images. We set batch size for training as 64. The base learning rate is set to 0.2, 0.1, 0.1 for CIFAR10,

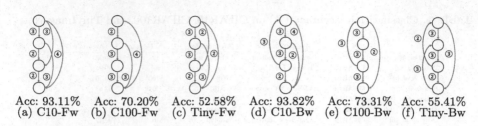

Acc: 93.11%   Acc: 70.20%   Acc: 52.58%   Acc: 93.82%   Acc: 73.31%   Acc: 55.41%
(a) C10-Fw   (b) C100-Fw   (c) Tiny-Fw   (d) C10-Bw   (e) C100-Bw   (f) Tiny-Bw

Fig. 6. Searched architecture examples (forward and backward configuration) for three benchmarks. Blue and red arrows denote forward connection and backward connection, respectively. The number on each arrow represents operations introduced in Fig. 5. (Color figure online)

CIFAR100, TinyImageNet, respectively. We use cosine learning rate scheduling [55]. Here, we set the total number of epochs to 300, 300, 200, for CIFAR10, CIFAR100, TinyImageNet, respectively. We set τ_m in Eq. 1 to $\frac{4}{3}$. We set α in Eq. 7 to $0.5 N_A^l$ to get similar sparsity scale in LIF neuron as a ReLU neuron. Also, we search 5000 architecture candidates from search space (We observe the accuracy saturates after 5000 samples, shown in Supplementary E). We use SpikingJelly [22] package for implementing an LIF neuron.

Architectures. Here, we provide details for architectures in Fig. 5. Note, we do not allow two nodes to have both forward and backward connections to ensure training convergence and stability. For the spike encoding layer, we use direct coding [85, 99, 104] where we pass the input image for T time-steps through the first convolution layer which generates spikes. The first neuron cell has C-channel input and C-channel output. Reduction cell consists of $Conv(C, 2C)$-$BN(2C)$-LIF followed by $AvgPool(2)$. The second neuron cell has $2C$-channel input and $2C$-channel output. Note, the structures of the first neuron cell and second neuron cell are identical. We set C to 256, 128, 128 for CIFAR10, CIFAR100, TinyImagNet, respectively. For vectorize block, we first apply $AvgPool(2)$ to the input feature and vectorize the output. Finally, the classifier consists of $Dropout(0.5)$-$FC(1024)$-$Voting\ layer$, where a voting layer is used to improve the robustness of classification [24].

5.2 Performance Comparison

Table 1 shows the performance comparison between our SNASNet founded by the proposed NAS algorithm and previous SNN models on three benchmarks. As our NAS approach has randomness, we run the same configuration 5 times and report the mean and standard deviation. In the table, "SNASNet-Fw" refers to our searched model with only forward connections and "SNASNet-Bw" denotes our searched model with both forward and backward connections. SNASNet-Fw achieves comparable performance with the previous works with extremely small timesteps. For example, our searched model achieves 70.06% with timestep 5 on CIFAR100, which is similar to the VGG16 model performance from Rathi

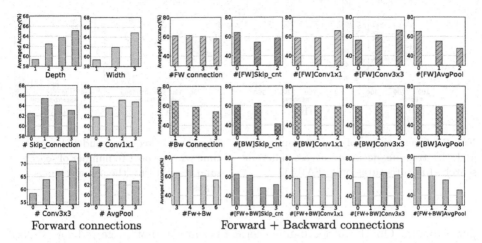

Fig. 7. Accuracy vs. cell attributes. **1st & 2nd columns:** Searching Fw connection only. **3rd–7th columns:** Searching both Fw and Bw connections. 1st, 2nd, 3rd rows show statistics of Fw, Bw, Fw+Bw, respectively.

et al. [68]. Note that, for CIFAR10, which is a relatively simple dataset, a few methods yield marginally better performance than SNASNet-Fw. Interestingly, compared to SNASNet-Fw, SNASNet-Bw improves the performance by 0.61%, 2.98%, and 1.79%, for CIFAR10, CIFAR100, and TinyImageNet, respectively. We note that SNASNet-Bw yields SOTA results across all datasets with only 5/8 timesteps. The results support our assertion that the representation power of SNNs can be enhanced by passing information through backward connections where temporal information is further exploited. We also illustrate the example of searched architecture cell found by our proposed NAS algorithm for each dataset in Fig. 6. Recently, Shu *et al.* [75] show that fast convergence ANN architectures bring smooth loss landscape and accurate gradient information, resulting in high test accuracy. We also found that our searched SNN architectures achieve fast convergence with high test accuracy, as shown in Fig. 8. By using this early stage information, there is a possibility of applying an evolutionary algorithm [70] to SNN searching in future works.

5.3   Experimental Analysis

Observations from Searched Cells. We provide several observations obtained from our searching algorithm. To this end, in Fig. 7, we ran 100 random searches on CIFAR100 and provide averaged accuracy with respect to the number of forward connections (Fw), backward connections (Bw), skip connections, Conv 3×3, Conv 1×1, Average pooling. The key observations are as follows. For **SNASNet with only forward connections**, (1) a deeper and wider cell improves performance, which implies that scaling up SNN is important (1st & 2nd columns in Fig. 7). (2) Convolutional layers are important for getting higher

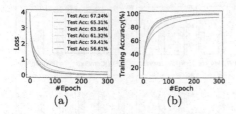
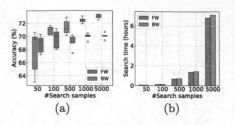

Fig. 8. Comparison of (a) training loss and (b) training accuracy across different searched architectures on CIFAR100.

Fig. 9. (a) Accuracy and (b) search time with respect to number of search samples. We run the same settings 5 times.

performance. On the other hand, average pooling is not preferred for SNNs. For **SNASNet with both forward and backward connections (3rd∼7th columns in Fig. 7)**, (1) The trend of forward connections (1st row) also prefer convolutional layers, which is similar to that of 1st row in Fig. 7. (2) As shown in the 2nd row, a small number of backward connections are preferred. Also, the type of connections does not affect the accuracy except for skip connection. (3) More than 2 backward skip connections degrade accuracy significantly. This implies that feedback without transformation (e.g., convolutional or pooling operation) deteriorates representation of SNNs. (4) Considering both forward and backward connections (3rd row), the total number of connections should be carefully designed.

Table 2. Transferability study of founded architectures. ΔAcc denotes the performance change compared to the best performed architecture shown in Fig. 6.

Celltype	Searching dataset	Train/test dataset	Accuracy (%)	ΔAcc (%)
Forward	CIFAR10	CIFAR100	69.98	−0.22
Forward	CIFAR10	TinyImageNet	52.02	−0.56
Forward	CIFAR100	CIFAR10	93.12	+0.01
Forward	CIFAR100	TinyImageNet	52.28	−0.30
Forward	TinyImageNet	CIFAR10	93.16	+0.05
Forward	TinyImageNet	CIFAR100	70.31	+0.11
Backward	CIFAR10	CIFAR100	73.19	−0.12
Backward	CIFAR10	TinyImageNet	54.61	−0.80
Backward	CIFAR100	CIFAR10	93.73	−0.09
Backward	CIFAR100	TinyImageNet	56.00	+0.59
Backward	TinyImageNet	CIFAR10	93.64	−0.18
Backward	TinyImageNet	CIFAR100	73.14	−0.17

Transferability of Searched Architecture. We conduct transferability analysis on searched SNN architecture in order to check the dependency of our searching method on the dataset. We search the optimal architecture on dataset A and train/test the searched architecture on dataset B ($A \neq B$). In Table 2, for both forward and backward configurations, we use the searched architecture (Fig. 6) for all experiments. Note, ΔAcc in 2 denotes the performance difference between the accuracy of the original searched architecture and transferred architecture. The results show that the searched SNASNets are surprisingly transferable across diverse datasets, which opens up the promising advantage of eliminating searching time for huge and complex datasets.

Analysis on Distance Metric. In our method, we use we propose Sparsity-Aware Hamming Distance (SAHD) where Hamming Distance (HD) is normalized based on the sparsity of the given two binary activation patterns. This effectively addresses a large variation of spike activation across data samples. We evaluate the performance of SNASNet according to the distance metric: HD vs. SAHD. In Table 3, we report the performance of SNASNet-Fw and SNASNet-Bw on CIFAR100. Here, we also run the search algorithm 5 times and report the mean and standard deviation. The results demonstrate that SAHD reveals better architecture with less standard deviation in terms of test accuracy for both SNASNet-Fw and SNASNet-Bw architectures.

Ablation on Number of Search Samples. In Fig. 9(a), we report the accuracy with respect to the number of search samples used in our searching algorithm. We change the number of search samples [50, 100, 500, 1000, 5000] on CIFAR100. The backward connection configuration (marked as red) shows higher variation as well as higher performance increase compared to that of the forward connection setting. This is because searching backward connections has larger search space than searching forward connections only. We also measure the computational time for searching in Fig. 9(b). We conduct the experiments on NVIDIA RTX 2080ti GPU and Intel(R) Xeon(R) Gold 6240 CPU @ 2.60 GHz processor. The results show that searching backward connection requires sightly longer time than searching forward connection.

Analysis on Timesteps. In Table 4, we report the performance on CIFAR100 with respect to the number of timesteps used in SNNs. Both SNASNet-Fw and SNASNet-Bw achieve performance gain with more number of timesteps. SNASNet-Fw and SNASNet-Bw with 20 timesteps have improved accuracy by 0.48% and 1.2% compared to 5 timesteps, respectively. Interestingly, the performance gain from SNASNet-Bw is larger than SNASNet-Fw. The results suggest that adding backward connections to SNNs effectively leverages the temporal information for improved learning, and thus supports the advantage of backward connections in SNNs.

Table 3. Performance comparison between HD and SAHD on CIFAR100.

Architecture	HD	SAHD
SNASNet-Fw	64.16 ± 2.02	70.06 ± 0.45
SNASNet-Bw	66.80 ± 1.73	73.04 ± 0.36

Table 4. Ablation studies on timesteps on CIFAR100.

Architecture	T = 5	T = 10	T = 15	T = 20
SNASNet-Fw	70.06	70.08	70.56	70.52
SNASNet-Bw	73.04	73.46	73.49	74.24

6   Conclusion

In this paper, we search better SNN architecture using the temporal activation pattern of initialized network. Our search space considers backward search connections in addition to forward connections, which brings the benefit of using temporal information. By achieving better performance than the previous works, we demonstrate that a new type of architecture is more suitable for SNNs where spikes convey information through multiple timesteps.

Acknowledgment. This work was supported in part by C-BRIC, a JUMP center sponsored by DARPA and SRC, Google Research Scholar Award, the National Science Foundation (Grant#1947826), TII (Abu Dhabi) and the DARPA AI Exploration (AIE) program.

References

1. Abdelfattah, M.S., Mehrotra, A., Dudziak, Ł., Lane, N.D.: Zero-cost proxies for lightweight NAS. arXiv preprint arXiv:2101.08134 (2021)
2. Baker, B., Gupta, O., Naik, N., Raskar, R.: Designing neural network architectures using reinforcement learning. arXiv preprint arXiv:1611.02167 (2016)
3. Bellec, G.: A solution to the learning dilemma for recurrent networks of spiking neurons. Nat. Commun. **11**(1), 1–15 (2020)
4. Bender, G., Kindermans, P.J., Zoph, B., Vasudevan, V., Le, Q.: Understanding and simplifying one-shot architecture search. In: International Conference on Machine Learning, pp. 550–559. PMLR (2018)
5. Brock, A., Lim, T., Ritchie, J.M., Weston, N.: Smash: one-shot model architecture search through hypernetworks. arXiv preprint arXiv:1708.05344 (2017)
6. Cai, H., Zhu, L., Han, S.: ProxylessNAS: direct neural architecture search on target task and hardware. arXiv preprint arXiv:1812.00332 (2018)
7. Cao, Y., Chen, Y., Khosla, D.: Spiking deep convolutional neural networks for energy-efficient object recognition. Int. J. Comput. Vision **113**(1), 54–66 (2015). https://doi.org/10.1007/s11263-014-0788-3
8. Chen, B., et al.: BN-NAS: neural architecture search with batch normalization. In: Proceedings of the IEEE/CVF International Conference on Computer Vision, pp. 307–316 (2021)
9. Chen, B., et al.: GLiT: neural architecture search for global and local image transformer. In: Proceedings of the IEEE/CVF International Conference on Computer Vision, pp. 12–21 (2021)

10. Chen, W., Gong, X., Wang, Z.: Neural architecture search on ImageNet in four GPU hours: a theoretically inspired perspective. arXiv preprint arXiv:2102.11535 (2021)

11. Chen, Y., Yang, T., Zhang, X., Meng, G., Xiao, X., Sun, J.: DetNAS: backbone search for object detection. Adv. Neural. Inf. Process. Syst. **32**, 6642–6652 (2019)

12. Christensen, D.V., et al.: 2022 roadmap on neuromorphic computing and engineering. Neuromorphic Comput. Eng. **2**, 022501 (2022)

13. Comsa, I.M., Fischbacher, T., Potempa, K., Gesmundo, A., Versari, L., Alakuijala, J.: Temporal coding in spiking neural networks with alpha synaptic function. In: ICASSP 2020–2020 IEEE International Conference on Acoustics, Speech and Signal Processing (ICASSP), pp. 8529–8533. IEEE (2020)

14. Demin, V., Nekhaev, D.: Recurrent spiking neural network learning based on a competitive maximization of neuronal activity. Front. Neuroinform. **12**, 79 (2018)

15. Deng, J., Dong, W., Socher, R., Li, L.J., Li, K., Fei-Fei, L.: ImageNet: a large-scale hierarchical image database. In: 2009 IEEE Conference on Computer Vision and Pattern Recognition, pp. 248–255. IEEE (2009)

16. Deng, S., Gu, S.: Optimal conversion of conventional artificial neural networks to spiking neural networks. arXiv preprint arXiv:2103.00476 (2021)

17. Deng, S., Li, Y., Zhang, S., Gu, S.: Temporal efficient training of spiking neural network via gradient re-weighting. arXiv preprint arXiv:2202.11946 (2022)

18. Diehl, P.U., Cook, M.: Unsupervised learning of digit recognition using spike-timing-dependent plasticity. Front. Comput. Neurosci. **9**, 99 (2015)

19. Diehl, P.U., Neil, D., Binas, J., Cook, M., Liu, S.C., Pfeiffer, M.: Fast-classifying, high-accuracy spiking deep networks through weight and threshold balancing. In: 2015 International Joint Conference on Neural Networks (IJCNN), pp. 1–8. IEEE (2015)

20. Dong, X., Yang, Y.: NAS-bench-201: extending the scope of reproducible neural architecture search. arXiv preprint arXiv:2001.00326 (2020)

21. Duan, Y., et al.: TransNAS-bench-101: improving transferability and generalizability of cross-task neural architecture search. In: Proceedings of the IEEE/CVF Conference on Computer Vision and Pattern Recognition, pp. 5251–5260 (2021)

22. Fang, W., et al.: Spikingjelly (2020). https://github.com/fangwei123456/spikingjelly

23. Fang, W., Yu, Z., Chen, Y., Huang, T., Masquelier, T., Tian, Y.: Deep residual learning in spiking neural networks. arXiv preprint arXiv:2102.04159 (2021)

24. Fang, W., Yu, Z., Chen, Y., Masquelier, T., Huang, T., Tian, Y.: Incorporating learnable membrane time constant to enhance learning of spiking neural networks. In: Proceedings of the IEEE/CVF International Conference on Computer Vision, pp. 2661–2671 (2021)

25. Garg, I., Chowdhury, S.S., Roy, K.: DCT-SNN: using DCT to distribute spatial information over time for low-latency spiking neural networks. In: Proceedings of the IEEE/CVF International Conference on Computer Vision, pp. 4671–4680 (2021)

26. Gong, X., Chang, S., Jiang, Y., Wang, Z.: AutoGAN: neural architecture search for generative adversarial networks. In: Proceedings of the IEEE/CVF International Conference on Computer Vision, pp. 3224–3234 (2019)

27. Gu, P., Xiao, R., Pan, G., Tang, H.: STCA: spatio-temporal credit assignment with delayed feedback in deep spiking neural networks. In: IJCAI, pp. 1366–1372 (2019)

28. Guo, Z., et al.: Single path one-shot neural architecture search with uniform sampling. In: Vedaldi, A., Bischof, H., Brox, T., Frahm, J.-M. (eds.) ECCV 2020. LNCS, vol. 12361, pp. 544–560. Springer, Cham (2020). https://doi.org/10.1007/978-3-030-58517-4_32
29. Han, B., Srinivasan, G., Roy, K.: RMP-SNN: residual membrane potential neuron for enabling deeper high-accuracy and low-latency spiking neural network. In: Proceedings of the IEEE/CVF Conference on Computer Vision and Pattern Recognition, pp. 13558–13567 (2020)
30. Hanin, B., Rolnick, D.: Complexity of linear regions in deep networks. In: International Conference on Machine Learning, pp. 2596–2604. PMLR (2019)
31. Hanin, B., Rolnick, D.: Deep ReLU networks have surprisingly few activation patterns (2019)
32. He, K., Zhang, X., Ren, S., Sun, J.: Delving deep into rectifiers: surpassing human-level performance on ImageNet classification. In: Proceedings of the IEEE International Conference on Computer Vision, pp. 1026–1034 (2015)
33. He, K., Zhang, X., Ren, S., Sun, J.: Deep residual learning for image recognition. In: CVPR, pp. 770–778 (2016)
34. Hu, S., et al.: DSNAS: direct neural architecture search without parameter retraining. In: Proceedings of the IEEE/CVF Conference on Computer Vision and Pattern Recognition, pp. 12084–12092 (2020)
35. Ioffe, S., Szegedy, C.: Batch normalization: accelerating deep network training by reducing internal covariate shift. arXiv preprint arXiv:1502.03167 (2015)
36. Izhikevich, E.M.: Simple model of spiking neurons. IEEE Trans. Neural Netw. **14**(6), 1569–1572 (2003)
37. Jia, S., Zhang, T., Cheng, X., Liu, H., Xu, B.: Neuronal-plasticity and reward-propagation improved recurrent spiking neural networks. Front. Neurosci. **15**, 205 (2021)
38. Jin, X., Rast, A., Galluppi, F., Davies, S., Furber, S.: Implementing spike-timing-dependent plasticity on spinnaker neuromorphic hardware. In: The 2010 International Joint Conference on Neural Networks (IJCNN), pp. 1–8. IEEE (2010)
39. Kim, Y., Panda, P.: Revisiting batch normalization for training low-latency deep spiking neural networks from scratch. arXiv preprint arXiv:2010.01729 (2020)
40. Kim, Y., Panda, P.: Optimizing deeper spiking neural networks for dynamic vision sensing. Neural Netw. **144**, 686–698 (2021)
41. Kim, Y., Panda, P.: Visual explanations from spiking neural networks using inter-spike intervals. Sci. Rep. **11**, 19037 (2021). https://doi.org/10.1038/s41598-021-98448-0
42. Kim, Y., Venkatesha, Y., Panda, P.: PrivateSNN: fully privacy-preserving spiking neural networks. arXiv preprint arXiv:2104.03414 (2021)
43. Krizhevsky, A., Hinton, G., et al.: Learning multiple layers of features from tiny images (2009)
44. Kundu, S., Datta, G., Pedram, M., Beerel, P.A.: Spike-thrift: towards energy-efficient deep spiking neural networks by limiting spiking activity via attention-guided compression. In: Proceedings of the IEEE/CVF Winter Conference on Applications of Computer Vision, pp. 3953–3962 (2021)
45. Kundu, S., Pedram, M., Beerel, P.A.: Hire-SNN: harnessing the inherent robustness of energy-efficient deep spiking neural networks by training with crafted input noise. In: Proceedings of the IEEE/CVF International Conference on Computer Vision, pp. 5209–5218 (2021)
46. Ledinauskas, E., Ruseckas, J., Juršėnas, A., Buračas, G.: Training deep spiking neural networks. arXiv preprint arXiv:2006.04436 (2020)

47. Lee, C., Sarwar, S.S., Panda, P., Srinivasan, G., Roy, K.: Enabling spike-based backpropagation for training deep neural network architectures. Front. Neurosci. **14**, 119 (2020)
48. Lee, J.H., Delbruck, T., Pfeiffer, M.: Training deep spiking neural networks using backpropagation. Front. Neurosci. **10**, 508 (2016)
49. Li, Y., Deng, S., Dong, X., Gong, R., Gu, S.: A free lunch from ANN: towards efficient, accurate spiking neural networks calibration. arXiv preprint arXiv:2106.06984 (2021)
50. Li, Y., Deng, S., Dong, X., Gu, S.: Converting artificial neural networks to spiking neural networks via parameter calibration. arXiv preprint arXiv:2205.10121 (2022)
51. Li, Y., Guo, Y., Zhang, S., Deng, S., Hai, Y., Gu, S.: Differentiable spike: rethinking gradient-descent for training spiking neural networks. Adv. Neural. Inf. Process. Syst. **34**, 23426–23439 (2021)
52. Liang, L., et al.: H2learn: high-efficiency learning accelerator for high-accuracy spiking neural networks. arXiv preprint arXiv:2107.11746 (2021)
53. Liu, C., et al.: Auto-DeepLab: hierarchical neural architecture search for semantic image segmentation. In: Proceedings of the IEEE/CVF Conference on Computer Vision and Pattern Recognition, pp. 82–92 (2019)
54. Liu, H., Simonyan, K., Yang, Y.: DARTs: differentiable architecture search. arXiv preprint arXiv:1806.09055 (2018)
55. Loshchilov, I., Hutter, F.: SGDR: stochastic gradient descent with warm restarts. arXiv preprint arXiv:1608.03983 (2016)
56. Lu, S., Sengupta, A.: Exploring the connection between binary and spiking neural networks. Front. Neurosci. **14**, 535 (2020)
57. Mellor, J., Turner, J., Storkey, A., Crowley, E.J.: Neural architecture search without training. In: International Conference on Machine Learning, pp. 7588–7598. PMLR (2021)
58. Montúfar, G., Pascanu, R., Cho, K., Bengio, Y.: On the number of linear regions of deep neural networks. arXiv preprint arXiv:1402.1869 (2014)
59. Mostafa, H.: Supervised learning based on temporal coding in spiking neural networks. IEEE Trans. Neural Net. Learn. Syst. **29**(7), 3227–3235 (2017)
60. Na, B., Mok, J., Park, S., Lee, D., Choe, H., Yoon, S.: AutoSNN: towards energy-efficient spiking neural networks. arXiv preprint arXiv:2201.12738 (2022)
61. Neftci, E.O., Mostafa, H., Zenke, F.: Surrogate gradient learning in spiking neural networks. IEEE Sign. Process. Mag. **36**, 61–63 (2019)
62. Panda, P., Aketi, S.A., Roy, K.: Toward scalable, efficient, and accurate deep spiking neural networks with backward residual connections, stochastic softmax, and hybridization. Front. Neurosci. **14**, 653 (2020)
63. Panda, P., Roy, K.: Learning to generate sequences with combination of Hebbian and non-Hebbian plasticity in recurrent spiking neural networks. Front. Neurosci. **11**, 693 (2017)
64. Park, S., Kim, S., Na, B., Yoon, S.: T2fSNN: deep spiking neural networks with time-to-first-spike coding. arXiv preprint arXiv:2003.11741 (2020)
65. Paszke, A., et al.: Automatic differentiation in PyTorch. In: NIPS-W (2017)
66. Pham, H., Guan, M., Zoph, B., Le, Q., Dean, J.: Efficient neural architecture search via parameters sharing. In: International Conference on Machine Learning, pp. 4095–4104. PMLR (2018)
67. Raghu, M., Poole, B., Kleinberg, J., Ganguli, S., Sohl-Dickstein, J.: On the expressive power of deep neural networks. In: International Conference on Machine Learning, pp. 2847–2854. PMLR (2017)

68. Rathi, N., Roy, K.: Diet-SNN: a low-latency spiking neural network with direct input encoding and leakage and threshold optimization. IEEE Trans. Neural Net. Learn. Syst. (2021)
69. Rathi, N., Srinivasan, G., Panda, P., Roy, K.: Enabling deep spiking neural networks with hybrid conversion and spike timing dependent backpropagation. arXiv preprint arXiv:2005.01807 (2020)
70. Real, E., Aggarwal, A., Huang, Y., Le, Q.V.: Regularized evolution for image classifier architecture search. In: Proceedings of the AAAI conference on artificial intelligence, vol. 33, pp. 4780–4789 (2019)
71. Roy, K., Jaiswal, A., Panda, P.: Towards spike-based machine intelligence with neuromorphic computing. Nature 575(7784), 607–617 (2019)
72. Rueckauer, B., Lungu, I.A., Hu, Y., Pfeiffer, M., Liu, S.C.: Conversion of continuous-valued deep networks to efficient event-driven networks for image classification. Front. Neurosci. 11, 682 (2017)
73. Sengupta, A., Ye, Y., Wang, R., Liu, C., Roy, K.: Going deeper in spiking neural networks: VGG and residual architectures. Front. Neurosci. 13, 95 (2019)
74. Shrestha, S.B., Orchard, G.: SLAYER: spike layer error reassignment in time. arXiv preprint arXiv:1810.08646 (2018)
75. Shu, Y., Wang, W., Cai, S.: Understanding architectures learnt by cell-based neural architecture search. arXiv preprint arXiv:1909.09569 (2019)
76. Siems, J., Zimmer, L., Zela, A., Lukasik, J., Keuper, M., Hutter, F.: NAS-bench-301 and the case for surrogate benchmarks for neural architecture search. arXiv preprint arXiv:2008.09777 (2020)
77. Simonyan, K., Zisserman, A.: Very deep convolutional networks for large-scale image recognition. In: ICLR (2015)
78. Tan, M., et al.: MnasNet: platform-aware neural architecture search for mobile. In: Proceedings of the IEEE/CVF Conference on Computer Vision and Pattern Recognition, pp. 2820–2828 (2019)
79. Venkatesha, Y., Kim, Y., Tassiulas, L., Panda, P.: Federated learning with spiking neural networks. arXiv preprint arXiv:2106.06579 (2021)
80. Wu, B., et al.: FBNet: hardware-aware efficient convnet design via differentiable neural architecture search. In: Proceedings of the IEEE/CVF Conference on Computer Vision and Pattern Recognition, pp. 10734–10742 (2019)
81. Wu, H., et al.: Training spiking neural networks with accumulated spiking flow. IJO 1(1) (2021)
82. Wu, J., Chua, Y., Zhang, M., Li, G., Li, H., Tan, K.C.: A tandem learning rule for effective training and rapid inference of deep spiking neural networks. arXiv e-prints pp. arXiv-1907 (2019)
83. Wu, J., Xu, C., Zhou, D., Li, H., Tan, K.C.: Progressive tandem learning for pattern recognition with deep spiking neural networks. arXiv preprint arXiv:2007.01204 (2020)
84. Wu, Y., Deng, L., Li, G., Zhu, J., Shi, L.: Spatio-temporal backpropagation for training high-performance spiking neural networks. Front. Neurosci. 12, 331 (2018)
85. Wu, Y., Deng, L., Li, G., Zhu, J., Xie, Y., Shi, L.: Direct training for spiking neural networks: faster, larger, better. In: Proceedings of the AAAI Conference on Artificial Intelligence, vol. 33, pp. 1311–1318 (2019)
86. Xie, S., Zheng, H., Liu, C., Lin, L.: SNAS: stochastic neural architecture search. arXiv preprint arXiv:1812.09926 (2018)

87. Xiong, H., Huang, L., Yu, M., Liu, L., Zhu, F., Shao, L.: On the number of linear regions of convolutional neural networks. In: International Conference on Machine Learning, pp. 10514–10523. PMLR (2020)
88. Xu, J., Zhao, L., Lin, J., Gao, R., Sun, X., Yang, H.: KNAS: green neural architecture search. In: International Conference on Machine Learning, pp. 11613–11625. PMLR (2021)
89. Xu, L., et al.: ViPNAS: efficient video pose estimation via neural architecture search. In: Proceedings of the IEEE/CVF Conference on Computer Vision and Pattern Recognition, pp. 16072–16081 (2021)
90. Yan, Z., Dai, X., Zhang, P., Tian, Y., Wu, B., Feiszli, M.: FP-NAS: fast probabilistic neural architecture search. In: Proceedings of the IEEE/CVF Conference on Computer Vision and Pattern Recognition, pp. 15139–15148 (2021)
91. Yang, T.J., Liao, Y.L., Sze, V.: NetAdaptV2: efficient neural architecture search with fast super-network training and architecture optimization. In: Proceedings of the IEEE/CVF Conference on Computer Vision and Pattern Recognition, pp. 2402–2411 (2021)
92. Yang, Y., You, S., Li, H., Wang, F., Qian, C., Lin, Z.: Towards improving the consistency, efficiency, and flexibility of differentiable neural architecture search. In: Proceedings of the IEEE/CVF Conference on Computer Vision and Pattern Recognition, pp. 6667–6676 (2021)
93. Yang, Z., et al.: HourNAS: extremely fast neural architecture search through an hourglass lens. In: Proceedings of the IEEE/CVF Conference on Computer Vision and Pattern Recognition, pp. 10896–10906 (2021)
94. Yao, M., et al.: Temporal-wise attention spiking neural networks for event streams classification. In: Proceedings of the IEEE/CVF International Conference on Computer Vision, pp. 10221–10230 (2021)
95. Ying, C., Klein, A., Christiansen, E., Real, E., Murphy, K., Hutter, F.: NAS-bench-101: towards reproducible neural architecture search. In: International Conference on Machine Learning, pp. 7105–7114. PMLR (2019)
96. Yousefzadeh, A., Stromatias, E., Soto, M., Serrano-Gotarredona, T., Linares-Barranco, B.: On practical issues for stochastic STDP hardware with 1-bit synaptic weights. Front. Neurosci. **12**, 665 (2018)
97. Zeng, D., Huang, Y., Bao, Q., Zhang, J., Su, C., Liu, W.: Neural architecture search for joint human parsing and pose estimation. In: Proceedings of the IEEE/CVF International Conference on Computer Vision, pp. 11385–11394 (2021)
98. Zhang, W., Li, P.: Spike-train level backpropagation for training deep recurrent spiking neural networks. arXiv preprint arXiv:1908.06378 (2019)
99. Zhang, W., Li, P.: Temporal spike sequence learning via backpropagation for deep spiking neural networks. arXiv preprint arXiv:2002.10085 (2020)
100. Zhang, X., Huang, Z., Wang, N., Xiang, S., Pan, C.: you only search once: single shot neural architecture search via direct sparse optimization. IEEE Trans. Pattern Anal. Mach. Intell. **43**(9), 2891–2904 (2020)
101. Zhang, X., et al.: DCNAS: densely connected neural architecture search for semantic image segmentation. In: Proceedings of the IEEE/CVF Conference on Computer Vision and Pattern Recognition, pp. 13956–13967 (2021)
102. Zhang, X., Hou, P., Zhang, X., Sun, J.: Neural architecture search with random labels. In: Proceedings of the IEEE/CVF Conference on Computer Vision and Pattern Recognition, pp. 10907–10916 (2021)

103. Zhao, Y., Wang, L., Tian, Y., Fonseca, R., Guo, T.: Few-shot neural architecture search. In: International Conference on Machine Learning, pp. 12707–12718. PMLR (2021)
104. Zheng, H., Wu, Y., Deng, L., Hu, Y., Li, G.: Going deeper with directly-trained larger spiking neural networks. arXiv preprint arXiv:2011.05280 (2020)
105. Zhong, Z., Yan, J., Wu, W., Shao, J., Liu, C.L.: Practical block-wise neural network architecture generation. In: Proceedings of the IEEE Conference on Computer Vision and Pattern Recognition, pp. 2423–2432 (2018)
106. Zoph, B., Le, Q.V.: Neural architecture search with reinforcement learning. arXiv preprint arXiv:1611.01578 (2016)
107. Zoph, B., Vasudevan, V., Shlens, J., Le, Q.V.: Learning transferable architectures for scalable image recognition. In: Proceedings of the IEEE Conference on Computer Vision and Pattern Recognition, pp. 8697–8710 (2018)

Where to Focus: Investigating Hierarchical Attention Relationship for Fine-Grained Visual Classification

Yang Liu[1], Lei Zhou[1], Pengcheng Zhang[1], Xiao Bai[1(✉)], Lin Gu[2,3], Xiaohan Yu[4], Jun Zhou[4], and Edwin R. Hancock[1,5]

[1] School of Computer Science and Engineering, State Key Laboratory of Software Development Environment, Jiangxi Research Institute, Beihang University, Beijing, China
baixiao@buaa.edu.cn
[2] RIKEN AIP, Tokyo, Japan
[3] The University of Tokyo, Tokyo, Japan
[4] Griffith University, Brisbane, Australia
[5] University of York, York, UK

Abstract. Object categories are often grouped into a multi-granularity taxonomic hierarchy. Classifying objects at coarser-grained hierarchy requires global and common characteristics, while finer-grained hierarchy classification relies on local and discriminative features. Therefore, humans should also subconsciously focus on different object regions when classifying different hierarchies. This granularity-wise attention is confirmed by our collected human real-time gaze data on different hierarchy classifications. To leverage this mechanism, we propose a Cross-Hierarchical Region Feature (CHRF) learning framework. Specifically, we first design a region feature mining module that imitates humans to learn different granularity-wise attention regions with multi-grained classification tasks. To explore how human attention shifts from one hierarchy to another, we further present a cross-hierarchical orthogonal fusion module to enhance the region feature representation by blending the original feature and an orthogonal component extracted from adjacent hierarchies. Experiments on five hierarchical fine-grained datasets demonstrate the effectiveness of CHRF compared with the state-of-the-art methods. Ablation study and visualization results also consistently verify the advantages of our human attention-oriented modules. The code and dataset are available at https://github.com/visiondom/CHRF.

Keywords: Fine-grained visual classification · Multi-granularity · Human attention · Orthogonal fusion

Y. Liu and L. Zhou—Equal contribution.

Supplementary Information The online version contains supplementary material available at https://doi.org/10.1007/978-3-031-20053-3_4.

S. Avidan et al. (Eds.): ECCV 2022, LNCS 13684, pp. 57–73, 2022.
https://doi.org/10.1007/978-3-031-20053-3_4

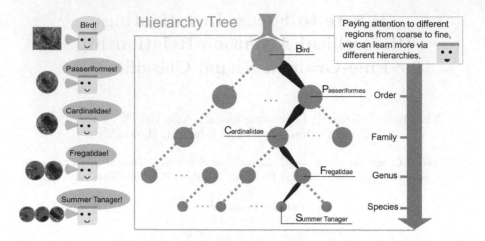

Fig. 1. Illustration of human attention behaviour for classification at different ranks. To recognize the *order* of a given bird image, humans generally glance at the entire bird, *i.e.*, large global attention that sufficiently discriminates categories of *orders*. When recognizing finer-grained categories, such as *genus* or *species*, humans ignore the shared characteristics in this *orders* and focus on smaller but significant local discriminative regions to find the minor inter-class differences between subordinate categories. (Color figure online)

1   Introduction

Fine-grained visual classification (FGVC) is more challenging than traditional image classification due to the highly similar appearance among subordinate categories. In the past decade, various approaches have been presented [2,23,36,43, 45] to learn the fine distinction between highly similar objects. Thanks to the powerful capability of deep neural networks on discriminative representation learning, deep model-based fine-grained methods [10,21,31,44] have achieved encouraging performance. However, most reported works ignore the multi-granularity relation among object categories, *e.g.*, different *orders* and *families* of birds, and directly train a classification model on one granularity or hierarchy.

The affinities of all the beings of the same class have sometimes been represented by a great tree[1]. Objects like animals, plants, cars, *etc.*, are often grouped into a taxon according to their shared morphological characteristics and given a taxonomic rank. Groups of a certain rank are aggregated to form a higher rank, thus creating a taxonomic hierarchy. Typically, closely related taxa under the same lower rank differ much less than more distantly related ones at higher levels. These hierarchical relationships are significant for designing computer vision models to solve the FGVC task. For example, to identify the *family* of a given bird, if its *order* is known, we then can focus on the differences between *families* that belonged to this *order* and ignore their common characteristics at the order

---

[1] Charles Darwin, On the Origin of Species.

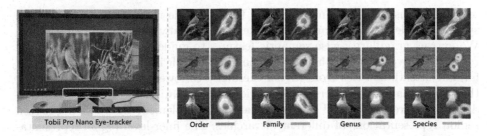

Fig. 2. Left: the eye-tracker device and classification game interface. Right: some samples of the collected human gaze on the CUB dataset [33]. From left to right are gaze data from the category hierarchy of *order*, *family*, *genus* and *species*, respectively.

rank, *i.e.*, more different discriminative regions should be paid attention to from coarse to fine levels. As illustrated in Fig. 1, the summer tanager, might be first classified to "passeriformes" according to their common characteristic perching-like shape, then grouped to "cardinalidae" with red belly, and finally classified to "summer tanager" due to the red crown and nape. In light of the taxonomic hierarchy, in this paper, we study the relationship of human attention for image classification at different granularities.

To investigate the attention mechanism of the human visual system when handling multi-granularity image classification, we designed a bird classification game at each category hierarchy of the Caltech-UCSD birds (CUB) dataset [33] following [22] to collect human gaze data for human attention monitoring. An eye-tracker is used to record participants' gaze when they classify the birds under different category hierarchies. We name the collected human gaze dataset Attention Reinforced Images on Species TaxonOmy (ARISTO). The detailed collection process is introduced in Appendix A. Figure 2 shows some samples of the ARISTO at different hierarchies. We can see that *at the coarser-level category hierarchy, humans prefer to glance at the entire bird, i.e., global attention. When classifying the finer-level categories, they attempt to find smaller local regions to distinguish the slight inter-class differences.* In addition, by observing the position of gaze points of the same image at different hierarchies, we can find the relationship between human attention at different category hierarchies: *the concerned regions at coarser-level classification tasks are usually different from the attention for finer-level classification.* This is because the attention of higher hierarchy often reflects the different attributes between the corresponding level category, while these attributes are common characteristics when classifying the sub-categories of one particular category. These results demonstrate that the human attention behavior on FGVC at different granularities coincides with the knowledge of taxonomic hierarchy.

Motivated by the adaptive human attention on different hierarchies, we propose a cross-hierarchical region feature (CHRF) learning framework to solve the FGVC problem at different granularities. There are two novel modules in the proposed framework: region feature mining (RFM) module and cross-hierarchical orthogonal fusion (COF) module. The RFM module mimics the human visual system that learns granularity-wise attention for individual category hierarchy. We extract granularity-wise semantic features to guide the learning of different region prototypes for each hierarchy. The COF module is designed to explore how human attention varies from higher hierarchy to lower one, further enhancing the discriminability of finer-grained region representation. Specifically, we introduce a feature orthogonal fusion operation to implement interaction between region representations of different hierarchies. The finer-level region representation can be disentangled by vector orthogonal decomposition with coarser-level representation, which outputs more discriminative features (orthogonal component) for the current hierarchy. Finally, we apply a fusion operation on the region representation and its orthogonal component.

Our main contributions can be summarized as follows: (1) We propose a cross-hierarchical region feature (CHRF) learning framework with two novel modules, *i.e.* the region feature mining and cross-hierarchical orthogonal fusion modules, to mimic human attention behavior towards improved FGVC at different granularities. (2) We design an image classification game that collects a human gaze dataset on the CUB at different category hierarchies. From the collected ARISTO dataset, we learn hierarchical relationships of human attention at different granularities, which are significant for the FGVC research. (3) Extensive experiments on five hierarchical fine-grained datasets show that our proposed CHRF can learn more discriminative representation on all hierarchies. The performance of CHRF is superior compared with other hierarchy-based methods and is also competitive among the state-of-the-art FGVC methods.

2   Related Work

2.1   Fine-Grained Visual Classification

Recently, the development of deep learning has led to remarkable breakthroughs in FGVC [3,36,40,44]. The primary stream methods of FGVC can be divided into two branches, *i.e.*, fine-grained feature learning [6,11,16,28] and discriminative part learning [1,10,15,21]. The former explores the invariant representation of images through end-to-end feature encoding. Methods with a bilinear structure [13,23,25] use high-order feature interactions to enhance the categorization and generalization abilities. However, the lack of spatial distributions of discriminative regions limits the performance of these feature learning methods when objects are severely deformed. On the other hand, methods based on part learning expect to locate the discriminative regions to help fine-grained recognition. Earlier researches in this direction [2,17,43] tend to improve classification performance by weak supervision of part or bounding box. However, the annotations for supervision are expensive to obtain. Therefore, some recent part-based works [9,20,38] use attention mechanisms to discover the distinguishable regions.

More recently, a few works [4,5] attempt to promote fine-grained classification by exploiting the multi-granularity category hierarchy. Chen *et al.* [5] introduced a hierarchical semantic embedding framework that used the predicted category score of the coarse level as the prior knowledge to predict the finer level sequentially. Chang *et al.* [4] designed a multiple label prediction model that exploits the inherent coarse-to-fine hierarchical relationship to perform hierarchy-wise feature disentanglement. Although the prior hierarchy relationship is available in these works, the essential multi-granularity classification mechanism of the human visual system is still not well-modelled in computer vision. Different from these works, we study the relationship of human attention for image classification at different granularities.

2.2   Human Attention in Vision

Many researchers [7,8,12,35] have exploited human attention behavior in different scenarios. Liu *et al.* [26] utilized human attention maps to guide the learning of attention maps for neural image caption. Huang *et al.* [18] proposed a hybrid model to predict human gaze by combining bottom-up visual saliency with task-dependent attention transition in egocentric videos. Liu *et al.* [27] tackled zero-shot recognition by learning discriminative attribute localization supervised by human attention when recognizing an unseen class. Human attention was also demonstrated to be able to enhance the medical application [19,34]. Rong *et al.* [32] exploited human attention as a data augmentation step to improve the accuracy of fine-grained classification. Yu *et al.* [42] proposed vision Transformer by simulating the glance and gaze behavior of humans when identifying objects in the natural scenario. Partially motivated by these works, in this paper we design a CHRF framework by mimicking the human attention behavior to solve the FGVC task at different granularities.

3   Approach

To classify images at different granularities, humans will focus on different regions of objects. A global observation is helpful to distinguish coarse-grained objects. However, when humans classify finer-grained objects, they tend to explore more local discriminative regions which may be ignored during coarser-grained classification. Motivated by the relationship between the observed regions from coarse to fine by the human visual system, we investigate the interaction among interested regions at different hierarchies.

Problem Definition. Different from most existing FGVC tasks [6,10,40,44], we follow a multi-grained classification setting [4,5]. For a given image $\mathbf{x}$, the multi-grained hierarchical labels, $\{y^1, y^2, ..., y^l, ..., y^L\}$, are available from coarse to fine. The motivation of this setting is to simulate humans to study the interactions of hierarchies under different granularity views. In this section, we propose a cross-hierarchical region feature (CHRF) learning framework to simultaneously perform classification at different category hierarchies.

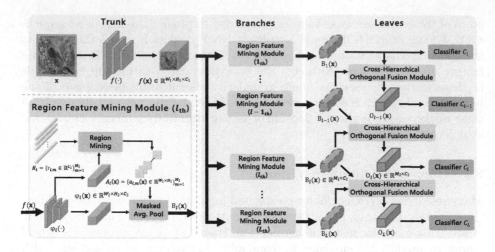

Fig. 3. An overview of the cross-hierarchical region feature learning (CHRF) framework, which consists of trunk, branches and leaves. The trunk is utilized to extract image features. Branches include L region feature mining (RFM) modules to mine different grained region representations. Leaves exploit the cross-hierarchical orthogonal fusion (COF) module to enhance the discriminability of the finer-grained representation by integrating the region representations of two adjacent hierarchies. The bottom left is the detailed RFM module. The COF module is shown in Fig. 4.

3.1   Overview

The overview of the proposed CHRF framework is depicted in Fig. 3. CHRF is a tree structure consisting of three parts, trunk, branches, and leaves. Given an image $\mathbf{x}$ with labels $\{y^1, y^2, ..., y^l, ..., y^L\}$, the trunk extracts image feature $f(\mathbf{x}) \in \mathbb{R}^{W_1 \times H_1 \times C_1}$ by a CNN $f(\cdot)$, where W_1, H_1 and C_1 denote the image feature's width, height and the number of channel, respectively.

Although $f(\mathbf{x})$ can describe the characteristics of $\mathbf{x}$, it lacks the insight in multi-granularity perspective. Therefore, we utilize the branches including L region feature mining (RFM) modules to mine the different grained region representations. Without loss of generality, we consider a multi-grained classification task with a category hierarchy of L levels. We use $1, 2, ..., l, ..., L$ to denote each level from coarse to fine. Each level contains one RFM module to simulate human cognitive behavior and find visual patterns corresponding to the level, *e.g.*, we will see the whole body of a bird or a butterfly in the order level, however, the head of the bird and the wing stripe of the butterfly will be focused on in the species level. Then the granularity-wise attention region representation $B_l(\mathbf{x}) \in \mathbb{R}^{M_l \times C_2}$ will be excavated, where M_l and C_2 denote the number of region at level l and the number of channels, respectively.

Leaves integrate the region representations of two adjacent levels through a cross-hierarchical orthogonal fusion (COF) module to enhance the finer-grained region representation. Our motivation of COF is to compare the difference between fine-grained observation and coarse-grained observation and improve the discriminability of the fine-grained representation. Specifically, for level l, COF takes as inputs $B_{l-1}(\mathbf{x})$ and $B_l(\mathbf{x})$ respectively produced by RFM_{l-1} and RFM_l and outputs the region orthogonal feature $O_l(\mathbf{x}) \in \mathbb{R}^{M_l \times C_2}$. For the most coarse-grained hierarchy, $i.e.$, level 1, we use the region representation B_1 and y^1 to directly learn the classifier C_1. The classification objective of the first hierarchy can be formulated as:

$$\mathcal{L}_{cls,1} = \mathcal{L}_{CE}\left(C_1(B_1), y^1\right) \tag{1}$$

where $\mathcal{L}_{CE}$ is the cross-entropy loss. For level l among 2 to L, the discriminative region orthogonal feature $O_l(\mathbf{x})$ and y^l are taken as inputs to the classifier C_l. The classification objective of the l-th hierarchy can be formulated as:

$$\mathcal{L}_{cls,l} = \mathcal{L}_{CE}\left(C_l(O_l), y^l\right), l = 2, 3, ..., L \tag{2}$$

The total classification loss function can be then written as:

$$\mathcal{L}_{cls} = \sum_{l=1}^{L} \mathcal{L}_{cls,l} \tag{3}$$

By minimizing the loss in Eq. (3), CHRF is expected to achieve two goals: 1) the fine-grained level can enhance the discriminability of the regional observation by finding the difference compared with the coarse-grained level during the forward procedure. 2) the coarse-grained level feature can obtain extra supplementary details from the fine-grained level through the backward procedure. By the interaction of regions among different hierarchies, both coarse and fine levels can gain a performance improvement.

3.2   Region Feature Mining Module

In light of the insight that humans will focus on different regions and different extents of a region when classifying images at multiple granularities [41], we simulate this human attention mechanism to study the region representations at different hierarchies. The detailed network structure of the RFM module is shown in the bottom left of Fig. 3.

   For the RFM of level l, we firstly extract granularity-wise semantic feature $\varphi_l(\mathbf{x}) \in \mathbb{R}^{W_2 \times H_2 \times C_2}$ by a CNN $\varphi_l(\cdot)$ from the image feature $f(\mathbf{x})$, where $\varphi_l(\cdot)$ is exclusive for the specific hierarchy. Specifically, a set of learnable region prototypes $R_l = \{r_{l,m} \in \mathbb{R}^{C_2}\}_{m=1}^{M_l}$ are introduced to discover M_l different regions of $\varphi_l(\mathbf{x})$, where $r_{l,m}$ denotes the m-th region prototype at level l. The feature vectors of $\varphi_l(\mathbf{x})$ are grouped into a series of related similarity map by calculating the dot product between the feature vector and region prototype. Then, we use a region mining operation implemented by batch normalization and ReLU activation to produce the region masks $A_l(\mathbf{x}) = \{a_{l,m}(\mathbf{x}) \in \mathbb{R}^{W_2 \times H_2}\}_{m=1}^{M_l}$. Finally, the vectors of semantic feature are weighted by the region masks and further aggregated to form region representation by global average pooling:

$$b_{l,m}(\mathbf{x}) = \frac{1}{W_2 H_2} \sum_{i=1}^{W_2} \sum_{j=1}^{H_2} a_{l,m}^{i,j}(\mathbf{x}) \varphi_l^{i,j}(\mathbf{x}) \tag{4}$$

where $b_{l,m}(\mathbf{x})$ denotes the m-th region representation and (i,j) denotes the spatial location. These region-level representations are futher concatenated to form the observation $B_l(\mathbf{x}) = [b_{l,1}(\mathbf{x}), b_{l,2}(\mathbf{x}), ..., b_{l,M_l}(\mathbf{x})]$ of level l. The observation B_l including M_l regions can describe the image's patterns from different views that is helpful to investigate the relationship of the region observations among multiple granularity levels.

Then, L region observations $B_1, B_2, ..., B_L$ are obtained from different granularity levels by branches. These multi-grained attentions contain the spatial location information and the extent of the regions which are similar to the human attention mechanism, $i.e.$, the coarser-grained focuses on less different spatial locations with larger extent. In contrast, the finer-grained focuses on more different spatial locations with smaller extent. For finer-grained classification, smaller local observations are discriminative, which are not necessarily emphasized in coarse-grained observation.

3.3   Cross-Hierarchical Orthogonal Fusion Module

When classifying images at category level l, humans tend to overlook the common properties of the same category at level $l - 1$ and pay more attention to the discriminative properties. We mimic this behavior to realize the interaction of the region representations of two adjacent levels. Inspired by [37,39], the discriminative features are expected to be disentangled from the finer-grained region representation by feature vector decomposition. Specifically, we design a COF module to improve the discriminability of region representations at different hierarchies.

The structure of COF is shown in Fig. 4(a). Firstly, the global observation $G_{l-1}(\mathbf{x}) \in \mathbb{R}^{1 \times C_2}$ of $B_{l-1}(\mathbf{x})$ is computed by average pooling operation:

$$G_{l-1}(\mathbf{x}) = \frac{1}{M_{l-1}} \sum_{m=1}^{M_{l-1}} b_{l-1,m}(\mathbf{x}) \tag{5}$$

Then, we calculate the projection $b_{l,m}^{proj}(\mathbf{x})$ of the m-th region representation $b_{l,m}(\mathbf{x})$ on the global observation. This operation can be written as:

$$b_{l,m}^{proj}(\mathbf{x}) = \frac{b_{l,m}(\mathbf{x}) \cdot G_{l-1}(\mathbf{x})}{|G_{l-1}(\mathbf{x})|^2} G_{l-1}(\mathbf{x}) \tag{6}$$

The projection contains redundant common properties of the m-th region representation of the finer-level. The discriminative region observation can be obtained by computing the orthogonal component:

$$b_{l,m}^{orth}(\mathbf{x}) = b_{l,m}(\mathbf{x}) - b_{l,m}^{proj}(\mathbf{x}) \tag{7}$$

A fusion operation is then used to enhance the discriminability of the region representation, which is demonstrated in Fig. 4(b), where we use $o_{l,m}^{optimal}$ to denote an optimal region representation for classification. To obtain a distinguishable

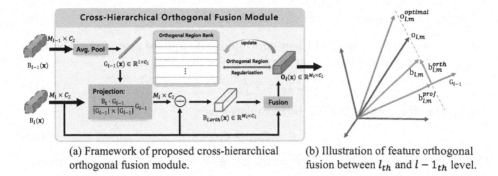

(a) Framework of proposed cross-hierarchical orthogonal fusion module.

(b) Illustration of feature orthogonal fusion between l_{th} and $l-1_{th}$ level.

Fig. 4. An illustration of the proposed cross-hierarchical orthogonal fusion module.

feature closer to $o_{l,m}^{optimal}$, we add a component to $b_{l,m}(\mathbf{x})$ along the direction of $b_{l,m}^{orth}(\mathbf{x})$. Therefore, the m-th region orthogonal feature can be calculated by:

$$o_{l,m}(\mathbf{x}) = b_{l,m}(\mathbf{x}) + \lambda b_{l,m}^{orth}(\mathbf{x}) \tag{8}$$

where λ is the influence factor controlling the degree of blending orthogonal component. We further analysis the fusion operation in Appendix B. Then, all orthogonal features are concatenated to form the whole region orthogonal feature $O_l(\mathbf{x}) = [o_{l,1}(\mathbf{x}), o_{l,2}(\mathbf{x}), ..., o_{l,M_l}(\mathbf{x})]$ of level l.

The region orthogonal features will be used next for classification. Furthermore, we introduce an orthogonal region bank to store the center representation $c_m^{y^l}$ of the orthogonal region for every category at level l. Inspired by [30], we design an orthogonal region regularization to make each region more discriminative, which can be written as:

$$\mathcal{L}_{orr,l} = \frac{1}{M_l} \sum_{m=1}^{M_l} \left(1 - \cos(o_{l,m}(\mathbf{x}), c_m^{y^l}) + \frac{1}{M_l - 1} \sum_{\substack{j=1 \\ j \neq m}}^{M_l} \left| \cos(o_{l,m}(\mathbf{x}), c_j^{y^l}) \right| \right)$$

$$= \frac{1}{M_l} \sum_{m=1}^{M_l} \left(1 - \cos(o_{l,m}(\mathbf{x}), c_m^{y^l}) \right) + \frac{1}{M_l(M_l - 1)} \sum_{m=1}^{M_l} \sum_{\substack{j=1 \\ j \neq m}}^{M_l} \left(\left| \cos(o_{l,m}(\mathbf{x}), c_j^{y^l}) \right| \right) \tag{9}$$

where $\cos(\cdot, \cdot)$ and $|\cdot|$ denote a cosine similarity and an absolute value operator, respectively. The first term makes the similarity between the region orthogonal feature and its center close to 1, which ensures clustering of the same region orthogonal feature. The second term makes the similarity close to 0, which ensures the orthogonality of different region orthogonal features to reduce their correlation, so that RFM can explore more different regions. The center representation $c_m^{y^l}$ of an orthogonal region is initialized from zero and optimized by momentum update:

$$c_m^{y^l} \leftarrow c_m^{y^l} + \beta \left(o_{l,m}(\mathbf{x}) - c_m^{y^l} \right) \tag{10}$$

where β is a momentum coefficient controlling the update rate of $c_m^{y^l}$. The total orthogonal region regularization can be written as:

$$\mathcal{L}_{orr} = \sum_{l=2}^{L} \mathcal{L}_{orr,l} \tag{11}$$

Then, the whole objective can be formulated as:

$$\mathcal{L} = \mathcal{L}_{cls} + \mathcal{L}_{orr} \tag{12}$$

The joint training establishes the relationship between hierarchies, thus improving discriminability of region representation.

4   Experiments and Analysis

In this section, we report comprehensive experiments to verify the effectiveness of our method. We analyse the influence of hierarchy interaction and compare our CHRF with baselines on five hierarchical fine-grained datasets. CHRF is also compared with the state-of-the-art fine-grained methods on three widely used FGVC datasets. Finally, we present additional experiments to demonstrate the consistency of results and human vision system in handling the hierarchical data. The implementation details are provided in Appendix C.

4.1   Datasets

CUB [33] is the most widely used benchmark for FGVC task. It contains $11,877$ images covering 200 species of birds. The dataset is divided into two sets including $5,994$ training images and $5,794$ test images. The 200 *species* of birds are grouped into 122 *genera*, 37 *families*, and 13 *orders* by a bird taxonomy hierarchy according to the ornithological systematics [5].

Butterfly-200 [5] is a newly released butterfly dataset, which has a hierarchical structure with 200 *species*, 116 *genera*, 23 *subfamilies*, and 5 *families* according to the insect taxonomy. The dataset contains $25,279$ images, including a training set of $5,135$ images, a validation set of $5,135$ images and a test set of $15,009$ images.

VegFru [14] is a dataset with fine-grained vegetables and fruits recognition covering 292 *subordinate* classes and 25 *upper-level* categories. VegFru dataset has $29,200$ images for training, $14,600$ for validation and $116,931$ for testing.

FGVC-Aircraft [29] contains 100 fine-grained aircraft *models*, which are grouped into 70 *families* and 30 *makers* by tracing superclasses in Wikipedia pages [4]. The dataset has $10,000$ images, $6,667$ are for training and $3,333$ for evaluation.

Stanford Cars [24] contains 196 car *models*, which can be re-organised into 9 *makers* by tracing superclasses in Wikipedia pages [4]. The dataset contains $16,185$ images, including $8,144$ images for training and $8,041$ images for testing.

Table 1. Comparison with different baselines on CUB, Butterfly-200 and VegFru under the multi-granularity setting. The best and the second best results are marked in red and blue.

Methods	CUB					Butterfly-200					VegFru		
	P_1	P_2	P_3	P_4	wAP	P_1	P_2	P_3	P_4	wAP	P_1	P_2	wAP
Baseline	98.5	95.4	91.6	85.4	88.9	98.9	97.4	94.4	84.3	88.8	90.6	88.5	88.7
Baseline++	98.6	95.5	91.4	85.3	88.8	98.9	97.3	94.2	84.4	88.8	90.8	88.8	89.0
HSE [5]	98.8	95.7	92.7	88.1	90.7	98.9	97.7	95.4	86.1	90.2	90.0	89.4	89.5
Ours-RF	98.7	95.7	92.8	87.2	90.3	98.9	97.8	95.3	86.5	90.4	92.0	90.6	90.7
Ours-CHRF	99.0	96.3	93.5	89.4	91.8	99.1	97.8	96.0	87.4	91.2	92.2	91.3	91.4

Table 2. Comparison with different baselines on CUB, FGVC-Aircraft and Stanford Cars under the multi-granularity setting. The best and the second best results are marked in red and blue.

Methods	CUB				FGVC-Aircraft				Stanford Cars		
	P_1	P_2	P_3	wAP	P_1	P_2	P_3	wAP	P_1	P_2	wAP
Baseline	98.5	95.7	85.4	87.6	95.9	93.8	91.5	93.0	96.7	93.5	93.6
Baseline++	98.6	95.5	85.3	87.5	96.0	94.1	91.9	93.3	96.9	93.4	93.6
FGN [4]	98.0	94.7	85.4	87.5	95.6	94.6	92.7	93.8	97.0	94.1	94.2
Ours-RF	98.7	96.0	87.2	89.1	96.4	95.2	92.5	94.0	97.2	94.1	94.2
Ours-CHRF	98.9	96.2	89.2	90.8	96.5	95.6	93.6	94.7	97.2	95.2	95.3

4.2 Hierarchy Interaction Analysis

Evaluation Metrics. Directly calculating the arithmetic mean of the accuracy across all hierarchies [4] cannot reasonably evaluate the overall performance of the model, since the classification difficulty at different hierarchies varies. Therefore, we propose a more convincing evaluation metric. First, we calculate the Top-1 precision of all hierarchies, respectively. Then, the hierarchical classification performance can be evaluated by the weighted average precision (wAP) of all hierarchies:

$$wAP = \sum_{l=1}^{L} \frac{class\_num_l}{\sum_{k=1}^{L} class\_num_k} P_l \tag{13}$$

where $class\_num_l$ and P_l denote the number of categories and Top-1 classification accuracy at level l, respectively. The finer-grained hierarchy contains more categories, so the performance of the finer-grained hierarchy should account for a larger proportion.

Compared Methods. To verify the effectiveness of CHRF and different modules, we compare them with several baseline methods. **Baseline** contains fundamental structures including $f(\cdot)$ and $\varphi(\cdot)$, which is similar to CHRF. The shared former network is frozen and the latter is learnable to adapt different hierarchies.

Baseline++ has the same structure as Baseline, but the parameters of $f(\cdot)$ are freed. **HSE** [5] also adopts a hierarchical structure for multi-granularity setting, which focuses on the influence of the prediction score of coarse hierarchy on the classification of fine hierarchy. **FGN** [4] investigates the impact of transfer between classification tasks at different granularities. **Ours-RF** is the Baseline model with the RFM module. **Ours-CHRF** is the full framework of our CHRF with hierarchy interaction. For fair comparisons, all methods were implemented with the same setting. For HSE, we show the results reported in [5]. For FGN, we re-produced the method and did experiments under the same setting as ours. We utilized the groups of CUB mentioned in [4].

Results and Ablation Study. The results are shown in Table 1 and Table 2. Baseline and Baseline++ exhibit similar performance under the metric of wAP on all datasets. We speculate that this is because the pre-trained $f(\cdot)$ can well extract visual feature representation. Thus, it is reasonable to fix the parameters of $f(\cdot)$ in our other models. When the RFM modules are added into Baseline, *i.e.* Ours-RF, the model extracts region representations to improve discrimination of different categories at all hierarchies and obtains 1.4%, 1.6%, 2.0%, 1.0%, and 0.6% improvement under wAP on all five datasets, respectively. Furthermore, compared with Ours-RF, Ours-CHRF can achieve 1.5%, 0.8%, 0.7%, 0.7%, and 1.1% wAP improvement on all five datasets, respectively. In the end, Ours-CHRF outperforms both HSE and FGN by a large margin.

Analysis. The experimental results show that our CHRF framework is effective in solving the FGVC task at different granularities. The proposed RFM and COF modules are the main technical contributions to ensure that the CHRF can mimic the human visual system, and the more discriminative regions are gradually focused on from coarse to fine. Different from other attention models [15, 21, 31], RFM explores granularity-wise attentions for different category hierarchies. On the coarser hierarchy, attention tends to be a global observation, so the improvement is not obvious. On finer hierarchy, attention tends to focus on more local regions, and more details are extracted, so Ours-RF has a significant improvement compared with the Baseline. Built on granularity-wise attention, COF investigates the interaction among attentions of different hierarchies. More discriminative regions of the finer hierarchy can be found by comparing coarse attention and fine attention. The interaction effectively boosts boost the classification accuracy of both coarse and fine granularity hierarchies.

Where to Focus? We visualize the attention maps of humans, Ours-RF, and Ours-CHRF in Fig. 5. By the region representations interaction through COF module, coarse-granularity and fine-granularity learn where to focus. Attention maps produced by Ours-RF and Ours-CHRF exhibit the consistent characteristic as human attentions, *i.e.*, global attentions are preferred to produce at coarser-granularity category hierarchy and more smaller discriminative local regions are

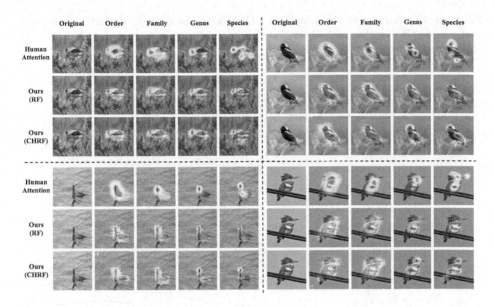

Fig. 5. Visualization of the attention maps from human, Ours-RF and Ours-CHRF on four hierarchies (*order, family, genus* and *species*) on the CUB dataset.

attempted to explore when classifying the finer-granularity categories. From the visualization results, we can see that the attentions of finer-granularity are usually different from the concerned regions of coarser-granularity. The common properties of the coarser-granularity are overlooked and the discriminative properties are concerned. In addition, attentions of Ours-CHRF are more distinct than Ours-RF for the discriminative regions mining at different hierarchies. This comparison validates the effectiveness of our COF module.

4.3   Evaluation on Traditional FGVC Setting

In this section, we also validate the effectiveness of our CHRF compared with recent state-of-the-art FGVC methods. We report the top-1 classification accuracy of CHRF at the bottom of the hierarchy. The results are shown in Table 3. For FGVC-Aircraft and Stanford Cars, CHRF outperforms all compared methods. For CUB, our CHRF can also achieve a competitive result which is only slightly lower than PMG. Notably, different from these methods, partial parameters of CHRF (*i.e.* $f(\cdot)$) are frozen. CHRF depends on the interaction among different hierarchies to improve the performance and achieve competitive results compared with state-of-the-art FGVC methods.

4.4   Further Analysis

Figure 6 shows the effect of the influence factor λ. We vary λ among $\{0.0, 0.2, 0.4, 0.6, 0.8\}$ to observe the performance changes. The best results are achieved for

Table 3. Comparison of the proposed CHRF with the state-of-the-art methods on traditional FGVC setting. The best and the second best results are marked in red and blue, respectively.

Methods	Accuracy (%)		
	CUB	FGVC-Aircraft	Stanford Cars
NTS-Net (ECCV'18) [40]	87.5	91.4	93.9
PC (ECCV'18) [11]	86.9	89.2	92.9
DCL (CVPR'19) [6]	87.8	93.0	94.5
S3N (ICCV'19) [9]	88.5	92.8	94.7
ACNet (CVPR'20) [21]	88.1	92.4	94.6
PMG (ECCV'20) [10]	89.6	93.4	95.1
SPS (ICCV'21) [16]	88.7	92.7	94.9
CHRF (Ours)	89.4	93.6	95.2

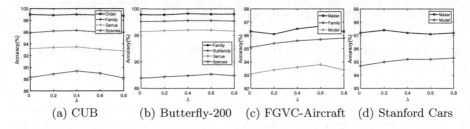

(a) CUB   (b) Butterfly-200   (c) FGVC-Aircraft   (d) Stanford Cars

Fig. 6. The effect of λ with different values on CUB, Butterfly-200, FGVC-Aircraft and Stanford Cars.

CUB and Cars datasets when λ is 0.4. For Butterfly-200 and Aircraft datasets, the best results are achieved when λ is 0.6. Thus, we set λ to 0.4 to achieve a trade-off performance on all datasets. Due to the length limitation of the paper, more analyses about region prototypes and orthogonal region regularization are given in Appendix C.

5   Conclusions

In this paper, we aim to solve the fine-grained visual classification task at different granularities. We study the relationship between hierarchical human attention by collecting human gaze data from a designed classification game. We designed a cross-hierarchical region feature learning framework to mimic human attention behavior that learns different discriminative representations for the corresponding category hierarchy. Extensive experiments on five hierarchical fine-grained datasets validate the superiority of the proposed human attention-oriented method. The code of our method and the collected human gaze dataset on four hierarchies of the CUB have been released. We believe there is tremendous potential for investigating the hierarchical human attention relationship for the multi-granularity image classification task.

Acknowledgement. This work was supported by JST, ACT-X Grant Number JPM-JAX190D, Japan and JST Moonshot R&D Grant Number JPMJMS2011.

References

1. Berg, T., Belhumeur, P.N.: POOF: part-based one-vs.-one features for fine-grained categorization, face verification, and attribute estimation. In: Proceedings of the IEEE Conference on Computer Vision and Pattern Recognition, pp. 955–962 (2013)
2. Chai, Y., Lempitsky, V., Zisserman, A.: Symbiotic segmentation and part localization for fine-grained categorization. In: Proceedings of the IEEE International Conference on Computer Vision, pp. 321–328 (2013)
3. Chang, D., et al.: The devil is in the channels: mutual-channel loss for fine-grained image classification. IEEE Trans. Image Process. **29**, 4683–4695 (2020)
4. Chang, D., Pang, K., Zheng, Y., Ma, Z., Song, Y.Z., Guo, J.: Your "flamingo" is my "bird": fine-grained, or not. In: Proceedings of the IEEE/CVF Conference on Computer Vision and Pattern Recognition, pp. 11476–11485 (2021)
5. Chen, T., Wu, W., Gao, Y., Dong, L., Luo, X., Lin, L.: Fine-grained representation learning and recognition by exploiting hierarchical semantic embedding. In: Proceedings of the 26th ACM International Conference on Multimedia, pp. 2023–2031 (2018)
6. Chen, Y., Bai, Y., Zhang, W., Mei, T.: Destruction and construction learning for fine-grained image recognition. In: Proceedings of the IEEE/CVF Conference on Computer Vision and Pattern Recognition, pp. 5157–5166 (2019)
7. Das, A., Agrawal, H., Zitnick, L., Parikh, D., Batra, D.: Human attention in visual question answering: do humans and deep networks look at the same regions? Comput. Vis. Image Underst. **163**, 90–100 (2017)
8. Ding, S., Qu, S., Xi, Y., Wan, S.: Stimulus-driven and concept-driven analysis for image caption generation. Neurocomputing **398**, 520–530 (2020)
9. Ding, Y., Zhou, Y., Zhu, Y., Ye, Q., Jiao, J.: Selective sparse sampling for fine-grained image recognition. In: Proceedings of the IEEE/CVF International Conference on Computer Vision, pp. 6599–6608 (2019)
10. Du, R., et al.: Fine-grained visual classification via progressive multi-granularity training of jigsaw patches. In: Vedaldi, A., Bischof, H., Brox, T., Frahm, J.-M. (eds.) ECCV 2020. LNCS, vol. 12365, pp. 153–168. Springer, Cham (2020). https://doi.org/10.1007/978-3-030-58565-5_10
11. Dubey, A., Gupta, O., Guo, P., Raskar, R., Farrell, R., Naik, N.: Pairwise confusion for fine-grained visual classification. In: Proceedings of the European Conference on Computer Vision, pp. 70–86 (2018)
12. Fan, D.P., Wang, W., Cheng, M.M., Shen, J.: Shifting more attention to video salient object detection. In: Proceedings of the IEEE/CVF Conference on Computer Vision and Pattern Recognition, pp. 8554–8564 (2019)
13. Gao, Y., Beijbom, O., Zhang, N., Darrell, T.: Compact bilinear pooling. In: Proceedings of the IEEE Conference on Computer Vision and Pattern Recognition, pp. 317–326 (2016)
14. Hou, S., Feng, Y., Wang, Z.: VegFru: a domain-specific dataset for fine-grained visual categorization. In: Proceedings of the IEEE International Conference on Computer Vision, pp. 541–549 (2017)

15. Hu, T., Qi, H., Huang, Q., Lu, Y.: See better before looking closer: weakly supervised data augmentation network for fine-grained visual classification. arXiv preprint arXiv:1901.09891 (2019)
16. Huang, S., Wang, X., Tao, D.: Stochastic partial swap: Enhanced model generalization and interpretability for fine-grained recognition. In: Proceedings of the IEEE/CVF International Conference on Computer Vision, pp. 620–629 (2021)
17. Huang, S., Xu, Z., Tao, D., Zhang, Y.: Part-stacked CNN for fine-grained visual categorization. In: Proceedings of the IEEE Conference on Computer Vision and Pattern Recognition, pp. 1173–1182 (2016)
18. Huang, Y., Cai, M., Li, Z., Sato, Y.: Predicting gaze in egocentric video by learning task-dependent attention transition. In: Proceedings of the European Conference on Computer Vision, pp. 754–769 (2018)
19. Huang, Y., et al.: Leveraging human selective attention for medical image analysis with limited training data. In: The British Machine Vision Conference (2021)
20. Huang, Z., Li, Y.: Interpretable and accurate fine-grained recognition via region grouping. In: Proceedings of the IEEE/CVF Conference on Computer Vision and Pattern Recognition, pp. 8662–8672 (2020)
21. Ji, R., et al.: Attention convolutional binary neural tree for fine-grained visual categorization. In: Proceedings of the IEEE/CVF Conference on Computer Vision and Pattern Recognition, pp. 10468–10477 (2020)
22. Karessli, N., Akata, Z., Schiele, B., Bulling, A.: Gaze embeddings for zero-shot image classification. In: Proceedings of the IEEE Conference on Computer Vision and Pattern Recognition, pp. 4525–4534 (2017)
23. Kong, S., Fowlkes, C.: Low-rank bilinear pooling for fine-grained classification. In: Proceedings of the IEEE Conference on Computer Vision and Pattern Recognition, pp. 365–374 (2017)
24. Krause, J., Stark, M., Deng, J., Fei-Fei, L.: 3D object representations for fine-grained categorization. In: Proceedings of the IEEE International Conference on Computer Vision Workshops, pp. 554–561 (2013)
25. Lin, T.Y., RoyChowdhury, A., Maji, S.: Bilinear CNN models for fine-grained visual recognition. In: Proceedings of the IEEE International Conference on Computer Vision, pp. 1449–1457 (2015)
26. Liu, C., Mao, J., Sha, F., Yuille, A.: Attention correctness in neural image captioning. In: Proceedings of the AAAI Conference on Artificial Intelligence (2017)
27. Liu, Y., et al.: Goal-oriented gaze estimation for zero-shot learning. In: Proceedings of the IEEE/CVF Conference on Computer Vision and Pattern Recognition, pp. 3794–3803 (2021)
28. Luo, W., et al.: Cross-X learning for fine-grained visual categorization. In: Proceedings of the IEEE/CVF International Conference on Computer Vision, pp. 8242–8251 (2019)
29. Maji, S., Rahtu, E., Kannala, J., Blaschko, M., Vedaldi, A.: Fine-grained visual classification of aircraft. arXiv preprint arXiv:1306.5151 (2013)
30. Ranasinghe, K., Naseer, M., Hayat, M., Khan, S., Khan, F.S.: Orthogonal projection loss. In: Proceedings of the IEEE/CVF International Conference on Computer Vision, pp. 12333–12343 (2021)
31. Rao, Y., Chen, G., Lu, J., Zhou, J.: Counterfactual attention learning for fine-grained visual categorization and re-identification. In: Proceedings of the IEEE/CVF International Conference on Computer Vision, pp. 1025–1034 (2021)
32. Rong, Y., Xu, W., Akata, Z., Kasneci, E.: Human attention in fine-grained classification. In: BMVC 2021 (2021)

33. Wah, C., Branson, S., Welinder, P., Perona, P., Belongie, S.: The caltech-UCSD birds-200-2011 dataset (2011)
34. Wang, S., Ouyang, X., Liu, T., Wang, Q., Shen, D.: Follow my eye: using gaze to supervise computer-aided diagnosis. IEEE Trans. Med. Imaging (2022)
35. Wang, W., Shen, J., Guo, F., Cheng, M.M., Borji, A.: Revisiting video saliency: a large-scale benchmark and a new model. In: Proceedings of the IEEE Conference on Computer Vision and Pattern Recognition, pp. 4894–4903 (2018)
36. Wang, Y., Morariu, V.I., Davis, L.S.: Learning a discriminative filter bank within a CNN for fine-grained recognition. In: Proceedings of the IEEE Conference on Computer Vision and Pattern Recognition, pp. 4148–4157 (2018)
37. Wu, A., Liu, R., Han, Y., Zhu, L., Yang, Y.: Vector-decomposed disentanglement for domain-invariant object detection. In: Proceedings of the IEEE/CVF International Conference on Computer Vision, pp. 9342–9351 (2021)
38. Xiao, T., Xu, Y., Yang, K., Zhang, J., Peng, Y., Zhang, Z.: The application of two-level attention models in deep convolutional neural network for fine-grained image classification. In: Proceedings of the IEEE Conference on Computer Vision and Pattern Recognition, pp. 842–850 (2015)
39. Yang, M., et al.: DOLG: single-stage image retrieval with deep orthogonal fusion of local and global features. In: Proceedings of the IEEE/CVF International Conference on Computer Vision, pp. 11772–11781 (2021)
40. Yang, Z., Luo, T., Wang, D., Hu, Z., Gao, J., Wang, L.: Learning to navigate for fine-grained classification. In: Proceedings of the European Conference on Computer Vision, pp. 420–435 (2018)
41. Yu, A., Grauman, K.: Fine-grained visual comparisons with local learning. In: Proceedings of the IEEE Conference on Computer Vision and Pattern Recognition, pp. 192–199 (2014)
42. Yu, Q., Xia, Y., Bai, Y., Lu, Y., Yuille, A.L., Shen, W.: Glance-and-gaze vision transformer. Adv. Neural Inf. Process. Syst. **34**, 12992–13003 (2021)
43. Zhang, N., Donahue, J., Girshick, R., Darrell, T.: Part-based R-CNNs for fine-grained category detection. In: Fleet, D., Pajdla, T., Schiele, B., Tuytelaars, T. (eds.) ECCV 2014. LNCS, vol. 8689, pp. 834–849. Springer, Cham (2014). https://doi.org/10.1007/978-3-319-10590-1_54
44. Zhao, Y., Yan, K., Huang, F., Li, J.: Graph-based high-order relation discovery for fine-grained recognition. In: Proceedings of the IEEE/CVF Conference on Computer Vision and Pattern Recognition, pp. 15079–15088 (2021)
45. Zheng, H., Fu, J., Zha, Z.J., Luo, J.: Looking for the devil in the details: learning trilinear attention sampling network for fine-grained image recognition. In: Proceedings of the IEEE/CVF Conference on Computer Vision and Pattern Recognition, pp. 5012–5021 (2019)

DaViT: Dual Attention Vision Transformers

Mingyu Ding[1], Bin Xiao[2(✉)], Noel Codella[2], Ping Luo[1(✉)], Jingdong Wang[3], and Lu Yuan[2]

[1] The University of Hong Kong, Pok Fu Lam, Hong Kong
mingyuding@hku.hk, pluo@cs.hku.hk
[2] Microsoft, Bellevue, USA
{bixi,ncodella,luyuan}@microsoft.com
[3] Baidu, Beijing, China

Abstract. In this work, we introduce Dual Attention Vision Transformers (DaViT), a simple yet effective vision transformer architecture that is able to capture global context while maintaining computational efficiency. We propose approaching the problem from an orthogonal angle: exploiting self-attention mechanisms with both *"spatial tokens"* and *"channel tokens"*. With spatial tokens, the spatial dimension defines the token scope, and the channel dimension defines the token feature dimension. With channel tokens, we have the inverse: the channel dimension defines the token scope, and the spatial dimension defines the token feature dimension. We further group tokens along the sequence direction for both spatial and channel tokens to maintain the linear complexity of the entire model. We show that these two self-attentions complement each other: (i) since each channel token contains an abstract representation of the entire image, the channel attention naturally captures global interactions and representations by taking all spatial positions into account when computing attention scores between channels; (ii) the spatial attention refines the local representations by performing fine-grained interactions across spatial locations, which in turn helps the global information modeling in channel attention. Extensive experiments show DaViT backbones achieve state-of-the-art performance on four different tasks. Specially, DaViT-Tiny, DaViT-Small, and DaViT-Base achieve 82.8%, 84.2%, and 84.6% top-1 accuracy on ImageNet-1K without extra training data, using 28.3M, 49.7M, and 87.9M parameters, respectively. When we further scale up DaViT with 1.5B weakly supervised image and text pairs, DaViT-Giant reaches 90.4% top-1 accuracy on ImageNet-1K. Code is available at https://github.com/microsoft/DaViT.

M. Ding—This work is done when Mingyu was an intern at Microsoft.

Supplementary Information The online version contains supplementary material available at https://doi.org/10.1007/978-3-031-20053-3_5.

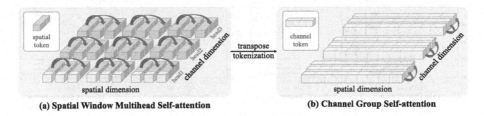

Fig. 1. (a) Spatial window multihead self-attention splits the spatial dimension into local windows, where each window contains multiple spatial tokens. Each token is also divided into multiple heads. (b) Channel group single-head self-attention groups channel tokens into multi groups. Attention is performed in each channel group with an entire image-level channel as a token. A channel-wise token that captures global information is also highlighted in (a). In this work, we alternately use these two types of attention to obtain both local fine-grained and global features.

1 Introduction

The global context is essential for many computer vision approaches, such as image classification and semantic segmentation. Convolutional neural networks (CNNs) [38] gradually obtain a global receptive field by multi-layer architectures and down-sampling operators. Recently, vision transformers [7,18], which directly capture long-range visual dependencies with a single self-attention layer, have drawn much attention. While these methods present strong capabilities to model the global context, their computational complexity grows quadratically with the token length, limiting their ability to scale up to high-resolution scenarios.

Designing an architecture that can capture global contexts while maintaining efficiency to learn from high-resolution inputs is still an open research problem. A substantial body of work has been dedicated to developing vision transformers toward this goal. iGPT [7] first utilized a standard transformer to solve vision tasks by treating the image as sequences of pixels and performing pixel-level interactions. After that, ViT [18] used non-overlapped image patches as tokens to model the relationship between small image patches instead of pixels, showing promising performance on middle-resolution tasks such as classification. To further reduce the computational cost, local attention [37,52,75] that limits attention in a spatially local window, and squeezed projection [55,58] that performs attention on downsampled tokens, were proposed. Though local attention methods benefit from linear complexity with the spatial size, operators like "Shift" [37], "Overlapping Patch" [55,58], "ConvFFN" [55,61,72] are indispensable to compensate for the loss of global contextual information.

The general pattern across all prior works is that they attain various tradeoffs between resolution, global context, and computational complexity: pixel-level [7] and patch-level [18,37,56,58] self-attentions suffer either the cost of quadratic computational overhead or loss of global contextual information. Beyond variations of pixel-level and patch-level self-attentions, can we design an image-level

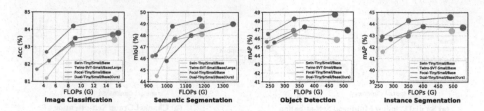

Fig. 2. Comparisons of the efficiency (*i.e.*, FLOPs) and performance (*e.g.*, Acc, mIoU, mAP) between the proposed approach and existing SoTA methods [9,37,65] on four computer vision tasks. Each method is represented by a circle, whose size represents the number of parameters. Our approach achieves superior performance under similar FLOPs than its counterparts on all four benchmarks.

self-attention mechanism that captures global information but is still efficient concerning the spatial size?

In this work, we introduce such a self-attention mechanism that is able to capture global context while maintaining computational efficiency. In addition to *"spatial tokens"* defined by existing works in Fig 1(a) representing the feature of an image patch, we introduce *"channel tokens"* by applying self-attention to the *transpose* of the token matrix, as shown in Fig 1(b). With channel tokens, the channel dimension defines the token scope, and the spatial dimension defines the token feature dimension. In this way, each channel token is global on the spatial dimension, containing an abstract representation of the entire image. Correspondingly, performing self-attention on such channel tokens further captures the global interaction by taking all spatial positions into account when computing attention scores between channels. Compared to conventional self-attention that performs global interactions over local pixels or patch tokens at a quadratic computational cost, the information exchange of channel self-attention is naturally imposed from a global perspective rather than a pixel/patch-wise one. Based on the global receptive field of the channel token, it fuses the representations to produce new global tokens and passes the information to the following layers. Thus, one can take such channel self-attention as a dynamic feature fusion over a series of abstract representations of the entire image.

Although this approach presents many advantages, a few challenges must be overcome. First, the computational complexity suddenly increases quadratically with the channel dimension, limiting the representation power of the layers. Inspired by spatial local attention [37,52,75], we propose *channel group attention* by dividing the feature channels into several groups and performing image-level interactions within each group. By group attention, we reduce the complexity to linear with respect to both the spatial and the channel dimensions. Since each channel token contains an abstract representation of the entire image, self-attention in this setting naturally captures the global interaction even we apply it locally along the channel dimensions.

Second, though channel-wise self-attention can capture global information easily, image-level tokens hinder local interactions across spatial locations. To solve this problem, we introduce Dual Attention Vision Transformers (DaViT) that alternately applies spatial window attention and channel group attention to capture both short-range and long-range visual dependencies, as shown in Fig. 1. Our results show that these two structures complement each other: the channel group attention provides a global receptive field on the spatial dimension and extracts high-level global-image representations by dynamic feature fusion across global channel tokens; the spatial window attention refines the local representations by performing fine-grained local interactions across spatial locations, which in turn helps the global information modeling in channel attention.

To summarize, we propose DaViT that contains two seamlessly integrated self-attentions: spatial window self-attention with *"spatial tokens"*, and channel group self-attention with *"channel tokens"*. The two forms of attention are complementary and alternatively arranged, providing both local fine-grained and global interactions in a computationally efficient manner. We evaluate the effectiveness of the proposed DaViT via comprehensive empirical studies on image classification, object detection, and segmentation. Results in Fig. 2 show that DaViT consistently outperforms the SoTA vision transformers across three benchmarks and four tasks with even fewer computational costs.

2 Related Work

Vision Transformers. Transformers [14,53] have dominated a wide range of natural language processing tasks. In computer vision, pioneering works iGPT [7] and ViT [18] apply attention directly to a sequence of image pixels or patches. Similarly, follow-up works [20,25,43,44,47,49,56,59,73] model global relationships on the patch-level tokens. All these works apply attention to capture interactions over all the local tokens, which can be pixel-level or patch-level. In this work, we model the global relationship from an orthogonal perspective and apply attention mechanisms to both spatial tokens as well as their transpose, which we refer to as image-level (global) channel tokens. In this manner, we capture both fine-grained structural patterns and global interactions.

Hierarchical Vision Transformers. Hierarchical designs are widely adopted to transformers [1,8,16,28,30–33,37,40,48,52,56,58,64,67,69,75,77,78] in vision. PVT [56] and CvT [58] perform attention on the squeezed tokens to reduce the computational cost. Swin Transformer [37], ViL [75], and HaloNet [52] apply local windows attention to the patch tokens, which capture fine-grained features and reduce the quadratic complexity to linear, but lose the ability of global modeling. To compensate for the loss of global context, Swin Transformer [37] conducts attention on the shifted local windows alternatively between consecutive blocks, and ViL [75] and HaloNet [52] play on overlapped windows. In this work, the proposed approach shares merits of hierarchical architectures and fine-grained local attention, meanwhile our proposed group channel attention still efficiently models the global context.

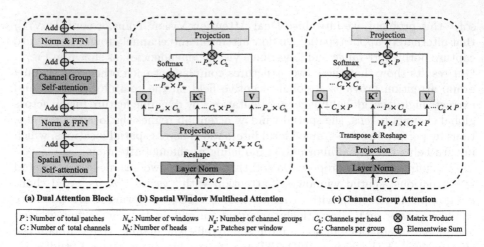

Fig. 3. Model architecture for our dual attention block. It contains two transformer blocks: spatial window self-attention and channel group self-attention blocks. By alternately using the two types of attention, our model enjoys the benefit of capturing both local fine-grained and global image-level interactions.

Channel-Wise Attentions. The author of [27] first proposes a Squeeze-and-Excitation (SE) block as channel-wise attention to re-calibrating the channel-wise features through the squeezed global feature. Other operators in CNNs related to our work are Dynamic Head [11] and DANet [19]. They apply attention along different feature dimensions on top of the CNN backbone for a specific task. Some transformer architectures involve channel-wise operations as well to reduce the computational costs. LambdaNetworks [2] first transforms the context into a linear function lambda that is applied to the corresponding query. XCiT [1] proposes cross-covariance attention (XCA) for efficient processing of high-resolution images. Similarly, CoaT [63] introduces a factorized attention mechanism that works efficiently in a multi-branch transformer backbone. We propose channel group attention to capture global information in transformers and demonstrate its power when combined with spatial window attention, forming our dual attention mechanism. Furthermore, we analyze in detail how our dual attention obtains global interactions as well as fine-grained local features.

3   Methodology

We propose Dual Attention Vision Transformers (DaViT), a clean, efficient, yet effective transformer backbone containing both local fine-grained features and global representations. In this section, we first introduce the hierarchical layout of our model. We then detail our channel group attention and the combination with spatial window attention [37].

3.1   Overview

We divide the model into four stages, where a patch embedding layer is inserted at the beginning of each stage. We stack our dual attention blocks in each stage with the resolution and feature dimension kept the same. Figure 3(a) illustrates the architecture of our dual attention block, consisting of a spatial window attention block and a channel group attention block.

Preliminaries. Let us assume a $\mathbb{R}^{P \times C}$ dimensional visual feature, where P is the number of total patches and C is the number of total channels. Simply applying the standard global self-attention leads to a complexity of $O(2P^2C + 4PC^2)$. It is defined as:

$$\mathcal{A}(\mathbf{Q}, \mathbf{K}, \mathbf{V}) = \text{Concat}(\text{head}_1, \dots, \text{head}_{N_h})$$
$$\text{where } \text{head}_i = \text{Attention}(\mathbf{Q}_i, \mathbf{K}_i, \mathbf{V}_i)$$
$$= \text{softmax}\left[\frac{\mathbf{Q}_i(\mathbf{K}_i)^{\text{T}}}{\sqrt{C_h}}\right] \mathbf{V}_i \qquad (1)$$

where $\mathbf{Q}_i = \mathbf{X}_i\mathbf{W}_i^Q$, $\mathbf{K}_i = \mathbf{X}_i\mathbf{W}_i^K$, and $\mathbf{V}_i = \mathbf{X}_i\mathbf{W}_i^V$ are $\mathbb{R}^{P \times C_h}$ dimensional visual features with N_h heads, $\mathbf{X}_i$ denotes the i_{th} head of the input feature and $\mathbf{W}_i$ denotes the projection weights of the i_{th} head for $\mathbf{Q}, \mathbf{K}, \mathbf{V}$, and $C = C_h * N_h$. Please note that the output projection $\mathbf{W}^O$ is omitted here. Considering P can be very large, e.g., 128×128, the computational cost is immoderate.

3.2   Spatial Window Attention

Window attention computes self-attention within local windows, as shown in Fig. 1(a). The windows are arranged to partition the image in a non-overlapping manner evenly. Supposing there are N_w different windows with each window containing P_w patches, where $P = P_w * N_w$. Then window attention can be represented by:

$$\mathcal{A}_{window}(\mathbf{Q}, \mathbf{K}, \mathbf{V}) = \{\mathcal{A}(\mathbf{Q}_j, \mathbf{K}_j, \mathbf{V}_j)\}_{j=0}^{N_w} \qquad (2)$$

where $\mathbf{Q}_j, \mathbf{K}_j, \mathbf{V}_j \in \mathbb{R}^{P_w \times C_h}$ are local window queries, keys, and values. The computational complexity of a window-based self-attention is $O(2PP_wC+4PC^2)$ with a linear complexity with the spatial size P. More details of window attention are shown in Fig. 3(b).

Though the computation is reduced, window attention loses the ability to model the global information. We will show that our proposed channel attention naturally solves this problem and mutually benefits with window attention.

3.3   Channel Group Attention

We visit self-attention from another perspective and propose channel-wise attention, as shown in Fig. 3(c). Previous self-attentions [7,37,52,53,58,74] in vision define tokens with pixels or patches, and gather the information along spatial dimensions. Instead of performing attention on pixel-level or patch-level, we apply attention mechanisms on the transpose of patch-level tokens. To obtain global information in the spatial dimension, we set the number of heads equal to 1. We argue that each transposed token abstracts the global information. In this way, channel tokens interact with global information on the channel dimension in linear spatial-wise complexity, as shown in Fig. 1(b).

Simply transposing the feature can obtain a vanilla channel-level attention with a complexity of $O(6PC^2)$. To further reduce the computational complexity, we group channels into multiple groups and perform self-attention within each group. Formally, let N_g denotes the number of groups and C_g denotes the number of channels in each group, we have $C = N_g * C_g$. In this way, our channel group attention is global, with image-level tokens interacting across a group of channels. It is defined as:

$$\mathcal{A}_{channel}(\mathbf{Q}, \mathbf{K}, \mathbf{V}) = \{\mathcal{A}_{group}(\mathbf{Q}_j, \mathbf{K}_j, \mathbf{V}_j)^T\}_{j=0}^{N_g}$$

$$\mathcal{A}_{group}(\mathbf{Q}_j, \mathbf{K}_j, \mathbf{V}_j) = \text{softmax}\left[\frac{\mathbf{Q}_j^T \mathbf{K}_j}{\sqrt{C_g}}\right] \mathbf{V}_j^T \qquad (3)$$

where $\mathbf{Q}_j, \mathbf{K}_j, \mathbf{V}_j \in \mathbb{R}^{P \times C_g}$ are grouped channel-wise image-level queries, keys, and values. Note that although we transpose the tokens in channel attention, the projection layers $\mathbf{W}$ and the scaling factor $\frac{1}{\sqrt{C_g}}$ remain performed and computed along the channel dimension, rather than the spatial one. Considering that the number of spatial patches varies with the image size, the above design ensures our model can generalize to any image size.

Complexity Analysis. Our channel group attention is performed on the image-level tokens across the channel dimension. Compared to window attention that produces an attention map with size $P_w \times P_w$, the channel-wise attention map is of $C_g \times C_g$-dimensional. The overall computational complexity of our model includes $O(2PC(P_w + C_g))$ for window and channel attentions, $O(8PC^2)$ for linear projections, and $O(16PC^2)$ for FFNs (expand ratio is 4). It can be seen that our dual attention is computationally efficient with linear complexity to both the spatial and channel dimensions. FFN dominates the number of FLOPs and model parameters. Considering our dual attention has both channel-wise and spatial-wise interactions, in this work, we conduct an initial exploration to show the potential of the pure-attention structure without FFNs. Details can be found in Appendix.

Global Interactions in Channel Attention. Channel attention naturally captures global information and interactions for visual recognition tasks. (i) After transposing the feature, each channel token itself is global on the spatial dimension, providing a global view of the image. (ii) Given C_g tokens with dimension P, the $C_g \times C_g$-dimensional attention map is computed by involving all spatial locations, i.e., $(C_g \times P) \cdot (P \times C_g)$. (iii) With such a global attentive map, channel attention fuses multiple global views of the image dynamically, producing

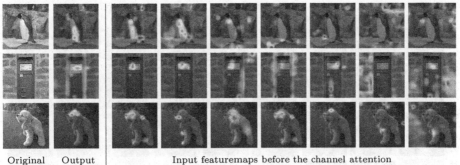

Original	Output	Input featuremaps before the channel attention
image	featuremap	(top-7 channels attending to the output channel, sorted by attention score)

Fig. 4. Illustrating how channel attention gathering global information by visualizing attended feature maps. The first and second columns denote the original image and a feature channel after our channel attention; while the other columns are the channel tokens with top-7 highest attention scores before the attention. Channel attention is able to select globally important regions and suppress background regions for better recognition. The third network stage of the classification model is used for visualization.

new global tokens and passing the information to the following spatial-wise layers. Compared to spatial-wise global attentions [18,49] that perform interactions across spatial locations, the information exchange of our channel self-attention is imposed from a global perspective rather than a patch-wise one, complementing the spatial window attention. Detailed analysis can be found in Sect. 4.

3.4   Model Instantiation

In this work, we follow the design strategy suggested by previous works [37,65]. Take an image with $H \times W$, a C-dimensional feature with a resolution of $\frac{H}{4} \times \frac{W}{4}$ is obtained after the first patch embedding layer. And its resolution is further reduced into $\frac{H}{8} \times \frac{W}{8}$, $\frac{H}{16} \times \frac{W}{16}$, and $\frac{H}{32} \times \frac{W}{32}$ with the feature dimension increasing to $2C$, $4C$, and $8C$ after the other three patch embedding layer, respectively. Here, our patch embedding layer is implemented by stride convolution. The convolutional kernels and stride values of our four patch embedding layers are $\{7, 2, 2, 2\}$ and $\{4, 2, 2, 2\}$, respectively.

We consider three different network configurations for image classification, objection detection, and segmentation:

- DaViT-Tiny: $C = 96, L = \{1, 1, 3, 1\}, N_g = N_h = \{3, 6, 12, 24\}$
- DaViT-Small: $C = 96, L = \{1, 1, 9, 1\}, N_g = N_h = \{3, 6, 12, 24\}$
- DaViT-Base: $C = 128, L = \{1, 1, 9, 1\}, N_g = N_h = \{4, 8, 16, 32\}$,

where L is the layer numbers, N_g is the number of groups in channel attention, and N_h is the number of heads in window attention for each stage.

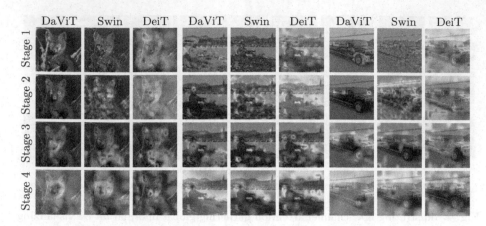

Fig. 5. Feature map visualization of our DaViT, Swin [37], and DeiT [49] at four different network stages (from top to bottom representing stages 1 to 4). DeiT [49] is divided into 4 stages by $2, 2, 6, 2$ layers, respectively. For all network stages, a random feature channel is visualized.

When more training data involved, we further scale up DaViT to large, huge, and giant size to validate the scaling ability of the proposed architecture for image classification:

- DaViT-Large: $C = 192, L = \{1, 1, 9, 1\}, N_g = N_h = \{6, 12, 24, 48\}$
- DaViT-Huge: $C = 256, L = \{1, 1, 9, 1\}, N_g = N_h = \{8, 16, 32, 64\}$
- DaViT-Giant: $C = 384, L = \{1, 1, 12, 3\}, N_g = N_h = \{12, 24, 48, 96\}$.

See Appendix for more details of model configurations.

4   Analysis

Interpretation of Global Interactions. Global interactions in transformers can be summarized into different types. Vanilla ViT [18] and DeiT [49] perform information exchange between different patches among the whole image; Focal Transformer [65] proposes interactions between tokens with different scales to get a larger receptive field; PVT [55] leverages a spatial reduction mechanism to obtain a coarse approximation of global attention; Swin [37] stacks multiple hierarchical layers to get global information eventually. Unlike them, a single block with our channel attention is able to learn the global interactions from another perspective by taking all spatial positions into account when computing the attention scores, as in $(C_g \times P) \cdot (P \times C_g)$. It captures the information from multiple global tokens, which represent different abstract views of the entire image. For example, different channels may contain information from different parts of an object; such part information can be aggregated into a global view.

Figure 4 illustrates how our channel attention works by visualizing the featuremaps before and after the attention. For each image in the first column, we randomly choose an output channel (the second column) in the third stage of the network and its corresponding top-7 relevant input channels for visualization. We can see that the channel attention fuses information from multiple tokens, selects globally important regions, and suppresses unimportant regions.

Relation to Swin and DeiT. To show the effectiveness of our dual self-attention, we make detailed comparisons with two representative clean baselines: Swin [37] with fine-grained local features, and DeiT [49] with global coarse features. Note that though our work and Swin both use window attention as a network element, the key design of Swin, *i.e.*, the use of "shifted window partitions" between successive layers to increase the receptive field, is not utilized in our work. We also simplifies its relative position encoding [10] with a depth-wise convolution before layernorm to get a cleaner structure for arbitrary input sizes. To further keep our architecture clean and efficient, we do not use additional operators like "Overlapping Patch" [55,58] and "ConvFFN" [61,72]. See Appendix for detailed throughput of our model compared with Swin.

Figure 5 shows the effectiveness of our channel group attention. We randomly visualize a feature channel in each stage of DaViT, Swin [37], and DeiT [49]. We observe that: (i) Swin captures fine-grained details but no focus in the first two stages as it lacks global information. It can not focus on the main object until the last stage. (ii) DeiT learns coarse-grained global features over the image but loses details hence difficult to focus on the main content. (iii) Our DaViT captures both short-range and long-range visual dependencies by combining two types of self-attention. It shows strong global modeling capabilities by finding out fine-grained details of the main content in stage 1, and further focusing on some keypoints in stage 2. It then gradually refines the regions of interest from both global and local perspectives for final recognition.

5   Experiments

We conduct experiments on ImageNet-1K image classification [13], COCO object detection [36], and ADE20K semantic segmentation [76]. Neither token labeling [29] nor distillation [49] is used in all experiments and comparisons.

5.1   Image Classification

We compare different methods on ImageNet-1K [13]. We implement our DaViT on the timm framework [57]. Following [15,35,37,58,75], we use the same set of data augmentation and regularization strategies used in [49] after excluding repeated augmentation [3,26] and exponential moving average (EMA) [41]. We train all the models for 300 epochs with a batch size 2048 and use AdamW [39] as the optimizer. The weight decay is set to 0.05 and the maximal gradient norm is clipped to 1.0. We use a simple triangular learning rate schedule [45] as in [51]. The stochastic depth drop rates are set to 0.1, 0.2, and 0.4 for our tiny, small, and base models, respectively. During training, we crop images randomly to 224×224, while a center crop is used during evaluation on the validation set.

Table 1. Comparison of image classification on ImageNet-1K for different models. All models are trained and evaluated with 224 × 224 resolution on ImageNet-1K by default, unless otherwise noted. For fair comparison, token labeling [29] and distillation [49] are not used for all models and their counterparts. † and ‡ denote the model is evaluated with resolution of 384 × 384 and 512 × 512, respectively.

Model	#Params (M)	FLOPs (G)	Top-1 (%)	Model	#Params (M)	FLOPs (G)	Top-1 (%)
ResNet-50 [24]	25.0	4.1	76.2	ResNet-152 [24]	60.0	11.0	78.3
DeiT-Small/16 [49]	22.1	4.5	79.8	PVT-Large [56]	61.4	**9.8**	81.7
PVT-Small [56]	24.5	3.8	79.8	DeiT-Base/16 [49]	86.7	17.4	81.8
ConvMixer-768/32 [51]	21.1	–	80.2	CrossViT-Base [5]	104.7	21.2	82.2
CrossViT-Small [5]	26.7	5.6	81.0	T2T-ViT-24 [68]	64.1	14.1	82.3
Swin-Tiny [37]	28.3	4.5	81.2	CPVT-Base [10]	88.0	17.6	82.3
CvT-13 [58]	**20.0**	4.5	81.6	TNT-Base [22]	65.6	14.1	82.8
CoAtNet-0 [12]	25.0	4.2	81.6	ViL-Base [75]	**55.7**	13.4	83.2
CaiT-XS-24 [50]	26.6	5.4	81.8	UFO-ViT-B [46]	64.0	11.9	83.3
ViL-Small [75]	24.6	5.1	82.0	Swin-Base [37]	87.8	15.4	83.4
PVTv2-B2 [55]	25.4	4.0	82.0	CaiT-M24 [50]	185.9	36.0	83.4
UFO-ViT-S [46]	21.0	**3.7**	82.0	NFNet-F0 [4]	71.5	12.4	83.6
Focal-Tiny [65]	29.1	4.9	82.2	PVTv2-B5 [55]	82.0	11.8	83.8
DaViT-Tiny (Ours)	28.3	4.5	**82.8**	Focal-Base [65]	89.8	16.0	83.8
ResNet-101 [24]	45.0	7.9	77.4	CoAtNet-2 [12]	75.0	15.7	84.1
PVT-Medium [56]	44.2	**6.7**	81.2	CSwin-B [17]	78.0	15.0	84.2
CvT-21 [58]	**32.0**	7.1	82.5	DaViT-Base (Ours)	87.9	15.5	**84.6**
UFO-ViT-M [46]	37.0	7.0	82.8	Pre-trained on ImageNet-22k			
Swin-Small [37]	49.6	8.7	83.1	Swin-Large [37] †	197.0	103.9	86.4
ViL-Medium [75]	39.7	9.1	83.3	CSWin-B [17] †	78.0	47.0	87.0
CaiT-S36 [50]	68.0	13.9	83.3	CSWin-L [17] †	173.0	96.8	87.5
CoAtNet-1 [12]	42.0	8.4	83.3	CoAtNet-3 [12] †	168.0	107.4	87.6
Focal-Small [65]	51.1	9.1	83.5	DaViT-Base (Ours) †	87.9	46.4	86.9
CSwin-S [17]	35.0	6.9	83.6	DaViT-Large (Ours) †	196.8	103.0	87.5
VAN-Large [21]	44.8	9.0	83.9	Pre-trained on 1.5B image and text pairs			
UniFormer-B [31]	50.0	8.3	83.9	DaViT-Huge (Ours) ‡	362	334	90.2
DaViT-Small (Ours)	49.7	8.8	**84.2**	DaViT-Giant (Ours) ‡	1437	1038	**90.4**

In Table 1, we summarize the results for baseline models and current state-of-the-art models on the image classification task. We can find our DaViT achieves new state-of-the-art and consistently outperforms other methods with similar model size (#Params.) and computational complexity (GFLOPs). Specifically, DaViT-Tiny, Small, and Base improve over the Swin Transformer [37] by 1.5%, 1.1%, and 1.2%, respectively. Notably, our DaViT-Small with 49.7M parameters reaches 84.2%, which surpasses all counterpart -Base models using much fewer parameters. For example, our DaViT-Small achieves 0.4% and 0.8% higher accuracy than Focal-Base and Swin-Base, respectively, using near half computations.

Following [18,37,58], when 13M images from ImageNet-22k [13] involved for pre-training, DaViT-Base and DaViT-Large obtained 86.9% and 87.5% top-1 accuracy, respectively. Furthermore, when we further scale up DaViT with 1.5B

Table 2. Comparisons with CNN and Transformer baselines and SoTA methods on COCO object detection. The box mAP (AP^b) and mask mAP (AP^m) are reported for RetinaNet and Mask R-CNN trained with 1× schedule. FLOPs are measured by 800 × 1280. More detailed comparisons with 3× schedule are in Table 3.

Backbone	FLOPs (G)	RetinaNet AP^b	Mask R-CNN AP^b	AP^m
ResNet-50 [24]	239/260	36.3	38.0	34.4
PVT-Small [56]	226/245	40.4	40.4	37.8
ViL-Small [75]	252/174	41.6	41.8	38.5
Swin-Tiny [37]	245/264	42.0	43.7	39.8
Focal-Tiny [65]	265/291	43.7	44.8	41.0
DaViT-Tiny (Ours)	244/263	**44.0**	**45.0**	**41.1**
ResNeXt101-32x4d [62]	319/340	39.9	41.9	37.5
PVT-Medium [56]	283/302	41.9	42.0	39.0
ViL-Medium [75]	339/261	42.9	43.4	39.7
Swin-Small [37]	335/354	45.0	46.5	42.1
Focal-Small [65]	367/401	45.6	47.4	42.8
DaViT-Small (Ours)	332/351	**46.0**	**47.7**	**42.9**
ResNeXt101-64x4d [62]	473/493	41.0	42.8	38.4
PVT-Large [56]	345/364	42.6	42.9	39.5
ViL-Base [75]	443/365	44.3	45.1	41.0
Swin-Base [37]	477/496	45.0	46.9	42.3
Focal-Base [65]	514/533	46.3	47.8	43.2
DaViT-Base (Ours)	471/491	**46.7**	**48.2**	**43.3**

privately collected weakly supervised image-text pairs data and pre-train DaViT with unified contrastive learning [66,70] approach, DaViT-Huge and DaViT-Giant reach 90.2% and 90.4% top-1 accuracy on ImageNet with 362M and 1.4B parameters, respectively.

5.2 Object Detection and Instance Segmentation

We benchmark our models on object detection with COCO 2017 [36]. The pre-trained models are used as visual backbones and then plugged into two representative pipelines, RetinaNet [35] and Mask R-CNN [23]. All models are pre-trained on ImageNet-1K [13] data, and are then trained on the COCO 2017 [36] training set. Results are reported on COCO 2017 [36] validation set. We follow the standard to use two training schedules, 1× schedule with 12 epochs and 3× schedule with 36 epochs. The same multi-scale training strategy as in [37] by randomly resizing the shorter side of the image to the range of [480, 800] is used. During training, we use AdamW [39] for optimization with initial learning rate 10^{-4} and weight decay 0.05. We use 0.1, 0.2, and 0.3 stochastic depth drop rates

Table 3. COCO object detection and segmentation results with RetinaNet [35] and Mask R-CNN [24]. All models are trained with 3× schedule and multi-scale inputs. The numbers before and after "/" at column 2 and 3 are the model size and complexity for RetinaNet and Mask R-CNN, respectively. FLOPs are measured by 800 × 1280.

Backbone	#Params (M)	FLOPs (G)	RetinaNet 3x						Mask R-CNN 3x					
			AP^b	AP^b_{50}	AP^b_{75}	AP_S	AP_M	AP_L	AP^b	AP^b_{50}	AP^b_{75}	AP^m	AP^m_{50}	AP^m_{75}
ResNet50 [24]	37.7/44.2	239/260	39.0	58.4	41.8	22.4	42.8	51.6	41.0	61.7	44.9	37.1	58.4	40.1
PVT-Small[56]	34.2/44.1	226/245	42.2	62.7	45.0	26.2	45.2	57.2	43.0	65.3	46.9	39.9	62.5	42.8
ViL-Small [75]	35.7/45.0	252/174	42.9	63.8	45.6	27.8	46.4	56.3	43.4	64.9	47.0	39.6	62.1	42.4
Swin-Tiny [37]	38.5/47.8	245/264	45.0	65.9	48.4	29.7	48.9	58.1	46.0	68.1	50.3	41.6	65.1	44.9
Focal-Tiny [65]	39.4/48.8	265/291	45.5	66.3	48.8	31.2	49.2	58.7	47.2	69.4	51.9	42.7	66.5	45.9
DaViT-Tiny (Ours)	38.5/47.8	244/263	46.5	68.1	49.6	32.3	50.6	59.9	47.4	69.5	52.0	42.9	66.8	46.4
ResNeXt101-32x4d [62]	56.4/62.8	319/340	41.4	61.0	44.3	23.9	45.5	53.7	44.0	64.4	48.0	39.2	61.4	41.9
PVT-Medium [56]	53.9/63.9	283/302	43.2	63.8	46.1	27.3	46.3	58.9	44.2	66.0	48.2	40.5	63.1	43.5
ViL-Medium [75]	50.8/60.1	339/261	43.7	64.6	46.4	27.9	47.1	56.9	44.6	66.3	48.5	40.7	63.8	43.7
Swin-Small [37]	59.8/69.1	335/354	46.4	67.0	50.1	31.0	50.1	60.3	48.5	70.2	53.5	43.3	67.3	46.6
Focal-Small [65]	61.7/71.2	367/401	47.3	67.8	51.0	31.6	50.9	61.1	48.8	70.5	53.6	43.8	67.7	47.2
DaViT-Small (Ours)	59.9/69.2	332/351	48.2	69.7	51.7	32.7	52.2	62.9	49.5	71.4	54.7	44.3	68.4	47.6
ResNeXt101-64x4d [62]	95.5/102	473/493	41.8	61.5	44.4	25.2	45.4	54.6	44.4	64.9	48.8	39.7	61.9	42.6
PVT-Large[56]	71.1/81.0	345/364	43.4	63.6	46.1	26.1	46.0	59.5	44.5	66.0	48.3	40.7	63.4	43.7
ViL-Base [75]	66.7/76.1	443/365	44.7	65.5	47.6	29.9	48.0	58.1	45.7	67.2	49.9	41.3	64.4	44.5
Swin-Base [37]	98.4/107.0	477/496	45.8	66.4	49.1	29.9	49.4	60.3	48.5	69.3	53.2	43.4	66.8	46.9
Focal-Base [65]	100.8/110.0	514/533	46.9	67.8	50.3	31.9	50.3	61.5	49.0	70.1	53.6	43.7	67.6	47.0
DaViT-Base (Ours)	98.5/107.3	471/491	48.7	70.0	52.3	33.7	52.8	62.9	49.9	71.5	54.6	44.6	68.8	47.8

to regularize the training for our tiny, small, and base models, respectively. The numbers of counterparts [37,75] are borrowed from [65].

In Table 2 and Table 3, we show the performance of our models against several state-of-the-art counterparts. The bbox mAP (AP^b) and mask mAP (AP^m) are reported. Results of 1× schedule shown in Table 2 have demonstrated the effectiveness of our method. We observe substantial gains across all settings and metrics compared with several strong transformer baselines.

To have more comprehensive comparisons, we further train our models with 3× schedule and show the detailed numbers, #parameters, and associated computational costs for RetinaNet and Mask R-CNN in Table 3. As we can see, even for the 3× schedule, our models can still achieve 1.5–2.9% gains on RetinaNet 3× and 1.0–1.4% gains on Mask R-CNN 3× over Swin Transformer models.

Moreover, from Table 3 we observe a saturated and even degraded mAP in Swin Transformer [37] and Focal Transformer [65] from small to base model, while the mAP of our model is continuously increased with larger model size, showing a better scale-up ability. Our base model outperforms the state-of-the-art [65] by 1.8% on RetinaNet 3× and 0.9% on Mask R-CNN 3×.

5.3   Semantic Segmentation on ADE20k

Besides the instance segmentation results above, we further evaluate our model on semantic segmentation, a task that usually requires high-resolution input and long-range interactions. We benchmark our method on ADE20K [76]. Specifically, we use UperNet [60] as the segmentation method and our DaViT as the backbone. We train three models with DaViT-Tiny, DaViT-Small, DaViT-Base,

Table 4. Comparison with SoTA methods for semantic segmentation on ADE20K [76] val set. Single-scale evaluation is used. FLOPs are measured by 512 × 2048.

Backbone	Method	#Params (M)	FLOPs (G)	mIoU (%)
Swin-Tiny [37]	UperNet [60]	60	945	44.5
PVT-Large [56]	SemanticFPN [34]	65	318	44.8
HRNet-w48 [54]	OCRNet [71]	71	664	45.7
Focal-Tiny [65]	UperNet [60]	62	998	45.8
XCiT-S12/16 [1]	UperNet [60]	52	–	45.9
Twins-SVT-Small [9]	UperNet [60]	54	912	46.2
DaViT-Tiny (Ours)	UperNet [60]	60	940	**46.3**
ResNet-101 [24]	UperNet [60]	86	1029	44.9
XCiT-S24/16 [1]	UperNet [60]	73	–	46.9
Swin-Small [37]	UperNet [60]	81	1038	47.6
Twins-SVT-Base [9]	UperNet [60]	88	1044	47.7
Focal-Small [65]	UperNet [60]	85	1130	48.0
ResNeSt-200 [74]	DLab.v3+ [6]	88	1381	48.4
DaViT-Small (Ours)	UperNet [60]	81	1030	**48.8**
Swin-Base [37]	UperNet [60]	121	1188	48.1
XCiT-M24/8 [1]	UperNet [60]	109	–	48.4
Twins-SVT-Large [9]	UperNet [60]	133	1188	48.8
ViT-Hybrid [42]	DPT [42]	124	1231	49.0
Focal-Base [65]	UperNet [60]	126	1354	49.0
DaViT-Base (Ours)	UperNet [60]	121	1175	**49.4**

respectively. For all models, we use a standard recipe by setting the input size to 512×512 and train the model for 160k iterations with batch size 16. All the models are pre-trained on ImageNet-1K [13] set. In Table 4, we show the comparisons to previous works. As we can see, our tiny, small, and base models consistently outperform recent SoTAs, such as 1.2–1.8% gains over Swin Transformers [37] with a similar number of parameters and FLOPs.

5.4 Ablation Study

Evaluation of Channel Group Attention at Different Stages. We make comparisons by inserting a dual attention block at different stages of a window transformer. From the quantitative results in Table 5, we observe: (i) The dual attention module consistently boosts performance at each stage. (ii) Dual attention in the second stage improves the most, as the earlier stage requires more global information. We speculate that the relatively small improvement in the first stage is that local texture features dominate the shallow part of the network. (iii) We achieve the best results when adding dual attention in all four stages.

Dual Attention Layout. We conduct experiments on the layout of our dual attention. There are three options with similar computations: (i) window atten-

Table 5. The effect of channel group attention at different network stages. Taking a transformer layout with all spatial window attention blocks as the baseline (n/a), we replace two spatial attention blocks at different stages with a dual attention block to show its effectiveness. The first two spatial attention blocks are selected in the third stage to compare with other stages fairly.

Stage	#Params (M)	FLOPs (G)	Top-1 (%)	Top-5 (%)
n/a	28.3	4.6	81.1	95.6
1	28.3	4.5	81.7	95.9
2	28.3	4.5	82.2	96.1
3	28.3	4.6	82.1	96.0
4	28.3	4.6	81.9	95.9
1–4	28.3	4.6	**82.8**	**96.2**

Table 6. Quantitative comparisons of different dual attention layouts on ImageNet.

Model	#Params (M)	FLOPs (G)	Top-1 (%)
Window → Channel	28.3	4.5	**82.8**
Channel → Window	28.3	4.5	82.6
Hybrid (parallel)	28.3	4.5	82.6

tion first; (ii) channel attention first; and (iii) two types of attention are paralleled arranged (*i.e.*, half of the token dims are used for channel attention, and the other half for spatial attention, then their outputs are concatenated and fed to an FFN). The comparison is shown in Table 6. We can see that the three strategies achieve similar performance, with 'window attention first' slightly better.

6 Conclusion

This work introduces the dual attention mechanism, containing spatial window attention and channel group attention, to capture global contexts while maintaining computational efficiency. We show that these two self-attentions complement each other. We further visualize how our channel group attention captures global interactions and demonstrate its effectiveness in various benchmarks.

Acknowledgement. Ping Luo is supported by the General Research Fund of HK No. 27208720, No. 17212120, and No. 17200622.

References

1. Ali, A., et al.: XCiT: cross-covariance image transformers. In: NeurIPS, vol. 34 (2021)

2. Bello, I.: Lambdanetworks: modeling long-range interactions without attention. arXiv preprint arXiv:2102.08602 (2021)
3. Berman, M., Jégou, H., Vedaldi, A., Kokkinos, I., Douze, M.: Multigrain: a unified image embedding for classes and instances. arXiv preprint arXiv:1902.05509 (2019)
4. Brock, A., De, S., Smith, S.L., Simonyan, K.: High-performance large-scale image recognition without normalization. arXiv Computer Vision and Pattern Recognition (2021)
5. Chen, C.F., Fan, Q., Panda, R.: CrossViT: cross-attention multi-scale vision transformer for image classification. In: ICCV (2021)
6. Chen, L.C., Zhu, Y., Papandreou, G., Schroff, F., Adam, H.: Encoder-decoder with Atrous separable convolution for semantic image segmentation. In: ECCV, pp. 801–818 (2018)
7. Chen, M., et al.: Generative pretraining from pixels. In: ICML, pp. 1691–1703 (2020)
8. Chen, Z., Xie, L., Niu, J., Liu, X., Wei, L., Tian, Q.: Visformer: the vision-friendly transformer. In: ICCV, pp. 589–598 (2021)
9. Chu, X., et al.: Twins: revisiting spatial attention design in vision transformers. arXiv preprint arXiv:2104.13840 (2021)
10. Chu, X., et al.: Conditional positional encodings for vision transformers. arxiv preprint arXiv:2102.10882 (2021)
11. Dai, X., et al.: Dynamic head: unifying object detection heads with attentions. In: CVPR, pp. 7373–7382 (2021)
12. Dai, Z., Liu, H., Le, Q., Tan, M.: CoAtNet: marrying convolution and attention for all data sizes. In: Advances in Neural Information Processing Systems, vol. 34 (2021)
13. Deng, J., Dong, W., Socher, R., Li, L.J., Li, K., Fei-Fei, L.: ImageNet: a large-scale hierarchical image database. In: CVPR, pp. 248–255. IEEE (2009)
14. Devlin, J., Chang, M.W., Lee, K., Toutanova, K.: BERT: pre-training of deep bidirectional transformers for language understanding. In: NAACL-HLT (1) (2019)
15. Ding, M., et al.: Learning versatile neural architectures by propagating network codes. In: ICLR (2022)
16. Ding, M., et al.: HR-NAS: Searching efficient high-resolution neural architectures with lightweight transformers. In: CVPR (2021)
17. Dong, X., et al.: CSWin transformer: a general vision transformer backbone with cross-shaped windows. arXiv preprint arXiv:2107.00652 (2021)
18. Dosovitskiy, A., et al.: An image is worth 16 × 16 words: transformers for image recognition at scale. In: ICLR (2021)
19. Fu, J., et al.: Dual attention network for scene segmentation. In: CVPR, pp. 3146–3154 (2019)
20. Graham, B.,et al.: LeViT: a vision transformer in convnet's clothing for faster inference. In: ICCV, pp. 12259–12269 (2021)
21. Guo, M.H., Lu, C.Z., Liu, Z.N., Cheng, M.M., Hu, S.M.: Visual attention network. arXiv preprint arXiv:2202.09741 (2022)
22. Han, K., Xiao, A., Wu, E., Guo, J., Xu, C., Wang, Y.: Transformer in transformer. In: NeurIPS, vol. 34 (2021)
23. He, K., Gkioxari, G., Dollár, P., Girshick, R.: Mask R-CNN. In: ICCV, pp. 2961–2969 (2017)
24. He, K., Zhang, X., Ren, S., Sun, J.: Deep residual learning for image recognition. In: CVPR, pp. 770–778 (2016)
25. Heo, B., Yun, S., Han, D., Chun, S., Choe, J., Oh, S.J.: Rethinking spatial dimensions of vision transformers. In: ICCV, pp. 11936–11945 (2021)

26. Hoffer, E., Ben-Nun, T., Hubara, I., Giladi, N., Hoefler, T., Soudry, D.: Augment your batch: improving generalization through instance repetition. In: CVPR, pp. 8129–8138 (2020)
27. Hu, J., Shen, L., Sun, G.: Squeeze-and-excitation networks. In: CVPR, pp. 7132–7141 (2018)
28. Huang, Z., Ben, Y., Luo, G., Cheng, P., Yu, G., Fu, B.: Shuffle transformer: rethinking spatial shuffle for vision transformer. arXiv preprint arXiv:2106.03650 (2021)
29. Jiang, Z.H., et al.: All tokens matter: token labeling for training better vision transformers. In: NeurIPS, vol. 34 (2021)
30. Li, C., et al.: BossNAS: exploring hybrid CNN-transformers with block-wisely self-supervised neural architecture search. In: ICCV, pp. 12281–12291 (2021)
31. Li, K., et al.: UniFormer: unifying convolution and self-attention for visual recognition. arXiv preprint arXiv:2201.09450 (2022)
32. Li, Y., et al.: Improved multiscale vision transformers for classification and detection. arXiv Computer Vision and Pattern Recognition (2021)
33. Li, Y., Zhang, K., Cao, J., Timofte, R., Van Gool, L.: LocalViT: bringing locality to vision transformers. arXiv preprint arXiv:2104.05707 (2021)
34. Lin, T.Y., Dollár, P., Girshick, R., He, K., Hariharan, B., Belongie, S.: Feature pyramid networks for object detection. In: CVPR, pp. 2117–2125 (2017)
35. Lin, T.Y., Goyal, P., Girshick, R., He, K., Dollár, P.: Focal loss for dense object detection. In: ICCV, pp. 2980–2988 (2017)
36. Lin, T.-Y., et al.: Microsoft COCO: common objects in context. In: Fleet, D., Pajdla, T., Schiele, B., Tuytelaars, T. (eds.) ECCV 2014. LNCS, vol. 8693, pp. 740–755. Springer, Cham (2014). https://doi.org/10.1007/978-3-319-10602-1_48
37. Liu, Z., et al.: Swin transformer: hierarchical vision transformer using shifted windows. In: ICCV (2021)
38. Liu, Z., Mao, H., Wu, C.Y., Feichtenhofer, C., Darrell, T., Xie, S.: A convnet for the 2020s. arXiv preprint arXiv:2201.03545 (2022)
39. Loshchilov, I., Hutter, F.: Decoupled weight decay regularization. arXiv preprint arXiv:1711.05101 (2017)
40. Pan, Z., Zhuang, B., Liu, J., He, H., Cai, J.: Scalable visual transformers with hierarchical pooling. arXiv preprint arXiv:2103.10619 (2021)
41. Polyak, B.T., Juditsky, A.B.: Acceleration of stochastic approximation by averaging. SIAM J. Control Optim. **30**(4), 838–855 (1992)
42. Ranftl, R., Bochkovskiy, A., Koltun, V.: Vision transformers for dense prediction. In: ICCV, pp. 12179–12188 (2021)
43. Riquelme, C., et al.: Scaling vision with sparse mixture of experts. In: NeurIPS, vol. 34 (2021)
44. Ryoo, M.S., Piergiovanni, A., Arnab, A., Dehghani, M., Angelova, A.: Token-learner: what can 8 learned tokens do for images and videos? arXiv Computer Vision and Pattern Recognition (2021)
45. Smith, L.N., Topin, N.: Super-convergence: very fast training of neural networks using large learning rates. In: Artificial Intelligence and Machine Learning for Multi-Domain Operations Applications, vol. 11006, p. 1100612. International Society for Optics and Photonics (2019)
46. Song, J.G.: UFO-ViT: high performance linear vision transformer without softmax. arXiv preprint arXiv:2109.14382 (2021)
47. Srinivas, A., Lin, T.Y., Parmar, N., Shlens, J., Abbeel, P., Vaswani, A.: Bottleneck transformers for visual recognition. In: CVPR, pp. 16519–16529 (2021)
48. Tang, S., Zhang, J., Zhu, S., Tan, P.: Quadtree attention for vision transformers. arXiv preprint arXiv:2201.02767 (2022)

49. Touvron, H., Cord, M., Douze, M., Massa, F., Sablayrolles, A., Jégou, H.: Training data-efficient image transformers & distillation through attention. In: ICML, pp. 10347–10357. PMLR (2021)
50. Touvron, H., Cord, M., Sablayrolles, A., Synnaeve, G., Jégou, H.: Going deeper with image transformers. arXiv preprint arXiv:2103.17239 (2021)
51. Trockman, A., Kolter, J.Z.: Patches are all you need? arXiv preprint arXiv:2201.09792 (2022)
52. Vaswani, A., Ramachandran, P., Srinivas, A., Parmar, N., Hechtman, B., Shlens, J.: Scaling local self-attention for parameter efficient visual backbones. In: CVPR, pp. 12894–12904 (2021)
53. Vaswani, A., et al.: Attention is all you need. In: NeurIPS (2017)
54. Wang, J., et al.: Deep high-resolution representation learning for visual recognition. IEEE TPAMI **43**, 3349–3364 (2020)
55. Wang, W., et al.: PVT v2: improved baselines with pyramid vision transformer. arXiv preprint arXiv:2106.13797 (2021)
56. Wang, W., et al.: Pyramid vision transformer: a versatile backbone for dense prediction without convolutions. In: ICCV (2021)
57. Wightman, R.: Pytorch image models. (cited on p.) (2019). https://github.com/rwightman/pytorch-image-models
58. Wu, H., et al.: CVT: introducing convolutions to vision transformers. arXiv preprint arXiv:2103.15808 (2021)
59. Wu, K., Peng, H., Chen, M., Fu, J., Chao, H.: Rethinking and improving relative position encoding for vision transformer. In: ICCV, pp. 10033–10041 (2021)
60. Xiao, T., Liu, Y., Zhou, B., Jiang, Y., Sun, J.: Unified perceptual parsing for scene understanding. In: ECCV, pp. 418–434 (2018)
61. Xie, E., Wang, W., Yu, Z., Anandkumar, A., Alvarez, J.M., Luo, P.: SegFormer: simple and efficient design for semantic segmentation with transformers. In: NeurIPS (2021)
62. Xie, S., Girshick, R., Dollár, P., Tu, Z., He, K.: Aggregated residual transformations for deep neural networks. In: CVPR, pp. 1492–1500 (2017)
63. Xu, W., Xu, Y., Chang, T., Tu, Z.: Co-scale conv-attentional image transformers. In: ICCV, pp. 9981–9990 (2021)
64. Xu, Y., Zhang, Q., Zhang, J., Tao, D.: ViTAE: vision transformer advanced by exploring intrinsic inductive bias. In: NeurIPS, vol. 34 (2021)
65. Yang, J., et al.: Focal self-attention for local-global interactions in vision transformers. arXiv preprint arXiv:2107.00641 (2021)
66. Yang, J., et al.: Unified contrastive learning in image-text-label space. In: Proceedings of the IEEE/CVF Conference on Computer Vision and Pattern Recognition (CVPR), pp. 19163–19173 (2022)
67. Yu, Q., Xia, Y., Bai, Y., Lu, Y., Yuille, A.L., Shen, W.: Glance-and-gaze vision transformer. In: NeurIPS, vol. 34 (2021)
68. Yuan, L., et al.: Tokens-to-token ViT: training vision transformers from scratch on imageNet. arXiv preprint arXiv:2101.11986 (2021)
69. Yuan, L., Hou, Q., Jiang, Z., Feng, J., Yan, S.: VOLO: vision outlooker for visual recognition. arXiv preprint arXiv:2106.13112 (2021)
70. Yuan, L., et al.: Florence: a new foundation model for computer vision. arXiv preprint arXiv:2111.11432 (2021)
71. Yuan, Y., Chen, X., Wang, J.: Object-contextual representations for semantic segmentation. arXiv preprint arXiv:1909.11065 (2019)
72. Yuan, Y., et al.: HRFormer: high-resolution transformer for dense prediction. In: NeurIPS (2021)

73. Zhai, X., Kolesnikov, A., Houlsby, N., Beyer, L.: Scaling vision transformers. arXiv Computer Vision and Pattern Recognition (2021)
74. Zhang, H., et al.: ResNest: split-attention networks. arXiv preprint arXiv:2004.08955 (2020)
75. Zhang, P., et al.: Multi-scale vision longformer: a new vision transformer for high-resolution image encoding. In: ICCV (2021)
76. Zhou, B., Zhao, H., Puig, X., Fidler, S., Barriuso, A., Torralba, A.: Scene parsing through ADE20K dataset. In: CVPR, pp. 633–641 (2017)
77. Zhou, D., et al.: DeepViT: towards deeper vision transformer. arXiv preprint arXiv:2103.11886 (2021)
78. Zhou, J., Wang, P., Wang, F., Liu, Q., Li, H., Jin, R.: ELSA: enhanced local self-attention for vision transformer. arXiv Computer Vision and Pattern Recognition (2021)

Optimal Transport for Label-Efficient Visible-Infrared Person Re-Identification

Jiangming Wang[1], Zhizhong Zhang[1(✉)], Mingang Chen[2], Yi Zhang[3],
Cong Wang[4], Bin Sheng[5], Yanyun Qu[6], and Yuan Xie[1(✉)]

[1] East China Normal University, Shanghai, China
51215901073@stu.ecnu.edu.cn, {zzzhang,yxie}@cs.ecnu.edu.cn
[2] Shanghai Development Center of Computer Software Technology, Shanghai, China
cmg@sscenter.sh.cn
[3] ZheJiang Lab, Hangzhou, China
zhangyi620@zhejianglab.com
[4] Huawei Technologies, Hangzhou, China
wangcong64@huawei.com
[5] Shanghai Jiao Tong University, Shanghai, China
shengbin@sjtu.edu.cn
[6] Xiamen University, Fujian, China
yyqu@xmu.edu.cnn

Abstract. Visible-infrared person re-identification (VI-ReID) has been
a key enabler for night intelligent monitoring system. However, the extensive laboring efforts significantly limit its applications. In this paper, we
raise a new label-efficient training pipeline for VI-ReID. Our observation
is: RGB ReID datasets have rich annotation information and annotating
infrared images is expensive due to the lack of color information. In our
approach, it includes two key steps: 1) We utilize the standard unsupervised domain adaptation technique to generate the pseudo labels for visible subset with the help of well-annotated RGB datasets; 2) We propose
an optimal-transport strategy trying to assign pseudo labels from visible to infrared modality. In our framework, each infrared sample owns
a label assignment choice, and each pseudo label requires unallocated
images. By introducing uniform sample-wise and label-wise prior, we
achieve a desirable assignment plan that allows us to find matched visible and infrared samples, and thereby facilitates cross-modality learning.
Besides, a prediction alignment loss is designed to eliminate the negative
effects brought by the incorrect pseudo labels. Extensive experimental
results on benchmarks demonstrate the effectiveness of our approach.
Code will be released at https://github.com/wjm-wjm/OTLA-ReID.

Keywords: VI-ReID · Optimal-transport · Label-efficient learning

---

Supplementary Information The online version contains supplementary material
available at https://doi.org/10.1007/978-3-031-20053-3_6.

1   Introduction

Visible-infrared person re-identification (VI-ReID) [3,19,27,29,31,37] has been a key enabler for night intelligent monitoring system. It aims to properly find the target visible/infrared images when given a query image from another modality. Due to the significant difference in sensing processes, visible-infrared heterogeneous images have large appearance variations. Therefore, it's very different from conventional visible ReID problem [38,41,42].

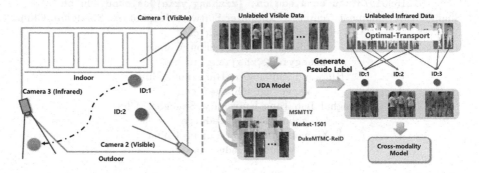

Fig. 1. Left: the real-life ReID application scenario. Right: Our proposed label efficient training pipeline.

Recently, impressive progress [24,34,36–38] in VI-ReID has been made to reduce the cross-modality variations. A common practice is to align the visible and infrared images on both image and feature level [34,36]. However, we have noticed that one of the important ingredient to their success is the availability of well-annotated training sets. These training sets need extensive labelling efforts, especially for infrared subsets due to lack of color information. Hence, a critical question comes up: Can we learn a cross-modality model only with one modal supervision or even without supervision?

To this end, we raise a new training pipeline towards label-efficient learning for VI-ReID. One key assumption of our approach is that only visible labels are accessible, or can be produced by self-training strategy from other visible datasets. This idea is inspired by the observation that: 1) The scale of existing cross-modality ReID dataset is relatively small, while visible ReID dataset has rich annotation information; 2) The cost of annotating infrared images is much more expensive, as it is difficult for annotators to recognize the identities without color information. In fact, this setting is also quite common in real-life scenario. For example, in a supermarket as shown in Fig. 1 left, there exits indoor and outdoor cameras which capture visible and infrared images, respectively. Hence, images from two modalities probably contain the same identity. But a ReID system is often deployed in the indoor scene (visible camera) but unprepared for the outdoor scene (infrared camera). It requires us to train a cross-modality model without infrared annotations, or directly avoid labour-extensive annotations by taking advantage of other well-annotated RGB datasets.

Driven by this analysis, our approach includes two key steps as shown in Fig. 1 right. Firstly, we utilize the standard UDA-ReID approach [12] to generate the pseudo labels for visible data by taking knowledge from the rich annotated dataset *e.g.*, Market-1501 [44], DukeMTMC-ReID [25], MSMT17 [32]. Secondly, to establish an explicit connection between cross-modality data, we propose an optimal-transport strategy for assigning the infrared images to the generated visible pseudo classes. In this module, each sample owns a label assignment choice viewed as supplier, and each label requires unallocated images viewed as demander. By introducing the uniform sample-wise and label-wise prior, we can achieve a desirable assignment plan that allows us to find truly matched visible and infrared samples. To eliminate the negative effects brought by the inaccurate supervised signals, we also propose a prediction alignment learning module, which in practice is a batch-level prediction mix-up and further facilitate the learning modality-invariant representations.

We conduct extensive experiments against state-of-the-arts of three categories (*i.e.*, fully-supervised, unsupervised learning and unsupervised domain adaption methods) on the widely adopted benchmarks for VI-ReID. We empirically find that 1) Taking knowledge from the rich annotated dataset is necessary for label-efficient VI-ReID; 2) Our approach achieves promising results, *i.e.*, 48.2% in term of Rank-1 accuracy on SYSU-MM01 with mere visible ground-truth labels and 29.9% without ground-truth labels. Our contributions can be summarized as follows:

- We propose a new label-efficient learning pipeline which roots from real-world scenario. By taking advantage of rich annotated visible dataset, we produce reliable pseudo labels for RGB images and these labels in turn allow us to train a cross-modality model.
- Two critical modules: Optimal-Transport Label Assignment module (OTLA) and Prediction Alignment Learning (PAL) are proposed. OTLA enables us to assign the infrared images to the generated visible pseudo classes, and thereby establish an explicit connection between visible and infrared data. PAL can reduce the negative effects brought by the inaccurate pseudo labels.
- We provide comprehensive evaluations on this challenge problem. Empirical results show that our approach achieves highly comparable results with fully supervised methods and outperforms recent UDA-ReID and USL-ReID methods.

2   Related Work

Visible-Infrared Person Re-Identification. Visible-infrared person ReID (VI-ReID) aims to match the person images between two modalities. Recently, some works [19,24,29,34,37] try to enhance the feature discrimination by using novel network structures (*e.g.*, graph convolution network and non-local module) or discovering nuanced but discriminative representation. While, another lines of novel works [3,15,30,31] attempt to excavate modality-invariant information by image generation. Besides, [5,18,39] have optimized metric learning items (*e.g.*, Triplet Loss) adapting to cross-modality learning.

Unsupervised Domain Adaptation Person Re-Identification. Unsupervised domain adaptation [23] aims to learn the knowledge of unlabeled target data with help of labeled source data. The recent application of UDA in ReID (UDA-ReID) can be regarded as an open set task, where label spaces between two domains are inconsistent. It can be roughly classified into three categories. The first category [21,47,48] attempts to reduce domain gap by digging up positive or negative pairs from labeled source data or unlabeled target data or both of them. The second category [9,11,12,43] has adopted unsupervised clustering methods. The last category [7,32,46] wants to learn domain invariant information by mutually generating images from source and target domain.

Unsupervised Learning Person Re-Identification. Unsupervised learning person ReID (USL-ReID) aims to train a model with only unlabeled data. But previous works often restrict the problem to a single modality ReID task. In this setting, most methods [8,12,17,28,35,45] are mainly based on pseudo labels, which establish a bridge with supervised manner. For example, two representative works [12,35] try to obtain pseudo labels with traditional clustering method, DBSCAN or K-means. Besides, some hierarchical clustering ways [17,45] are designed to obtain high-quality pseudo labels.

Optimal Transport. Optimal transport (OT) [4] theory has obtained an increasing attention in the field of machine learning, which is often used to find correspondences with learnable features or measure the distribution distance. M. Asano *et al.* [1] has extended OT to self-supervised learning. In this framework, they alternate between the following two steps: 1) Making use of Sinkhorn-Knopp algorithm to produce pseudo labels for unlabeled data. 2) Doing classification with current pseudo labels. In fact, [1] is a clustering based self-supervised approach, which aims to find a good pretraining model. By contrast, we apply OT for a global data-label assignment problem.

Summary. By reviewing recent studies, VI-ReID often requires extensive labelling efforts. However, collecting a well annotated dataset is time-consuming and laborious. Besides, most UDA-ReID and USL-ReID methods restrict their studies to single modality problem, which can't meet the challenges posed by VI-ReID. Towards the label-efficient learning, Liang *et al.* [16] firstly designed an unsupervised framework by taking advantage of the clustering process. But it is sub-optimal since the rich annotated visible data is not utilized and the heterogeneous pseudo labels is also not well aligned. Considering the above problems, we divide label-efficient learning of VI-ReID into two parts: 1) Producing accurate pseudo visible labels by using recent well-established UDA-ReID or USL-ReID methods. 2) Formulating an optimal-transport task inspired by [1] so as to assign infrared data to visible pseudo classes.

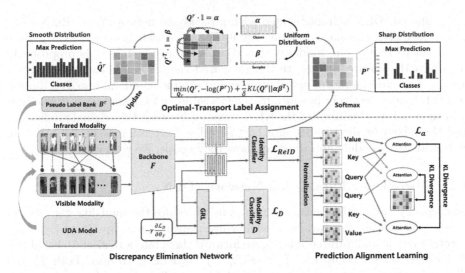

Fig. 2. The pipeline of our framework. Left Bottom: we first use an UDA model to generate the pseudo labels for visible images. Then we take both visible and infrared data into Discrepancy Elimination Network. Upper: The identity prediction of infrared images are sent into Optimal-Transport Label Assignment to assign labels. Right Bottom: The identity predictions are also forwarded into Prediction Alignment Learning to align the mixed predictions, so as to reduce the effects from incorrect pseudo labels.

3 Methodology

3.1 Problem Formulation and Overview

Suppose we are given a collection $\mathcal{X} = \{\mathcal{V}, \mathcal{R}\}$ consisting of cross-modality pedestrian images. $\mathcal{V} = \{\boldsymbol{x}_i^v\}_{i=1}^{N_v}$ and $\mathcal{R} = \{\boldsymbol{x}_i^r\}_{i=1}^{N_r}$ denote the visible and infrared images with N_v and N_r samples, respectively. To learn a cross-modality model only with one modal supervision or even without supervision, a natural idea is to utilize the supervision from the well annotated visible ReID dataset. Intuitively, these labeled data allow us to take advantage of UDA-ReID [9,11,12,21,40,43], and hence enable us to produce reliable pseudo labels $\mathcal{Y} = \{\boldsymbol{y}_i^v\}$ for visible subset $\mathcal{V}$. In our implementation, we adopt the SOTA clustering based method SpCL [12] to generate $\mathcal{Y}$, by taking RGB dataset *e.g.*, Market-1501 [44], DukeMTMC-ReID [25], MSMT17 [32] as the source domain, and $\mathcal{V}$ in visible-infrared dataset as the target domain. Since the data in both domains are homogeneous RGB images, falling in the scope of standard UDA-ReID problem, we can obtain relatively reliable pseudo labels.

In the second stage, infrared images are required to be assigned to the generated pseudo labels for cross-modality training. To this end, three key components: Discrepancy Elimination Network (DEN), Optimal-Transport Label Assignment module (OTLA), and Prediction Alignment Learning module (PAL) are proposed. DEN is implemented with a backbone network (*e.g.*, ResNet-50) and a modality classifier (bottom left in Fig. 2), which is served as a feature extractor to reduce the modality gap. OTLA (upper in Fig. 2) is proposed to transport the infrared images to the generated visible pseudo classes. By introducing class-wised uniform distribution $\boldsymbol{\alpha}$ and sample-wised uniform distribution $\boldsymbol{\beta}$, OTLA can effectively produce matched visible and infrared data. PAL (bottom right in Fig. 2) minimizes the KL-divergence between the original predictions and the mixed predictions using a batch-level self-attention technique. We will elaborate each module and illustrate how they cooperate with each other.

3.2 Discrepancy Elimination Network (DEN)

Discrepancy elimination network enables us to reduce the modality gap, served as a strong baseline for learning modality-invariant features. Specifically, given a batch of visible and infrared images, we forward them into a ResNet-50 backbone $\boldsymbol{F}$ for feature extraction, *i.e.*, $\boldsymbol{f}_i^v = \boldsymbol{F}(\boldsymbol{x}_i^v)$, $\boldsymbol{f}_i^r = \boldsymbol{F}(\boldsymbol{x}_i^r)$. To make both $\boldsymbol{f}_i^v$ and $\boldsymbol{f}_i^r$ modality-invariant, we deploy a modality classifier $\boldsymbol{D}$ to determine which modality the feature comes from. The learning objective is thus formulated as:

$$\mathcal{L}_D = \max_{\boldsymbol{F}} \min_{\boldsymbol{D}} \mathbb{E}_{\boldsymbol{f}_i^v}[\log(1 - \boldsymbol{D}(\boldsymbol{f}_i^v)] + \mathbb{E}_{\boldsymbol{f}_i^r}[\log(\boldsymbol{D}(\boldsymbol{f}_i^r)]. \tag{1}$$

Note that Eq. (1), in fact, is an adversarial loss widely used in the field of domain adaptation. We achieve Eq. (1) by using a gradient reversal layer (GRL) [10]. During the forward propagation, GRL acts as an identity transform. In the back propagation, GRL flips the gradient of modality classifier (*i.e.* multiply gradient by $-\gamma$) and passes it to the preceding layer. To design DEN, we experimentally find that GRL would degrade the performance in the fully-supervised VI-ReID, but is effective in semi-supervised/unsupervised case. DEN appears to be able to reduce modality discrepancy, especially in the absence of accurate guidance.

3.3 Optimal-Transport Label Assignment (OTLA)

To train a discriminative model for VI-ReID, only using generated pseudo labels $\boldsymbol{y}_i^v$ for visible data is insufficient. For example, Triplet Loss [26] is widely used in VI-ReID community, and its common step is to choose the positive and negative samples to construct the triplet. However, without the matched infrared and visible data, triplet loss can hardly promote the cross-modality matching performance. A intuitive solution is to use the self-training technique to assign labels for infrared images. However, if we send the features $\boldsymbol{f}_i^v$ and $\boldsymbol{f}_i^r$ into an identity classifier, and use the pseudo visible label $\boldsymbol{y}_i^v$ with standard cross-entropy and triplet loss to optimize it:

$$\mathcal{L}_{\text{V-ReID}} = \mathcal{L}_{\text{Tri}}^v + \mathcal{L}_{\text{CE}}^v, \tag{2}$$

it will lead a so-called degeneration of classifier problem. In this case, most infrared samples are assembled in a few classes. This phenomenon may not happen in single modality training, because Eq.(2) encourages the classifier pay more attention on the visible data while neglecting the discrimination in infrared images. So, if we follow the self-training methods [9], using the maximum value of classifier output p_i^r or clustering result as the infrared labels, the cross-modality learning would be significantly biased to visible data.

To solve such issue, we propose an Optimal-Transport Label Assignment (OTLA) module to find infrared samples associated with visible data. Inspired by [1], we formulate the label assignment task as an optimal transport problem. In our framework, the infrared samples are viewed as suppliers, while the pseudo labels are considered as demands. The goal is to transport samples in suppliers to demands at the lowest cost via an optimal plan Q^r. To prevent the degeneration of classifier, we start from two intuitions: first, each infrared image owns an assignment choice that corresponds to a generated pseudo label; second, each generated pseudo label owns approximately the same number of infrared images.

To this end, we define a supplier vector $\alpha \in \mathbb{R}^{N_r}$ indicating that each sample owns a label assignment choice, and a demander vector $\beta \in \mathbb{R}^{N_p}$ indicating the desired assigned results. Besides, let $P^r \in \mathbb{R}^{N_r \times N_p}$ denote the softmax output of classifier for the infrared images, where N_p stands for the total number of identities. We use P^r to act as as a kind of cost measuring the difficulty of each image assigned to the identity. Thus we can define a label assignment objective:

$$\min_{Q^r} \langle Q^r, -\log(P^r) \rangle + \frac{1}{\delta} KL(Q^r || \alpha \beta^T).$$

$$\text{s.t.} \begin{cases} Q^r \mathbb{1} = \alpha, & \alpha = \mathbb{1} \cdot \frac{1}{N_r}, \\ Q^{r^T} \mathbb{1} = \beta, & \beta = \mathbb{1} \cdot \frac{1}{N_p}, \end{cases} \tag{3}$$

where $Q^r \in \mathbb{R}^{N_r \times N_p}$ represents the plan used for pseudo label assignment, $\langle \cdot \rangle$ denotes the Frobenius dot-product, δ is a hyper-parameter, and KL denotes the KL-divergence. In essence, Eq. (3) is a transport problem, and also a trade-off between prediction and smooth assignment. α and β represent the class-wise prior uniform distribution vector and the sample-wise prior uniform distribution vector, respectively. Through them, the infrared samples can be forced to be assigned to equally-sized subsets, avoiding samples are grouped together.

However, traditional approaches are not applicable to solve this transport objective due to the large amount of data points and identities. Instead, such constraint leads us to adopt the Sinkhorn-Knopp algorithm [4]. As a result, the optimal solution $\hat{Q}^r$ can be achieved through the iteratively conducted Sinkhorn-Knopp algorithm with a simple matrix scaling operation:

$$\forall i : \alpha_i \leftarrow [(P^r)^\delta \beta]_i^{-1} \quad \forall j : \beta_j \leftarrow [\alpha^T (P^r)^\delta]_j^{-1}, \tag{4}$$

where initialize α with $\frac{1}{N_r} \cdot \mathbb{1}$ and β with $\frac{1}{N_p} \cdot \mathbb{1}$. When the iteration meets the termination conditions or exceeds the maximum number, the auxiliary vectors α and β are fixed. One primary advantage of this approach is it can equivalently convert Eq. (3) as:

$$Q^r = \text{diag}(\alpha)(P^r)^\delta \text{diag}(\beta), \tag{5}$$

Algorithm 1. Label-efficient VI-ReID

Require: Unlabeled visible-infrared data $\{\mathcal{V}, \mathcal{R}\}$, other labeled visible data $\{\mathcal{V}'\}$.

1: Using $\mathcal{V}'$ and $\mathcal{V}$ to generate reliable pseudo labels $\{y_i^v\}$ by SpCL [12].
2: Initialize pseudo label bank $\boldsymbol{B}^r$ for all infrared data.
3: **for** $epoch = 1 : M$ **do**
4:     **for** $batch = 1 : N$ **do**
5:         According to $\{y_i^v\}$ and $\boldsymbol{B}^r$ sample a batch of visible and infrared data.
6:         Calculate $\mathcal{L}_{\text{ReID}}$, $\mathcal{L}_D$, $\mathcal{L}_a$ with $\{y_i^v\}$ and $\boldsymbol{B}^r$ and update the parameters.
7:     **end for**
8:     Extracting prediction $\boldsymbol{P}^r$ for all infrared data.
9:     Initialize $\boldsymbol{\alpha}^0$ with $\frac{1}{N_r} \cdot \mathbb{1}$ and $\boldsymbol{\beta}^0$ with $\frac{1}{N_p} \cdot \mathbb{1}$.
10:    **while** $\|\boldsymbol{\alpha}^k - \boldsymbol{\alpha}^k\|_1 < \epsilon$ **do**
11:        $\forall i : \boldsymbol{\alpha}_i^k \leftarrow [(\boldsymbol{P}^r)^\delta \boldsymbol{\beta}^{k-1}]_i^{-1}$ $\forall j : \boldsymbol{\beta}_j^k \leftarrow [\boldsymbol{\alpha}^{k-1^T}(\boldsymbol{P}^r)^\delta]_j^{-1}$.
12:    **end while**
13:    $\boldsymbol{Q}^r = \text{diag}(\boldsymbol{\alpha})(\boldsymbol{P}^r)^\delta \text{diag}(\boldsymbol{\beta})$.
14:    Using $\boldsymbol{Q}^r$ to update $\boldsymbol{B}^r$.
15: **end for**

---

where $\text{diag}(\cdot)$ denotes the square diagonal matrix with the elements of vector on the main diagonal.

On this basis, we reassign each sample with the class-wise and sample-wise smooth prior, and hold a pseudo label bank $\boldsymbol{B}^r$ according to the maximum value of optimal plan $\hat{\boldsymbol{Q}}^r$ to store the assigned results. This bank is updated epoch by epoch, and then assigns a reliable label for each infrared image. Finally, we use the pseudo labels of both visible and infrared data for training a standard VI-ReID model with cross-entropy and triplet loss. Our experimental results show that the identities of $\{x_i^r\}_{i=1}^m$ and $\{x_i^v\}_{i=1}^m$ can gradually coincide with each other, and the computational cost of assignment is extremely low.

3.4 Prediction Alignment Learning (PAL)

With the help of pseudo labels, we can sample the cross-modality images belong to the same identity to construct triplet, enabling us to complete the cross modality training. However, there are still incorrect labels harming the training process. To eliminate the negative effects brought by incorrect labels, we propose a batch-level prediction mix-up, which aligns the prediction distributions between modalities from a batch perspective.

Specifically, for a batch of samples, we first normalize the prediction of classifier to obtain $\boldsymbol{S}^v \in \mathbb{R}^{B \times N_p}$ and $\boldsymbol{S}^r \in \mathbb{R}^{B \times N_p}$, where the superscript v/r represents visible/infrared modality and B is the number of visible/infrared images. Note that in order to adopt the triplet loss, we typically sample equal-sized cross-modality images according to the pseudo labels and hence the size of $\boldsymbol{S}^r$ and $\boldsymbol{S}^v$ are the same. To encourage the classifier to make consistent predictions on these sampled images, we conduct self-attention by taking $\boldsymbol{S}^v$ as query, and

S^r as key and value. Formally, we have:

$$S^{vr} = \text{softmax}\left(S^v(S^r)^T\right)S^r. \tag{6}$$

After that, we compute the KL divergence between the source prediction S^{vr} and the target prediction S^v to get the alignment loss:

$$\mathcal{L}_a^{vr} = KL(S^v||S^{vr}). \tag{7}$$

Intuitively, Eq. (7) forces the visible prediction fused with infrared images to be consistent with S^v. Even though there unfortunately exists an incorrect label, self-attention would eliminate its negative effect by emphasising the truly-related samples while neglecting the incorrect ones, by promoting the instance-level alignment to batch-level alignment. This strategy is like the mix-up technique by fusing samples from two modalities in a batch. The mixed prediction is hence encouraged to filter the outliers and reduce the prediction gap between two modalities.

Due to the more noise in S^r, it is not wise to design a symmetric loss $\mathcal{L}_a^{rv}$, which may bring permutation to the training process. Instead, we define two mixed prediction S^{rr} and S^{rv}:

$$\begin{aligned} S^{rr} &= \text{softmax}\left(S^r(S^r)^T\right)S^r, \\ S^{rv} &= \text{softmax}\left(S^r(S^v)^T\right)S^v. \end{aligned} \tag{8}$$

With them, we can finally obtain another alignment loss:

$$\mathcal{L}_a^{rv} = KL(S^{rv}||S^{rr}). \tag{9}$$

The reason for this design is that two mixed predictions are less effected by the incorrect labels. Based on the above analysis, the proposed prediction alignment loss $\mathcal{L}_a$ is formulated as:

$$\mathcal{L}_a = \lambda_a^{vr}\mathcal{L}_a^{vr} + \lambda_a^{rv}\mathcal{L}_a^{rv}. \tag{10}$$

where λ_a^{vr} and λ_a^{rv} are the coefficients (set to 0.1 and 0.5 in our experiments).

3.5   Optimization

The training process is summarized in Algorithm 1. The total training loss $\mathcal{L}$ can be formulated as follows:

$$\mathcal{L} = \mathcal{L}_{\text{ReID}} + \lambda_1\mathcal{L}_D + \lambda_2\mathcal{L}_a. \tag{11}$$

where $\mathcal{L}_{\text{ReID}}$ denotes the standard cross-entropy and triplet loss of both modalities, λ_1 and λ_2 are trade-off hyperparameters (empirically set them to 1.0).

4   Experiments

In this section, we conduct extensive experiments to provide a basic yet comprehensive evaluation on this new challenge problem. We report the results under two experimental settings *i.e.,* unsupervised VI-ReID (USVI-ReID, visible labels are generated by SpCL [12]), semi-supervised VI-ReID (SSVI-ReID, with ground-truth visible labels). For USVI-ReID and SSVI-ReID, any ground-truth label of infrared images is **inaccessible** during the training process.

4.1   Experimental Settings

Datasets. The proposed methods are evaluated on two widely adopted benchmarks **SYSU-MM01** [33] and **RegDB** [22]. Specifically, SYSU-MM01 is a large-scale dataset which is collected by four RGB and two infrared cameras from both indoor and outdoor environments. It composed of 287,628 visible images and 15,792 infrared images for 491 different identities. RegDB is collected by two aligned cameras (one visible and one infrared), and it includes 412 identities, where each identity has 10 infrared images and 10 visible images.

Evaluation Metrics. On both datasets, we follow the popular protocols [37] for evaluation, in which cumulative match characteristic (CMC) and mean average precision (mAP) are adopted. SYSU-MM01 contains two different testing settings, *i.e., all-search* and *indoor-search* mode. For all-search mode, the gallery consists of all visible images (captured by CAM1, CAM2, CAM3, CAM4) and the query is composed of all infrared samples (captured by CAM5, CAM6). For indoor-search mode, images captured only from indoor scene are adopted, excluding CAM4 and CAM5. On both search mode, the proposed method is evaluated under single-shot setting. For RegDB [22], we report the average result by randomly splitting of training and testing set 10 times.

4.2   Implementation Details

Training. We implement our model using MindSpore and PyTorch on one NVIDIA TITAN RTX. The batch size is fixed to 64 for all experiments. With the pseudo labels, in a batch we sample 4 different identities, and each identity includes 8 visible images and 8 infrared images. The model is optimized by Adam optimizer with an initial learning rate of 3.5×10^{-3}. The learning rate is incorporated with a warm-up strategy [20] and decays 10 times at the 20-th and the 50-th epoch. The total of training epochs is set to 80. All the pedestrian images are resized to 288×144. The margin ρ of triplet loss is set to 0.3. The δ of OTLA is fixed to 25. In the training stage, the input images are randomly flipped and erased with 50% probability, while visible images are extra randomly grayscale with 50% probability.

Critical Architectures. We adopt ResNet-50 [13] pretrained on ImageNet [6] as backbone, where last stride size of is set to 1. The modality classifier in DEN is

Table 1. Comparisons with SOTA methods on SYSU-MM01 (single-shot) and RegDB, including unsupervised domain adaptation ReID (UDA-ReID), unsupervised ReID (USL-ReID), fully-supervised VI-ReID (SVI-ReID) and unsupervised VI-ReID (USVI-ReID). All methods are measured by CMC(%) and mAP(%). † indicates we re-implement the result with official code. ‡ indicates the results are copied from [16].

Settings			SYSU-MM01				RegDB			
			All search		Indoor search		Visible2Thermal		Thermal2Visible	
Type	Method	Venue	Rank-1	mAP	Rank-1	mAP	Rank-1	mAP	Rank-1	mAP
UDA-ReID	SSG‡ [9]	ICCV'19	2.3	12.7	–	–	2.2	2.9	–	–
	ECN‡ [47]	CVPR'19	8.1	5.0	–	–	1.9	3.2	–	–
	D-MMD† [21]	ECCV'20	12.5	10.4	19.0	15.4	2.2	3.7	2.0	3.6
	MMT† [11]	ICLR'20	13.9	8.4	21.0	15.3	5.3	7.1	11.0	12.1
	SpCL(UDA)† [12]	NIPS'20	15.1	6.5	19.5	12.1	3.3	4.3	8.4	9.5
	GLT† [43]	CVPR'21	7.7	9.5	12.1	18.0	2.9	4.5	6.3	7.6
USL-ReID	BUC† [17]	AAAI'19	8.2	3.2	12.5	6.0	4.7	4.5	8.8	6.0
	SpCL(USL)† [12]	NIPS'20	18.7	11.4	27.1	20.9	20.6	17.3	19.0	16.6
	MetaCam† [35]	CVPR'21	14.7	9.3	23.9	17.1	23.1	17.5	20.9	16.5
	HCD† [45]	ICCV'21	18.0	17.9	24.4	28.8	10.8	12.3	12.4	13.7
SVI-ReID	JSIA-ReID [29]	AAAI'20	38.1	36.9	43.8	52.9	48.5	49.3	48.1	48.9
	Hi-CMD [3]	CVPR'20	34.9	35.9	–	–	70.9	66.0	–	–
	AGW [38]	TPAMI'21	47.5	47.7	54.17	63.0	70.1	66.4	70.5	65.9
	NFS [2]	CVPR'21	56.9	55.5	62.8	69.8	80.5	72.1	78.0	69.8
	LbA [24]	ICCV'21	55.4	54.1	58.5	66.3	74.2	67.6	72.4	65.5
	CAJL [36]	ICCV'21	69.9	66.9	76.3	80.4	85.0	79.1	84.8	77.8
	MPANet [34]	CVPR'21	70.6	68.2	76.7	81.0	83.7	80.9	82.8	80.7
USVI-ReID	H2H [16]	TIP'21	25.5	25.2	–	–	14.1	12.3	13.9	12.7
	Ours	–	29.9	27.1	29.8	38.8	32.9	29.7	32.1	28.6
SSVI-ReID	Ours	–	48.2	43.9	47.4	56.8	49.9	41.8	49.6	42.8

implemented with three FC layers and a BN layer [14] is added before the output. The GRL [10] is a non-parametric module and $\gamma = 2/(1 + \exp(-\tau \frac{iter}{maxiter})) - 1$ controls the scale of the reversed gradient. τ is fixed to 10 and $maxiter$ is set to 10000. The $iter$ linearly increases as the training goes on.

4.3 Main Results

We compare our approach with four related ReID settings to demonstrate its effectiveness, *i.e.*, fully-supervised VI-ReID (SVI-ReID), unsupervised VI-ReID (USVI-ReID), unsupervised domain adaptation ReID (UDA-ReID) and unsupervised learning ReID (USL-ReID). For UDA-ReID methods, we use ground-truth labeled visible data as source domain and unlabeled infrared data as target domain. For USL-ReID methods, we use both unlabeled visible and infrared data to train the model. The main results are shown in Table 1.

Comparison with Unsupervised Methods. H2H [16] is a representative unsupervised VI-ReID method most relevant with our approach. However, it ignores the rich annotated visible data and the heterogeneous pseudo labels are

Table 2. Ablation study in terms of CMC(%) and mAP(%) on SYSU-MM01.

Order	Approach				All search							
					USVI-ReID				SSVI-ReID			
	$\mathcal{L}_{\text{V-ReID}}$	$\mathcal{L}_D$	$\mathcal{L}_a$	$OTLA$	Rank-1	Rank-10	Rank-20	mAP	Rank-1	Rank-10	Rank-20	mAP
1	✓	–	–	–	12.62	41.91	57.27	12.73	12.25	46.49	62.24	14.66
2	✓	✓	–	–	16.62	49.91	64.53	15.94	23.69	59.56	73.10	24.71
3	✓	–	✓	–	12.65	42.39	57.03	12.81	13.86	46.67	61.87	14.72
4	✓	✓	–	✓	20.90	59.53	73.86	19.83	33.89	73.89	85.49	32.44
5	✓	–	✓	✓	19.64	61.16	77.31	19.74	36.31	77.31	86.93	34.66
6	✓	✓	✓	✓	29.98	71.79	83.85	27.13	48.15	85.30	92.64	43.86

not well aligned, leading to a inferior performance. Other unsupervised methods are designed for single-modality ReID task, so it is somewhat unfair to directly compare them, since most of them don't consider the cross-modality discrepancy. We report here because very few methods have studied this problem before.

Comparison with Unsupervised Domain Adaptation Methods. It appears that recent state-of-the-art UDA-ReID methods cannot effectively deal with the huge modality discrepancy. Notice that the supervised signal used in UDA-ReID is even stronger than ours, but the highest accuracy is much lower than our method. That indicates our approach is able to learn robust multi-modality representation, significantly outperforming all UDA-ReID methods. On the other hand, USL-ReID methods appear to achieve better results than UDA-ReID approaches. We conjecture this is because most UDA-ReID methods [9,11,21,43] rely heavily on the labeled source domain which drives the model to overfit on visible data. However, USL-ReID methods tend to fuse two modal data so as to achieve better results than UDA-ReID methods.

Comparison with Fully-Supervised Methods. Surprisingly, our approach only with ground-truth visible data outperforms several fully-supervised VI-ReID methods on SYSU-MM01 dataset, and achieves closed results on RegDB. Such phenomenon indicates label information of infrared images could be learned from optimal transport assignment. Besides, we should admit there is still a large gap between our method and SOTA fully-supervised results.

4.4 Ablation Study

In this subsection, we conduct ablation study to show the effectiveness of each component in our approach. We firstly clarify various settings. $OTLA$ indicate whether the OTLA mechanism is used. $\mathcal{L}_{\text{V-ReID}}$ is visible basic ReID loss functions defined in Sect. 3. As shown in Table 2, the main observations are:

(1) The modality classifier in semi-supervised setting works well, which brings improvement of 11.44%@Rank-1 and 10.05%@mAP (see 1st row and 2nd row). When combined with $OTLA$ and $\mathcal{L}_a$, it also boosts huge performance of unsupervised setting (see 5th and 6th row).

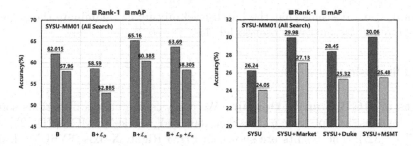

Fig. 3. Left: The supervised ablation results of discriminative loss $\mathcal{L}_D$ and prediction alignment loss $\mathcal{L}_a$ (**B** means baseline model). Right: The effects of source RGB datasets.

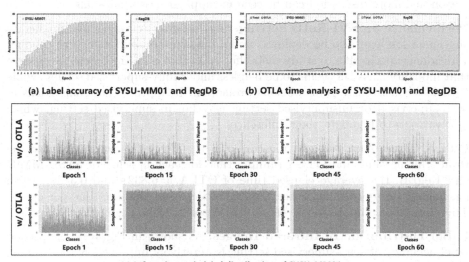

Fig. 4. Left upper: infrared pseudo label assignment accuracy of semi-supervised setting produced by OTLA epoch by epoch. Right upper: the elapsed time of OTLA and total training process in each epoch on SYSU-MM01 and RegDB. Bottom: the assigned infrared label distribution as the training goes on (green area means pseudo label distribution w/OTLA, red area means pseudo label distribution w/o OTLA). (Color figure online)

(**2**) Though noisy in the first few epochs, the pseudo labels for infrared images can be gradually rectified through the proposed OTLA (see Fig. 4 Left Upper). It also lays a crucial and solid foundation, where removing this technique leads to a dramatic performance drop (see 2nd row and 4th row, 3rd row and 5th row).

(**3**) Prediction alignment learning loss significantly boosts the performance when combined with $OTLA$ and $\mathcal{L}_D$ (see Fig. 5, 4th row and 6th row). That indicates a further promotion would be expected when aligning the predictions between two modalities. It seems that the batch-level mix-up can eliminate the negative effects brought by incorrect pseudo labels.

4.5 Discussion

Effects of RGB Source Domain. We analysis the effects of various source RGB domains in SpCL (*e.g.,* Market-1501 [44], DukeMTMC-ReID [25] and MSMT17 [32]). The results are shown in Fig. 3 Right. X-axis 'SYSU' indicates we use the USL mode of SpCL to generate the pseudo labels and hence only the SYSU-MM01 data is involved for training. It seems that using annotated visible data achieves better results and Market-1501 is the most effective domain. The reason and more discussion can be seen in supplementary materials.

Performance on SVI-ReID Setting. Since modality classifier and prediction alignment loss can also be deployed under fully-supervised setting, we conduct additional experiments to study their effects. As shown in Fig. 3 Left, we observe that modality classifier seems to be helpless under fully-supervised setting, while PAL loss consistently gains obvious promotion. It appears that some tricks in semi-supervised or unsupervised setting may fail in supervised setting, which motivates us to highlight their differences.

OTLA Time Analysis. As illustrated in the Fig. 4 (b), we summarize the total training time and OTLA running time for each epoch. For SYSU-MM01 and RegDB, the average elapsed time of OTLA is 6.832 s and 0.353 s, which has merely occupied 2.293% and 0.639% of the total training time per epoch. Therefore, the computational cost of OTLA seems to be negligible.

Label Distribution of Infrared Images. As shown in Fig. 4(a), the pseudo label accuracy of semi-supervised setting is iteratively improved as the training continues. It can achieve about 50% accuracy on SYSU-MM01 and 30% accuracy on RegDB. From Fig. 4(c), it seems that OTLA can alleviate the degeneration of the classifier as training goes on. Without OTLA the degradation of classifier is significant, *i.e.,* the pseudo label distribution is sharp during the training, indicating that the classifier can not distinguish the identities of infrared images.

Visualization of Prediction Alignment Learning. We visualize the attention map to help understand the influence of prediction alignment learning. As shown in Fig. 5, we draw the attention coefficients $A^{V2I} = \text{softmax}(S^v(S^r)^T)$ and $A^{I2I} = \text{softmax}(S^r(S^r)^T)$ in PAL. To show its effectiveness, we also visualize the binary matrices C^{V2I} and C^{I2I} using ground-truth labels in the upper of Fig. 5, where 1 (fill color) indicates two samples share same identity, and 0 (not fill color) otherwise. From this figure, we can find that the learned attention matrices are consistent with the binary ground-truth label accuracy matrices, which indicates our prediction alignment mechanism can more or less filter the incorrect labels and align the cross-modality predictions.

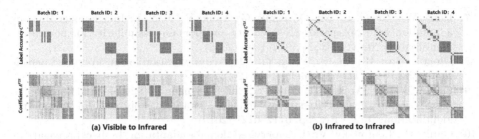

Fig. 5. Visualization of self-attention matrix in prediction alignment learning with random batches. (a) Visible to Infrared. (b) Infrared to Infrared. The upper figures are ground-truth binary matrices and the bottom are our learned attention map in PAL.

5 Conclusion

In this paper, we raise a novel label-efficient learning pipeline for VI-ReID, where the visible labels can be produced by UDA-ReID approach with the help of rich annotated RGB datasets. In this setting, we propose a Discrepancy Elimination Network to reduce modality gap. An Optimal-Transport Label Assignment mechanism is designed to uniformly assign labels for infrared images and thereby connect two kinds of modal data. We also propose a Prediction Alignment Learning to eliminate the negative effect brought by incorrect assignment. Extensive experimental results highlight the state-of-the-art performance of our approach. Finally, we hope our study can help researchers to understand the VI-ReID problem from a new perspective.

Acknowledgements. This work is supported by grants from the National Key Research and Development Program of China (2021ZD0111000), National Natural Science Foundation of China No.62106075, 62176092, Shanghai Science and Technology Commission No.21511100700, Natural Science Foundation of Shanghai (20ZR1417700), CAAI-Huawei MindSpore Open Fund.

References

1. Asano, Y.M., Rupprecht, C., Vedaldi, A.: Self-labelling via simultaneous clustering and representation learning. In: ICLR (2020)
2. Chen, Y., Wan, L., Li, Z., Jing, Q., Sun, Z.: Neural feature search for RGB-infrared person re-identification. In: CVPR, pp. 587–597 (2021)
3. Choi, S., Lee, S., Kim, Y., Kim, T., Kim, C.: Hi-CMD: hierarchical cross-modality disentanglement for visible-infrared person re-identification. In: CVPR, pp. 10257–10266 (2020)
4. Cuturi, M.: Sinkhorn distances: lightspeed computation of optimal transport. In: NIPS, vol. 26, pp. 2292–2300 (2013)
5. Dai, P., Ji, R., Wang, H., Wu, Q., Huang, Y.: Cross-modality person re-identification with generative adversarial training. In: IJCAI, vol. 1, p. 6 (2018)
6. Deng, J., Dong, W., Socher, R., Li, L.J., Li, K., Fei-Fei, L.: ImageNet: a large-scale hierarchical image database. In: CVPR, pp. 248–255. IEEE (2009)

7. Deng, W., Zheng, L., Ye, Q., Kang, G., Yang, Y., Jiao, J.: Image-image domain adaptation with preserved self-similarity and domain-dissimilarity for person re-identification. In: CVPR, pp. 994–1003 (2018)
8. Ding, Y., Fan, H., Xu, M., Yang, Y.: Adaptive exploration for unsupervised person re-identification. TOMM **16**(1), 1–19 (2020)
9. Fu, Y., Wei, Y., Wang, G., Zhou, Y., Shi, H., Huang, T.S.: Self-similarity grouping: a simple unsupervised cross domain adaptation approach for person re-identification. In: CVPR, pp. 6112–6121 (2019)
10. Ganin, Y., Lempitsky, V.: Unsupervised domain adaptation by backpropagation. In: ICML, pp. 1180–1189. PMLR (2015)
11. Ge, Y., Chen, D., Li, H.: Mutual mean-teaching: pseudo label refinery for unsupervised domain adaptation on person re-identification. In: ICLR (2020)
12. Ge, Y., Zhu, F., Chen, D., Zhao, R., Li, H.: Self-paced contrastive learning with hybrid memory for domain adaptive object re-id. In: NIPS (2020)
13. He, K., Zhang, X., Ren, S., Sun, J.: Deep residual learning for image recognition. In: CVPR, pp. 770–778 (2016)
14. Ioffe, S., Szegedy, C.: Batch normalization: accelerating deep network training by reducing internal covariate shift. In: ICML, pp. 448–456. PMLR (2015)
15. Li, D., Wei, X., Hong, X., Gong, Y.: Infrared-visible cross-modal person re-identification with an x modality. In: AAAI, vol. 34, pp. 4610–4617 (2020)
16. Liang, W., Wang, G., Lai, J., Xie, X.: Homogeneous-to-heterogeneous: unsupervised learning for RGB-infrared person re-identification. TIP **30**, 6392–6407 (2021)
17. Lin, Y., Dong, X., Zheng, L., Yan, Y., Yang, Y.: A bottom-up clustering approach to unsupervised person re-identification. In: AAAI, vol. 33, pp. 8738–8745 (2019)
18. Liu, H., Tan, X., Zhou, X.: Parameter sharing exploration and hetero-center triplet loss for visible-thermal person re-identification. TMM **23**, 4414–4425 (2020)
19. Lu, Y., et al.: Cross-modality person re-identification with shared-specific feature transfer. In: CVPR, pp. 13379–13389 (2020)
20. Luo, H., et al.: A strong baseline and batch normalization neck for deep person re-identification. TMM **22**(10), 2597–2609 (2019)
21. Mekhazni, D., Bhuiyan, A., Ekladious, G., Granger, E.: Unsupervised domain adaptation in the dissimilarity space for person re-identification. In: Vedaldi, A., Bischof, H., Brox, T., Frahm, J.-M. (eds.) ECCV 2020. LNCS, vol. 12372, pp. 159–174. Springer, Cham (2020). https://doi.org/10.1007/978-3-030-58583-9_10
22. Nguyen, D.T., Hong, H.G., Kim, K.W., Park, K.R.: Person recognition system based on a combination of body images from visible light and thermal cameras. Sensors **17**(3), 605 (2017)
23. Pan, S.J., Yang, Q.: A survey on transfer learning. TKDE **22**(10), 1345–1359 (2009)
24. Park, H., Lee, S., Lee, J., Ham, B.: Learning by aligning: visible-infrared person re-identification using cross-modal correspondences. In: CVPR, pp. 12046–12055 (2021)
25. Ristani, E., Solera, F., Zou, R., Cucchiara, R., Tomasi, C.: Performance measures and a data set for multi-target, multi-camera tracking. In: Hua, G., Jégou, H. (eds.) ECCV 2016. LNCS, vol. 9914, pp. 17–35. Springer, Cham (2016). https://doi.org/10.1007/978-3-319-48881-3_2
26. Schroff, F., Kalenichenko, D., Philbin, J.: FaceNet: a unified embedding for face recognition and clustering. In: CVPR, pp. 815–823 (2015)
27. Tian, X., Zhang, Z., Lin, S., Qu, Y., Xie, Y., Ma, L.: Farewell to mutual information: variational distillation for cross-modal person re-identification. In: CVPR, pp. 1522–1531 (2021)

28. Wang, D., Zhang, S.: Unsupervised person re-identification via multi-label classification. In: CVPR, pp. 10981–10990 (2020)
29. Wang, G.A., et al.: Cross-modality paired-images generation for RGB-infrared person re-identification. In: AAAI, vol. 34, pp. 12144–12151 (2020)
30. Wang, G., Zhang, T., Cheng, J., Liu, S., Yang, Y., Hou, Z.: RGB-infrared cross-modality person re-identification via joint pixel and feature alignment. In: CVPR, pp. 3623–3632 (2019)
31. Wang, Z., Wang, Z., Zheng, Y., Chuang, Y.Y., Satoh, S.: Learning to reduce dual-level discrepancy for infrared-visible person re-identification. In: CVPR, pp. 618–626 (2019)
32. Wei, L., Zhang, S., Gao, W., Tian, Q.: Person transfer GAN to bridge domain gap for person re-identification. In: CVPR, pp. 79–88 (2018)
33. Wu, A., Zheng, W.S., Yu, H.X., Gong, S., Lai, J.: RGB-infrared cross-modality person re-identification. In: ICCV (2017)
34. Wu, Q., et al.: Discover cross-modality nuances for visible-infrared person re-identification. In: CVPR, pp. 4330–4339 (2021)
35. Yang, F., et al.: Joint noise-tolerant learning and meta camera shift adaptation for unsupervised person re-identification. In: CVPR, pp. 4855–4864 (2021)
36. Ye, M., Ruan, W., Du, B., Shou, M.Z.: Channel augmented joint learning for visible-infrared recognition. In: ICCV, pp. 13567–13576 (2021)
37. Ye, M., Shen, J., J. Crandall, D., Shao, L., Luo, J.: Dynamic dual-attentive aggregation learning for visible-infrared person re-identification. In: Vedaldi, A., Bischof, H., Brox, T., Frahm, J.-M. (eds.) ECCV 2020. LNCS, vol. 12362, pp. 229–247. Springer, Cham (2020). https://doi.org/10.1007/978-3-030-58520-4_14
38. Ye, M., Shen, J., Lin, G., Xiang, T., Shao, L., Hoi, S.C.: Deep learning for person re-identification: a survey and outlook. TPAMI **44**, 2872–2893 (2021)
39. Ye, M., Wang, Z., Lan, X., Yuen, P.C.: Visible thermal person re-identification via dual-constrained top-ranking. In: IJCAI, vol. 1, p. 2 (2018)
40. Zhai, Y., Ye, Q., Lu, S., Jia, M., Ji, R., Tian, Y.: Multiple expert brainstorming for domain adaptive person re-identification. In: Vedaldi, A., Bischof, H., Brox, T., Frahm, J.-M. (eds.) ECCV 2020. LNCS, vol. 12352, pp. 594–611. Springer, Cham (2020). https://doi.org/10.1007/978-3-030-58571-6_35
41. Zhang, Z., Xie, Y., Li, D., Zhang, W., Tian, Q.: Learning to align via wasserstein for person re-identification. TIP **29**, 7104–7116 (2020)
42. Zhang, Z., Xie, Y., Zhang, W., Tang, Y., Tian, Q.: Tensor multi-task learning for person re-identification. TIP **29**, 2463–2477 (2019)
43. Zheng, K., Liu, W., He, L., Mei, T., Luo, J., Zha, Z.J.: Group-aware label transfer for domain adaptive person re-identification. In: CVPR, pp. 5310–5319 (2021)
44. Zheng, L., Shen, L., Tian, L., Wang, S., Wang, J., Tian, Q.: Scalable person re-identification: a benchmark. In: ICCV, pp. 1116–1124 (2015)
45. Zheng, Y., et al.: Online pseudo label generation by hierarchical cluster dynamics for adaptive person re-identification. In: CVPR, pp. 8371–8381 (2021)
46. Zhong, Z., Zheng, L., Li, S., Yang, Y.: Generalizing a person retrieval model hetero- and homogeneously. In: ECCV, pp. 172–188 (2018)
47. Zhong, Z., Zheng, L., Luo, Z., Li, S., Yang, Y.: Invariance matters: exemplar memory for domain adaptive person re-identification. In: CVPR, pp. 598–607 (2019)
48. Zhong, Z., Zheng, L., Luo, Z., Li, S., Yang, Y.: Learning to adapt invariance in memory for person re-identification. TPAMI **43**(8), 2723–2738 (2020)

Locality Guidance for Improving Vision Transformers on Tiny Datasets

Kehan Li[1], Runyi Yu[1], Zhennan Wang[2], Li Yuan[1,2(✉)], Guoli Song[2], and Jie Chen[1,2(✉)]

[1] School of Electronic and Computer Engineering, Peking University, Beijing, China
[2] Peng Cheng Laboratory, Shenzhen, China
yuanli-ece@pku.edu.cn, chenj@pcl.ac.cn

Abstract. While the Vision Transformer (VT) architecture is becoming trendy in computer vision, pure VT models perform poorly on tiny datasets. To address this issue, this paper proposes the locality guidance for improving the performance of VTs on tiny datasets. We first analyze that the local information, which is of great importance for understanding images, is hard to be learned with limited data due to the high flexibility and intrinsic globality of the self-attention mechanism in VTs. To facilitate local information, we realize the locality guidance for VTs by imitating the features of an already trained convolutional neural network (CNN), inspired by the built-in local-to-global hierarchy of CNN. Under our dual-task learning paradigm, the locality guidance provided by a lightweight CNN trained on low-resolution images is adequate to accelerate the convergence and improve the performance of VTs to a large extent. Therefore, our locality guidance approach is very simple and efficient, and can serve as a basic performance enhancement method for VTs on tiny datasets. Extensive experiments demonstrate that our method can significantly improve VTs when training from scratch on tiny datasets and is compatible with different kinds of VTs and datasets. For example, our proposed method can boost the performance of various VTs on tiny datasets (*e.g.*, 13.07% for DeiT, 8.98% for T2T and 7.85% for PVT), and enhance even stronger baseline PVTv2 by 1.86% to 79.30%, showing the potential of VTs on tiny datasets. The code is available at https://github.com/lkhl/tiny-transformers.

1 Introduction

Recently, models based on the self-attention mechanism have been widely used in visual tasks and demonstrated surprising performance, making it an alternative to convolution [3,5,9,46]. Of these models, ViT [9] is the first full-transformer model for image classification, which can outperform CNNs when large training

---

K. Li, R. Yu—Equal contribution.

Supplementary Information The online version contains supplementary material available at https://doi.org/10.1007/978-3-031-20053-3_7.

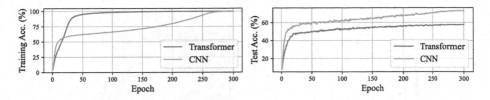

Fig. 1. Training accuracy (left) and test accuracy (right) when training CNN and Transformer on CIFAR-100 dataset. Compared with the CNN, the Transformer fits the training set faster but has lower test accuracy, due to the difficulty of learning the local information with the globality of the self-attention mechanism.

data is available. Based on ViT, a lot of works modify it and make it more adaptable to image data, which makes it possible for training Vision Transformer (VT) from scratch on medium-sized datasets (*e.g.*, ImageNet-1K [7] with 1.3 million samples) [26,33,38,45,51].

However, it is still difficult to train VTs from scratch on tiny datasets with a normal training policy [25]. To be more intuitive, we train a visual transformer T2T-ViT-14 [51] on CIFAR-100 dataset with weak data augmentations (including padding and random cropping), where only 50,000 training samples are available. The results in Fig. 1 show that the accuracy on the training set increases rapidly to 100% yet the accuracy on the test set can only reach about 58%, showing obvious overfitting. A commonly used method to address this issue is pretraining model on large datasets. However, this pretraining-finetuning paradigm has several limitations. Firstly, large-scale datasets are naturally lacking in some specific domains like medical image [30,53,55]. Secondly, the model must be able to fit both the large pre-trained dataset and the small target dataset, constraining the flexibility of model designing [18]. Finally, the pre-training on a large dataset with a large model is computationally expensive. It is unacceptable that we need to retrain a new model on large dataset, even if the model architecture changes only a little, which is sometimes inevitable for specific tasks [24,34].

Aiming to find a more efficient way to make VTs work well on tiny datasets, we start with analyzing why pre-training works. To do this, we compare the self-attention statistics of VTs with and without ImageNet [7] pre-training. We employ the attention distance following [35] and the attention map by Attention Rollout [1] as the self-attention statistics, which are commonly used for analyzing self-attention mechanism [9,35]. The attention distance given in Fig. 2(a) is obtained by weighted averaging the distance between any two tokens through their attention intensity, representing the mean distance of each token to aggregate information. The attention map given in Fig. 2(b) shows the attention matrix $q \cdot v$ of the center token. By analyzing the attention distance in Fig. 2(a), we find that the VT with pre-training learns to assign attention rationally. By rationally, we mean that the shallow blocks focus more on the local and the deep blocks focus more on the global. However, all blocks of the VT without pre-training only focus on the global. On the other hand, the attention map in Fig. 2(b) shows that the VT with pre-training progressively finds the rela-

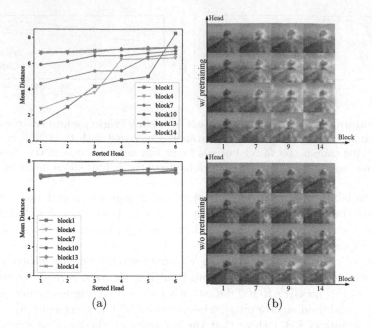

Fig. 2. Comparison of the self-attention statistics between the model with pre-training (top) and the model without pre-training (bottom). (a) Attention distance [9,35] in different blocks. The abscissa represents the sorted attention heads. The small distance means that it is focused on the local information, and the large distance means that it is focused on the global information. (b) Self-attention map obtained by Attention Rollout [40]. The columns represent sorted blocks and the rows represent sorted heads.

tionships and finally focuses on the correct positions, while the VT without pre-training starts paying relatively fixed and uniform attention from the middle blocks. Based on these observations, we conclude that pre-training on a relatively large dataset can learn hierarchical information from locality to globality, which makes pre-trained models easier to understand images than models trained from scratch. Unfortunately, small datasets are not sufficient to extract hierarchical information for VTs.

To address these limitations, we present the locality guidance for improving the performance of VTs on tiny datasets, which helps the VTs capture the hierarchical information effectively and efficiently, as an alternative to the costly pre-training. Our proposed locality guidance is realized through the regularization provided by convolution, motivated by the inherent local-to-global hierarchy of convolutional neural network (CNN) [22]. Specifically, we employ an already trained lightweight CNN on the same dataset to distill the VT in hidden layers. Therefore, there are two tasks for the VT. One is to imitate the features generated by the CNN (*i.e.*, receive the guidance), and the other is to learn by itself from the supervised information. The imitation task is auxiliary and thus does not impair the strong learning ability of VTs.

The efficiency of our method is reflected in three aspects. a) Since the feature imitation is just used as an auxiliary task to guide the VT, the performance of the CNN will not be the bottleneck for the VT, and therefore it is possible to utilize a lightweight model and low image resolution, making the computational cost of CNN as small as possible. b) Information from the CNN is only needed when training, thus there is no extra computational cost when inference. c) Our method can largely accelerate the convergence and reduce the training time of the VT.

The proposed method shows its effectiveness on various types of VT and datasets. On CIFAR-100 dataset [31], our method achieves 13.07% improvement for the DeiT [38] baseline and improves a stronger baseline PVTv2 by 1.86% to 79.30%, demonstrating the potential of using VTs on tiny datasets as the alternatives to CNN. Moreover, we adopt our method on Chaoyang dataset [55] and show its practicality and validity on medical imaging, where the large-scale dataset for pre-training is hard to obtain. These experiments show that our locality guidance method is generally useful and can advance the wider application of transformers in vision tasks.

2   Related Work

Vision Transformers. Transformer, a model mainly based on self-attention mechanism, is first proposed by Vaswani et al. [40] for machine translation and is widely used in natural language processing tasks [4,8] and cross-modal tasks [23, 47,49]. ViT [9] is the first pure visual transformer model to process images, and can outperform CNNs on image classification task with large-scale training data [9]. However, when massive training data is not available, ViT can not perform well [10,25]. Aiming to train from scratch and surpass CNNs on medium datasets (e.g., ImageNet-1K [7]), there are lots of improved models based on ViT, including adopting a hierarchical structure [16,26,42,43,51,54], introducing inductive bias [33,38,45,50], performing self-attention locally [26,52,54], etc. But for tiny datasets, most of these methods still perform poorly.

Hybrid of Convolution and Self-attention. Introducing the convolutional inductive bias to transformers has been proved effective in visual tasks. To make use of both the locality of convolution and the globality of self-attention, Peng et al. [33] build a hybrid model including a CNN branch, a transformer branch and feature coupling units. Yuan et al. [50] incorporate convolution in tokenization module and feed-forward module of transformer block, while Wu et al. [45] introduce convolution when embedding tokens and calculating q, k, v. Unlike these methods which modify the structure of VT to incorporate convolution, we keep the pure VT structure unchanged. We just employ CNN as a regularizer to guide the feature learning of VT. Therefore, our method is very simple and easy to implement, and can be used in a plug-and-play fashion. Moreover, we also show that our method can be combined with them to further improve the performance.

Vision Transformers on Tiny Datasets. There are only a few studies focusing on how to use VTs on tiny datasets [12,25,38]. Liu et al. [25] propose an auxiliary self-supervised task for encouraging VTs to learn spatial relations within an image, making the VT training much more robust when training data is scarce. Hassani et al. [12] focus on the structure design for tiny datasets, which includes exploiting small patch size, introducing convolution in shallow layers and discarding the *classification* token. We argue that exploiting small patch size will bring quadratic computational complexity increases which are unacceptable when the size of the image is large. Touvron et al. [38] adopt a longer training schedule of 7200 epochs for the VT on CIFAR-10 dataset to obtain a good result. In contrast, our proposed locality guidance for VT achieves significant performance improvements on tiny datasets while employing only 100/300 epochs.

Knowledge Distillation. Our method is also related to knowledge distillation, which is first proposed by Hinton et al. [17] and becomes a commonly used technology for model compression and acceleration [14,29,41,44]. The knowledge to be distilled can be divided into three kinds [11], *i.e.*, response-based knowledge [17,19], feature-based knowledge [14,20,36,48] and relation-based knowledge [32,39]. Our method is highly related to feature-based knowledge distillation, or also feature imitation [41], which is first defined in Fitnets [36]. Following Fitnets, there are many variants of representing knowledge, *e.g.*, attention map [20], truncated SVD [48], average pooling [6], *etc.* Most applications of knowledge distillation are based on the setting of a strong teacher model and a weak student model, to achieve model compression and acceleration. Different from them, our goal of using CNN teacher is providing the locality guidance for the VT, making the learning process on tiny datasets easier so that the VT can be trained better. In our setting, the performance of the teacher will not be the performance bottleneck of the VT, since the VT is still learning by itself and can play to the advantage of the transformer. Therefore, a lightweight CNN teacher would suffice. A recent proposed method DeiT [38] also uses knowledge distillation, which makes the VT learn the classification results of the CNN teacher. However, a CNN of comparable size to the VT is required in DeiT. By comparison, our method can achieve much higher performance with just a lightweight CNN.

3   Method

In this section, we first formulate the overall training procedure of the proposed method, followed by the detailed designs of our method which consist of the guidance positions and the architecture of the guidance model.

3.1   The Overall Approach

To improve the poor performance as well as speed up the convergence of VTs when training from scratch on tiny datasets, we propose to provide locality guidance for VTs to aid in the process of learning local information. As shown in

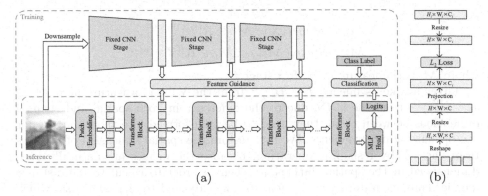

(a)   (b)

Fig. 3. Illustration of the proposed method. (a) The process of our method. There are two tasks when training. A lightweight CNN trained on the same dataset is used to help the VT to learn local information and the VT also learns from the supervision of class labels. (b) The details of feature guidance. Transformations in both spatial and channel dimensions are performed to align features from different models and L_2 Loss is used to reduce the distance between the transformed features.

Fig. 3, we introduce a lightweight CNN trained on the same dataset that the VT used. During training, there are mainly two tasks. Firstly, the semantic gaps between token sequences from different layers of the VT and the features from the CNN are forced to be close to some extent. This procedure is implemented by feature alignment in both spatial and channel dimensions and a feature distance metric as the loss function to be optimized, motivated by feature-based knowledge distillation [2,15,36,37,41]. Secondly, the VT learns knowledge by itself through the supervision of class labels, so that it can understand the images in its own way. The proposed method is aimed at how to train a VT effectively and efficiently on tiny datasets, so we just modify the training process and there are no additional designs in the structure of the VT. In addition, the CNN is no longer needed during inference.

Feature Alignment. A typical VT consists of two parts, the patch embedding module and a series of stacking transformer encoder blocks. The patch embedding module blocks the image and performs a linear projection to generate tokens. Each transformer encoder block contains a multi-head self-attention layer and a two-layer MLP for processing information of tokens. For the input image $X \in \mathbf{R}^{H \times W \times 3}$, the information flow of VT can be formulated as

$$
\begin{aligned}
\mathcal{T}_0 &= PatchEmbedding(X), \ \mathcal{T}_0 \in \mathbf{R}^{L \times C}, \\
\mathcal{T}_i &= Block_i(\mathcal{T}_{i-1}), \ \mathcal{T}_i \in \mathbf{R}^{L \times C},
\end{aligned}
\tag{1}
$$

where $\mathcal{T}_0$ is the initial token sequence produced from the image, $\mathcal{T}_i$ is the token sequence after transformer encoder block i, L is the number of tokens and C is the embedding dimension.

A CNN is usually composed of multiple stages. As the depth increases, the resolution gradually decreases. The information flow of CNN can be formulated as

$$\mathcal{M}_1 = Stage_1(X), \ \mathcal{M}_1 \in \boldsymbol{R}^{H_1 \times W_1 \times C_1},$$
$$\mathcal{M}_i = Stage_i(\mathcal{M}_{i-1}), \ \mathcal{M}_i \in \boldsymbol{R}^{H_i \times W_i \times C_i}, \tag{2}$$

where $\mathcal{M}_i$ is the feature map after stage i.

Given a token sequence $\mathcal{T}_i \in \boldsymbol{R}^{L \times C}$ from the VT and a feature map $\mathcal{M}_j \in \boldsymbol{R}^{H_j \times W_j \times C_j}$ from the CNN, due to the difference in both spatial and channel dimensions between them, they need to be transformed into the same size for the optimization convenience. We first restore the spatial dimension of features from the VT by reshaping operation, because the images are naturally two-dimensional in the spatial dimension. Then in order to calculate the distance metric more accurately, the two features are adjusted to the same size, which is the largest length and width of them. We employ the linear up-sampling to implement the resizing operation. These spatial feature alignment operations are formulated as follows

$$\hat{T}_i = Reshape(\mathcal{T}_i), \ \hat{T}_i \in \boldsymbol{R}^{H_t \times W_t \times C},$$
$$\hat{H} = \max(H_t, H_j), \ \hat{W} = \max(W_t, W_j),$$
$$\hat{F}_{vt} = Resize(\hat{T}_i), \ \hat{F}_{vt} \in \boldsymbol{R}^{\hat{H} \times \hat{W} \times C}, \tag{3}$$
$$F_{cnn} = Resize(\mathcal{M}_j), \ F_{cnn} \in \boldsymbol{R}^{\hat{H} \times \hat{W} \times C_j},$$

where $\hat{F}_{vt}$ and F_{cnn} are the spatially transformed features from the VT and the CNN, respectively.

For the alignment of channel dimension, a learnable point-wise linear projection are performed on the features from VT

$$F_{vt} = Linear(\hat{F}_{vt}), \ F_{vt} \in \boldsymbol{R}^{\hat{H} \times \hat{W} \times C_j}, \tag{4}$$

where $Linear$ is the learnable linear projection, which is implemented by 1×1 convolution. The linear projection acts as not only a transformation to align the channel dimension, but also a simple yet effective way to prevent the VT from learning the same features as the CNN, which may lead to a performance bottleneck. To do this, the learning of VT is flexible and the capability of the VT will not be limited by the CNN. It is also applicable to use other channel dimension transformation functions that do not align features forcibly in this framework (e.g., attention map [20], similarity matrix [39]), but the learnable linear projection is simpler and more flexible, which is shown in ablation study of Sect. 4.3.

Dual-task Learning Paradigm. With the two one-to-one sets of transformed features $\{F_{vt}^i \,|\, i = 1, 2, \cdots, k\}$ and $\{F_{cnn}^j \,|\, j = 1, 2, \cdots, k\}$, we use L_2 distance metric to realize feature guidance

$$L_{guidance} = \sum_{i=1}^{k} \frac{1}{\hat{H}_i \cdot \hat{W}_i} ||F_{vt}^i - F_{cnn}^i||_F^2. \tag{5}$$

where k is the number of features chosen to perform guidance. Then the total loss can be formulated as

$$L = L_{cls} + \beta L_{guidance}, \tag{6}$$

where L_{cls} is the cross-entropy loss for classification task. The final loss consists of two parts, corresponding to the two tasks, in which L_{cls} allows the VT to learn by itself while $L_{guidance}$ forces the VT to imitate the features learned by the CNN for the purpose of incorporating local information better. Under such a dual-task setting the VT is able to express as its own way instead of just copying the features learned by the CNN, so that the performance of the CNN is not a decisive factor for the performance of VT, making it unnecessary to adopt a large-capacity CNN, which is proved by our experiments in Sect. 4.3. The hyperparameter β is used to balance imitation and self-learning and we show its influence through ablation study in Sect. 4.3.

3.2 Guidance Positions

We now detail the rule of constructing the two one-to-one feature sets, *i.e.*, deciding the positions to perform guidance both in the VT and the CNN. The two feature sets are defined as

$$\begin{aligned} S_T &= \{\mathcal{T}_{i_1}, \mathcal{T}_{i_2}, \cdots, \mathcal{T}_{i_k}\}, \ \mathcal{T}_{i.} \in \mathbf{R}^{L \times C}, \\ S_C &= \{\mathcal{M}_{j_1}, \mathcal{M}_{j_2}, \cdots, \mathcal{M}_{j_k}\}, \ \mathcal{M}_{j.} \in \mathbf{R}^{H_{j_k} \times W_{j_k} \times C_{j_k}}, \end{aligned} \tag{7}$$

where $i_1, i_2, \cdots, i_k$ and $j_1, j_2, \cdots, j_k$ are the indexes of blocks or stages in the VT and the CNN, respectively. It is worth noting that information in one layer is produced based on previous layers in both the VT and the CNN, due to a feed-forward structure. Therefore, indexes of features in the VT and the CNN should have the same relative position (*e.g.*, $i_1, i_2, \cdots, i_k$ should be monotonically increasing if $j_1, j_2, \cdots, j_k$ are monotonically increasing). Based on this rule, as well as making use of the information learned by the CNN as much as possible, we select the features after each stage of the CNN and the features uniformly distributed within a specific depth of the VT correspondingly to implement guidance through the loss function shown in Eq. (5). The regulation of choosing features can be summarized as

$$\begin{aligned} j_k &= k, \\ i_k &= \lfloor (k-1) \cdot \frac{R \cdot N_T - 1}{N_C - 1} \rfloor + 1, \end{aligned} \tag{8}$$

where $k \in \{x \mid 1 \leq x \leq N_C, x \in \mathbf{Z}\}$ is the index of the selected feature. N_T and N_C are the number of blocks or stages in VT and CNN, respectively. R is a hyperparameter to control the depth of performing guidance in the VT. We provide further experimental results to compare different choices in ablation study in Sect. 4.3.

3.3   Architecture of the CNN

Unlike most applications of knowledge distillation which focus on transferring the knowledge of a strong teacher model to a weak student model to realize model compression, our method aims at realizing locality guidance from the teacher, rather than totally transferring the features of the teacher. Under our framework, the VT will learn by itself through the supervision of class labels, while the CNN just provides some guidance on locality for the VT. Therefore, the weak CNN will not be a performance bottleneck for the strong VT.

In order to achieve an efficient training process, we chose a lightweight CNN model ResNet-56 [13], which has only 0.86M parameters. What's more, the inputs of the CNN are low resolution images. With these two designs, we obtain a weak CNN that even performs worse than some VTs. Even if the weak CNN performs poorly, we show that different VTs can perform significantly better than both the weak CNN and the VT baselines in different levels, requiring only a small amount of computational overhead. We provide ablation study to prove that CNNs with different sizes can provide guidance on local information to the VT and help VT make great progress on tiny datasets. In other words, the capability of the CNN will not be the performance bottleneck, reflecting the effectiveness and the efficiency of our framework.

4   Experiments

In this section, we demonstrate the effectiveness and efficiency of our approach on image classification task. Firstly, we evaluate different VTs' performance on various datasets with and without our method, and compare the method with two other similar ones. Then, we explore the effect of our method via visualization same as in Sect. 1. At last, we provide ablation studies to discuss the design of our method.

4.1   Main Results

Datasets. We evaluate our method on CIFAR-100 [31] dataset (with 50,000 training samples and 10,000 test samples for 100 classes) and Oxford Flowers [21] dataset (with 2,040 training samples and 6,149 test samples for 102 classes) of natural image domain. Furthermore, we also explore its performance on Chaoyang [55] dataset (with 4021 training samples and 2139 test samples for 4 classes) of medical image domain, in which large-scale datasets and pre-trained models are hard to obtain, making it a practical application domain for our method.

Models. To illustrate the generality, we test our method for different kinds of VTs including pure transformer architectures (DeiT [38], T2T [51]), hierarchical architectures (PVT [42], PiT [16]), and architectures with convolutional inductive bias (PVTv2 [43], ConViT [10]).

Table 1. Results of different VTs and datasets. As shown here, our method can be generalized to different VTs and datasets, and we make VTs to be effective options even on tiny datasets. What's more, it's worth mentioning that all VTs perform significantly better than the CNN guidance model.

Model	Top-1 Acc.		
	CIFAR-100	Flowers	Chaoyang
Guidance model			
ResNet-56 [13] (32 res.)	70.43	59.83	78.12
CNN Baseline			
ResNet-18 [13] (224 res.)	79.00	69.23	84.71
Pure transformer			
DeiT-Ti [38]	65.08	50.06	82.00
DeiT-Ti + $L_{guidance}$	78.15 (+**13.07**)	68.50 (+**18.44**)	84.20 (+2.20)
T2T-ViT-7 [51]	69.37	65.20	80.74
T2T-ViT-7 + $L_{guidance}$	78.35 (+8.98)	68.97 (+3.77)	82.89 (+2.15)
Transformer with hierarchy structure			
PiT-Ti [16]	73.58	56.40	82.70
PiT-Ti + $L_{guidance}$	78.48 (+4.90)	68.32 (+11.92)	83.78 (+1.08)
PVT-Ti [42]	69.22	62.32	73.68
PVT-Ti + $L_{guidance}$	77.07 (+7.85)	70.61 (+8.29)	**85.65** (+**11.97**)
Transformer with convolutional inductive bias			
PVTv2-B0 [43]	77.44	67.51	82.05
PVTv2-B0 + $L_{guidance}$	**79.30** (+1.86)	**72.34** (+4.83)	84.25 (+2.20)
ConViT-Ti [10]	75.32	57.51	82.47
ConViT-Ti + $L_{guidance}$	78.95 (+3.63)	67.04 (+9.53)	84.10 (+1.63)

Implementation Details. We adopt the training settings used by Liu et al. [25] for all VTs. Specifically, we employ the AdamW [28] optimizer with an initial learning rate of 5e−4 and a weight decay of 0.05. The learning rate is finally reduced to 5e−6 following the cosine learning rate policy [27]. All VTs are trained for 300 epochs (with linear warm-up for 20 epochs) on 224 × 224 resolution images if not specified. The hyperparameter R of our method is fixed to 1.0 for convenience, while β is selected for different VTs, which is discussed in detail through ablation study. Considering the efficiency, we choose ResNet-56 [13] as the guidance model and train it on 32 × 32 resolution images. For the CNN baseline ResNet-18 [13], we train it with the same setting of VTs for fair comparison, except that we use the SGD optimizer with an initial learning rate of 0.1 and a weight decay of 5e−4. We choose the smallest variant for all VTs, in order to match the size of the CNN baseline. Further implementation details are provided in supplementary material.

Table 2. Results of training for 100/300 epochs. It is possible to achieve excellent results in shorter training schedule with our method, demonstrating its efficiency.

Model	Top-1 Acc.				
	Baseline	100 Epoches		300 Epoch	
DeiT-Tiny	65.08	77.29	+12.21	78.15	+13.07
T2T-ViT-7	69.37	77.16	+7.79	78.35	+8.98
PiT-Tiny	73.58	77.61	+4.03	78.48	+4.90
PVT-Tiny	69.22	76.20	+6.98	77.07	+7.85

Table 3. Comparison with the method of Liu et al. [25] (100 epochs). Our method achieves better performance.

Model	Method	Top-1 Acc.			
		CIFAR-100		Flowers	
T2T-ViT-14	baseline	65.16	–	31.73	–
	L_{drloc} [25]	68.03	+2.87	34.35	+2.62
	Ours	**77.84**	**+12.68**	**67.71**	**+35.98**
CvT-13	baseline	73.50	–	54.29	–
	L_{drloc} [25]	74.51	+1.01	56.29	+2.00
	Ours	**76.55**	**+3.05**	**65.13**	**+10.84**

Results. Table 1 shows the experimental results of different kinds of VTs on various datasets. We find that our method gets different degrees of improvement for different VTs. The pure transformer models perform the worst since the self-attention mechanism lacks distance limitation and our method brings surprising improvements to these models. The VTs with convolutional inductive bias show not bad performance, and our method can make these strong baselines even better, which shows the potential of using VTs on small datasets to be another choice besides CNN. Meanwhile, it is worth noting that our method can also be generalized to medical image domain, in which training from scratch on small datasets is inevitable. To summarize, our approach improves different VTs by substantial margins on small datasets and makes it possible for VTs to surpass CNNs.

To prove the role of proposed locality guidance in accelerating convergence, we also train these VTs with shorter schedule on CIFAR-100 dataset. The experimental results are given in Table 2. Even with only 1/3 training epochs, our method can largely improve the baseline, demonstrating the efficiency. However, it is reasonable that a bigger improvement can be achieved with more training epochs.

Table 3 compares our method with the method of Liu et al. [25], which designs an additional self-supervised task parallel with the supervised classification task. Their self-supervised task is defined as predicting the distance in 2D space of

Table 4. Comparison with Touvron et al. [38]. Our method reaches higher performance.

Student model	Teacher model	Method	Top-1 Acc.
DeiT-Tiny (65.08)	ResNet-56(70.43)	DeiT-Soft	66.92 (+1.84)
		DeiT-Hard	73.25 (+8.17)
		Ours	78.15 (+13.07)

Table 5. Comparison of attention distance. The VTs with locality guidance learn to pay more attention to locality than those ones trained from scratch.

Model	DeiT	T2T	PiT	PVT	PVTv2	ConViT
w/o $L_{guidance}$	0.0336	0.0338	0.0421	0.2590	0.2622	0.0250
w/ $L_{guidance}$	0.0185	0.0181	0.0293	0.2059	0.2568	0.0171

any two tokens, aiming to constrain the globality of VTs. We argue that there are two shortcomings of this approach. Firstly, a recent research [35] points out that ViT highly maintains spatial location information, so this self-supervised task may be too easy for VTs. Secondly, only implementing this task at the last layer of VTs makes it hard for shallow layers to catch information, and thus it will lead to a limited boost. As shown in Table 3, with the hierarchical locality guidance of CNN, our method improves VTs more significantly.

Table 4 compares our method with the method of Touvron et al. [38], which distills the knowledge of CNNs from logits. Although it is originally used in medium-size datasets, we make a comparison between them since they both introduce knowledge distillation and CNNs. The main difference lies in the aim of introducing knowledge distillation, which provides a kind of guidance in our method and learns the classification results of the CNN in DeiT, respectively. Thus in our method, only a lightweight CNN is required. Comparing the experimental results under the same setting, the performance boost in DeiT is still limited, though the distillation method of DeiT seems effective. With our method, the performance of the VT can surpass the CNN guidance model a lot, proving that the weak CNN guidance model won't be the performance bottleneck for the VT. Besides, additional *distill* token in DeiT, which will increase the computational cost during inference, is not necessary in our method.

4.2 Discussion

The purpose of our method is to simplify the process of learning locality for VT. To prove that it does achieve such a purpose, we compare the attention statistics with or without our method via the same approaches in Sect. 1. In addition, we calculate the attention distance averaging on each head and each layer. All the results shown in this section are produced on CIFAR-100 test set. The attention distance given in Table 5 shows that the VTs with locality guidance learn to pay

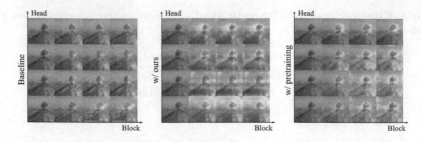

Fig. 4. Comparison of attention map. The attention map of VT with locality guidance (center) present similar to the ones of the pre-trained model (right) and are more reasonable than the ones of baseline (left).

more attention to locality than those ones trained from scratch. By checking the attention maps of T2T-ViT-14 [51] shown in Fig. 4, we find that the VT can learn more meaningful and generalizable information after adding locality guidance and the attended scope is expanded firstly and then focused on region of interests gradually. In summary, our method can play a similar role as pretraining to simplify the learning process of VTs. Moreover, the VT acts in its own way thanks to the dual-task setting. As a result, the proposed method achieves significant improvements for VTs on tiny datasets.

4.3   Ablation Study

To defend the design options in our method, we perform ablation studies on the guidance positions, the hyperparameter β used to balance imitation and self-learning, the channel transformation function and the complexity of the CNN model. All results shown in this section are based on DeiT-Tiny, CIFAR-100 dataset and training schedule of 100 epochs.

Table 6 shows the influence of different guidance positions. It can be concluded that completely utilizing the features of the CNN is important to achieve remarkable improvement. We also observe that R is related to the depth of the features from the CNN. For example, it is optimal to set $R = 1.0$ while all the features from the CNN are selected, and $R = 0.5$ or $R = 0.75$ while 2/3 of the features are selected. This can be interpreted as that the VTs understand images in a hierarchical way similar to CNNs, so that the guidance may be ambiguous when the features from the CNN are misaligned or missing.

To verify the impact of hyperparameter β, we adopt different β evenly distributed in $[0, 3.0]$. The experimental results in Table 7 demonstrate the role of β for balancing imitation and self-learning. The imitation signal will be too weak if β is too small, leading to that the VT can not receive enough guidance on locality. Our method can show a significant performance improvement when β is within a suitable range.

We implement different transformation functions to replace the learnable linear projection in Eq. (4), which aligns the channel dimension of features from

Table 6. Ablation study results on guidance position. The ratio R in Eq. (8) is related to the utilization rate of the CNN. It is optimal to utilize all features from the CNN.

CNN Layers	R	VT Layers	Top-1 Acc.
(1, 2, 3)	0.25	(1, 2, 3)	70.56
	0.50	(1, 3, 6)	75.26
	0.75	(1, 5, 9)	76.43
	1.00	(1, 6, 12)	**77.29**
(1, 2)	0.25	(1, 3)	65.93
	0.50	(1, 6)	67.44
	0.75	(1, 9)	**68.01**
	1.00	(1, 12)	67.08

Table 7. Ablation study results on the factor β in Eq. (6).

Table 8. Ablation on the transformation in Eq. (4).

Table 9. Ablation on the complexity of the guidance model by changing the number of layers.

β	Acc.	β	Acc.	Method	Acc.	CNN Model	CNN Acc.	VT Acc.
0.0	65.08	2.0	77.00	None	65.08	None	-	65.08
0.5	70.88	2.5	**77.29**	AT[20]	73.51	ResNet-20	62.91	72.91
1.0	74.91	3.0	77.18	SP[39]	67.36	ResNet-56	70.43	**77.29**
1.5	76.37			Linear	**77.29**	ResNet-110	**74.70**	76.62

different models. We test each transformation function with the corresponding optimal β. The experimental results given in Table 8 show that different transformation functions are feasible under our framework. Although different transformation functions express the information in different ways, they all play a common role to guide the VT to understand image information more easily. Nonetheless, the Attention [20] and the Similarity [39] methods perform not so well, due to the fixed form. The adopted learnable linear projection is more flexible and achieves the largest improvement.

As for the guidance model, we apply three CNNs which have the same architecture but different number of layers. From Table 9 we can find that even though the three CNNs show a huge performance gap, the difference between improvements for VT brought by them is relatively small. This phenomenon reveals that our method acts as a guidance for the VT to learn locality, rather than fully transferring the knowledge of the CNN, which allows our method to become very efficient by using lightweight CNNs.

5   Conclusion

In this paper, we introduce an effective and efficient method, which significantly improves the performance of VTs on tiny datasets. It is usually difficult to learn locality in an image for VTs when training from scratch with limited data. To this end, we propose to provide locality guidance by imitating the features learned by a lightweight CNN. Meanwhile, VTs also learn by themselves through supervision to act in a suitable way for them. Extensive experiments confirm the applicability of our method in both natural image domain and medical image domain, as well as for different VTs. We hope that our approach will advance the wider application of transformers on vision tasks, especially for the tiny datasets.

Acknowledgements. This work is supported by the Nature Science Foundation of China (No.61972217, No.62081360152, No.62006133), Natural Science Foundation of Guangdong Province in China (No.2019B1515120049, 2020B11113 40056). Li Yuan is supported in part by PKU-Shenzhen Start-Up Research Fund (1270110283).

References

1. Abnar, S., Zuidema, W.: Quantifying attention flow in transformers. In: Proceedings of the 58th Annual Meeting of the Association for Computational Linguistics, pp. 4190–4197 (2020)
2. Ahn, S., Hu, S.X., Damianou, A., Lawrence, N.D., Dai, Z.: Variational information distillation for knowledge transfer. In: Proceedings of the IEEE/CVF Conference on Computer Vision and Pattern Recognition, pp. 9163–9171 (2019)
3. Arnab, A., Dehghani, M., Heigold, G., Sun, C., Lučić, M., Schmid, C.: ViViT: a video vision transformer. In: Proceedings of the IEEE/CVF International Conference on Computer Vision, pp. 6836–6846 (2021)
4. Brown, T., et al.: Language models are few-shot learners. In: Advances in Neural Information Processing Systems, vol. 33, pp. 1877–1901 (2020)
5. Carion, N., Massa, F., Synnaeve, G., Usunier, N., Kirillov, A., Zagoruyko, S.: End-to-end object detection with transformers. In: Vedaldi, A., Bischof, H., Brox, T., Frahm, J.-M. (eds.) ECCV 2020. LNCS, vol. 12346, pp. 213–229. Springer, Cham (2020). https://doi.org/10.1007/978-3-030-58452-8_13
6. Changyong, S., Peng, L., Yuan, X., Yanyun, Q., Longquan, D., Lizhuang, M.: Knowledge squeezed adversarial network compression. arXiv preprint arXiv:1904.05100 (2019)
7. Deng, J., Dong, W., Socher, R., Li, L.J., Li, K., Fei-Fei, L.: ImageNet: a large-scale hierarchical image database. In: 2009 IEEE Conference on Computer Vision and Pattern Recognition, pp. 248–255. IEEE (2009)
8. Devlin, J., Chang, M.W., Lee, K., Toutanova, K.: BERT: pre-training of deep bidirectional transformers for language understanding. arXiv preprint arXiv:1810.04805 (2018)
9. Dosovitskiy, A., et al.: An image is worth 16x16 words: transformers for image recognition at scale. arXiv preprint arXiv:2010.11929 (2020)
10. d'Ascoli, S., Touvron, H., Leavitt, M.L., Morcos, A.S., Biroli, G., Sagun, L.: ConViT: improving vision transformers with soft convolutional inductive biases. In: International Conference on Machine Learning, pp. 2286–2296. PMLR (2021)
11. Gou, J., Yu, B., Maybank, S.J., Tao, D.: Knowledge distillation: a survey. Int. J. Comput. Vis. **129**(6), 1789–1819 (2021)
12. Hassani, A., Walton, S., Shah, N., Abuduweili, A., Li, J., Shi, H.: Escaping the big data paradigm with compact transformers. arXiv preprint arXiv:2104.05704 (2021)

13. He, K., Zhang, X., Ren, S., Sun, J.: Deep residual learning for image recognition. In: Proceedings of the IEEE Conference on Computer Vision and Pattern Recognition, pp. 770–778 (2016)
14. He, T., Shen, C., Tian, Z., Gong, D., Sun, C., Yan, Y.: Knowledge adaptation for efficient semantic segmentation. In: Proceedings of the IEEE/CVF Conference on Computer Vision and Pattern Recognition, pp. 578–587 (2019)
15. Heo, B., Lee, M., Yun, S., Choi, J.Y.: Knowledge transfer via distillation of activation boundaries formed by hidden neurons. In: Proceedings of the AAAI Conference on Artificial Intelligence, vol. 33, pp. 3779–3787 (2019)
16. Heo, B., Yun, S., Han, D., Chun, S., Choe, J., Oh, S.J.: Rethinking spatial dimensions of vision transformers. In: Proceedings of the IEEE/CVF International Conference on Computer Vision, pp. 11936–11945 (2021)
17. Hinton, G., Vinyals, O., Dean, J.: Distilling the knowledge in a neural network. arXiv preprint arXiv:1503.02531 (2015)
18. Ke, A., Ellsworth, W., Banerjee, O., Ng, A.Y., Rajpurkar, P.: CheXtransfer: performance and parameter efficiency of ImageNet models for chest x-ray interpretation. In: Proceedings of the Conference on Health, Inference, and Learning, pp. 116–124 (2021)
19. Kim, S.W., Kim, H.E.: Transferring knowledge to smaller network with class-distance loss (2017)
20. Komodakis, N., Zagoruyko, S.: Paying more attention to attention: improving the performance of convolutional neural networks via attention transfer. In: ICLR (2017)
21. Krizhevsky, A., Hinton, G., et al.: Learning multiple layers of features from tiny images (2009)
22. Lee, H., Grosse, R., Ranganath, R., Ng, A.Y.: Unsupervised learning of hierarchical representations with convolutional deep belief networks. Commun. ACM 54(10), 95–103 (2011)
23. Li, H., Li, X., Karimi, B., Chen, J., Sun, M.: Joint learning of object graph and relation graph for visual question answering. arXiv preprint arXiv:2205.04188 (2022)
24. Li, Z., Peng, C., Yu, G., Zhang, X., Deng, Y., Sun, J.: DetNet: design backbone for object detection. In: Proceedings of the European Conference on Computer Vision (ECCV), pp. 334–350 (2018)
25. Liu, Y., Sangineto, E., Bi, W., Sebe, N., Lepri, B., Nadai, M.: Efficient training of visual transformers with small datasets. In: Advances in Neural Information Processing Systems, vol. 34 (2021)
26. Liu, Z., et al.: Swin transformer: hierarchical vision transformer using shifted windows. In: Proceedings of the IEEE/CVF International Conference on Computer Vision, pp. 10012–10022 (2021)
27. Loshchilov, I., Hutter, F.: Sgdr: Stochastic gradient descent with warm restarts. arXiv preprint arXiv:1608.03983 (2016)
28. Loshchilov, I., Hutter, F.: Decoupled weight decay regularization. arXiv preprint arXiv:1711.05101 (2017)
29. Luo, P., Zhu, Z., Liu, Z., Wang, X., Tang, X.: Face model compression by distilling knowledge from neurons. In: Thirtieth AAAI Conference on Artificial Intelligence (2016)
30. Menze, B.H.: The multimodal brain tumor image segmentation benchmark (brats). IEEE Trans. Med. Imaging 34(10), 1993–2024 (2014)
31. Nilsback, M.E., Zisserman, A.: Automated flower classification over a large number of classes. In: 2008 Sixth Indian Conference on Computer Vision, Graphics & Image Processing, pp. 722–729. IEEE (2008)

32. Passalis, N., Tzelepi, M., Tefas, A.: Heterogeneous knowledge distillation using information flow modeling. In: Proceedings of the IEEE/CVF Conference on Computer Vision and Pattern Recognition, pp. 2339–2348 (2020)

33. Peng, Z., et al.: Conformer: local features coupling global representations for visual recognition. In: Proceedings of the IEEE/CVF International Conference on Computer Vision, pp. 367–376 (2021)

34. Qiao, S., Chen, L.C., Yuille, A.: Detectors: detecting objects with recursive feature pyramid and switchable atrous convolution. In: Proceedings of the IEEE/CVF Conference on Computer Vision and Pattern Recognition, pp. 10213–10224 (2021)

35. Raghu, M., Unterthiner, T., Kornblith, S., Zhang, C., Dosovitskiy, A.: Do vision transformers see like convolutional neural networks? In: Advances in Neural Information Processing Systems, vol. 34 (2021)

36. Romero, A., Ballas, N., Kahou, S.E., Chassang, A., Gatta, C., Bengio, Y.: FitNets: hints for thin deep nets. arXiv preprint arXiv:1412.6550 (2014)

37. Shen, Z., He, Z., Xue, X.: Meal: multi-model ensemble via adversarial learning. In: Proceedings of the AAAI Conference on Artificial Intelligence, vol. 33, pp. 4886–4893 (2019)

38. Touvron, H., Cord, M., Douze, M., Massa, F., Sablayrolles, A., Jégou, H.: Training data-efficient image transformers & distillation through attention. In: International Conference on Machine Learning, pp. 10347–10357. PMLR (2021)

39. Tung, F., Mori, G.: Similarity-preserving knowledge distillation. In: Proceedings of the IEEE/CVF International Conference on Computer Vision, pp. 1365–1374 (2019)

40. Vaswani, A., et al.: Attention is all you need. In: Advances in Neural Information Processing Systems, vol. 30 (2017)

41. Wang, T., Yuan, L., Zhang, X., Feng, J.: Distilling object detectors with fine-grained feature imitation. In: Proceedings of the IEEE/CVF Conference on Computer Vision and Pattern Recognition, pp. 4933–4942 (2019)

42. Wang, W., et al.: Pyramid vision transformer: a versatile backbone for dense prediction without convolutions. In: Proceedings of the IEEE/CVF International Conference on Computer Vision, pp. 568–578 (2021)

43. Wang, W., et al.: PVTv2: improved baselines with pyramid vision transformer. Comput. Vis. Media 8(3), 1–10 (2022)

44. Wu, A., Zheng, W.S., Guo, X., Lai, J.H.: Distilled person re-identification: towards a more scalable system. In: Proceedings of the IEEE/CVF Conference on Computer Vision and Pattern Recognition, pp. 1187–1196 (2019)

45. Wu, H., et al.: CvT: introducing convolutions to vision transformers. In: Proceedings of the IEEE/CVF International Conference on Computer Vision, pp. 22–31 (2021)

46. Xie, E., Wang, W., Yu, Z., Anandkumar, A., Alvarez, J.M., Luo, P.: SegFormer: simple and efficient design for semantic segmentation with transformers. In: Advances in Neural Information Processing Systems, vol. 34 (2021)

47. Yang, Z., et al.: Tap: text-aware pre-training for text-VQA and text-caption. In: Proceedings of the IEEE/CVF Conference on Computer Vision and Pattern Recognition, pp. 8751–8761 (2021)

48. Yim, J., Joo, D., Bae, J., Kim, J.: A gift from knowledge distillation: fast optimization, network minimization and transfer learning. In: Proceedings of the IEEE Conference on Computer Vision and Pattern Recognition, pp. 4133–4141 (2017)

49. Yu, Z., Yu, J., Cui, Y., Tao, D., Tian, Q.: Deep modular co-attention networks for visual question answering. In: Proceedings of the IEEE/CVF Conference on Computer Vision and Pattern Recognition, pp. 6281–6290 (2019)

50. Yuan, K., Guo, S., Liu, Z., Zhou, A., Yu, F., Wu, W.: Incorporating convolution designs into visual transformers. In: Proceedings of the IEEE/CVF International Conference on Computer Vision, pp. 579–588 (2021)

51. Yuan, L., et al.: Tokens-to-token ViT: training vision transformers from scratch on imagenet. In: Proceedings of the IEEE/CVF International Conference on Computer Vision, pp. 558–567 (2021)

52. Yuan, L., Hou, Q., Jiang, Z., Feng, J., Yan, S.: Volo: vision outlooker for visual recognition. arXiv preprint arXiv:2106.13112 (2021)

53. Zbontar, J., et al.: fastMRI: an open dataset and benchmarks for accelerated MRI. arXiv preprint arXiv:1811.08839 (2018)

54. Zhang, Z., Zhang, H., Zhao, L., Chen, T., Arık, S.O., Pfister, T.: Nested hierarchical transformer: towards accurate, data-efficient and interpretable visual understanding. In: AAAI Conference on Artificial Intelligence (AAAI) (2022)

55. Zhu, C., Chen, W., Peng, T., Wang, Y., Jin, M.: Hard sample aware noise robust learning for histopathology image classification. IEEE Trans. Med. Imaging 41, 881–894 (2021)

Neighborhood Collective Estimation for Noisy Label Identification and Correction

Jichang Li[1,2] , Guanbin Li[1(✉)] , Feng Liu[3] , and Yizhou Yu[2(✉)]

[1] Sun Yat-sen University, Guangzhou 510006, China
csjcli@connect.hku.hk, liguanbin@mail.sysu.edu.cn
[2] The University of Hong Kong, Hong Kong, China
yizhouy@acm.org
[3] Deepwise AI Lab, Beijing, China
liufeng@deepwise.com

Abstract. Learning with noisy labels (LNL) aims at designing strategies to improve model performance and generalization by mitigating the effects of model overfitting to noisy labels. The key success of LNL lies in identifying as many clean samples as possible from massive noisy data, while rectifying the wrongly assigned noisy labels. Recent advances employ the predicted label distributions of individual samples to perform noise verification and noisy label correction, easily giving rise to confirmation bias. To mitigate this issue, we propose Neighborhood Collective Estimation, in which the predictive reliability of a candidate sample is re-estimated by contrasting it against its feature-space nearest neighbors. Specifically, our method is divided into two steps: 1) Neighborhood Collective Noise Verification to separate all training samples into a clean or noisy subset, 2) Neighborhood Collective Label Correction to relabel noisy samples, and then auxiliary techniques are used to assist further model optimization. Extensive experiments on four commonly used benchmark datasets, i.e., CIFAR-10, CIFAR-100, Clothing-1M and Webvision-1.0, demonstrate that our proposed method considerably outperforms state-of-the-art methods.

Keywords: Learning with noisy labels · Neighborhood collective estimation · Confirmation bias

1 Introduction

Deep neural networks (DNNs) have achieved significant success in computer vision tasks, such as image classification [1,5,18,22,41,51], *etc.* However, they rely heavily on tremendous quantities of high-quality manual annotations. To

Supplementary Information The online version contains supplementary material available at https://doi.org/10.1007/978-3-031-20053-3_8.

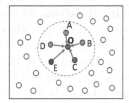

Fig. 1. An illustration to exemplify our basic idea. Samples distributed within the dotted circle, including the candidate sample, Point O, and its nearest neighbors, *i.e.*, Point A, B, C, D and E are close to each other in the feature-space neighborhood. Different colors indicate different labels (either predicted label or given groundtruth label). In the noise verification stage, a given label of the candidate (Point O) is considered noisy if there is a huge inconsistency between the label distributions of the candidate and its nearest neighbors; and otherwise, the candidate is considered as a clean sample. Likewise, in the noise correction stage, a noisy sample discards the given noisy label and is relabeled through a neighborhood collective estimation process involving its contrastive neighbors

alleviate the need for extensive human annotations while improving the generalization capability of deep neural networks, learning with noisy labels (LNL) has been proposed to effectively leverage large-scale yet poorly-annotated datasets while mitigating the effects of model overfitting to noisy labels.

To tackle the challenges imposed by LNL, previous works have proposed massive strategies [10, 19, 32, 39, 47], including noisy label correction [3, 24], noisy label or sample rejection [14, 15, 19, 47], and noisy sample reweighing [12, 35, 42]. The mainstream pipeline first uses noise verification strategies to separate the original training set into a clean set and a noisy set, which contain training samples with clean labels and noisy labels respectively, in order to diminish the effect of noisy labels during model training. Then, (un)supervised learning or semi-supervised learning (SSL) based techniques are adopted to correct noisy labels and further optimize the classification model by regarding the clean set and noisy set as labeled and unlabeled samples respectively. In this scheme, original noisy labels are simply discarded for their high chances to be incorrect, avoiding the negative effect of noisy label memorization in the trained model.

In the context of learning with noisy labels, there may exist classes with imbalanced noisy or clean samples, especially in real-world noisy datasets such as Clothing-1M [45] and Webvision-1.0 [23]. For instance, there might be a relatively high proportion of noisy labels in some hard-to-annotate classes; on the other hand, a trained model may produce low-confident predictions on a relatively high proportion of hard-to-learn clean samples in some classes, making existing noise identification algorithms incorrectly identify them as noisy samples. As a result, noise accumulation may take place implicitly in such classes, making the trained model produce unreliable label predictions. The above scenarios could make an LNL algorithm fall into the so-called confirmation bias [2, 40], which causes the algorithm to favor incorrect training labels that have been confirmed with predicted labels in earlier training iterations. In this context, relying too much on the potentially biased label predictions for individual training samples would increase the risk of incorrectly identifying noisy labels in the noise verification stage. Moreover, confirmation bias also exists in the subsequent noise correction stage, where SSL or other methods, such as label-guessing [19,30,50] and label re-assignment [47], construct pseudo-labels for unlabeled samples in the noisy set using potentially biased label predictions. Apparently, model training in the optimization stage would strengthen this bias as more confident but incorrect predictions would defy new changes, and subsequently even deteriorate model performance in high noise ratio scenarios.

We are inspired by the premise of contrastive learning that samples from the same class should have higher similarity in the feature space than those from different classes [9,29,31]. Therefore, we approach learning with noisy labels from a different perspective and propose Neighborhood Collective Estimation (NCE), in which we re-estimate the predictive reliability of a candidate sample by contrasting it against its feature-space nearest neighboring samples. Herein, we borrow the concept from contrastive learning, and then name such neighboring samples of the candidate as contrastive neighbors. Leveraging contrastive neighbors enriches the predictive information associated with the candidate and also makes such information relatively unbiased, thereby improving the accuracy of noisy label identification and correction. Figure 1 displays the basic idea of the proposed method.

Specifically, to abide by the mainstream LNL pipeline, we divide our method into two steps: 1) Neighborhood Collective Noise Verification (NCNV) to separate all training samples into a clean set and a noisy set, 2) Neighborhood Collective Label Correction (NCLC) to relabel noisy samples. In the NCNV stage, a candidate sample is considered noisy when there is a huge inconsistency between the one-hot vector of the given label of the candidate and the label distributions of its contrastive neighbors predicted using the trained model. In the NCLC stage, we only relabel noisy samples whose predicted label distribution is sufficiently similar to the given labels of neighboring clean samples, and the corrected label of a noisy sample is related to a weighted combination of the given labels of neighboring clean samples. Once we have identified clean samples and relabeled noisy ones, we leverage off-the-shelf and well-established techniques, such as mixup regularization [49] and consistency regularization [36], to perform further SSL-based model training.

In summary, the main contributions are as follows.

- We propose Neighborhood Collective Estimation for learning with noisy labels, which leverages contrastive neighbors to obtain richer and relatively unbiased predictive information for candidate samples and thus mitigates confirmation bias.
- Concretely, we design two steps called Neighborhood Collective Noise Verification and Neighborhood Collective Label Correction to identify clean samples and relabel noisy ones respectively.

– We evaluate our method on four widely used LNL benchmark datasets, *i.e.*, CIFAR-10 [16], CIFAR-100 [16], Clothing-1M [45] and Webvision-1.0 [23], and the results demonstrate that our proposed method considerably outperforms state-of-the-art LNL methods.

2 Related Work

In this section, we focus on noise verification and label correction that are means involved in current dominant pipeline to address the LNL problem.

2.1 Noise Verification

Noise verification involves sample selection to choose and remove noisy labels within the training datasets. Proper noise verification strategies are necessary and several earlier works [10,15,48] have shown that samples with smaller cross-entropy loss are prone to hold clean labels, assuming that deep neural networks prefer to memorize simple patterns first rather than overfit to noisy labels. Also, some recently superior methods made efforts to model per-sample loss distributions with Beta Mixture Models (BMM) [26] or Gaussian Mixture Models (GMM) [34] to separate noisy labels from all the training samples [3,13,19,30,46,50]. However, based on the predicted label distributions of individual candidate samples to identify the training samples, the above-stated noise verification strategies tend to fall into confirmation bias. Previous works have also attempted to identify noisy labels by leveraging neighborhood information. They either use neighborhood samples to remove noisy labels or re-weight them [4,32,43,44,52]. For example, Bahri *et al.* [4] proposed to identify noisy label by searching nearest neighbors based on the model predictions of a KNN classifier, while Zhu *et al.* [52] uses feature-space neighbors to help estimate a noise transition matrix. In our work, we employ neighborhood collective estimation to realize both the identification and correction of noise labels, and make the two promote each other, to achieve better noise label learning.

2.2 Label Correction

To alleviate the effect of noisy memorization, noisy labels are discarded simply, and then label correction is adopted to relabel unlabeled samples [19,25,30,37,47,50]. This aims to give reliable pseudo-labels and support subsequent model training so as to achieve better performance. For example, "SELFIE" proposed by Song *et al.* [37] tried to perform label correction by considering model predictions from past selecting clean labels. Also, Li *et al.* [19] "co-guessed" pseudo-labels for unlabeled (noisy) samples via ensembling predictions of coupled networks, while Yao *et al.* [47] employed label re-assignment to provide pseudo-labels with the predictions of a temporally averaged model. Different from those as mentioned above, we correct noisy labels with the aid of neighboring labeled samples. This can relatively avoid confirmation bias that derives from model predictions at individual samples.

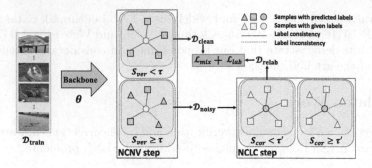

Fig. 2. Our proposed steps for learning with noisy labels. Triangles and squares represent contrastive neighbors from two different classes while circles denote the candidate samples in various steps. We assume the candidates belong to the class represented by the squares. In this work, we design two steps called Neighborhood Collective Noise Verification (NCNV) and Neighborhood Collective Label Correction (NCLC) to identify clean samples and relabel noisy ones respectively. Both steps leverage contrastive neighbors to obtain richer and relatively unbiased predictive information for candidate samples and thus mitigate confirmation bias

3   The Proposed Method

Problem Formulation. Learning with noisy labels seeks an optimal model trained with a large-scale noisy dataset $\mathcal{D}_{\mathbf{train}} = \{(x_i, y_i)\}_{i=1}^{N}$, where N is the number of sample-label pairs and each pair consists of a training sample x_i and its associated label y_i over C classes while whether the given label is noisy or clean is unknown. During the training process, a sample is fed into a model being trained, that is parameterized by θ and contains a feature extractor Φ and a classifier with a softmax layer, to obtain its corresponding feature representation $\Phi(x_i)$ and class probabilities $p(y|x_i)$ respectively.

Contrastive Neighbors. We contrast a candidate sample against its feature-space nearest neighbors to enrich and diversify predictive information of the candidate. Such nearest neighbors are called contrastive neighbors in this paper. First, to compute feature similarity between a candidate sample x_i and one of its feature-space neighbors x_j, we define a similarity function:

$$d(x_i, x_j) = \frac{\Phi(x_i)^\top \Phi(x_j)}{\|\Phi(x_i)\|\|\Phi(x_j)\|}, \tag{1}$$

where $d(\cdot, \cdot)$ denotes the cosine distance metric. Then, we set up a pairwise connection between the two samples and quantify the discrepancy between their label distributions through the Jensen-Shannon (JS) divergence as follows,

$$J(p_i, p_j) = \frac{1}{2} KL(p_i \| \frac{p_i + p_j}{2}) + \frac{1}{2} KL(p_j \| \frac{p_i + p_j}{2}), \tag{2}$$

where $KL(\cdot||\cdot)$ represents the Kullback-Leibler (KL) divergence, and for sample x_i (or x_j), in different contexts, p_i (or p_j) represents either its probabilistic label distribution predicted using a trained model or its given ground-truth label. $J(\cdot, \cdot)$ returns values in the range of [0,1], and the use of JS divergence allows us to measure the discrepancy between the probabilistic label distributions of different samples. $J(p_i, p_j) \rightarrow 0$ indicates that the label distributions of p_i and p_j are very similar while $J(p_i, p_j) \rightarrow 1$ means the label distributions of these two samples are of great difference.

Overview. In this paper, we propose Neighborhood Collective Estimation (NCE) to tackle learning with noisy labels. In detail, we first propose Neighborhood Collective Noise Verification (NCNV) to identify noisy labels in $\mathcal{D}_{\mathbf{train}}$ and divide $\mathcal{D}_{\mathbf{train}}$ into clean subset $\mathcal{D}_{\mathbf{clean}}$ and noisy subset $\mathcal{D}_{\mathbf{noisy}}$. Then, we propose Neighborhood Collective Label Correction (NCLC) to relabel selected samples from $\mathcal{D}_{\mathbf{noisy}}$ and form a new subset $\mathcal{D}_{\mathbf{relab}}$. Finally, we leverage auxiliary techniques to perform model fine-tuning so as to further optimize our model. The diagram and the training procedure of our proposed model have been summarized in Fig. 2 and Algorithm 1, respectively.

Algorithm 1: Learning with Noisy Labels based on Neighborhood Collective Estimation

---

Input: Dataset $\mathcal{D}_{\mathbf{train}}$; Number of training epochs T_{tr}; Number of warm-up epochs T_{wu}; Learning rate η

Output: Optimal model parameter θ

1   **for** $t \rightarrow 1 \cdots T_{tr}$ **do**
2   **if** $t < T_{wu}$ **then**
      /* The warm-up step.   */
3   WarmUp($\mathcal{D}_{\mathbf{train}}$; θ).   // Initialize the model with a "WarmUp" function.
4   **else**
      /* The NCNV step.   */
5   Use Eq. (5) to split $\mathcal{D}_{\mathbf{train}}$ into clean samples $\mathcal{D}_{\mathbf{clean}}$ and noisy ones $\mathcal{D}_{\mathbf{noisy}}$.
      /* The NCLC step.   */
6   Use Eq. (9) to relabel a subset of samples from $\mathcal{D}_{\mathbf{noisy}}$ and form a new subset $\mathcal{D}_{\mathbf{relab}}$.
      /* The model fine-tuning step.   */
7   Randomly sample mini-batches from $\mathcal{D}_{\mathbf{clean}}$ and $\mathcal{D}_{\mathbf{relab}}$.
8   Update model parameter θ by applying SGD with η to Eq. (13).

3.1   Neighborhood Collective Noise Verification

In an effort to identify label noise for the task of LNL, most recent research establish sample selection criteria on the basis of predicted label distributions of individual samples [3,10,15,19,48], thus it is hard for them to avoid confirmation bias. Aiming at mitigating such bias, we formulate a novel noise verification function that determines whether a candidate is a noisy sample or not through the estimation of its label inconsistency score, which measures the degree of inconsistency between the label distributions of the candidate sample and its contrastive neighbors. Specifically, given a candidate sample-label pair $(x^{(c)}, y^{(c)}) \in \mathcal{D}_{\mathbf{train}}$, we first find its K nearest neighbors in the feature space using the cosine similarity in Eq. (1) and then declare them as contrastive neighbors, as formulated below.

$$\{x_k^{(c)}\}, k = 1, \cdots, K \leftarrow \mathbf{KNN}(x^{(c)}; \mathcal{D}_{\mathbf{train}}; K), \tag{3}$$

where $\mathbf{KNN}(x^{(c)}; \mathcal{D}_{\mathbf{train}}; K)$ is a function that returns K most similar samples in $\mathcal{D}_{\mathbf{train}}$ for the candidate sample $x^{(c)}$. Note that $x^{(c)}$ is temporarily removed from $\mathcal{D}_{\mathbf{train}}$ at this moment.

Then, the neighborhood-based label inconsistency score for the given label of the candidate can be defined as follows,

$$S_{ver}(x^{(c)}, y^{(c)}) = \frac{1}{K} \sum_{k=1}^{K} J(p_y(y^{(c)}), p(y|x_k^{(c)})), \tag{4}$$

where $p_y(y^{(c)})$ is the one-hot vector for the given ground-truth label $y^{(c)}$ of the candidate sample and $p(y|x_k^{(c)})$ stands for the probabilistic label distribution of the k-th contrastive neighbor predicted using a classification model trained with all original samples including both clean and noisy ones. Here, instead of the model prediction at the candidate sample, we make use of model predictions at its contrastive neighbors, implicitly diversifying the predictive information of the candidate sample and making it relatively unbiased.

After computing the label inconsistency score for every candidate sample, we observe that if the given ground-truth label of a candidate sample is significantly different from the model prediction of its contrastive neighbor samples, i.e., of large inconsistency, then the given label is very likely to be a noisy label. Therefore, by setting a threshold τ, we can classify candidate sample $x^{(c)}$ as a noisy sample if $S_{ver}(x^{(c)}, y^{(c)}) \geq \tau$, and otherwise, a clean one. To this end, we can obtain $\mathcal{D}_{\mathbf{clean}}$ and $\mathcal{D}_{\mathbf{noisy}}$ as follows,

$$\begin{aligned} \mathcal{D}_{\mathbf{clean}} &\leftarrow \{(x_i, y_i) \,|\, S_{ver}(x_i, y_i) < \tau, \forall (x_i, y_i) \in \mathcal{D}_{\mathbf{train}}\}, \\ \mathcal{D}_{\mathbf{noisy}} &\leftarrow \{(x_i,) \,|\, S_{ver}(x_i, y_i) \geq \tau, \forall (x_i, y_i) \in \mathcal{D}_{\mathbf{train}}\}. \end{aligned} \tag{5}$$

3.2 Neighborhood Collective Label Correction

After the neighborhood collective noise verification (NCNV) stage, we treat samples from $\mathcal{D}_{\mathbf{clean}}$ and $\mathcal{D}_{\mathbf{noisy}}$ as labeled and unlabeled samples respectively by simply discarding noisy labels to prevent noise memorization in the resulted classification model. To leverage the unlabeled samples, some studies have taken pseudo-labeling based methods to mine discriminative cues for model training [19,32,47], yet all of them resort to model predictions at individual unlabeled samples, again tracing back to the unavoidable bias. On the contrary, we set up neighborhood collective label correction (NCLC) stage, which corrects noisy labels by relying on neighboring clean samples to obtain more reliable and relatively unbiased pseudo-labels.

As in the NCNV stage, we first find K contrastive neighbors for each noisy sample $x^{(u)} \in \mathcal{D}_{\mathbf{noisy}}$ according to the ranked feature similarities between $x^{(u)}$ and its neighbors, as formulated below. At this time, we require all its contrastive neighbors to belong to the clean set $\mathcal{D}_{\mathbf{clean}}$.

$$\{(x_k^{(u)}, y_k^{(u)})\}, k = 1, \cdots, K \leftarrow \mathbf{KNN}(x^{(u)}; \mathcal{D}_{\mathbf{clean}}; K), \qquad (6)$$

where $(x_k^{(u)}, y_k^{(u)})$ is a sample-label pair from $\mathcal{D}_{\mathbf{clean}}$. Unlike the NCNV stage, the ground-truth label information of contrastive neighbors is required in this stage.

Afterwards, we perform the following label consistency check between each candidate sample and its contrastive neighbors to mine those noisy samples that are similar to their neighboring samples in both the feature and label space,

$$S_{cor}(x^{(u)}) = \frac{1}{K} \sum_{k=1}^{K} J(p(y|x^{(u)}), p_y(y_k^{(u)})), \qquad (7)$$

where $J(p(y|x^{(u)}), p_y(y_k^{(u)}))$ computes the discrepancy between the probabilistic label distribution of the candidate sample $x^{(u)}$ predicted using the trained classification model, and the one-hot vector for the given ground-truth label of its k-th contrastive neighbor. A large $S_{cor}(x^{(u)})$ indicates that the predicted label of the candidate sample is highly dissimilar to the clean and definite labels of its contrastive neighbors, suggesting that the candidate sample may lie near the decision boundary of the model. To be safe, we drop such candidate noisy samples if $S_{cor}(x^{(u)}) \geq \tau'$, where a second threshold τ' is used. In contrast, a candidate sample that satisfies $S_{cor}(x^{(u)}) < \tau'$ is more likely to be farther away from the decision boundary and could derive a more reliable pseudo-label from its contrastive neighbors. Therefore, we define a label correction function to generate a new label for such a noisy sample as follows,

$$\mathbf{Correct}(x^{(u)}) = \arg\max_{c} \sum_{k=1}^{K} w(x^{(u)}; k) \cdot p_y(y_k^{(u)}), \qquad (8)$$

where we use $w(x^{(u)}; k) = 1 - J(p(y|x^{(u)}), p_y(y_k^{(u)}))$ to approximate the probability that the candidate sample belongs to the same class as its k-th contrastive neighbor, and $c = 1, \cdots, C$ indicates the c-th component of a label distribution vector has the maximum value. For convenience, we set $\hat{y}^{(u)} = \mathbf{Correct}(x^{(u)})$.

Finally, we define a new sample collection that contains all relabeled noisy samples as follows,

$$\mathcal{D}_{\mathbf{relab}} \leftarrow \{(x_i, \hat{y}_i) | \hat{y}_i = \mathbf{Correct}(x_i), S_{cor}(x_i) < \tau', \forall x_i \in \mathcal{D}_{\mathbf{noisy}}\}. \qquad (9)$$

3.3 Training Objectives

Once we have the clean set $\mathcal{D}_{\mathbf{clean}}$ and relabeled set $\mathcal{D}_{\mathbf{relab}}$ respectively from the NCNV and NCLC steps, we use both datasets together to further optimize the classification model through fine-tuning. Auxiliary techniques are incorporated during model optimization. Since the initial classification model trained using both clean and noisy samples memorizes noisy labels during its training process and Mixup [49] can effectively attenuate such noise memorization, we first employ the mixup regularization to construct augmented samples through linear combinations of existing samples from $\mathcal{D}_{\mathbf{clean}}$.

Given two existing samples (x_i, y_i) and (x_j, y_j) from $\mathcal{D}_{\mathbf{clean}}$, an augmented sample $(\tilde{x}, \tilde{y})$ can be generated as follows,

$$\tilde{x} = \lambda x_i + (1 - \lambda)x_j, \tilde{y} = \lambda p_y(y_i) + (1 - \lambda)p_y(y_j), \tag{10}$$

where $\lambda \sim Beta(\alpha)$ is a mixup ratio and α is a scalar parameter of Beta distribution. The cross-entropy loss applied to B augmented samples in each mini-batch is defined as follows,

$$\mathcal{L}^{mix} = -\sum_{b=1}^{B} \tilde{y}_b \log p(y|\tilde{x}_b). \tag{11}$$

In the NCLC stage, more reliable pseudo-labels are assigned to noisy samples farther away from the decision boundary. To leverage these relabeled samples during model optimization, we apply consistency regularization to them to further enhance the robustness of the model [8]. Label consistency is a good choice to achieve this goal because it encourages the fine-tuned model to produce the same output when there are minor perturbations in the input [36]. In practice, we enforce label consistency through the following loss:

$$\mathcal{L}^{lab} = -\sum_{b'=1}^{B'} p_y(y_{b'}) \log p(y|\mathbf{Aug}(x_{b'})), \tag{12}$$

where B' relabeled samples $(x_{b'}, y_{b'}) \in \mathcal{D}_{\mathbf{relab}}$ are chosen in each iteration, $p_y(y_{b'})$ is the one-hot vector of the pseudo-label of $x_{b'}$, $\mathbf{Aug}(\cdot)$ denotes the function that perturbs the chosen samples using Autoaugment technique proposed in [7], and $p(y|\mathbf{Aug}(x_{b'}))$ is the predicted label distribution of the perturbed sample. Proved by our experiments, this label consistency loss can be also applied to the selected clean samples from $\mathcal{D}_{\mathbf{clean}}$, especially under low noise ratios, to better boost the performance of the model.

As stated above, the overall loss function for final model fine-tuning is a combination of the cross-entropy and label consistency losses,

$$\mathcal{L}^{overall} = \mathcal{L}^{mix} + \gamma\mathcal{L}^{lab}, \tag{13}$$

where γ is a trade-off scalar to balance those two loss terms.

Table 1. Test accuracy (%) of our method (NCE) and existing state-of-the-art methods on the CIFAR-10 and CIFAR-100 datasets. (Mean accuracy and 95% confidence interval over 3 trails)

Dataset	CIFAR-10					CIFAR-100			
Noise type	Symmetric				Assymetric	Symmetric			
Method/Noise ratio	0.2	0.5	0.8	0.9	0.4	0.2	0.5	0.8	0.9
Cross-Entropy [19]	86.8	79.4	62.9	42.7	85.0	62.0	46.7	19.9	10.1
F-correction [33]	86.8	79.8	63.3	42.9	87.2	61.5	46.6	19.9	10.2
Co-teaching+ [48]	89.5	85.7	67.4	47.9	–	65.6	51.8	27.9	13.7
PENCIL [17]	92.4	89.1	77.5	58.9	88.5	69.4	57.5	31.1	15.3
LossModelling [3]	94.0	92.0	86.8	69.1	87.4	73.9	66.1	48.2	24.3
DivideMix [19]	96.1	94.6	93.2	76.0	93.4	77.3	74.6	60.2	31.5
ELR [24]	95.8	94.8	93.3	78.7	93.0	77.6	73.6	60.8	33.4
ProtoMix [21]	95.8	94.3	92.4	75.0	91.9	79.1	74.8	57.7	29.3
NGC [44]	95.9	94.5	91.6	80.5	90.6	79.3	75.9	62.7	29.8
NCE(best)	**96.2** ±0.09	**95.3** ±0.12	**93.9** ±0.22	**88.4** ±0.98	**94.5** ±0.70	**81.4** ±0.37	**76.3** ±0.28	**64.7** ±0.56	**41.1** ±0.54
NCE(last)	96.0 ±0.22	95.2 ±0.23	93.6 ±0.30	88.0 ±1.21	94.2 ±0.96	81.0 ±0.27	75.3 ±0.07	64.5 ±0.86	40.7 ±0.42

Table 2. Test accuracy (%) of our method (NCE) and existing state-of-the-art methods on the Clothing-1M dataset.

Meta-L. [20]	DivideMix [19]	ELR [24]	ELR+ [24]	NestedCoT. [6]	AugDesc [30]	NCE
73.5	74.8	72.9	74.8	74.9	75.1	**75.3**

4 Experiments

4.1 Experimental Setup

Implementation. We highlight the effectiveness of our proposed NCE method on four standard LNL benchmark datasets: CIFAR-10 [16], CIFAR-100 [16], Clothing-1M [45] and Webvision-1.0 [23]. To be fair, we follow most details of the training and evaluation processes from the previous work "DivideMix" [19], such as network architectures, confidence penalty for asymmetric noise, and so on. Our code is publicly available at https://github.com/lijichang/LNL-NCE.

CIFAR-10 and CIFAR-100 are two classic synthetic datasets for the LNL problem. We follow "DivideMix" [19] to create the noisy types, *i.e.*, "Symmetry" and "Asymmetry", and to set noise ratios, namely "0.20", "0.50", "0.80" and "0.90" for "Symmetry", and "0.40" for "Asymmetry". Similar to existing works [19,24,44], we also select PreAct Resnet [11] as the model backbone for CIFAR-10/CIFAR-100. Then we train it using a SGD optimizer with a momentum of 0.9 and a weight decay of 5×10^{-4} respectively. To better initialize our model, we set a warm-up step to perform supervised training on the model over all available samples using a standard cross-entropy loss. For effectiveness, this step is assigned a training period $T_{wu} = 10$ (or 30) for CIFAR-10 (or CIFAR-100). For adapting to diverse scenarios, we empirically set τ to 0.75 on CIFAR-10 or 0.90 on CIFAR-100, while τ' are usually set as 2×10^{-3} and 1×10^{-2} on CIFAR-10 and CIFAR-100, respectively. With respect to other hyper-parameters that are involved in NCE on CIFAR-10/CIFAR-100, we set $K = 20, T_{tr} = 300, \gamma = 1.0, \eta = 0.02, B = 128, B' = 128$ and $\alpha = 4$.

Clothing-1M and Webvision-1.0 are two large-scale real-world noisy datasets. Clothing-1M contains one million samples grabbed from the online shopping websites and Webvision-1.0 only uses top-50 classes originating from the Google image Subset of Webvision [23]. For Webvision-1.0, the results are reported from testing our model on both the WebVision validation set and the ImageNet ILSVRC12 validation set [38].

Baselines. We compare NCE with the following state-of-the-art algorithms to address the LNL problem on CIFAR-10 and CIFAR-100: "Cross-Entropy" [19], "F-correction" [33], "Co-teaching+" [48], "PENCIL" [17], "LossModelling" [3], "DivideMix" [19], "ELR" [24], "ProtoMix" [21] and "NGC" [44]. Herein, "Cross-Entropy" trains the model only with a supervised cross-entropy loss over training samples along with given noisy labels, and its results are copied from "DivideMix". Besides methods stated above, we perform our comparison on Clothing-1M with previous methods, including "Meta-Learning" [20], "ELR+" [24], "NestedCoTeaching" [6] and "AugDesc" [30], where the augmentation strategy of our method on this dataset refers to that of "AugDesc" for comparison fairness. Moreover, we evaluate the proposed approach on Webvision-1.0 by newly adding "Decoupling" [28], "MentorNet" [15], and "Co-teaching" [10].

4.2 Comparisons with the State of the Art

Synthetic Noisy Datasets. CIFAR-10 and CIFAR-100 are two representative synthetic LNL benchmark datasets and we report results on these datasets in Table 1. For fair comparison, we follow all the settings in [19,44]. We can see that our NCE outperforms all existing state-of-the-art methods on CIFAR-10 and CIFAR-100 under all settings of symmetric (from 20% to 90%) and asymmetric (40% only) label noise ratio. In particular, on CIFAR-10, our method surpasses the best performing baselines by 7.9% and 1.1% at the highest symmetric and asymmetric noise ratios, respectively. In addition, in comparison to the performance of existing algorithms on CIFAR-100, NCE achieves the highest classification accuracy under all four noise ratio settings by exceeding the second best by 2.1%, 0.4%, 2.0% and 7.7%, respectively.

Real-World Noisy Datasets. To further verify the effectiveness of the proposed NCE method, we also conduct experiments on real-world noisy datasets,

Table 3. Top-1 and top-5 test accuracy (%) of our method (NCE) and existing state-of-the-art methods on the Webvision and ImageNet ILSVRC12 validation sets. The models are trained on the training set of the Webvision-1.0 dataset

Method	WebVision		ILSVRC12	
	top-1	top-5	top-1	top-5
F-correction [33]	61.1	82.7	57.4	82.4
Decoupling [28]	62.5	84.7	58.3	82.3
MentorNet [15]	63.0	81.4	57.8	79.9
Co-teaching [10]	63.6	85.2	61.5	84.7
DivideMix [19]	77.3	91.6	75.2	90.8
ELR [24]	76.3	91.3	68.7	87.8
ELR+ [24]	77.8	91.7	70.3	89.8
NGC [44]	79.2	91.8	74.4	91.0
NCE	**79.5**	**93.8**	**76.3**	**94.1**

Table 4. Ablation study of our method (NCE) on the CIFAR-10 and CIFAR-100 datasets under multiple label noise ratios. "repl." is an abbreviation for "replaced", and $\mathcal{L}^{ce}$ means the model is trained on the clean samples using a cross-entropy loss. (Only one of three trails is selected for comparison in our NCE method)

M-(#)	Dataset	CIFAR-10			CIFAR-100		Mean
	Noise type	Symmetric		Assymetric	Symmetric		
	Method/Noise ratio	0.5	0.8	0.4	0.5	0.8	
1	NCE	95.3	94.1	94.6	76.1	65.2	85.1
2	NCE repl. NCNV w/GMM	94.8	79.0	89.7	75.8	56.8	79.2
3	NCE repl. NCLC w/CT(0.95)	94.3	86.1	90.1	76.0	58.7	81.0
4	NCE repl. NCNV w/GMM & w/o $\mathcal{L}^{lab}$	91.2	78.8	87.3	71.4	49.7	75.7
5	NCE w/o $\mathcal{L}^{lab}$	92.5	86.7	92.6	74.4	57.9	80.8
6	NCE repl. $\mathcal{L}^{mix}$ w/$\mathcal{L}^{ce}$	93.3	78.5	89.0	73.2	55.2	77.8
7	NCE repl. perturbed w/unperturbed in Eq. (12)	93.6	89.4	90.5	72.5	56.1	80.4

namely Clothing-1M and Webvision-1.0. Table 2 and Table 3 show performance comparisons between NCE and existing algorithms when these two are respectively used as the training set. We can observe that NCE achieves the highest accuracy on Clothing-1M and an improvement of 0.2% over "AugDesc", the best performing method among existing ones. Likewise, on the challenging Webvision-1.0, NCE again achieves higher performance than most existing methods in terms of top-1 and top-5 accuracy. These results further verify that our proposed approach can effectively perform well on the real-world noisy datasets.

4.3 Analysis

To provide insights on how effectively each component of our algorithm works, we conduct an ablation study by removing or replacing individual components. Results of this ablation study are summarized in Table 4 and Fig. 3. Also, as displayed in and Fig. 4, we perform feature visualization to further analyze the proposed algorithm. All experiments are performed on both CIFAR-10 and CIFAR-100 datasets.

Effectiveness of NCNV Step. To examine the effectiveness of the NCNV step in identifying clean/noisy labels, we replace NCNV with a well-known GMM-based strategy proposed in "DivideMix" [19]. In Table 4, a comparison between row M-(1) and row M-(2) reveals that our NCNV step significantly outperforms the GMM-based strategy because the former is capable of identifying clean labels of harder samples. Specifically, Fig. 3(a) and (b) show the power of our NCNV step in handling "hard" classes and "hard" samples in the clean subset. A class is considered "hard" when multiple methods have an overall low clean sample identification accuracy in the class, while a "hard" sample has a low probability (confidence) associated with its predicted class label. As Fig. 3(a) shows, our method achieves higher sensitivity on "hard" classes, *i.e.* "cat", "bird" and "deer", where both methods have the lowest identification accuracy. In addition, Fig. 3(b) also shows that our NCNV step works significantly better on "hard" samples, whose predicted class labels are associated with a low probability (confidence).

Effectiveness of NCLC Step. To better understand the performance of the NCLC step in label correction, we replace NCLC with an existing label correction scheme, called Confidence Thresholding (CT) [36], which relabels such samples whose pseudo-labels have a confidence value exceeding a predefined threshold, *e.g.*, 0.95. According to row M-(3) of Table 4, NCLC clearly outperforms CT under all noise ratio settings. In detail, Fig. 3(c) and (d) reveal that CT works with few pseudo-labels in the early epochs. This is because, at that moment, the model cannot fit the training samples well and thus unlabeled samples with low-confidence predictions (< 0.95) would not be assigned pseudo-labels. Afterwards, although plenty of unlabeled samples are given pseudo-labels as model training goes on, the label correction accuracy drops at the same time. Ultimately, it leads to lower performance than NCLC, which, on the other hand, obtains more reliable pseudo-labels for unlabeled (noisy) points.

Necessity of Mixup Regularization. To verify the importance of the mixup regularization, we remove it from our algorithm and then perform standard supervision over clean samples. As shown in row M-(6) of Table 4, this change causes very serious performance degradation, indicating that the mixup regularization is able to effectively attenuate noise memorization.

Necessity of Consistency Regularization. To investigate the effectiveness of consistency regularization over unlabeled (noisy) samples, we conduct two experiments. First, we disable $\mathcal{L}^{lab}$, meaning that the model is only trained over

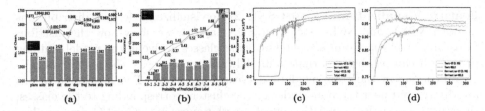

Fig. 3. Analysis of ablation study results. **(a)** The accuracy of clean sample identification in various classes. **(b)** The accuracy of clean sample identification vs. the probability (confidence) of predicted class label. **(c)** The evolution of the numbers of pseudo-labels and correct pseudo-labels over epochs. **(d)** The evolution of label correction accuracy and test classification accuracy over epochs. The experiments for (a) and (b) are performed on CIFAR-10 and CIFAR-100 respectively with the same noise profile (Noise ratio: 0.80; Noise type: Symmetric). The blue bars represent the distribution of clean samples. (c) and (d) describe the same experiment, where we analyze the label correction performance of NCLC and Confidence Thresholding (*i.e.*, CT(0.95)) on CIFAR-10 (Noise ratio: 0.50; Noise type: Symmetric) (Color figure oniline)

(a) NCNV step, Epoch=30 (b) NCNV step, Epoch=60 (c) NCNV step, Epoch=300 (d) NCLC step, Epoch=300

Fig. 4. Feature visualization using t-SNE. We choose 10 representative classes on CIFAR-100 (Noise ratio: 0.80; Noise type: Symmetric). **(a)**–**(c)** show how the distributions of misidentifications in the NCNV step evolve during model training. They are involved in samples from $\mathcal{D}_{\mathbf{train}}$ corresponding to each representative class. In these subfigures, points in black are misclassified samples, such as clean (or noisy) samples misclassified as noisy (or clean) ones, in the training data, while samples in purple are correctly identified ones. The accuracy of training sample identification in (a)–(c) is 82.2%, 94.7% and 95.2%, respectively. **(d)** shows the feature distributions of unlabeled (noisy) samples in $\mathcal{D}_{\mathbf{noisy}}$ corresponding to 10 classes in the NCLC step, and points in bright colors, black and grey respectively denote correctly relabeled samples, mis-relabeled ones and dropped ones (Colour figure online)

all clean samples. By comparing row M-(5) with row M-(1) in Table 4, we observe that the performance under all noise ratios drops by 1.7% to 7.6%, suggesting that this consistency loss is important for the performance of the model, especially when the noise ratio is high. In the second experiment, we replace the perturbed samples used in Eq. (12) with unperturbed ones to examine the need of sample perturbations. As shown in row M-(7) of Table 4, the average accuracy drops considerably by 4.7%. This demonstrates that sample perturbations in Eq. (12) play a significant role in realizing the full potential of consistency regularization.

Feature Visualization. We use t-SNE [27] to visualize the feature distributions in both NCNV and NCLC steps. In Fig. 4(a)–(c), we show how the distributions of misidentified samples across diverse classes evolve in the model training process. It can be observed that as model training proceeds, the number of misclassifications in the training data decreases gradually. The misclassifications are distributed near the boundaries of the clusters corresponding to the classes, showing a good noise verification effect. Furthermore, in the NVLC step, as illustrated in Fig. 4(d), most well-relabeled samples are located in the core regions of the clusters, while the mis-relabeled points and dropped ones are closer to the boundaries of the clusters or peripheral areas between different clusters. This meets our assumption stated in Sect. (3.2) that a candidate sample in the NVLC step that satisfies Eq. (9) is more likely to be farther away from the decision boundary of the model and could derive a more reliable pseudo-label.

5 Conclusions

In this paper, we have introduced a novel method called Neighborhood Collective Estimation (NCE) to tackle the problem of learning with noisy labels. In this method, we re-estimate the predictive reliability of a candidate sample by contrasting it against its feature-space nearest neighbors. This can enrich and diversify predictive information associated with the candidate and also makes such information relatively unbiased. The accuracy of noisy label identification and correction can thus be improved, facilitating subsequent model training. In detail, NCE consists of two steps, 1) Neighborhood Collective Noise Verification (NCNV) for separating all training data into clean samples and noisy ones, and 2) Neighborhood Collective Label Correction (NCLC) for relabeling noisy samples. Extensive experiments and a thorough ablation study have confirmed the superiority of our proposed method.

Acknowledgements. This work was supported in part by the Guangdong Basic and Applied Basic Research Foundation (No. 2020B1515020048), in part by the National Natural Science Foundation of China (No. 61976250, No. U1811463), in part by the Guangzhou Science and technology project (No. 202102020633), and in part by Hong Kong Research Grants Council through Research Impact Fund (Grant R-5001-18).

References

1. Algan, G., Ulusoy, I.: Image classification with deep learning in the presence of noisy labels: a survey. Knowl. Based Syst. **215**, 106771 (2021)
2. Arazo, E., Ortego, D., Albert, P., O'Connor, N.E., McGuinness, K.: Pseudo-labeling and confirmation bias in deep semi-supervised learning. In: 2020 International Joint Conference on Neural Networks (IJCNN). IEEE (2020)
3. Arazo, E., Ortego, D., Albert, P., O'Connor, N., McGuinness, K.: Unsupervised label noise modeling and loss correction. In: International Conference on Machine Learning, pp. 312–321. PMLR (2019)

4. Bahri, D., Jiang, H., Gupta, M.: Deep k-NN for noisy labels. In: III, H.D., Singh, A. (ed.) Proceedings of the 37th International Conference on Machine Learning, Proceedings of Machine Learning Research, vol. 119, pp. 540–550. PMLR (2020)

5. Bendre, N., Marín, H.T., Najafirad, P.: Learning from few samples: a survey. arXiv preprint arXiv:2007.15484 (2020)

6. Chen, Y., Shen, X., Hu, S.X., Suykens, J.A.: Boosting co-teaching with compression regularization for label noise. In: CVPR Learning from Limited and Imperfect Data (L2ID) workshop (2021)

7. Cubuk, E.D., Zoph, B., Mane, D., Vasudevan, V., Le, Q.V.: Autoaugment: learning augmentation strategies from data. In: Proceedings of the IEEE/CVF Conference on Computer Vision and Pattern Recognition, pp. 113–123 (2019)

8. Englesson, E., Azizpour, H.: Consistency regularization can improve robustness to label noise. arXiv preprint arXiv:2110.01242 (2021)

9. Gunel, B., Du, J., Conneau, A., Stoyanov, V.: Supervised contrastive learning for pre-trained language model fine-tuning. In: International Conference on Learning Representations (2020)

10. Han, B., et al.: Co-teaching: robust training of deep neural networks with extremely noisy labels. In: NeurIPS, pp. 8535–8545 (2018)

11. He, K., Zhang, X., Ren, S., Sun, J.: Identity mappings in deep residual networks. In: Leibe, B., Matas, J., Sebe, N., Welling, M. (eds.) ECCV 2016. LNCS, vol. 9908, pp. 630–645. Springer, Cham (2016). https://doi.org/10.1007/978-3-319-46493-0_38

12. Huang, L., Zhang, C., Zhang, H.: Self-adaptive training: beyond empirical risk minimization. In: Advances in Neural Information Processing Systems, vol. 33 (2020)

13. Huang, Z., et al.: Learning with noisy correspondence for cross-modal matching. In: Advances in Neural Information Processing Systems, vol. 34, pp. 29406–29419 (2021)

14. Jiang, L., Huang, D., Liu, M., Yang, W.: Beyond synthetic noise: deep learning on controlled noisy labels. In: International Conference on Machine Learning, pp. 4804–4815. PMLR (2020)

15. Jiang, L., Zhou, Z., Leung, T., Li, L.J., Fei-Fei, L.: MentorNet: learning data-driven curriculum for very deep neural networks on corrupted labels. In: International Conference on Machine Learning, pp. 2304–2313. PMLR (2018)

16. Krizhevsky, A.: Learning multiple layers of features from tiny images. Master's thesis, University of Tront (2009)

17. Kun, Y., Jianxin, W.: Probabilistic end-to-end noise correction for learning with noisy labels. In: The IEEE Conference on Computer Vision and Pattern Recognition (CVPR) (2019)

18. Li, J., Li, G., Shi, Y., Yu, Y.: Cross-domain adaptive clustering for semi-supervised domain adaptation. In: Proceedings of the IEEE/CVF Conference on Computer Vision and Pattern Recognition (CVPR), pp. 2505–2514 (2021)

19. Li, J., Socher, R., Hoi, S.C.: Dividemix: learning with noisy labels as semi-supervised learning. arXiv preprint arXiv:2002.07394 (2020)

20. Li, J., Wong, Y., Zhao, Q., Kankanhalli, M.S.: Learning to learn from noisy labeled data. In: Proceedings of the IEEE/CVF Conference on Computer Vision and Pattern Recognition, pp. 5051–5059 (2019)

21. Li, J., Xiong, C., Hoi, S.C.: Learning from noisy data with robust representation learning. In: Proceedings of the IEEE/CVF International Conference on Computer Vision (ICCV), pp. 9485–9494 (2021)

22. Li, W., Li, F., Luo, Y., Wang, P., et al.: Deep domain adaptive object detection: a survey. In: 2020 IEEE Symposium Series on Computational Intelligence (SSCI), pp. 1808–1813. IEEE (2020)

23. Li, W., Wang, L., Li, W., Agustsson, E., Gool, L.V.: Webvision database: visual learning and understanding from web data. Arxiv Preprint (2017)

24. Liu, S., Niles-Weed, J., Razavian, N., Fernandez-Granda, C.: Early-learning regularization prevents memorization of noisy labels. In: Advances in Neural Information Processing Systems, vol. 33 (2020)

25. Ma, X., et al.: Dimensionality-driven learning with noisy labels. In: Dy, J., Krause, A. (eds.) Proceedings of the 35th International Conference on Machine Learning, Proceedings of Machine Learning Research, vol. 80, pp. 3355–3364. PMLR (2018)

26. Ma, Z., Leijon, A.: Bayesian estimation of beta mixture models with variational inference. IEEE Trans. Pattern Anal. Mach. Intell. **33**(11), 2160–2173 (2011)

27. Van der Maaten, L., Hinton, G.: Visualizing data using t-SNE. J. Mach. Learn. Res. **9**(11), 2579–2605 (2008)

28. Malach, E., Shalev-Shwartz, S.: Decoupling" when to update" from" how to update". In: Advances in Neural Information Processing Systems , vol. 30, pp. 960–970 (2017)

29. Mikolov, T., Sutskever, I., Chen, K., Corrado, G.S., Dean, J.: Distributed representations of words and phrases and their compositionality. In: Burges, C.J.C., Bottou, L., Welling, M., Ghahramani, Z., Weinberger, K.Q. (eds.) Advances in Neural Information Processing Systems, vol. 26. Curran Associates, Inc. (2013). https://proceedings.neurips.cc/paper/2013/file/9aa42b31882ec039965f3c4923ce901b-Paper.pdf

30. Nishi, K., Ding, Y., Rich, A., Hollerer, T.: Augmentation strategies for learning with noisy labels. In: Proceedings of the IEEE/CVF Conference on Computer Vision and Pattern Recognition, pp. 8022–8031 (2021)

31. Oord, A.v.d., Li, Y., Vinyals, O.: Representation learning with contrastive predictive coding. arXiv preprint arXiv:1807.03748 (2018)

32. Ortego, D., Arazo, E., Albert, P., O'Connor, N.E., McGuinness, K.: Multi-objective interpolation training for robustness to label noise. In: Proceedings of the IEEE/CVF Conference on Computer Vision and Pattern Recognition, pp. 6606–6615 (2021)

33. Patrini, G., Rozza, A., Krishna Menon, A., Nock, R., Qu, L.: Making deep neural networks robust to label noise: a loss correction approach. In: Proceedings of the IEEE Conference on Computer Vision and Pattern Recognition, pp. 1944–1952 (2017)

34. Permuter, H., Francos, J., Jermyn, I.: A study of gaussian mixture models of color and texture features for image classification and segmentation. Pattern Recogn. **39**(4), 695–706 (2006)

35. Ren, M., Zeng, W., Yang, B., Urtasun, R.: Learning to reweight examples for robust deep learning. In: International Conference on Machine Learning, pp. 4334–4343. PMLR (2018)

36. Sohn, K., et al.: Fixmatch: simplifying semi-supervised learning with consistency and confidence. In: Advances in Neural Information Processing Systems, vol. 33 (2020)

37. Song, H., Kim, M., Lee, J.G.: Selfie: refurbishing unclean samples for robust deep learning. In: International Conference on Machine Learning, pp. 5907–5915. PMLR (2019)

38. Szegedy, C., Ioffe, S., Vanhoucke, V., Alemi, A.A.: Inception-v4, inception-ResNet and the impact of residual connections on learning. In: Thirty-first AAAI Conference on Artificial Intelligence (2017)
39. Tanaka, D., Ikami, D., Yamasaki, T., Aizawa, K.: Joint optimization framework for learning with noisy labels. In: Proceedings of the IEEE Conference on Computer Vision and Pattern Recognition, pp. 5552–5560 (2018)
40. Tarvainen, A., Valpola, H.: Mean teachers are better role models: weight-averaged consistency targets improve semi-supervised deep learning results. In: Proceedings of the 31st International Conference on Neural Information Processing Systems, pp. 1195–1204 (2017)
41. Van Engelen, J.E., Hoos, H.H.: A survey on semi-supervised learning. Mach. Learn. **109**(2), 373–440 (2020)
42. Wang, Y., et al.: Iterative learning with open-set noisy labels. In: Proceedings of the IEEE Conference on Computer Vision and Pattern Recognition, pp. 8688–8696 (2018)
43. Wu, P., Zheng, S., Goswami, M., Metaxas, D.N., Chen, C.: A topological filter for learning with label noise. In: Advances in Neural Information Processing Systems, vol. 33 (2020)
44. Wu, Z.F., Wei, T., Jiang, J., Mao, C., Tang, M., Li, Y.F.: NGC: a unified framework for learning with open-world noisy data (2021)
45. Xiao, T., Xia, T., Yang, Y., Huang, C., Wang, X.: Learning from massive noisy labeled data for image classification. In: 2015 IEEE Conference on Computer Vision and Pattern Recognition (CVPR), pp. 2691–2699 (2015)
46. Yang, M., Huang, Z., Hu, P., Li, T., Lv, J., Peng, X.: Learning with twin noisy labels for visible-infrared person re-identification. In: Proceedings of the IEEE/CVF Conference on Computer Vision and Pattern Recognition, pp. 14308–14317 (2022)
47. Yao, Y., et al.: Jo-SRC: a contrastive approach for combating noisy labels. In: Proceedings of the IEEE/CVF Conference on Computer Vision and Pattern Recognition, pp. 5192–5201 (2021)
48. Yu, X., Han, B., Yao, J., Niu, G., Tsang, I., Sugiyama, M.: How does disagreement help generalization against label corruption? In: International Conference on Machine Learning, pp. 7164–7173. PMLR (2019)
49. Zhang, H., Cisse, M., Dauphin, Y.N., Lopez-Paz, D.: mixup: beyond empirical risk minimization. arXiv preprint arXiv:1710.09412 (2017)
50. Zheltonozhskii, E., Baskin, C., Mendelson, A., Bronstein, A.M., Litany, O.: Contrast to divide: self-supervised pre-training for learning with noisy labels. arXiv preprint arXiv:2103.13646 (2021)
51. Zhou, H.Y., Chen, X., Zhang, Y., Luo, R., Wang, L., Yu, Y.: Generalized radiograph representation learning via cross-supervision between images and free-text radiology reports. Nat. Mach. Intell. **4**(1), 32–40 (2022)
52. Zhu, Z., Song, Y., Liu, Y.: Clusterability as an alternative to anchor points when learning with noisy labels. In: International Conference on Machine Learning, pp. 12912–12923. PMLR (2021)

Few-Shot Class-Incremental Learning via Entropy-Regularized Data-Free Replay

Huan Liu[1,2]([✉]) [ID], Li Gu[1] [ID], Zhixiang Chi[1] [ID], Yang Wang[1,3] [ID],
Yuanhao Yu[1] [ID], Jun Chen[2] [ID], and Jin Tang[1]

[1] Noah's Ark Lab, Huawei Technologies, Shenzhen, China
liuh127@mcmaster.ca
{li.gu,zhixiang.chi,yang.wang3,yuanhao.yu,tangjin}@huawei.com
[2] McMaster University, Hamilton, Canada
[3] University of Manitoba, Winnipeg, Canada
chenjun@mcmaster.ca

Abstract. Few-shot class-incremental learning (FSCIL) has been proposed aiming to enable a deep learning system to incrementally learn new classes with limited data. Recently, a pioneer claims that the commonly used replay-based method in class-incremental learning (CIL) is ineffective and thus not preferred for FSCIL. This has, if truth, a significant influence on the fields of FSCIL. In this paper, we show through empirical results that adopting the data replay is surprisingly favorable. However, storing and replaying old data can lead to a privacy concern. To address this issue, we alternatively propose using data-free replay that can synthesize data by a generator without accessing real data. In observing the effectiveness of uncertain data for knowledge distillation, we impose entropy regularization in the generator training to encourage more uncertain examples. Moreover, we propose to relabel the generated data with one-hot-like labels. This modification allows the network to learn by solely minimizing the cross-entropy loss, which mitigates the problem of balancing different objectives in the conventional knowledge distillation approach. Finally, we show extensive experimental results and analysis on CIFAR-100, miniImageNet and CUB-200 to demonstrate the effectiveness of our proposed one.

1 Introduction

Recently, there has been a tremendous success in using deep learning technologies [18] in large-scale image recognition tasks. Despite the remarkable success, they usually train a neural network to learn a mapping on a large amount of data. The model is then fixed and cannot be changed according to the users' needs. In

Supplementary Information The online version contains supplementary material available at https://doi.org/10.1007/978-3-031-20053-3_9.

contrast, humans can continually learn new knowledge throughout their lifetime. Inspired by this human capability, class-incremental learning (CIL) has been introduced to allow the neural network to continually update after new classes or environments are encountered. Despite the practical value of CIL, it usually suffers severely from the well-known catastrophic forgetting issue [13], especially when the old model is fine-tuned only with a large amount of new data. CIL assumes that we have enough training data for each new class. In real-world applications, this assumption is not practical since it is expensive to collect a large number of examples for each new class. In this paper, we consider the more realistic setting, i.e., few-shot class incremental learning (FSCIL). FSCIL aims to design learning systems that can incrementally learn new classes with limited data. This problem is more challenging than CIL since a system can easily overfit very few new examples and severely forget the old knowledge.

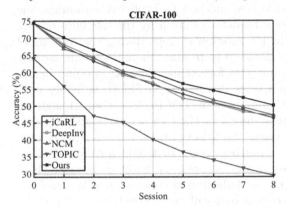

Fig. 1. The comparison between TOPIC [27] and three replay-based methods, i.e. iCaRL [22], NCM [15] and DeepInversion [30]. Our approach is also included for reference.

A naive way to address the FSCIL problem is to directly apply the commonly used approaches in the CIL, such as data replay [22]. Current literature demonstrates several ways for addressing the FSCIL problem, but none of them attempts to apply the replay-based method. One possible reason is that the pioneer [27] emphasizes the defectiveness of adopting data replay in addressing FSCIL. The authors denote that vanilla data replay can cause a significant problem of imbalance [15] and thus is not preferred in FSCIL as new classes are learned with very limited data. Extensive experiments also shows that several replay-based CIL approaches performs extremely bad in FSCIL. The strong conclusion might prevent the researchers from exploring the line of approaches further. Intuitively, data replay is conceptually suitable for addressing the kind of incremental learning problem. To confirm our intuition, we re-implement several replay-based CIL methods under the setting of FSCIL and carefully tune their performance to the best. Somewhat surprisingly, we find through experimental results that the affirmation of the TOPIC [27] is **not true.** Fig. 1 presents the comparison between TOPIC and replay-based approaches, from which we can observe that all the replay-based approaches outperform TOPIC [27] by a significant margin. This evidence attracts our interest in exploring a specific design for FSCIL using data replay. However, another concern might arise as the replay of previous real data is not permitted in many computer vision applications since it can violate legality concerns.

Recently, DeepInversion [30] has been proposed in addressing CIL without violating the legality issues. It learns to optimize random noises to photo-realistic images by inverting a reference network without accessing the real data. However, this approach leverages a constraint that generated images should strictly belong to a particular class with high confidence. In FSCIL, since the incremental classes only provide limited data examples, the network's predictions of these few-shot learned classes are usually uncertain. Therefore, it can be expected that only a small collection of images that represent part of the class identities can be generated for replay using [30]. As a result, DeepInversion is not suitable for FSCIL.

In this paper, we propose a replay-based method in FSCIL under the data-free setting. In observing the fact that distilling knowledge using uncertain data is more effective since they are usually close to the model's decision boundaries [20], we introduce an entropy-regularized method to explicitly encourage the replayed data to be close to decision boundaries given by the reference model. This is achieved by maximizing the information entropy during the training of the generator for data replay. This allows us to produce more uncertain data for effective knowledge distillation to mitigate forgetting. However, we find in our experiments that using vanilla knowledge distillation in FSCIL is highly non-trivial, which is consistent with the analysis in TOPIC [27]. Even though we can carefully tune the current replay-based method to achieve satisfying performance (as is shown in Fig. 1), tuning the hyper-parameters is a cumbersome task in general. For example, the hyper-parameter to weight for cross-entropy loss and knowledge distillation loss should be precisely selected. Because there is a dilemma to balance between the contribution of cross-entropy loss and KL divergence loss when using replayed data to distill knowledge from an old model to a new one. Specifically, the learning rate required to minimize cross-entropy loss is usually large, while a large learning rate can potentially cause instability when minimizing KL divergence. To address this issue, we propose re-labelling the generated data samples by one-hot-like labels using the old model and adding the generated data pairs together with novel real data to the current dataset. Then, we can solely adopt the cross-entropy loss to alleviate forgetting and simultaneously learn new classes.

In summary, we have the following contributions:

- Through experiments, we point out a misleading conclusion in the current literature that data replay is not preferred for FSCIL. Our re-implementation of several replay-based approaches demonstrates that data replay is actually effective.
- We propose to introduce data-free replay in handling FSCIL problem. Thanks to the nature of data-free replay, we can replay observed data without violating legality concerns.

- We improve the current data-free replay method by introducing an entropy term to penalize the generator's training and introduce re-label generated data to avoid the problem of balancing between different loss functions in the typical knowledge distillation. Our method demonstrates that it is possible and even preferred to adopt a replay-based method in FSCIL.
- Extensive experiments show that we achieve state-of-the-art performance for the FSCIL setting.

2 Related Works

2.1 Class-Incremental Learning

Recently, extensive attention has been attracted to enabling artificial intelligent systems to learn incrementally. In this paper, we focus on methods that address the class-incremental learning problem. iCaRL [22] incrementally learn nearest-neighbor classifier to predict novel classes and store real data of old classes against forgetting via knowledge distillation. However, this approach violates data privacy. EEIL [3] design an end-to-end learning system for incremental learning, where a cross-entropy loss and knowledge distillation loss are respectively adopted to learn novel classes to preserve old knowledge. NCM [15] introduces cosine normalization to balance between the classifier for previous and novel data. Besides, inspired by the remarkable progress in self-supervised visual representation learning [1,2,6,7,12,19] propose to enable continual learning without labeled data. In this paper, we aim to address a more realistic and challenging problem, i.e., few-shot class incremental learning (FSCIL). Unlike the typical class-incremental learning with numerous data for new classes' training, there are limited samples to be provided for training new classes under FSCIL.

2.2 Few-Shot Class-Incremental Learning

The problem of few-shot class-incremental learning (FSCIL) is firstly introduced in TOPIC [27]. It proposes a single neural gas (NG) network to stabilize feature typologies for observed classes and implement to grow NG to adapt to new training data. Recently, many works have been proposed aiming to address this problem. [32] propose a self-promoted prototype refinement mechanism to explicitly consider the dependencies among classes, which results in an extensible feature representation. To further leverage the benefits from re-projected features, a dynamic relation projection module is designed to update prototypes using relational metrics. [8] introduce a mixture of subspace-based method with synthetic feature generation, where the catastrophic forgetting problem is handled using a mixture of subspace and synthetic feature generation can help alleviate the over-fitting problem of novel classes. [31] introduce a pseudo incremental learning paradigm incorporating meta-learning approach to enable the graph network to update the classifier according to the global context of all classes. [9]

proposes a bi-level optimization technique to learn how to incrementally learn in the setting of FSCIL. Despite the success of these approaches, we notice that the replay-based method is under-studied.

2.3 Data-Free Knowledge Distillation

Data-free replay has been proven effective in dealing with the incremental learning problem. There are two lines of works that synthesize data of old classes. The first line of research [10,24,25] requires a generator to be trained on the original image samples. However, this setting is not preferred as the generator must be stored and transmitted to the next training session. Our method is proposed following the second line of generative replay that only uses a trained network as a reference to synthesize pseudo images. DeepInversion [30] propose to 'invert' an already-trained network to synthesize images of particular classes starting from random noises. [4,20] alternatively uses a GAN architecture to synthesize images, where they fix a trained network as a discriminator and optimize a generator to derive images that can be adopted to distill knowledge from the fixed network to a new network. Recently, [26,29,30] have integrated the idea of generative reply into addressing class-incremental learning problem using Deep-Inversion. However, due to the more challenging setting of FSCIL, these approaches cannot be simply migrated to handle the few-shot scenario.

3 Preliminaries

In this section, we formally describe the problem setting of few-shot class-incremental learning (FSCIL). We also introduce data-free replay, which is the basis of our approach.

3.1 Problem Setting

FSCIL aims to enable a learning system to continually learn novel classes from very few data examples. The problem is defined as follows. Let $\{\mathcal{D}_{train}^0, \mathcal{D}_{train}^1, ..., \mathcal{D}_{train}^N\}$ and $\{\mathcal{D}_{test}^0, \mathcal{D}_{test}^1, ..., \mathcal{D}_{test}^N\}$ respectively denote the collection of training datasets and testing datasets, where N is the total number of learning sessions. The class labels of each session are disjoint. Following the setting in [27], $\mathcal{D}_{train}^0$ is the base training dataset. The base training set contains a large number of classes where each class has enough training samples. For each subsequent session i ($i = 1, 2, ..., N$), the corresponding training set $\mathcal{D}_{train}^i$ only contains a small number of classes where each class only has very few training examples. At the ith session, only $\mathcal{D}_{train}^i$ can be accessed for training. After the i-th session, the model is evaluated on its performance in recognizing all object classes that have appeared so far. In other words, the test dataset $\mathcal{D}_{test}^i$ contains examples of all object classes that have appeared in $\{\mathcal{D}_{train}^0, \mathcal{D}_{train}^1, ..., \mathcal{D}_{train}^i\}$.

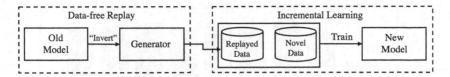

Fig. 2. Overview of our system. We first train a generator to synthesize old samples given an old model. Then, the replayed data together with novel data are used to train a new model.

3.2 Data-Free Replay

Here, we briefly show the procedures of training a generator for synthesizing critical samples of observed classes.

Given a trained model $\mathcal{T}(\cdot; \theta)$, our goal is to train a generator $\mathcal{G}(\cdot; \theta_G)$ that can synthesize critical samples for replay purpose. We follow [20] to train the generator by including an auxiliary model $\mathcal{A}(\cdot; \theta_A)$ as a helper to assist the convergence of the generator. Specifically, there are two phases in training the generator, i.e., the knowledge transferring phase and the generator evolving phase. In the knowledge transferring phase, the generator takes a noise vector $z \sim \mathcal{N}(0, I)$ and outputs a generated image x. Then, each sample x is fed into the original model $\mathcal{T}(\cdot; \theta)$ and the auxiliary model $\mathcal{A}(\cdot; \theta_A)$, where the input sample is mapped to logit o and o_A (i.e., inputs of softmax function), respectively. We optimize on the auxiliary model to let its outputs match the original model using the following loss:

$$\mathcal{L}_A = ||\mathcal{T}(\mathcal{G}(z)) - \mathcal{A}(\mathcal{G}(z))||_2^2 \tag{1}$$

Here, the primary purpose of this update is to enable the auxiliary model to be close to the original model. Then we conduct the generator evolving phase. In this phase, the goal is to optimize the generator so that it can produce more critical samples for knowledge transfer. To achieve this, we optimize the generator using the following loss:

$$\mathcal{L}_G = -||\mathcal{T}(\mathcal{G}(z)) - \mathcal{A}(\mathcal{G}(z))||_2^2 \tag{2}$$

By maximizing the distance between the outputs of the old model and the auxiliary model, we push the generator to produce samples that are hard to be learned by the auxiliary model. We alternate between the knowledge transferring phase and the generator evolving phase. The generator can finally produce more critical examples for transferring knowledge. Note that we adopt mean square error (MSE) as objective in both phases other than KL divergence adopted in [20], because logit matching has better generalization capacity [16].

In [20], the authors also indicate that the uncertain samples (i.e. those with less confident predictions) are usually close to the boundary decisions of the original model. This property has important implication in FSCIL as models learned with few-shot examples often assign low confidence to an input image. By observing that, we propose using information entropy to quantify the confidence and impose an entropy regularization to explicitly encourage the generator to produce more uncertain data.

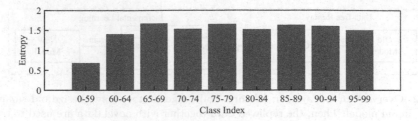

Fig. 3. The average entropy of network outputs in different classes. Classes 0–59 are the base classes, where all data samples are available for training. Classes 60–99 are the incrementally learned classes, where each class has 5 training images. The few-shot learned classes (60–99) have higher entropy than the regularly trained classes (0–59). The experiment is conducted on CIFAR-100.

4   Methodology

In this section, we present our data-free replay approach in addressing the FSCIL problem. Figure 2 shows an overview of our approach at a particular session i. Given the old model from the previous session, we first "invert" the old model to obtain a generator. The generator is used to synthesize examples of classes that have appeared in the previous sessions $\{0, 1, ..., i - 1\}$. These synthetic examples will be used for replay in order to alleviate the catastrophic forgetting issue. The training at the i-th session is performed using both those synthetic examples and the training examples for new classes in this session. However, we have found that a naive application of data-free replay does not work well since the synthesized examples are often far away from any decision boundaries. As a result, they do not have much influence on the learned model. Instead, we introduce entropy-regularized data-free replay to explicitly encourage the generator to synthesize examples that are close to decision boundaries. Then, we show our incremental learning algorithm that uses the replayed data samples.

4.1   Entropy-Regularized Data-Free Replay

Information entropy is a well-defined measurement for uncertainty. High entropy denotes low confidence and vise versa. In a few-shot incrementally trained model, the high entropy response of input usually can be identified as the case that the input is on its decision boundary [20] or is learned in a few-shot incremental session (i.e. not in base classes). To demonstrate this phenomenon, we show the output entropy of a continually learned model [31] in Fig. 3. We can observe that the classes trained using a large amount of data (0–59) maintain a low entropy, while all few-shot learned classes (60–99) have a high entropy on test images. This indicates that the network cannot assign confident predictions to images of few-shot learned classes. Motivated by this observation, we propose an entropy regularization to guide the generator to synthesize uncertain images. Specifically, we optimize the generator to maximize the entropy of predictions

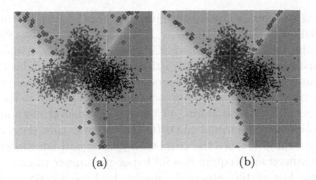

(a)   (b)

Fig. 4. Toy example to illustrate the generated data (yellow crosses). (a) shows the data generated using a normal generator. (b) shows the case when the generator is trained with entropy constraint. Red, green, and blue points are the real data. The background shows the decision boundaries of the model trained on real data. (Color figure online)

from the original model. we measure the Shannon entropy of each prediction using:

$$H(\hat{y}) = -\sum_c p(o^c) \log p(o^c) \tag{3}$$

where c denote the class index and $p(o^c)$ represents the probability. Since our objective is to maximize the entropy of the teacher's prediction to the generated image, during the generator evolving phase, Eq. 2 becomes:

$$\mathcal{L}_G^* = -||\mathcal{T}(\mathcal{G}(z)) - \mathcal{A}(\mathcal{G}(z))||_1 - H(\mathcal{T}(\mathcal{G}(z))) \tag{4}$$

We use the toy experiment proposed by [20] to illustrate the effects of our entropy regularization in Fig. 5. Thanks to the proposed entropy regularization, we can observe that the generated samples (yellow crosses) are more likely to lie on the high-entropy regions (decision boundaries) (Fig. 4).

4.2   Learning Incrementally with Uncertain Data

Given an old model learned on previous session $i - 1$ with parameters θ_{i-1}, our goal is to add linear classifier nodes parameterized by $\theta_i^{l^*}$ for new session and update the evolved model $\mathcal{T}_i(\cdot; \theta_i)$ using both generated data and novel data. Note that a new model on current session i is initialized by the following parameters:

$$\theta_i = \{\theta_{i-1}^b, \theta_{i-1}^l, \theta_i^{l^*}\} \tag{5}$$

where θ_{i-1}^b and θ_{i-1}^l are respectively the parameters of old backbone and old linear classifier, i.e., $\theta_{i-1} = \{\theta_{i-1}^b, \theta_{i-1}^l\}$. $\theta_i^{l^*}$ is randomly initialized.

Intuitively, with the old data samples replayed by our generator, we can go against forgetting in incremental learning by distilling the knowledge from the old model to a new one. A simple way to achieve this is that we can let a new model imitate the output of the old one given generated data following the vanilla knowledge distillation pipeline. However, it is non-trivial to adopt the knowledge distillation method in addressing the FSCIL problem directly. Although we show in Fig. 1 that using vanilla knowledge distillation with replayed data can achieves good performance, we also find in the process of re-implementation that the performance of current replay-based approaches is very sensitive to the selection of hyper-parameters. A careless tuning of these replay-based methods can easily result in the opposite conclusion (TOPIC [27] denotes that data replay is not preferred.). For example, since the cross-entropy loss and knowledge distillation loss are less balanced and require careful hyper-parameter tuning, it makes the training process less stable, especially under the few-shot scenario. To alleviate the burden, we introduce to re-label the generated data with one-hot-like labels. Then, we can use the generated data together with the novel data to train an evolved network by minimizing cross-entropy solely. Specifically, unlike the vanilla knowledge distillation, we alternatively assign hard labels to the generated images and eliminate the KL divergence loss. Given a synthetic image x^* and its pseudo label $\mathcal{T}_{i-1}(x^*)$ produced by the old model, we assign a one-hot label $y^* \in \{0, 1, 2, ..., C - 1\}$ to x^* using the following equation, where C is the total number of classes.

$$y^* \leftarrow argmax(\mathcal{T}_{i-1}(x^*)) \tag{6}$$

The generated image pairs $\{X^*, Y^*\}$ as the representative of old classes can be added to the dataset of the current session. We thus form a new training set on the current session by:

$$\mathcal{D}^i_{train^*} = \mathcal{D}^i_{train} \cup \{X^*, Y^*\} \tag{7}$$

Then, we can sample data pair $\{x, y\}$ from $\mathcal{D}^i_{train^*}$ to train current model $\mathcal{T}_i(\cdot; \theta_i)$ using cross-entropy $\mathcal{L}_{CE}(s, y)$, where s denotes the final probability vector given by cosine classifier [15]. Note that re-labeling uncertain data with one-hot-like labels does not change the fact that the uncertain data is hard to be classified and important for transferring knowledge from an old model to a new one. It is shown in [5,11] that using uncertain data (*hard data*) can improve training efficiency.

It is also worth mentioning that most of the current methods [8,32] conduct incremental learning on a fixed backbone θ^b_0 that is trained on the initial session. The trivial solution is sometimes beneficial because updating the backbone parameters in FSCIL can let the network easily over-fit on a few examples and forget the old mapping. However, keeping the backbone fixed can usually lead to defective model generalization on novel classes, as the backbone cannot provide discriminative features to novel classes. Thanks to our data replay, with the availability of both replayed data and novel data, we can fine-tune all the old parameters $\{\theta^b_{i-1}, \theta^l_{i-1}\}$ and update new task-specific parameters $\{\theta^{l^*}_i\}$ using:

$$\{\theta_{i-1}^b, \theta_{i-1}^l\} = \{\theta_{i-1}^b, \theta_{i-1}^l\} - \lambda_1 \frac{\partial \mathcal{L}_{CE}(s, y)}{\partial \{\theta_{i-1}^b, \theta_{i-1}^l\}}$$

$$\theta_i^{l^*} = \theta_i^{l^*} - \lambda_2 \frac{\partial \mathcal{L}_{CE}(s, y)}{\partial \theta_i^{l^*}} \tag{8}$$

where λ_1 and λ_2 denotes the learning rates for fine-tuning old parameters and updating new parameters. After training, the new model of current session is parameterized by $\theta_i = \{\theta_i^b, \theta_i^l\}$, where $\theta_i^b = \theta_{i-1}^b$ and $\theta_i^l = \{\theta_{i-1}^l \theta_i^{l^*}\}$. Due to the page limit, the overall algorithm is shown in the Appendix.

5   Experiments

In this section, we show the performance and several properties of our method through extensive experiments.

5.1   Datasets

We follow TOPIC [27] to conduct experiments on three widely used datasets including CIFAR-100 [17], miniImageNet [23] and CUB-200 [28].

CIFAR-100 consists of 60,000 32×32 color images in 100 classes, where the base training set contains 60 classes and incremental datasets are the collection of images from the remaining 40 classes. Each incremental dataset includes a total of 5 classes where each class has 5 training images.

MiniImageNet contains 100 classes that are sampled from the ILSVRC-12 dataset [23]. All images are 84×84 color images. The first 60 classes form the base dataset, and the remaining 40 classes are divided into 8 incremental sessions. Each incremental session is a 5-way 5-shot task.

CUB-200 is a classification dataset containing 200 bird species. There are a total of 11,788 images for 200 classes, where the first 100 classes form our base dataset and the remaining 100 classes form 10 incremental sessions. In each incremental session, each class has 10 images with a resolution of 224×224.

5.2   Implementation Details

Backbone Network. We implement our classification network by selecting from the off-the-shelf structures following TOPIC [27]. Specifically, we adopt ResNet20 [14] as the backbone for the experiments on CIFAR-100 and use ResNet18 [14] for the experiments on miniImageNet and CUB-200. We use the same network structure for the main network $\mathcal{T}$ and the auxiliary network $\mathcal{A}$. The generator of DCGAN [21] is adopted for replaying observed data in all the experiments.

Table 1. Comparison with the state-of-the-art methods on CIFAR-100, miniImageNet and CUB-200 datasets. Top rows are the CIL methods, and bottom rows are the FSCIL methods. * indicates our implementation of the methods under the FSCIL setting. + indicates the results reported in TOPIC [27]. Other results are copied from the corresponding papers.

CIFAR-100

Methods	Sessions									Average Acc	Final Impro.
	0	1	2	3	4	5	6	7	8		
iCaRL+ [22]	64.10	53.28	41.69	34.13	27.93	25.06	20.41	15.48	13.73	32.87	+36.41
iCaRL* [22]	74.4	67.67	63.26	59.68	56.29	53.48	50.93	48.76	46.37	57.87	+2.9
NCM+ [15]	64.10	53.05	43.96	36.97	31.61	26.73	21.23	16.78	13.54	34.22	+36.60
NCM* [15]	74.4	66.9	64.13	60.25	58.37	54.87	51.74	49.53	47.21	58.60	+2.17
DeepInv* [30]	74.4	68.22	64.37	59.09	56.87	52.26	50.77	48.21	47.08	57.92	+2.85
TOPIC+ [27]	64.10	55.88	47.07	45.16	40.11	36.38	33.96	31.55	29.37	42.62	+20.77
Zhu et al.[32]	64.10	65.86	61.36	57.34	53.69	50.75	48.58	45.66	43.25	54.51	+6.89
Cheraghian et al.[8]	62.00	57.00	56.7	52.00	50.60	48.8	45.00	44.00	41.64	50.86	+8.5
CEC [31]	73.07	68.88	65.26	61.19	58.09	55.57	53.22	51.34	49.14	59.53	+1.00
Ours	**74.4**	**70.2**	**66.54**	**62.51**	**59.71**	**56.58**	**54.52**	**52.39**	**50.14**	**60.77**	–

miniImageNet

Methods	Sessions									Average Acc	Final Impro.
	0	1	2	3	4	5	6	7	8		
iCaRL+ [22]	61.31	46.32	42.49	37.63	30.49	24.00	20.89	18.80	17.21	33.24	+31.0
iCaRL* [22]	71.84	63.82	59.43	56.88	53.14	50.06	48.37	45.89	44.13	54.84	+3.18
NCM+ [15]	61.31	47.80	39.31	31.91	25.68	21.35	18.67	17.24	14.17	30.83	+34.04
NCM* [15]	71.84	66.52	62.18	57.93	54.02	50.89	47.26	45.83	42.36	55.43	+2.59
DeepInv* [30]	71.84	64.87	61.43	58.46	56.62	52.21	49.42	47.26	45.06	56.35	+1.67
TOPIC+ [27]	61.31	50.09	45.17	41.16	37.48	35.52	32.19	29.46	24.42	39.64	+23.79
Zhu et al.[32]	61.45	63.80	59.53	55.53	52.50	49.60	46.69	43.79	41.92	52.75	+6.29
Cheraghian et al.[8]	61.40	59.80	54.20	51.69	49.45	48.00	45.20	43.80	42.1	50.63	+6.11
CEC [31]	72.00	66.83	62.97	59.43	56.70	53.73	51.19	49.24	47.63	57.75	+0.58
Ours	**71.84**	**67.12**	**63.21**	**59.77**	**57.01**	**53.95**	**51.55**	**49.52**	**48.21**	**58.02**	–

CUB-200

Methods	Sessions											Average Acc	Final Impro.
	0	1	2	3	4	5	6	7	8	9	10		
iCaRL+ [22]	68.68	52.65	48.61	44.16	36.62	29.52	27.83	26.26	24.01	23.89	21.16	36.67	+31.23
iCaRL* [22]	75.9	63.32	60.08	57.89	53.89	51.76	48.88	47.76	44.92	43.18	41.37	53.54	+7.98
NCM+ [15]	68.68	57.12	44.21	28.78	26.71	25.66	24.62	21.52	20.12	20.06	19.87	32.49	+32.52
NCM* [15]	75.9	65.89	57.73	52.08	48.36	43.38	39.59	36.02	33.68	32.01	30.87	46.86	+14.66
DeepInv* [30]	75.90	70.21	65.36	60.14	58.79	55.88	53.21	51.27	49.38	47.11	45.67	57.54	+3.98
TOPIC+ [27]	68.68	62.49	54.81	49.99	45.25	41.40	38.35	35.36	32.22	28.31	26.28	43.92	+17.58
Zhu et al.[32]	68.68	61.85	57.43	52.68	50.19	46.88	44.65	43.07	40.17	39.63	37.33	49.32	+15.06
Cheraghian et al.[8]	68.78	59.37	59.32	54.96	52.58	49.81	48.09	46.32	44.33	43.43	43.23	51.84	+9.16
CEC [31]	75.85	71.94	68.50	63.50	62.43	58.27	57.73	55.81	54.83	53.52	52.28	61.33	+0.11
Ours	**75.90**	**72.14**	**68.64**	**63.76**	**62.58**	**59.11**	**57.82**	**55.89**	**54.92**	**53.58**	**52.39**	**61.52**	–

Training Details. For all the experiments, we follow [27] to conduct training on base classes for 100 epochs using SGD with momentum and a batch size of 128. The learning rate is initialized to 0.1 with decay by a factor of 0.1 at epoch 60 and 70. We train the generator for 300 epochs at the beginning of each incremental session using Adam optimizer. The initial learning rate for updating the auxiliary network and the generator is set to 0.001 and 0.1, respectively. Learning rate decay is used on epochs 100, 150, and 200 by a factor of 0.1 for the auxiliary network and the generator. We then conduct incremental learning

Table 2. Ablation studies on CIFAR-100. We research the effects of adopting *entropy regularization* (ER), *re-labeling* (RL) and *backbone fine-tuning* (BF).

ER	RL	BF	Sessions									Average
			0	1	2	3	4	5	6	7	8	Acc
	✓	✓	74.4	70.02	66.24	62.27	59.38	56.01	53.76	51.78	49.50	60.39
✓		✓	74.4	69.32	65.78	61.65	58.32	55.27	53.19	50.88	48.92	59.74
✓	✓		74.4	69.45	65.92	61.59	58.66	55.53	53.24	51.14	49.13	59.90
✓	✓	✓	**74.4**	**70.2**	**66.54**	**62.51**	**59.71**	**56.58**	**54.52**	**52.39**	**50.14**	**60.77**

on a new model initialized by the old one using both the generated data and novel data. The quantity of generated data is the same as the number of training samples for all experiments. The learning rate λ_1 of backbone and old classifier is set to 0.0001, $\lambda_2 = 0.1$ for new nodes. Each incremental learning stage lasts for 40 epochs, with the learning rate decayed at 10-th and 30-th epochs. Data augmentations, such as random crop, random scale, and random flip, are adopted at training time.

5.3 Re-implementation of Replay-based Methods

To confirm our intuition that data replay can be used in FSCIL, we re-implement two replay-based approaches (i.e., iCaRL [22] and NCM [15]) under our setting. Table 1 presents the comparison between our obtained results (marked with *) and that reported in TOPIC [27] (marked with +). The comparison shows that the performance of replay-based CIL methods is actually competitive under the FSCIL setting. The two methods outperform several state-of-the-arts by a significant margin. For example, the NCM [15] outperform TOPIC [27], zhu et al. [32], and Cheraghian et al. [8] by 17.71%, 3.83% and 5.44% on CIFAR-100. This fact indicates that data replay is indeed preferred and can potentially be adopted to address the FSCIL problem.

5.4 Main Results and Comparison

We conduct comparison with several methods, including three replay-based methods (i.e., iCaRL [22], NCM [15] and DeepInversion (DeepInv) [30]) and four FSCIL methods (i.e., TOPIC [27], Zhu et.al [32], Cheraghian et.al [8] and CEC [31]). Table 1 summarizes the top-1 accuracy and average accuracy on all three benchmarks. Our main observations are as follows.

- Our method outperforms all the state-of-the-art on all three benchmarks across all sessions. The comparisons with the most recent method [8] illustrate the superiority of our proposed one. Specifically, our method achieves a final accuracy improvement over Cheraghian et al. [8] by 8.5%, 6.11% and 9.16% on CIFAR-100, miniImageNet and CUB-200, respectively. We outperform the existing state-of-the-art method (CEC [31]) by 1.00%, 0.58%, and

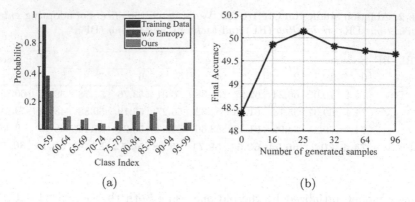

(a)   (b)

Fig. 5. (a) shows the label distribution of training data and generated data. (b) shows the average accuracy of the proposed method given different number of replayed data per batch.

0.11%. The superior performance of our approach further proves the effectiveness of adopting data replay in handling FSCIL problem.

- Despite replay-based methods performing well, we still outperform them by a large margin. Since all the replayed-based methods are proposed to handle class-incremental learning and not specifically designed to address FSCIL, the performance of them is somewhat limited. In contrast, our method can successfully incorporate data replay in FSCIL.

5.5   Analysis

Importance of Different Components. We firstly conduct ablation studies to reveal the effectiveness of different components in our proposed method. To be specific, we analyze the effects of *entropy regularization* (ER) in Sect. 4.1, re-labeling (RL) in Sect. 4.2 and backbone fine-tuning (BF) in Sect. 4.2. The results are illustrated in Table 2. It can be observed that the method with all the proposed components outperforms the others. By further comparing the full solution to the methods that are removed by one component, we can have several observations. 1) By removing the entropy regularization (shown in the first row in Table 2), we notice that the final accuracy decreases. This shows that it is desirable to generate uncertain data for replay. 2) By removing the re-labeling of generated data and alternately following the vanilla knowledge distillation using KL divergence as distillation loss, we can observe from the second row of Table 2 that the performance drops significantly. This indicates the original knowledge distillation method is not appropriate for solving the specific problem. 3) We can see the benefit from updating our backbone parameters. Usually, simply updating the parameters of the backbone network is harmful, as the backbone can quickly over-fit on the few samples during incremental learning. Our data-free replay naturally inherits the advantage of fine-tuning, which allows a model to learn new classes as well as avoid forgetting. Thus, we can observe the improvements of adopting backbone fine-tuning by comparing the last two rows in Table 2.

Label Distribution of Generated Data. As is denoted in Sect. 4.1, our proposed entropy regularizer can encourage the generator to synthesize much data of few-shot learned classes. However, since the incremental classes are trained using very limited data samples, it is somewhat doubtful that the generator can synthesize sufficient data for the new classes. To address this concern and further disclose the property of our approach, we show in Fig. 5(a) to illustrate the label distribution of the real data and our generated data. Besides, we also include the results produced by the generator without using our proposed entropy regularizer. It can be observed that using entropy regularizer can encourage the generator to synthesize more samples belonging to the few-shot learned classes. In contrast, the generator trained without entropy regularizer tends to synthesize more images belonging to base classes.

Analysis of Number of Generated Data. Fig. 5(b) shows the impact of adopting different numbers of generated samples in our proposed method. It illustrates that the performance of our method is maximized when the quantity of replayed data is the same as the training data (in CIFAR-100, each incremental session provides 25 training images.). Using smaller or larger quantities of the replayed data can jeopardize the overall performance mainly because of the adverse effects of the imbalance [15]. A small number of replayed data might not be sufficient against forgetting, while too much replayed old data can potentially hinder the network from adapting to new classes. Note that we do not fix the input noise vectors across batches. This allows the generator to synthesize more diverse data samples of the observed classes.

Analysis of Data-Free Replay. In addition to the adopted method [20], DeepInversion [30] provides an alternative solution to data-free replay. Here, we study the effect of replacing our adopted replay method with DeepInversion.

Table 3 summarizes the results. First, by comparing the first row with the second row, we can observe that using DeepInversion with our re-labeling and backbone fine-tuning can significantly boost its performance. Second, the comparison of the last two rows illustrates that our data replay approach is more suitable for FSCIL. Specifically, our method outperforms the case using DeepInversion by 1.66% in terms of final accuracy. The potential issue of DeepInversion is that it encourages the generated data to have confident predictions by the old model. Due to the fact that certain predictions are relatively rare under the few-shot setting, the generated data might be

Table 3. The impact of adopting DeepInversion (DI) as data-free replay method.

Method	Session 0	Session 8	Average Acc	Final Impro
DeepInv	74.4	47.08	57.92	+2.85
DeepInv+Ours	74.4	48.48	59.11	+1.66
Ours	74.4	50.14	60.77	–

ineffective. Another issue we have observed for DeepInversion is that the data generation process is time-consuming.This is also confirmed in [30]. In contrast, our generator can replay data very efficiently once it is trained to be ready.

6   Conclusion

In this paper, we first disclose that data replay can be adopted in addressing FSCIL problem. Then we propose a novel approach to denote the effectiveness of using data replay in FSCIL. To address the privacy concern of vanilla data replay, we introduce the data-free replay scheme for synthesizing old samples. By observing that the prediction of the classification model becomes uncertain under the few-shot incremental setting, we propose an entropy regularization on the training of the generator. We then design a new method to learn from the uncertain data via re-labeling against forgetting issues. Extensive comparison with the state-of-the-arts illustrates that our approach achieves the best performance for avoiding forgetting and quickly adapting to new classes.

Limitation. Difficulties might occur when training the generator on large-scaled datasets, potentially jeopardizing replayed data quality.

References

1. Caron, M., Misra, I., Mairal, J., Goyal, P., Bojanowski, P., Joulin, A.: Unsupervised learning of visual features by contrasting cluster assignments. Adv. Neural. Inf. Process. Syst. **33**, 9912–9924 (2020)
2. Caron, M., et al.: Emerging properties in self-supervised vision transformers. In: Proceedings of the IEEE/CVF International Conference on Computer Vision, pp. 9650–9660 (2021)
3. Castro, F.M., Marín-Jiménez, M.J., Guil, N., Schmid, C., Alahari, K.: End-to-end incremental learning. In: European Confererence on Computer Vison (2018)
4. Chen, H., et al.: Data-free learning of student networks. In: IEEE International Conference on Computer Vision (2019)
5. Chen, K., Chen, Y., Han, C., Sang, N., Gao, C.: Hard sample mining makes person re-identification more efficient and accurate. Neurocomputing **382**, 259–267 (2020)
6. Chen, T., Kornblith, S., Norouzi, M., Hinton, G.: A simple framework for contrastive learning of visual representations. In: International Conference on Machine Learning, pp. 1597–1607. PMLR (2020)
7. Chen, X., Fan, H., Girshick, R., He, K.: Improved baselines with momentum contrastive learning. arXiv preprint arXiv:2003.04297 (2020)
8. Cheraghian, A., et al.: Synthesized feature based few-shot class-incremental learning on a mixture of subspaces. In: IEEE International Conference on Computer Vision (2021)
9. Chi, Z., Gu, L., Liu, H., Wang, Y., Yu, Y., Tang, J.: MetaFSCIL: a meta-learning approach for few-shot class incremental learning. In: IEEE/CVF Conference on Computer Vision and Pattern Recognition, pp. 14166–14175 (2022)
10. Cong, Y., Zhao, M., Li, J., Wang, S., Carin, L.: Gan memory with no forgetting. In: Advances in Neural Information Processing Systems (2020)

11. Felzenszwalb, P.F., Girshick, R.B., McAllester, D., Ramanan, D.: Object detection with discriminatively trained part-based models. IEEE Trans. Pattern Anal. Mach. Intell. **32**(9), 1627–1645 (2009)
12. Fini, E., da Costa, V.G.T., Alameda-Pineda, X., Ricci, E., Alahari, K., Mairal, J.: Self-supervised models are continual learners. In: Proceedings of the IEEE/CVF Conference on Computer Vision and Pattern Recognition, pp. 9621–9630 (2022)
13. French, R.M.: Catastrophic forgetting in connectionist networks. Trends Cogn. Sci. **3**(4), 128–135 (1999)
14. He, K., Zhang, X., Ren, S., Sun, J.: Deep residual learning for image recognition. In: IEEE/CVF Conference on Computer Vision and Pattern Recognition (2016)
15. Hou, S., Pan, X., Loy, C.C., Wang, Z., Lin, D.: Learning a unified classifier incrementally via rebalancing. In: IEEE/CVF Conference on Computer Vision and Pattern Recognition (2019)
16. Kim, T., Oh, J., Kim, N.Y., Cho, S., Yun, S.Y.: Comparing kullback-leibler divergence and mean squared error loss in knowledge distillation. In: International Joint Conference on Artificial Intelligence (2021)
17. Krizhevsky, A., Hinton, G., et al.: Learning multiple layers of features from tiny images (2009)
18. LeCun, Y., Bengio, Y., Hinton, G.: Deep learning. Nature **521**(7553), 436–444 (2015)
19. Liang, H., et al.: Self-supervised spatiotemporal representation learning by exploiting video continuity. In: Proceedings of the AAAI Conference on Artificial Intelligence, vol. 36, pp. 1564–1573 (2022)
20. Micaelli, P., Storkey, A.J.: Zero-shot knowledge transfer via adversarial belief matching. In: Advances in Neural Information Processing Systems (2019)
21. Radford, A., Metz, L., Chintala, S.: Unsupervised representation learning with deep convolutional generative adversarial networks. In: International Conference on Learning Representations (2016)
22. Rebuffi, S.A., Kolesnikov, A., Sperl, G., Lampert, C.H.: iCaRL: incremental classifier and representation learning. In: IEEE/CVF Conference on Computer Vision and Pattern Recognition (2017)
23. Russakovsky, O.: ImageNet large scale visual recognition challenge. Int. J. Comput. Vis. **115**(3), 211–252 (2015)
24. Shankarampeta, A.R., Yamauchi, K.: Few-shot class incremental learning with generative feature replay. In: International Conference on Pattern Recognition Applications and Methods, pp. 259–267 (2021)
25. Shin, H., Lee, J.K., Kim, J., Kim, J.: Continual learning with deep generative replay. In: Advances in Neural Information Processing Systems (2017)
26. Smith, J., Hsu, Y.C., Balloch, J., Shen, Y., Jin, H., Kira, Z.: Always be dreaming: a new approach for data-free class-incremental learning. In: IEEE International Conference on Computer Vision (2021)
27. Tao, X., Hong, X., Chang, X., Dong, S., Wei, X., Gong, Y.: Few-shot class-incremental learning. In: IEEE/CVF Conference on Computer Vision and Pattern Recognition (2020)
28. Wah, C., Branson, S., Welinder, P., Perona, P., Belongie, S.: The caltech-UCSD birds-200-2011 dataset (2011)
29. Xin, X., Zhong, Y., Hou, Y., Wang, J., Zheng, L.: Memory-free generative replay for class-incremental learning. arXiv preprint arXiv:2109.00328 (2021)
30. Yin, H., et al.: Dreaming to distill: data-free knowledge transfer via deepinversion. In: IEEE/CVF Conference on Computer Vision and Pattern Recognition (2020)

31. Zhang, C., Song, N., Lin, G., Zheng, Y., Pan, P., Xu, Y.: Few-shot incremental learning with continually evolved classifiers. In: IEEE/CVF Conference on Computer Vision and Pattern Recognition (2021)
32. Zhu, K., Cao, Y., Zhai, W., Cheng, J., Zha, Z.J.: Self-promoted prototype refinement for few-shot class-incremental learning. In: IEEE/CVF Conference on Computer Vision and Pattern Recognition (2021)

Anti-retroactive Interference for Lifelong Learning

Runqi Wang[1], Yuxiang Bao[1], Baochang Zhang[1(✉)], Jianzhuang Liu[2], Wentao Zhu[3], and Guodong Guo[4]

[1] Beihang University, Beijing, China
{runqiwang,bczhang}@buaa.edu.cn
[2] Huawei Noah's Ark Lab, Shenzhen, China
[3] Kuaishou Technology, Beijing, China
[4] Institute of Deep Learning, Baidu Research, Beijing, China

Abstract. Humans can continuously learn new knowledge. However, machine learning models suffer from drastic dropping in performance on previous tasks after learning new tasks. Cognitive science points out that the competition of similar knowledge is an important cause of forgetting. In this paper, we design a paradigm for lifelong learning based on meta-learning and associative mechanism of the brain. It tackles the problem from two aspects: extracting knowledge and memorizing knowledge. First, we disrupt the sample's background distribution through a background attack, which strengthens the model to extract the key features of each task. Second, according to the similarity between incremental knowledge and base knowledge, we design an adaptive fusion of incremental knowledge, which helps the model allocate capacity to the knowledge of different difficulties. It is theoretically analyzed that the proposed learning paradigm can make the models of different tasks converge to the same optimum. The proposed method is validated on the MNIST, CIFAR100, CUB200 and ImageNet100 datasets. The code is available at https://github.com/bhrqw/ARI.

Keywords: Lifelong learning · Meta learning · Background attack · Associative learning

1 Introduction

A standard benchmark for success in artificial intelligence is the ability to emulate human learning. However, at the current stage, the machine does not really understand what it has learned. It may just do rote memorization, which overlooks a critical characteristic of human learning: being robust to changing tasks and sequential experience. Future learning machines should be able to adapt to

---

Supplementary Information The online version contains supplementary material available at https://doi.org/10.1007/978-3-031-20053-3_10.

S. Avidan et al. (Eds.): ECCV 2022, LNCS 13684, pp. 163–178, 2022.
https://doi.org/10.1007/978-3-031-20053-3_10

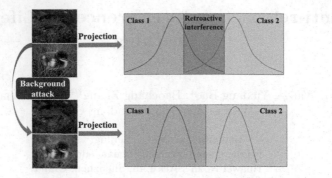

Fig. 1. In lifelong learning, the knowledge in the present stage competes with the previous memory and interferes with the previous learning, especially when the knowledge is similar. Therefore, we attack similar contents in both tasks to change the data distribution and avoid retroactive interference.

the ever-changing world. They should continuously learn new tasks without forgetting previously learned ones. Although many learning paradigms have been proposed, such as lifelong learning (LLL) [2,21], these problems have not been addressed well. Many researchers are brute-force and idealized in the construction of model training. In pedagogy and psychology, human learning and the cognitive process have been widely discussed, among which there are many theories worthy of reference. The learning process of new tasks results in catastrophic forgetting [10] of previous knowledge due to **retroactive interference** [25], which means that the content of later learning competes with the previous memory and interferes with the previous learning. This kind of competition causes confusion and forgetting of knowledge. This problem can be solved by capturing critical points of knowledge and removing redundant content to avoid the competition of knowledge, which is termed filter efficiency [27] in pedagogy. In the computer vision task of classification, different categories of images might have the same or similar backgrounds, such as a bicycle and a dog on a lawn. Machine learning models may mistake lawn features for bicycle features or dog features, which creates unnecessary memory competition in learning new knowledge.

In order to solve the problem of forgetting in the process of learning new tasks in a deep learning model, we propose a lifelong learning paradigm based on meta-learning and associative learning. We divide the model into two stages: extracting intra-class features and fusing inter-class features. In the first stage, we hope to avoid retroactive interference by reducing the competition between old and new knowledge. We need to accurately capture the critical knowledge of new tasks and focus on learning it, which can effectively avoid confusion of knowledge. In this way, incremental knowledge can complement rather than compete with existing knowledge. It is an anthropomorphic process that associates the original images with the foreground of the images, i.e., only learning the critical knowledge of the new task as a complement to the knowledge base. In this way, model information redundancy can be avoided, which is consistent with the machine learning theory in [19]. In order to realize this idea, we present a background attack method to attack the samples adversarially. Through the spatial attention mechanism, the importance map of the image can be obtained. We believe that areas of low importance level in an image do not belong to the necessary information of its class, which may cause information redundancy and competition between classes as shown in Fig. 1. Therefore, we carry out an adversarial attack on non-critical areas, (*i.e.*, the background) and blur the data distribution in these areas, thus weakening the model's learning of unimportant information.

In the second stage, we combine the existing model with the model just learned. It is different from conventional incremental learning that updates the pre-trained model directly, which is easy to cause catastrophic damage to the model's weight distribution. We organize the knowledge to learn into different tasks, just like the chapters of a textbook. Each task is learned separately, and an independent model is outputted. Specifically, when learning a new task, a small number of samples are extracted from previous tasks for review, and then the models corresponding to these tasks are fused, which is consistent with Ausubel's theory [3] that points out that the most important thing in learning is whether the knowledge learned can form a system, *i.e.*, to complete the deduction of knowledge from the individual to the whole. Following this process, we chose a meta-training based method to generate models, which will be described in Sect. 3. To this end, we propose a novel task-specific fusion method, and show that our training process can ensure that these different models are converged to a common optimal one to reduce the information loss. Our contributions are summarized as follows:

- We combine the adversarial attack with meta-learning to extract features. The adversarial attack is performed on the image background to reinforce the model's attention to critical features.
- Based on human cognition, a new lifelong learning paradigm, *Anti-Retroactive Interference for lifelong learning* (ARI), is established to ensure that the machine learning model can integrate incremental knowledge more effectively. It is analyzed that the fusion method in ARI can ensure that the task-specific models are converged to the same optimal model to reduce the information loss caused by fusion.
- The proposed method is validated on the MNIST, CIFAR100, CUB200 and ImageNet100 datasets, and state-of-the-art results are obtained on all the benchmarks.

2   Related Work

2.1   Lifelong Learning

So far, lifelong learning methods can be divided into three groups. The first one is based on regularization. LwF [16] preserves the ancient knowledge by adding a distillation loss. In addition, the distillation loss is implemented by [4, 22, 36] to reduce forgetting. [30,36] propose bias correction strategies whereby the model can perform equally well on current and older classes by re-balancing the final fully-connected layer. EWC [13] computes synaptic importance offline by calculating a Fisher information matrix. E-MAS-SDC proposed by [32] estimates the drift of previous tasks during the training of new tasks to make semantic drift compensation. RRR in [7] tries to save the correct attentions of previous images to avoid the attentions being affected by other tasks. The second group is about expanding the model with progressive learning and designing binary masks that directly map each task to the corresponding model architecture. MARK [12] keeps a set of shared weights among tasks. These shared weights are envisioned as a common knowledge base used to learn new tasks and enriched with new knowledge as the model learns new tasks. In [1], each convolutional layer is equipped with task-specific gating modules, selecting specific filters for a given task. The shortcomings of these methods are the extra model complexity and the need for a practical scheme to calculate the mask precisely. The third group is replay based and it gets popular recently. Replay based approaches are ideally suitable for lifelong learning in which tasks are added in turn. iTAML [21] introduces a meta-learning approach that seeks to maintain an equilibrium between all the encountered tasks, in the sense that it is unbiased towards class samples of majority and simultaneously minimizes forgetting.

2.2   Adversarial Training

Though the success of deep learning models has been demonstrated on various computer vision tasks, they are sensitive to adversarial attacks [9]. An imperceptible perturbation added to inputs may cause undesirable outputs. The Fast Gradient Sign Method (FGSM) is proposed in [8] to generate adversarial examples with a single gradient step. To defend the attacks, many methods have been proposed to defend against them. The most common method is adversarial training [15,18,26] with adversarial examples added to the training data. In this paper, we introduce adversarial training to the meta-learning process to obtain a robust model that can extract good features from very few available samples.

3   Proposed Method

We adopt a task-incremental learning setup where the model continuously learns new tasks, each containing a fixded number of novel classes. During the training process of task n, we have access to $\mathbb{M}_{n-1}$ and $\mathbb{D}_n$ where $\mathbb{M}_{n-1}$ is an exampler memory containing a small number of samples for old tasks, and $\mathbb{D}_n$ is the training data for task n, which contains pairs $(\mathbf{x}_i, y_i)$, with $\mathbf{x}_i$ being an image of class $y_i \in R_n$. Using $\mathbb{M}_{n-1}$ to train task n is a form of meta-learning. We define the set of classes on task n as $R_n = \{r_{n,1}, r_{n,2}, ..., r_{n,m}\}$, where $r_{n,1}$ is the first class in task n, and m is the number of classes in task n. Different tasks do not contain the same class: $R_t \cap R_s = \varnothing, t \neq s$. After learning all the tasks, we evaluate the learned model on all tasks $R = \cup_i R_i$.

Algorithm 1: Associative learning with background attack

Input: Training data $\mathbf{x}$;
Hyper-parameters: Epoch number S, $\varepsilon = \frac{8}{255}$;
Initialize model parameters $\boldsymbol{\theta}$;
Output: The network model;
Train an architecture for S epochs:
$t = 0$;
while $(t \leq S)$ **do**
> # First inference:
> Input $\mathbf{x}$;
> According to [29], calculate the spatial attention $\mathbf{A}$;
> Return $\mathbf{A}$;
> #Back propagation:
> According to Eq. 2, calculate $\mathbf{x}'$;
> # Second inference:
> Input $\mathbf{x}'$;
> #Back propagation:
> Update parameters $\boldsymbol{\theta}$;
> $t \leftarrow t + 1$.

end

3.1 Extracting Intra-Class Features

Lifelong learning requires the model to retain previous knowledge and learn new knowledge. However, if the previous and new knowledge have similar characteristics, it is easy to cause forgetting. Data are labeled for different classes according to different object features, but the background information is ignored, which may mislead the model's incremental learning. In order to eliminate similar characteristics between different classes and prevent retroactive interference, we design associative learning with background attack. This approach involves two processes. In the first process, the model learns from the original image to obtain the background region and conduct adversarial attack on it. This attack can disturb the distribution of the background and strengthen the feature extraction on the critical region of the image. In the second process, the model is trained with the attacked images. This approach associates the objects with different backgrounds, which avoids the negative effect of background on few-shot learning. Therefore, the model can effectively avoid over-fitting by associative learning.

In adversarial training, we need to add perturbation to the images, which can increase the robustness of the model. However, now we use a background mask $\mathbf{B}$ to guide the model to attack the background regions of the images. The mask $\mathbf{B}$ has three forms:

$$\mathbf{B} = 1 - \mathbf{A}, \quad \mathbf{B} = 1 - \mathbf{A} \circ \mathbf{A}, \quad \mathbf{B} = \frac{1}{\mathbf{A}}, \tag{1}$$

where $\mathbf{A} \in \mathbb{R}^{s \times s}$ denotes the spatial attention obtained by [29], $\circ$ denotes the Hadamard product, $\mathbf{B} \in \mathbb{R}^{s \times s}$ is the mask for focusing on the background, and

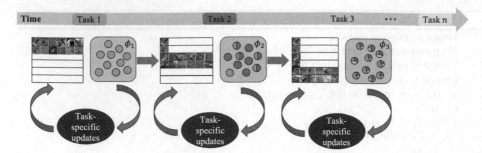

Fig. 2. We design a serial learning structure for lifelong learning. A small-scale rehearsal memory of the previous tasks is also used to fine-tune the new model to adapt to the new task.

$s \times s$ is the size of the image. In order to widen the distance between important and unimportant information in the attention and guide the background attack, we use the three forms of $\mathbf{B}$ in Eq. 1, making the unimportant regions (corresponding more to the background) prominent. Therefore, the attack guided by $\mathbf{B}$ tends to be more selective on the background.

We formulate the background attack model as:

$$\mathbf{x}' = \mathbf{x} + \mathbf{B} \circ \zeta = \mathbf{x} + \mathbf{B} \circ (\varepsilon \mathbf{sgn}(\nabla_{\mathbf{x}} G(\boldsymbol{\theta}, \mathbf{x}, y))), \tag{2}$$

where $\mathbf{x} \in \mathbb{R}^{s \times s}$ is the clean input and $\mathbf{x}'$ is the adversarial counterpart. ζ denotes the global perturbation of the clean input $\mathbf{x}$ which is designed based on [8]. y denotes the label of the input $\mathbf{x}$. ε is the perturbation bound, $\boldsymbol{\theta}$ denotes the parameters of the deep model, and G is the cross-entropy function.

The algorithm of the associative learning with adversarial background attack is listed in Algorithm 1, which associates clean input $\mathbf{x}$ with various adversarial inputs $\mathbf{x}'$. After the adversarial training with $\mathbf{x}'$, the model learns to be robust to the distribution shift [34] of background and thus can focus more on the foreground (object) features, reducing forgetting as shown in Fig. 1. Experimental verification is shown in Sect. 4.4.

3.2 Generating and Fusing Task-Specific Models

The adversarial images after the background attack are used as input to participate in training. Lifelong learning is a scenario in which tasks are entered serially. The base model should contain information about all learned tasks after learning a new task, as shown in Fig. 2, in which ϕ_n denotes the base model after learning task n. The process of learning a new task is embedded in the task-specific updating. When updating in a new task, our meta-learning approach involves three phases: (1) generating task-specific models for all the seen tasks, (2) fusing the task-specific models into the base model, and (3) meta-training the base model, as shown in Fig. 3.

Algorithm 2: Training in task n

Input: $\mathbb{D}_n$, $\mathbb{M}_{n-1}$, ϕ_{n-1};

Hyper-parameters: task number n, epoch number S, image number J_i of task i, $i \in [1, n]$;

Output: The base model ϕ_n;

\# Train an architecture for S epochs;

$\phi_b^0 = \phi_{n-1}$, $t = 1$;

while $(t \leq S)$ **do**

    for $i = 1$ **to** n **do**

        $\{\hat{y}_j^i\}_{j=1}^{J_i} \leftarrow \phi_b^{t-1}\left(\{\mathbf{x}_j^i\}_{j=1}^{J_i}\right)$;

        $loss \leftarrow$ **Eq. 7**;

    end

    $\phi_i^t \leftarrow$ **Optimizer**$(\phi_b^{t-1}, loss)$;

    $\phi_f^t \leftarrow$ **Fusion**$[\phi_1^t, ..., \phi_n^t, \phi_b^{t-1}]$;

    $\phi_b^t \leftarrow \gamma\phi_f^t + (1 - \gamma)\phi_b^{t-1}$;

    $t \leftarrow t + 1$;

end

$\phi_n \leftarrow$ **Meta train** (ϕ_b^S).

Generating Task-Specific Models. We randomly sample a mini-batch $\mathbb{B}_n = \{(\mathbf{x}_k, y_k)\}_{k=1}^{K_n}$ from the current task n training data $\mathbb{D}_n$ and the memory bank $\mathbb{M}_{n-1}$, which contains a few samples for old tasks. $\mathbf{x}_k$ and y_k are the training images and their labels, respectively, and K_n is the image number of the batch. Therefore, the mini-batch of data for task-specific updates, as shown in Fig. 3, is represented as:

$$\mathbb{B}_n \sim \mathbb{D}_n \cup \mathbb{M}_{n-1}. \tag{3}$$

We sample the training data according to the tasks to construct $\mathbb{B}_\mu^i = \{(\mathbf{x}_j^i, y_j^i)\}_{j=1}^{J_i}$ for training the task-specific models ϕ_i, $i \in [1, n]$, where J_i is the image number of task i. The loss function in the task-specific updating is the binary cross-entropy loss with a regularizer from **dif**, which is defined next in Eq. 6. The binary cross-entropy is:

$$L(\phi_i(\{\mathbf{x}_j^i\}), \{y_j^i\}) = -\frac{1}{J_i}\sum_{j=1}^{J_i}(y_j^i \cdot \log\left(\phi_i\left(\mathbf{x}_j^i\right)\right) + \left(1 - y_j^i\right) \cdot \log(1 - \log(\phi_i(\mathbf{x}_j^i)))). \tag{4}$$

This helps to obtain task-specific models ϕ_i, thus providing a better estimate for gradient updates in the current task-specific training (described next) to obtain a base model. The training process of the specific tasks, *i.e.*, phase 1 in Fig. 3, is shown in the for-loop of Algorithm 2, which generates n independent models. In Algorithm 2, the Optimizer denotes some optimizer such as SGD. The function Fusion is described next (Eq. 9). ϕ_i^t is the task-specific model i at epoch t, and ϕ_b^t is the base model at epoch t. All these models $\phi_1, ..., \phi_n, \phi_b$ have the same structure.

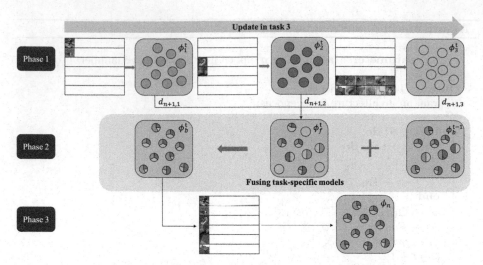

Fig. 3. Taking task 3 for example, the task-specific updating is divided into three phases. In phase 1, task-specific model training is carried out. It is noteworthy that only a small amount of previous task samples are used in the current training. In phase 2, task-specific models are fused. In phase 3, meta-training is performed on the fused model to obtain the incremental base model of task 3.

Fusing Task-Specific Models. We combine the task-specific models ϕ_i^t generated during phase 1 to the base model ϕ_n in phase 2 of Fig. 3. We denote the set of the models at epoch t as:

$$\Phi^t = \{\phi_1^t, ..., \phi_n^t, \phi_b^{t-1}\}. \tag{5}$$

Due to the task-specific models being generated by different tasks, there may be large differences between their parameter values, which causes information loss in model fusion. We adopt a new strategy to use the Manhattan distance between a task-specific model and the base model as the fusion weight. When the gap between the two models is larger, the fusion weight is larger. The weight coefficients are calculated as follows. First, we define

$$\textbf{dif} = \begin{bmatrix} 0 & d_{1,2} & \cdots & d_{1,n+1} \\ d_{2,1} & 0 & & d_{2,n+1} \\ \vdots & & \ddots & \vdots \\ d_{n+1,1} & d_{n+1,2} & \cdots & 0 \end{bmatrix}, \tag{6}$$

where $d_{1,2}$ denotes the Manhattan distance between ϕ_1^t and ϕ_2^t, and $d_{1,n+1}$ denotes the Manhattan distance between ϕ_1^t and ϕ_b^{t-1}. Considering the goal of model fusion is to minimize the differences among task-specific models and produce a fused model that performs well across tasks, we formulate the loss as two parts, the regularizer based on **dif** and the binary cross-entropy as shown in Eq. 4.

$$loss = L\left(\hat{y}_j^i, y_j^i\right) + \sum_{a=1}^{i+1}\sum_{b=1}^{i+1} |d_{a,b}|^2. \tag{7}$$

To ensure that the sum of weights equals 1, each row of **dif** is transformed by the softmax function as:

$$\mathbf{dif}^* = \begin{bmatrix} d_{1,1}^* & d_{1,2}^* & \cdots & d_{1,n+1}^* \\ d_{2,1}^* & d_{2,2}^* & & d_{2,n+1}^* \\ \vdots & & \ddots & \vdots \\ d_{n+1,1}^* & d_{n+1,2}^* & \cdots & d_{n+1,n+1}^* \end{bmatrix}. \tag{8}$$

Finally, the fused model is formulated as:

$$\phi_f^t = \sum_{i=1}^{n+1}(d_{n+1,i}^* \cdot \phi_i^t), \tag{9}$$

where $\phi_{n+1}^t = \phi_b^{t-1}$. The reason we take the elements of the last row of $\mathbf{dif}^*$ as the weights is that the base model could adopt the knowledge from the task-specific models as much as possible. Thus more weights should be given to the task-specific model with a larger difference from the base model.

The fusion model is combined with ϕ_b^{t-1} to form a new base model ϕ_b^t:

$$\phi_b^t = \gamma\phi_f^t + (1-\gamma)\phi_b^{t-1}, \tag{10}$$

where γ is a hyper-parameter that controls the speed of learning new information, *i.e.*, for higher γ the model prefers to learn new information and forget the old, and with smaller γ it learns little new knowledge.

Due to the regularization from **dif**, after a sufficient number of iterations, in the sense that t is large enough, the differences among the task-specific and base models $\{\phi_1^t, ..., \phi_n^t, \phi_b^{t-1}\}$ is decreasing gradually and all the models tend to have the same weights. In the supplementary material, we provide evidence to analyze that all the models converge to the same optimal weights. Moreover, an experiment is conducted in the ablation study to verify the convergence. When all the models, $\phi_1, ..., \phi_n, \phi_b$ are ideally optimized to the same model, they share the same knowledge, thus eliminating information loss in the task-specific model fusion.

Meta-training the Base Model. In phase 3 of Fig. 3, take a small number of samples from all learned tasks to form $\mathbb{M}_n$. $\mathbb{M}_n$ is used for meta-training of ϕ_b^S to further optimize the distribution of model parameters. After meta-training, ϕ_b^S is the model ϕ_n that learned task n.

4   Experiments and Results

We conduct experiments on several common datasets, including MNIST [33], CIFAR100 [14], CUB200 [28] and ImageNet100 which is a subset of ISLVRC 2012 [23]. We also perform ablation study to analyze different components of our approach.

4.1 Datasets

MNIST. MNIST contains 60k images of handwritten numbers in the training set and 10k samples in the test set. All the images are 28 × 28 pixels. In our experiment, MNIST is divided into 5 tasks with 2 classes per task.

CIFAR100. CIFAR100 consists of 60k pictures of 32 × 32 color images from 100 classes. Each class has 500 training and 100 testing samples. 100 classes are split into 10 tasks with 10 classes in each task.

CUB200. CUB200 contains 200 classes of birds with 11,788 images in total. The training set and the test set consist of 5994 and 5794 images, respectively. The 200 bird classes are split into 6 tasks in our experiment.

ImageNet100. ImageNet100, as a subset of ILSVRC2012, contains 100 classes and 130 thousand samples of 224 × 224 color images. Each class has about 1,300 training and 50 test samples. We split ImageNet100 into 10 tasks.

4.2 Implementation Details

Network Architecture. For MNIST, a two-layer MLP is selected as the model. For CIFAR100 and CUB200, the network is $(ResNet - 18(1/3))$ which is a reduced version of ResNet-18. For ImageNet100, the original ResNet-18 is used in the experiment. All the architectures used are added the spatial attention mechanism after the first layer.

Training Details. For MNIST, each incremental training has 20 epochs. The initial learning rate is set to 0.1 and reduced to 1/2 of the previous learning rate after 5, 10, and 15 epochs. The weight decay is set to 0, the batch size is 256, and $\gamma = 0.1$. The optimizer is SGD.

For CIFAR100, each incremental training has 70 epochs. The initial learning rate starts from 0.01 and is reduced to 1/5 of the previous learning rate after 30 and 60 epochs. The weight decay is set to 0, the batch size is 512, and $\gamma = 0.1$. The optimizer is set to RAdam [21].

For CUB200 and ImageNet100, each incremental task is trained for 100 epochs. The learning rate starts from 0.1 initially and is reduced to 1/10 of the previous learning rate after 40, 70, and 90 epochs. The weight decay is set to 0, the batch size is 512, and $\gamma = 0.1$. The optimizer is RAdam [21].

For a fair comparison, we set the rehearsal memory size as 2,000 for MNIST and CIFAR100. For CUB200 and Imagenet100, the memory size is set as 3000. The perturbation bound $\epsilon = \frac{8}{255}$ and step size of $\frac{2}{255}$ is set for all the benchmarks.

4.3 Results and Comparison

In this section, we report the results on MNIST, CIFAR100, CUB200 and ImageNet100, and compare our ARI method with the state-of-the-art methods.

Small Scale. The compared typical lifelong learning approaches include Memory Aware Synapses (MAS) [2], LwF [16], Synaptic Intelligence (SI) [33], Elastic Weight Consolidation (EWC) [13], Gradient Episodic Memory (GEM) [17], Deep Generative Replay (DGR) [24] and Incremental Task-Agnostic Meta learning (iTAML) [21]. As shown in Fig. 4, ARI outperforms all the others. Its average classification accuracy of 5 tasks is around 98.91%.

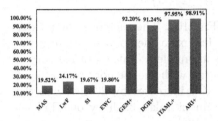 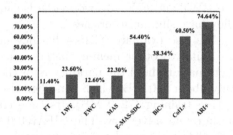

Fig. 4. Comparison results on the MNIST dataset. "+" indicates that the method is memory-based.

Fig. 5. The average classification accuracy on CUB200, with 6 tasks learned incrementally. "+" indicates that the method is memory-based.

Medium Scale. ARI attains significant advantages on CIFAR100 compared with other state-of-the-art approaches. For the 10-task lifelong learning, as shown in Table 1 ARI achieves the classification accuracy of 80.88% which surpasses all the previous methods.

Table 1. Comparison among different lifelong learning methods on CIFAR100. The accuracy of task t is the average accuracy of all $1, 2, .., t$ tasks.

Dataset	Methods	Task 1	Task 2	Task 3	Task 4	Task 5	Task 6	Task 7	Task 8	Task 9	Task 10
CIFAR100	DMC [35]	88.11%	76.30%	67.53%	62.19%	57.85%	52.87%	48.59%	43.88%	40.32%	36.28%
	LwF [16]	89.30%	70.13%	54.25%	45.78%	39.83%	36.08%	31.67%	28.86%	24.37%	23.86%
	SI [33]	88.85%	51.76%	40.35%	33.66%	32.01%	29.87%	27.71%	25.97%	24.31	23.51%
	EWC [13]	88.98%	52.37%	48.37%	38.26%	31.64%	26.14%	21.88%	19.94%	18.76%	16.03%
	MAS [2]	88.16%	42.31%	36.16%	35.89%	33.29%	25.97%	21.77%	18.84%	18.11%	15.86%
	RWalk [5]	89.57%	55.12%	40.19%	32.54%	29.13%	25.89%	23.61%	21.84%	19.32%	17.91%
	iCARL [22]	88.74%	78.13%	72.39%	67.23%	63.69%	60.18%	56.35%	54.38%	51.87%	49.46%
	Bic [30]	–	84.70%	–	71.60%	–	63.68%	–	58.12%	–	53.74%
	iTAML [21]	**89.15%**	**89.03%**	**87.32%**	**86.18%**	**84.31%**	**82.12%**	80.65%	79.06%	78.42%	77.79%
	ARI	88.60%	86.90%	85.77%	84.55%	83.10%	81.75%	**81.57%**	**80.98%**	**80.20%**	**80.88%**

We calculate the metrics BWT [17] and FWT [17] to measure forgetting and learning. As shown in Table 2, although the BWT value of GEM is the highest, its accuracy (65.4%) is much lower than ours (80.88%). As mentioned in [17],

Table 2. Comparison of forgetting metrics on CIFAR100.

	UCIR	GEM	PODNet [6]	iTAML	iTAML+RRR	ARI
BWT	−8.5%	**1.2%**	−16.3%	−11.5%	−8.5%	−7.5%
FWT	−5.56%	0.47%	−5.58%	0.14%	0.77%	**1.18%**

the BWT and FWT of two methods can indicate their performances only when they have similar accuracies.

We also evaluate ARI's efficiency on CIFAR100. The memory complexity is similar to other memory-based methods. Its extra memory addition is the dictionary to hold the parameters of the specific models. This extra memory is only about 100 MB, which is negligible compared with the memory requirement during training (7200 MB). Its time complexity increases by 20% due to the background adversary. The CIFAR100 experiment takes 3.3 h by one TITAN XP when total epochs = 70 and batch size = 512.

In Fig. 5, We compare different methods on CUB200 with 6 incremental tasks where BiC [30] and CoIL [37] are memory-based methods. ARI surpasses CoIL by 14.14%, which illustrates that ARI is less prone to catastrophic forgetting.

Large Scale. We compare ARI with the state-of-the-art algorithms on the large scale dataset ImageNet100. The comparison results are listed in Table 3, where Mem% denotes the proportion of the memory size $\mathbb{M}$ in the Imagenet100 training set. ARI outperforms Fixed representations (FixedRep) and other methods of lifelong learning. ARI increases the accuracy on ImageNet100 by 5.22% (from 74.10% to 79.32%).

Table 3. Comparison of different approaches on ImageNet100.

Datasets	Methods	Accuracy	Mem%
ImageNet100	iCaRL [22]	63.50%	2%
	UCIR [11]	69.09%	2%
	MARK [12]	69.43%	10%
	DER [31]	66.70%	2%
	RPSnet [20]	74.10%	2%
	ARI	**79.32%**	3%

The above results illustrate ARI's consistent effectiveness and superiority on small, medium, and large scale datasets over other methods.

4.4   Ablation Study

In this section, we conduct extensive experiments to verify the effects of the proposed background attack and task-specific model fusion.

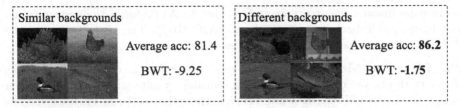

Fig. 6. Similar characteristics lead to the forgetting of lifelong learning.

Similar Characteristics Lead to Forgetting. First we provide a toy experiment to demonstrate that retroactive interference leads to forgetting, as shown in Fig. 6. We construct a dataset with 10 categories, each containing 100 training and 50 test images. We replace the training image backgrounds with similar backgrounds but do not change the test images. We form 5 tasks, each with 2 categories. Average accuracy and BWT are evaluated after all tasks are trained, and the result is compared with its counterpart from the original training images with different backgrounds. The results show that similar characteristics cause forgetting.

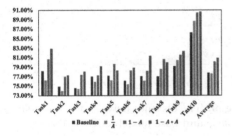

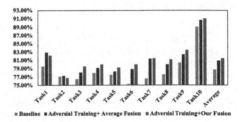

Fig. 7. The impacts of various types of background mask on the lifelong learning process on CIFAR100. The baseline is the model without the attack.

Fig. 8. The classification accuracy in lifelong learning process on CIFAR100. The baseline is the same model but without the attack and with average model fusion.

The Effects of Different B. During the adversarial training process, we apply different ways to make background attacks. We set the mask $\mathbf{B}$ as $(\frac{1}{\mathbf{A}})$, $(1 - \mathbf{A})$ and $(1 - \mathbf{A} \circ \mathbf{A})$, and perform experiments respectively. As shown in Fig. 7, the performance varies according to the background mask $\mathbf{B}$. The results performed by $(1 - \mathbf{A} \circ \mathbf{A})$ are better than other methods. In order to analyze the cause of the various impact, we randomly sample 5 attention masks and list their distributions in Table 4. Since the masks have values close to 0, the attack with $\mathbf{B} = (\frac{1}{\mathbf{A}})$ would be so huge that it decreases the robustness of the model. Moreover, because the values are closer to 1 than to 0, $\mathbf{B} = (1 - \mathbf{A} \circ \mathbf{A})$ can widen the distance between foreground and background more effectively than $\mathbf{B} = 1 - \mathbf{A}$.

In our experiments, the attack using $\mathbf{B} = (1 - \mathbf{A} \circ \mathbf{A})$ performs the best, meaning that it can guide background attack more effectively. The visualization results of $\mathbf{A}$ and $\mathbf{B}$ are presented in the supplementary material.

The Effects of Model Fusion. To verify the effect of our proposed model fusion method, we compare the lifelong learning results with and without our model fusion on CIFAR100 while keeping the other settings unchanged. The results are shown in Fig. 8. It could be observed that our fusion operation makes the learning better incrementally. To verify whether the task-specific models tend to be similar, we test the values of **dif**. In Fig. 9, we intercept the 90 – 100 epochs on the CUB200 benchmark. The task number n equals 6 as shown in Eq. 6. The vertical axis represents the distances between task-specific models and the base model. As the training progresses, the distance gradually converges to 0. Through our model fusion method, different task-specific models can converge to the optimal one, thus eliminating information loss and retroactive interference in the task-specific model fusion, which illustrates the effectiveness of our method.

Table 4. We conduct 5 tests and analyze the data distribution of $\mathbf{A}$. *std* denotes the standard deviation. The majority of the values are closer to 1 than to 0.

	Test1	Test2	Test3	Test4	Test5
$[0, 0.3)$	2.03%	1.19%	4.22%	2.62%	1.72%
$[0.3, 0.5)$	7.62%	5.86%	17.43%	12.62%	4.65%
$[0.5, 0.7)$	75.03%	29.42%	59.59%	55.43%	81.93%
$[0.7, 1]$	15.32%	63.54%	18.76%	29.33%	11.70%
std	14.35%	13.72%	17.48%	15.14%	14.52%

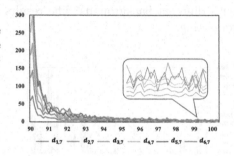

Fig. 9. The distance between task-specific models and base model on CUB200.

5   Conclusion

Lifelong learning aims to learn a single model that can continuously adapt to the new knowledge without overriding existing knowledge. We develop a meta-learning approach to train a base model which can be efficiently optimized for lifelong learning. First, a background attack method is introduced to extract critical features and avoid retroactive interference. Then, an adaptive weight fusion mechanism is presented according to the distances between the base and the task-specific models. Our experiments demonstrate consistent improvements across a range of classification datasets, including ImageNet100, CUB200, CIFAR100, and MNIST.

Acknowledgements. This work was supported in part by the National Natural Science Foundation of China under Grant 62076016.

References

1. Abati, D., Tomczak, J., Blankevoort, T., Calderara, S., Cucchiara, R., Bejnordi, B.E.: Conditional channel gated networks for task-aware continual learning. In: CVPR (2020)
2. Aljundi, R., Babiloni, F., Elhoseiny, M., Rohrbach, M., Tuytelaars, T.: Memory aware synapses: learning what (not) to forget. In: Ferrari, V., Hebert, M., Sminchisescu, C., Weiss, Y. (eds.) ECCV 2018. LNCS, vol. 11207, pp. 144–161. Springer, Cham (2018). https://doi.org/10.1007/978-3-030-01219-9_9
3. Ausubel, D.P., Fitzgerald, D.: The role of discriminability in meaningful learning and retention. J. Educ. Psychol. **52**(5), 266 (1961)
4. Castro, F.M., Marín-Jiménez, M.J., Guil, N., Schmid, C., Alahari, K.: End-to-end incremental learning. In: Ferrari, V., Hebert, M., Sminchisescu, C., Weiss, Y. (eds.) ECCV 2018. LNCS, vol. 11216, pp. 241–257. Springer, Cham (2018). https://doi.org/10.1007/978-3-030-01258-8_15
5. Chaudhry, A., Dokania, P.K., Ajanthan, T., Torr, P.H.S.: Riemannian walk for incremental learning: understanding forgetting and intransigence. In: Ferrari, V., Hebert, M., Sminchisescu, C., Weiss, Y. (eds.) ECCV 2018. LNCS, vol. 11215, pp. 556–572. Springer, Cham (2018). https://doi.org/10.1007/978-3-030-01252-6_33
6. Douillard, A., Cord, M., Ollion, C., Robert, T., Valle, E.: PODNet: pooled outputs distillation for small-tasks incremental learning. In: Vedaldi, A., Bischof, H., Brox, T., Frahm, J.-M. (eds.) ECCV 2020. LNCS, vol. 12365, pp. 86–102. Springer, Cham (2020). https://doi.org/10.1007/978-3-030-58565-5_6
7. Ebrahimi, S., et al.: Remembering for the right reasons: explanations reduce catastrophic forgetting. In: ICLR (2021)
8. Goodfellow, I.J., Shlens, J., Szegedy, C.: Explaining and harnessing adversarial examples. In: ICLR (2015)
9. Goodfellow, I., Bengio, Y., Courville, A.: Deep Learning. MIT Press, Cambridge (2016)
10. Hadsell, R., Rao, D., Rusu, A.A., Pascanu, R.: Embracing change: continual learning in deep neural networks. Trends in Cogn. Sci. **24**, 1028–1040 (2020)
11. Hou, S., Pan, X., Loy, C.C., Wang, Z., Lin, D.: Learning a unified classifier incrementally via rebalancing. In: CVPR (2019)
12. Hurtado, J., Raymond-Saez, A., Soto, A.: Optimizing reusable knowledge for continual learning via metalearning. In: NeurIPS (2021)
13. Kirkpatrick, J., et al.: Overcoming catastrophic forgetting in neural networks. Proc. Natl. Acad. Sci. **114**(13), 3521–3526 (2017)
14. Krizhevsky, A., Hinton, G., et al.: Learning multiple layers of features from tiny images. Technical report (2009)
15. Kurakin, A., Goodfellow, I., Bengio, S.: Adversarial examples in the physical world. In: ICLR (2016)
16. Li, Z., Hoiem, D.: Learning without forgetting. IEEE Trans. Pattern Anal. Mach. Intell. **40**(12), 2935–2947 (2017)
17. Lopez-Paz, D., Ranzato, M.: Gradient episodic memory for continual learning. In: NeurIPS (2017)
18. Na, T., Ko, J.H., Mukhopadhyay, S.: Cascade adversarial machine learning regularized with a unified embedding. In: ICLR (2017)
19. Peng, H., Long, F., Ding, C.: Feature selection based on mutual information criteria of max-dependency, max-relevance, and min-redundancy. IEEE Trans. Pattern Anal. Mach. Intell. **27**, 1226–1238 (2005)

20. Rajasegaran, J., Hayat, M., Khan, S.H., Khan, F.S., Shao, L.: Random path selection for continual learning. In: NeurIPS (2019)
21. Rajasegaran, J., Khan, S., Hayat, M., Khan, F.S., Shah, M.: iTAML: an incremental task-agnostic meta-learning approach. In: CVPR (2020)
22. Rebuffi, S.A., Kolesnikov, A., Sperl, G., Lampert, C.H.: iCARL: incremental classifier and representation learning. In: CVPR (2017)
23. Russakovsky, O., et al.: ImageNet large scale visual recognition challenge. Int. J. Comput. Vision **115**(3), 211–252 (2015)
24. Shin, H., Lee, J.K., Kim, J., Kim, J.: Continual learning with deep generative replay. In: NeurIPS (2017)
25. Sternberg, R.J., Sternberg, K., Mio, J.: Cognitive Psychology. Cengage Learning Press, Boston (2012)
26. Tramèr, F., Boneh, D., Kurakin, A., Goodfellow, I., Papernot, N., McDaniel, P.: Ensemble adversarial training: attacks and defenses. In: ICLR (2018)
27. Vogel, E.K., McCollough, A.W., Machizawa, M.G.: Neural measures reveal individual differences in controlling access to working memory. Nature **438**(7067), 500–503 (2005)
28. Wah, C., Branson, S., Welinder, P., Perona, P., Belongie, S.: The caltech-UCSD birds-200. Technical report CNS-TR-2010-001 (2011)
29. Woo, Sanghyun, Park, Jongchan, Lee, Joon-Young., Kweon, In So.: CBAM: convolutional block attention module. In: Ferrari, Vittorio, Hebert, Martial, Sminchisescu, Cristian, Weiss, Yair (eds.) ECCV 2018. LNCS, vol. 11211, pp. 3–19. Springer, Cham (2018). https://doi.org/10.1007/978-3-030-01234-2_1
30. Wu, Y., et al.: Large scale incremental learning. In: CVPR (2019)
31. Yan, S., Xie, J., He, X.: DER: Dynamically expandable representation for class incremental learning. In: CVPR (2021)
32. Yu, L., et al.: Semantic drift compensation for class-incremental learning. In: CVPR (2020)
33. Zenke, F., Poole, B., Ganguli, S.: Continual learning through synaptic intelligence. In: ICML (2017)
34. Zhang, C., et al.: Delving deep into the generalization of vision transformers under distribution shifts. arXiv (2021)
35. Zhang, J., et al.: Class-incremental learning via deep model consolidation. In: WACV (2020)
36. Zhao, B., Xiao, X., Gan, G., Zhang, B., Xia, S.T.: Maintaining discrimination and fairness in class incremental learning. In: CVPR (2020)
37. Zhou, D., Ye, H., Zhan, D.: Co-transport for class-incremental learning. In: ACM MM (2021)

Towards Calibrated Hyper-Sphere Representation via Distribution Overlap Coefficient for Long-Tailed Learning

Hualiang Wang[1,3], Siming Fu[1], Xiaoxuan He[1], Hangxiang Fang[1], Zuozhu Liu[1,2], and Haoji Hu[1(✉)]

[1] College of Information Science and Electronic Engineering, Zhejiang University, Hangzhou, China
{hualiang_wang,fusiming,Xiaoxiao_He,fhx,chuhp,haoji_hu}@zju.edu.cn
[2] ZJU-UIUC Institute, Zhejiang University, Hangzhou, China
zuozhuliu@intl.zju.edu.cn
[3] Angelalign Inc., Shanghai, China

Abstract. Long-tailed learning aims to tackle the crucial challenge that head classes dominate the training procedure under severe class imbalance in real-world scenarios. However, little attention has been given to how to quantify the dominance severity of head classes in the representation space. Motivated by this, we generalize the cosine-based classifiers to a von Mises-Fisher (vMF) mixture model, denoted as vMF classifier, which enables to quantitatively measure representation quality upon the hyper-sphere space via calculating distribution overlap coefficient. To our knowledge, this is the first work to measure representation quality of classifiers and features from the perspective of distribution overlap coefficient. On top of it, we formulate the inter-class discrepancy and class-feature consistency loss terms to alleviate the interference among the classifier weights and align features with classifier weights. Furthermore, a novel post-training calibration algorithm is devised to zero-costly boost the performance via inter-class overlap coefficients. Our method outperforms previous work with a large margin and achieves state-of-the-art performance on long-tailed image classification, semantic segmentation, and instance segmentation tasks (e.g., we achieve 55.0% overall accuracy with ResNetXt-50 in ImageNet-LT). Our code is available at https://github.com/VipaiLab/vMF_OP.

Keywords: von Mises-Fisher Distribution · Distribution overlap coefficient · Long-tailed learning · Representation learning

---

H. Wang and S. Fu—These authors contributed equally.

Supplementary Information The online version contains supplementary material available at https://doi.org/10.1007/978-3-031-20053-3_11.

S. Avidan et al. (Eds.): ECCV 2022, LNCS 13684, pp. 179–196, 2022.
https://doi.org/10.1007/978-3-031-20053-3_11

1   Introduction

Most real-world data comes with a long-tailed nature: a few head classes contribute the majority of data, while most tail classes comprise relatively few data.An undesired phenomenon is models [2,36,42] trained with long-tailed data perform better on head classes while exhibiting extremely low accuracy on tail ones.

To remedy it, one of the mainstream insights works on devising balanced classifiers [16,44,45] against imbalanced data. The cosine-based classifier discards the norms that have been proven to be larger on head classes [53]. The τ-norm classifier [16] manually shrinks the discrepancy among the norms of classifier weights through a τ-normalization function. In addition, some works [2,13,23,32] attach extra margin or scale terms on output scores to prompt classifiers to focus on data-scarce classes. Another prevailing method devotes to learning discriminative features using imbalanced data [5,31,34,43,51]. Range loss [51] is proposed to enlarge the inter-class feature distance and reduce the intra-class feature variation within the mini-batch data. Unsupervised discovery (UD) [43] uses self-supervised learning to help the model highlight tail classes from the feature level. In addition, LDA [31] transfers the learned feature distribution from the training domain to an ideal balanced domain.

While achieving promising performance, there lack of measures to quantitatively evaluate to what extent these classifiers or features can achieve the presumed "balanced" classifiers or "discriminative" features. Hence, one cannot measure how severely head classes dominate the features and classifiers in the high-dimensional representation space, resulting in confusions to guide further optimization for improved long-tailed learning.

To this end, we first extend cosine-based classifier as a von Mises-Fisher (vMF) distribution mixture model on hyper-sphere, denoted as the vMF classifier. Second, based on the representation space constructed by the vMF classifier, we mathematically define a novel measure between two probability density fuctions, denoted as distribution overlap coefficient o_Λ, to quantify to what extent the classifiers are "balanced" or features are "discriminative". A high o_Λ means that the two distributions (classes) are severely intertwined together. We suppose that o_Λ among classes in a "balance" classifier should be low enough, i.e., one class is not overwhelmingly dominated by other ones. "Discriminative" features means o_Λ between features and the corresponding classifier weights is high enough, i.e., features are well matched with correct classes.

On top of o_Λ, we provide an explicit optimization objective to boost the representation quality on hyper-sphere, i.e., to allow classifier weights to be distributed separately while aligning the weights of classifiers with features. Specifically, we propose two loss terms: the inter-class discrepancy and class-feature consistency loss. The first one minimizes the overlap among classifier weights, and the second one maximizes the overlap between features and the corresponding classifier weights. To further ease dominance of the head classes in classification decisions during inference, we develop a post-training calibration algorithm for classifier at zero cost based on the learned class-wise overlap coefficients.

We extensively validate our model on three typical visual recognition tasks, including image classification on benchmarks (ImageNet-LT [25] and iNaturalist2018 [39]), semantic segmentation on ADE20K dataset [55], and instance segmentation on LVIS-v1.0 dataset [9]. The experimental results and ablative study demonstrate our method consistently outperforms the state-of-the-art approaches on all the benchmarks.

Summary of Contributions:

- To the best of our acknowledge, we are the first in long-tailed learning to define the distribution overlap coefficient to evaluate representation quality for features and the proposed vMF classifiers.
- We formulate overlap-based inter-class discrepancy and class-feature consistency loss terms to alleviate the interference among the classifier weights and align features with classifier weights.
- We develop a post-training calibration algorithm for classifier at zero cost based on the learned class-wise overlap coefficients to ease dominance of the head classes in classification decisions during inference.
- Our models outperform previous work with a large margin and achieve state-of-the-art performance on long-tailed image classification, semantic segmentation and instance segmentation tasks.

2   Related Works

Classifier Design for Deep Long-Tailed Learning. In generic visual problems [11,54], the common practice of deep learning is to use linear classifier. However, long-tailed class imbalance often results in larger classifier weight norms for head classes than tail classes, which makes the linear classifier easily biased to dominant classes. To address long-tailed class imbalance, researchers design different types of classifiers. Scale-invariant cosine classifier [44] is proposed, where both the classifier weights and sample features are normalized. The τ-normalized classifier [16] rectifies the imbalance of decision boundaries by introducing the τ temperature factor for normalization [48]. Realistic taxonomic classifier (RTC) [45] addresses the issue with hierarchical classification where different samples are classified adaptively at different hierarchical levels. GistNet classifier [24] leverages the over-fitting to the popular classes to transfer class geometry from popular to few-shot classes. Causal classifier [37] records the bias by computing the exponential moving average features during training, and then removes the bad causal effect by subtracting the bias from prediction logits during inference.

Representation Learning for Long-Tailed Learning. Existing representation learning methods for long-tailed learning mainly focus on metric learning, prototype learning. Metric learning based methods [17,34,41] explore distance-based losses to learn a more discriminative feature space. LMLE [14] introduces a quintuple loss to learn representations that maintain both inter-cluster and

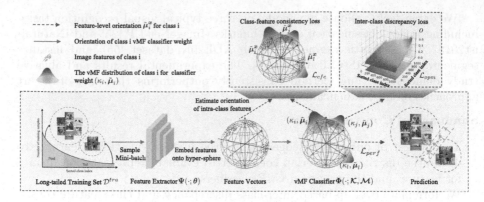

Fig. 1. Overview of our proposed method during the training period. **Bottom box** consists of the following steps in sequence: sampling a mini-batch images $\mathcal{B}$ from training set $\mathcal{D}^{tra}$, learning features by the feature extractor $\Psi(\cdot; \theta)$, embedding features onto hyper-sphere, predicting output via our proposed vMF classifier $\Phi(\cdot; \mathcal{K}, \mathcal{M})$ and calculating the performance loss value. **Upper boxes** introduce our proposed the class-feature consistency loss term $\mathcal{L}_{cfc}$ and inter-class discrepancy loss term $\mathcal{L}_{icd}$.

inter-class margins. Prototype learning based methods [26,58] seek to learn class-specific feature prototypes to enhance long-tailed learning performance. Open long-tailed recognition (OLTR) [26] innovatively explores the idea of feature prototypes to handle long-tailed recognition in an open world. Self-supervised pre-training (SSP) [47] uses self-supervised learning for model pre-training, followed by standard training on long-tailed data.

von Mises-Fisher Distribution. In directional statistics, the von Mises-Fisher distribution [15] is a probability distribution on the hyper-sphere. There are a lot of methods built on von Mises-Fisher distribution in machine learning and deep learning. The vMF Mixture Model (vMFMM) [10] proposes SFR model which assumes that the facial features are unit vectors and distributed according to a mixture of vMFs. The vMF k-means algorithm [28] is proposed based on the mixture vMF distribution to unsupervisedly evaluate the compactness and orientation of clusters. More recently, the t-vMF similarity [19] rebuilds the classifier by the proposed similarity based on vMF distribution to regularize features within deteriorated data. Sphere Confidence Face [20] minimizes KL divergence between spherical Dirac delta and r-radius vMF to achieve superior performance on face uncertainty learning.

Different from all them, to our best acknowledge, we are the first to quantify the distribution overlap coefficient between vMF distributions. Benefiting from it, we conduct a series of comprehensive and in-depth analyses to explore how to achieve high-quality representation space built upon vMF distribution.

3   Methodology

First, we briefly review the canonical pipeline of long-tailed learning, exemplified by long-tailed image classification, and elaborate on our proposed vMF classifier.

Afterward, we mathematically define the distribution overlap coefficient. On top of it, we further present the proposed the inter-class discrepancy loss and class-feature consistency loss terms. Finally, a post-training calibration algorithm is devised to zero-costly boost performance.

3.1   Build vMF Classifier on Hyper-Sphere

Let $\mathcal{D}^{tra} = \{I^l, y^l\}$, $l \in \{1, \cdots, N\}$ be the training set, where I^l denotes an image sample and $y^l = i$ indicates it belongs to class i. Let C be the total numbers of classes, n_i be the number of samples in class i, where $\sum_{i=1}^{C} n_i = N$. The class prior distribution on training set can be defined as $p_{\mathcal{D}}^{tra}(i) = n_i/N$.

As shown in Fig. 1, given a pair (I^l, y^l) sampled from a mini-batch $\mathcal{B} \subset \mathcal{D}^{tra}$, feature vector $\boldsymbol{x}^l = \boldsymbol{\Psi}(I^l; \boldsymbol{\theta}) \in \mathbb{R}^{1 \times d}$ is extracted by the feature extractor $\boldsymbol{\Psi}(\cdot; \boldsymbol{\theta})$, of which learnable parameter $\boldsymbol{\theta}$ is instantiated by a neural network (e.g., ResNet). Then $\boldsymbol{x}^l$ is projected onto the unit hyper-sphere $\mathbb{S}^{d-1}$ via $\tilde{\boldsymbol{x}}^l = \boldsymbol{x}^l/\|\boldsymbol{x}^l\|_2$ and subsequently fed into the vMF classifier.

We depict the classifier with C classes as a mixture model with C von Mises-Fisher distributions on $\mathbb{S}^{d-1}$, each class containing two variables: the compactness $\kappa_i \in \mathbb{R}^+$ and the unit orientation vector $\tilde{\boldsymbol{\mu}}_i \in \mathbb{R}^{1 \times d}$. Consequently, vMF classifier is well-defined as $\boldsymbol{\Phi}(\cdot; \mathcal{K}, \mathcal{M})$, where $\mathcal{K} = \{\kappa_1, ..., \kappa_C\}$ and $\mathcal{M} = \{\tilde{\boldsymbol{\mu}}_1, ..., \tilde{\boldsymbol{\mu}}_C\}$ are learnable compactness and orientation vectors for C classes, respectively. The probability density function (PDF) $p(\tilde{\boldsymbol{x}}|\kappa_i, \tilde{\boldsymbol{\mu}}_i)$ of i-th class is mathematically defined as:

$$p(\tilde{\boldsymbol{x}}|\kappa_i, \tilde{\boldsymbol{\mu}}_i) = C_d(\kappa_i)e^{\kappa_i \cdot \tilde{\boldsymbol{x}}\tilde{\boldsymbol{\mu}}_i^\top} = \frac{\kappa_i^{\frac{d}{2}-1}}{(2\pi)^{\frac{d}{2}} \cdot I_{\frac{d}{2}-1}(\kappa_i)}e^{\kappa_i \cdot \tilde{\boldsymbol{x}}\tilde{\boldsymbol{\mu}}_i^\top}, \tag{1}$$

where $I_v(\kappa)$ is the modified Bessel function [18] of the first kind of real order v and $C_d(\kappa)$ is a normalization constant.

From the view of Bayes Theorem [29], given the class prior distribution $p_{\mathcal{D}}^{tra}(i)$ and $p(\tilde{\boldsymbol{x}}^l|\kappa_i, \tilde{\boldsymbol{\mu}}_i)$, the probability p_i^l for I^l belonging to class i can be formulated by the posterior probability $p(y^l = i|\tilde{\boldsymbol{x}}^l)$ as:

$$p_i^l = p(y^l = i|\tilde{\boldsymbol{x}}^l) = \frac{p_{\mathcal{D}}^{tra}(i) \cdot p(\tilde{\boldsymbol{x}}^l|\kappa_i, \tilde{\boldsymbol{\mu}}_i)}{\sum_{j=1}^{C} p_{\mathcal{D}}^{tra}(j) \cdot p(\tilde{\boldsymbol{x}}^l|\kappa_j, \tilde{\boldsymbol{\mu}}_j)}. \tag{2}$$

Equation 2 is the formulation of our vMF classifier. Our vMF classifer degrades to a balanced cosine classifier [32] with a temperature σ, when $\kappa_i = const\ \sigma, \forall i \in [1, C]$.

The performance loss $\mathcal{L}_{perf}$ of the mini-batch $\mathcal{B}$ is calculated by the cross-entropy function as follows:

$$\mathcal{L}_{perf} = -\frac{1}{N'}\sum_{l=1}^{N'}\sum_{i=1}^{C} \mathbb{1}[y^l = i] \cdot \log p_i^l, \tag{3}$$

Table 1. Derivatives for compactness and orientation of vMF classifier.

	∂o_Λ	$\partial \log p_i^l$
$\partial \kappa_i$	$o_\Lambda^2 \cdot \frac{\partial A_d(\kappa_i)}{\partial \kappa_i} \cdot (\kappa_j \cdot \tilde{\boldsymbol{\mu}}_i \tilde{\boldsymbol{\mu}}_j^\top - \kappa_i)$	$(1 - p_i^l) \cdot (\tilde{\boldsymbol{x}}^l \tilde{\boldsymbol{\mu}}_i^\top - A_d(\kappa_i))$
$\partial \kappa_j$	$o_\Lambda^2 \cdot (A_d(\kappa_i) \cdot \tilde{\boldsymbol{\mu}}_i \tilde{\boldsymbol{\mu}}_j^\top - A_d(\kappa_j))$	$-p_j^l \cdot (\tilde{\boldsymbol{x}}^l \tilde{\boldsymbol{\mu}}_j^\top - A_d(\kappa_j))$
$\partial \tilde{\boldsymbol{\mu}}_i$	$o_\Lambda^2 \cdot \kappa_j \cdot A_d(\kappa_i) \cdot \tilde{\boldsymbol{\mu}}_j$	$(1 - p_i^l) \cdot \kappa_i \cdot \tilde{\boldsymbol{x}}$
$\partial \tilde{\boldsymbol{\mu}}_j$	$o_\Lambda^2 \cdot \kappa_j \cdot A_d(\kappa_i) \cdot \tilde{\boldsymbol{\mu}}_i$	$-p_j^l \cdot \kappa_j \cdot \tilde{\boldsymbol{x}}$

where $\mathbb{1}[y = i]$ is the binary indicator that denotes whether the corresponding image comes from the i-th class and N' is the number of samples in a mini-batch. The total loss $\mathcal{L}$ for mini-batch $\mathcal{B}$ in one iteration is calculated as:

$$\mathcal{L} = \mathcal{L}_{perf} + \lambda \cdot (\mathcal{L}_{icd} + \mathcal{L}_{cfc}), \tag{4}$$

where $\mathcal{L}_{icd}$ and $\mathcal{L}_{cfc}$ are proposed additional loss terms to regularize feature and classifier, which will be introduced in the subsequent subsection. λ is a hyperparameter to adjust the weight of additional loss terms.

3.2 Quantify Distribution Overlap Coefficient on Hyper-Sphere

As aforementioned, we geometrically depict the classifier as a set of vMF distributions on $\mathbb{S}^{d-1}$. The distribution overlap coefficient [7] is mathematically explained as the area of intersection between two probability density functions. Based on it, we mathematically quantify distribution overlap coefficient to measure the intersection degree of two classes (vMF distribution) in the $\mathcal{S}^{d-1}$. In this paper, we provide the analytic expression o_Λ based on Kullback-Leibler divergence [30] for the vMF distribution [8]. Specifically, o_Λ is defined as:

$$o_\Lambda(\kappa_i, \kappa_j, \tilde{\boldsymbol{\mu}}_i, \tilde{\boldsymbol{\mu}}_j) = \frac{1}{1 + KL\{p(\tilde{\boldsymbol{x}}|\kappa_i, \tilde{\boldsymbol{\mu}}_i), p(\tilde{\boldsymbol{x}}|\kappa_j, \tilde{\boldsymbol{\mu}}_j)\}}, \tag{5}$$

where $KL\{p(\tilde{\boldsymbol{x}}|\kappa_i, \tilde{\boldsymbol{\mu}}_i), p(\tilde{\boldsymbol{x}}|\kappa_j, \tilde{\boldsymbol{\mu}}_j)\}$ is the Kullback-Leibler divergence between two vMF distributions, abbreviated as KL_{ij}:

$$
\begin{aligned}
KL_{ij} &= -\int_{\tilde{\boldsymbol{x}}} p(\tilde{\boldsymbol{x}}|\kappa_i, \tilde{\boldsymbol{\mu}}_i) \cdot \ln \frac{p(\tilde{\boldsymbol{x}}|\kappa_j, \tilde{\boldsymbol{\mu}}_j)}{p(\tilde{\boldsymbol{x}}|\kappa_i, \tilde{\boldsymbol{\mu}}_i)} \, d\tilde{\boldsymbol{x}} \\
&= \ln \frac{C_d(\kappa_i)}{C_d(\kappa_j)} \cdot \underbrace{\int_{\tilde{\boldsymbol{x}}} C_d(\kappa_i) \cdot e^{\kappa_i \cdot \tilde{\boldsymbol{x}} \tilde{\boldsymbol{\mu}}_i^\top} \, d\tilde{\boldsymbol{x}}}_{=1} \\
&\quad + (\underbrace{\int_{\tilde{\boldsymbol{x}}} \tilde{\boldsymbol{x}} \cdot C_d(\kappa_i) \cdot e^{\kappa_i \cdot \tilde{\boldsymbol{x}} \tilde{\boldsymbol{\mu}}_i^\top} \, d\tilde{\boldsymbol{x}}}_{=\mathbb{E}[\tilde{\boldsymbol{x}}] = A_d(\kappa_i) \cdot \tilde{\boldsymbol{\mu}}_i})(\kappa_i \cdot \tilde{\boldsymbol{\mu}}_i^\top - \kappa_j \cdot \tilde{\boldsymbol{\mu}}_j^\top) \\
&= \ln \frac{C_d(\kappa_i)}{C_d(\kappa_j)} + A_d(\kappa_i) \cdot (\kappa_i - \kappa_j \tilde{\boldsymbol{\mu}}_i \tilde{\boldsymbol{\mu}}_j^\top),
\end{aligned}
\tag{6}
$$

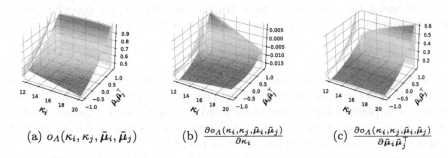

(a) $o_\Lambda(\kappa_i, \kappa_j, \tilde{\mu}_i, \tilde{\mu}_j)$ (b) $\dfrac{\partial o_\Lambda(\kappa_i, \kappa_j, \tilde{\mu}_i, \tilde{\mu}_j)}{\partial \kappa_i}$ (c) $\dfrac{\partial o_\Lambda(\kappa_i, \kappa_j, \tilde{\mu}_i, \tilde{\mu}_j)}{\partial \tilde{\mu}_i \tilde{\mu}_j^\top}$

Fig. 2. Visualization of overlap coefficient $o_\Lambda(\kappa_i, \kappa_j, \tilde{\mu}_i, \tilde{\mu}_j)$ and partial derivatives for κ_i and $\tilde{\mu}_i \tilde{\mu}_j^\top$. To exhibit them in 3D coordination, κ_j is fixed to a certain value, instantiated as 16. κ_i and $\tilde{\mu}_i \tilde{\mu}_j^\top$ ($\tilde{\mu}_i \in \mathbb{R}^{1 \times 512}$) are uniformly sampled 100 values from range $[12, 20]$ and range $[-1, 1]$, respectively.

where $A_d(\kappa_i) = I_{d/2}(\kappa_i)/I_{d/2-1}(\kappa_i)$ is non-decreasing and $0 < A_d(\kappa_i) < 1$. $\mathbb{E}[\tilde{x}]$ is the expectation vector for $\tilde{x} \sim p(\tilde{x} | \kappa_i, \tilde{\mu}_i)$ [33]. Generally $0 < o_\Lambda \leq 1$. $o_\Lambda = 1$ (i.e., $\kappa_i = \kappa_j$ and $\tilde{\mu}_i \tilde{\mu}_j^\top = 1$) means they are completely congruent. $o_\Lambda \to 0$ indicates there is nearly no intersection between two distributions.

The derivatives of κ_i, κ_j, $\tilde{\mu}_i$ and $\tilde{\mu}_j$ for o_Λ are listed as the Col 1 of Table 1. And visualization for them is demonstrated in Fig. 2. Specifically, the partial derivative with respect to $\tilde{\mu}_i \tilde{\mu}_j^\top$ is non-negative.

The partial derivatives with respect to κ_i or κ_j are non-monotonous. An empirical conclusion is that κ_i and κ_j need to be kept at the same order of magnitude to achieve guaranteed performance, when using o_Λ as the optimization objective.

3.3 Improve Representation of Feature and Classifier via o_Λ

Inter-class Discrepancy Loss. To achieve the discriminative representation space in long-tailed learning, we seek to optimize our vMF classifier via shrinking the overlap among classes as much as possible to alleviate the overwhelm of the head classes on the tail ones. We denote the above optimization objective as the inter-class discrepancy loss term $\mathcal{L}_{icd}$, which acts function on the weights $\mathcal{K}$ and $\mathcal{M}$ of the vMF classifier.

First, we measure the average overlap coefficient o_i among class i and all the other classes, formulated by:

$$o_i = \frac{1}{C-1} \sum_{j=1, j \neq i}^{C} o_\Lambda(\kappa_i, \kappa_j, \tilde{\mu}_i, \tilde{\mu}_j). \qquad (7)$$

Furthermore, we define the inter-class discrepancy loss term $\mathcal{L}_{icd}$ as:

$$\mathcal{L}_{icd} = \frac{1}{C} \sum_{i=1}^{C} o_i, \qquad (8)$$

The proposed $\mathcal{L}_{icd}$ minimizes the average distribution overlap coefficient to regularize distributions, contributing to a more distinction-prone classifier on $\mathbb{S}^{d-1}$.

Class-Feature Consistency Loss. In addition, the poorly matching between the feature vectors and the corresponding classifier weights derives unsatisfied performance, especially for the sample-starved classes. Class-feature consistency loss term $\mathcal{L}_{cfc}$ is proposed to alleviate the above issue by aligning features with the corresponding classifier weights as far as possible.

Specifically, we first fit the class-wise feature distribution $(\kappa^x, \tilde{\boldsymbol{\mu}}^x)$ within the mini-batch $\mathcal{B}$. The class set involved in $\mathcal{B}$ is denote as $\mathcal{C}'$. For a certain class $i \in \mathcal{C}'$, the feature-level orientation vector $\tilde{\boldsymbol{\mu}}_i^x$ is defined as:

$$\tilde{\boldsymbol{\mu}}_i^x = \frac{\sum_{l=1,y^l=i}^{N'} \boldsymbol{x}^l}{\| \sum_{l=1,y^l=i}^{N'} \boldsymbol{x}^l \|_2}. \tag{9}$$

Considering that the compactness κ is over-sensitive to sample number and intractable to be estimated [10], κ is shared between the feature and the corresponding classifier weight, i.e., feature-level compactness κ_i^x for class i is equal to κ_i. Then, $\mathcal{L}_{cfc}$ is formulated as following:

$$\mathcal{L}_{cfc} = \mathbb{E}_{i \in \mathcal{C}'}[1 - o_\Lambda(\kappa_i, \kappa_i^x, \tilde{\boldsymbol{\mu}}_i, \tilde{\boldsymbol{\mu}}_i^x)], \tag{10}$$

where $\mathbb{E}$ indicates the average function. $\mathcal{L}_{cfc}$ is, in effect, equivalent to maximizing the distribution overlap coefficient between features and the corresponding classifier weights.

3.4   Calibrate Classifier Weight Beyond Training via o_Λ

Despite exerting additional loss terms to regularize features and classifiers, the overwhelm of the head classes on the tail ones is, in effect, tough to eradicate under a highly imbalanced dataset. We visualize the compactness of the classifier and the average overlap coefficients from a well-trained model, as demonstrated in Col 1 of Fig. 3. The head classes share larger compactness and smaller overlap coefficients, however, the case for tail ones is reversed.

A general summary of the calibration strategy is that increase the compactness for classes that are severely overlapped with other classes. Specifically, given a well-trained vMF classifier $\Phi(\cdot; \mathcal{K}, \mathcal{M})$, we first apply Eq. 7 to obtain the average overlap coefficient for each class, denoted as $\mathcal{O} = \{o_1, ..., o_C\}$. Then we use a maximum-minimum normalization strategy to reconcile $\mathcal{O}$ to the same value range as $\mathcal{K}$, to make sure that both are on the same order of magnitude by:

$$\hat{o}_i = \frac{o_i - o^{min}}{o^{max} - o^{min}} \cdot (\kappa^{max} - \kappa^{min}) + \kappa^{min}, \tag{11}$$

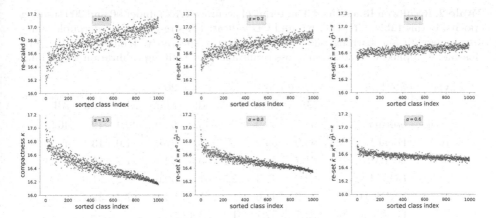

Fig. 3. The calibrated compactness of vMF classifier (trained on ImageNet-LT with ResNetXt-50 feature extractor). Under different α settings, we adjust κ via Eq. 11 and Eq. 12. Each picture represents the value of re-scaled $\hat{\mathcal{K}}$ when α equals to the corresponding value. When $\alpha = 0$, it indicates $\hat{\kappa}_i = \hat{o}_i$, while $\alpha = 1$, $\hat{\kappa}_i = \kappa_i$.

where o^{max} and o^{min} are maximum and minimum values of set $\mathcal{O}$, respectively, as well as κ^{max} and κ^{min}. We reset compactness vector as $\hat{\mathcal{K}} = \{\hat{\kappa}_1, ..., \hat{\kappa}_C\}$, formulated as following:

$$\hat{\kappa}_i = \kappa_i^{\alpha} \cdot \hat{o}_i^{1-\alpha}, \tag{12}$$

$\alpha \in [0, 1]$ is a hyper-parameter to balance the importance contribution to the re-scaled $\hat{\mathcal{K}}$ as shown in Fig. 3. In the inference period, we comply with a canonical assumption that the classes on the test set follow the uniform distribution, i.e., $p_{\mathcal{D}}^{test}(i) = 1/C$. Consequently, we replace $p_{\mathcal{D}}^{tra}(i)$ by $p_{\mathcal{D}}^{test}(i)$ in Eq. 2, and the vMF classifier is calibrated as $\Phi(\cdot; \hat{\mathcal{K}}, \mathcal{M})$.

Moreover, our post-training calibration algorithm is capable of extending to several wide-used classifiers for cost-free performance boosting. Next, we instantiate how to apply the algorithm above to calibrate the weights of τ-norm [16], causal classifiers [38] and linear classifiers. Given the weight vector $\boldsymbol{w}_i^{\tau}$ of class i from a well-trained τ-norm classifier $\boldsymbol{W}^{\tau}$, we equivalently convert $\boldsymbol{w}_i^{\tau}$ into compactness $\kappa_i = \|\boldsymbol{w}_i^{\tau}\|_2^{1-\tau}$ and orientation vector $\tilde{\mu}_i = \boldsymbol{w}_i^{\tau}/\|\boldsymbol{w}_i^{\tau}\|_2$. After calibration via Eq. 11 and Eq. 12, $\boldsymbol{w}_i^{\tau}$ is rebuilt by producting orientation vector and re-balanced compactness together. Along the same lines, the weight vector $\boldsymbol{w}_i^{cau}$ for a well-trained causal classifier $\boldsymbol{W}^{cau}$ is converted to $\kappa_i = \|\boldsymbol{w}_i^{cau}\|_2/(\|\boldsymbol{w}_i^{cau}\|_2+\gamma)$ and $\tilde{\mu}_i = \boldsymbol{w}_i^{cau}/\|\boldsymbol{w}_i^{cau}\|_2$. The weight vector $\boldsymbol{w}_i^{lin}$ for a well-trained linear classifier $\boldsymbol{W}^{lin}$ is converted to $\kappa_i = \|\boldsymbol{w}_i^{lin}\|_2$ and $\tilde{\mu}_i = \boldsymbol{w}_i^{lin}/\|\boldsymbol{w}_i^{lin}\|_2$. γ and τ are both the hyper-parameters for classifiers above. (Detail proofs in Appendix **A.2**)

4   Experiments

In this section, we conduct a series of experiments to validate the effectiveness of our method. Below we present our experimental analysis and ablation study on the image classification task in Sect. 4.1, followed by our results on semantic segmentation task and instance segmentation task in Sect. 4.2.

188   H. Wang et al.

Table 2. Results on ImageNet-LT in terms of accuracy (Acc) under 90 and 200 training epochs. In this table, CR, DT, RL and CD indicate class re-balancing, decouple training, representation learning and classifier design, respectively. † indicates only vMF classifier is applied w/o additional loss terms and post-training calibration algorithm.

Type	Method	90 epochs				200 epochs			
		Many	Med	Few	All	Many	Med	Few	All
Baseline	Softmax	66.5	39.0	8.6	45.5	66.9	40.4	12.6	46.8
CR	Focal Loss [23]	66.9	39.2	9.2	45.8	67.0	41.0	13.1	47.2
	BALMS [32]	61.7	48.0	29.9	50.8	62.4	47.7	32.1	51.2
	LDAM [2]	62.3	47.4	32.5	51.1	60.0	49.2	31.9	51.1
	LADE [13]	62.2	48.6	31.8	51.5	63.1	47.7	32.7	51.6
	DisAlign [50]	62.7	52.1	31.4	53.4	–	–	–	–
DT	IB-CRT [16]	62.6	46.2	26.7	49.9	64.2	46.1	26.0	50.3
	CB-CRT [16]	62.4	39.3	14.9	44.9	60.9	36.9	13.5	43.0
	MiSLAS [54]	62.1	48.9	31.6	51.4	65.3	50.6	33.0	53.4
	xERM$_{TDE}$ [57]	–	–	–	–	68.6	50.0	27.5	54.1
RL	OLTR [26]	58.2	45.5	19.5	46.7	62.9	44.6	18.8	48.0
	SSP [47]	65.6	49.6	30.3	53.1	67.3	49.1	28.3	53.3
	DRO-LT [34]	–	–	–	–	64.0	49.8	33.1	53.5
	PaCo [5]	59.7	51.7	36.6	52.7	63.2	51.6	39.2	54.4
CD	τ-norm [16]	61.8	46.2	27.4	49.6	–	–	–	–
	TDE [38]	63.0	48.5	31.4	51.8	64.9	46.9	28.1	51.3
	Ours†	64.2	49.8	26.9	52.2	65.9	50.5	28.1	53.4
	Ours	**64.2**	**51.4**	**31.8**	**53.7**	**65.1**	**52.8**	**34.2**	**55.0**

4.1 Long-Tailed Image Classification Task

Datasets and Setup. We perform experiments on long-tailed image classification datasets, including the ImageNet-LT [25] and iNaturalist2018 [39].

- ImageNet-LT is a long-tailed version of the ImageNet dataset by sampling a subset following the Pareto distribution with power value 6. It contains 115.8K images from 1,000 categories, with class cardinality ranging from 5 to 1,280.
- iNaturalist2018 is the largest dataset for long-tailed visual recognition. It contains 437.5K images from 8,142 categories. It is extremely imbalanced with an imbalance factor of 512.

Experimental Details. For image classification on ImageNet-LT, we implement all experiments in PyTorch. Following [5,13,38], we use ResNetXt-50 [46] as the feature extractor for all methods. We conduct model training with the SGD optimizer based on batch size 512, momentum 0.9. In both training epochs

Table 3. Benchmarking on iNaturalists2018 in accuracy (%). DT, CD and RL indicate decouple training, classifier design and representation learning, respectively.

Type	Method	iNaturalist2018			
		Many	Med	Few	All
Baseline	CE	72.2	63.0	57.2	61.7
DT	Decoupling [16]	65.6	65.3	65.5	65.6
	BBN [56]	49.4	70.8	65.3	66.3
CD	TDE [38]	–	–	–	68.7
	τ-norm [16]	65.6	65.3	65.5	65.6
RL	TSC [21]	72.6	70.6	67.8	69.7
	DisAlign [50]	69.0	71.1	70.2	70.6
	Ours	**72.8**	**71.7**	**70.0**	**71.0**

(90 and 200 training epochs), the learning rate is decayed by a cosine scheduler [27]. On iNaturalist2018 [39] dataset, we use ResNet-50 [46] as the feature extractor for all methods with 200 training epochs, with the same experimental parameters set for the other. By default, learnable κ for all categories are initialized as 16 and λ is 0.2. Moreover, we use the same basic data augmentation (i.e., random resize and crop to 224, random horizontal flip, color jitter, and normalization) for all methods.

Comparison with State of the Arts. In our paper, the comparison methods use single models. Note that there are also ensemble models for long-tailed classification, e.g., RIDE [42] and TADE [52]. For fair comparisons, following xERM [57], we will not include their results in the experiments. Table 2 shows the long-tailed results on ImageNet-LT. We adopt the performance data from the deep long-tailed survey [53] for various methods at 90 and 200 training epochs to make a fair comparison. Our approach achieves 53.7% and 55.0% in overall accuracy, which outperforms the state-of-the-art methods by a significant margin at 90 and 200 training epochs, respectively. Compared with representation learning methods, our method surpasses SSP by 0.6% (53.7% vs 53.1%) at 90 training epochs and outperforms SSP by 1.7% (55.0% vs 53.3%) at 200 training epochs. In addition, our method obtains higher performance by 1.0% (53.7% vs 52.7%) and 0.6% (55.0% vs 54.4%) comparing to PaCo at 90 and 200 training epochs, respectively. We observe that our vMF classifier (w/o proposed additional loss terms and post-training calibration algorithm) still achieves better performance than previous classifier design strategies, i.e., our vMF classifier surpasses τ-norm and TDE which by 2.6% (52.2% vs 49.6%) and 0.4% (52.2% vs 51.8%) at 90 epochs. Moreover, our vMF classifier performs better when training 200 epochs than 90 epochs (53.4% vs 52.2%), in contrast to TDE (51.3% vs 51.8%). This shows that our vMF classifier has more potential to fit data better and learn better representations.

Table 4. Performance of semantic segmentation on ADE20K and instance segmentation on LVIS-v1.0. R-50 and R-101 denote ResNet-50 and ResNet-101, respectively. 'Cascade-R101' is for Cascade Mask R-CNN [1].

Model	Method	ADE20K		Model	Method	LVIS-v1.0	
		mIoU	mAcc			AP	AP_b
OCRNet	Baseline	40.8	50.9	Cascade (R101)	Cross-Entropy	22.6	25.2
(HRNet-W18)	**Ours**	**41.5**	**52.9**		De-confound [38]	23.5	25.8
DeepLabV3+	Baseline	44.9	55.0		TDE [38]	27.1	30.0
(R-50)	DisAlign [50]	45.7	**57.3**		EQL v2 [35]	28.8	32.3
	Ours	**45.9**	57.0		DisAlign [50]	28.9	32.7
DeepLabV3+	Baseline	46.4	56.7		BAGS [22]	27.9	31.5
(R-101)	DisAlign [50]	47.1	59.5		Seesaw Loss [40]	29.6	32.5
	Ours	**47.2**	**59.8**		**Ours**	**29.8**	**32.9**

Furthermore, Table 3 presents the experimental results on the naturally-skewed dataset iNaturalist2018. Compared with the improvement brought by representation learning and classifier design approaches, our method achieves competitive result (71.0%) consistently.

4.2 Long-Tailed Semantic and Instance Segmentation Task

To further validate our method, we conduct comprehensive experiments on the semantic and instance segmentation datasets, i.e., ADE20K [55] and LVIS-v1.0 [9].

Dataset and Setup

- ADE20K is a scene parsing dataset covering 150 fine-grained semantic concepts and it is one of the most challenging semantic segmentation datasets. The training set contains 20,210 images with 150 semantic classes. The validation and test set contain 2,000 and 3,352 images respectively.
- LVIS-v1.0 contains 1230 categories with both bounding box and instance mask annotations. LVIS-v1.0 divides all categories into 3 groups based on the number of images that contain those categories: frequent (>100 images), common (11–100 images) and rare (<10 images). We train the models with 57K train images and report the accuracy on 5K val images.

Experimental Details. We evaluate our method using two wide-adopted segmentation models (OCRNet [49] and DeepLabV3+ [4]) based on different backbone networks. We initialize the backbones using the models pre-trained on ImageNet [6] and the framework randomly. All models are trained with an image

Table 5. Ablation on our proposed two loss terms and the loss weight λ. 'None' indicates only the performance loss term is applied to train model. '0.1' means λ is set as 0.1.

Additional Loss	All	Many	Med.	Few
Baseline	51.8	62.6	48.9	31.3
None	52.2	64.2	49.8	26.9
0.2, $\mathcal{L}_{icd}$	52.9	64.2	49.8	31.7
0.2, $\mathcal{L}_{cfc}$	53.1	65.3	50.4	27.9
0.2, $\mathcal{L}_{icd}$, $\mathcal{L}_{cfc}$	**53.5**	**65.4**	**50.8**	**29.1**
0.1, $\mathcal{L}_{icd}$, $\mathcal{L}_{cfc}$	53.2	65.0	50.7	27.9
0.4, $\mathcal{L}_{icd}$, $\mathcal{L}_{cfc}$	52.6	64.9	50.1	26.8
0.3, $\mathcal{L}_{icd}$, $\mathcal{L}_{cfc}$	53.2	65.1	50.8	28.0

Table 6. Ablation on the hyper-parameter α of post-training calibration algorithm with different classifiers. ‡ indicates the corresponding classifier is calibrated under the optimal α.

$\mathcal{K}$	All	Many	Med.	Few
Linear	43.2	66.2	35.4	6.0
Linear ‡	48.3	60.9	46.4	19.9
τ-norm [16]	48.6	69.9	42.5	10.1
τ-norm [16] ‡	53.0	66.5	50.2	24.1
Causal [38]	49.0	69.6	43.0	12.2
Causal [38] ‡	50.9	69.0	45.8	17.5
Ours	53.5	65.4	50.8	29.1
Ours ‡	**53.7**	**63.9**	**51.5**	**32.4**

size of 512×512 and 160K iterations in total. We train the models using Adam optimizer with the initial learning rate 0.01, weight decay 0.0005 and momentum 0.9. Furthermore, We implement our method on LVIS-v1.0 with mmdetection [3] and train Mask R-CNN [12] with random sampler by 2x training schedule. The model is trained with batch size of 16 for 24 epochs. The optimizer is SGD with momentum 0.9 and weight decay 0.0001. The initial learning rate is 0.02 with 500 iterations' warm up. For above two tasks, we set the optimal configuration in our experiments that is all learnable $\mathcal{K}$ are initialized to 16.

Comparison with State of the Arts. For the semantic segmentation task, The numerical results and comparison with other peer methods are reported in left part of Table 4. Our method achieves 0.7% (41.5% vs 40.8%) improvement in mIoU using OCRNet with HRNet-W18. Moreover, our method outperforms the baseline with large at 1.0% (45.9% vs 44.9%) in mIoU using DeeplabV3+ with ResNet-50 when the iteration is 160K. Even with a stronger backbone: ResNet-101, our method also achieves 0.8% (47.2% vs 46.4%) mIoU improvement than baseline. For the instance segmentation task, we report quantitative results and compare our method with recent work in the right part of Table 3. Our method can achieve 29.8% in AP and 32.9% in AP_b when applied to the Cascade-R101. Apart from the CE loss baseline, we further compare our method with recent designs for long-tailed instance segmentation. Our method surpasses Seesaw Loss by 0.2% (29.8% vs 29.6%) AP, and surpasses DisAlign by 0.9% (29.8% vs 28.9%) AP, which reveals the effectiveness of our method (Table 6).

4.3   Ablation Study

We conduct ablation study on ImageNet-LT dataset to further understand the hyper-parameters of our methods and the effect of each proposed component.

Ablation Study on Two Additional Loss Terms and the Loss Weight λ. Firstly, we evaluate the effectiveness of the proposed $\mathcal{L}_{icd}$ and $\mathcal{L}_{cfc}$. Setting $\lambda = 0.2$ and initializing $\kappa = 16$, we train vMF classifier w/o additional loss terms, w/ $\mathcal{L}_{icd}$, w/ $\mathcal{L}_{cfc}$ and w/ both of them, respectively. Experimental results are reported in Row 1–4 of Table 5. Our baseline is the balanced cosine classifier [32]. Conclusions are **(1)**. Giving additional surveillance via $\mathcal{L}_{icd}$ is beneficial to the performance on tail classes. It can be seen from the second and third rows in the Table 5. The performance of the tail of the loss term has been greatly improved (26.9% vs 31.7%). **(2)**. $\mathcal{L}_{cfc}$ gains the non-trival performance improvements on all classes. **(3)**. Simultaneously adopting the above two loss terms further improves the accuracy by 1.3%, further widening the performance gap up to 1.7% compared with the baseline. Secondly, we conduct four experiments on different λ. Row 5–8 of Table 5 show $\lambda = 0.2$ is the optimal setting.

Ablation Study on Post-calibration Algorithm with Different Classifier To verify the versatility of our post-training calibration algorithm, we perform it on our vMF, linear, τ-norm ($\tau = 0.7$, optimal setting in [16]) and causal [38] classifiers, following Sect. 3.4. All of them have trained on ImageNet-LT with ResNetXt-50. We set the hyper-parameter α in the interval 0 to 1 with a stride of 0.1 and take the eleven sets of values to conduct ablation experiments on above classifiers. For linear classifier, the optimal $\alpha = 0.7$, where our algorithm improves allover accuracy performance by 5.1%. For τ-norm classifier and causal classifier, under the optimal $\alpha = 0.1$, the allover accuracy is improved by 4.4% and 1.9%. When $\alpha = 0.2$, our vMF classifier achieves highest accuracy 53.7%. The reason for slight improvement on ours may be because it has already learned with proposed loss terms ($\mathcal{L}_{cfc}$ and $\mathcal{L}_{icd}$) that are also based on distribution overlap coefficient.

5   Conclusions

In this paper, we extend cosine-based classifiers as a vMF distribution mixture model on hyper-sphere, denoted as the vMF classifier. Benefiting from the representation space constructed by the vMF classifier, we define the distribution overlap coefficient to measure the representation quality for features and classifiers. Based on distribution overlap coefficient, we formulate the inter-class discrepancy and class-feature consistency loss terms to alleviate the interference among the classifier weights and align features with classifier weights. Furthermore, we develop a novel post-training calibration algorithm to zero-costly boost the performance. Our method outperforms previous work with a large margin and achieves state-of-the-art performance on long-tailed image classification, semantic segmentation, and instance segmentation tasks.

Acknowledgments. This work is supported by the National Natural Science Foundation of China (U21B2004), the Zhejiang Provincial key RD Program of China (2021C01119) , and the Zhejiang University-Angelalign Inc. R & D Center for Intelligent Healthcare.

References

1. Cai, Z., Vasconcelos, N.: Cascade r-cnn: high quality object detection and instance segmentation. IEEE Trans. Pattern Anal. Mach. Intell. **43**(5), 1483–1498 (2019)
2. Cao, K., Wei, C., Gaidon, A., Arechiga, N., Ma, T.: Learning imbalanced datasets with label-distribution-aware margin loss. Adv. Neural Inf. Process. Syst. **32** (2019)
3. Chen, K., et al.: Mmdetection: open mmlab detection toolbox and benchmark. arXiv preprint arXiv:1906.07155 (2019)
4. Chen, L.C., Zhu, Y., Papandreou, G., Schroff, F., Adam, H.: Encoder-decoder with atrous separable convolution for semantic image segmentation. In: Proceedings of the European Conference on Computer Vision (ECCV), pp. 801–818 (2018)
5. Cui, J., Zhong, Z., Liu, S., Yu, B., Jia, J.: Parametric contrastive learning (2021)
6. Deng, J., Dong, W., Socher, R., Li, L.J., Li, K., Fei-Fei, L.: Imagenet: a large-scale hierarchical image database. In: 2009 IEEE Conference on Computer Vision and Pattern Recognition, pp. 248–255 (2009)
7. Dhaker, H., Ngom, P., Mbodj, M.: Overlap coefficients based on kullback-leibler divergence: exponential populations case. Int. J. Appl. Math. Res. **6**(4) (2017)
8. Diethe, T.: A note on the kullback-leibler divergence for the von mises-fisher distribution. arXiv preprint arXiv:1502.07104 (2015)
9. Gupta, A., Dollar, P., Girshick, R.: Lvis: a dataset for large vocabulary instance segmentation. In: Proceedings of the IEEE/CVF Conference on Computer Vision and Pattern Recognition, pp. 5356–5364 (2019)
10. Hasnat, M., Bohné, J., Milgram, J., Gentric, S., Chen, L., et al.: von mises-fisher mixture model-based deep learning: application to face verification. arXiv preprint arXiv:1706.04264 (2017)
11. He, K., Fan, H., Wu, Y., Xie, S., Girshick, R.: Momentum contrast for unsupervised visual representation learning. In: Proceedings of the IEEE/CVF Conference on Computer Vision and Pattern Recognition, pp. 9729–9738 (2020)
12. He, K., Gkioxari, G., Dollár, P., Girshick, R.: Mask r-cnn. In: Proceedings of the IEEE International Conference on Computer Vision, pp. 2961–2969 (2017)
13. Hong, Y., Han, S., Choi, K., Seo, S., Kim, B., Chang, B.: Disentangling label distribution for long-tailed visual recognition. In: Proceedings of the IEEE/CVF Conference on Computer Vision and Pattern Recognition, pp. 6626–6636 (2021)

14. Huang, C., Li, Y., Loy, C.C., Tang, X.: Learning deep representation for imbalanced classification. In: Proceedings of the IEEE Conference on Computer Vision and Pattern Recognition, pp. 5375–5384 (2016)
15. Jupp, P.E., Mardia, K.V.: Maximum likelihood estimators for the matrix von mises-fisher and bingham distributions. Ann. Stat. **7**(3), 599–606 (1979)
16. Kang, B., et al.: Decoupling representation and classifier for long-tailed recognition (2019)
17. Kang, B., Li, Y., Xie, S., Yuan, Z., Feng, J.: Exploring balanced feature spaces for representation learning. In: International Conference on Learning Representations (2021)
18. Kent, J.: Some probabilistic properties of bessel functions. Ann. Probabil., 760–770 (1978)
19. Kobayashi, T.: t-vmf similarity for regularizing intra-class feature distribution. In: 2021 IEEE/CVF Conference on Computer Vision and Pattern Recognition (CVPR), pp. 6612–6621 (2021)
20. Li, S., Xu, J., Xu, X., Shen, P., Li, S., Hooi, B.: Spherical confidence learning for face recognition. In: Proceedings of the IEEE/CVF Conference on Computer Vision and Pattern Recognition, pp. 15629–15637 (2021)
21. Li, T., et al.: Targeted supervised contrastive learning for long-tailed recognition. In: Proceedings of the IEEE/CVF Conference on Computer Vision and Pattern Recognition, pp. 6918–6928 (2022)
22. Li, Y., et al.: Overcoming classifier imbalance for long-tail object detection with balanced group softmax. In: Proceedings of the IEEE/CVF Conference on Computer Vision and Pattern Recognition, pp. 10991–11000 (2020)
23. Lin, T.Y., Goyal, P., Girshick, R., He, K., Dollár, P.: Focal loss for dense object detection. In: Proceedings of the IEEE International Conference on Computer Vision, pp. 2980–2988 (2017)
24. Liu, B., Li, H., Kang, H., Hua, G., Vasconcelos, N.: Gistnet: a geometric structure transfer network for long-tailed recognition. In: Proceedings of the IEEE/CVF International Conference on Computer Vision, pp. 8209–8218 (2021)
25. Liu, Z., Miao, Z., Zhan, X., Wang, J., Gong, B., Yu, S.X.: Large-scale long-tailed recognition in an open world. In: IEEE Conference on Computer Vision and Pattern Recognition (CVPR) (2019)
26. Liu, Z., Miao, Z., Zhan, X., Wang, J., Gong, B., Yu, S.X.: Large-scale long-tailed recognition in an open world. In: Proceedings of the IEEE/CVF Conference on Computer Vision and Pattern Recognition, pp. 2537–2546 (2019)
27. Loshchilov, I., Hutter, F.: SGDR: stochastic gradient descent with warm restarts. arXiv preprint arXiv:1608.03983 (2016)
28. Mash'al, M., Hosseini, R.: K-means++ for mixtures of von mises-fisher distributions. In: 2015 7th Conference on Information and Knowledge Technology (IKT), pp. 1–6. IEEE (2015)
29. Nicholls, E., Stark, A.: Bayes' theorem. Med. J. Aust. **2**(26), 1335–1339 (1971)
30. Papadopoulos, C.I.: On the Kullback-Leibler information measure and statistical inference. Wayne State University (1971)
31. Peng, Z., Huang, W., Guo, Z., Zhang, X., Jiao, J., Ye, Q.: Long-tailed distribution adaptation. In: Proceedings of the 29th ACM International Conference on Multimedia, pp. 3275–3282 (2021)
32. Ren, J., Yu, C., Ma, X., Zhao, H., Yi, S., et al.: Balanced meta-softmax for long-tailed visual recognition. Adv. Neural Inf. Process. Syst. **33**, 4175–4186 (2020)

33. Romanazzi, M.: Discriminant analysis with high dimensional von mises-fisher distributions. In: 8th Annual International Conference on Statistics, pp. 1–16. Athens Institute for Education and Research (2014)
34. Samuel, D., Chechik, G.: Distributional robustness loss for long-tail learning. In: Proceedings of the IEEE/CVF International Conference on Computer Vision (ICCV) (2021)
35. Tan, J., Lu, X., Zhang, G., Yin, C., Li, Q.: Equalization loss v2: a new gradient balance approach for long-tailed object detection. In: Proceedings of the IEEE/CVF Conference on Computer Vision and Pattern Recognition, pp. 1685–1694 (2021)
36. Tan, J., et al.: Equalization loss for long-tailed object recognition. In: Proceedings of the IEEE/CVF Conference on Computer Vision and Pattern Recognition, pp. 11662–11671 (2020)
37. Tang, K., Huang, J., Zhang, H.: Long-tailed classification by keeping the good and removing the bad momentum causal effect. In: NeurIPS (2020)
38. Tang, K., Huang, J., Zhang, H.: Long-tailed classification by keeping the good and removing the bad momentum causal effect. Adv. Neural Inf. Process. Syst. **33**, 1513–1524 (2020)
39. Van Horn, G., et al.: The inaturalist species classification and detection dataset. In: Proceedings of the IEEE Conference on Computer Vision and Pattern Recognition, pp. 8769–8778 (2018)
40. Wang, J., et al.: Seesaw loss for long-tailed instance segmentation. In: Proceedings of the IEEE Conference on Computer Vision and Pattern Recognition (2021)
41. Wang, P., Han, K., Wei, X.S., Zhang, L., Wang, L.: Contrastive learning based hybrid networks for long-tailed image classification. In: Proceedings of the IEEE/CVF Conference on Computer Vision and Pattern Recognition, pp. 943–952 (2021)
42. Wang, X., Lian, L., Miao, Z., Liu, Z., Yu, S.: Long-tailed recognition by routing diverse distribution-aware experts. In: International Conference on Learning Representations (2021)
43. Weng, Z., Ogut, M.G., Limonchik, S., Yeung, S.: Unsupervised discovery of the long-tail in instance segmentation using hierarchical self-supervision. In: Proceedings of the IEEE/CVF Conference on Computer Vision and Pattern Recognition, pp. 2603–2612 (2021)
44. Wu, T., Liu, Z., Huang, Q., Wang, Y., Lin, D.: Adversarial robustness under long-tailed distribution (2021)
45. Wu, T.Y., Morgado, P., Wang, P., Ho, C.H., Vasconcelos, N.: Solving long-tailed recognition with deep realistic taxonomic classifier
46. Xie, S., Girshick, R., Dollár, P., Tu, Z., He, K.: Aggregated residual transformations for deep neural networks. arXiv preprint arXiv:1611.05431 (2016)
47. Yang, Y., Xu, Z.: Rethinking the value of labels for improving class-imbalanced learning. Adv. Neural Inf. Process. Syst. **33**, 19290–19301 (2020)
48. Ye, H.J., Chen, H.Y., Zhan, D.C., Chao, W.L.: Identifying and compensating for feature deviation in imbalanced deep learning (2020)
49. Yuan, Y., Wang, J.: Ocnet: object context network for scene parsing (2018)
50. Zhang, S., Li, Z., Yan, S., He, X., Sun, J.: Distribution alignment: a unified framework for long-tail visual recognition. In: Proceedings of the IEEE/CVF Conference on Computer Vision and Pattern Recognition, pp. 2361–2370 (2021)
51. Zhang, X., Fang, Z., Wen, Y., Li, Z., Qiao, Y.: Range loss for deep face recognition with long-tailed training data. In: Proceedings of the IEEE International Conference on Computer Vision, pp. 5409–5418 (2017)

52. Zhang, Y., Hooi, B., Hong, L., Feng, J.: Test-agnostic long-tailed recognition by test-time aggregating diverse experts with self-supervision. arXiv preprint arXiv:2107.09249 (2021)
53. Zhang, Y., Kang, B., Hooi, B., Yan, S., Feng, J.: Deep long-tailed learning: a survey. arXiv preprint arXiv:2110.04596 (2021)
54. Zhong, Z., Cui, J., Liu, S., Jia, J.: Improving calibration for long-tailed recognition. In: Proceedings of the IEEE/CVF Conference on Computer Vision and Pattern Recognition, pp. 16489–16498 (2021)
55. Zhou, B., Zhao, H., Puig, X., Fidler, S., Barriuso, A., Torralba, A.: Scene parsing through ade20k dataset. In: Proceedings of the IEEE Conference on Computer Vision and Pattern Recognition, pp. 633–641 (2017)
56. Zhou, B., Cui, Q., Wei, X.S., Chen, Z.M.: BBN: bilateral-branch network with cumulative learning for long-tailed visual recognition. In: Proceedings of the IEEE/CVF Conference on Computer Vision and Pattern Recognition, pp. 9719–9728 (2020)
57. Zhu, B., Niu, Y., Hua, X.S., Zhang, H.: Cross-domain empirical risk minimization for unbiased long-tailed classification. In: AAAI Conference on Artificial Intelligence (2022)
58. Zhu, L., Yang, Y.: Inflated episodic memory with region self-attention for long-tailed visual recognition. In: Proceedings of the IEEE/CVF Conference on Computer Vision and Pattern Recognition, pp. 4344–4353 (2020)

Dynamic Metric Learning
with Cross-Level Concept Distillation

Wenzhao Zheng[1,2], Yuanhui Huang[1,2], Borui Zhang[1,2], Jie Zhou[1,2],
and Jiwen Lu[1,2(✉)]

[1] Department of Automation, Tsinghua University, Beijing, China
{zhengwz18,huang-yh18,zhang-br21}@mails.tsinghua.edu.cn
[2] Beijing National Research Center for Information Science and Technology,
Beijing, China
{jzhou,lujiwen}@tsinghua.edu.cn

Abstract. A good similarity metric should be consistent with the
human perception of similarities: a sparrow is more similar to an owl
if compared to a dog but is more similar to a dog if compared to a car.
It depends on the semantic levels to determine if two images are from
the same class. As most existing metric learning methods push away
interclass samples and pull closer intraclass samples, it seems contradictory if the labels cross semantic levels. The core problem is that a
negative pair on a finer semantic level can be a positive pair on a coarser
semantic level, so pushing away this pair damages the class structure
on the coarser semantic level. We identify the negative repulsion as the
key obstacle in existing methods since a positive pair is always positive for coarser semantic levels but not for negative pairs. Our solution,
cross-level concept distillation (CLCD), is simple in concept: we only
pull closer positive pairs. To facilitate the cross-level semantic structure
of the image representations, we propose a hierarchical concept refiner
to construct multiple levels of concept embeddings of an image and then
pull closer the distance of the corresponding concepts. Extensive experiments demonstrate that the proposed CLCD method outperforms all
other competing methods on the hierarchically labeled datasets. Code is
available at: https://github.com/wzzheng/CLCD.

1 Introduction

Measuring the similarity between images is a crucial step in the field of computer vision. Modern methods use deep neural networks such as Convolutional
Neural Networks (CNNs) [22,43,48] or Vision Transformers (ViTs) [7,12,33] to
extract an embedding vector to represent an image for similarity computing. The
design of the model architecture is crucial, but how to train this model matters
equally. As a widely used learning paradigm, deep metric learning aims to learn

---

Supplementary Information The online version contains supplementary material
available at https://doi.org/10.1007/978-3-031-20053-3_12.

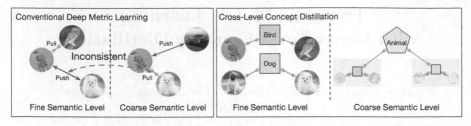

Fig. 1. The motivation of the proposed CLCD method. Conventional deep metric learning pulls closer samples from the same class and pushes away samples from different classes. This results in conflicts if we consider the class of images from different semantic levels. A pair image may be deemed dissimilar at a fine semantic level but similar at a coarse semantic level. To address this, we construct a hierarchy of concept embeddings and propose a CLCD method to distill higher-level concepts using the corresponding lower-level concepts. (Best viewed in color.)

a discriminative embedding by reducing the distance between samples from the same class and enlarging the distance between samples from different classes, which has benefited various tasks including image retrieval [13,30,38,45], face recognition [23,41], and person re-identification [5,42,51,66].

Humans perceive concepts in a hierarchical way. We first recognize a sparrow as an animal, then as a bird, and finally as an owl. When we consider the similarities between images, the result varies at different semantic levels. A sparrow is more similar to an owl when compared to a dog, but is more similar to a dog than to a car. Therefore, the objective of deep metric learning, pulling closer positive pairs and pushing away negative pairs, seems reasonable within a single semantic level, but conflicts emerge when considering multiple semantic levels, as shown in Fig. 1. The sparrow-dog pair should be pushed away in a fine semantic level but instead should be pulled closer in a coarse semantic level. Sun *et al.* [47] recently identified this issue and formulated the dynamic metric learning (DyML) problem, where an image is assigned three labels in the coarse, middle, and fine level, respectively. The goal is to retrieve the correct samples with the same labels in all three semantic levels. They also proposed a recipe for this problem by setting increasing similarity margins to separate the positive and negative pair in the fine, middle, and coarse levels. They need to manually set a fixed margin to separate concepts from different levels, leading to rigid concept scopes at each semantic level.

Our solution, on the other hand, is free of hand-crafted margins. Given that the conflicts result from the positive attraction and negative repulsion across different semantic levels, we propose to completely discard the latter for pure harmony. That is, we only pull closer positive pairs, which is simple in concept but non-trivial to implement. To put this into practice, we propose a cross-level concept distillation (CLCD) method, which simultaneously learns multiple-level concept embeddings to guide the training of the image embedding. Specifically, we employ a hierarchical concept refiner to extract multiple concepts corresponding to different semantic levels for each image. We represent each concept using an embedding vector with the same size as the image embedding and treat the image embedding as a concept of instance level. We propose a cross-level concept distillation method to pull closer the cross-level concepts of two images under the finest semantic level that they have the same label. The proposed CLCD avoids the cross-level conflict by only pulling closer positive samples and achieves discriminativeness by the hierarchical concept refining. We conduct extensive experiments on the three dynamic metric learning datasets: DyML-Animal, DyML-Vehicle, and DyML-Products [47], which show that our proposed CLCD achieves the best performance. We also demonstrate that a simple positive attraction loss in the proposed manner is effective to learn a discriminative embedding space and achieves comparable performance under the conventional deep metric learning setting on the widely-used CUB-200-2011 [50] dataset for image retrieval.

2   Related Work

Deep Metric Learning: Deep metric learning aims at learning a discriminative embedding space where intraclass distances are small and interclass distances are large. Existing methods achieve this by imposing different restrictions on the embedding space. A number of works directly constrain the distances between sample pairs [2,11,15,17,41,44,45,53,54,59]. For example, Schroff *et al.* [41] employed a triplet loss acting on three samples to enforce a margin on the distance between the positive pair and the negative pair. Sohn *et al.* [44] extended the triplet loss to an N-Pair loss which simultaneously constrains the relations between $N + 1$ samples from different classes. The vast number of combinations of samples causes the sampling of informative tuples to be an important component for deep metric learning. Some methods addressed this by using a carefully designed sampling strategy [16,21,24,41,57,60,62] or synthesis generation method [13,28,31,64,65], while other works reduced the sampling complexity by representing each class using proxies and instead restrict the relations between samples and proxies [9,11,27,32,34,39,52].

Most existing deep metric learning only consider the semantic similarity under a certain semantic level and a direct extension of existing methods leads to cross-level conflicts of pulling closer and pushing away the same pair of samples. Some methods [26,36,37] employ hyperbolic embeddings to effectively represent hierarchically structured data, yet they still cannot avoid the cross-level conflicts during training. This motivates Sun *et al.* [47] to formulate a dynamic metric learning task to consider the similarity measure under different semantic levels. They further proposed a Cross-Scale Learning (CSL) method to enforce increasing margins between the similarities between positive pairs and negative pairs for coarser and coarser semantic levels. They rely on manually set margins to differentiate concepts at different semantic levels. Differently, the proposed CLCD employs a hierarchical concept refiner to adaptively distill concepts by summarizing the corresponding lower-level concepts. In addition, SimSiam learns unsupervised image representations using only positive pairs. We demonstrate that only using positive attraction is also effective for supervised learning and further extend it to dynamic metric learning.

Hierarchical Image Classification: Another related area is the hierarchical image classification (HIC), which aims to predict the correct labels across different semantic levels for an image [10,14,19,55,58]. It can be seen as a special case for multi-task learning [4] if we regard the multiple classification problems as different tasks. Most methods perform this task during training in order to better leverage the hierarchical annotations provided by various datasets [8,29] to improve the performance on the finest-level classification. For example, Verma *et al.* [49] added coarse-level metric matrices to obtain fine-grained-level metric matrices for hierarchical classification. Dutt *et al.* [14] proposed a partially merged network architecture to jointly learn classifiers at different semantic levels and employed a probability adjustment procedure to improve the performance. Yan *et al.* [58] designed a hierarchical deep convolutional neural network to complete the coarse and fine classification task progressively.

The task of hierarchical image classification is essentially different from dynamic metric learning. While HIC only requires the model to correctly predict the labels of different semantic levels, DyML further requires the model to obtain a single representation for an image so that it can properly reflect the similarities between images across semantic levels.

3   Proposed Approach

In this section, we first formulate the problem of dynamic metric learning and identify the cross-level conflicts caused by existing methods. We then present the proposed hierarchical concept refiner and cross-level concept distillation method as the two main components of our CLCD method.

3.1   Dynamic Metric Learning

For a set of images $\mathbf{X} = \{\mathbf{x}_1, \mathbf{x}_2, \cdots, \mathbf{x}_N\}$, conventional metric learning only assumes a single label l_i for each image $\mathbf{x}_i$. Deep metric learning employs a deep network to obtain an n-dimentsion embedding $\mathbf{y} \in \mathbb{R}^d$ and then imposes discriminative constraints on the Euclidean distances between image embeddings:

$$\begin{cases} \text{Positive attraction (PA): } \min d(\mathbf{y}_i, \mathbf{y}_j), & \text{if } l_i = l_j, \\ \text{Negative repulsion (NR): } \max d(\mathbf{y}_i, \mathbf{y}_j), & \text{if } l_i \neq l_j, \end{cases} \tag{1}$$

where $d(\cdot, \cdot)$ denotes the Euclidean distance.

This seems reasonable for images with a single label, but what if an image is assigned multiple hierarchical labels at different semantic levels? This is common in reality, for example, a Ferrari can be classified as a car or a vehicle if we consider it at different semantic levels. Considering this, Sun *et al.* [47] formulates the dynamic metric learning (DyML) problem, aiming at learning an embedding space where images can be correctly retrieved across multiple semantic labels.

Formally, each image $\mathbf{x}_i$ is assigned a label set of K labels $\{l_i^1, \cdots, l_i^K\}$, where K is the number of the concerned semantic levels. We further assume a hierarchical structure in each label set, i.e., the coarser-level labels of two images are always the same if they share a label at a certain level:

$$l_i^k = l_j^k, \quad \forall k > t, \quad \text{if} \ \exists \ l_i^t = l_j^t. \tag{2}$$

This is reasonable since a coarse concept (e.g., animal) should include the fine concepts (e.g., bird, dog). We can then define the finest semantic level $\alpha(\mathbf{x}_i, \mathbf{x}_j)$ where two images share the same label:

$$\alpha(\mathbf{x}_i, \mathbf{x}_j) = \begin{cases} \arg\min_k (l_i^k = l_j^k), & \text{if} \ \exists \ l_i^k = l_j^k, \\ K+1, & \text{if} \ l_i \neq l_j \ \forall \ k, \end{cases} \tag{3}$$

The objective of DyML can be then formulated as:

$$d(\mathbf{y}_a, \mathbf{y}_p) < d(\mathbf{y}_a, \mathbf{y}_n), \quad \text{if} \ \alpha(\mathbf{x}_a, \mathbf{x}_p) < \alpha(\mathbf{x}_a, \mathbf{x}_n). \tag{4}$$

Despite the hierarchical structure of each label set, it is still possible for two images to have different fine-level labels but share a coarse-level label, i.e., $l_i^s \neq l_j^s$ but $l_i^t = l_j^t$ if $s < t$. Therefore, directly extending the objective of conventional deep metric learning (1) to multiple semantic levels would cause the NR under a fine level to be contradictory to the PA under a coarse level, rendering the learning process less effective.

To address this, Sun et al. [47] present a recipe by enforcing different margins between for negative pairs at different semantic levels:

$$d(\mathbf{y}_a, \mathbf{y}_p) + m(\alpha(\mathbf{x}_a, \mathbf{x}_n)) \leq d(\mathbf{y}_a, \mathbf{y}_n), \tag{5}$$

where $\alpha(\mathbf{x}_a, \mathbf{x}_p) = 1$, and $m(\cdot)$ is a positive monotonically increasing function.

Intuitively, it requires the dissimilar pairs at coarser levels to be separated with a larger margin. However, it requires a manual setting of the margins and enforces a handcrafted prior on the distances between concepts. Our solution is, on the other hand, free of margins: we only pull closer positive pairs.

3.2 Hierarchical Concept Refiner

To address the cross-level positive attraction and negative repulsion conflict dilemma, we propose an alternative solution to completely discard the negative repulsion at all layers. However, directly pulling closer positive pairs without the regularization of the reverse effect of negative repulsion, the trained model will quickly collapse to a trivial model that represents all images in a single point in the embedding space.

To avoid this, we propose to instead restrict the distances between concepts, where each concept corresponds to a label as well as a semantic level. We represent each concept using a vector $\mathbf{c}$ called the concept embedding. As each image is assigned a set of labels with a hierarchy structure, we propose a hierarchical concept refiner R to distill concepts directly from images, as shown in Fig. 2. The refiner R takes as input the image embedding $\mathbf{y}$ and outputs a set of concepts corresponding to each semantic level:

$$R(\mathbf{y}) = \{\mathbf{c}^0, \mathbf{c}^1, \mathbf{c}^2, \cdots, \mathbf{c}^K\}, \tag{6}$$

where $\mathbf{c} \in \mathbb{R}^n$ has the same dimension with the image embedding $\mathbf{y}$. For convenience, we also regard the image (and possibly its variants with different data augmentations) as a concept at the finest semantic level, i.e., $\mathbf{c}^0 = \mathbf{y}$.

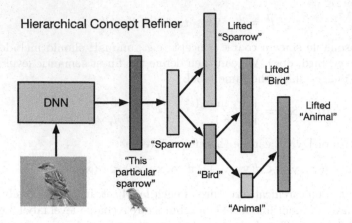

Fig. 2. Illustration of the proposed hierarchical concept refiner. For each image, we first use a deep neural network to obtain an image embedding and then employ a series of encoders to refine a hierarchy of meta-concept embeddings with decreasing dimensions. Finally, we use a set of decoders to map the meta-embeddings to the image embedding space for the sake of direct comparison. (Best viewed in color.)

Considering the hierarchical structure of labels, we design the refiner R accordingly in a hierarchical manner. Since a coarse concept may correspond to multiple concepts at a finer level, we refine the concepts progressively from fine level to coarse level. That is, we first discard certain information to purify an image to a fine concept, and then discard more information to purify the fine concept to a more coarse concept. We continue this process until we obtain a pure coarsest concept. For example, for an image of a sparrow, we first discard the sparrow-specific information to obtain the concept "bird", and then further discard the bird-specific information to obtain the concept "animal". On the other hand, we can add certain information to specify an "animal" concept to a "bird", and further specify it to a "sparrow".

Formally, we employ a series of fully connected layers with decreasing output dimensions to obtain a meta-concept embedding $\widetilde{\mathbf{c}}^i$ at each semantic level.

$$\begin{cases} \widetilde{\mathbf{c}}^0 = \mathbf{c}^0 = \mathbf{y} \in \mathbb{R}^n, \\ E_i(\widetilde{\mathbf{c}}^k) = \widetilde{\mathbf{c}}^{k+1} \in \mathbb{R}^{\beta(k+1)}, \quad k = 0, 1, \cdots, K-1, \end{cases} \tag{7}$$

where $\beta(\cdot)$ is a monotonically decreasingly function. We use $\beta(k) = \frac{n}{2^k}$ in this work, but other choices are also possible.

To enable direct comparison between concepts, we use a set of decoders to map the meta-concept embedding back to the n-dimension embedding space:

$$D_i(\widetilde{\mathbf{c}}^k) = \mathbf{c}^k \in \mathbb{R}^n, \quad k = 1, 2, \cdots, K. \tag{8}$$

Since we do not provide additional specific information to the decoders, the decoders only interpret a concept in a larger space but do not specify a concept to a finer one.

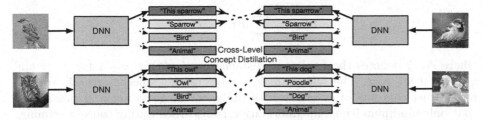

Fig. 3. The framework of the proposed CLCD method. We learn each concept by distilling information from its affiliated lower-level concepts. Having obtained the set of hierarchical concept embeddings for each image, we constrain the distance between the lower-level concept of one image and the higher-level concept of another image if they are from the same class at the higher semantic level. (Best viewed in color.)

Using the proposed hierarchical concept refiner, we can predict the concepts of an image at different semantic levels and represent them in the same space for further relational constraints.

3.3 Cross-Level Concept Distillation

The hierarchical design of the proposed concept refiner naturally constrain finer-level coarser-level concepts to contain less information and thereby to be more general, but how to learn each concept embedding remains challenging.

A straightforward way is to pull closer the distance between the corresponding positive concept embeddings at the same semantic level:

$$L_{naive} = d(\mathbf{c}_i^k, \mathbf{c}_j^k), \quad \text{if} \quad l_i^k = l_j^k. \tag{9}$$

However, the learning process in this way is only aware of same-level concepts and unaware of the lower-level concepts. The concept refiner is then able to bypass the distillation of lower-level concepts and only enforces relations between same-level concepts, ignoring the cross-level concept hierarchically structural relations.

Instead, we think that the formation of a concept requires examining a set of lower-level concepts and then summarizing their common grounds. For example, the "bird" concept should be able to access all the affiliated finer concepts such as "sparrow", "owl", and "pigeon", and then be distilled as a "bird" concept.

Motivated by this, we propose cross-level concept distillation to constrain the relations between cross-level concepts to learn the hierarchical concept refiner, as shown in Fig. 3. We further propose two strategies to refine the concept: adjacent concept refining (ACR) and instance-based concept refining (ICR). For ACR, we distill a higher-level concept by considering the corresponding adjacent level concepts. For ICR, we distill a high-level concept from all the corresponding instances that share this concept. Both strategies exploit the cross-level concept relations to distill new concepts, which only differ in extracting concepts from already constructed concepts or directly from instances.

For both strategies, we impose two constraints to learn the concept refiner. The first self-aware loss requires the multi-level concept embeddings of an image to reconstruct its lower-level concept embedding:

$$L_{self} = \sum_{k=1}^{K} d(\mathbf{c}^{\gamma(k)}, \mathbf{c}^k), \tag{10}$$

where $d(\cdot, \cdot)$ denotes the Euclidean distance,, and $\gamma(k) = k - 1$ for ACR and $\gamma(k) = 0$ for ICR. The self-aware loss requires the concept of each level to reconstruct concepts of lower levels of the same image as much as possible so that only minimum irrelevant information is discarded during concept refining.

The self-aware loss alone is not enough to distill a concept, since we need to discard more information to construct a higher-level concept. Therefore, we further employ an inter-distillation loss to force a concept to only preserve the common knowledge that defines itself. We reduce the distance between the cross-level concepts of two images if they share the same label at a certain level:

$$L_{inter} = \sum_{j:\alpha(\mathbf{x}_i, \mathbf{x}_j) = k} d(\mathbf{c}_i^{\gamma(k)}, \mathbf{c}_j^k) + d(\mathbf{c}_i^k, \mathbf{c}_j^{\gamma(k)}). \tag{11}$$

The inter-distillation loss encourage each concept to discard more information to purify irrelevant knowledge, while the self-aware loss constrains each concept to preserve the instance information as much as possible. The two losses enforce the concept refiner to extract the most relevant information that defines a concept.

The abandonment of negative repulsion avoids the cross-level conflicts, but the absence of a counter-force could easily cause the model to collapse, bringing challenges to the optimization process. Motivated by the stop-gradient technique employed in a number of self-supervised methods [3,6,18], we detach the lower-level concept embeddings in the loss and only use them as targets: The overall objective of the CLCD can be formulated as:

$$
\begin{aligned}
L &= L_{self} + L_{inter}, \\
&= \sum_{k=1}^{K} d(\text{detach}(\mathbf{c}^{\gamma(k)}), \mathbf{c}^k) + \sum_{j:\alpha(\mathbf{x}_i, \mathbf{x}_j) = k} (d(\text{detach}(\mathbf{c}_i^{\gamma(k)}), \mathbf{c}_j^k) + d(\text{detach}(\mathbf{c}_i^k), \mathbf{c}_j^{\gamma(k)})), \tag{12}
\end{aligned}
$$

where $\text{detach}(x)$ denotes the detach operation where the gradients do not pass through x during back-propagation.

Our CLCD refines the multi-level concepts progressively in a hierarchical way and employs a cross-level distillation method to learn the concepts. The concepts at all semantic levels are learned jointly to preserve the hierarchical structure of the labels, which implicitly constrain the image embedding to share similar hierarchical distances with other semantically varied images.

3.4   Discussions

The Preventing of Collapsing: Why using a stop-gradient operation can prevent collapsing remains a mystery in the literature [3,6,18]. One hypothesis is that the stop-gradient operation transforms the optimization into an implicit alternating optimization between two sets of variables. Applying the stop-gradient to the lower-level concept in our case converts it into a fixed target during each iteration, where the targets are probably different for different concepts thanks to the curse of dimensionality [1]. See Chen *et al.* [6] for more details.

Adaptive Learning of the Concept Scope: Though our method does not explicitly push away negative pairs of concepts, the distances between negative pairs are naturally increased due to the clustering of intraclass concepts. Existing methods manually set a margin to control the scope of each concept. We argue that different concepts may occupy regions with different areas in the embedding space. For example, even at the same semantic level, the concept "animal" contains more diverse lower-level concepts than the concept "vehicle", and thus should spread out more. The proposed CLCD method adaptively learns the scope for each concept by using the cross-level concept distillation to train the concept encoders and decoders. The more diverse concepts are more difficult to compress, thereby being encoded to a larger area in order for the decoder to (attempt to) reconstruct the lower-level concepts.

Sampling of Mini-batches: The proposed inter-distillation loss (11) acts on pairs of positive concepts at multiple semantic levels, yet the number of negative pairs is far larger than that of the positive pairs, bringing challenges to the sampling process. To achieve balanced learning of all concepts, we employ a hierarchical sampling strategy to guarantee the existence of positive pairs across all the semantic levels. To sample a mini-batch of B images with a label set of K levels, we first sample $\frac{B}{2^K}$ K-level labels, and then for each k-level label, we randomly select two $(k-1)$-level labels until reaching the first (finest) level, where we sample two images.

4   Experiments

In this section, we conduct extensive experiments to evaluate the performance of the proposed CLCD method on the dynamic metric learning task, which aims to learn a versatile similarity metric that is able to perform well across different semantic sales. We demonstrate that using a simple positive attraction loss under our framework achieves comparable performance on the conventional deep metric learning setting. We additional provide an in-depth experimental analysis to demonstrate the effectiveness of our framework.

4.1   Datasets

We follow existing work to conduct experiments on the three dynamic metric learning datasets: DyML-Vehicle, DyML-Animal, and DyML-Product [47]. The images in each dataset are labeled with three hierarchical labels corresponding to three semantic scales (i.e., coarse, middle, and fine). We follow existing work to perform the dataset split for fair comparisons. Specifically, the class labels for the coarse scale on the training and test split have a low intersection, while the training and test labels are disjoint for the middle and fine scale. We detail the dataset setting in the supplementary material.

4.2 Evaluation Protocol

To evaluate the performance of the learned metric across all the semantic levels, we first test the performance under each semantic level and then compute the average of all levels. Specifically, we adopt the widely used Recall@Ks and mean Average Precision (mAP) for the image retrieval tasks under each level. The recall@Ks compute the percentage of images in the query set that has at least one correct retrieved sample with the sample label from the K nearest neighbors in the gallery set. The mAP first computes the average precision score for each correct retrieved sample for a ranked list in the query set and then takes the mean across all the samples in the query set. Note we omit the average set intersection (ASI) metric used in the original paper [47] as the computing requires the ground truth ranking list of each image which is not provided in the datasets.

4.3 Implementation Details

We conducted all the experiments using the PyTorch package. We followed Sun *et al.* [47] to adopt the ResNet-34 as the backbone CNN model, where uses the ImageNet-1K [40] pretrained weights on the DyML-Vehicle and DyML-Product datasets and randomly initialized weights on the DyML-Animal dataset. Following the backbone CNN, we added an adaptive max pooling layer a randomly initialized fully connected layer to obtain a 512-dimension image embedding, and set the concept embedding sizes to 256, 128, and 64 for the fine, middle, and coarse semantic levels, respectively. We then added an L2-normalization layer after each image embedding and concept embedding before distance computation. We normalized all the images to 256×256 as inputs to the CNN model. For training, we performed data augmentation to images with random cropping to 227×227 and random horizontal mirror with a possibility of 0.5. We set the learning rate to 10^{-5} for the backbone CNN, 10^{-4} for the following fully connected layer, and 10^{-2} for the encoders and decoders. We only use the refiner and the multi-level concepts during training and simply use the image representation $\mathbf{y}$ from the backbone during evaluation. The multi-level concepts serve as targets to train the image representation and are discarded after training.

4.4 Main Results

We compare our CLCD with all the methods provided by the dynamic metric learning benchmark [47] as shown in Table 1, including the cross-level deep metric learning method CSL [47], conventional deep metric learning methods (the triplet loss [41], the Multi-Sim loss [54], and the N-Pair loss [44]), and classification methods (the softmax loss, CosFace [52], and the circle loss [46]).

Table 1. Experimental results (%) of the proposed CLCD method compared with existing methods on the DyML task.

	DyML-Vehicle				DyML-Animal				DyML-Product			
	mAP	R@1	R@10	R@20	mAP	R@1	R@10	R@20	mAP	R@1	R@10	R@20
Triplet	10.0	13.8	52.6	65.1	11.0	18.2	55.5	66.3	9.3	11.2	43.6	53.3
Multi-Sim	10.4	17.4	56.0	67.9	11.6	16.7	53.5	64.8	10.0	12.7	45.7	56.4
N-Pair	10.5	16.4	55.7	68.1	30.3	39.6	69.6	78.8	15.3	20.3	55.5	65.6
Softmax	12.0	22.9	61.6	72.9	25.8	49.6	81.7	88.8	26.1	50.2	81.6	87.7
Cosface	12.0	22.9	62.1	73.4	28.4	45.1	75.7	83.3	25.0	49.3	81.3	87.7
Circle	12.1	23.5	62.0	73.3	30.6	41.5	72.2	80.3	15.0	26.7	61.5	70.3
CSL	12.1	25.2	64.2	75.0	31.0	52.3	81.7	88.3	28.7	54.3	83.1	89.4
CLCD-ACR	16.0	42.9	74.0	84.1	**36.0**	**57.1**	**85.2**	**90.1**	29.4	58.8	86.2	90.7
CLCD-ICR	**16.6**	**43.7**	**75.4**	**86.3**	35.7	56.0	84.8	89.7	**30.2**	**59.5**	**87.1**	**92.1**

Table 2. Experimental results using pretrained weights on the DyML-Animal dataset.

Methods	mAP	R@1	R@10	R@20
CLCD-ACR pretrained	55.1	83.0	96.8	98.6
CLCD-ICR pretrained	**55.4**	**83.3**	**97.0**	**98.7**

We see that the proposed method achieves the best performance on all three DyML datasets without negative repulsion. This is because our CLCD only imposes positive attraction on the concepts from different semantic levels, which avoids the cross-level conflicts and is able to adaptively learn the concept scope at each semantic level. Also, we observe that the ICR strategy for concept distillation attains better performance on the DyML-Vehicle and DyML-Product datasets but lower performance on the DyML-Animal dataset.

4.5   Experimental Analysis

Analysis of ACR and ICR: We first studied why ICR performs worse than ACR on DyML-Animal but better on DyML-Vehicle and DyML-Product. The hypothesized factor is whether to use pre-trained weights, as we followed the benchmark setting to use randomly initialized weights on DyML-Animal. We thus conducted an experiment to also use pre-trained weights on DyML-Animal, as shown in Table 2. We see that ICR outperforms ACR in this case, which is the same to the results on the other datasets.

Performance Analysis at Different Semantic Levels: To further analyze the effectiveness of our method, we present the results of the proposed CLCD-ICR on each semantic level compared with CosFace [52] and CSL [47], as shown in Table 3. We see that despite achieving better overall performance, our method does not perform the best on all the semantic levels. Specifically, the CSL method

Table 3. Experimental results (%) at all the semantic levels of the proposed CLCD method compared with existing methods.

Method	Level	DyML-Vehicle		DyML-Animal		DyML-Product	
		mAP	R@1	mAP	R@1	mAP	R@1
Cosface	Fine	–	–	8.7	18.3	11.1	20.3
	Middle	–	–	28.4	46.6	16.9	47.6
	Coarse	–	–	48.2	70.5	47.1	80.0
	Overall	–	–	28.4	45.1	25.0	49.3
CSL	Fine	–	–	10.3	25.3	15.6	26.2
	Middle	–	–	30.1	53.9	20.1	53.2
	Coarse	–	–	52.7	77.7	50.4	83.7
	Overall	–	–	31.0	52.3	28.7	54.3
CLCD	Fine	3.8	12.6	13.8	28.9	13.9	29.4
	Middle	10.5	30.7	35.6	59.0	22.4	59.2
	Coarse	35.6	75.3	57.7	80.1	54.2	89.8
	Overall	16.6	43.7	35.7	56.0	30.2	59.5

Table 4. Comparisons of whether to use negative repulsion on DyML-Product.

Method	Fine level		Middle level		Coarse level		Overall	
	mAP	R@1	mAP	R@1	mAP	R@1	mAP	R@1
CLCD w/ NP	**16.2**	**27.5**	19.7	51.8	52.1	86.9	29.3	55.4
CLCD	13.9	29.4	**22.4**	**59.2**	**54.2**	**89.8**	**30.2**	**59.5**

outperforms our method at the fine level on the DyML-Product dataset, while our method achieves higher results on the middle and coarse levels. We think this is because the absence of the negative repulsion in our method compromises the discriminativeness of the image embedding space for a more flexible scope of each concept. To validate this hypothesis, we add the negative repulsion only on the fine level, as shown in Table 4. We see that negative repulsion helps on the fine level but reduces the performance on the other levels. Therefore, the adaptively learned concept scopes are more important on higher semantic levels which are more probable to contain different numbers of sub-concepts. The use of fixed hand-crated margins in CSL enforces each concept to occupy the same area of region in the embedding space regardless of the concept scope, which may damage the generalization ability of the learned metric.

Conventional Metric Learning without Negative Repulsion: To demonstrate the effectiveness of only using a positive attraction loss to learn the embedding space, we applied our method to the conventional metric learning setting on the CUB-200-2011 [50] dataset, where only one level of concept is present in the data. We simplified the proposed CLCD method to a vanilla version (CLCD-V), where only one encoder and decoder are used to refine a single concept embed-

Table 5. Experimental results (%) of for conventional deep metric learning.

	Concatenated (512-dim)			Separated (128-dim)		
	P@1	RP	MAP@R	P@1	RP	MAP@R
Pretrained	51.05	24.85	14.21	50.54	25.12	14.53
Contrastive [20]	**68.13 ± 0.31**	37.24 ± 0.28	26.53 ± 0.29	59.73 ± 0.40	31.98 ± 0.29	21.18 ± 0.28
Triplet [56]	64.24 ± 0.26	34.55 ± 0.24	23.69 ± 0.23	55.76 ± 0.27	29.55 ± 0.16	18.75 ± 0.15
ProxyNCA [34]	65.69 ± 0.43	35.14 ± 0.26	24.21 ± 0.27	57.88 ± 0.30	30.16 ± 0.22	19.32 ± 0.21
Margin [57]	64.37 ± 0.18	34.59 ± 0.16	23.71 ± 0.16	55.56 ± 0.16	29.32 ± 0.15	18.51 ± 0.13
N. Softmax [63]	65.65 ± 0.30	35.99 ± 0.15	25.25 ± 0.13	58.75 ± 0.19	31.75 ± 0.12	20.96 ± 0.11
CosFace [52]	67.32 ± 0.32	**37.49 ± 0.21**	**26.70 ± 0.23**	59.63 ± 0.36	31.99 ± 0.22	21.21 ± 0.22
ArcFace [9]	67.50 ± 0.25	37.31 ± 0.21	26.45 ± 0.20	**60.17 ± 0.32**	**32.37 ± 0.17**	**21.49 ± 0.16**
FastAP [2]	63.17 ± 0.34	34.20 ± 0.20	23.53 ± 0.20	55.58 ± 0.31	29.72 ± 0.16	19.09 ± 0.16
SNR [61]	66.44 ± 0.56	36.56 ± 0.34	25.75 ± 0.36	58.06 ± 0.39	31.21 ± 0.28	20.43 ± 0.28
MS [54]	65.04 ± 0.28	35.40 ± 0.12	24.70 ± 0.13	57.60 ± 0.24	30.84 ± 0.13	20.15 ± 0.14
MS+Miner [54]	67.73 ± 0.18	37.37 ± 0.19	26.52 ± 0.18	59.41 ± 0.30	31.93 ± 0.15	21.01 ± 0.14
SoftTriple [39]	67.27 ± 0.39	37.34 ± 0.19	26.51 ± 0.20	59.94 ± 0.33	32.12 ± 0.14	21.31 ± 0.14
CLCD-V	67.13 ± 0.24	37.17 ± 0.17	26.49 ± 0.25	59.97 ± 0.24	31.33 ± 0.11	21.26 ± 0.13

ding. We then simply use the distance between an image embedding with its positive concept embedding as the loss function to train the model.

For fair comparisons with existing deep metric learning losses, we adopted the recent proposed experimental settings [35] including using the ImageNet-1K [40] pretrained BN-Inception [25], smaller batch size, and strict dataset split. See Musgrave et al. [35] for more details. We strictly followed these protocols by implementing our method using the provided code[1]. Table 5 shows the performance of various loss functions. We observe that using a simple positive attraction loss achieves comparable performance with the other losses, which all impose both positive attraction and negative repulsion on the image embeddings. The results demonstrate that the proposed CLCD method is able to learn a discriminative embedding space despite the absence of negative repulsion. Our method implicitly pushes away negative pairs in an adaptive manner free from handcrafted margins, which we found affect the performance of the contrastive loss, the triplet loss, the margin loss largely.

Ablation Study: We conduct an ablation study to analyze the effectiveness of each component in the proposed CLCD method on the DyML-Vehicle dataset, as shown in Table 6. Asymmetry denotes we only pull closer the concept embedding of one image to the image embedding of another positive sample but not always the other way around. Random sampling means that we randomly select images from the dataset to construct a mini-batch. Intra-level represents using (9) as the loss function to pull closer positive concept embeddings at the same semantic level. W/o stop-gradient means we do not use the stop-gradient operation in our method.

---

[1] https://github.com/KevinMusgrave/pytorch-metric-learning.

Table 6. Ablation study of different settings on DyML-Vehicle.

Setting	mAP	R@1	R@10	R@20
Asymmetry	14.9	40.1	72.3	83.2
Random sampling	10.2	30.6	62.6	78.8
Intra-level	12.4	34.3	67.9	80.0
W/o stop-gradient	1.3	10.2	23.6	73.3
CLCD	**16.6**	**43.7**	**75.4**	**86.3**

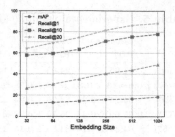

Fig. 4. Effect of different embedding sizes.

We see that Asymmetry attains slightly lower performance resulting from the possible inaccurate estimates of the backward gradient due to the lack of comparisons. Random sampling also leads to compromised performance and much lower convergence speed, since we can only find very few positive pairs in each mini-batch especially for the finest level, due to the vast number of classes. Using the intra-level positive pulling loss also achieves poor performance as each concept cannot see the relevant concepts from the lower levels and thus is not able to reflect their common grounds. The absence of the stop-gradient operation leads to model collapse. To further understand how the stop-gradient operation works, we conducted an experiment where we initialized all the embeddings to a fixed point so that the targets are the same for different concepts. We observe that the training collapses even with the stop-gradient operation. This verifies the significance of using different targets and further backs up the hypothesis [6].

Effect of Embedding Dimension: We conduct an experiment on the DyML-Vehicle dataset with different dimensions of the image embedding size, as shown in Fig. 4. The dimension of each meta-concept embedding is proportionally resized according to that of the image embedding. We see that using a larger embedding dimension generally improves the performance across all the semantic levels due to the better representation ability. Note that the output feature after the pooling layer of the ResNet-34 model used in the experiments had a dimension of 512, but uplifting it into a 1024-dimension embedding as the image representation still improves the performance.

5   Conclusion

In this paper, we have presented a cross-level concept distillation method for dynamic metric learning. We employ a hierarchical concept refiner to obtain a series of concept embeddings for an image and distill higher-level concepts using lower-level concepts. We only impose constraints on the cross-level positive concept pairs to avoid the possible conflicts across semantic levels. We have evaluated our method under the dynamic metric learning setting which shows that the proposed CLCD outperforms all other existing methods. We also conducted experiments under the conventional deep metric learning setting to further verify the effectiveness of only pulling closer positive pairs. In the future, it is interesting to apply our method to semi-supervised learning, where we can regard the instance-level and class-level labels as concepts from different semantic levels.

Acknowledgements. This work was supported in part by the National Key Research and Development Program of China under Grant 2017YFA0700802, in part by the National Natural Science Foundation of China under Grant 62125603 and Grant U1813218, in part by a grant from the Beijing Academy of Artificial Intelligence (BAAI).

References

1. Bellman, R.: Dynamic programming. Science **153**(3731), 34–37 (1966)
2. Cakir, F., He, K., Xia, X., Kulis, B., Sclaroff, S.: Deep metric learning to rank. In: CVPR, pp. 1861–1870 (2019)
3. Caron, M., Misra, I., Mairal, J., Goyal, P., Bojanowski, P., Joulin, A.: Unsupervised learning of visual features by contrasting cluster assignments. In: NeurIPS (2020)
4. Caruana, R.: Multitask learning. Mach. Learn. **28**(1), 41–75 (1997)
5. Chen, W., Chen, X., Zhang, J., Huang, K.: Beyond triplet loss: a deep quadruplet network for person re-identification. In: CVPR, pp. 1320–329 (2017)
6. Chen, X., He, K.: Exploring simple siamese representation learning. In: CVPR, pp. 15750–15758 (2021)
7. Chu, X., et al.: Twins: revisiting the design of spatial attention in vision transformers (2021)
8. Deng, J., Dong, W., Socher, R., Li, L.J., Li, K., Fei-Fei, L.: Imagenet: a large-scale hierarchical image database. In: CVPR, pp. 248–255 (2009)
9. Deng, J., Guo, J., Xue, N., Zafeiriou, S.: Arcface: additive angular margin loss for deep face recognition. In: CVPR, pp. 4690–4699 (2019)
10. Dhall, A., Makarova, A., Ganea, O., Pavllo, D., Greeff, M., Krause, A.: Hierarchical image classification using entailment cone embeddings. In: CVPRW, pp. 836–837 (2020)
11. Do, T.T., Tran, T., Reid, I., Kumar, V., Hoang, T., Carneiro, G.: A theoretically sound upper bound on the triplet loss for improving the efficiency of deep distance metric learning. In: CVPR, pp. 10404–10413 (2019)
12. Dosovitskiy, A., et al.: An image is worth 16×16 words: transformers for image recognition at scale. In: ICLR (2020)
13. Duan, Y., Zheng, W., Lin, X., Lu, J., Zhou, J.: Deep adversarial metric learning. In: CVPR, pp. 2780–2789 (2018)
14. Dutt, A., Pellerin, D., Quénot, G.: Improving hierarchical image classification with merged cnn architectures. In: Proceedings of the 15th International Workshop on Content-Based Multimedia Indexing, pp. 1–7 (2017)
15. Elezi, I., Vascon, S., Torcinovich, A., Pelillo, M., Leal-Taixé, L.: The group loss for deep metric learning. In: Vedaldi, A., Bischof, H., Brox, T., Frahm, J.-M. (eds.) ECCV 2020. LNCS, vol. 12352, pp. 277–294. Springer, Cham (2020). https://doi.org/10.1007/978-3-030-58571-6_17
16. Ge, W., Huang, W., Dong, D., Scott, M.R.: Deep metric learning with hierarchical triplet loss. In: ECCV, pp. 269–285 (2018)
17. Ghosh, S., Singh, R., Vatsa, M.: On learning density aware embeddings. In: CVPR, pp. 4884–4892 (2019)
18. Grill, J.B., et al.: Bootstrap your own latent: a new approach to self-supervised learning. arXiv abs/2006.07733 (2020)

19. Guo, Y., Liu, Y., Bakker, E.M., Guo, Y., Lew, M.S.: Cnn-rnn: a large-scale hierarchical image classification framework. Multimedia Tools Appl. **77**(8), 10251–10271 (2018)
20. Hadsell, R., Chopra, S., LeCun, Y.: Dimensionality reduction by learning an invariant mapping. In: CVPR, pp. 1735–1742 (2006)
21. Harwood, B., Kumar B G, V., Carneiro, G., Reid, I., Drummond, T.: Smart mining for deep metric learning. In: ICCV, pp. 2840–2848 (2017)
22. He, K., Zhang, X., Ren, S., Sun, J.: Deep residual learning for image recognition. In: CVPR, pp. 770–778 (2016)
23. Hu, J., Lu, J., Tan, Y.P.: Discriminative deep metric learning for face verification in the wild. In: CVPR, pp. 1875–1882 (2014)
24. Huang, C., Loy, C.C., Tang, X.: Local similarity-aware deep feature embedding. In: NeurIPS, pp. 1262–1270 (2016)
25. Ioffe, S., Szegedy, C.: Batch normalization: accelerating deep network training by reducing internal covariate shift. In: ICML, pp. 448–456 (2015)
26. Khrulkov, V., Mirvakhabova, L., Ustinova, E., Oseledets, I., Lempitsky, V.: Hyperbolic image embeddings. In: CVPR, pp. 6418–6428 (2020)
27. Kim, S., Kim, D., Cho, M., Kwak, S.: Proxy anchor loss for deep metric learning. In: CVPR, pp. 3238–3247 (2020)
28. Ko, B., Gu, G.: Embedding expansion: augmentation in embedding space for deep metric learning. In: CVPR, pp. 7255–7264 (2020)
29. Krizhevsky, A., Hinton, G., et al.: Learning multiple layers of features from tiny images (2009)
30. Law, M.T., Urtasun, R., Zemel, R.S.: Deep spectral clustering learning. In: ICML, pp. 1985–1994 (2017)
31. Lin, X., Duan, Y., Dong, Q., Lu, J., Zhou, J.: Deep variational metric learning. In: ECCV, pp. 689–704 (2018)
32. Liu, W., Wen, Y., Yu, Z., Li, M., Raj, B., Song, L.: Sphereface: deep hypersphere embedding for face recognition. In: CVPR, pp. 6738–6746 (2017)
33. Liu, Z., et al.: Swin transformer: hierarchical vision transformer using shifted windows (2021)
34. Movshovitz-Attias, Y., Toshev, A., Leung, T.K., Ioffe, S., Singh, S.: No fuss distance metric learning using proxies. In: ICCV, pp. 360–368 (2017)
35. Musgrave, K., Belongie, S., Lim, S.-N.: A metric learning reality check. In: Vedaldi, A., Bischof, H., Brox, T., Frahm, J.-M. (eds.) ECCV 2020. LNCS, vol. 12370, pp. 681–699. Springer, Cham (2020). https://doi.org/10.1007/978-3-030-58595-2_41
36. Nickel, M., Kiela, D.: Poincaré embeddings for learning hierarchical representations. In: NeurIPS, vol. 30 (2017)
37. Nickel, M., Kiela, D.: Learning continuous hierarchies in the lorentz model of hyperbolic geometry. In: ICML, pp. 3779–3788 (2018)
38. Opitz, M., Waltner, G., Possegger, H., Bischof, H.: Deep metric learning with bier: boosting independent embeddings robustly. TPAMI **42**, 276–290 (2018)
39. Qian, Q., Shang, L., Sun, B., Hu, J.: Softtriple loss: deep metric learning without triplet sampling. In: ICCV (2019)
40. Russakovsky, O., et al.: Imagenet large scale visual recognition challenge. IJCV **115**(3), 211–252 (2015)
41. Schroff, F., Kalenichenko, D., Philbin, J.: Facenet: a unified embedding for face recognition and clustering. In: CVPR, pp. 815–823 (2015)
42. Shi, H., et al.: Embedding deep metric for person re-identification: a study against large variations. In: Leibe, B., Matas, J., Sebe, N., Welling, M. (eds.) ECCV 2016.

LNCS, vol. 9905, pp. 732–748. Springer, Cham (2016). https://doi.org/10.1007/978-3-319-46448-0_44

43. Simonyan, K., Zisserman, A.: Very deep convolutional networks for large-scale image recognition. arXiv abs/1409.1556 (2014)

44. Sohn, K.: Improved deep metric learning with multi-class n-pair loss objective. In: NeurIPS, pp. 1857–1865 (2016)

45. Song, H.O., Xiang, Y., Jegelka, S., Savarese, S.: Deep metric learning via lifted structured feature embedding. In: CVPR, pp. 4004–4012 (2016)

46. Sun, Y., et al.: Circle loss: a unified perspective of pair similarity optimization. In: CVPR, pp. 6398–6407 (2020)

47. Sun, Y., et al.: Dynamic metric learning: towards a scalable metric space to accommodate multiple semantic scales. In: CVPR, pp. 5393–5402 (2021)

48. Szegedy, C., et al.: Going deeper with convolutions. In: CVPR, pp. 1–9 (2015)

49. Verma, N., Mahajan, D., Sellamanickam, S., Nair, V.: Learning hierarchical similarity metrics. In: CVPR, pp. 2280–2287 (2012)

50. Wah, C., Branson, S., Welinder, P., Perona, P., Belongie, S.J.: The Caltech-UCSD Birds-200-2011 dataset. Technical Report. CNS-TR-2011-001, California Institute of Technology (2011)

51. Wang, F., Zuo, W., Lin, L., Zhang, D., Zhang, L.: Joint learning of single-image and cross-image representations for person re-identification. In: CVPR, pp. 1288–1296 (2016)

52. Wang, H., et al.: Cosface: large margin cosine loss for deep face recognition. In: CVPR, pp. 5265–5274 (2018)

53. Wang, J., Zhou, F., Wen, S., Liu, X., Lin, Y.: Deep metric learning with angular loss. In: ICCV, pp. 2593–2601 (2017)

54. Wang, X., Han, X., Huang, W., Dong, D., Scott, M.R.: Multi-similarity loss with general pair weighting for deep metric learning. In: CVPR, pp. 5022–5030 (2019)

55. Wang, Y., Hu, B.G.: Hierarchical image classification using support vector machines. In: ACCV, pp. 23–25 (2002)

56. Weinberger, K.Q., Saul, L.K.: Distance metric learning for large margin nearest neighbor classification. JMLR 10(2), 207–244 (2009)

57. Wu, C.Y., Manmatha, R., Smola, A.J., Krähenbühl, P.: Sampling matters in deep embedding learning. In: ICCV, pp. 2859–2867 (2017)

58. Yan, Z., et al.: Hd-cnn: hierarchical deep convolutional neural networks for large scale visual recognition. In: ICCV, pp. 2740–2748 (2015)

59. Yu, B., Tao, D.: Deep metric learning with tuplet margin loss. In: ICCV, pp. 6490–6499 (2019)

60. Yu, R., Dou, Z., Bai, S., Zhang, Z., Xu, Y., Bai, X.: Hard-aware point-to-set deep metric for person re-identification. In: ECCV, pp. 188–204 (2018)

61. Yuan, T., Deng, W., Tang, J., Tang, Y., Chen, B.: Signal-to-noise ratio: a robust distance metric for deep metric learning. In: CVPR, pp. 4815–4824 (2019)

62. Yuan, Y., Yang, K., Zhang, C.: Hard-aware deeply cascaded embedding. In: ICCV, pp. 814–823 (2017)

63. Zhai, A., Wu, H.Y.: Classification is a strong baseline for deep metric learning. arXiv abs/1811.12649 (2018)

64. Zhao, Y., Jin, Z., Qi, G.J., Lu, H., Hua, X.S.: An adversarial approach to hard triplet generation. In: ECCV, pp. 501–517 (2018)

65. Zheng, W., Chen, Z., Lu, J., Zhou, J.: Hardness-aware deep metric learning. In: CVPR, pp. 72–81 (2019)

66. Zhou, J., Yu, P., Tang, W., Wu, Y.: Efficient online local metric adaptation via negative samples for person re-identification. In: ICCV, pp. 2420–2428 (2017)

MENet: A Memory-Based Network with Dual-Branch for Efficient Event Stream Processing

Linhui Sun[1,2], Yifan Zhang[1,2(✉)], Ke Cheng[1,2], Jian Cheng[1,2], and Hanqing Lu[1,2]

[1] Institute of Automation, Chinese Academy of Sciences, Beijing 100190, China
{sunlinhui2018,chengke2017}@ia.ac.cn,
{yfzhang,jcheng,luhq}@nlpr.ia.ac.cn
[2] School of Artificial Intelligence, University of Chinese Academy of Sciences, Beijing 100049, China

Abstract. Event cameras are bio-inspired sensors that asynchronously capture per-pixel brightness change and trigger a stream of events instead of frame-based images. Each event stream is generally split into multiple sliding windows for subsequent processing. However, most existing event-based methods ignore the motion continuity between adjacent spatiotemporal windows, which will result in the loss of dynamic information and additional computational costs. To efficiently extract strong features for event streams containing dynamic information, this paper proposes a novel memory-based network with dual-branch, namely MENet. It contains a base branch with a full-sized event point-wise processing structure to extract the base features and an incremental branch equipped with a light-weighted network to capture the temporal dynamics between two adjacent spatiotemporal windows. For enhancing the features, especially in the incremental branch, a point-wise memory bank is designed, which sketches the representative information of event feature space. Compared with the base branch, the incremental branch reduces the computational complexity up to 5 times and improves the speed by 19 times. Experiments show that MENet significantly reduces the computational complexity compared with previous methods while achieving state-of-the-art performance on gesture recognition and object recognition.

Keywords: Event-based model · Dual-branch structure · Memory bank

1 Introduction

Event cameras [4,30,49] are novel sensors that represent visual information by sparse and asynchronous events. Different from traditional cameras that record synchronized frames at a fixed low-rate (typically less than 60 frames per second), event cameras trigger an individual event asynchronously when the brightness

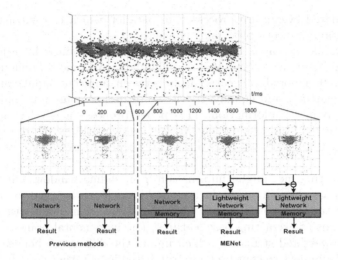

Fig. 1. Top: The event stream of an arm roll gesture is shown in the time-width-height space, in which the red dots represent that the polarity of an event is positive and the blue dots represent negative polarity. **Bottom:** The way to process adjacent windows of previous methods and that of the proposed MENet, respectively. Note that for intuitively representing the events contained in sliding windows, we transform it into a frame-based form by compressing the time dimension.

change on a pixel exceeds a preset threshold at a high rate. Each event encodes the pixel location, trigger time, and polarity of the brightness change. Compared with traditional cameras, event cameras exhibit four attractive properties. Firstly, event cameras are low latency, because they trigger event immediately when the intensity change exceeds the threshold. Secondly, event cameras only transmit changed information, thus they are low power. Thirdly, the high temporal resolution (μs) of event-based data can avoid motion blur. Fourthly, event cameras have a high dynamic range (140 dB vs 60 dB of traditional cameras), thus they can acquire information under challenging lighting conditions. These characteristics bring advantages to event cameras over traditional cameras when facing tasks that require low latency, low power, robustness to high-speed motion and variant illumination. Therefore, event cameras are widely used in many applications, such as object recognition [7,43,58], gesture recognition [1,3,64], pose relocalization [40,55], 3D reconstruction [11,23,52], autonomous driving [10,33], optical flow estimation [46,67], video reconstruction [19,45,54], etc.

To take the advantage of event-based data in downstream tasks, extracting meaningful features efficiently and effectively from the event stream is one of the key steps. Some previous methods [1,31,55] proposed to operate on the event-based data through event-by-event processing. However, processing each event serially will accumulate a large time consumption and an event alone can not provide enough information. Therefore, following other methods [8,12,33,40,59], this paper operates on groups of events contained in sliding windows. In this way, the accumulated events are processed in parallel, which can extract sufficient information and improve processing efficiency.

However, as shown in Fig. 1, the information contained in adjacent windows is continuous and some of it is redundant. And most previous methods [8,12,33,40,59] ignored the correlation between adjacent inputs and process them independently and equally. It will cause useless computational costs and the loss of dynamic information. This paper proposes a novel memory-based network with dual-branch, namely MENet, which utilizes the dynamic correlation between adjacent windows and avoids repeated extraction of redundant information.

For extracting meaningful information from sliding windows effectively and efficiently, a base branch and an incremental branch are designed to form a dual-branch structure. The base branch with a full-sized event point-wise processing structure, aims at extracting base features. The incremental branch is equipped with a light-weighted structure, which inputs the differences between two spatiotemporal windows to capture temporal dynamics. Furthermore, for obtaining high-quality differences between adjacent windows, a double polarities calculation method is proposed, which only records the changed event information between two windows and retains the low power characteristic of event-based data. Thanks to the proposed dual-branch structure and the double polarities calculation method, the inference accuracy and efficiency are both improved.

For utilizing the information extracted by the base branch to enhance features, a point-wise memory bank is proposed, which aims at sketching the representative information of the event feature space. For gesture recognition, the memory bank records the motion pattern of each action, while for object recognition, it records discrimination information among categories. Therefore, through adaptively recalling the information stored in the memory, both the base branch and incremental branch can perform feature enhancement to improve accuracy.

The contributions of this paper are summarized as follows:

1. We propose a MENet with dual-branch to utilize the correlation between adjacent spatiotemporal windows to improve feature extraction efficiency and prediction accuracy. The base branch with a full-sized event point-wise processing structure extracts base features, while the light-weighted incremental branch captures temporal dynamics between adjacent windows.
2. We propose a double polarities calculation method that calculates the high-quality differences between adjacent windows with little time consumption.
3. We introduce a point-wise memory bank to MENet for recording representative information of the event feature space, which can be recalled adaptively to further enhance features for improving estimation accuracy.
4. Experiments show that the MENet achieves state-of-the-art results on gesture recognition and object recognition while significantly reducing the computational complexity with respect to previous methods.

2   Related Work

2.1   Event-Based Representations

According to the number of events processed simultaneously, event-based methods can be divided into two categories. The first type operates on an event-by-event basis, which can update the estimation upon the arrival of a single event. For event-by-event processing, event-based data can be compressed into a 2D map, namely time surface (TS) [27], in which each pixel records the timestamp of the most recent event. Although the representation of TS is applied in many tasks [32,39,58,66], their ability will degrade on dealing with textured scenes [38], in which pixels spike frequently. In addition to the TS-based methods, Spiking Neural Networks (SNNs) [31,41,43] are adopted to process a single event, which is also bio-inspired designed. However, the training phase of SNNs is difficult because the output spikes are non-differentiable. Besides, Li *et al.* [62] proposed a graph-based method to process single event asynchronously. Sekikawa *et al.* [55] designed a recursive and event-wise manner to process event streams. Although these methods can respond immediately when a new event arrives, the serial processing of event data will accumulate a large time consumption due to the high time dimension characteristic of events.

The other type of method operates on sliding windows containing groups of events, which are obtained by splitting event streams with a fixed time interval or event number. For utilizing existing methods based on deep neural networks (DNNs), some methods [8,40,53] compressed sliding windows into 2D frames. Such intuitive expression retains the spatial information about scene edges, thus it can be applied in low-level and mid-level problems [2,13,44]. However, these methods discard the sparsity nature of events and quantify the timestamps. For improving the temporal resolution, events are converted into 3D voxel grids [6,35,67]. However, the computation of 3D convolution is expensive. Different from these methods that use alternative representations, some methods treated groups of events as event clouds [3,9,37,54] to retain the high temporal resolution characteristic of them. Benosman *et al.* [21] computed the dense visual flow by introducing plane fitting. Wang *et al.* [59] utilized PointNet++ [50] for gesture recognition, which aggregated local and global features. However, these methods ignore the correlation between adjacent windows and just process them independently and equally, which will cause useless computational costs and the loss of dynamic information. Therefore, the proposed MENet introduces a dual-branch structure to utilize the relationship between adjacent windows.

2.2   Memory-Based Networks

Recently, memory networks have been introduced in many computer vision tasks, such as anomaly detection [14,47], few-shot learning [5,20,68], video captioning [48], video prediction [29], etc. For a memory module, how to update important information to memory and how to recall effective content from memory are critical issues. Weston *et al.* [60] firstly proposed an additional memory component to deal with the task of question answer, which overcomes the drawback of limited memory of recurrent networks (RNNs). Huang *et al.* [17] introduced a self-supervised memory module to record the prototypical patterns of rain degradations for image deraining. To utilize long-term context for short-term image prediction, Lee *et al.* [29] introduced a long-term motion context memory (LMC-Memory) with an additional matrix, which is updated through back-propagation. For understanding the unstructured documents, the Key-Value Memory Network [36] utilized key memory to infer the weight of the corresponding value memory to obtain the fused features. For sketching the representative information of the event feature space, we introduce a memory bank to event-based data, which only utilizes information extracted by the base branch to update memory and can be adaptively recalled to improve the prediction accuracy.

3 Event Camera Model

Event cameras capture the change in logarithmic brightness signal $L(u_i, t_i) = logI(u_i, t_i)$ of each pixel $u_i = (x_i, y_i)$. Let ΔL denotes the change at pixel location (x_i, y_i) between timestamp t_i and t_{i-1}:

$$\Delta L = L(u_i, t_i) - L(u_i, t_{i-1}) \tag{1}$$

When ΔL exceeds a preset threshold C, an event will be triggered asynchronously. Each event $e_i = (x_i, y_i, t_i, p_i)$ encodes the pixel location (x_i, y_i), trigger time t_i, and polarity of the brightness change $p_i \in \{-1, 1\}$.

$$p = \begin{cases} 1, \Delta L \geqslant C \\ -1, \Delta L \leqslant -C \end{cases} \tag{2}$$

An asynchronous event stream can be split into multiple sliding windows with a fixed time interval T or event number N_{num}:

$$\begin{cases} S_k^T = \{e_i | i = j, ..., j + n(j)\} \\ S_k^N = \{e_i | i = j, ..., j + N_{num}\} \end{cases} \tag{3}$$

where S_k^T and S_k^N represent kth sliding window based on T or N_{num}, respectively. $n(j)$ represents the number of events between the time of the first event in the kth sliding window t_j and the time $(t_j + T)$. In this paper, sliding windows are obtained based on a fixed time interval, and the step size is set as $T/2$.

4 Method

For effectively and efficiently extracting meaningful information contained in event streams, this paper proposes a novel memory-based network with dual-branch, namely MENet, as illustrated in Fig. 2. In order to utilize the correlation

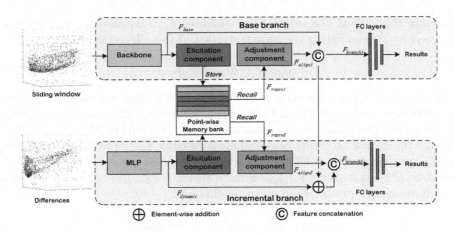

Fig. 2. Overview of the proposed MENet. The upper path is the base branch utilized to extract base features. The lower branch is the incremental branch used for capturing the temporal dynamics between adjacent spatiotemporal windows. The point-wise memory bank is introduced to sketch representative information of the event feature space.

between adjacent spatiotemporal windows, a dual-branch structure (Sect. 4.1) is introduced. In addition, we propose a double polarities calculation method to obtain high-quality differences between two adjacent windows (Sect. 4.2). Furthermore, a point-wise memory bank is introduced to sketch the representative information of the event feature space, which can be adaptively recalled to perform feature enhancement (Sect. 4.3). In Sect. 4.4, the details of the training and testing strategies will be described.

4.1 Dual-Branch Structure

The proposed MENet adopts a dual-branch structure, including a base branch and an incremental branch, as illustrated in Fig. 2. Taking PointNet++ [50] as the backbone, the base branch introduces an elicitation component and an adjustment component for memory feature extraction and feature alignment, as illustrated in the upper path of Fig. 2. Considering that each sliding window contains rich dynamic information and the information contained in adjacent spatiotemporal windows is correlated, a light-weighted incremental branch is proposed to capture the temporal dynamics between two adjacent windows while avoiding repeated extraction of redundant information. As illustrated in the lower path of Fig. 2, the incremental branch adopts a multi-layer-perceptron (MLP) block consisting of four layers to extract dynamic features. And the elicitation component and adjustment component are also introduced.

The base branch takes a sliding window as input. The base features F_{base} are extracted by the backbone, which is then input into the elicitation component for memory feature extraction. Through memory bank, the representative features F_{repre1} are recalled and will be aligned with F_{base} by the adjustment component to obtain the aligned features F_{align1}. Features $F_{branch1}$ used for predicting is obtained by concatenating the base features and the aligned features:

$$F_{branch1} = F_{base} ©F_{align1} \tag{4}$$

where © is the feature concatenation operation. The incremental branch takes the differences win_{diff} between the previous window and the current input window as input. The temporal dynamics $F_{dynamic}$ is captured by MLP block. Then through the elicitation component and memory bank, the representative features F_{repre2} are adaptively recalled. The adjustment component is also introduced to obtain aligned features F_{align2}. Finally, features $F_{branch2}$ of the incremental branch utilized to predict results can be obtained:

$$F_{branch2} = F_{align2} ©(F_{pre} \oplus F_{dynamic}) \tag{5}$$

where F_{pre} represents the features of the previous window used for predicting and $\oplus$ is the element-wise addition operation.

In addition, in inference, N_{win} sliding windows are regarded as a processing package. Only $1/N_{win}$ of sliding windows will go through the base branch, and the rest will be processed by the light-weighted incremental branch, which reduces the computational complexity.

4.2   Double Polarities Calculation Method

A direct way to obtain the differences between two adjacent windows is to directly subtract the unordered event clouds of the previous window win_{pre} from the clouds of the current one win_{curr}. However, this approach ignores the location and timestamp of each event, which will obtain low-quality differences. Besides, due to the high time resolution of events, obtaining the differences strictly according to the timestamp and space location will bring huge time consumption and memory usage. Therefore, in order to efficiently and effectively calculate the differences win_{diff} between two adjacent windows, a double polarities calculation method is proposed, which can be divided into four steps.

1. The previous sliding window win_{pre} is compressed into an edge frame ($W \times H \times 2$). The two channels of each pixel record the number of corresponding events with positive polarity or negative polarity, respectively. Therefore, the edge frame records the histograms of positive events and negative events:

$$h^+(x, y) = \sum_{e_k \in win_{pre}, p_k = +1} \delta(x - x_k, y - y_k) \tag{6}$$

where $h^+(x, y)$ represents the histogram of positive events. e_k means a single event belongs to win_{pre}. δ is the Kronecker delta. The histogram h^- of negative events can be obtained through a similar way with $p_k = -1$. Stacking the h^+ and h^- will obtain the edge frame.

2. Based on the first step, an edge frame $(W \times H \times 2)$ are produced for the current input window win_{curr}. And a time frame $(W \times H \times 2)$ is produced, in which each pixel records the timestamp of the most recent event.
3. The edge frame of win_{pre} is subtracted from that of win_{curr}. The position of the results whose values larger than 0 are recorded. According to the position and results, the location (x, y) and cumulative polarity p are obtained. And the corresponding timestamp t can be obtained from the time frame.
4. Finally, based on the location, cumulative polarity, and timestamp of events, the differences win_{diff} between two adjacent windows in the form of event clouds will be obtained, which contains the additional events that occur in win_{curr}, compared with win_{pre}.

Through the double polarities calculation method, high-quality differences between adjacent windows only recording changed event information is obtained efficiently and effectively, which retains the low power characteristic of event-based data. Taking such differences as input, the incremental branch can capture temporal dynamics of two windows, which provides guidance for prediction.

4.3 Point-Wise Memory Bank

Features extracted by the base branch represent the complete high-level semantics of the input window. Based on these features, the representative information of event feature space can be sketched by introducing a memory bank, which can be adaptively recalled to enhance features. Considering the form of memory features extracted by the elicitation component, we propose a point-wise memory bank with a matrix form, $M \in \mathbb{R}^{N \times C^m}$ with N points and C^m channels, which can be updated through back-propagation. For only recording the representative information of the base features, the memory bank is stored and recalled by the base branch, while the incremental branch only involves the recall operation.

Let $m_i \in \mathbb{R}^{C^m}$ represent an item of the memory bank M and $f_j^{mem1} \in \mathbb{R}^{C^m}$ is a row vector of features $F_{mem1} \in \mathbb{R}^{N_1 \times C^m}$ extracted from the elicitation component. For the base branch, the addressing vector $a^{ddr} \in \mathbb{R}^N$ will be firstly calculated, in which each scalar a_i^{ddr} represents an attention weight for the corresponding memory item m_i:

$$a_i^{ddr} = \frac{exp((f_j^{mem1})^T, m_i)}{\sum_{k=1}^{N} exp((f_j^{mem1})^T, m_k)} \tag{7}$$

where $exp(\cdot)$ represents softmax function. For each query f_j^{mem1}, the relevant representative information can be recalled from memory by weighting the item m_i with the corresponding weight a_i^{ddr}:

$$f_j^{repre1} = \sum_{i=1}^{N} a_i^{ddr} m_i \tag{8}$$

The representative features $F_{repre1} = \{f_j^{repre1}\}_{j=1}^{N_1} \in \mathbb{R}^{N_1 \times C^m}$ can be obtained by positioning each feature f_j^{repre1}.

For the incremental branch, the same operations as the base branch will be performed, including using the elicitation component to extract memory features, calculating the addressing vector for recalling the memory, and utilizing the adjustment component to align features, except performing the back-propagate to the memory. By only using the results of the base branch to perform back-propagation on the memory, the representative information of the event feature space can be adaptively recorded into the memory bank.

4.4   Training and Testing Strategies

In the training process, two adjacent windows win_{pre} and win_{curr} will be input into MENet. win_{pre} is input into the base branch to perform prediction, and the estimation error is used to update the parameters of the base branch and memory bank. The incremental branch takes the differences win_{diff} between win_{pre} and win_{curr} as input to capture temporal dynamics between two windows. For gesture recognition and object recognition, the cross-entropy loss function with label smoothing is adopted. To improve training efficiency, the result prediction and parameters updating of the two branches are performed in parallel.

In the testing stage, N_{win} consecutive windows belonging to the same event stream are regarded as a processing package. For taking advantage of the dual-branch structure, only the first window of the package will go through the base branch, while the rest windows will calculate the differences with the previous one and use the incremental branch for prediction. In this way, the incremental branch further exerts its advantages, and the captured temporal dynamics can provide guidance for subsequent prediction.

5   Experiments

5.1   Experimental Setup

Datasets. We evaluate our methods on four commonly used datasets, DVS128 Gesture Dataset [1], N-Cars [58], CIFAR10-DVS [15], and MNIST-DVS [42]. The DVS128 Gesture Dataset is collected from 29 subjects under 3 kinds of light conditions and records 1342 instances of 11 gestures. The N-Cars dataset is a benchmark for car recognition, which contains 12,336 car samples and 11693 background samples. Different from the first two datasets, CIFAR10-DVS and MNIST-DVS are converted from the frame-based datasets. The CIFAR10-DVS dataset collects 10000 samples for 10 categories, which is converted from CIFAR10 [25]. In MNIST-DVS, 10000 samples chosen from MNIST [28] are displayed at three different scales, thus it contains 30000 samples in total.

Implementation Details. The base branch adopts the first three set abstraction levels of PointNet++ [50] as the backbone, with three fully connected (FC) layers [512, 256, K] for prediction (K means the number of categories). For efficiency, the elicitation component adopts a simplified set abstraction level [50]

($SA(32, 0.2, [512, 256, 64])$), which selects 32 points from input, forms 32 local regions with ball radius 0.2 and encodes local regions into features by three FC layers. The adjustment component utilizes a lightweight MLP only containing two layers ([128, 256]). For the incremental branch, a MLP consisting of four layers ([64, 256, 512, 1024]) is adopted for feature extraction, and a MLP containing 2 layers ([256, 512]) is utilized for the adjustment component. The structure of the elicitation component and FC layers of the incremental branch are the same as the base branch. The matrix size of the point-wise memory bank is 16×64. The proposed method is implemented by PyTorch, which is trained on a Tesla K80 GPU. The batch size is set as 24 and the Adam [24] optimizer is adopted with an initial learning rate of 0.001 multiplied by 0.5 after 20 epochs.

Metrics. For object recognition and gesture recognition, prediction accuracy is adopted as the evaluation metric. In addition, the giga floating-point operations of the network (GFLOPs), the million floating-point operations per sliding window (MFLOPs/win), and the million floating-point operations per event (MFLOPs/event) are used for evaluating the computational complexity.

5.2   Ablation Study

For verifying the improvement of accuracy brought by the proposed adjustment component, point-wise memory bank, and double polarities calculation method, as well as the reduction of computational complexity and time consumption brought by the dual-branch structure, we conduct ablation experiments on the DVS128 Gesture Dataset [1]. Since the average duration of each event stream is $6s$, the fixed time interval is set as $T = 0.5s$ for producing sliding windows. In addition, for improving processing efficiency and considering that meaningful events have the characteristic of aggregation, each window is sampled 512 events randomly in the time dimension for processing.

Table 1. Contribution of the proposed adjustment component and the point-wise memory bank, evaluated on the DVS128 Gesture Dataset.

Method	Adjustment Component	Point-wise Memory bank	Accuracy %
MENet	✗	✓	97.34
	✓	✗	96.96
	✓	✓	**98.86**

Adjustment Component and Point-Wise Memory Bank. For verifying the effectiveness of adjustment component and memory bank, we conduct experiments on two additional structures. The first structure removes the adjustment component from MENet, and the second removes the memory bank but

Table 2. Contribution of the proposed double polarities calculation method, evaluated on the DVS128 Gesture Dataset.

Method	Double polarities calculation	Sub-diff.	Accuracy %
MENet	×	✓	97.34
	✓	×	**98.86**

Table 3. The average time and MFLOPs of the base branch and the incremental branch for processing a single sliding window.

Method	Branch	MFLOPs/win	Time (ms)
MENet	Base branch	4732	288
	Incremental branch	**1045**	**15**

retains elicitation component and adjustment component. As shown in Table 1, removing either the adjustment component or memory bank will both decrease accuracy. The results confirm that the memory bank can sketch representative information of event feature space for feature enhancement, and the adjustment component can align recalled memory features with features extracted by branch.

Double Polarities Calculation Method. Table 2 confirms the effect of the proposed calculation method, and both the models adopt memory bank and adjustment component. In Table 2, Sub-diff represents that the differences between two windows are obtained by directly subtracting the unordered event clouds of the previous window from the clouds of the current input one. The results show that even though taking the rough differences calculated by Sub-diff as input, the incremental branch can still capture useful information and obtain an accuracy of 97.34%. When higher quality differences calculated by the proposed calculation method are obtained, the accuracy is increased by 1.52%. The results confirm that the double polarities calculation method can obtain meaningful differences to assist incremental branch to obtain temporal dynamics between two adjacent spatiotemporal windows.

Computational Complexity and Time Consumption. For utilizing the correlation between two spatiotemporal windows and avoiding repeated extraction of redundant information, MENet adopts a dual-branch structure. For verifying the efficiency improvement brought by the incremental branch, we record the average time and MFLOPs required by the base branch and incremental branch to process a sliding window, as shown in Table 3. Compared with the base branch, the incremental branch reduces the MFLOPs/win by nearly 5 times and speeds up by 19 times. In testing, N_{win} sliding windows are treated as a processing package, as mentioned in Sect. 4.4. Table 4 evaluates the impact of choosing different N_{win} on MFLOPs/win, inference time of processing a single window, and accuracy. As shown in Table 4, as N_{win} increases, both MFLOPs/win and

Table 4. The MFLOPs, inference time, and accuracy of choosing different N_{win}.

N_{win}	MFLOPs/win	Time (ms)	Accuracy (%)
2	2889	151.5	98.11
4	2003	85.0	**98.86**
6	1708	64.1	98.48
8	1561	53.2	96.59
10	1450	45.0	95.07
12	1376	39.5	94.31

inference time are reduced due to the low computational complexity of the incremental branch. The best result is achieved by setting the N_{win} as 4, and when $N_{win} = 6$, MENet also achieves a competitive accuracy.

It is worth noting that the accuracy shows a trend of rising first and then falling, with the increase of N_{win}. There are reasons for this phenomenon. Taking differences between adjacent windows as input, the incremental branch can model the motion information contained in the two windows. Then, features of the previous window will be used for prediction of the current one, which accumulates the motion information. The accumulation of motion context in a short time period can provide guidance for estimation. Therefore, as N_{win} increases, the accuracy first shows an upward trend. However, in the long-term accumulation of motion context, events in the front window have a weak connection with the events in the back. When N_{win} is too large, part of the accumulated motion context may even introduce noise for prediction, thus the accuracy decreases.

5.3   Object Recognition

The experiments are conducted on three commonly used object recognition datasets. Since the average duration of each event stream in the CIFAR10-DVS dataset is $1.2s$, the fixed time interval is set as $200ms$. Each window is randomly sampled 4096 events. In addition, for verifying the effect of the proposed pointwise memory bank on object recognition, two additional structures are proposed, including MENet-single without incremental branch and Single-nomem further removing the memory bank. These two structures are evaluated on MNIST-DVS and N-Cars, in which each stream is sampled 512 or 1024 events, respectively.

Comparison with State of the Art. Table 5 compares the proposed Single-nomem and MENet-single with previous methods on MNIST-DVS and N-Cars. Firstly, compared with Single-nomem, MENet-single improves accuracy by 0.77% and 1.92% with almost the same computational complexity. The results confirm that the proposed memory bank stores representative information of event feature space, and the features recalled from it contains discrimination information of categories, which improves the accuracy with very low computational complexity. Secondly, previous methods have achieved high accuracy on

Table 5. Comparison with different methods on the MNIST-DVS dataset and N-Cars dataset. Red and blue represent the best and the second best result, respectively.

Methods	Representation	MNIST-DVS		N-Cars	
		Accracy%	MFLOPs/event	Accuracy%	MFLOPs/event
Shi *et al.* [56]	Spike	78.1	–	–	–
H-First [43]	Spike	59.5	-	56.1	–
HATS [58]	TimeSurface	98.4	-	90.2	–
HOTS [27]	TimeSurface	80.3	26	62.4	14.0
DART [51]	TimeSurface	98.5	–	–	–
LIAF-Net [61]	Frame	99.1	–	–	–
YOLE [7]	VoxelGrid	96.1	-	92.7	328.1
Asynet [35]	VoxelGrid	**99.4**	112	**94.4**	21.5
Bi *et al.* [3]	Graph	98.6	–	91.4	–
EvS-S [62]	Graph	99.1	15.2	93.1	6.1
Dominic *et al.* [18]	Point-clouds	99.1	–	–	–
Single-nomem	Point-clouds	98.8	9.2	93.4	4.6
MENet-single	Point-clouds	99.57	9.2	95.32	4.6

these two datasets, but the MENet-single further improves performance with the lowest computational complexity. Compared with two competitive methods, Asynet [35] and EvS-S [62] which process events asynchronously, MENet-single improves accuracy by 0.17% and 0.47% while reducing MFLOPs/event by nearly 12 times and 1.6 times on MNIST-DVS, respectively. On N-Cars, the accuracy is improved by 0.92% and 2.22% with reducing MFLOPs/event by 4.7 times and 1.3 times. The results confirm that by taking event clouds as input, the proposed method can process multiple events in parallel and extract the rich information contained in events effectively. Moreover, compared with the other methods in Table 5, MENet-single uses fewer events and achieves higher accuracy, which also confirms that the proposed method is effective and efficient.

In Table 6, compared with other methods on CIFAR10-DVS, MENet achieves the best performance with the lowest computational complexity. Compared with two competitive methods LIAF-Net [61] and TA-SNN [64], MENet improves accuracy by 3.7% and 2.1%, respectively. These two methods both compressed event stream into frames and utilized SNN-based model. Experimental results prove that MENet retains the high time resolution characteristic of event-based data and the incremental branch can effectively capture the rich temporal dynamics contained in event data. Therefore, MENet can greatly improve accuracy while reducing computational complexity.

5.4   Gesture Recognition

As set in the ablation study, in DVS128 Gesture Dataset [1], the fixed time interval is $T = 0.5s$. For each sliding window, 512 events are sampled for processing.

Table 6. Comparison with different methods on the CIFAR10-DVS dataset. Red and blue represent the best and the second best result, respectively.

Methods	Representation	Accuracy (%)	MFLOPs/event	GFLOPs
STBP-tdBN [65]	Spike	67.8	–	–
HOTS [27]	TimeSurface	27.1	26	–
HATS [58]	TimeSurface	52.4	–	–
DART [51]	TimeSurface	65.8	–	–
Asynet [35]	VoxelGrid	66.3	103	–
Kugele *et al.* [26]	Frame	66.7	–	8.8
LIAF-Net [61]	Frame	70.4	–	**7.1**
TA-SNN [64]	Frame	**72.0**	–	–
EvS-S [62]	Graph	68.0	33.2	–
Dominic *et al.* [18]	Point-clouds	56.6	–	–
MENet	Point-clouds	74.1	0.9	3.7

Comparison with State of the Art. In Table 7, compared with MENet-single, MENet achieves a better result (98.86% vs 98.11%), while the speed is increased by 3 times and computational complexity is reduced by 2 times. In addition, compared with other methods that have achieved high accuracy, MENet achieves a new state-of-the-art result while significantly reducing the computational complexity. Although TA-SNN adopts a small time interval $dt = 10$ ms to generate the frames and processes all events contained in the window, MENet also achieves a better result (98.86% vs 98.61%). In addition, compared with LIAF-Net [61], MENet improves accuracy by 1.3% and reduces the GFLOPs by 7.8 times. These experimental results prove once again that MENet can effectively and efficiently utilize the dynamic information contained in event streams.

Table 7. Comparison with different methods on the DVS128 Gesture Dataset. Red and blue represent the best and the second best result, respectively.

Methods	Representation	Accuracy (%)	GFLOPs
Slayer [57]	Spike	93.64	–
Amir *et al.* [1]	Spike	94.59	–
SpArNet [22]	Spike	95.10	–
STBP-tdBN [65]	Spike	96.87	–
Bi *et al.* [3]	Graph	97.20	13.7
Wang *et al.* [59]	Point-clouds	95.32	–
PAT [63]	Point-clouds	96.00	–
Kugele *et al.* [26]	Frame	95.56	15.0
Massa *et al.* [34]	Frame	89.64	–
LIF-Net [16]	Frame	93.40	–
LIAF-Net [61]	Frame	97.56	13.6
TA-SNN [64]	Frame	**98.61**	–
MENet-single	Point-clouds	98.11	**4.73**
MENet	Point-clouds	98.86	2.00

6   Conclusion

This paper proposes a novel memory-based network with dual-branch for efficiently and effectively processing event-based data, namely MENet. For utilizing the correlation between adjacent windows and avoiding repeated extraction of redundant information, MENet contains two branches. The first one is the base branch which aims at extracting base features, while the second one is the incremental branch with a light-weighted structure for capturing temporal dynamics between two adjacent spatiotemporal windows. In addition, for calculating the differences between two adjacent windows to capture meaningful information, a double polarities calculation method is proposed. Furthermore, a point-wise memory bank is introduced to sketch the representative information of event feature space for feature enhancement. Experimental results show that the proposed dual-branch structure can reduce computational complexity and time consumption while improving accuracy, and the proposed double polarities calculation method and the point-wise memory bank can play their roles.

Acknowledgments. This work was supported in part by the National Key Research and Development Program of China under Grant 2020AAA0103402, Jiangsu Key Research and Development Plan (No. BE2021012-2), and NSFC 61876182, 61906195.

References

1. Amir, A., et al.: A low power, fully event-based gesture recognition system. In: 2017 IEEE Conference on Computer Vision and Pattern Recognition, CVPR 2017, Honolulu, HI, USA, 21–26 July 2017, pp. 7388–7397. IEEE Computer Society (2017). https://doi.org/10.1109/CVPR.2017.781

2. Bardow, P., Davison, A.J., Leutenegger, S.: Simultaneous optical flow and intensity estimation from an event camera. In: 2016 IEEE Conference on Computer Vision and Pattern Recognition, CVPR 2016, Las Vegas, NV, USA, 27–30 June 2016, pp. 884–892. IEEE Computer Society (2016). https://doi.org/10.1109/CVPR.2016.102

3. Bi, Y., Chadha, A., Abbas, A., Bourtsoulatze, E., Andreopoulos, Y.: Graph-based spatial-temporal feature learning for neuromorphic vision sensing. CoRR abs/1910.03579 (2019). http://arxiv.org/abs/1910.03579

4. Brandli, C., Berner, R., Yang, M., Liu, S., Delbrück, T.: A 240 × 180 130 db 3 μs latency global shutter spatiotemporal vision sensor. IEEE J. Solid State Circuits **49**(10), 2333–2341 (2014). https://doi.org/10.1109/JSSC.2014.2342715

5. Cai, Q., Pan, Y., Yao, T., Yan, C., Mei, T.: Memory matching networks for one-shot image recognition. In: 2018 IEEE Conference on Computer Vision and Pattern Recognition, CVPR 2018, Salt Lake City, UT, USA, 18–22 June 2018, pp. 4080–4088. Computer Vision Foundation/IEEE Computer Society (2018). https://doi.org/10.1109/CVPR.2018.00429

6. Cannici, M., Ciccone, M., Romanoni, A., Matteucci, M.: Asynchronous convolutional networks for object detection in neuromorphic cameras. In: IEEE Conference on Computer Vision and Pattern Recognition Workshops, CVPR Workshops 2019, Long Beach, CA, USA, 16–20 June 2019, pp. 1656–1665. Computer Vision Foundation/IEEE (2019). https://doi.org/10.1109/CVPRW.2019.00209

7. Cannici, M., Ciccone, M., Romanoni, A., Matteucci, M.: Attention mechanisms for object recognition with event-based cameras. In: IEEE Winter Conference on Applications of Computer Vision, WACV 2019, Waikoloa Village, HI, USA, 7–11 January 2019, pp. 1127–1136. IEEE (2019). https://doi.org/10.1109/WACV.2019.00125

8. Cannici, M., Ciccone, M., Romanoni, A., Matteucci, M.: A differentiable recurrent surface for asynchronous event-based data. In: Vedaldi, A., Bischof, H., Brox, T., Frahm, J.-M. (eds.) ECCV 2020. LNCS, vol. 12365, pp. 136–152. Springer, Cham (2020). https://doi.org/10.1007/978-3-030-58565-5_9

9. Chen, J., Meng, J., Wang, X., Yuan, J.: Dynamic graph CNN for event-camera based gesture recognition. In: IEEE International Symposium on Circuits and Systems, ISCAS 2020, Sevilla, Spain, 10–21 October 2020, pp. 1–5. IEEE (2020). https://doi.org/10.1109/ISCAS45731.2020.9181247

10. Cheng, W., Luo, H., Yang, W., Yu, L., Chen, S., Li, W.: DET: a high-resolution DVS dataset for lane extraction. In: IEEE Conference on Computer Vision and Pattern Recognition Workshops, CVPR Workshops 2019, Long Beach, CA, USA, 16–20 June 2019, pp. 1666–1675. Computer Vision Foundation/IEEE (2019). https://doi.org/10.1109/CVPRW.2019.00210

11. Gallego, G., Rebecq, H., Scaramuzza, D.: A unifying contrast maximization framework for event cameras, with applications to motion, depth, and optical flow estimation. In: 2018 IEEE Conference on Computer Vision and Pattern Recognition, CVPR 2018, Salt Lake City, UT, USA, 18–22 June 2018, pp. 3867–3876. Computer Vision Foundation/IEEE Computer Society (2018). https://doi.org/10.1109/CVPR.2018.00407

12. Gehrig, D., Loquercio, A., Derpanis, K.G., Scaramuzza, D.: End-to-end learning of representations for asynchronous event-based data. In: 2019 IEEE/CVF International Conference on Computer Vision, ICCV 2019, Seoul, Korea (South), 27 October–2 November 2019, pp. 5632–5642. IEEE (2019). https://doi.org/10.1109/ICCV.2019.00573

13. Gehrig, D., Rebecq, H., Gallego, G., Scaramuzza, D.: Eklt: asynchronous photometric feature tracking using events and frames. Int. J. Comput. Vision **128**, 601–618 (2019)

14. Gong, D., Liu, L., Le, V., Saha, B., Mansour, M.R., Venkatesh, S., van den Hengel, A.: Memorizing normality to detect anomaly: memory-augmented deep autoencoder for unsupervised anomaly detection. In: 2019 IEEE/CVF International Conference on Computer Vision, ICCV 2019, Seoul, Korea (South), 27 October–2 November 2019, pp. 1705–1714. IEEE (2019). https://doi.org/10.1109/ICCV.2019.00179

15. Li, H., Liu, H., Ji, X., Li, G., Shi, L.: Cifar10-dvs: an event-stream dataset for object classification. Front. Neurosci. **11**, 309 (2017)

16. He, W., et al.: Comparing snns and rnns on neuromorphic vision datasets: similarities and differences. CoRR abs/2005.02183 (2020). https://arxiv.org/abs/2005.02183

17. Huang, H., Yu, A., He, R.: Memory oriented transfer learning for semi-supervised image deraining. In: IEEE Conference on Computer Vision and Pattern Recognition, CVPR 2021, virtual, 19–25 June 2021, pp. 7732–7741. Computer Vision Foundation/IEEE (2021)

18. Jack, D., Maire, F., Denman, S., Eriksson, A.: Sparse convolutions on continuous domains for point cloud and event stream networks. In: Ishikawa, H., Liu, C.-L., Pajdla, T., Shi, J. (eds.) ACCV 2020. LNCS, vol. 12622, pp. 400–416. Springer, Cham (2021). https://doi.org/10.1007/978-3-030-69525-5_24

19. Jiang, Z., Zhang, Y., Zou, D., Ren, J.S.J., Lv, J., Liu, Y.: Learning event-based motion deblurring. In: 2020 IEEE/CVF Conference on Computer Vision and Pattern Recognition, CVPR 2020, Seattle, WA, USA, 13–19 June 2020, pp. 3317–3326. Computer Vision Foundation/IEEE (2020). https://doi.org/10.1109/CVPR42600.2020.00338, https://openaccess.thecvf.com/content_CVPR_2020/html/Jiang_Learning_Event-Based_Motion_Deblurring_CVPR_2020_paper.html

20. Kaiser, L., Nachum, O., Roy, A., Bengio, S.: Learning to remember rare events. In: 5th International Conference on Learning Representations, ICLR 2017, Toulon, France, 24–26 April 2017, Conference Track Proceedings. OpenReview.net (2017). https://openreview.net/forum?id=SJTQLdqlg

21. Khairallah, M.Z., Bonardi, F., Roussel, D., Bouchafa, S.: PCA event-based optical flow for visual odometry. CoRR abs/2105.03760 (2021). https://arxiv.org/abs/2105.03760

22. Khoei, M.A., Yousefzadeh, A., Pourtaherian, A., Moreira, O., Tapson, J.: Sparnet: sparse asynchronous neural network execution for energy efficient inference. In: 2nd IEEE International Conference on Artificial Intelligence Circuits and Systems, AICAS 2020, Genova, Italy, 31 August–2 September 2020, pp. 256–260. IEEE (2020). https://doi.org/10.1109/AICAS48895.2020.9073827

23. Kim, H., Leutenegger, S., Davison, A.J.: Real-time 3D reconstruction and 6-DoF tracking with an event camera. In: Leibe, B., Matas, J., Sebe, N., Welling, M. (eds.) ECCV 2016. LNCS, vol. 9910, pp. 349–364. Springer, Cham (2016). https://doi.org/10.1007/978-3-319-46466-4_21

24. Kingma, D.P., Ba, J.: Adam: a method for stochastic optimization. In: Bengio, Y., LeCun, Y. (eds.) 3rd International Conference on Learning Representations, ICLR 2015, San Diego, CA, USA, 7–9 May 2015, Conference Track Proceedings (2015). http://arxiv.org/abs/1412.6980

25. Krizhevsky, A.: Learning multiple layers of features from tiny images, pp. 32–33 (2009). https://www.cs.toronto.edu/kriz/learning-features-2009-TR.pdf

26. Kugele, A., Pfeil, T., Pfeiffer, M., Chicca, E.: Efficient processing of spatio-temporal data streams with spiking neural networks. Front. Neuroscie. **14**, 439 (2020). https://doi.org/10.3389/fnins.2020.00439, https://www.frontiersin.org/article/10.3389/fnins.2020.00439

27. Lagorce, X., Orchard, G., Galluppi, F., Shi, B.E., Benosman, R.: HOTS: a hierarchy of event-based time-surfaces for pattern recognition. IEEE Trans. Pattern Anal. Mach. Intell. **39**(7), 1346–1359 (2017). https://doi.org/10.1109/TPAMI.2016.2574707

28. Lecun, Y., Bottou, L., Bengio, Y., Haffner, P.: Gradient-based learning applied to document recognition. Proc. IEEE **86**(11), 2278–2324 (1998). https://doi.org/10.1109/5.726791

29. Lee, S., Kim, H.G., Choi, D.H., Kim, H., Ro, Y.M.: Video prediction recalling long-term motion context via memory alignment learning. In: IEEE Conference on Computer Vision and Pattern Recognition, CVPR 2021, virtual, 19–25 June 2021, pp. 3054–3063. Computer Vision Foundation/IEEE (2021)

30. Lichtsteiner, P., Posch, C., Delbrück, T.: A 128×128 120 db 15 μs latency asynchronous temporal contrast vision sensor. IEEE J. Solid State Circuits **43**(2), 566–576 (2008). https://doi.org/10.1109/JSSC.2007.914337

31. Liu, Q., Ruan, H., Xing, D., Tang, H., Pan, G.: Effective AER object classification using segmented probability-maximization learning in spiking neural networks. In: The Thirty-Fourth AAAI Conference on Artificial Intelligence, AAAI 2020, The Thirty-Second Innovative Applications of Artificial Intelligence Conference, IAAI 2020, The Tenth AAAI Symposium on Educational Advances in Artificial Intelligence, EAAI 2020, New York, NY, USA, 7–12 February 2020, pp. 1308–1315. AAAI Press (2020). https://aaai.org/ojs/index.php/AAAI/article/view/5486

32. Manderscheid, J., Sironi, A., Bourdis, N., Migliore, D., Lepetit, V.: Speed invariant time surface for learning to detect corner points with event-based cameras. In: IEEE Conference on Computer Vision and Pattern Recognition, CVPR 2019, Long Beach, CA, USA, 16–20 June 2019, pp. 10245–10254. Computer Vision Foundation/IEEE (2019). https://doi.org/10.1109/CVPR.2019.01049

33. Maqueda, A.I., Loquercio, A., Gallego, G., García, N., Scaramuzza, D.: Event-based vision meets deep learning on steering prediction for self-driving cars. In: 2018 IEEE Conference on Computer Vision and Pattern Recognition, CVPR 2018, Salt Lake City, UT, USA, 18–22 June 2018, pp. 5419–5427. Computer Vision Foundation/IEEE Computer Society (2018). https://doi.org/10.1109/CVPR.2018.00568, http://openaccess.thecvf.com/content_cvpr_2018/html/Maqueda_Event-Based_Vision_Meets_CVPR_2018_paper.html

34. Massa, R., Marchisio, A., Martina, M., Shafique, M.: An efficient spiking neural network for recognizing gestures with a DVS camera on the loihi neuromorphic processor. CoRR abs/2006.09985 (2020). https://arxiv.org/abs/2006.09985

35. Messikommer, N., Gehrig, D., Loquercio, A., Scaramuzza, D.: Event-based asynchronous sparse convolutional networks. In: Vedaldi, A., Bischof, H., Brox, T., Frahm, J.-M. (eds.) ECCV 2020. LNCS, vol. 12353, pp. 415–431. Springer, Cham (2020). https://doi.org/10.1007/978-3-030-58598-3_25

36. Miller, A.H., Fisch, A., Dodge, J., Karimi, A., Bordes, A., Weston, J.: Key-value memory networks for directly reading documents. In: Su, J., Carreras, X., Duh, K. (eds.) Proceedings of the 2016 Conference on Empirical Methods in Natural Language Processing, EMNLP 2016, Austin, Texas, USA, 1–4 November 2016, pp. 1400–1409. The Association for Computational Linguistics (2016). https://doi.org/10.18653/v1/d16-1147

37. Mitrokhin, A., Hua, Z., Fermüller, C., Aloimonos, Y.: Learning visual motion segmentation using event surfaces. In: 2020 IEEE/CVF Conference on Computer Vision and Pattern Recognition, CVPR 2020, Seattle, WA, USA, 13–19 June 2020, pp. 14402–14411. Computer Vision Foundation/IEEE (2020). https://doi.org/10.1109/CVPR42600.2020.01442

38. Mueggler, E., Bartolozzi, C., Scaramuzza, D.: Fast event-based corner detection. In: British Machine Vision Conference 2017, BMVC 2017, London, UK, 4–7 September 2017. BMVA Press (2017). https://www.dropbox.com/s/vicqrsz0yicq65c/0070.pdf?dl=1

39. Munda, G., Reinbacher, C., Pock, T.: Real-time intensity-image reconstruction for event cameras using manifold regularisation. Int. J. Comput. Vision **126**(12), 1381–1393 (2018). https://doi.org/10.1007/s11263-018-1106-2

40. Nguyen, A., Do, T., Caldwell, D.G., Tsagarakis, N.G.: Real-time 6dof pose relocalization for event cameras with stacked spatial LSTM networks. In: IEEE Conference on Computer Vision and Pattern Recognition Workshops, CVPR Workshops 2019, Long Beach, CA, USA, 16–20 June 2019, pp. 1638–1645. Computer Vision Foundation/IEEE (2019). https://doi.org/10.1109/CVPRW.2019.00207

41. Orchard, G., Benosman, R., Etienne-Cummings, R., Thakor, N.V.: A spiking neural network architecture for visual motion estimation. In: 2013 IEEE Biomedical Circuits and Systems Conference (BioCAS), Rotterdam, The Netherlands, 31 October–2 November 2013, pp. 298–301. IEEE (2013). https://doi.org/10.1109/BioCAS.2013.6679698

42. Orchard, G., Jayawant, A., Cohen, G., Thakor, N.: Converting static image datasets to spiking neuromorphic datasets using saccades (2015)

43. Orchard, G., Meyer, C., Etienne-Cummings, R., Posch, C., Thakor, N.V., Benosman, R.: Hfirst: a temporal approach to object recognition. IEEE Trans. Pattern Anal. Mach. Intell. **37**(10), 2028–2040 (2015). https://doi.org/10.1109/TPAMI.2015.2392947

44. Pan, L., Liu, M., Hartley, R.: Single image optical flow estimation with an event camera. In: 2020 IEEE/CVF Conference on Computer Vision and Pattern Recognition, CVPR 2020, Seattle, WA, USA, 13–19 June 2020, pp. 1669–1678. Computer Vision Foundation/IEEE (2020). https://doi.org/10.1109/CVPR42600.2020.00174

45. Pan, L., Scheerlinck, C., Yu, X., Hartley, R., Liu, M., Dai, Y.: Bringing a blurry frame alive at high frame-rate with an event camera. In: IEEE Conference on Computer Vision and Pattern Recognition, CVPR 2019, Long Beach, CA, USA, 16–20 June 2019, pp. 6820–6829. Computer Vision Foundation/IEEE (2019). https://doi.org/10.1109/CVPR.2019.00698

46. Paredes-Vallés, F., Scheper, K.Y.W., de Croon, G.C.H.E.: Unsupervised learning of a hierarchical spiking neural network for optical flow estimation: from events to global motion perception. IEEE Trans. Pattern Anal. Mach. Intell. **42**(8), 2051–2064 (2020). https://doi.org/10.1109/TPAMI.2019.2903179

47. Park, H., Noh, J., Ham, B.: Learning memory-guided normality for anomaly detection. In: 2020 IEEE/CVF Conference on Computer Vision and Pattern Recognition, CVPR 2020, Seattle, WA, USA, 13–19 June 2020, pp. 14360–14369. Computer Vision Foundation/IEEE (2020). https://doi.org/10.1109/CVPR42600.2020.

01438, https://openaccess.thecvf.com/content_CVPR_2020/html/Park_Learning_Memory-Guided_Normality_for_Anomaly_Detection_CVPR_2020_paper.html

48. Pei, W., Zhang, J., Wang, X., Ke, L., Shen, X., Tai, Y.: Memory-attended recurrent network for video captioning. In: IEEE Conference on Computer Vision and Pattern Recognition, CVPR 2019, Long Beach, CA, USA, 16–20 June 2019, pp. 8347–8356. Computer Vision Foundation / IEEE (2019). https://doi.org/ 10.1109/CVPR.2019.00854, http://openaccess.thecvf.com/content_CVPR_2019/ html/Pei_Memory-Attended_Recurrent_Network_for_Video_Captioning_CVPR_ 2019_paper.html

49. Posch, C., Matolin, D., Wohlgenannt, R.: A QVGA 143 db dynamic range frame-free PWM image sensor with lossless pixel-level video compression and time-domain CDS. IEEE J. Solid State Circuits 46(1), 259–275 (2011). https://doi. org/10.1109/JSSC.2010.2085952

50. Qi, C.R., Yi, L., Su, H., Guibas, L.J.: Pointnet++: Deep hierarchical feature learning on point sets in a metric space. In: Guyon, I., von Luxburg, U., Bengio, S., Wallach, H.M., Fergus, R., Vishwanathan, S.V.N., Garnett, R. (eds.) Advances in Neural Information Processing Systems 30: Annual Conference on Neural Information Processing Systems 2017, Long Beach, CA, USA, 4–9 December 2017, pp. 5099–5108 (2017)

51. Ramesh, B., Yang, H., Orchard, G., Thi, N.A.L., Zhang, S., Xiang, C.: DART: distribution aware retinal transform for event-based cameras. IEEE Trans. Pattern Anal. Mach. Intell. 42(11), 2767–2780 (2020). https://doi.org/10.1109/TPAMI. 2019.2919301

52. Rebecq, H., Gallego, G., Mueggler, E., Scaramuzza, D.: EMVS: event-based multi-view stereo—3D reconstruction with an event camera in real-time. Int. J. Comput. Vision 126(12), 1394–1414 (2017). https://doi.org/10.1007/s11263-017-1050-6

53. Rebecq, H., Ranftl, R., Koltun, V., Scaramuzza, D.: Events-to-video: bringing modern computer vision to event cameras. In: IEEE Conference on Computer Vision and Pattern Recognition, CVPR 2019, Long Beach, CA, USA, 16–20 June 2019, pp. 3857–3866. Computer Vision Foundation/IEEE (2019). https://doi.org/10.1109/ CVPR.2019.00398

54. Rebecq, H., Ranftl, R., Koltun, V., Scaramuzza, D.: High speed and high dynamic range video with an event camera. IEEE Trans. Pattern Anal. Mach. Intell. 43(6), 1964–1980 (2021). https://doi.org/10.1109/TPAMI.2019.2963386

55. , Sekikawa, Y., Hara, K., Saito, H.: Eventnet: asynchronous recursive event processing. In: IEEE Conference on Computer Vision and Pattern Recognition, CVPR 2019, Long Beach, CA, USA, 16–20 June 2019, pp. 3887–3896. Computer Vision Foundation/IEEE (2019). https://doi.org/10.1109/CVPR.2019.00401

56. Shi, C., Li, J., Wang, Y., Luo, G.: Exploiting lightweight statistical learning for event-based vision processing. IEEE Access 6, 19396–19406 (2018). https://doi. org/10.1109/ACCESS.2018.2823260

57. Shrestha, S.B., Orchard, G.: SLAYER: spike layer error reassignment in time. CoRR abs/1810.08646 (2018). http://arxiv.org/abs/1810.08646

58. Sironi, A., Brambilla, M., Bourdis, N., Lagorce, X., Benosman, R.: HATS: histograms of averaged time surfaces for robust event-based object classification. In: 2018 IEEE Conference on Computer Vision and Pattern Recognition, CVPR 2018, Salt Lake City, UT, USA, 18–22 June 2018, pp. 1731–1740. Computer Vision Foundation/IEEE Computer Society (2018). https://doi.org/10.1109/CVPR.2018. 00186

59. Wang, Q., Zhang, Y., Yuan, J., Lu, Y.: Space-time event clouds for gesture recognition: From RGB cameras to event cameras. In: IEEE Winter Conference on Applications of Computer Vision, WACV 2019, Waikoloa Village, HI, USA, 7–11 January 2019, pp. 1826–1835. IEEE (2019). https://doi.org/10.1109/WACV.2019.00199

60. Weston, J., Chopra, S., Bordes, A.: Memory networks. In: Bengio, Y., LeCun, Y. (eds.) 3rd International Conference on Learning Representations, ICLR 2015, San Diego, CA, USA, 7–9 May 2015, Conference Track Proceedings (2015). http://arxiv.org/abs/1410.3916

61. Wu, Z., Zhang, H., Lin, Y., Li, G., Wang, M., Tang, Y.: Liaf-net: leaky integrate and analog fire network for lightweight and efficient spatiotemporal information processing. CoRR abs/2011.06176 (2020). https://arxiv.org/abs/2011.06176

62. Li, Y., Zhou, H., Yang, B.: Graph-based asynchronous event processing for rapid object recognition. In: ICCV, pp. 934–943 (2021)

63. Yang, J., Zhang, Q., Ni, B., Li, L., Liu, J., Zhou, M., Tian, Q.: Modeling point clouds with self-attention and gumbel subset sampling. In: IEEE Conference on Computer Vision and Pattern Recognition, CVPR 2019, Long Beach, CA, USA, 16–20 June 2019, pp. 3323–3332. Computer Vision Foundation/IEEE (2019). https://doi.org/10.1109/CVPR.2019.00344

64. Yao, M., et al.: Temporal-wise attention spiking neural networks for event streams classification. CoRR abs/2107.11711 (2021). https://arxiv.org/abs/2107.11711

65. Zheng, H., Wu, Y., Deng, L., Hu, Y., Li, G.: Going deeper with directly-trained larger spiking neural networks. CoRR abs/2011.05280 (2020). https://arxiv.org/abs/2011.05280

66. Zhou, Y., Gallego, G., Shen, S.: Event-based stereo visual odometry. IEEE Trans. Rob. **37**(5), 1433–1450 (2021). https://doi.org/10.1109/TRO.2021.3062252

67. Zhu, A.Z., Yuan, L., Chaney, K., Daniilidis, K.: Unsupervised event-based learning of optical flow, depth, and egomotion. In: IEEE Conference on Computer Vision and Pattern Recognition, CVPR 2019, Long Beach, CA, USA, 16–20 June 2019, pp. 989–997. Computer Vision Foundation/IEEE (2019). https://doi.org/10.1109/CVPR.2019.00108, http://openaccess.thecvf.com/content_CVPR_2019/html/Zhu_Unsupervised_Event-Based_Learning_of_Optical_Flow_Depth_and_Egomotion_CVPR_2019_paper.html

68. Zhu, L., Yang, Y.: Inflated episodic memory with region self-attention for long-tailed visual recognition. In: 2020 IEEE/CVF Conference on Computer Vision and Pattern Recognition, CVPR 2020, Seattle, WA, USA, 13–19 June 2020, pp. 4343–4352. Computer Vision Foundation/IEEE (2020). https://doi.org/10.1109/CVPR42600.2020.00440

Out-of-distribution Detection
with Boundary Aware Learning

Sen Pei[1,2](✉), Xin Zhang[1,2], Bin Fan[4], and Gaofeng Meng[1,2,3](✉)

[1] NLPR, Institute of Automation, Chinese Academy of Sciences, Beijing, China
gfmeng@nlpr.ia.ac.cn
[2] School of Artificial Intelligence, University of Chinese Academy of Sciences, Beijing, China
peisen2020@ia.ac.cn
[3] CAIR, HK Institute of Science and Innovation, Chinese Academy of Sciences, Beijing, China
[4] University of Science and Technology Beijing, Beijing, China

Abstract. There is an increasing need to determine whether inputs are out-of-distribution (OOD) for safely deploying machine learning models in the open world scenario. Typical neural classifiers are based on the closed world assumption, where the training data and the test data are drawn $i.i.d.$ from the same distribution, and as a result, give over-confident predictions even faced with OOD inputs. For tackling this problem, previous studies either use real outliers for training or generate synthetic OOD data under strong assumptions, which are either costly or intractable to generalize. In this paper, we propose boundary aware learning (**BAL**), a novel framework that can learn the distribution of OOD features adaptively. The key idea of BAL is to generate OOD features from trivial to hard progressively with a generator, meanwhile, a discriminator is trained for distinguishing these synthetic OOD features and in-distribution (ID) features. Benefiting from the adversarial training scheme, the discriminator can well separate ID and OOD features, allowing more robust OOD detection. The proposed BAL achieves *state-of-the-art* performance on classification benchmarks, reducing up to 13.9% FPR95 compared with previous methods.

Keywords: OOD detection, Boundary aware learning, GAN

1 Introduction

Deep convolutional neural networks are one of the basic architectures in deep learning, and they have achieved great success in modern computer vision tasks. However, the over-confidence issue of OOD data has always been with CNN which harms its generalization performance seriously. In previous research, neural networks have been proved to generalize well when the test data is drawn $i.i.d.$ from the same distribution as the training data, i.e., the ID data. However,

---

Supplementary Information The online version contains supplementary material available at https://doi.org/10.1007/978-3-031-20053-3_14.

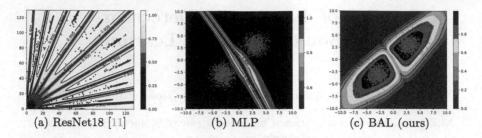

(a) ResNet18 [11]   (b) MLP   (c) BAL (ours)

Fig. 1. Over-confidence issue in typical classification nets. (a): A ResNet18 trained on MNIST. The number of neurons of its penultimate layer is set to 2 for feature visualization. The **blue points** are feature representations of *ID* data. The background color represents confidence score given by the ResNet18. It is shown that the region far from the blue points gets high confidence score. (b): Classification on two gaussian distribution with a MLP. The green points are training data. It can be seen the classification net gives *OOD* regions high confidence which is abnormal. (c): Boundary aware learning (BAL) gives *ID* regions much higher confidence than *OOD* regions. More visualization results are shown in the Appendix Fig. 7. (Color figure online)

when deep learning models are deployed in an open world scenario, the input samples can be *OOD* data and therefore should be handled cautiously.

Generally, there are two major challenges for improving the robustness of models: adversarial examples and *OOD* examples. As pointed out in [10], adding very small perturbations to the input can fool a well-trained classification net, and these modified inputs are the so-called adversarial examples. Another problem is how to detect *OOD* examples that are drawn far away from the training data. The trained neural networks often produce very high confidence to these *OOD* samples which has raised concerns for AI Safety [4] in many applications, which is the so-called over-confidence issue [28]. As shown in Fig. 1 (a), a trained ResNet18 is used for extracting features from the MNIST dataset, and the blue points indicate feature representations of *ID* data. It can be found that almost the whole feature space is assigned with high confidence score but the *ID* data only concentrates in some narrow regions densely.

Previous studies have proposed different approaches for detecting *OOD* samples to improve the robustness of classifiers. In [12], a max-softmax method is proposed for identifying *OOD* samples. Further, in ODIN [25], temperature scaling and input pre-processing are introduced for improving the confidence scores of *ID* samples. In [38], convolutional prototype learning is proposed for image classification which shows effectiveness in *OOD* detection and class-incremental learning. In [7], it points out that the outputs of softmax can not represent the confidence of neural net actually, and thus, a new branch is separated for confidence estimation independently. All these previous works have brought many different perspectives and inspirations for solving the open world recognition tasks. However, these methods pay limited attention to the learning of *OOD* features which is a key factor in *OOD* detection. The neural networks can better detect *OOD* samples if they are supervised by the *trivial* and *hard OOD* information, and that's why we argue OOD feature learning is important for OOD uncertainty estimation.

In this paper, we attribute the reason of poor OOD detection performance to the fact that the traditional classification networks can not perceive the boundary of ID data due to lack of OOD supervision, as illustrated in Fig. 1 (a) and (b). Consequently, this paper focuses on how to generate synthetic OOD information that supervises the learning of classifiers. The key idea of our proposed boundary aware learning (**BAL**) is to generate synthetic OOD features from trivial to hard gradually via a generator. At the same time, a discriminator is trained to distinguish ID and OOD features. Powered by this adversarial training phase, the discriminator can well separate ID and OOD features. The key contributions of this work can be summarized as follows:

- A boundary aware learning framework is proposed for improving the rejection ability of neural networks while maintaining the classification performance. BAL can be combined with mainstream CNN architectures easily.
- We use a GAN to learn the distribution of OOD features adaptively step by step without introducing any assumptions about the distribution of ID features. Alongside, we propose an efficient method called RSM (Representation Sampling Module) to sample synthetic *hard* OOD features.
- We test the proposed BAL on several datasets with different CNN architectures, the results suggest that BAL significantly improves the performance of OOD detection, achieving *state-of-the-art* performance and allowing more robust classification in the open world scenario.

2   Related Work

OOD Detection with Softmax-Based Scores. In [12], a baseline approach to detect OOD inputs named max-softmax is proposed, and the metrics of evaluating OOD detectors are defined properly. Following this, inspired by [10], ODIN [25] and generalized ODIN [15] are proposed for improving the detection ability of max-softmax using temperature scaling, input pre-processing, and confidence decomposition. In [3,24], these studies argue that the feature maps from the penultimate layer of neural networks are not suitable for detecting outliers, and thus, they use the features from a well-chosen layer and adopt some metrics such as Euclidean distance, Mahalanobis distance, and OSVM [34]. In [7], a branch is separated for confidence regression since the outputs of softmax can not well represent the confidence of neural networks. More recently, GradNorm [17] finds that the magnitude of gradients is higher in ID than that of OOD, making it informative for OOD detection. In [26], energy score derived from discriminative models is used for OOD detection which also brings some improvement.

OOD Detection with Synthetic Data. These kinds of methods usually use the ID samples to generate fake OOD samples, and then, train a $(C+1)$ classifier which can improve the rejection ability of neural nets. [35] treats the OOD samples as two types, one indicates these samples that are close to but outside the *ID* manifold, and the other is these samples which lie on the *ID* boundary. This work uses Variational AutoEncoder [33] to generate such data for training. In [23], the authors argue that samples lie on the boundary of *ID* manifold can be treated as *OOD* samples, and they use GAN [9] to generate these data. The proposed joint training method of confident classifier and adversarial generator inspires our work. It can not be ignored that the methods mentioned above are only suitable for small toy datasets, and the joint training method harms the classification performance of neural nets. Further, in [6], the study points out that AutoEncoder can reconstruct the *ID* samples with much less error than *OOD* examples, allowing more effective detection with taking reconstruction error into consideration. Very recently, a newly proposed VOS [8] introduces the *OOD* detection into object detection tasks, and its main focus is still the *OOD* feature generation. In these previous works, the features of each category from penultimate layer of CNN are assumed to follow a multivariate gaussian distribution. We argue and verify that this assumption is not reasonable. Our proposed BAL uses a GAN to learn the *OOD* distribution adaptively without making assumptions, and the experimental results show that BAL outperforms gaussian assumption based methods significantly.

Improving Detection Robustness with Model Ensembles. In [21], the authors initialize different parameters for neural networks randomly, and the bagging sampling method is used for generating training data. Similarly, in [31], the features from different layers of neural networks are used for identifying *OOD* samples. The defined higher order Gram Matrices in this work yield better *OOD* detection performance. More recently, [32] converts the labels of training data into different word embeddings using *GloVe* [29] and *FastText* [18] as the supervision to gain diversity and redundancy, the semantic structure improves the robustness of neural networks.

OOD **Detection with Auxiliary Supervision.** In [30], the authors argue that the likelihood score is heavily affected by the population level background statistics, and thus, they propose a likelihood ratio method to deal with background and semantic targets in image data. In [14], the study finds that self-supervision can benefit the robustness of recognition tasks in a variety of ways. In [40], a residual flow method is proposed for learning the distribution of feature space of a pre-trained deep neural network which can help to detect *OOD* examples. The latest work in [36] treats *ood* samples as *near-OOD* and *far-OOD* samples, it argues that contrastive learning can capture much richer features which improve the performance in detecting *near-OOD* samples. In [13], the author uses auxiliary datasets served as *OOD* data for improving the anomaly detection ability of neural networks. Generally, these kinds of methods use some prior information to supervise the learning of *OOD* detector.

3   Preliminaries

Problem Statement. This work considers the problem of separating *ID* and *OOD* samples. Suppose P_{in} and P_{out} are distributions of *ID* and *OOD* data,

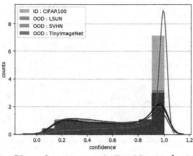 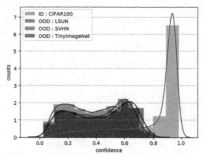

(a) Classification with ResNet18 [11]   (b) Classification with BAL (ours)

Fig. 2. Confusion between *ID* and *OOD* data. (a): In typical classifiers, the *ID* and *OOD* data are confused, and both of them get very high confidence scores. (b): With the proposed BAL, the *OOD* data is assigned with much lower confidence, allowing more effective *OOD* detection.

$X = \{x_1, x_2, ..., x_N\}$ are images randomly sampled from these two distributions. This task aims to give lower confidence of image x_i sampled from P_{out} while higher to that of P_{in}. Typically, *OOD* detection can be formulated as a binary classification problem. With a chosen threshold γ and confidence score $S(x)$, input is judged as *OOD* data if $S(x) < \gamma$ otherwise *ID*. Figure 2 (a) shows the traditional classifiers can not capture the *OOD* uncertainty, and as a result, produce over-confident predictions on *OOD* data. Figure 2 (b) shows an ideal case where *ID* data gets higher score than *OOD*. Methods that aim to boost the performance of *OOD* detection should use no data labeled as *OOD* explicitly.

Methodology. For a given image x, its corresponding feature representation f can be got from the penultimate layer of a pre-trained neural network, and based on the total probability theorem, we have:

$$P(w|f) = P(w|f \in \mathcal{M}_f) \cdot P(f \in \mathcal{M}_f|f)$$
$$+ P(w|f \notin \mathcal{M}_f) \cdot P(f \notin \mathcal{M}_f|f) \tag{1}$$

where w is the category label of *ID* data, and $\mathcal{M}_f$ represents the manifold of *ID* features. Typical neural networks have no access to *OOD* data, therefore the softmax output is actually the conditional probability assuming the inputs are *ID* data, i.e., $P(w|f \in \mathcal{M}_f)$. Empirically, since the *OOD* data has quite different semantic meanings compared with *ID* data, it is reasonable to approximate $P(w|f \notin \mathcal{M}_f)$ to 0. Then, we have:

$$P(w|f) \approx P(w|f \in \mathcal{M}_f) \cdot P(f \in \mathcal{M}_f|f) \tag{2}$$

It tells that the approximation of posterior can be formulated as the product of outputs from pre-trained classifiers and the probability f belongs to $\mathcal{M}_f$. The proposed BAL aims to estimate $P(f \in \mathcal{M}_f|f)$ with features from the penultimate layer of pre-trained CNN.

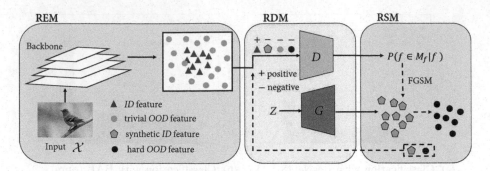

Fig. 3. The proposed BAL framework. The *ID* features are extracted from pre-trained classifier. The trivial *OOD* features are uniformly sampled in feature space. The *hard OOD* features are generated using FGSM method. All features except *ID* feature are treated as *OOD* when training the discriminator. $\mathcal{M}_f$ is the manifold of *ID* features. REM, RSM and RDM are representation extraction module, representation sampling module and representation discrimination module respectively.

4 Boundary Aware Learning

The proposed boundary aware learning framework contains three modules as illustrated in Fig. 3. These modules handle the following problems: **(I)** Representation Extraction Module (REM): how to generate trivial *OOD* features to supervise the learning of conditional discriminator; **(II)** Representation Sampling Module (RSM): how to generate synthetic *hard OOD* features to enhance the discrimination ability of conditional discriminator step by step; **(III)** Representation Discrimination Module (RDM): how to make the conditional discriminator aware the boundary of *ID* features.

4.1 Representation Extraction Module (REM)

This module handles the problem of how to generate trivial synthetic *OOD* features. As in prior works, we use the outputs of penultimate layer in CNN to represent the input images. In the following parts, $\mathcal{H}$ and h are used to indicate the pre-trained classification net with and without the top classification layer, and θ is the pre-trained weights. Formally, the feature f of an input image x is:

$$f = h(x; \theta) \tag{3}$$

During training, image x and its corresponding label c are sampled from dataset $\mathcal{X}$. We get an *ID* feature-label pair $\langle f, c \rangle$ with Eq. (3). For generating trivial synthetic *OOD* features, we sample data in feature space uniformly. Given a batch features $\{f_1, f_2, f_3, ..., f_k\}$, the length of each feature vector f_i is m. We first calculate the minimal and maximal bound in m-dimensional space that contains all features within this batch. For $j \in \{1, 2, 3, ..., m\}$, we have:

$$R_{\min}^{(j)} = \min_{1 \le i \le k} f_i^{(j)}, \quad R_{\max}^{(j)} = \max_{1 \le i \le k} f_i^{(j)} \tag{4}$$

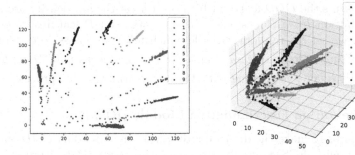

Fig. 4. Feature distribution in penultimate layer of CNN. Left: Classification on MNIST with ResNet18, the penultimate layer has 2 neuros for visualization. Right: Same as the left, the penultimate layer has 3 neurons. There is a large deviation between the distribution of *ID* feature and a multivariate gaussian. Moreover, it is clear that *ID* features densely distribute at some narrow regions in feature space.

Consequently, the batch-wise lower and upper bound of feature vectors are obtained as follows:

$$a = (R_{\min}^{(1)}, R_{\min}^{(2)}, ..., R_{\min}^{(m)})^T, \quad b = (R_{\max}^{(1)}, R_{\max}^{(2)}, ..., R_{\max}^{(m)})^T \tag{5}$$

We use $\mathbb{U}(a,b)$ to indicate a batch-wise uniform distribution in feature space. Randomly sampled feature $\hat{f}$ from $\mathbb{U}(a,b)$ is treated as a negative sample with a randomly generated label $\hat{c}$. The negative pair is expressed as $\langle \hat{f}, \hat{c} \rangle$. We give the reasons of uniform sampling: **(a)** It can not be guaranteed that features from the penultimate layer of CNN follow a multivariate gaussian distribution no matter in low dimensional space or higher feature space. For verifying this idea, we set the penultimate layer of CNN to have two and three neurons for feature visualization, the results shown in Fig. 4 indicate the unreasonableness of this assumption. **(b)** *ID* features densely distribute in some narrow regions which means the most samples from uniform sampling are *OOD* data. Conflicts may happen when $\hat{f}$ is close to *ID* and $\hat{c}$ does match with $\hat{f}$, the RDM deals with these conflicts.

4.2   Representation Sampling Module (RSM)

This module is used for generating *hard OOD* features. For noise z sampled from normal distribution P_z, its corresponding synthetic *ID* feature f can be got by $G(z,c)$ where c is a conditional label. Since the generator G is trained for generating *ID* data, the feature f is much closer to *ID* instead of *OOD*. With Fast Gradient Sign Method [10], we push the feature f towards the boundary of *ID* manifold which gets a much lower score from discriminator.

$$\tilde{f} = f - \epsilon \frac{\partial D(f;c)}{\partial f} \approx f - \epsilon \operatorname{sgn}(\frac{\partial D(f;c)}{\partial f}) \tag{6}$$

$$\tilde{z} = z - \epsilon \frac{\partial D(f;c)}{\partial z} = z - \epsilon \frac{\partial D(G(z;c);c)}{\partial G(z;c)} \frac{\partial G(z;c)}{\partial z} \tag{7}$$

where $\tilde{f}$ represents the OOD feature which scatters at the low density area of ID feature distribution P_f. $\tilde{z}$ can be used for generating OOD features by $G(\tilde{z};c)$. In particular, we set ϵ a random variable which follows a gaussian distribution for improving the diversity of sampling. $\langle \tilde{f}, \tilde{c} \rangle$ is treated as *hard OOD* feature pair because its quality is growing with the adversarial training process.

4.3   Representation Discrimination Module (RDM)

This module aims to make the discriminator aware the boundary of ID features. The generator with FGSM is used for generating *hard OOD* representations while the discriminator is used for separating ID and OOD features. The noise vector z is sampled from a normal distribution P_z. The features of training images from REM follow a distribution P_f. For learning the boundary of ID data via discriminator, we propose **shuffle loss** and **uniform loss**. The shuffle loss makes the discriminator aware the category of each ID cluster in feature space, and the uniform loss makes the discriminator aware the boundary of each ID feature cluster.

Shuffle Loss. In each batch of the training data, we get feature-label pairs like $\langle f, c \rangle$. In a conditional GAN, these $\langle f, c \rangle$ pairs are treated as positive samples. With a shuffle function $T(\cdot)$, the positive pair $\langle f, c \rangle$ is transformed to a negative pair $\langle f, \tilde{c} \rangle$ where $\tilde{c} = T(c) \neq c$ is a mismatched label with feature f. The discriminator is expected to identify these mismatch pairs as OOD data for awareness of category label, and the classification loss is the so called **shuffle loss** as below:

$$L_s = \mathbb{E}_{P_f}(\log D(f;T(c)) - \log D(f;c)) \tag{8}$$

Uniform Loss. We get positive pair $\langle f, c \rangle$ and negative pair $\langle \hat{f}, \hat{c} \rangle$ from REM. It is mentioned before that conflicts may happen when $\hat{f}$ is close to some ID feature clusters and the randomly generated label $\hat{c}$ dose match with them. For tackling this issue, we strengthen the memory of discriminator about positive pair $\langle f, c \rangle$ while weaken that about negative pair $\langle \hat{f}, \hat{c} \rangle$. We force the discriminator to maximize $D(f;c)$ for remembering positive pairs, meanwhile, a hyperparameter λ_c is used to mitigate the negative effects of conflicts. The **uniform loss** is defined as follows:

$$L_u = \lambda_c \cdot \mathbb{E}_{P_U} \log D(\hat{f};\hat{c}) - \mathbb{E}_{P_f} \log D(f;c) \tag{9}$$

Alongside, the *hard OOD* features from RSM introduce no conflicts, and they are treated as negative OOD pairs for calculating uniform loss when training discriminator. Formally, the loss function L_d for conditional discriminator can be formulated as below:

$$L_t = -\mathbb{E}_{P_f} \log D(f;c) - \mathbb{E}_{P_z} \log(1 - D(G(z);c)) \tag{10}$$
$$L_d = L_t + L_s + L_u \tag{11}$$

where L_t is the loss of discriminator in a vanilla conditional GAN. A well trained discriminator is a binary classifier for separating *ID* and *OOD* features. In the process of training generator, we add a regularization term to accelerate the convergence. The loss function of generator is written as:

$$L_g = \mathbb{E}_{P_z} \log(1 - D(G(z;c);c)) + \lambda(\min_{f_c \in \mathcal{M}_c} ||f_c - G(z;c)||_1) \qquad (12)$$

where $||\cdot||_1$ indicates the L1 norm, $\mathcal{M}_c$ is the set of *ID* features with label c, and λ is a balance hyperparameter. The regularization term reduces the difference between synthetic features and the real. We set λ to 0.01 in our experiments. In the process of training generator, the label c is generated randomly.

Generally, the BAL framework only trains the conditional GAN while keeping the pre-trained classification net unchanged. The confidence score outputted by a trained discriminator is treated as $P(f \in \mathcal{M}_f|f)$. Based on Eq. (2), the approximation of posteriori is formulated as the product of outputs from pre-trained classification net and discriminator. The training and inference pipeline is shown in Algorithm 1. Code is available at: `https://github.com/ForeverPs/BAL`

Algorithm 1: *OOD* Detection with Boundary Aware Learning

Input: pre-trained network $\mathcal{H}$ (backbone h) on *ID* data with parameter θ,
      initial generator G, initial discriminator D, *ID* dataset $\mathcal{X}$
Output: *OOD* discriminator D, synthetic *ID* generator G

1   **while** *Training* **do**
2   # Discriminator training;
3   Sample a batch data x from $\mathcal{X}$;
4   Get the corresponding feature vectors : $f = h(x;\theta)$;
5   Calculate the lower and upper bound of f with Eqs. (4,5);
6   Transform the positive pairs $\langle f,c \rangle$ into negative pairs $\langle f, T(c) \rangle$;
7   Sample *trivial* and *hard OOD* feature pairs $\langle \hat{f}, \hat{c} \rangle$ via uniform sampling and
       RSM;
8   Calculate the shuffle loss L_s, the uniform loss L_u, and the vanilla loss L_t
       with Eqs. (8,9,10);
9   Update the parameters of D with gradient descent method.
10   # Generator training;
11   Sample noise z from normal distribution;
12   Get the features conditioned by random labels : $G(z;c)$;
13   Calculate the loss function of generator with Eq. (12);
14   Update the parameters of G with gradient descent method.

15   **while** *Inference* **do**
16   Get feature vector : $\hat{f} = h(\hat{x};\theta)$;
17   Get predict label and corresponding confidence: $p_1, \hat{c} = \mathcal{H}(\hat{x};\theta)$;
18   Get *ID* confidence score : $p_2 = D(\hat{f}, \hat{c})$;
19   Perform *OOD* detection with $p_1 \cdot p_2$ under a chosen threshold.

---

5 Experiments

In this section, we validate the proposed BAL on several image classification datasets and neural net architectures. Experimental setup is described in Sect. 5.1 and Sect. 5.2, evaluation metrics are detailed in Appendix Sect. 6.10 and ablation study is described in Sect. 5.3. We report the main results and metrics in Sect. 5.4. Visualization of synthetic *OOD* data is given in Sect. 5.5.

5.1 Dataset

MNIST [22]: A database of handwritten digits in total 10 categories, has a training set of 60k examples, and a test set of 10k examples.

Fashion-MNIST [37]: A dataset contains grayscale images of fashion products from 10 categories, has a training set of 60k images, and a test set of 10k images.

Omniglot [20]: A dataset that contains 1623 different handwritten characters from 50 different alphabets. In this work, we treat Omniglot as *OOD* data.

CIFAR-10 and CIFAR-100 [19]: The former one contains 60k colour images in 10 classes, with 6k images per class. The latter one also contains 60k images but in 100 classes, with 600 images per class.

TinyImageNet [5]: A dataset contains 120k colour images in 200 classes, with 600 images per class.

SVHN [27] and **LSUN** [39]: The former one contains colour images of street view house number. The latter one is a large-scale scene understanding dataset.

5.2 Experimental Setup

Softmax Baseline. ResNet [11] and DenseNet [16] are used as backbones, and they are trained with an Adam optimizer using cross-entropy loss in total of 300 epochs. Images from MNIST, Fashion-MNIST and Omniglot are resized to 28 × 28 with only one channel. Other datasets are resized to 32 × 32 with RGB channels. For MNIST, Fashion-MNIST and Omniglot, ResNet18 is used as the feature extractor. For any other datasets, ResNet34 and DenseNet-BC with 100 layers are used for feature extraction.

GCPL. We use distance-based cross-entropy loss and prototype loss as mentioned in [38]. The hyperparameter λ (weight of prototype loss) is set to 0.01.

ODIN and Generalized ODIN. Parameters (T, ϵ) are provided in Table 7.

AEC. This method uses reconstruction error to detect outliers. We reproduce it following the details in [6]. See Appendix Fig. 7 for more details.

Table 1. Ablation on different combinations of loss functions. All networks are trained with the training set of CIFAR-10, and **no** OOD data is used. λ_c in uniform loss L_u is set to 0.7. It can be seen that the proposed shuffle loss and uniform loss enhance the ability for detecting outliers.

	↑ AUPR$_{in}$	↑ AUPR$_{out}$	↑ AUROC	↓ FPR 95
Softmax baseline	95.3	92.2	94.1	41.1
BAL (L_t)	97.0	96.0	96.6	17.9
BAL ($L_t + L_s$)	97.1	96.2	96.6	9.3
BAL ($L_t + L_u$)	97.2	96.3	96.7	8.1
BAL ($L_t + L_s + L_u$)	**98.2**	**98.0**	**97.0**	**5.0**

Table 2. Ablation on parameter λ_c. All networks are trained with the training set of CIFAR-10, and **no** OOD data is used. In the following experiments, if not specified, λ_c is set to 0.7 throughout.

λ_c	0.1	0.3	0.5	0.7	0.9
AUROC	94.8	95.2	96.7	**97.0**	96.2
AUPR$_{in}$	95.3	95.3	97.1	**98.2**	96.3
AUPR$_{out}$	92.1	93.4	96.9	**98.0**	97.1

5.3 Ablation Study

Ablation on Proposed Loss Functions. We compare different loss functions proposed in BAL. Specifically, we use DenseNet-BC as the feature extractor. CIFAR-10 is set as ID data while TinyImageNet is set as OOD data. We consider four combinations of proposed loss functions: L_t, $L_t + L_s$, $L_t + L_u$ and $L_t + L_s + L_u$. The details of pre-mentioned loss functions can be found in Eqs. (8-10). For uniform loss L_u, we set the hyperparameter λ_c to 0.7. The results are summarized in Table 1, where BAL with shuffle loss and uniform loss outperforms the alternative combinations. Compared to max-softmax, BAL reduces FPR95 up to 36.1%.

Ablation on λ_c in uniform loss. We test the sensitivity of λ_c in Eq. (9). CIFAR-10 and TinyImageNet are set as ID and OOD respectively. DenseNet-BC is used as the backbone. The ablation results shown in Table 2 demonstrate that with the increasing of λ_c, AUPR$_{out}$ of neural networks increases synchronously which means the classifier can aware more OOD data. In particular, using λ_c as 0.7 yields both better ID and OOD detection performance.

Ablation on OOD Synthesis Sampling Methods. We consider different trivial OOD feature sampling methods. As described in Sect. 4.1, the distribution of features in convolutional layer is usually assumed to follow a multivariate gaussian distribution. Therefore, the low density area of each category is treated as OOD region. We argue this assumption is not reasonable enough because: **(I)**

Table 3. Ablation on BAL with different sampling methods. The values in the table are AUROC. Both uniform and gaussian sampling are performed within BAL framework.

feature dim	2	64	256	512	1024
BAL (Gaussian)	94.3	96.4	96.9	98.1	98.5
BAL (Uniform)	96.5	97.0	97.3	98.1	**98.8**

Table 4. Detecting *OOD* samples on MNIST, Fashion-MNIST and Omniglot with ResNet18. We use the mixture of two datasets as *OOD* samples.

ID	MNIST				F-MNIST			
OOD	F-MNIST & Omniglot				MNIST & Omniglot			
Methods	Softmax baseline [12]/ODIN [25]/GCPL [38]/**BAL(ours)**							
↑ Cls Acc	**99.43**	**99.43**	99.23	**99.43**	**91.51**	**91.51**	90.93	**91.51**
↓ Det Err	4.14	5.01	4.77	**3.06**	32.42	19.14	30.73	**7.10**
↓ FPR 95	3.29	5.03	4.54	**1.11**	59.84	33.27	56.45	**9.20**
↑ AUROC	97.66	97.94	97.96	**99.32**	89.44	93.45	81.79	**97.82**
↑ AUPR$_{in}$	97.22	97.42	98.14	**99.46**	90.80	94.28	72.40	**98.31**
↑ AUPR$_{out}$	97.24	97.64	97.35	**99.09**	86.20	91.36	82.38	**96.95**

From Fig. 1 (a) and Fig. 4, we can see that in low dimensional feature space, the conditional distribution of each category has a great deviation with multivariate gaussian distribution; **(II)** In high dimensional space, the distribution of *ID* features is extremely sparse, therefore it is hard to estimate the probability density of assumed gaussian distribution accurately; **(III)** It is costly to calculate the mean vector μ and covariance matrix Σ of multivariate gaussian distribution in high dimensional feature space; **(IV)** Inefficient sampling. It is of low efficiency since the probability density needs to be calculated for each synthetic sample. Without introducing any strong assumptions about the *ID* features, we verify that the naive uniform sampling together with a GAN framework can model the *OOD* feature distribution effectively. We still use CIFAR-10 and TinyImageNet as *ID* and *OOD* data. We compare uniform sampling and gaussian sampling in feature space. The dimensionality of features is controlled by setting different number of neurons in the penultimate fully connected layer. The ablation results are shown in Table 3. It is clear that BAL with uniform sampling outperforms gaussian sampling in both low and high dimensional space.

5.4   Detection Results

We detail the main experimental results on several datasets with ResNet18, ResNet34, and DenseNet-BC. For CIFAR-10, CIFAR-100, and SVHN, we use the pre-trained ResNet-34 and DenseNet-BC, and for MNIST, Fashion-MNIST, and Omniglot, we train the ResNet18 from scratch.

Table 5. Main *OOD* detection results. We use C-10, C-100, TIN, D-BC and R-34 to represent CIFAR-10, CIFAR-100, TinyImageNet, DenseNet-BC and ResNet-34.

ID	OOD	↓ FPR at 95% TPR					↑ AUPR in					↑ AUPR out				
		Softmax baseline [12]/AEC [6]/ODIN [25]/Generalized ODIN [15]/**BAL(ours)**														
C-10 D-BC	SVHN	59.8	57.2	63.6	44.2	**32.6**	91.9	92.3	89.1	94.6	**99.7**	87.0	92.5	83.9	88.7	**99.7**
	LSUN	33.4	27.6	5.6	5.2	**4.7**	96.4	97.3	98.9	99.0	**99.5**	94.0	96.3	98.7	**98.9**	98.9
	TIN	41.1	35.1	10.5	9.3	**5.0**	95.3	96.2	98.1	97.9	**98.2**	92.2	94.0	97.8	97.4	**98.0**
C-10 R-34	SVHN	67.5	57.2	64.4	12.7	**11.3**	92.2	93.4	85.8	94.5	**95.5**	84.9	84.5	81.8	93.4	**97.4**
	LSUN	54.6	34.6	26.2	21.3	**15.8**	92.3	91.8	93.7	**94.0**	93.9	88.5	92.1	93.8	93.9	**94.1**
	TIN	55.3	28.7	28.0	27.4	**21.6**	92.4	93.1	94.0	**94.3**	93.9	88.3	90.1	92.9	92.7	**93.8**
C-100 D-BC	SVHN	73.3	63.2	60.9	31.9	**21.5**	85.9	89.3	90.2	90.7	**91.5**	78.5	86.7	85.2	89.5	**92.8**
	LSUN	83.3	66.0	58.4	23.9	**11.3**	72.4	87.4	85.0	88.1	**89.3**	65.4	84.9	82.0	87.6	**88.7**
	TIN	82.4	59.7	56.9	22.7	**12.0**	73.0	83.7	84.7	86.5	**91.5**	67.4	82.9	83.0	84.3	**90.6**
C-100 R-34	SVHN	79.7	76.5	76.5	31.2	**17.3**	81.5	82.5	73.8	85.3	**87.1**	74.5	79.6	74.2	85.1	**89.3**
	LSUN	81.2	52.1	54.6	27.1	**18.7**	76.0	80.0	82.4	89.0	**91.5**	70.1	78.4	84.1	**89.0**	88.7
	TIN	79.6	55.3	50.6	29.7	**22.5**	79.2	87.1	86.8	89.3	**91.6**	72.3	85.6	87.0	88.0	**89.8**
SVHN D-BC	LSUN	22.9	22.7	22.1	18.7	**16.4**	96.7	95.4	95.3	97.2	**98.5**	88.0	88.7	**89.3**	86.3	89.3
	C-10	30.7	20.1	24.7	20.3	**12.1**	95.4	93.2	92.5	96.0	**97.3**	88.5	84.7	81.7	84.2	**89.9**
	TIN	21.2	18.6	19.9	15.2	**11.7**	97.0	96.1	95.5	97.3	**98.5**	88.9	90.7	90.1	**91.6**	90.6
SVHN R-34	LSUN	25.7	21.0	22.2	18.1	**13.5**	93.8	91.3	91.3	96.4	**97.8**	84.6	86.5	85.9	89.4	**92.1**
	C-10	21.7	19.5	20.0	16.7	**14.8**	94.8	92.0	91.9	97.0	**97.6**	86.4	87.3	87.1	88.2	**89.0**
	TIN	21.0	19.3	18.0	15.4	**14.3**	95.4	93.4	93.5	96.8	**98.2**	86.9	88.5	88.6	**89.4**	89.4

Results on MNIST, Fashion-MNIST, and Omniglot. We observe the effects of BAL in two groups. In the first group, MNIST is *ID* data, and the mixture of Fashion-MNIST and Omniglot is *OOD* data. In the second group, Fashion-MNIST is *ID* data while MNIST and Omniglot are *OOD* data. For simplicity, Cls Acc and Det Err are used to represent Classification Accuracy and Detection Error. For ODIN, temperature (T) and magnitude (ϵ) are 10 and 5e-4 respectively. The results summarized in Table 4 tell that BAL is effective on image classification benchmark, particularly, BAL reduces FPR95 up to 24.1% compared with ODIN in the second group.

Results on CIFAR-10, CIFAR-100, and SVHN. We consider sufficient experimental settings in this part for testing the generalization ability of BAL. The pre-trained ResNet-34 and DenseNet-BC on CIFAR-10, CIFAR-100 and SVHN come from [1]. The main results on image classification tasks are summarized in Table 5, where BAL demonstrates superior performance compared with the mainstream methods under different experimental settings. Optimal temperature (T) and magnitude (ϵ) are searched for ODIN in each group. Specifically, BAL reports a decline of FPR95 up to 13.9% compared with Generalized ODIN.

5.5 Visualization of *trivial* and *hard OOD* features

We show the visualization results of *trivial OOD* features from uniform sampling and the *hard OOD* features from generator via FGSM in Fig. 5. We set the

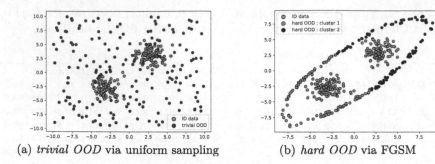

(a) *trivial OOD* via uniform sampling   (b) *hard OOD* via FGSM

Fig. 5. Synthetic *OOD* in raw data space. When the dimensionality of raw data space is high, we have to perform sampling in feature space as shown in Algorithm 1.

Fig. 6. *OOD* detection in open world scenario. Two columns on the left: classification results on *ID* data. Two columns on the right: classification results on *OOD* images from ImageNet. **Green:** max-softmax baseline. **Pink:** the proposed BAL. The threshold for distinguish *ID* and *OOD* is set to 0.60 . It is shown that BAL reduces the false positives among classification results. The image with macarons is a failure case where BAL misclassifies it as a dog. (Color figure online)

training data as two gaussian distributions with dimensionality $m = 2$. We use a MLP with three layers as the classifier. The discriminator and generator only use fully connected layers. In the adversarial training process, we sample data in raw data space uniformly since the dimensionality of raw data is fairly low. The other training details are the same as pipeline shown in Algorithm 1. We also report the classification results on dogs vs. cats [2]. The images from ImageNet are treated as *OOD* data. The top-1 classification results of BAL and Softmax baseline are given in Fig. 6.

6   Conclusion

In this paper, we propose using **BAL** to learn the distribution of *OOD* features adaptively. No strong assumptions about the *ID* features are introduced. We use a simple uniform sampling method combined with a GAN framework can generate *OOD* features in very high quality progressively. BAL has been proved to generalize well across different datasets and architectures. Experimental results on image classification benchmarks promise the *state-of-the-art* performance. The ablation study also shows BAL is stable with different parameter settings.

Acknowledgments. This research was supported by the National Key Research and Development Program of China under Grant No. 2020AAA0109702, the National Natural Science Foundation of China under Grants 61976208, and the InnoHK project.

References

1. https://github.com/facebookresearch/odin
2. https://www.kaggle.com/c/dogs-vs-cats
3. Abdelzad, V., Czarnecki, K., Salay, R., Denouden, T., Vernekar, S., Phan, B.: Detecting out-of-distribution inputs in deep neural networks using an early-layer output. CoRR abs/1910.10307 (2019). http://arxiv.org/abs/1910.10307
4. Amodei, D., Olah, C., Steinhardt, J., Christiano, P.F., Schulman, J., Mané, D.: Concrete problems in AI safety. CoRR abs/1606.06565 (2016). http://arxiv.org/abs/1606.06565
5. Deng, J., Dong, W., Socher, R., Li, L.J., Li, K., Fei-Fei, L.: Imagenet: a large-scale hierarchical image database. In: 2009 IEEE Conference on Computer Vision and Pattern Recognition, pp. 248–255. IEEE (2009)
6. Denouden, T., Salay, R., Czarnecki, K., Abdelzad, V., Phan, B., Vernekar, S.: Improving reconstruction autoencoder out-of-distribution detection with mahalanobis distance. CoRR abs/1812.02765 (2018). http://arxiv.org/abs/1812.02765
7. DeVries, T., Taylor, G.W.: Learning confidence for out-of-distribution detection in neural networks. Stat **1050**, 13 (2018)
8. Du, X., Wang, Z., Cai, M., Li, Y.: Vos: learning what you don't know by virtual outlier synthesis. In: Proceedings of the International Conference on Learning Representations (2022)
9. Goodfellow, I., et al.: Generative adversarial nets. Adv. Neural Inf. Process. Syst. **27** (2014)
10. Goodfellow, I.J., Shlens, J., Szegedy, C.: Explaining and harnessing adversarial examples. In: Bengio, Y., LeCun, Y. (eds.) 3rd International Conference on Learning Representations, ICLR 2015, San Diego, CA, USA, 7–9 May 2015, Conference Track Proceedings (2015). http://arxiv.org/abs/1412.6572
11. He, K., Zhang, X., Ren, S., Sun, J.: Deep residual learning for image recognition. In: Proceedings of the IEEE Conference on Computer Vision and Pattern Recognition, pp. 770–778 (2016)
12. Hendrycks, D., Gimpel, K.: A baseline for detecting misclassified and out-of-distribution examples in neural networks. In: Proceedings of International Conference on Learning Representations (2017)
13. Hendrycks, D., Mazeika, M., Dietterich, T.: Deep anomaly detection with outlier exposure. In: Proceedings of the International Conference on Learning Representations (2019)
14. Hendrycks, D., Mazeika, M., Kadavath, S., Song, D.: Using self-supervised learning can improve model robustness and uncertainty. In: Advances in Neural Information Processing Systems (NeurIPS) (2019)

15. Hsu, Y.C., Shen, Y., Jin, H., Kira, Z.: Generalized odin: detecting out-of-distribution image without learning from out-of-distribution data. In: Proceedings of the IEEE/CVF Conference on Computer Vision and Pattern Recognition, pp. 10951–10960 (2020)
16. Huang, G., Liu, Z., Van Der Maaten, L., Weinberger, K.Q.: Densely connected convolutional networks. In: Proceedings of the IEEE Conference on Computer Vision and Pattern Recognition, pp. 4700–4708 (2017)
17. Huang, R., Geng, A., Li, Y.: On the importance of gradients for detecting distributional shifts in the wild. Adv. Neural Inf. Process. Syst. **34** (2021)
18. Joulin, A., Grave, E., Bojanowski, P., Douze, M., Jégou, H., Mikolov, T.: Fasttext.zip: compressing text classification models. arXiv preprint arXiv:1612.03651 (2016)
19. Krizhevsky, A., Hinton, G., et al.: Learning multiple layers of features from tiny images (2009)
20. Lake, B.M., Salakhutdinov, R., Tenenbaum, J.B.: Human-level concept learning through probabilistic program induction. Science **350**(6266), 1332–1338 (2015)
21. Lakshminarayanan, B., Pritzel, A., Blundell, C.: Simple and scalable predictive uncertainty estimation using deep ensembles. Adv. Neural Inf. Process. Syst. **30** (2017)
22. LeCun, Y.: The mnist database of handwritten digits. http://yann.lecun.com/exdb/mnist/ (1998)
23. Lee, K., Lee, H., Lee, K., Shin, J.: Training confidence-calibrated classifiers for detecting out-of-distribution samples. In: 6th International Conference on Learning Representations, ICLR 2018, Vancouver, BC, Canada, 30 April–3 May 2018, Conference Track Proceedings. OpenReview.net (2018). https://openreview.net/forum?id=ryiAv2xAZ
24. Lee, K., Lee, K., Lee, H., Shin, J.: A simple unified framework for detecting out-of-distribution samples and adversarial attacks. Adv. Neural Inf. Process. Syst. **31** (2018)
25. Liang, S., Li, Y., Srikant, R.: Enhancing the reliability of out-of-distribution image detection in neural networks. In: 6th International Conference on Learning Representations, ICLR 2018, Vancouver, BC, Canada, 30 April–3 May 2018, Conference Track Proceedings. OpenReview.net (2018). https://openreview.net/forum?id=H1VGkIxRZ
26. Liu, W., Wang, X., Owens, J., Li, Y.: Energy-based out-of-distribution detection. Adv. Neural Inf. Process. Syst. **33**, 21464–21475 (2020)
27. Netzer, Y., Wang, T., Coates, A., Bissacco, A., Wu, B., Ng, A.: Reading digits in natural images with unsupervised feature learning. In: NIPS (2011)
28. Nguyen, A., Yosinski, J., Clune, J.: Deep neural networks are easily fooled: High confidence predictions for unrecognizable images. In: Proceedings of the IEEE Conference on Computer Vision and Pattern Recognition, pp. 427–436 (2015)
29. Pennington, J., Socher, R., Manning, C.: Glove: global vectors for word representation. vol. 14, pp. 1532–1543 (2014). https://doi.org/10.3115/v1/D14-1162
30. Ren, J., et al.: Likelihood ratios for out-of-distribution detection. Adv. Neural Inf. Process. Syst. **32** (2019)
31. Sastry, C.S., Oore, S.: Detecting out-of-distribution examples with in-distribution examples and gram matrices. CoRR abs/1912.12510 (2019). http://arxiv.org/abs/1912.12510
32. Shalev, G., Adi, Y., Keshet, J.: Out-of-distribution detection using multiple semantic label representations. Adv. Neural Inf. Process. Syst. **31** (2018)

33. Sohn, K., Lee, H., Yan, X.: Learning structured output representation using deep conditional generative models. In: Cortes, C., Lawrence, N., Lee, D., Sugiyama, M., Garnett, R. (eds.) Advances in Neural Information Processing Systems, vol. 28. Curran Associates, Inc. (2015). https://proceedings.neurips.cc/paper/2015/file/8d55a249e6baa5c06772297520da2051-Paper.pdf
34. Tax, D.M.J., Duin, R.P.W.: Support vector domain description (1999)
35. Vernekar, S., Gaurav, A., Abdelzad, V., Denouden, T., Salay, R., Czarnecki, K.: Out-of-distribution detection in classifiers via generation. CoRR abs/1910.04241 (2019). http://arxiv.org/abs/1910.04241
36. Winkens, J., Bunel, R.: Contrastive training for improved out-of-distribution detection. CoRR abs/2007.05566 (2020). https://arxiv.org/abs/2007.05566
37. Xiao, H., Rasul, K., Vollgraf, R.: Fashion-mnist: a novel image dataset for benchmarking machine learning algorithms. CoRR abs/1708.07747 (2017). http://arxiv.org/abs/1708.07747
38. Yang, H., Zhang, X., Yin, F., Liu, C.: Robust classification with convolutional prototype learning. In: 2018 IEEE Conference on Computer Vision and Pattern Recognition, CVPR 2018, Salt Lake City, UT, USA, 18–22 June 2018, pp. 3474–3482. Computer Vision Foundation/IEEE Computer Society (2018). https://doi.org/10.1109/CVPR.2018.00366, http://openaccess.thecvf.com/content_cvpr_2018/html/Yang_Robust_Classification_With_CVPR_2018_paper.html
39. Yu, F., Zhang, Y., Song, S., Seff, A., Xiao, J.: LSUN: construction of a large-scale image dataset using deep learning with humans in the loop. CoRR abs/1506.03365 (2015). http://arxiv.org/abs/1506.03365
40. Zisselman, E., Tamar, A.: Deep residual flow for out of distribution detection. In: Proceedings of the IEEE/CVF Conference on Computer Vision and Pattern Recognition, pp. 13994–14003 (2020)

Learning Hierarchy Aware Features for Reducing Mistake Severity

Ashima Garg[✉], Depanshu Sani, and Saket Anand

Indraprastha Institute of Information Technology, Delhi, India
{ashimag,depanshus,anands}@iiitd.ac.in

Abstract. Label hierarchies are often available apriori as part of biological taxonomy or language datasets WordNet. Several works exploit these to learn hierarchy aware features in order to improve the classifier to make semantically meaningful mistakes while maintaining or reducing the overall error. In this paper, we propose a novel approach for learning *Hierarchy Aware Features (HAF)* that leverages classifiers at each level of the hierarchy that are constrained to generate predictions consistent with the label hierarchy. The classifiers are trained by minimizing a Jensen-Shannon Divergence with target soft labels obtained from the fine-grained classifiers. Additionally, we employ a simple geometric loss that constrains the feature space geometry to capture the semantic structure of the label space. HAF is a *training time* approach that improves the mistakes while maintaining top-1 error, thereby, addressing the problem of cross-entropy loss that treats all mistakes as equal. We evaluate HAF on three hierarchical datasets and achieve state-of-the-art results on the iNaturalist-19 and CIFAR-100 datasets. The source code is available at https://github.com/07Agarg/HAF.

1 Introduction

Conventional classifiers trained with the cross-entropy loss treat all misclassifications equally. However, certain categories may be more semantically related to each other than to other categories, implying that some classification mistakes may be more *severe* than others. For instance, an autonomous vehicle confusing a `car` for a `truck` is not as severe as mistaking a `pedestrian` for `road`, where the latter mistake could lead to a catastrophe. Similarly, falsely identifying a `pine tree` with an `oak tree` is less severe than identifying it as a `rose`. Classifiers trained to make mistakes with lower severity could benefit and are often critical in many real-world applications.

The severity of a mistake is typically defined based on some notion of semantic similarity between class labels. For example, a taxonomic hierarchy tree defined over the class labels can express specific semantic relationships between classes

Supplementary Information The online version contains supplementary material available at https://doi.org/10.1007/978-3-031-20053-3_15.

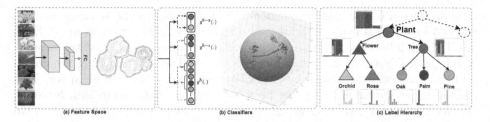

(a) Feature Space   (b) Classifiers   (c) Label Hierarchy

Fig. 1. Overview of HAF. We propose a probabilistic approach using to learn *hierarchy-aware features* that respect the label hierarchy in the feature space and thereby make semantically meaningful mistakes. We train separate classifiers, with a shared feature space, for each level of the label hierarchy. We model the relationship between the fine-grained classes and their respective coarser classes using the label hierarchy and impose consistency constraints on the probability distributions. We further impose simple geometric constraints on the weight vectors of classifiers from different levels to align the weight vectors of fine-grained classes with their corresponding weight vectors of coarser-classes.

through its tree structure, thus enabling an ordering of classes. This ordering was obtained using the lowest common ancestor (LCA) measure in [4,14]. These hierarchies are often readily available in the class label space as part of language datasets like WordNet [19] or from biological taxonomies, e.g., the one used with the iNaturalist-19 dataset [25].

Bertinetto et al. [4] proposed approaches to reduce the severity of mistakes by employing hierarchy-sensitive adaptations of the cross-entropy loss. They reported reduction in the mistake severity based on the average hierarchical distance of top-k predictions at the cost of an increased top-1 error, with the trade-off being controlled by a hyperparameter. A more desirable solution would be the one that reduces the severity of mistakes while maintaining or reducing the overall top-1 error. Karthik et al. [14] highlighted this trade-off and pointed out that the classical approach of Conditional Risk Minimization (CRM) could reduce the mistake severity without a significant change in the top-1 error. Moreover, CRM is a test-time intervention that applies post-hoc corrections on the class likelihoods using the LCA measure between classes. Despite its simplicity, the CRM approach is versatile and its effectiveness is remarkable. In Sect. 4, we show that CRM, when combined with other approaches, almost always improves the mistake severity, without a significant impact on the top-1 error.

While CRM improves the quality of prediction errors, being a test-time approach, it does not affect the model. Consequently, the learned representations are inherently inadequate because the cross-entropy loss function ignores all semantic structure in the label space and treats each class independently. To overcome this limitation, the hierarchical cross-entropy (HXE) loss was proposed in [4], which essentially amounts to a weighted combination of the cross-entropy loss applied at different levels of the hierarchy[1]. Chang et al. [7] pointed out that

---

[1] See the supplementary material for a derivation.

training with a coarse class cross-entropy loss deteriorates the accuracy at fine-grained levels. This is likely the reason why both variants proposed in [4], HXE and the soft-labels loss, result in a trade-off between top-1 error and the severity of mistakes. Chang et al. [7] mitigate this trade-off by disentangling the coarse and the fine-grained features by explicitly partitioning the feature space. This disentangling approach proved to be successful for small hierarchies, however, the feature vector partitioning limits its scalability to larger hierarchies. We argue that for addressing the problem of mistake severity, while maintaining the top-1 error, it is important to learn a feature space that captures the structure available in the label space. To this end, we propose learning a *hierarchy-aware feature* (HAF) space that is explicitly trained to inherit the hierarchical structure of the labels.

We observe that a hierarchy-aware feature space should enable classification at *all* levels of the hierarchy, and simultaneously lead to a lower mistake severity at the finest level. The label hierarchy structure constrains the coarse-level class labels to be a composition of *disjoint* sets of its sub-classes in the hierarchy. We exploit two key properties of the classifiers acting on the feature space to help inherit this compositional structure from the label space.

First, we train a classifier using the fine-grained cross-entropy and use its predictions to obtain target soft labels (Fig. 1) for training the coarse-level auxiliary classifiers. The coarse-level classifiers minimize the Jensen-Shannon divergence (JSD) between their predictions and the target soft labels. This loss avoids the use of hard labels at coarser levels and thus serves as a consistency regularization for the fine-grained classifier, which in turn leads to improved mistake severity without compromising the top-1 error. We take this approach to avoid the pitfall highlighted in [7], which states that fine-grained features can lead to better coarse-grained predictions, however, explicitly using cross-entropy loss for coarse-level classifiers leads to feature spaces that worsens the performance at a finer granularity. Second, we impose geometric consistency constraints on the classifier weight vectors that align sub-classes belonging to the same super-class (Fig. 1(b)). The resulting loss promotes a feature space (Fig. 1(a)) that respects the semantic hierarchy of the label space (Fig. 1(c)). We present further details of the loss terms in Sect. 3. We summarize our contributions below.

- We introduce a novel approach for learning a *hierarchy-aware feature* (HAF) space by inheriting the structure of the label space. We design the loss functions that impose probabilistic and geometric constraints between coarse and fine level classifiers.
- We empirically demonstrate that HAF scales well with large label hierarchies and reduces mistake severity while maintaining the top-1 fine-grained error.

2   Related Work

Several works exploit the hierarchical taxonomy of the data for image classification for visual [4,7,14] and text [18] data, multi-label classification tasks [27], image retrieval [2,29], object recognition [22], and recently to improve semi-supervised approaches [12,24]. We discuss some of the important works that are closely related with our objective.

Label-Embedding Methods. These methods model the class relationships using soft-embeddings. DeViSE [10] maximizes the cosine similarity between the embeddings of an image extracted from a pretrained visual model and the embeddings of label obtained using pretrained word2vec model on Wikipedia. Liu et al. [17] exploit hyperbolic geometry to learn the hierarchical representations. Similar to DeViSE [10], they minimize the Poincaré distance between the Poincaré label embeddings [20] and the image features embeddings. Barz & Denzler [2] map the embeddings onto a unit hypersphere and use LCA to encode the hierarchical distances. Bengio et al. [3] impose the structure over the classes and fastens learning to embed in low dimensional space to model semantic relationships between classes. Bertinetto et al. [4] proposed Soft-labels that uses the soft-targets encoded with inter-class semantic information based on LCA.

Hierarchical-Architecture Based Methods. Wu et al. [28] jointly optimize multi-task loss function wherein cross-entropy loss is applied at each hierarchical level. Recently, Chang et al. [7] established that jointly optimizing fine-grained with coarse-grained recognition in vanilla framework deteriorates performance on fine-grained classification. The authors proposed architecture for multi-granularity classification with independent level-specific classifiers. Redmon et al. [22] proposed a probabilistic model, YOLOv2, for object detection and classification, where softmax is applied at every coarse-category level to address the mutual exclusion of all the classes in conventional softmax classifier.

Hierarchical-Loss Based Methods. Bertinetto et al. [4] proposed another approaches - hierarchical cross-entropy (HXE). HXE is a probabilistic approach that optimizes a loss function based on conditional probabilities, where predictions for a particular class is conditioned on the parent-class probabilities. Brust & Denzler et al. [6] proposed a conditional probability classifier for DAGs. Bilal et al. [5] proposed hierarchical-aware convolutional neural networks by adding branches to the intermediate network pipeline. In [16], authors use prototypical network which uses softmax over distances between the features to the class prototypes, along with a regularization term that encourages the class prototypes to follow the relationship in label hierarchy. Our work is in line with this body of research. We study a different probabilistic model and propose a loss function based on that model. In HAF, we explicitly define class prototypes at every level and take a different approach for arrangement of these prototype vectors.

Cost Based Methods. Another line of research is based on assigning different costs depending on the types of misclassification [1]. Deng et al. [8] proposed to use *mean classification cost* to make hierarchy-aware predictions by penalizing the mistakes based on the hierarchies. [9,26] used semantic hierarchy to design cost matrix optimizing accuracy-specificity trade-offs between the level of abstraction of the selected class while selecting the best in specificity. These methods include both internal and leaf nodes in the cost matrix. While Karthik et al. [14] study conditional risk minimization (CRM) on similar lines to [8], an inference-time approach that weighs the predictions based on the cost matrix defined using LCA distances among the leaf nodes. HAF also fits in this framework. However, unlike CRM [14], HAF is a training-time approach to learn feature embeddings such that they are hierarchically meaningful.

3   HAF: Proposed Approach

Consider a label hierarchy tree with $H+1$ levels, where the root is at level-0, and $h \in [1, \ldots, H]$ denote the hierarchical level with $h=1$ and $h=H$ the coarsest and finest levels respectively. We ignore the root node for our purposes as it denotes the universal super-set containing all classes. Let $\mathcal{X} = \{\mathbf{x}_i, y_i^h | i = 1, \ldots, N\}$ be the set of N images and their respective ground-truth labels at level h. We denote the common feature extractor $f_\phi(\cdot)$, which is implemented using some backbone neural network and is parameterized by ϕ. As illustrated in Fig. 1, we use classifiers at each level of the hierarchy in training HAF and denote the level-h classifier as $g^h(\cdot)$ parameterized by the weight matrix $\mathbf{W}^h$. The resulting prediction probabilities are denoted by $p^h(\widehat{y}_i^h | \mathbf{x}_i; \mathbf{W}^h) = g^h(f_\phi(\mathbf{x}_i))$, where $\widehat{y}_i^h$ is the label predicted for $\mathbf{x}_i$ by $g^h(\cdot)$ and can take class labels from the set of classes at level-h as $\mathcal{C}^h = \left\{\bigcup_{i=1}^{|A|} A_i, \bigcup_{i=1}^{|B|} B_i, \bigcup_{i=1}^{|C|} C_i, \ldots\right\}$, where we define the set of classes at level-$(h-1)$ as $\mathcal{C}^{h-1} = \{A, B, C, \ldots\}$. With a slight abuse of notation, here we use A to denote a super-class label at level-$(h-1)$ and the set of its sub-classes $\{A_1, A_2, \ldots\}$ at level-h.

3.1   Fine Grained Cross-Entropy ($L_{CE_{fine}}$)

We use the ground truth labels only at the finest level of the hierarchy and apply the cross-entropy loss to train the level-H classifier, i.e., $g^H(\cdot)$. The fine-grained cross-entropy loss for a sample is given by

$$L_{CE_{fine}} = -\sum_{c \in \mathcal{C}^H} \mathbf{1}\left[y_i^H = c\right] \log\left(p^H(\widehat{y}_i^H = c | \mathbf{x}_i; \mathbf{W}^H)\right) \tag{1}$$

where $\mathbf{1}[\cdot]$ serves as an indicator function and takes a value of one when the argument is true, else zero.

3.2   Soft Hierarchical Consistency (L_{shc})

For making better mistakes, we want the classifiers at all levels to use the same feature space and yet make predictions consistent with the label hierarchy. While it is natural to use the cross-entropy loss for training the classifiers at all levels, as noted in [7] and observed during our initial experiments, this choice of loss compromises the fine-grained accuracy. Instead, we enforce the consistency across classifiers at different levels by using soft labels and a symmetric entropy-based loss function. We minimize the Jensen-Shannon Divergence (JSD) [11] between the predictions of a coarse classifier $g^{h-1}(\cdot)$ and the soft labels obtained from the next fine-level classifier $g^h(\cdot)$. As defined above, for a given class label $A \in \mathcal{C}^{h-1}$, let $P[\widehat{y}^{h-1} = A|\mathbf{x}_i]$ denote the probability of the sample $\mathbf{x}_i$ belonging to the class A, which is computed as

$$P\left[\widehat{y}_i^{h-1} = A|\mathbf{x}_i\right] = \sum_{k=1}^{|A|} p^h(\widehat{y}_i^h = A_k|\mathbf{x}_i; \mathbf{W}^h) \qquad (2)$$

The probabilities $P[c], \forall c \in \mathcal{C}^{h-1}$ are concatenated together to construct the probability vector $\widehat{p}^{h-1}(\widehat{y}_i^{h-1}|\mathbf{x}_i)$, which is used as the soft label for $\mathbf{x}_i$. This soft label generation process is illustrated in Fig. 2.

The JSD is minimized between the soft labels and the predictions from the classifier $g^h(\cdot)$. For convenience, we use p_i^h to refer to $p^h(\widehat{y}_i^h|x_i; \mathbf{W}^h)$ and similarly $\widehat{p}_i^h$ for the corresponding soft label. The JSD based total Soft Hierarchical Consistency is computed by summing the pairwise losses across the levels

$$L_{shc} = \sum_{h=1}^{H-1} JS^h\left(p_i^h||\widehat{p}_i^h\right) = \frac{1}{2}\sum_{h=1}^{H-1}(\mathrm{KL}(p_i^h||m) + \mathrm{KL}(\widehat{p}_i^h||m)) \qquad (3)$$

where $m = \frac{1}{2}(p_i^h + \widehat{p}_i^h)$ and $\mathrm{KL}(\cdot||\cdot)$ refers to Kullback-Leibler divergence.

It is important to highlight the key difference between the soft labels generated above and those defined in [4]. The latter are designed using the LCA-based distance between classes, whereas our choice of soft labels can be interpreted as a *learned* label-smoothing that better regularizes the coarse-level classifiers. Yuan et al. [30] make a similar argument about label smoothing in the context of knowledge distillation. The use of a symmetric loss like in Eq. (3) further enables the classifiers at both levels to jointly drive the feature space learning. This behavior of the coarse classifiers improving the performance of the finer-level classifiers is analogous to the Reversed Knowledge Distillation (Re-KD) setting as presented in [30], where the authors showed that a student ($g^{h-1}(\cdot)$) is capable of improving the performance of the teacher ($g^h(\cdot)$).

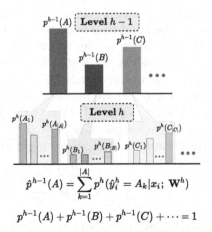

$$\widehat{p}^{h-1}(A) = \sum_{k=1}^{|A|} p^h(\widehat{y}_i^h = A_k|x_i; \mathbf{W}^h)$$

$$p^{h-1}(A) + p^{h-1}(B) + p^{h-1}(C) + \cdots = 1$$

Fig. 2. Constructing the soft labels for training the coarse-level classifiers. The super-class target probability is the sum of its sub-classes' predicted probability. The colors indicate the class relationships across levels $h-1$ and h.

3.3   Margin Loss (L_m)

While L_{shc} improves the mistake severity (as we show in Sect. 5) successfully by virtue of better regularization, it does not directly encourage discrimination between coarse-level classes. Therefore, we use a pairwise margin-based loss to promote a more discriminative feature space. We use this loss over coarser levels $h \in \mathcal{H}$ where $\mathcal{H}$ is $[k, H-1]$ and k ranges from $[1, H-1]$. For a given batch of samples, we create pairs of samples that have dissimilar labels at a level h, i.e., $\mathcal{B}^h = \{(i,j)|y_i^h \neq y_j^h\}$. Then we compute the margin loss over the batch as

$$L_m = \sum_{h \in \mathcal{H}} \sum_{(i,j) \in \mathcal{B}^h} \max\left(0, m - \text{JS}^h(p_i^h \| p_j^h)\right) \tag{4}$$

where p_i^h is the softmax probability generated by $g^h(f_\phi(\mathbf{x}_i))$ and m is the margin. The margin loss is only applied to the coarser levels of the hierarchy, as the cross-entropy loss of (1) is sufficient for fine-grained discrimination.

3.4   Geometric Consistency (L_{gc})

HAF uses classifiers at all the levels of hierarchy. In a hierarchy-aware feature space, the weight vectors of the coarse class and its fine-grained classes should be correlated. The losses introduced in the previous subsections impose probabilistic consistency across the classifier predictions, and only indirectly affect the feature space geometry. In order to better orient the feature space to inherit the label space hierarchy, we use a geometric consistency loss. As before, let $A \in \mathcal{C}^{h-1}$ be a given super-class and its sub-classes be $A_k \in \mathcal{C}^h$, $k = 1, \ldots, |A|$. Let the weight vector corresponding to the super-class A be $\mathbf{w}_A^{h-1}$ and similarly the weight vectors corresponding to the sub-classes be $\mathbf{w}_{A_k}^h$. Note that the classifier $g^{h-1}(\cdot)$ is defined by the weight matrix $\mathbf{W}^{h-1}$, which is obtained by stacking the weight vectors $\mathbf{w}_c$, $c \in \mathcal{C}^{h-1}$. We further constrain each weight vector to be unit norm $\|\mathbf{w}_c^h\|_2 = 1, \forall c, h$, across all classifiers. For the super-class $A \in \mathcal{C}^{h-1}$, we define the target weight vector as $\widehat{\mathbf{w}}_A^{h-1} = \widetilde{\mathbf{w}}_A^{h-1}/\|\widetilde{\mathbf{w}}_A^{h-1}\|_2$, where $\widetilde{\mathbf{w}}_A^{h-1} = \sum_{k=1}^{|A|} \mathbf{w}_{A_k}^h$. Thus, the Geometric Consistency loss to be minimized is

$$L_{gc} = \sum_{h=1}^{H-1} \sum_{c \in \mathcal{C}^h} \left(1 - \cos\left(\mathbf{w}_c^h, \widehat{\mathbf{w}}_c^h\right)\right) \tag{5}$$

where $\cos\left(\mathbf{w}_c^h, \widehat{\mathbf{w}}_c^h\right)$ refers to the cosine similarity between the weight vectors $\mathbf{w}_c^h$ and $\widehat{\mathbf{w}}_c^h$.

Finally, the total loss is given by $L_{total} = L_{CE_{fine}} + L_{shc} + L_m + L_{gc}$.

4   Experiments and Results

4.1   Experimental Setup

Datasets. We present the evaluation of HAF approach on the CIFAR-100 [15], iNaturalist-19 [25] and tieredImageNet-H [23] datasets. We follow the hierarchical taxonomy as is in [16] for CIFAR-100, and [4] for iNaturalist-19 and tieredImageNet-H. In all the three datasets, Level-0 has only one node, i.e., the root node. Therefore, we only consider the bottom H hierarchical levels. Similar to [4], we compute the distance between any two nodes by finding the minimum distance between the node and their Lowest Common Ancestor (LCA). Table 1 summarizes the dataset statistics.

Table 1. Statistics of the datasets.

	Train	Val	Test	#Classes	#Levels
CIFAR-100	45,000	5,000	10,000	100	6
iNaturalist-19	187,385	40,121	40,737	1010	8
TieredImageNet-H	425,600	15,200	15,200	608	13

Baselines. We directly compare HAF with the baseline cross-entropy, Barz & Denzler's [2], YOLO-v2 [22], both approaches of Bertinetto et al's [4] work - soft-labels and HXE, and the recently proposed CRM-based method from [14]. We also compare with recently proposed Chang et al.'s [7] multi-task framework for classification with different granularities. For fair comparisons, we re-run all the experiments with the same codebase under the new best hyperparameter settings for all the methods and report mean and standard deviation of each experiment averaged over three-different seeds.

Evaluation Metrics. We use the same evaluation metrics as Bertinetto et al. [4]; Karthik et al. [14]. We report the following three metrics: i) top-1 error, ii) average mistakes severity, i.e., average LCA-based distance between the ground-truth and predicted class label for *only* incorrectly classified samples, and iii) average hierarchical distance @k, i.e., average distance from the LCA of ground-truth label and k most likely predictions for *all* the samples.

4.2 Training Configurations

We adopt the Wideresnet-28-2 [31] backbone for evaluation on the CIFAR-100 dataset. For the iNaturalist-19 and tieredImageNet-H datasets, we use the ImageNet pretrained ResNet-18 [13] backbone with an additional fully-connected (FC) layer of 600 hidden units. Chang et al. [7] only employ this fully connected layer for facilitating disentanglement, however, we use this additional layer as part of the backbone for consistency across all the methods. Classifiers for each hierarchical level follow this layer. We train all the models with a batch size of 256. We use a fixed margin m of 3.0 across all the datasets defined in Eq. (4) and create a total of 256 dissimilar pairs from a batch of data. For CIFAR-100, we employ `RandomPadandCrop(32)` and `RandomFlip()` for augmentation. For iNaturalist-19 and tieredImagenet-H, we use `RandomHorizontalFlip()` followed by `RandomResizedCrop()` as carried out in [4].

We find the training strategy (learning rate and optimizer) of Chang et al. [7] to give optimal results on both CIFAR-100 and iNaturalist-19 datasets on the baseline cross-entropy. This training strategy with the SGD optimizer boosts the performance of cross-entropy on iNaturalist-19 as opposed to the ones reported using Adam optimizer in [4]. We obtain the best results for CIFAR-100 and iNaturalist-19 using the SGD optimizer on all methods, except for soft-labels and HXE where Adam [21] performs the best. For the methods trained with SGD, we set different learning rates for the backbone network and the FC layer as 0.01 and 0.1 respectively, following [7]. For training with soft-labels and HXE with Adam optimizer, using a hyperparameter sweep we find that the model performs the best with learning rate as 1e−3 and 1e−4 for CIFAR-100 and iNaturalist-19 respectively. We train all the models on tieredImageNet-H for 120 epochs with a learning rate of 1e−5. Unlike other datasets, we employ the Adam optimizer for tieredImageNet-H as it performed better than the SGD optimizer.

4.3   Results

Tables 2, 3 and 4 present the comparisons of our proposed technique with the baselines on CIFAR-100, iNaturalist-19, and tieredImageNet-H respectively. Karthik et al. [14] apply the CRM technique on the baseline cross-entropy. Since CRM is a test-time approach that reweighs the probability distribution of samples obtained from any trained model, it can be applied to all other approaches. Therefore, in each of the Tables 2–4, we group the results to report evaluation metrics with and without using CRM at test-time. We re-emphasize that the goal of the problem is to improve the hierarchical metrics by maintaining or improving the top-1 error. Towards this goal, in each table, we highlight the competitive methods (rows) on the top-1 error with lightgreen . Among these competitive methods, we highlight the best-performing entries for each metric with green . On CIFAR-100 (Table 2), baseline cross-entropy, Chang et al. [7] and HAF and their counterparts using CRM are competitive methods on top-1 error. However, HAF and HAF + CRM outperforms all other hierarchical metrics without compromising top-1 error. We observe similar trends on iNaturalist-19 (Table 3), where HAF , and HAF + CRM are the only competitive *training method* to cross-entropy, which maintain the top-1 error and yet improve the hierarchical metrics. On tieredImageNet-H (Table 4), baseline cross-entropy, HXE $\alpha = 0.1$, Soft-labels $\beta = 30$, and HAF are competitive for both, top-1 error and hierarchical metrics. However, HAF is the best performing method on hier dist@20.

It is worth pointing out that Chang et al.'s [7] method does not scale well with increasing number of hierarchical levels. For CIFAR-100 with six levels, the accuracy is competitive with cross-entropy, however, with both iNat and tieredImageNet-H, which have 8 and 13 levels, the top-1 error worsens. This is not unexpected as the feature vector is divided based on number of levels. While increasing the feature space may be a reasonable solution to maintain performance, it may not be straightforward to decide the feature vector size for each level, especially for hierarchies that may be skewed. On the contrary, HAF is

Table 2. Results comparing top-1 error (%) and hierarchical metrics on the test set of *CIFAR-100*. Results in the *Top* block are reported without using CRM [14] technique and *Bottom* block are reported using CRM. Rows highlighted with lightgreen are competitive methods in top-1 error (%). Of these competitive methods, we highlight the best performing entries for each metric with green .

Method	Top-1 Error(↓)	Mistakes severity(↓)	Hier dist@1(↓)	Hier dist@5(↓)	Hier dist@20(↓)
			Without CRM		
Cross-Entropy	22.27 ± 0.001	2.35 ± 0.024	0.52 ± 0.003	2.24 ± 0.007	3.17 ± 0.007
Barz & Denzler	31.69 ± 0.004	2.36 ± 0.025	0.75 ± 0.012	1.25 ± 0.364	2.49 ± 0.004
YOLO-v2 [22]	32.03 ± 0.006	3.72 ± 0.022	1.19 ± 0.019	2.85 ± 0.010	3.39 ± 0.0109
HXE α = 0.1 [4]	28.41 ± 0.003	2.43 ± 0.004	0.69 ± 0.008	2.08 ± 0.008	3.02 ± 0.012
HXE α = 0.6 [4]	30.42 ± 0.003	2.29 ± 0.008	0.7 ± 0.008	1.76 ± 0.007	2.79 ± 0.008
Soft-labels β = 30 [4]	26.99 ± 0.003	2.38 ± 0.004	0.64 ± 0.008	1.39 ± 0.027	2.79 ± 0.005
Soft-labels β = 4 [4]	32.15 ± 0.008	2.21 ± 0.037	0.71 ± 0.024	1.23 ± 0.018	2.23 ± 0.008
Chang et al. [7]	21.94 ± 0.002	2.32 ± 0.005	0.51 ± 0.005	2.06 ± 0.018	3.08 ± 0.007
HAF	22.27 ± 0.001	2.24 ± 0.014	0.50 ± 0.003	1.41 ± 0.007	2.64 ± 0.002
			With CRM		
Cross-Entropy [14]	22.23 ± 0.001	2.31 ± 0.033	0.51 ± 0.006	1.11 ± 0.006	2.18 ± 0.002
YOLO-v2	32.01 ± 0.006	3.72 ± 0.020	1.19 ± 0.021	3.17 ± 0.003	3.64 ± 0.004
HXE (α=0.1)	28.41 ± 0.003	2.42 ± 0.005	0.69 ± 0.007	1.24 ± 0.005	2.24 ± 0.005
HXE (α=0.6)	30.46 ± 0.003	2.28 ± 0.009	0.69 ± 0.009	1.22 ± 0.007	2.22 ± 0.004
Soft-labels (β = 30)	27.17 ± 0.004	2.36 ± 0.001	0.64 ± 0.008	1.20 ± 0.005	2.22 ± 0.003
Soft-labels (β = 4)	32.73 ± 0.007	2.21 ± 0.023	0.72 ± 0.017	1.23 ± 0.011	2.23 ± 0.006
Chang et al. [7]	21.92 ± 0.001	2.27 ± 0.009	0.50 ± 0.003	1.10 ± 0.002	2.18 ± 0.002
HAF	22.31 ± 0.001	2.23 ± 0.018	0.50 ± 0.003	1.10 ± 0.003	2.17 ± 0.003

Table 3. Results comparing top-1 error(%) and hierarchical metrics on the test set of *iNaturalist-19*. Results in the *Top* block are reported without using CRM [14] technique and *Bottom* block are reported using CRM. Rows highlighted with lightgreen are competitive methods in top-1 error (%). Of these competitive methods, we highlight the best performing entries for each metric with green .

Method	Top-1 Error(↓)	Mistakes severity(↓)	Hier dist@1(↓)	Hier dist@5(↓)	Hier dist@20(↓)
			Without CRM		
Cross-Entropy	36.44 ± 0.061	2.39 ± 0.007	0.87 ± 0.004	1.97 ± 0.002	3.25 ± 0.002
Barz & Denzler [2]	62.63 ± 0.278	1.99 ± 0.008	1.24 ± 0.005	1.49 ± 0.005	1.97 ± 0.005
YOLO-v2 [22]	44.37 ± 0.106	2.42 ± 0.003	1.08 ± 0.004	1.90 ± 0.003	2.87 ± 0.010
HXE α = 0.1 [4]	41.48 ± 0.204	2.41 ± 0.009	1.00 ± 0.005	1.77 ± 0.011	2.69 ± 0.021
HXE α = 0.6 [4]	45.45 ± 0.014	2.24 ± 0.006	1.02 ± 0.003	1.70 ± 0.005	2.55 ± 0.005
Soft-labels β = 30 [4]	41.67 ± 0.134	2.32 ± 0.010	0.97 ± 0.006	1.50 ± 0.006	2.23 ± 0.005
Soft-labels β = 4 [4]	74.70 ± 0.212	1.82 ± 0.005	1.36 ± 0.004	1.49 ± 0.003	1.96 ± 0.004
Chang et al. [7]	37.23 ± 0.175	2.28 ± 0.006	0.85 ± 0.004	1.75 ± 0.005	3.02 ± 0.008
HAF	36.4 ± 0.092	2.28 ± 0.012	0.83 ± 0.002	1.62 ± 0.002	2.55 ± 0.003
			With CRM		
Cross-Entropy [14]	36.51 ± 0.083	2.33 ± 0.001	0.85 ± 0.002	1.32 ± 0.001	1.86 ± 0.002
YOLO-v2	45.17 ± 0.046	2.43 ± 0.001	1.10 ± 0.001	1.50 ± 0.001	1.99 ± 0.002
HXE α=0.1	41.47 ± 0.220	2.38 ± 0.011	0.99 ± 0.008	1.41 ± 0.006	1.93 ± 0.005
HXE α=0.6	45.60 ± 0.017	2.21 ± 0.008	1.01 ± 0.003	1.40 ± 0.004	1.40 ± 0.004
Soft-labels β = 30	41.99 ± 0.126	2.31 ± 0.009	0.97 ± 0.007	1.40 ± 0.005	1.91 ± 0.005
Soft-labels β = 4	77.34 ± 0.262	2.06 ± 0.012	1.60 ± 0.007	1.72 ± 0.008	2.14 ± 0.007
Chang et al. [7]	37.31 ± 0.145	2.24 ± 0.008	0.84 ± 0.002	1.30 ± 0.002	1.84 ± 0.002
HAF	36.48 ± 0.095	2.25 ± 0.012	0.82 ± 0.003	1.29 ± 0.004	1.84 ± 0.002

Table 4. Results comparing top-1 error(%) and hierarchical metrics on the test set of *tieredImageNet-H*. The *Top* block reports results without using CRM [14] and the *Bottom* block are reported using CRM. Rows highlighted with lightgreen are competitive methods in top-1 error (%). Of these methods, we highlight the best performing entries for each metric with green .

Method	Top-1 error(↓)	Mistakes severity(↓)	Hier dist@1(↓)	Hier dist@5(↓)	Hier dist@20(↓)
			Without CRM		
Cross-Entropy	30.60 ± 0.030	7.05 ± 0.010	2.16 ± 0.006	5.67 ± 0.003	7.17 ± 0.003
Barz & Denzler [2]	39.73 ± 0.240	6.80 ± 0.019	2.70 ± 0.022	5.48 ± 0.271	6.21 ± 0.005
YOLO-v2 [22]	33.37 ± 0.082	7.02 ± 0.004	2.34 ± 0.016	5.85 ± 0.011	7.43 ± 0.016
DeViSE [10]	36.75 ± 0.090	6.87 ± 0.017	2.52 ± 0.009	5.57 ± 0.005	6.98 ± 0.005
HXE $\alpha = 0.1$ [4]	30.72 ± 0.036	7.00 ± 0.019	2.15 ± 0.005	5.62 ± 0.008	7.08 ± 0.015
HXE $\alpha = 0.6$ [4]	34.50 ± 0.007	6.73 ± 0.014	2.32 ± 0.003	5.48 ± 0.001	6.78 ± 0.003
Soft-labels $\beta = 30$ [4]	30.53 ± 0.194	7.05 ± 0.009	2.15 ± 0.013	5.66 ± 0.002	7.14 ± 0.008
Soft-labels $\beta = 4$ [4]	38.99 ± 0.105	6.60 ± 0.024	2.57 ± 0.004	5.13 ± 0.002	6.21 ± 0.001
Chang et al. [7]	33.46 ± 0.026	6.99 ± 0.010	2.34 ± 0.006	5.75 ± 0.005	7.34 ± 0.010
HAF	30.50 ± 0.010	7.03 ± 0.024	2.14 ± 0.008	5.62 ± 0.011	6.99 ± 0.009
			With CRM		
Cross-Entropy [14]	30.67 ± 0.020	6.99 ± 0.007	2.14 ± 0.006	4.95 ± 0.002	6.11 ± 0.001
YOLO-v2	33.98 ± 0.099	6.99 ± 0.011	2.38 ± 0.012	5.05 ± 0.001	6.17 ± 0.001
HXE $\alpha = 0.1$	30.80 ± 0.079	6.95 ± 0.021	2.14 ± 0.005	4.94 ± 0.003	6.11 ± 0.002
HXE $\alpha = 0.6$	34.68 ± 0.003	6.69 ± 0.007	2.32 ± 0.001	4.99 ± 0.005	6.13 ± 0.003
Soft-labels $\beta = 30$	30.69 ± 0.125	6.99 ± 0.007	2.15 ± 0.008	4.95 ± 0.001	6.11 ± 0.001
Soft-labels $\beta = 4$	82.72 ± 0.079	7.54 ± 0.001	6.24 ± 0.005	6.94 ± 0.005	7.25 ± 0.002
Chang et al. [7]	33.73 ± 0.033	6.93 ± 0.015	5.02 ± 0.007	2.34 ± 0.002	6.15 ± 0.001
HAF	30.63 ± 0.007	6.97 ± 0.024	2.14 ± 0.008	4.95 ± 0.004	6.11 ± 0.001

independent of the number of hierarchical levels used despite using hierarchical classifiers at each level. We also note that the CRM approach fails to improve Soft-labels $\beta=4$. This is perhaps because the label distribution is very flat for smaller β values, leading to predictions with low confidence, which CRM could not help rectify.

4.4   Coarse Classification Accuracy

We also report comparisons over the coarse classification accuracy at all hierarchical levels. The learned feature representations guided with label hierarchies is expected to follow the structure of label hierarchies in the feature space. Such a feature space must restrict the confusions within their respective coarse classes, thereby, increasing the coarse-classification accuracy. We map the target labels and the predicted labels from the finest-level classifier to their respected coarse classes to evaluate the performance of the models on other hierarchical levels using coarse-classification accuracy. The results are reported in the Fig. 3. On both CIFAR-100 and iNaturalist-19, HAF outperforms all the other baseline methods. On tieredImageNet-H, HAF has comparable performance with the Soft-labels $\beta = 30$, HXE $\alpha = 0.1$, and HXE $\alpha = 0.6$.

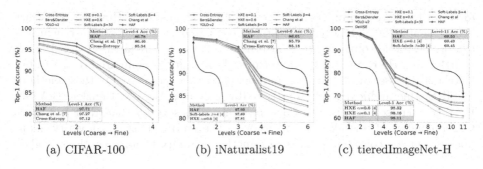

Fig. 3. Coarse-level top-1 accuracy for each dataset. Level = 1 is the coarsest level.

5 Analysis

5.1 Ablation Study

In order to assess the contributions of each loss function used in our proposed approach, we present in Table 5, the results obtained with different variants of HAF on CIFAR-100 and iNaturalist19 datasets respectively. It is evident that different variants of HAF perform slightly better than the cross-entropy baseline but HAF outperforms all the other variants. We can thus conclude that all the components of the loss function are significant and complementary for the overall performance of HAF.

Table 5. Ablative study comparing top-1 error(%) and hierarchical metrics on the test sets of *CIFAR-100* (top) and *iNaturalist-19* (bottom).

Method	Loss function $L_{CE_{fine}}$	L_{shc}	L_{gc}	L_m	Top-1 error($\downarrow$)	Mistakes severity($\downarrow$)	Hier Dist@1($\downarrow$)	Hier Dist@5($\downarrow$)	Hier Dist@20($\downarrow$)
Cross-entropy	✓	-	-	-	22.11	2.37	0.52	2.24	3.16
Variant of HAF	✓	✓	-	-	22.70	2.36	0.54	1.61	2.78
Variant of HAF	✓	✓	✓	-	22.35	2.32	0.52	1.66	2.87
Variant of HAF	✓	✓	-	✓	22.12	2.24	0.5	1.44	2.61
HAF	✓	✓	✓	✓	22.25	2.22	0.49	1.40	2.64
Cross-entropy	✓	-	-	-	36.48	2.39	0.87	1.97	3.25
Variant of HAF	✓	✓	-	-	36.23	2.34	0.85	1.73	2.81
Variant of HAF	✓	✓	✓	-	36.60	2.32	0.85	1.71	2.73
Variant of HAF	✓	✓	-	✓	36.34	2.31	0.84	1.76	2.91
HAF	✓	✓	✓	✓	36.47	2.27	0.83	1.62	2.56

5.2 Mistakes Severity Plots

We plot histograms to compare HAF with the baselines depicting the distribution of mistakes at different hierarchical levels. We present them for each dataset in Fig. 4. Mistakes at hierarchical distance 1 refers to the mistakes with LCA=1. On CIFAR-100, HAF has the lowest mistake severity compared to all the methods and has number of mistakes comparable to cross-entropy at all levels except for level-1, where Chang et al. [7] generates fewer mistakes. However, HAF has lesser number of high severity mistakes compared to Chang et al. [7] which is a more desirable solution. On iNaturalist-19 dataset, soft-labels $\beta = 4$, Barz & Denzler, and HXE $\alpha = 0.6$ has lower mistake severity as compared to HAF , but HAF makes lesser or nearly equal number of mistakes compared to these methods at all the hierarchical levels. On tieredImageNet-H, Barz & Denzler, DeViSE, HXE $\alpha = 0.6$, soft-labels $\beta = 4$ has lower mistakes severity than HAF but much larger number of mistakes at every level. The metric 'mistakes severity' alone does not give a complete picture of a method's ability to improve the mistakes.

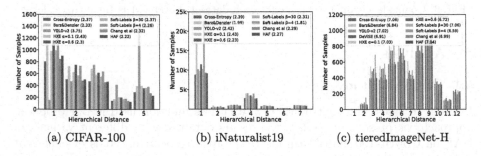

(a) CIFAR-100   (b) iNaturalist19   (c) tieredImageNet-H

Fig. 4. Mistakes severity plot showing distributions of mistakes at each level for each dataset. Numbers in the bracket denote the mistake severity of the method.

5.3   Discussion: Hierarchical Metrics

We discuss the inadequacy of the hierarchical metrics that have been proposed thus far. Figure 5 plots the histogram of the smallest possible LCA for all classes of the tieredImageNet-H dataset. Most classes have a minimum LCA greater than one, which indicates a skewed hierarchy tree, in turn explaining the high values of the hierarchical metrics in Table 4 across all methods. When these metrics are averaged over samples, the resulting

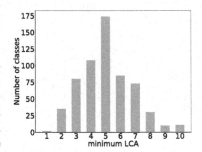

Fig. 5. Number of classes with minimum LCA for tieredImageNet-H dataset.

change turns out to be very small, as observed by the reported standard deviations in Tables 2, 3 and 4. This problem of large values persists in all LCA-based metrics, and is dependent on the label hierarchy tree.

As is depicted above in Fig. 4, mistakes severity favours the model with the reduction of *average* LCA over the mistakes, implying that this metric may prefer a model with a large number of low-severity mistakes. Karthik et. al [14] highlights the problems with mistakes severity. They overcome this drawback by using average hierarchical distance@1. However, we also note the problem with average hierarchical distance@1 metric. It is an average LCA distance of *all* the samples from ground-truth to the top-1 predictions. This average includes as many zeros as the number of correct predictions (since the LCA distance for a correct prediction is 0). Therefore, it favours models that make fewer overall mistakes and thus fails to adequately capture the notion of a mistake's severity.

An ideal method is the one that improves the mistakes severity metric while maintaining (or improving) the top-1 error, i.e., the sum of LCA of mistakes should reduce while maintaining (or improving) the total number of errors. On the CIFAR-100 dataset, we note that with a minimal drop in the top-1 accuracy, there is nearly 5% improvement in reducing the sum of LCA of mistakes using HAF + CRM as compared to 2.17% using cross-entropy + CRM. Similarly, on iNaturalist-19, HAF + CRM minimizes the sum of LCA of mistakes by 5.68% compared to 2% on cross-entropy + CRM. We present a more detailed analysis of these metrics in the supplementary material and defer the design for a more appropriate metric to measure mistake severity for future work.

6   Conclusion

In this paper, we introduced a novel approach to learn a hierarchy-aware feature space, which can preserve or improve the top-1 error and yet reduce the severity of mistakes. Our approach uses auxiliary classifiers at each level of the hierarchy that are trained by minimizing a Jensen-Shannon Divergence with target soft labels derived from finer-grained predictions of the samples. This training strategy regularizes the fine-grained classifier to make more consistent predictions with the coarser level classifiers, leading to a reduction in severity of mistakes. We further impose geometric consistency constraints between coarse and fine classifiers that leads to better alignment of the feature space distributions of the sub-classes with that of their super-classes. Without any additional hyperparameters, we simply trained our models with these loss functions and showed a reduction in mistake severity without trading off the top-1 error. We reported results from extensive experiments over three large datasets with varying levels of hierarchy and showed the strengths of our proposed method. We also presented an analysis of the commonly used hierarchical metrics and highlighted their limitations. We note that there exist recent works that leverage non-Euclidean spaces to learn appropriate embeddings for hierarchical data. However, much of the recent work on evaluating mistake severity is restricted to Euclidean feature spaces, and we present our analysis in the same space. Nonetheless, we conjecture that the nature of our contributions in this paper, i.e., losses that impose probabilistic and geometric constraints, would also extend to non-Euclidean spaces like hyperbolic feature spaces and would serve as a promising direction for future work.

Acknowledgement. Ashima Garg was supported by SERB, Govt. of India, under grant no. CRG/2020/006049. Depanshu Sani was supported by Google's AI for Social

Good "Impact Scholars" program, 2021. Saket Anand gratefully acknowledges for the partial support from the Infosys Center for Artificial Intelligence at IIIT-Delhi.

References

1. Abe, N., Zadrozny, B., Langford, J.: An iterative method for multi-class cost-sensitive learning. In: Proceedings of the Tenth ACM SIGKDD International Conference on Knowledge Discovery and Data Mining, pp. 3–11 (2004)
2. Barz, B., Denzler, J.: Hierarchy-based image embeddings for semantic image retrieval. In: 2019 IEEE Winter Conference on Applications of Computer Vision (WACV), pp. 638–647. IEEE (2019)
3. Bengio, S., Weston, J., Grangier, D.: Label embedding trees for large multi-class tasks. In: Lafferty, J., Williams, C., Shawe-Taylor, J., Zemel, R., Culotta, A. (eds.) Advances in Neural Information Processing Systems, vol. 23. Curran Associates Inc. (2010). https://proceedings.neurips.cc/paper/2010/file/06138bc5af6023646ede0e1f7c1eac75-Paper.pdf
4. Bertinetto, L., Mueller, R., Tertikas, K., Samangooei, S., Lord, N.A.: Making better mistakes: leveraging class hierarchies with deep networks. In: Proceedings of the IEEE/CVF Conference on Computer Vision and Pattern Recognition (CVPR) (2020)
5. Bilal, A., Jourabloo, A., Ye, M., Liu, X., Ren, L.: Do convolutional neural networks learn class hierarchy? IEEE Trans. Visual Comput. Graph. **24**(1), 152–162 (2017)
6. Brust, C.-A., Denzler, J.: Integrating domain knowledge: using hierarchies to improve deep classifiers. In: Palaiahnakote, S., Sanniti di Baja, G., Wang, L., Yan, W.Q. (eds.) ACPR 2019. LNCS, vol. 12046, pp. 3–16. Springer, Cham (2020). https://doi.org/10.1007/978-3-030-41404-7_1
7. Chang, D., Pang, K., Zheng, Y., Ma, Z., Song, Y.Z., Guo, J.: Your "flamingo" is my "bird": fine-grained, or not. In: Proceedings of the IEEE/CVF Conference on Computer Vision and Pattern Recognition, pp. 11476–11485 (2021)
8. Deng, J., Berg, A.C., Li, K., Fei-Fei, L.: What does classifying more than 10,000 image categories tell us? In: Daniilidis, K., Maragos, P., Paragios, N. (eds.) ECCV 2010. LNCS, vol. 6315, pp. 71–84. Springer, Heidelberg (2010). https://doi.org/10.1007/978-3-642-15555-0_6
9. Deng, J., Krause, J., Berg, A.C., Fei-Fei, L.: Hedging your bets: optimizing accuracy-specificity trade-offs in large scale visual recognition. In: 2012 IEEE Conference on Computer Vision and Pattern Recognition, pp. 3450–3457. IEEE (2012)
10. Frome, A., et al.: Devise: a deep visual-semantic embedding model. In: Burges, C.J.C., Bottou, L., Welling, M., Ghahramani, Z., Weinberger, K.Q. (eds.) Advances in Neural Information Processing Systems, vol. 26. Curran Associates Inc. (2013). https://proceedings.neurips.cc/paper/2013/file/7cce53cf90577442771720a370c3c723-Paper.pdf
11. Fuglede, B., Topsoe, F.: Jensen-shannon divergence and hilbert space embedding. In: International Symposium on Information Theory, 2004. ISIT 2004. Proceedings, p. 31. IEEE (2004)
12. Garg, A., Bagga, S., Singh, Y., Anand, S.: Hiermatch: leveraging label hierarchies for improving semi-supervised learning. In: Proceedings of the IEEE/CVF Winter Conference on Applications of Computer Vision, pp. 1015–1024 (2022)
13. He, K., Zhang, X., Ren, S., Sun, J.: Deep residual learning for image recognition. In: Proceedings of the IEEE Conference on Computer Vision and Pattern Recognition, pp. 770–778 (2016)

14. Karthik, S., Prabhu, A., Dokania, P.K., Gandhi, V.: No cost likelihood manipulation at test time for making better mistakes in deep networks. In: International Conference on Learning Representations (2021). https://openreview.net/forum?id=193sEnKY1ij

15. Krizhevsky, A.: Learning multiple layers of features from tiny images. Technical report (2009)

16. Landrieu, L., Garnot, V.S.F.: Leveraging class hierarchies with metric-guided prototype learning. In: British Machine Vision Conference (BMVC) (2021)

17. Liu, S., Chen, J., Pan, L., Ngo, C.W., Chua, T.S., Jiang, Y.G.: Hyperbolic visual embedding learning for zero-shot recognition. In: Proceedings of the IEEE/CVF Conference on Computer Vision and Pattern Recognition, pp. 9273–9281 (2020)

18. Mao, Y., Tian, J., Han, J., Ren, X.: Hierarchical text classification with reinforced label assignment. In: Proceedings of the 2019 Conference on Empirical Methods in Natural Language Processing and the 9th International Joint Conference on Natural Language Processing (EMNLP-IJCNLP), pp. 445–455 (2019)

19. Miller, G.A.: WordNet: An Electronic Lexical Database. MIT press (1998)

20. Nickel, M., Kiela, D.: Poincaré embeddings for learning hierarchical representations. In: Advances in Neural Information Processing Systems 30 (2017)

21. Reddi, S.J., Kale, S., Kumar, S.: On the convergence of adam and beyond. In: International Conference on Learning Representations (2018). https://openreview.net/forum?id=ryQu7f-RZ

22. Redmon, J., Farhadi, A.: Yolo9000: better, faster, stronger. In: Proceedings of the IEEE Conference on Computer Vision and Pattern Recognition, pp. 7263–7271 (2017)

23. Ren, M., et al.: Meta-learning for semi-supervised few-shot classification. In: Proceedings of 6th International Conference on Learning Representations ICLR (2018)

24. Su, J., Maji, S.: Semi-supervised learning with taxonomic labels. In: British Machine Vision Conference (BMVC) (2021)

25. Van Horn, G., et al.: The inaturalist species classification and detection dataset. In: Proceedings of the IEEE Conference on Computer Vision and Pattern Recognition, pp. 8769–8778 (2018)

26. Wang, Y., Wang, Z., Hu, Q., Zhou, Y., Su, H.: Hierarchical semantic risk minimization for large-scale classification. In: IEEE Transactions on Cybernetics (2021)

27. Wehrmann, J., Cerri, R., Barros, R.: Hierarchical multi-label classification networks. In: International Conference on Machine Learning, pp. 5075–5084. PMLR (2018)

28. Wu, H., Merler, M., Uceda-Sosa, R., Smith, J.R.: Learning to make better mistakes: semantics-aware visual food recognition. In: Proceedings of the 24th ACM international conference on Multimedia, pp. 172–176 (2016)

29. Yang, Z., Bastan, M., Zhu, X., Gray, D., Samaras, D.: Hierarchical proxy-based loss for deep metric learning. In: Proceedings of the IEEE/CVF Winter Conference on Applications of Computer Vision, pp. 1859–1868 (2022)

30. Yuan, L., Tay, F.E., Li, G., Wang, T., Feng, J.: Revisiting knowledge distillation via label smoothing regularization. In: Proceedings of the IEEE/CVF Conference on Computer Vision and Pattern Recognition (CVPR) (2020)

31. Zagoruyko, S., Komodakis, N.: Wide residual networks. In: Richard C. Wilson, E.R.H., Smith, W.A.P. (eds.) Proceedings of the British Machine Vision Conference (BMVC), pp. 87.1–87.12. BMVA Press (2016). https://doi.org/10.5244/C.30.87

Learning to Detect Every Thing
in an Open World

Kuniaki Saito[1]($\boxtimes$), Ping Hu[1], Trevor Darrell[2], and Kate Saenko[1,3]

[1] Boston University, Boston, USA
keisaito@bu.edu
[2] University of California, Berkeley, USA
[3] MIT-IBM Watson AI Lab., Cambridge, USA

Abstract. Many open-world applications require the detection of novel objects, yet state-of-the-art object detection and instance segmentation networks do not excel at this task. The key issue lies in their assumption that regions without any annotations should be suppressed as negatives, which teaches the model to treat any unannotated (hidden) objects as background. To address this issue, we propose a simple yet surprisingly powerful data augmentation and training scheme we call Learning to Detect Every Thing (LDET). To avoid suppressing hidden objects, we develop a new data augmentation method, BackErase, which pastes annotated objects on a background image sampled from a small region of the original image. Since training solely on such synthetically-augmented images suffers from domain shift, we propose a multi-domain training strategy that allows the model to generalize to real images. LDET leads to significant improvements on many datasets in the open-world instance segmentation task, outperforming baselines on cross-category generalization on COCO, as well as cross-dataset evaluation on UVO, Objects365, and Cityscapes. https://ksaito-ut.github.io/openworld_ldet/.

Keyword: Open world instance segmentation

1 Introduction

Humans routinely encounter new tools, foods, or animals, and perceive the novel objects as *objects* despite having never seen them before. Unlike humans, current state-of-the-art detection and segmentation methods [20,29,31,35,36] have difficulty recognizing novel objects as *objects* because these methods are designed with a closed-world assumption. Their training aims to localize known (annotated) objects while regarding unknown (unannotated) objects as *background*. This causes the models to fail in locating novel objects and learning general *objectness*. One way to deal with this challenge is to create a dataset with an

Supplementary Information The online version contains supplementary material available at https://doi.org/10.1007/978-3-031-20053-3_16.

Fig. 1. In an open world detection task, the model must locate and segment all objects in the image irrespective of categories used for training. **Left**: We propose a new multi-domain training scheme using real images and augmented images with "erased" background. **Right**: When training on COCO [30] and testing on UVO [41], our detector correctly localizes many objects that are not labeled in COCO with the help of our new data augmentation and training scheme.

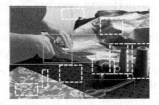 

Fig. 2. **Hidden objects**: Existing datasets do not exhaustively label all objects, leading to detectors that are ill-prepared to propose boxes for long-tail categories. Colored boxes are annotated boxes while white-dashed boxes are potential background regions. Many white-dashed regions locate objects, but are regarded as background during training. This can suppress the objectness of novel objects. (Color figure online)

exhaustive annotation of every single object in each image. However, creating such datasets is very expensive. In fact, many public datasets [15,30,44] for object detection and instance segmentation do not label all objects in an image (Fig. 2).

Failing to learn general objectness can cause issues in many applications. For instance, embodied AI (e.g., robotics, autonomous driving) requires localizing objects unseen during training. Autonomous driving systems need to detect novel objects in front of the vehicle to avoid accidents, though identifying the category is not necessarily required. In addition, zero-shot, and few-shot detection have to localize objects unseen during training. Open-world instance segmentation [41] aims to localize and segment novel objects, but the state-of-the-art model [20] does not perform well as shown in [41].

The failure of current state-of-the-art models is partly due to the training pipeline, *i.e.*, regarding all regions that are not annotated as the foreground objects as background. Even if the background includes *hidden* objects-background objects that are visible but unlabeled-as in Fig. 2, the models are trained not to detect them, which prevents them from learning general objectness. To address this, Kim *et al.* [26] proposed to learn the localization quality of region proposals instead of classifying them as foreground vs. background. Their approach samples object proposals close to the ground truth and learns to estimate the corresponding localization quality. While partially mitigating the issue, this approach still needs to carefully set the overlap threshold for positive/negative sampling and risks suppressing hidden objects as non-objects.

To improve open-world instance segmentation, we propose a simple, yet effective, learning framework along with a new data augmentation method, called *Learning to Detect Every Thing (LDET)*. To eliminate the risk of suppressing hidden objects, we copy foreground objects using their mask annotation and paste them onto a background image. The background image is synthesized by resizing a cropped patch. By keeping the cropped patch small, we make it unlikely that the resulting synthesized images contain any hidden objects. However, this background creation process makes synthesized images look very different from real images, *e.g.*, the background tends to have only low-frequency content. Thus, a detector naively trained on such images performs poorly. To overcome this limitation, we decouple the training into two parts: 1) training background and foreground region classification and localization heads with synthesized images, and 2) learning a mask head with real images. We show that such hybrid training on both domains but with a shared backbone makes the model invariant to the domain shift between augmented and real images.

LDET demonstrates remarkable gains in open-world instance segmentation and detection. On COCO [30], LDET trained on VOC categories improves the average recall by 12.8 points when evaluated on non-VOC categories. Surprisingly, LDET achieves significant improvements in detecting novel objects without requiring additional annotation, *e.g.*, LDET trained only on VOC categories (20 classes) in COCO outperforms Mask RCNN trained on all COCO categories (80 classes) when evaluating average recall on UVO [41]. As shown in Fig. 1, LDET can generate precise object proposals as well as find many objects in the scene.

Our contributions are summarized as follows:

- We propose LDET, a simple framework for open-world instance segmentation which is applicable to both one-stage and two-stage detectors and consists of 1) a special type of data augmentation and 2) decoupled training
- We demonstrate that both (1) and (2) are crucial to achieving good performance in open-world instance segmentation.
- LDET outperforms state-of-the-art methods in all settings including cross-category settings on COCO and cross-dataset setting on COCO-to-UVO, COCO-to-Object365, and Cityscapes-to-Mapillary.

2   Related Work

Region Proposals. Unsupervised region proposal generation used to be a standard approach to localize objects in a scene [1,2,39,45]. These approaches localize objects in a class-agnostic way, but employ hand-crafted features (*i.e.*, color contrast, edge, *etc.*) to capture general objectness.

Closed-World Object Detection. Much effort has been spent on supervised object detection with a closed world assumption [16, 18, 19, 31, 35, 36]. The ability to detect known objects has been improving with better architecture designs [5, 10, 28] or objectives [29]. Also, localizing objects given a few training examples or semantic information is becoming a popular research topic [3, 25]. However, these attempts are still constrained by the taxonomy defined by the dataset. Our model can detect more categories than defined by the dataset, which can be very useful in few-shot or zero-shot object detection.

Open-World Object Detection/Segmentation. Open-world recognition problems are gaining attention in image classification, object detection, and segmentation [4, 6, 11]. Especially, many methods have been proposed for open-set image classification, where the goal is to separate novel categories from known categories given a closed-set training set [4, 32, 34, 38, 43]. On the contrary, the goal of open-world instance segmentation is to detect and segment all objects in a scene without distinguishing novel objects from seen ones. We acknowledge that there is ambiguity in the definition of "object", and follow [41] during evaluation.

Wang *et al.* [41] recently published the first benchmark dataset for open-set instance segmentation, which includes various categories from YouTube videos. However, from a methodological perspective, open-world object detection and segmentation remain understudied despite the importance of the task. Hu *et al.* and Kuo *et al.* [22, 27] proposed approaches for predicting masks of various objects, but they require bounding boxes from classes of interest. Jaiswal *et al.* [23] trained a detector in an adversarial manner to learn class-invariant objectness. Joseph *et al.* [24] proposed a semi-supervised learning approach for open-world detection, which regards regions that are far from ground truth boxes but have a high objectness score as hidden foreground objects. Kim *et al.* [26] employed localization quality estimation with the claim that the estimation strategy is more generalizable in open-world instance segmentation. Note that this is a concurrent work.

The core of the open-world detection problem lies in the detector training pipeline: regarding hidden objects as background. This training scheme is common in both two-stage and one-stage detectors. However, none of the approaches listed above solves this issue. Our approach takes the first step in addressing background suppression via novel data augmentation strategies and shows remarkable improvements over baselines despite its simplicity.

Copy-Paste Augmentation. Pasting foreground objects on a background is a widely used technique in many vision applications [12, 17, 40]. Recently, copy-and-paste augmentation was shown to be a very useful technique in instance segmentation [13, 14, 17]. Dwibedi *et al.* [14] proposed to synthesize an instance segmentation dataset by pasting object instances on diverse backgrounds and trained on the augmented images in addition to the original dataset. Dvornik *et al.* [13] considered modeling the visual context to paste the objects

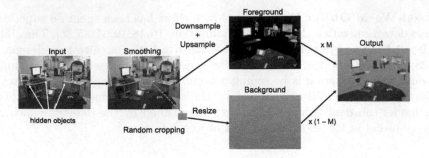

Fig. 3. Our augmentation strategy creates images without hidden objects by upscaling small regions to use as background.

while Ghiasi *et al.* [17] showed that pasting objects randomly is good enough to provide solid gains. These methods still assume a closed-world setting, whereas our task is the open-world instance segmentation problem. There are two technical differences compared to these methods. First, our augmentation samples background images from a small region of an original image to create a background unlikely to have any objects. This pipeline is designed to circumvent suppressing hidden objects as background and does not require any external background data as used in [14]. Second, we decouple the training into two parts, which is also key to achieving a well-performing open-world detection model. In contrast, all of the existing approaches above simply train on synthesized images.

3   Learning to Detect Every Thing

In this section, we describe the proposed LDET scheme for open-world instance segmentation. During training, we are given an instance segmentation dataset with annotations of known classes. In testing, the model is required to locate objects of unknown classes.

Mask-RCNN [20] serves as the base model, but our method is applicable to different architectures such as RetinaNet [29] and TensorMask [7]. We describe details of the data generation process (Fig. 3) and training scheme (Fig. 5) below.

3.1   Data Augmentation: Background Erasing (BackErase)

We propose a new data augmentation to mitigate the bias induced by unlabeled objects prevalent in most training sets. These hidden objects are not given annotation because they do not belong to known classes or are overlooked by annotators. We propose to synthesize fully labeled training images. Using the instance mask, we crop only the annotated foreground regions and paste them on the synthesized background canvas. These synthesized images have fully labeled objects and lead to objectness detectors that generalize better to open world settings.

Fig. 4. Examples of original inputs (odd columns) and synthesized image (even columns). Masked regions are highlighted with colors (odd columns). Using small regions as background avoids the risk of having hidden objects in the background. We achieve to suppress unlabeled objects present in the background. (Color figure online)

Background Region Sampling. First, we apply Gaussian smoothing to the input image before cropping the foreground and background region, and denote the smoothed image as I_1. By smoothing the whole image before this operation, we expect to reduce the discrepancy in high-frequency content between the foreground and background images.

Then, we randomly crop a small region from I_1, where width and height of the region is set as $\frac{1}{8}$ of the original image's. We resize it to the same size as the input image to serve as a background canvas, which we denote as I_2. Cropping a small region entails a much lower risk of including hidden background objects compared to using the original background. Even if it happens to include unannotated objects, drastically upscaling the patch makes the objects' appearance very different, as shown in examples in Fig. 4. We vary the scale of the background canvas in experiments (See Table 4).

Blending Pasted Objects. To avoid the model learning to separate background and foreground by the difference in frequency information, foreground objects are downsampled and resized to the original size. Then, the foreground objects are pasted on the canvas. To insert copied objects into an image, we use the binary mask (M) of pasted objects using ground-truth annotations and compute the new image as $I_1 \times M + I_2 \times (1 - M)$. We apply a Gaussian filter to the binary mask to smooth the edges of the copied objects. Examples of synthesized images using the COCO dataset with 80 categories are illustrated in Fig. 4. Note that even in datasets with dense annotations like COCO, many objects are not annotated, and our augmentation effectively removes such hidden objects from the background. We do not claim that details such as smoothing and resizing operations are necessarily optimal for open-world instance segmentation, but empirically find they work well.

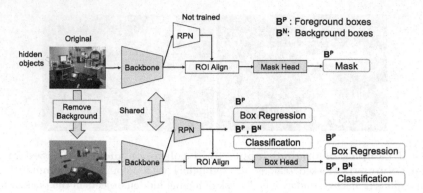

Fig. 5. Training pipeline. Given an original input image and the synthesized image, we train the detector on the mask loss computed on the original image, while classification and regression losses are applied to the synthesized image.

3.2 Decoupled Multi-domain Training

Simply training a detector on the synthesized images in the conventional way [20] does not work well due to the domain shift (See Table 3). Since real images and our synthesized images have very distinct content and layout, a detector trained on our synthesized data does not generalize well to real images. In this section, we propose a simple yet effective approach to mitigate this issue. We solve the shift by computing mask loss on real images while calculating detection loss on synthesized images. Because the backbone is trained on both the synthetic and real domains, it learns an invariance between real and augmented object regions. Even though the losses are different for the two domains, they are highly correlated, which makes the backbone network adapted to real images on both tasks. The entire training pipeline is summarized in Fig. 5.

Typically, the training objectives for instance segmentation models consist of two major terms: object detection loss and instance mask loss. In methods like Mask RCNN [20], the object detection loss is composed of a region proposal classification loss and a box regression loss, which are used to train both the region proposal network (RPN) and the region of interest (ROI) heads. For simplicity, we unify the objectives for RPN and ROI as one loss.

Each predicted box B_i includes predictions for a box location $\hat{t}_i$, objectness score $\hat{y}_i$, and mask prediction $\hat{m}_i$. During training, B_i comes with corresponding ground truth, t_i, y_i, and m_i. Let B^p and B^n, the positive (foreground) and negative (background) boxes, denote a set of boxes with $y = 1$ and $y = 0$ respectively. The label of positive or negative, y, is decided based on the Intersection over Union (IoU) with the nearest bounding box during training, $e.g.$, regions with IoU smaller/larger than 0.5 are background/foreground respectively in the case of ROI head. Note that, in general, the proposal classification loss is computed for both positive and negative boxes, $B = B^p \cup B^n$, while the box regression and mask loss are computed for B^p.

We highlight that B^n from synthetic images (I_S) are unlikely to contain unlabeled objects due to our augmentation while unlabeled objects can be present in those from real images (I_R). Given this fact, the detection loss should be computed on boxes of I_S. However, training only on I_S will not make the model generalizable to I_R since I_R and I_S look very different. Then, to bridge the domain gap between I_S and I_R, we propose to compute the instance mask loss on I_R. Why does the mask loss help to mitigate the gap w.r.t. the detection task? Mask prediction aims to separate background and foreground pixels within a foreground bounding box whereas the box classification decides the objectness for one box. The two tasks are very similar in that both attempt to separate background and foreground samples except that the mask loss is computed only for B^p. Then, the mask loss training signal, which should be useful to solve the detection task for I_R, is propagated to a deep backbone network shared among the region proposal network, bounding box head, and mask head. The features obtained from the backbone will improve the performance of the box head in I_R. Furthermore, the model will not learn to suppress unlabeled objects by using the mask loss because the loss is computed on foreground boxes only. In summary, the use of mask loss on real images will make the backbone network adapted to real images without suppressing unlabeled objects.

Specifically, the loss is computed as follows:

$$\sum_{B_i \in B_{aug}^p} L_{reg}(\hat{t}_i, t_i) + \sum_{B_i \in B_{aug}} L_{cls}(\hat{y}_i, y_i) + \sum_{B_i \in B_{real}^p} L_{mask}(\hat{m}_i, m_i) \qquad (1)$$

where L_{reg}, L_{cls}, and L_{mask} indicate the regression, object classification, and mask loss respectively. Note that B_{aug} and B_{real} are used to differentiate the boxes from synthetic and real images.

Class Agnostic Inference. Since our goal is to detect objects in a scene without classifying them into closed-set classes, class agnostic inference is preferred. We apply a class agnostic inference method to a class discriminative object detector. Given the classification output of a region, we sum up all scores of (known) foreground classes, deeming the result as an objectness score. Mask and box regression are performed for the class with the maximum score.

4 Experiments

We evaluate LDET on two settings of open-world instance segmentation: *Cross-category* and *Cross-dataset*. The Cross-category setting is based on the COCO [30] dataset, where we split annotated classes into known and unknown classes, train models on known ones, and evaluate detection/segmentation performance on unknown and on all classes separately. Since the model can be exposed to a new environment and encounter novel instances, the Cross-dataset setting evaluates models' ability to generalize to new datasets. For this purpose, we adopt either COCO [30] or Cityscapes [9] as a training source, with UVO [41], Obj365 [37] and Mappilary Vista [33] as the test datasets.

Table 1. Results of VOC → COCO generalization. LDET outperforms all baselines and shows large improvements compared to Mask RCNN.

Method	Non-VOC						All			
	Box			Mask			Box		Mask	
	AP	AR_{10}	AR_{100}	AP	AR_{10}	AR_{100}	AR_{10}	AR_{100}	AR_{10}	AR_{100}
Mask RCNN [20]	1.5	8.8	10.9	0.7	7.2	9.1	19.3	23.1	16.7	19.9
Mask RCNN[P]	3.4	8.7	10.7	2.2	7.2	8.9	19.1	23.0	16.5	19.8
Mask RCNN[S]	1.1	13.2	18.0	0.6	11.3	15.8	21.7	27.4	19.2	24.4
LDET	**5.0**	**18.2**	**30.8**	**4.7**	**16.3**	**27.4**	**24.4**	**36.8**	**22.4**	**33.1**

Fig. 6. Visualization in VOC to Non-VOC in COCO dataset. Top: Mask RCNN. Bottom: LDET. Note that training categories do not include giraffe, trash box, pen, kite, and floats. LDET detects many novel objects better than Mask RCNN.

Implementation. Detectron2 [42] is used to implement LDET. Mask R-CNN [20] with ResNet-50 [21] as feature pyramid [28] is used unless otherwise specified. Following [41], we utilize the standard hyperparameters of Mask R-CNN [20] as defined in Detectron2; more details *e.g.*, hyper-parameters are in the appendix.

Baselines. Since open-world instance segmentation is a new task, we develop several baselines as follows (see appendix for more details.)

1) Mask R-CNN. We adopt the default model without changing any objectives or input data. Comparison to this baseline will reveal the difference from standard training.

2) Mask RCNN[S]. We avoid sampling background regions with hidden objects by sampling background boxes from the regions mostly inside the ground truth boxes. We assume that these regions are less likely to contain hidden objects. We compute the area of intersection with ground truth boxes over the area of the proposal box and sample background boxes with a large value of this criterion.

3) Mask RCNN[P]. Inspired by [24], we implement a pseudo-labeling based open-set instance segmentation baseline. The idea is to assign pseudo-labels of foreground classes to the background regions (IoU with GT < 0.5) that have

Table 2. AR on top- and worst-5 classes detected by Mask RCNN baseline in VOC → Non-VOC.

Method	Top-5					Worst-5				
	Bear	Bed	Microwave	Elephant	t-bear	Carrot	Tie	Skis	Broccoli	Donut
Mask RCNN	**78.6**	45.2	36.5	28.6	20.3	0.4	0.4	1.2	1.2	1.2
LDET	76.5	**57.6**	**59.5**	**67.2**	**45.9**	**6.2**	**1.9**	**8.1**	**8.3**	**15.7**

Table 3. Ablation study of data and training method in VOC → Non-VOC.
We change the data used to compute detection and mask loss. Training only on synthetic data does not perform well while LDET, which is trained on both data with decoupled training, performs the best.

Method	Box		Mask		Box		
	Real	Synth	Real	Synth	AR_{10}	AR_{100}	AR0.5
Plain	✓		✓		8.8	10.9	19.1
Synth Only		✓			1.6	4.3	11.7
Synth Only*		✓		✓	3.0	9.5	23.8
LDET		✓	✓		**18.2**	**30.8**	**53.2**

high objectness scores. A model is trained to minimize the box classification loss on pseudo-labels.

Evaluation. In this work, Average Recall (AR) is mainly employed for performance evaluation following [41]. When class labels are available, we compute AR for each class given the objectness score and average over all classes as done in the standard COCO evaluation protocol. Unless otherwise specified, AR is computed following the COCO evaluation protocol, $i.e.$, AR at 100 detections. Average precision (AP) is computed in a class agnostic way.

4.1   Cross-category Generalization

Setup. We split the COCO dataset into 20 seen (VOC) classes and 60 unseen (non-VOC) classes. We train a model only on the annotation of seen classes. The hyper-parameters of baselines and LDET are chosen based on the performance of the randomly selected 20 Non-VOC classes. Then, the whole validation split of COCO is adopted for evaluation. To better understand the results, we report AR on two settings $i.e.$, 60 non-VOC classes only (novel class evaluation) and all 80 classes (generalized evaluation). In evaluating AR in novel class evaluation, we do not count the "seen class" detection boxes into the budget of the recall when computing the score. This is to avoid evaluating recall on seen-class objects.

Comparison with Baselines. As shown in Table 1, our method outperforms baselines in all metrics with a large margin. The difference is more evident in the results on non-VOC classes. In this setting, the ratio of unlabeled objects regarded as background in the proposal sampling for roi head is 17.4%. The number indicates that the probability that an unlabeled object is regarded as a background region in each forward. Some visualizations are available in Fig. 6. Mask RCNN tends to overlook non-VOC class objects even when they are in the dominant and salient region, *e.g.*, *trash can* (leftmost column) and *giraffes* (second leftmost column). On the other hand, LDET generalizes well to novel objects such as *comb, towel, giraffes, pen, phone, kites,* and *floats.* Table 2 describes AR of top- and worst-5 classes in Mask RCNN. Mask RCNN outperforms LDET on *bear* probably because there are several categories similar to *bear*, *e.g.*, *dog* and *horse* or maybe because there are no 'bear' hidden objects. Although both LDET and the baseline do not excel at detecting classes whose appearance is dissimilar to VOC classes, LDET outperforms Mask RCNN.

Ablation Study for Learning Objectives. Table 3 shows an ablation study of training data and objectives. If a model learns only from synthetic data (Synth Only), it fails to detect and segment objects. Interestingly, adding the synthetic mask loss on top of the synthetic detection data (Synth Only*) improves the performance. This supports our claim that mask prediction and detection tasks are highly correlated. Adding the mask loss even for synthetic data provides a better understanding of the location of the objects and improves performance. Computing detection loss of synthetic data and mask loss on real data obtains the best results. These results indicate that our proposed decoupled training is very suitable for the open-world instance segmentation and detection task.

Visualization of the Learnt Objectness Map. Fig. 7 visualizes the confidence scores map of the region proposal network, computed by averaging outputs from all feature pyramids. Models trained only on synthetic data (first and second from the leftmost) cannot separate foreground and background well though they seem to cover many foreground objects. While the model trained only with real data (second from rightmost) suppresses the score for many objects, LDET (rightmost) correctly captures objectness for diverse objects, *e.g.*, it captures objectness well in an image crowded with objects in the first row. The mask loss on real images helps the detector to separate foreground and background well.

Size of Background Regions. The size of background regions is important in our data augmentation: a larger background region can include more hidden objects. We analyze the effect of the region's size in Table 4, wherein improvements with the smaller size are significant. There are two possible reasons; 1) smaller backgrounds prevent sampling hidden objects, 2) since we downsample a whole image to align with the size of the background region, each object loses category-specific information, which leads the detector to learn category-invariant objectness. We leave the detailed analysis for future work.

Table 4. Varying the size of background regions. 2^{-m} indicates cropping background region with 2^{-m} of width and height of an input image. Sampling background from smaller region tends to improve AR.

Background ratio	AP	AR_{10}	AR_{100}	AR_{small}	AR_{medium}	AR_{large}
2^{-1}	**5.2**	16.8	26.2	17.0	27.0	40.6
2^{-2}	5.0	16.5	25.9	17.3	27.1	38.9
2^{-3}	5.0	18.2	30.8	18.8	34.6	44.5
2^{-4}	**5.2**	17.5	31.8	20.1	35.8	45.6
2^{-5}	4.9	18.4	**33.7**	21.1	38.4	**49.7**
2^{-6}	5.0	**19.0**	33.7	**22.1**	**39.1**	48.2

Table 5. Comparison between region proposal network and region of interest head.

Method	Detector	AR_{10}	AR_{50}	AR_{100}
Plain	RPN	**11.0**	**19.4**	**22.9**
Plain	ROI	8.8	10.8	10.9
LDET	RPN	15.4	26.4	30.8
LDET	ROI	**18.2**	**28.0**	30.8

Table 6. Results on RetinaNet and TensorMask

Detector	Method	AR_{10}	AR_{50}	AR_{100}
RetinaNet	Plain	9.9	15.7	17.8
	LDET	**15.3**	**26.7**	**31.0**
TensorMask	Plain	10.6	17.6	19.7
	LDET	**16.3**	**26.8**	**31.1**

External Data for Background. Using an external background dataset is an alternative way to synthesize background regions. In this experiment, we use DTD [8] (texture image dataset). The background region is replaced with a randomly cropped patch from DTD dataset, and a model is trained in the same way as LDET. See the appendix for more details of training. The resulting AR is 26.7 (LDET − 3.1) in bounding box localization. The dataset includes a considerable number of objects despite being primarily a texture dataset, which is probably the cause of degradation in AR.

Region Proposal Network (RPN) and Region of Interest (ROI) Head. RPN and ROI heads are compared in Table 5. In Mask RCNN, RPN covers more novel objects, which means ROI learns to suppress many novel objects. In contrast, ROI of LDET is comparable or better than RPN in all metrics.

One-Stage Detectors. We evaluate LDET on one-stage detectors, RetinaNet [29] and TensorMask [7] in Table 6. See appendix for the details of the experiment. LDET shows clear gains over the baseline, which shows that LDET is a universal approach that can be integrated into diverse detectors.

| Input | Detect on Synth | Detect on Synth
Mask on Synth | Detect on Real
Mask on Real | Detect on Synth
Mask on Real |

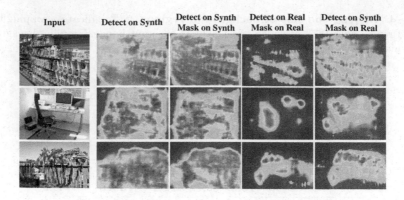

Fig. 7. Objectness map (RPN score) visualization w.r.t. different data used to compute detection and mask loss. A model only with the detection loss for synthetic data (leftmost) does not suppress background regions well. Adding mask loss on real data (rightmost) captures objectness of various categories whereas a plain model (second from the right) suppresses many objects.

Table 7. Results of COCO → UVO generalization. Top rows: Models trained on VOC-COCO. Bottom rows: Models trained on COCO. LDET demonstrates high AP and AR in all cases compared to baselines.

Method	Train	Box					Mask				
		AP	AR	AR$_{small}$	AR$_{med}$	AR$_{large}$	AP	AR	AR$_{small}$	AR$_{med}$	AR$_{large}$
Mask RCNN	VOC (COCO)	19.8	30.0	10.7	21.3	43.0	15.5	23.9	9.2	18.5	32.8
Mask RCNN[P]		19.2	30.1	10.6	21.3	43.3	15.4	24.1	9.4	18.4	33.2
Mask RCNN[S]		19.7	32.0	10.0	23.3	46.0	14.1	25.9	9.5	20.2	35.4
LDET		**22.4**	**43.7**	**24.7**	**39.9**	**52.9**	**18.4**	**36.0**	**22.1**	**34.8**	**41.4**
Mask RCNN	COCO	25.3	42.3	22.2	38.3	52.0	20.6	35.9	19.6	33.9	42.6
Mask RCNN[P]		24.4	41.9	22.3	37.8	51.5	20.1	35.4	19.7	33.6	41.8
Mask RCNN[S]		23.4	40.5	17.6	34.9	52.3	18.0	34.7	16.6	31.5	42.8
LDET		**25.8**	**47.5**	**29.1**	**44.8**	**55.6**	**21.9**	**40.7**	**26.8**	**40.0**	**45.7**

Table 8. Results of COCO → Obj365 generalization. Improvement on Mask RCNN is shown next to each result in the row of LDET. LDET outperforms all baselines and showing large improvements on Mask RCNN.

Method	Non-COCO					All			
	AP	AR	AR$_{small}$	AR$_{med}$	AR$_{large}$	AR	AR$_{small}$	AR$_{med}$	AR$_{large}$
Mask RCNN [20]	11.9	34.4	21.2	36.0	45.8	38.5	24.0	40.1	50.2
Mask RCNN[P]	11.8	32.7	17.5	33.5	47.1	38.6	24.5	39.8	50.8
Mask RCNN[S]	10.9	34.6	21.9	35.7	46.6	35.9	18.9	36.6	50.2
LDET	**12.9**	**38.9**	**25.5**	**41.8**	**50.2**	**41.1**	**26.1**	**43.8**	**52.8**

Table 9. Results of Cityscapes → Mappilary Vista generalization. LDET is effective for autonomous driving dataset. $AR_{0.5}$ denotes AR with IoU threshold $= 0.5$

Method	Box				Mask			
	AP	AR_{10}	AR_{100}	$AR_{0.5}$	AP	AR_{10}	AR_{100}	$AR_{0.5}$
Mask RCNN	8.2	7.7	11.1	20.2	7.3	6.1	8.4	16.3
Mask RCNN^P	6.9	7.4	10.8	19.3	7.5	5.5	7.9	16.3
Mask RCNN^S	8.3	6.7	13.3	26.9	6.3	5.5	10.2	21.0
LDET	**8.5**	**8.0**	**14.0**	**28.0**	**7.8**	**6.7**	**10.6**	**21.8**

Fig. 8. Visualization of results for models trained on COCO. Top: Mask RCNN. Bottom: LDET.

4.2 Cross-Dataset Generalization

COCO to UVO. We utilize UVO [41], which covers many categories outside COCO as 57% object instances do not belong to any of the 80 COCO classes. Since UVO is based on Youtube videos, the appearance is very different from COCO *e.g.*, some videos are egocentric views and have significant motion blur. We test models trained on the COCO-VOC split or the whole COCO. The validation split is used to measure the performance. Since this dataset does not provide class labels, we evaluate the performance in a class-agnostic way. As shown in Table 7, in both COCO-VOC and COCO settings, LDET outperforms baselines with a large margin. Note that our VOC-COCO model outperforms Mask RCNN trained on COCO in many metrics. This indicates the remarkable label efficiency of LDET in open-world instance segmentation. Unlike the result in VOC-NonVOC experiment, the AP of Mask RCNN^S drops compared to Mask RCNN, probably because their region sampling leads to imbalanced sampling for regions with different scales.

COCO to Obj365. We evaluate models on the validation split of Obj365 [37] detection dataset, wherein 60% object instances do not belong to any of the 80 COCO classes. We test models trained on the whole coco, and evaluation is done in the way as cross-category setting. As shown in Table 8, in both non-COCO categories and all categories, LDET outperforms all baselines. This result confirms that LDET is generalizable to detect various categories of objects.

Cityscape to Mapillary. We examine performance in autonomous driving scenes. Detectors are trained on Cityscape [9] (8 foreground classes, *person, rider, car, truck, bus, train, motorcycle,* and *bicycles*) and tested on the validation set of Mapillary Vistas [33] with 35 foreground classes including not only vehicles, but also animals, *trash can, mailbox,* and so on. In Table 9, LDET shows solid gains over baselines, though this setting is very challenging. Note that the model is trained only on 8 classes and is required to generalize to all the 35 classes in the test data, which explains the lower performance compared to experiments on COCO. The result demonstrates that LDET generalizes to datasets other than COCO and could be useful for autonomous driving systems.

Visualization. As Fig. 1 shows, the Mask RCNN detector fails in localizing objects different from the 80 training categories, while our detector shows surprisingly good generalization. For example, in the second leftmost row, it recognizes a character drawn on the wall, which is clearly outside COCO categories. Figure 8 visualizes additional examples from UVO and COCO.

5   Conclusion

In this paper, we presented a simple approach, LDET, for the challenging task of open-world instance segmentation. LDET builds on existing detectors but augments data with synthetic images with no hidden objects in the background and trains on real and synthesized images in a decoupled way. LDET demonstrates strong performance on a benchmark dataset of open-world instance segmentation and promising results on autonomous driving datasets. We hope that LDET becomes a simple baseline and accelerates further research in this area. Although its performance is much better than baselines, LDET still fails to detect some novel objects. If the appearance of novel objects is distinct from known objects, LDET and most baselines may miss them. Also, experiments on Cityscapes (Table 9) indicate the importance of covering various categories in training data.

Acknowledgments. This work was supported by DARPA LwLL and NSF Award No. 1535797. We thank Donghyun Kim and Piotr Teterwak for giving valuable feedback on the draft.

References

1. Alexe, B., Deselaers, T., Ferrari, V.: Measuring the objectness of image windows. IEEE TPAMI **34**(11), 2189–2202 (2012)
2. Arbeláez, P., Pont-Tuset, J., Barron, J.T., Marques, F., Malik, J.: Multiscale combinatorial grouping. In: CVPR, pp. 328–335 (2014)
3. Bansal, A., Sikka, K., Sharma, G., Chellappa, R., Divakaran, A.: Zero-shot object detection. In: ECCV, pp. 384–400 (2018)
4. Bendale, A., Boult, T.E.: Towards open set deep networks. In: CVPR, pp. 1563–1572 (2016)

5. Cai, Z., Vasconcelos, N.: Cascade r-cnn: delving into high quality object detection. In: CVPR, pp. 6154–6162 (2018)
6. Cen, J., Yun, P., Cai, J., Wang, M.Y., Liu, M.: Deep metric learning for open world semantic segmentation. In: ICCV (2021)
7. Chen, X., Girshick, R., He, K., Dollar, P.: Tensormask: a foundation for dense object segmentation. In: ICCV (2019)
8. Cimpoi, M., Maji, S., Kokkinos, I., Mohamed, S., Vedaldi, A.: Describing textures in the wild. In: CVPR, pp. 3606–3613 (2014)
9. Cordts, M., et al.: The cityscapes dataset for semantic urban scene understanding. In: CVPR (2016)
10. Dai, J., et al.: Deformable convolutional networks. In: ICCV, pp. 764–773 (2017)
11. Dhamija, A., Gunther, M., Ventura, J., Boult, T.: The overlooked elephant of object detection: open set. In: WACV, pp. 1021–1030 (2020)
12. Dosovitskiy, A., et al.: Flownet: learning optical flow with convolutional networks. In: ICCV, pp. 2758–2766 (2015)
13. Dvornik, N., Mairal, J., Schmid, C.: Modeling visual context is key to augmenting object detection datasets. In: ECCV, pp. 364–380 (2018)
14. Dwibedi, D., Misra, I., Hebert, M.: Cut, paste and learn: surprisingly easy synthesis for instance detection. In: Proceedings of the IEEE International Conference on Computer Vision, pp. 1301–1310 (2017)
15. Everingham, M., Van Gool, L., Williams, C.K., Winn, J., Zisserman, A.: The pascal visual object classes (voc) challenge. IJCV **88**(2), 303–338 (2010)
16. Felzenszwalb, P.F., Girshick, R.B., McAllester, D.: Cascade object detection with deformable part models. In: CVPR, pp. 2241–2248. IEEE (2010)
17. Ghiasi, G., et al.: Simple copy-paste is a strong data augmentation method for instance segmentation. In: CVPR, pp. 2918–2928 (2021)
18. Girshick, R.: Fast r-cnn. In: ICCV, pp. 1440–1448 (2015)
19. Girshick, R., Donahue, J., Darrell, T., Malik, J.: Rich feature hierarchies for accurate object detection and semantic segmentation. In: CVPR, pp. 580–587 (2014)
20. He, K., Gkioxari, G., Dollár, P., Girshick, R.: Mask r-cnn. In: ICCV (2017)
21. He, K., Zhang, X., Ren, S., Sun, J.: Deep residual learning for image recognition. In: CVPR (2016)
22. Hu, R., Dollár, P., He, K., Darrell, T., Girshick, R.: Learning to segment every thing. In: CVPR, pp. 4233–4241 (2018)
23. Jaiswal, A., Wu, Y., Natarajan, P., Natarajan, P.: Class-agnostic object detection. In: WACV, pp. 919–928 (2021)
24. Joseph, K., Khan, S., Khan, F.S., Balasubramanian, V.N.: Towards open world object detection. In: CVPR, pp. 5830–5840 (2021)
25. Kang, B., Liu, Z., Wang, X., Yu, F., Feng, J., Darrell, T.: Few-shot object detection via feature reweighting. In: ICCV, pp. 8420–8429 (2019)
26. Kim, D., Lin, T.Y., Angelova, A., Kweon, I.S., Kuo, W.: Learning open-world object proposals without learning to classify. arXiv preprint arXiv:2108.06753 (2021)
27. Kuo, W., Angelova, A., Malik, J., Lin, T.Y.: Shapemask: learning to segment novel objects by refining shape priors. In: ICCV, pp. 9207–9216 (2019)
28. Lin, T.Y., Dollár, P., Girshick, R., He, K., Hariharan, B., Belongie, S.: Feature pyramid networks for object detection. In: CVPR, pp. 2117–2125 (2017)
29. Lin, T.Y., Goyal, P., Girshick, R., He, K., Dollár, P.: Focal loss for dense object detection. In: ICCV, pp. 2980–2988 (2017)

30. Lin, T.-Y., et al.: Microsoft COCO: common objects in context. In: Fleet, D., Pajdla, T., Schiele, B., Tuytelaars, T. (eds.) ECCV 2014. LNCS, vol. 8693, pp. 740–755. Springer, Cham (2014). https://doi.org/10.1007/978-3-319-10602-1_48

31. Liu, W., Anguelov, D., Erhan, D., Szegedy, C., Reed, S., Fu, C.-Y., Berg, A.C.: SSD: single shot multibox detector. In: Leibe, B., Matas, J., Sebe, N., Welling, M. (eds.) ECCV 2016. LNCS, vol. 9905, pp. 21–37. Springer, Cham (2016). https://doi.org/10.1007/978-3-319-46448-0_2

32. Liu, Z., Miao, Z., Zhan, X., Wang, J., Gong, B., Yu, S.X.: Large-scale long-tailed recognition in an open world. In: CVPR, pp. 2537–2546 (2019)

33. Neuhold, G., Ollmann, T., Rota Bulo, S., Kontschieder, P.: The mapillary vistas dataset for semantic understanding of street scenes. In: ICCV, pp. 4990–4999 (2017)

34. Perera, P., et al.: Generative-discriminative feature representations for open-set recognition. In: CVPR, pp. 11814–11823 (2020)

35. Redmon, J., Divvala, S., Girshick, R., Farhadi, A.: You only look once: unified, real-time object detection. In: CVPR (2016)

36. Ren, S., He, K., Girshick, R., Sun, J.: Faster r-cnn: towards real-time object detection with region proposal networks. In: NeurIPS (2015)

37. Shao, S., et al.: Objects365: a large-scale, high-quality dataset for object detection. In: ICCV, pp. 8430–8439 (2019)

38. Tack, J., Mo, S., Jeong, J., Shin, J.: Csi: novelty detection via contrastive learning on distributionally shifted instances. arXiv preprint arXiv:2007.08176 (2020)

39. Uijlings, J.R., Van De Sande, K.E., Gevers, T., Smeulders, A.W.: Selective search for object recognition. IJCV **104**(2), 154–171 (2013)

40. Varol, G., et al.: Learning from synthetic humans. In: CVPR (2017)

41. Wang, W., Feiszli, M., Wang, H., Tran, D.: Unidentified video objects: a benchmark for dense, open-world segmentation. arXiv preprint arXiv:2104.04691 (2021)

42. Wu, Y., Kirillov, A., Massa, F., Lo, W.Y., Girshick, R.: Detectron2 (2019). https://github.com/facebookresearch/detectron2

43. Yoshihashi, R., Shao, W., Kawakami, R., You, S., Iida, M., Naemura, T.: Classification-reconstruction learning for open-set recognition. In: CVPR, pp. 4016–4025 (2019)

44. Zhou, B., Zhao, H., Puig, X., Fidler, S., Barriuso, A., Torralba, A.: Scene parsing through ade20k dataset. In: CVPR, pp. 633–641 (2017)

45. Zitnick, C.L., Dollár, P.: Edge boxes: locating object proposals from edges. In: Fleet, D., Pajdla, T., Schiele, B., Tuytelaars, T. (eds.) ECCV 2014. LNCS, vol. 8693, pp. 391–405. Springer, Cham (2014). https://doi.org/10.1007/978-3-319-10602-1_26

KVT: k-NN Attention for Boosting Vision Transformers

Pichao Wang[✉], Xue Wang, Fan Wang, Ming Lin, Shuning Chang, Hao Li,
and Rong Jin

Alibaba Group, Hangzhou, China
{pichao.wang,xue.w,fan.w,ming.l,shuning.csn,lihao.lh,
jinrong.jr}@alibaba-inc.com

Abstract. Convolutional Neural Networks (CNNs) have dominated
computer vision for years, due to its ability in capturing locality and
translation invariance. Recently, many vision transformer architectures
have been proposed and they show promising performance. A key component in vision transformers is the fully-connected self-attention which
is more powerful than CNNs in modelling long range dependencies. However, since the current dense self-attention uses all image patches (tokens)
to compute attention matrix, it may neglect locality of images patches
and involve noisy tokens (e.g., clutter background and occlusion), leading
to a slow training process and potential degradation of performance. To
address these problems, we propose the k-NN attention for boosting vision
transformers. Specifically, instead of involving all the tokens for attention
matrix calculation, we only select the top-k similar tokens from the keys
for each query to compute the attention map. The proposed k-NN attention naturally inherits the local bias of CNNs without introducing convolutional operations, as nearby tokens tend to be more similar than others.
In addition, the k-NN attention allows for the exploration of long range
correlation and at the same time filters out irrelevant tokens by choosing
the most similar tokens from the entire image. Despite its simplicity, we
verify, both theoretically and empirically, that k-NN attention is powerful
in speeding up training and distilling noise from input tokens. Extensive
experiments are conducted by using 11 different vision transformer architectures to verify that the proposed k-NN attention can work with any
existing transformer architectures to improve its prediction performance.
The codes are available at https://github.com/damo-cv/KVT.

1 Introduction

Traditional CNNs provide state of the art performance in vision tasks, due to
its ability in capturing locality and translation invariance, while transformer [53]

P. Wang and X. Wang—The first two authors contribute equally.

Supplementary Information The online version contains supplementary material
available at https://doi.org/10.1007/978-3-031-20053-3_17.

S. Avidan et al. (Eds.): ECCV 2022, LNCS 13684, pp. 285–302, 2022.
https://doi.org/10.1007/978-3-031-20053-3_17

is the de-facto standard for natural language processing (NLP) tasks thanks to its advantages in modelling long-range dependencies. Recently, various vision transformers [16,24,41,51,52,55,59,69–71] have been proposed by building pure or hybrid transformer models for visual tasks. Inspired by the transformer scaling success in NLP tasks, vision transformer converts an image into a sequence of image patches (tokens), with each patch encoded into a vector. Since self-attention in the transformer is position agnostic, different positional encoding methods [11,14,16] have been developed, and in [8,59] their roles have been replaced by convolutions. Afterwards, all tokens are fed into stacked transformer encoders for feature learning, with an extra *CLS* token [14,16,51] or global average pooling (GAP) [8,41] for final feature representation. Compared with CNNs, transformer-based models explicitly exploit global dependencies and demonstrate comparable, sometimes even better, results than highly optimised CNNs [26,47].

Albeit achieving its initial success, vision transformers suffer from slow training. One of the key culprits is the fully-connected self-attention, which takes all the tokens to calculate the attention map. The dense attention not only neglects the locality of images patches, an important feature of CNNs, but also involves noisy tokens into the computation of self-attention, especially in the situations of cluttered background and occlusion. Both issues can slow down the training significantly [12,14]. Recent works [8,59,69] try to mitigate this problem by introducing convolutional operators into vision transformers. Despite encouraging results, these studies fail to resolve the problem fundamentally from the transformer structure itself, limiting their success. In this study, we address the challenge by directly attacking its root cause, i.e. the fully-connected self-attention.

To this end, we propose the k-NN attention to replace the fully-connected attention. Specifically, we do not use all the tokens for attention matrix calculation, but only select the top-k similar tokens from the sequence for each query token to compute the attention map. The proposed k-NN attention not only naturally inherits the local bias of CNNs as the nearby tokens tend to be more similar than others, but also builds the long range dependency by choosing the most similar tokens from the entire image. Compared with convolution operator which is an aggregation operation built on Ising model [43] and the feature of each node is aggregated from nearby pixels, in the k-NN attention, the aggregation graph is no longer limited by the spatial location of nodes but is adaptively computed via attention maps, thus, the k-NN attention can be regarded as a relieved version of local bias. The similar idea is proposed in [75] where the k-NN attention is mostly evaluated on NLP tasks. Despite the similarity in terms of the calculation of top-k, our work focuses on the recent vision transformers, makes a deep theoretical understanding and presents a thoroughly analysis by defining several metrics. We verify, both theoretically and empirically, that k-NN attention is effective in speeding up training and distilling noisy tokens of vision transformers. Eleven different available vision transformer architectures are adopted to verify the effectiveness of the proposed k-NN attention.

2 Related Work

2.1 Self-attention

Self-attention [53] has demonstrated promising results on NLP related tasks, and is making breakthroughs in speech and computer vision. For time series modeling, self-attention operates over sequences in a step-wise manner. Specifically, at every time-step, self-attention assigns an attention weight to each previous input element and uses these weights to compute the representation of the current time-step as a weighted sum of the past inputs. Besides the vanilla self-attention, many efficient transformers [50] have been proposed. Among these efficient transformers, sparse attention and local attention are one of the main streams, which are highly related to our work. Sparse attention can be further categorized into data independent (fixed) sparse attention [1,9,29,72] and content-based sparse attention [13,34,45,48]. Local attention [40–42] mainly considers attending only to a local window size. Our work is also content-based attention, but compared with previous works [13,34,45,48], our k-NN attention has its merits for vision domain. For example, compared with routing transformer [45] that clusters both queries and keys, our k-NN attention equals only clustering keys by assigning each query as the cluster center, making the quantization more continuous which is a better fitting of image domain; compared with reformer [34] which adopts complex hashing attention that cannot guarantee each bucket contain both queries and keys, our k-NN attention can guarantee that each query has number k keys for attention computing. In addition, our k-NN attention is also a generalized local attention, but compared with local attention, our k-NN attention not only enjoys the locality but also empowers the ability of global relation mining.

2.2 Transformer for Vision

Transformer [53] is an effective sequence-to-sequence modeling network, and it has achieved state-of-the-art results in NLP tasks with the success of BERT [15]. Due to its great success, it has also be exploited in computer vision community, and 'Transformer in CNN' becomes a popular paradigm [2,4,7,25,36,37,58,80]. ViT [16] leads the other trend to use 'CNN in Transformer' paradigm for vision tasks [27,35,62,66,68]. Even though ViT has been proved compelling in vision recognition, it has several drawbacks when compared with CNNs: large training data, fixed position embedding, rigid patch division, coarse modeling of inner patch feature, single scale, unstable training process, slow speed training, easily fitting data and poor generalization, shallow & narrow architecture, and quadratic complexity. To deal with these problems, many variants have been proposed [17,19,20,30,32,44,56,57,64,67,74,78,79]. For example, DeiT [51] adopts several training techniques and uses distillation to extend ViT to a data-efficient version; CPVT [11] proposes a conditional positional encoding that is adaptable to arbitrary input sizes; CvT [59], CoaT [63] and Visformer [8] safely remove the position embedding by introducing convolution operations; T2T ViT [70], CeiT [69], and CvT [59] try to deal with the rigid patch division by introducing convolution operation for patch sequence generation; Focal Transformer [65] makes each token attend its closest surrounding tokens at fine granularity and the tokens far away at coarse granularity; TNT [24] proposes the pixel embedding to model the inner patch feature; PVT [55], Swin Transformer [41], MViT [18], ViL [73], CvT [59], PiT [28], LeViT [22], CoaT [63], and Twins [10] adopt multi-scale technique for rich feature learning; DeepViT [77], CaiT [52], and PatchViT [21] investigate the unstable training problem, and propose the re-attention, re-scale and anti-over-smoothing techniques respectively for stable training; to accelerate the convergence of training, ConViT [14], PiT [28], CeiT [69], LocalViT [38] and Visformer [8] introduce convolutional bias to speedup the training; conv-stem is adopted in LeViT [22], EarlyConv [60], CMT [23], VOLO [71] and ScaledReLU [54] to improve the robustness of training ViTs; LV-ViT [31] adopts several techniques including MixToken and Token Labeling for better training and feature generation; T2T ViT [70], DeepViT [77] and CaiT [52] try to train deeper vision transformer models; T2T ViT [70], ViL [73] and CoaT [63] adopt efficient transformers [50] to deal with the quadratic complexity; To further exploit the capacities of vision transformer, OmniNet [49], CrossViT [6] and So-ViT [61] propose the dense omnidirectional representations, coarse-fine-grained patch fusion and cross covariance pooling of visual tokens, respectively. However, all of these works adopt the fully-connected self-attention which will bring the noise or irrelevant tokens for computing and slow down the training of networks. In this paper, we propose an efficient sparse attention, called k-NN attention, for boosting vision transformers. The proposed k-NN attention not only inherits the local bias of CNNs but also achieves the ability of global feature exploitation. It can also speed up the training and achieve better performance.

3 k-NN Attention

3.1   Vanilla Attention

For any sequence of length n, the vanilla attention in the transformer is the dot product attention [53]. Following the standard notation, the attention matrix $A \in \mathbb{R}^{n \times n}$ is defined as:

$$A = \text{softmax}\left(\frac{QK^\top}{\sqrt{d}}\right),$$

where $Q \in \mathbb{R}^{n \times d}$ denotes the queries while $K \in \mathbb{R}^{n \times d}$ denotes the keys, and d represents the dimension. By multiplying the attention weights A with the values $V \in \mathbb{R}^{n \times d}$, the new values $\hat{V}$ are calculated as:

$$\hat{V} = AV.$$

The intuitive understanding of the attention is the weighted average over the old ones, where the weights are defined by the attention matrix A. In this paper, we consider the Q, K and V are generated via the linear projection of the input token matrix X:

$$Q = XW_Q, \quad K = XW_K, \quad V = XW_V,$$

where $X \in \mathbb{R}^{n \times d_m}$, $W_Q, W_K, W_V \in \mathbb{R}^{d_m \times d}$ and d_m is the input token dimension.

One shortcoming with fully-connected self-attention is that irrelevant tokens, even though assigned with smaller weights, are still taken into consideration when updating the representation V, making it less resilient to noises in V. This shortcoming motivates us to develop the k-NN attention.

3.2 k-NN Attention

Instead of computing the attention matrix for all the query-key pairs as in vanilla attention, we select the top-k most similar keys and values for each query in the k-NN attention. There are two versions of k-NN attention, as described below.

Slow Version: For the i-th query, we first compute the Euclidean distance against all the keys, and then obtain its k-nearest neighbors $\mathcal{N}_i^k$ and $\mathcal{N}_i^v$ from keys and values , and lastly calculate the scaled dot product attention as:

$$A_i = \text{softmax} \left(\frac{\langle q_i, (k_{j_1}, ..., k_{j_l}, ..., k_{j_k}) \rangle}{\sqrt{d}} \right), k_{j_l} \in \mathcal{N}_i^k.$$

The shape of final attention matrix is $A^{knn} \in \mathbb{R}^{n \times k}$, and the new values $\hat{V}^{knn}$ is the same size of values $\hat{V}$. The slow version is the exact definition of k-NN attention, but it is extremely slow because for each query it has to compute distances for different k keys.

Fast Version: As the computation of Euclidean distance against all the keys for each query is slow, we propose a fast version of k-NN attention. The key idea is to take advantage of matrix multiplication operations. Same as vanilla attention, all the queries and keys are calculated by the dot product, and then row-wise top-k elements are selected for softmax computing. The procedure can be formulated as:

$$\hat{V}^{knn} = \text{softmax} \left(\mathcal{T}_k \left(\frac{QK^\top}{\sqrt{d}} \right) \right) \cdot V,$$

where $\mathcal{T}_k (\cdot)$ denotes the row-wise top-k selection operator:

$$[\mathcal{T}_k(A)]_{ij} = \begin{cases} A_{ij} & A_{ij} \in \text{top-k(row } j) \\ -\infty & \text{otherwise.} \end{cases}$$

3.3   Theoretical Analysis on k-NN Attention

In this section, we will show theoretically that despite its simplicity, k-NN attention is powerful in speeding up network training and in distilling noisy tokens. All the proof of the lemmas are provided in the supplementary.

Convergence Speed-up. Compared to CNNs, the fully-connected self-attention is able to capture long range dependency. However, the price to pay is that the dense self-attention model requires to mix each image patch with every other patch in the image, which has potential to mix irrelevant information together, e.g. the foreground patches may be mixed with background patches through the self-attention. This defect could significantly slow down the convergence as the goal of visual object recognition is to identify key visual patches relevant to a given class.

To see this, we consider the model with only learnable parameters W_Q, W_K in attention layers and adopting Adam optimizer [33]. According to Theorem 4.1 in [33], Adam's convergence is proportional to $\mathcal{O}\left(\alpha^{-1}(G_\infty + 1) + \alpha G_\infty\right)$, where α is the learning rate and G_∞ is an element-wise upper bound on the magnitude of the batch gradient[1]. Let f_i be the loss function corresponding to batch i. Via chain rule of derivative, the gradient w.r.t the W_Q in a self-attention block can be represented as $\nabla_{W_Q} f_i = F_i(\hat{V}^{knn}) \cdot \frac{\partial \hat{V}^{knn}}{\partial W_Q}$, where $F_i(\hat{V}^{knn})$ is a matrix output function. Since the possible value of $\hat{V}^{knn}$ is a subset of its fully-connected counterpart, the upper bound of on the magnitude of $F_i(\hat{V}^{knn})$ is no larger than the full attention. We then introduce the weighed covariate matrix of patches to characterize the scale of $\frac{\partial \hat{V}^{knn}}{\partial W_Q}$ in the following lemma.

Lemma 1. *(Informal) Let $\hat{V}_l^{knn}$ be the l-th row of the $\hat{V}^{knn}$. We have*

$$\frac{\partial \hat{V}_l^{knn}}{\partial W_Q} \propto Var_{a_l}(x) \ and \ \frac{\partial \hat{V}_l^{knn}}{\partial W_K} \propto Var_{a_l}(x),$$

where $Var_{a_l}(x)$ is the covariate matrix on patches $\{x_1, ..., x_n\}$ with probability from l-th row of the attention matrix.
The same is true for $\hat{V}$ of the fully-connected self-attention.

Since k-NN attention only uses patches with large similarity, its $Var_{a_l}(x)$ will be smaller than that computed from the fully-connected attention. As indicated in Lemma 1, $\frac{\partial \hat{V}^{knn}}{\partial W_Q}$ is proportional to variance $Var_{a_l}(x)$ and thus the scale of $\nabla_{W_Q} f_i$ becomes smaller in k-NN attention. Similarly, the scale of $\nabla_{W_K} f_i$ is also smaller in k-NN attention. Therefore, the element-wise upper bound on batch gradient G_∞ in Adam analysis is also smaller for k-NN attention. For the same learning rate, the k-NN attention yields faster convergence. It is particularly significant at the beginning of training. This is because, due to the random initialization, we expect a relatively small difference in similarities between patches, which essentially makes self-attention behave like "global average". It will take multiple iterations for Adam to turn the "global average" into the real function of self-attention. In Table 2 and Fig. 2, we numerically verify the training efficiency of k-NN attention as opposed to the fully-connected attention.

---

[1] Theorem 4.1 in [33] describes the upper bound for regrets (the gap on loss function value between the current step parameters and optimal parameters). One can telescope it to the average regrets to consider the Adam's convergence.

Noisy Patch Distillation. As already mentioned before, the fully-connected self-attention model may mix irrelevant patches with relevant ones, particularly at the beginning of training when similarities between relevant patches are not significantly larger than those for irrelevant patches. k-NN attention is more effective in identifying noisy patches by only considering the top k most similar patches. To formally justify this point, we consider a simple scenario where all the patches are divided into two groups, the group of relevant patches and the group of noisy patches. All the patches are sampled independently from unknown distributions. We assume that all relevant patches are sampled from distributions with the same shared mean, which is different from the means of distributions for noisy patches. It is important to know that although distributions for the relevant patches share the mean, those relevant patches can look quite differently, due to the large variance in stochastic sampling. In the following Lemma, we will show that the k-NN attention is more effective in distilling noises for the relevant patches than the fully-connected attention.

Lemma 2 (informal). *We consider the self-attention for query patch l. Let's assume the patch $\boldsymbol{x}_i$ are bounded with mean $\boldsymbol{\mu}_i$ for $i = 1, 2, ..., n$, and ρ_k is the ratio of the noisy patches in all selected patches. Under mild conditions, the follow inequality holds with high probability:*

$$\left\| \hat{\boldsymbol{V}}_l^{knn} - \boldsymbol{\mu}_l \boldsymbol{W}_V \right\|_\infty \leq \mathcal{O}(k^{-1/2} + c_1 \rho_k),$$

where c_1 is a positive number.

In the above lemma, the quantity $\left\| \hat{\boldsymbol{V}}_l^{knn} - \boldsymbol{\mu}_l \boldsymbol{W}_V \right\|_\infty$ measures the distance between $\hat{\boldsymbol{V}}_l^{knn}$, representation vector updated by the k-NN attention, and its mean $\boldsymbol{\mu}_l \boldsymbol{W}_V$. We now consider two cases: the normal k-NN attention with appropriately chosen k, and fully-connected attention with $k = n$. In the first case, with appropriately chosen k, we should have most of the selected patches coming from the relevant group, implying a small ρ_k. By combining with the fact that k is decently large, we expect a small upper bound for the distance $\left\| \hat{\boldsymbol{V}}_l^{knn} - \boldsymbol{\mu}_l \boldsymbol{W}_V \right\|_\infty$, indicating that k-NN attention is powerful in distilling noise. For the case of fully-connected attention model, i.e. $k = n$, it is clearly that $\rho_n \approx 1$, leading to a large distance between transformed representation $\hat{\boldsymbol{V}}_l$ and its mean, indicating that fully-connected attention model is not very effective in distilling noisy patches, particularly when noise is large.

Besides the instance with low signal-noise-ratio, the instance with a large volume of backgrounds can also be hard. In the next lemma, we show that under a proper choice of k, with a high probability the k-NN attention will be able to select all meaningful patches.

Lemma 3 (informal). *Let $\mathcal{M}^*$ be the index set contains all patches relevant to query $\boldsymbol{q}_l$. Under mild conditions, there exist $c_2 \in (0, 1)$ such that with high probability, we have*

$$\sum_{i=1}^{n} \mathbb{1}(\boldsymbol{q}_l \boldsymbol{k}_i^\top \geq \min_{j \in \mathcal{M}^*} \boldsymbol{q}_l \boldsymbol{k}_j^\top) \leq \mathcal{O}(nd^{-c_2}).$$

The above lemma shows that if we select the top $\mathcal{O}(nd^{-c_2})$ elements, with high probability, we will be able to eliminate almost all the irrelevant noisy patches, without losing any relevant patches. Numerically, we verify the proper k gains better performance (e.g., Fig. 1) and for the hard instance k-NN gives more accurate attention regions. (e.g., Fig. 4 and Fig. 5).

4   Experiments for Vision Transformers

In this section, we replace the dense attention with k-NN attention on the existing vision transformers for image classification to verify the effectiveness of the proposed method. The recent DeiT [51] and its variants, including T2T ViT [70], TNT [24], PiT [28], Swin [41], CvT [59], So-ViT [61], Visformer [8], Twins [10], Dino [3] and VOLO [71], are adopted for evaluation. These methods include both supervised methods [8,10,24,28,41,51,59,61,70,71] and self-supervised method [3]. Ablation studies are provided to further analyze the properties of k-NN attention.

4.1   Experimental Settings

We perform image classification on the standard ILSVRC-2012 ImageNet dataset [46]. In our experiments, we follow the experimental setting of original official released codes. For fair comparison, we only replace the vanilla attention with proposed k-NN attention. Unless otherwise specified, the fast version of k-NN attention is adopted for evaluation. To speed up the slow version, we develop the CUDA version k-NN attention. As for the value k, different architectures are assigned with different values. For DeiT [51], So-ViT [61], Dino [3], CvT [59], TNT [24] PiT [28] and VOLO [71], as they directly split an input image into rigid tokens and there is no information exchange in the token generation stage, we suppose the irrelevant tokens are easy to filter, and tend to assign a smaller k compared with these complicated token generation methods [8,10,41,70]. Specifically, we assign k to approximate $\frac{n}{2}$ at each scale stage; for these complicated token generation methods [8,10,41,70], we assign a larger k which is approximately $\frac{2}{3}n$ or $\frac{4}{5}n$ at each scale stage.

4.2   Results on ImageNet

Table 1 shows top-1 accuracy results on the ImageNet-1K validation set by replacing the dense attention with k-NN attention using eleven different vision transformer architectures. From the Table we can see that the proposed k-NN attention improves the performance from 0.2% to 0.8% for both global and local vision transformers. It is worth noting that on ImageNet-1k dataset, it is very hard to improve the accuracy after 85%, but our k-NN attention can still consistently improve the performance even without model size increase.

Table 1. The k-NN attention performance on ImageNet-1K validation set. "!" means we pretrain the model with 300 epochs and finetune the pretrained model for 100 epoch for linear eval, following the instructions of Dino training and evaluation; "→ k-NN Attn" represents replacing the vanilla attention with proposed k-NN attention;→ k-NN Attn-slow means adopting the slow version.

Arch.	Model	Input	Params	GFLOPs	Top-1
Transformers (Supervised)	DeiT-Tiny [51]	224^2	5.7 M	1.3	72.2%
	DeiT-Tiny [51] → k-NN Attn	224^2	5.7 M	1.3	73.0%
	DeiT-Tiny [51] → k-NN Attn-slow	224^2	5.7 M	1.3	73.0%
	So-ViT-7 [61]	224^2	5.5 M	1.3	76.2%
	So-ViT-7 [61] → k-NN Attn	224^2	5.5 M	1.3	77.0%
Transformers (Supervised)	Visformer-Tiny [8]	224^2	10 M	1.3	78.6%
	Visformer-Tiny [8] → k-NN Attn	224^2	10 M	1.3	79.0%
Transformers (Supervised)	CvT-13 [59]	224^2	20 M	4.6	81.6%
	CvT-13 [59] → k-NN Attn	224^2	20 M	4.6	81.9%
	DeiT-Small [51]	224^2	22 M	4.6	79.8%
	DeiT-Small [51] → k-NN Attn	224^2	22 M	4.6	80.1%
	TNT-Small [24]	224^2	24 M	5.2	81.5%
	TNT-Small [24] → k-NN Attn	224^2	24 M	5.2	81.9%
	VOLO-D1 [71]	384^2	27 M	22.8	85.2%
	VOLO-D1 [71] → k-NN Attn	384^2	27 M	22.8	85.4%
	Swin-Tiny [41]	224^2	28 M	4.5	81.2%
	Swin-Tiny [41] → k-NN Attn	224^2	28 M	4.5	81.3%
	T2T-ViT-t-19 [70]	224^2	39 M	9.8	82.2%
	T2T-ViT-t-19 [70] → k-NN Attn	224^2	39 M	9.8	82.7%
Transformers (Supervised)	Dino-Small [3]!	224^2	22 M	4.6	76.0%
	Dino-Small [3]! → k-NN Attn	224^2	22 M	4.6	76.2%
Transformers (Supervised)	Twins-SVT-Base [10]	224^2	56 M	8.3	83.2%
	Twins-SVT-Base [10] → k-NN Attn	224^2	56 M	8.3	83.4%
	PiT-Base [28]	224^2	74 M	12.5	82.0%
	PiT-Base [28] → k-NN Attn	224^2	74 M	12.5	82.6%
	VOLO-D3 [71]	448^2	86 M	67.9	86.3%
	VOLO-D3 [71] → k-NN Attn	448^2	86 M	67.9	**86.5%**

4.3 The Impact of Number k

The only parameter for k-NN attention is k, and its impact is analyzed in Fig. 1. As shown in the figure, for DeiT-Tiny, $k = 100$ is the best, where the total number of tokens $n = 196$ (14 × 14), meaning that k approximates half of n; for CvT-13, there are three scale stages with the number of tokens $n_1 = 3136$, $n_2 = 784$ and $n_3 = 196$, and the best results are achieved when the k in each stage is assigned to 1600/400/100, which also approximate half of n in each stage; for Visformer-Tiny, there are two scale stages with the number of tokens $n_1 = 196$ and $n_2 = 49$, and the best results are achieved when k in each stage is assigned to 150/45, as there are more than 21 conv layers for token generation and the information in each token are already mixed, making it hard to distinguish the irrelevant tokens, thus larger values of k are desired; for PiT-Base, there are three scale stages with the number of tokens $n_1 = 961$, $n_2 = 256$ and $n_3 = 64$, and the optimal values of k also approximate the half of n. Please note that, we do not perform exhaustive search for the optimal choice of k, instead, a general rule as below is sufficient: $k \approx \frac{n}{2}$ at each scale stage for simple token generation methods and $k \approx \frac{2}{3}n$ or $\frac{4}{5}n$ for complicated token generation methods at each scale stage.

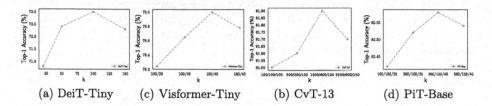

(a) DeiT-Tiny   (c) Visformer-Tiny   (b) CvT-13   (d) PiT-Base

Fig. 1. The impact of k on DeiT-Tiny, Visformer-Tiny, CvT-13 and PiT-Base.

4.4   Convergence Speed of k-NN Attention

In Table 2, we investigate the convergence speed of k-NN attention. Three methods are included for comparison, i.e. DeiT-Small [51], CvT-13 [59] and T2T-ViT-t-19 [70]. From the Table we can see that the convergence speed of k-NN attention is faster than full-connected attention, especially in the early stage of training. These observations reflect that removing the irrelevant tokens benefits the convergence of neural networks training.

Table 2. Ablation study on the convergence speed of k-NN attention.

Epoch	Top-1 accuracy					
	DeiT-S	DeiT-S $\rightarrow$ k	CvT-13	CvT-13 $\rightarrow$ k	T2T-ViT-t-19	T2T-ViT-t-19 $\rightarrow$ k
10	29.1%	31.3%	51.4%	54.2%	0.52%	0.68%
30	54.4%	55.4%	65.4%	68.1%	63.0%	63.2%
50	60.9%	62.0%	68.1%	70.5%	73.8%	74.4%
70	65.0%	65.8%	69.9%	72.2%	76.9%	77.3%
90	67.7%	68.2%	71.0%	73.0%	78.4%	78.6%
120	69.9%	70.7%	72.4%	73.7%	79.7%	80.0%
150	72.4%	72.4%	74.4%	74.9%	80.7%	80.9%
200	75.5%	75.7%	77.3%	77.7%	82.0%	82.3%
300	79.8%	80.0%	81.6%	81.9%	81.3%	81.7%

4.5   Other Properties of k-NN Attention

To analyze other properties of k-NN attention, four quantitative metrics are defined as follows.

Layer-wise Cosine Similarity Between Tokens: Following [21] this metric is defined as:

$$\text{CosSim}(\mathbf{t}) = \frac{1}{n(n-1)} \sum_{i \neq j} \frac{t_i^T t_j}{\|t_i\| \|t_j\|},$$

where t_i represents the i-th token in each layer and $\|\cdot\|$ denotes the Euclidean norm. This metric implies the convergence speed of the network.

Layer-wise Standard Deviation of Attention Weights: Given a token t_i and its softmax attention weight $\text{sfm}(t_i)$, the standard deviation of the softmax attention weight $\text{std}(\text{sfm}(t_i))$ is defined as the second metric. For multi-head attention, the standard deviations over all heads are averaged. This metric represents the degree of training stability.

Ratio Between the Norms of Residual Activations and Main Branch: The ratio between the norm of the residual activations and the norm of the activations of the main branch in each layer is defined as $\|f_l(t)\| / \|t\|$, where $f_l(t)$ can be the attention layer or the FFN layer. This metric denotes the information preservation ability of the network.

Nonlocality: following [14], the nonlocality is defined by summing, for each query patch i, the distances $\|\delta_{ij}\|$ to all the key patches j weighted by their attention score $\boldsymbol{A}_{ij}$. The number obtained over the query patch is averaged to obtain the nonlocality metric of head h, which can the be averaged over the attention heads to obtain the nonlocality of the whole layer l:

$$D_{loc}^{l,h} := \frac{1}{L} \sum_{ij} \boldsymbol{A}_{ij}^{h,l} \|\delta_{ij}\|, D_{loc}^{l} := \frac{1}{N_h} \sum_{h} D_{loc}^{l,h},$$

where D_{loc} is the number of patches between the center of attention and the query patch; the further the attention heads look from the query patch, the higher the nonlocality.

Comparisons of the four metrics on DeiT-tiny without distillation token are shown in Fig. 2 and Fig. 3. From Fig. 2 (a) we can see that by using k-NN attention, the averaged cosine similarity is larger than that of using dense self-attention, which reflects that the convergence speed is faster for k-NN attention. Figure 2 (b) shows that the averaged standard deviation of k-NN attention is smoother than that of fully-connected self-attention, and the smoothness will help make the training more stable. Figure 2 (c) and (d) show the ratio between the norms of residual activations and main branch are consistent with each other for k-NN attention and dense attention, which indicates that there is nearly no information lost in k-NN attention by removing the irrelevant tokens. Figure 3 shows that, with k-NN attention, lower layers tend to focus more on the local areas (with more lines being pushed toward the bottom area in Fig. 3), while

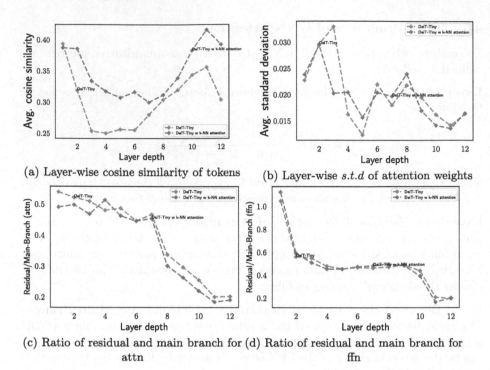

(a) Layer-wise cosine similarity of tokens   (b) Layer-wise *s.t.d* of attention weights

(c) Ratio of residual and main branch for (d) Ratio of residual and main branch for
attn   ffn

Fig. 2. The properties of k-NN attention. Blue and red dotted lines represent the metrics for k-NN attetion and the original fully-connected self-attention, respectively. (Color figure online)

the higher layers still maintain their capability of extracting global information. Additionally, it is also observed that the non-locality of different layers is spreading more evenly, indicating that they can explore a larger variety of dependencies at different ranges.

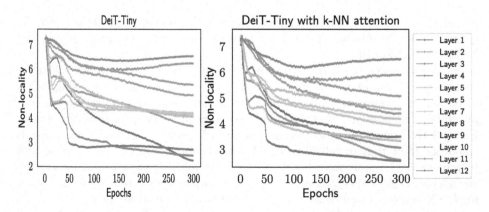

Fig. 3. The nonlocality of DeiT-Tiny. It is plotted averaged over all the images from training set of ImageNet-1k.

4.6 Comparisons with Temperature in Softmax

k-NN attention effectively zeros the bottom $N - k$ tokens out of the attention calculation. How does this compare with introducing a temperature parameter to softmax over the attention values? We compare our k-NN attention with temperature t in softmax as softmax(attn/t). The performance over the t is shown in Table 3. From the Table we can see that small t makes the training crash due to large value of attention values; the performance increases a little bit to 72.5 (baseline 72.2) with t assigned to appropriate values. The k-NN attention is more robust compared with temperature in softmax, and achieves much better performance, 73.0 (k-NN attention) vs 72.5 (best performance for temperature in softmax).

Table 3. The Top-1 (%) over the temperature t in softmax.

t	0.05	0.1	0.25	0.75	2	4	8	16
Top-1 (%)	Crash	Crash	72.0	72.5	72.5	72.5	72.5	72.1

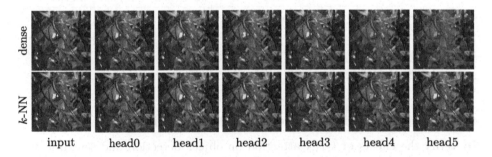

Fig. 4. Self-attention heads from the last layer.

4.7 Visualization

Figure 4 visualizes the self-attention heads from the last layer on Dino-Small [3]. We can see that different heads attend to different semantic regions of an image. Compared with dense attention, the k-NN attention filters out most irrelevant information from background regions which are similar to the foreground, and successfully concentrates on the most informative foreground regions. Images from different classes are visualized in Fig. 5 using Transformer Attribution method [5] on DeiT-Tiny. It can be seen that the k-NN attention is more concentrated and accurate, especially in the situations of cluttered background and occlusion.

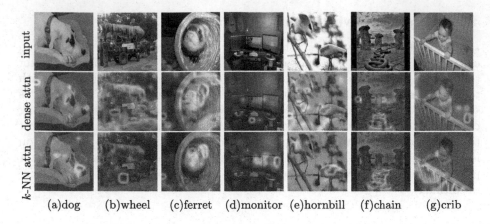

Fig. 5. Visualization using Transformer Attribution [5].

Table 4. Object detection and Segmentation results for Swin-Tiny and Twins-SVT-Base with/without k-NN attention on the COCO and ADE20K validation sets. All the models are pretrained on ImageNet-1k.

Backbone	COCO		ADE20K	
	Method	mAP(box)	Method	mIoU
Swin-T	Mask R-CNN 3x	46.0	UPerNet	44.5
Swin-T-k-NN	Mask R-CNN 3x	46.2	UPerNet	44.7
Twins-SVT-Base	Mask R-CNN 1x	45.2	UPerNet	47.4
Twins-SVT-Base-k-NN	Mask R-CNN 1x	45.6	UPerNet	47.9

4.8   Object Detection and Semantic Segmentation

To verify the effects of k-NN attention on object detection and semantic segmentation tasks, the widely-used COCO [39] and ADE20K [76] are adopted for evaluation. We adopt Swin-Tiny [41] and Twins-SVT-Base [10] for comparisons due to the well released codes, and the results are shown in Table 4. From the Table we can see that by replacing the vanilla attention with our k-NN attention, the performance increases with almost no overhead.

5   Conclusion

In this paper, we propose an effective k-NN attention for boosting vision transformers. By selecting the most similar keys for each query to calculate the attention, it screens out the most ineffective tokens. The removal of irrelevant tokens speeds up the training. We theoretically prove its properties in speeding up training, distilling noises without losing information, and increasing the performance by choosing a proper k. Several vision transformers are adopted to verify the effectiveness of the k-NN attention.

References

1. Beltagy, I., Peters, M.E., Cohan, A.: Longformer: the long-document transformer. arXiv preprint arXiv:2004.05150 (2020)
2. Carion, N., Massa, F., Synnaeve, G., Usunier, N., Kirillov, A., Zagoruyko, S.: End-to-end object detection with transformers. In: Vedaldi, A., Bischof, H., Brox, T., Frahm, J.-M. (eds.) ECCV 2020. LNCS, vol. 12346, pp. 213–229. Springer, Cham (2020). https://doi.org/10.1007/978-3-030-58452-8_13
3. Caron, M., et al.: Emerging properties in self-supervised vision transformers. arXiv preprint arXiv:2104.14294 (2021)
4. Chang, S., Wang, P., Wang, F., Li, H., Feng, J.: Augmented transformer with adaptive graph for temporal action proposal generation. arXiv preprint arXiv:2103.16024 (2021)
5. Chefer, H., Gur, S., Wolf, L.: Transformer interpretability beyond attention visualization. In: CVPR (2021)
6. Chen, C.F., Fan, Q., Panda, R.: Crossvit: cross-attention multi-scale vision transformer for image classification. arXiv preprint arXiv:2103.14899 (2021)
7. Chen, X., Yan, B., Zhu, J., Wang, D., Yang, X., Lu, H.: Transformer tracking. In: CVPR (2021)
8. Chen, Z., Xie, L., Niu, J., Liu, X., Wei, L., Tian, Q.: Visformer: the vision-friendly transformer. arXiv preprint arXiv:2104.12533 (2021)
9. Child, R., Gray, S., Radford, A., Sutskever, I.: Generating long sequences with sparse transformers. arXiv preprint arXiv:1904.10509 (2019)
10. Chu, X., et al.: Twins: revisiting spatial attention design in vision transformers. arXiv preprint arXiv:2104.13840 (2021)
11. Chu, X., Zhang, B., Tian, Z., Wei, X., Xia, H.: Do we really need explicit position encodings for vision transformers? arXiv preprint arXiv:2102.10882 (2021)
12. Cordonnier, J.B., Loukas, A., Jaggi, M.: On the relationship between self-attention and convolutional layers. In: ICLR (2019)
13. Correia, G.M., Niculae, V., Martins, A.F.: Adaptively sparse transformers. In: EMNLP, pp. 2174–2184 (2019)
14. d'Ascoli, S., Touvron, H., Leavitt, M., Morcos, A., Biroli, G., Sagun, L.: Convit: improving vision transformers with soft convolutional inductive biases. arXiv preprint arXiv:2103.10697 (2021)
15. Devlin, J., Chang, M.W., Lee, K., Toutanova, K.: Bert: pre-training of deep bidirectional transformers for language understanding. arXiv preprint arXiv:1810.04805 (2018)
16. Dosovitskiy, A., et al.: An image is worth 16x16 words: transformers for image recognition at scale. arXiv preprint arXiv:2010.11929 (2020)
17. El-Nouby, A., et al.: Xcit: cross-covariance image transformers. arXiv preprint arXiv:2106.09681 (2021)
18. Fan, H., Xiong, B., Mangalam, K., Li, Y., Yan, Z., Malik, J., Feichtenhofer, C.: Multiscale vision transformers. arXiv preprint arXiv:2104.11227 (2021)
19. Fang, J., Xie, L., Wang, X., Zhang, X., Liu, W., Tian, Q.: Msg-transformer: exchanging local spatial information by manipulating messenger tokens. arXiv preprint arXiv:2105.15168 (2021)
20. Gao, P., Lu, J., Li, H., Mottaghi, R., Kembhavi, A.: Container: context aggregation network. arXiv preprint arXiv:2106.01401 (2021)
21. Gong, C., Wang, D., Li, M., Chandra, V., Liu, Q.: Improve vision transformers training by suppressing over-smoothing. arXiv preprint arXiv:2104.12753 (2021)

22. Graham, B., et al.: Levit: a vision transformer in convnet's clothing for faster inference. arXiv preprint arXiv:2104.01136 (2021)
23. Guo, J., Han, K., Wu, H., Xu, C., Tang, Y., Xu, C., Wang, Y.: Cmt: convolutional neural networks meet vision transformers. arXiv preprint arXiv:2107.06263 (2021)
24. Han, K., Xiao, A., Wu, E., Guo, J., Xu, C., Wang, Y.: Transformer in transformer. arXiv preprint arXiv:2103.00112 (2021)
25. Han, L., Wang, P., Yin, Z., Wang, F., Li, H.: Exploiting better feature aggregation for video object detection. In: ACM MM (2020)
26. He, K., Zhang, X., Ren, S., Sun, J.: Deep residual learning for image recognition. In: CVPR (2016)
27. He, S., Luo, H., Wang, P., Wang, F., Li, H., Jiang, W.: Transreid: transformer-based object re-identification. arXiv preprint arXiv:2102.04378 (2021)
28. Heo, B., Yun, S., Han, D., Chun, S., Choe, J., Oh, S.J.: Rethinking spatial dimensions of vision transformers. arXiv preprint arXiv:2103.16302 (2021)
29. Ho, J., Kalchbrenner, N., Weissenborn, D., Salimans, T.: Axial attention in multi-dimensional transformers. arXiv preprint arXiv:1912.12180 (2019)
30. Huang, Z., Ben, Y., Luo, G., Cheng, P., Yu, G., Fu, B.: Shuffle transformer: rethinking spatial shuffle for vision transformer. arXiv preprint arXiv:2106.03650 (2021)
31. Jiang, Z., et al.: Token labeling: training a 85.5% top-1 accuracy vision transformer with 56m parameters on imagenet. arXiv preprint arXiv:2104.10858 (2021)
32. Jonnalagadda, A., Wang, W., Eckstein, M.P.: Foveater: foveated transformer for image classification. arXiv preprint arXiv:2105.14173 (2021)
33. Kingma, D.P., Ba, J.: Adam: a method for stochastic optimization. arXiv preprint arXiv:1412.6980 (2014)
34. Kitaev, N., Kaiser, L., Levskaya, A.: Reformer: the efficient transformer. arXiv preprint arXiv:2001.04451 (2020)
35. Li, W., Liu, H., Ding, R., Liu, M., Wang, P.: Lifting transformer for 3D human pose estimation in video. arXiv preprint arXiv:2103.14304 (2021)
36. Li, X., Hou, Y., Wang, P., Gao, Z., Xu, M., Li, W.: Transformer guided geometry model for flow-based unsupervised visual odometry. Neural Comput. Appl. **33**(13), 8031–8042 (2021). https://doi.org/10.1007/s00521-020-05545-8
37. Li, X., Hou, Y., Wang, P., Gao, Z., Xu, M., Li, W.: Trear: transformer-based RGB-D egocentric action recognition. arXiv preprint arXiv:2101.03904 (2021)
38. Li, Y., Zhang, K., Cao, J., Timofte, R., Van Gool, L.: Localvit: bringing locality to vision transformers. arXiv preprint arXiv:2104.05707 (2021)
39. Lin, T.-Y., et al.: Microsoft COCO: common objects in context. In: Fleet, D., Pajdla, T., Schiele, B., Tuytelaars, T. (eds.) ECCV 2014. LNCS, vol. 8693, pp. 740–755. Springer, Cham (2014). https://doi.org/10.1007/978-3-319-10602-1_48
40. Liu, P.J., et al.: Generating Wikipedia by summarizing long sequences. In: ICLR (2018)
41. Liu, Z., et al.: Swin transformer: hierarchical vision transformer using shifted windows. arXiv preprint arXiv:2103.14030 (2021)
42. Luong, M.T., Pham, H., Manning, C.D.: Effective approaches to attention-based neural machine translation. In: EMNLP (2015)
43. Pai, S.: Convolutional neural networks arise from Ising models and restricted Boltzmann machines
44. Rao, Y., Zhao, W., Liu, B., Lu, J., Zhou, J., Hsieh, C.J.: Dynamicvit: efficient vision transformers with dynamic token sparsification. arXiv preprint arXiv:2106.02034 (2021)
45. Roy, A., Saffar, M., Vaswani, A., Grangier, D.: Efficient content-based sparse attention with routing transformers. Trans. Assoc. Comput. Linguist. **9**, 53–68 (2021)

46. Russakovsky, O., et al.: ImageNet large scale visual recognition challenge. Int. J. Comput. Vis. **115**(3), 211–252 (2015). https://doi.org/10.1007/s11263-015-0816-y
47. Tan, M., Le, Q.: Efficientnet: rethinking model scaling for convolutional neural networks. In: ICML (2019)
48. Tay, Y., Bahri, D., Yang, L., Metzler, D., Juan, D.C.: Sparse sinkhorn attention. In: ICML (2020)
49. Tay, Y., et al.: Omninet: omnidirectional representations from transformers. arXiv preprint arXiv:2103.01075 (2021)
50. Tay, Y., Dehghani, M., Bahri, D., Metzler, D.: Efficient transformers: a survey. arXiv preprint arXiv:2009.06732 (2020)
51. Touvron, H., Cord, M., Douze, M., Massa, F., Sablayrolles, A., Jégou, H.: Training data-efficient image transformers & distillation through attention. arXiv preprint arXiv:2012.12877 (2020)
52. Touvron, H., Cord, M., Sablayrolles, A., Synnaeve, G., Jégou, H.: Going deeper with image transformers. arXiv preprint arXiv:2103.17239 (2021)
53. Vaswani, A., et al.: Attention is all you need. In: NIPS (2017)
54. Wang, P., et al.: Scaled relu matters for training vision transformers. arXiv preprint arXiv:2109.03810 (2021)
55. Wang, W., et al.: Pyramid vision transformer: a versatile backbone for dense prediction without convolutions. arXiv preprint arXiv:2102.12122 (2021)
56. Wang, W., Yao, L., Chen, L., Cai, D., He, X., Liu, W.: Crossformer: a versatile vision transformer based on cross-scale attention. arXiv preprint arXiv:2108.00154 (2021)
57. Wang, Y., Huang, R., Song, S., Huang, Z., Huang, G.: Not all images are worth 16x16 words: dynamic vision transformers with adaptive sequence length. arXiv preprint arXiv:2105.15075 (2021)
58. Wang, Y., et al.: End-to-end video instance segmentation with transformers. In: CVPR (2021)
59. Wu, H., et al.: Cvt: introducing convolutions to vision transformers. arXiv preprint arXiv:2103.15808 (2021)
60. Xiao, T., Singh, M., Mintun, E., Darrell, T., Dollár, P., Girshick, R.: Early convolutions help transformers see better. arXiv preprint arXiv:2106.14881 (2021)
61. Xie, J., Zeng, R., Wang, Q., Zhou, Z., Li, P.: So-vit: mind visual tokens for vision transformer. arXiv preprint arXiv:2104.10935 (2021)
62. Xu, T., Chen, W., Wang, P., Wang, F., Li, H., Jin, R.: Cdtrans: cross-domain transformer for unsupervised domain adaptation. arXiv preprint arXiv:2109.06165 (2021)
63. Xu, W., Xu, Y., Chang, T., Tu, Z.: Co-scale conv-attentional image transformers. arXiv preprint arXiv:2104.06399 (2021)
64. Xu, Y., et al.: Evo-vit: sow-fast token evolution for dynamic vision transformer. arXiv preprint arXiv:2108.01390 (2021)
65. Yang, J., et al.: Focal self-attention for local-global interactions in vision transformers. arXiv preprint arXiv:2107.00641 (2021)
66. Yin, Z., et al.: Transfgu: a top-down approach to fine-grained unsupervised semantic segmentation. In: European Conference on Computer Vision (2022)
67. Yu, Q., Xia, Y., Bai, Y., Lu, Y., Yuille, A., Shen, W.: Glance-and-gaze vision transformer. arXiv preprint arXiv:2106.02277 (2021)
68. Yu, Z., Li, X., Wang, P., Zhao, G.: Transrppg: remote photoplethysmography transformer for 3D mask face presentation attack detection. arXiv preprint arXiv:2104.07419 (2021)

69. Yuan, K., Guo, S., Liu, Z., Zhou, A., Yu, F., Wu, W.: Incorporating convolution designs into visual transformers. arXiv preprint arXiv:2103.11816 (2021)
70. Yuan, L., et al.: Tokens-to-token vit: training vision transformers from scratch on imagenet. arXiv preprint arXiv:2101.11986 (2021)
71. Yuan, L., Hou, Q., Jiang, Z., Feng, J., Yan, S.: Volo: vision outlooker for visual recognition. arXiv preprint arXiv:2106.13112 (2021)
72. Zaheer, M., et al.: Big bird: transformers for longer sequences. arXiv preprint arXiv:2007.14062 (2020)
73. Zhang, P., et al.: Multi-scale vision longformer: a new vision transformer for high-resolution image encoding. arXiv preprint arXiv:2103.15358 (2021)
74. Zhang, Z., Zhang, H., Zhao, L., Chen, T., Pfister, T.: Aggregating nested transformers. arXiv preprint arXiv:2105.12723 (2021)
75. Zhao, G., Lin, J., Zhang, Z., Ren, X., Su, Q., Sun, X.: Explicit sparse transformer: concentrated attention through explicit selection. arXiv preprint arXiv:1912.11637 (2019)
76. Zhou, B., et al.: Semantic understanding of scenes through the ADE20K dataset. Int. J. Comput. Vis. **127**(3), 302–321 (2018). https://doi.org/10.1007/s11263-018-1140-0
77. Zhou, D., et al.: Deepvit: towards deeper vision transformer. arXiv preprint arXiv:2103.11886 (2021)
78. Zhou, D., et al.: Refiner: refining self-attention for vision transformers. arXiv preprint arXiv:2106.03714 (2021)
79. Zhou, J., Wang, P., Wang, F., Liu, Q., Li, H., Jin, R.: Elsa: enhanced local self-attention for vision transformer. arXiv preprint arXiv:2112.12786 (2021)
80. Zou, C., et al.: End-to-end human object interaction detection with hoi transformer. In: CVPR (2021)

Registration Based Few-Shot Anomaly Detection

Chaoqin Huang[1,3,4], Haoyan Guan[2], Aofan Jiang[1], Ya Zhang[1,3(✉)],
Michael Spratling[2], and Yan-Feng Wang[1,3(✉)]

[1] Cooperative Medianet Innovation Center, Shanghai Jiao Tong University,
Shanghai, China
{huangchaoqin,stillunnamed,ya_zhang,
wangyanfeng}@sjtu.edu.cn
[2] King's College London, London, UK
{haoyan.guan,michael.spratling}@kcl.ac.uk
[3] Shanghai Artificial Intelligence Laboratory, Shanghai, China
[4] National University of Singapore, Singapore, Singapore

Abstract. This paper considers few-shot anomaly detection (FSAD), a
practical yet under-studied setting for anomaly detection (AD), where
only a limited number of normal images are provided for each category at
training. So far, existing FSAD studies follow the one-model-per-category
learning paradigm used for standard AD, and the inter-category commonality has not been explored. Inspired by how humans detect anomalies, *i.e.,* comparing an image in question to normal images, we here leverage registration, an image alignment task that is inherently generalizable
across categories, as the proxy task, to train a category-agnostic anomaly
detection model. During testing, the anomalies are identified by comparing the registered features of the test image and its corresponding support
(normal) images. As far as we know, this is the first FSAD method that
trains a single generalizable model and requires no re-training or parameter fine-tuning for new categories. Experimental results have shown that
the proposed method outperforms the state-of-the-art FSAD methods
by 3%–8% in AUC on the MVTec and MPDD benchmarks. Source code
is available at: https://github.com/MediaBrain-SJTU/RegAD.

Keywords: Anomaly detection · Few-shot learning · Registration

1 Introduction

Anomaly detection (AD), with a wide range of applications such as defect detection [24], medical diagnosis [44], and autonomous driving [10], has received quite
some attention in the computer vision community over the last decades. With
the ambiguous definition of "anomaly", *i.e.,* samples that do not conform to the
"normal", it is impossible to train with an exhaustive set of anomalous samples.
As a result, recent studies on anomaly detection have largely been devoted to

Supplementary Information The online version contains supplementary material
available at https://doi.org/10.1007/978-3-031-20053-3_18.

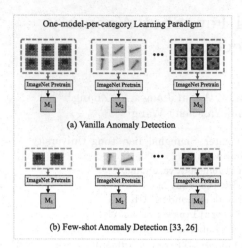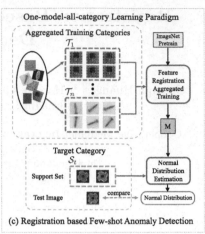

Fig. 1. Different from (a) vanilla AD, and (b) existing FSAD methods under the one-model-per-category learning paradigm, the proposed method (c) leverages feature registration as a category-agnostic approach for FSAD, under the one-model-all-category learning paradigm. Trained with aggregated data of multiple categories, the model is directly applicable to novel categories without any parameter fine-tuning, with the only need to estimate the normal feature distribution given the corresponding support set.

unsupervised learning, *i.e.*, learning with only the "normal" samples. Through modeling the normal distribution with one-class classification [30,35,43], reconstruction [13,18,39,47], or self-supervised learning tasks [12,33,42,45], many AD methods detect anomalies by identifying samples with different distributions than the model.

Most existing AD methods have focused on training a dedicated model for each category (Fig. 1 (a)). However, in real-world scenarios such as defect detection, given hundreds of industrial products to handle, it is not cost-effective to collect a large training set for each product, not to mention the need for many time-sensitive applications. A couple of studies [29,36] have recently explored a special, yet practical, setting of AD, *i.e.*, few-shot anomaly detection (FSAD), where only a limited number of normal images are provided for each category at training (Fig. 1 (b)). The few-shot learning of anomaly detection has been approached with strategies to reduce the demand on training samples, such as radical data augmentation with multiple transformations [36] or a lighter estimator for the normal distribution estimation [29]. *However, such approaches still follow the one-model-per-category learning paradigm and fail to leverage the inter-category commonality.*

This paper aims to explore a new paradigm for FSAD, by learning a common model shared among multiple categories and also generalizable to novel categories, and inspired by how human beings detect anomalies. In fact, when a human is asked to search for the anomaly in an image, a simple strategy one may adopt is to compare the sample to a normal one to find the difference. As long as one knows how to compare two images, the actual semantics of the images does not matter anymore. To achieve such a human-like comparison process, we resort to registration, a process of transforming different images into one coordinate system in order to better enable comparison [4,25,46]. Registration is particularly suitable for FSAD, as *registration is expected to be category-agnostic and thus generalizable across categories, allowing the model to be adaptable to novel categories without the necessity of parameter fine-tuning.*

Figure 1 (c) provides an overview of the proposed Registration based few-shot Anomaly Detection (RegAD) framework. To train a category-agnostic anomaly detection model, we leverage registration, a task that is inherently generalizable across categories, as the proxy task. A Siamese network [5] with three spatial transformer network [19] blocks is employed as the registration network (see Fig. 2). For better robustness, instead of registering the images pixel-by-pixel as typical registration methods [25], here we propose a feature-level registration loss by maximizing the cosine similarity of features from the same category, which may be deemed as a relaxed version of the pixel-wise registration loss. Normal images from different categories are used together to aggregately train the model, with two images from the same category randomly selected as a training pair. Such aggregated training procedure is adopted so as to enable the trained registration model to be category-agnostic. At test time, a support set of a few normal samples is provided for the target category, together with each test sample. It is straightforward to identify anomalies by comparing the registered features of the test image and the corresponding support (normal) images. Given the support set, the normal distribution of registered features for the target category is estimated with a statistical-based distribution estimator [8]. Test samples that are out of the statistical normal distribution are considered anomalies. In this way, the model quickly adapts to novel categories by simply estimating its normal feature distribution without any parameter fine-tuning.

To validate the effectiveness of RegAD, we experiment with two challenging benchmark datasets for industrial defect detection, MVTec AD [2] and MPDD [20]. Our experimental results have shown that RegAD outperforms the state-of-the-art FSAD methods [29,36], achieving improvements of 5.1%, 6.9%, and 8.0% in AUC on MVTec, and improvements of 3.2%, 5.0%, and 3.4% in AUC on MPDD, for 2-shot, 4-shot, and 8-shot scenarios, respectively.

The main contributions of the paper are summarised as follows:

- We introduce feature registration as a category-agnostic approach for few-shot anomaly detection (FSAD). To our best of knowledge, it is the first FSAD method that trains a single generalizable model and requires no re-training or parameter fine-tuning for new categories.
- Extensive experiments on recent benchmark datasets have shown that the proposed RegAD outperforms the state-of-the-art FSAD methods on both the anomaly detection and anomaly localization tasks.

2 Related Work

2.1 Anomaly Detection

AD is a task where training datasets contain only normal data. To better estimate the normal distributions, one-class classification based approaches tend to depict the normal data directly with statistical approaches [9,26,30,35]. Self-supervised based approaches are trained using only normal data, and then make inferences by assuming that anomalous data performs differently. In this domain, reconstruction [1,13,17,32,34,39,40,47] is the most popular self-supervision. Some approaches [12,33,42] introduce other self-supervisions, *e.g.*, [12] applies dozens of image geometric transforms for transformation classification; [42] proposes a restoration framework for attribute restoration. Recent AD methods usually use feature embeddings extracted from a pre-trained deep neural network. Feature embedding is mostly used as an input for a traditional machine learning algorithm or statistical metrics such as the Mahalanobis distance [8]. The network used as a feature extractor can be trained from scratch [43], while several methods [8,14,21,28,45] have also achieved state-of-the-art results using models pre-trained on the ImageNet dataset [31]. This paper differs from these previous works by focusing on FSAD, where only a few normal images are available.

2.2   Few-Shot Learning

Few-shot learning (FSL) aims to adapt to novel classes with a few annotated examples. Representative FSL methods can be categorized into metric learning, generation, and optimization. Metric learning approaches [15,37,38] learn to calculate a feature space that classifies an unseen sample based on its nearest example category. Generation methods [6,22,41] enhance the novel class performance by generating its images or features. Optimization methods [11,27] learn commonalities among different categories and explore efficient optimization strategies for novel classes based on these commonalities. In this paper, the proposed method predicts 'normal' or 'anomaly' for a new category. In contrast to previous work on FSL, both training data and support set only have positive (normal) examples without any negative (anomaly) samples.

2.3   Few-Shot Anomaly Detection

FSAD aims to indicate anomalies with only a few normal samples as the support images for target categories. TDG [36] proposes a hierarchical generative model that captures the multi-scale patch distribution of each support image. They use multiple image transformations and optimize discriminators to distinguish between real and fake patches, as well as between different transformations applied to the patches. The anomaly score was obtained by aggregating the patch-based votes of the correct transformations. DiffNet [29] leverages the descriptiveness of features extracted by convolutional neural networks to estimate their density using a normalizing flow, which is a tool well-suited to estimate distributions from a few support samples. Metaformer [39] can be applied to the FSAD, although an additional large-scale dataset, MSRA10K [7], should be used during its entire meta-training procedure (beyond parameter pre-training), together with additional pixel-level annotations. In this paper, we design registration based FSAD to learn the category-agnostic feature registration, enabling the model to detect anomalies in new categories given a few normal images without fine-tuning.

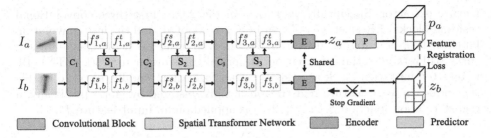

Fig. 2. The model architecture of the proposed RegAD. Given paired images from the same category, features are extracted by three convolutional residual blocks each followed by a spatial transformer network. A Siamese network acts as the feature encoder, supervised by a registration loss for feature similarity maximization.

3   Problem Setting

We first formally define the problem setting for the proposed few-shot anomaly detection. Given a training set consisting of only normal samples of n categories, i.e., $\mathcal{T}_{train} = \bigcup_{i=1}^{n} \mathcal{T}_i$, where the subset $\mathcal{T}_i$ consists of normal samples from the category c_i, $(i = 1, 2, \cdots, n)$, we want to train a category-agnostic anomaly detection model. At test time, given a normal or anomalous image from a target category c_t $(t \notin \{1, 2, \cdots, n\})$ and its associated support set $\mathcal{S}_t$ consisting of k normal samples from the target category c_t, the trained category-agnostic anomaly detection model should predict whether the image is anomalous or not.

For FSAD, we attempt to detect anomalies from test samples of unseen/novel categories using only a few normal images as the support set. The key challenges lie in: (i) $\mathcal{T}_{train}$ has only access to normal samples from multiple known categories (e.g., different objects or textures), without any image-level or pixel-level annotations, (ii) the test data is from an unseen/novel category, and (iii) only a few normal samples from the target category c_t are available, making it hard to estimate the normal distribution of the target category c_t.

4   Method

Motivated by how humans detect anomalies, the feature registration is used as a generalization paradigm for FSAD. During the training procedure, we leverage an anomaly-free feature registration network to learn category-agnostic feature registration. During testing, given the support set of a few normal images, the normal distribution of registered features for the target category is estimated with a statistical-based distribution estimator. Test samples that are out of the learned statistical normal distribution are considered anomalies.

4.1   Feature Registration Network

Given a pair of images I_a and I_b randomly selected from a same category in the training set $\mathcal{T}_{train}$, a ResNet-type convolutional network [16] is leveraged as the feature extractor. Specifically, as shown in Fig. 2, the first three convolutional residual blocks of ResNet, C_1, C_2, and C_3, are adopted, and the last convolution block in ResNet's original design is discarded, in order to ensure that final features still retain spatial information. A spatial transformer network (STN) [19] is inserted into each block as a feature transformation module, so as to enable the model to learn feature registration flexibly, inspired by [45]. Specifically, a transformation function S_i ($i = 1, 2, 3$) is applied on an input feature f_i^s:

$$\begin{pmatrix} x_i^t \\ y_i^t \end{pmatrix} = S_i(f_i^s) = A_i \begin{pmatrix} x_i^s \\ y_i^s \\ 1 \end{pmatrix} = \begin{bmatrix} \theta_{11} & \theta_{12} & \theta_{13} \\ \theta_{21} & \theta_{22} & \theta_{23} \end{bmatrix} \begin{pmatrix} x_i^s \\ y_i^s \\ 1 \end{pmatrix}, \tag{1}$$

where (x_i^t, y_i^t) are the target coordinates of output feature f_i^t, (x_i^s, y_i^s) are the same points in the source coordinates of input feature f_i^s and A_i is the affine transformation matrix. The module S_i is used to learn the mappings from features of convolutional block C_i with the same tiny architecture as used in [19].

Given paired extracted features $f_{3,a}^t$ and $f_{3,b}^t$ as the final transformation outputs, we design the feature encoder as a Siamese network [3]. A Siamese network is a parameter-sharing neural network applied on multiple inputs. To avoid the collapsing problem when optimized without negative pairs, inspired by SimSiam [5], features are processed by the same encoder network E followed by a prediction head P applied on one branch. A stop-gradient operation is applied on the other branch, as shown in Fig. 2, which is critical to prevent such collapsing solutions. Denote $p_a \triangleq P(E(f_{3,a}))$ and $z_b \triangleq E(f_{3,b})$, a negative cosine similarity loss is applied:

$$\mathcal{D}(p_a, z_b) = -\frac{p_a}{||p_a||_2} \cdot \frac{z_b}{||z_b||_2}, \tag{2}$$

where $|| \cdot ||_2$ is a L_2 norm. Instead of registering the images pixel-by-pixel, here we use a feature-level registration loss which may be deemed as a relaxed version of the pixel-wise registration constraints for better robustness. Finally, following SimSiam [5], a symmetrized feature registration loss is defined as:

$$\mathcal{L} = \frac{1}{2}(\mathcal{D}(p_a, z_b) + \mathcal{D}(p_b, z_a)). \tag{3}$$

Discussion. Features from the proposed method retain relatively complete spatial information, since we adopt the first three convolutional blocks of ResNet as the backbone without global average pooling, followed by a convolutional encoder and predictor architecture, but not the MLP architecture in SimSiam [5]. Thus Eq. (3) should be computed by averaging cosine similarity scores at every spatial pixel. Features containing spatial information are beneficial for the AD task, which needs to provide anomaly score maps as prediction results. Different from SimSiam [5], which defines the inputs as two augmentations of one image and maximizes their similarity to enhance the model representation, the proposed feature registration leverages two different images as inputs and maximizes the similarity between the features to learn the registration.

4.2   Normal Distribution Estimation

To perform testing, it is assumed that the feature registration ability can generalize to the target category, and the learned feature registration model is applied to the support set $\mathcal{S}_t$ for the target category without parameter fine-tuning. Multiple data augmentations are applied to the support images, consistent with [36]. As the two branches of the Siamese network are exactly the same, only one branch feature is used for the normal distribution estimation. After achieving the registered features, a statistical-based estimator [8] is used to estimate the normal distribution of target category features, which uses multivariate Gaussian distributions to get a probabilistic representation of the normal class. Suppose an image is divided into a grid of $(i, j) \in [1, W] \times [1, H]$ positions where $W \times H$ is the resolution of features used to estimate the normal distribution. At each patch position (i, j), let $F_{ij} = \{f_{ij}^k, k \in [1, N]\}$ be the registered features from N augmented support images. f_{ij} is the aggregated features at patch position (i, j), achieved by concatenating the three STN outputs at the corresponding position with upsampling operations to match their sizes. By the assumption that F_{ij} is generated by $\mathcal{N}(\mu_{ij}, \Sigma_{ij})$, the sample covariance is:

$$\Sigma_{ij} = \frac{1}{N-1} \sum_{k=1}^{N} \left(f_{ij}^k - \mu_{ij} \right) \left(f_{ij}^k - \mu_{ij} \right)^{\mathrm{T}} + \epsilon I, \tag{4}$$

where μ_{ij} is the sample mean of F_{ij}, and the regularization term ϵI makes the sample covariance matrix full rank and invertible. Finally, each possible patch position is associated with a multivariate Gaussian distribution.

Discussion. Data augmentations are widely adopted in AD, and especially in FSAD, including TDG [36] and DiffNet [29]. However, most methods simply apply the data augmentations on both the support and test images without any exploration of the impact. In this paper, we emphasize that data augmentation plays a very important role in expanding the support set, which is beneficial for the normal distribution estimation. Specifically, we adopt augmentations including rotation, translation, flipping, and graying for each image in the support set $\mathcal{S}_t$. Other augmentations like mixup and cutpaste are not considered since they seem more suitable for simulating anomalies [21]. We conduct the possible combinations of all these augmentations for each sample in the support set, which jointly combine into a larger support set. We conduct the normal distribution estimation on such an augmented support set. We study the impacts of different augmentations in the supplementary material.

4.3   Inference

During inference, test samples that are out of the normal distribution are considered anomalies. For each test image in $\mathcal{T}_{test}$, we use the Mahalanobis distance $\mathcal{M}(f_{ij})$ to give an anomaly score to the patch in position (i, j), where

$$\mathcal{M}(f_{ij}) = \sqrt{(f_{ij} - \mu_{ij})^T \Sigma_{ij}^{-1} (f_{ij} - \mu_{ij})}. \tag{5}$$

The matrix of Mahalanobis distances $\mathcal{M} = (\mathcal{M}(f_{ij}))_{1 \leqslant i \leqslant W, 1 \leqslant j \leqslant H}$ forms an anomaly map. Three inverse affine transformations corresponding to the three STN modules are applied to this anomaly map to get the final anomaly score map $\mathcal{M}_{final}$ aligned with the original image. High scores in this map indicate the anomalous areas. The final anomaly score of the entire image is the maximum of anomaly map $\mathcal{M}_{final}$. Compared with [29,36], RegAD cancels the data augmentation of the test images which reduces the inference computational costs.

5   Experiments

5.1   Experimental Setups

Datasets. We experiment on two challenging real-world benchmark datasets for AD [2,20], which are both related to industrial defect detection.

- **MVTec** [2]: MVTec comprises 15 categories with 3629 images for training and validation and 1725 images for testing. The training set contains only of normal images without defects. The test set contains both images with various kinds of defects (anomaly) and defect-free images (normal). On average five per category, 73 different defect types are given. All images are in the resolution range between 700×700 and 1024×1024 pixels. Pixel-wise ground truth labels for each defective image region are provided.
- **MPDD** [20]: MPDD is a newly proposed dataset focused specifically on defect detection during painted metal part fabrication, containing 6 classes of metal parts. Images are captured under the conditions of various spatial orientations, positions, and distances of multiple objects, concerning different light intensities and a non-homogeneous background.

For each dataset, we conduct experiments on two different experimental settings. (i) **Aggregated training** on multiple categories and then adapting to unseen categories, and (ii) **Individual training** only with the support set for each category.

Competing Methods. We consider two state-of-the-art FSAD approaches, TDG [36] and DiffNet [29]. These two methods both train models individually for each category (setting (ii)). Results are reproduced using the official source code. Considering that our method uses data from multiple categories, for fairness of comparison, we extend them to leverage the same amount of data (setting (i)). A pre-training procedure is added to these methods, where data from multiple categories are used to pre-train the transformation classifier for TDG or initialize the normalizing flow-based estimator for DiffNet. The corresponding methods are TDG+ and DiffNet+. We also evaluate RegAD under the individual training setting, and denote the corresponding method as RegAD-L. We compare with some state-of-the-art vanilla AD methods, such as GANomaly [1], ARNet [42], MKD [33], CutPaste [21], FYD [45], PaDiM [8], PatchCore [28] and CflowAD [14]. These methods use the whole normal dataset for their training, so they can be deemed as the upper bound on FSAD performance.

Table 1. Results of k-shot anomaly detection on the MVTec dataset, comparing with state-of-the-art methods. Results are listed as the average AUC in % of 10 runs and are marked individually for each category. A macro-average score over all categories is also reported in the last row. The best-performing method is in bold.

Category	k = 2			k = 4			k = 8		
	TDG+ [36]	DiffNet+ [29]	RegAD (ours)	TDG+ [36]	DiffNet+ [29]	RegAD (ours)	TDG+ [36]	DiffNet+ [29]	RegAD(ours)
Bottle	69.3	99.3	**99.4**	69.6	99.3	**99.4**	70.3	99.4	**99.8**
Cable	68.3	**85.3**	65.1	70.3	**85.2**	76.1	74.7	**87.9**	80.6
Capsule	55.1	**73.0**	67.5	47.6	**80.3**	72.4	44.7	**78.6**	76.3
Carpet	66.2	78.4	**96.5**	68.7	78.6	**97.9**	78.2	78.5	**98.5**
Grid	83.8	62.1	**84.0**	86.2	60.5	**91.2**	87.6	78.5	**91.5**
Hazelnut	67.2	94.9	**96.0**	71.2	**95.8**	95.8	82.8	**97.9**	96.5
Leather	93.6	90.7	**99.4**	93.2	91.2	**100**	93.5	92.2	**100**
Metal Nut	67.1	61.9	**91.4**	69.2	67.3	**94.6**	68.7	67.6	**98.3**
Pill	69.2	**83.2**	81.3	64.7	**84.0**	80.8	67.9	**82.1**	80.6
Screw	**98.8**	73.4	52.5	**98.8**	72.5	56.6	**99.0**	75.0	63.4
Tile	86.3	**97.0**	94.3	87.2	**98.0**	95.5	87.4	**99.6**	97.4
Toothbrush	54.4	60.8	**86.6**	57.8	62.5	**90.9**	57.6	60.8	**98.5**
Transistor	55.9	61.8	**86.0**	67.7	62.2	**85.2**	71.5	63.3	**93.4**
Wood	98.4	98.1	**99.2**	98.3	96.4	**98.6**	98.4	99.4	99.4
Zipper	64.4	**89.2**	86.3	65.3	84.8	**88.5**	66.3	87.3	**94.0**
Average	73.2	80.6	**85.7**	74.4	81.3	**88.2**	76.6	83.2	**91.2**

Evaluation Protocols. We quantify the model performance using the area under the Receiver Operating Characteristic (ROC) curve metric (AUC), which is commonly adopted as the performance measurement for AD tasks. The image-level AUC and the pixel-level AUC are used for anomaly detection and anomaly localization respectively.

Model Configuration and Training Details. An ImageNet pre-trained ResNet-18 [16] is used as the backbone, followed by a convolutional-based encoder and predictor. To retain the spatial information, the encoder contains three 1×1 convolutional layers, while the predictor contains two 1×1 convolutional layers, without any pooling operation. We train models on 224×224 images on one NVIDIA GTX 3090. We update the parameters using momentum SGD with a learning rate of 0.0001 for 50 epochs, with a batch size of 32. A single cycle of cosine learning rate is used as the decay schedule.

5.2   Comparison with State-of-the-Art Methods

Comparison with Few-Shot Anomaly Detection Methods. Experiments were conducted using the leave-one-out setting, *i.e.*, a target category was chosen to be tested, while other categories in the dataset are used for training. Table 1 and Table 2 show the comparison results on MVTec and MPDD, respectively, under the experimental setting (i). RegAD achieves an improvement of 5.1%, 6.9%, 8.0% in average AUC on MVTec, and an improvement of 3.2%, 5.0%, 3.4% in average AUC on MPDD, over DiffNet+ [29], with 2-shot, 4-shot, and 8-shot scenarios, respectively. Also, with one-shot, RegAD achieves 82.4% and 57.8% AUC on MVtec and MPDD respectively.

Table 2. Results of k-shot anomaly detection on the MPDD dataset, comparing with state-of-the-art methods. Results are listed as the average AUC in % of 10 runs and are marked individually for each category. A macro-average score over all categories is also reported in the last row. The best-performing method is in bold.

Category	$k=2$			$k=4$			$k=8$		
	TDG+ [36]	DiffNet+ [29]	RegAD (ours)	TDG+ [36]	DiffNet+ [29]	RegAD (ours)	TDG+ [36]	DiffNet+ [29]	RegAD (ours)
Bracket black	46.4	56.7	**63.3**	48.8	59.9	**63.8**	51.0	**69.7**	67.3
Bracket brown	54.9	**61.3**	59.4	57.5	64.2	**66.1**	65.4	66.3	**69.6**
Bracket white	**64.0**	42.2	55.6	**65.4**	51.8	59.3	66.8	**69.1**	61.4
Connector	53.1	54.1	**73.0**	55.8	54.8	**77.2**	62.9	54.5	**84.9**
Metal plate	91.8	**96.8**	61.7	95.1	**98.2**	78.6	98.4	**98.8**	80.2
Tubes	51.8	49.8	**67.1**	58.5	50.7	**67.5**	64.9	52.6	**67.9**
Average	60.3	60.2	**63.4**	63.5	63.3	**68.3**	68.2	68.5	**71.9**

Table 3. Results of anomaly detection on the MVTec and MPDD datasets under two different experimental settings (i) and (ii), comparing with state-of-the-art few-shot anomaly detection methods on $k = 2, 4, 8$. Results are listed as the macro-average AUC in % over all categories in each dataset of 10 runs. The best-performing method for each experimental setting is in bold.

Methods	ImageNet pretrain	Aggregated training	Time of adaptation	MVTec			MPDD		
				$k=2$	$k=4$	$k=8$	$k=2$	$k=4$	$k=8$
TDG [36]	✓	✗	–	71.2	72.7	75.2	57.3	60.4	64.4
DiffNet [29]	✓	✗	–	80.5	80.8	82.9	**58.4**	**61.2**	**66.5**
RegAD-L (ours)	✓	✗	–	**81.5**	**84.9**	**87.4**	50.8	54.2	61.1
TDG+ [36]	✓	✓	1559.76s	73.2	74.4	76.6	60.3	63.5	68.2
DiffNet+ [29]	✓	✓	357.75s	80.6	81.3	83.2	60.2	63.3	68.5
RegAD (ours)	✓	✓	4.47s	**85.7**	**88.2**	**91.2**	**63.4**	**68.3**	**71.9**

RegAD is tested without any parameter fine-tuning, which may not guarantee the best performance for every category, while other baselines have unfair advantages in that they tune the parameters for each category. In 9 out of the 15 categories, RegAD outperforms all the other baselines. RegAD also achieves the least standard deviation (10.94) for the 15 categories when k=8, compared to TDG+ (15.20) and DiffNet+ (13.11), suggesting its better generalizability across different categories. Also, although using different training settings, for MVTec (k=8), RegAD achieves 91.2% AUC, with an ≈3% improvement compared with Metaformer [39] which uses an additional large-scale dataset, MSRA10K [7], during its entire training procedure.

Discussion. Adaptation time is important for real-world applications of FSAD. The procedures of fine-tuning for both TDG+ and DiffNet+ are time-consuming since they update the models for many epochs, while RegAD has the fastest adaptation speed since it is based on a statistical estimator which needs only one inference for each support image. In Table 3, we report the adaptation times for each method, by averaging the results for $k = 2, 4, 8$ on both the MVTec and

Table 4. Results of anomaly detection and anomaly localization on the MVTec and MPDD datasets, comparing with state-of-the-art vanilla AD methods. Results are listed as AUC in % as the macro-average score over all categories in each dataset.

Methods	Data	ImageNet pretrain	Backbone	MVTec		MPDD	
				Image	Pixel	Image	Pixel
RegAD (k = 4)	4 images	✓	Res18	88.2	95.8	68.8	93.9
RegAD (k = 8)	8 images	✓	Res18	91.2	96.7	71.9	95.1
RegAD (k = 16)	16 images	✓	Res18	92.7	96.6	75.3	96.3
RegAD (k = 32)	32 images	✓	Res18	94.6	96.9	76.8	96.3
GANomaly [1]	Full data	✗	UNet	80.5	–	64.8	–
ARNet [42]	Full data	✗	UNet	83.9	–	69.7	–
MKD [33]	Full data	✓	Res18	87.7	90.7	–	–
CutPaste [21]	Full data	✓	Res18	95.2	96.0	–	–
FYD [45]	Full data	✓	Res18	97.3	97.4	–	–
PaDiM [8]	Full data	✓	WRN50	97.9	97.5	74.8	96.7
PatchCore [28]	Full data	✓	WRN50	99.1	98.1	82.1	95.7
CflowAD [14]	Full data	✓	WRN50	98.3	98.6	86.1	97.7

MPDD datasets. Compared with TDG+ (1559.76s) and DiffNet+ (357.75s), the proposed RegAD has the fastest adaptation speed (4.47s).

Table 3 also compares these methods under experimental setting (ii), where we train the models individually using the support images for each category. RegAD-L means RegAD with individual training on one category only. Assuming that features pre-trained by ImageNet are fully representative, we simply fine-tune features using limited support images. Thus, we conduct the fine-tuning procedures directly under an ImageNet pre-training backbone for all methods. All methods use the same ImageNet pre-training backbone to have a fair comparison. In this setting, RegAD-L outperforms both TDG and DiffNet on the MVTec dataset. DiffNet performs better than the proposed method on the MPDD dataset. However, compared with RegAD-L, the proposed RegAD improves a lot, showing the effectiveness of the proposed feature registration aggregated training procedure on multiple categories.

Comparison with Vanilla Anomaly Detection Methods. The state-of-the-art vanilla AD methods use the whole normal dataset for their training and train a separate model for each category, so their performance can be seen as the upper bound for FSAD. We consider methods including GANomaly [1], ARNet [42], MKD [33], CutPaste [21], FYD [45], PaDiM [8], PatchCore [28] and CflowAD [14]. Results in Table 4 show that the proposed RegAD reaches competitive performance even compared with vanilla AD methods that are based on extensive normal data. For example, with only 4 support images, the proposed

Table 5. Ablation studies of k-shot anomaly detection and localization on the MVTec and MPDD datasets. Modules of 'A', 'F', and 'S' mean the augmentations for the support set, the feature registration aggregated training, and the spatial transformer networks (STN), respectively. Results are listed as the macro-average AUC in % over all categories in each dataset of 10 runs. The best-performing method is in bold.

Modules			MVTec						MPDD					
			Image			Pixel			Image			Pixel		
A	F	S	$k=2$	$k=4$	$k=8$	$k=2$	$k=4$	$k=8$	$k=2$	$k=4$	$k=8$	$k=2$	$k=4$	$k=8$
			74.7	78.0	80.5	88.6	90.5	92.1	49.6	53.7	55.5	89.5	91.2	92.0
✓			81.5	84.9	87.4	93.3	94.7	95.5	50.8	54.2	61.1	92.4	93.3	93.9
		✓	78.0	80.9	83.1	90.8	92.5	94.0	53.9	55.5	57.2	91.5	92.2	93.0
	✓	✓	79.1	82.9	84.9	90.5	93.3	94.3	57.6	60.9	62.7	91.0	91.8	93.0
✓	✓		83.0	86.4	89.3	**94.7**	**95.9**	96.6	52.8	57.7	64.8	**93.3**	**94.1**	94.4
✓	✓	✓	**85.7**	**88.2**	**91.2**	94.6	95.8	**96.7**	**63.4**	**68.8**	**71.9**	93.2	93.9	**95.1**

Table 6. Ablation studies of different transformation versions of STN modules on MVTec and MPDD for anomaly detection with $k = 2$. T, R means translation, and rotation, respectively. Results are listed as the macro-average AUC in % over all categories in each dataset of 10 runs. The best-performing method is in bold.

Data	no STN	T	R	Scale	Shear	R+scale	T+scale	T+R	T+R+scale	Affine
MVTec	83.0	84.5	85.0	84.9	84.9	**85.7**	84.9	84.2	84.9	84.5
MPDD	52.8	62.3	57.7	59.2	59.0	61.5	61.8	61.0	61.7	**63.4**

method (88.2% AUC) outperforms MKD (87.7%) with the same ImageNet pre-trained backbone, and with 32 support images its AUC increases to 94.6%.

5.3 Ablation Studies

Experiments were performed to evaluate the contribution made by individual components of the proposed method. Results of ablation studies for k-shot anomaly detection and localization on the MVTec and MPDD datasets are shown in Table 5. Modules of 'A', 'F', and 'S' mean the augmentations for support sets, the feature registration aggregated training on multiple categories, and the spatial transformer networks (STN), respectively. Results in Table 5 show that:

(i) **Augmentations.** The proposed support set augmentations are shown to be essential for both detection and localization. With $k = \{2, 4, 8\}$, the AUC is improved for 6.8%, 6.9%, 6.9% on MVTec and for 1.2%, 0.5%, 0.6% on MPDD, respectively. We further presents the ablation studies of comparing different augmentation methods for support images in the supplementary material.

(ii) **Feature Registration Aggregated Training.** The feature registration aggregated training on multiple categories is effective both with and without support image augmentations. It shows that the proposed feature registration is beneficial for estimating the normal distribution. As shown in Table 5, with

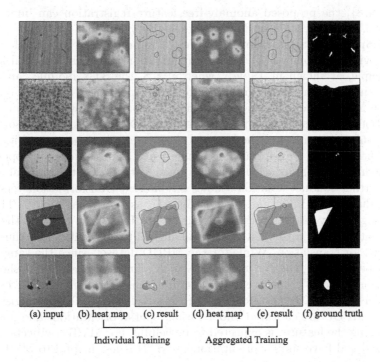

(a) input   (b) heat map   (c) result   (d) heat map   (e) result   (f) ground truth

Individual Training   Aggregated Training

Fig. 3. Qualitative results of anomaly localization for RegAD on the MVTec dataset (top three rows) and the MPDD dataset (bottom two rows) for several cases, including localization results with individual training and aggregated training. Results from (e) show better performance than results from (c), showing the effectiveness of the proposed feature registration aggregated training procedure.

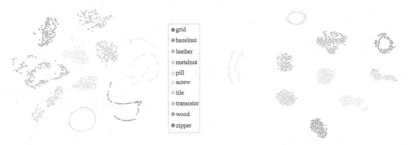

(a) Without Feature Registration   (b) With Feature Registration

Fig. 4. Visualization, using t-SNE, of the features learned from the MVTec dataset, using (a) the baseline without the feature registration, and (b) the proposed method with the feature registration. The same t-SNE optimization iterations are used in each case. Results show that features with registration are more compact within each category, and more separated from different categories.

$k = \{2, 4, 8\}$, the proposed anomaly-free feature registration can improve the AUC by 3.3%, 2.9%, 2.6% on MVTec, respectively.

(iii) **Spatial Transformer Modules.** The proposed STN module is good for improving the ability of the feature registration and thus beneficial for AD. For example, as shown in Table 5, when $k = 8$, the STN module can further improve the performance from 89.3% to 91.2% on MVTec and from 64.8% to 71.9% on MPDD. However, models with STN modules show similar pixel-level localization performance with models without STN modules. The reason comes from the information lost of the inverse transformation operation and its imprecision. These inverse transformations are designed as post-processing operations to rematch the spatial location of transformed features and the original images.

We further conduct ablation studies on different transformation versions of STN modules on MVTec and MPDD for AD, as shown in Table 6. The best performing STN version is rotation+scale on MVTec, which matches the observation that samples in this dataset are all aligned to the center, and thus, there is no need for translation. While for the MPDD dataset, since the samples are not well be centered, the version of STN with affine transformations shows the best performance. STN is used as a feature transformation module, enabling the model to implicitly transform the images to facilitate feature registration. Images in MPDD are captured under various spatial orientations and positions, thus aligning the features is expected to be helpful. For MVTec, objects are well centralized and have similar orientations, so STN is less helpful to MVTec.

5.4 Visualization Analysis

To qualitatively analyze how the proposed feature registration approach improves the anomaly localization performance, we visualize the results of some cases from the MVTec and MPDD datasets. It can be seen from the results in Fig. 3 that the localization produced by RegAD using aggregated training (column e) is closer to the ground truth (column f) than that produced by the individual training baseline (column c). This illustrates the effectiveness of the proposed feature registration training procedure on multiple categories.

We also use t-SNE [23] to visualize the features learned on the MVTec dataset, as shown in Fig. 4. Each dot here represents an augmented normal sample from the test set. It can be seen that the proposed feature registration makes the features more compact within each category, and pushes away features of different categories, which is desirable for the benefit of estimating the normal distribution for each category.

6 Conclusion

This paper proposes an FSAD method utilizing registration, a task inherently generalizable across categories, as the proxy task. Given only a few normal samples for each category, we trained a category-agnostic feature registration network with the aggregated data. This model is shown to be directly generalizable to new categories, requiring no re-training or parameter fine-tuning. The anomalies are identified by comparing the registered features of the test image and its corresponding support (normal) images. For both anomaly detection and anomaly localization, the method is shown to be competitive, even compared with vanilla AD methods that are trained with much larger volumes of data. The impressive results suggest a high potential for the proposed method to be applicable in real-world anomaly detection environments.

Acknowledgments. This work is supported by the National Key Research and Development Program of China (No. 2020YFB1406801), 111 plan (No. BP0719010), and STCSM (No. 18DZ2270700), and State Key Laboratory of UHD Video and Audio Production and Presentation.

References

1. Akcay, S., Atapour-Abarghouei, A., Breckon, T.P.: GANomaly: semi-supervised anomaly detection via adversarial training. In: Jawahar, C.V., Li, H., Mori, G., Schindler, K. (eds.) ACCV 2018. LNCS, vol. 11363, pp. 622–637. Springer, Cham (2019). https://doi.org/10.1007/978-3-030-20893-6_39
2. Bergmann, P., Fauser, M., Sattlegger, D., Steger, C.: MVTec AD–a comprehensive real-world dataset for unsupervised anomaly detection. In: Proceedings of the IEEE/CVF Conference on Computer Vision and Pattern Recognition (CVPR), pp. 9592–9600 (2019)
3. Bromley, J., Guyon, I., LeCun, Y., Säckinger, E., Shah, R.: Signature verification using a "Siamese" time delay neural network. Adv. Neural Inf. Process. Syst. (NeurIPS) **6** (1993)
4. Brown, L.G.: A survey of image registration techniques. ACM Comput. Surv. **24**(4), 325–376 (1992)
5. Chen, X., He, K.: Exploring simple Siamese representation learning. In: Proceedings of the IEEE/CVF Conference on Computer Vision and Pattern Recognition (CVPR), pp. 15750–15758 (2021)
6. Chen, Z., Fu, Y., Zhang, Y., Jiang, Y.G., Xue, X., Sigal, L.: Multi-level semantic feature augmentation for one-shot learning. IEEE Trans. Image Process. **28**(9), 4594–4605 (2019)
7. Cheng, M.M., Mitra, N.J., Huang, X., Torr, P.H., Hu, S.M.: Global contrast based salient region detection. IEEE Trans. Pattern Anal. Mach. Intell. **37**(8), 569–582 (2014)
8. Defard, T., Setkov, A., Loesch, A., Audigier, R.: PaDiM: a patch distribution modeling framework for anomaly detection and localization. In: Del Bimbo, A., et al. (eds.) ICPR 2021. LNCS, vol. 12664, pp. 475–489. Springer, Cham (2021). https://doi.org/10.1007/978-3-030-68799-1_35
9. Eskin, E.: Anomaly detection over noisy data using learned probability distributions. In: International Conference on Machine Learning (ICML) (2000)
10. Eykholt, K., et al.: Robust physical-world attacks on deep learning visual classification. In: Proceedings of the IEEE/CVF Conference on Computer Vision and Pattern Recognition (CVPR), pp. 1625–1634 (2018)
11. Finn, C., Abbeel, P., Levine, S.: Model-agnostic meta-learning for fast adaptation of deep networks. In: International Conference on Machine Learning (ICML), pp. 1126–1135 (2017)
12. Golan, I., El-Yaniv, R.: Deep anomaly detection using geometric transformations. Adv. Neural Inf. Process. Syst. (NeurIPS) **31** (2018)

13. Gong, D., et al.: Memorizing normality to detect anomaly: memory-augmented deep autoencoder for unsupervised anomaly detection. In: Proceedings of the IEEE/CVF International Conference on Computer Vision (ICCV), pp. 1705–1714 (2019)
14. Gudovskiy, D., Ishizaka, S., Kozuka, K.: CFLOW-AD: real-time unsupervised anomaly detection with localization via conditional normalizing flows. In: Proceedings of the IEEE/CVF Winter Conference on Applications of Computer Vision (WACV), pp. 98–107 (2022)
15. He, J., Hong, R., Liu, X., Xu, M., Wang, M.: Revisiting deep local descriptor for improved few-shot classification. In: 30th International Joint Conference on Artificial Intelligence (IJCAI), pp. 3420–3426 (2021)
16. He, K., Zhang, X., Ren, S., Sun, J.: Deep residual learning for image recognition. In: Proceedings of the IEEE/CVF Conference on Computer Vision and Pattern Recognition (CVPR), pp. 770–778 (2016)
17. Huang, C., Xu, Q., Wang, Y., Wang, Y., Zhang, Y.: Self-supervised masking for unsupervised anomaly detection and localization. IEEE Transactions on Multimedia (2022)
18. Huang, C., Ye, F., Zhao, P., Zhang, Y., Wang, Y., Tian, Q.: ESAD: end-to-end semi-supervised anomaly detection. In: The 32nd British Machine Vision Conference (BMVC) (2022)
19. Jaderberg, M., Simonyan, K., Zisserman, A., et al.: Spatial transformer networks. Adv. Neural Inf. Process. Syst. (NeurIPS) **28** (2015)
20. Jezek, S., Jonak, M., Burget, R., Dvorak, P., Skotak, M.: Deep learning-based defect detection of metal parts: evaluating current methods in complex conditions. In: International Congress on Ultra Modern Telecommunications and Control Systems and Workshops (ICUMT), pp. 66–71. IEEE (2021)
21. Li, C.L., Sohn, K., Yoon, J., Pfister, T.: CutPaste: self-supervised learning for anomaly detection and localization. In: Proceedings of the IEEE/CVF Conference on Computer Vision and Pattern Recognition (CVPR), pp. 9664–9674 (2021)
22. Liu, J., Sun, Y., Han, C., Dou, Z., Li, W.: Deep representation learning on long-tailed data: a learnable embedding augmentation perspective. In: Proceedings of the IEEE/CVF Conference on Computer Vision and Pattern Recognition (CVPR), pp. 2970–2979 (2020)
23. Van der Maaten, L., Hinton, G.: Visualizing data using t-SNE. J. Mach. Learn. Res. **9**(11), 2579–2605 (2008)
24. Matsubara, T., Tachibana, R., Uehara, K.: Anomaly machine component detection by deep generative model with unregularized score. In: 2018 International Joint Conference on Neural Networks (IJCNN), pp. 1–8. IEEE (2018)
25. Peng, H., et al.: BrainAligner: 3D registration atlases of drosophila brains. Nat. Methods **8**(6), 493–498 (2011)
26. Rahmani, M., Atia, G.K.: Coherence pursuit: fast, simple, and robust principal component analysis. IEEE Trans. Signal Process. **65**(23), 6260–6275 (2017)
27. Ravi, S., Larochelle, H.: Optimization as a model for few-shot learning. In: International Conference on Learning Representations (ICLR) (2017)
28. Roth, K., Pemula, L., Zepeda, J., Schölkopf, B., Brox, T., Gehler, P.: Towards total recall in industrial anomaly detection. In: Proceedings of the IEEE/CVF Conference on Computer Vision and Pattern Recognition (CVPR), pp. 14318–14328 (2022)
29. Rudolph, M., Wandt, B., Rosenhahn, B.: Same same but DifferNet: semi-supervised defect detection with normalizing flows. In: Proceedings of the

IEEE/CVF Winter Conference on Applications of Computer Vision (WACV), pp. 1907–1916 (2021)

30. Ruff, L., et al.: Deep one-class classification. In: International Conference on Machine Learning (ICML), pp. 4393–4402 (2018)
31. Russakovsky, O., et al.: ImageNet large scale visual recognition challenge. Int. J. Comput. Vis. **115**(3), 211–252 (2015). https://doi.org/10.1007/s11263-015-0816-y
32. Sabokrou, M., Khalooei, M., Fathy, M., Adeli, E.: Adversarially learned one-class classifier for novelty detection. In: Proceedings of the IEEE/CVF Conference on Computer Vision and Pattern Recognition (CVPR), pp. 3379–3388 (2018)
33. Salehi, M., Sadjadi, N., Baselizadeh, S., Rohban, M.H., Rabiee, H.R.: Multiresolution knowledge distillation for anomaly detection. In: Proceedings of the IEEE/CVF Conference on Computer Vision and Pattern Recognition (CVPR), pp. 14902–14912 (2021)
34. Schlegl, T., Seeböck, P., Waldstein, S.M., Schmidt-Erfurth, U., Langs, G.: Unsupervised anomaly detection with generative adversarial networks to guide marker discovery. In: Niethammer, M., et al. (eds.) IPMI 2017. LNCS, vol. 10265, pp. 146–157. Springer, Cham (2017). https://doi.org/10.1007/978-3-319-59050-9_12
35. Schölkopf, B., Platt, J.C., Shawe-Taylor, J., Smola, A.J., Williamson, R.C.: Estimating the support of a high-dimensional distribution. Neural Comput. **13**(7), 1443–1471 (2001)
36. Sheynin, S., Benaim, S., Wolf, L.: A hierarchical transformation-discriminating generative model for few shot anomaly detection. In: Proceedings of the IEEE/CVF International Conference on Computer Vision (ICCV), pp. 8495–8504 (2021)
37. Snell, J., Swersky, K., Zemel, R.: Prototypical networks for few-shot learning. Adv. Neural Inf. Process. Syst. (NeurIPS) **30** (2017)
38. Sung, F., Yang, Y., Zhang, L., Xiang, T., Torr, P.H., Hospedales, T.M.: Learning to compare: relation network for few-shot learning. In: Proceedings of the IEEE/CVF Conference on Computer Vision and Pattern Recognition (CVPR), pp. 1199–1208 (2018)
39. Wu, J.C., Chen, D.J., Fuh, C.S., Liu, T.L.: Learning unsupervised metaformer for anomaly detection. In: Proceedings of the IEEE/CVF International Conference on Computer Vision (ICCV), pp. 4369–4378 (2021)
40. Xia, Y., Cao, X., Wen, F., Hua, G., Sun, J.: Learning discriminative reconstructions for unsupervised outlier removal. In: Proceedings of the IEEE/CVF International Conference on Computer Vision (ICCV), pp. 1511–1519 (2015)
41. Yang, S., Liu, L., Xu, M.: Free lunch for few-shot learning: distribution calibration. In: International Conference on Learning Representations (ICLR) (2021)
42. Ye, F., Huang, C., Cao, J., Li, M., Zhang, Y., Lu, C.: Attribute restoration framework for anomaly detection. IEEE Trans. Multimedia **24**, 116–127 (2022)
43. Yi, J., Yoon, S.: Patch SVDD: patch-level SVDD for anomaly detection and segmentation. In: Proceedings of the Asian Conference on Computer Vision (ACCV) (2020)
44. Zhang, J., et al.: Viral pneumonia screening on chest X-ray images using confidence-aware anomaly detection. IEEE Trans. Med. Imaging **40**(3), 879–890 (2021)
45. Zheng, Y., Wang, X., Deng, R., Bao, T., Zhao, R., Wu, L.: Focus your distribution: coarse-to-fine non-contrastive learning for anomaly detection and localization. arXiv preprint arXiv:2110.04538 (2021)
46. Zitová, B., Flusser, J.: Image registration methods: a survey. Image Vis. Comput. **21**(11), 977–1000 (2003)
47. Zong, B., et al.: Deep autoencoding gaussian mixture model for unsupervised anomaly detection. In: International Conference on Learning Representations (ICLR) (2018)

Improving Robustness by Enhancing Weak Subnets

Yong Guo$^{(\boxtimes)}$, David Stutz , and Bernt Schiele

Max Planck Institute for Informatics, Saarland Informatics Campus, Saarbrücken, Germany
{yongguo,david.stutz,schiele}@mpi-inf.mpg.de

Abstract. Despite their success, deep networks have been shown to be highly susceptible to perturbations, often causing significant drops in accuracy. In this paper, we investigate model robustness on perturbed inputs by studying the performance of internal sub-networks (subnets). Interestingly, we observe that most subnets show particularly poor robustness against perturbations. More importantly, these weak subnets are correlated with the overall lack of robustness. Tackling this phenomenon, we propose a new training procedure that **identifies and enhances weak subnets (EWS) to improve robustness**. Specifically, we develop a search algorithm to find particularly weak subnets and explicitly strengthen them via knowledge distillation from the full network. We show that EWS greatly improves both robustness against corrupted images as well as accuracy on clean data. Being complementary to popular data augmentation methods, EWS consistently improves robustness when combined with these approaches. To highlight the flexibility of our approach, we combine EWS also with popular adversarial training methods resulting in improved adversarial robustness.

Keywords: Model robustness · Training method · Sub-networks

1 Introduction

Since 2012, when AlexNet won the first place in the ImageNet competition [46], deep (convolutional) networks [48] have been producing state-of-the-art results in many challenging tasks [35,49]. Recent work, however, highlights how brittle these models are when applied to images with simple corruptions, such as noise, blur, and pixelation [38]. In fact, these corruptions cannot fool the human vision system but often severely hamper the accuracy of deep networks [37,38]. Among an increasing body of work on developing robust models, data augmentation is particularly popular and effective. For example, AutoAugment [21], AugMix [40] or DeepAugment [37] improve the robustness against corrupted examples alongside the clean accuracy.

Complementary to this line of research, we study the robustness of nowadays overparameterized networks by analyzing their internal sub-networks (subnets). While it is well-known that few well-performing subnets, i.e., "winning tickets", exist within these large networks [27,50,73], the role of the remaining subnets in terms of robustness

---

Supplementary Information The online version contains supplementary material available at https://doi.org/10.1007/978-3-031-20053-3_19.

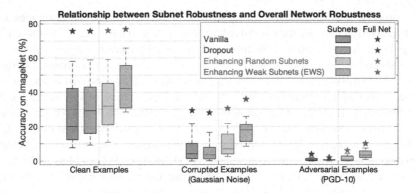

Fig. 1. On ImageNet, we plot accuracies on clean and perturbed examples for a standard ResNet-50 (blue stars) and 1K randomly sampled subnets (blue box plot) corresponding to 70% of the paths/channels each. On clean examples (left), subnets perform significantly worse than the overall network, with average accuracy reducing to roughly 20%. On examples perturbed with Gaussian (middle) or adversarial (right) noise, overall accuracy reduces severely alongside subnet accuracy, suggesting that *weak subnets* are responsible for this lack of robustness. By identifying and enhancing these weak subnets (EWS, red), we can improve robustness significantly. Importantly, we search for particularly weak subnets in order to enhance them through knowledge distillation, while encouraging distributed representations through dropout [76] (violet) or improving *random* subnets (green) does not improve accuracy or robustness as much. (Color figure online)

remains unexplored. In this paper, we find that most of these subnets perform rather poorly. Moreover, this is strongly correlated with the network's overall performance and becomes particularly apparent on corrupted or adversarial examples. As illustrated in Fig. 1, for a standard ResNet-50 [35] on ImageNet [67], the network's accuracy (blur star) reduces significantly alongside the severely degraded subnets' accuracy (blue box) when facing perturbed examples, e.g., with Gaussian noise. Note that the blue box illustrates the performance range of 1K randomly sampled subnets, each corresponding to 70% of the overall network, and the mean performance (blue line in box) is at the lower end of this range. Overall, this leads us to the hypothesis that these *weak subnets* are, to some degree, responsible for the lack of robustness of the overall network.

In order to test this hypothesis and improve robustness, we intend to enhance subnet performance. Interestingly, dropout [76] can be regarded as a particular approach to construct and train subnets by randomly dropping the internal connections. Unfortunately, as shown in Fig. 1, it only slightly improves the subnets on clean data but yields much worse performance on perturbed data. It is worth noting that, the correlation between subnet and full network still holds, i.e., better subnets (blue boxes > violet boxes) always come along with better full network (blue stars > violet stars) on perturbed data (middle and right of Fig. 1). Thus, regarding this correlation, how to effectively improve subnets becomes an important problem to boost the overall robustness against perturbations.

Contributions: To address this, we propose to directly and very explicitly identify and improve weak subnets instead of the random ones, which is proved to be a more effective way (see Fig. 1 and Table 5). Specifically, we make three key contributions:

(1) We propose a novel robust training method which identifies and **enhances weak subnets (EWS)** to improve the overall robustness of the full network. *(2)* To this end, we develop a search algorithm that obtains weak subnets by identifying particularly weak paths/channels inside the full network. Given a weak subnet, its performance is further enhanced by distilling knowledge from the full network. This approach is not only very scalable, it also adds negligible computational overhead (see results in Sect. 5.1). Note that identifying particularly weak subnets is crucial as shown in Fig. 1 where enhancing *random* subnets has little effect (red stars and boxes > green stars and boxes). *(3)* In experiments, we apply EWS on top of state-of-the-art data augmentation schemes to improve accuracy and corruption robustness on CIFAR-10/100-C and ImageNet-C [37]. Moreover, we also demonstrate the generality of our approach for improving adversarial robustness on top of recent adversarial training methods. Importantly, our approach is complementary to all these methods and improves consistently across a wide range of approaches. Our code is available at https://github.com/guoyongcs/EWS.

2   Related Work

Despite their outstanding performance, deep networks are not robust to image corruptions [37]. To address this, recent work explores re-calibrating batch normalization statistics [6,59,71], utilizing the frequency domain [68], or using vision transformers [57] to improve corruption robustness. However, data augmentation methods such as [11,21,28,37,40,66,69] represent the most prominent and successful line of work, ranging from simple Gaussian noise augmentation [66], over well-known schemes such as AutoAugment [21] to strategies specifically targeted towards corruption robustness such as AugMix [40] or DeepAugment [37].

Besides random corruptions, deep networks are susceptible to adversarial examples [29,79]. While plenty of approaches for defending against adversarial examples have been proposed [1,5,7,17,31,60,64,74,84,86], adversarial training (AT) has become the de facto standard [56]. This is also because other methods have repeatedly been "broken" using stronger or adaptive attacks, e.g., see [3,12–15,20,26,54,58]. Thus, recent work concentrates on various variants of AT: [90] adds an additional Kullback-Leibler term, [39] incorporates a complementary self-supervised loss, [2,16] use additional unlabeled examples. Many more variants exploring, e.g., instance-adaptive threat models [4,25], additional regularizers [8,51,61,61,63,75,80,88], curriculum training [10,85], weight perturbations [77,82], among many others [19,43,47,81,91–93], have been proposed. Moreover, AT has also been applied to corruption robustness [44,55].

Complementary to the above lines of research, existing work [24,50,72] have shown the existence of particularly strong/robust subnets inside a large model. However, the impact of the remaining weak subnets on the overall robustness has not been investigated. Interestingly, as shown by Fig. 1, we observe that the majority of subnets are particularly weak and there is a clear correlation between the performance of subnets and overall robustness. This motivates us to explicitly enhance these weak subnets. To achieve this goal, our method is also inspired by recent work on neural architecture search (NAS) [9,18,34,52,95] and knowledge distillation (KD) [41,94]. Unlike existing NAS methods, we focus on improving the robustness of deep models and exploit

NAS techniques to find weak subnets which may hamper the overall performance. Once we find these weak subnets, we seek to further enhance them using a KD loss, similar to learning lightweight student models in model compression [30,53,78].

3   EWS: Training by Enhancing Weak Subnets

This paper studies the robustness of deep, over-parameterized networks to image perturbations through the lens of subnets defined by a subselection of internal blocks/channels. After arguing that the robustness of subnets has a large impact on overall performance in Sect. 3.1, we seek to improve robustness through a novel training procedure: identifying and enhancing weak subnets through knowledge distillation, as summarized in Fig. 3. Specifically, in Sect. 3.2, we first discuss the construction and search of particularly weak subnets along with the motivation for strengthening them. Here, we present an effective and scalable search algorithm to find weak subnets. In Sect. 3.3, we then integrate the found weak subnets into our training procedure to explicitly enhance them. Our procedure is summarized in Algorithm 1. In this paper, we mainly concentrate on improving robustness to corrupted images, e.g., with noise or blur, on standard benchmarks such as CIFAR-10-C and ImageNet-C [37]. Besides, we also highlight the flexibility of our method by applying it on top of adversarial training [56].

3.1   Subnet Construction and Impact on Overall Performance

We intend to investigate the robustness of deep networks from the perspective of subnets. To this end, we define subnets as follows: Given a full (convolutional feedforward) network M, we construct a set of subnets $\alpha \in \Omega$ where Ω denotes the space of all the possible subnets of M. In this paper, we particularly consider deep models that consist of a stack of basic blocks, e.g., ResNets [35]. Actually, our approach can easily be adapted to any other architectures since most popular designs (e.g., MobileNet [42,70] and ResNeXt [83]) can be also decomposed into the basic units defined in Fig. 2. Without loss of generality, we allow each basic block i to have a specific number of paths n_i and each layer j in a block to have a specific number of channels c_j. For example, a basic residual block [35] contains $n_i = 2$ paths (i.e., the residual path and the skip connection). As shown in Fig. 2, we construct subnets by selecting a subset of paths and channels in each block and layer, respectively. Given a subnet width $\rho \in (0, 1)$, we select roughly $\rho \cdot n_i$ paths in each block i and $\rho \cdot c_j$ channels for each layer j. For example, $\rho = 0.7$ denotes selecting 70% of paths and channels.

We further investigate the impact of subnets on the overall performance. In Fig. 1, we quantify the robustness of such subnets ($\rho = 0.7$) on corrupted and adversarial examples: Even on *clean* examples (left) where the full network tends to make correct predictions with relatively high accuracy (blue star), more than 50% of the subnets yield an accuracy below 20% (blue box). On corrupted or adversarial examples (middle and right), this phenomenon is further emphasized. More critically, as the performance of subnets deteriorates on such perturbed examples, the network's overall performance also reduces significantly. It is worth noting that, each subnet can be regarded as an indicator to show whether the corresponding parameters inside the full model are well

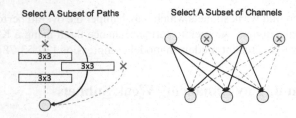

Fig. 2. We construct subnets by selecting a subset of paths (left) and channels (right) in each block of the network. Left: An example for a basic block with multiple paths where only one path is kept (in **bold**). Right: In the convolutional (fully connected) layers of each block, we select a subset of channels (in **bold**). This approach is applied block-by-block, layer-by-layer using a fixed fraction of paths/channels to be selected.

learned or not. In this sense, one may easily improve the overall performance if we put more focus on these "weak" parameters during training. This motivates us to explicitly find and enhance these weak subnets. However, we emphasize that merely training random subnets, e.g., dropout [76] (violet in Fig. 1), does *not* contribute to the improved robustness.

3.2 Finding Particularly Weak Subnets

In order to improve subnet performance and following Fig. 3, our proposed EWS has two core components: finding particular weak subnets and strengthening their performance. Regarding the first component (Fig. 3, left), given a search space Ω, the easiest way to identify/enhance such subnets is by random sampling, i.e., randomly selecting blocks and channels for a given ρ. However, Fig. 1 (green) shows that improving the performance of random subnets during training (as described in detail in Sect. 3.3) does not result in significantly more robust subnets (box plot) or improved overall performance (star). Instead, we propose a novel search algorithm that finds particularly poor subnets α, as evaluated based on their classification accuracy $R(\alpha)$. Following [33,62], the accuracy can be approximated based on a batch of sampled data in each iteration. To be specific, we learn a policy π_θ, parameterized by θ, and use it to generate candidates of weak subnets, i.e., $\alpha \sim \pi_\theta$, as identified based on particularly low accuracy. To learn the policy, we build a controller model to produce candidate subnets by minimizing the accuracy $R(\alpha)$ in expectation. Formally, we solve the following optimization problem

$$\min_\theta \mathbb{E}_{\alpha\sim\pi_\theta}\left[R(\alpha)\right].\tag{1}$$

The controller's parameters can be updated using policy gradient based on a mini-batch of sampled subnets (see the supplementary material for details). This is made explicit in the first part (Lines 3–7) of Algorithm 1.

Architecture of the Controller Model. Since a network like ResNet can be represented by a series of tokens [62], the subnet generation task can be viewed as a sequential decision making problem. Following [33,62], we build an LSTM-based [32] controller model to learn the policy π_θ. Specifically, the controller takes an initial hidden state (kept constant during training) as input and sequentially predicts the selected

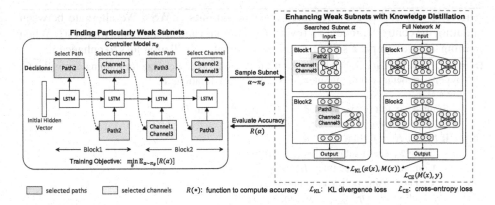

Fig. 3. Overview of our proposed **enhancing weak subnets (EWS)** training procedure. During training, we alternatingly perform subnet search based on a controller model (left) and train the full network with an additional distillation loss (right). As illustrated, the controller is trained using policy gradient every K iterations, while the full network can be any state-of-the-art network such as ResNets [35]. The distillation loss enforces predictions of the full network and the found weak subnet to be similar to improve subnet performance. We refer to Algorithm 1 for a detailed description.

paths/channels for each block/layer, as illustrated exemplarily in Fig. 3 (left). Specifically, for each block, we first select a subset of paths and subsequently select a subset of channels for each layer in the selected paths. We emphasize that the controller model scales linearly with the overall network and is easily applicable to a wide range of architectures. Please refer to our supplementary for further details.

3.3 EWS: Enhancing Weak Subnets with Knowledge Distillation

In the second step of EWS, corresponding to Fig. 3 (right) and based on the found weak subnets $\alpha \sim \pi_\theta$, we use a distillation loss to enhance subnet performance and thereby aim to improve the overall robustness of the full network. Let x be a training example with its label y. Besides the standard cross-entropy (CE) loss, we introduce an additional Kullback-Leibler (KL) divergence loss between the full network's predictions $M(x)$ and the subnet's predictions $\alpha(x)$. This can be thought of as distilling knowledge from the full network into the subnet and is meant to enhance the selected particularly weak subnets. Overall, the loss function to be minimized becomes

$$\mathcal{L}(x,y) = \mathcal{L}_{\mathrm{CE}}\big(M(x),y\big) + \underbrace{\lambda\mathcal{L}_{\mathrm{KL}}\big(\alpha(x), M(x)\big)}_{\text{enhance weak subnet}}, \tag{2}$$

where λ is a trade-off parameter determining the importance of enhancing weak subnets (see impact of λ in Sect. 5.1). While other losses for improving weak subnets are possible, e.g., a CE loss with the true labels $\mathcal{L}_{\mathrm{CE}}\big(\alpha(x), y\big)$, we found that distillation with the KL divergence works best in practice (see supplementary for details). We emphasize that our method is very flexible in that it can easily be combined with different losses and is entirely complementary to data augmentation approaches.

Algorithm 1. Training by **enhancing weak subnets (EWS)**: We alternate between updating the controller model π_θ (every K iterations) and updating the model M. When training M, we sample a subnet $\alpha \sim \pi_\theta$ and exploit a distillation loss to enhance it.

Require: Training data $\mathcal{D}$, batch size for training model N, batch size for training controller C, hyper-parameter λ, training interval K, number of iterations T
1: **for** $t = 1, \cdots, T$ **do**
2:     Sample a batch of examples $\mathbb{B} = \{(x_i, y_i)\}_{i=1}^N$ from $\mathcal{D}$
3:     // *Update the controller every K iterations*
4:     **if** $t \bmod K = 0$ **then**
5:         Sample a set of subnets $\{\alpha_i\}_{i=1}^C$ from π_θ
6:         Compute subnet accuracy $R(\alpha)$ on $\mathbb{B}$
7:         Update θ using policy gradient:
$$\theta \leftarrow \theta + \eta \tfrac{1}{C} \sum_{i=1}^C \nabla_\theta \log \pi_\theta(\alpha_i) R(\alpha_i)$$
8:     **end if**
9:     // *Train the full model while enhancing weak subnets*
10:     Sample a weak subnet $\alpha \sim \pi_\theta$
11:     Update w using gradient descent:
$$w \leftarrow w - \eta \tfrac{1}{N} \sum_{i=1}^N \left(\nabla_w \mathcal{L}_{\text{CE}}(M(x_i), y_i) + \lambda \nabla_w \mathcal{L}_{\text{KL}}(\alpha(x_i), M(x_i)) \right)$$
12: **end for**

As indicated in Algorithm 1, it is worth noting that, once we update the model parameters, the previously learned controller π_θ is outdated. This is problematic as the sampled subnets $\alpha \sim \pi_\theta$ might not be particularly weak anymore. Therefore, the model and controller are updated in an alternating fashion. However, we found that it is not necessary to update the controller model in each iteration. Instead, we only update the controller every K iterations where $K = 1$ represents fully alternating training, while $K \gg 1$ updates the controller more rarely. This also reduces the computational overhead of our methods significantly. As discussed in detail in Sect. 5.1, we find that $K = 10$ works very well in practice and leads to a negligible computational overhead.

3.4   Combining EWS with Adversarial Training

We further demonstrate the flexibility of EWS by combining it with adversarial training to improve adversarial robustness. Instead of identifying weak subnets by accuracy, we now consider *robust* accuracy on adversarial examples. Similarly, we enhance these subnets using a distillation loss on adversarial examples instead of the clean ones.

Searching for *Adversarially* Weak Subnets. Here, we seek to find subnets that are vulnerable to adversarial examples. We follow [56] and compute adversarial L_∞ perturbations by maximizing cross-entropy loss. Specifically, we construct the perturbed data as $x' = \arg\max_{\|x-x'\|_p \le \epsilon} \mathcal{L}_{\text{CE}}(M(x'), y)$. While other objectives are possible, this is commonly achieved using projected gradient ascent (PGD), where the projection reduces to a simple clamping operation for ensuring $\|x - x'\| \le \epsilon$. Finally, to find adversarially vulnerable subnets, we replace the (clean) accuracy in Eq. (1) with the adversarial accuracy. We also note that the adversarial examples are computed with respect to the full model M and re-computed every iteration. Again, we follow Algorithm 1 and train the controller using policy gradient.

Adversarially Enhancing Weak Subnets. With the found weak subnets, we again enhance them to improve the overall adversarial robustness. Following the vanilla adversarial training [56], we optimize the cross-entropy loss on adversarial examples:

$$\min_{w} \mathbb{E}_{(x,y)\sim\mathcal{D}}\left[\mathcal{L}(x',y)\right] \quad \text{where } x' = \argmax_{\|x-x'\|_p\le\epsilon} \mathcal{L}_{\text{CE}}(M(x'),y). \tag{3}$$

Again, we additionally introduce a distillation-based KL divergence loss to enhance the subnets, following Sect. 3.3 above. Formally, the loss in Equation (3) becomes

$$\mathcal{L}(x',y) = \mathcal{L}_{\text{CE}}(M(x'),y) + \underbrace{\lambda\mathcal{L}_{\text{KL}}\big(\alpha(x'),M(x')\big)}_{\text{enhance subnet on x'}} \tag{4}$$

Note that the KL divergence is computed on the predictions $M(x')$ and $\alpha(x')$ based on the adversarial examples x'. As before, λ determines the importance of weak subnet performance. Even though this formulation follows vanilla adversarial training, our approach generalizes easily to other variants, including TRADES [89] where an additional loss on clean examples is minimized. In such cases, the KL divergence used for distillation is also computed on clean examples (see supplementary for more details). Additionally applying weight perturbations [82] or using additional unlabeled examples [16] is possible as well (see Table 4). While Fig. 1 only considers a model trained without adversarial examples, i.e., following Sect. 3.3, enhancing subnets during training clearly has a positive impact on robustness against adversarial examples (e.g., PGD ones as computed in [56]). Thus, we expect a similarly positive impact when explicitly finding and enhancing adversarially vulnerable subnets during adversarial training.

4   Experiments

In the following, we demonstrate that EWS allows to train more accurate and robust models, as tested mainly against corrupted examples in Sect. 4.1. Besides the standard training settings, we emphasize that EWS can be successfully used in a complementary fashion on top of popular data augmentation schemes, including AutoAugment [21], AugMix [40] or DeepAugment [37]. Moreover, we also show that EWS easily generalizes to adversarial training without significant modifications and greatly improves the adversarial robustness in Sect. 4.2. We provide additional ablations in Sect. 5.

4.1   Improving Corruption Robustness

We start by training our EWS on standard benchmark datasets, i.e., CIFAR-10 [45], CIFAR-100 [45], and ImageNet [23], and testing on both clean test examples and the corrupted ones, namely CIFAR-10-C, CIFAR-100-C, and ImageNet-C. On CIFAR-10-C and CIFAR-100-C, we report the test error on clean or corrupted examples. On ImageNet-C, in contrast, we report the mean corruption error (mCE) [38]. We also consider ImageNet-P which evaluates the prediction stability on videos using mean flip rate (mFR). For all the metrics, *lower is better*. In all the experiments, by default, we set $K = 10$, $\lambda = 1$, and $\rho = 0.7$ for our EWS.

Table 1. Clean and corrupted test error on CIFAR-10(-C) and CIFAR-100(-C). Our proposed EWS approach not only improves clean test error, but also consistently reduces corrupted test error as highlighted in **bold** on top of different data augmentation schemes.

Method		CIFAR-10		CIFAR-100	
		Clean Error (%) ↓	Corruption Error (%) ↓	Clean Error (%) ↓	Corruption Error (%) ↓
Standard	Vanilla	5.32 (-0.00)	26.46 (-0.00)	23.45 (-0.00)	50.76 (-0.00)
	Dropout	5.16 (-0.16)	26.17 (-0.29)	23.19 (-0.26)	50.43 (-0.33)
	EWS	**4.44 (-0.88)**	**24.94 (-1.52)**	**22.41 (-1.04)**	**40.08 (-1.68)**
AutoAugment	Vanilla	4.05 (-0.00)	16.19 (-0.00)	23.02 (-0.00)	44.37 (-0.00)
	Dropout	3.91 (-0.14)	16.04 (-0.15)	22.84 (-0.18)	44.09 (-0.28)
	EWS	**3.23 (-0.82)**	**14.31 (-1.88)**	**22.16 (-0.86)**	**42.40 (-1.97)**
AugMix	Vanilla	4.35 (-0.00)	13.57 (-0.00)	22.45 (-0.00)	38.28 (-0.00)
	Dropout	4.19 (-0.16)	13.44 (-0.13)	22.11 (-0.34)	37.97 (-0.31)
	EWS	**3.76 (-0.59)**	**10.80 (-2.77)**	**21.81 (-0.64)**	**35.24 (-3.04)**

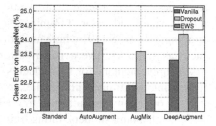 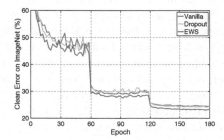

Fig. 4. *Left:* Comparisons of clean top-1 test error on ImageNet. EWS consistently reduces error across diverse augmentation schemes. *Right:* Training curves in terms of top-1 test error on ImageNet using the standard data augmentation scheme. Clearly, the improvement of EWS can be observed throughout training.

Results on CIFAR. We compare different training methods based on a ResNet-50 model with 400 training epochs. Besides the standard training method, we also compare our method with Dropout [76]. By default, we use random cropping and horizontal flipping as the standard data augmentation. Moreover, we consider state-of-the-art augmentation methods that are commonly used to improve robustness, such as AutoAugment [21] and AugMix [40]. Note that our EWS is complementary to these methods and does not require any modifications.

Table 1 shows that EWS is able to improve both clean and corrupted test errors over all three data augmentation schemes, i.e., "standard", AutoAugment and AugMix. For example, on CIFAR-10, we are able to improve the clean accuracy over AugMix by 0.59% and significantly reduce the corruption error by 2.77%. Moreover, we also observe a similar performance improvement on CIFAR-100. To be specific, our EWS reduces the corruption error by 3.04% for AugMix while improving the clean accuracy by 0.64% on CIFAR-100. Note that the improvement is also significant for AutoAugment and the standard data augmentation, i.e., with the improvement of 1.88% and 1.52% on CIFAR-10, and the improvement of 1.97% and 1.68% on CIFAR-100.

Table 2. Corruption error on ImageNet-C. We consider the mean corruption error (mCE) as well as the individual ones. In all data augmentation settings, EWS reduces mCE significantly. We just report Dropout for the standard setting as it usually worsens mCE on top of complex augmentation and put the full comparisons in our supplementary.

Method		mCE ↓	Gauss.	Shot	Imp.	Defoc.	Glass	Mot.	Zoom	Snow	Frost	Fog	Bright	Contra.	Elas.	Pixel	JPEG
Standard	Vanilla	76.5 (-0.0)	80	82	83	75	89	78	80	78	75	66	**57**	71	85	77	77
	Dropout	76.5 (-0.0)	77	79	80	78	90	79	87	**77**	77	67	58	**70**	84	75	76
	EWS	**75.1 (-1.4)**	**75**	**76**	**77**	**73**	**87**	**77**	**79**	80	**73**	**65**	58	73	**83**	**74**	**75**
AutoAugment	Vanilla	72.7 (-0.0)	69	68	72	**77**	83	80	81	79	75	64	56	70	88	57	**71**
	EWS	**71.7 (-1.0)**	**67**	**68**	**71**	78	**82**	**78**	**79**	**78**	**73**	64	**55**	**69**	**86**	**56**	72
AugMix	Vanilla	68.4 (-0.0)	65	66	67	70	**80**	66	66	75	72	67	58	**58**	79	69	**69**
	EWS	**67.5 (-0.9)**	**64**	**63**	**63**	**70**	81	**65**	**66**	**72**	**70**	**64**	**57**	63	79	**64**	70
DeepAugment	Vanilla	60.4 (-0.0)	49	50	47	59	73	65	76	64	**60**	58	51	61	76	48	67
	EWS	**58.7 (-1.7)**	**48**	**48**	**47**	**58**	**72**	**58**	**62**	**63**	62	58	**50**	**56**	**74**	**47**	**62**

Table 3. Mean flip rate (mFR) on ImageNet-P, testing stability of predictions on (corrupted) videos. In line with Table 2, EWS improves consistently over all considered data augmentation schemes and nearly all corruption types. Similar to Table 2, Dropout did not improve over AutoAugment, AugMix or DeepAugment.

Method		mFR ↓	Gaussian	Shot	Motion	Zoom	Snow	Bright	Translate	Rotate	Tilt	Scale
Standard	Vanilla	58.0 (-0.0)	**59**	58	64	72	63	62	**44**	52	57	**48**
	Dropout	57.8 (-0.2)	62	59	65	52	48	58	63	57	44	72
	EWS	**56.1 (-1.9)**	62	**55**	**62**	49	**45**	**52**	64	52	**42**	71
AutoAugment	Vanilla	51.7 (-0.0)	50	45	57	**68**	63	53	40	**44**	50	46
	EWS	**50.4 (-1.3)**	**48**	**44**	**53**	70	**62**	**52**	**36**	45	**49**	**45**
AugMix	Vanilla	37.4 (-0.0)	46	41	**30**	47	38	46	**25**	**32**	35	33
	EWS	**36.6 (-0.8)**	**45**	**39**	31	**42**	**33**	**43**	39	35	**27**	**32**
DeepAugment	Vanilla	32.1 (-0.0)	29	28	**25**	41	31	43	27	31	33	33
	EWS	**30.9 (-1.2)**	**28**	**26**	**25**	**40**	**28**	**41**	**26**	**30**	**32**	33

We emphasize that the improvement gets more significant with more complex data augmentation. This highlights that EWS is entirely complementary to state-of-the-art data augmentation. Furthermore, our method outperforms Dropout in all settings. As Dropout can be interpreted as randomly selecting channels in the preceding layers, it is a natural baseline to compare our EWS against. In addition, we also compare with a pruning based method CARDs [24] that yields state-of-the-art results on CIFAR-10-C. We highlight that, with AugMix, our EWS yields a larger relative improvement than CARDs [24] (2.77% vs 1.50%, see more details in our supplementary).

Results on ImageNet. Again, we adopt a ResNet-50 as the baseline model. Following [40], we use the learning rate warm-up for the first 5 epochs and train the model for 180 epochs in total. In addition to AutoAugment and Augmix, we consider a stronger augmentation scheme DeepAugment [37] designed for ImageNet.

In Fig. 4 (left), we first show that EWS consistently improves clean error on top of all considered data augmentation schemes. When equipped with AugMix, our EWS yields the best error of 22.1% across all the considered settings. The improvement of EWS can be also observed throughout the whole training process, as illustrated for the

Table 4. Clean and robust test error, i.e., on adversarial examples generated using PGD-20 and AutoAttack, for three different architectures: PreAct ResNet-18, WRN-28-10 and WRN-34-10. We consider "vanilla" AT and TRADES as well as their AWP variants as the baselines. We also highlight the improvement against AutoAttack in parentheses. * denotes the models trained with additional 500K unlabeled data [16]. Across all the settings, EWS reduces both the robust test error and the clean error.

Method		PreAct ResNet-18			WRN-28-10			WRN-34-10		
		Clean ↓	PGD-20 ↓	AA ↓	Clean ↓	PGD-20 ↓	AA ↓	Clean ↓	PGD-20 ↓	AA ↓
AT	Vanilla [56]	17.54	49.18	52.96 (-0.00)	14.89	45.17	47.81 (-0.00)	14.74	45.39	47.47 (-0.00)
	EWS	16.85	47.99	51.84 (-1.12)	14.57	44.24	47.17 (-0.64)	14.33	44.04	46.58 (-0.89)
	AWP [82]	19.59	46.01	51.43 (-0.00)	15.89	42.93	46.41 (-0.00)	14.17	41.89	45.96 (-0.00)
	AWP-EWS	19.25	44.98	50.48 (-0.95)	15.81	41.72	45.58 (-0.83)	14.21	41.07	45.29 (-0.67)
TRADES	Vanilla [89]	17.42	46.88	50.84 (-0.00)	15.50	44.11	47.40 (-0.00)	15.32	43.84	46.89 (-0.00)
	EWS	17.10	45.73	49.67 (-1.17)	15.09	43.45	46.72 (-0.68)	14.56	43.13	46.06 (-0.83)
	AWP [82]	18.27	45.36	49.62 (-0.00)	14.84	41.25	44.86 (-0.00)	15.55	40.85	43.90 (-0.00)
	AWP-EWS	17.67	44.20	48.58 (-1.04)	14.30	40.40	44.22 (-0.64)	14.13	40.05	43.17 (-0.73)
TRADES-AWP*		17.13	43.68	48.37 (-0.00)	13.37	38.51	41.97 (-0.00)	12.73	35.97	40.74 (-0.00)
TRADES-AWP-EWS*		16.62	42.33	47.23 (-1.14)	12.59	37.60	41.23 (-0.74)	11.90	35.19	40.05 (-0.69)

standard data augmentation scheme in Fig. 4 (right). More critically, in Table 2 and 3 we focus on the significant robustness improvements on ImageNet-C and ImageNet-P through EWS. Specifically, we consistently reduce mCE by $> 0.9\%$ across different augmentation schemes on ImageNet-C. We also highlight that EWS improves results across most included corruption types. Regarding ImageNet-P, these observations are further confirmed. For example, EWS reduces the mean flip rate (mFR) from 32.1% to 30.9% (1.2% improvement) on top of DeepAugment. Overall, these results indicate that improving the performance of subnets through EWS boosts clean and corrupted error across a range of state-of-the-art data augmentation schemes.

4.2 Improving Adversarial Robustness

Besides corruption robustness, on CIFAR-10, we also apply EWS on top of several popular adversarial training approaches, including vanilla adversarial training (AT) [56], TRADES [89], AT with adversarial weight perturbations (AT-AWP) [82], and using additional unlabeled examples [16]. Our setup follows the settings of [65]. For AWP, we follow the hyper-parameters of the original paper [82]. Note that combinations with these approaches are also possible, e.g., TRADES with AWP *and* EWS, highlighting the flexibility of EWS. We consider PreAct ResNet-18 [36], WRN-28-10 and WRN-34-10 [87] and employ early stopping [65]. We train and evaluate using an ϵ of $8/255$. During training we use 10 iterations of PGD. At test time, we evaluate models under AutoAttack (AA) [20] and PGD with 20 iterations.

In Table 4, our EWS consistently yield significant improvement in term of adversarial robustness across both architectures and adversarial training variants. For example, considering vanilla AT, EWS reduces clean error of PreAct ResNet-18 by 1.19% and robust error against AA by 1.12%. While the improvement gets slightly smaller for larger models, i.e., WRN-28-10 and WRN-34-10, EWS improves both clean and

Table 5. Clean and corrupted test error on CIFAR-10 and CIFAR-10-C. We compare our search method with random search and an L_1-norm based heuristic method. While randomly selecting subnets to improve already reduces both clean and corrupted error, finding particularly weak subnets obtains the lowest errors.

Method	Clean error (%) ↓	Corruption error (%) ↓
Baseline	5.32	26.46
Random search	4.49	25.81
L_1-norm selection	4.37	25.45
Ours	**4.12**	**24.94**

robust error consistently. On a WRN-34-10, the improvement in robust error is still 0.89%. We highlight that we can yield a similar improvement of 0.77% against AA when we consider stronger training tricks specified by [60], i.e., additionaly using label smoothing and Softplus (see more details in the supplementary). This improvement also generalizes to TRADES and AWP both of which generally improve adversarial robustness. Moreover, EWS is able to improve over TRADES and AWP when using additional pseudo-labeled training examples, which performs best in our experiments. Here, EWS reduces the robust test error from 40.74% to 40.05% (0.69% improvement). At the same time, EWS also reduces the clean error by 0.83%. EWS improving over AWP also indicates that utilizing adversarial weight perturbations [82] *on* weak subnets instead of the overall network is more beneficial. We also compare our method with a very recent adversarial training method LBGAT [22]. We show that, using the same settings of LBGAT [22], EWS yields better adversarial robustness and clean accuracy than LBGAT on both CIFAR-10 and CIFAR-100. We put the detailed comparisons in supplementary due to page limit. Overall, these experiments highlight the generality of our method, improving not only corruption robustness but also adversarial robustness.

5   Ablation and Discussions

In the following, we present further ablation experiments and discussions. Specifically, in Sect. 5.1, we demonstrate that finding particularly weak subnets is important and discuss training cost as well as hyper-parameters. This also shows that computational overhead is minimal, even for adversarial training. Furthermore, we study the weight of the distillation loss λ and the width of the selected subnets ρ. Finally, in Sect. 5.2, we show that EWS allows to analyze the vulnerability of individual blocks and layers.

5.1   Search Strategies and Hyper-Parameters

We perform ablations on CIFAR-10(-C) regarding our search strategy and hyper-parameters. For all the experiments, we use a ResNet-50 and adopt the same settings as before.

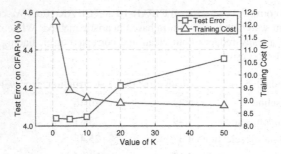

Fig. 5. We plot (clean) test error on CIFAR-10 (blue) and training cost in hours (red) against the controller training interval K, see Algorithm 1. Clearly, increasing K reduces training cost significantly. At the same time, clean error reduces significantly for $K \leq 10$. In practice, $K = 10$ yields a good trade-off and only introduces little computational overhead (roughly 3%) for both corruption and adversarial experiments. (Color figure online)

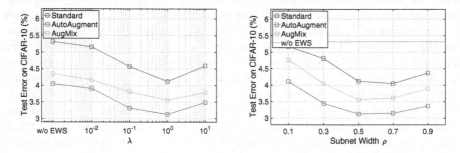

Fig. 6. Clean test error on CIFAR-10 plotted against the weight of the distillation loss (left, see Algorithm 1) and the subnet width ρ (right). *Left:* Across all tested data augmentation schemes, including AutoAugment and AugMix, $\lambda = 1$ performs best. *Right:* Too small or too large subnets during training reduce the benefit of EWS. We found that $\rho = 0.5$ and $\rho = 0.7$ perform best in most cases.

Search Strategies. In Table 5, we conduct an ablation study to investigate the effectiveness of our search method. We compare our method to two baselines: random search selects subnets entirely at random; and L_1-norm selection chooses the channels/paths with lowest L_1-norm of weights. For simplicity, we compare clean and corrupted test error on CIFAR-10(-C). Since the randomly sampled subnets may contain some weak components, we are able to reduce both the clean and corrupted error. Using L_1-norm is a simple heuristic to find weaker subnets than random search. This can be seen by a slightly reduced clean and corrupted error. Nevertheless, the L_1-norm may not be highly correlated with accuracy and the search results are often suboptimal. In contrast, our method yields the lowest clean and corrupted errors as the controller directly finds subnets with low accuracy. This also confirms our results in Fig. 1.

Training Interval K and Training Cost. As detailed in Sect. 3.3 and Algorithm 1, we train the controller model every K iterations. Thus, we expect a trade-off between train-

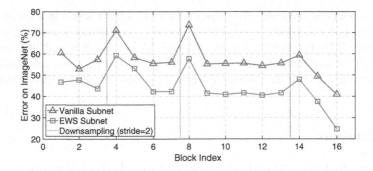

Fig. 7. Test error on ImageNet when constructing subnets by randomly selecting 50% of paths/channels in a specific block while keeping the rest unchanged. The results are averaged across 100 sampled subnets. The dotted line marks the position of downsampling operation. Clearly, blocks *after* downsampling blocks are most vulnerable and the last two blocks are least vulnerable. In all cases, EWS reduces error on subnets significantly. (Color figure online)

ing cost and performance: a stronger controller model should improve performance, but needs to be updated more often (i.e., lower K) which, however, increases the training cost. As shown in Fig. 5, gradually increasing K greatly reduces the training cost. Note that we obtain promising results for $K \leq 10$ but observe a significant increase of test error when $K > 10$. We observe that $K = 10$ also works well for ImageNet(-C) and the data dependent tuning is not necessary. This justifies our choice of $K = 10$ which also results in small computational overhead of roughly 3% on the adversarial training settings.

Weight of Distillation Loss. In Fig. 6 (left), we change the value of λ in Eqn. (2). Note that $\lambda = 0$ corresponds to training *without* EWS. Larger λ, in contrast, increases the effect of EWS, i.e., trying to enhance weak subnets more aggressively. Given a set of values $\lambda \in \{0, 0.001, 0.01, 0.1, 1, 10\}$, we gradually reduce clean test error up until $\lambda = 1$. Larger values will result in a small performance degradation. However, even $\lambda = 10$ still outperforms training without EWS. This generalizes across all considered data augmentation schemes, including AutoAugment and AugMix.

Subnet Width. In Fig. 6 (right), we investigate the impact of subnet width ρ on the performance improvement obtained using EWS. To this end, we consider a set of candidate widths $\rho \in \{0.1, 0.3, 0.5, 0.7, 0.9\}$. We suspect that very small subnets ($\rho = 0.1$) cause the distillation loss $\mathcal{L}_{\mathrm{KL}}\big(\alpha(x), M(x)\big)$ to be very large, hampering the training process. When we increase ρ to 0.5 or 0.7, EWS yields significantly better results. For a larger $\rho \geq 0.9$, the distillation loss can be very small, performance drops again.

5.2   Vulnerability of Blocks and Layers

As mentioned in Sect. 3.1, we construct subnets by selecting a subset of paths and channels. This also allows us to investigate the vulnerability of each block. To this end, we construct subnets by randomly selecting a subset of paths/channels in a specific block, while keeping all other blocks unchanged. In Fig. 7, we report test error on ImageNet when randomly sampling 100 subnets for each block. We observed that the blocks behind the downsampling operation (dotted lines) tend to be more vulnerable. More critically, EWS consistently reduces test error across all blocks compared to standard training.

6   Conclusion

In this paper, we described the phenomenon that most subnets of deep networks perform rather poorly, especially on perturbed examples. Interestingly, these weak subnets are highly correlated with the lack of robustness of the full model. To address this issue, we focused on improving model robustness by identifying and enhancing these particularly weak subnets. This leads to our proposed training method, EWS, which specifically employs a search algorithm to find weak subnets and then strengthens them through knowledge distillation. With minimal computational overhead, EWS can be applied on top of popular data augmentation schemes as well as adversarial training variants. Experiments show that EWS improves robustness consistently over these methods.

References

1. Akhtar, N., Mian, A.: Threat of adversarial attacks on deep learning in computer vision: a survey. IEEE Access **6**, 14410–14430 (2018)
2. Alayrac, J., Uesato, J., Huang, P., Fawzi, A., Stanforth, R., Kohli, P.: Are labels required for improving adversarial robustness? Adv. Neural Inf. Process. Syst. **32** (2019)
3. Athalye, A., Carlini, N.: On the robustness of the CVPR 2018 white-box adversarial example defenses. arXiv preprint arXiv:1804.03286 (2018)
4. Balaji, Y., Goldstein, T., Hoffman, J.: Instance adaptive adversarial training: improved accuracy tradeoffs in neural nets. arXiv preprint arXiv:1910.08051 (2019)
5. Barreno, M., Nelson, B., Sears, R., Joseph, A.D., Tygar, J.D.: Can machine learning be secure? In: Proceedings of the 2006 ACM Symposium on Information, Computer and Communications Security, pp. 16–25 (2006)
6. Benz, P., Zhang, C., Karjauv, A., Kweon, I.: Revisiting batch normalization for improving corruption robustness. In: Proceedings of the IEEE/CVF Winter Conference on Applications of Computer Vision, pp. 494–503 (2020)
7. Biggio, B., Roli, F.: Wild patterns: ten years after the rise of adversarial machine learning. Pattern Recognit. **84**, 317–331 (2018)
8. Bui, A., et al.: Improving adversarial robustness by enforcing local and global compactness. In: Vedaldi, A., Bischof, H., Brox, T., Frahm, J.-M. (eds.) ECCV 2020. LNCS, vol. 12372, pp. 209–223. Springer, Cham (2020). https://doi.org/10.1007/978-3-030-58583-9_13
9. Cai, H., Zhu, L., Han, S.: ProxylessNAS: direct neural architecture search on target task and hardware. arXiv preprint arXiv:1812.00332 (2019)
10. Cai, Q., Liu, C., Song, D.: Curriculum adversarial training. In: IJCAI, pp. 3740–3747 (2018)
11. Calian, D.A., et al.: Defending against image corruptions through adversarial augmentations. arXiv preprint arXiv:2104.01086 (2021)
12. Carlini, N.: Is AmI (attacks meet interpretability) robust to adversarial examples? arXiv preprint arXiv:1902.02322 (2019)

13. Carlini, N., Wagner, D.: Adversarial examples are not easily detected: bypassing ten detection methods. In: Proceedings of the 10th ACM Workshop on Artificial Intelligence and Security, pp. 3–14 (2017)
14. Carlini, N., Wagner, D.A.: Defensive distillation is not robust to adversarial examples. arXiv preprint arXiv:1607.04311 (2016)
15. Carlini, N., Wagner, D.A.: Magnet and "efficient defenses against adversarial attacks" are not robust to adversarial examples. arXiv preprint arXiv:1711.08478 (2017)
16. Carmon, Y., Raghunathan, A., Schmidt, L., Duchi, J.C., Liang, P.: Unlabeled data improves adversarial robustness. Adv. Neural Inf. Process. Syst. **32** (2019)
17. Chaubey, A., Agrawal, N., Barnwal, K., Guliani, K.K., Mehta, P.: Universal adversarial perturbations: a survey. arXiv preprint arXiv:2005.08087 (2020)
18. Chen, Y., et al.: Contrastive neural architecture search with neural architecture comparators. In: Proceedings of the IEEE/CVF Conference on Computer Vision and Pattern Recognition, pp. 9502–9511 (2021)
19. Cheng, M., Lei, Q., Chen, P., Dhillon, I.S., Hsieh, C.: CAT: customized adversarial training for improved robustness. arXiv preprint arXiv:2002.06789 (2020)
20. Croce, F., Hein, M.: Reliable evaluation of adversarial robustness with an ensemble of diverse parameter-free attacks. In: International Conference on Machine Learning, pp. 2206–2216. PMLR (2020)
21. Cubuk, E.D., Zoph, B., Mane, D., Vasudevan, V., Le, Q.V.: AutoAugment: learning augmentation policies from data. arXiv preprint arXiv:1805.09501 (2019)
22. Cui, J., Liu, S., Wang, L., Jia, J.: Learnable boundary guided adversarial training. In: Proceedings of the IEEE/CVF International Conference on Computer Vision, pp. 15721–15730 (2021)
23. Deng, J., Dong, W., Socher, R., Li, L.J., Li, K., Fei-Fei, L.: ImageNet: a large-scale hierarchical image database. In: 2009 IEEE Conference on Computer Vision and Pattern Recognition, pp. 248–255 (2009)
24. Diffenderfer, J., Bartoldson, B., Chaganti, S., Zhang, J., Kailkhura, B.: A winning hand: compressing deep networks can improve out-of-distribution robustness. Adv. Neural. Inf. Process. Syst. **34**, 664–676 (2021)
25. Ding, G.W., Sharma, Y., Lui, K.Y.C., Huang, R.: MMA training: direct input space margin maximization through adversarial training. arXiv preprint arXiv:1812.02637 (2020)
26. Engstrom, L., Ilyas, A., Athalye, A.: Evaluating and understanding the robustness of adversarial logit pairing. arXiv preprint arXiv:1807.10272 (2018)
27. Jonathan, F., Michael, C.: The lottery ticket hypothesis: training pruned neural networks. In: Proceedings of the 7th International Conference on Learning Representations (ICLR). New Orleans, Louisiana, pp. 1–42 (2019)
28. Geirhos, R., Rubisch, P., Michaelis, C., Bethge, M., Wichmann, F.A., Brendel, W.: ImageNet-trained CNNs are biased towards texture; increasing shape bias improves accuracy and robustness. arXiv preprint arXiv:1811.12231 (2019)
29. Goodfellow, I.J., Shlens, J., Szegedy, C.: Explaining and harnessing adversarial examples. arXiv preprint arXiv:1412.6572 (2014)
30. Gou, J., Yu, B., Maybank, S.J., Tao, D.: Knowledge distillation: a survey. Int. J. Comput. Vis. **129**(6), 1789–1819 (2021). https://doi.org/10.1007/s11263-021-01453-z
31. Gowal, S., Qin, C., Uesato, J., Mann, T.A., Kohli, P.: Uncovering the limits of adversarial training against norm-bounded adversarial examples. arXiv preprint arXiv:2010.03593 (2020)
32. Graves, A.: Long short-term memory. In: Supervised Sequence Labelling with Recurrent Neural Networks. Studies in Computational Intelligence, vol. 385, pp. 37–45. Springer, Heidelberg (2012). https://doi.org/10.1007/978-3-642-24797-2_4

33. Guo, Y., et al.: Breaking the curse of space explosion: towards efficient NAS with curriculum search. In: International Conference on Machine Learning, pp. 3822–3831. PMLR (2020)
34. Guo, Y., et al.: Towards accurate and compact architectures via neural architecture transformer. In: IEEE Transactions on Pattern Analysis and Machine Intelligence (PAMI) (2021)
35. He, K., Zhang, X., Ren, S., Sun, J.: Deep residual learning for image recognition. In: Proceedings of the IEEE Conference on Computer Vision and Pattern Recognition (CVPR), pp. 770–778 (2016)
36. He, K., Zhang, X., Ren, S., Sun, J.: Identity mappings in deep residual networks. In: Leibe, B., Matas, J., Sebe, N., Welling, M. (eds.) ECCV 2016. LNCS, vol. 9908, pp. 630–645. Springer, Cham (2016). https://doi.org/10.1007/978-3-319-46493-0_38
37. Hendrycks, D., et al.: The many faces of robustness: a critical analysis of out-of-distribution generalization. In: Proceedings of the IEEE/CVF International Conference on Computer Vision (ICCV), pp. 8340–8349 (2021)
38. Hendrycks, D., Dietterich, T.G.: Benchmarking neural network robustness to common corruptions and perturbations. arXiv preprint arXiv:1903.12261 (2019)
39. Hendrycks, D., Mazeika, M., Kadavath, S., Song, D.: Using self-supervised learning can improve model robustness and uncertainty. Adv. Neural Inf. Process. Syst. 32 (2019)
40. Hendrycks, D., Mu, N., Cubuk, E.D., Zoph, B., Gilmer, J., Lakshminarayanan, B.: AugMix: a simple data processing method to improve robustness and uncertainty. arXiv preprint arXiv:1912.02781 (2020)
41. Hinton, G., Vinyals, O., Dean, J.: Distilling the knowledge in a neural network. In: NeurIPS Deep Learning and Representation Learning Workshop (2014)
42. Howard, A.G., et al.: MobileNets: efficient convolutional neural networks for mobile vision applications. arXiv preprint arXiv:1704.04861 (2017)
43. Jeddi, A., Shafiee, M.J., Wong, A.: A simple fine-tuning is all you need: towards robust deep learning via adversarial fine-tuning. arXiv preprint arXiv:2012.13628 (2020)
44. Kireev, K., Andriushchenko, M., Flammarion, N.: On the effectiveness of adversarial training against common corruptions. In: Uncertainty in Artificial Intelligence, pp. 1012–1021. PMLR (2021)
45. Krizhevsky, A., Hinton, G.: Learning multiple layers of features from tiny images (2009)
46. Krizhevsky, A., Sutskever, I., Hinton, G.E.: ImageNet classification with deep convolutional neural networks. In: NeurIPS, pp. 1097–1105 (2012)
47. Lamb, A., Verma, V., Kannala, J., Bengio, Y.: Interpolated adversarial training: achieving robust neural networks without sacrificing too much accuracy. In: Proceedings of the 12th ACM Workshop on Artificial Intelligence and Security (AISec), pp. 95–103 (2019)
48. LeCun, Y., et al.: Backpropagation applied to handwritten zip code recognition. Neural Comput. 1(4), 541–551 (1989)
49. Lee, C.Y., Xie, S., Gallagher, P., Zhang, Z., Tu, Z.: Deeply-supervised nets. In: Artificial Intelligence and Statistics (AISTATS), pp. 562–570. PMLR (2015)
50. Li, B., et al.: Towards practical lottery ticket hypothesis for adversarial training. arXiv preprint arXiv:2003.05733 (2020)
51. Li, Y., et al.: Towards robustness of deep neural networks via regularization. In: Proceedings of the IEEE/CVF International Conference on Computer Vision (ICCV), pp. 7496–7505 (2021)
52. Liu, H., Simonyan, K., Yang, Y.: DARTS: differentiable architecture search. arXiv preprint arXiv:1806.09055 (2019)
53. Liu, J., et al.: Discrimination-aware network pruning for deep model compression. IEEE Trans. Pattern Anal. Mach. Intell. 44(8), 4035–4051 (2020)
54. Liu, Y., Zhang, W., Li, S., Yu, N.: Enhanced attacks on defensively distilled deep neural networks. arXiv preprint arXiv:1711.05934 (2017)

55. Madaan, D., Shin, J., Hwang, S.J.: Learning to generate noise for robustness against multiple perturbations. arXiv preprint arXiv:2006.12135 (2020)
56. Madry, A., Makelov, A., Schmidt, L., Tsipras, D., Vladu, A.: Towards deep learning models resistant to adversarial attacks. arXiv preprint arXiv:1706.06083 (2018)
57. Mao, X., et al.: Towards robust vision transformer. In: Proceedings of the IEEE/CVF Conference on Computer Vision and Pattern Recognition, pp. 12042–12051 (2021)
58. Mosbach, M., Andriushchenko, M., Trost, T.A., Hein, M., Klakow, D.: Logit pairing methods can fool gradient-based attacks. arXiv preprint arXiv:1810.12042 (2018)
59. Nado, Z., Padhy, S., Sculley, D., D'Amour, A., Lakshminarayanan, B., Snoek, J.: Evaluating prediction-time batch normalization for robustness under covariate shift. arXiv preprint arXiv:2006.10963 (2020)
60. Pang, T., Yang, X., Dong, Y., Su, H., Zhu, J.: Bag of tricks for adversarial training. arXiv preprint arXiv:2010.00467 (2021)
61. Pang, T., Yang, X., Dong, Y., Xu, T., Zhu, J., Su, H.: Boosting adversarial training with hypersphere embedding. Adv. Neural. Inf. Process. Syst. **33**, 7779–7792 (2020)
62. Pham, H., Guan, M.Y., Zoph, B., Le, Q.V., Dean, J.: Efficient neural architecture search via parameter sharing. In: International Conference on Machine Learning, pp. 4092–4101 (2018)
63. He, Z., Rakin, A.S., Fan, D.: Parametric noise injection: trainable randomness to improve deep neural network robustness against adversarial attack. In: Proceedings of the IEEE/CVF Conference on Computer Vision and Pattern Recognition, pp. 588–597 (2019)
64. Rebuffi, S.A., Gowal, S., Calian, D.A., Stimberg, F., Wiles, O., Mann, T.: Fixing data augmentation to improve adversarial robustness. arXiv preprint arXiv:2103.01946 (2021)
65. Rice, L., Wong, E., Kolter, J.Z.: Overfitting in adversarially robust deep learning. In: International Conference on Machine Learning (ICML), pp. 8093–8104. PMLR (2020)
66. Rusak, E., et al.: A simple way to make neural networks robust against diverse image corruptions. In: Vedaldi, A., Bischof, H., Brox, T., Frahm, J.-M. (eds.) ECCV 2020. LNCS, vol. 12348, pp. 53–69. Springer, Cham (2020). https://doi.org/10.1007/978-3-030-58580-8_4
67. Russakovsky, O., et al.: ImageNet large scale visual recognition challenge. Int. J. Comput. Vis. **115**(3), 211–252 (2015). https://doi.org/10.1007/s11263-015-0816-y
68. Saikia, T., Schmid, C., Brox, T.: Improving robustness against common corruptions with frequency biased models. In: Proceedings of the IEEE/CVF International Conference on Computer Vision, pp. 10211–10220 (2021)
69. Salman, H., Ilyas, A., Engstrom, L., Kapoor, A., Madry, A.: Do adversarially robust ImageNet models transfer better? Adv. Neural. Inf. Process. Syst. **33**, 3533–3545 (2020)
70. Sandler, M., Howard, A., Zhu, M., Zhmoginov, A., Chen, L.C.: MobileNetV2: inverted residuals and linear bottlenecks. In: Proceedings of the IEEE Conference on Computer Vision and Pattern Recognition (CVPR), pp. 4510–4520 (2018)
71. Schneider, S., Rusak, E., Eck, L., Bringmann, O., Brendel, W., Bethge, M.: Improving robustness against common corruptions by covariate shift adaptation. Adv. Neural. Inf. Process. Syst. **33**, 11539–11551 (2020)
72. Sehwag, V., Wang, S., Mittal, P., Jana, S.: HYDRA: pruning adversarially robust neural networks. Adv. Neural. Inf. Process. Syst. **33**, 19655–19666 (2020)
73. Sehwag, V., Wang, S., Mittal, P., Jana, S.: On pruning adversarially robust neural networks. arXiv preprint arXiv:2002.10509 (2020)
74. Silva, S.H., Najafirad, P.: Opportunities and challenges in deep learning adversarial robustness: a survey. arXiv preprint arXiv:2007.00753 (2020)
75. Singla, S., Feizi, S.: Second-order provable defenses against adversarial attacks. In: International Conference on Machine Learning (ICML), pp. 8981–8991. PMLR (2020)
76. Srivastava, N., Hinton, G.E., Krizhevsky, A., Sutskever, I., Salakhutdinov, R.: Dropout: a simple way to prevent neural networks from overfitting. J. Mach. Learn. Res. **15**(1), 1929–1958 (2014)

77. Stutz, D., Hein, M., Schiele, B.: Relating adversarially robust generalization to flat minima. In: Proceedings of the IEEE/CVF International Conference on Computer Vision (ICCV), pp. 7807-7817 (2021)

78. Sun, S., Cheng, Y., Gan, Z., Liu, J.: Patient knowledge distillation for BERT model compression. arXiv preprint arXiv:1908.09355 (2019)

79. Szegedy, C., et al.: Intriguing properties of neural networks. arXiv preprint arXiv:1312.6199 (2013)

80. Wan, W., Chen, J., Yang, M.-H.: Adversarial training with bi-directional likelihood regularization for visual classification. In: Vedaldi, A., Bischof, H., Brox, T., Frahm, J.-M. (eds.) ECCV 2020. LNCS, vol. 12369, pp. 785–800. Springer, Cham (2020). https://doi.org/10.1007/978-3-030-58586-0_46

81. Wang, H., Chen, T., Gui, S., Hu, T., Liu, J., Wang, Z.: Once-for-all adversarial training: in-situ tradeoff between robustness and accuracy for free. Adv. Neural. Inf. Process. Syst. **33**, 7449–7461 (2020)

82. Wu, D., Xia, S.T., Wang, Y.: Adversarial weight perturbation helps robust generalization. Adv. Neural. Inf. Process. Syst. **33**, 2958–2969 (2020)

83. Xie, S., Girshick, R., Dollár, P., Tu, Z., He, K.: Aggregated residual transformations for deep neural networks. In: Proceedings of the IEEE Conference on Computer Vision and Pattern Recognition, pp. 1492–1500 (2017)

84. Xu, H., et al.: Adversarial attacks and defenses in images, graphs and text: a review. Int. J. Autom. Comput. **17**, 151–178 (2019). https://doi.org/10.1007/s11633-019-1211-x

85. Yu, H., Liu, A., Liu, X., Yang, J., Zhang, C.: Towards noise-robust neural networks via progressive adversarial training (2019)

86. Yuan, X., He, P., Zhu, Q., Bhat, R.R., Li, X.: Adversarial examples: attacks and defenses for deep learning. IEEE Trans. Neural Netw. Learn. Syst. **30**(9), 2805–2824 (2019)

87. Zagoruyko, S., Komodakis, N.: Wide residual networks. arXiv preprint arXiv:1605.07146 (2016)

88. Zhang, H., Wang, J.: Defense against adversarial attacks using feature scattering-based adversarial training. Adv. Neural Inf. Process. Syst. **32** (2019)

89. Zhang, H., Yu, Y., Jiao, J., Xing, E., El Ghaoui, L., Jordan, M.: Theoretically principled tradeoff between robustness and accuracy. In: International Conference on Machine Learning (ICML), pp. 7472–7482. PMLR (2019)

90. Zhang, H., Yu, Y., Jiao, J., Xing, E.P., Ghaoui, L.E., Jordan, M.I.: Theoretically principled trade-off between robustness and accuracy. In: International Conference on Machine Learning (ICML), pp. 7472–7482. PMLR (2019)

91. Zhang, H., Chen, H., Song, Z., Boning, D., Dhillon, I.S., Hsieh, C.J.: The limitations of adversarial training and the blind-spot attack. arXiv preprint arXiv:1901.04684 (2019)

92. Zhang, J., et al.: Attacks which do not kill training make adversarial learning stronger. In: International Conference on Machine Learning (ICML), pp. 11278–11287. PMLR (2020)

93. Zi, B., Zhao, S., Ma, X., Jiang, Y.: Revisiting adversarial robustness distillation: robust soft labels make student better. In: Proceedings of the IEEE/CVF International Conference on Computer Vision (ICCV), pp. 16443–16452 (2021)

94. Zi, B., Zhao, S., Ma, X., Jiang, Y.G.: Revisiting adversarial robustness distillation: robust soft labels make student better. In: CVPR (2021)

95. Zoph, B., Le, Q.V.: Neural architecture search with reinforcement learning. arXiv preprint arXiv:1611.01578 (2017)

Learning Invariant Visual Representations for Compositional Zero-Shot Learning

Tian Zhang[1] , Kongming Liang[1(✉)] , Ruoyi Du[1] , Xian Sun[2],
Zhanyu Ma[1] , and Jun Guo[1]

[1] Pattern Recognition and Intelligent System Laboratory, School of Artificial
Intelligence, Beijing University of Posts and Telecommunications, Beijing, China
{zhangtian1874,liangkongming,duruoyi,mazhanyu,guojun}@bupt.edu.cn
[2] Aerospace Information Research Institute, Chinese Academy of Sciences,
Beijing, China
sunxian@aircas.ac.cn

Abstract. Compositional Zero-Shot Learning (CZSL) aims to recognize novel compositions using knowledge learned from seen attribute-object compositions in the training set. Previous works mainly project an image and a composition into a common embedding space to measure their compatibility score. However, both attributes and objects share the visual representations learned above, leading the model to exploit spurious correlations and bias towards seen pairs. Instead, we reconsider CZSL as an out-of-distribution generalization problem. If an object is treated as a domain, we can learn object-invariant features to recognize the attributes attached to any object reliably. Similarly, attribute-invariant features can also be learned when recognizing the objects with attributes as domains. Specifically, we propose an invariant feature learning framework to align different domains at the representation and gradient levels to capture the intrinsic characteristics associated with the tasks. Experiments on three CZSL benchmarks demonstrate that the proposed method significantly outperforms the previous state-of-the-art.

Keywords: Compositional Zero-Shot Learning · Out-of-distribution generalization · Invariant feature learning

1 Introduction

Humans can easily generalize the *red* state from *apples* to *tomatoes* even if no images of *red tomatoes* have been seen. Since visual concepts follow the long tailed distribution, the instances of most concepts are rarely presented in the real world scenario. Therefore, the ability to generalize the learned knowledge to novel concepts is of vital importance for human to recognize a large number of concepts and is considered as one of the hallmarks of human intelligence [22,29].

T. Zhang and K. Liang—Equal contribution; codes are available at https://github.com/PRIS-CV/IVR.

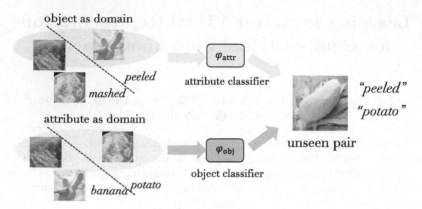

Fig. 1. The illustration of our motivation. Ellipses represent corresponding domains. The samples in one ellipse belong to the same domain, the samples outside the ellipse belong to other domains. And the dotted lines represent category decision boundaries within decoupled feature space.

The goal of Compositional Zero-Shot Learning (CZSL) is to build a model that can learn the attributes and objects from seen compositions and generalize them well to unseen compositions. For instance, the model trained with images of *red apples* and *green tomatoes* can correctly predict images of *red tomatoes*.

Previous works [19, 21, 22, 24] in CZSL mainly project image features and attribute-object composition features into a common embedding space and constrain the features belonging to the same concept to be closer. Specifically, the current state-of-the-art method [21] use cosine similarity to calculate the compatibility score of images and compositions in the embedding space. Since the features are learned in a composition way, they are not disentangled for attribute and object which makes the model over-rely on a limited number of attribute-object pairs in the training process. For instance, when machines had only seen *red apples*, they might easily misidentify *red tomatoes* as *red apples* since classifier had prone to spuriously correlate *red* with *apple*. Machine learning models are data-driven and typically require samples of various perspectives and lighting. This makes them often rely on spurious features [1, 2, 14, 33, 43] unrelated to the core concept and lose generalization performance [10], especially in zero-shot learning scenarios. Therefore, recognizing attributes and objects independently may actually assist the model in achieving better performance.

In this paper, we leverage the idea of Domain Generalization (DG) to improve the ability of the model to generalize to unknown compositions. Most deep learning methods work well under the *i.i.d.* assumption that training and testing data are independently and identically distributed [4, 27]. However, this assumption does not always hold true in reality. When the probability distributions of training and testing data are different, the performance of deep learning models is often degraded due to the domain shift [31, 38]. DG trains model only with data from the source domain, making it generalize well to the unseen arbitrary target domain. For instance, given a training set consisting of *photos, cartoon images* and *paintings*, DG requires training a model to have promising performance in classifying *sketches*, which are significantly different from the images in the training set. Most of the work alleviates domain shift by aligning feature distributions of the source with target domains, resulting in domain-invariant features.

Since a domain is composed of data that are sampled from a distribution [38], the Compositional Zero-Shot Learning task is analogous to two DG sub-tasks in essence, by taking objects or attributes as domains. As shown in the Fig. 1, in the case of treating objects as domains, if the model learns the attributes of *mashed* and *peeled* in the *banana* domain, then we expect that it can also reliably recognize the attribute of *peeled* when generalized to the *potato* domain. Similarly, in the case of treating attributes as domains, if the model learns the objects of *banana* and *potato* in the *mashed* domain, it should recognize the object of *potato* when generalized to the *peeled* domain. Eventually, the model is able to successfully recognize the unseen pairs (*peeled potato*). We simulate a domain generalization scenario by designing a triplet input network. To decouple the highly-coupled features, we construct two branches, the object-domain branch and the attribute-domain branch. For the object-domain branch, our goal is to accurately recognize the attribute regardless of object labels. We learn consistency at the representation level by discarding object-specific channels. Moreover, we minimize the gradient differences of attribute prediction in different object domains to achieve gradient-level consistency. For the attribute-domain branch, we learn attribute-invariant features in the same way. Finally, by penalizing domain-specific power of features, we discover invariant mechanisms in the data which are hard to vary across examples and thus learn the optimal attribute classifier and object classifier.

The contributions of the paper are summarized below. (1) To the best of our knowledge, we are the first to solve the Compositional Zero-Shot Learning task from a Domain Generalization perspective. In other words, the compositional learning problem is transformed into a domain-shift problem. (2) We treat attributes or objects as domains and align different domains to learn domain-invariant features, thus improving the generalization performance of the model to recognize unseen pairs. (3) We prove the effectiveness of our method through abundant experiments.

2   Related Works

2.1   Compositional Zero-Shot Learning

Compositional Zero-Shot Learning (CZSL) is a special case of Zero-Shot Learning (ZSL) [25,40,41]. Given a training set containing a set of attribute-object compositions, CZSL aims to recognize unknown compositions of these attributes and objects at inference time. Part of the work proposes to learn classifiers for individual concepts and combine them to recognize integrated concepts. Chen et al. [8] deduce unobserved attribute-object pairs through tensor decomposition during training. Misra et al. [22] consider compositionality and contextuality as the key to solving CZSL, and they merge classifiers for primitive concepts into classifiers for composite concepts. A most popular line of work involves embedding attribute-object compositions into a feature space. Nagarajan et al. [24] argue that objects are entities while attributes are properties of the objects and consider the composition of attributes and objects as a learned transformation. Wei et al. [39] model the attribute-object relationships within the feature space based on a GAN framework. Li et al. [19] propose symmetry as an essential principle for attribute-object transformations and introduce group theory as an axiomatic foundation to satisfy the specific principles of nature. Mancini et al. [21] propose a new open world setting for CZSL task where the prior knowledge of unseen compositions is not provided. Instead, other works learn the joint compatibility between the input image and the attribute-object pair. Purushwalkam et al. [29] train a set of network modules jointly with a gating network to produce features that indicate compatibility between the input image and the concept. Atzmon et al. [3] describe CZSL from a causal perspective and try to find which intervention cause the image. Unlike these works, we focus on the independence between the sub-concepts and learn an attribute classifier and object classifier that can be generalized to new compositions.

2.2 Domain Generalization

In reality, the distribution of training and test sets is often different, leading to model performance degradation. This problem is known as out-of-distribution generalization or domain generalization [5,23,45]. Since the generalization ability of the model often depends on the quantity and quality of training data [38], one line of work increases the diversity of existing training data through data augmentation and data generation to learn more general representations. Qiao et al. [30] leverage Wasserstein Auto-Encoders (WAE) [37] to help generate samples that retain semantics and have large domain transportation. Shankar et al. [34] introduce a domain classifier to expand the training data by disturbing the input data. Carlucci et al. [6] enrich the understanding of the data by solving puzzle problems, allowing the model to induce invariance and regularity autonomously. A different line of work uses domain alignment techniques or feature disentanglement to learn domain-invariant features. Sun et al. [36] conduct domain alignment by matching the mean and variance of representations in different domains. Li et al. [18] use Maximum Mean Discrepancy (MMD) to align different domains to obtain domain-invariant representation. Peng et al. [27] decouple features into domain-invariant features, domain-specific features, and class-irrelevant features through adversarial learning. Huang et al. [12] propose a self-challenge mechanism, which iteratively discards the dominant features activated on the training data. Kim et al. [15] propose self-supervised contrastive regularization to map the latent representations of the positive pair samples close together. In this paper, we mainly leverage the idea of exploring invariance in DG to enhance the performance of the CZSL task (Fig. 3).

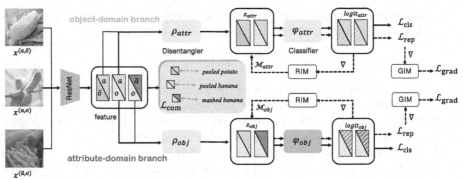

a: peeled ā: mashed o: banana ō: potato ⟶: first forward --→: second forward ∇: gradient

Fig. 2. Overview of the proposed framework. We construct object-domain branch and attribute-domain branch. In the object-domain branch, we execute consistent alignment across different object domains so that the model learns the essential characteristics of the attribute. The same for the attribute-domain branch.

3 Methods

In typical CZSL, we have access to all the attributes and objects, while only part of attribute-object compositions can be obtained in the training phase. The goal is to recognize unknown compositions of individual attribute and object concepts. Composing the learned knowledge into unseen compositions heavily relies on out-of-distribution generalization ability [1,14,16,17,33]. Therefore, we formalize the CZSL problem into two domain generalization sub-tasks, in which we consider attributes as domains to recognize objects and vice versa. Then, two types of invariant mechanisms are proposed to remove the spurious domain-specific features and improve the generalization ability of the model.

An overview of our proposed framework is shown in Fig. 2. In the following sections, we first introduce the visual and composition embedding learning procedure. Then we present how the visual features are decomposed and processed by representation and gradient invariant mechanisms in sequential. Finally, we describe the training and inference methodologies.

3.1 Visual and Composition Embedding

We need to train a model that learns a mapping from a set of images X to a set of compositions $Y = Y_{attr} \times Y_{obj}$, where Y_{attr} is a set of attribute labels and Y_{obj} is a set of object labels. The composition label is divided into $Y = Y_s \cup Y_u$, where Y_s is the set of seen compositions during training and Y_u is the set of unseen compositions for the validation and test sets, with $Y_s \cap Y_u = \emptyset$. Given an image $x \in X$ in the training set and its corresponding label $y \in Y_s$, we first use a pre-trained network $f(\cdot)$ (e.g., ResNet-18 [11]) to extract its visual embedding. Then, the composition embedding function $g(\cdot)$ projects the combined concepts y into a common semantic space. The composition classification loss can be obtained by minimizing the distance between the two embedding features,

$$h_{comp}(x, y) = d_{cos}(f(x), g(y)), \tag{1}$$

where $d_{cos}(\cdot, \cdot)$ is the cosine distance of the input two embeddings. The distance in the embedding space represents the compatibility of the input image and the attribute-object composition. Therefore, the smaller the distance is, the higher probability that the composition exists in the image [24].

However, the visual representations learned in the above manner are shared by both attributes and objects, which may lead the model exploiting spurious correlations and bias the model against seen pairs. In this work, we utilize invariant feature learning to decouple attributes and objects from a domain generalization perspective. The learned invariant features explore the independence between attribute and object concepts and prove to be effective to complement the conventional visual embedding.

3.2   Decomposing Visual Features

In order to conduct the invariant feature learning for CZSL, we need to decompose the visual features into two parts by considering object and attribute as domain respectively. Here, we design a triplet input network with $x^{a,\bar{o}}$, $x^{a,o}$ and $x^{\bar{a},o}$ as inputs to diversify the inter-domain variation, where $a, \bar{a} \in Y_{attr}$ denote different attributes, and $o, \bar{o} \in Y_{obj}$ denote different objects, e.g., $x^{(a,\bar{o})}$ represents an image of different object with the same attribute as $x^{(a,o)}$. We denote the composition set of a triplet input as $\mathcal{C} = \{(a, \bar{o}), (a, o), (\bar{a}, o)\}$. And the classification task set is denoted as $\mathcal{T} = \{attr, obj\}$.

The extracted visual features from the pre-trained network $f(\cdot)$ are directly fed into two individual MLPs, attribute disentangler $\rho_{attr}(\cdot)$ and object disentangler $\rho_{obj}(\cdot)$. For $i \in \mathcal{C}$ and $j \in \mathcal{T}$, the image features of x^i can be decoupled as $z_j^i = \rho_j(f(x^i))$. Given the cross entropy loss function $l(\cdot, \cdot)$, the attribute and object classification loss can be defined as,

$$L_{cls} = \sum_{i \in \mathcal{C}} \sum_{j \in \mathcal{T}} l(\varphi_j(z_j^i; \theta_j), y_j^i), \tag{2}$$

where $\varphi_j(\cdot)$ denotes the classifier of task j which predict classification labels over the decomposed visual features. θ_j represents the parameters of classifier $\varphi_j(\cdot)$.

3.3   Learning Invariant Features for CZSL

A notion of invariance implies something that stays the same while something else changes [26]. Capturing invariance helps model learn the core features related to the label. Returning to the previous example, the explanations to distinguish *tomatoes* from *apples* should be invariant, no matter whether the *tomatoes* are *red* or *green*. Therefore, we leverage invariant feature learning to capture the invariance of objects when attributes change or vice versa. Finally the learned invariant features of attributes and objects can be generalized to novel compositions.

When the model takes $x^{(a,o)}$ and $x^{(a,\bar{o})}$ as inputs, we construct a scenario that recognize attribute concept with object as domain. Similarly, with $x^{(a,o)}$ and $x^{(\bar{a},o)}$ as inputs, we construct a scenario that recognize object concept in terms of attribute as domain. Our goal is to recognize an attribute associated with any objects and recognize an object described by any attributes. To improve the generalization performance of the model, we explicitly promote invariance to disentangle spurious features at representation level and gradient level.

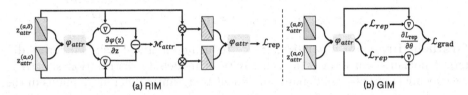

(a) RIM   (b) GIM

Fig. 3. Consider the object-domain branch with the representations $z_{attr}^{(a,o)}$ and $z_{attr}^{(a,\bar{o})}$. (a) In the representation invariant mechanism (RIM), we learn object-irrelevant attribute features at the representation level by filtering out object-specific channels. (b) In the gradient invariant mechanism (GIM), we learn object-irrelevant attribute features at the gradient level by minimizing the distance between gradients of different object domains.

Representation Invariant Learning. To learn an invariant classifier that helps with generalizing to new domain, we explore invariance at the representation level to pull together samples with the same class from different domains in the feature space. In other words, learn a model that maps different domains to a single statistical distribution [2,33].

Firstly, we calculate the gradient of prediction results over the different domains with respect to the representation,

$$g_j^i = \frac{\partial([\varphi_j(z_j^i; \theta_j)]^\top \cdot y_j^i)}{\partial z_j^i}. \tag{3}$$

The representations associated with the similar gradients indicate intrinsic characteristic of attribute concepts that are invariant to object factors or vice versa. Thus we calculate the absolute value of the difference between the two gradients,

$$\Delta g_{attr} = \left| g_{attr}^{(a,o)} - g_{attr}^{(a,\bar{o})} \right|, \quad \Delta g_{obj} = \left| g_{obj}^{(a,o)} - g_{obj}^{(\bar{a},o)} \right|. \tag{4}$$

The semantic channels with small difference can be regarded as object-invariant feature channels of attribute and attribute-invariant feature channels of object. We sort the difference from the largest to the smallest, taking the value at α percent, and denoted as t^α. Then we construct a mask that shares the same dimension with the representation as follows. For the kth element,

$$m_j(k) = \begin{cases} 0, & \text{if } \Delta g_j(k) \geq t^\alpha \\ 1, & \text{else} \end{cases}. \tag{5}$$

By overwriting the mask to the original representation, the network filters out domain-specific feature channels to learn the domain-invariant feature,

$$\hat{z}_j^i = z_j^i \odot m_j. \tag{6}$$

Then we computes the cross entropy loss with the object-irrelevant attribute-specific representation and the attribute-irrelevant object-specific representation,

$$L_{rep} = l(\varphi_{attr}(\hat{z}_{attr}^{(a,o)}; \theta_{attr}), y_{attr}^{(a,o)}) + l(\varphi_{attr}(\hat{z}_{attr}^{(a,\bar{o})}; \theta_{attr}), y_{attr}^{(a,\bar{o})}) \\ + l(\varphi_{obj}(\hat{z}_{obj}^{(a,o)}; \theta_{obj}), y_{obj}^{(a,o)}) + l(\varphi_{obj}(\hat{z}_{obj}^{(\bar{a},o)}; \theta_{obj}), y_{obj}^{(\bar{a},o)}). \tag{7}$$

Gradient Invariant Learning. Since reducing empirical risk [44] across different domains can reduce the sensitivity of models to distribution shift [17], we execute gradient-level domain alignment to optimize different domains in the same direction, which will penalize the network to minimize the dispersion of gradients in different domains to capture invariance. The objective of enhancing gradient consistency is to find local or global minimum in the loss space across all of the training domains and let the network share similar Hessians for different domains [33].

We calculate the gradient of attribute prediction results to attribute classifier in different object domains as well as the gradient of object prediction results to object classifier in different attribute domains as follows,

$$G_j^i = \frac{\partial l(\varphi_j(\hat{z}_j^i; \theta_j), y_j^i)}{\partial \theta_j}. \tag{8}$$

The gradient represents the optimal path. It is easier to obtain invariant predictions in different domains by encouraging the same optimization paths in all domains [35]. In order to align different domains at the gradient level and learn the invariance associated with label, we penalize the domain prediction ability by minimizing the Euclidean distance $d_{euc}(\cdot, \cdot)$ between the two gradients as shown below,

$$L_{grad} = d_{euc}(G_{attr}^{(a,o)}, G_{attr}^{(a,\bar{o})}) + d_{euc}(G_{obj}^{(a,o)}, G_{obj}^{(\bar{a},o)}). \tag{9}$$

We measure the alignment by calculating the Euclidean distances of gradients across different domains. In addition, cosine distance is also considered to measure the alignment of domains in the ablation experiment (see Sect. 4.6).

By introducing these regularizing terms, we can adaptively look for domain-specific channels and discard them, forcing the network to find an invariant relationship between the input image and the label at the representation-level consistency. We also conduct all the domains optimized in the same direction at the gradient-level consistency. Finally, we get decoupled attribute features and object features, which will improve the predictive performance of the model in unseen compositions.

3.4   Training and Inference

For training, we borrow from previous works using the composition classification loss in embedding learning to explore the dependence between attributes and objects,

$$L_{comp} = \sum_{i \in C} h_{comp}(x^i, y^i). \tag{10}$$

Simultaneously, we employ invariant feature learning to decouple attributes and objects to explore their independence. Finally, the objective of optimization can be expressed as,

$$L = L_{comp} + L_{cls} + \lambda_1 L_{rep} + \lambda_2 L_{grad}, \tag{11}$$

where λ_1 and λ_2 are trade-off parameters.

During inference, given an image in the test set, we project it into the common embedding space. The distance between visual embedding features and all candidate pair vectors is calculated and sorted to obtain a pair score predicted in the form of coupling. On the other hand, we use classifiers to predict attributes and objects separately in a decoupled manner and combine the predicted results into a pair score. The final prediction result is obtained by adding the two pair scores, which will improve the performance of the model for both seen and unseen pairs.

4   Experiments

4.1   Datasets

Mit-States [13] and UT-Zappos50K [42] are two benchmark datasets widely used in CZSL task.

After careful observation of the dataset, we also discover three significant problems. First, because Mit-States is labelled automatically using early image search engine technology [3], it contains much noise. For example, there is an image labelled *pierced bear*, but it is actually a brown ceramic pot. Second, the existence of both super-classes and sub-classes in this dataset, such as *animal* and *horse*, as well as *fruit* and *apple*, can create ambiguity. Thirdly, the semantic expression of some attributes is not clear enough. For example, *big bear* and *large bear* are precisely the same from the picture. In light of these issues, we believe that the Mit-States dataset is too noisy to evaluate effectively. Therefore, we use UT-Zappos50K, Clothing16K, and AO-CLEVr for the experiment.

UT-Zappos50K [42] is a fine-grained shoes dataset which contains about 33k images with 12 object classes and 16 attribute classes. The object concepts are mainly the types of shoes (e.g. heels, slippers), while the attribute concepts are mainly the material of shoes (e.g. canvas, leather). Following the generalized evaluation protocol proposed by [29], we test on both seen and unseen pairs. We adopt the standard split from [21, 29], the training set has about 23k images belonging to 83 attribute-object pairs. The validation set has about 3k images consisting of 15 seen pairs and 15 unseen pairs. And the test set has about 3k images consisting of 18 seen pairs and 18 unseen pairs.

Clothing16K[1] was initially a dataset used for multi-label classification in Kaggle competitions with 8 object classes and 9 attribute classes. The object concepts are mainly the types of clothing (e.g. shirt, pants), while the attribute concepts are mainly the clothing colour(e.g. black, green). We find that the attributes and objects of this dataset are very distinct and almost contain no noise, which is very suitable for the CZSL task. Therefore, we split the dataset by ourselves following the generalized ZSL principle [29]. The training set has about 7k images in 18 attribute-object pairs. The validation set consists of 10 seen pairs and 10 unseen pairs with a total of about 5k images. And the test set consists of 9 seen pairs and 8 unseen pairs with a total of about 3k images.

AO-CLEVr [3] is a synthetic dataset consisting of 3 object classes (e.g. sphere, cube, cylinder) and 8 attribute classes (e.g. yellow, gray), with 24 compositional classes in total. We also split the dataset following the generalized ZSL principle [29]. The training set has about 103k images in 16 attribute-object pairs. The validation set consists of 4 seen pairs and 4 unseen pairs with a total of about 39k images. And the test set has about 38k images from 4 seen pairs and 4 unseen pairs.

4.2 Metric

Following [21,29], we test the performance by the accuracy of their top-1 prediction for recognizing seen pairs (*Seen*) and unseen pairs (*Unseen*) in the validation set and test set. To account for the inherent bias towards seen pairs, we follow Chao et al. [7] to add a calibration bias term to the unseen pairs to balance the seen-unseen accuracy. When the calibration value is positive, the prediction accuracy of the unseen pair will be high, and when the calibration value is negative, the model tends to have a bias towards seen pairs. As the candidate value changes, a curve can be drawn with the accuracy of seen pairs on the X-axis and unseen pairs on the Y-axis. We report the Area Under Curve (*AUC*) to evaluate the overall performance. We also consider the best harmonic mean (*HM*) of seen accuracy and unseen accuracy defined as $2(Seen * Unseen)/(Seen + Unseen)$ in this curve, which can penalize the large performance discrepancies between two quantities and as such enables the model to verify performance on both seen and unseen pairs simultaneously.

4.3 Implementation Details

Following [21,29], we use ResNet-18 [11] pretrained on ImageNet [9] as the feature extractor. For a fair comparison with prior works, we do not finetune this network. The extracted 512-dimension features are mapped into a common embedding space through an image embedding function consists of 2 fully-connected layers. Then, we build an attribute disentangler and an object disentangler with a fully-connected layer to map the features into attribute subspace

---

[1] https://www.kaggle.com/kaiska/apparel-dataset.

and object subspace respectively. Finally, an attribute classifier and an object classifier implemented by a fully-connected layer are trained to recognize concepts respectively. Simultaneously, we map concatenated compositional text features into the common embedded space. We use Adam optimizer with a initial learning rate set to 0.001 and a weight decay set to 5×10^{-5}. The λ_1 and λ_2 in Eqs. (11) are respectively set to 1 and 10 in all experiments.

4.4 Compared Methods

We compare our work with several methods.

(1) LE+ [24] uses GloVe [28] word vectors to represent attribute and object concepts and trains the neural network to project the concatenated concept features and visual features to a joint embedding space.
(2) AttrAsOp [24] treats the attribute as a matrix operator and treats the object as a vector. Then conducts attribute-conditioned transformations to learn unseen attribute-object pairs.
(3) SymNet [19] considers the symmetry principle in the attribute-object composition process and introduces group theory as a foundation for axiomatics.
(4) TMN [29] trains a set of network modules jointly with a gating network where the compositional reasoning task is divided into sub-tasks that multiple small networks can solve in a semantic concept space.
(5) CompCos [21] proposes an open world setting where all the compositions of attributes and objects could potentially exist. A feasible strategy is proposed to remove the impossible compositions.
(6) VisProd [20]. Unlike the above methods, VisProd does not model the composition explicitly but imposes attribute classifier and object classifier independently over the image features. The prediction result of a composition is the product of the probability of each element: $P(c) = P(a) \times P(o)$.

4.5 Quantitative Result

We summarize the results for our method and other methods on the three datasets in Table 1. Our method outperforms almost all reported results. Compared with the accuracy of seen pairs, our method improves the accuracy of unseen pairs to a greater extent. This is because our method inevitably loses the spurious correlation between attributes and objects while learning them independently. In other words, it hurts the model's bias against the seen pairs. Although the ability of model to recognize seen pairs is weak, HM and AUC, the metrics of comprehensive recognition ability, increased. The experimental result sufficiently proves the superiority of our proposed method.

Figure 4 shows the unseen-seen accuracy curve on the UT-Zappos50K and Clothing16K dataset. With the increase of calibration value, the classification accuracy of seen pairs decreases while that of unseen pairs increases. This is a general and essential trade-off when learning models that are robust for interventions [32]. Compared to other methods, our method keeps a better balance

Table 1. Comparative experiment between recent methods with our method on UT-Zappos50K, Clothing16K, and AO-CLEVr.

Method	UT-Zappos50K				Clothing16K				AO-CLEVr			
	Seen	Unseen	HM	AUC	Seen	Unseen	HM	AUC	Seen	Unseen	HM	AUC
LE+ [24]	53.0	61.9	41.0	25.7	93.9	88.3	77.4	76.0	95.7	99.2	92.3	93.5
AttrAsOp [24]	59.8	54.2	40.8	25.9	95.1	80.1	60.0	58.7	95.5	85.5	64.8	65.8
SymNet [19]	49.8	57.4	40.4	23.4	95.7	90.2	73.4	75.2	87.1	97.8	71.8	74.2
VisProd [20]	56.6	60.2	43.7	28.1	96.4	91.4	74.7	77.5	91.9	98.2	71.3	75.6
TMN [29]	58.7	60.0	45.0	29.3	94.9	89.7	80.9	79.5	96.1	93.9	86.9	87.1
CompCos [21]	**59.8**	62.5	43.1	28.7	96.9	93.0	83.9	84.7	96.3	99.1	94.5	94.2
Ours	56.9	**65.5**	**46.2**	**30.6**	**96.9**	**94.6**	**86.3**	**87.0**	**97.1**	**99.3**	**95.1**	**95.6**

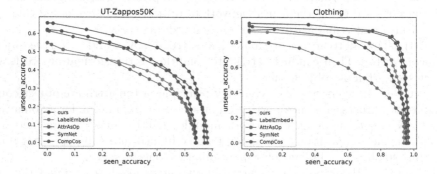

Fig. 4. Unseen-seen accuracy on UT-Zappos50K and Clothing16K under various calibration biases.

between seen and unseen pairs on both datasets, which leads to better performance.

Overall, the results on these challenging datasets strongly support our idea of leveraging invariant mechanisms to decouple attributes and objects effectively. Learning attributes and objects in a decoupled way may discourage certain types of correlations [3], so the model can not benefit from them when the test and training distributions are the same, that is, recognizing seen pairs. However, when recognizing unseen pairs, where the test and training distributions are different, our method of improving generalization performance can come into play without taking advantage of these spurious correlations.

4.6   Ablation Study

To verify the effect of each proposed component, we conduct ablation experiments on the UT-Zappos50K and Clothing16K datasets. As shown in Table 2, when only compositional classification loss (denoted as "L_{comp}") is applied, the model have a positive bias towards the seen pairs because of the dependence between objects and attributes. When the concepts are learned in a decoupled way using attribute and object classifiers (denoted as "L_{cls}"), the model is

Table 2. Analysis of each component on UT-Zappos50K and Clothing16K.

Method	UT-Zappos50K				Clothing16K			
	Seen	Unseen	HM	AUC	Seen	Unseen	HM	AUC
L_{comp}	**58.4**	58.0	43.5	27.8	96.9	91.8	81.6	82.9
L_{cls}	56.0	63.5	44.0	27.7	95.1	93.5	82.2	83.2
$L_{cls}+L_{comp}$	57.0	63.4	44.2	28.8	96.2	93.7	84.7	84.8
$L_{cls}+L_{comp}+L_{rep}$	55.9	65.5	45.3	29.8	96.7	94.0	85.3	85.3
$L_{cls}+L_{comp}+L_{grad}$	56.6	64.4	46.1	30.0	**97.2**	94.2	85.6	86.3
$L_{cls}+L_{comp}+L_{rep}+L_{grad}$	56.9	**65.5**	**46.2**	**30.6**	96.9	**94.6**	**86.3**	**87.0**

Table 3. Analysis of parameter α on UT-Zappos50K and Clothing16K.

α	UT-Zappos50K				Clothing16K			
	Seen	Unseen	HM	AUC	Seen	Unseen	HM	AUC
1/6	56.9	**65.5**	**46.2**	**30.6**	96.8	94.4	86.4	86.6
1/4	56.3	65.0	45.5	29.9	**96.9**	**94.6**	86.3	**87.0**
1/3	**57.5**	63.4	45.2	29.2	96.8	94.5	86.4	86.6
1/2	53.6	65.4	44.4	28.5	96.8	93.9	**86.7**	86.5

Table 4. Analysis of distance function on UT-Zappos50K and Clothing16K.

Distance Function	UT-Zappos50K				Clothing16K			
	Seen	Unseen	HM	AUC	Seen	Unseen	HM	AUC
Euclidean	56.9	**65.5**	**46.2**	**30.6**	96.9	94.6	**86.3**	**87.0**
Cosine	**58.3**	62.6	44.2	28.6	96.7	94.3	85.0	85.9

biased towards unseen pairs since the correlation between attributes and objects is removed. The utilization of representation invariant mechanism (denoted as "L_{rep}") can help the model to discard domain-specific spurious features at the representation level, thus improving the performance of the model. When the gradient invariant mechanism (denoted as "L_{grad}") is employed, the gradients of different domains are optimized in the same direction. Through these two invariant learning mechanisms, the model can learn the optimal attribute classifier and object classifier, which remarkably improves the comprehensive performance of the model.

Effect of Parameter α. The scale parameter α is employed to control the proportion of discarding in Eqs. (5). We select α in $\{\frac{1}{6}, \frac{1}{4}, \frac{1}{3}, \frac{1}{2}\}$ and report the performance of the model in Table 3. For the UT-Zappos50K dataset, the optimal performances can be observed when α is set to $\frac{1}{6}$. For the Clothing16K dataset, the optimal performances can be observed when α is set to $\frac{1}{4}$. A suitable α

Fig. 5. Qualitative results of retrieving *nubuck sandals, leather sandals, nubuck ankle-boots, leather ankle-boots* in UT-Zappos50K and *black dress, blue dress, red hoodie, pink hoodie* in Clothing16K.

can subtly discard domain-specific features and help the model generalize from known concepts to unseen ones by using domain-invariant features.

Effect of distance function. In the gradient invariant mechanism, we use Euclidean distance to measure the distance between gradients in different domains. In addition, our method also works with cosine distance. As shown in Table 4, the performance of Euclidean distance is better than cosine distance, probably because we pay more attention to the absolute numerical differences between gradients.

4.7 Image Retrieval

To qualitatively evaluate our method, we further report image retrieval results. Figure 5 shows examples of retrieving images. The query is made up of attribute text and object text. We choose compositions of different objects with the same attribute and compositions of different attributes with the same object. For UT-Zappos50K and Clothing16K datasets, our method can retrieve a certain number of correct samples in the top-5, indicating that our method can solve the combinatorial generalization problem.

5 Conclusions

In reality, there are many situations where data distribution is different during training and testing. Inspired by the idea of exploring domain invariance in the DG task, we propose the representation invariant mechanism and gradient invariant mechanism to find essential features of attributes and objects, and finally learn attribute and object classifiers that can be generalized to any new composition. The limitation of our method is that it can be challenging to decouple attributes or objects when they can only form one composition in the training set. At this point, the model is more likely to overfit to the seen pairs.

In the future, we will delve into studying the core features of such concepts. Besides, we will also explore the application of generalization ideas to multiple sub-concept composition scenarios and even other avenues of research.

Acknowledgement. This work was supported in part by National Natural Science Foundation of China (NSFC) No. 61922015, 62106022, U19B2036, and in part by Beijing Natural Science Foundation Project No. Z200002.

References

1. Ahuja, K., et al.: Invariance principle meets information bottleneck for out-of-distribution generalization. NeurIPS **34**, 3438–3450 (2021)
2. Arjovsky, M., Bottou, L., Gulrajani, I., Lopez-Paz, D.: Invariant risk minimization. arXiv preprint arXiv:1907.02893 (2019)
3. Atzmon, Y., Kreuk, F., Shalit, U., Chechik, G.: A causal view of compositional zero-shot recognition. NeurIPS **33**, 1462–1473 (2021)
4. Bengio, Y., et al.: A meta-transfer objective for learning to disentangle causal mechanisms. arXiv preprint arXiv:1901.10912 (2019)
5. Blanchard, G., Lee, G., Scott, C.: Generalizing from several related classification tasks to a new unlabeled sample. NeurIPS (2011)
6. Carlucci, F.M., D'Innocente, A., Bucci, S., Caputo, B., Tommasi, T.: Domain generalization by solving jigsaw puzzles. In: CVPR (2020)
7. Chao, W.-L., Changpinyo, S., Gong, B., Sha, F.: An empirical study and analysis of generalized zero-shot learning for object recognition in the wild. In: Leibe, B., Matas, J., Sebe, N., Welling, M. (eds.) ECCV 2016. LNCS, vol. 9906, pp. 52–68. Springer, Cham (2016). https://doi.org/10.1007/978-3-319-46475-6_4
8. Chen, C.Y., Grauman, K.: Inferring analogous attributes. In: CVPR, pp. 200–207 (2014)
9. Deng, J., Dong, W., Socher, R., Li, L.J., Li, K., Fei-Fei, L.: ImageNet: a large-scale hierarchical image database. In: CVPR, pp. 248–255 (2009)
10. Geirhos, R., Rubisch, P., Michaelis, C., Bethge, M., Wichmann, F.A., Brendel, W.: ImageNet-trained CNNs are biased towards texture; increasing shape bias improves accuracy and robustness. arXiv preprint arXiv:1811.12231 (2018)
11. He, K., Zhang, X., Ren, S., Sun, J.: Deep residual learning for image recognition. In: CVPR, pp. 770–778 (2016)
12. Huang, Z., Wang, H., Xing, E.P., Huang, D.: Self-challenging improves cross-domain generalization. In: Vedaldi, A., Bischof, H., Brox, T., Frahm, J.-M. (eds.) ECCV 2020. LNCS, vol. 12347, pp. 124–140. Springer, Cham (2020). https://doi.org/10.1007/978-3-030-58536-5_8
13. Isola, P., Lim, J.J., Adelson, E.H.: Discovering states and transformations in image collections. In: CVPR, pp. 1383–1391 (2015)
14. Khezeli, K., Blaas, A., Soboczenski, F., Chia, N., Kalantari, J.: On invariance penalties for risk minimization. arXiv preprint arXiv:2106.09777 (2021)
15. Kim, D., Yoo, Y., Park, S., Kim, J., Lee, J.: Selfreg: self-supervised contrastive regularization for domain generalization. In: ICCV, pp. 9619–9628 (2021)
16. Koyama, M., Yamaguchi, S.: Out-of-distribution generalization with maximal invariant predictor. ICLR (2021)
17. Krueger, D., et al.: Out-of-distribution generalization via risk extrapolation (rex). In: ICML, pp. 5815–5826 (2021)

18. Li, H., Pan, S.J., Wang, S., Kot, A.C.: Domain generalization with adversarial feature learning. In: CVPR (2018)
19. Li, Y.L., Xu, Y., Mao, X., Lu, C.: Symmetry and group in attribute-object compositions. In: CVPR (2020)
20. Lu, C., Krishna, R., Bernstein, M., Fei-Fei, L.: Visual relationship detection with language priors. In: Leibe, B., Matas, J., Sebe, N., Welling, M. (eds.) ECCV 2016. LNCS, vol. 9905, pp. 852–869. Springer, Cham (2016). https://doi.org/10.1007/978-3-319-46448-0_51
21. Mancini, M., Naeem, M.F., Xian, Y., Akata, Z.: Open world compositional zero-shot learning. In: CVPR (2021)
22. Misra, I., Gupta, A., Hebert, M.: From red wine to red tomato: composition with context. In: CVPR, pp. 1160–1169 (2017)
23. Muandet, K., Balduzzi, D., Schölkopf, B.: Domain generalization via invariant feature representation. In: ICML, pp. 10–18 (2013)
24. Nagarajan, T., Grauman, K.: Attributes as operators: factorizing unseen attribute-object compositions. In: ECCV (2018)
25. Palatucci, M., Pomerleau, D., Hinton, G.E., Mitchell, T.M.: Zero-shot learning with semantic output codes. NeurIPS (2009)
26. Parascandolo, G., Neitz, A., Orvieto, A., Gresele, L., Schölkopf, B.: Learning explanations that are hard to vary. arXiv preprint arXiv:2009.00329 (2020)
27. Peng, X., Huang, Z., Sun, X., Saenko, K.: Domain agnostic learning with disentangled representations. In: ICML, pp. 5102–5112 (2019)
28. Pennington, J., Socher, R., Manning, C.D.: Glove: global vectors for word representation. In: EMNLP, pp. 1532–1543 (2014)
29. Purushwalkam, S., Nickel, M., Gupta, A., Ranzato, M.: Task-driven modular networks for zero-shot compositional learning. In: ICCV (2019)
30. Qiao, F., Zhao, L., Peng, X.: Learning to learn single domain generalization. In: CVPR (2020)
31. Quiñonero-Candela, J., Sugiyama, M., Schwaighofer, A., Lawrence, N.D.: Dataset Shift in Machine Learning. MIT Press (2008)
32. Rothenhäusler, D., Meinshausen, N., Bühlmann, P., Peters, J.: Anchor regression: heterogeneous data meet causality. J. Royal Stat. Soc.: Ser. B (Stat. Methodol.) **83**(2), 215–246 (2021)
33. Shahtalebi, S., Gagnon-Audet, J.C., Laleh, T., Faramarzi, M., Ahuja, K., Rish, I.: Sand-mask: an enhanced gradient masking strategy for the discovery of invariances in domain generalization. arXiv preprint arXiv:2106.02266 (2021)
34. Shankar, S., Piratla, V., Chakrabarti, S., Chaudhuri, S., Jyothi, P., Sarawagi, S.: Generalizing across domains via cross-gradient training. arXiv preprint arXiv:1804.10745 (2018)
35. Shi, Y., et al.: Gradient matching for domain generalization. arXiv preprint arXiv:2104.09937 (2021)
36. Sun, B., Saenko, K.: Deep CORAL: correlation alignment for deep domain adaptation. In: Hua, G., Jégou, H. (eds.) ECCV 2016. LNCS, vol. 9915, pp. 443–450. Springer, Cham (2016). https://doi.org/10.1007/978-3-319-49409-8_35
37. Tolstikhin, I., Bousquet, O., Gelly, S., Schoelkopf, B.: Wasserstein auto-encoders. arXiv preprint arXiv:1711.01558 (2017)
38. Wang, J., Lan, C., Liu, C., Ouyang, Y., Zeng, W., Qin, T.: Generalizing to unseen domains: a survey on domain generalization. arXiv preprint arXiv:2103.03097 (2021)

39. Wei, K., Yang, M., Wang, H., Deng, C., Liu, X.: Adversarial fine-grained composition learning for unseen attribute-object recognition. In: ICCV, pp. 3741–3749 (2019)
40. Xian, Y., Lorenz, T., Schiele, B., Akata, Z.: Feature generating networks for zero-shot learning. In: CVPR, pp. 5542–5551 (2018)
41. Xian, Y., Schiele, B., Akata, Z.: Zero-shot learning-the good, the bad and the ugly. In: CVPR, pp. 4582–4591 (2017)
42. Yu, A., Grauman, K.: Fine-grained visual comparisons with local learning. In: CVPR, pp. 192–199 (2014)
43. Zhang, H., Zhang, Y.F., Liu, W., Weller, A., Schölkopf, B., Xing, E.P.: Towards principled disentanglement for domain generalization. arXiv preprint arXiv:2111.13839 (2021)
44. Zhang, H., Cisse, M., Dauphin, Y.N., Lopez-Paz, D.: mixup: beyond empirical risk minimization. arXiv preprint arXiv:1710.09412 (2017)
45. Zhou, K., Liu, Z., Qiao, Y., Xiang, T., Change Loy, C.: Domain generalization: a survey. arXiv preprint arXiv:2103.02503 (2021)

Improving Covariance Conditioning of the SVD Meta-layer by Orthogonality

Yue Song$^{(\boxtimes)}$ (iD), Nicu Sebe, and Wei Wang

DISI, University of Trento, 38123 Trento, Italy
yue.song@unitn.it
https://github.com/KingJamesSong/OrthoImproveCond

Abstract. Inserting an SVD meta-layer into neural networks is prone to make the covariance ill-conditioned, which could harm the model in the training stability and generalization abilities. In this paper, we systematically study how to improve the covariance conditioning by enforcing orthogonality to the Pre-SVD layer. Existing orthogonal treatments on the weights are first investigated. However, these techniques can improve the conditioning but would hurt the performance. To avoid such a side effect, we propose the Nearest Orthogonal Gradient (NOG) and Optimal Learning Rate (OLR). The effectiveness of our methods is validated in two applications: decorrelated Batch Normalization (BN) and Global Covariance Pooling (GCP). Extensive experiments on visual recognition demonstrate that our methods can simultaneously improve the covariance conditioning and generalization. Moreover, the combinations with orthogonal weight can further boost the performances.

Keywords: Differentiable SVD · Covariance conditioning · Orthogonality constraint

1 Introduction

The Singular Value Decomposition (SVD) can factorize a matrix into orthogonal eigenbases and non-negative singular values, serving as an essential step for many matrix operations. Recently in computer vision and deep learning, many approaches integrated the SVD as a meta-layer in the neural networks to perform some differentiable spectral transformations, such as the matrix square root and inverse square root. The applications arise in a wide range of methods, including Global Covariance Pooling (GCP) [13,29,44], decorrelated Batch Normalization (BN) [20,22,45], Whitening an Coloring Transform (WCT) for universal style transfer [8,30,55], and Perspective-n-Point (PnP) problems [4,6,11].

For the input feature map $\mathbf{X}$ passed to the SVD meta-layer, one often first computes the covariance of the feature as $\mathbf{X}\mathbf{X}^T$. This can ensure that the covariance matrix is both symmetric and positive semi-definite, which does not involve

---

Supplementary Information The online version contains supplementary material available at https://doi.org/10.1007/978-3-031-20053-3_21.

any negative eigenvalues and leads to the identical left and right eigenvector matrices. However, it is observed that inserting the SVD layer into deep models would typically make the covariance very ill-conditioned [44], resulting in deleterious consequences on the stability and optimization of the training process. For a given covariance $\mathbf{A}$, its conditioning is measured by the condition number:

$$\kappa(\mathbf{A}) = \sigma_{max}(\mathbf{A})\sigma_{min}^{-1}(\mathbf{A}) \tag{1}$$

where $\sigma(\cdot)$ denotes the eigenvalue of the matrix. Mathematically speaking, the condition number measures how sensitive the SVD is to the errors of the input. Matrices with low condition numbers are considered **well-conditioned**, while matrices with high condition numbers are said to be **ill-conditioned**. Specific to neural networks, the ill-conditioned covariance matrices are harmful to the training process in several aspects, which we will analyze in detail later.

This phenomenon was first observed in the GCP methods by [44], and we found that it generally extrapolates to other SVD-related tasks, such as decorrelated BN. Figure 1 depicts the covariance conditioning of these two tasks throughout the training. As can be seen, the integration of the SVD layer makes the generated covariance very ill-conditioned ($\approx 1e12$ for decorrelated BN and $\approx 1e16$ for GCP). By contrast, the conditioning of the approximate solver (Newton-Schulz iteration [19]) is about $1e5$ for decorrelated BN and is around $1e15$ for GCP, while the standard BN only has a condition number of $1e3$.

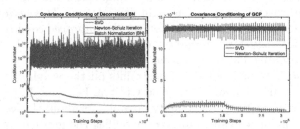

Fig. 1. The covariance conditioning of the SVD meta-layer during the training process in the tasks of decorrelated BN (*left*) and GCP (*Right*). The decorrelated BN is based on ResNet-50 and CIFAR100, while ImageNet and ResNet-18 are used for the GCP.

Ill-conditioned covariance matrices can harm the training of the network in both the forward pass (FP) and the backward pass (BP). For the FP, mainly the SVD solver is influenced in terms of stability and accuracy. Since the ill-conditioned covariance has many trivially-small eigenvalues, it is difficult for an SVD solver to accurately estimate them and large round-off errors are likely to be triggered, which might hurt the network performances. Moreover, the very imbalanced eigenvalue distribution can easily make the SVD solver fail to converge and cause the training failure [44,54]. For the BP, as pointed out in [20,27,56], the feature covariance is closely related to the Hessian matrix during the backpropagation. Since the error curvature is given by the eigenvalues of the Hessian matrix [48], for the ill-conditioned Hessian, the Gradient Descent (GD) step would bounce back and forth in high curvature directions (large eigenvalues) and make slow progress in low curvature directions (small eigenvalues). As a consequence, the ill-conditioned covariance could cause slow convergence and oscillations in the optimization landscape. The generalization abilities of a deep model are thus harmed.

Due to the data-driven learning nature and the highly non-linear transform of deep neural networks, directly giving the analytical form of the covariance conditioning is intractable. Some simplifications have to be performed to ease the investigation. Since the covariance is generated and passed from the previous layer, the previous layer is likely to be the most relevant to the conditioning. Therefore, we naturally limit our focus to the Pre-SVD layer, *i.e.*, the layer before the SVD layer. To further simplify the analysis, we study the Pre-SVD layer in two consecutive training steps, which can be considered as a mimic of the whole training process. Throughout the paper, we mainly investigate some meaningful manipulations on the weight, the gradient, and the learning rate of the Pre-SVD layer in two sequential training steps. *Under our Pre-SVD layer simplifications, one promising direction to improve the conditioning is enforcing orthogonality on the weights.* Orthogonal weights have the norm-preserving property, which could improve the conditioning of the feature matrix. This technique has been widely studied in the literature of stable training and Lipschitz networks [33,43,52]. We select some representative methods and validate their effectiveness in the task of decorrelated BN. Our experiment reveals that these orthogonal techniques can greatly improve the covariance conditioning, but could only bring marginal performance improvements and even slight degradation. *This indicates that when the representation power of weight is limited, the improved conditioning does not necessarily lead to better performance. Orthogonalizing only the weight is thus insufficient to improve the generalization.*

Instead of seeking orthogonality constraints on the weights, we propose our Nearest Orthogonal Gradient (NOG) and Optimal Learning Rate (OLR). These two techniques explore the orthogonality possibilities about the learning rate and the gradient. More specifically, our NOG modifies the gradient of the Pre-SVD layer into its nearest-orthogonal form and keeps the GD direction unchanged. On the other hand, the proposed OLR dynamically changes the learning rate of the Pre-SVD layer at each training step such that the updated weight is as close to an orthogonal matrix as possible. The experimental results demonstrate that the proposed two techniques not only significantly improve the covariance conditioning but also bring obvious improvements in the validation accuracy of both GCP and decorrelated BN. Moreover, when combined with the orthogonal weight treatments, the performance can have further improvements.

The main contributions and findings are summarized below:

- We systematically study the problem of how to improve the covariance conditioning of the SVD meta-layer. We propose our Pre-SVD layer simplification to investigate this problem from the perspective of orthogonal constraints.
- We explore different techniques of orthogonal weights to improve the covariance conditioning. Our experiments reveal that these techniques could improve the conditioning but would harm the generalization abilities due to the limitation on the representation power of weight.

- We propose the nearest orthogonal gradient and optimal learning rate. The experiments on GCP and decorrelated BN demonstrate that these methods can attain better covariance conditioning and improved generalization. Their combinations with weight treatments can further boost the performance.

2   Related Work

In this section, we introduce the related work in differentiable matrix decomposition and the orthogonality in neural networks which could be relevant in improving the covariance conditioning.

2.1   Differentiable Matrix Decomposition

The differentiable matrix decomposition is widely used in neural networks as a spectral meta-layer. Ionescu *et al.* [24,25] first propose the theory of matrix back-propagation and laid a foundation for the follow-up research. In deep neural networks, the transformation of matrix square root and its inverse are often desired due to the appealing spectral property. Their applications cover a wide range of computer vision tasks [45,46]. To avoid the huge time consumption of the SVD, some iterative methods are also developed to approximate the solution [19,45,46]. In [8,20–23,45], the inverse square root is used in the ZCA whitening transform to whiten the feature map, which is also known as the decorrelated BN. The Global Covariance Pooling (GCP) models [13,28,29,44,47,53,58] compute the matrix square root of the covariance as a spectral normalization, which achieves impressive performances on some recognition tasks, including large-scale visual classification [29,44,45,58], fine-grained visual categorization [28,29,47], and video action recognition [13]. The Whitening and Coloring Transform (WCT), which uses both the matrix square root and inverse square root, is usually adopted in some image generation tasks such as neural style transfer [30,55], image translation [9,51], and domain adaptation [1,10]. In the geometric vision problems, the differentiable SVD is usually applied to estimate the fundamental matrix and the camera pose [6,11,38]. Besides the SVD-based factorization, differentiating Cholesky decomposition [35] and some low-rank decomposition is used to approximate the attention mechanism [14,31,59] or to learn the constrained representations [7,60].

2.2   Orthogonality in Neural Network

Orthogonal weights have the benefit of the norm-preserving property, *i.e.,* the relation $\|\mathbf{WA}\|_F = \|\mathbf{A}\|_F$ holds for any orthogonal $\mathbf{W}$. When it comes to deep neural networks, such a property can ensure that the signal stably propagates through deep networks without either exploding or vanishing gradients [3,15], which could speed up convergence and encourage robustness and generalization. In general, there are three ways to enforce orthogonality to a layer: orthogonal weight initialization [33,40,57], orthogonal regularization [2,37,39,52], and explicit orthogonal weight via Carley transform or matrix exponential [32,43,49]. Among these techniques, orthogonal regularization and orthogonal weight are most commonly used as they often bring some practical improvements in generalization. Since the covariance is closely related to the weight matrix of the Pre-SVD layer, enforcing the orthogonality constraint could help to improve the covariance conditioning of the SVD meta-layer. We will choose some representative methods and validate their impact in Sect. 4.2.

Notice that the focus of existing literature is different from our work. The orthogonality constraints are often used to improve the Lipschitz constants of the neural network layers, which is expected to improve the visual quality in image generation [5,34], to allow for better adversarial robustness [43,50], and to improve generalization abilities [41,52]. Our work is concerned with improving the covariance conditioning and generalization performance. Moreover, the orthogonality literature mainly investigates how to enforce orthogonality to weight matrices, whereas less attention is put on the gradient and learning rate. In Sect. 5, we will explore such possibilities and propose our solutions: nearest orthogonal gradient and optimal learning rate which is optimal in the sense that the updated weight is as close to an orthogonal matrix as possible.

3   Background: SVD Meta-layer

This section presents the background knowledge about the propagation rules of the SVD meta-layer.

3.1   Forward Pass

Given the reshape feature $\mathbf{X} \in \mathbb{R}^{d \times N}$ where d denotes the feature dimensionality (*i.e.*, the number of channels) and N represents the number of features (*i.e.*, the product of spatial dimensions of features), an SVD meta-layer first computes the sample covariance as:

$$\mathbf{P} = \mathbf{XJX}^T, \mathbf{J} = \frac{1}{N}(\mathbf{I} - \frac{1}{N}\mathbf{11}^T) \tag{2}$$

where $\mathbf{J}$ represents the centering matrix, $\mathbf{I}$ denotes the identity matrix, and $\mathbf{1}$ is a column vector whose values are all ones, respectively. The covariance is always positive semi-definite (PSD) and does not have any negative eigenvalues. Afterward, the eigendecomposition is performed using the SVD:

$$\mathbf{P} = \mathbf{U\Lambda U}^T, \ \mathbf{\Lambda} = \text{diag}(\lambda_1, \ldots, \lambda_d) \tag{3}$$

where $\mathbf{U}$ is the orthogonal eigenvector matrix, $\text{diag}(\cdot)$ denotes transforming a vector to a diagonal matrix, and $\mathbf{\Lambda}$ is the diagonal matrix in which the eigenvalues are sorted in a non-increasing order *i.e.*, $\lambda_i \geq \lambda_{i+1}$. Then depending on the application, the matrix square root or the inverse square root is calculated as:

$$\mathbf{Q} \triangleq \mathbf{P}^{\frac{1}{2}} = \mathbf{U\Lambda}^{\frac{1}{2}}\mathbf{U}^T, \mathbf{\Lambda}^{\frac{1}{2}} = \text{diag}(\lambda_1^{\frac{1}{2}}, \ldots, \lambda_d^{\frac{1}{2}})$$
$$\mathbf{S} \triangleq \mathbf{P}^{-\frac{1}{2}} = \mathbf{U\Lambda}^{-\frac{1}{2}}\mathbf{U}^T, \mathbf{\Lambda}^{-\frac{1}{2}} = \text{diag}(\lambda_1^{-\frac{1}{2}}, \ldots, \lambda_d^{-\frac{1}{2}}) \tag{4}$$

The matrix square root $\mathbf{Q}$ is often used in GCP-related tasks [29,44,58], while the application of decorrelated BN [20,42] widely applies the inverse square root $\mathbf{S}$. In certain applications such as WCT, both $\mathbf{Q}$ and $\mathbf{S}$ are required.

3.2   Backward Pass

Let $\frac{\partial l}{\partial \mathbf{Q}}$ and $\frac{\partial l}{\partial \mathbf{S}}$ denote the partial derivative of the loss l w.r.t to the matrix square root $\mathbf{Q}$ and the inverse square root $\mathbf{S}$, respectively. Then the gradient passed to the eigenvector is computed as:

$$\frac{\partial l}{\partial \mathbf{U}}\Big|_{\mathbf{Q}} = (\frac{\partial l}{\partial \mathbf{Q}} + (\frac{\partial l}{\partial \mathbf{Q}})^T)\mathbf{U}\mathbf{\Lambda}^{\frac{1}{2}}, \quad \frac{\partial l}{\partial \mathbf{U}}\Big|_{\mathbf{S}} = (\frac{\partial l}{\partial \mathbf{S}} + (\frac{\partial l}{\partial \mathbf{S}})^T)\mathbf{U}\mathbf{\Lambda}^{-\frac{1}{2}} \tag{5}$$

Notice that the gradient equations for $\mathbf{Q}$ and $\mathbf{S}$ are different. For the eigenvalue, the gradient is calculated as:

$$\frac{\partial l}{\partial \mathbf{\Lambda}}\Big|_{\mathbf{Q}} = \frac{1}{2}\mathrm{diag}(\lambda_1^{-\frac{1}{2}},\dots,\lambda_d^{-\frac{1}{2}})\mathbf{U}^T\frac{\partial l}{\partial \mathbf{Q}}\mathbf{U}, \quad \frac{\partial l}{\partial \mathbf{\Lambda}}\Big|_{\mathbf{S}} = -\frac{1}{2}\mathrm{diag}(\lambda_1^{-\frac{3}{2}},\dots,\lambda_d^{-\frac{3}{2}})\mathbf{U}^T\frac{\partial l}{\partial \mathbf{S}}\mathbf{U}$$
$$\tag{6}$$

Subsequently, the derivative of the SVD step can be calculated as:

$$\frac{\partial l}{\partial \mathbf{P}} = \mathbf{U}((\mathbf{K}^T \circ (\mathbf{U}^T\frac{\partial l}{\partial \mathbf{U}})) + (\frac{\partial l}{\partial \mathbf{\Lambda}})_{\mathrm{diag}})\mathbf{U}^T \tag{7}$$

where $\circ$ denotes the matrix Hadamard product, and the matrix $\mathbf{K}$ consists of entries $K_{ij} = 1/(\lambda_i - \lambda_j)$ if $i \neq j$ and $K_{ij} = 0$ otherwise. This step is the same for both $\mathbf{Q}$ and $\mathbf{S}$. Finally, we have the gradient passed to the feature $\mathbf{X}$ as:

$$\frac{\partial l}{\partial \mathbf{X}} = (\frac{\partial l}{\partial \mathbf{P}} + (\frac{\partial l}{\partial \mathbf{P}})^T)\mathbf{X}\mathbf{J} \tag{8}$$

With the above rules, the SVD function can be easily inserted into any neural networks and trained end-to-end as a meta-layer.

4   Pre-SVD Layer and Weight Treatments

In this section, we first motivate our simplification of the Pre-SVD layer, and then validate the efficacy of some representative weight treatments.

4.1   Pre-SVD Layer Simplification

The neural network consists of a sequential of non-linear layers where the learning of each layer is data-driven. Stacking these layers leads to a highly non-linear and complex transform, which makes directly analyzing the covariance conditioning intractable. To solve this issue, we have to perform some simplifications.

Our simplifications involve limiting the analysis only to the layer previous to the SVD layer (which we dub as the Pre-SVD layer) in two consecutive training steps. The Pre-SVD layer directly determines the conditioning of the generated covariance, while the two successive training steps are a mimic of the whole training process. The idea is to simplify the complex transform by analyzing the sub-model (two layers) and the sub-training (two steps), which can be considered as an "abstract representation" of the deep model and its complete training.

Let $\mathbf{W}$ denote the weight matrix of the Pre-SVD layer. Then for the input $\mathbf{X}_l$ passed to the layer, we have:

$$\mathbf{X}_{l+1} = \mathbf{W}\mathbf{X}_l + \mathbf{b} \tag{9}$$

where $\mathbf{X}_{l+1}$ is the feature passed to the SVD layer, and $\mathbf{b}$ is the bias vector. Since the bias $\mathbf{b}$ has a little influence here, we can sufficiently omit it for simplicity. The covariance in this step is computed as $\mathbf{W}\mathbf{X}_l\mathbf{X}_l^T\mathbf{W}^T$. After the BP, the weight matrix is updated as $\mathbf{W} - \eta\frac{\partial l}{\partial \mathbf{W}}$ where η denotes the learning rate of the layer. Let $\mathbf{Y}_l$ denote the passed-in feature of the next training step. Then the covariance is calculated as:

$$
\begin{aligned}
\mathbf{C} &= \left((\mathbf{W} - \eta\frac{\partial l}{\partial \mathbf{W}}) \cdot \mathbf{Y}_l\right)\left((\mathbf{W} - \eta\frac{\partial l}{\partial \mathbf{W}}) \cdot \mathbf{Y}_l\right)^T \\
&= (\mathbf{W} - \eta\frac{\partial l}{\partial \mathbf{W}})\mathbf{Y}_l\mathbf{Y}_l^T(\mathbf{W} - \eta\frac{\partial l}{\partial \mathbf{W}})^T \\
&= \mathbf{W}\mathbf{Y}_l\mathbf{Y}_l^T\mathbf{W}^T - \eta\frac{\partial l}{\partial \mathbf{W}}\mathbf{Y}_l\mathbf{Y}_l^T\mathbf{W}^T - \eta\mathbf{W}\mathbf{Y}_l\mathbf{Y}_l^T(\frac{\partial l}{\partial \mathbf{W}})^T + \eta^2\frac{\partial l}{\partial \mathbf{W}}\mathbf{Y}_l\mathbf{Y}_l^T(\frac{\partial l}{\partial \mathbf{W}})^T
\end{aligned}
\tag{10}
$$

where $\mathbf{C}$ denotes the generated covariance of the second step. Now the problem becomes how to stop the new covariance $\mathbf{C}$ from becoming worse-conditioned than $\mathbf{W}\mathbf{X}_l\mathbf{X}_l^T\mathbf{W}^T$. In Eq. (10), three variables could influence the conditioning: the weight $\mathbf{W}$, the gradient of the last step $\frac{\partial l}{\partial \mathbf{W}}$, and the learning rate η of this layer. Among them, the weight $\mathbf{W}$ seems to be the most important as it contributes to three terms of Eq. (10). Moreover, the first term $\mathbf{W}\mathbf{Y}_l\mathbf{Y}_l^T\mathbf{W}^T$ computed by $\mathbf{W}$ is not attenuated by η or η^2 like the other terms. Therefore, it is natural to first consider manipulating $\mathbf{W}$ such that the conditioning of $\mathbf{C}$ could be improved.

4.2   General Treatments on Weights

In the literature of enforcing orthogonality to the neural network, there are several techniques to improve the conditioning of the weight $\mathbf{W}$. Now we introduce some representatives methods and validate their impacts.

Spectral Normalization (SN). In [34], the authors propose a normalization method to stabilize the training of generative models [16] by dividing the weight matrix with its largest eigenvalue. The process is defined as:

$$\mathbf{W}/\sigma_{max}(\mathbf{W}) \tag{11}$$

Such a normalization can ensure that the spectral radius of $\mathbf{W}$ is always 1, i.e., $\sigma_{max}(\mathbf{W}) = 1$. This could help to reduce the conditioning of the covariance since we have $\sigma_{max}(\mathbf{W}\mathbf{Y}_l) = \sigma_{max}(\mathbf{Y}_l)$ after the spectral normalization.

Orthogonal Loss (OL). Besides limiting the spectral radius of $\mathbf{W}$, enforcing orthogonality constraint could also improve the covariance conditioning. As orthogonal matrices are norm-preserving (*i.e.*, $||\mathbf{W}\mathbf{Y}_l||_F = ||\mathbf{W}||_F$), lots of methods have been proposed to encourage orthogonality on weight matrices for more stable training and better signal-preserving property [2,36,43,49,52]. One common technique is to apply *soft* orthogonality [52] by the following regularization:

$$l = ||\mathbf{W}\mathbf{W}^T - \mathbf{I}||_F \tag{12}$$

This extra loss is added in the optimization objective to encourage more orthogonal weight matrices. However, since the constraint is achieved by regularization, the weight matrix is not exactly orthogonal at each training step.

Orthogonal Weights (OW). Instead of applying *soft* orthogonality by regularization, some methods can explicitly enforce *hard* orthogonality to the weight matrices [43,49]. The technique of [43] is built on the mathematical property: for any skew-symmetric matrix, its matrix exponential is an orthogonal matrix.

$$\exp(\mathbf{W} - \mathbf{W}^T)\exp(\mathbf{W} - \mathbf{W}^T)^T = \mathbf{I} \tag{13}$$

where the operation of $\mathbf{W} - \mathbf{W}^T$ is to make the matrix skew-symmetric, *i.e.*, the relation $\mathbf{W} - \mathbf{W}^T = -(\mathbf{W} - \mathbf{W}^T)^T$ always holds. Then $\exp(\mathbf{W} - \mathbf{W}^T)$ is used as the weight. This technique explicitly constructs the weight as an orthogonal matrix. The orthogonal constraint is thus always satisfied during the training.

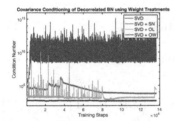

Fig. 2. The covariance conditioning during the training process. All the weight treatments can improve the conditioning.

Table 1. Performance of different weight treatments on ResNet-50 and CIFAR100 based on 10 runs.

Methods	mean $\pm$ std	min
SVD	19.99 ± 0.16	19.80
SVD + SN	19.94 ± 0.33	19.60
SVD + OL	$\mathbf{19.73 \pm 0.28}$	$\mathbf{19.54}$
SVD + OW	20.06 ± 0.17	19.94
Newton-Schulz iteration	19.45 ± 0.33	19.01

We apply the above three techniques in the experiment of decorrelated BN. Figure 2 displays the covariance conditioning throughout the training, and Table 1 presents the corresponding validation errors. As can be seen, all of these techniques attain much better conditioning, but the performance improvements are not encouraging. The SN reduces the conditioning to around 10^5, while the validation error marginally improves. The *soft* orthogonality by the OL brings slight improvement on the performance despite some variations in the conditioning. The conditioning variations occur because the orthogonality constraint by regularization is not strictly enforced. Among the weight treatments, the *hard* orthogonality by the OW achieves the best covariance conditioning, continuously maintaining the condition number around 10^3 throughout the training. However, the OW slightly hurts the validation error. This implies that better covariance conditioning does not necessarily correspond to the improved performance, and orthogonalizing only the weight cannot improve the generalization. *We conjecture that enforcing strict orthogonality only on the weight might limit its representation power.* Nonetheless, as will be discussed in Sect. 5.1, the side effect can be canceled when we simultaneously orthogonalize the gradient.

5   Nearest Orthogonal Gradient and Optimal Learning Rate

In this section, we introduce our proposed two techniques on modifying the gradient and learning rate of the Pre-SVD layer. Their combinations with the weight treatments are also discussed.

5.1   Nearest Orthogonal Gradient (NOG)

As discussed in Sect. 4.1, the covariance conditioning is also influenced by the gradient $\frac{\partial l}{\partial \mathbf{W}}$. However, existing literature mainly focuses on orthogonalizing the weights. To make the gradient also orthogonal, we propose to find the nearest-orthogonal gradient of the Pre-SVD layer. Different matrix nearness problems have been studied in [18], and the nearest-orthogonal problem is defined as:

$$\min_{\mathbf{R}} || \frac{\partial l}{\partial \mathbf{W}} - \mathbf{R} ||_{\mathrm{F}} \ subject \ to \ \mathbf{R}\mathbf{R}^T = \mathbf{I} \tag{14}$$

where $\mathbf{R}$ is the seeking solution. To obtain such an orthogonal matrix, we can construct the error function as:

$$e(\mathbf{R}) = Tr\left((\frac{\partial l}{\partial \mathbf{W}} - \mathbf{R})^T (\frac{\partial l}{\partial \mathbf{W}} - \mathbf{R}) \right) + Tr\left(\mathbf{\Sigma} \mathbf{R}^T \mathbf{R} - \mathbf{I} \right) \tag{15}$$

where $Tr(\cdot)$ is the trace measure, and $\mathbf{\Sigma}$ denotes the symmetric matrix Lagrange multiplier. The closed-form solution is given by:

$$\mathbf{R} = \frac{\partial l}{\partial \mathbf{W}} \left((\frac{\partial l}{\partial \mathbf{W}})^T \frac{\partial l}{\partial \mathbf{W}} \right)^{-\frac{1}{2}} \tag{16}$$

The detailed derivation is given in the supplementary material. If we have the SVD of the gradient ($\mathbf{U}\mathbf{S}\mathbf{V}^T = \frac{\partial l}{\partial \mathbf{W}}$), the solution can be further simplified as:

$$\mathbf{R} = \mathbf{U}\mathbf{S}\mathbf{V}^T (\mathbf{V}\mathbf{S}^{-1}\mathbf{V}^T) = \mathbf{U}\mathbf{V}^T \tag{17}$$

As indicated above, the nearest orthogonal gradient is achieved by setting the singular value matrix to the identity matrix, *i.e.*, setting $\mathbf{S}$ to $\mathbf{I}$. Notice that only the gradient of Pre-SVD layer is changed, while that of the other layers is not modified. Our proposed NOG can bring several practical benefits.

Orthogonal Constraint and Optimal Conditioning. The orthogonal constraint is exactly enforced on the gradient as we have $(\mathbf{UV}^T)^T\mathbf{UV}^T = \mathbf{I}$. Since we explicitly set all the singular values to 1, the optimal conditioning is also achieved, $i.e.$, $\kappa(\frac{\partial l}{\partial \mathbf{W}}) = 1$. This could help to improve the conditioning.

Keeping Gradient Descent Direction Unchanged. In the high-dimensional optimization landscape, the many curvature directions (GD directions) are characterized by the eigenvectors of gradient ($\mathbf{U}$ and $\mathbf{V}$). Although our modification changes the gradient, the eigenvectors and the GD directions are untouched. In other words, our NOG only adjusts the step size in each GD direction. This indicates that the modified gradients will not harm the network performances.

Combination with Weight Treatments. Our orthogonal gradient and the previous weight treatments are complementary. They can be jointly used to simultaneously orthogonalize the gradient and weight. In the following, we will validate their joint impact on the conditioning and performance.

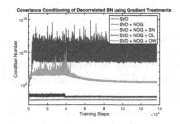

Fig. 3. The covariance conditioning during the training process using orthogonal gradient and combined weight treatments.

Table 2. Performance of gradient and weight treatments on ResNet-50 and CIFAR100. Each result is based on 10 runs.

Methods	mean $\pm$ std	min
SVD	19.99 ± 0.16	19.80
SVD + NOG	19.43 ± 0.24	19.15
SVD + NOG + SN	19.43 ± 0.21	19.20
SVD + NOG + OL	20.14 ± 0.39	19.54
SVD + NOG + OW	$\mathbf{19.22 \pm 0.28}$	$\mathbf{18.90}$
Newton-Schulz iteration	19.45 ± 0.33	19.01

Figure 3 and Table 2 present the covariance conditioning of decorrelated BN and the corresponding validation errors, respectively. As we can observe, solely using the proposed NOG can largely improve the covariance conditioning, decreasing the condition number from 10^{12} to 10^6. Though this improvement is not as significant as the orthogonal constraints ($e.g.$, OL and OW), our NOG can benefit more the generalization abilities, leading to the improvement of validation error by 0.6%. Combining the SN with our NOG does not lead to obvious improvements in either the conditioning or validation errors, whereas the joint use of NOG and OL harms the network performances. This is because the orthogonality constraint by loss might not be enforced under the gradient manipulation. When our NOG is combined with the OW, the side effect of using only OW is eliminated and the performance is further boosted by 0.3%. This phenomenon demonstrates that when the gradient is orthogonal, applying the orthogonality constraint to the weight could also be beneficial to the generalization.

5.2   Optimal Learning Rate (OLR)

So far, we only consider orthogonalizing $\mathbf{W}$ and $\frac{\partial l}{\partial \mathbf{W}}$ separately, but how to jointly optimize $\mathbf{W} - \eta \frac{\partial l}{\partial \mathbf{W}}$ has not been studied yet. Actually, it is desired to choose an appropriate learning rate η such that the updated weight is close to an orthogonal matrix. To this end, we need to achieve the following objective:

$$\min_{\eta} \|(\mathbf{W} - \eta \frac{\partial l}{\partial \mathbf{W}})(\mathbf{W} - \eta \frac{\partial l}{\partial \mathbf{W}})^T - \mathbf{I}\|_{\mathrm{F}} \tag{18}$$

This optimization problem can be more easily solved in the vector form. Let $\mathbf{w}$, $\mathbf{i}$, and $\mathbf{l}$ denote the vectorized $\mathbf{W}$, $\mathbf{I}$, and $\frac{\partial l}{\partial \mathbf{W}}$, respectively. Then we construct the error function as:

$$e(\eta) = \left((\mathbf{w} - \eta \mathbf{l})^T (\mathbf{w} - \eta \mathbf{l}) - \mathbf{i}\right)^T \left((\mathbf{w} - \eta \mathbf{l})^T (\mathbf{w} - \eta \mathbf{l}) - \mathbf{i}\right) \tag{19}$$

Expanding and differentiating the equation w.r.t. η lead to:

$$\frac{de(\eta)}{d\eta} \approx -4\mathbf{w}\mathbf{w}^T \mathbf{l}^T \mathbf{w} + 4\eta \mathbf{w}\mathbf{w}^T \mathbf{l}^T \mathbf{l} + 8\eta \mathbf{l}^T \mathbf{w}\mathbf{l}^T \mathbf{w} = 0$$

$$\eta^\star \approx \frac{\mathbf{w}^T \mathbf{w} \mathbf{l}^T \mathbf{w}}{\mathbf{w}^T \mathbf{w} \mathbf{l}^T \mathbf{l} + 2\mathbf{l}^T \mathbf{w} \mathbf{l}^T \mathbf{w}} \tag{20}$$

where some higher-order terms are neglected. The detailed derivation is given in the supplementary material. Though the proposed OLR yields the updated weight nearest to an orthogonal matrix theoretically, the value of $\eta^\star$ is unbounded for arbitrary $\mathbf{w}$ and $\mathbf{l}$. Directly using $\eta^\star$ might cause unstable training. To avoid this issue, we propose to use the OLR only when its value is smaller than the learning rate of other layers. Let lr denote the learning rate of the other layers. The switch process can be defined as:

$$\eta = \begin{cases} \eta^\star & if \ \eta^\star < lr \\ lr & otherwise \end{cases} \tag{21}$$

Combination with Weight/Gradient Treatments. When either the weight or the gradient is orthogonal, our OLR needs to be carefully used. When only $\mathbf{W}$ is orthogonal, $\mathbf{w}^T \mathbf{w}$ is a small constant and it is very likely to have $\mathbf{w}^T \mathbf{w} \ll \mathbf{l}^T \mathbf{w}$. Consequently, we have $\mathbf{w}^T \mathbf{w} \mathbf{l}^T \mathbf{w} \ll \mathbf{l}^T \mathbf{w} \mathbf{l}^T \mathbf{w}$ and $\eta^\star$ will attenuate to zero. Similarly for orthogonal gradient, we have $\mathbf{w}^T \mathbf{w} \mathbf{l}^T \mathbf{w} \ll \mathbf{l}^T \mathbf{w} \mathbf{l}^T \mathbf{l}$ and this will cause $\eta^\star$ close to zero. Therefore, the proposed OLR cannot work when either the weight or gradient is orthogonal. Nonetheless, we note that if both $\mathbf{W}$ and $\frac{\partial l}{\partial \mathbf{W}}$ are orthogonal, our $\eta^\star$ is bounded. Specifically, we have:

Proposition 1. *When both $\mathbf{W}$ and $\frac{\partial l}{\partial \mathbf{W}}$ are orthogonal, $\eta^\star$ is both upper and lower bounded. The upper bound is $\frac{N^2}{N^2+2}$ and the lower bound is $\frac{1}{N^2+2}$ where N denotes the row dimension of $\mathbf{W}$.*

We give the detailed proof in the supplementary material. Obviously, the upper bound of $\eta^\star$ is smaller than 1. For the lower bound, since the row dimension of N is often large (*e.g.*, 64), the lower bound of $\eta^\star$ can be according very small (*e.g.*, $2e-4$). This indicates that our proposed OLR could also give a small learning rate even in the later stage of the training process.

In summary, the optimal learning rate is set such that the updated weight is optimal in the sense that it become as close to an orthogonal matrix as possible. In particular, it is suitable when both the gradient and weight are orthogonal.

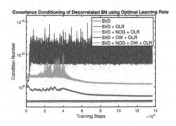

Fig. 4. The covariance conditioning during the training process using optimal learning rate and hybrid treatments.

Table 3. Performance of optimal learning rate and hybrid treatments on ResNet-50 and CIFAR100 based on 10 runs.

Methods	mean $\pm$ std	min
SVD	19.99 ± 0.16	19.80
SVD + OLR	19.50 ± 0.39	18.95
SVD + NOG + OLR	19.77 ± 0.27	19.36
SVD + OW + OLR	20.61 ± 0.22	20.43
SVD + NOG + OW +OLR	$\mathbf{19.05 \pm 0.31}$	**18.77**
Newton-Schulz iteration	19.45 ± 0.33	19.01

We give the covariance conditioning and the validation errors of our OLR in Fig. 4 and in Table 3, respectively. Our proposed OLR significantly reduces the condition number to 10^4 and improves the validation error by 0.5%. When combined with either orthogonal weight or orthogonal gradient, there is a slight degradation on the validation errors. This meets our expectation as $\eta^\star$ would attenuate to zero in both cases. However, when both $\mathbf{W}$ and $\frac{\partial l}{\partial \mathbf{W}}$ are orthogonal, jointly using our OLR achieves the best performance, outperforming only OLR by 0.5% and beating OW+NOG by 0.2%. This observation confirms that the proposed OLR works well for simultaneously orthogonal $\mathbf{W}$ and $\frac{\partial l}{\partial \mathbf{W}}$.

6   Experiments

We validate the proposed approaches in two applications: GCP and decorrelated BN. These two tasks are very representative because they have different usages of the SVD meta-layer. The GCP uses the matrix square root, while the decorrelated BN applies the inverse square root. In addition, the models of decorrelated BN often insert the SVD meta-layer at the beginning of the network, whereas the GCP models integrate the layer before the FC layer.

6.1   Decorrelated Batch Normalization

Table 4 compares the performance of each method on CIFAR10/CIFAR100 [26] based on ResNet-50 [17]. Both of our NOG and OLR achieve better performance

Table 4. Performance comparison of different decorrelated BN methods on CIFAR10/CIFAR100 [26] based on ResNet-50 [17]. We report each result based on 10 runs. The best four results are highlighted in red, **blue**, green, and cyan respectively.

Methods	CIFAR10		CIFAR100	
	mean ± std	min	mean ± std	min
SVD	4.35 ± 0.09	4.17	19.99 ± 0.16	19.80
SVD + Spectral Norm (SN)	4.31 ± 0.10	4.15	19.94 ± 0.33	19.60
SVD + Orthogonal Loss (OL)	4.28 ± 0.07	4.23	19.73 ± 0.28	19.54
SVD + Orthogonal Weight (OW)	4.42 ± 0.09	4.28	20.06 ± 0.17	19.94
SVD + Nearest Orthogonal Gradient (NOG)	4.15 ± 0.06	4.04	19.43 ± 0.24	19.15
SVD + Optimal Learning Rate (OLR)	4.23 ± 0.17	**3.98**	19.50 ± 0.39	18.95
SVD + NOG + OW	**4.09 ± 0.07**	4.01	**19.22 ± 0.28**	18.90
SVD + NOG + OW + OLR	3.93 ± 0.09	3.85	19.05 ± 0.31	18.77
Newton-Schulz iteration	4.20 ± 0.11	4.11	19.45 ± 0.33	19.01

than other weight treatments and the SVD. Moreover, when hybrid treatments are adopted, we can observe step-wise steady improvements on the validation errors. Among these techniques, the joint usage of OLR with NOG and OW achieves the best performances across metrics and datasets, outperforming the SVD baseline by 0.4% on CIFAR10 and by 0.9% on CIFAR100. This demonstrates that these treatments are complementary and can benefit each other.

Table 5. Performance comparison of different GCP methods on ImageNet [12] based on ResNet-18 [17]. The failure times denote the total times of non-convergence of the SVD solver during one training process. The best four results are highlighted in red, **blue**, green, and cyan respectively.

Method	Failure Times	Top-1 Acc. (%)	Top-5 Acc. (%)
SVD	5	73.13	91.02
SVD + Spectral Norm (SN)	2	73.28 (↑ 0.2)	91.11 (↑ 0.1)
SVD + Orthogonal Loss (OL)	1	71.75 (↓ 1.4)	90.20 (↓ 0.8)
SVD + Orthogonal Weight (OW)	2	73.07 (↓ 0.1)	90.93 (↓ 0.1)
SVD + Nearest Orthogonal Gradient (NOG)	1	73.51 (↑ 0.4)	91.35 (↑ 0.3)
SVD + Optimal Learning Rate (OLR)	0	73.39 (↑ 0.3)	91.26 (↑ 0.2)
SVD + NOG + OW	0	**73.71 (↑ 0.6)**	**91.43 (↑ 0.4)**
SVD + NOG + OW + OLR	0	73.82 (↑ 0.7)	91.57 (↑ 0.6)
Newton-Schulz iteration	0	73.36 (↑ 0.2)	90.96 (↓ 0.1)

6.2   Global Covariance Pooling

Table 5 presents the total failure times of the SVD solver in one training process and the validation accuracy on ImageNet [12] based on ResNet-18 [17].

The results are very coherent with our experiment of decorrelated BN. Among the weight treatments, the OL and OW hurt the performance, while the SN improves that of SVD by 0.2%. Our proposed NOG and OLR outperform the weight treatments and improve the SVD baseline by 0.4% and by 0.3%, respectively. Moreover, the combinations with the orthogonal weight further boost the performance. Specifically, combining NOG and OW surpasses the SVD by 0.6%. The joint use of OW with NOG and OLR achieves the best performance among all the methods and beats the SVD by 0.7%.

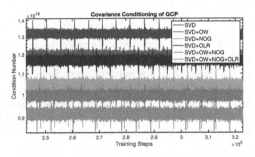

Fig. 5. The covariance conditioning of GCP methods in the later stage of the training. The periodic spikes are caused by the evaluation on the validation set after every epoch.

Figure 5 depicts the covariance conditioning in the later training stage. Our OLR and the OW both reduce the condition number by around 1e15, whereas the proposed NOG improves the condition number by 2e15. When hybrid treatments are used, combining NOG and OW attains better conditioning than the separate usages. Furthermore, simultaneously using all the techniques leads to the best conditioning and improves the condition number by 5e15.

The covariance conditioning of GCP tasks is not improved as much as that of decorrelated BN. This might stem from the unique architecture of GCP models: the covariance is directly used as the final representation and fed to the FC layer. We conjecture that this setup might cause the covariance to have a high condition number. The approximate solver (Newton-Schulz iteration) does not have well-conditioned matrices either ($\approx$1e15), which partly supports our conjecture.

7 Conclusion and Future Work

In this paper, we explore different approaches to improve the covariance conditioning of the SVD meta-layer. Existing treatments on orthogonal weight are first studied. Our experiments reveal that these techniques could improve the conditioning but might hurt the performance due to the limitation on the representation power. To avoid the side effect of orthogonal weight, we propose the nearest orthogonal gradient and the optimal learning rate, both of which could simultaneously attain better covariance conditioning and improved generalization abilities. Moreover, their combinations with orthogonal weight further boost the performance. In future work, we would like to study the problem of ill-conditioned covariance from other perspectives and extend our proposed techniques to other SVD-related methods.

Acknowledgement. This research was supported by the EU H2020 projects AI4Media (No. 951911) and SPRING (No. 871245).

References

1. Abramov, A., Bayer, C., Heller, C.: Keep it simple: image statistics matching for domain adaptation. arXiv preprint arXiv:2005.12551 (2020)
2. Bansal, N., Chen, X., Wang, Z.: Can we gain more from orthogonality regularizations in training deep networks? In: NeurIPS (2018)
3. Bengio, Y., Simard, P., Frasconi, P.: Learning long-term dependencies with gradient descent is difficult. IEEE Trans. Neural Netw. **5**(2), 157–166 (1994)
4. Brachmann, E., et al.: DSAC-differentiable RANSAC for camera localization. In: CVPR (2017)
5. Brock, A., Donahue, J., Simonyan, K.: Large scale GAN training for high fidelity natural image synthesis. In: ICLR (2019)
6. Campbell, D., Liu, L., Gould, S.: Solving the blind perspective-n-point problem end-to-end with robust differentiable geometric optimization. In: Vedaldi, A., Bischof, H., Brox, T., Frahm, J.-M. (eds.) ECCV 2020. LNCS, vol. 12347, pp. 244–261. Springer, Cham (2020). https://doi.org/10.1007/978-3-030-58536-5_15
7. Chan, T.H., Jia, K., Gao, S., Lu, J., Zeng, Z., Ma, Y.: PCANet: a simple deep learning baseline for image classification? IEEE TIP **24**(12), 5017–5032 (2015)
8. Chiu, T.Y.: Understanding generalized whitening and coloring transform for universal style transfer. In: ICCV (2019)
9. Cho, W., Choi, S., Park, D.K., Shin, I., Choo, J.: Image-to-image translation via group-wise deep whitening-and-coloring transformation. In: CVPR (2019)
10. Choi, S., Jung, S., Yun, H., Kim, J.T., Kim, S., Choo, J.: RobustNet: improving domain generalization in urban-scene segmentation via instance selective whitening. In: CVPR (2021)
11. Dang, Z., Yi, K.M., Hu, Y., Wang, F., Fua, P., Salzmann, M.: Eigendecomposition-free training of deep networks for linear least-square problems. TPAMI **43**(9), 3167–3182 (2020)
12. Deng, J., Dong, W., Socher, R., Li, L.J., Li, K., Fei-Fei, L.: ImageNet: a large-scale hierarchical image database. In: CVPR (2009)
13. Gao, Z., Wang, Q., Zhang, B., Hu, Q., Li, P.: Temporal-attentive covariance pooling networks for video recognition. In: NeurIPS (2021)
14. Geng, Z., Guo, M.H., Chen, H., Li, X., Wei, K., Lin, Z.: Is attention better than matrix decomposition? In: ICLR (2021)
15. Glorot, X., Bengio, Y.: Understanding the difficulty of training deep feedforward neural networks. In: AISTATS (2010)
16. Goodfellow, I., et al.: Generative adversarial nets. In: NeurIPS (2014)
17. He, K., Zhang, X., Ren, S., Sun, J.: Deep residual learning for image recognition. In: CVPR (2016)

18. Higham, N.J.: Matrix Nearness Problems and Applications. Princeton, Citeseer (1988)
19. Higham, N.J.: Functions of Matrices: Theory and Computation. SIAM, Philadelphia (2008)
20. Huang, L., Yang, D., Lang, B., Deng, J.: Decorrelated batch normalization. In: CVPR (2018)
21. Huang, L., Zhao, L., Zhou, Y., Zhu, F., Liu, L., Shao, L.: An investigation into the stochasticity of batch whitening. In: CVPR (2020)
22. Huang, L., Zhou, Y., Liu, L., Zhu, F., Shao, L.: Group whitening: Balancing learning efficiency and representational capacity. In: CVPR (2021)
23. Huang, L., Zhou, Y., Zhu, F., Liu, L., Shao, L.: Iterative normalization: Beyond standardization towards efficient whitening. In: CVPR (2019)
24. Ionescu, C., Vantzos, O., Sminchisescu, C.: Matrix backpropagation for deep networks with structured layers. In: ICCV (2015)
25. Ionescu, C., Vantzos, O., Sminchisescu, C.: Training deep networks with structured layers by matrix backpropagation. arXiv preprint arXiv:1509.07838 (2015)
26. Krizhevsky, A.: Learning multiple layers of features from tiny images. Master's thesis, University of Tront (2009)
27. LeCun, Y.A., Bottou, L., Orr, G.B., Müller, K.-R.: Efficient BackProp. In: Montavon, G., Orr, G.B., Müller, K.-R. (eds.) Neural Networks: Tricks of the Trade. LNCS, vol. 7700, pp. 9–48. Springer, Heidelberg (2012). https://doi.org/10.1007/978-3-642-35289-8_3
28. Li, P., Xie, J., Wang, Q., Gao, Z.: Towards faster training of global covariance pooling networks by iterative matrix square root normalization. In: CVPR (2018)
29. Li, P., Xie, J., Wang, Q., Zuo, W.: Is second-order information helpful for large-scale visual recognition? In: ICCV (2017)
30. Li, Y., Fang, C., Yang, J., Wang, Z., Lu, X., Yang, M.H.: Universal style transfer via feature transforms. In: NeurIPS (2017)
31. Lu, J., et al.: SOFT: softmax-free transformer with linear complexity. In: NeurIPS (2021)
32. Maduranga, K.D., Helfrich, K.E., Ye, Q.: Complex unitary recurrent neural networks using scaled Cayley transform. In: AAAI (2019)
33. Mishkin, D., Matas, J.: All you need is a good init. In: ICLR (2016)
34. Miyato, T., Kataoka, T., Koyama, M., Yoshida, Y.: Spectral normalization for generative adversarial networks. In: ICLR (2018)
35. Murray, I.: Differentiation of the cholesky decomposition. arXiv preprint arXiv:1602.07527 (2016)
36. Pascanu, R., Mikolov, T., Bengio, Y.: On the difficulty of training recurrent neural networks. In: ICML (2013)
37. Qi, H., You, C., Wang, X., Ma, Y., Malik, J.: Deep isometric learning for visual recognition. In: ICML. PMLR (2020)
38. Ranftl, R., Koltun, V.: Deep fundamental matrix estimation. In: ECCV (2018)
39. Rodríguez, P., Gonzalez, J., Cucurull, G., Gonfaus, J.M., Roca, X.: Regularizing CNNs with locally constrained decorrelations. In: ICLR (2016)
40. Saxe, A.M., McClelland, J.L., Ganguli, S.: Exact solutions to the nonlinear dynamics of learning in deep linear neural networks. In: ICLR (2014)
41. Sedghi, H., Gupta, V., Long, P.M.: The singular values of convolutional layers. In: ICLR (2018)
42. Siarohin, A., Sangineto, E., Sebe, N.: Whitening and coloring batch transform for GANs. In: ICLR (2018)

43. Singla, S., Feizi, S.: Skew orthogonal convolutions. In: ICML (2021)
44. Song, Y., Sebe, N., Wang, W.: Why approximate matrix square root outperforms accurate SVD in global covariance pooling? In: ICCV (2021)
45. Song, Y., Sebe, N., Wang, W.: Fast differentiable matrix square root. In: ICLR (2022)
46. Song, Y., Sebe, N., Wang, W.: Fast differentiable matrix square root and inverse square root. arXiv preprint arXiv:2201.12543 (2022)
47. Song, Y., Sebe, N., Wang, W.: On the eigenvalues of global covariance pooling for fine-grained visual recognition. IEEE TPAMI (2022)
48. Sutskever, I., Martens, J., Dahl, G., Hinton, G.: On the importance of initialization and momentum in deep learning. In: ICML (2013)
49. Trockman, A., Kolter, J.Z.: Orthogonalizing convolutional layers with the Cayley transform. In: ICLR (2020)
50. Tsuzuku, Y., Sato, I., Sugiyama, M.: Lipschitz-margin training: scalable certification of perturbation invariance for deep neural networks. In: NeurIPS (2018)
51. Ulyanov, D., Vedaldi, A., Lempitsky, V.: Improved texture networks: maximizing quality and diversity in feed-forward stylization and texture synthesis. In: CVPR (2017)
52. Wang, J., Chen, Y., Chakraborty, R., Yu, S.X.: Orthogonal convolutional neural networks. In: CVPR (2020)
53. Wang, Q., Xie, J., Zuo, W., Zhang, L., Li, P.: Deep CNNs meet global covariance pooling: better representation and generalization. TPAMI 43(8), 2582–2597 (2020)
54. Wang, W., Dang, Z., Hu, Y., Fua, P., Salzmann, M.: Robust differentiable SVD. TPAMI (2021)
55. Wang, Z., et al.: Diversified arbitrary style transfer via deep feature perturbation. In: CVPR (2020)
56. Wiesler, S., Ney, H.: A convergence analysis of log-linear training. In: NeurIPS (2011)
57. Xiao, L., Bahri, Y., Sohl-Dickstein, J., Schoenholz, S., Pennington, J.: Dynamical isometry and a mean field theory of CNNs: how to train 10,000-layer vanilla convolutional neural networks. In: ICML. PMLR (2018)
58. Xie, J., Zeng, R., Wang, Q., Zhou, Z., Li, P.: So-ViT: Mind visual tokens for vision transformer. arXiv preprint arXiv:2104.10935 (2021)
59. Xiong, Y., et al.: Nyströmformer: A nyström-based algorithm for approximating self-attention. In: AAAI (2021)
60. Yang, Y., Sun, J., Li, H., Xu, Z.: ADMM-Net: a deep learning approach for compressive sensing MRI. arXiv preprint arXiv:1705.06869 (2017)

Out-of-Distribution Detection
with Semantic Mismatch Under Masking

Yijun Yang⬤, Ruiyuan Gao⬤, and Qiang Xu$^{(\boxtimes)}$⬤

CUhk REliable Computing Laboratory (CURE Lab.), Department of Computer
Science and Engineering, The Chinese University of Hong Kong,
Hong Kong S.A.R., China
{yjyang,rygao,qxu}@cse.cuhk.edu.hk

Abstract. This paper proposes a novel out-of-distribution (OOD)
detection framework named MOODCAT for image classifiers. MOODCAT
masks a random portion of the input image and uses a generative model
to synthesize the masked image to a new image conditioned on the classification result. It then calculates the semantic difference between the
original image and the synthesized one for OOD detection. Compared to
existing solutions, MOODCAT naturally learns the semantic information
of the in-distribution data with the proposed mask and conditional synthesis strategy, which is critical to identify OODs. Experimental results
demonstrate that MOODCAT outperforms state-of-the-art OOD detection solutions by a large margin. Our code is available at https://github.
com/cure-lab/MOODCat.

Keywords: OOD detection · Robust AI · Generative model

1 Introduction

Deep neural networks (DNNs) are trained under a "close-world" assumption [12,23], where all the samples fed to the model are assumed to follow a
narrow semantic distribution. However, when deployed in the wild, the model
is exposed to an "open-world" with all kinds of inputs not necessarily following
this distribution [9]. Such out-of-distribution (OOD) samples with significantly
different semantics may mislead DNN models and generate wrong prediction
results with extremely high confidence, thereby hindering DNN's deployment
safety [1,7,14,15,33].

To distinguish OOD samples from the in-distribution (In-D) data, some propose to reuse the features extracted from the original DNN model to tell the
difference [15,26–28,42,43]. However, such a feature-sharing strategy inevitably
results in the trade-off between the prediction accuracy for In-D samples and the
OOD detection capabilities. There are also various density-based OOD detection methods [3,35,36], which try to model the In-D data with probabilistic

Supplementary Information The online version contains supplementary material
available at https://doi.org/10.1007/978-3-031-20053-3_22.

measures such as energy and likelihood. However, the trustworthiness of these measures is not guaranteed [21]. Another popular OOD detection mechanism uses generative models (e.g., variational autoencoder (VAE)) to reconstruct the input [6,38]. Based on the assumption that In-D data can be well reconstructed while OODs cannot since they are not seen during training, one could measure the distance between the original input and the reconstructed one and detect OOD with a threshold. However, this assumption is not sound. There are cases where OODs are faithfully reconstructed with the generative models, causing misjudgements [21].

In this paper, we propose a novel distance-based OOD detection framework, named *Masked OOD Catcher* (MOODCAT), wherein we consider the semantic mismatch under masking as the distance metric. Specifically, for image classifiers, we first randomly mask a portion of the input image, use a generative model to synthesize the masked image to a new image conditioned on the classification result, and then calculate the semantic difference between the original image and the synthesized one for OOD detection.

Our insight is that, the classification result carries discriminative semantic information and it imposes strong constraints onto the synthesis procedure, especially when trying to recover the masked portions. With MOODCAT, for correctly classified In-D data, the generative model can use the unmasked region to make up the masked part with sufficient training. In contrast, for OOD samples that are semantically different, the synthesized image based on the classification result tends to be dramatically different, especially for the masked region.

MOODCAT is a standalone OOD detector, and it does not require fine-tuning the original classifier. Consequently, it can be combined with any classifier to equip it with OOD detection capability without affecting its accuracy. We perform comprehensive evaluations on standard OOD detection benchmarks [44] with six datasets and four detection settings. Results show that our method can outperform state-of-the-art (SOTA) solutions by a large margin. We summarize the contributions of this work in the following:

- We propose a novel OOD detection framework by identifying semantic mismatch under masking, MOODCAT. To the best of our knowledge, this is the first work that *explicitly* considers semantics information for OOD detection.
- We present a novel masking and conditional synthesis flow in MOODCAT, and investigate various masking strategies and conditional generator designs for OOD detection.
- To tell the semantic difference between the original image and the synthesized one, we employ an anomalous scoring model composed of various quality assessment metrics (e.g., DISTS [8] and LPIPS [52]) and a newly-proposed conditional binary classifier.

The rest of the paper is constructed as follows. Section 2 surveys related OOD detection methods. We detail our proposed MOODCAT framework in Sect. 3. Section 4 presents our experimental results and the corresponding ablation studies. Finally, Sect. 5 concludes this paper.

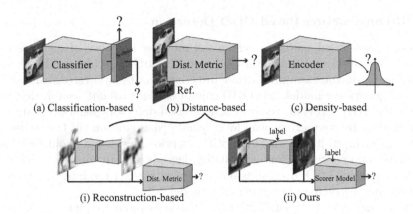

Fig. 1. Comparison of OOD Detection Methods. MOODCAT is a distance-based solution, and it relies on conditional image synthesis rather than reconstruction.

2   Related Work

2.1   Existing OOD Detection Methods

In general, OOD detection methods can be categorized into: classification-based, density-based and distance-based methods [45].

Classification-based methods derive OOD scores based on the output of DNNs, as shown in Fig. 1(a). Maximum Softmax Probability (MSP) [15] simply uses the maximum softmax probability as the indicator of In-D data. ODIN [26] is applies a temperature scaling to the softmax value for OOD detection. Follow-up works include methods based on the output of DNNs [27,28,42,43], the gradient of DNNs [19] and data generation or augmentation [40,41]. Although simple to implement, most of them alter the training process of the original classifier, thereby reducing the classification accuracy for In-D samples.

Density-based methods usually apply some probabilistic models for the distribution of In-D samples and regard test data in low-density regions as OOD [3,25,36], as shown in Fig. 1(c). Some methods in this category also resort to generative models [35] to learn the distribution of data. However, recent research found that the learned density model may assign high likelihood value to some OODs, since the obtained likelihood could be dominated by low-level features such as location and variance instead of the high-level semantics, which is related to the specific network architecture and data used for learning [3,30].

Distance-based methods consider that OODs should be relatively far away from In-Ds. They either calculate the centroids of In-D classes in the feature space [18,49] (Fig. 1(b)) or reconstruct the input itself (Sect. 2.2, Fig. 1(i)) for OOD detection. However, for high-level semantic features, their assumption for distance disparity may not hold, and high reconstruction quality cannot ensure In-Ds. In this paper, we use conditional synthesis on masked images to highlight the semantics difference in the image space.

2.2   Reconstruction-Based OOD Detection

Reconstruction-based methods, which fall into the category of distance-based methods, are closely related to the proposed MOODCAT technique. These methods are based on the assumption that In-D data can be well-reconstructed from a trained generative model, but OOD cannot as they are not seen during training (see Fig. 1(i)). Previous reconstruction-based detectors generally distinguish OOD samples by comparing pixel-level quality "degradation" of the reconstruction for given input [6,38]. However, without prior-knowledge about OOD samples, there is no guarantee for such quality degradation. In contrast, MOODCAT tries to synthesize In-D images instead of reconstructing the inputs, which is in line with the objective of the generative model.

The framework of MOODCAT (Fig. 1(ii)) is inspired by [46], which detects adversarial examples (AE) by generating synthesized images conditioned on the output of the misled classifier. AE detection is quite different from OOD detection because adversarial examples are In-D samples with imperceptible perturbations. The classification label itself is sufficient to train the generative model to differentiate AEs and benign samples. This is not the case for OOD samples, which motivates the proposed MOODCAT solution for OOD detection, as detailed in Sect. 3.

2.3   OOD Detection with External OOD Data

Recently, some researchers propose to involve data from other datasets to simulate OOD samples for model training. Representative "OOD-aware" techniques include Outlier Exposure (OE) [16], Maximum Classifier Discrepancy (MCD) [48], and Unsupervised Dual Grouping (UDG) [44]. OE relies on large-scale purified OOD samples, whereas MCD and UDG only need extra unlabeled data, which contains both In-D and OOD data. However, all of them are classification-based methods, where external data are used to train a modified classifier model. Following the same unlabeled extra data setting of MCD and UDG, we present that including extra training data (In-D, OOD mixture) into the training process can further improve MOODCAT's performance. Since our MOODCAT works independently with the original classifiers, MOODCAT will not degrade the accuracy of the original classifiers. We provide the detailed description in Sect. 3.6 and experimental results in Sect. 4.

2.4   Open Set Recognition

A similar problem to OOD detection is the so-called Open Set Recognition (OSR) problem, which aims to distinguish the known and unknown classes [34,45]. Several existing works [10,11,31,34] targeted on OSR also employ generative models, whereas differ from MOODCAT significantly. Specifically, OSRCI [31] uses Generative Adversarial Network (GAN) as data augmentation to train the classifier; C2AE [34] and CVAECapOSR [11] are conditional VAE/Autoencoder-based detectors. C2AE identifies outliers based on reconstruction errors, and

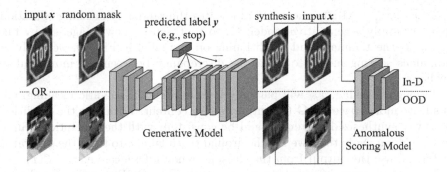

Fig. 2. Pipeline of MOODCAT. We first mask a portion of the input image. Next, a generative model synthesizes the masked image to a new image conditioned on y, and then an anomalous scoring model measures the semantic difference between the input image and the synthesized one for OOD detection.

requires K-time inference to give the final decision. In contrast, MOODCAT infers once and makes the decision based on semantic contradiction. CVAECapOSR use Conditional VAE (CVAE) to model the distribution of In-D samples and detect outliers at latent space (i.e., without using the generator), whereas MOODCAT detects at image space.

3   Proposed Method

3.1   Design Goals

This work considers the scenario where we have an In-D data trained classifier ($\mathcal{C}$), which needs to be deployed in the wild. Consequently, the classifier will be threatened by OOD samples. We aim at building an OOD detection method, which can identify the OOD samples effectively without compromising the classification accuracy of the classifier. Our model is assumed to have access to the predicted label, y, but we do not modify any part of the classifier, including but may not limit to the architecture and the trained weights. As a result, our method can be a plug-and-play detector that easily cooperates with classifiers.

3.2   Method Overview

As pointed out by [45], OOD samples ($x_o \in \mathcal{O}$) are defined by label-shifted samples or samples with non-overlapping labels w.r.t the training data, or In-Ds ($x_{in} \in \mathcal{I}$). Hence, the semantics of any OOD sample contradicts with any In-D sample. This is the observation that motivates us to design a framework for OOD detection by spotlighting their semantic discrepancy.

Figure 2 depicts the overview of our method. The proposed Masked Out-of-Distribution Catcher (MOODCAT) contains three stages: *randomly masking, generative synthesis* and *scoring*. Specifically, we first randomly mask the input image x as $x_m = \mathbf{M}(x)$, where $\mathbf{M}(\cdot)$ indicates the randomly masking operation. Then, we apply a generative model, $\mathbf{G}$, to synthesize a new image, x', by taking x_m as the template and conditioning on the label y. Finally, we apply an anomalous scoring model to judge the discrepancy between the input and its synthesis.

Through masking, x_m will partially lose its original semantic meaning, and thus leave more space for $\mathbf{G}$ to synthesize new content. With y as the condition, the newly synthesized content should be consistent with the semantic meaning indicated by y. Note that, we use the ground truth label y to train the generative model and use the output from the classifier when inference, i.e., $y = \mathcal{C}(x)$.

Here, we analyze different situations with In-D or OOD samples. On the one hand, if an In-D sample x_{in} comes, the predicted label y matches x_{in}'s intrinsic semantic meaning appropriately. Although the input image, $x_{in \cdot m}$, is partially masked, there should be some visual clue related to its semantic meaning, e.g., wings of a bird or paws of a dog. As a result, $\mathbf{G}$ can synthesize x'_{in} quite faithful to x_{in}. As exemplified in the upper half of Fig. 2, the synthesis of the "stop" sign can be very close to the original input. On the other hand, when it comes to an OOD sample x_o, the predicted label provided by the classifier is irreverent to x_o's semantic meaning. Even with x_o as a template, the generative model will try its best to synthesize contents related to the semantic label. As a result, the mismatch of semantic meaning between input and label can be spotlighted by the discrepancy between input and its synthesis. As the example shows in the lower part in Fig. 2, if an OOD sample (car) is wrongly predicted as a "stop" sign. The synthesis will be highly related to the "stop" sign rather than the original image.

Through such conditional synthesis, we can spotlight the discrepancy caused by OOD samples. Thus OODs can be easily distinguished by comparing the pair of input with its synthesis, (x, x').

3.3   Masking Mechanism

In MOODCAT, the generative model uses the input image as a template and synthesizes an image with the same semantic meaning as the given label. A high-quality synthesis can better highlight the contradiction. However, due to the intrinsic contradiction between the input image and the label for OOD, too much information from the input image can degrade the quality of generation. Therefore, we propose to apply masking on x to remove some redundant information while leaving more space for the generative model to synthesize.

The use of masking follows the key motivation of MOODCAT in OOD detection, which applies generation for synthesis rather than reconstruction. Previous reconstruction-based methods (e.g., [6,38]) tend to reconstruct the image based on pixel-level dependency. In practice, the assumption that an OOD sample cannot be reconstructed well may not hold since they do not consider any semantics. However, our generative model aims at semantic synthesis. The masking mechanism can cooperate with the predicted label from the classifier to spotlight the contradiction caused by OOD.

The contribution of randomly masking is twofold: **1)** masking the input image can encourage the generative model to better depict the semantic meaning of the given label on the synthesis, especially to an OOD sample; **2)** masking, as a typical data augmentation method, can encourage the encoder to summarize the features of the input from a holistic perspective, thus improve the quality of synthesis, especially when synthesizing with In-Ds as templates. Obviously, the above two aspects both contribute to apart the behavior of In-D and OOD. As a result, a large discrepancy lies in the OOD sample and its synthesis.

3.4   Generative Model

The Generative model is responsible for generating a synthesis by taking both the masked input x_m and the pre-assigned semantic label y into consideration. As shown in Fig. 2, we select the Encoder ($\mathbf{E}$) and Decoder ($\mathbf{D}$) architecture as the generative model, i.e. $\mathbf{G} = \mathbf{E} \cdot \mathbf{D}$. This architecture is inspired by [46]. The encoder $\mathbf{E}$ acts as a feature extractor (as shown by the gray part in Fig. 2). By taking the masked image x_m as input, $\mathbf{E}$ is expected to capture necessary low-level features and encoder them as a latent vector, $z = \mathbf{E}(x_m)$. As done by VAE [20], we use the KL Divergence to regulate the latent vector z, which can be formulated as Eq. (1).

$$\mathcal{L}_{KLD} = D_{KL}[\mathcal{N}(\mu(x_m), \Sigma(x_m)) \| \mathcal{N}(0, 1)], \qquad (1)$$

where $\mathcal{N}(\mu, \Sigma)$ indicates the Gaussian distribution with respect to μ and Σ. We use the reparameterization trick from VAE on the latent variable z during training, $z = \mu(x_m) + \Sigma(x_m) \cdot \epsilon$, where $\epsilon \sim \mathcal{N}(0, 1)$.

The decoder, $\mathbf{D}$, is trained to generate a synthesis $x' = \mathbf{D}(z, y)$. The given semantic label y is used to control the semantic meaning of the synthesis, while z is used to provide low-level features from the template image x. This synthetic target is fulfilled through the class-conditional batch normalization layer [5]. This layer is usually used in conditional image generation [29,51]. Since the normalization is determined by the given semantic label y, the semantic meaning of the synthesis can be highly dependent on it. As a result, if the semantic meaning of x is consistent with y (in the case of In-D samples), the synthesis can be highly close to x. However, if input an OOD sample, the semantic contradiction between the input image and the label will lead the synthesis to be far away from the input image, thus spotlighting the contradiction.

We implement $\mathbf{D}$ based on the generator architecture proposed in [2]. We apply the classic ℓ_1, ℓ_2 and $\mathcal{SSIM}$ [37] as part of loss items to constrain that x' resembles x. Furthermore, we adopt the U-net based discriminator [39] to operate an adversarial loss on the training process to further improve the quality of the synthetic image. Compared with the vanilla discriminator, this U-net based one can additionally provide a per-pixel real/fake map to locate the fake parts in the image. Therefore, the generative model can be trained to focus on both local and global features with more realistic details. Due to space limitations, we detailed the training process and corresponding objective functions of $\mathbf{G}$ in Appendix.

3.5   Anomalous Scoring Model

As analyzed in the former sections, MOODCAT can generate high-quality synthe-ses in terms of similarity for In-D samples, but not for OOD samples. To distin-guish OODs from In-Ds, we develop an anomalous scoring model. The proposed anomalous scoring model is built on two types of scorers: one is the *conditional binary classifier*, and the other is *Image Quality Assessment models* (IQA) [52]. Both can provide assessments of the syntheses by referring to input images.

Conditional Binary Classifier. Identifying the semantic mismatch lies between OOD and its synthesis can be seen as a binary classification task. With the trained generative model, we can train a binary classifier for this in a super-vised way. This is feasible because the binary classifier can learn to identify OODs by the similarity between the given image and its conditional synthesis. We also provide the semantic label to the classifier for judgement, this can further ease the distinguishing procedure.

Note that, we do not rely on OOD data through training. To mitigate the lack of OOD samples during training, we leverage the In-D samples with the synthetic results under mismatched labels to simulate the behavior of OOD samples. As a result, the binary classifier can learn to identify the semantic mismatch, which is the spotlighted feature for OOD samples. Moreover, we condition the binary classifier on the semantic label via the projection layer [29]. With the prior knowledge of the class, the binary classifier can learn a fine-grained decision boundary for each class, leading to better performance.

Another good property of this training strategy is that there is no need for specific information from the DNN model, here the classifier ($\mathcal{C}$), to be protected. Actually, the judgement of the binary classifier is only conditioned on given label, which is independent of the DNN model. Therefore, the trained conditional binary classifier can fit various DNN models in a plug-and-play manner.

Figure 3 demonstrates the train-ing process of the proposed condi-tional binary classifier, $\mathcal{C}_b$. *hinge loss* serves as the objective, as formu-lated in Eq. (2), where the x'_y indi-cates the synthesis generated under the groundtruth label y of x, and the (x, x'_y) is used as the positive pair. $x'_{y'}$ depicts the synthesis gener-ated under a randomly sampled mis-matched semantic label $y' \neq y$, then $(x, x'_{y'})$ is used as the negative pair during training. During inference, $\mathcal{C}_b$ is used to score the input image pair. The score can be used to flag OOD samples by a given threshold.

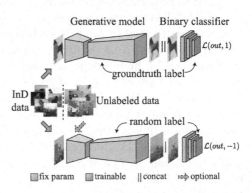

Fig. 3. Training pipeline of the proposed Conditional Binary Classifier.

$$\mathcal{L}_{\mathcal{C}_b} = ReLU(1 - \mathcal{C}_b((x, x'_y), y)) + ReLU(1 + \mathcal{C}_b((x, x'_{y'}), y')) \qquad (2)$$

Image Quality Assessment Models. IQA models [52] are widely adopted to evaluate the perceptual quality of a synthesis by referring to the source image in many computer vision tasks, such as denoising, super-resolution and compression. Here, we apply IQA models as the perceptual metric for the quality of synthesis, forming part of our anomalous scoring model. Since our generative model has already highlighted the contradiction caused by OOD through conditional synthesis, IQA models can be directly applied for detection.

In all, the *Conditional Binary Classifier* and *IQA* models work in a cascade way, where any scorer flags an OOD can lead to the final rejection. Different scoring mechanisms can evaluate the quality of generation from different perspectives, thus supporting each other for better performance than anyone alone.

3.6 Learning with Unlabeled Data

Recently, researchers have shown that including OOD data into the training process can improve the performance of OOD detection [16, 48]. However, they may rely on well labeled data that need to manually identify In-D and OOD elements[1], e.g., [16]. On the contrary, unlabeled data can be easily collected from various sources with little cost. Actually, MOODCAT can be further improved with unlabeled data.

The Conditional Binary Classifier introduced in Sect. 3.5 is trained by treating In-D data with synthesis of mismatched semantic labels as negative pairs. This procedure can be directly combined with external data. Note that, our negative pair only require that the semantic label used for synthesis is different from that of input image. To eliminate possible In-D samples from unlabeled data, we can apply a classifier trained with In-D data to generate pseudo label for unlabeled data. Then, during training, when we randomly sample the mismatched semantic label, we uniformly sample from all possible labels other than the pseudo label. In this way, the sampled semantic label is ensured to be mismatched for both OOD and some possible In-D data from the unlabeled data. Therefore, all of them can be utilized correctly to improve the performance of MOODCAT.

4 Experiments

4.1 Evaluation Settings

Benchmarks. We evaluate MOODCAT on the most recent semantic OOD detection benchmarks, SC-OOD benchmarks [44]. SC-OOD benchmarks provide extensive semantic-level OOD detection settings for evaluation. Specifically, from SC-OOD, images from different datasets are filtered to ensure that only those containing different semantic meanings are considered as OOD samples.

---

[1] Note that, images from another dataset are not necessarily to be OOD w.r.t semantic meaning [44].

SC-OOD focus on the semantic difference between samples, thus being more practical for the real-world model deployment than other previous OOD benchmarks [15,16,26], which are built by setting one dataset as In-D and all others as OOD.

Datasets. Following the settings in [44], we employ CIFAR-10 [22], CIFAR-100 [22] as In-D samples, respectively, and others as OOD samples. When setting CIFAR-10 as In-D, we employ six datasets as OOD datasets, including SVHN [32], CIFAR-100 [22], TEXTURE [4], PLACES365 [53], LSUN [47] and TINY-IMAGENET [24]. For CIFAR-100 benchmarks, the OOD datasets are the same as that of CIFAR-10, except for swapping CIFAR-100 for CIFAR-10 as OOD.

4.2   Evaluation Metrics

We employ FPR@TPR95%, AUROC, AUPR, and Classification Accuracy as the evaluation metrics following [28,44]. In this paper, unless otherwise specified, we denote the In-D as Positive (P), and the OOD as Negative (N).

FPR@TPR95% presents the False Positive Rate (FPR) when the True Positive Rate (TPR) equals 95%. This metric reflects the ratio of falsely identified OOD when most of In-D samples are correctly recognized.

AUROC. The Area Under Receiver Operating Characteristic curve (AUROC) is an overall evaluation metric to reflect the detection capability of a detector.

AUPR-In. AUPR calculates the Area Under the Precision-Recall curve. AUPR is a complementary metric that reflects the impact of imbalanced datasets. For AUPR-In metric, In-D samples are denoted as positive samples.

AUPR-Out indicates the same measure as AUPR-In mentioned above, whereas the OOD samples are deemed as positive during calculating AUPR-Out.

Classification Accuracy presents the classifier's performance on the In-D samples. It indicates the impact on the original classifier caused by OOD detector.

4.3   Experimental Results

We evaluate MOODCAT with two settings: **1)** MOODCAT trained with In-D dataset only; **2)** MOODCAT trained with external unlabeled data (Sect. 3.6). We report the results in Table 1 and Table 2, respectively. Experiments are performed with ResNet18 [13] classifier[2] for fair comparison.

Main Results. As shown in Table 1 and Table 2, experimental results indicate that MOODCAT outperforms or at least on par with SOTA methods on CIFAR-10/CIFAR-100 benchmarks without/with external training data. Since our method detects OODs relying on their semantic-level mismatching instead of low-level distribution shift, the performance of MOODCAT is stable across various OODs. As a plug-and-play model, MOODCAT causes no classifier performance degradation.

Table 1. OOD Detection Performance on Cifar-10 as In-D without using external OOD data for training. All the values are in percentages. ↑/↓ indicates higher/lower value is better. The best results are in **bold**. We also add our results with external data in gray.

Detection methods	OOD	FPR@ TPR95% ↓	AUROC ↑	AUPR In ↑	AUPR Out ↑	Classification accuracy ↑
ODIN [26]	Svhn	52.27	83.26	63.76	92.60	**95.02**
	Cifar-100	61.19	78.40	73.21	80.99	**95.02**
	Tiny-ImageNet	59.09	79.69	79.34	77.52	**92.54**
	Texture	42.52	84.06	86.01	80.73	**95.02**
	Lsun	47.85	84.56	81.56	85.58	**95.02**
	Places365	53.94	82.01	54.92	93.30	**93.87**
	Mean/Std	52.00	82.00/2.48	73.13/11.79	85.12/6.59	**94.42/1.03**
EBO [28]	Svhn	**30.56**	92.08	80.95	96.28	**95.02**
	Cifar-100	56.98	79.65	75.09	81.23	**95.02**
	Tiny-ImageNet	57.81	81.65	81.80	78.75	**92.54**
	Texture	52.11	80.70	83.34	75.20	**95.02**
	Lsun	50.56	85.04	82.80	85.29	**95.02**
	Places365	52.16	83.86	58.96	93.90	**93.87**
	Mean/Std	50.03	83.83/4.51	77.16/9.40	85.11/8.44	**94.42/1.03**
Ours	Svhn	**37.72**/24.27	**92.99**/95.93	**87.43**/92.98	**96.70**/98.05	**95.02**
	Cifar-100	**42.32**/39.92	**89.88**/91.45	**89.75**/91.54	**90.24**/91.73	**95.02**
	Tiny-ImageNet	**40.60**/32.41	**90.57**/93.34	**90.59**/93.63	**90.76**/93.41	**92.54**
	Texture	**26.12**/6.86	**94.15**/98.69	**96.33**/99.29	**91.68**/97.71	**95.02**
	Lsun	**43.86**/33.31	**90.61**/93.40	**91.07**/93.85	**90.02**/93.22	**95.02**
	Places365	**42.34**/35.51	**90.16**/92.77	**75.28**/82.25	**96.83**/94.82	**93.87**
	Mean	**38.83**/28.71	**91.39**/94.27	**88.40**/92.26	**92.71**/94.82	**94.42**
	Std	–	**1.75**/2.61	**7.07**/5.57	**3.20**/2.56	**1.03**

Cifar-10 *Benchmark*. Table 1 reports the detection performance of ODIN [26], EBO [28] and MoodCat on Cifar-10 benchmarks. ODIN and EBO are developed without external OOD data. When comparing these two methods, we implemented MoodCat in the same setting. We additionally report results with external data for training to show the improvements. As shown in Table 1, MoodCat outperforms ODIN and EBO in most cases. For example, for the AUROC, which reflects the overall performance of a detector, MoodCat outperforms baselines on all six OOD benchmarks. Furthermore, MoodCat presents a more stable performance across all OOD datasets. As for statistics, we report the standard deviation (Std) for each metric[3]. As in Table 1, the Std of MoodCat can be much lower than baselines. To be more specific, EBO performs quite well when encounter OODs sourcing from Svhn (AUROC = 92.08%), but when it comes to Cifar-100, the AUROC drops by 12% to 79.65%. On the contrary, the AUROC for MoodCat are all around a high mean value. This stability may due to that MoodCat utilize semantic information, which is exactly the definition

---

[2] For more results under other classifier architectures (WRN28 [50], DenseNet [17]), please refer to Appendix.

[3] FPR@TPR95% is only a single point on the PR curve. It may not reflect the overall performance in terms of standard deviation.

Table 2. OOD Detection Performance on CIFAR-100 as In-D with TINY-IMAGENET as external data for training. All the values are in percentages. ↑/↓ indicates higher/lower value is better. The best results are in **bold**. We also add our results without external data in gray.

Detection methods	OOD	FPR@ TPR95% ↓	AUROC ↑	AUPR In ↑	AUPR Out ↑	Classification accuracy ↑
MCD [48]	SVHN	85.82	76.61	65.50	85.52	68.80
	CIFAR-10	87.74	73.15	76.51	67.24	68.80
	TINY-IMAGENET	84.46	75.32	85.11	59.49	62.21
	TEXTURE	83.97	73.46	83.11	56.79	08.80
	LSUN	86.08	74.05	84.21	58.62	67.51
	PLACES365	82.74	76.30	61.15	87.19	70.47
	Mean/Std	85.14	74.82/1.47	75.93/10.31	69.14/13.81	67.77/2.88
OE [16]	SVHN	68.87	84.23	75.11	91.41	70.49
	CIFAR-10	79.72	78.92	81.95	74.28	70.49
	TINY-IMAGENET	83.41	76.99	86.36	60.56	63.69
	TEXTURE	86.56	73.89	84.48	54.84	70.49
	LSUN	83.53	77.10	86.28	60.97	69.89
	PLACES365	78.24	79.62	67.13	88.89	72.02
	Mean/Std	80.06	78.46/3.46	80.22/**7.66**	71.83/15.58	69.51/2.94
UDG [44]	SVHN	60.00	88.25	**81.46**	93.63	68.51
	CIFAR-10	83.35	76.18	78.92	71.15	68.51
	TINY-IMAGENET	81.73	77.18	86.00	61.67	61.80
	TEXTURE	75.04	79.53	87.63	65.49	68.51
	LSUN	78.70	76.79	84.74	63.05	67.10
	PLACES365	73.89	79.87	65.36	89.60	69.83
	Mean/Std	75.45	79.63/4.48	80.69/8.14	74.10/14.01	67.38/**2.87**
Ours	SVHN	58.16/**51.60**	87.38/**88.99**	78.25/80.89	93.81/**94.81**	76.65
	CIFAR-10	54.31/**50.17**	85.91/**87.76**	86.27/**88.18**	85.91/**87.79**	76.65
	TINY-IMAGENET	55.33/**46.07**	86.95/**89.42**	87.55/**89.73**	86.67/**89.28**	69.56
	TEXTURE	46.70/**42.22**	89.20/**90.56**	93.48/**94.43**	83.28/**85.13**	76.65
	LSUN	53.43/**47.85**	87.98/**89.96**	88.82/**90.33**	87.32/**89.23**	76.10
	PLACES365	54.20/**47.72**	87.41/**89.30**	71.68/**74.83**	95.78/**96.48**	77.56
	Mean	53.69/**47.61**	87.47/**89.33**	84.34/**86.40**	88.80/**90.45**	75.53
	Std	–	0.95/**1.09**	7.19/7.94	4.33/**4.89**	2.96

of OOD. Comparing to the classification features or other low-level features, the semantic contradiction exists more generally.

As discussed in Sect. 3.6, MOODCAT can be equipped with external OOD data for better detection ability. In Table 1, we report the performance for MOODCAT using TINY-IMAGENET as external unlabeled training data in external unlabeled training data in gray. These results evidence the effectiveness of the training strategy with external data for MOODCAT, where significant performance improvements can be found. Due to space limitation, for this setting, we only compare results with baselines on CIFAR-100 (see below) and leave that on CIFAR-10 benchmarks in Appendix.

CIFAR-100 *Benchmark.* OE [16], MCD [48] and UDG [44] rely on TINY-IMAGENET as external OOD data for training. We use them as baselines to show the effectiveness of MooDCAT under this setting. Note that MooDCAT treats all external data as unlabeled during training.

Table 2 shows the results on CIFAR-100 benchmarks. As can be seen, though taking advantage of external data, MCD, OE and UDG suffer from the complicated CIFAR-100 dataset. By contrast, MooDCAT's performance on CIFAR-100 is comparable with that on CIFAR-10 against same OOD shown in Table 1. This is due to MooDCAT's detection mechanism, which relying on the semantic mismatch. Even when the In-D dataset becomes complicated, the semantic mismatch in OODs is still obvious. For methods detect OODs based on DNN-extracted features, e.g. MCD, OE, UDG, they may suffer from poor decision boundaries as the number of classes increases. Similarly as in the case on CIFAR-10, to show the effectiveness of the proposed training strategy with external data, we also report the performance for MooDCAT without external data in external unlabeled training data in gray. The improvement can be seen on all metrics across all OOD settings. For space limitation, we leave the comparison on CIFAR-100 benchmarks without external data in Appendix.

4.4   Comparison with Open Set Recognition Methods

The experimental protocol in OSR is to randomly selecting K classes from a specific n-class dataset as "known" classes and the left $n - K$ as "unknown" classes. To make a fair comparison, we retrain MooDCAT under the experimental settings in CVAECapOSR [11], where only 4 or 6 classes from CIFAR-10 are used for training. We report AUROC scores in Table 3, and the results for other methods are from CVAECapOSR [11]. As can be seen, MooDCAT outperforms these methods in all three settings, especially in the original CIFAR setting, where MooDCAT outperforms the second best method about 6%.

Table 3. Comparison with Open Set Recognition methods. AUROC scores on the detection of known and unknown classes. CIFAR indicates splitting CIFAR-10 to 6 known classes, and 4 unknown. CIFAR $+N$ samples known 4 classes form CIFAR-10, N unknown classes from CIFAR-100. The **bold** indicates the best. For more details about dataset splits, please refer to CVAECapOSR [11].

Method	CIFAR	CIFAR +10	CIFAR +50
OSRCI [31]	$69.9_{\pm 3.8}$	83.8	82.7
C2AE [34]	$71.1_{\pm 0.8}$	$81.0_{\pm 0.5}$	$80.3_{\pm 0.0}$
CVAECapOSR [11]	$83.5_{\pm 2.3}$	$88.8_{\pm 1.9}$	$88.9_{\pm 1.7}$
MooDCAT (ours)	$\mathbf{89.48}_{\pm 0.50}$	$\mathbf{89.36}_{\pm 0.74}$	$\mathbf{89.23}_{\pm 0.19}$

Table 4. OOD Detection Performance under different combinations of anomalous scorers. MOODCAT is trained on CIFAR-10 (In-D) without external data. OODs are from CIFAR-100. All the values are in percentages. ↑/↓ indicates the higher/lower value is better. The best results are in **bold**.

Anomalous scorer	FPR@TPR95% ↓	AUROC ↑	AUPR-In ↑	AUPR-Out↑
C_b	42.80	89.13	88.58	89.85
$LPIPS$	76.62	73.93	72.68	73.23
$DISTS$	82.03	72.14	71.83	70.35
$C_b + LPIPS$	42.14	89.49	89.18	90.11
$C_b + DISTS$	42.31	89.35	89.09	89.98
$LPIPS + DISTS$	76.06	74.78	74.25	73.86
$C_b + LPIPS + DISTS$	**41.95**	**89.57**	**89.30**	**90.16**

4.5 Ablation Study

In this section, we first analyze the effectiveness of every anomalous scorer and how scorers cooperate to achieve the final decent performance. Then we conduct experiments on masking, and give insights on masking's effectiveness.

Anomalous Scoring Model. Table 4 summarizes the performances of every scorer, every two scorers and all three scorers working together. As can be seen in Table 4, the $C_b + LPIPS + DISTS$ combination wins the best detection performance in terms of all evaluation metrics, which means our proposed C_b has a high flexibility to cooperate with IQA models (see Sect. 3.5). We can also observe that coupling scorers usually lead to a better detection capability than that of any single scorer within the coupling. However, adding extra scorers inevitably increases computational and memory overheads. The cost of basic version of MOODCAT, i.e. C_b, **E**, **D**, is relatively small, i.e. Params 4.552M, MACs 0.408G, when compared to that of the widely adopted classifier architectures, e.g., ResNet50 (Params 23.251M, MACs 1.305G). Due to space limitations, we detail the computational and memory costs of MOODCAT and those of the baselines in the Appendix. In practice, MOODCAT can achieve appropriate detection ability, by tailoring scorers in MOODCAT's anomalous scoring model according to the application scenario, i.e. trade-off between the performance and costs, and we discussed this part in Appendix.

Masking. To evidence the effectiveness of masking holistically, we conduct another ablation study without masking in training. As shown in Table 5, the masking scheme indeed plays an important role in the performance of MOOD-CAT. Due to space limitation, we leave the ablation study on masking style in Appendix.

Label Conditioning. As for evaluating label conditioning, we degrade the cGAN to vanilla GAN without conditions. Table 6 reports this ablation study. We can see that our conditioning mechanism outperforms the unconditioned

Table 5. Ablation study on Masking. We set the masking ratio as 0.3 for "Fixed High Ratio" and "Patched", 0.1 for "Fixed Low Ratio", and that of "Randomly" varies from 0.1 to 0.3. MOODCAT employs the **Randomly** masking style.

Training	Inference	FPR@95 ↓	AUROC ↑	AUPR In ↑	AUPR Out ↑
w/o mask	w/o mask	40.67	90.79	90.91	90.88
	Randomly	$38.57_{\pm0.75}$	$90.99_{\pm0.18}$	$90.85_{\pm0.21}$	$91.31_{\pm0.19}$
with mask	w/o mask	37.74	91.52	91.5	91.77
	Fix Low Ratio	37.5	91.64	91.6	91.9
	Fix High Ratio	36.16	91.44	91.03	91.9
	Randomly	$\mathbf{36.15}_{\pm0.94}$	$\mathbf{91.78}_{\pm0.17}$	$\mathbf{91.68}_{\pm0.24}$	$\mathbf{92.08}_{\pm0.14}$

Table 6. Ablation study on label conditioning

In-data	Methods	FPR@95 ↓	AUROC ↑	AUPR In ↑	AUPR Out ↑
Cifar10 In-D	**ours**	**41.95**	**89.57**	**89.30**	**90.16**
Cifar100 OOD	uncond.	86.94	63.62	71.26	63.01
Cifar100 In-D	**ours**	**50.17**	**87.76**	**88.18**	**87.79**
Cifar10 OOD	uncond.	96.74	52.48	56.29	71.24

scheme by a large margin. As analyzed in Sect. 3.2, the conditioning spotlights the semantic discrepancy between In-D and OOD to facilitate OOD detection.

5 Conclusion

In this paper, we propose a novel plug-and-play OOD detection method for image classifiers, MOODCAT, wherein we consider the semantic mismatch under masking as the distance metric. MOODCAT naturally learns the semantic information from the in-distribution data with the proposed mask and conditional synthesis framework. Experimental results demonstrate significantly better OOD detection capabilities of MOODCAT over SOTA solutions.

Acknowledgements. We appreciate the reviewers for their thoughtful comments and efforts towards improving this paper. This work was supported in part by General Research Fund of Hong Kong Research Grants Council (RGC) under Grant No. 14203521 and No. 14205420.

References

1. Amodei, D., Olah, C., Steinhardt, J., Christiano, P., Schulman, J., Mané, D.: Concrete problems in AI safety. arXiv preprint arXiv:1606.06565 (2016)
2. Brock, A., Donahue, J., Simonyan, K.: Large scale GAN training for high fidelity natural image synthesis. In: International Conference on Learning Representations (2018)

3. Choi, H., Jang, E., Alemi, A.A.: WAIC, but why? Generative ensembles for robust anomaly detection. arXiv preprint arXiv:1810.01392 (2018)
4. Cimpoi, M., Maji, S., Kokkinos, I., Mohamed, S., Vedaldi, A.: Describing textures in the wild. In: Proceedings of the IEEE Conference on Computer Vision and Pattern Recognition (CVPR) (2014)
5. De Vries, H., Strub, F., Mary, J., Larochelle, H., Pietquin, O., Courville, A.C.: Modulating early visual processing by language. In: Advances in Neural Information Processing Systems, vol. 30 (2017)
6. Denouden, T., Salay, R., Czarnecki, K., Abdelzad, V., Phan, B., Vernekar, S.: Improving reconstruction autoencoder out-of-distribution detection with Mahalanobis distance. arXiv preprint arXiv:1812.02765 (2018)
7. Dietterich, T.G.: Steps toward robust artificial intelligence. AI Mag. **38**(3), 3–24 (2017)
8. Ding, K., Ma, K., Wang, S., Simoncelli, E.P.: Image quality assessment: unifying structure and texture similarity. IEEE Trans. Pattern Anal. Mach. Intell. **44**(5), 2567–2581 (2022)
9. Drummond, N., Shearer, R.: The open world assumption. In: eSI Workshop: The Closed World of Databases Meets the Open World of the Semantic Web, vol. 15 (2006)
10. Ge, Z., Demyanov, S., Chen, Z., Garnavi, R.: Generative openmax for multi-class open set classification. In: British Machine Vision Conference 2017. British Machine Vision Association and Society for Pattern Recognition (2017)
11. Guo, Y., Camporese, G., Yang, W., Sperduti, A., Ballan, L.: Conditional variational capsule network for open set recognition. In: Proceedings of the IEEE/CVF International Conference on Computer Vision, pp. 103–111 (2021)
12. He, K., Zhang, X., Ren, S., Sun, J.: Delving deep into rectifiers: surpassing human-level performance on imagenet classification. In: Proceedings of the IEEE International Conference on Computer Vision, pp. 1026–1034 (2015)
13. He, K., Zhang, X., Ren, S., Sun, J.: Deep residual learning for image recognition. In: Proceedings of the IEEE Conference on Computer Vision and Pattern Recognition, pp. 770–778 (2016)
14. Hein, M., Andriushchenko, M., Bitterwolf, J.: Why ReLU networks yield high-confidence predictions far away from the training data and how to mitigate the problem. In: Proceedings of the IEEE/CVF Conference on Computer Vision and Pattern Recognition, pp. 41–50 (2019)
15. Hendrycks, D., Gimpel, K.: A baseline for detecting misclassified and out-of-distribution examples in neural networks. In: 5th International Conference on Learning Representations (ICLR) (2017)
16. Hendrycks, D., Mazeika, M., Dietterich, T.: Deep anomaly detection with outlier exposure. In: International Conference on Learning Representations (2018)
17. Huang, G., Liu, Z., Pleiss, G., Van Der Maaten, L., Weinberger, K.: Convolutional networks with dense connectivity. IEEE Trans. Pattern Anal. Mach. Intell. 1 (2019)
18. Huang, H., Li, Z., Wang, L., Chen, S., Zhou, X., Dong, B.: Feature space singularity for out-of-distribution detection. In: Proceedings of the Workshop on Artificial Intelligence Safety (SafeAI) (2021)
19. Huang, R., Geng, A., Li, Y.: On the importance of gradients for detecting distributional shifts in the wild. In: Advances in Neural Information Processing Systems, vol. 34 (2021)
20. Kingma, D.P., Welling, M.: Auto-encoding variational Bayes. In: 2nd International Conference on Learning Representations (ICLR) (2014)

21. Kirichenko, P., Izmailov, P., Wilson, A.G.: Why normalizing flows fail to detect out-of-distribution data. In: Advances in Neural Information Processing Systems, vol. 33, pp. 20578–20589 (2020)
22. Krizhevsky, A., Hinton, G., et al.: Learning multiple layers of features from tiny images (2009)
23. Krizhevsky, A., Sutskever, I., Hinton, G.E.: ImageNet classification with deep convolutional neural networks. In: Advances in Neural Information Processing Systems, vol. 25, pp. 1106–1114 (2012)
24. Le, Y., Yang, X.: Tiny ImageNet visual recognition challenge. CS 231N **7**(7), 3 (2015)
25. Lee, K., Lee, K., Lee, H., Shin, J.: A simple unified framework for detecting out-of-distribution samples and adversarial attacks. In: Advances in Neural Information Processing Systems, vol. 31 (2018)
26. Liang, S., Li, Y., Srikant, R.: Enhancing the reliability of out-of-distribution image detection in neural networks. In: 6th International Conference on Learning Representations, ICLR 2018 (2018)
27. Lin, Z., Roy, S.D., Li, Y.: MOOD: multi-level out-of-distribution detection. In: Proceedings of the IEEE/CVF Conference on Computer Vision and Pattern Recognition, pp. 15313–15323 (2021)
28. Liu, W., Wang, X., Owens, J., Li, Y.: Energy-based out-of-distribution detection. In: Advances in Neural Information Processing Systems, vol. 33, pp. 21464–21475. Curran Associates, Inc. (2020)
29. Miyato, T., Koyama, M.: cGANs with projection discriminator. In: International Conference on Learning Representations (2018)
30. Nalisnick, E., Matsukawa, A., Teh, Y.W., Gorur, D., Lakshminarayanan, B.: Do deep generative models know what they don't know? In: International Conference on Learning Representations (2019)
31. Neal, L., Olson, M., Fern, X., Wong, W.-K., Li, F.: Open set learning with counterfactual images. In: Ferrari, V., Hebert, M., Sminchisescu, C., Weiss, Y. (eds.) ECCV 2018. LNCS, vol. 11210, pp. 620–635. Springer, Cham (2018). https://doi.org/10.1007/978-3-030-01231-1_38
32. Netzer, Y., Wang, T., Coates, A., Bissacco, A., Wu, B., Ng, A.Y.: Reading digits in natural images with unsupervised feature learning. In: NIPS Workshop on Deep Learning and Unsupervised Feature Learning 2011 (2011)
33. Nguyen, A., Yosinski, J., Clune, J.: Deep neural networks are easily fooled: high confidence predictions for unrecognizable images. In: Proceedings of the IEEE Conference on Computer Vision and Pattern Recognition, pp. 427–436 (2015)
34. Oza, P., Patel, V.M.: C2AE: class conditioned auto-encoder for open-set recognition. In: Proceedings of the IEEE/CVF Conference on Computer Vision and Pattern Recognition, pp. 2307–2316 (2019)
35. Pidhorskyi, S., Almohsen, R., Doretto, G.: Generative probabilistic novelty detection with adversarial autoencoders. In: Advances in Neural Information Processing Systems, vol. 31 (2018)
36. Ren, J., et al.: Likelihood ratios for out-of-distribution detection. In: Advances in Neural Information Processing Systems, vol. 32 (2019)
37. Sara, U., Akter, M., Uddin, M.S.: Image quality assessment through FSIM, SSIM, MSE and PSNR-a comparative study. J. Comput. Commun. **7**(3), 8–18 (2019)
38. Schlegl, T., Seeböck, P., Waldstein, S.M., Schmidt-Erfurth, U., Langs, G.: Unsupervised anomaly detection with generative adversarial networks to guide marker discovery. In: Niethammer, M., et al. (eds.) IPMI 2017. LNCS, vol. 10265, pp. 146–157. Springer, Cham (2017). https://doi.org/10.1007/978-3-319-59050-9_12

39. Schonfeld, E., Schiele, B., Khoreva, A.: A U-Net based discriminator for generative adversarial networks. In: Proceedings of the IEEE/CVF Conference on Computer Vision and Pattern Recognition, pp. 8207–8216 (2020)
40. Sricharan, K., Srivastava, A.: Building robust classifiers through generation of confident out of distribution examples. arXiv preprint arXiv:1812.00239 (2018)
41. Vernekar, S., Gaurav, A., Abdelzad, V., Denouden, T., Salay, R., Czarnecki, K.: Out-of-distribution detection in classifiers via generation. arXiv preprint arXiv:1910.04241 (2019)
42. Wang, H., Liu, W., Bocchieri, A., Li, Y.: Can multi-label classification networks know what they don't know? In: Advances in Neural Information Processing Systems, vol. 34 (2021)
43. Wang, Y., Li, B., Che, T., Zhou, K., Liu, Z., Li, D.: Energy-based open-world uncertainty modeling for confidence calibration. In: Proceedings of the IEEE/CVF International Conference on Computer Vision, pp. 9302–9311 (2021)
44. Yang, J., et al.: Semantically coherent out-of-distribution detection. In: Proceedings of the IEEE/CVF International Conference on Computer Vision, pp. 8301–8309 (2021)
45. Yang, J., Zhou, K., Li, Y., Liu, Z.: Generalized out-of-distribution detection: a survey. arXiv preprint arXiv:2110.11334 (2021)
46. Yang, Y., Gao, R., Li, Y., Lai, Q., Xu, Q.: What you see is not what the network infers: detecting adversarial examples based on semantic contradiction. In: Network and Distributed System Security Symposium (NDSS) (2022)
47. Yu, F., Seff, A., Zhang, Y., Song, S., Funkhouser, T., Xiao, J.: LSUN: construction of a large-scale image dataset using deep learning with humans in the loop (2016)
48. Yu, Q., Aizawa, K.: Unsupervised out-of-distribution detection by maximum classifier discrepancy. In: Proceedings of the IEEE/CVF International Conference on Computer Vision (ICCV) (2019)
49. Zaeemzadeh, A., Bisagno, N., Sambugaro, Z., Conci, N., Rahnavard, N., Shah, M.: Out-of-distribution detection using union of 1-dimensional subspaces. In: Proceedings of the IEEE/CVF Conference on Computer Vision and Pattern Recognition, pp. 9452–9461 (2021)
50. Zagoruyko, S., Komodakis, N.: Wide residual networks. In: British Machine Vision Conference 2016. British Machine Vision Association (2016)
51. Zhang, H., Goodfellow, I., Metaxas, D., Odena, A.: Self-attention generative adversarial networks. In: International Conference on Machine Learning (2019)
52. Zhang, R., Isola, P., Efros, A.A., Shechtman, E., Wang, O.: The unreasonable effectiveness of deep features as a perceptual metric. In: Proceedings of the IEEE Conference on Computer Vision and Pattern Recognition, pp. 586–595 (2018)
53. Zhou, B., Lapedriza, A., Khosla, A., Oliva, A., Torralba, A.: Places: a 10 million image database for scene recognition. IEEE Trans. Pattern Anal. Mach. Intell. **40**(6), 1452–1464 (2017)

Data-Free Neural Architecture Search via Recursive Label Calibration

Zechun Liu[1,2], Zhiqiang Shen[1,2,3(✉)], Yun Long[4], Eric Xing[2,3],
Kwang-Ting Cheng[1], and Chas Leichner[4]

[1] Hong Kong University of Science and Technology, Hong Kong, China
zliubq@connect.ust.hk, zhiqiangshen0214@gmail.com, timcheng@ust.hk
[2] Carnegie Mellon University, Pittsburgh, USA
epxing@cs.cmu.edu
[3] Mohamed bin Zayed University of Artificial Intelligence,
Abu Dhabi, UAE
[4] Google Research, Mountain View, USA
{longy,cleichner}@google.com

Abstract. This paper aims to explore the feasibility of neural architecture search (NAS) given only a pre-trained model without using any original training data. This is an important circumstance for privacy protection, bias avoidance, etc., in real-world scenarios. To achieve this, we start by synthesizing usable data through recovering the knowledge from a pre-trained deep neural network. Then we use the synthesized data and their predicted soft labels to guide NAS. We identify that the quality of the synthesized data will substantially affect the NAS results. Particularly, we find NAS requires the synthesized images to possess enough semantics, diversity, and a minimal domain gap from the natural images. To meet these requirements, we propose recursive label calibration to encode more relative semantics in images, as well as regional update strategy to enhance the diversity. Further, we use input and feature-level regularization to mimic the original data distribution in latent space and reduce the domain gap. We instantiate our proposed framework with three popular NAS algorithms: DARTS, ProxylessNAS and SPOS. Surprisingly, our results demonstrate that the architectures discovered by searching with our synthetic data achieve accuracy that is comparable to, or even higher than, architectures discovered by searching from the original ones, for the first time, deriving the conclusion that NAS can be done effectively with no need of access to the original or called natural data if the synthesis method is well designed. Code and models are available at: https://github.com/liuzechun/Data-Free-NAS.

1 Introduction

Neural architecture search (NAS) has demonstrated substantial success in automating the design of neural networks [1,11,14,20,21,26,35]. A typical NAS

This work is done when Zechun Liu is an intern at Google Research.

Supplementary Information The online version contains supplementary material available at https://doi.org/10.1007/978-3-031-20053-3_23.

algorithm usually involves three core components: a search space, a search algorithm, and a set of training data. The majority of researches in NAS focuses on search space design [15,30] or exploring superior search algorithms [4,27]. While, in this study, we investigate the feasibility of performing neural architecture search without accessing the original training data. We assume that we only have a pre-trained model, and the original dataset is not accessible during the neural architecture search process. This is a common and useful circumstance that is needed to be solved urgently for privacy protection, bias avoidance, etc. We call this *data-free NAS*, a practical task for application scenarios in which privacy or logistical concerns restrict sharing of the original training data but permit sharing of a model trained by such data for NAS. Also, models are usually smaller in size than large-scale datasets, which makes them easier to exchange and store.

Conducting NAS without data is challenging. Traditional NAS relies on the input images to train and rank different architectures. A natural image dataset contains semantic patterns and inter-class relationships, which are helpful in guiding architecture search. For scenarios where the original data is not accessible, we first need to synthesize an image dataset from the model pre-trained on the original data, and use such a synthesized dataset for conducting architecture search. This, however, raises a crucial question: how do we synthesize an image dataset that has the important search-relevant attributes or properties of the original data for effective NAS without using any of the original data?

Currently, data-free NAS is an under-explored task that requires unique understanding of the particular synthesized data. In this work, we empirically identify three attributes that NAS in data-free scenario requires the synthesized images to have: (i) rich semantic information, (ii) sufficient image diversity, and (iii) a minimized domain gap with the original data. Rich semantic information ensures the classification task on the synthesized images is as complex as that of the original training images. High image diversity prevents the NAS algorithms from overfitting to the synthesized data and producing trivial solutions. A minimized domain gap makes certain that architectures found by searching over the synthesized data also can perform well on the original data.

To fulfill these requirements, we propose a novel image synthesis method for promoting the effectiveness of architecture search procedure. As shown in Fig. 1, we synthesize the images using gradient descent with respect to class labels. We observe that conducting NAS on data synthesized from one-hot labels leads to overfitting and the models searched by the NAS algorithms fail to generalize to the original training data. This issue is caused by one-hot labels' limitation of being unable to capture the full set of semantic relationships between classes in the original training data. For instance, the synthesized images will be confidently classified as a single class (*e.g.*, "coffee mug") but with no trace of similarity to other relevant classes (*e.g.*, "cup"). To avoid this, we propose *recursive label calibration* for finding semantically-significant soft labels.

As shown in Fig. 1(a), we use logits derived from the pre-trained model as the class labels during the image synthesis process. Starting from a hard label, i.e., one-hot distribution, we recursively apply this labeling process to successive

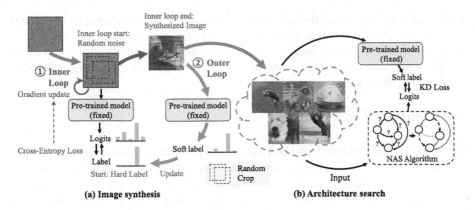

Fig. 1. The proposed data-free NAS framework consists of two stages: (a) image synthesis using recursive label calibration, and regional update; (b) running an architecture search using the synthesized images. Specifically, the image synthesis stage consists of an **Inner Loop** and an **Outer Loop**. The **Inner Loop** starts with a random noise input, which is then updated with the gradient computed from the cross-entropy loss (CE-loss). The inner loop ends when random noise converges to a batch of synthesized images. Then in the **Outer Loop**, we infer the predictions of the synthesized images using the pre-trained model and use these predictions as the soft labels for synthesizing the next batch of images. See Sect. 3 for details.

batches of images to amplify the representation of classes which are semantically related to the original target class while only weakly presented in the initial image synthesis. We show that images synthesized using recursive label calibration are more diverse and can better capture semantic relationships that exist in the original training data. In order to further improve the diversity, we propose a novel regional gradient updating scheme on synthesized images to match the random crop augmentation in training NAS.

We show that, the architecture accuracy rankings on the data synthesized with the proposed method produce more consistent correlation with the rankings on the original data. In turn, NAS on our synthesized data discovers the searched architecture with much higher accuracy. We demonstrate the feasibility of our data-free NAS conversion on three prevalent NAS algorithms: a reinforcement-learning-based algorithm (ProxylessNAS [4]), an evolution-based algorithm (Single Path One-Shot [8]) and a gradient-based algorithm (DARTS [15]).

We make four major contributions in this paper:

- We reveal, for the first time, that it is feasible to search architectures without relying on the original training data and propose a framework for data-free NAS.
- We identify properties of synthesized images that NAS requires, and propose a data synthesis method that uses recursive label calibration and regional update to generate images with sufficiently high diversity from the information stored in a pre-trained model for effective NAS.

- We validate the generalization ability of data-free NAS by integrating it with three different NAS algorithms and demonstrating competitive results.
- We further extend the scope of our data synthesis method and demonstrate that it also outperforms prior approaches for the data-free pruning and knowledge transfer tasks.

2   Related Work

Generative adversarial networks (GAN) [2,33] can generate images with high fidelity, but still need real images as a reference while training the generator, which is not fully data-free. Recently, Chen et al. [5] and Xu et al. [28] proposed to use a generator to synthesize images from a pre-trained model and simultaneously train the student network. Further, Yin et al. [29] proposed to synthesize images from the pre-trained teacher network using regularization terms and Jensen-Shannon divergence loss. However, such method is a general design without explicitly considering the requirements for architecture search and also ignoring the crucial factors like the semantic diversity in the latent feature and image spaces. In this work, we propose recursive label calibration and regional update to generate more diverse and semantically meaningful images to fulfill the demand of neural architecture search.

Neural Architecture Search (NAS) is a tool for automatic discovery of optimized neural network architectures under various practical constraints. To conduct NAS, it normally requires a search space, a search algorithm and a set of training data. Current NAS research mainly focuses on improving the search algorithms [1,20,34,35], designing the search space [7,21,30], reducing the search cost [3,4,11,15,19] and integrating direct metrics with the search process [8,27]. To our best knowledge, there is no previous literature directly studying the problem of data-free NAS. Thus, our work has many practical and useful guidelines on this problem for future research. One prior work [13] may be the closest one to ours, it proposed to conduct NAS without human-annotated labels. In our study, we take one step further and attempt to answer the question of whether NAS can be conducted even without the original data at all.

3   Our Method

In data-free neural architecture search, as we have no access to the original data $\mathbf{X} \in \mathbb{R}^{w \times h}$, we aim to use synthesized data $\hat{\mathbf{X}} \in \mathbb{R}^{w \times h}$ to search for the high-performing architecture $\mathbf{A}^*$ in the search space of $\mathcal{S}$, with the NAS algorithm minimizing the loss:

$$\mathbf{A}^* = \underset{\mathbf{A} \in \mathcal{S}}{\text{argmin}} \ \mathcal{L}(\mathbf{A}|\hat{\mathbf{X}}). \tag{1}$$

In this way, we target at finding an architecture that achieves high performance when evaluated on the target data $\mathcal{X}$:

$$\mathbf{A}^* \approx \underset{\mathbf{A} \in \mathcal{S}}{\text{argmax}} \ \mathbf{Acc}_{\text{eval}}(\mathbf{A}|\mathbf{X}). \tag{2}$$

This requires the synthesized images to be semantically meaningful, diverse, and have a minimum domain gap with target data (*i.e.*, $\hat{\mathbf{X}} \sim \mathbf{X}$) to ensure that the architecture rankings on the synthesized images align well with the rankings on original data. Such that we can conduct data-free NAS by integrating the synthesized data and their corresponding soft labels with existing NAS algorithms.

3.1 Data Synthesis

We optimize the classification (cross-entropy) loss between the pre-trained model's prediction $\mathbf{M}_{\mathrm{pretrained}}(\hat{\mathbf{X}})$ on the synthesized data and the target label y:

$$\min_{\hat{\mathbf{X}}} \mathcal{L}_{CE}(\mathbf{M}_{\mathbf{pretrained}}(\hat{\mathbf{X}}), \mathbf{y}), \tag{3}$$

where $\mathcal{L}_{CE}$ denotes the classification loss (*i.e.*, cross-entropy loss) and $\hat{\mathbf{X}}$ denotes input "image".

Specifically, since one-hot label $\mathbf{y}$ is unable to capture the underlying class relationship, we propose recursive label calibration to automatically learn the semantically-related soft labels $\hat{\mathbf{y}}$ and use $\hat{\mathbf{y}}$ for image synthesis. Furthermore, we propose a novel regional update scheme to improve the diversity of generated images.

Regularization (i) *Input-level Regularization:*
As a natural image taken from a real scene is unlikely to sharply vary in value between adjacent pixels, following [17], we impose a regularization term $\mathcal{L}_{input}$ to penalize the overall variance in the synthesized data:

$$\mathcal{L}_{input} = \sum_{i,j}((\hat{\mathbf{X}}_{(i+1,j)} - \hat{\mathbf{X}}_{(i,j)})^2 + (\hat{\mathbf{X}}_{(i,j+1)} - \hat{\mathbf{X}}_{(i,j)})^2) \tag{4}$$

where i, j denotes the index of each pixel in the image.
(ii) *Feature-level Regularization:*
Further, we impose a regularization term to align the high-level feature map statistics with the target images by enforcing the synthesized images to produce similar statistics in the feature maps as statistics calculated and stored in each BN layer of the pre-trained model, as [29].

$$\mathcal{L}_{feat} = \sum_{l}(||\mathbf{E}_l(\hat{\mathbf{X}}) - \mathbf{E}_l(\mathbf{X})||_2 + ||\mathbf{Var}_l(\hat{\mathbf{X}}) - \mathbf{Var}_l(\mathbf{X})||_2) \tag{5}$$

Here, $\mathbf{E}_l(\hat{\mathbf{X}})$ and $\mathrm{Var}_l(\hat{\mathbf{X}})$ denote the mean and variance of the feature map of synthesized images in the lth convolutional layer, $\mathbf{E}_l(\mathbf{X})$ and $\mathrm{Var}_l(\mathbf{X})$ denote the historical mean and variance of target images, which are stored in Batch-Norm [10] of the pre-trained model.

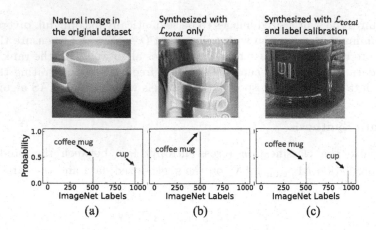

Fig. 2. The pre-trained model's prediction on the input image. (a) Natural image in the category *"coffee mug"*. Its prediction contains a peak at *"coffee mug"* and another peak value in the related class *"cup"*. (b) The image synthesized *w.r.t.* the *"coffee mug"* class as a one-hot hard label. The pre-trained model only strongly predicts this image as *"coffee mug"*. Meanwhile, there is a pattern on the surface of the mug that resembles coffee. (c) The image synthesized using recursive label calibration. It automatically identifies *"cup"* as a related class for the image synthesized *w.r.t.* the *"coffee mug"* category. The image looks more natural as well.

Recursive Label Calibration. Importantly, we observe that the pre-trained model's prediction on a natural image will spread as a distribution of logits, with the maximum value being the target class and other several peaks landing at similar classes, shown in Fig. 2(a).

Thus, for encouraging synthesized images to model higher-level class correlation and to capture more subtle semantic information, we want the targets of synthesized images to be a distribution of semantically-related classes. Considering no original images are available, we cannot obtain the relationship between classes directly. However, we make an important observation that the pre-trained model's prediction on the image synthesized with respect to the hard label also has fractional logits spread between semantically similar classes. But these logits are too weak to be reflected in the synthetic images. Thus, we propose recursive label calibration to amplify this distribution, which utilizes the soft prediction of the previously synthesized image as the new targets,

$$\hat{\mathbf{y}}_{t-1} = \mathbf{M}_{\mathbf{pretrained}}(\hat{\mathbf{X}}_{t-1}), \tag{6}$$

replacing the hard label y in Eq. 3 to guide the image synthesizing process:

$$\hat{\mathbf{X}}_t^* = \min_{\hat{\mathbf{X}}} \mathcal{L}_{CE}(\mathbf{M}_{\mathbf{pretrained}}(\hat{\mathbf{X}}_t), \hat{\mathbf{y}}_{t-1}) \tag{7}$$

as also illustrated in Fig. 3.

After visualizing the images synthesized with recursive label calibration, we confirm that these images do learn the semantic relationships among classes. As

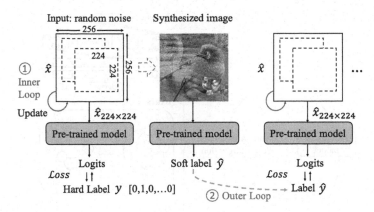

Fig. 3. An illustration of the proposed regional update scheme and recursive label calibration for image synthesis. In every iteration of the generation process, a 224×224 region is randomly cropped from the 256×256 input and we update the selected region using gradients calculated *w.r.t.* Eq. 3. After an image is synthesized, we use the pre-trained model's prediction on the synthesized image as the soft label for computing the cross-entropy loss with the output logits of the next image batch.

shown in Fig. 2(b), the image synthesized without label calibration is overconfident at the prediction of the "coffee mug" class. While in Fig. 2(c), the prediction of the image synthesized with recursive label calibration automatically learns that "coffee mug" and "cup" are two related classes. Recursive label calibration encourages the synthesized images to learn class relationships as natural images instead of over-fitting to a single class, which in turn allows the synthesized images to encode more semantic information.

In addition, the prediction of the most related classes differs between synthetic image batches due to stochasticity in the synthesis process. Since each synthesis target is now a weighted combination of related classes rather than a single class, the number of distinct targets is greatly increased. More targets lead to more diversity in the images synthesized from these targets and produce a synthesized dataset that better resembles the natural training set. We show that higher similarity between synthetic and natural dataset leads to consistency in evaluation accuracy between architectures trained on original data and the synthetic data.

Regional Update Scheme. To further enhance synthesized image diversity, we propose a regional update scheme for synthesis process. The regional update is formulated as:

$$\mathbf{G}_{\hat{\mathbf{X}}} = \nabla_{\hat{\mathbf{X}}} \mathcal{L}_{CE}(\mathbf{M}_{\mathbf{pretrained}}(\hat{\mathbf{X}}_{w,h \in \mathbf{R}_{\mathbf{selected}}}), \mathbf{y}), \tag{8}$$

Instead of generating the images with the size required for forward computation in the neural network, *e.g.*, 224×224 for ImageNet dataset, we enlarge the size of the input tensor $\hat{\mathbf{X}}$, *e.g.*, 256×256 for ImageNet dataset. In every iteration,

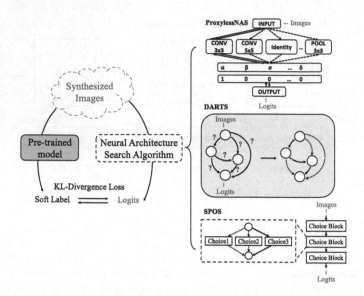

Fig. 4. The proposed data-free neural architecture search framework using the synthesized images. We replace the original ones with the synthesized images and use the soft labels to compute the KL-divergence loss with the output logits of NAS.

we randomly select a sub-region $\mathbf{R_{selected}}$, *e.g.*, 224×224 as the input to the pre-trained model and calculate the gradients $\mathbf{G_{\hat{x}}}$. We only update the selected region, leaving the pixels outside of that region unchanged, as also shown in Fig. 3. This proposed regional update during image synthesis reflects the random crop data augmentation during training, which greatly increases the amount of trainable data and enhances the image diversity. Additionally, it can encourage the translation-invariance in the synthesized images.

3.2   Architecture Search

After extracting the classification-relevant information from the pre-trained model by constructing a synthetic dataset, we use that dataset to conduct neural architecture search. Figure 4 illustrates the proposed data-free neural architecture search framework: data-free NAS can be applied to an existing NAS algorithm by replacing the natural training data with synthetic data, and the classification labels with soft labels from pre-trained model. We instantiate data-free NAS with three prevalent NAS algorithms: ProxylessNAS [4], DARTS [15] and SPOS [8], which are reinforcement-learning-based, gradient-based and evolution-based respectively:

The gradient-based neural architecture search jointly learn the architecture parameter $\boldsymbol{\alpha}$ and the SuperNet weights $\mathbf{W}$, aiming to find $\boldsymbol{\alpha}^*$ that minimizes the validation loss $\mathcal{L}_{val}$, with weights $\mathbf{W}^*$ in the SuperNet obtained by minimizing the training loss $\mathcal{L}_{train}$ [15].

$$\min_{\alpha} \quad \mathcal{L}_{val}(\mathbf{W}^*(\alpha), \alpha) \tag{9}$$

$$\text{s.t.} \quad \mathbf{W}^*(\alpha) = \operatorname*{argmin}_{\mathbf{W}} \mathcal{L}_{train}(\mathbf{W}, \alpha) \tag{10}$$

The reinforcement-learning-based method use the policy gradient to update the architecture parameters $\mathbf{g}$ to maximize the reward R [4].

$$\mathcal{L}(\alpha) = \mathbb{E}_{\mathbf{g} \sim \alpha}[R(\mathbf{A_g})], \tag{11}$$

$$\nabla_\alpha \mathcal{L}(\alpha) = \mathbb{E}_{\mathbf{g} \sim \alpha}[R(\mathbf{A_g}) \nabla_\alpha \log(\mathbf{p}(\mathbf{g}))], \tag{12}$$

where $\mathbf{g}$ denotes the binary gates of choosing certain masks with probability $\mathbf{p}$.

The evolution-based search in SPOS disentangled SuperNet training and architectural parameter optimization. Specifically for SuperNet training:

$$\mathbf{W}^*(\alpha) = \operatorname*{argmin}_{\mathbf{W}}, \mathbb{E}_{\alpha \sim \Gamma(\mathbf{A})} \mathcal{L}_{train}(\mathbf{W}, \alpha), \tag{13}$$

where $\mathbf{W}$ denotes the SuperNet weights, α denotes the architecture parameters and $\Gamma(\mathbf{A})$ is the probability distribution of architecture sampling. After the supernet is trained, the weights can be used for evolutionary search in the second separate step.

In the search phase, data-free NAS explores the pre-defined search space using the same search algorithm as the NAS algorithm it integrates. Instead of using the original data for ranking different architectures, we show that data-free NAS can reliably estimate the ranking with synthetic data generated with the proposed method. Further, we show that these architectural rankings are consistent with rankings on the original data, meaning that data-free NAS algorithms can discover architectures that achieve high accuracy when evaluated on the target data.

4   Experiments

To verify the effectiveness of our proposed data synthesis method for NAS, we first conduct consistency experiments, showing that with the proposed data synthesis method, the synthesized dataset possesses high correlation with the original data. Then, with these synthetic data, we demonstrate the feasibility of data-free NAS in discovering the architectures that perform competitively when evaluated on the target data. Further, we show that our synthesized data is also helpful in enhancing the accuracy of other tasks like data-free pruning and knowledge transfer and outperforms previous works. Lastly, we visualize the synthetic data in Sec. *Visualization*, and find that the proposed recursive label calibration and regional update scheme can largely improve the semantic diversity of the synthetic data and helps capture the underlying class relationships.

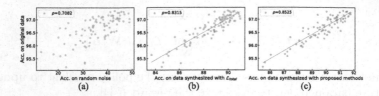

Fig. 5. Correlation between the accuracy of the architectures sampled from the DARTS [15] search space on the original CIFAR-10 data and different sources of synthetic data (including random noise). Here, ρ denotes Spearman's rank correlation.

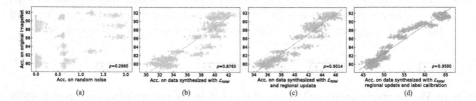

Fig. 6. Accuracy correlation on the SPOS [8] search space between original ImageNet *vs.* random noise as well as data synthesized with different methods. ρ denotes Spearman's rank correlation.

4.1   Consistency Exploration

We conduct the consistency experiments on two search spaces: the DARTS search space [15], and the Single Path One-Shot (SPOS) search space [8]. The term *consistency* refers to the accuracy correlation between the architectures trained on the synthetic data and the original data.

DARTS Search Space on CIFAR-10 Dataset. For DARTS search space, we randomly sample 100 architectures, and train each architecture from scratch using original CIFAR-10 data, synthetic data, or random noise separately and report the architecture's accuracy when evaluated on original CIFAR-10 validation dataset. Figure 5 shows the correlation between the accuracy of architectures trained on synthetic data and the original data. Spearman's Rank Correlation [25], denoted as "ρ", is calculated in order to quantify the correlations between accuracy on synthesized and original data. From Fig. 5(a) we can see that the overall accuracy of the network trained on the random noise is lower than 50% and the ranking is highly noisy, the random noise can hardly guide NAS for finding a high-quality architecture. In contrast, synthesized data improves the correlation compared to random noise and recursive label calibration further enhances the correlation. This correlation supports our belief that a NAS algorithm applied on the good synthetic data is likely to discover architectures that perform well on the original data.

Table 1. Comparison between data-free DARTS and other NAS algorithms on CIFAR-10. † denotes using cutout.

Methods	Top-1 err (%)	Params (M)	Data for NAS
NASNet-A† [35]	2.65	3.3	CIFAR-10
BlockQNN [32]	3.54	39.8	CIFAR-10
AmoebaNet-A† [20]	3.12	3.1	CIFAR-10
PNAS [14]	3.41 ± 0.09	3.2	CIFAR-10
ENAS† [19]	2.89	4.6	CIFAR-10
Random search† [15]	3.29 ± 0.15	3.2	CIFAR-10
DARTS† [15]	2.76 ± 0.09	3.3	CIFAR-10
Data-free DARTS	**2.68 ± 0.09**	3.3	**Synthesized data**

Table 2. Generalization of architecture searched with data-free DARTS [15] from CIFAR-10 to ImageNet.

Methods	Top-1 err (%)	Params (M)	Data for NAS
DARTS [15]	26.7	4.7	ImageNet
Data-free DARTS	**26.4**	4.7	**Synthesized data**

SPOS Search Space on ImageNet Dataset. We use the SPOS [8] search space to explore the more challenging task of architecture search on the large-scale ImageNet dataset. We randomly sample 1000 architectures from the SPOS search space, then evaluate their accuracy. As shown in Fig. 6(a), for the large-scale ImageNet, simply using the random noise results in a totally uncorrelated accuracy between original and the "noise data", the images synthesized with the regularization term produce an improved correlation compared to random noise, which, however, is still not sufficient for performing architecture search, as shown in Fig. 6(b). The proposed recursive label calibration and regional update scheme further improve the correlation with ρ increasing from 0.87 to 0.96, in Fig. 6(d), showing that the images synthesized with the proposed method produce a more correlated architecture ranking, which better guarantees the architecture searched on the synthesized dataset will achieve high accuracy on the target dataset.

4.2 Search Results

We investigate the effectiveness and generality of our data-free neural architecture search framework by testing it with three prevalent neural architecture search algorithms: DARTS [15], SPOS [8] and ProxylessNAS [4].

Implementation Details
Our experiments on DARTS are targeted at classification over CIFAR-10 [12] dataset and our experiments on SPOS and ProxylessNAS are targeted at classification over ImageNet [22] dataset. More experimental details can be referred to our Appendix.

Z. Liu et al.

Table 3. Comparison between data-free SPOS, original SPOS [8] as well as other baseline results. "All choice" refers to the baseline algorithm where the same operation is chosen for all layers. "All Choice _3, _5, _7" denotes choosing only a ShuffleNet [31] block with 3 × 3, 5 × 5, or 7 × 7 convolution, respectively. "Choice _x" denotes using the Xception block [6].

Methods	Top-1 err (%)	FLOPs (M)	Data for NAS
all choice _3	26.6	324	ImageNet
all choice _5	26.5	321	ImageNet
all choice _7	26.4	327	ImageNet
all choice _x	26.5	326	ImageNet
Random Select	~26.3	~320	ImageNet
Random Search	26.2	323	ImageNet
SPOS [8]	**25.7**	319	ImageNet
Data-free SPOS	25.8	316	**Synthesized data**

Table 4. Comparison between RL-based ProxylessNAS integrated with our data-free NAS framework and the original ProxylessNAS. We choose the targeting metrics as FLOPs.

Methods	Top-1 err (%)	FLOPs (M)	Data for NAS
ProxylessNAS [4]	24.4	467	ImageNet
Data-free ProxylessNAS	**24.2**	465	**Synthesized data**

Instantiations

Data-Free DARTS: The architecture found by using DARTS with the data synthesized with the proposed method achieves 2.68% test error. As shown in Table 1, this is comparable to the architecture found when using DARTS with the original CIFAR-10 data. The search result of using data synthesized without label calibration is comparable to random search. This shows that the proposed synthesis method generates data with high correlation to the original CIFAR-10 data, which provides a basis for searching architectures on synthetic data that achieve high performance when evaluated on the original data. Further, the architecture discovered from the data synthesized with label calibration also generalizes well to the ImageNet dataset and achieves slightly higher accuracy than original DARTS, shown in Table 2.

Data-Free Single Path One-Shot: As shown in Table 3, compared to data synthesized without label calibration, the data synthesized with label calibration provides better guidance and results in higher final accuracy. The architecture discovered using synthesized data with label calibration achieves 74.2% top-1 accuracy. This accuracy is comparable to the results obtained by the SPOS search on the original ImageNet. This result also far exceeds random search as well as the baseline method of choosing the same operation for all layers, demonstrating the feasibility of using synthetic images for data-free NAS on a large-scale dataset.

Table 5. Comparison for data-free pruning on ResNet-50 structure.

Methods	Data type	Top-1 err (%)	FLOPs (G)
ImageNet	Original	23.4	4.1
BigGAN [2]	GAN synthesized	37.0	~1.2
DI [29]	Synthesized	44.1	~1.2
ADI [29]	Synthesized	39.3	~1.2
Ours	Synthesized	**36.5**	**1.0**

Table 6. The top-1 error of data-free knowledge transfer using ResNet-34 as the pre-trained teacher model for synthesize images and train a ResNet-18 student model from scratch for CIFAR-10.

Methods	Noise	DeepDream [17]	DAFL [5]	ADI [29]	Ours
Top-1 err (%)	86.39	70.02	7.78	6.74	**5.97**

Data-Free ProxylessNAS: We adopt the RL-based ProxylessNAS targeting at the FLOPs constraint. Table 4 shows that ProxylessNAS, when integrated with our data-free framework, also achieves accuracy comparable to Proxyless-NAS searching on the original data.

4.3   Extension Tasks

Data-Free Pruning: We show that the proposed data-free NAS can be applied to pruning tasks via integrating with a search-based pruning method, MetaPruning [16]. We use synthesized ImageNet images to guide MetaPruning for finding the best pruning ratio in each layer and train the searched pruned network from scratch also with the synthesized images. Results in Table 5 show that our data-free pruning achieves much higher accuracy than the previous state-of-the-art data-free pruning [29]. It further surpasses pruning using GAN-synthesized images. See the appendix for full training details.

Data-Free Knowledge Transfer: The synthesized images can also serve as a foundation for knowledge transfer from a pre-trained teacher to the student network through training the student network from scratch with knowledge distillation [9,18,23,24] on the synthesized images. Compared to the previous state-of-the-art data-free learning methods [5,29], we achieve higher knowledge transfer accuracy when the target dataset is CIFAR-10 or ImageNet, as shown in Table 6 and 7. Full training details are included in the appendix.

4.4   Visualization

In Fig. 7, we can observe that images synthesized with regularization terms only have homogeneous color palettes and similar backgrounds, but when using the

Table 7. Data-free knowledge transfer on ImageNet from pre-trained ResNet-50 to the same network initialized from scratch.

Methods	Data type	Data amount	Epochs	Top-1 err (%)
ImageNet	Original	1.3M	250	23.4
BigGAN [2]	GAN synthesized	215K	90	36.0
ADI [29]	Synthesized	140K	250	26.2
Ours	Synthesized	140K	250	**25.9**
Ours	Synthesized	140K	500	**24.8**

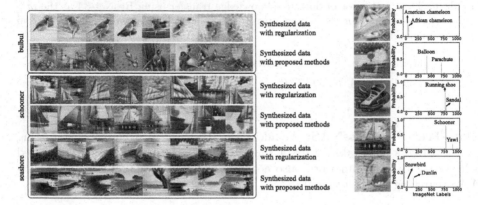

Fig. 7. Synthesized 256 × 256 images with ResNet-50 optimized on ImageNet as the pre-trained network. We visualize three classes (*"blublu"*, *"schooner"* and *"seashore"*) with different data synthesis methods.

Fig. 8. Recursive label calibration automatically learns semantically-related labels for the synthetic images.

proposed label calibration and regional update scheme for synthesis, the images exhibit more diverse feature and look more realistic. Figure 8 further shows a promising finding that the images synthesized with recursive label calibration do capture the underlining class relationships in a similar manner to the natural images. These attributes produce a good accuracy correlation between architectures trained on synthesized images and natural images which in turn contributes to the success of data-free NAS.

5   Conclusion

We have presented a novel framework that can conduct neural architecture search (NAS) without access to the original data. In order to perform data-free NAS, we developed a new recursive label calibration method and regional update strategy which automatically discover and encode the relationships between classes in soft labels and generate images *w.r.t.* these soft labels, while preserving the diversity of generated images. We demonstrate the effectiveness of our proposed method with three typical NAS algorithms. Our experimental results show that using the recovered data from a pre-trained model, NAS algorithms using our data synthesis method can obtain performance comparable to NAS algorithms using the original training data. This verifies that it is feasible to conduct NAS without original data if the synthesis method is well designed. In addition, we demonstrate that our synthetic data can produce state-of-the-art results for data-free pruning as well as knowledge transfer.

References

1. Baker, B., Gupta, O., Naik, N., Raskar, R.: Designing neural network architectures using reinforcement learning. arXiv preprint arXiv:1611.02167 (2016)
2. Brock, A., Donahue, J., Simonyan, K., et al.: Large scale GAN training for high fidelity natural image synthesis. arXiv preprint arXiv:1809.11096 (2018)
3. Brock, A., Lim, T., Ritchie, J.M., Weston, N.: SMASH: one-shot model architecture search through hypernetworks. arXiv preprint arXiv:1708.05344 (2017)
4. Cai, H., Zhu, L., Han, S., et al.: ProxylessNAS: direct neural architecture search on target task and hardware. arXiv preprint arXiv:1812.00332 (2018)
5. Chen, H., et al.: Data-free learning of student networks. In: Proceedings of the IEEE International Conference on Computer Vision, pp. 3514–3522 (2019)
6. Chollet, F.: Xception: deep learning with depthwise separable convolutions. In: Proceedings of the IEEE Conference on CVPR, pp. 1251–1258 (2017)
7. Dai, X., et al.: ChamNet: towards efficient network design through platform-aware model adaptation. arXiv preprint arXiv:1812.08934 (2018)
8. Guo, Z., et al.: Single path one-shot neural architecture search with uniform sampling. arXiv preprint arXiv:1904.00420 (2019)
9. Hinton, G., Vinyals, O., Dean, J.: Distilling the knowledge in a neural network. arXiv preprint arXiv:1503.02531 (2015)
10. Ioffe, S., Szegedy, C.: Batch normalization: accelerating deep network training by reducing internal covariate shift. arXiv preprint arXiv:1502.03167 (2015)
11. Jin, H., Song, Q., Hu, X.: Efficient neural architecture search with network morphism. arXiv preprint arXiv:1806.10282 (2018)
12. Krizhevsky, A., Hinton, G.: Learning multiple layers of features from tiny images. Technical report, Citeseer (2009)
13. Liu, C., Dollár, P., He, K., Girshick, R., Yuille, A., Xie, S.: Are labels necessary for neural architecture search? arXiv preprint arXiv:2003.12056 (2020)
14. Liu, C., et al.: Progressive neural architecture search. In: Ferrari, V., Hebert, M., Sminchisescu, C., Weiss, Y. (eds.) ECCV 2018. LNCS, vol. 11205, pp. 19–35. Springer, Cham (2018). https://doi.org/10.1007/978-3-030-01246-5_2
15. Liu, H., Simonyan, K., Yang, Y., et al.: DARTS: differentiable architecture search. In: International Conference on Learning Representations (2019)
16. Liu, Z., et al.: MetaPruning: meta learning for automatic neural network channel pruning. In: Proceedings of ICCV, pp. 3296–3305 (2019)
17. Mordvintsev, A., Olah, C., Tyka, M., et al.: Inceptionism: going deeper into neural networks (2015)
18. Müller, R., Kornblith, S., Hinton, G.: When does label smoothing help? In: NeurIPS (2019)
19. Pham, H., Guan, M.Y., Zoph, B., Le, Q.V., Dean, J.: Efficient neural architecture search via parameter sharing. arXiv preprint arXiv:1802.03268 (2018)

20. Real, E., Aggarwal, A., Huang, Y., Le, Q.V.: Regularized evolution for image classifier architecture search. arXiv preprint arXiv:1802.01548 (2018)
21. Real, E., et al.: Large-scale evolution of image classifiers. In: Proceedings of the 34th International Conference on Machine Learning, vol. 70, pp. 2902–2911. JMLR.org (2017)
22. Russakovsky, O., et al.: ImageNet large scale visual recognition challenge. Int. J. Comput. Vis. **115**(3), 211–252 (2015). https://doi.org/10.1007/s11263-015-0816-y
23. Shen, Z., He, Z., Xue, X.: MEAL: multi-model ensemble via adversarial learning. In: Proceedings of the AAAI Conference on Artificial Intelligence, vol. 33, pp. 4886–4893 (2019)
24. Shen, Z., Liu, Z., Xu, D., Chen, Z., Cheng, K.T., Savvides, M.: Is label smoothing truly incompatible with knowledge distillation: an empirical study. In: International Conference on Learning Representations (2021)
25. Spearman, C.: The proof and measurement of association between two things (1961)
26. Tan, M., Chen, B., Pang, R., Vasudevan, V., Le, Q.V.: MnasNet: platform-aware neural architecture search for mobile. arXiv preprint arXiv:1807.11626 (2018)
27. Wu, B., et al.: FBNet: hardware-aware efficient convnet design via differentiable neural architecture search. arXiv preprint arXiv:1812.03443 (2018)
28. Xu, S., et al.: Generative low-bitwidth data free quantization. arXiv preprint arXiv:2003.03603 (2020)
29. Yin, H., et al.: Dreaming to distill: data-free knowledge transfer via deepinversion. In: Proceedings of the CVPR, pp. 8715–8724 (2020)
30. Ying, C., Klein, A., Christiansen, E., Real, E., Murphy, K., Hutter, F.: NAS-Bench-101: towards reproducible neural architecture search. In: International Conference on Machine Learning, pp. 7105–7114 (2019)
31. Zhang, X., Zhou, X., Lin, M., Sun, J.: ShuffleNet: an extremely efficient convolutional neural network for mobile devices. In: Proceedings of the IEEE Conference on Computer Vision and Pattern Recognition, pp. 6848–6856 (2018)
32. Zhong, Z., et al.: BlockQNN: efficient block-wise neural network architecture generation. arXiv preprint arXiv:1808.05584 (2018)
33. Zhu, J.Y., Park, T., Isola, P., Efros, A.A.: Unpaired image-to-image translation using cycle-consistent adversarial networks. In: Proceedings of the IEEE International Conference on Computer Vision, pp. 2223–2232 (2017)
34. Zoph, B., Le, Q.V.: Neural architecture search with reinforcement learning. arXiv preprint arXiv:1611.01578 (2016)
35. Zoph, B., Vasudevan, V., Shlens, J., Le, Q.V.: Learning transferable architectures for scalable image recognition. In: Proceedings of the IEEE Conference on Computer Vision and Pattern Recognition, pp. 8697–8710 (2018)

Learning from Multiple Annotator Noisy Labels via Sample-Wise Label Fusion

Zhengqi Gao[1]([✉]), Fan-Keng Sun[1], Mingran Yang[1], Sucheng Ren[2],
Zikai Xiong[1], Marc Engeler[3], Antonio Burazer[3], Linda Wildling[3],
Luca Daniel[1], and Duane S. Boning[1]

[1] Massachusetts Institute of Technology, Cambridge, MA 02139, USA
zhengqi@mit.edu
[2] South China University of Technology, Guangzhou, China
[3] Takeda Pharmaceuticals Co., Ltd., Zurich, Switzerland

Abstract. Data lies at the core of modern deep learning. The impressive performance of supervised learning is built upon a base of massive accurately labeled data. However, in some real-world applications, accurate labeling might not be viable; instead, multiple noisy labels (instead of one accurate label) are provided by several annotators for each data sample. Learning a classifier on such a noisy training dataset is a challenging task. Previous approaches usually assume that all data samples share the same set of parameters related to annotator errors, while we demonstrate that label error learning should be both annotator and data sample dependent. Motivated by this observation, we propose a novel learning algorithm. The proposed method displays superiority compared with several state-of-the-art baseline methods on MNIST, CIFAR-100, and ImageNet-100. Our code is available at: https://github.com/zhengqigao/Learning-from-Multiple-Annotator-Noisy-Labels.

1 Introduction

In addition to improved neural network architectures (e.g., residual connections [10], batch-norm [11]), the prevalence and success of modern deep learning are attributed to the availability of large datasets (e.g., CIFAR-100 [15], COCO [17], ImagNet [4]). The massive amount of labeled data plays a critical role in the training of deep neural networks under a supervised learning setting. Thanks to the efforts of many researchers, access to these accurately labeled data is so convenient that we often take them for granted.

However, in many real-world applications, large numbers of accurate labels are not available or practicable to generate. Instead, only multiple noisy labels for data samples are gathered, due to economic limitations. Consider the need for training data to support a binary labeling (i.e., good or bad) neural network of drug vial images in an automated visual inspection system for pharmaceutical

---

Supplementary Information The online version contains supplementary material available at https://doi.org/10.1007/978-3-031-20053-3_24.

S. Avidan et al. (Eds.): ECCV 2022, LNCS 13684, pp. 407–422, 2022.
https://doi.org/10.1007/978-3-031-20053-3_24

products. Training dataset generation involves labeling of a set of collected vial images (with and without defects) by a modest number of highly trained human experts. Because visual acuity, conditions, and expertise can vary among experts, not all experts will agree on labels. As a result, golden labels are not always available. Instead, we seek to take maximal advantage of the available labels from these multiple annotators.

This problem corresponds to a supervised classification task on a training dataset with multiple noisy labels available for each data point. To address this problem, a naive approach is to aggregate labels for each sample via a weighted summation, followed by a vanilla training procedure on the weighted aggregate. When all elements of the weight vector are equal, this approach is known as majority voting [19]. More sophisticated approaches have been proposed over the past several decades. The first major category, built on Bayesian methods [13, 19,24], has been dominant before the era of deep learning. In these methods, a probabilistic model is first defined and the maximum likelihood estimation or the maximum-a-posteriori solution is found by leveraging the expectation maximization (EM) algorithm. The second category, which is learning-based, has emerged more recently. For instance, WDN [9] generalizes the idea of majority voting by learning the *weight vector* instead of directly setting all its entries to a single constant. In contrast, rather than using a weight vector, MBEM [14] introduces an annotator-specific *confusion matrix* to mimic the labeling process of each annotator, and embeds this into the training of the classifier using an EM framework. Later, the authors in [23] proposed to learn the annotator confusion matrices by a novel loss function involving trace regularization (referred to as TraceReg in our paper).

However, these previous methods adopt assumptions – that all data samples share a single annotator weight vector, or that the same set of confusion matrices apply to all data samples – that can be overly limiting, as will be demonstrated in this paper. Motivated by this observation, we propose a new learning algorithm to jointly learn sample-wise weight vectors and sample-wise annotator confusion matrices, and thus make label fusion possible. Specifically, for any input data sample, our neural network outputs its label prediction, an annotator weight vector, and a set of confusion matrices. To carry out the training process to learn these values, a novel loss function is proposed. Furthermore, for practical utility, we take advantage of the Birkhoff-von Neumann theorem and matrix decomposition technique so that only a small set of coefficients can be learned to approximate the set of confusion matrices. To exhibit our method's superior performance, we compare it with several state-of-the-art baseline methods on MNIST, CIFAR-100, and ImageNet-100.

2   Preliminaries

2.1   Related Works

Multi-label Classification. Generally, multi-label classification refers to the classification problem where multiple (valid) labels are assigned to each instance.

For example, in the movie genre classification problem, one movie could belong to each of action, comedy, and fiction classes at the same time. One intuitive way to solve this problem is converting to several separate binary classification problems. Specifically, if there are R distinct classes that one instance could belong to, we assign a set of binary labels $\{y^{(r)} \in \{0,1\}\}_{r=1}^R$ to the instance $\mathbf{x}$, where R is the total number of classes and the r-th label represents whether the sample belongs to the r-th class or not. The same formalism can be adopted in our problem, but we now interpret R as the number of annotators and notice that $y^{(r)}$ resides in $\{0,1,\cdots,K-1\}$ (instead of $\{0,1\}$) for a K-class classification problem. One subtle difference is that in our problem each instance has only one correct label, i.e., ideally, the provided labels $\{y^{(r)}\}_{r=1}^R$ should be identical for a specific sample $\mathbf{x}$ (i.e., $y^{(1)} = y^{(2)} = \cdots = y^{(R)}$). However, in multi-label classification, $y^{(1)}$ could be different from $y^{(2)}$ in principle, with both labels being correct.

Learning with Noisy Labels. In a conventional K-class classification setting, 'noisy label' refers to the fact that the label y assigned to the instance $\mathbf{x}$ might be corrupted. Learning with noisy labels has been a hot topic for the past several years and various methods have been proposed [1,3,8,12,18,20–22,25]. These methods can be generally grouped into two categories [1]: (i) model-based approaches, and (ii) model-free approaches. Model-based approaches attempt to find the underlying noise structure and eliminate its impact from the observed data, while model-free approaches aim to achieve label noise robustness without explicitly modeling the noise [1]. To name one example for each kind, the noisy channel approach [18] assumes a noisy channel on top of a base classifier [1]. It will learn the noise structure in the training phase and thus the base classifier can be trained using the processed clean labels. On the other hand, many model-free approaches focus on designing loss functions robust to the noise [3,8]. For instance, the authors in [8] show that mean absolute value of error (MAE) is more resilient to noise, compared with the commonly used categorical cross entropy loss.

In our problem, we have multiple noisy labels provided by different annotators which might be consistent or inconsistent. Majority voting [19] simply aggregates all labels via a weighted summation over one-hot-encoded annotator labels with a $1/R$ constant weight vector, while WDN [9] automatically learns the weight vector. On the other hand, MBEM [14] and TraceReg [23] both introduce the concept of a per-annotator confusion matrix to model the labeling of each annotator. In what follows, we demonstrate that the data sample-independent assumption used in these methods is overly restrictive, and justify why an alternative data sample-dependent configuration is intriguing.

2.2   Motivations

Formally, we consider a supervised K-class classification problem on a given dataset $\mathcal{D} = \{(\mathbf{x}_n, y_n^{(r)}) \,|\, n = 1,2,\cdots,N, r = 1,2,\cdots,R\}$, where $(\mathbf{x}_n, y_n^{(r)})$ denotes the n-th input feature and its corresponding label from the r-th annotator, N and R respectively represent the number of samples and annotators.

In our paper, when the bold symbol $\mathbf{y}_n^{(r)} \in \mathbb{R}^K$ is presented, it denotes the one-hot-encoding of $y_n^{(r)} \in \{0, 1, \cdots, K-1\}$.

Two sorts of parameters are usually exploited in previous relevant work. The first one is a weight vector $\mathbf{w} \in \mathbb{R}^R$ used by majority voting and WDN [9]. Namely, they use $\mathbf{w}$ to weight the opinions of annotators and assume that the golden (one-hot-encoded) label $\mathbf{y}_n^{\star}$ can be approximated by a weighted summation of all annotators' labels $\mathbf{y}_n^{\text{targ}}$:

$$\mathbf{y}_n^{\star} \approx \mathbf{y}_n^{\text{targ}} = [\mathbf{y}_n^{(1)}, \mathbf{y}_n^{(2)}, \cdots, \mathbf{y}_n^{(R)}] \cdot \mathbf{w} \quad \forall n \in \{1, 2, \cdots, N\} \tag{1}$$

where $\mathbf{w}$ is set as a constant vector with all elements equal to $1/R$ in soft majority voting [19], and with variable elements that are automatically learned in WDN [9]. Note that in both approaches, one single $\mathbf{w}$ is shared among all N samples. However, we argue that this modeling assumption can be too strong in some cases, such as the example shown in the blue box of Fig. 1. Specifically, consider two annotators on the MNIST dataset. Because of personal writing and perception habits, the first and second annotators, AnT-1 and AnT-2, might erroneously assign label '6' to an image of '5', and label '2' to an image of '1', respectively. Thus, for an input image of '6', the weight vector should be more biased towards the second annotator AnT-2 (say $\mathbf{w} = [0.3, 0.7]^T$) since in this case the first annotator AnT-1 is more likely to provide a problematic label. Alternatively, when the input image shows '1', the weight vector should rely more on the first annotator (say with weights $\mathbf{w} = [0.7, 0.3]^T$). This example implies that the weight vector should be different for different input images (i.e., sample-wise) when considering the reliability of annotators.

Other works such as MBEM [14] and TraceReg [23], instead of resorting to a weight vector $\mathbf{w}$, introduce a set of annotator confusion matrices $\{\mathbf{P}^{(r)} \in \mathbb{R}^{K \times K}\}_{r=1}^R$ to mimic the labeling processes of annotators. Specifically, the entry on the i-th row and j-th column $P_{ij}^{(r)}$ represents the probability that the r-th annotator returns label i, given that the golden label $y_n^{\star}$ equals j:

$$P_{ij}^{(r)} = \Pr[y_n^{(r)} = i \,|\, y_n^{\star} = j] \quad \forall n \in \{1, 2, \cdots, N\} \tag{2}$$

These works assume that the probability of the r-th annotator corrupting the label is independent of the input data point, and thus all samples share the same confusion matrix for the given annotator. However, similar to the case of $\mathbf{w}$, this assumption can also be too restrictive, as demonstrated in the yellow box of Fig. 1. This example indicates that the confusion matrix $\mathbf{P}^{(2)}$ of a single annotator AnT-2 should be different for different input images $\mathbf{x}_1$ and $\mathbf{x}_2$. Motivated by the observations that the annotator weight vector and annotator confusion matrix should be sample-wise, we propose our method in the next section.

3   Proposed Approach

To begin with, we assume that for each input $\mathbf{x}_n$, knowing the confusion matrix $\mathbf{P}_n^{(r)} \in \mathbb{R}^{K \times K}$ can eliminate the bias (e.g., writing or recognition habit in our example) of the r-th annotator and yield a clean soft label:

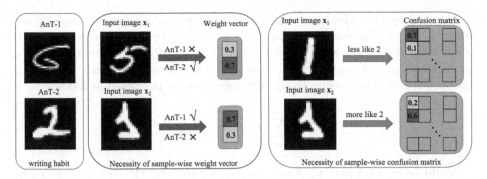

Fig. 1. An illustration of why weight vector and confusion matrix need to be sample-wise using MNIST dataset. (i) The orange box contains examples of the first and second annotator writing '6' and '2', respectively. (ii) In the blue box, when input image $\mathbf{x}_1$ is provided, AnT-1 might assign label '6' due to his/her writing habit, while AnT-2 provides the correct label 5. Thus in this case, the weight vector should emphasize on AnT-2. Alternatively, the weight vector should emphasize on AnT-1 when $\mathbf{x}_2$ is given. (iii) In the yellow box, we only consider AnT-2. When $\mathbf{x}_1$ is given, it looks less like digit '2', thus $P_{21}^{(2)} = \Pr[y_1^{(2)} = 2|y_1^\star = 1]$ is small (say 0.1). Yet when $\mathbf{x}_2$ is provided, $P_{21}^{(2)} = \Pr[y_1^{(2)} = 2|y_1^\star = 1]$ will be large (say 0.6). (Color figure online)

$$\mathbf{y}_n^{(r),\text{cln}} = \mathbf{P}_n^{(r)}\,\mathbf{y}_n^{(r)} \tag{3}$$

where $\{\mathbf{P}_n^{(r)}\}_{r=1}^R$ will be learned by the network. Note that in our definition of confusion matrix, the entry on the i-th row and j-th column of $\mathbf{P}_n^{(r)}$ represents the probability of $y_n^{(r),\text{cln}} = i$ given $y_n^{(r)} = j$, i.e., $\Pr[y_n^{(r),\text{cln}} = i \,|\, y_n^{(r)} = j]$. Our definition differs from that of MBEM [14] or TraceReg [23] given by Eq. (2). We emphasize that $\mathbf{y}_n^{(r)} \in \mathbb{R}^K$ is one-hot-encoded and only one of its entries is 1, while $\mathbf{y}_n^{(r),\text{cln}} \in \mathbb{R}^K$ is a soft stochastic vector, which can be regarded as the clean label after removing the annotator's bias.

Once the confusion matrix $\mathbf{P}_n^{(r)}$ is learned, we can use the clean label $\mathbf{y}_n^{(r),\text{cln}}$ to guide the training of a neural network by KL divergence. In this situation, a natural thought would be to use their weighted summation with $\mathbf{w}_n \in \mathbb{R}^R$ as the coefficient to approximate the true label:

$$\mathbf{y}_n^\star \approx \mathbf{y}_n^{\text{targ}} = [\mathbf{y}_n^{(1),\text{cln}}, \mathbf{y}_n^{(2),\text{cln}}, \cdots, \mathbf{y}_n^{(R),\text{cln}}] \cdot \mathbf{w}_n \tag{4}$$

where $\mathbf{w}_n$ is also learned by the network. An advantage of learning from multiple clean labels in this approach is that $\mathbf{y}_n^{\text{targ}}$ becomes more stable. Intuitively, when $\mathbf{P}_n^{(r)}$ is sufficiently good, $\{\mathbf{y}_n^{(r),\text{cln}}\}_{r=1}^R$ can be regarded as R i.i.d. samples drawn from $P(Y|X = \mathbf{x}_n)$. Thus, the weighted summation of $\mathbf{y}_n^{(r),\text{cln}}$ is closer to the expected $\mathbf{y}_n^\star$ compared to using only one clean label, i.e., $\mathbb{E}[(\mathbf{y}_n^{\text{targ}} - \mathbf{y}_n^\star)^2] = \frac{1}{N}\mathbb{E}[(\mathbf{y}_n^{(1),\text{cln}} - \mathbf{y}_n^\star)^2]$. In a nutshell, for each input $\mathbf{x}_n$, if $\mathbf{P}_n^{(r)}$ and $\mathbf{w}_n$ are available, then we can obtain $\mathbf{y}_n^{\text{targ}}$ by Eq. (3)–(4) and minimize the KL divergence between it and the neural network's label prediction $\mathbf{f}(\mathbf{x}_n)$.

Inspired by this idea, our model architecture and learning framework are shown in Fig. 2. For each input $\mathbf{x}_n$, it is first fed into a deep neural network to obtain a good high-level representation, followed by three separate MLPs, outputting a set of confusion matrices $\{\mathbf{P}_n^{(r)}\}_{r=1}^{R}$, a weight vector $\mathbf{w}_n$, and a class prediction $\mathbf{f}(\mathbf{x}_n)$, respectively. The loss function is defined as follows:

$$\mathcal{L} = \frac{1}{N} \sum_{n=1}^{N} \mathcal{L}_{KL}(\mathbf{f}(\mathbf{x}_n), \mathbf{y}_n^{\text{targ}}) \tag{5}$$

It should be noticed that $\mathbf{y}_n^{\text{targ}}$ is a function of $\mathbf{w}_n$ and $\{\mathbf{P}_n^{(r)}\}_{r=1}^{R}$ as shown in Eq. (3) and (4). Thus, the loss function $\mathcal{L}$ is a composite function with variables $\mathbf{f}(\mathbf{x}_n)$, $\{\mathbf{P}_n^{(r)}\}_{r=1}^{R}$, and $\mathbf{w}_n$, for $n = 1, 2, \ldots, N$. These variables are what we will learn simultaneously via training the model in Fig. 2.

Although intuitive, further thought reveals that the above loss is insufficient. Let us provide an example of achieving minimum loss $\mathcal{L} = 0$, but it is completely meaningless. Consider all entries on the first row of $\mathbf{P}_n^{(r)}$ equal to 1 for any n and r. Then, no matter what $\mathbf{w}_n$ is, the network always returns the prediction $\mathbf{f}(\mathbf{x}_n) = [1, 0, \cdots, 0]^T$ no matter what the input is. This network can achieve zero loss, but obviously it is an undesired trivial solution. The essence of the problem is that we attempt to learn the annotators' biases (and thus the clean labels) along with learning the label prediction, but the critical parameters $\{\mathbf{P}_n^{(r)}\}_{r=1}^{R}$ are free to vary, which can lead to bizarre clean labels.

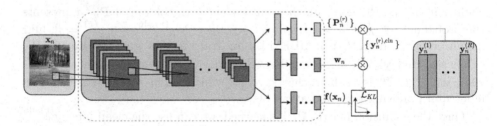

Fig. 2. Training flow of our proposed method. The trainable neural network is highlighted by the dashed line. The set of confusion matrices, weight vector, and the class prediction vector share the same representation extraction network shown in the orange box. The green and purple arrows correspond to Eq. (3) and (4), respectively. During training, all paths are active, while in inference time, only the bottom blue path is active and the label prediction $\mathbf{f}(\mathbf{x}_n)$ is used. (Color figure online)

To overcome this, we invoke some facts about the confusion matrices so that they can be formulated as constraints and imposed on $\{\mathbf{P}_n^{(r)}\}_{r=1}^{R}$. Recall in the above illustrating example, that setting the first row of all $\mathbf{P}_n^{(r)}$ equal to 1 is to say that the clean labels always indicate the first class no matter what the annotator's labels are for all annotators on all data samples. In reality, the annotators will typically not be that bad at labeling. To encode a preference toward the provided annotator labels, we revise the loss as follows:

$$\mathcal{L} = \frac{1}{N} \sum_{n=1}^{N} \left\{ \mathcal{L}_{KL}(\mathbf{f}(\mathbf{x}_n), \mathbf{y}_n^{\text{targ}}) + \frac{\lambda}{R} \mathbf{u}^T \tilde{\mathbf{D}}^2 \mathbf{u} \right\} \tag{6}$$

where $\tilde{\mathbf{D}} = \text{Diag}[\mathbf{I} - \mathbf{P}_n^{(r)}] \in \mathbb{R}^{K \times K}$, $\mathbf{u} \in \mathbb{R}^K$ represents a column vector with all elements equal to 1, and λ is a user-defined hyper-parameter. Intuitively, this quadratic term encourages the diagonal elements in $\mathbf{P}_n^{(r)}$ to be large (i.e., approaching to 1 from below). Namely, we have implicitly assumed that annotators won't provide completely erroneous labels, considering our definition of confusion matrix. As will be visualized in the TwoMoon example, the introduction of this quadratic term prevents the occurrence of pathological $\mathbf{P}_n^{(r)}$, and thus produces a meaningful trained network.

The training flow presented so far still has a memory problem. Namely, as shown in Fig. 2, there are $RK^2 + R + K \approx \mathcal{O}(RK^2)$ outputs for one input during training, which is orders larger than that (i.e., $\mathcal{O}(K)$) of a conventional neural network in the K-class classification problem. Carefully examining the training flow reveals that the memory bottleneck lies in the set of confusion matrices, which might also be a key reason why previous works have not adopted sample-wise confusion matrices. To properly address this issue, we first notice that $\mathbf{P}_n^{(r)}$ satisfies two conditions: (i) all entries are between 0 and 1, and (ii) the summation of entries in each column equals 1. The matrix satisfying the above two requirements is known as singly stochastic [2]. Built upon this, if the row summation also equals 1, then the matrix is doubly stochastic [6]. Furthermore, the Birkhoff-von Neumann theorem [5] states that any $K \times K$ doubly stochastic matrix can be decomposed into a convex combination of permutation matrices $\{\mathbf{B}_m \in \mathbb{R}^{K \times K}\}_{m=1}^{M}$, where M is the number of basis matrices. Consequently, we impose an additional constraint that our $\mathbf{P}_n^{(r)}$ be doubly stochastic so that the theorem can be applied. Under this constraint, the network does not need to output $\mathbf{P}_n^{(r)}$, but only the coefficients $\mathbf{c}_n^{(r)} = [c_{n,1}^{(r)}, c_{n,2}^{(r)}, \cdots, c_{n,M}^{(r)}]^T \in \mathbb{R}^M$ instead. When it is needed, we can recover $\mathbf{P}_n^{(r)}$ by:

$$\mathbf{P}_n^{(r)} \approx c_{n,1}^{(r)} \mathbf{B}_1 + c_{n,1}^{(r)} \mathbf{B}_2 + \cdots c_{n,M}^{(r)} \mathbf{B}_M \tag{7}$$

We employ this idea in our training flow to reduce the memory requirement, as shown in Fig. 3(b). Specifically, the number M of basis matrices is treated as a hyper-parameter, and the permutation matrices $\{\mathbf{B}_m\}_{m=1}^M$ are randomly generated before training and fixed for later use. The coefficient $\mathbf{c}_n^{(r)}$ is produced after a Softmax activation to guarantee its entries no smaller than zero and all sum to one. Essentially, we shrink the exploration space of the confusion matrix $\mathbf{P}_n^{(r)}$ as shown in Fig. 3(a). Representing $\mathbf{P}_n^{(r)}$ by a convex combination of fixed permutation matrices and introducing the quadratic term into the loss function can be regarded as two techniques to regularize the confusion matrices.

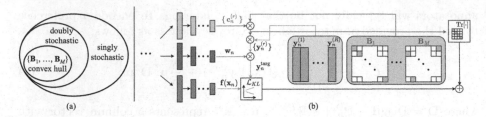

Fig. 3. (a) A Venn Diagram shows the relationship among the convex hull of $\mathbf{B}_m$, doubly stochastic matrix, and singly stochastic matrix. (b) Our improved training flow. The red, green and purple arrows correspond to Eq. (7), (3) and (4), respectively. (Color figure online)

For an intuitive understanding of our approach, we perform some visualizations on the TwoMoon toy example [7,26]. We generate 20,000 samples on the XY-plane and specify their golden labels according to which branch (i.e., upper or lower) the samples lie in. Assume that two annotators respectively view the data from horizontal and vertical perspectives. For instance, the first annotator AnT-1 assigns label 1 to samples with X-coordinates less than zero, and label 0 to those larger than zero. See Fig. 4 for an illustration of the generated data and labels. Next, we divide data into training and test dataset according to the ratio 4:1. In the training dataset, only annotators' labels are provided, while the golden labels are available in the test dataset. Note that TwoMoon is a binary classification task (i.e., $K = 2$) and that only two 2×2 permutation matrices exist, so we can use two basis matrices $\{\mathbf{B}_1, \mathbf{B}_2\}$ to approximate the confusion matrix. A three-layer MLP is used as the backbone model. In one experiment running, the classifier obtained by learning from AnT-1's labels alone attains 66.51% test accuracy, and that from AnT-2's labels alone is 83.67%. Moreover, due to the nature of AnT-1's and AnT-2's labels, the decision boundary of these two classifiers are vertical and horizontal, respectively. On the other hand, the classifier obtained via our method achieves 86.70% test accuracy and the decision boundary, as shown in Fig. 5(a), is curved, neither vertical nor horizontal anymore.

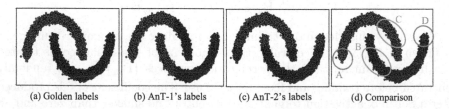

(a) Golden labels   (b) AnT-1's labels   (c) AnT-2's labels   (d) Comparison

Fig. 4. The modified TwoMoon toy example. Red and blue dots represent label 1 and 0, respectively. In (d), the regions where AnT-1 is wrong while AnT-2 is correct are marked with pink circles B and C. Similarly, orange circles A and D denote where AnT-1 is correct while AnT-2 is wrong. The remaining regions are those where both annotators are wrong or correct simultaneously. (Color figure online)

To verify that our method comes to effect, another necessary action is to examine whether the resulting weight vectors and confusion matrices are indeed sample-dependent. Figure 5(b) plots the heatmap of the weight associated with AnT-1. Matching it with Fig. 4(d), we see that the region B and C have smaller weights than 0.5. That coincides with our intuition: because region B and C correspond to where AnT-1 is wrong while AnT-2 is correct, the weight vector should incline more to AnT-2. Applying the same reasoning, we expect region A and D are painted with light color in Fig. 5(b). We notice that D matches our expectation while A does not. Moreover, in Fig. 5(c), we do witness that the places corresponding to region B and C have darker color than that of D; while the place of region A should be light colored, it is dark in reality. This discrepancy between our solution (Fig. 5) and the real case (Fig. 4) might be attributed to two reasons: (i) the assumption of annotator labels being not too bad is violated in this example considering that there are places where both annotators are wrong, and generally (ii) the discrepancy is inevitable due to the nature of the inverse problem. Namely, the real case is only one possible scenario (or local optimum) among many that could be reached via minimizing our loss function. With our hyper-parameter setting, we currently reach the solution shown in Fig. 5. Nevertheless, the most important observation is that different colors (i.e., sample-dependent parameters) do indeed appear, which is our main proposition. Since our concern here is not to precisely recover the generating function, but rather to have a more accurate classifier, the example still demonstrates the potential of our method.

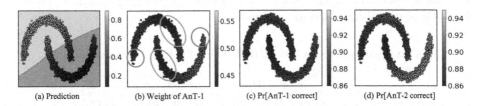

(a) Prediction   (b) Weight of AnT-1   (c) Pr[AnT-1 correct]   (d) Pr[AnT-2 correct]

Fig. 5. (a) Prediction heatmap and classification boundary of our learned classifier. (b) Heatmap of the first element in $\mathbf{w}_n \in \mathbb{R}^2$. (c) Heatmap of the diagonal elements in $\mathbf{P}_n^{(1)} \in \mathbb{R}^{2\times 2}$. (d) Heatmap of the diagonal elements in $\mathbf{P}_n^{(2)} \in \mathbb{R}^{2\times 2}$. Specifically, when the annotator's label is 0, we plot the first diagonal element, while if it is 1, we plot the second. Namely, the heatmap represents the probability that the annotator's label is correct.

4 Numerical Results

4.1 MNIST

Synthesis Method. The MNIST dataset is a collection of handwritten digits with 10 classes [16]. We divide all images into a training dataset, a validation dataset, and a test dataset containing 55,000, 5,000, and 10,000 images, respectively. We note that no well-known public datasets suit our purpose (i.e., data with annotator identification) in the community, so that the existing literature all uses some sort of annotator synthesis method. For example, MBEM [14] and TraceReg [23] use a 'hammer-spammer' synthesis rule, assuming that each annotator is either a hammer, always returning golden labels, or a spammer, randomly choosing labels in a uniform way. However, it appears to us that bad annotators are generally better than randomly picking labels and good annotators sometimes also make mistakes. Thus, in our experiment, we synthesize three annotators according to the following rule: We assume that for each of these annotators, there exists one 'weakness' image that the annotator cannot identify. For the images whose Euclidean distance to the 'weakness' image are smaller than a threshold ϵ, the annotator will randomly pick another class label different from the golden one, in a uniform way. Otherwise, the annotator will provide the correct label.

Setting. For comparison purpose, besides training with solely one single annotator's labels, we also implement majority voting, TraceReg [23], MBEM [14], and WDN [9] as baselines. We choose LeNet [16] as the backbone model, set the number of epochs to 40, learning rate to 0.01, and use SGD with momentum as the optimizer. For our method, we randomly generate 20 (i.e., $M = 20$) base permutation matrices to approximate the confusion matrices, and set the hyper-parameter λ in Eq. (6) to 1.0. Following the setting of TraceReg [23], we assume that golden labels are available in the validation dataset, so that validation can be used to compare models among different training epochs and select the optimal model for a specific method.

Table 1. Accuracies (%) on MNIST under different annotator skills ϵ

	$\epsilon = 30$	$\epsilon = 31$	$\epsilon = 32$	$\epsilon = 33$	$\epsilon = 34$	$\epsilon = 35$
w/AnT-1's	80.79	75.67	67.48	59.49	47.63	43.06
w/AnT-2's	66.53	57.47	49.25	41.42	33.68	25.99
w/AnT-3's	48.35	40.75	33.01	27.08	21.25	16.25
Mjv	87.72	80.35	74.47	67.15	56.75	44.46
TraceReg	85.98	76.91	70.47	62.38	51.52	40.09
MBEM	83.30	74.66	66.35	56.52	49.36	36.65
WDN	81.09	72.16	64.32	52.90	44.50	32.00
Ours	**92.49**	**80.67**	**76.76**	**70.44**	**61.19**	**46.21**
w/true label	99.20	99.20	99.20	99.20	99.20	99.20

Results. The accuracies of different optimal models yielded by different methods on the test dataset are reported in Table 1. All results are reported by averaging five independent experiments, and the left plot of Fig. 6 visualizes these results. Our method outperforms all other methods and is the closest to training with true golden labels (i.e., the upper bound) under all different annotator skills. Moreover, at $\epsilon = 30$, our method achieves 4.77% more accuracy compared to the second best method. It is worth mentioning that in some cases, TraceReg [23] and MBEM [14] perform even worse than majority voting, which seems contradictory to what they report. However, this is because our annotator synthesis method is different from theirs, and we hypothesize that their method might not perform well under a sample-dependent synthesis (as in our case) due to the assumption of sample-independent weight vector or confusion matrix. We perform further experiments under their synthesis method; for this and further discussion, please refer to the supplementary material.

In the right plot of Fig. 6, we show model accuracy on the validation dataset as a function of the number of epochs. As classification on MNIST is rather easy, all methods converge quickly after only a few epochs. We see that our method is almost consistently better than all other methods among all epochs.

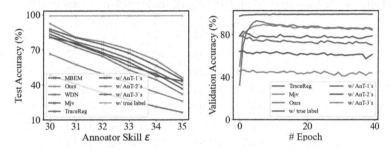

Fig. 6. MNIST test cases. Left: Test accuracy is plotted versus different annotator skills. Right: During the training phase of one experiment with $\epsilon = 30$, the validation accuracy is plotted as a function of the number of epochs. Since MBEM [14] has an additional loop (corresponding to EM algorithm) outside the training of classifier, it has been omitted from the figure. WDN [9] is omitted for a similar reason.

4.2 CIFAR-100

Setting. CIFAR-100 [15] is a collection of 32×32 RGB images with 100 classes. We divide all images into a training dataset, a validation dataset and a test dataset containing 40,000, 10,000, and 10,000 images, respectively. Following the synthesize method described in the previous subsection, we create three annotators AnT-1, AnT-2 and AnT-3. We select ResNet18 as the backbone model. Note that we have reduced the convolution kernel size to 3×3 to suit the case of 32×32 RGB input. We choose SGD with momentum as the optimizer, set learning rate to 0.1, and number of epochs to 200. For our method, the hyper-parameter λ is set to 1.0, and since now the number of classes K is 100, we randomly generate 150 (i.e., $M = 150$) base permutation matrices to approximate the confusion matrix.

Results. Table 2 reports the test accuracies of different methods on CIFAR-100 under different expert skills ϵ. With ϵ increasing, the annotators' labels become worse and all methods' accuracies drop. Moreover, it is interesting to note that when $\epsilon = 24$, the test accuracy obtained with a model trained solely on AnT-3's labels is better than all other baselines except our method. As shown in the left plot of Fig. 7, our method always achieves the highest accuracy among all other baselines under different ϵ. For instance, when $\epsilon = 22$, our method attains 5.74% more accuracy compared to the second best method. Moreover, as shown in the right plot of Fig. 7, our method (i.e., green line) is consistently better than other baselines after about 30 epochs, and it is even comparable to training with true labels (i.e., red line) at around 50 to 100 epochs. A few ablation studies (such as varying λ, only using $\mathbf{w}_n$ or $\mathbf{P}_n^{(r)}$, using pretrained neural networks as annotators) are performed in the supplementary.

Table 2. Accuracies (%) on CIFAR-100 under different expert skills ϵ

	$\epsilon = 20$	$\epsilon = 21$	$\epsilon = 22$	$\epsilon = 23$	$\epsilon = 24$
w/AnT-1's	62.05	58.98	54.02	50.27	42.97
w/AnT-2's	40.64	32.26	25.04	16.99	11.67
w/AnT-3's	63.07	58.33	58.74	53.68	50.42
Mjv	65.06	60.97	57.22	52.25	46.77
TraceReg	67.16	65.51	57.70	48.96	42.79
MBEM	64.75	62.69	57.37	55.02	49.74
WDN	66.92	63.37	58.42	53.97	48.17
Ours	**70.05**	**67.83**	**64.48**	**60.12**	**54.77**
w/true label	73.24	73.24	73.24	73.24	73.24

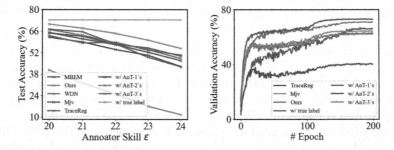

Fig. 7. CIFAR-100 test cases. Left: Test accuracy is plotted versus different annotator skills. Right: During the training phase of one experiment with $\epsilon = 20$, the validation accuracy is plotted as a function of the number of epochs. (Color figure online)

4.3   ImageNet-100

Setting. To make the total running time affordable, we conduct the experiment on a well-known subset of ImageNet, ImageNet-100, in this example. It is a subset of ImageNet dataset [4], containing 100 random classes and a total of 135,000 images. We divide all images into a training dataset, a validation dataset and a test dataset with ratio of 25:1:1. Following the synthesize method described in previous section, we create three annotators AnT-1, AnT-2, and AnT-3. We choose ResNet18 as the backbone model and SGD with momentum as the optimizer. We set learning rate to 0.1 and number of epoch to 200. For our method, we set the hyper-parameter λ to 1.0 and randomly generate $M = 150$ permutation matrices as bases.

Results. Table 3 reports the test accuracy of different methods on ImageNet-100 under expert skill ϵ. Our method outperforms all baselines under this setting, and is consistently better than other baselines after around 50 epochs as shown in Fig. 8. Moreover, in this example, we observe that our method achieves more accuracy improvement compared to that in MNIST or CIFAR-100.

Table 3. Accuracies (%) on ImageNet-100 under different expert skills ϵ

	$\epsilon = 580$	$\epsilon = 600$	$\epsilon = 620$	$\epsilon = 650$	$\epsilon = 680$
w/AnT-1's	38.36	34.25	28.24	22.71	15.81
w/AnT-2's	34.72	30.75	24.50	17.91	12.70
w/AnT-3's	56.35	52.62	47.16	40.41	34.86
Mjv	53.83	46.67	41.13	35.90	29.83
TraceReg	58.51	55.13	48.90	43.07	36.54
MBEM	45.18	39.12	32.90	26.14	20.06
WDN	56.03	51.86	46.90	37.94	31.65
Ours	**73.34**	**70.59**	**68.91**	**62.72**	**54.93**
w/true label	74.26	74.26	74.26	74.26	74.26

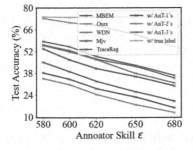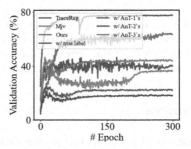

Fig. 8. ImageNet-100 test cases. Left: Test accuracy is plotted versus different annotator skills. Right: During the training phase of one experiment with $\epsilon = 20$, the validation accuracy is plotted as a function of the number of epochs.

5 Conclusions and Future Work

Limitations and Future Work. Here we discuss the limitations of our method and potential future work. First, even with the matrix decomposition method, the number of our neural network outputs is still on the order of $\mathcal{O}(RM)$. Although we can choose $M \sim \mathcal{O}(K)$, the complexity remains linear in R. This is not a problem when R is small (e.g., $R = 3$ in our experiments), while complexity may be a concern when there are many annotators. However, MBEM [14] has demonstrated its validity in this situation. Future work could explore extensions to our proposed method for the large R case.

In addition to scalability, another direction worth exploration is dealing with missing annotator labels, as MBEM [14] and TraceReg [23] do. Namely, an annotator might not provide labels for all data samples, and sometimes some labels might be missing. The MBEM [14] and TraceReg [23] frameworks implicitly handle this situation. However, it is less clear how our method could efficiently address such scenarios. One possible approach would be using a mask operation in Eq. (3). Namely, we could add a vector $\mathbf{s}_n^{(r)} \in \mathbb{R}^K$ ahead of $\mathbf{P}_n^{(r)}$ on the right hand side of the equation. If the r-th annotator does not provide a label for the n-th data, then the elements of $\mathbf{s}_n^{(r)}$ are set to all zeros, otherwise, all ones. However, this method might be inefficient if each annotator only provides labels for a small subset of all images (i.e., annotators' labels are sparse). A related avenue is to explore if we could use such sparsity to address the scalability issue.

Conclusions. In this paper, we propose a novel method to learn a classifier given a noisy training dataset, in which each data point has several labels from multiple annotators. Our key idea is to make the weight vectors and the confusion matrices data-dependent. Moreover, we realize two regularization methods for the confusion matrix to guide the training process: one is to include a quadratic term inside the loss function, and the other is to confine the confusion matrix as a convex combination of permutation matrices. Our visualization on the TwoMoon dataset verifies that the learned parameters are indeed sample-wise, and our numerical results on MNIST, CIFAR-100 and ImageNet-100 demonstrate that our method outperforms various state-of-the-art methods.

Acknowledgements. This research was supported in part by Millennium Pharmaceuticals, Inc. (a subsidiary of Takeda Pharmaceuticals). The authors also acknowledge helpful feedback from the reviewers. Zhengqi Gao would like to thank Alex Gu, Suvrit Sra, Zichang He and Hangyu Lin for useful discussions, and Zihui Xue for her support.

References

1. Algan, G., Ulusoy, I.: Image classification with deep learning in the presence of noisy labels: a survey. Knowl.-Based Syst. **215**, 106771 (2021)
2. Asmussen, S.: Applied Probability and Queues, vol. 51. Springer, New York (2003). https://doi.org/10.1007/b97236

3. Charoenphakdee, N., Lee, J., Sugiyama, M.: On symmetric losses for learning from corrupted labels. In: International Conference on Machine Learning, pp. 961–970 (2019)
4. Deng, J., Dong, W., Socher, R., Li, L.J., Li, K., Fei-Fei, L.: ImageNet: a large-scale hierarchical image database. In: IEEE Conference on Computer Vision and Pattern Recognition, pp. 248–255 (2009)
5. Dufossé, F., Uçar, B.: Notes on Birkhoff-von Neumann decomposition of doubly stochastic matrices. Linear Algebra Appl. **497**, 108–115 (2016)
6. Gagniuc, P.: Markov Chains: From Theory to Implementation and Experimentation. Wiley, Hoboken (2017)
7. Gao, Z., Ren, S., Xue, Z., Li, S., Zhao, H.: Training-free robust multimodal learning via sample-wise Jacobian regularization (2022)
8. Ghosh, A., Kumar, H., Sastry, P.: Robust loss functions under label noise for deep neural networks. In: Proceedings of the AAAI Conference on Artificial Intelligence, vol. 31 (2017)
9. Guan, M., Gulshan, V., Dai, A., Hinton, G.: Who said what: modeling individual labelers improves classification. In: Proceedings of the AAAI Conference on Artificial Intelligence, vol. 32 (2018)
10. He, K., Zhang, X., Ren, S., Sun, J.: Deep residual learning for image recognition. In: 2016 IEEE Conference on Computer Vision and Pattern Recognition, pp. 770–778 (2016)
11. Ioffe, S., Szegedy, C.: Batch normalization: accelerating deep network training by reducing internal covariate shift. CoRR (2015)
12. Jiang, L., Zhou, Z., Leung, T., Li, L.J., Fei-Fei, L.: MentorNet: learning data-driven curriculum for very deep neural networks on corrupted labels. In: International Conference on Machine Learning, pp. 2304–2313 (2018)
13. Kajino, H., Tsuboi, Y., Sato, I., Kashima, H.: Learning from crowds and experts. In: Workshops at the Twenty-Sixth AAAI Conference on Artificial Intelligence (2012)
14. Khetan, A., Lipton, Z.C., Anandkumar, A.: Learning from noisy singly-labeled data. In: International Conference on Learning Representations (2018)
15. Krizhevsky, A., Hinton, G., et al.: Learning multiple layers of features from tiny images (2009)
16. Lecun, Y., Bottou, L., Bengio, Y., Haffner, P.: Gradient-based learning applied to document recognition. Proc. IEEE **86**(11), 2278–2324 (1998)
17. Lin, T.-Y., et al.: Microsoft COCO: common objects in context. In: Fleet, D., Pajdla, T., Schiele, B., Tuytelaars, T. (eds.) ECCV 2014. LNCS, vol. 8693, pp. 740–755. Springer, Cham (2014). https://doi.org/10.1007/978-3-319-10602-1_48
18. Patrini, G., Rozza, A., Krishna Menon, A., Nock, R., Qu, L.: Making deep neural networks robust to label noise: a loss correction approach. In: Proceedings of the IEEE Conference on Computer Vision and Pattern Recognition, pp. 1944–1952 (2017)
19. Raykar, V.C., et al.: Supervised learning from multiple experts: whom to trust when everyone lies a bit. In: Proceedings of the 26th Annual International Conference on Machine Learning, pp. 889–896 (2009)
20. Reed, S., Lee, H., Anguelov, D., Szegedy, C., Erhan, D., Rabinovich, A.: Training deep neural networks on noisy labels with bootstrapping. arXiv preprint arXiv:1412.6596 (2014)
21. Song, H., Kim, M., Park, D., Shin, Y., Lee, J.G.: Learning from noisy labels with deep neural networks: a survey. arXiv preprint arXiv:2007.08199 (2020)

22. Tanaka, D., Ikami, D., Yamasaki, T., Aizawa, K.: Joint optimization framework for learning with noisy labels. In: Proceedings of the IEEE Conference on Computer Vision and Pattern Recognition, pp. 5552–5560 (2018)
23. Tanno, R., Saeedi, A., Sankaranarayanan, S., Alexander, D.C., Silberman, N.: Learning from noisy labels by regularized estimation of annotator confusion. In: Proceedings of the IEEE/CVF Conference on Computer Vision and Pattern Recognition, pp. 11244–11253 (2019)
24. Whitehill, J., Wu, T.F., Bergsma, J., Movellan, J., Ruvolo, P.: Whose vote should count more: optimal integration of labels from labelers of unknown expertise. In: Advances in Neural Information Processing Systems, vol. 22, pp. 2035–2043 (2009)
25. Xiao, T., Xia, T., Yang, Y., Huang, C., Wang, X.: Learning from massive noisy labeled data for image classification. In: Proceedings of the IEEE Conference on Computer Vision and Pattern Recognition, pp. 2691–2699 (2015)
26. Xue, Z., Ren, S., Gao, Z., Zhao, H.: Multimodal knowledge expansion. In: Proceedings of the IEEE/CVF International Conference on Computer Vision, pp. 854–863 (2021)

Acknowledging the Unknown for Multi-label Learning with Single Positive Labels

Donghao Zhou[1,2], Pengfei Chen[3], Qiong Wang[1], Guangyong Chen[4(✉)], and Pheng-Ann Heng[1,5]

[1] Guangdong Provincial Key Laboratory of Computer Vision and Virtual Reality Technology, Shenzhen Institute of Advanced Technology, Chinese Academy of Sciences, Shenzhen, China
dh.zhou@siat.ac.cn
[2] University of Chinese Academy of Sciences, Beijing, China
[3] Tencent Technology, Shenzhen, China
[4] Zhejiang Lab, Hangzhou, China
gychen@zhejianglab.com
[5] The Chinese University of Hong Kong, Hong Kong, China

Abstract. Due to the difficulty of collecting exhaustive multi-label annotations, multi-label datasets often contain partial labels. We consider an extreme of this weakly supervised learning problem, called single positive multi-label learning (SPML), where each multi-label training image has only one positive label. Traditionally, all unannotated labels are assumed as negative labels in SPML, which introduces false negative labels and causes model training to be dominated by assumed negative labels. In this work, we choose to treat all unannotated labels from an alternative perspective, i.e. acknowledging they are unknown. Hence, we propose entropy-maximization (EM) loss to attain a special gradient regime for providing proper supervision signals. Moreover, we propose asymmetric pseudo-labeling (APL), which adopts asymmetric-tolerance strategies and a self-paced procedure, to cooperate with EM loss and then provide more precise supervision. Experiments show that our method significantly improves performance and achieves state-of-the-art results on all four benchmarks. Code is available at https://github.com/Correr-Zhou/SPML-AckTheUnknown.

Keywords: Weakly supervised learning · Single positive multi-label learning · Entropy maximization · Pseudo-labeling

1 Introduction

Each image is assumed to associate with only one label in *multi-class* classification, while the real world is closer to being *multi-label*, since multiple objects

Supplementary Information The online version contains supplementary material available at https://doi.org/10.1007/978-3-031-20053-3_25.

		person	dog	bus	bicycle	apple	boat	laptop	couch
(a)		✓	✗	✓	✓	✗	✗	✗	✗
(b)		✓	✗	?	✓	?	✗	?	?
(c)		✓	?	?	?	?	?	?	?

Fig. 1. Example of the image with (a) full annotations, (b) partial annotations, and (c) "singe positive" annotations. In single positive multi-label learning (SPML), for this image, only one positive label (*person*) is annotated, and the other labels (*dog, bus, bicycle*, etc.) remain unannotated

are inherently contained in a realistic scene [51]. Along with the wide adoption of deep learning, recent years have witnessed great progress in multi-label classification [26,33,52]. Unfortunately, it is excessively laborious to collect exhaustive multi-label annotations for a large-scale image dataset [8]. The major reasons are that the number of potential labels for an image can be large [27] and human annotators tend to ignore rare or small objects [48], which could cause a large amount of label noise. In fact, some publicly available multi-label datasets, including MS-COCO [25] and Open Images [19], are considered to contain only partial labels of images [14]. Therefore, it is of scientific interest to explore multi-label learning with partially labeled datasets.

In this paper, we focus on an extreme of this weakly supervised learning problem in multi-label classification called *single positive multi-label learning* (*SPML*) [7], where only one single positive label (and no other positive or negative labels) is annotated for each training image (see Fig. 1). SPML is a worth-exploring variant of multi-label learning for the following reasons: First, this is a common setting in numerous practical scenarios. For instance, when collecting images from the web, the only annotated positive label of an image is from its query [22]. Second, some multi-class datasets like ImageNet [35] actually contain images that associates with more than one label [2,38,42], while the multi-class training fashion penalizes any predictions beyond the single annotated label [51]. Third, in-depth research of multi-label learning with this minimal supervision could significantly relax the annotation requirement of large-scale multi-label datasets, which helps to reduce expensive annotation costs [9].

Due to the lack of supervision from all negative labels and most positive labels, SPML remains a challenging problem. Unfortunately, if ignoring unannotated labels, the model trained with only positive labels would collapse to a trivial solution. Since negative labels are generally the overwhelming majority of multi-label annotations, the traditional method is to assume all unannotated labels are negative to provide supervision signals, which is commonly regarded as the baseline of SPML [7]. However, this assumption would introduce false negative labels and make model training be dominated by assumed negative labels, which damages model generalization and causes a substantial performance drop. Therefore, unannotated labels should be *properly treated* in model training. In this work, instead of making any unrealistic assumptions, we choose to treat all unannotated labels from a quite different perspective in SPML, i.e. *acknowledging the fact that they are unknown*, and propose a simple but efficient method in response to the issues above. Our main contributions are summarized as follows:

1. Motivated by the idea of acknowledging the unknown, we propose a novel loss function called *entropy-maximization (EM) loss* for SPML, which aims to maximize the entropy of predicted probabilities for unannotated labels. Besides, we reveal the mechanism of EM loss with gradient-based analysis, which demonstrates that EM loss is capable of tackling inherent issues of the traditional method due to its special gradient regime.
2. For more precise supervision, we propose *asymmetric pseudo-labeling (APL)* to cooperate with EM loss. Considering the positive-negative label imbalance of unannotated labels, APL adopts asymmetric-tolerance strategies for positive and negative pseudo-labels with a self-paced procedure, which can generate highly accurate pseudo-labels to further boost performance.
3. Experiments performed on four popular multi-label datasets, i.e. PASCAL VOC [10], MS-COCO [25], NUS-WIDE [6], and CUB [43], show that our method achieves state-of-the-art results on all four benchmarks. Moreover, detailed ablation study and further analysis verified the effectiveness and rationality of the proposed method.

2   Related Work

Multi-label Learning with Weak Supervision. There are several multi-label tasks similar to single positive multi-label learning (SPML). Multi-label learning with missing labels (MLML) assumes that some labels are annotated and the others are "missing" for each training image [40]. Different methods have been proposed for MLML, including treating missing labels as negative ones [29,39,44,47], label matrix completion [3,4,50], learning image-label similarities [14], etc. Semi-supervised multi-label learning (SSML) assumes training data is a subset of images with exhaustive labels and a large number of images without any labels [27]. Common solutions to SSML include non-negative matrix factorization [28], label propagation [45], aligning image features [46], etc. However, these two tasks are quite different from SPML, where all training images are labeled but each one only contains one positive label. Within the limit of this special setting, most standard methods of these two tasks, like consistency regularization [37] and learning label correlations [9,53], are not applicable to SPML.

Entropy Min-/Maximization. The idea of entropy min-/maximization has been widely exploited in various fields. Grandvalet et al. proposed entropy minimization regularization for semi-supervised learning [11], and Pereyra et al. have shown that penalizing low entropy also acts as a strong regularizer in multi-class classification [32]. In domain adaptation, entropy min-/maximization has been adopted to adversarially optimize the model [36] and learn from target domain data [49]. Besides, entropy maximization has been shown to improve exploration in reinforcement learning [30]. To the best of our knowledge, our entropy-maximization (EM) loss is the *first* loss function to utilize entropy maximization for unannotated labels and demonstrate its effectiveness.

Pseudo-Labeling. The goal of pseudo-labeling is to assign labels to under-labeled samples with a trained model [20]. There are many methods to implement pseudo-labeling, including exploiting neighborhood graphs [15], performing clustering [41], estimating prediction uncertainty [9,34], etc. However, existing pseudo-labeling techniques fail to consider the positive-negative label imbalance of unannotated labels in SPML, which would result in a large amount of label noise. By adopting asymmetric-tolerance strategies for positive and negative pseudo-labels, our asymmetric pseudo-labeling (APL) can significantly reduce wrong pseudo-labels, allowing for better performance.

3   Methodology

In this section, we start by giving a formal definition of single positive multi-label learning (SPML) in Sect. 3.1. Then, we would introduce our entropy-maximization (EM) loss designed for SPML in Sect. 3.2. Finally, we would describe the proposed asymmetric pseudo-labeling (APL) in Sect. 3.3.

3.1   Problem Definition

Let $\mathcal{D} = \{(\mathbf{x}^{(n)}, \mathbf{y}^{(n)})\}_{n=1}^{N}$ denotes a partially labeled multi-label dataset with N images, where each image $\mathbf{x}^{(n)}$ from input space $\mathcal{X}$ is associated with a vector of labels $\mathbf{y}^{(n)}$ from the label space $\mathcal{Y} = \{-1, 0, 1\}^C$ with C classes. Let $y_c^{(n)}$ be the c-th entry of $\mathbf{y}^{(n)}$, where $y_c^{(n)} = 1$ indicates $\mathbf{x}^{(n)}$ is relevant to the c-th class (i.e. $\mathbf{x}^{(n)}$ contains a positive label of the c-th class) and $y_c^{(n)} = -1$ otherwise. Besides, $y_c^{(n)} = 0$ indicates that the label of the c-th class is unannotated for $\mathbf{x}^{(n)}$. In SPML, $\mathbf{y}^{(n)}$ satisfies $y_c^{(n)} \in \{0, 1\}$ and $\sum_{c=1}^{C} \mathbb{1}_{[y_c^{(n)}=1]} = 1$, where $\mathbb{1}_{[\cdot]}$ denotes the indicator function, meaning that only one positive label (and no other positive or negative labels) is annotated for each training image.

The goal of SPML is to learn a mapping function $f : \mathcal{X} \to \mathcal{Y}'$ from $\mathcal{D}$, where $\mathcal{Y}' = \{-1, 1\}^C$ is the ground-truth label space for $\mathcal{X}$. Defining f as a deep model $f(\cdot; \mathbf{w})$ with the weights $\mathbf{w}$, the standard training approach is to treat each label prediction as an independent binary classification and solve $\hat{\mathbf{w}} = \arg\min_{\mathbf{w}} \frac{1}{N} \sum_{n=1}^{N} \mathcal{L}(\mathbf{f}^{(n)}, \mathbf{y}^{(n)})$, where $\mathbf{f}^{(n)} = f(\mathbf{x}^{(n)}; \mathbf{w}) \in [0, 1]^C$ denotes the predicted probabilities for $\mathbf{x}^{(n)}$ activated by the sigmoid function, and $\mathcal{L} : [0, 1]^C \times \mathcal{Y} \to \mathbb{R}$ denotes a loss function that can handle labels $\mathbf{y}^{(n)}$. Let $f_c^{(n)}$ denotes the c-th entry of $\mathbf{f}^{(n)}$.

3.2   Entropy-Maximization Loss

Since negative labels are generally the overwhelming majority of multi-label annotations, the widely recognized baseline of SPML is *assuming-negative (AN)*

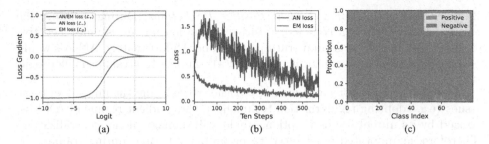

Fig. 2. (a): Gradients of $\mathcal{L}_+$, $\mathcal{L}_-$ and $\mathcal{L}_\varnothing$. For fair comparison, α of $\mathcal{L}_\varnothing$ is set to 1. (b): Training losses (averaged in 3 runs) of annotated positive labels (i.e. $\mathcal{L}_+$) on VOC from the model trained with AN and EM loss, where α is also set to 1. Note that $\mathcal{L}_+$ of AN loss is more unstable and would increase in early training. (c): Proportions of unannotated positive and negative labels of each class on COCO

loss [7], which assumes all unannotated labels as negative ones for training. Given a image-label pair $(\mathbf{x}^{(n)}, \mathbf{y}^{(n)})$, AN loss is defined as

$$\mathcal{L}_{\mathrm{AN}}(\mathbf{f}^{(n)}, \mathbf{y}^{(n)}) = -\frac{1}{C} \sum_{c=1}^{C} [\mathbb{1}_{[y_c^{(n)}=1]} \log(f_c^{(n)}) + \mathbb{1}_{[y_c^{(n)}=0]} \log(1 - f_c^{(n)})]. \quad (1)$$

To better understand the influence of AN loss on model training, we perform gradient-based analysis for AN loss, which is commonly used to deeply study loss functions [24,33]. For convenience, let $g = g_c^{(n)}$ denotes the output logit of the c-th class for $\mathbf{x}^{(n)}$, $p = 1/(1 + e^{-g})$ (i.e. the sigmoid function) denotes the predicted probability, and $\mathcal{L}_+ = -\log(p)$ (resp. $\mathcal{L}_- = -\log(1 - p)$) denotes the loss of the annotated positive label (resp. assumed negative label) in AN loss. The gradients of AN loss for the logit g are

$$\begin{cases} \dfrac{\partial \mathcal{L}_+}{\partial g} = \dfrac{\partial \mathcal{L}_+}{\partial p} \dfrac{\partial p}{\partial g} = \dfrac{-e^{-g}}{1 + e^{-g}}, & y_c^{(n)} = 1, \\[3mm] \dfrac{\partial \mathcal{L}_-}{\partial g} = \dfrac{\partial \mathcal{L}_-}{\partial p} \dfrac{\partial p}{\partial g} = \dfrac{1}{1 + e^{-g}}, & y_c^{(n)} = 0, \end{cases} \quad (2)$$

which shows that AN loss utilizes the same gradient regime for $\mathcal{L}_+$ and $\mathcal{L}_-$ (see Fig. 2(a)). Thus, the model trained with AN loss would treat annotated positive labels and assumed negative labels equally during training, which would result in bad performance in SPML due to the following issues:

1. *Dominance of Assumed Negative Labels*: For each training sample, assumed negative labels are $C - 1$ times more than annotated positive ones. Hence, affected by the same gradient regime, the model training would be dominated by assumed negative labels until they are well fitted, which hinders the model from learning from annotated positive labels (see Fig. 2(b)).
2. *Introduced Label Noise*: It is unavoidable that there are positive labels wrongly assumed as negative ones in AN loss. Due to the same gradient regime, false negative labels and true positive labels would severely confuse the model.

3. *Over-Suppression for Confident Positive Predictions*: During training, the model may output a confident positive prediction for an assumed negative label that may be a ground-truth positive one. Unfortunately, AN loss would provide a large gradient for it (see Fig. 2(a)), aiming to attain a smaller logit.

Despite there are some common approaches to reducing the impacts of these issues (e.g. adopting regularization techniques), the gradient regime of AN loss, caused by its unrealistic assumption, would still damage model generalization. Therefore, unannotated labels need to be properly treated during training, or more specifically, be treated with *a better gradient regime*. Instead of assuming they are negative, we choose to treat them from an alternative perspective, i.e. acknowledging they are unknown. Motivated by that, we propose *entropy-maximization (EM) loss* for SPML, which is defined as

$$\mathcal{L}_{\text{EM}}(\mathbf{f}^{(n)}, \mathbf{y}^{(n)}) = -\frac{1}{C} \sum_{c=1}^{C} [\mathbb{1}_{[y_c^{(n)}=1]} \log(f_c^{(n)}) + \mathbb{1}_{[y_c^{(n)}=0]} \alpha H(f_c^{(n)})], \quad (3)$$

$$H(f_c^{(n)}) = -[f_c^{(n)} \log(f_c^{(n)}) + (1 - f_c^{(n)}) \log(1 - f_c^{(n)})], \quad (4)$$

where α is a hyperparameter to down-weight the strength of entropy maximization. Note that EM loss adopts entropy maximization as a *separate* loss term (instead of an extra auxiliary regularizer) for unannotated labels to independently provide supervision signals for them, which is a unique loss design.

Likewise, we reveal the mechanism of EM loss by analyzing its gradients. Let $\mathcal{L}_\varnothing = \alpha[p \log p + (1 - p) \log (1 - p)]$ denotes the loss of the unannotated label in EM loss. The gradients of EM loss for the logit g are

$$\begin{cases} \dfrac{\partial \mathcal{L}_+}{\partial g} = \dfrac{\partial \mathcal{L}_+}{\partial p} \dfrac{\partial p}{\partial g} = \dfrac{-e^{-g}}{1 + e^{-g}}, & y_c^{(n)} = 1, \\[3ex] \dfrac{\partial \mathcal{L}_\varnothing}{\partial g} = \dfrac{\partial \mathcal{L}_\varnothing}{\partial p} \dfrac{\partial p}{\partial g} = \dfrac{-\alpha e^{-g} \log e^{-g}}{(1 + e^{-g})^2}, & y_c^{(n)} = 0, \end{cases} \quad (5)$$

which shows that EM loss utilizes the same gradient regime as AN loss for annotated positive labels and adopts a quite different one for unannotated labels (see Fig. 2(a)). Compared with AN loss, the special gradient regime of EM loss can lead to the following beneficial training behaviours (see Appendix B for additional empirical evidence of these claims):

1. *Learning from Annotated Labels Preferentially*: In early training, the model would produce ambiguous predictions before being well trained, i.e. predicted probabilities (resp. output logits) would be near 0.5 (resp. 0). At this time, the gradients of $\mathcal{L}_+$ (resp. $\mathcal{L}_\varnothing$) would be relatively large (resp. small) (see Fig. 2(a)), leading the model to preferentially learn from annotated positive labels (see Fig. 2(b)). Unlike simply down-weighting $\mathcal{L}_-$, EM loss tends to keep the predictions of unannotated labels ambiguous, and thus is capable of providing small gradients for them throughout training.

Algorithm 1. Asymmetric Pseudo-Labeling

Input: Training set $\mathcal{D}$ and model f_{T_w} trained with Eq. 3 for T_w epochs
Parameter: Total training epoch T_t, sample proportion $\theta\%$ and loss weight β
Output: Well-trained model f_i

1: $i \leftarrow T_w$, $\theta'\% \leftarrow \theta\%/(T_t - T_w)$
2: **repeat**
3:    Generate pseudo-labels using f_i by following Eq. 6
4:    Train f_{i+1} from f_i with Eq. 8
5:    $i \leftarrow i + 1$
6: **until** early stopping **or** $i = T_t$
7: **return** f_i

---

2. *Mitigating the Effect of Label Noise*: There are no positive labels wrongly regarded as negative ones in EM loss, which prevents the model from producing incorrect negative predictions. Moreover, though unannotated positive labels still exist, the model trained with EM loss would mainly focus on the annotated ones due to the special gradient regime.
3. *Maintaining Confident Positive Predictions*: After preferentially learning from annotated positive labels, the model is more likely to output confident positive predictions for potential positive labels. When the logit is large enough, the gradient of $\mathcal{L}_{\varnothing}$ would decline and even approach 0 as the logit goes larger (see Fig. 2(a)), which helps to maintain these confident positive predictions.

3.3 Asymmetric Pseudo-labeling

Exploiting a better gradient regime, the model trained with EM loss can produce more distinguishable predictions for unannotated positive and negative labels (see Fig. 4(a) and (b)). According to these informative predictions, we can assign pseudo-labels to partially labeled images, aiming to provide more precise supervision for the model and then further improve its performance. Generally, pseudo-labeling is performed by setting a predefined rule to select potential positive or negative labels, e.g. setting a score threshold [20] or sample proportion [5]. In pseudo-labeling, there is a natural trade-off between the provided supervision and the introduced noise, since generating more pseudo-labels is often accompanied by introducing more noise. Specifically, adopting a *low-tolerance* strategy (high score threshold or low sample proportion) would provide less accurate pseudo-labels, whereas adopting a *high-tolerance* strategy (low score threshold or high sample proportion) would introduce more noisy pseudo-labels.

Different from the other tasks, in SPML, the amounts of unannotated positive and negative labels are quite imbalanced on most classes (see Fig. 2(c), refer to Appendix F.1 for more examples). Considering this enormous imbalance, we choose to treat positive and negative pseudo-labels with *asymmetric tolerance* and thus propose *asymmetric pseudo-labeling (APL)* to cooperate with EM loss, aiming to generate relatively sufficient and accurate pseudo-labels. For negative pseudo-labels, APL adopts a *high-tolerance* strategy with a high sample proportion $\theta\% = 90\%$, which means that 90% of unannotated labels on a class could be selected as negative pseudo-labels at most during training. For positive ones, APL directly ignores them to avoid introducing any noisy positive pseudo-labels that would significantly reduce performance (see Fig. 3(b)), which can be regarded as an extreme *low-tolerance* strategy.

As shown in Algorithm 1, after warm-up for T_w epochs, pseudo-labels would be generated for subsequent epochs until training is over, which is equivalent to exploiting them to gradually fine-tune the model. Moreover, inspired by self-paced learning [18], instead of generating all the pseudo-labels at once time, APL would progressively generate more confident ones of them. Specifically, negative pseudo-labels are generated with a sample proportion $\theta'\% = \theta\%/(T_t - T_w)$ in each epoch, where T_t is the total training epoch. For the c-th class, APL firstly sorts the predicted probability set $U_c = \{f_c^{(n)} | y_c^{(n)} = 0, n = 1, 2, ..., N\}$ in ascending order. Then, APL assigns negative pseudo-labels of the c-th class to the images with the $\theta'\%$ lowest predicted probabilities in U_c. For an partially labeled image $\mathbf{x}^{(n)}$, negative pseudo-labels are generated by following

$$y_c^{(n)} \triangleq -\mathbb{1}_{[f_c^{(n)} \in U_c']}, \quad \forall c \in \{c | y_c^{(n)} = 0\}, \tag{6}$$

where $U_c' \subset U_c$ denotes the $\theta'\%$ lowest predicted probability subset of U_c, and $y_c^{(n)} \triangleq -1$ means that $\mathbf{x}^{(n)}$ is assigned the negative pseudo-label of the c-th class. Moreover, instead of assigning hard labels to images, APL records $s_c^{(n)} \triangleq f_c^{(n)}$ as soft labels for them to mitigate the effect of noisy negative pseudo-labels. Thus, the loss term of the negative pseudo-label is

$$\mathcal{L}_*(f_c^{(n)}, s_c^{(n)}) = s_c^{(n)} \log(f_c^{(n)}) + (1 - s_c^{(n)}) \log(1 - f_c^{(n)}). \tag{7}$$

As for the remaining unannotated labels, we still provide supervision signals for them by entropy maximization. Finally, adopting β as a hyperparameter to down-weight $\mathcal{L}_*$, EM loss combined with APL is formulated as

$$\mathcal{L}_{\text{EM+APL}}(\mathbf{f}^{(n)}, \mathbf{y}^{(n)}) = -\frac{1}{C} \sum_{c=1}^{C} [\mathbb{1}_{[y_c^{(n)}=1]} \log(f_c^{(n)}) + \mathbb{1}_{[y_c^{(n)}=0]} \alpha H(f_c^{(n)})$$

$$+ \mathbb{1}_{[y_c^{(n)}=-1]} \beta \mathcal{L}_*(f_c^{(n)}, s_c^{(n)})]. \tag{8}$$

4   Experiments

4.1   Experimental Setup

Datasets. Since there are no existing datasets totally in line with the setting of single positive multi-label learning (SPML), following [7], we use popular large-scale multi-label datasets to simulate "single positive" datasets by discarding annotations, which can guarantee access to all ground-truth labels for analyzing training phenomena and evaluating performance. Specifically, after withholding 20% of the training images for validation, we randomly select one positive label to keep and treat the other labels are unannotated ones for each training image, which is performed once for each dataset. Note that the validation and test sets remain fully labeled. We use PASCAL VOC 2012 (VOC) [10], MS-COCO 2014 (COCO) [25], NUS-WIDE (NUS) [6], and CUB-200-2011 (CUB) [43] in our experiments. More dataset descriptions are contained in Appendix C.1.

Implementation Details. For fair comparison, we follow the main implementation of [7]. Specifically, ResNet-50 [12] pretrained on the ImageNet [35] is adopted as the backbone, followed by global average pooling [23] and a $2048 \times C$ fully connection layer that outputs the predicted probabilities of C classes. All input images are resized to 448×448, and the training images are horizontally flipped with a probability of 0.5 for data augmentation. For each method, we conduct a grid search of batch sizes in $\{8, 16\}$ and learning rates in $\{1e-2, 1e-3, 1e-4, 1e-5\}$, and then select the hyperparameters with the best mean average precision (mAP) on the validation set. Moreover, we use Adam [17] as our optimizer to train all models for 10 epochs, and early stopping is performed when mAP on the validation set descends. Each experiment runs three times, and the mean and standard deviations of mAP are reported.

Comparing Methods. We compare our method to the following methods: AN loss (assuming-negative loss), EntMin (entropy minimization regularization) [11], Focal loss [24], ASL (asymmetric loss) [33], ROLE (regularized online label estimation) [7], and ROLE+LI (ROLE combined with the "LinearInit") [7]. Besides, we also compare our method to the baseline (i.e. AN loss) with the following improvement: DW (down-weighting $\mathcal{L}_-$), L1R/L2R (l_1/l_2 regularization), LS (label smoothing), and N-LS (label smoothing for only $\mathcal{L}_-$). Moreover, we also report the performance of the models trained with binary cross-entropy (BCE) loss on the fully labeled dataset and on a special partially labeled dataset (i.e. 1 P. & All N. in Table 1). To simulate the lacking of positive supervision, BCE loss would ignore all unannotated labels (i.e. their losses are not computed) in the latter case. Refer to Appendix C.2 and C.3 for the details of the comparing methods and the hyperparameters of each method respectively.

4.2   Results and Discussion

The experimental results on four SPML benchmarks are reported in Table 1. It can be observed that the assumption of AN loss (i.e. assuming all unannotated labels are negative) causes a significant performance drop, e.g. 9.81% and 12.59% mAP decrements than being trained with full annotations (i.e. All P. & All N.) on NUS and CUB respectively. When adopting some improvement on AN loss, the impact of this assumption can be mitigated. Down-weighting $\mathcal{L}_-$ of Eq. 1 can help to achieve competitive performance on CUB, and label smoothing is more useful on VOC. Note that adopting label smoothing for only assumed negative labels can achieve better performance, which verifies the importance of learning

Table 1. Experimental results of our method and the comparing methods on four SPML benchmarks. The best performance of the methods in the SPML setting (i.e. 1 P. & 0 N.) is marked in bold and the second best is marked in italic

Ann. labels	Methods	VOC	COCO	NUS	CUB
All P. & All N.	BCE loss	89.42 ± 0.27	76.78 ± 0.13	52.08 ± 0.20	30.90 ± 0.64
1 P. & All N.	BCE loss	87.60 ± 0.31	71.39 ± 0.19	46.45 ± 0.27	20.65 ± 1.11
1 P. & 0 N.	AN loss	85.89 ± 0.38	64.92 ± 0.19	42.27 ± 0.56	18.31 ± 0.47
	DW	86.98 ± 0.36	67.59 ± 0.11	45.71 ± 0.23	19.15 ± 0.56
	L1R	85.97 ± 0.31	64.44 ± 0.20	42.15 ± 0.46	17.59 ± 1.82
	L2R	85.96 ± 0.36	64.41 ± 0.24	42.72 ± 0.12	17.71 ± 1.79
	LS	87.90 ± 0.21	67.15 ± 0.13	43.77 ± 0.29	16.26 ± 0.45
	N-LS	88.12 ± 0.32	67.15 ± 0.10	43.86 ± 0.54	16.82 ± 0.42
	EntMin	53.16 ± 2.81	32.52 ± 5.55	19.38 ± 3.64	13.08 ± 0.15
	Focal loss	87.59 ± 0.58	68.79 ± 0.14	47.00 ± 0.14	19.80 ± 0.30
	ASL	87.76 ± 0.51	68.78 ± 0.32	46.93 ± 0.30	18.81 ± 0.48
	ROLE	87.77 ± 0.22	67.04 ± 0.19	41.63 ± 0.35	13.66 ± 0.24
	ROLE+LI	88.26 ± 0.21	69.12 ± 0.13	45.98 ± 0.26	14.86 ± 0.72
1 P. & 0 N.	EM loss	*89.09 ± 0.17*	*70.70 ± 0.31*	*47.15 ± 0.11*	*20.85 ± 0.42*
	EM loss+APL	**89.19 ± 0.31**	**70.87 ± 0.23**	**47.59 ± 0.22**	**21.84 ± 0.34**

from annotated positive labels. Whereas, a common regularization technique, i.e. l_1/l_2 regularization, seems to under-perform in the SPML setting.

As for the other comparing methods, Focal loss and ASL can achieve good performance on NUS and CUB, which can reduce the effect of the dominance of assumed negative labels but still can not address this issue well. The state-of-the-art method of SPML (i.e. ROLE), which adopts a jointly trained label estimator to perform label estimation during training, has competitive performance in SPML, e.g. achieving 88.77% mAP on VOC. Moreover, the "LinearInit" training fashion can be integrated with ROLE to further improve its performance. However, this state-of-the-art method still achieves a poor classification result on CUB. It is worth noting that entropy minimization regularization, which is the opposite of our entropy maximization (EM) loss, achieves badly poor and unstable results on all datasets. It demonstrates that this widely adopted method of semi-supervised learning does not applicable to SPML, since only positive labels are annotated for multi-label training images in this special setting.

It can be observed that our EM loss, which adopts entropy maximization for unannotated labels, outperforms the existing methods on all four SPML benchmarks, e.g. achieving 89.09% and 70.70% mAP on VOC and COCO respectively. Note that ROLE uses a learnable label matrix to act as the label estimator, which significantly increases the memory consumption during training. Moreover, this method requires access to the average number of positive labels, which is practically unavailable in the SPML setting. Compared with ROLE, our EM loss is cost-free and does not introduce any extra learnable parameters in light of

Table 2. Left: Experimental results of AN loss, ROLE, and EM loss on VOC with different backbones. Right: Precision (averaged in 3 runs) of pseudo-labels generated by APL cooperating with AN and EM loss on four multi-label datasets

Methods	ResNet-34	ResNet-50	ResNet-101
AN loss	84.60 ± 0.29	85.89 ± 0.38	86.59 ± 0.19
ROLE	85.44 ± 0.16	87.77 ± 0.22	88.37 ± 0.07
EM loss	$\mathbf{86.58 \pm 0.25}$	$\mathbf{89.09 \pm 0.17}$	$\mathbf{88.80 \pm 0.11}$

Losses	VOC	COCO	NUS	CUB
AN loss	96.44%	96.32%	98.16%	89.82%
EM loss	**99.57%**	**99.67%**	**99.89%**	**91.58%**

Table 3. Experimental results of APL and the pseudo-labeling variants on CUB. ✓ indicates that the corresponding technique are adopted. Note that the first row denotes that pseudo-labeling is not performed and the last row is our APL

High prop.	Soft label	DW	Pos. PL	mAP
				20.85 ± 0.42
	✓	✓		20.95 ± 0.34
✓		✓		20.99 ± 0.38
✓	✓			21.00 ± 0.44
✓	✓	✓	✓	20.82 ± 0.68
✓	✓	✓		$\mathbf{21.84 \pm 0.34}$

its simplicity. Besides, the model trained with EM loss can even outperform the model trained with additional supervision (i.e. 1 P. & All N.) in three benchmarks (i.e. VOC, NUS, and CUB). Moreover, it can also be observed that asymmetric pseudo-labeling (APL) can further boost the performance of the model trained with EM loss, and finally our EM loss+APL achieves state-of-the-art results on all four benchmarks. Especially, EM loss+APL can achieve a 6.98% mAP increment than ROLE+LI on CUB, and achieves 89.19% mAP on VOC, which even approaches the result of being trained with full annotations.

4.3   Ablation Study

Robustness of EM Loss to α. To investigate how performance is affected by α, we present the experimental results of EM loss with different α in Fig. 3(a). The performance has a peak at $\alpha = 0.2$ on VOC and an improper α might cause a performance drop. However, the variation range of mAP remains slight and EM loss can still achieve relatively high performance with different α. Especially, EM loss with all different α can still outperform AN loss, and even approaches the result of being trained with full annotations (i.e. BCE loss) when $\alpha = 0.2$, showing that performance can be improved by selecting a proper α.

Effectiveness of EM Loss on Different Backbones. To study the impact of the special gradient regime of EM loss when the scale of the deep model varies, we

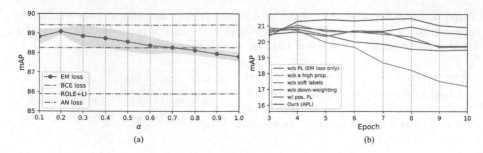

Fig. 3. (a): Experimental results (averaged in 3 runs) of EM loss with different α on VOC. (b): Performance curves (averaged in 3 runs) of APL and its variants on CUB. Note that the x-axis ticks start by 3 since the first 3 epochs are for warm-up

consider ResNet with different depths (i.e. ResNet-34, ResNet-50, and ResNet-101) as backbones to be trained with EM loss. As reported in Table 2, EM loss achieves the best performance on these backbones as we expect. However, the performance of EM loss on ResNet-50 is even better than on ResNet-101, which can be reserved as an interesting work for further exploration.

Evaluation of APL. We perform detailed ablation study for APL (see Fig. 3(b) and Table 3). Specifically, we remove or add several key components of APL to obtain the following five variants: 1) w/o pseudo-labeling: the model is trained only with EM loss. 2) w/o a high sample proportion: $\theta\%$ is set to 10%. 3) w/o soft labels: the pseudo-labeled samples are assigned hard pseudo-labels. 4) w/o down-weighting: β is set to 1. 5) w/ positive pseudo-labeling: positive pseudo-labeling is also performed in the same way as negative pseudo-labeling, and its sample proportion is set to 10%. The results on the test set of CUB show that APL can achieve more stable training and each component adopted by APL contributes to performance improvement (see Appendix D for detailed analysis). Moreover, we report the precision of pseudo-labels generated by APL (see Table 2, we disable early stopping for fair comparison), which shows that APL can generate pseudo-labels with high precision ($\approx$99%) in EM loss on most datasets. Though unannotated labels are already assumed as negative ones in AN loss, we also try adopting APL in AN loss to select potential ground-truth negative labels for reference, showing the effectiveness of asymmetric-tolerance strategies and the capability of EM loss to reduce false negative predictions.

4.4   Further Analysis

Class-Wise Performance Improvement. To investigate whether EM loss is beneficial to most classes of the "single positive" datasets, we report class-wise average precision (AP) improvement of EM loss (over AN loss) on the test sets of VOC and COCO. As shown in Fig. 4(c), our EM loss can improve performance on most classes, or more specifically, on 95% classes of VOC and 93.75% classes of COCO, which demonstrates its general effectiveness.

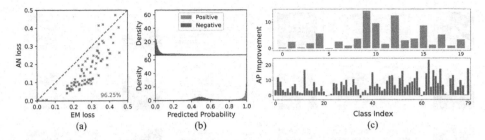

Fig. 4. (a): Wasserstein distances between the distributions of the predicted probabilities for unannotated positive and negative labels on the training set of COCO, where each point indicates one class. We present the proportion of points that are under the red line. (b): Densities of predicted probabilities on the most common "person" class of the test set of COCO, produced by the models trained with AN (*top*) and EM (*bottom*) loss. (c): Class-wise AP improvement of EM loss on VOC (*top*) and COCO (*bottom*) (Color figure online)

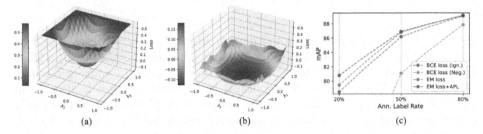

Fig. 5. (a) and (b): 3D visualization of loss landscapes around the minima of the models trained with AN and EM loss on VOC respectively. Note that we set the z-axis to the same scale for comparing the sharpness. (c): Comparison of our method and two baselines in the MLML setting. We randomly discard a percentage of annotations per image as done in [9] to simulate MLML datasets

Distinguishability of Model Predictions. A well-generalizing model should be able to produce informative predictions for unannotated labels, i.e. the predicted probabilities of unannotated positive and negative labels are more distinguishable. The divergences between these predicted probabilities can be quantitatively calculated by the Wasserstein distance. As shown in Fig. 4(a), the model trained with EM loss usually achieves a much larger Wasserstein distance, which means that it can yield more distinguishable predictions on most classes. Furthermore, we also visualize the predicted probabilities on the test set. For the most common "person" class of COCO, as shown in Fig. 4(b), EM loss also contributes to more distinguishable predictions for the test images. We also provide more visualization results of other classes in Appendix F.2.

Generalization Evaluation by Loss Landscapes. Considering the sharpness of loss minima, we can further explore why EM loss helps to better generalization. Given established principles of statistics and information theory, the study in [1]

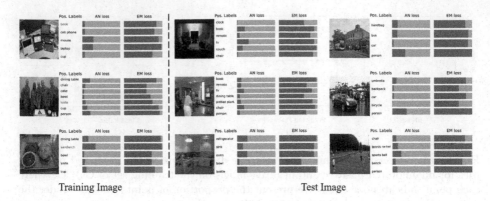

Training Image   Test Image

Fig. 6. Examples of training and test images of COCO. Note that the annotated positive labels are marked in red for each training image, and the blue bars indicate the predicted probabilities produced by the models trained with AN and EM loss (Color figure online)

shows that a flat minimum has lower mutual information between training data and model parameters and thus leads to better generalization. Several previous works [13,16,31] also show that a flat minimum can make the converged model generalize well. Using the technique in [21], we visualize the loss landscapes in Fig. 5. It can be observed that the model trained with AN (resp. EM) loss would converge to a sharp (resp. flatter) minimum, which further explains why the model trained with EM loss can acquire better generalization.

Qualitative Results. As shown in Fig. 6, we can observe that the model trained with AN loss would produce low predicted probabilities for almost all unannotated positive labels, especially for small and rare objects in the images. Besides, the predictions of the test images also show that AN loss would severely damage model generalization. However, the model trained with EM loss can produce relatively confident positive predictions for positive labels of training and test images, even for those small and rare objects, which further demonstrates the remarkable effectiveness of EM loss.

Performance in a More General Scenario. Our work focuses on learning from single positive labels, but we are curious about whether it can perform well in a more general setting, i.e. multi-label learning with missing labels (MLML). Thus, we report the preliminary experimental results in Fig. 5. Note that the baselines are BCE loss with unannotated labels being ignored or regarded as negative ones and EM loss acts like BCE loss with unannotated labels being supervised by entropy maximization in MLML. We find that our method can still achieve performance improvement, which shows that it can be generalized to other similar tasks and is well worth further exploration in the future.

5   Conclusions

In this paper, we aim to solve an extreme variant of multi-label learning called single positive multi-label learning (SPML) which is a challenging but under-explored problem. Instead of assuming all unannotated labels are negative as traditionally done, we choose to treat them from an alternative perspective, i.e. acknowledging they are unknown. Hence, we propose entropy-maximization (EM) loss and asymmetric pseudo-labeling (APL) for SPML. Experiments show that our method achieves state-of-the-art results on all four benchmarks. We believe that our method can serve as a stronger baseline for SPML and expect this paper can motivate more future work of weakly supervised learning.

Acknowledgements. This work is supported by the National Key R&D Program of China (2022YFE0200700), the National Natural Science Foundation of China (Project No. 62006219 and No. 62072452), the Natural Science Foundation of Guangdong Province (2022A1515011579), and the Hong Kong Innovation and Technology Fund (Project No. GHP/110/19SZ and ITS/170/20).

References

1. Achille, A., Soatto, S.: Emergence of invariance and disentanglement in deep representations. J. Mach. Learn. Res. **19**(1), 1947–1980 (2018)
2. Beyer, L., Hénaff, O.J., Kolesnikov, A., Zhai, X., van den Oord, A.: Are we done with ImageNet? arXiv preprint arXiv:2006.07159 (2020)
3. Cabral, R., De la Torre, F., Costeira, J.P., Bernardino, A.: Matrix completion for weakly-supervised multi-label image classification. IEEE Trans. Pattern Anal. Mach. Intell. **37**(1), 121–135 (2014)
4. Cabral, R.S., Torre, F., Costeira, J.P., Bernardino, A.: Matrix completion for multi-label image classification. In: Advances in Neural Information Processing Systems, pp. 190–198 (2011)
5. Chen, X., et al.: Self-PU: self boosted and calibrated positive-unlabeled training. In: International Conference on Machine Learning, pp. 1510–1519. PMLR (2020)
6. Chua, T.S., Tang, J., Hong, R., Li, H., Luo, Z., Zheng, Y.: NUS-WIDE: a real-world web image database from national university of Singapore. In: Proceedings of the ACM International Conference on Image and Video Retrieval, pp. 1–9 (2009)
7. Cole, E., Mac Aodha, O., Lorieul, T., Perona, P., Morris, D., Jojic, N.: Multi-label learning from single positive labels. In: Proceedings of the IEEE/CVF Conference on Computer Vision and Pattern Recognition, pp. 933–942 (2021)
8. Deng, J., Russakovsky, O., Krause, J., Bernstein, M.S., Berg, A., Fei-Fei, L.: Scalable multi-label annotation. In: Proceedings of the SIGCHI Conference on Human Factors in Computing Systems, pp. 3099–3102 (2014)
9. Durand, T., Mehrasa, N., Mori, G.: Learning a deep convnet for multi-label classification with partial labels. In: Proceedings of the IEEE/CVF Conference on Computer Vision and Pattern Recognition, pp. 647–657 (2019)
10. Everingham, M., Winn, J.: The PASCAL visual object classes challenge 2012 (VOC2012) development kit. Pattern Analysis, Statistical Modelling and Computational Learning, Technical report **8**, 5 (2011)

11. Grandvalet, Y., Bengio, Y.: Semi-supervised learning by entropy minimization. In: Advances in Neural Information Processing Systems, vol. 17 (2004)
12. He, K., Zhang, X., Ren, S., Sun, J.: Deep residual learning for image recognition. In: Proceedings of the IEEE Conference on Computer Vision and Pattern Recognition, pp. 770–778 (2016)
13. Hochreiter, S., Schmidhuber, J.: Flat minima. Neural Comput. 9(1), 1–42 (1997)
14. Huynh, D., Elhamifar, E.: Interactive multi-label CNN learning with partial labels. In: Proceedings of the IEEE/CVF Conference on Computer Vision and Pattern Recognition, pp. 9423–9432 (2020)
15. Iscen, A., Tolias, G., Avrithis, Y., Chum, O.: Label propagation for deep semi-supervised learning. In: Proceedings of the IEEE/CVF Conference on Computer Vision and Pattern Recognition (CVPR), June 2019
16. Keskar, N.S., Mudigere, D., Nocedal, J., Smelyanskiy, M., Tang, P.T.P.: On large-batch training for deep learning: generalization gap and sharp minima. arXiv preprint arXiv:1609.04836 (2016)
17. Kingma, D.P., Ba, J.: Adam: a method for stochastic optimization. arXiv preprint arXiv:1412.6980 (2014)
18. Kumar, M., Packer, B., Koller, D.: Self-paced learning for latent variable models. In: Advances in Neural Information Processing Systems, vol. 23, pp. 1189–1197 (2010)
19. Kuznetsova, A., et al.: The open images dataset V4. Int. J. Comput. Vis. 128(7), 1956–1981 (2020). https://doi.org/10.1007/s11263-020-01316-z
20. Lee, D.H., et al.: Pseudo-label: the simple and efficient semi-supervised learning method for deep neural networks. In: Workshop on Challenges in Representation Learning, ICML, vol. 3, p. 896 (2013)
21. Li, H., Xu, Z., Taylor, G., Studer, C., Goldstein, T.: Visualizing the loss landscape of neural nets. arXiv preprint arXiv:1712.09913 (2017)
22. Li, W., et al.: WebVision challenge: visual learning and understanding with web data. arXiv preprint arXiv:1705.05640 (2017)
23. Lin, M., Chen, Q., Yan, S.: Network in network. arXiv preprint arXiv:1312.4400 (2013)
24. Lin, T.Y., Goyal, P., Girshick, R., He, K., Dollár, P.: Focal loss for dense object detection. In: Proceedings of the IEEE International Conference on Computer Vision, pp. 2980–2988 (2017)
25. Lin, T.-Y., et al.: Microsoft COCO: common objects in context. In: Fleet, D., Pajdla, T., Schiele, B., Tuytelaars, T. (eds.) ECCV 2014. LNCS, vol. 8693, pp. 740–755. Springer, Cham (2014). https://doi.org/10.1007/978-3-319-10602-1_48
26. Liu, S., Zhang, L., Yang, X., Su, H., Zhu, J.: Query2Label: a simple transformer way to multi-label classification. arXiv preprint arXiv:2107.10834 (2021)
27. Liu, W., Wang, H., Shen, X., Tsang, I.: The emerging trends of multi-label learning. IEEE Trans. Pattern Anal. Mach. Intell. 44(11), 7955–7974 (2021)
28. Liu, Y., Jin, R., Yang, L.: Semi-supervised multi-label learning by constrained non-negative matrix factorization. In: AAAI, vol. 6, pp. 421–426 (2006)
29. Mahajan, D., et al.: Exploring the limits of weakly supervised pretraining. In: Ferrari, V., Hebert, M., Sminchisescu, C., Weiss, Y. (eds.) ECCV 2018. LNCS, vol. 11206, pp. 185–201. Springer, Cham (2018). https://doi.org/10.1007/978-3-030-01216-8_12
30. Mnih, V., et al.: Asynchronous methods for deep reinforcement learning. In: International Conference on Machine Learning, pp. 1928–1937. PMLR (2016)
31. Neyshabur, B., Bhojanapalli, S., McAllester, D., Srebro, N.: Exploring generalization in deep learning. arXiv preprint arXiv:1706.08947 (2017)

32. Pereyra, G., Tucker, G., Chorowski, J., Kaiser, Ł., Hinton, G.: Regularizing neural networks by penalizing confident output distributions. arXiv preprint arXiv:1701.06548 (2017)
33. Ridnik, T., et al.: Asymmetric loss for multi-label classification. In: Proceedings of the IEEE/CVF International Conference on Computer Vision, pp. 82–91 (2021)
34. Rizve, M.N., Duarte, K., Rawat, Y.S., Shah, M.: In defense of pseudo-labeling: an uncertainty-aware pseudo-label selection framework for semi-supervised learning. arXiv preprint arXiv:2101.06329 (2021)
35. Russakovsky, O., et al.: ImageNet large scale visual recognition challenge. Int. J. Comput. Vis. **115**(3), 211–252 (2015). https://doi.org/10.1007/s11263-015-0816-y
36. Saito, K., Kim, D., Sclaroff, S., Darrell, T., Saenko, K.: Semi-supervised domain adaptation via minimax entropy. In: Proceedings of the IEEE/CVF International Conference on Computer Vision (ICCV), October 2019
37. Sajjadi, M., Javanmardi, M., Tasdizen, T.: Regularization with stochastic transformations and perturbations for deep semi-supervised learning. In: Lee, D., Sugiyama, M., Luxburg, U., Guyon, I., Garnett, R. (eds.) Advances in Neural Information Processing Systems, vol. 29. Curran Associates, Inc. (2016)
38. Stock, P., Cisse, M.: ConvNets and ImageNet beyond accuracy: understanding mistakes and uncovering biases. In: Ferrari, V., Hebert, M., Sminchisescu, C., Weiss, Y. (eds.) ECCV 2018. LNCS, vol. 11210, pp. 504–519. Springer, Cham (2018). https://doi.org/10.1007/978-3-030-01231-1_31
39. Sun, C., Shrivastava, A., Singh, S., Gupta, A.: Revisiting unreasonable effectiveness of data in deep learning era. In: Proceedings of the IEEE International Conference on Computer Vision, pp. 843–852 (2017)
40. Sun, Y.Y., Zhang, Y., Zhou, Z.H.: Multi-label learning with weak label. In: Twenty-Fourth AAAI Conference on Artificial Intelligence (2010)
41. Taherkhani, F., Dabouei, A., Soleymani, S., Dawson, J., Nasrabadi, N.M.: Self-supervised Wasserstein pseudo-labeling for semi-supervised image classification. In: Proceedings of the IEEE/CVF Conference on Computer Vision and Pattern Recognition (CVPR), pp. 12267–12277, June 2021
42. Tsipras, D., Santurkar, S., Engstrom, L., Ilyas, A., Madry, A.: From ImageNet to image classification: contextualizing progress on benchmarks. In: International Conference on Machine Learning, pp. 9625–9635. PMLR (2020)
43. Wah, C., Branson, S., Welinder, P., Perona, P., Belongie, S.: The Caltech-UCSD Birds-200-2011 dataset. Technical report, California Institute of Technology (2011)
44. Wang, J., Yang, Y., Mao, J., Huang, Z., Huang, C., Xu, W.: CNN-RNN: a unified framework for multi-label image classification. In: Proceedings of the IEEE Conference on Computer Vision and Pattern Recognition, pp. 2285–2294 (2016)
45. Wang, L., Ding, Z., Fu, Y.: Adaptive graph guided embedding for multi-label annotation. In: IJCAI (2018)
46. Wang, L., Liu, Y., Qin, C., Sun, G., Fu, Y.: Dual relation semi-supervised multi-label learning. In: Proceedings of the AAAI Conference on Artificial Intelligence, vol. 34, pp. 6227–6234 (2020)
47. Wang, Q., Shen, B., Wang, S., Li, L., Si, L.: Binary codes embedding for fast image tagging with incomplete labels. In: Fleet, D., Pajdla, T., Schiele, B., Tuytelaars, T. (eds.) ECCV 2014. LNCS, vol. 8690, pp. 425–439. Springer, Cham (2014). https://doi.org/10.1007/978-3-319-10605-2_28
48. Wolfe, J.M., Horowitz, T.S., Kenner, N.M.: Rare items often missed in visual searches. Nature **435**(7041), 439–440 (2005)

49. Wu, X., Zhou, Q., Yang, Z., Zhao, C., Latecki, L.J., et al.: Entropy minimization vs. diversity maximization for domain adaptation. arXiv preprint arXiv:2002.01690 (2020)
50. Xu, M., Jin, R., Zhou, Z.H.: Speedup matrix completion with side information: application to multi-label learning. In: Advances in Neural Information Processing Systems, pp. 2301–2309 (2013)
51. Yun, S., Oh, S.J., Heo, B., Han, D., Choe, J., Chun, S.: Re-labeling ImageNet: from single to multi-labels, from global to localized labels. In: Proceedings of the IEEE/CVF Conference on Computer Vision and Pattern Recognition, pp. 2340–2350 (2021)
52. Zhu, K., Wu, J.: Residual attention: a simple but effective method for multi-label recognition. In: Proceedings of the IEEE/CVF International Conference on Computer Vision, pp. 184–193 (2021)
53. Zhu, Y., Kwok, J.T., Zhou, Z.H.: Multi-label learning with global and local label correlation. IEEE Trans. Knowl. Data Eng. **30**(6), 1081–1094 (2017)

AutoMix: Unveiling the Power of Mixup for Stronger Classifiers

Zicheng Liu[1,2], Siyuan Li[1,2], Di Wu[1,2], Zihan Liu[1,2], Zhiyuan Chen[2], Lirong Wu[1,2], and Stan Z. Li[2(✉)]

[1] Zhejiang University, Hangzhou 310000, China
{liuzicheng,lisiyuan,wudi,liuzihan,
chenzhiyuan,wulirong,stan.z.li}@westlake.edu.cn
[2] AI Lab, School of Engineering, Westlake University, Hangzhou 310000, China

Abstract. Data mixing augmentation have proved to be effective for improving the generalization ability of deep neural networks. While early methods mix samples by hand-crafted policies (*e.g.*, linear interpolation), recent methods utilize saliency information to match the mixed samples and labels via complex offline optimization. However, there arises a trade-off between precise mixing policies and optimization complexity. To address this challenge, we propose a novel automatic mixup (AutoMix) framework, where the mixup policy is parameterized and serves the ultimate classification goal directly. Specifically, AutoMix reformulates the mixup classification into two sub-tasks (*i.e.*, mixed sample generation and mixup classification) with corresponding sub-networks and solves them in a bi-level optimization framework. For the generation, a learnable lightweight mixup generator, Mix Block, is designed to generate mixed samples by modeling patch-wise relationships under the direct supervision of the corresponding mixed labels. To prevent the degradation and instability of bi-level optimization, we further introduce a momentum pipeline to train AutoMix in an end-to-end manner. Extensive experiments on nine image benchmarks prove the superiority of AutoMix compared with state-of-the-arts in various classification scenarios and downstream tasks.

Keywords: Data augmentation · Mixup · Image classification

1 Introduction

Recent years have witnessed the great success of Deep Neural Networks (DNNs) in various tasks, such as image processing [43,44,56,63,65], graph learning [3,55,58], and video processing [7,26,28,29]. Most of these successes can be attributed to the use of complex network architectures with numerous parameters and a sufficient amount of data. However, when the data is insufficient, models with high

---

Z. Liu and S. Li—Equal contribution.

Supplementary Information The online version contains supplementary material available at https://doi.org/10.1007/978-3-031-20053-3_26.

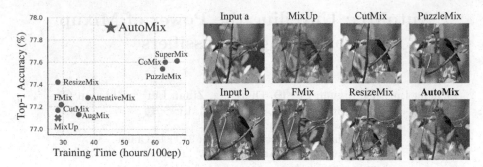

Fig. 1. The plot of efficiency *vs.* accuracy on ImageNet-1k and visualization of mixup methods. AutoMix improves performance without the heavy computational overhead.

complexity, *e.g.*, Transformer-based networks [9,47], are prone to over-fitting and overconfidence [14], resulting in poor generalization abilities [1,42,53].

To improve the generalization of DNNs, a series of data mixing augmentation techniques emerged. As shown in Fig. 1, MixUp [64] generates augmented samples via a linear combination of corresponding data pairs; CutMix [61] designs a patch replacement strategy that randomly replaces a patch in an image with patches from the other image. However, these *hand-crafted* methods [11,15,50] cannot guarantee mixed samples containing target objects and might cause the *label mismatch* problem. Subsequently, [37,48,52] try to guide CutMix by saliency information to relieve this problem. Recently, *optimization-based* methods try to solve the problem by searching an approximate mixing policy [8,21,22] based on portfolio optimization, *e.g.*, maximizing the saliency regions to confirm the co-presence of the targets in the mixed samples. Although they design more precise mixing policies than *head-crafted* methods, their indirect optimization and heavy computational overhead limit the algorithms' efficiency. Evidently, it is not efficient to transform the mixup policy from a random linear interpolation to a complex portfolio optimization problem.

This paper mainly discusses two questions: **(1) how to design an accurate mixing policy and serve directly to the mixup classification objective; (2) how to solve generation-classification optimization problems efficiently instead of portfolio optimizations.** As a basis for solving these two issues, we first reformulate the mixup training into two sub-tasks, mixed sample generation and mixup classification. Then, we propose a novel automatic mixup framework (AutoMix) that generates accurate mixed samples by a generation sub-network, Mix Block (MB), with a good complexity-accuracy trade-off. Specifically, MB is a cross-attention-based module that dynamically selects discriminative pixels based on feature maps of the sample pair to match the corresponding mixed labels. However, MB may collapse into trivial solutions when optimized jointly with the classification encoder due to a gradient entanglement problem. Thus, Momentum Pipeline (MP) is further introduced to stabilize AutoMix and decouple the training process of this bi-level optimization problem. Comprehensive experiments on eight classification benchmarks (CIFAR-10/100,

Tiny-ImageNet, ImageNet-1k, CUB-200, FGVC-Aircraft, iNaturalist2017/2018, and Place205) and eight network architectures show that AutoMix consistently outperforms state-of-the-art mixup methods across different tasks. We further provide an extensive analysis to verify the effectiveness of proposed components and the robustness of hyper-parameters. Our main contributions are three-fold:

- From a fresh perspective, we divide the mixup training into bi-level subtasks: mixed sample generation and mixup classification, and regard the generation as an auxiliary task to the classification. We unify them into a framework named AutoMix to optimize the mixup policy in an end-to-end manner.
- A novel Mix Block is designed for mixed sample generation. The combination of Mix Block and Momentum Pipeline optimizes the two sub-tasks in a decoupled manner and improves mixup training accuracy and stability.
- AutoMix surpasses counterparts significantly on various classification scenarios based on eight popular network architectures and downstream tasks.

2   Preliminaries

Mixup Training. We first consider the general image classification task with k different classes: given a finite set of n samples $X = [x_i]_{i=1}^n \in \mathbb{R}^{n \times W \times H \times C}$ and their ground-truth class labels $Y = [y_i]_{i=1}^n \in \mathbb{R}^{n \times k}$, encoded by a one-hot vector $y_i \in \mathbb{R}^k$. We seek the mapping from the data x_i to its class label y_i modeled by a deep neural network $f_\theta : x \longmapsto y$ with network parameters θ by optimizing a classification loss $\ell(.)$, say the cross entropy (CE) loss,

$$\ell_{CE}(f_\theta(x), y) = -y \log f_\theta(x), \tag{1}$$

Then we consider the mixup classification task: given a sample mixup function h, a label mixup function g, and a mixing ratio λ sampled from $Beta(\alpha, \alpha)$ distribution, we can generate the mixup data X_{mix} with $x_{mix} = h(x_i, x_j, \lambda)$ and the mixup label Y_{mix} with $y_{mix} = g(y_i, y_j, \lambda)$. Similarly, we learn $f_\theta : x_{mix} \longmapsto y_{mix}$ by mixup cross-entropy (MCE) loss,

$$\ell_{MCE} = \lambda \ell_{CE}(f_\theta(x_{mix}), y_i) + (1 - \lambda)\ell_{CE}(f_\theta(x_{mix}), y_j), \tag{2}$$

Mixup Reformulation. Comparing Eq. 1 and Eq. 2, the mixup training has the following features: (1) extra mixup policies, g and h, are required to generate X_{mix} and Y_{mix}. (2) the classification performance of f_θ depends on the generation policy of mixup. Naturally, we can split the mixup task into two complementary sub-tasks: (i) mixed sample generation and (ii) mixup classification. Notice that the sub-task (i) is subordinate to (ii) because the final goal is to obtain a stronger classifier. Therefore, from this perspective, we regard the mixup generation as an auxiliary task for the classification task. Since g is generally designed as a linear interpolation, i.e., $g(y_i, y_j, \lambda) = \lambda y_i + (1 - \lambda)y_j$, h becomes the key function to determine the performance of the model. Generalizing previous offline methods, we define a parametric mixup policy h_ϕ as the

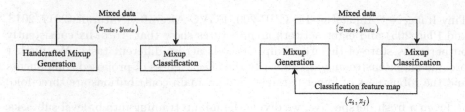

Fig. 2. The difference between AutoMix and offline approaches. **Left**: Offline mixup methods, where a fixed mixup policy generates mixed samples for the classifier to learn from. **Right**: AutoMix, where the mixup policy is trained with the feature map.

sub-task with another set of parameters ϕ. The final goal is to optimize ℓ_{MCE} given θ and ϕ as below:

$$\min_{\theta,\,\phi} \ell_{MCE}\Big(f_\theta\big(h_\phi(x_i, x_j, \lambda)\big), g(y_i, y_j, \lambda)\Big), \tag{3}$$

Offline Mixup Limits the Power of Mixup. Keep the reformulation in mind, the previous methods focus on manually designing $h(\cdot)$ in an offline and non-parametric manner based on their prior hypotheses, or arguably, such mixup policies are separated from the ultimate optimization of the model, e.g., an optimization algorithm with the goal of maximizing saliency information. Specifically, they build an implicit connection between the two sub-tasks, as shown in the left of Fig. 2. Therefore, the mixed samples generated from these offline mixup policies could be redundant or mislead the training. To address this, we propose AutoMix, *which combines these two sub-tasks in a mutually beneficial manner and unveils the power of mixup.*

3   AutoMix

We build a bridge between the mixup generation and classification task with a unified optimization framework named as AutoMix to improve the mixup training efficiency. In this framework, the proposed Mix Block (MB) and Momentum

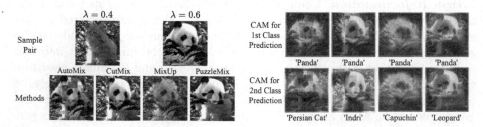

Fig. 3. Illustration of *label mismatch* by visualizing mixed samples and class activation mapping (CAM) [41] on 'Panda' and 'Persian Cat'. From top to bottom rows, we show the original images, mixed images, CAM for top-2 predicted classes, respectively.

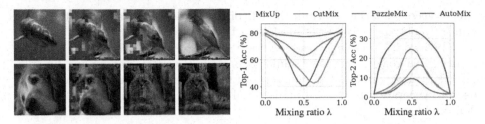

Fig. 4. Left: AutoMix samples with different λ (0, 0.3, 0.7, 1). **Right**: Top-1 accuracy of mixed data. Prediction is counted as correct if the top-1 prediction belongs to $\{y_i, y_j\}$; Top-2 accuracy is calculated by counting the top-2 predictions are equal to $\{y_i, y_j\}$.

Pipeline (MP) in AutoMix not only can generate semantic mixed samples but reduces computational overhead significantly. A comparison overview with offline approaches is presented in Fig. 2.

3.1   Label Mismatch: MixBlock

In Fig. 3, we further examined that offline approaches are incapable of addressing the *label mismatch* issue in mixup training. It is difficult for offline methods to preserve the discriminative features in the mixed sample if detach from the final optimization goal. As a result, the prediction of the accuracy of the mixed sample is limited (see the right of Fig. 4). This paper presents a parametric mixup generation function named Mix Block (MB) $\mathcal{M}_\phi$ for learning a mixup policy without requiring extensive saliency computation. $\mathcal{M}_\phi$ generates a pixel-wise mixup mask $s \in \mathbb{R}^{H \times W}$ for the pairs of input images, where $s_{w,h} \in [0, 1]$. We regard the mask-based mixup policy as an adaptive selection process in terms of λ, which can automatically select the discriminative patches from sample pairs to generate label-matched mixed samples. Thus, the core of $\mathcal{M}_\phi$ is the devised λ embedded cross-attention mechanism to learn the pixel-level proportional relationships in a given data pair. To do so, the deep feature maps z from f_θ with rich spatial and semantic information can be utilized to *bootstrap the two sub-tasks of mixup*. Additionally, to facilitate the capture of task-relevant information in the generated mixed samples, the $\mathcal{M}_\phi$ training is directly supervised by the target loss, ℓ_{MCE}, in an end-to-end manner.

Parametric Mixup Generation. The generation task can be formulated as a dynamic regression problem: given a sample pair (x_i, x_j) and a mixing ratio λ, MB predicts the probability that each pixel (or patch) on x_{mix} belongs to x_i according to the feature map pair (z_i, z_j) and mixing ratio λ. The overall parametric mixup function of AutoMix can be formulated as follows:

$$h_\phi(x_i, x_j, \lambda) = \mathcal{M}_\phi(z_{i,\lambda}^l, z_{j,1-\lambda}^l) \odot x_i + (1 - \mathcal{M}_\phi(z_{i,\lambda}^l, z_{j,1-\lambda}^l)) \odot x_j, \quad (4)$$

where $\odot$ denotes element-wise product; z_λ^l is λ embedded feature map at l-th layer. As shown in the right of Fig. 5, we first embed λ with the l-th feature map in a simple and efficient way by concatenating, $z_\lambda^l = \mathrm{concat}(z, \lambda)$, whose effectiveness has been shown in the left of Fig. 4. As we can see from Eq. 4, our aim is to obtain a pixel-level mask s in the input space from $\mathcal{M}_\phi(\cdot)$ based on λ embedded $z_{i,\lambda}^l$ and $z_{j,1-\lambda}^l$ to generate semantic mixed samples. In order to achieve this goal, a pair-wise similarity matrix P and an upsampling function $U(\cdot)$ is required. Due to the symmetry of mixup, i.e., the sum of the two masks used to generate a mixed sample is equal to 1, for x_i of a pair (x_i, x_j), we can denote $\mathcal{M}_\phi : z_{i,\lambda}^l, z_{j,1-\lambda}^l \longrightarrow s_i$,

$$s_i = U\Big(\sigma\big(P(z_{i,\lambda}^l, z_{j,1-\lambda}^l) \otimes W_Z\, z_{i,\lambda}^l\big)\Big), \qquad (5)$$

where W_Z is a linear transformation matrix; σ is the Sigmoid activation function, which is used to probabilize the mask; and s_i is the $H \times W$ mask we are looking for. By multiplying P and the value embedding, $W_Z z_{i,\lambda}^l$, the discriminative features in $x_{i,\lambda}$ relative to $x_{j,1-\lambda}$ are then selected. Symmetrically, the mask s_j for x_j can be calculated in this way, $s_j = 1 - s_i$. Furthermore, the similarity matrix P has to consider both λ information and relative relationships in a sample pair, thus the *cross-attention mechanism* is introduced to achieve this purpose. When x_i in a sample pair (x_i, x_j) is taken as the input, a mask can be generated dynamically from corresponding $z_{i,\lambda}^l$ and P matrix. Formally, our cross-attention can be formulated as:

$$P(z_{i,\lambda}^l, z_{j,1-\lambda}^l) = \text{softmax}\Big(\frac{(W_P z_{i,\lambda}^l)^T \otimes W_P z_{j,1-\lambda}^l}{C(z_{i,\lambda}^l, z_{j,1-\lambda}^l)}\Big), \qquad (6)$$

where W_P denotes shared linear transformation matrices (e.g., 1×1 convolution), $\otimes$ denotes matrix multiplication, and $C(z_{i,\lambda}^l, z_{j,1-\lambda}^l)$ is a normalization factor. Notice that P is the row normalized pair-wise similarity matrix between every spatial position on $z_{i,\lambda}^l$ and $z_{j,1-\lambda}^l$. Similarly, if we take $z_{j,1-\lambda}^l$ as the value, then the mask can be computed by transposing P and $s_i = 1 - s_j$.

AutoMix in End-to-End Training. The framework is shown in Fig. 5, given a set of labeled data $\mathcal{D} = \{(x_i, y_i)\}_{i=1}^n$ and the corresponding l-th layer feature map $\mathcal{Z} = \{z_i^l\}_{i=1}^n$, $\mathcal{M}_\phi$ is nested in encoder for optimization. Under the supervision of the same loss ℓ_{MCE}, the encoder is trained using the mixed sample generated by $\mathcal{M}_\phi$, which in turn uses backbone's feature to generate the mixed sample. To enable $\mathcal{M}_\phi$ to find the λ correspondence between the x_{mix} and y_{mix} at the early stage of training, our auxiliary loss is proposed:

$$\ell_\lambda = \gamma \max\Big(\|\lambda - \frac{1}{HW}\sum_{h,w} s_{i,h,w}\| - \epsilon, 0\Big), \qquad (7)$$

where γ is a loss weight linearly decreased to 0 during training. We set the initial γ to 0.1 and $\epsilon = 0.1$. Notice that AutoMix uses standard cross-entropy loss ℓ_{CE} as default. ℓ_{CE} loss facilitates the backbone to provide a stable feature map at the early stage so that speeds up $\mathcal{M}_\phi$ converges. To differentiate the function

Fig. 5. The **left** diagram represents the five key steps of AutoMix. (1) Extract feature map $\mathcal{Z}$ from the frozen encoder k. (2) Mix Block $\mathcal{M}_\phi$ generates mixed samples by using $\mathcal{Z}$ and mixup ratio $\lambda \in [0,1]$. (3) and (4) Decoupled training $\mathcal{M}_\phi$ and encoder q via *stop gradient*, the blue and green lines indicate the encoder training and the $\mathcal{M}_\phi$ training, correspondingly. (5) Update the k's parameters through momentum moving. The **right** diagram is the architecture of proposed $\mathcal{M}_\phi$. (Color figure online)

of ℓ_{MCE}, *cls* denotes classification task for training encoder and *gen* denotes generation task for training $\mathcal{M}_\phi$. AutoMix can be optimized by a joint loss:

$$\mathcal{L}(\theta, \phi) = \underbrace{\ell_{CE} + \ell_{MCE}^{cls}}_{classification} + \underbrace{\ell_{MCE}^{gen} + \ell_\lambda}_{generation}. \qquad (8)$$

Obviously, the purpose of the classification task is to optimize θ while the generation task is to optimize ϕ. Therefore, this is a typical bi-level optimization problem. Although $\mathcal{M}_\phi$ does not need extra computational overhead to maximize the saliency information, using SGD to directly update the nested θ and ϕ will lead to instability. To address this problem properly, we use the momentum pipeline to decouple the training of θ and ϕ. As indicated in Eq. 8, though the same ℓ_{MCE} is used, the focus of each is different.

3.2   Bi-level Optimization: Momentum Pipeline

Although MB is designed to be lightweight and efficient, it also poses a bi-level optimization problem with *gradient entanglement*. Experiments demonstrate that the entanglement problem may cause $\mathcal{M}_\phi$ trapped into a trivial solution (degraded to MixUp, in Fig. 6). $\mathcal{M}_\phi$ with a much smaller parameters than the encoder will be disturbed by the classification task when optimizing both the two sub-tasks at the same time. MB thus cannot generate semantic mixed samples stably and eventually collapse. According to Eq. 3 and Eq. 8, for each

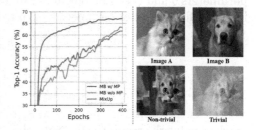

Fig. 6. Accuracy on Tiny-ImageNet and different results of the mixed sample. Momentum pipeline decoupled mixup generation and classification, which mitigates the trivial solution problem.

448   Z. Liu et al.

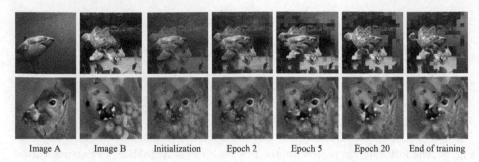

| Image A | Image B | Initialization | Epoch 2 | Epoch 5 | Epoch 20 | End of training |

Fig. 7. Visualization of mixed samples generated by $\mathcal{M}_\phi$ with $\lambda = 0.5$ at different training periods on ImageNet-1k (100 epochs in total). It is worth noting that $\mathcal{M}_\phi$ is able to generate mixed samples stably and converge quickly with the addition of MP.

iteration, the gradient entanglement problem of $\mathcal{L}^{cls}$ in $\mathcal{M}_\phi$ can be formulated as

$$\nabla_\phi \mathcal{L}_{MCE}^{cls} \propto \nabla_\phi h_\phi(x_i, x_j, \lambda) \odot f'_\theta(h_\phi(x_i, x_j, \lambda)). \tag{9}$$

It is notable that the instability of f_θ may result in a vicious cycle of the joint training. As a consequence, the primary goal of getting the Eq. 3 operating well is to ensure that f_θ outputs stable features and, to the extent possible, that ϕ and θ can focus on their own tasks in the case of using the same loss. Inspired by methods in self-supervised learning [13,16], they adopted momentum pipeline (MP) to avoid the feature collapse and realized that the teacher network f_{θ_k} of the Siamese network shows more stable performance than student network f_{θ_q}. Along this path, we designed a new MP for decoupling the nested bi-level optimization problem of AutoMix: the student network f_{θ_q} focuses on the classification task, while the stable teacher network f_{θ_k} is connected with $\mathcal{M}_\phi$ to perform generation task. Moreover, optimizing Eq. 8 with batch approach requires X_{mix} generated by f_{θ_k} and $\mathcal{M}_\phi$ first and then using X_{mix} to optimize f_{θ_q}. By analogy, referring to the Expectation-Maximization (EM) algorithm, the two sets of parameters θ and ϕ can be optimized in an alternating way by the designed MP, i.e., first fix one set of parameters optimizing the other:

$$\theta_q^t \leftarrow \underset{\theta}{\arg\min} \ \mathcal{L}(\theta_q^{t-1}, \phi^{t-1}), \tag{10}$$

$$\phi^t \leftarrow \underset{\phi}{\arg\min} \ \mathcal{L}(\theta_k^t, \phi^{t-1}), \tag{11}$$

where t is the iteration step, θ_q and θ_k represent the parameters of student and teacher network, respectively. Note that f_{θ_q} and f_{θ_k} share the same network structure with the same initialized parameters, but f_{θ_k} is updated via an exponential moving average (EMA) strategy [36] from f_{θ_q}:

$$\theta_k \leftarrow m\theta_k + (1-m)\theta_q, \tag{12}$$

where $m \in [0, 1)$ is the momentum coefficient. It is worthy to notice that *MP not only solves optimization instability but also significantly speeds up and stabilizes the convergence of AutoMix*. In Fig. 7, $\mathcal{M}_\phi$ gets close to convergence in the first few epochs and consistently delivers high-quality mixed samples to f_θ. Moreover, detailed AutoMix architecture and pseudo code are provided in Appendix.

4   Experiments

We evaluate AutoMix in three aspects: (1) Image classification in various scenarios based on various network architectures, (2) Robustness against corruptions and adversarial samples, and (3) Transfer learning capacities to downstream tasks.

4.1   Evaluation on Image Classification

This subsection demonstrates performance gains of AutoMix for various classification tasks on **eight classification benchmarks**, including CIFAR-10/100 [23], Tiny-ImageNet [5], ImageNet-1k [39], CUB-200-2011 (CUB) [51], FGVC-Aircraft (Aircraft) [34], iNaturalist2017/2018 (iNat2017/2018) [20], and Place205 [66]. We verify generalizabilities of AutoMix for **eight network architectures**, the experiments adopt popular ConvNets, including ResNet (R) [17], Wide-ResNet (WRN) [62], ResNeXt (32x4d) (RX) [59], MobileNet.V2 [40], EfficientNet [45], and ConvNeXt [31], and Transformer-based architectures (DeiT [47] and Swin Transformer (Swin) [30]) as backbone networks. For a fair comparison, we use open-source codebase OpenMixup [25] for most mixup methods: (i) *hand-crafted* methods: Mixup [64], CutMix [61], ManifoldMix [50], Aug-Mix [19], AttentiveMix [52], SaliencyMix [48], FMix [15], and ResizeMix [37]; (ii) *optimization-based* methods: PuzzleMix [22], Co-Mixup [21], and Super-Mix [8]. Notice that AugMix is reproduced by timm [54], * denotes open-source arXiv preprint work, and methods without source codes (AlignMix [49] and TransMix [2]) are not compared. All mixup methods use the optimal α among $\{0.2, 0.5, 1, 2, 4\}$, while the rest of hyper-parameters follow the original paper. AutoMix uses the same set of hyper-parameters in all experiments: $\alpha = 2$, the feature layer $l = 3$, the momentum coefficient in MP starts from $m = 0.999$ and is increased to 1 in a cosine curve. As for all classification results, we report the *mean* performance of 3 trials where the *median* of top-1 test accuracy in the last 10 training epochs is recorded for each trial, and **bold** and blue denote the best and second best results.

Table 1. Top-1 accuracy (%)↑ of various algorithms based on ResNet variants for small-scale classification on CIFAR-10/100 and Tiny-ImageNet datasets.

Method	CIFAR-10		CIFAR-100			Tiny-ImageNet	
	R-18	RX-50	R-18	RX-50	WRN-28-8	R-18	RX-50
Vanilla	95.50	96.23	78.04	81.09	81.63	61.68	65.04
MixUp	96.62	97.30	79.12	82.10	82.82	63.86	66.36
CutMix	96.68	97.01	78.17	81.67	84.45	65.53	66.47
ManifoldMix	96.71	97.33	80.35	82.88	83.24	64.15	67.30
SaliencyMix	96.53	97.18	79.12	81.53	84.35	64.60	66.55
FMix*	96.58	96.76	79.69	81.90	84.21	63.47	65.08
PuzzleMix	97.10	97.27	81.13	82.85	85.02	65.81	67.83
Co-Mixup	97.15	97.32	81.17	82.91	85.05	65.92	68.02
ResizeMix*	96.76	97.21	80.01	81.82	84.87	63.74	65.87
AutoMix	**97.34**	**97.65**	**82.04**	**83.64**	**85.18**	**67.33**	**70.72**
Gain	+0.19	+0.32	+0.87	+0.76	+0.13	+1.41	+2.70

Small-Scale Datasets

Settings. On CIFAR-10/100, `RandomFlip` and `RandomCrop` with 4 pixels padding for 32 × 32 resolutions are basic data augmentations, and we use the following training settings: SGD optimizer with SGD weight decay of 0.0001, the momentum of 0.9, the batch size of 100, and training 800 epochs; the basic learning rate is 0.1 adjusted by Cosine Scheduler [32]. On Tiny-ImageNet, the basic augmentations include `RandomFlip` and `RandomResizedCrop` for 64 × 64 resolutions, and we use the similar training ingredients as CIFAR except for the basic learning rate of 0.2 and training 400 epochs. CIFAR version of ResNet variants [17] are used, *i.e.*, replacing the 7 × 7 convolution and MaxPooling by a 3 × 3 convolution.

Classification. Table 1 shows small-scale classification results on CIFAR-10/100 and Tiny datasets. Compared to the previous state-of-the-art methods, AutoMix consistently surpasses ManifoldMix (+0.32–1.94%), PuzzleMix (+0.16–0.91%), and Co-Mixup (+0.13–0.87%) based on various architectures on CIFAR.

Calibration. DNNs tend to predict over-confidently in classification tasks [46], mixup methods can significantly alleviate this problem. To verify the calibration ability of AutoMix, we evaluate popular mixup algorithms by the expected calibration error (ECE) [14] on CIFAR-100, *i.e.*, the absolute discrepancy between accuracy and confidence. As shown in Fig. 8, AutoMix achieved the best calibration effect among all competitors with the ECE error rate of 2.3%.

Table 2. Top-1 accuracy (%)↑ of image classification based on ResNet variants on ImageNet-1k using PyTorch-style 100-epoch and 300-epoch training procedures.

Methods	PyTorch 100 epochs					PyTorch 300 epochs			
	R-18	R-34	R-50	R-101	RX-101	R-18	R-34	R-50	R-101
Vanilla	70.04	73.85	76.83	78.18	78.71	71.83	75.29	77.35	78.91
MixUp	69.98	73.97	77.12	78.97	79.98	71.72	75.73	78.44	80.60
CutMix	68.95	73.58	77.17	78.96	80.42	71.01	75.16	78.69	80.59
ManifoldMix	69.98	73.98	77.01	79.02	79.93	71.73	75.44	78.21	80.64
SaliencyMix	69.16	73.56	77.14	79.32	80.27	70.21	75.01	78.46	80.45
FMix*	69.96	74.08	77.19	79.09	80.06	70.30	75.12	78.51	80.20
PuzzleMix	70.12	74.26	77.54	79.43	80.53	71.64	75.84	78.86	80.67
ResizeMix*	69.50	73.88	77.42	79.27	80.55	71.32	75.64	78.91	80.52
AutoMix	**70.50**	**74.52**	**77.91**	**79.87**	**80.89**	**72.05**	**76.10**	**79.25**	**80.98**
Gain	+0.38	+0.26	+0.37	+0.44	+0.34	+0.22	+0.26	+0.34	+0.31

ImageNet Datasets

Settings. In the more challenging large-scale classification scenarios, mixup methods are widely used, especially for recently proposed Transformer-based networks. We evaluate AutoMix and popular mixup variants on ImageNet-1k using three popular training procedures: (a) PyTorch-style setting trains 100 or 300 epochs by SGD optimizer with the batch size of 256, the basic learning rate of 0.1, the SGD weight decay of 0.0001, and the SGD momentum of 0.9, which is the standard benchmarks for mixup methods [37,61]; (b) DeiT setting trains 300 epochs by AdamW optimizer [33] with the batch size of 1024, the basic learning rate of 0.001, and the weight decay of 0.05; (c) timm [54] RSB A2/A3 settings train 300/100 epochs by LAMB optimizer [60] with the batch size of 2048, the basic learning rate of 0.005/0.008, and the weight decay of 0.02. More detailed ingredients and hyper-parameters are provided in Appendix. These three settings adopt the basic data augmentations (`RandomResizedCrop` and `RandomFlip`) for 224 × 224 resolutions with Cosine Scheduler by default, (b) and (c) use RandAugment [6] for better performances.

Classification. Table 2 and Fig. 1 show regular image classification results using *only one mixup methods*: AutoMix consistently outperforms previous

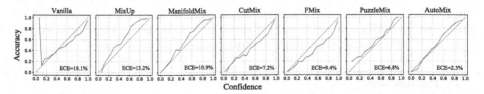

Fig. 8. *Calibration* plots of Mixup variants and AutoMix on CIFAR-100 using ResNet-18. The red line indicates the expected prediction tendency. (Color figure online)

452   Z. Liu et al.

Table 3. Top-1 accuracy (%)↑ of various algorithms based on ResNet variants on fine-grained and scenic classification datasets.

Method	CUB-200		FGVC-Aircraft		iNat2017		iNat2018		Place205	
	R-18	RX-50	R-18	RX-50	R-50	RX-101	R-50	RX-101	R-18	R-50
Vanilla	77.68	83.01	80.23	85.10	60.23	63.70	62.53	66.94	59.63	63.10
MixUp	78.39	84.58	79.52	85.18	61.22	66.27	62.69	67.56	59.33	63.01
CutMix	78.40	85.68	78.84	84.55	62.34	67.59	63.91	69.75	59.21	63.75
ManifoldMix	79.76	86.38	80.68	86.60	61.47	66.08	63.46	69.30	59.46	63.23
SaliencyMix	77.95	83.29	80.02	84.31	62.51	67.20	64.27	70.01	59.50	63.33
FMix*	77.28	84.06	79.36	86.23	61.90	66.64	63.71	69.46	59.51	63.63
PuzzleMix	78.63	84.51	80.76	86.23	62.66	67.72	64.36	70.12	59.62	63.91
ResizeMix*	78.50	84.77	78.10	84.08	62.29	66.82	64.12	69.30	59.66	63.88
AutoMix	**79.87**	**86.56**	**81.37**	**86.72**	**63.08**	**68.03**	**64.73**	**70.49**	**59.74**	**64.06**
Gain	+0.11	+0.18	+0.61	+0.12	+0.42	+0.31	+0.37	+0.37	+0.08	+0.15

state-of-the-art methods with light/median/heavy ResNet architectures, *e.g.*, +0.26~0.44% for 100 epochs and +0.22~0.34% for 300 epochs. More results related to Transformer-based architectures are presented in Appendix A.3.

4.2 Evaluation on Fine-Grained and Scenic Classification

Small-Scale Datasets. We first perform small-scale fine-grained classification following transfer learning settings on CUB-200 and Aircraft: training 200 epochs by SGD optimizer with the initial learning rate of 0.001, the weight decay of 0.0005, the batch size of 16, using the standard augmentations as in Sect. 4.1; the official PyTorch pre-trained models on ImageNet-1k are adopted as initialization. Table 3 shows that AutoMix achieves the best performance and noticeably improves the vanilla (2.19%/3.55% on CUB-200 and 1.14%/1.62% on Aircraft), which verifies that AutoMix has strong adaptability to more challenging scenarios.

Large-Scale Datasets. Then, we adopt similar settings as (a) in Sect. 4.1 with the total epoch of 100 epochs (training from scratch) on large-scale datasets based on ResNet variants. As for the imbalanced and long-tail fine-grained recognition tasks on iNat2017/2018, Table 3 shows that AutoMix surpasses the previous best methods and improves the vanilla by large margins (2.74%/4.33% on iNat2017 and 2.20%/3.55% on iNat2018), which demonstrates that AutoMix can alleviate the long-tail and imbalance issues. As for scenic classification on Place205, AutoMix still sets state-of-the-art performances. Therefore, we can conclude that AutoMix can adapt to more challenging scenarios.

4.3 Robustness

We first evaluate robustness against corruptions on CIFAR-100-C [18], which is designed for evaluating the corruption robustness and provides 19 different

Table 4. Top-1 accuracy (%)↑ and FGSM error (%)↓ on CIFAR-100 based on ResNeXt-50 (32x4d) trained 400 epochs.

	Clean acc (%)↑	Corruption acc (%)↑	FGSM error (%)↓
Vanilla	80.24	51.71	63.92
MixUp	82.44	58.10	56.60
CutMix	81.09	49.32	76.84
AugMix	81.18	66.54	55.59
PuzzleMix	82.76	57.82	63.71
AutoMix	**83.13**	**58.35**	**55.34**

Table 5. Transfer learning of object detection task with Faster-RCNN on Pascal VOC and COCO datasets.

Methods	VOC mAP	COCO		
		mAP	AP_{50}^{bb}	AP_{75}^{bb}
Vanilla	81.0	38.1	59.1	41.8
Mixup	80.7	37.9	59.0	41.7
CutMix	81.9	38.2	59.3	42.0
PuzzleMix	81.9	38.3	59.3	42.1
ResizeMix	82.1	38.4	59.4	42.1
AutoMix	**82.4**	**38.6**	**59.5**	**42.2**

Table 6. MaxBoxAcc (%)↑ for the WSOL task on CUB-200 based on ResNet variants.

Backbone	Vanilla	Mixup	CutMix	FMix*	PuzzleMix	Co-Mixup	**Ours**
R-18	49.91	48.62	51.85	50.30	53.95	54.13	**54.46**
RX-50	53.38	50.27	57.16	59.80	59.34	59.76	**61.05**

corruptions (*e.g.*, noise, blur, and digital corruption, *etc.*) AugMix [19] is proposed to improve robustness against natural corruptions by minimizing Jensen-Shannon divergence (JSD) between logits of a clean image and two AugMix images. However, the improvement of AugMix is very limited on clean data. In Table 4, AutoMix shows a consistent top level in both clean and corruption data. We further study robustness against the FGSM [12] white box attack of $8/255$ ℓ_∞ epsilon ball following [64], and AutoMix outperforms previous methods in Table 4.

4.4 Transfer Learning

Weakly Supervised Object Localization. Following CutMix, we also evaluate AutoMix on the weakly supervised object localization (WSOL) task on CUB-200 in Table 6, which aims to localize objects of interest without bounding boxes supervision. We use CAM to extract attention maps, and calculate the maximal box accuracy with a threshold $\delta \in \{0.3, 0.5, 0.7\}$, following MaxBoxAccV2 [4].

Object Detection. We then evaluate transferable abilities of the learned features to object detection task with Faster R-CNN [38] on PASCAL VOC *trainval07+12* [10] and COCO *train2017* [27] based on Detectron2 [57]. We fine-tune Faster R-CNN with R50-C4 pre-trained on ImageNet-1k with mixup methods on VOC (24k iterations) and COCO (2× schedule). Table 5 shows that AutoMix achieves better performances than previous cutting-based mixup variants.

4.5 Ablation Study

We conduct an ablation study to prove that each component of AutoMix plays an essential role to make the framework operate properly. Three main questions are answered here: (1) Are the modules in MB effective? (2) How many gains can MB bring without EMA and CE? (3) Is AutoMix robust to hyperparameters?

(1) Cross-attention mechanism enables MB to capture the task-relevant pixels between two samples, which is the core design of MB to generate useful mixed masks. Based on this, λ embedding and ℓ_λ encourage MB to learn proportional correspondence on a different scale. Without these modules, the performance drops by almost 4% (66.83% vs. 70.72%), as shown in Fig. 7. (2) In Table 8, we show that the EMA and CE adopted in the MP improves performance of MB by ensuring training stability, however CE is not as effective for other mixup methods. Most importantly, without these them, i.e. EMA and CE, we show MB still delivers significant gains (e.g. +2.29% and +2.21% on CIFAR-100 and Tiny). Note that $m = 0$ indicates removing EMA, which means f_{θ_k} is a copy of f_{θ_q} with the same weights. Therefore, we can confirm the effectiveness of $\mathcal{M}_\phi$. (3) AutoMix has two core hyper-parameters, α and l, which are fixed for all experiments. A larger α facilitates MB to learn intra-class relationships. Figure 9 shows that AutoMix with $\alpha = 2$ as default achieves the best performances on various datasets. The feature layer l_3 makes a good trade-off between the performance and complexity, as shown in Table 9.

5 Related Work

MixUp [64], the first mixing-based data augmentation algorithm, was proposed to generate mixed samples with mixed labels by convex interpolations of any two samples and their unique one-hot labels. ManifoldMix [50] extends MixUp to the hidden space of DNNs and [11,49] improves ManifoldMix. CutMix [61] incorporates the Dropout strategy into the mixup strategy and proposes a mixing strategy based on the patch of the image, i.e., randomly replacing a local rectangular area in images. Based on CutMix, AttentiveMix [52] and SaliencyMix [48] guide mixing patches by saliency regions in the image (based on CAM or a saliency detector) to obtain mixed samples with more class-relevant information; ResizeMix [37] maintains the information integrity by replacing one resized image directly into a rectangular area of another image. Furthermore, PuzzleMix [22] and Co-Mixup [21] propose combinatorial optimization strategies to find optimal mixup masks by maximizing the saliency information.

Table 7. Ablation of modules in MixBlock.

Module	Tiny-ImageNet	
	R-18	RX-50
(random grids)	64.40	66.83
+cross attention	66.87	69.76
+λ embedding	67.15	70.41
+ℓ_λ	**67.33**	**70.72**

Table 8. Ablation of the proposed momentum pipeline (MP) and the cross-entropy loss l_{CE} (CE) based on ResNet-18.

Modules	CIFAR-100			Tiny-ImageNet			ImageNet-1k		
	MixUp	CutMix	$\mathcal{M}_\phi$	MixUp	CutMix	$\mathcal{M}_\phi$	MixUp	CutMix	$\mathcal{M}_\phi$
(none)	79.12	78.17	79.46	63.39	64.40	64.84	69.98	68.95	70.04
+MP (m = 0)	–	–	81.75	–	–	67.05	–	–	70.41
+MP	**80.82**	79.57	81.93	66.02	**65.72**	67.19	**70.13**	70.02	70.45
+MP+CE	80.41	**79.64**	**82.04**	**66.10**	65.05	**67.33**	70.10	**70.04**	**70.50**

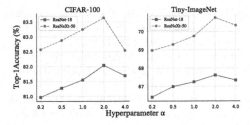

Fig. 9. Ablation of hyperparameter α of AutoMix on CIFAR-100 and Tiny-ImageNet.

Table 9. Ablation of feature layer l on Tiny-ImageNet, reporting top-1 Acc (%)$\uparrow$ *vs.* params (M)$\downarrow$ *vs.* the total training time (hours)$\downarrow$.

	R-18			RX-50		
	Acc (%)	Params	Time	Acc (%)	Params	Time
Mixup	63.86	11.27	20	66.36	23.38	113
l_1	67.30	11.38	67	70.70	23.80	413
l_2	67.27	11.39	41	70.43	23.86	252
l_3	**67.33**	11.44	34	**70.72**	24.84	196
l_4	67.32	11.64	28	70.67	27.99	174

6   Conclusion

In this paper, we propose an *AutoMix* framework, which optimizes both the mixed sample generation task and the mixup classification task in a momentum training pipeline. Without adding cost to inference, AutoMix can generate semantic samples with adaptive masks. Extensive experiments have shown the effectiveness and excellent generalizability of AutoMix on broad datasets. On top of that, we also outperformed other mixup algorithms when comparing with robustness and localization tasks as well. Furthermore, the proposed momentum training pipeline serves a significant improvement in convergence speed and overall performance.

Acknowledgement. This work is supported by the Science and Technology Innovation 2030- Major Project (No. 2021ZD0150100) and National Natural Science Foundation of China (No. U21A20427).

References

1. Bishop, C.M.: Pattern Recognition and Machine Learning. Springer, New York (2006)
2. Chen, J.N., Sun, S., He, J., Torr, P., Yuille, A., Bai, S.: TransMix: attend to mix for vision transformers (2021)
3. Cheng, Z., et al.: Physical attack on monocular depth estimation with optimal adversarial patches (2022)
4. Choe, J., Oh, S.J., Lee, S., Chun, S., Akata, Z., Shim, H.: Evaluating weakly supervised object localization methods right. In: Proceedings of the IEEE/CVF Conference on Computer Vision and Pattern Recognition, pp. 3133–3142 (2020)
5. Chrabaszcz, P., Loshchilov, I., Hutter, F.: A downsampled variant of ImageNet as an alternative to the CIFAR datasets. arXiv preprint arXiv:1707.08819 (2017)
6. Cubuk, E.D., Zoph, B., Shlens, J., Le, Q.V.: RandAugment: practical automated data augmentation with a reduced search space. In: Proceedings of the IEEE/CVF Conference on Computer Vision and Pattern Recognition Workshops, pp. 702–703 (2020)
7. Cui, Y., Yan, L., Cao, Z., Liu, D.: TF-Blender: temporal feature blender for video object detection. In: Proceedings of the IEEE/CVF International Conference on Computer Vision (ICCV), pp. 8138–8147 (2021)

8. Dabouei, A., Soleymani, S., Taherkhani, F., Nasrabadi, N.M.: SuperMix: supervising the mixing data augmentation. In: Proceedings of the IEEE/CVF Conference on Computer Vision and Pattern Recognition, pp. 13794–13803 (2021)

9. Dosovitskiy, A., et al.: An image is worth 16 × 16 words: transformers for image recognition at scale. In: International Conference on Learning Representations (ICLR) (2021)

10. Everingham, M., Van Gool, L., Williams, C.K., Winn, J., Zisserman, A.: The pascal visual object classes (VOC) challenge. Int. J. Comput. Vis. **88**(2), 303–338 (2010). https://doi.org/10.1007/s11263-009-0275-4

11. Faramarzi, M., Amini, M., Badrinaaraayanan, A., Verma, V., Chandar, S.: PatchUp: a regularization technique for convolutional neural networks. arXiv preprint arXiv:2006.07794 (2020)

12. Goodfellow, I.J., Shlens, J., Szegedy, C.: Explaining and harnessing adversarial examples. In: International Conference on Learning Representations (ICLR) (2015)

13. Grill, J.B., et al.: Bootstrap your own latent: a new approach to self-supervised learning. In: Advances in Neural Information Processing Systems (NeurIPS) (2020)

14. Guo, C., Pleiss, G., Sun, Y., Weinberger, K.Q.: On calibration of modern neural networks. In: International Conference on Machine Learning, pp. 1321–1330. PMLR (2017)

15. Harris, E., Marcu, A., Painter, M., Niranjan, M., Hare, A.P.B.J.: FMix: enhancing mixed sample data augmentation, **2**(3), 4. arXiv preprint arXiv:2002.12047 (2020)

16. He, K., Fan, H., Wu, Y., Xie, S., Girshick, R.: Momentum contrast for unsupervised visual representation learning. In: Proceedings of the IEEE/CVF Conference on Computer Vision and Pattern Recognition, pp. 9729–9738 (2020)

17. He, K., Zhang, X., Ren, S., Sun, J.: Deep residual learning for image recognition. In: Proceedings of the Conference on Computer Vision and Pattern Recognition (CVPR), pp. 770–778 (2016)

18. Hendrycks, D., Dietterich, T.: Benchmarking neural network robustness to common corruptions and perturbations. arXiv preprint arXiv:1903.12261 (2019)

19. Hendrycks, D., Mu, N., Cubuk, E.D., Zoph, B., Gilmer, J., Lakshminarayanan, B.: AugMix: a simple data processing method to improve robustness and uncertainty. arXiv preprint arXiv:1912.02781 (2019)

20. Horn, G.V., et al.: The iNaturalist species classification and detection dataset. In: Proceedings of the Conference on Computer Vision and Pattern Recognition (CVPR) (2018)

21. Kim, J.H., Choo, W., Jeong, H., Song, H.O.: Co-Mixup: saliency guided joint mixup with supermodular diversity. arXiv preprint arXiv:2102.03065 (2021)

22. Kim, J.H., Choo, W., Song, H.O.: Puzzle Mix: exploiting saliency and local statistics for optimal mixup. In: International Conference on Machine Learning, pp. 5275–5285. PMLR (2020)

23. Krizhevsky, A., Hinton, G., et al.: Learning multiple layers of features from tiny images (2009)

24. Krizhevsky, A., Sutskever, I., Hinton, G.E.: ImageNet classification with deep convolutional neural networks. In: Advances in Neural Information Processing Systems, pp. 1097–1105 (2012)

25. Li, S., Liu, Z., Wu, D.: OpenMixup: open mixup toolbox and benchmark for visual representation (2022). https://github.com/Westlake-AI/openmixup

26. Li, S., Zhang, Z., Liu, Z., Wang, A., Qiu, L., Du, F.: TLPG-Tracker: joint learning of target localization and proposal generation for visual tracking. In: Proceedings of the 29th International Joint Conference on Artificial Intelligence (IJCAI), pp. 708–715 (2020)

27. Lin, T.-Y., et al.: Microsoft COCO: common objects in context. In: Fleet, D., Pajdla, T., Schiele, B., Tuytelaars, T. (eds.) ECCV 2014. LNCS, vol. 8693, pp. 740–755. Springer, Cham (2014). https://doi.org/10.1007/978-3-319-10602-1_48

28. Liu, D., Cui, Y., Tan, W., Chen, Y.: SG-Net: spatial granularity network for one-stage video instance segmentation. In: Proceedings of the IEEE/CVF Conference on Computer Vision and Pattern Recognition (CVPR), pp. 9816–9825 (2021)

29. Liu, D., Cui, Y., Yan, L., Mousas, C., Yang, B., Chen, Y.: DenserNet: weakly supervised visual localization using multi-scale feature aggregation. In: Proceedings of the AAAI Conference on Artificial Intelligence, no. 7, pp. 6101–6109 (2021)

30. Liu, Z., et al.: Swin transformer: hierarchical vision transformer using shifted windows. In: International Conference on Computer Vision (ICCV) (2021)

31. Liu, Z., Mao, H., Wu, C.Y., Feichtenhofer, C., Darrell, T., Xie, S.: A convnet for the 2020s (2022)

32. Loshchilov, I., Hutter, F.: SGDR: stochastic gradient descent with warm restarts. arXiv preprint arXiv:1608.03983 (2016)

33. Loshchilov, I., Hutter, F.: Decoupled weight decay regularization. In: International Conference on Learning Representations (ICLR) (2019)

34. Maji, S., Rahtu, E., Kannala, J., Blaschko, M., Vedaldi, A.: Fine-grained visual classification of aircraft. arXiv preprint arXiv:1306.5151 (2013)

35. Paszke, A., et al.: PyTorch: an imperative style, high-performance deep learning library. In: Advances in Neural Information Processing Systems (NeurIPS) (2019)

36. Polyak, B.T., Juditsky, A.B.: Acceleration of stochastic approximation by averaging. SIAM J. Control. Optim. **30**(4), 838–855 (1992)

37. Qin, J., Fang, J., Zhang, Q., Liu, W., Wang, X., Wang, X.: ResizeMix: mixing data with preserved object information and true labels. arXiv preprint arXiv:2012.11101 (2020)

38. Ren, S., He, K., Girshick, R., Sun, J.: Faster R-CNN: towards real-time object detection with region proposal networks. arXiv preprint arXiv:1506.01497 (2015)

39. Russakovsky, O., et al.: ImageNet large scale visual recognition challenge. Int. J. Comput. Vis. **115**, 211–252 (2015). https://doi.org/10.1007/s11263-015-0816-y

40. Sandler, M., Howard, A., Zhu, M., Zhmoginov, A., Chen, L.C.: MobileNetV2: inverted residuals and linear bottlenecks. In: Proceedings of the IEEE Conference on Computer Vision and Pattern Recognition (CVPR) (2018)

41. Selvaraju, R.R., Cogswell, M., Das, A., Vedantam, R., Parikh, D., Batra, D.: Grad-CAM: visual explanations from deep networks via gradient-based localization. arXiv preprint arXiv:1610.02391 (2019)

42. Srivastava, N., Hinton, G., Krizhevsky, A., Sutskever, I., Salakhutdinov, R.: Dropout: a simple way to prevent neural networks from overfitting. J. Mach. Learn. Res. **15**(1), 1929–1958 (2014)

43. Tan, C., Gao, Z., Wu, L., Li, S., Li, S.Z.: Hyperspherical consistency regularization. In: Proceedings of the IEEE/CVF Conference on Computer Vision and Pattern Recognition (CVPR), pp. 7244–7255 (2022)

44. Tan, C., Xia, J., Wu, L., Li, S.Z.: Co-learning: learning from noisy labels with self-supervision. In: Proceedings of the 29th ACM International Conference on Multimedia, pp. 1405–1413 (2021)

45. Tan, M., Le, Q.V.: EfficientNet: rethinking model scaling for convolutional neural networks. In: International Conference on Machine Learning (ICML) (2019)

46. Thulasidasan, S., Chennupati, G., Bilmes, J., Bhattacharya, T., Michalak, S.: On mixup training: improved calibration and predictive uncertainty for deep neural networks. arXiv preprint arXiv:1905.11001 (2019)

47. Touvron, H., Cord, M., Douze, M., Massa, F., Sablayrolles, A., Jegou, H.: Training data-efficient image transformers & distillation through attention. In: International Conference on Machine Learning (ICML), pp. 10347–10357 (2021)
48. Uddin, A., Monira, M., Shin, W., Chung, T., Bae, S.H., et al.: SaliencyMix: a saliency guided data augmentation strategy for better regularization. arXiv preprint arXiv:2006.01791 (2020)
49. Venkataramanan, S., Avrithis, Y., Kijak, E., Amsaleg, L.: AlignMix: improving representation by interpolating aligned features (2021)
50. Verma, V., et al.: Manifold mixup: better representations by interpolating hidden states. In: International Conference on Machine Learning, pp. 6438–6447 (2019)
51. Wah, C., Branson, S., Welinder, P., Perona, P., Belongie, S.: The Caltech-UCSD Birds-200-2011 dataset. California Institute of Technology (2011)
52. Walawalkar, D., Shen, Z., Liu, Z., Savvides, M.: Attentive cutmix: an enhanced data augmentation approach for deep learning based image classification. In: ICASSP 2020–2020 IEEE International Conference on Acoustics, Speech and Signal Processing (ICASSP), pp. 3642–3646 (2020)
53. Wan, L., Zeiler, M., Zhang, S., Le Cun, Y., Fergus, R.: Regularization of neural networks using dropconnect. In: International Conference on Machine Learning, pp. 1058–1066. PMLR (2013)
54. Wightman, R., Touvron, H., Jégou, H.: ResNet strikes back: an improved training procedure in timm (2021)
55. Wu, L., Lin, H., Tan, C., Gao, Z., Li, S.Z.: Self-supervised learning on graphs: contrastive, generative, or predictive. IEEE Trans. Knowl. Data Eng. (2021)
56. Wu, L., Yuan, L., Zhao, G., Lin, H., Li, S.Z.: Deep clustering and visualization for end-to-end high-dimensional data analysis. IEEE Trans. Neural Netw. Learn. Syst. (2022)
57. Wu, Y., Kirillov, A., Massa, F., Lo, W.Y., Girshick, R.: Detectron2 (2019). https://github.com/facebookresearch/detectron2
58. Xia, J., Zhu, Y., Du, Y., Li, S.Z.: Pre-training graph neural networks for molecular representations: retrospect and prospect. In: ICML 2022 2nd AI for Science Workshop (2022)
59. Xie, S., Girshick, R., Dollár, P., Tu, Z., He, K.: Aggregated residual transformations for deep neural networks. In: Proceedings of the IEEE Conference on Computer Vision and Pattern Recognition, pp. 1492–1500 (2017)
60. You, Y., et al.: Large batch optimization for deep learning: training BERT in 76 minutes. In: International Conference on Learning Representations (ICLR) (2020)
61. Yun, S., Han, D., Oh, S.J., Chun, S., Choe, J., Yoo, Y.: CutMix: regularization strategy to train strong classifiers with localizable features. In: Proceedings of the International Conference on Computer Vision (ICCV), pp. 6023–6032 (2019)
62. Zagoruyko, S., Komodakis, N.: Wide residual networks. In: Proceedings of the British Machine Vision Conference (BMVC) (2016)
63. Zang, Z., et al.: DLME: deep local-flatness manifold embedding (2022)
64. Zhang, H., Cisse, M., Dauphin, Y.N., Lopez-Paz, D.: mixup: beyond empirical risk minimization. arXiv preprint arXiv:1710.09412 (2017)
65. Zhao, Z., Wu, Z., Zhuang, Y., Li, B., Jia, J.: Tracking objects as pixel-wise distributions (2022)
66. Zhou, B., Lapedriza, A., Xiao, J., Torralba, A., Oliva, A.: Learning deep features for scene recognition using places database. In: Advances in Neural Information Processing Systems (NeurIPS), pp. 487–495 (2014)

MaxViT: Multi-axis Vision Transformer

Zhengzhong Tu[1,2]([⊠]), Hossein Talebi[1], Han Zhang[1], Feng Yang[1],
Peyman Milanfar[1], Alan Bovik[2], and Yinxiao Li[1]

[1] Google Research, Mountain View, USA
[2] University of Texas at Austin, Austin, USA
zhengzhong.tu@utexas.edu

Abstract. Transformers have recently gained significant attention in the computer vision community. However, the lack of scalability of self-attention mechanisms with respect to image size has limited their wide adoption in state-of-the-art vision backbones. In this paper we introduce an efficient and scalable attention model we call multi-axis attention, which consists of two aspects: blocked local and dilated global attention. These design choices allow global-local spatial interactions on arbitrary input resolutions with only linear complexity. We also present a new architectural element by effectively blending our proposed attention model with convolutions, and accordingly propose a simple hierarchical vision backbone, dubbed MaxViT, by simply repeating the basic building block over multiple stages. Notably, MaxViT is able to "see" globally throughout the entire network, even in earlier, high-resolution stages. We demonstrate the effectiveness of our model on a broad spectrum of vision tasks. On image classification, MaxViT achieves state-of-the-art performance under various settings: without extra data, MaxViT attains 86.5% ImageNet-1K top-1 accuracy; with ImageNet-21K pre-training, our model achieves 88.7% top-1 accuracy. For downstream tasks, MaxViT as a backbone delivers favorable performance on object detection as well as visual aesthetic assessment. We also show that our proposed model expresses strong generative modeling capability on ImageNet, demonstrating the superior potential of MaxViT blocks as a universal vision module. The source code and trained models will be available at https://github.com/google-research/maxvit.

Keywords: Transformer · Image classification · Multi-axis attention

1 Introduction

Convolutional Neural Networks (ConvNets) have been the dominant architectural design choice for computer vision [26,41,65,66] since AlexNet [41]. ConvNets continue to excel on numerous vision problems by going deeper [65],

---

Supplementary Information The online version contains supplementary material available at https://doi.org/10.1007/978-3-031-20053-3_27.

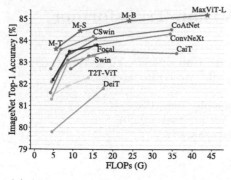 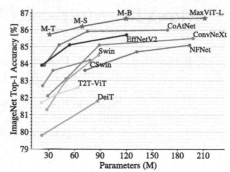

(a) Accuracy vs. FLOPs performance scaling curve under ImageNet-1K training setting at input resolution 224×224.

(b) Accuracy vs. Parameters scaling curve under ImageNet-1K fine-tuning setting allowing for higher sizes (384/512).

Fig. 1. Performance comparison of MaxViT with state-of-the-art vision Transformers on ImageNet-1K. Our model shows superior performance in terms of both accuracy *vs.* computation and accuracy *vs.* parameters tradeoff.

wider [64,66], adding dense connections [32], efficient separable convolutions [30, 61], atrous convolutions [8], using encoder-decoder frameworks [58], and even introducing modern micro-design components [50]. Meanwhile, as inspired by the evolution of self-attention models like Transformers [75] in natural language processing [18,42,54,89], numerous researchers have started to introduce attention mechanisms into vision [6,78]. The Vision Transformer (ViT) [20] is perhaps the first fully Transformer-based architecture for vision, whereby image patches are simply regarded as sequences of words and a transformer encoder is applied on these visual tokens. When pre-trained on large-scale datasets [63], ViT can achieve compelling results on image recognition.

However, it has been observed that without extensive pre-training [20,71] ViT underperforms on image recognition. This is due to the strong model capacity of Transformers, that is imbued with less inductive bias, which leads to over-fitting. To properly regularize the model capacity and improve its scalability, numerous subsequent efforts have studied sparse Transformer models tailored for vision tasks such as local attention [14,43,49,88]. These methods typically re-introduce hierarchical architectures to compensate for the loss of non-locality. The Swin Transformer [49] is one such successful attempt to modify Transformers by applying self-attention on shifted non-overlapping windows. For the first time, this approach outperformed ConvNets on the ImageNet benchmark with a pure vision Transformer. Despite having more flexibility and generalizability than the full attention used in ViT, window-based attention has been observed to have limited model capacity due to the loss of non-locality, and henceforth scales unfavorably on larger data regimes such as ImageNet-21K and JFT [17]. However, acquiring global interactions via full-attention at early or high-resolution stages in a hierarchical network is computationally heavy, as the attention operator requires quadratic complexity. How to efficiently incorporate global and local interactions to balance the model capacity and generalizability under a computation budget still remains challenging.

In this paper, we present a new type of Transformer module, called multi-axis self-attention (Max-SA), that capably serves as a basic architecture component which can perform both local and global spatial interactions in a single block. Compared to full self-attention, Max-SA enjoys greater flexibility and efficiency, *i.e.*, naturally adaptive to different input lengths with linear complexity; in contrast to (shifted) window/local attention, Max-SA allows for stronger model capacity by proposing a global receptive field. Moreover, with merely linear complexity, Max-SA can be used as a general stand-alone attention module in any layer of a network, even in earlier, high-resolution stages.

To demonstrate its effectiveness and universality, we further design a simple but effective vision backbone called **Multi-axis Vision Transformer (MaxViT)** by hierarchically stacking repeated blocks composed of Max-SA and convolutions. While our proposed model belongs to the category of hybrid vision Transformers, MaxViT distinguishes from previous approaches [17,83] in that we strive for simplicity, by designing a basic block unifying convolution, local, and global attention, then simply repeating it. Our experiments shows that the MaxViT significantly improves upon state-of-the-art (SOTA) performance under all data regimes for a broad range of visual tasks including classification, object detection and segmentation, image aesthetics assessment, and image generation. Specifically, as Fig. 1 shows, MaxViT outperforms all recent Transformer-based models in regards to both accuracy *vs.* FLOPs and accuracy *vs.* parameter curves. Our contributions are:

- A generic strong Transformer backbone, **MaxViT**, that can capture both local and global spatial interactions throughout every stage of the network.
- A novel stand-alone multi-axis attention module composed of blocked local and dilated global attention, enjoying global perception in linear complexity.
- We demonstrate large amounts of design choices including number of layers, layouts, the use of MBConv, *etc.* . with extensive ablation studies, that eventually converge towards our final modular design, the MaxViT-Block.
- Our extensive experiments show that MaxViT achieves SOTA results under various data regimes for a broad range of tasks including image classification, object detection, image aesthetic assessment, and image generation.

2   Related Work

Convolutional Networks. Since AlexNet [41], convolutional neural networks (ConvNets) have been used as *de facto* solutions to almost all vision tasks [7,11,26,32,44,68,79,80,93] before the "Roaring 20s" [50]. Phenomenal architectural improvements have been made in the past decade: residual [26] and dense connections [32], fully-convolutional networks [51], encoder-decoder schemes [58], feature pyramids [45], increased depths and widths [65], spatial-

and channel-wise attention models [31,81], non-local interactions [78], to name a few. A remarkable recent work ConvNeXt [50] has re-introduced core designs of vision Transformers and shown that a 'modernized' pure ConvNet can achieve performance comparable to Transformers on broad vision tasks.

Transformers in Vision. Transformers were originally proposed for natural language processing [75]. The debut of the Vision Transformer (ViT) [20] in 2020 showed that pure Transformer-based architectures are also effective solutions for vision problems. The elegantly novel view of ViT that treats image patches as visual words has stimulated explosive research interest in visual Transformers. To account for locality and 2D nature of images, the Swin Transformer aggregates attention in shifted windows in a hierarchical architecture [49]. More recent works have been focused on improving model and data efficiency, including sparse attention [1,19,55,76,85,88], improved locality [24,90], pyramidal designs [22,77, 86], improved training strategies [3,71,72,94], *etc.* We refer readers to dedicated surveys [38,38] of vision Transformers for a comprehensive review.

Hybrid Models. Pure Transformer-based vision models have been observed to generalize poorly due to relatively less inductive bias [17,20,71]. Vision Transformers also exhibit substandard optimizability [83]. An intriguingly simple improvement is to adopt a hybrid design of Transformer and convolution layers such as using a few convolutions to replace the coarse patchify stem [17,83]. A broad range of works fall into this category, either explicitly hybridized [4,17,21,22,82,83,87] or in an implicit fashion [14,49].

Transformer for GANs. Transformers have also proven effective in generative adversarial networks (GANs) [23]. TransGAN [35] built a pure Transformer GAN with a careful design of local attention and upsampling layers, demonstrating effectiveness on small scale datasets [16,40]. GANformer [33] explored efficient global attention mechanisms to improve on StyleGAN [36] generator. HiT [92] presents an efficient Transformer generator based on local-global attention that can scale up to 1K high-resolution image generation.

3   Method

Inspired by the sparse approaches presented in [73,92], we introduce a new type of attention module, dubbed blocked multi-axis self-attention (Max-SA), by decomposing the fully dense attention mechanisms into two sparse forms – window attention and grid attention – which reduces the quadratic complexity of vanilla attention to linear, without any loss of non-locality. Our sequential design offers greater simplicity and flexibility, while performing even better than previous methods – each individual module can be used either standalone or combined in any order (Tables 7, 8 and 9), whereas parallel designs [73,92] offer no such benefits. Because of the flexibility and scalability of Max-SA, we are able to build a novel vision backbone, which we call MaxViT, by simply stacking alternative layers of Max-SA with MBConv [30] in a hierarchical architecture, as shown in Fig. 2. MaxViT benefits from global and local receptive fields throughout the

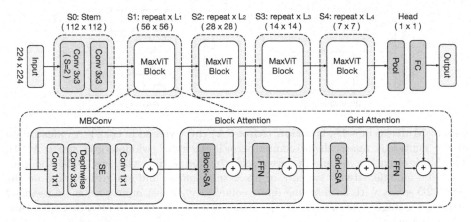

Fig. 2. MaxViT architecture. We follow a typical hierarchical design of ConvNet practices (e.g., ResNet) but instead build a new type of basic building block that unifies MBConv, block, and grid attention layers. Normalization and activation layers are omitted for simplicity.

entire network, from shallow to deep stages, demonstrating superior performance in regards to both model capacity and generalization abilities.

3.1 Attention

Self-attention allows for spatial mixing of entire spatial (or sequence) locations while also benefiting from content-dependent weights based on normalized pairwise similarity. The standard self-attention defined in [20,75] is location-unaware, *i.e.*, non-translation equivariant, an important inductive bias imbued in ConvNets. Relative self-attention [17,35,49,62] has been proposed to improve on vanilla attention by introducing a relative learned bias added to the attention weights, which has been shown to consistently outperform original attention on many vision tasks [17,35,49]. In this work, we mainly adopt the pre-normalized relative self-attention defined in [17] as the key operator in MaxViT.

3.2 Multi-axis Attention

Global interaction is one of the key advantages of self-attention as compared to local convolution. However, directly applying attention along the entire space is computationally infeasible as the attention operator requires quadratic complexity. To tackle this problem, we present a multi-axis approach to decompose the full-size attention into two sparse forms – local and global – by simply decomposing the spatial axes. Let $X \in \mathbb{R}^{H \times W \times C}$ be an input feature map. Instead of applying attention on the flattened spatial dimension HW, we block the feature into a tensor of shape $(\frac{H}{P} \times \frac{W}{P}, P \times P, C)$, representing partitioning into non-overlapping windows, each of size $P \times P$. Applying self-attention on the

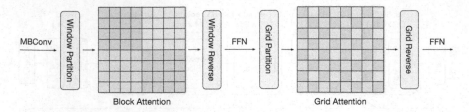

Fig. 3. Multi-axis self-attention (Max-SA) (best viewed in color). An illustration of the multi-axis approach for computing self-attention (window/grid size is 4×4). The block-attention module performs self-attention within windows, while the grid-attention module attends globally to pixels in a sparse, uniform grid overlaid on the entire 2D space, with both having linear complexity against input size, as we use fixed attention footage. The same colors are spatially mixed by the self-attention operation. (Color figure online)

local spatial dimension *i.e.*, $P \times P$, is equivalent to attending within a small window [49]. We will use this **block attention** to conduct local interactions.

Despite bypassing the notoriously heavy computation of full self-attention, local-attention models have been observed to underfit on huge-scale datasets [17, 20]. Inspired by block attention, we present a surprisingly simple but effective way to gain sparse global attention, which we call **grid attention**. Instead of partitioning feature maps using fixed window size, we grid the tensor into the shape $(G \times G, \frac{H}{G} \times \frac{W}{G}, C)$ using a fixed $G \times G$ uniform grid, resulting in windows having adaptive size $\frac{H}{G} \times \frac{W}{G}$. Employing self-attention on the decomposed grid axis *i.e.*, $G \times G$, corresponds to dilated, global spatial mixing of tokens. By using the same *fixed* window and grid sizes (we use $P = G = 7$ following Swin [49]), we can fully balance the computation between local and global operations, both having only linear complexity with respect to spatial size or sequence length. Note that our proposed Max-SA module can be a drop-in replacement of the Swin attention module [49] with exactly the same number of parameters and FLOPs. Yet it enjoys *global interaction* capability without requiring masking, padding, or cyclic-shifting, making it more implementation friendly, preferable to the shifted window scheme [49]. For instance, the multi-axis attention can be easily implemented with `einops` [57] without modifying the original attention operation (see Appendix). It is worth mentioning that our proposed multi-axis attention (Max-SA) is fundamentally different from the axial-attention models [28,76]. Please see Appendix for a detailed comparison.

MaxViT Block. We sequentially stack the two types of attentions to gain both local and global interactions in a single block, as shown in Fig. 3. Note that we also adopt typical designs in Transformers [20,49], including Layer-Norm [2], Feedforward networks (FFNs) [20,49], and skip-connections. We also add a MBConv block [30] with squeeze-and-excitation (SE) module [31] prior to the multi-axis attention, as we have observed that using MBConv together with attention further increases the generalization as well as the trainability of the

ÅÅÅ ÅÅÅÅÅ ÅÅ ÅÅÅ ÅÅ ÅÅ ÅÅÅÅÅÅ

Table 1. MaxViT architecture variants. B and C denotes number of blocks and number of channels for each stage. We set each attention head to 32 for all attention layers. For MBConv, we always use expansion rate 4 and shrinkage rate 0.25 in SE [31], following [17,69,70]. We use two Conv layers in the stem.

Stage	Size	MaxViT-T	MaxViT-S	MaxViT-B	MaxViT-L	MaxViT-XL
S0: Conv-stem	1/2	B=2 C=64	B=2 C=64	B=2 C=64	B=2 C=128	B=2 C=192
S1: MaxViT-Block	1/4	B=2 C=64	B=2 C=96	B=2 C=96	B=2 C=128	B=2 C=192
S2: MaxViT-Block	1/8	B=2 C=128	B=2 C=192	B=6 C=192	B=6 C=256	B=6 C=384
S3: MaxViT-Block	1/16	B=5 C=256	B=5 C=384	B=14 C=384	B=14 C=512	B=14 C=768
S4: MaxViT-Block	1/32	B=2 C=512	B=2 C=768	B=2 C=768	B=2 C=1024	B=2 C=1536

network [83]. Using MBConv layers prior to attention offers another advantage, in that depthwise convolutions can be regarded as conditional position encoding (CPE) [15], making our model free of explicit positional encoding layers. Note that our proposed stand-alone multi-axis attention may be used together or in isolation for different purposes – block attention for local interaction, and grid attention for global mixing. These elements can be easily plugged into many vision architectures, especially on high-resolution tasks that can benefit by global interactions with affordable computation.

3.3 Architecture Variants

We designed a series of extremely simple architectural variants to explore the effectiveness of our proposed MaxViT block, as shown in Fig. 2. We use a hierarchical backbone similar to common ConvNet practices [17,26,50,70] where the input is first downsampled using Conv3x3 layers in stem stage (S0). The body of the network contains four stages (S1-S4), with each stage having half the resolution of the previous one with a doubled number of channels (hidden dimension). In our network, we employ *identical* MaxViT blocks throughout the entire backbone. We apply downsampling in the Depthwise Conv3x3 layer of the first MBConv block in each stage. The expansion and shrink rates for inverted bottleneck [30] and squeeze-excitation (SE) [31] are 4 and 0.25 by default. We set the attention head size to be 32 for all attention blocks. We scale up the model by increasing block numbers per stage B and the channel dimension C. We summarize the architectural configurations of the MaxViT variants in Table 1.

4   Experiments

We validated the efficacy of our proposed model on various vision tasks: ImageNet classification [41], image object detection and instance segmentation [46], image aesthetics/quality assessment [52], and unconditional image generation [23]. More experimental details can be found in the Appendix.

Table 2. Performance comparison under ImageNet-1K setting. Throughput is measured on a single V100 GPU with batch size 16, following [49,50,70].

	Model	Eval size	Params	FLOPs	Throughput (image/s)	IN-1K top-1 acc.
ConvNets	•EffNet-B6 [69]	528	43M	19.0G	96.9	84.0
	•EffNet-B7 [69]	600	66M	37.0G	55.1	84.3
	•RegNetY-16 [53]	224	84M	16.0G	334.7	82.9
	•NFNet-F0 [5]	256	72M	12.4G	533.3	83.6
	•NFNet-F1 [5]	320	132M	35.5G	228.5	84.7
	•EffNetV2-S [70]	384	24M	8.8G	666.6	83.9
	•EffNetV2-M [70]	480	55M	24.0G	280.7	85.1
	•ConvNeXt-S [50]	224	50M	8.7G	447.1	83.1
	•ConvNeXt-B [50]	224	89M	15.4G	292.1	83.8
	•ConvNeXt-L [50]	224	198M	34.4G	146.8	84.3
ViTs	∘ViT-B/32 [20]	384	86M	55.4G	85.9	77.9
	∘ViT-B/16 [20]	384	307M	190.7G	27.3	76.5
	∘DeiT-B [71]	384	86M	55.4G	85.9	83.1
	∘CaiT-M24 [72]	224	186M	36.0G	-	83.4
	∘CaiT-M24 [72]	384	186M	116.1G	-	84.5
	∘DeepViT-L [94]	224	55M	12.5G	-	83.1
	∘T2T-ViT-24 [90]	224	64M	15.0G	-	82.6
	∘Swin-S [49]	224	50M	8.7G	436.9	83.0
	∘Swin-B [49]	384	88M	47.0G	84.7	84.5
	∘CSwin-B [19]	224	78M	15.0G	250	84.2
	∘CSwin-B [19]	384	78M	47.0G	-	85.4
	∘Focal-S [88]	224	51M	9.1G	-	83.5
	∘Focal-B [88]	224	90M	16.0G	-	83.8
Hybrid	◇CvT-21 [82]	384	32M	24.9G	-	83.3
	◇CoAtNet-2 [17]	224	75M	15.7G	247.7	84.1
	◇CoAtNet-3 [17]	224	168M	34.7G	163.3	84.5
	◇CoAtNet-3 [17]	384	168M	107.4G	48.5	85.8
	◇CoAtNet-3 [17]	512	168M	203.1G	22.4	86.0
	◇MaxViT-T	224	31M	5.6G	349.6	83.62
	◇MaxViT-S	224	69M	11.7G	242.5	84.45
	◇MaxViT-B	224	120M	23.4G	133.6	84.95
	◇MaxViT-L	224	212M	43.9G	99.4	85.17
	◇MaxViT-T	384	31M	17.7G	121.9	83.62
	◇MaxViT-S	384	69M	36.1G	82.7	85.24
	◇MaxViT-B	384	120M	74.2G	45.8	85.74
	◇MaxViT-L	384	212M	133.1G	34.3	86.34
	◇MaxViT-T	512	31M	33.7G	63.8	85.72
	◇MaxViT-S	512	69M	67.6G	43.3	86.19
	◇MaxViT-B	512	120M	138.5G	24.0	86.66
	◇MaxViT-L	512	212M	245.4G	17.8	**86.70**

Table 3. Performance comparison for large-scale data regimes: ImageNet-21K and JFT pretrained models.

	Model	Eval size	Params	FLOPs	IN-1K top-1 acc.	
					21K→1K	JFT→1K
ConvNets	•BiT-R-101x3 [39]	384	388M	204.6G	84.4	-
	•BiT-R-152x4 [39]	480	937M	840.5G	85.4	-
	•EffNetV2-L [70]	480	121M	53.0G	86.8	-
	•EffNetV2-XL [70]	512	208M	94.0G	87.3	-
	•ConvNeXt-L [50]	384	198M	101.0G	87.5	-
	•ConvNeXt-XL [50]	384	350M	179.0G	87.8	-
	•NFNet-F4+ [5]	512	527M	367G	-	89.20
ViTs	○ViT-B/16 [20]	384	87M	55.5G	84.0	-
	○ViT-L/16 [20]	384	305M	191.1G	85.2	-
	○ViT-L/16 [20]	512	305M	364G	-	87.76
	○ViT-H/14 [20]	518	632M	1021G	-	88.55
	○HaloNet-H4 [74]	512	85M	-	85.8	-
	○SwinV2-B [49]	384	88M	-	87.1	-
	○SwinV2-L [49]	384	197M	-	87.7	-
Hybrid	◇CvT-W24 [82]	384	277M	193.2G	87.7	-
	◇R+ViT-L/16 [20]	384	330M	-	-	87.12
	◇CoAtNet-3 [17]	384	168M	107.4G	87.6	88.52
	◇CoAtNet-3 [17]	512	168M	214G	87.9	88.81
	◇CoAtNet-4 [17]	512	275M	360.9G	88.1	89.11
	◇CoAtNet-5 [17]	512	688M	812G	-	**89.77**
	◇MaxViT-B	384	119M	74.2G	88.24	88.69
	◇MaxViT-L	384	212M	128.7G	88.32	89.12
	◇MaxViT-XL	384	475M	293.7G	**88.51**	89.36
	◇MaxViT-B	512	119M	138.3G	88.38	88.82
	◇MaxViT-L	512	212M	245.2G	88.46	89.41
	◇MaxViT-XL	512	475M	535.2G	**88.70**	**89.53**

4.1   Image Classification on ImageNet-1K

ImageNet-1K. We show in Table 2 the performance comparisons on ImageNet-1K classification. Under the basic 224 × 224 setting, MaxViT outperformed the most recent strong hybrid model CoAtNet by a large margin across the entire FLOPs spectrum, as shown in Fig. 1a. The MaxViT-L model sets a new performance record of 85.17% at 224 × 224 training without extra training strategies, outperforming CoAtNet-3 by 0.67%. In regards to throughput-accuracy

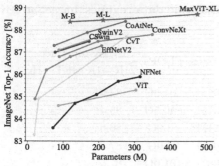 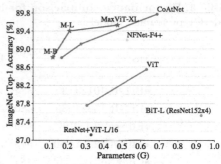

(a) Accuracy vs. Params performances for ImageNet-21K pre-trained models.

(b) Accuracy vs. Params scaling curve for JFT-300M pre-trained models.

Fig. 4. Performance comparison on large-scale pre-trained models. MaxViT shows superior scaling performance under both ImageNet-21K and JFT-300M pre-trained settings.

trade-offs at 224^2, MaxViT-S obtains 84.45% top-1 accuracy, 0.25% higher than CSWin-B and 0.35% higher than CoAtNet-2 with comparable throughput.

When fine-tuned at higher resolutions (384/512), MaxViT continues to deliver high performance compared to strong ConvNet and Transformer competitors: (1) at 384^2, MaxViT-B attains 86.34% top-1 accuracy, outperforming EfficientNetV2-L by 0.64%; (2) when fine-tuned at 512^2, our MaxViT-L (212M) achieves top-1 accuracy 86.7%, setting new SOTA performance on ImageNet-1K under the normal training setting. As Fig. 1 shows, MaxViT scales much better than SOTA vision Transformers on the ImageNet-1K trained model scale.

ImageNet-21K. Table 3 shows the results of models pre-trained on ImageNet-21K. Remarkably, the MaxViT-B model achieves 88.38% accuracy, outperforming the previous best model CoAtNet-4 by 0.28% using only 43% of parameter count and 38% of FLOPs, demonstrating greater parameter and computing efficiency. Figure 4a visualizes the model size comparison – MaxViT scales significantly better than previous attention-based models of similar complexities, across the board. Additionally, the MaxViT-XL model achieves new SOTA performance, an accuracy of 88.70% when fine-tuned at resolution 512 × 512.

JFT-300M. We also trained our model on a larger-scale proprietary dataset JFT-300M which contains ∼300 million weakly labeled images. As shown in Table 3 and Fig. 4b, our model is also scalable to massive scale training data – MaxViT-XL achieves a high accuracy of 89.53% with 475 million parameters, outperforming previous models under comparable model sizes. Due to resource limitations, we leave experiments on billion-parameter-scale models on planet-scale datasets (*e.g.*, JFT-3B [91]) as future work.

Table 4. Comparison of two-stage object detection and instance segmentation on COCO2017. All models are pretrained on ImageNet-1K.

Backbone	Resolution	AP	AP_{50}	AP_{75}	AP^m	AP^m_{50}	AP^m_{75}	FLOPs	Pars.
•ResNet-50 [26]	1280×800	46.3	64.3	50.5	40.1	61.7	43.4	739G	82M
•X101-32 [84]	1280×800	48.1	66.5	52.4	41.6	63.9	45.2	819G	101M
•X101-64 [84]	1280×800	48.3	66.4	52.3	41.7	64.0	45.1	972G	140M
•ConvNeXt-T [50]	1280×800	50.4	69.1	54.8	43.7	66.5	47.3	741G	-
•ConvNeXt-S [50]	1280×800	51.9	70.8	56.5	45.0	68.4	49.1	827G	-
•ConvNeXt-B [50]	1280×800	52.7	71.3	57.2	45.6	68.9	49.5	964G	-
○Swin-T [49]	1280×800	50.4	69.2	54.7	43.7	66.6	47.3	745G	86M
○Swin-S [49]	1280×800	51.9	70.7	56.3	45.0	68.2	48.8	838G	107M
○Swin-B [49]	1280×800	51.9	70.5	56.4	45.0	68.1	48.9	982G	145M
○UViT-T [12]	896×896	51.1	70.4	56.2	43.6	67.7	47.2	613G	47M
○UViT-S [12]	896×896	51.4	70.8	56.2	44.1	68.2	48.0	744G	54M
○UViT-B [12]	896×896	52.5	72.0	57.6	44.3	68.7	48.3	975G	74M
○As-ViT-L [13]	1024×1024	52.7	72.3	57.9	45.2	69.7	49.8	1094G	139M
◇MaxViT-T	896×896	52.1	71.9	56.8	44.6	69.1	48.4	475G	69M
◇MaxViT-S	896×896	53.1	72.5	58.1	45.4	69.8	49.5	595G	107M
◇MaxViT-B	896×896	**53.4**	**72.9**	**58.1**	**45.7**	**70.3**	**50.0**	856G	157M

4.2   Object Detection and Instance Segmentation

Setting. We evaluated the MaxViT architectures on the COCO2017 [46] object bounding box detection and instance segmentation tasks with a two-stage framework [56]. On the object detection task, a feature-pyramid architecture [45] was employed to boost different levels of objectiveness. In the instance segmentation task, a well-known Cascade Mask-RCNN framework [25] was employed. The dataset contains 118K training and 5K validation samples. For all the compared models, the backbones are first pretrained using ImageNet-1K. The pretrained models are then used to finetune on the detection and segmentation tasks.

Results on COCO. As shown in Table 4, AP, AP_{50}, and AP_{75} are reported for comparison. The parameters and FLOPs are also reported as a reference for model complexity. The MaxViT backbone models, used in object detection and segmentation tasks, outperform all other backbones by large margins, including Swin, ConvNeXt, and UViT at various model sizes with respect to both accuracy and efficiency. Note that MaxViT-S outperforms other base-level models (*e.g.*, Swin-B, UViT-B), with about 40% less computational cost.

4.3   Image Aesthetic Assessment

Setting. We train and evaluate the MaxViT model on the AVA benchmark [52] which contains 255K images with aesthetics scores rated by amateur photographers. Similar to [67], we split the dataset into 80%/20% training and test

Table 5. Image aesthetic assessment results on the AVA benchmark [52]. PLCC and SRCC represent the Pearson's linear and Spearman's rank correlation coefficients.

Model	Res.	Pars.	PLCC↑	SRCC↑
•NIMA [67]	224	56M	0.636	0.612
•EffNet-B0 [69]	224	5.3M	0.642	0.620
•AFDC[9]	224	44.5M	0.671	0.649
∘ViT-S/32 [37]	384	22M	0.665	0.656
∘ViT-B/32 [37]	384	88M	0.664	0.664
∘MUSIQ [37]	224–512	27M	0.720	0.706
◇MaxViT-T	224	31M	0.707	0.685
◇MaxViT-T	384	31M	0.736	0.699
◇MaxViT-T	512	31M	**0.745**	**0.708**

Table 6. Comparison of image generation on ImageNet. ‡ used a pre-trained ImageNet classifier.

Model	FID↓	IS↑
•GAN [23]	54.17	14.01
•PacGAN2 [47]	57.51	13.50
•MGAN [29]	50.90	14.44
•LogoGAN [59]‡	38.41	18.86
•SS-GAN [10]	43.87	-
•SC GAN [48]	40.30	15.82
•ConvNet-R_1 [92]	37.18	19.55
∘HiT [92] (32.9M)	30.83	21.64
◇MaxViT (18.6M)	**30.77**	**22.58**

sets. We followed [67] and used the normalized Earth Mover's Distance as our training loss. We trained MaxViT at three different input resolutions: 224^2, 384^2 and 512^2, initialized with ImageNet-1K pre-trained weights.

Results on AVA. To evaluate and compare our model against existing methods, we present a summary of our results in Table 5. For similar input resolutions, the proposed MaxViT-T model outperforms existing image aesthetic assessment methods. As the input resolution increases, the performance improves, benefiting from its strong non-local capacity. Also, MaxViT shows better linear correlation compared to the SOTA method [37] which uses multi-resolution inputs.

4.4   Image Generation

Setting. We evaluate the generative ability of MaxViT blocks to generate images of 128×128 resolution on ImageNet-1K. We choose the unconditional image generation to focus on the performance of different generators in GANs. We use the Inception Score (IS) [60] and the Fréchet Inception Distance (FID) [27] as quantitative evaluation metrics. 50,000 samples were randomly generated to calculate the FID and IS scores. We compared MaxViT against HiT [92], a SOTA generative Transformer model, which uses attention at low resolutions (e.g., 32, 64), and using implicit neural functions at high resolutions (e.g., 128). By contrast, MaxViT uses the proposed MaxViT block at every resolution. Note that we use an inverse block order (GA-BA-Conv) as we found it to perform better (see Table 8). Since Batch Normalization [34,92] achieves better results on image generation, we replaced all Layer Norm with Batch Norm under this setting.

Results on ImageNet-1K. The results are shown in Table 6. Our MaxViT achieved better FID and IS with significantly lower number of parameters. These results demonstrate the effectiveness of MaxViT blocks for generation tasks. More details of the generative experiment can be found in Appendix.

Table 7. Effects of global grid-attention. Ablate-S1 means we remove grid-attention in stage 1 while Replace-S1 means replacing grid-attention with block-attention.

Model	Pars.	FLOPs	Top-1 Acc.
MaxViT-T	30.9M	5.6G	83.62
Ablate-S1	30.8M	5.3G	83.36(-0.26)
Ablate-S2	30.5M	5.3G	83.38(-0.24)
Ablate-S3	26.9M	4.9G	83.00(-0.62)
Replace-S1	30.9M	5.6G	83.49(-0.13)
Replace-S2	30.9M	5.6G	83.41(-0.22)
Replace-S3	30.9M	5.6G	83.40(-0.23)

Table 8. Block order study. C, BA, GA represent MBConv, block-, and grid-attention respectively.

Model	Pars.	FLOPs	Top-1 acc.
C-BA-GA	30.9M	5.6G	83.62
C-GA-BA	30.9M	5.6G	83.54(-0.08)
BA-C-GA	31.1M	5.3G	83.07(-0.55)
BA-GA-C	31.1M	5.3G	83.02(-0.60)
GA-C-BA	31.1M	5.3G	83.08(-0.54)
GA-BA-C	31.1M	5.3G	83.03(-0.59)

GAN experiments			
Model	Pars.	FID↓	IS↑
GA-BA-C	18.6M	30.77	22.68
C-BA-GA	18.6M	31.40	21.49(-1.19)

Table 9. Ablation of MBConv. Ablate-S1 means we delete MBConv layers in stage 1. Note that the network will also be smaller if we ablate MBConv layers in some stage.

Model	Pars.	FLOPs	Top-1 acc.
MaxViT-T	30.9M	5.6G	83.62
Ablate-S1	30.8M	5.2G	83.24(-0.38)
Ablate-S2	30.5M	5.4G	83.02(-0.60)
Ablate-S3	27.6M	5.1G	82.65(-0.97)
Ablate-S4	25.7M	5.4G	83.09(-0.53)

Table 10. Sequential *vs.* parallel. We compared our model with modified parallel multi-axis scheme *Paral-**.

Model	Pars.	FLOPs	Top-1 acc.
MaxViT-T	30.9M	5.6G	83.62
Paral-T	34.5M	6.2G	82.64(-0.98)
MaxViT-S	68.9M	11.7G	84.45
Paral-S	76.9M	13.0G	83.45(-1.00)
MaxViT-B	119.4M	24.2G	84.95
Paral-B	133.4M	26.9G	83.70(-1.25)
MaxViT-L	211.8M	43.9G	85.17
Paral-L	236.6M	48.8G	83.54(-1.63)

4.5 Ablation Studies

In this section, we ablate important design choices in MaxViT on ImageNet-1K image classification. We use the MaxViT-T model trained for 300 epochs by default and report top-1 accuracy on ImageNet-1K. Except for the ablated design choice, we used the same training configurations, unless stated otherwise.

Global Grid-Attention. One of our main contributions is the grid-attention module, which allows for sparse global interactions at linear time, enabling our model to capture global information at all stages. We conducted two ablations to understand its gain: 1) completely removed global attention at each stage; 2) replaced grid attention with block attention to retain the same parameter count and FLOPs. As Table 7 shows, enabling global attention at earlier stages can further boost performance over using only local attention or convolutions.

MBConv Layer. We also ablated the usage of MBConv layers in MaxViT by removing all MBConv in each stage. Note that we should also consider the reduction of parameter count and FLOPs when removing the MBConv layers. Plus, Stage 3 has 5 blocks whereas other stages have only 2. As Table 9 shows, the usage of MBConv layers in MaxViT significantly boosts performance.

Block Order Study. We present three different modules to build the MaxViT block – MBConv, block-, and grid-attention – which captures spatial interactions from local to global. To investigate the most effective way to combine them, we evaluated the MaxViT-T model using all 6 permutations. We always apply downsampling in the first layer, which might cause a minor model size difference. We can observe from Table 8 that placing MBConv before attention layers is almost always better than other combinations. The reason might be that it is more suitable to get local features/patterns in early layers, then aggregate them globally, which is aligned with existing hybrid models [17,83], which puts Conv layers in front of attention. In generative experiments (Sect. 4.4), however, we found the best order to be from global to local: GA-BA-C. We hypothesize that it may be advantageous for generation tasks to first obtain the overall structures correct with global processing blocks (*i.e.*, grid-attention layers), then fill in finer details using local processing blocks (*i.e.*, MBConv).

Sequential *vs*. Parallel. In our approach, we sequentially stack the multi-axis attention modules following [49,76], while there also exist other models that adopt a parallel design [73,92]. In this ablation, we compare our sequential Max-SA against parallel branches containing block- and grid-attention respectively. Note that we use an input projection to double the channels, then split the heads to feed the two branches in order to remain similar complexity to MaxViT, and an output projection that reduces the concatenated branches. We did rough parameter tuning and found that an initial learning rate of 10^{-3} performs significantly better than 3×10^{-3} for parallel models. We use all the same parameters except the learning rate. As Table 10 shows, our sequential approach remarkably outperforms parallel counterparts with fewer parameters and computation. The reason may be that the parallel designs learn complementary cues with less interactions between them, whereas our sequential stack is able to learn more powerful fusions between local and global layers.

Vertical Layout. We further examine our vertical layout design, *i.e.*, the number of blocks each stage. We compared our design against the choice of Swin/ConvNeXt [49,50]. We change MaxViT-T and -S to blocks $B = (2, 2, 6, 2)$, and MaxViT-B, -L to have blocks $B = (2, 2, 18, 2)$ strictly following the stage ratio of Swin [49]. It may be seen from Fig. 5 that our layout performed comparably to Swin for small models, but scales significantly better for larger models.

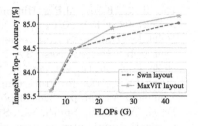

Fig. 5. Vertical layout ablation. Our model scales better than Swin layeout [49].

5   Discussion and Conclusion

While recent works in the 2020s s have arguably shown that ConvNets and vision Transformers can achieve similar performance on image recognition, our work presents a unified design that takes advantages of the best of both worlds – efficient convolution and sparse attention – and demonstrates that a model built on top, namely MaxViT, can achieve state-of-the-art performance on a variety of vision tasks, and more importantly, scale extremely well to massive scale data sizes. Even though we present our model in the context of vision tasks, the proposed multi-axis approach can easily extend to language modeling to capture both local and global dependencies in linear time. We also look forward to studying other forms of sparse attention in higher-dimensional or multi-modal signals such as videos, point clouds, and vision-languages.

Societal Impact. Investigating the performance and scalability of large model designs would consume considerable computing resources. These efforts can contribute to increased carbon emissions, which could hence raise environmental concerns. However, the proposed model offers strong modular candidates that expand the network's design space for future efforts on automated architectural design. If trained improperly, the proposed model may express bias and fairness issues. The proposed generative model can be abused to generate misleading media and fake news. These issues demand caution in future related research.

Acknowledgment. We thank Xianzhi Du and Wuyang Chen for extensive help on experiments. We also thank Hanxiao Liu, Zihang Dai, Anurag Arnab, Huiwen Chang, Junjie Ke, Mauricio Delbracio, Sungjoon Choi, and Irene Zhu for valuable discussions and help.

References

1. Arnab, A., Dehghani, M., Heigold, G., Sun, C., Lučić, M., Schmid, C.: Vivit: a video vision transformer. In: Proceedings of the IEEE/CVF International Conference on Computer Vision, pp. 6836–6846 (2021)

2. Ba, J.L., Kiros, J.R., Hinton, G.E.: Layer normalization. arXiv preprint arXiv:1607.06450 (2016)
3. Bello, I., et al.: Revisiting resnets: improved training and scaling strategies. Adv. Neural. Inf. Process. Syst. **34**, 22614–22627 (2021)
4. Bello, I., Zoph, B., Vaswani, A., Shlens, J., Le, Q.V.: Attention augmented convolutional networks. In: Proceedings of the IEEE/CVF International Conference on Computer Vision, pp. 3286–3295 (2019)
5. Brock, A., De, S., Smith, S.L., Simonyan, K.: High-performance large-scale image recognition without normalization. In: International Conference on Machine Learning, pp. 1059–1071. PMLR (2021)
6. Carion, N., Massa, F., Synnaeve, G., Usunier, N., Kirillov, A., Zagoruyko, S.: End-to-end object detection with transformers. In: Vedaldi, A., Bischof, H., Brox, T., Frahm, J.-M. (eds.) ECCV 2020. LNCS, vol. 12346, pp. 213–229. Springer, Cham (2020). https://doi.org/10.1007/978-3-030-58452-8_13
7. Chen, L.H., Bampis, C.G., Li, Z., Norkin, A., Bovik, A.C.: Proxiqa: a proxy approach to perceptual optimization of learned image compression. IEEE Trans. Image Process. **30**, 360–373 (2020)
8. Chen, L.C., Papandreou, G., Kokkinos, I., Murphy, K., Yuille, A.L.: DeepLab: semantic image segmentation with deep convolutional nets, atrous convolution, and fully connected CRFs. IEEE Trans. Pattern Anal. Mach. Intell. **40**(4), 834–848 (2017)
9. Chen, Q., et al.: Adaptive fractional dilated convolution network for image aesthetics assessment. In: Proceedings of the IEEE/CVF Conference on Computer Vision and Pattern Recognition, pp. 14114–14123 (2020)
10. Chen, T., Zhai, X., Ritter, M., Lucic, M., Houlsby, N.: Self-supervised GANs via auxiliary rotation loss. In: Proceedings of the IEEE/CVF Conference on Computer Vision and Pattern Recognition, pp. 12154–12163 (2019)
11. Chen, W.T., Huang, Z.K., Tsai, C.C., Yang, H.H., Ding, J.J., Kuo, S.Y.: Learning multiple adverse weather removal via two-stage knowledge learning and multi-contrastive regularization: toward a unified model. In: Proceedings of the IEEE/CVF Conference on Computer Vision and Pattern Recognition, pp. 17653–17662 (2022)
12. Chen, W., et al.: A simple single-scale vision transformer for object localization and instance segmentation. CoRR abs/2112.09747 (2021). arxiv.org/abs/2112.09747
13. Chen, W., Huang, W., Du, X., Song, X., Wang, Z., Zhou, D.: Auto-scaling vision transformers without training. arXiv preprint arXiv:2202.11921 (2022)
14. Chu, X., et al.: Twins: revisiting the design of spatial attention in vision transformers. In: Advances in Neural Information Processing Systems, vol. 34 (2021)
15. Chu, X., et al.: Conditional positional encodings for vision transformers. arXiv preprint arXiv:2102.10882 (2021)
16. Coates, A., Ng, A., Lee, H.: An analysis of single-layer networks in unsupervised feature learning. In: Gordon, G., Dunson, D., Dudík, M. (eds.) Proceedings of the Fourteenth International Conference on Artificial Intelligence and Statistics. Proceedings of Machine Learning Research, Fort Lauderdale, FL, USA, 11–13 April 2011, vol. 15, pp. 215–223. PMLR (2011). http://proceedings.mlr.press/v15/coates11a.html
17. Dai, Z., Liu, H., Le, Q., Tan, M.: Coatnet: marrying convolution and attention for all data sizes. In: Advances in Neural Information Processing Systems, vol. 34 (2021)

18. Devlin, J., Chang, M.W., Lee, K., Toutanova, K.: Bert: pre-training of deep bidirectional transformers for language understanding. arXiv preprint arXiv:1810.04805 (2018)
19. Dong, X., et al.: Cswin transformer: a general vision transformer backbone with cross-shaped windows. arXiv preprint arXiv:2107.00652 (2021)
20. Dosovitskiy, A., et al.: An image is worth 16x16 words: transformers for image recognition at scale. arXiv preprint arXiv:2010.11929 (2020)
21. d'Ascoli, S., Touvron, H., Leavitt, M.L., Morcos, A.S., Biroli, G., Sagun, L.: Convit: improving vision transformers with soft convolutional inductive biases. In: International Conference on Machine Learning, pp. 2286–2296. PMLR (2021)
22. Fan, H., et al.: Multiscale vision transformers. In: Proceedings of the IEEE/CVF International Conference on Computer Vision, pp. 6824–6835 (2021)
23. Goodfellow, I., et al.: Generative adversarial nets. In: Advances in Neural Information Processing Systems, vol. 27 (2014)
24. Han, K., Xiao, A., Wu, E., Guo, J., Xu, C., Wang, Y.: Transformer in transformer. In: Advances in Neural Information Processing Systems, vol. 34 (2021)
25. He, K., Gkioxari, G., Dollár, P., Girshick, R.: Mask R-CNN. In: 2017 IEEE International Conference on Computer Vision (ICCV), pp. 2980–2988 (2017). https://doi.org/10.1109/ICCV.2017.322
26. He, K., Zhang, X., Ren, S., Sun, J.: Deep residual learning for image recognition. In: Proceedings of the IEEE Conference on Computer Vision and Pattern Recognition, pp. 770–778 (2016)
27. Heusel, M., Ramsauer, H., Unterthiner, T., Nessler, B., Hochreiter, S.: GANs trained by a two time-scale update rule converge to a local nash equilibrium. In: NeurIPS, pp. 6629–6640 (2017)
28. Ho, J., Kalchbrenner, N., Weissenborn, D., Salimans, T.: Axial attention in multi-dimensional transformers. arXiv preprint arXiv:1912.12180 (2019)
29. Hoang, Q., Nguyen, T.D., Le, T., Phung, D.: Mgan: training generative adversarial nets with multiple generators. In: International Conference on Learning Representations (2018)
30. Howard, A.G., et al.: Mobilenets: efficient convolutional neural networks for mobile vision applications. arXiv preprint arXiv:1704.04861 (2017)
31. Hu, J., Shen, L., Sun, G.: Squeeze-and-excitation networks. In: Proceedings of the IEEE Conference on Computer Vision and Pattern Recognition, pp. 7132–7141 (2018)
32. Huang, G., Liu, Z., Van Der Maaten, L., Weinberger, K.Q.: Densely connected convolutional networks. In: Proceedings of the IEEE Conference on Computer Vision and Pattern Recognition, pp. 4700–4708 (2017)
33. Hudson, D.A., Zitnick, L.: Generative adversarial transformers. In: International Conference on Machine Learning, pp. 4487–4499. PMLR (2021)
34. Ioffe, S., Szegedy, C.: Batch normalization: accelerating deep network training by reducing internal covariate shift. In: International Conference on Machine Learning, pp. 448–456. PMLR (2015)
35. Jiang, Y., Chang, S., Wang, Z.: TransGAN: two pure transformers can make one strong GAN, and that can scale up. In: Advances in Neural Information Processing Systems, vol. 34 (2021)
36. Karras, T., Laine, S., Aittala, M., Hellsten, J., Lehtinen, J., Aila, T.: Analyzing and improving the image quality of stylegan. In: Proceedings of the IEEE/CVF Conference on Computer Vision and Pattern Recognition, pp. 8110–8119 (2020)

37. Ke, J., Wang, Q., Wang, Y., Milanfar, P., Yang, F.: Musiq: multi-scale image quality transformer. In: Proceedings of the IEEE/CVF International Conference on Computer Vision, pp. 5148–5157 (2021)
38. Khan, S., Naseer, M., Hayat, M., Zamir, S.W., Khan, F.S., Shah, M.: Transformers in vision: a survey. ACM Comput. Surv. (CSUR) (2021)
39. Kolesnikov, A., et al.: Big transfer (BiT): general visual representation learning. In: Vedaldi, A., Bischof, H., Brox, T., Frahm, J.-M. (eds.) ECCV 2020. LNCS, vol. 12350, pp. 491–507. Springer, Cham (2020). https://doi.org/10.1007/978-3-030-58558-7_29
40. Krizhevsky, A., Hinton, G., et al.: Learning multiple layers of features from tiny images (2009)
41. Krizhevsky, A., Sutskever, I., Hinton, G.E.: Imagenet classification with deep convolutional neural networks. In: Advances in Neural Information Processing Systems, vol. 25 (2012)
42. Lan, Z., Chen, M., Goodman, S., Gimpel, K., Sharma, P., Soricut, R.: Albert: a lite bert for self-supervised learning of language representations. arXiv preprint arXiv:1909.11942 (2019)
43. Li, Y., Zhang, K., Cao, J., Timofte, R., Van Gool, L.: LocalViT: bringing locality to vision transformers. arXiv preprint arXiv:2104.05707 (2021)
44. Li, Y., Jin, P., Yang, F., Liu, C., Yang, M.H., Milanfar, P.: COMISR: compression-informed video super-resolution. In: Proceedings of the IEEE/CVF International Conference on Computer Vision, pp. 2543–2552 (2021)
45. Lin, T.Y., Dollár, P., Girshick, R.B., He, K., Hariharan, B., Belongie, S.J.: Feature pyramid networks for object detection. In: 2017 IEEE Conference on Computer Vision and Pattern Recognition (CVPR), pp. 936–944 (2017)
46. Lin, T.-Y., et al.: Microsoft COCO: common objects in context. In: Fleet, D., Pajdla, T., Schiele, B., Tuytelaars, T. (eds.) ECCV 2014. LNCS, vol. 8693, pp. 740–755. Springer, Cham (2014). https://doi.org/10.1007/978-3-319-10602-1_48
47. Lin, Z., Khetan, A., Fanti, G., Oh, S.: Pacgan: the power of two samples in generative adversarial networks. In: Advances in Neural Information Processing Systems, vol. 31 (2018)
48. Liu, S., Wang, T., Bau, D., Zhu, J.Y., Torralba, A.: Diverse image generation via self-conditioned GANs. In: Proceedings of the IEEE/CVF Conference on Computer Vision and Pattern Recognition, pp. 14286–14295 (2020)
49. Liu, Z., et al.: Swin transformer: hierarchical vision transformer using shifted windows. In: Proceedings of the IEEE/CVF International Conference on Computer Vision, pp. 10012–10022 (2021)
50. Liu, Z., Mao, H., Wu, C.Y., Feichtenhofer, C., Darrell, T., Xie, S.: A convnet for the 2020s. arXiv preprint arXiv:2201.03545 (2022)
51. Long, J., Shelhamer, E., Darrell, T.: Fully convolutional networks for semantic segmentation. In: Proceedings of the IEEE Conference on Computer Vision and Pattern Recognition, pp. 3431–3440 (2015)
52. Murray, N., Marchesotti, L., Perronnin, F.: AVA: a large-scale database for aesthetic visual analysis. In: 2012 IEEE Conference on Computer Vision and Pattern Recognition, pp. 2408–2415. IEEE (2012)
53. Radosavovic, I., Kosaraju, R.P., Girshick, R., He, K., Dollár, P.: Designing network design spaces. In: Proceedings of the IEEE/CVF Conference on Computer Vision and Pattern Recognition, pp. 10428–10436 (2020)
54. Raffel, C., et al.: Exploring the limits of transfer learning with a unified text-to-text transformer. arXiv preprint arXiv:1910.10683 (2019)

55. Rao, Y., Zhao, W., Liu, B., Lu, J., Zhou, J., Hsieh, C.J.: DynamicViT: efficient vision transformers with dynamic token sparsification. In: Advances in Neural Information Processing Systems, vol. 34 (2021)
56. Ren, S., He, K., Girshick, R., Sun, J.: Faster R-CNN: towards real-time object detection with region proposal networks. In: Cortes, C., Lawrence, N., Lee, D., Sugiyama, M., Garnett, R. (eds.) Advances in Neural Information Processing Systems, vol. 28. Curran Associates, Inc. (2015). http://proceedings.neurips.cc/paper/2015/file/14bfa6bb14875e45bba028a21ed38046-Paper.pdf
57. Rogozhnikov, A.: Einops: clear and reliable tensor manipulations with einstein-like notation. In: International Conference on Learning Representations (2022). https://openreview.net/forum?id=oapKSVM2bcj
58. Ronneberger, O., Fischer, P., Brox, T.: U-Net: convolutional networks for biomedical image segmentation. In: Navab, N., Hornegger, J., Wells, W.M., Frangi, A.F. (eds.) MICCAI 2015. LNCS, vol. 9351, pp. 234–241. Springer, Cham (2015). https://doi.org/10.1007/978-3-319-24574-4_28
59. Sage, A., Agustsson, E., Timofte, R., Van Gool, L.: Logo synthesis and manipulation with clustered generative adversarial networks. In: Proceedings of the IEEE Conference on Computer Vision and Pattern Recognition, pp. 5879–5888 (2018)
60. Salimans, T., et al.: Improved techniques for training GANs. In: NeurIPS (2016)
61. Sandler, M., Howard, A., Zhu, M., Zhmoginov, A., Chen, L.C.: MobileNetV2: inverted residuals and linear bottlenecks. In: Proceedings of the IEEE Conference on Computer Vision and Pattern Recognition, pp. 4510–4520 (2018)
62. Shaw, P., Uszkoreit, J., Vaswani, A.: Self-attention with relative position representations. arXiv preprint arXiv:1803.02155 (2018)
63. Sun, C., Shrivastava, A., Singh, S., Gupta, A.: Revisiting unreasonable effectiveness of data in deep learning era. In: Proceedings of the IEEE International Conference on Computer Vision, pp. 843–852 (2017)
64. Szegedy, C., Ioffe, S., Vanhoucke, V., Alemi, A.A.: Inception-v4, inception-resnet and the impact of residual connections on learning. In: Thirty-First AAAI Conference on Artificial Intelligence (2017)
65. Szegedy, C., et al.: Going deeper with convolutions. In: Proceedings of the IEEE Conference on Computer Vision and Pattern Recognition, pp. 1–9 (2015)
66. Szegedy, C., Vanhoucke, V., Ioffe, S., Shlens, J., Wojna, Z.: Rethinking the inception architecture for computer vision. In: Proceedings of the IEEE Conference on Computer Vision and Pattern Recognition, pp. 2818–2826 (2016)
67. Talebi, H., Milanfar, P.: NIMA: neural image assessment. IEEE Trans. Image Process. 27(8), 3998–4011 (2018)
68. Talebi, H., Milanfar, P.: Learning to resize images for computer vision tasks. In: Proceedings of the IEEE/CVF International Conference on Computer Vision, pp. 497–506 (2021)
69. Tan, M., Le, Q.: Efficientnet: rethinking model scaling for convolutional neural networks. In: International Conference on Machine Learning, pp. 6105–6114. PMLR (2019)
70. Tan, M., Le, Q.: EfficientNetV2: smaller models and faster training. In: International Conference on Machine Learning, pp. 10096–10106. PMLR (2021)
71. Touvron, H., Cord, M., Douze, M., Massa, F., Sablayrolles, A., Jégou, H.: Training data-efficient image transformers & distillation through attention. In: International Conference on Machine Learning, pp. 10347–10357. PMLR (2021)
72. Touvron, H., Cord, M., Sablayrolles, A., Synnaeve, G., Jégou, H.: Going deeper with image transformers. In: Proceedings of the IEEE/CVF International Conference on Computer Vision, pp. 32–42 (2021)

73. Tu, Z., et al.: Maxim: multi-axis MLP for image processing. arXiv preprint arXiv:2201.02973 (2022)
74. Vaswani, A., Ramachandran, P., Srinivas, A., Parmar, N., Hechtman, B., Shlens, J.: Scaling local self-attention for parameter efficient visual backbones. In: Proceedings of the IEEE/CVF Conference on Computer Vision and Pattern Recognition, pp. 12894–12904 (2021)
75. Vaswani, A., et al.: Attention is all you need. In: Advances in Neural Information Processing Systems, vol. 30 (2017)
76. Wang, H., Zhu, Y., Green, B., Adam, H., Yuille, A., Chen, L.-C.: Axial-DeepLab: stand-alone axial-attention for panoptic segmentation. In: Vedaldi, A., Bischof, H., Brox, T., Frahm, J.-M. (eds.) ECCV 2020. LNCS, vol. 12349, pp. 108–126. Springer, Cham (2020). https://doi.org/10.1007/978-3-030-58548-8_7
77. Wang, W., et al.: Pyramid vision transformer: a versatile backbone for dense prediction without convolutions. In: Proceedings of the IEEE/CVF International Conference on Computer Vision, pp. 568–578 (2021)
78. Wang, X., Girshick, R., Gupta, A., He, K.: Non-local neural networks. In: Proceedings of the IEEE Conference on Computer Vision and Pattern Recognition, pp. 7794–7803 (2018)
79. Wang, Y., et al.: Rich features for perceptual quality assessment of UGC videos. In: Proceedings of the IEEE/CVF Conference on Computer Vision and Pattern Recognition, pp. 13435–13444 (2021)
80. Whang, J., Delbracio, M., Talebi, H., Saharia, C., Dimakis, A.G., Milanfar, P.: Deblurring via stochastic refinement. In: Proceedings of the IEEE/CVF Conference on Computer Vision and Pattern Recognition, pp. 16293–16303 (2022)
81. Woo, S., Park, J., Lee, J.Y., Kweon, I.S.: CBAM: convolutional block attention module. In: Proceedings of the European Conference on Computer Vision (ECCV), pp. 3–19 (2018)
82. Wu, H., et al.: CVT: introducing convolutions to vision transformers. In: Proceedings of the IEEE/CVF International Conference on Computer Vision, pp. 22–31 (2021)
83. Xiao, T., Dollar, P., Singh, M., Mintun, E., Darrell, T., Girshick, R.: Early convolutions help transformers see better. In: Advances in Neural Information Processing Systems, vol. 34 (2021)
84. Xie, S., Girshick, R., Dollár, P., Tu, Z., He, K.: Aggregated residual transformations for deep neural networks. In: Proceedings of the IEEE Conference on Computer Vision and Pattern Recognition, pp. 1492–1500 (2017)
85. Xu, R., Tu, Z., Xiang, H., Shao, W., Zhou, B., Ma, J.: CoBEVT: cooperative bird's eye view semantic segmentation with sparse transformers. arXiv preprint arXiv:2207.02202 (2022)
86. Xu, R., Xiang, H., Tu, Z., Xia, X., Yang, M.H., Ma, J.: V2X-ViT: vehicle-to-everything cooperative perception with vision transformer. arXiv preprint arXiv:2203.10638 (2022)
87. Xu, W., Xu, Y., Chang, T., Tu, Z.: Co-scale conv-attentional image transformers. In: Proceedings of the IEEE/CVF International Conference on Computer Vision, pp. 9981–9990 (2021)
88. Yang, J., et al.: Focal self-attention for local-global interactions in vision transformers. arXiv preprint arXiv:2107.00641 (2021)
89. Yang, Z., Dai, Z., Yang, Y., Carbonell, J., Salakhutdinov, R.R., Le, Q.V.: XLNet: generalized autoregressive pretraining for language understanding. In: Advances in Neural Information Processing Systems, vol. 32 (2019)

90. Yuan, L., et al.: Tokens-to-token VIT: training vision transformers from scratch on imagenet. In: Proceedings of the IEEE/CVF International Conference on Computer Vision, pp. 558–567 (2021)
91. Zhai, X., Kolesnikov, A., Neil, H., Beyer, L.: Scaling vision transformers. arXiv preprint arXiv:2106.04560 (2021)
92. Zhao, L., Zhang, Z., Chen, T., Metaxas, D., Zhang, H.: Improved transformer for high-resolution GANs. In: Advances in Neural Information Processing Systems, vol. 34 (2021)
93. Zhao, Z., Wu, Z., Zhuang, Y., Li, B., Jia, J.: Tracking objects as pixel-wise distributions. arXiv preprint arXiv:2207.05518 (2022)
94. Zhou, D., et al.: DeepViT: towards deeper vision transformer. arXiv preprint arXiv:2103.11886 (2021)

ScalableViT: Rethinking the Context-Oriented Generalization of Vision Transformer

Rui Yang[1], Hailong Ma[2(✉)], Jie Wu[2(✉)], Yansong Tang[1], Xuefeng Xiao[2], Min Zheng[2], and Xiu Li[1(✉)]

[1] Tsinghua Shenzhen International Graduate School, Tsinghua University, Beijing, China
r-yang20@mails.tsinghua.edu.cn, {tang.yansong,li.xiu}@sz.tsinghua.edu.cn
[2] ByteDance Inc., Beijing, China
{mahailong.1206,wujie.10,xiaoxuefeng.ailab,zhengmin.666}@bytedance.com

Abstract. The vanilla self-attention mechanism inherently relies on pre-defined and steadfast computational dimensions. Such inflexibility restricts it from possessing context-oriented generalization that can bring more contextual cues and global representations. To mitigate this issue, we propose a Scalable Self-Attention (SSA) mechanism that leverages two scaling factors to release dimensions of *query*, *key*, and *value* matrices while unbinding them with the input. This scalability fetches context-oriented generalization and enhances object sensitivity, which pushes the whole network into a more effective trade-off state between accuracy and cost. Furthermore, we propose an Interactive Window-based Self-Attention (IWSA), which establishes interaction between non-overlapping regions by re-merging independent *value* tokens and aggregating spatial information from adjacent windows. By stacking the SSA and IWSA alternately, the **Scalable Vision Transformer** (ScalableViT) achieves state-of-the-art performance on general-purpose vision tasks. For example, ScalableViT-S outperforms Twins-SVT-S by **1.4%** and Swin-T by **1.8%** on ImageNet-1K classification.

Keywords: Vision transformer · Self-attention mechanism · Classification · Detection · Semantic segmentation

1 Introduction

Convolutional Neural Networks (CNNs) dominated the computer vision field last few years, which attributes to their capacity in modeling realistic images from

---

R. Yang and H. Ma—Equal contribution.
R. Yang—This work was partly done while Rui Yang interned at ByteDance. Code: https://github.com/Yangr116/ScalableViT.

Supplementary Information The online version contains supplementary material available at https://doi.org/10.1007/978-3-031-20053-3_28.

Fig. 1. Visualization for feature maps in the Vision Transformer. We show the feature maps after the second Transformer blocks in Window-based Self-Attention (WSA) [5,24] and Scalable Self-Attention (SSA). The activation from WSA is discontinuous because of a limited mapping dimension. SSA ($r_c \equiv 1$) reduces computational overhead while retaining a global perception, ensuring its feature map is nearly continuous. $r_c \equiv 1$ denotes no scaling factors in the channel dimension. SSA introduces scale factors to spatial and channel dimensions, modeling a holistic representation and a context-oriented generalization.

a local to global perception. Although they have been widely applied in various vision tasks, there are still deficiencies in global visual perception. This global view is essential for downstream tasks, such as object detection and semantic segmentation. Recently, ViT [10] and its follow-ups [5,24,31,36] employed transformer encoders to address the image task and achieved comparable performance against their CNN counterparts because of the global receptive field. However, the global perception of the Transformer entails an unaffordable computation since self-attention (the primary operation of the Transformer) is quadratically computed on the whole sequence. To alleviate this overhead, typical Swin transformer [24] employed Window-based Self-Attention (WSA), which partitioned a feature map into many non-overlapped sub-regions and enabled it to process large-scale images with linear complexity. They also proposed a novel Shifted Window-based Self-Attention (SWSA) to compensate for losses of potential long-range dependency. Twins [5] combined the WSA with Global Sub-sampled Attention (GSA) for better performance.

To gain an insight into the WSA [5,24], we visualize feature maps after the second block. As shown in Fig. 1, features captured by the WSA are dispersed, and their responses incline to partial rather than object-oriented. It may attribute to an invariably fixed dimension that results in limited learning ability, thereby the final performance of the model being highly determined by the difficulty of input data. To alleviate this problem, we develop a novel self-attention mechanism, termed Scalable Self-Attention (SSA), which simultaneously introduces two scaling factors (r_n and r_c) to spatial and channel dimensions. Namely, SSA selectively applies these factors to *query*, *key*, and *value* matrices (Q, K, and V), ensuring the dimension is more elastic and no longer deeply bound by the input. On the one hand, SSA aggregates redundant tokens with similar semantic information to a more compact one via spatial scalability. Consequently, unnecessary intermediate multiplication operations are eliminated, and the computational complexity is reduced significantly. In the third row of Fig. 1, we can easily observe that spatial scalability can bring nearly contiguous visual modeling for objects, but some contextual cues are still lost. Hence, on the other hand, we expand the channel dimension to learn a more graphic representation. As depicted in the last row of Fig. 1, SSA successfully obtains complete object activation while maintaining context-oriented generalization via channel scalability. For instance, the contextual cues of the cat in the last column are represented in detail. Such scaling factors also restore the output dimension to align with the input, which makes the residual connection feasible.

Moreover, we propose an Interactive Window-based Self-Attention (IWSA) that consists of a regular WSA and a local interactive module (LIM). The IWSA establishes information connections by re-merging independent *value* tokens and aggregating spatial information from adjacent windows. Therefore, it no longer limits the self-attention to local windows, particularly non-overlapping windows. Such characteristic enhances the desired global receptive field and takes good advantage of the most significant superiority of the Transformer in a single layer. The effectiveness of LIM for WSA is validated in Table 5b. To achieve a more efficient backbone for general vision tasks, we adopt a hierarchical design [14,29] and propose a new Vision Transformer architecture, termed **ScalableViT**, which alternately arranges IWSA and SSA blocks in each stage.

Main contributions of our ScalableViT lie in two aspects:

- For the global self-attention, we propose SSA to supply context-oriented generalization in the vanilla self-attention block, which significantly reduces computational overhead without sacrificing contextual expressiveness.
- For the local self-attention, we design LIM to enhance the global perception ability of WSA.

Both SSA and IWSA can model long-range dependency in a single layer instead of stacking more self-attention layers; hence, the ScalableViT is more suitable for visual tasks. We employ ScalableViT on several vision tasks, including image-level classification on ImageNet [8], pixel-level object detection and instance segmentation on COCO [23], and semantic segmentation on ADE20K [47]. Extensive experiments demonstrate that the ScalableViT outperforms other state-of-the-art Vision Transformers with similar or less computational cost. For example, ScalableViT-S achieves **+1.4%** gains against Twins-SVT-S and **+1.8%** gains against Swin-T on ImageNet-1K classification.

2   Related Work

The Transformer architecture [33] has become a common template for natural language processing (NLP) tasks due to its solid global modeling capabilities and convenient parallelization ability. Inspired by this, many researchers tried to equip CNNs with the self-attention to modulate and augment outputs of convolutions [2,39,43]. DETR [3] employed the self-attention mechanism to model relations between objects for end-to-end detection. Others [1,18,37] combined self-attention with convolutions for full-image contextual information. Recently, the emergence of ViT [10], DeiT [31], and a series of follow-ups [5,9,24,35,38,44,45] proved the bright prospect of the Vision Transformer.

2.1   Vision Transformer

ViT [10] applied standard Transformer encoders to build a convolution-free image classifier by decomposing the image into a sequence of non-overlapping patches directly. Although it harvested promising results, a gap still existed between data-hungry Transformers and top-performing CNNs [30] when only training on the midsize ImageNet-1K [8] from scratch. In order to bridge this gap, DeiT [31] proposed a token-based distillation procedure and a data-efficient training strategy to optimize the Transformer effectively. Later, the follow-ups improved different aspects of the ViT, making them more suitable for vision tasks. T2T-ViT [45] optimized the tokenization by concatenating the neighboring tokens into one token. DynamicViT [28] pruned the tokens of less importance in a dynamic way for a better lightweight module. Cvt [38], CeiT [44] incorporated the convolution designs into the self-attention or the FFN to enhance the locality. CPVT [6] utilized the implicit position representation ability from convolutions (with zero padding) to encode the conditional position information for inputs with the arbitrary size. Then, hierarchical pyramid structures [5,9,24,35] were performed by progressively shrinking the number of tokens and replacing the class token with the average pooling. Thus, the Transformer, supported by multi-level features [21], can handle object detection and image segmentation tasks conveniently. In this paper, we develop a Vision Transformer, ScalableViT, which achieves a better accuracy and cost trade-off on visual tasks.

2.2   Local Self-attention

The computational complexity of the self-attention mechanism is a barrier that confines it in only downsampled feature maps or small images. Thus, several previous studies [15,16,18,26,34] proposed decomposing the global self-attention into much paralleled local self-attention to handle expensive computation burdens. However, this local self-attention limits the receptive field that is critical to dense predict tasks. [18,34] proposed generating the sparse attention map on a criss-cross path to realize global interaction. [16] captured the information from all the other positions via interlacing elements between different local windows. HaloNet [32] used the overlapped local windows to add the interactions between

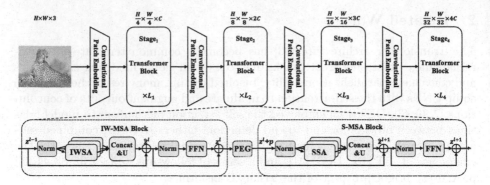

Fig. 2. The architecture of the ScalableViT. IW-MSA and S-MSA, the multi-head format of IWSA and SSA, are organized alternately in each stage. A PEG [6] is placed between two blocks in the front of each stage to encode implicit position information dynamically.

independent windows. After ViT [10] showed competitiveness, several follow-ups [5,17,24,46] applied the self-attention within non-overlapped local windows for linear computational complexity. To compensate for lost information, Swin Transformer [24] introduced a novel shifted window strategy, and Twins Transformer [5] baked sparse global attention [35] after WSA. We design the IWSA, which can aggregate information from a collection of discrete *value* tokens and enable local self-attention to model long-range dependency in a single block.

3   Method

In this section, we elaborately introduce the architecture of ScalableViT and mainly focus on SSA and IWSA mechanisms. SSA simultaneously introduces different scale factors into spatial and channel dimensions to maintain context-oriented generalization while reducing computational overhead. IWSA enhances the receptive field of local self-attention by aggregating information from a set of discrete *value* tokens. Both have linear computational complexity and can learn long-range dependency in a single layer.

3.1   Overall Architecture

The architecture of ScalableViT is illustrated in Fig. 2. For an input image with size $H \times W \times 3$, a convolutional patch embedding layer (7×7, stride 4) is used to obtain a collection of tokens ($\frac{H}{4} \times \frac{W}{4}$) and project the channel dimension to C. Then, these initial tokens will pass through four stages which contain a series of Transformer blocks. Between two adjacent stages, another convolutional patch embedding layer (3×3, stride 2) is utilized to merge tokens and

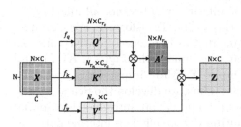

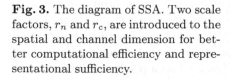

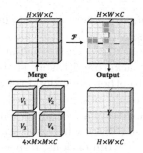

Fig. 3. The diagram of SSA. Two scale factors, r_n and r_c, are introduced to the spatial and channel dimension for better computational efficiency and representational sufficiency.

Fig. 4. The diagram of LIM. It merges a series of discrete V_i by the function $\mathcal{F}$, and outputs an interacted Y.

double the channel dimension. For the ith stage, there are $\frac{H}{2^{i+1}} \times \frac{W}{2^{i+1}}$ input tokens with $2^{i-1}C$ channels and L_i Transformer blocks. As a result, the quantity of tokens will eventually be reduced to $\frac{H}{32} \times \frac{W}{32}$. This architecture enables us to obtain a hierarchical representation similar to the typical backbones based on CNNs [14,29]. This merit allows ScalableViT to naturally migrate to various vision tasks, such as object detection and segmentation. In each stage, we devise an alternate arrangement of IW-MSA and S-MSA blocks to organize the topological structure. In the front of each stage, a position encoding generator (PEG) [6] is inserted between two Transformer blocks to generate position embedding dynamically.

3.2 Scalable Self-attention

Self-attention is a critical mechanism in the Transformer, and the vanilla self-attention can be calculated as:

$$Z = A(X)V(X) = Softmax(\frac{Q(X)K(X)^T}{\sqrt{d_k}})V(X), \tag{1}$$

where $A(X)$ is the attention matrix of the input X; $Q(X), K(X), V(X) \in \mathbb{R}^{N \times C}$ are the *query*, *key*, and *value* matrices; d_k is the channel dimension of *query* or *key* matrix; N is the number of tokens in each matrix, and C is the channel dimension. The original self-attention mechanism obtains a global receptive field by establishing associations between all input tokens, which is a vital advantage of the Transformer over CNNs. However, it has quadratic computational overhead with N, leading to inefficiency in the intermediate multiplication operations.

Generally, there is much homologous information in natural images, but vanilla self-attention still calculates their similarity. Notably, not all information is necessary to calculate self-attention in the Vision Transformer. For example, similar background tokens should be aggregated as one representative token to attend to other foreground tokens. Namely, the dimension of $Q(X)$, $K(X)$, and $V(X)$ should not be bounded with the input X. More importantly, the fixed dimension results in limited learning ability. Thus, we develop the Scalable Self-Attention (SSA), where two scaling factors (r_n and r_c) are introduced to spatial and channel dimensions, respectively, resulting a more efficient intermediate calculation than the vanilla one. As illustrated in Fig. 3, the spatial dimension N and channel dimension C are selectively scaled to $N \times r_n$ and $C \times r_c$, respectively, by three transformation functions $f_q(\cdot)$, $f_k(\cdot)$, and $f_v(\cdot)$. These scaling factors can also restore the output dimension to align with the input, making the subsequent FFN layers and residual connections feasible. As a result, the intermediate dimension is more elastic and no longer deeply bound with the input X. The model can reap context-oriented generalization while dwindling computational overhead significantly. SSA can be naturally written as:

$$Z' = A'(X)V'(X) = Softmax(\frac{Q'(X)K'(X)^T}{\sqrt{d'_k}})V'(X), \tag{2}$$

$$Q'(X) = f_q(X), \quad K'(X) = f_k(X), \quad V'(X) = f_v(V), \tag{3}$$

where $Q'(X) \in \mathbb{R}^{N \times Cr_c}, K'(X) \in \mathbb{R}^{Nr_n \times Cr_c}, V'(X) \in \mathbb{R}^{Nr_n \times C}$ are the scaled *query*, *key* and *value* matrices of the input $X \in \mathbb{R}^{H \times W \times C}$; $A'(X) \in \mathbb{R}^{N \times Nr_n}$ is the scaled attention matrix; Z' is the weighted sum of $V'(X)$. The transformation $f_q(\cdot)$ scales the channel dimension of *query* from C to C_{r_c}. $f_k(\cdot)$ is the scaling function for *key*, which scales the spatial dimension from N to N_{r_n} while scaling the channel dimension from C to C_{r_c}. $f_v(\cdot)$ is the scaling function for *value*, which scales the spatial dimension from N to N_{r_n}. Hence, some unnecessary intermediate multiplication is decreased significantly. The computation complexity of the proposed SSA is equal to $\mathcal{O}(NN_{r_n}C + NN_{r_n}C_{r_c})$ that is linear with the input size ($N = H \times W$). For utility and briefness, three transformations are operated by convolutions and cooperates with linear projections to get the scaled *query*, *key*, and *value* matrices. The efficient SSA does not change the size of Z and can be expanded to the Scalable Multi-Head Self-Attention (S-MSA) easily.

More importantly, the introduced spatial and channel scalability can bring context-oriented generalization (see Fig. 1). If only spatial scalability is introduced ($r_c \equiv 1$), there would realize nearly contiguous visual modeling for objects but a lack of critical graphic representation. When further introducing channel scalability, SSA can successfully maintain contextual cues and obtain complete object activation, which is essential in visual tasks. The values of these two scaling factors vary with model configurations and different network stages. As the network gradually deepens, the quantity of tokens shrinks, and the degree of redundancy is also dropped. Thus, r_n is largen with the stage depth. Similarly, the channel dimension does not always mismatch with spatial dimension in the self-attention operation. Thus, we set $r_c \geq 1$ in ScalableViT-S and ScalableViT-B. Because of a too-large channel dimension, we set $r_c \leq 1$ in ScalableViT-L. Details about two scale factors are displayed in Table 1.

3.3   Interactive Window-Based Self-attention

Besides the efficient self-attention [35], earlier researches have developed the local self-attention [5,24] to avoid the quadratic computational complexity with the number of tokens. For example, WSA divides an image $(H \times W \times C)$ into multiple partial windows which contains $M \times M$ tokens. Then, the self-attention would be calculated in every isolated window and produce a set of discrete outputs $\{Z_n\}_{n=1}^{\frac{H}{M} \times \frac{W}{M}}$, where Z_n can be calculated as:

$$Z_n = A_n(X_n)V_n(X_n) = Softmax(\frac{Q_n(X_n)K_n(X_n)^T}{\sqrt{d_k}})V_n(X_n), \qquad (4)$$

in which $X_n \in \Omega_n^{M \times M \times C}$ is the partial window field; $Q_n(X_n), K_n(X_n), V_n(X_n) \in \mathbb{R}^{M^2 \times C}$ are the *query*, *key*, and *value* matrices of the discrete window X_n, respectively. d_k is equal to the channel dimension of discrete *query/key* tokens. Finally, a collection of discrete $\{Z_n\}_{n=1}^{\frac{H}{M} \times \frac{W}{M}}$ is merged back to $Z \in \mathbb{R}^{N \times C}$. Thus, for an image, the computational complexity of attention would be reduced from $\mathcal{O}(2H^2W^2C)$ to $\mathcal{O}(2M^2HWC)$. The WSA can be suitable for various vision tasks that require high-resolution input due to its linear complexity.

However, such computationally efficient WSA yields a feature map with an integrated shape but isolated activation (see Fig. 1), which ascribed to the missed global receptive field in a single layer. This is far from the initial aims of self-attention. To alleviate above problem, we propose Interactive Window-based Self-Attention (IWSA) that incorporates a local interactive module (LIM) into WSA, as illustrated in Fig. 4. After getting a collection of discrete *values* $\{V_n(X_n)\}_{n=1}^{\frac{H}{M} \times \frac{W}{M}}$, the LIM reshapes them into $M \times M \times C$ and merges them into a shape-integrated *value* map $V \in \mathbb{R}^{H \times W \times C}$. Subsequently, a function $\mathcal{F}(x)$ is employed to establish marriages and connections between adjacent $V_n(X_n)$s. As a result, the output $Y = \mathcal{F}(V)$ is an integrated feature map with global information. Finally, this feature map is added on Z as the final output Z'. Without loss of generality, the IWSA is calculated as:

$$Z' = Z + \mathcal{F}(V), \qquad (5)$$

where $Z \in \mathbb{R}^{N \times C}$ is merged by a set of $\{Z_n\}_{n=1}^{\frac{H}{M} \times \frac{W}{M}}$. In order to be implemented friendly, a depth-wise convolution with zero padding is employed to take the place of function $\mathcal{F}(x)$. If the kernel size of this depth-wise convolution is $k \times k$ (set to 3 by default), the computational cost from the LIM is negligible in practice. Additionally, [19] demonstrated that the convolution with zero padding could

Table 1. Detailed configurations of ScalableViT series. r_c and r_n are scale factors for the channel and the spatial dimensions, respectively. '#Blocks' and '#Heads' refer to the number of blocks ($[L_1, L_2, L_3, L_4]$) and heads in four stages, respectively. '#Channels' refers to the channel dimension of the first stage.

Models	#Channels	#Blocks	#Heads	r_c	r_n
ScalableViT-S	64	[2,2,20,2]	[2,4,8,16]	[1.25,1.25,1.25,1.0]	$[\frac{1}{64}, \frac{1}{16}, \frac{1}{4}, 1]$
ScalableViT-B	96	[2,2,14,6]	[3,6,12,24]	[2.0,1.25,1.25,1.0]	$[\frac{1}{64}, \frac{1}{16}, \frac{1}{4}, 1]$
ScalableViT-L	128	[2,6,12,4]	[4,8,16,32]	[0.25,0.5,1.0,1.0]	$[\frac{1}{64}, \frac{1}{16}, \frac{1}{4}, 1]$

implicitly encode position information through experiments. Thus, IWSA allows self-attention to benefit from the translation invariance. Furthermore, IWSA can be easily expanded to Interactive Window-based Multi-head Self-Attention (IW-MSA) format easily if calculated in different heads.

CoaT [42] also introduced a depth-wise convolution into self-attention. However, they only considered the convolution as a positional encoding method and inserted it deeply into the calculation. If this convolution is expanded into the WSA, it would be limited in the discrete $V_n(X_n)$, which is denoted as local enhanced module (LEM). Differently, we regard our LIM as a matchmaker, which is applied on the spliced *value* map V and parallels with self-attention. By making the sufficient ablation study in Sect. 4.4, we demonstrate that LIM is capable of delivering stable improvements, especially for downstream tasks.

3.4 Position Encoding

Besides the position information introduced by LIM, we utilize the positional encoding generator (PEG) [6], composed of a convolution layer with fixed weights, to acquire implicit positional information. As illustrated in Fig. 2, it is plugged between two consecutive Transformer blocks, with only one in the front of each stage. After the PEG, input tokens are sent to subsequent blocks where position bias could enable the Transformer to realize the input permutation.

3.5 Architecture Variants

In order to fairly compare with other models under similar computation complexity, we set three models: ScalableViT-S, ScalableViT-B, and ScalableViT-L. The detailed configurations are provided in Table 1, where r_c and r_n denote expansion or reduction factors for channel and spatial dimensions, respectively, as described in Sect. 3.2. Due to the varying representational capability, we set different r_c for three models. Additionally, the number of blocks, channels, and heads varies with the computational cost.

4   Experiments

In the following, we compare the proposed model with other state-of-the-art works on ImageNet-1K [8], COCO [23], and ADE20K [47]. Then, we conduct ablation studies on the upgraded parts to verify their effectiveness.

4.1   Image Classification on ImageNet-1K

Settings. Image classification experiments are conducted on the ImageNet-1K [8] dataset. All settings mainly follow DeiT [31]. During training, we apply data augmentation and regularization strategies in [31]. We employ the AdamW optimizer [25] to train models for 300 epochs from scratch. The learning rate is set to 0.001 initially and varies with the cosine scheduler. The global batchsize is set to 1024 on 8 V100 GPUs. During testing on the validation set, the shorter side of an input image is first resized to 256, and a center crop of 224×224 is used to evaluate the classification accuracy.

Result. Classification results on ImageNet-1K are reported in Table 2, where all models are divided into small (around 4G), base (around 9G), and large (around 15G) levels according to computation complexity (FLOPs). ScalableViT-S with a two-layer head outperforms comparable models (1.4% better than Twins-SVT-S, and 1.8% better than Swin-T). Moreover, it can even approach or exceed other base models. For the base level, ScalableViT-B surpasses Twins-SVT-B by 0.9% and SWin-S by 1.1% with similar FLOPs. ScalableViT-L also achieves a prominent accuracy-cost trade-off. Additionally, our ScalableViT outperforms the EfficientNet by 0.2%, 0.5%, and 0.4% under three magnitude receptively.

4.2   Object Detection on COCO

Settings. Object detection experiments are conducted on COCO 2017 [23] dataset. We verify the model effectiveness on RetinaNet [22] and Mask R-CNN [13] detection frameworks using the MMDetection [4]. Before training, we initialize the backbone with the weight pre-trained on ImageNet-1K, FPN with Xavier [11] scheme, and other new layers with Normal scheme ($std = 0.01$). All models utilize the same settings as [5]: AdamW [25] optimizer, $1\times$ (12 epochs), and $3\times$ (36 epochs) schedules with a global batchsize of 16 on 8 GPUs. For the $1\times$ schedule, the short side of images is resized to 800 pixels, and the long side is never more than 1333 pixels. The learning rate is declined at the 8th and 11th epoch with a decay rate of 0.1. For the $3\times$ schedule, we adopt the multi-scale training, which randomly resizes the short side of images within the range of [480, 800] while keeping the longer side at most 1333. The learning rate is declined at the 27th and 33rd with a decay rate of 0.1.

Result. We present results of RetinaNet and Mask R-CNN frameworks in Table 3, where AP^b and AP^m refer to box mAP and mask mAP, respectively. For object detection with RetinaNet, ScalableViT performs a notable advantage against its CNN and Transformer counterparts. With the $1\times$ schedule, our

Table 2. Comparison with different state-of-the-art backbones on ImageNet-1K classification. Except for EfficientNet, other models are trained and evaluated on 224 × 224 input size. Top-1 refers to top-1 accuracy (%).

Method	#Param.	FLOPs	Top-1	Method	#Param.	FLOPs	Top-1
ConvNet				Transformer			
RegNetY-4G [27]	21M	4.0G	80.0	T2T-ViT-19 [45]	39M	8.9G	81.9
RegNetY-8G [27]	39M	8.0G	81.7	CoaT(S) [42]	22M	12.6G	82.1
RegNetY-16G [27]	84M	16.0G	82.9	CoaT-Lite(M) [42]	45M	9.8G	83.6
EfficientNet-B4 [30]	19M	4.2G	82.9	PVT-Medium [35]	44M	6.7G	81.2
EfficientNet-B5 [30]	30M	9.9G	83.6	Swin-S [24]	50M	8.7G	83.0
EfficientNet-B6 [30]	43M	19.0G	84.0	CvT-21 [38]	32M	7.1G	82.5
Transformer				Twins-SVT-B [5]	56M	8.6G	83.2
DeiT-Small/16 [31]	22M	4.6G	79.9	CrossFormer-B [36]	52M	9.2G	83.4
T2T-ViT-14 [45]	22M	5.2G	81.5	**ScalableViT-B(ours)**	81M	8.6G	**84.1**
TNT-S [12]	24M	5.2G	81.3	Deit-Base/16 [31]	86M	17.6G	81.8
CoaT-Lite(S) [42]	20M	4.0G	81.9	T2T-ViT-24 [45]	64M	14.1G	82.3
PVT-Small [35]	25M	3.8G	79.8	TNT-B [12]	66M	14.1G	82.8
Swin-T [24]	29M	4.5G	81.3	PVT-Large [35]	61M	9.8G	81.7
CvT-13 [38]	20M	4.5G	81.6	Swin-B [24]	88M	15.4G	83.3
Twins-SVT-S [5]	24M	2.9G	81.7	Twins-SVT-L [5]	99M	15.1G	83.7
CrossFormer-S [36]	31M	4.9G	82.5	CrossFormer-L [36]	92M	16.1G	84.0
ScalableViT-S(ours)	32M	4.2G	**83.1**	**ScalableViT-L(ours)**	104M	14.7G	**84.4**

ScalableViT brings 7.3–8.9 AP^b against ResNet at comparable settings. Compared with the popular Swin and Twins Transformers, our ScalableViT performs 3.5–3.7 AP^b and 0.5–2.2 AP^b improvements, respectively. With the 3× schedule, our ScalableViT still achieves competitive performance. For Mask R-CNN, our ScalableViT-S outperforms ResNet-50 by 7.8 AP^b and 7.3 AP^m with the 1× schedule. ScalableViT-S achieves 3.6 AP^b and 2.6 AP^m gains than Swin-T. With the 3× schedule, ScalableViT-S brings 7.7 AP^b and 6.5 AP^m against ResNet-50. Similarly, it also surpasses Swin-T and Twins-SVT-S Transformers. Under base level, there is also a similar improvement, demonstrating its stronger context-oriented generalization. Additionally, Fig. 5 depicts some qualitative object detection and instance segmentation results from ScalableViT-S-based RetinaNet and Mask R-CNN, which show that contextual representation from the backbone enables the model to detect objects better.

4.3 Semantic Segmentation on ADE20K

Settings. Semantic segmentation experiments are conducted on the challenging ADE20K [47] dataset. We use the typical Semantic FPN [20] and the UperNet [40] as segmentation frameworks to evaluate our models. We use the MMSegmentation [7] to implement all related experiments, and the settings follow [5,24,35]. For the Semantic FPN, we train 80K iterations with a batch size 16 on 4 GPUs. For the UperNet, we train 160K iterations with a batch size 16 on 8 GPUs. During training, we first resize the short side of input images to 512 pixels, and the long side is never more than 2048 pixels, then they are

Table 3. Results on COCO object detection using the RetinaNet [22] and Mask R-CNN [13] framework. 1× refers to 12 epochs, and 3× refers to 36 epochs. MS means multi-scale training. AP^b and AP^m denotes box mAP and mask mAP, respectively. FLOPs are measured at resolution 800×1280.

Backbone	#Param (M)	FLOPs (G)	RetinaNet 1×						RetinaNet 3× + MS					
			AP^b	AP^b_{50}	AP^b_{75}	AP^b_S	AP^b_M	AP^b_L	AP^b	AP^b_{50}	AP^b_{75}	AP^b_S	AP^b_M	AP^b_L
ResNet50 [14]	38	239	36.3	55.3	38.6	19.3	40.0	48.8	39.0	58.4	41.8	22.4	42.8	51.6
PVT-Small [35]	34	226	40.4	61.3	43.0	25.0	42.9	55.7	42.2	62.7	45.0	26.2	45.2	57.2
Swin-T [24]	39	245	41.5	62.1	44.2	25.1	44.9	55.5	43.9	64.8	47.1	28.4	47.2	57.8
Twins-SVT-S [5]	34	210	43.0	64.2	46.3	28.0	46.4	57.5	45.6	67.1	48.6	29.8	49.3	60.0
CrossFormer-S [36]	41	272	44.4	65.8	47.4	28.2	48.4	59.4	—	—	—	—	—	—
ScalableViT-S(ours)	36	238	**45.2**	**66.5**	**48.4**	**29.2**	**49.1**	**60.3**	**47.8**	**69.2**	**51.2**	**31.4**	**51.5**	**63.4**
ResNet101 [14]	58	315	38.5	57.8	41.2	21.4	42.6	51.1	40.9	60.1	44.0	23.7	45.0	53.8
PVT-Medium [35]	54	283	41.9	63.1	44.3	25.0	44.9	57.6	43.2	63.8	46.1	27.3	46.3	58.9
Swin-T [24]	60	335	44.5	65.7	47.5	27.4	48.0	59.9	46.3	67.4	49.8	31.1	50.3	60.9
Twins-SVT-B [5]	67	326	45.3	66.7	48.1	28.5	48.9	60.6	46.9	68.0	50.2	31.7	50.3	61.8
CrossFormer-B [36]	62	389	**46.2**	**67.8**	**49.5**	**30.1**	**49.9**	**61.8**	—	—	—	—	—	—
ScalableViT-B(ours)	85	330	45.8	67.3	49.2	29.9	49.5	61.0	**48.0**	**69.3**	**51.4**	**32.8**	**51.6**	**62.4**

Backbone	#Param. (M)	FLOPs (G)	Mask R-CNN 1×						Mask R-CNN 3× + MS					
			AP^b	AP^b_{50}	AP^b_{75}	AP^m	AP^m_{50}	AP^m_{75}	AP^b	AP^b_{50}	AP^b_{75}	AP^m	AP^m_{50}	AP^m_{75}
ResNet50 [14]	44	260	38.0	58.6	41.4	34.4	55.1	36.7	41.0	61.7	44.9	37.1	58.4	40.1
PVT-Small [35]	44	245	40.4	62.9	43.8	37.8	60.1	40.3	43.0	65.3	46.9	39.9	62.5	42.8
Swin-T [24]	48	264	42.2	64.4	46.2	39.1	64.6	42.0	46.0	68.2	50.2	41.6	65.1	44.8
Twins-SVT-S [5]	44	228	43.4	66.0	47.3	40.3	63.2	43.4	46.8	69.2	51.2	42.6	66.3	45.8
CoaT-Lite(S) [42]	40	—	45.2	—	—	40.7	—	—	45.7	—	—	41.1	—	—
CrossFormer-S [36]	50	301	45.4	**68.0**	49.7	41.4	**64.8**	44.6	—	—	—	—	—	—
ScalableViT-S(ours)	46	256	**45.8**	67.6	**50.0**	**41.7**	64.7	**44.8**	**48.7**	**70.1**	**53.6**	**43.6**	**67.2**	**47.2**
ResNet101 [14]	63	336	40.4	61.1	44.2	36.4	57.7	38.8	42.8	63.2	47.1	38.5	60.1	41.3
PVT-Medium [35]	64	302	42.0	64.4	45.6	39.0	61.6	42.1	44.2	66.0	48.2	40.5	63.1	43.5
Swin-S [24]	69	354	44.8	66.6	48.9	40.9	63.4	44.2	48.5	70.2	53.5	43.3	67.3	46.6
Twins-SVT-B [5]	76	340	45.2	67.6	49.3	41.5	64.5	44.8	48.0	69.5	52.7	43.0	66.8	46.6
CoaT(S) [42]	42	—	46.5	—	—	41.8	—	—	**49.0**	—	—	43.7	—	—
CrossFormer-B [36]	72	408	**47.2**	**69.9**	**51.8**	**42.7**	**66.6**	**46.2**	—	—	—	—	—	—
ScalableViT-B(ours)	95	349	46.8	68.7	51.5	42.5	65.8	45.9	**49.0**	**70.3**	**53.6**	43.8	**67.4**	**47.5**

Fig. 5. Qualitative results based on ScalableViT-S. (a), (b) and (c) are yielded by RetinaNet [22], Mask R-CNN [13], and Semantic FPN [20], respectively.

Table 4. Results on ADE20K segmentation using the Semantic FPN [20] and Uper-Net [40] framework. FLOPs are measured at resolution 512×2048. MS refers to the test time augmentation, including flip and multi-scale test.

Backbone	Semantic FPN 80k			UperNet 160k		
	#Param.	FLOPs	mIoU(%)	#Param.	FLOPs	mIoU/MS mIoU(%)
ResNet50 [14]	29M	183G	36.7	—	—	—/—
PVT-Small [35]	28M	161G	39.8	—	—	—/—
Swin-T [24]	32M	182G	41.5	60M	945G	44.5/45.8
Twins-SVT-S [5]	28M	144G	43.2	54M	901G	46.2/47.1
CrossFormer-S [36]	34M	221G	**46.0**	62M	980G	47.6/48.4
ScalableViT-S(ours)	30M	174G	44.9	57M	931G	**48.5/49.4**
ResNet101 [14]	48M	260G	38.8	86M	1092G	—/44.9
PVT-Medium [35]	48M	219G	41.6	—	—	—/—
Swin-S [24]	53M	274G	45.2	81M	1038G	47.6/49.5
Twins-SVT-B [5]	60M	261G	45.3	89M	1020G	47.7/48.9
CrossFormer-B [36]	56M	331G	47.7	84M	1090G	**49.7/50.6**
ScalableViT-B(ours)	79M	270G	**48.4**	107M	1029G	49.5/50.4
ResNeXt101-64×4d [41]	86M	—	40.2	—	—	—/—
PVT-Large [35]	65M	283G	42.1	—	—	—/—
Swin-B [24]	91M	422G	46.0	121M	1188G	48.1/49.7
Twins-SVT-L [5]	104M	404G	46.7	133M	1164G	48.8/50.2
CrossFormer-L [36]	95M	497G	48.7	126M	1258G	**50.4/51.4**
ScalableViT-L(ours)	105M	402G	**49.4**	135M	1162G	49.8/50.7

randomly cropped to 512×512. During testing, we resize input images as the training phase but without cropping. We also use the test time augmentation for UperNet, including multi-scale test ($[0.5, 0.75, 1.0, 1.25, 1.5, 1.75] \times$ resolution) and flip.

Result. Table 4 reports the segmentation results. For the Semantic FPN, our ScalableViT outperforms Swin Transformer by +3.4 mIoU, +3.2 mIoU, and +3.4 mIoU, respectively, under three FLOPs levels. Compared with CrossFormer-S [36], ScalableViT-S performs a modest mIoU but has a fewer computation. When equipped into the UperNet, the ScalableViT achieves +4 mIoU, +1.9 mIoU, and +1.6 mIoU gains than Swin Transformer under different model sizes. The same competitive results are achieved when test time augmentation is adopted. In addition, ScalableViT-S outperforms CrossFormer-S by +0.9 mIoU and achieves comparable performance on the base and large size. Figure 5(c) shows some qualitative results from ScalableViT-S-based Semantic FPN on validation split. These results indicate that the ScalableViT can obtain high-quality semantic segmentation results under contextual-oriented generalization.

4.4 Ablation Study

Analysis for Self-attention Mechanisms. Our ScalableViT contains two important designs: SSA and IWSA. We ablate their benefits in Table 5a. Firstly, all attention modules in ScalableViT-S are replaced with the regular window-based self-attention (WSA). Although WSA achieves 82.4% top-1 accuracy, the

Table 5. Ablation study for different self-attention mechanisms and LIM using ScalableViT-S. Top-1 refers to top-1 accuracy (%) on ImageNet-1K. Semantic segmentation results are yielded from Semantic FPN on ADE20K.

(a) Analysis for different self-attention mechanisms.

Method	#Param.	FLOPs	Top-1	mIoU(%)
WSA	30M	4.3G	82.4	38.9
IWSA	30M	4.3G	82.9	43.5
SSA	34M	4.1G	82.9	44.4
SSA ($r_c \equiv 1$)	32M	3.9G	82.6	43.7
SWSA & SSA	32M	4.2G	82.9	—
SSA & IWSA	32M	4.2G	83.0	—
IWSA & SSA	32M	4.2G	**83.1**	44.9

(b) Analysis for local interactive module and positional encoding generator.

PEG	LEM	LIM	#Param.	FLOPs	Top-1	mIoU(%)
			32M	4.2G	82.7	41.7
✓			32M	4.2G	82.9	43.2
	✓		32M	4.2G	82.8	—
		✓	32M	4.2G	**83.0**	**43.7**
✓	✓		32M	4.2G	83.0	—
✓		✓	32M	4.2G	**83.1**	**44.9**

Table 6. Comparison speed with state-of-the-art models.

Method	#Param.	FLOPs	Top-1	throughput(img/s)
Swin-T [24]	29M	4.5G	81.3	975.0
Swin-S [24]	50M	8.7G	83.0	589.2
CrossFormer-S [36]	31M	4.9G	82.5	859.0
ScalableViT-S(**ours**)	32M	4.2G	**83.1**	832.9

dispersed feature (see Fig. 1) hinders it from better performance on the downstream visual task. Then, we substituted all attention modules with our IWSA and SSA, respectively. Both of them outperform WSA 0.4% top-1 accuracy. More importantly, they bring +4.6 mIoU and +5.5 mIoU improvements on ADE20K because of the ability modeling long-range dependency. With spatial scalability ($r_c \equiv 1$), SSA only achieve 82.6% top-1 accuracy and 43.7 mIoU. Thus, the context-oriented generalization from the cooperation between spatial and channel scalability plays a critical role in visual tasks. Additionally, we examine the topology by rearranging IWSA and SSA. Results demonstrate that prioritizing IWSA followed by SSA performs best. We also compare IWSA with SWSA [24] in ScalableViT, where our IWSA is more appropriate than SWSA.

Speed Analysis. Following [24], we measure throughput of the ScalableViT-S on single 3090 GPU with a batch size of 64 in Table 6. ScalableViT-S achieves 859.0 img/s, which perform better speed-accuracy trade-offs than Swin-S.

Effectiveness of Local Interactive Module. We examine the effectiveness of LIM in Table 5b. The ScalableViT-S without position encoding generator (PEG), locally enhanced module (LEM), or LIM is regarded as a baseline model which achieves 82.7% top-1 accuracy on ImageNet. Then, three modules are inserted and yield +0.2%, +0.1%, and +0.3% gains than baseline, respectively. It demonstrates that the reasonable convolution can help the model perform better. Due to the window connection, LIM outperforms LEM by +0.2% top-1 accuracy, proving the significance of the information interaction. Additionally, we combine PEG with LEM or LIM, whose results are better than only using a single module. Note that the combination of PEG and LIM outperforms the

PEG and LEM under the same overhead. LIM aims to bring global perception into the single Transformer block. Its effectiveness is greatly demonstrated on downstream tasks. Using Semantic FPN with ScalableViT-S on ADE20K, LIM obtains +2.0 mIoU, and associating PEG with LIM brings +3.2 mIoU gains.

5 Conclusion

In this paper, we have presented a Vision Transformer backbone named ScalableViT, composed of two highly effective self-attention mechanisms (SSA and IWSA). SSA employs two cooperated scaling factors in spatial and channel dimensions for context-oriented generalization, which maintains more contextual cues and learns graphic representations. IWSA develops a local interactive module to establish information connections between independent windows. Both of them owns the capability to model long-range dependency in a single layer. The proposed ScalableViT alternately stakes these two self-attention modules. It pushes the whole framework into a more effective trade-off state and achieves state-of-the-art performance on various vision tasks.

Acknowledgements. This work was supported by the National Key R&D Program of China 505 (Grant No. 2020AAA0108303), the National Natural Science Foundation of China (Grant No. 41876098) and the Shenzhen Science and Technology Project (Grant No. JCYJ20200109143041798).

References

1. Bello, I., Zoph, B., Le, Q., Vaswani, A., Shlens, J.: Attention augmented convolutional networks. In: ICCV, pp. 3285–3294. IEEE (2019)
2. Cao, Y., Xu, J., Lin, S., Wei, F., Hu, H.: GCNet: non-local networks meet squeeze-excitation networks and beyond. In: ICCV, pp. 1971–1980 (2019)
3. Carion, N., Massa, F., Synnaeve, G., Usunier, N., Kirillov, A., Zagoruyko, S.: End-to-end object detection with transformers. In: Vedaldi, A., Bischof, H., Brox, T., Frahm, J.-M. (eds.) ECCV 2020. LNCS, vol. 12346, pp. 213–229. Springer, Cham (2020). https://doi.org/10.1007/978-3-030-58452-8_13
4. Chen, K., et al.: MMDetection: open MMLab detection toolbox and benchmark. arXiv preprint arXiv:1906.07155 (2019)
5. Chu, X., et al.: Twins: revisiting the design of spatial attention in vision transformers. arXiv preprint arXiv:2104.13840 (2021)
6. Chu, X., et al.: Conditional positional encodings for vision transformers. arXiv preprint arXiv:2102.10882 (2021)
7. Contributors, M.: MMSegmentation: OpenMMLab semantic segmentation toolbox and benchmark (2020). https://github.com/open-mmlab/mmsegmentation
8. Deng, J., Dong, W., Socher, R., Li, L., Li, K., Fei-Fei, L.: Imagenet: a large-scale hierarchical image database. In: CVPR, pp. 248–255 (2009)
9. Dong, X., et al.: CSWin transformer: a general vision transformer backbone with cross-shaped windows. arXiv preprint arXiv:2107.00652 (2021)
10. Dosovitskiy, A., et al.: An image is worth 16x16 words: transformers for image recognition at scale. In: ICLR (2021)

11. Glorot, X., Bengio, Y.: Understanding the difficulty of training deep feedforward neural networks. In: Teh, Y.W., Titterington, D.M. (eds.) Proceedings of the Thirteenth International Conference on Artificial Intelligence and Statistics, vol. 9, pp. 249–256 (2010)

12. Han, K., Xiao, A., Wu, E., Guo, J., Xu, C., Wang, Y.: Transformer in transformer. arXiv preprint arXiv:2103.00112 (2021)

13. He, K., Gkioxari, G., Dollár, P., Girshick, R.B.: Mask R-CNN. IEEE TPAMI **42**(2), 386–397 (2020)

14. He, K., Zhang, X., Ren, S., Sun, J.: Deep residual learning for image recognition. In: CVPR, pp. 770–778. IEEE Computer Society (2016)

15. Hu, H., Zhang, Z., Xie, Z., Lin, S.: Local relation networks for image recognition. In: ICCV, pp. 3463–3472 (2019)

16. Huang, L., Yuan, Y., Guo, J., Zhang, C., Chen, X., Wang, J.: Interlaced sparse self-attention for semantic segmentation. arXiv preprint arXiv:1907.12273 (2019)

17. Huang, Z., Ben, Y., Luo, G., Cheng, P., Yu, G., Fu, B.: Shuffle transformer: rethinking spatial shuffle for vision transformer. arXiv preprint arXiv:2106.03650 (2021)

18. Huang, Z., Wang, X., Huang, L., Huang, C., Wei, Y., Liu, W.: CCNet: criss-cross attention for semantic segmentation. In: ICCV, pp. 603–612 (2019)

19. Islam, M.A., Jia, S., Bruce, N.D.B.: How much position information do convolutional neural networks encode? In: ICLR (2020)

20. Kirillov, A., Girshick, R.B., He, K., Dollár, P.: Panoptic feature pyramid networks. In: CVPR, pp. 6399–6408 (2019)

21. Lin, T., Dollár, P., Girshick, R.B., He, K., Hariharan, B., Belongie, S.J.: Feature pyramid networks for object detection. In: CVPR, pp. 936–944 (2017)

22. Lin, T., Goyal, P., Girshick, R.B., He, K., Dollár, P.: Focal loss for dense object detection. IEEE TPAMI **42**(2), 318–327 (2020)

23. Lin, T.-Y., et al.: Microsoft COCO: common objects in context. In: Fleet, D., Pajdla, T., Schiele, B., Tuytelaars, T. (eds.) ECCV 2014. LNCS, vol. 8693, pp. 740–755. Springer, Cham (2014). https://doi.org/10.1007/978-3-319-10602-1_48

24. Liu, Z., et al.: Swin transformer: hierarchical vision transformer using shifted windows. arXiv preprint arXiv:2103.14030 (2021)

25. Loshchilov, I., Hutter, F.: Decoupled weight decay regularization. In: ICLR (2019)

26. Parmar, N., Ramachandran, P., Vaswani, A., Bello, I., Levskaya, A., Shlens, J.: Stand-alone self-attention in vision models. In: NeurIPS, pp. 68–80 (2019)

27. Radosavovic, I., Kosaraju, R.P., Girshick, R.B., He, K., Dollár, P.: Designing network design spaces. In: CVPR, pp. 10425–10433 (2020)

28. Rao, Y., Zhao, W., Liu, B., Lu, J., Zhou, J., Hsieh, C.J.: Dynamicvit: efficient vision transformers with dynamic token sparsification. arXiv preprint arXiv:2106.02034 (2021)

29. Simonyan, K., Zisserman, A.: Very deep convolutional networks for large-scale image recognition. In: Bengio, Y., LeCun, Y. (eds.) ICLR (2015)

30. Tan, M., Le, Q.V.: Efficientnet: rethinking model scaling for convolutional neural networks. In: Chaudhuri, K., Salakhutdinov, R. (eds.) Proceedings of the 36th International Conference on Machine Learning, ICML, vol. 97, pp. 6105–6114 (2019)

31. Touvron, H., Cord, M., Douze, M., Massa, F., Sablayrolles, A., Jégou, H.: Training data-efficient image transformers & distillation through attention. In: Proceedings of the 38th International Conference on Machine Learning, ICML, vol. 139, pp. 10347–10357 (2021)

32. Vaswani, A., Ramachandran, P., Srinivas, A., Parmar, N., Hechtman, B.A., Shlens, J.: Scaling local self-attention for parameter efficient visual backbones. In: CVPR, pp. 12894–12904 (2021)
33. Vaswani, A., et al.: Attention is all you need. In: NeurIPS, pp. 5998–6008 (2017)
34. Wang, H., Zhu, Y., Green, B., Adam, H., Yuille, A., Chen, L.-C.: Axial-DeepLab: stand-alone axial-attention for panoptic segmentation. In: Vedaldi, A., Bischof, H., Brox, T., Frahm, J.-M. (eds.) ECCV 2020. LNCS, vol. 12349, pp. 108–126. Springer, Cham (2020). https://doi.org/10.1007/978-3-030-58548-8_7
35. Wang, W., et al.: Pyramid vision transformer: a versatile backbone for dense prediction without convolutions. arXiv preprint arXiv:2102.12122 (2021)
36. Wang, W., et al.: Crossformer: a versatile vision transformer hinging on cross-scale attention. arXiv preprint arXiv:2108.00154 (2021)
37. Wang, X., Girshick, R.B., Gupta, A., He, K.: Non-local neural networks. In: CVPR, pp. 7794–7803 (2018)
38. Wu, H., et al.: CVT: introducing convolutions to vision transformers. arXiv preprint arXiv:2103.15808 (2021)
39. Xia, X., et al.: TRT-ViT: TensorRT-oriented vision transformer. arXiv preprint arXiv:2205.09579 (2022)
40. Xiao, T., Liu, Y., Zhou, B., Jiang, Y., Sun, J.: Unified perceptual parsing for scene understanding. In: Ferrari, V., Hebert, M., Sminchisescu, C., Weiss, Y. (eds.) ECCV 2018. LNCS, vol. 11209, pp. 432–448. Springer, Cham (2018). https://doi.org/10.1007/978-3-030-01228-1_26
41. Xie, S., Girshick, R.B., Dollár, P., Tu, Z., He, K.: Aggregated residual transformations for deep neural networks. In: CVPR, pp. 5987–5995 (2017)
42. Xu, W., Xu, Y., Chang, T., Tu, Z.: Co-scale conv-attentional image transformers. arXiv preprint arXiv:2104.06399 (2021)
43. Yin, M., et al.: Disentangled non-local neural networks. In: Vedaldi, A., Bischof, H., Brox, T., Frahm, J.-M. (eds.) ECCV 2020. LNCS, vol. 12360, pp. 191–207. Springer, Cham (2020). https://doi.org/10.1007/978-3-030-58555-6_12
44. Yuan, K., Guo, S., Liu, Z., Zhou, A., Yu, F., Wu, W.: Incorporating convolution designs into visual transformers. arXiv preprint arXiv:2103.11816 (2021)
45. Yuan, L., et al.: Tokens-to-token ViT: training vision transformers from scratch on imagenet. arXiv preprint arXiv:2101.11986 (2021)
46. Yuan, Y., et al.: HRFormer: high-resolution transformer for dense prediction. arXiv preprint arXiv:2110.09408 (2021)
47. Zhou, B., et al.: Semantic understanding of scenes through the ADE20K dataset. Int. J. Comput. Vis. 127(3), 302–321 (2019)

Three Things Everyone Should Know About Vision Transformers

Hugo Touvron[1,2(✉)], Matthieu Cord[2], Alaaeldin El-Nouby[1,3], Jakob Verbeek[1], and Hervé Jégou[1]

[1] Meta AI, Fundamental AI Research (FAIR), Paris, France
[2] Sorbonne University, Paris, France
htouvron@fb.com
[3] INRIA, Paris, France

Abstract. After their initial success in natural language processing, transformer architectures have rapidly gained traction in computer vision, providing state-of-the-art results for tasks such as image classification, detection, segmentation, and video analysis. We offer three insights based on simple and easy to implement variants of vision transformers. (1) The residual layers of vision transformers, which are usually processed sequentially, can to some extent be processed efficiently in parallel without noticeably affecting the accuracy. (2) Fine-tuning the weights of the attention layers is sufficient to adapt vision transformers to a higher resolution and to other classification tasks. This saves compute, reduces the peak memory consumption at fine-tuning time, and allows sharing the majority of weights across tasks. (3) Adding MLP-based patch preprocessing layers improves Bert-like self-supervised training based on patch masking. We evaluate the impact of these design choices using the ImageNet-1k dataset, and confirm our findings on the ImageNet-v2 test set. Transfer performance is measured across six smaller datasets.

Keywords: Image classification · Transformers · Self-supervised learning

1 Introduction

Since its introduction the Transformer architecture [66] has become the dominant architecture in natural language processing tasks, replacing previously popular recurrent architectures. The vision transformer [16] (ViT) is a simple adaptation of transformers to computer vision tasks like image classification: the input image is divided into non-overlapping patches, which are fed to a vanilla transformer architecture, after a linear patch projection layer. In contrast to networks built from convolutional layers, transformers offer parallel processing and a complete field-of-view in a single layer. Along with other attention-based architectures,

Supplementary Information The online version contains supplementary material available at https://doi.org/10.1007/978-3-031-20053-3_29.

see e.g. [4,7], transformers have recently substantially influenced the design of computer vision architectures. Many modern architectures in computer vision directly inherit parts of their design from this work, or are at least inspired by the recent findings resulting from transformers [7,16,62]. This has led to significant progress on different computer vision tasks, ranging from object detection and segmentation [18] and video analysis [1,19] to image generation [9,31].

While vision transformers have led to considerable progress, the optimization of their design and training procedures have only been explored to a limited extent. In this paper, we offer three insights on training vision transformers.

1. Parallel vision transformers. Several works [20,75] advocate the interest shallower networks for reasons ranging from lower latency to easier optimization. We propose a very simple way to achieve this with ViTs. Let us denote by MHSA the multi-headed self-attention residual block, and by FFN the residual feedforward network. Starting from a sequential architecture depicted as follows,

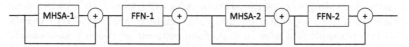

we parallelize the architecture by reorganizing the same blocks by pairs,

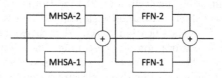

which can be done for any different numbers of parallel blocks. This produces an architecture with the same number of parameters and compute, while being wider and shallower. This design allows for more parallel processing, easing optimization and reducing latency depending on the implementation.

In Sect. 3, we experimentally analyse the performance of this parallel construction, and in particular how it affects the accuracy in comparison to the sequential baseline. The parallel version becomes a compelling option if deep enough. In some cases, we observe improvements in accuracy resulting from an easier optimization. Regarding the latency on GPUs, we observe reductions in the case of small batch sizes.[1]

2. Fine-tuning attention is all you need. It is common practice to pre-train networks before fine-tuning them on a target task. This is the standard approach underpinning transfer learning, where one leverages a large generic dataset like ImageNet [56] when the number of images is limited for the target task [50,73]. Another context is the one of changing resolution. Typically one would train at a lower resolution than the one employed at inference time. This saves resources, but additionally it reduces the discrepancy of scale between train and test images that results from data augmentation [65]. In Sect. 4 we show that, in the case of

---

[1] We have not found any papers in the literature analyzing the effect of width versus depth for ViT on common GPUs and CPUs.

ViT, it is mostly sufficient to fine-tune only the multi-head attention layers and freeze the feedforward network (FFN) layers. This saves compute and reduces the memory peak during training. Importantly this allows the same FFN weights, which dominate the number of parameters, to be used for multiple tasks. The impact on accuracy is statistically not significant when fine-tuning for different image resolutions. For large models, the impact on accuracy is limited when considering transfer to other classification tasks.

3. Patch preprocessing with masked self-supervised learning. The first layers of a transformer have a relatively local span [11], suggesting that they mostly behave like convolutions. Some recent hybrid architectures [18,21,23] preprocess their input images with a convolutional stem, to improve accuracy and training stability [71]. However, preprocessing images with convolutions is *a priori* not compatible with the recent and successful mask-based self-supervised learning approaches, like BeiT [3] or MAE [24]. The convolutions propagate information across patches, impeding the masked prediction task.

In Sect. 5, we propose a simple way to adapt mask-based self-supervised training methods with patch pre-processing, by applying the masking after the patch pre-processing. However, our analysis reveals that existing convolutional stems are not effective when combined with BeiT. To address this issue, we introduce a hierarchical MLP (hMLP) stem that interleaves MLP layers and patch aggregation operations, and prohibits any communication between patches. Our experiments show that this choice is effective and able to leverage the benefit of both BeiT self-supervised pre-training and patch pre-processing. Moreover, our hMLP-stem is also effective for ViT in the supervised case: it is on par with the best convolutional stem of our comparison [21].

2   Background

In this section, we discuss related work in common with our different contributions. We also introduce the baseline ViT models considered in this study and how they are trained. In subsequent sections, we discuss related work that is more specific to each of our three specific contributions.

2.1   Related Work

Attention-based models, and in particular transformers [66], have been rapidly adopted in neural networks handling text [6,12,40,52,66], speech [33,44], and even for more complex tasks such as function integration or solving differential equation [37]. In computer vision, DeTR [7] and Vision Transformers [16] (ViT) have deeply influenced the design of architectures in a short period of time. Most of the architectures introduced since ViT can be regarded as some form of hybridisation of transformers with convolutional neural networks, as illustrated by the hierarchical transformers [19,21,41,67], or conversely by convolutional neural networks with design elements inspired from ViT [42,63], or even multi-layer perceptrons adopting designs inspired by transformers [14,39,47,60,61].

In our case we build upon the basic ViT design of Dosovitskiy. Its design is governed by a small hyper-parameter space, and as such is less engineered than some recent follow-up architectures. With a proper training procedure [58,62,69], it achieves interesting performance/complexity trade-offs. It is also versatile: it can be effectively combined with hierarchical detection or segmentation frameworks [18]. Importantly, in spite of limited built-in priors, it has demonstrated great potential when combined with self-supervised learning, either with contrastive methods [8,10] or for reconstruction-based techniques like BeiT [3] or other forms of masked auto-encoders [15,17,24,68,72,76].

2.2   Experimental Setting

ViT Models. We consider the vanilla ViT models initially introduced by Dosovitskiy et al. [16] as well as the smaller ones proposed by Touvron et al. [62]. Therefore we use the initial pooling method that is based on a so-called class token. We only consider transformers operating on 16×16 patches. Decreasing this patch size improves the results but significantly increases the model complexity.

Training Procedure. To prevent overfitting, we adopt an existing training setting, namely the A2 procedure of Wightman et al. [69]. It uses a binary cross entropy loss and fixes the setting of most of the hyper-parameters. Wightman et al.'s A2 procedure was originally designed for training ResNet-50 models, and requires a few modifications when adopting it for ViTs to get strong performance and ensure sufficient stability:

- *The learning rate* should be reduced compared to ResNet-50. We set it to $lr = 4.10^{-3}$ for ViT-Ti and ViT-S and to $lr = 3.10^{-3}$ for ViT-B and ViT-L.
- *Stochastic depth drop-rate sd:* we adjust it per model following Touvron et al. [64]. It is not used for ViT-Ti. We fix $sd = 0.05$ for Vit-S, $sd = 0.1$ for ViT-B and $sd = 0.4$ for Vit-L.

We observe that LayerScale [64] significantly improves the performance when training large models, and that in that case a longer training is also beneficial. Therefore in addition to our main baseline where we train during 300 epochs without LayerScale, like in DeiT and in the A2 procedure of Wightman et al. [69], we consider another one that is trained for 400 epochs with LayerScale (LS).

Evaluation. Unless specified otherwise, we train our models on the ImageNet-1k dataset [56], and evaluate the top-1 accuracy on its validation set. All experiments are carried with seed 0. Since we have adjusted a low number of hyper-parameters, and since we share them across models except stochastic depth, we do not expect much overfitting. Nevertheless we also evaluate our models with the same metric on ImageNet-V2 [55] (matched frequency), which provides a separate test set, to provide a complementary view on the results.

Table 1. Baseline models and their performance on ImageNet1k-val top1 accuracy at resolution 224×224. We adopt common models with their default parametrization: Vit-B and Vit-L [16] and Vit-Ti and ViT-S [62], all with patch size of 16×16. Baseline results trained with or without LayerScale [64], and for 300 or 400 epochs of training.

Model	Depth	Width	Heads	Params $(\times 10^6)$	Flops $(\times 10^9)$	Speed (im/s)	300 epochs		400 ep.+LS	
							val	v2	val	v2
ViT-Ti/16	12	192	3	5.7	1.3	3796	72.7	60.3	73.5	61.4
ViT-S/16	12	384	6	22.1	4.6	1827	79.7	68.5	80.7	69.3
ViT-B/16	12	768	12	86.6	17.6	799	82.2	71.2	82.7	72.2
ViT-L/16	24	1024	16	304.4	61.6	277	83.0	72.4	84.0	73.7

2.3 Baselines

We report the results of our baseline in Table 1. With the few adaptations that we have done, our training procedure outperforms existing ones for supervised training for the model sizes that we consider, see Appendix A (Table 8). Note that all our models use a patch size of 16×16 as in Dosovitskiy et al. [16]. Unless specified, our experiments are carried out with images of size 224×224.

3   Depth vs Width: Parallel ViT

A recurrent debate in neural architecture design is on how to balance width versus depth. The first successful neural networks on Imagenet [35,57] were not very deep, for instance the 22-layer GoogleNet [59] was regarded as deep in 2014's standards. This has changed with ResNets [25,26], for which going deeper was hindering significantly less the optimization due to the residual connections. After its introduction, some researchers have investigated alternative choices for trading depth against width [13,30,75], like Wide Residual Networks [75].

Recently, there has been a renewed interest for wider architectures with attention [20,38]. For instance the Non-deep Networks [20] proposes an architecture with several parallel branches whose design is more complex. In our work, we aim at proposing a much simpler and flexible alternative that builds upon a regular ViT in a more straightforward manner.

3.1   Preliminary Discussion on Width Versus Depth for ViT

The ViT architecture of Dosovitskiy et al. [16] is parametrized by three quantities: the width (i.e., the working dimensionality d), the depth, and the number of heads. We do not discuss the latter. Increasing depth or width increases the capacity of the model and usually its accuracy. For the most common ViT models that we report in Table 1 [16,62], width and height are scaled together. Below, we discuss the different pros and cons for favoring width versus depth.

Parametrization & Optimization. The compositionality of the layers is better with deeper networks. This was one of the decisive advantage of ResNet once optimization issues were solved by residual connections. Yet too much depth hinders optimization, even with residual connections. Some solutions have been proposed to address this issue for ViTs [64], showing that transformers benefit from depth when trained with improved optimization procedure.

Separability. In image classification, the spatial features are ultimately projected [35] or pooled [25] into a high-dimensional latent vector that is subsequently fed to a linear classifier. The dimensionality of this vector should be high enough so that the classes are linearly separable. Hence it is typically larger for tasks involving many classes. For instance in ResNet-50 it has dimension 512 when applied to CIFAR, but 2048 for ImageNet. In ViT, the width is identical to the working dimensionality of each patch, and is typically smaller than with ResNet, possibly limiting the separation capabilities. Besides, a larger dimension of the latent vector tend to favor overfitting. In this regard the compromise between capacity and overfitting is subtle and depends size of the training set [58].

Complexity. In ViT, the different complexity measures are affected differently by width and depth. Ignoring the patch pre-processing and final classification layer, which contribute to complexity in a negligible manner, then we have:

- *The number of parameters* is proportional to depth and a quadratic function of the width.
- *The compute,* as determined by FLOPS, is similarly proportional to the depth and quadratic in width.
- *The peak memory usage at inference time* is constant when increasing the depth for a fixed width, but it is quadratic as a function of width.
- *The latency* of wide architectures is in theory better as they are more parallel, but actual speedups depend on implementation and hardware.

3.2   Parallelizing ViT

We propose and analyze flattening vision transformers by grouping layers following the scheme presented in the introduction. Let us consider a sequence of transformer blocks defined by the functions $\mathrm{mhsa}_l(\cdot)$, $\mathrm{ffn}_l(\cdot)$, $\mathrm{mhsa}_{l+1}(\cdot)$ and $\mathrm{ffn}_{l+1}(\cdot)$. Instead of sequentially processing the input x_l in four steps as done in the usual implementation:

$$\begin{aligned} x'_{l+1} &= x_l + \mathrm{mhsa}_l(x_l), & x_{l+1} &= x'_{l+1} + \mathrm{ffn}_l(x'_{l+1}), \\ x'_{l+2} &= x_{l+1} + \mathrm{mhsa}_{l+1}(x_{l+1}), & x_{l+2} &= x'_{l+2} + \mathrm{ffn}_{l+1}(x'_{l+2}), \end{aligned} \tag{1}$$

we replace this composition by two parallel operations:

$$\begin{aligned} x_{l+1} &= x_l + \mathrm{mhsa}_{l,1}(x_l) + \mathrm{mhsa}_{l,2}(x_l), \\ x_{l+2} &= x_{l+1} + \mathrm{ffn}_{l,1}(x_{l+1}) + \mathrm{ffn}_{l,2}(x_{l+1}). \end{aligned} \tag{2}$$

This reduces the depth by two for a given number of MHSA and FFN blocks. Conversely, there is twice the amount of processing in parallel. The intuition behind this parallelization is as follows: as networks get deeper, the contribution of any residual block $r(\cdot)$, be it mhsa$(\cdot)$ or ffn$(\cdot)$, becomes increasingly smaller with respect to the overall function. Therefore, the approximation $\forall r, r' \ r'(x + r(x)) \approx r'(x)$ becomes increasingly satisfactory, and it is easy to check that if this approximation is true, Eq. (1) and (2) are equivalent.

Our strategy is different from taking transformers with a larger working dimensionality, which leads to different trade-offs between accuracy, parameters, memory and FLOPS, as discussed in our experiments. In contrast to increasing the working dimension, which increases the complexity quadratically as discussed above, our modification is neutral with respect to parameter and compute.

Depending on whether we effectively parallelize the processing, the peak memory usage at inference time and the latency are modified. Note that rather than just two, we can choose to process any number of blocks in parallel; falling back to the sequential design if we process a single block in each layer.

3.3 Experiments

Notation. We adopt the standard naming convention of previous work [16,62] to use the postfixes Ti/S/B/L to identify the working dimensionality of the models, i.e., the column "width" in Table 1. We append the depth N to indicate variations on the number of pairs of layers (MHSA, FFN) [64]. For instance, ViT-B24 has the same width as a ViT-B12 but with twice the depth, i.e., 24 pairs of MHSA and FFN layers instead of 12. For our parallel models, we specify both the depth and the number of parallel branches: ViT-B12×2 has twice the number of residual modules as a ViT-B12. It includes a total of $12 \times 2 = 24$ pairs of MHSA and FFN layers. Therefore it has the same complexity as the ViT-B24 model (a.k.a. ViT-B24×1).

Comparison of Sequential and Parallel ViTs. In Fig. 1, we compare the performance of sequential and parallel models of a fixed complexity. We fix the total number of blocks, i.e. pairs of MHSA and FFN layers, which determines the number of parameters and FLOPS, and we consider different possible of branches that leads to the same total number of blocks. For instance 36 can be obtained as the sequential ViT 36 × 1, or the parallel ViTs 18 × 2, 12 × 3 or 9 × 4.

We observe that, amongst the parallel and sequential models, the best performance is obtained with two parallel branches for all tested model capacities. The performance is comparable between the S20 × 3 and S30 × 2 for ViT-S60, but generally using more than two parallel branches is not favorable in terms of accuracy and we do not discuss them further. Note that Fig. 1 compares ViT models with a relatively large number of blocks (36 and 60). This is the case where sequential models are relatively difficult to optimize due to their depth. The parallel models with two branches are easier to train, while being deep enough to benefit from layer compositionality.

In Fig. 2, we consider models with only 24 pairs (MHSA,FFN) and a varying width. Here we observe that the smallest models ViT-Ti and ViT-S are better in

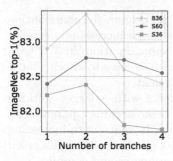

Fig. 1. Impact of the parallelism on performance for a given model size (ViT-S36, -S60 and -B36) and 1–4 parallel branches.

Table 2. Impact of the training on parallel and sequential models.

Model	Number of Epochs	LS	ImNet top1 -val	-v2
	300	✗	82.9	72.2
sequential:	300	✓	83.9	73.2
ViT-B36x1	400	✗	83.4	72.5
	400	✓	84.1	73.9
	300	✗	83.3	72.4
parallel:	300	✓	83.8	73.3
ViT-B18x2	400	✗	83.4	73.1
	400	✓	84.1	73.5

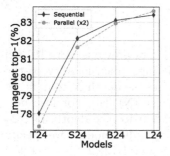

Fig. 2. Impact of model width (T:192, S:384, B:768, L:1024). We train the two L24 with LS to avoid optimization issues.

Table 3. Comparison of parallel models with more blocks with models with a higher working dimensionality. L24×1, B36×1 and B18×2 trained with LS.

Model	#params ($\times 10^6$)	Flops ($\times 10^9$)	Mem. (MB)	ImNet top1 -val	-v2
B12×1	86.6	17.6	2077	$82.2_{\pm 0.06}$	$71.0_{\pm 0.26}$
S48×1	85.9	18.3	1361	82.3	72.0
S24×2	85.9	18.3	1433	82.6	72.3
L24×1	304.4	61.6	3788	83.4	73.3
B36×1	256.7	52.5	3071	83.9	73.2
B18×2	256.7	52.5	3217	83.8	73.3

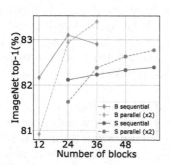

Fig. 3. Sequential vs. parallel ViT-S and -B when varying the number of blocks.

Table 4. Throughput for ViT-S18×2 and ViT-B18×2 (im/s). With parallel ViT, the residual blocks can be processed either sequentially (seq) or in parallel (par).

batch size	ViT-S18x2 seq	par	best	gain	ViT-B18x2 seq	par	best	gain
1	44	61	61	38%	42	61	61	45%
2	84	123	123	46%	80	117	117	47%
4	168	245	245	46%	155	187	187	21%
8	334	474	474	42%	230	211	230	0%
16	569	518	569	0%	266	231	266	0%
32	616	556	616	0%	276	245	276	0%
64	647	575	647	0%	286	248	286	0%

their sequential version. This is because are easy to optimize up to 24 layers. The B24×1 and B12×2 achieve comparable performance. In contrast, the ViT-L12×2 is stronger than its sequential counterpart, which is more difficult to optimize even though we used LS for this size; without LS its performance is 83% at 300 epochs.

In Fig. 3, we compare the performance of sequential and parallel as a function of the number of blocks for ViT-S and ViT-B. Our observations concur with our previous findings: the parallel version is more helpful for the deeper and higher capacity models that are more difficult to optimize; our parallelization scheme alleviates this issue.

Impact of Optimization. In Table 2, we provide results with LayerScale [64], which helps the optimization of the biggest models. It improves the performance of both sequential and parallel models, which end up approximately on par. Hence, for models big enough and with proper optimization, sequential and parallel ViTs are roughly equivalent.

Increasing the Number of Modules or the Working Dimensionality? Table 3 provides a comparison between different ViT architectures: sequential, parallel, and with larger working dimensionality. We approximately adjust the complexity in terms of parameters and FLOPS, yet this means that ViT models with larger working dimensionality have a higher peak memory usage with typical implementation. In both tested settings the sequential and parallel models yield substantially higher accuracy than the models with larger working dimensionality. The sequential and parallel models are comparable with 36 blocks. The parallel model is better in the case of 48 blocks due to the increased depth of the sequential model.

Latency. On a commodity V100 GPUs, we observe a significant speed-up in the case of per-sample processing, with also some gains for small batch sizes with relatively small models, see Table 4. This comparison is based on a simple implementation of our parallel architecture, which is suboptimal due to the lack of a specific CUDA kernel. Overall our measurements suggest specific hardware or kernels are required to obtain compelling benefits in terms of throughput.

4   Fine-Tuning Attention is All You Need

In this section we focus on fine-tuning ViT models, either to adapt the model to larger image resolutions or to address different downstream classification tasks. In particular, we consider an approach where we only fine-tune the weights corresponding to the MHSA layer, see Fig. 4. We analyse the impact in terms of prediction accuracy and savings in processing complexity, peak memory usage and parameter count. As we will see, our choice is significantly better than alternative ones, such as fine-tuning the parameter-heavy FFN layers.

It is common to train networks at lower resolution and fine-tuning it at a higher target resolution. This saves a significant amount of compute at training time, and typically also improves the accuracy of the network at the target

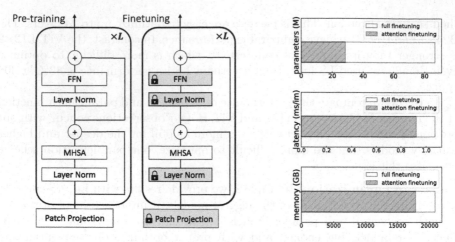

Fig. 4. Fine-tuning the weights of the self-attention layer only (middle panel) leads to savings during fine-tuning in peak memory usage and computational cost. It also leads to important savings in the number of parameters when a model is fine-tuned for multiple resolutions or multiple downstream classification tasks.

resolution [65]. This is because it reduces the discrepancy between the scale of the images seen at train and at test time that is induced by common data augmentation. Fine-tuning is also the paradigm associated with foundation models in general and to the concept of transfer learning itself [22,50,73]. A recent line of work explores adaptation of pre-trained models with various types of adapter modules with a small amount of task-specific parameters [5,29,45,46,51,54]. In our work, instead, we focus on fine-tuning vanilla ViTs.

Fine-Tuning at Different Resolutions. In Table 5, we report results with fine-tuning ViT-S, ViT-B and ViT-L at 384×384 resolution for models pre-trained at 224×224. Solely fine-tuning the MHSA weights provides results that are within standard deviation (± 0.1) from a full fine-tuning both on ImageNet-val and ImageNet-V2. This is not the case when fine-tuning the FFN layers, while these contain twice the number of parameters of MHSA. Note, our pre-trained models have been trained long enough (400 epochs) to ensure convergence.

There are only advantages to use this approach when fine-tuning at higher resolution as opposed to doing a full fine-tuning, as we get substantial savings in terms of parameters, latency, and peak memory usage for free, see Fig. 4 (right panels). First, the fine-tuning stage requires 10% less memory on the GPU, which is especially interesting in the context of high-resolution fine-tuning where the higher images require more memory. The training is also 10% faster, as less gradients are computed. Finally, the attention weights correspond to approximately one third of the weights. Therefore, if one wants to use multiple models fine-tuned for different input resolutions, we save 66% of the storage for each additional model.

Table 5. Comparison of full finetuning of all weight (full), finetuning of the MHSA layer weights only (attn) and of the FFN layer only (ffn) when adapting models at resolution 384 × 384 on ImageNet-1k from model pre-trained at 224 × 224. We compare finetuning with SGD and AdamW [43] optimizers.

	ImageNet1k-val top1 acc.							ImageNet1k-V2 top1 acc.					
Model	AdamW↑384			SGD↑384			Model	AdamW↑384			SGD↑384		
	full	attn	ffn	full	attn	ffn		full	attn	ffn	full	attn	ffn
ViT-S	**82.7**	82.5	82.2	**82.6**	82.3	82.0	ViT-S	**72.5**	72.4	71.6	**72.5**	72.2	71.1
ViT-B	**84.3**	**84.3**	84.1	**84.3**	84.2	84.0	ViT-B	73.7	**74.0**	73.6	**74.0**	73.9	73.7
ViT-L	**85.5**	**85.5**	85.2	**85.4**	85.3	85.1	ViT-L	**75.5**	75.4	75.2	**75.6**	75.1	75.0

Fine-Tuning on Different Datasets. We now evaluate our approach when transferring ViTs pre-trained on ImageNet to different downstream classification tasks by fine-tuning. We consider public benchmarks whose characteristics and references are given in Appendix B.

In Table 6 we report the performance for different fine-tuning strategies. Here we make different observations. First, for the **smallest datasets**, namely CARS and Flowers, fine-tuning only the MHSA layers is an excellent strategy. In most cases it is even better than full-tuning. Our interpretation is that restricting the number of weights has a regularizing effect. The conclusion is more mixed with the **largest datasets**, in particular iNaturalist, where we observe a significant gap between the full fine-tuning and our solution for the ViT-S. This could be expected: in this case there are more images to learn from and new classes

Table 6. Transfer learning experiments: we compare fine-tuning the full model, or only the attention or ffn layers on six transfer learning dataset with three different ViT models pre-trained on ImageNet-1k.

Model	Finetuning			INAT-18	INAT-19	CIFAR-10	CIFAR-100	CARS	Flowers
	full	attn	ffn						
ViT-S	✓	✗	✗	**68.0**	**73.9**	**98.9**	**90.5**	89.7	96.8
	✗	✓	✗	60.6	68.7	98.7	89.1	**89.8**	**96.9**
	✗	✗	✓	64.4	72.5	**98.9**	90.1	88.3	96.1
ViT-B	✓	✗	✗	**74.1**	**78.2**	**99.3**	**92.5**	92.7	97.8
	✗	✓	✗	71.1	75.7	99.2	91.8	**92.8**	**98.5**
	✗	✗	✓	73.3	77.3	**99.3**	92.1	88.9	97.5
ViT-L	✓	✗	✗	**75.9**	**79.7**	**99.3**	**93.2**	**93.8**	98.3
	✗	✓	✗	75.3	78.7	99.2	92.7	**93.8**	**98.4**
	✗	✗	✓	75.4	79.3	99.2	93.0	93.0	97.6

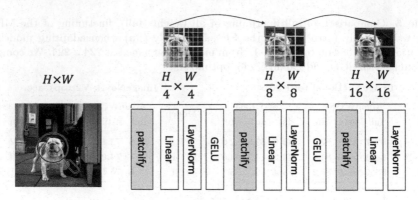

Fig. 5. Design of our hMLP-stem: we start from subpatches and progressively merge them with linear layers interleaved by GELU non-linearities. The design of our stem is such that the patches are processed independently. Hence it commutes with masking.

that were not seen before the fine-tuning stage. Restricting the fine-tuning to MHSA layer allows modifying only a relatively small number of parameters. FFN layers have twice more weights and leads to better results in that case. This limitation tends to disappear with the **larger ViT-L models**, for which the capacity of the MHSA is much larger and therefore sufficient. Our strategy is typically interesting for foundation models, which are very large models that are fine-tuned on a variety of downstream tasks.

5   Patch Preprocessing for Self-supervised Learning

The original ViT paper [16] considered to include convolution instead of patch projection in the network design. Several recent papers [21,23,67,70,71,74] advocate this choice to include a small pre-processing network in the architecture, instead of a simple patch projection. Most of the pre-processing subnetworks that have been considered are based on convolutions, and are often referred to as "convolutional stems". Small transformers have also been considered [74].

While these patch pre-processing designs have been developed to improve accuracy and/or stability, there are some remaining questions regarding their design and flexibility. First, it is not clear which is the most effective when combined with a vanilla transformer. Second, to our knowledge there is no work addressing the problem of their compatibility with self-supervised methods based on patch masking, and in particular on Bert-like auto-encoders such as BeiT [3].

In this section we try to answer these questions. We compare several existing pre-processing designs in terms of accuracy and compute and evaluate them in combination with BeiT, using the codebase release by the authors of BeiT. The only change we make is to train the tokenizer on ImageNet-1k, rather than using the one from DALL-E [53] used in BeiT which is trained on a proprietary dataset comprised of 250 million images. In this manner, pre-training is based on

Table 7. Patch pre-processing: Performance in top1 accuracy with for a ViT-B12. All models are (1) trained 300 epochs in the supervised case; (2) pre-trained during 300 epochs and fine-tuned 100 epochs when used with BeiT. We report the result of a ViT-B13 to provide the performance of a vanilla transformer with more FLOPS. We measure the standard deviation for the two linear stem baselines and our hMLP stem on 5 runs. The other measurements are made with the fixed seed 0.

Stem type	norm.	NL	GFLOPS	ImNet1k supervised		BeiT+FT
				acc. -val	acc. -v2	ImNet-val
Linear: ViT-B12 [16]	–	–	17.58	$82.20_{\pm0.06}$	71.0	$83.05_{\pm0.08}$
	BN	–	17.58	82.31	71.0	82.98
	–	GELU	17.58	81.55	70.5	83.09
	BN	GELU	17.58	82.38	70.7	82.99
Linear: ViT-B13	–	–	19.04	$82.35_{\pm0.12}$	71.3	$83.26_{\pm0.06}$
Conv: LeViT [21]	BN	GELU	19.07	**82.57**	71.0	83.04
	LN	GELU	19.07	**82.50**	70.9	83.06
Local transformer [23]			19.12	82.26	70.6	82.38
hMLP (ours)	BN	GELU	17.73	$\mathbf{82.54}_{\pm0.09}$	71.5	$\mathbf{83.43}_{\pm0.10}$
	LN	GELU	17.73	$\mathbf{82.50}_{\pm0.07}$	71.0	$83.24_{\pm0.09}$

ImageNet-1k only. This permits reproducible experimentation and fair comparison, and gives equivalent results [49]. Since existing convolutional designs are not satisfactory in combination with masking, we first introduce our own design.

Our hierarchical MLP (hMLP) stem is depicted in Fig. 5. All patches are processed independently with linear layers interleaved with non-linearities and renormalization. Its design is guided by our motivation to remove any interaction between the different 16×16 patches during the pre-processing stage. Even if we mask a patch, it does not create any artifacts resulting from the convolution overlapping with other patches, as it is the case with existing designs. Therefore, with our hMLP solution, we can equivalently mask the patches before or after the patch-processing stage. Note that, although patches are processed independently, our hMLP-stem is equivalent to a convolutional stem in which the size of the convolutional kernel and its stride are matched, and in practice we implement it with convolutional layers, see our code in Appendix C.

In short, we start from small 2×2 patches, and gradually increase their size until they reach 16×16. Each increase of the patch size is denoted by "*patchify*" in Fig. 5, in spirit of hierarchical transformer designs like Swin-Transformers [41]. The patches are projected with a linear projection and normalized before we apply a GELU non-linearity [27]. For the normalization, we consider and evaluate two choices: either we use batch-normalization (BN) [32] or layer-normalization (LN) [2]. While the BN offers better trade-offs, LN is of interest when used with small batch sizes: it works well even with a single image per batch, as often used in object detection.

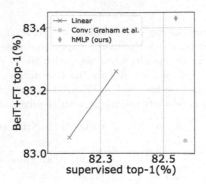

Fig. 6. Performance of patch pre-processing in the supervised and BeiT+FT settings. Our hMLP stem performs well in both cases, improving the accuracy compared to linear projection (shown for B12 and B13) without significantly increasing the complexity (+0.8% FLOPS compared to the ViT-B12 in the bottom-left corner). In contrast, the convolutional stem only improves the performance in the supervised case, while significantly increasing complexity (+7.5% FLOPS).

In contrast with existing stems from the literature, our hMLP design does not significantly increase the compute requirement. For instance, ViT-B, requires FLOPS is 17.73 GFLOPS with our design. This adds less than 1% of compute compared to using the usual linear projection stem.

Stem Comparison in Supervised Learning. In Table 7 we provide a comparison between different stem designs. We have selected several prototypical designs from the literature for which the code is available online. In addition to our hMLP stem, we have considered some variations over the standard linear projection to evaluate the influence of the non-linearities and normalization. For the standard linear stem, we also consider a ViT-B13 including an extra pair (MHSA, FFN) to allow more direct comparisons with other stems with more FLOPS. In this comparison the most effective existing design is the one of LeViT [21]. The improvements with respect to the linear baseline are significant considering the standard deviation, even when taking into account the extra layer of ViT-B13 to compare with an similar number of FLOPS. Our hMLP stem obtains a comparable performance but with lower complexity, and without any interaction between the 16 × 16 patches.

Results with BeiT Training. We report the results with BeiT, fine-tuned on ImageNet-val, in the right-most column of Table 7. We use the code of BeiT [3] with their training procedure, which includes LayerScale and a relatively elaborated fine-tuning procedure. As one can see, existing stems do not provide any improvement compared to the linear baseline, while adding compute. In contrast, our design is effective and provides an improvement of +0.3/+0.4 top1 accuracy compared to the baseline, which is significant considering the measured standard deviations in the results. The interest of hMLP in the context of masked self-supervised learning is clear in Fig. 6, where we plot the performance, averaged over 5 seeds for our method, in the supervised case versus the one with BeiT.

6   Conclusion

In this paper, we looked at three different topics related to Vision Transformers. First, we investigated a simple but effective way to parallelize them, showing a viable alternative to increase capacity without significantly increasing the working dimensionality. Whether this simple parallel design principle can be applied to other architectures is an exploration left for future work. Second, we considered different fine-tuning strategies and showed that fine-tuning the self-attention layer is sufficient in the context of resolution fine-tuning. This can also be interesting when transferring to other downstream classification tasks, especially when fine-tuning large models or/and transferring to a dataset with few training images. Last, we introduced a simple patch pre-processing stem, which processes patches independently across multiple linear layers interleaved with non-linearities and patch aggregation. It is especially useful when combined with mask-based self-supervised learning such as BeiT.

Acknowledgement. We thank Francisco Massa for valuable discussions and insights about optimizing the implementation of block parallelization.

References

1. Arnab, A., Dehghani, M., Heigold, G., Sun, C., Lučić, M., Schmid, C.: ViVit: a video vision transformer. In: Proceedings of the IEEE/CVF International Conference on Computer Vision, pp. 6836–6846 (2021)
2. Ba, J.L., Kiros, J.R., Hinton, G.E.: Layer normalization. arXiv preprint arXiv:1607.06450 (2016)
3. Bao, H., Dong, L., Wei, F.: BEiT: BERT pre-training of image transformers. arXiv preprint arXiv:2106.08254 (2021)
4. Bello, I., Zoph, B., Vaswani, A., Shlens, J., Le, Q.V.: Attention augmented convolutional networks. In: Proceedings of the IEEE/CVF International Conference on Computer Vision, pp. 3286–3295 (2019)
5. Berriel, R., et al.: Budget-aware adapters for multi-domain learning. In: Proceedings of the IEEE/CVF International Conference on Computer Vision, pp. 382–391 (2019)
6. Brown, T.B., et al.: Language models are few-shot learners. arXiv preprint arXiv:2005.14165 (2020)
7. Carion, N., Massa, F., Synnaeve, G., Usunier, N., Kirillov, A., Zagoruyko, S.: End-to-end object detection with transformers. In: Vedaldi, A., Bischof, H., Brox, T., Frahm, J.-M. (eds.) ECCV 2020. LNCS, vol. 12346, pp. 213–229. Springer, Cham (2020). https://doi.org/10.1007/978-3-030-58452-8_13
8. Caron, M., et al.: Emerging properties in self-supervised vision transformers. arXiv preprint arXiv:2104.14294 (2021)
9. Chang, H., Zhang, H., Jiang, L., Liu, C., Freeman, W.T.: MaskGIT: masked generative image transformer. arXiv preprint arXiv:2202.04200 (2022)

10. Chen, X., Xie, S., He, K.: An empirical study of training self-supervised vision transformers. In: Proceedings of the IEEE/CVF International Conference on Computer Vision, pp. 9640–9649 (2021)
11. d'Ascoli, S., Touvron, H., Leavitt, M.L., Morcos, A.S., Biroli, G., Sagun, L.: ConViT: improving vision transformers with soft convolutional inductive biases. In: International Conference on Machine Learning, pp. 2286–2296. PMLR (2021)
12. Devlin, J., Chang, M.W., Lee, K., Toutanova, K.: BERT: pre-training of deep bidirectional transformers for language understanding. In: NAACL (2019)
13. Ding, X., Zhang, X., Ma, N., Han, J., Ding, G., Sun, J.: RepVGG: making VGG-style convnets great again. In: Proceedings of the IEEE/CVF Conference on Computer Vision and Pattern Recognition, pp. 13733–13742 (2021)
14. Ding, X., Zhang, X., Han, J., Ding, G.: RepMLP: re-parameterizing convolutions into fully-connected layers for image recognition. arXiv preprint arXiv:2105.01883 (2021)
15. Dong, X., et al.: PeCo: perceptual codebook for BERT pre-training of vision transformers. arXiv preprint arXiv:2111.12710 (2021)
16. Dosovitskiy, A., et al.: An image is worth 16x16 words: transformers for image recognition at scale. In: International Conference on Learning Representations (2021)
17. El-Nouby, A., Izacard, G., Touvron, H., Laptev, I., Jegou, H., Grave, E.: Are large-scale datasets necessary for self-supervised pre-training? arXiv preprint arXiv:2112.10740 (2021)
18. El-Nouby, A., et al.: XCiT: cross-covariance image transformers. In: NeurIPS (2021)
19. Fan, H., et al.: Multiscale vision transformers. arXiv preprint arXiv:2104.11227 (2021)
20. Goyal, A., Bochkovskiy, A., Deng, J., Koltun, V.: Non-deep networks. arXiv preprint arXiv:2110.07641 (2021)
21. Graham, B., et al.: LeViT: a vision transformer in convnet's clothing for faster inference. arXiv preprint arXiv:2104.01136 (2021)
22. Guo, Y., Shi, H., Kumar, A., Grauman, K., Simunic, T., Feris, R.S.: SpotTune: transfer learning through adaptive fine-tuning. In: Proceedings of the IEEE/CVF Conference on Computer Vision and Pattern Recognition, pp. 4805–4814 (2019)
23. Han, K., Xiao, A., Wu, E., Guo, J., Xu, C., Wang, Y.: Transformer in transformer. arXiv preprint arXiv:2103.00112 (2021)
24. He, K., Chen, X., Xie, S., Li, Y., Dollár, P., Girshick, R.: Masked autoencoders are scalable vision learners. arXiv preprint arXiv:2111.06377 (2021)
25. He, K., Zhang, X., Ren, S., Sun, J.: Deep residual learning for image recognition. In: Proceedings of the IEEE Conference on Computer Vision and Pattern Recognition, pp. 770–778 (2016)
26. He, K., Zhang, X., Ren, S., Sun, J.: Identity mappings in deep residual networks. arXiv preprint arXiv:1603.05027 (2016)
27. Hendrycks, D., Gimpel, K.: Gaussian error linear units (GELUs). arXiv preprint arXiv:1606.08415 (2016)
28. Horn, G.V., et al.: The inaturalist challenge 2017 dataset. arXiv preprint arXiv:1707.06642 (2017)
29. Houlsby, N., et al.: Parameter-efficient transfer learning for NLP. In: International Conference on Machine Learning, pp. 2790–2799. PMLR (2019)
30. Huang, G., Sun, Yu., Liu, Z., Sedra, D., Weinberger, K.Q.: Deep networks with stochastic depth. In: Leibe, B., Matas, J., Sebe, N., Welling, M. (eds.) ECCV

2016. LNCS, vol. 9908, pp. 646–661. Springer, Cham (2016). https://doi.org/10.1007/978-3-319-46493-0_39

31. Hudson, D.A., Zitnick, C.L.: Generative adversarial transformers. In: International Conference on Machine Learning, pp. 4487–4499. PMLR (2021)

32. Ioffe, S., Szegedy, C.: Batch normalization: accelerating deep network training by reducing internal covariate shift. In: International Conference on Machine Learning, pp. 448–456. PMLR (2015)

33. Karita, S., Chen, N., Hayashi, T., et al.: A comparative study on transformer vs RNN in speech applications. arXiv preprint arXiv:1909.06317 (2019)

34. Krause, J., Stark, M., Deng, J., Fei-Fei, L.: 3D object representations for fine-grained categorization. In: IEEE Workshop on 3D Representation and Recognition (2013)

35. Krizhevsky, A., Sutskever, I., Hinton, G.: ImageNet classification with deep convolutional neural networks. Commun. ACM **60**(6), 84–90 (2012)

36. Krizhevsky, A.: Learning multiple layers of features from tiny images. Tech. rep., CIFAR (2009)

37. Lample, G., Charton, F.: Deep learning for symbolic mathematics. arXiv preprint arXiv:1912.01412 (2019)

38. Li, X., Wang, W., Hu, X., Yang, J.: Selective kernel networks. In: Proceedings of the IEEE/CVF Conference on Computer Vision and Pattern Recognition, pp. 510–519 (2019)

39. Liu, H., Dai, Z., So, D.R., Le, Q.V.: Pay attention to MLPs. arXiv preprint arXiv:2105.08050 (2021)

40. Liu, Y., et al.: RoBERTa: a robustly optimized BERT pretraining approach. arXiv preprint arXiv:1907.11692 (2019)

41. Liu, Z., et al.: Swin transformer: hierarchical vision transformer using shifted windows. arXiv preprint arXiv:2103.14030 (2021)

42. Liu, Z., Mao, H., Wu, C.Y., Feichtenhofer, C., Darrell, T., Xie, S.: A convnet for the 2020s. arXiv preprint arXiv:2201.03545 (2022)

43. Loshchilov, I., Hutter, F.: Fixing weight decay regularization in Adam. arXiv preprint arXiv:1711.05101 (2017)

44. Lüscher, C., Beck, E., Irie, K., et al.: RWTH ASR systems for LibriSpeech: hybrid vs attention. In: Interspeech (2019)

45. Mahabadi, R.K., Ruder, S., Dehghani, M., Henderson, J.: Parameter-efficient multi-task fine-tuning for transformers via shared hypernetworks. In: ACL/IJCNLP (2021)

46. Mancini, M., Ricci, E., Caputo, B., Bulò, S.R.: Adding new tasks to a single network with weight transformations using binary masks. In: European Conference on Computer Vision Workshops (2018)

47. Melas-Kyriazi, L.: Do you even need attention? A stack of feed-forward layers does surprisingly well on ImageNet. arXiv preprint arXiv:2105.02723 (2021)

48. Nilsback, M.E., Zisserman, A.: Automated flower classification over a large number of classes. In: Proceedings of the Indian Conference on Computer Vision, Graphics and Image Processing (2008)

49. Nouby, A.E., Izacard, G., Touvron, H., Laptev, I., Jégou, H., Grave, E.: Are large-scale datasets necessary for self-supervised pre-training? arXiv preprint arXiv:2112.10740 (2021)

50. Oquab, M., Bottou, L., Laptev, I., Sivic, J.: Learning and transferring mid-level image representations using convolutional neural networks. In: Proceedings of the IEEE Conference on Computer Vision and Pattern Recognition, pp. 1717–1724 (2014)

51. Pfeiffer, J., Rücklé, A., Poth, C., Kamath, A., Vulic, I., Ruder, S., Cho, K., Gurevych, I.: AdapterHub: A framework for adapting transformers. In: EMNLP (2020)

52. Radford, A., Wu, J., Child, R., Luan, D., Amodei, D., Sutskever, I.: Language models are unsupervised multitask learners. OpenAI blog **1**(8), 9 (2019)

53. Ramesh, A., et al.: Zero-shot text-to-image generation. arXiv preprint arXiv:2102.12092 (2021)

54. Rebuffi, S.A., Bilen, H., Vedaldi, A.: Efficient parametrization of multi-domain deep neural networks. Proceedings of the IEEE Conference on Computer Vision and Pattern Recognition, pp. 8119–8127 (2018)

55. Recht, B., Roelofs, R., Schmidt, L., Shankar, V.: Do ImageNet classifiers generalize to ImageNet? In: International Conference on Machine Learning, pp. 5389–5400. PMLR (2019)

56. Russakovsky, O., et al.: ImageNet large scale visual recognition challenge. Int. J. Comput. Vis. **115**(3), 211–252 (2015). https://doi.org/10.1007/s11263-015-0816-y

57. Simonyan, K., Zisserman, A.: Very deep convolutional networks for large-scale image recognition. In: International Conference on Learning Representations (2015)

58. Steiner, A., Kolesnikov, A., Zhai, X., Wightman, R., Uszkoreit, J., Beyer, L.: How to train your ViT? Data, augmentation, and regularization in vision transformers. arXiv preprint arXiv:2106.10270 (2021)

59. Szegedy, C., et al.: Going deeper with convolutions. In: Proceedings of the IEEE Conference on Computer Vision and Pattern Recognition, pp. 1–9 (2015)

60. Tolstikhin, I., et al.: MLP-Mixer: an all-MLP architecture for vision. arXiv preprint arXiv:2105.01601 (2021)

61. Touvron, H., et al.: ResMLP: feedforward networks for image classification with data-efficient training. arXiv preprint arXiv:2105.03404 (2021)

62. Touvron, H., Cord, M., Douze, M., Massa, F., Sablayrolles, A., Jégou, H.: Training data-efficient image transformers & distillation through attention. In: International Conference on Machine Learning, pp. 10347–10357. PMLR (2021)

63. Touvron, H., et al.: Augmenting convolutional networks with attention-based aggregation. arXiv preprint arXiv:2112.13692 (2021)

64. Touvron, H., Cord, M., Sablayrolles, A., Synnaeve, G., Jégou, H.: Going deeper with image transformers. In: Proceedings of the IEEE/CVF International Conference on Computer Vision, pp. 32–42(2021)

65. Touvron, H., Vedaldi, A., Douze, M., Jegou, H.: Fixing the train-test resolution discrepancy. Adv. Neural Inf. Process. Syst. **32** (2019)

66. Vaswani, A., et al.: Attention is all you need. Adv. Neural Inf. Process. Syst. **30** (2017)

67. Wang, W., et al.: Pyramid vision transformer: a versatile backbone for dense prediction without convolutions. arXiv preprint arXiv:2102.12122 (2021)

68. Wei, C., Fan, H., Xie, S., Wu, C.Y., Yuille, A., Feichtenhofer, C.: Masked feature prediction for self-supervised visual pre-training. arXiv preprint arXiv:2112.09133 (2021)

69. Wightman, R., Touvron, H., Jégou, H.: ResNet strikes back: an improved training procedure in timm. arXiv preprint arXiv:2110.00476 (2021)

70. Wu, H., et al.: CvT: introducing convolutions to vision transformers. arXiv preprint arXiv:2103.15808 (2021)

71. Xiao, T., Singh, M., Mintun, E., Darrell, T., Dollár, P., Girshick, R.B.: Early convolutions help transformers see better. arXiv preprint arXiv:2106.14881 (2021)

72. Xie, Z., et al.: SimMIM: a simple framework for masked image modeling. arXiv preprint arXiv:2111.09886 (2021)
73. Yosinski, J., Clune, J., Bengio, Y., Lipson, H.: How transferable are features in deep neural networks? arXiv preprint arXiv:1411.1792 (2014)
74. Yuan, L., et al.: Tokens-to-Token ViT: training vision transformers from scratch on ImageNet. arXiv preprint arXiv:2101.11986 (2021)
75. Zagoruyko, S., Komodakis, N.: Wide residual networks. arXiv preprint arXiv:1605.07146 (2016)
76. Zhou, J., et al.: iBOT: image BERT pre-training with online tokenizer. International Conference on Learning Representations (2022)

DeiT III: Revenge of the ViT

Hugo Touvron[1,2(✉)], Matthieu Cord[2], and Hervé Jégou[1]

[1] Meta AI, Fundamental AI Research (FAIR), Paris, France
htouvron@fb.com
[2] Sorbonne University, Paris, France

Abstract. A Vision Transformer (ViT) is a simple neural architecture amenable to serve several computer vision tasks. It has limited built-in architectural priors, in contrast to more recent architectures that incorporate priors either about the input data or of specific tasks. Recent works show that ViTs benefit from self-supervised pre-training, in particular BerT-like pre-training like BeiT.

In this paper, we revisit the supervised training of ViTs. Our procedure builds upon and simplifies a recipe introduced for training ResNet-50. It includes a new simple data-augmentation procedure with only 3 augmentations, closer to the practice in self-supervised learning. Our evaluations on Image classification (ImageNet-1k with and without pre-training on ImageNet-21k), transfer learning and semantic segmentation show that our procedure outperforms by a large margin previous fully supervised training recipes for ViT. It also reveals that the performance of our ViT trained with supervision is comparable to that of more recent architectures. Our results could serve as better baselines for recent self-supervised approaches demonstrated on ViT.

1 Introduction

After their vast success in NLP, transformers models [54] and their derivatives are increasingly popular in computer vision. They are now used in image classification [12], detection & segmentation [2], video analysis, etc. In particular, the vision transformers (ViT) of Dosovistky et al. [12] are a reasonable alternative to convolutional architectures. This supports the adoption of transformers as a general architecture able to learn convolutions as well as longer range operations through the attention process [4,7]. In contrast, convolutional networks [20,27,29,40] implicitly offer built-in translation invariance. As a result their training does not have to learn this prior. It is therefore not surprising that hybrid architectures that include convolution converge faster than ViTs [17].

Because they incorporate as priors only the co-localisation of pixels in patches, transformers have to learn about the structure of images while optimizing the model such that it processes the input with the objective of solving

Supplementary Information The online version contains supplementary material available at https://doi.org/10.1007/978-3-031-20053-3_30.

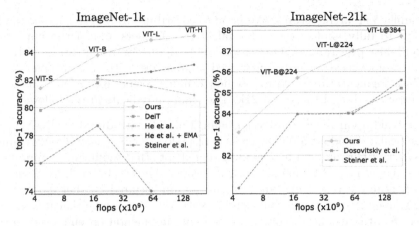

Fig. 1. Comparison of training recipes. *Left:* vanilla vision transformers trained on ImageNet-1k and evaluated at resolution 224 × 224. *Right:* pre-trained on ImageNet-21k at 224 × 224 and finetuned on ImageNet-1k at resolution 224 × 224 or 384 × 384.

a given task. This can be either reproducing labels in the supervised case, or other proxy tasks in the case of self-supervised approaches.

Nevertheless, despite their huge success, there has been only few works in computer vision studying how to efficiently train vision transformers, and in particular on a midsize dataset like ImageNet-1k. Since the work of Dosovistky et al. [12], the training procedures are mostly variants from the proposal of Touvron et al. [47] and Steiner et al. [41]. In contrast, multiple works have proposed alternative architectures by introducing pooling, more efficient attention, or hybrid architectures re-incorporating convolutions and a pyramid structure. These new designs, while being particularly effective for some tasks, are less general. One difficult question is whether the improved performance is due to a specific architectural design, or because it facilitates the optimization.

Recently, self-supervised approaches inspired by the popular BerT pre-training have raised hopes for a BerT moment in computer vision. There are some analogies between the fields of NLP and computer vision, starting with the transformer architecture itself. However, these fields are not identical in every way: The modalities processed are of different nature (continuous versus discrete). Computer vision offer large annotated databases like ImageNet [39], and fully supervised pre-training on ImageNet is effective for handling different downstream tasks such as transfer learning [36] or semantic segmentation.

Without further work on fully supervised approaches on ImageNet it is difficult to conclude if the intriguing performance of self-supervised approaches like BeiT [1] is due to the training, e.g. data augmentation, regularization, optimization, or to an underlying mechanism that is capable of learning more general implicit representations. In this paper, we do not pretend to answer this difficult question, but we want to feed this debate by renewing the training procedure for vanilla ViT architectures. We hope to contribute to a better understanding on how to fully exploit the potential of transformers and of the importance of BerT-like pre-training. Our work builds upon the recent state of the art on fully supervised and self-supervised approaches, with new insights regarding data-augmentation. We propose new training recipes for vision transformers on ImageNet-1k and ImageNet-21k. The main ingredients are as follows:

- We build upon the work of Wightman et al. [56] introduced for ResNet50. In particular we adopt a binary cross entropy loss for Imagenet1k only training. We adapt this method by including ingredients that significantly improve the training of large ViT [50], namely stochastic depth [24] and LayerScale [50].
- **3-Augment**: is a simple data augmentation inspired by that employed for self-supervised learning. Surprisingly, with ViT we observe that it works better than the usual automatic/learned data-augmentation employed to train vision transformers like RandAugment [5].
- **Simple Random Cropping** is more effective than Random Resize Cropping when pre-training on a larger set like ImageNet-21k.
- **A lower resolution** at training time. This choice reduces the train-test discrepancy [52] but has not been much exploited with ViT. We observe that it also has a regularizing effect for the largest models by preventing overfitting. For instance, for a target resolution of 224×224, a ViT-H pre-trained at resolution 126×126 (81 tokens) achieves a better performance on ImageNet-1k than when pre-training at resolution 224×224 (256 tokens). This is also less demanding at pre-training time, as there are 70% fewer tokens. From this perspective it offers similar scaling properties as mask-autoencoders [19].

Our "new" training strategies do not saturate with the largest models, making another step beyond the Data-Efficient Image Transformer (DeiT) by Touvron et al. [47]. As a result, we obtain a competitive performance in image classification and segmentation, even when compared to recent popular architectures such as SwinTransformers [31] or modern convnet architectures like ConvNext [32]. Below we point out a few interesting outcomes.

- We leverage models with more capacity even on midsize datasets. For instance, we reach 85.2% top-1 accuracy when training a ViT-H on ImageNet1k only, which is an improvement of +5.1% over the best ViT-H with supervised training procedure reported in the literature at resolution 224×224.
- Our training procedure for ImageNet-1k allow us to train a **billion-parameter ViT-H** (52 layers) without any hyper-parameter adaptation, just using the same stochastic depth drop-rate as for the ViT-H. It attains 84.9% at 224×224, i.e., +0.2% higher than the corresponding ViT-H trained in the same setting.
- Without sacrificing performance, we **divide by more than 2** the number of GPUs required and the training time for ViT-H, making it effectively possible to train such models with a reduced amount of resources. This is thanks to our pre-training at lower resolution, which reduces the peak memory.

- For ViT-B and Vit-L models, our supervised training approach is on par with BerT-like self-supervised approaches [1,19] with their default setting and when using the same level of annotations and less epochs, both for the tasks of image classification and of semantic segmentation.
- With this improved training procedure, a vanilla ViT closes the gap with recent state-of-the art architectures, often offering better compute/performance trade-offs. Our models are also comparatively better on the additional test set ImageNet-V2 [38], which indicates that our trained models generalize better to another validation set than most prior works.
- An ablation on the effect of the crop ratio employed in transfer learning classification tasks. We observe that it has a noticeable impact on the performance but that the best value depends a lot on the target dataset/task.

2   Related Work

Vision Transformers. were introduced by Dosovitskiy et al. [12]. This architecture, which derives from the transformer by Vaswani et al. [54], is now used as an alternative to convnets in many tasks: image classification [12,47], detection [2,31], semantic segmentation [1,31] video analysis [16,34], to name only a few. This greater flexibility typically comes with the downside that they need larger datasets, or the training must be adapted when the data is scarcer [13,47]. Many variants have been introduced to reduce the cost of attention by introducing for example more efficient attention [15,16,31] or pooling layers [21,31,55]. Some papers re-introduce spatial biases specific to convolutions within hybrid architectures [17,57,59]. These models are less general than vanilla transformers but generally perform well in certain computer vision tasks, because their architectural priors reduce the need to learn from scratch the task biases. This is especially important for smaller models, where specialized models do not have to devote some capacity to reproduce known priors such as translation invariance. The models are formally less flexible but they do not require sophisticated training procedures.

Training Procedures: The first procedure proposed in the ViT paper [12] was mostly effective for larger models trained on large datasets. In particular the ViT were not competitive with convnets when trained from scratch on ImageNet. Touvron et al. [47] showed that by adapting the training procedure, it is possible to achieve a performance comparable to that of convnets with Imagenet training only. After this Data Efficient Image Transformer procedure (DeiT), only few adaptations have been proposed to improve the training vision transformers. Steiner et al. [41] published a complete study on how to train vision transformers on different datasets by doing a complete ablation of the different training components. Their results on ImageNet [39] are slightly inferior to those of DeiT but they report improvements on ImageNet-21k compared to Dosovitskiy et al. [12]. The self-supervised approach referred to as masked auto-encoder (MAE) [19] proposes an improved supervised baseline for the larger ViT models.

BerT Pre-training: In the absence of a strong fully supervised training procedure, BerT [9]-like approaches that train ViT with a self-supervised proxy objective, followed by full finetuning on the target dataset, seem to be the best paradigm to fully exploit the potential of vision transformers. Indeed, BeiT [1] or MAE [19] significantly outperform the fully-supervised approach, especially for the largest models. Nevertheless, to date these approaches have mostly shown their interest in the context of mid-size datasets. For example MAE [19] report its most impressive results when pre-training on ImageNet-1k with a full finetuning on ImageNet-1k. When pre-training on ImageNet-21k and finetuning on ImageNet-1k, BeiT [1] requires a full 90-epochs finetuning on ImageNet-21k followed by another full finetuning on ImageNet-1k to reach its best performance, suggesting that a large labeled dataset is needed so that BeiT realizes its best potential. A recent work suggests that such auto-encoders are mostly interesting in a data starving context [14], but this questions their advantage in the case where more labelled data is actually available.

Data-Augmentation: For supervised training, the community commonly employs data-augmentations offered by automatic design procedures such as RandAugment [5] or Auto-Augment [6]. These data-augmentations seem to be essential for training vision transformers [47]. Nevertheless, papers like TrivialAugment [33] and Uniform Augment [30] have shown that it is possible to reach interesting performance levels when simplifying the approaches. However, these approaches were initially optimized for convnets. In our work, we propose to go further in this direction and drastically limit and simplify data-augmentation: we introduce a data-augmentation policy that employs only 3 different transformations randomly drawn with uniform probability. That's it!

3   Revisit Training and Pre-training for Vision Transformers

In this section, we present our training procedure for vision transformers and compare it with existing approaches. The detail the ingredients and hyperparameters ingredients in Table 8 in Appendix A.1. Building upon Wightman et al. [56] and Touvron et al. [47], we introduce several changes that have a significant impact on the final model accuracy.

3.1   Regularization and Loss

Stochastic depth is a regularization that is especially useful for training deep networks. We use a uniform drop rate across all layers and adapt it according to the model size [50]. Table 9 (Appendix A) gives the drop-rate per model.

LayerScale. We use LayerScale [50]. This method was introduced to facilitate the convergence of deep transformers. With our training procedure, we do not have convergence problems, however we observe that LayerScale allows our models to attain a higher accuracy for the largest models. In the original paper [50],

Table 1. Ablation of our data-augmentation strategy with ViT-B on ImageNet-1k.

Data-Augmentation				ImageNet-1k		
ColorJitter	Grayscale	Gaussian Blur	Solarization	Val	Real	V2
0.3	✗	✗	✗	81.4	86.1	70.3
0.3	✓	✗	✗	81.0	86.0	69.7
0.3	✓	✓	✗	82.7	87.6	**72.7**
0.3	✓	✓	✓	**83.1**	**87.7**	72.6
0.0	✓	✓	✓	**83.1**	**87.7**	72.0

the initialization of LayerScale is adapted according to the depth. In order to simplify the method we use the same initialization (10^{-4}) for all our models.

Binary Cross Entropy. Wigthman et al. [56] adopt a binary cross-entropy (BCE) loss instead of the more common cross-entropy (CE) to train ResNet-50. They conclude that the gains are limited compared to the CE loss but that this choice is more convenient when employed with Mixup [61] and CutMix [60]. For larger ViTs and with our training procedure on ImageNet-1k, the BCE loss provides us a significant improvement in performance, see an ablation in Table 3. We did not achieve compelling results during our exploration phase on ImageNet21k, and therefore keep CE when pre-training with this dataset as well as for the subsequent fine-tuning.

3.2   Data-Augmentation

Since the advent of AlexNet, there has been significant modifications to the data-augmentation procedures employed to train neural networks. Interestingly, the same data augmentation, like RandAugment [5], is widely employed for ViT while their policy was initially learned for convnets. Given that the architectural priors and biases are quite different in these architectures, the augmentation policy may not be adapted, and possibly overfitted considering the large amount of choices involved in their selection. We therefore revisit this prior choice.

3-Augment: We propose a simple data augmentation inspired by what is used in self-supervised learning (SSL). We consider the following transformations:

- Grayscale: This favors color invariance and give more focus on shapes.
- Solarization: This adds strong noise on the colour to be more robust to the variation of colour intensity and so focus more on shape.
- Gaussian Blur: In order to slightly alter details in the image.

For each image, we select only one of this data-augmentation with a uniform probability over 3 different ones. In addition to these 3 aumgnentations choices, we include the common color-jitter and horizontal flip. Figure 2 illustrates the different augmentations used in our 3-Augment approach. In Table 1 we provide an ablation on our different data-augmentation components.

3.3   Cropping

Random Resized Crop (RRC) was introduced in the GoogleNet [42] paper. It serves as a regularisation to limit model overfitting, while favoring that the decision done by the model is invariant to a certain class of transformations. This data augmentation was deemed important on Imagenet1k to prevent overfitting, which happens to occur rapidly with modern large models.

This cropping strategy however introduces some discrepancy between train and test images in terms of the aspect ratio and the apparent size of objects [52]. Since ImageNet-21k includes significantly more images, it is less prone to overfitting. Therefore we question whether the benefit of the strong RRC regularization compensates for its drawback when training on larger sets.

Simple Random Crop (SRC)   is a much simpler way to extract crops. It is similar to the original cropping choice proposed in AlexNet [27]: We resize the image such that the smallest side matches the training resolution. Then we apply a reflect padding of 4 pixels on all sides, and finally we apply a square Crop of training size randomly selected along the x-axis of the image.

Figure 7 vizualizes cropping boxes sampled for RRC and SRC. RRC provides a lot of diversity and very different sizes for crops. In contrast SRC covers a much larger fraction of the image overall and preserve the aspect ratio, but offers less diversity: The crops overlaps significantly. As a result, when training on ImageNet-1k the performance is better with the commonly used RRC. For instance a ViT-S reduces its top-1 accuracy by -0.9% if we do not use RRC.

However, in the case of ImageNet-21k ($\times 10$ bigger than ImageNet-1k), there is less risk of overfitting and increasing the regularisation and diversity offered by RRC is less important. In this context, SRC offers the advantage of reducing the discrepancy in apparent size and aspect ratio. More importantly, it gives a higher chance that the actual label of the image matches that of the crop: RRC is relatively aggressive in terms of cropping and in many cases the labelled object is not even present in the crop, as shown in Fig. 3 where some of the crops do not contain the labelled object. For instance, with RRC there is a crop no zebra in

Original   Gauss. Blurr   Grayscale   Solarization

Fig. 2. Illustration of the 3 type of data-augmentations used in 3-Augment.

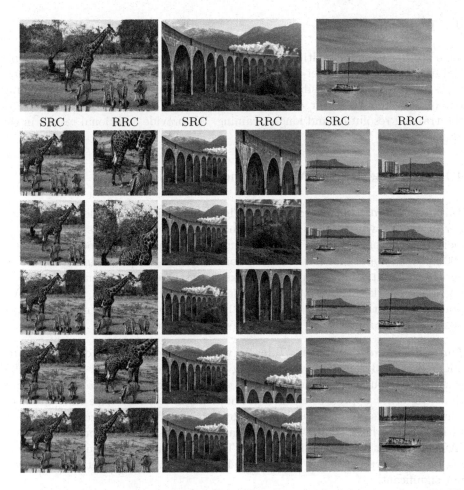

Fig. 3. Illustration of Random Resized Crop (RRC) and Simple Random Crop (SRC). The usual RRC is a more aggressive data-augmentation than SRC: It has a more important regularizing effect and avoids overfitting by giving more variability to the images. At the same time it introduces a discrepancy of scale and aspect-ratio. It also leads to labeling errors, for instance when the object is not in the cropped region (e.g., train or boat). On ImageNet-1k this regularization is overall regarded as beneficial. However our experiments show that it is detrimental on ImageNet-21k, which is less prone to overfitting.

the left example, or no train in three of the crops from the middle example. This is more unlikely to happen with SRC, which covers a much larger fraction of the image pixels. In the supplemental material, in Table 16 we provide an ablation of random resized crop on ImageNet-21k, where we see that these observations translate as a significant gain in performance.

4   Experiments

This section includes multiple experiments in image classification, with a special emphasis on ImageNet-1k [8,38,39]. We also report results for downstream tasks in fine-grained classification and segmentation. We include a large number of ablations to better analyze different effects, such as the importance of the training resolution and longer training. We provide additional results in the appendices.

4.1   Training Recipes Ablation and Comparison

Impact of Training Duration. In Fig. 4 we provide an ablation on the number of epochs, which shows that ViT models do not saturate as rapidly as the DeiT training procedure [47] when we increase the number of epochs beyond the 400 epochs adopted for our baseline. For ImageNet-21k pre-training, we use 90 epochs for pre-training as in a few works [31,48]. We finetune during 50 epochs on ImageNet-1k [48] and marginally adapt the stochastic depth parameter. We point out that this choice is mostly for the sake of consistency across models: we observe that training 30 epochs also provides similar results.

Data-Augmentation. In Table 2 we compare our handcrafted data-augmentation 3-Augment with existing augmentation methods. With the ViT architecture, our data-augmentation is the most effective while being simpler than the other approaches. Since previous augmentations were introduced on convnets, we also provide results for a ResNet-50. In this case, previous augmentation policies have similar (RandAugment, Trivial-Augment) or better results (Auto-Augment) on the validation set. This is no longer the case when evaluating on the independent set V2, for which the Auto-Augment better accuracy is not significant.

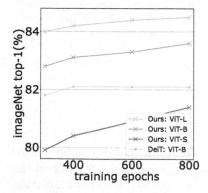

Fig. 4. Accuracy on ImageNet-1k only at resolution 224 × 224 with our training recipes and a different number of epochs.

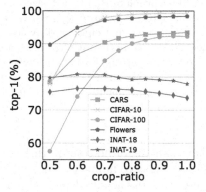

Fig. 5. Transfer learning performance on 6 datasets with different test-time crop ratio. ViT-B pre-trained at resolution 224.

Table 2. Comparison of our simple 3-Augment with existing data-augmentation used with self-supervised learning.

Method	Learned	#DA	Model	ImageNet-1k Val Real V2
Auto-Augment (AutoAug [6])	✓	14	ResNet50	79.7 85.6 67.9
			ViT-B	82.8 87.5 71.9
			ViT-L	84.0 **88.6** 74.0
RandAugment (RandAug [5])	✓	14	ResNet50	79.5 85.5 67.6
			ViT-B	82.7 87.4 72.2
			ViT-L	84.0 88.3 73.8
Trivial-Augment [33]	✗	14	ResNet50	79.5 85.4 67.6
			ViT-B	82.3 87.0 71.2
			ViT-L	83.6 88.1 73.7
3-Augment (3aug: *ours*)	✗	3	ResNet50	79.4 85.5 67.8
			ViT-B	**83.1 87.7 72.6**
			ViT-L	**84.2 88.6 74.3**

Table 3. Ablation of training components with training at resolution 224×224 on ImageNet-1k, evaluated on different sets.

Model	Loss	LS	Augm.	Epochs	ImageNet-1k val real v2
ViT-S	CE	✗	RandAug	300	79.8 85.3 68.1
	BCE	✗	RandAug	300	79.8 85.9 68.2
	BCE	✓	RandAug	300	80.1 **86.1** 69.1
	BCE	✓	RandAug	400	**80.7** 86.0 69.3
	BCE	✓	3-Augment	400	80.4 **86.1 69.7**
ViT-B	CE	✗	RandAug	300	80.9 85.5 68.5
	BCE	✗	RandAug	300	82.2 87.2 71.4
	BCE	✓	RandAug	300	82.5 87.5 71.4
	BCE	✓	RandAug	400	82.7 87.4 72.2
	BCE	✓	3-Augment	400	**83.1 87.7 72.6**
ViT-L	BCE	✗	RandAug	300	83.0 87.9 72.4
	BCE	✗	RandAug	400	83.3 87.7 72.5
	BCE	✓	RandAug	400	84.0 88.3 73.8
	BCE	✓	3-Augment	400	**84.2 88.6 74.3**

Comparison with Previous Training Recipes for ViT. In Fig. 1, we compare training procedures used to pre-train the ViT architecture either on ImageNet-1k and ImageNet-21k. Our procedure outperforms existing recipes with a large margin. For instance, with ImageNet-21k pre-training we have an improvement of +3.0% with ViT-L in comparison to the best approach. Similarly, when training from scratch on ImageNet-1k we improve the accuracy by +2.1% for ViT-H compared to the previous best approach, and by +4.3% with the best approach that does not use EMA. See also detailed results in appendices.

4.2   Image Classification

ImageNet-1k. In Table 4 we compare ViT architectures trained with our training recipes on ImageNet-1k with other architectures. We include a comparison with the recent SwinTransformers [31] and ConvNeXts [32].

Overfitting Evaluation. The comparison between ImageNet-val and -v2 is a way to quantify overfitting [53], or at least the better capability to generalize in a nearby setting without any fine-tuning[1]. In Fig. 6 we plot ImageNet-val top-1 accuracy vs ImageNet-v2 top-1 accuracy in order to evaluate how the models performed when evaluated on a test set never seen at validation time. Our models overfit significantly less than all other models considered, especially

---

[1] Note, the measures are less robust with -V2 as the number of test images is 10000 instead of 50000 for Imagenet-val, leading to a standard deviation around 0.2%.

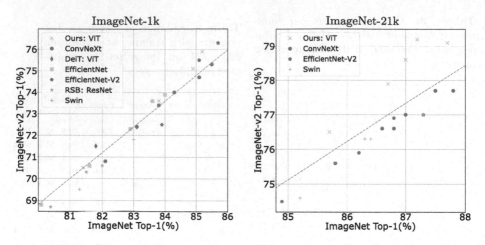

Fig. 6. Generalization experiment: top-1 accuracy on ImageNet1k-val vs ImageNet-v2 for models in Table 13 and Table 14. We display a linear interpolation of all points in order to compare the level of overfitting for the different models.

on ImageNet-21k. This is a good behaviour that validates the fact that our restricted choice of hyper-parameters and variants in our recipe does not lead to (too much) overfitting.

ImageNet-21k. In Table 4 (right columns), we compare ViT pre-trained on ImageNet-21k with our training recipe then finetuned on ImageNet-1k. We can observe that the findings are similar to what we obtained on ImageNet-1k only.

Comparison with BerT-like Pre-training. In Table 5 we compare ViT models trained with our training recipes with ViT trained with different BerT-like approaches. We observe that for an equivalent number of epochs our approach gives comparable performance on ImageNet-1k and better on ImageNet-v2 as well as in segmentation on Ade. For BerT like pre-training we compare our method with MAE [19] and BeiT [1] because they remain relatively simple approaches with very good performance. As our approach does not use distillation or multi-crops we have not made a comparison with approaches such as PeCo [11] which use an auxiliary model as a psycho-visual loss and iBoT [63], which uses multi-crop and an exponential moving average of the model.

Transfer Learning. In order to evaluate the quality of the ViT models learned through our training procedure we evaluated them with transfer learning tasks. We focus on the performance of ViT models pre-trained on ImageNet-1k only at resolution 224 × 224 during 400 epochs on the 6 datasets shown in Table 10. Our results are presented in Table 6. In Fig. 5 we measure the impact of the crop ratio at inference time on transfer learning results. We observe that on iNaturalist this parameter has a significant impact on the performance. As recommended

Table 4. Classification on ImageNet-1k. We compare architectures with comparable FLOPs and number of parameters. All models are evaluated with pre-training on ImageNet-1k (INet-1k) or on ImageNet-21k (INet-21k) without distillation nor self-supervised pre-training. We report Top-1 accuracy on the validation set of ImageNet-1k and ImageNet-V2 with different measure of complexity: throughput, FLOPs, number of parameters and peak memory usage. The throughput and peak memory are measured on a single V100-32GB GPU with batch size fixed to 256 and mixed precision. For Swin-L we decrease the batch size to 128 in order to avoid out of memory error and re-estimate the memory consumption. ↑R indicates that the model is fine-tuned at the target resolution R. See Tables 13 and 14 in appendix for more comparisons.

Architecture	nb params ($\times 10^6$)	throughput (im/s)	FLOPs ($\times 10^9$)	Peak Mem (MB)	INet-1k pretr.		INet-21k pretr.	
					Top-1	V2	Top-1	V2
"Traditional" ConvNets								
EfficientNetV2-S↑384 [44]	21.5	874	8.5	4515	83.9	74.0	84.9	74.5
EfficientNetV2-M↑480 [44]	54.1	312	25.0	7127	85.1	75.5	86.2	75.9
EfficientNetV2-L↑480 [44]	118.5	179	53.0	9540	85.7	76.3	86.8	76.9
EfficientNetV2-XL↑512 [44]	208.1	–	94.0	–	–	–	87.3	77.0
Patch-based ConvNets								
ConvNeXt-B [32]	88.6	563	15.4	3029	83.8	73.4	85.8	75.6
ConvNeXt-B↑384 [32]	88.6	190	45.1	7851	85.1	74.7	86.8	76.6
ConvNeXt-L [32]	197.8	344	34.4	4865	84.3	74.0	86.6	76.6
ConvNeXt-L↑384 [32]	197.8	115	101	11938	85.5	75.3	87.5	77.7
ConvNeXt-XL [32]	350.2	241	60.9	6951	–	–	87.0	77.0
ConvNeXt-XL↑384 [32]	350.2	80	179.0	16260	–	–	87.8	77.7
Vision transformers derivative								
Swin-B [31]	87.8	532	15.4	4695	83.5	–	85.2	74.6
Swin-B↑384 [31]	87.9	160	47.0	19385	84.5	–	86.4	76.3
Swin-L [31]	196.5	337	34.5	7350	–	–	86.3	76.3
Swin-L↑384 [31]	196.7	100	103.9	33456	–	–	87.3	77.0
Vanilla vision transformers								
ViT-B/16 [41]	86.6	831	17.6	2078	79.8	–	84.0	–
ViT-B/16↑384 [41]	86.7	190	55.5	8956	81.6	–	85.5	–
ViT-L/16 [41]	304.4	277	61.6	3789	75.7	–	84.0	–
ViT-L/16↑384 [41]	304.8	67	191.1	12866	77.2	–	85.5	–
Our vanilla vision transformers								
ViT-S	22.0	1891	4.6	987	81.4	70.5	83.1	73.8
ViT-B	86.6	831	17.6	2078	83.8	73.6	85.7	76.5
ViT-B↑384	86.9	190	55.5	8956	85.0	74.8	86.7	77.9
ViT-L	304.4	277	61.6	3789	84.9	75.1	87.0	78.6
ViT-L↑384	304.8	67	191.2	12866	85.8	76.7	87.7	79.1
ViT-H	632.1	112	167.4	6984	85.2	75.9	87.2	79.2

in the paper Three Things [49] we finetune only the attention layers for transfer learning experiments on Flowers.

Semantic Segmentation. We evaluate our ViT baselines models (400 epochs schedules for ImageNet-1k models and 90 epochs for ImageNet-21k models) with semantic segmentation experiments on ADE20k dataset [62]. For the training, we adopt the same schedule as in Swin: 160k iterations with UperNet [58]. At

Table 5. Comparison of self-supervised pre-training with our approach. As our approach is fully supervised, this table is given as an indication. All models are evaluated at resolution 224×224. We report Image classification results on ImageNet val, real and v2 in order to evaluate overfitting. $^{(21k)}$ indicate a finetuning with labels on ImageNet-21k and $^{(1k)}$ indicate a finetuning with labels on ImageNet-1k. * design the improved setting of MAE using pixel (w/ norm) loss.

Pretrained data	Model	Method	# pre-training epochs	# finetuning epochs	ImageNet val	Real	V2
INET-1k	ViT-B	BeiT	300	$100^{(1k)}$	82.9	-	-
			800	$100^{(1k)}$	83.2	-	-
		MAE*	1600	$100^{(1k)}$	83.6	88.1	73.2
		Ours	$400^{(1k)}$	$20^{(1k)}$	83.5	88.0	72.8
			$800^{(1k)}$	$20^{(1k)}$	**83.8**	**88.2**	**73.6**
	ViT-L	BeiT	800	$30^{(1k)}$	85.2	-	-
		MAE	400	$50^{(1k)}$	84.3	-	-
			800	$50^{(1k)}$	84.9	-	-
			1600	$50^{(1k)}$	85.1	-	-
		MAE*	1600	$50^{(1k)}$	**85.9**	**89.4**	**76.5**
		Ours	$400^{(1k)}$	$20^{(1k)}$	84.5	88.8	75.1
			$800^{(1k)}$	$20^{(1k)}$	84.9	88.7	75.1
INET-21k	ViT-B	BeiT	150	$50^{(1k)}$	83.7	88.2	73.1
			$150 + 90^{(21k)}$	$50^{(1k)}$	85.2	89.4	75.4
		Ours	$90^{(21k)}$	$50^{(1k)}$	85.2	89.4	76.1
			$240^{(21k)}$	$50^{(1k)}$	**85.7**	**89.5**	**76.5**
	ViT-L	BeiT	150	$50^{(1k)}$	86.0	89.6	76.7
			$150 + 90^{(21k)}$	$50^{(1k)}$	**87.5**	**90.1**	**78.8**
		Ours	$90^{(21k)}$	$50^{(1k)}$	86.8	89.9	78.3
			$240^{(21k)}$	$50^{(1k)}$	87.0	90.0	78.6

Table 6. We compare Transformers based models on different transfer learning tasks with ImageNet-1k pre-training. We report results with our default training on ImageNet-1k (400 epochs at resolution 224 × 224). We also report results with convnets for reference. For consistency we keep our crop ratio equal to 1.0 on all datasets. Other works use 0.875, which is better for iNat-19 and iNat-18, see Fig. 5.

Model	CIFAR-10	CIFAR-100	Flowers	Cars	iNat-18	iNat-19
Grafit ResNet-50 [51]	-	-	98.2	92.5	69.8	75.9
ResNet-152 [3]	-	-	-	-	69.1	-
ViT-B/16 [12]	98.1	87.1	89.5	-	-	-
ViT-L/16 [12]	97.9	86.4	89.7	-	-	-
ViT-B/16 [41]	-	87.8	96.0	-	-	-
ViT-L/16 [41]	-	86.2	91.4	-	-	-
DeiT-B	99.1	90.8	98.4	92.1	73.2	77.7
Ours ViT-S	98.9	90.6	96.4	89.9	67.1	72.7
Ours ViT-B	99.3	92.5	98.6	93.4	73.6	78.0
Ours ViT-L	**99.3**	**93.4**	**98.9**	**94.5**	**75.6**	**79.3**

Table 7. ADE20k semantic segmentation performance using UperNet [58] (in comparable settings [10,15,31]). All models are pre-trained on ImageNet-1k except models with † symbol that are pre-trained on ImageNet-21k. We report the pre-training resolution used on ImageNet-1k and ImageNet-21k.

Backbone	Pre-training resolution	#params ($\times 10^6$)	FLOPs ($\times 10^9$)	Single scale mIoU	Multi-scale mIoU
ResNet50	224×224	66.5	–	42.0	–
DeiT-S	224×224	52.0	1099	–	44.0
XciT-T12/16	224×224	34.2	874	41.5	–
XciT-T12/8	224×224	33.9	942	43.5	–
Swin-T	224×224	59.9	945	44.5	46.1
Our ViT-T	224×224	10.9	148	40.1	41.8
Our ViT-S	224×224	41.7	588	**45.6**	**46.8**
XciT-M24/16	224×224	112.2	1213	47.6	–
XciT-M24/8	224×224	110.0	2161	48.4	–
PatchConvNet-B60	224×224	140.6	1258	48.1	48.6
PatchConvNet-B120	224×224	229.8	1550	49.4	50.3
MAE ViT-B	224×224	127.7	1283	48.1	–
Swin-B	384×384	121.0	1188	48.1	49.7
Our ViT-B	224×224	127.7	1283	49.3	50.2
Our ViT-L	224×224	353.6	2231	**51.5**	**52.0**
PatchConvNet–B60†	224×224	140.6	1258	50.5	51.1
PatchConvNet-L120†	224×224	383.7	2086	52.2	52.9
Swin-B† (640×640)	224×224	121.0	1841	50.0	51.6
Swin-L† (640×640)	224×224	234.0	3230	–	53.5
Our ViT-B†	224×224	127.7	1283	51.8	52.8
Our ViT-B†	384×384	127.7	1283	53.4	54.1
Our ViT-L†	224×224	353.6	2231	53.8	54.7
Our ViT-L†	320×320	353.6	2231	**54.6**	**55.6**

test time we evaluate with a single scale and multi-scale. See Appendix B for more details. Our results are reported in Table 7. We observe that vanilla ViTs trained with our training recipes have a better FLOPs-accuracy trade-off than recent architectures like XCiT or Swin.

5   Conclusion

This paper makes a simple contribution: it proposes improved baselines for vision transformers trained in a supervised fashion that can serve (1) as a comparison basis for new architectures; (2) for other training approaches such as those based on self-supervised learning. We hope that this strong baseline will serve the community effort in making progress on learning foundation models that could serve many tasks. Our experiments have also gathered a few insights on how to train ViT for larger models with reduced resources without hurting accuracy, allowing us to train a one-billion parameter model with 4 nodes of 8 GPUs.

References

1. Bao, H., Dong, L., Wei, F.: BEiT: BERT pre-training of image transformers. arXiv preprint arXiv:2106.08254 (2021)
2. Carion, N., Massa, F., Synnaeve, G., Usunier, N., Kirillov, A., Zagoruyko, S.: End-to-end object detection with transformers. In: Vedaldi, A., Bischof, H., Brox, T., Frahm, J.-M. (eds.) ECCV 2020. LNCS, vol. 12346, pp. 213–229. Springer, Cham (2020). https://doi.org/10.1007/978-3-030-58452-8_13
3. Chu, P., Bian, X., Liu, S., Ling, H.: Feature space augmentation for long-tailed data. arXiv preprint arXiv:2008.03673 (2020)
4. Cordonnier, J.B., Loukas, A., Jaggi, M.: On the relationship between self-attention and convolutional layers. arXiv preprint arXiv:1911.03584 (2019)
5. Cubuk, E.D., Zoph, B., Shlens, J., Le, Q.V.: RandAugment: practical automated data augmentation with a reduced search space. arXiv preprint arXiv:1909.13719 (2019)
6. Cubuk, E.D., Zoph, B., Mané, D., Vasudevan, V., Le, Q.V.: AutoAugment: learning augmentation policies from data. arXiv preprint arXiv:1805.09501 (2018)
7. d'Ascoli, S., Touvron, H., Leavitt, M.L., Morcos, A.S., Biroli, G., Sagun, L.: ConViT: improving vision transformers with soft convolutional inductive biases. In: ICML (2021)
8. Deng, J., Dong, W., Socher, R., Li, L.J., Li, K., Fei-Fei, L.: ImageNet: a large-scale hierarchical image database. In: Conference on Computer Vision and Pattern Recognition, pp. 248–255 (2009)
9. Devlin, J., Chang, M.W., Lee, K., Toutanova, K.: BERT: pre-training of deep bidirectional transformers for language understanding. In: NAACL (2019)
10. Dong, X., et al.: CSWin transformer: a general vision transformer backbone with cross-shaped windows. arXiv preprint arXiv:2107.00652 (2021)
11. Dong, X., et al.: PeCo: perceptual codebook for BERT pre-training of vision transformers. arXiv preprint arXiv:2111.12710 (2021)
12. Dosovitskiy, A., et al.: An image is worth 16×16 words: transformers for image recognition at scale. In: International Conference on Learning Representations (2021)
13. El-Nouby, A., Izacard, G., Touvron, H., Laptev, I., Jegou, H., Grave, E.: Are large-scale datasets necessary for self-supervised pre-training? arXiv preprint arXiv:2112.10740 (2021)
14. El-Nouby, A., Neverova, N., Laptev, I., Jégou, H.: Training vision transformers for image retrieval. arXiv preprint arXiv:2102.05644 (2021)

15. El-Nouby, A., et al.: XCiT: cross-covariance image transformers. arXiv preprint arXiv:2106.09681 (2021)
16. Fan, H., et al.: Multiscale vision transformers. arXiv preprint arXiv:2104.11227 (2021)
17. Graham, B., et al.: LeViT: a vision transformer in convnet's clothing for faster inference. arXiv preprint arXiv:2104.01136 (2021)
18. Han, K., Xiao, A., Wu, E., Guo, J., Xu, C., Wang, Y.: Transformer in transformer. arXiv preprint arXiv:2103.00112 (2021)
19. He, K., Chen, X., Xie, S., Li, Y., Doll'ar, P., Girshick, R.B.: Masked autoencoders are scalable vision learners. arXiv preprint arXiv:2111.06377 (2021)
20. He, K., Zhang, X., Ren, S., Sun, J.: Deep residual learning for image recognition. In: Conference on Computer Vision and Pattern Recognition (2016)
21. Heo, B., Yun, S., Han, D., Chun, S., Choe, J., Oh, S.J.: Rethinking spatial dimensions of vision transformers. arXiv preprint arXiv:2103.16302 (2021)
22. Horn, G.V., et al: The iNaturalist species classification and detection dataset. arXiv preprint arXiv:1707.06642 (2017)
23. Horn, G.V., et al.: The inaturalist challenge 2018 dataset. arXiv preprint arXiv:1707.06642 (2018)
24. Huang, G., Sun, Yu., Liu, Z., Sedra, D., Weinberger, K.Q.: Deep networks with stochastic depth. In: Leibe, B., Matas, J., Sebe, N., Welling, M. (eds.) ECCV 2016. LNCS, vol. 9908, pp. 646–661. Springer, Cham (2016). https://doi.org/10.1007/978-3-319-46493-0_39
25. Kolesnikov, A., et al.: Big transfer (bit): general visual representation learning. arXiv preprint arXiv:1912.11370 **6**, 3 (2019)
26. Krause, J., Stark, M., Deng, J., Fei-Fei, L.: 3D object representations for fine-grained categorization. In: IEEE Workshop on 3D Representation and Recognition (2013)
27. Krizhevsky, A., Sutskever, I., Hinton, G.: ImageNet classification with deep convolutional neural networks. In: NeurIPS (2012)
28. Krizhevsky, A.: Learning multiple layers of features from tiny images. Technical report, CIFAR (2009)
29. LeCun, Y., Bottou, L., Bengio, Y., Haffner, P.: Gradient-based learning applied to document recognition. Proc. IEEE **86**(11), 2278–2324 (1998)
30. LingChen, T.C., Khonsari, A., Lashkari, A., Nazari, M.R., Sambee, J.S., Nascimento, M.A.: UniformAugment: a search-free probabilistic data augmentation approach. arXiv preprint arXiv:2003.14348 (2020)
31. Liu, Z., et al.: Swin transformer: hierarchical vision transformer using shifted windows. arXiv preprint arXiv:2103.14030 (2021)
32. Liu, Z., Mao, H., Wu, C.Y., Feichtenhofer, C., Darrell, T., Xie, S.: A convnet for the 2020s. arXiv preprint arXiv:2201.03545 (2022)
33. Müller, S., Hutter, F.: TrivialAugment: tuning-free yet state-of-the-art data augmentation. arXiv preprint arXiv:2103.10158 (2021)
34. Neimark, D., Bar, O., Zohar, M., Asselmann, D.: Video transformer network. arXiv preprint arXiv:2102.00719 (2021)
35. Nilsback, M.E., Zisserman, A.: Automated flower classification over a large number of classes. In: Proceedings of the Indian Conference on Computer Vision, Graphics and Image Processing (2008)
36. Oquab, M., Bottou, L., Laptev, I., Sivic, J.: Learning and transferring mid-level image representations using convolutional neural networks. In: Conference on Computer Vision and Pattern Recognition (2014)

37. Radosavovic, I., Kosaraju, R.P., Girshick, R.B., He, K., Dollár, P.: Designing network design spaces. In: Conference on Computer Vision and Pattern Recognition (2020)
38. Recht, B., Roelofs, R., Schmidt, L., Shankar, V.: Do ImageNet classifiers generalize to ImageNet? In: International Conference on Machine Learning (2019)
39. Russakovsky, O., et al.: ImageNet large scale visual recognition challenge. Int. J. Comput. Vision **115**(3), 211–252 (2015)
40. Simonyan, K., Zisserman, A.: Very deep convolutional networks for large-scale image recognition. In: International Conference on Learning Representations (2015)
41. Steiner, A., Kolesnikov, A., Zhai, X., Wightman, R., Uszkoreit, J., Beyer, L.: How to train your ViT? Data, augmentation, and regularization in vision transformers. arXiv preprint arXiv:2106.10270 (2021)
42. Szegedy, C., et al.: Going deeper with convolutions. In: Conference on Computer Vision and Pattern Recognition (2015)
43. Tan, M., Le, Q.V.: EfficientNet: rethinking model scaling for convolutional neural networks. arXiv preprint arXiv:1905.11946 (2019)
44. Tan, M., Le, Q.V.: EfficientNetV2: smaller models and faster training. In: International Conference on Machine Learning (2021)
45. Tolstikhin, I., et al.: MLP-mixer: an all-MLP architecture for vision. arXiv preprint arXiv:2105.01601 (2021)
46. Touvron, H., et al.: ResMLP: feedforward networks for image classification with data-efficient training. arXiv preprint arXiv:2105.03404 (2021)
47. Touvron, H., Cord, M., Douze, M., Massa, F., Sablayrolles, A., Jégou, H.: Training data-efficient image transformers & distillation through attention. In: International Conference on Machine Learning (2021)
48. Touvron, H., et al.: Augmenting convolutional networks with attention-based aggregation. arXiv preprint arXiv:2112.13692 (2021)
49. Touvron, H., Cord, M., El-Nouby, A., Verbeek, J., J'egou, H.: Three things everyone should know about vision transformers. arXiv preprint arXiv:2203.09795 (2022)
50. Touvron, H., Cord, M., Sablayrolles, A., Synnaeve, G., Jégou, H.: Going deeper with image transformers. In: International Conference on Computer Vision (2021)
51. Touvron, H., Sablayrolles, A., Douze, M., Cord, M., Jégou, H.: Grafit: learning fine-grained image representations with coarse labels. In: International Conference on Computer Vision (2021)
52. Touvron, H., Vedaldi, A., Douze, M., Jegou, H.: Fixing the train-test resolution discrepancy. In: Neurips (2019)
53. Touvron, H., Vedaldi, A., Douze, M., Jégou, H.: Fixing the train-test resolution discrepancy: FixEfficientNet. arXiv preprint arXiv:2003.08237 (2020)
54. Vaswani, A., et al.: Attention is all you need. In: NeurIPS (2017)
55. Wang, W., et al.: Pyramid vision transformer: a versatile backbone for dense prediction without convolutions. arXiv preprint arXiv:2102.12122 (2021)
56. Wightman, R., Touvron, H., Jégou, H.: ResNet strikes back: an improved training procedure in TIMM. arXiv preprint arXiv:2110.00476 (2021)
57. Wu, H., et al.: CVT: introducing convolutions to vision transformers. arXiv preprint arXiv:2103.15808 (2021)
58. Xiao, T., Liu, Y., Zhou, B., Jiang, Y., Sun, J.: Unified perceptual parsing for scene understanding. In: Ferrari, V., Hebert, M., Sminchisescu, C., Weiss, Y. (eds.) ECCV 2018. LNCS, vol. 11209, pp. 432–448. Springer, Cham (2018). https://doi.org/10.1007/978-3-030-01228-1_26

59. Xiao, T., Singh, M., Mintun, E., Darrell, T., Dollár, P., Girshick, R.: Early convolutions help transformers see better. arXiv preprint arXiv:2106.14881 (2021)
60. Yun, S., Han, D., Oh, S.J., Chun, S., Choe, J., Yoo, Y.: CutMix: regularization strategy to train strong classifiers with localizable features. arXiv preprint arXiv:1905.04899 (2019)
61. Zhang, H., Cissé, M., Dauphin, Y.N., Lopez-Paz, D.: Mixup: beyond empirical risk minimization. arXiv preprint arXiv:1710.09412 (2017)
62. Zhou, B., Zhao, H., Puig, X., Fidler, S., Barriuso, A., Torralba, A.: Scene parsing through ADE20K dataset. In: Conference on Computer Vision and Pattern Recognition (2017)
63. Zhou, J., et al.: iBOT: image BERT pre-training with online tokenizer. arXiv preprint arXiv:2111.07832 (2021)

MixSKD: Self-Knowledge Distillation from Mixup for Image Recognition

Chuanguang Yang[1,2], Zhulin An[1(✉)], Helong Zhou[3], Linhang Cai[1,2], Xiang Zhi[1,2], Jiwen Wu[1], Yongjun Xu[1], and Qian Zhang[3]

[1] Institute of Computing Technology, Chinese Academy of Sciences, Beijing, China
{yangchuanguang,anzhulin,cailinhang19g,zhixiang20g,xyj}@ict.ac.cn
[2] University of Chinese Academy of Sciences, Beijing, China
[3] Horizon Robotics, Beijing, China
{helong.zhou,qian01.zhang}@horizon.ai

Abstract. Unlike the conventional Knowledge Distillation (KD), Self-KD allows a network to learn knowledge from itself without any guidance from extra networks. This paper proposes to perform Self-KD from image Mixture (MixSKD), which integrates these two techniques into a unified framework. MixSKD mutually distills feature maps and probability distributions between the random pair of original images and their mixup images in a meaningful way. Therefore, it guides the network to learn cross-image knowledge by modelling supervisory signals from mixup images. Moreover, we construct a self-teacher network by aggregating multi-stage feature maps for providing soft labels to supervise the backbone classifier, further improving the efficacy of self-boosting. Experiments on image classification and transfer learning to object detection and semantic segmentation demonstrate that MixSKD outperforms other state-of-the-art Self-KD and data augmentation methods. The code is available at https://github.com/winycg/Self-KD-Lib.

Keywords: Self-Knowledge Distillation · Mixup · Image recognition

1 Introduction

Knowledge Distillation (KD) [15] is an effective paradigm to enable a given student network to generalize better under the guidance of a pre-trained high-performance teacher. The seminal KD guides the student to mimic the predictive class probability distributions (also namely *soft labels*) generated from the teacher. Interestingly, although the soft label assigns probabilities to incorrect classes, the relative probability distribution also encodes meaningful information on similarity among various categories [46]. The soft label has been widely demonstrated as dark knowledge to enhance the student's performance [15,46].

Supplementary Information The online version contains supplementary material available at https://doi.org/10.1007/978-3-031-20053-3_31.

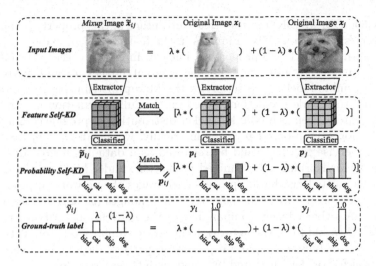

Fig. 1. Overview of the basic idea about our proposed MixSKD.

The conventional KD [15, 30, 38, 39, 43] relies on a pretrained teacher to provide soft labels. Thus the two-stage process increases the training pipeline and is time-consuming. Recent studies of *Self-KD* have illuminated that a network can distill its own knowledge to teach itself without a pretrained teacher. However, exploring knowledge from the network itself is a non-trivial problem. Existing Self-KD works often employ *auxiliary architecture* [18, 31, 51–53] or *data augmentation* [37, 48] to capture additional knowledge to enhance the network. The auxiliary-architecture-based method often appends extra branches to the backbone network. Self-KD regularizes these branches and the backbone network to generate similar predictions via knowledge transfer [31, 52]. Another vein is to mine meaningful knowledge from external data augmentations. Data-augmentation-based methods aim to regularize the consistent predictions between distorted versions of the same instance [37] or two instances from the same class [48]. A common point of previous Self-KD methods is that the mined supervisory signal, *e.g.* soft label, is generated from an individual input sample.

In contrast, we propose incorporating **Self-KD** with image **Mix**ture (namely MixSKD) into a unified framework. Image mixture has been developed as an advanced data augmentation called Mixup [50]. Mixup performs pixel-wise image mixture between two randomly sampled images x_i and x_j to construct a virtual sample $\tilde{x}_{ij}$. The virtual sample's label $\tilde{y}_{ij}$ is a linear interpolation between the one-hot ground-truth labels of y_i and y_j with the same mixture proportion. Additional Mixup images introduce more samples in the input space by randomly fusing different images. This allows Self-KD to distill richer knowledge towards image mixture over the independent samples. The success behind Mixup is to encourage the network to favour simple linear behaviours in-between training samples [50]. Our MixSKD further takes advantage of this property by modelling supervisory signals from Mixup images in the feature and probability space.

As shown in Fig. 1, we propose to linearly interpolate the probability distributions p_i and p_j inferred from the original images x_i and x_j to model the soft ensemble label p_{ij} to supervise the Mixup distribution $\tilde{p}_{ij}$. Intuitively, p_{ij} encodes the crude predictions based on the full information in two original images. It can be seen as a pseudo teacher distribution to provide comprehensive knowledge for Mixup-based $\tilde{p}_{ij}$. Symmetrically, we also regard $\tilde{p}_{ij}$ as the soft label to supervise p_{ij}. $\tilde{p}_{ij}$ could be regarded as a data-augmented distribution to refine p_{ij} for learning robust mixed predictions under Mixup and avoid overfitting. The mutual distillation process encourages the network to produce consistent predictions between the pair of original images (x_i, x_j) and their Mixup image $\tilde{x}_{ij}$. Another efficacy compared with the conventional Mixup training is that Self-KD would force the network to generate similar wrong predictions over incorrect classes between p_{ij} and $\tilde{p}_{ij}$. This property of dark knowledge may also be a critical factor demonstrated by previous KD research [46].

Inspired by [31,38,39,52], we append auxiliary feature alignment modules for transforming the feature maps from shallow layers to match the hierarchy with the final feature map. We match these feature maps between the pair of original images (x_i, x_j) and their Mixup image $\tilde{x}_{ij}$ via Self-KD, as shown in Fig. 1. Motivated by [36], we propose an adversarial feature Self-KD method that utilizes l_2 loss to force the feature maps to be close and a discriminator loss to simultaneously increase the difficulty of mimicry. This process encourages the network to learn common semantics between matched feature maps. We further attach auxiliary classifiers to these hidden feature maps to output probability distributions and perform probability Self-KD. This further regularizes the consistency of intermediate information.

Over the training graph, we also construct a self-teacher to supervise the final classifier of the backbone network. The self-teacher aggregates all intermediate feature maps and uses a linear classifier to provide meaningful soft labels. The soft label is informative since it assembles all feature information across the network. During the training phase, we introduce auxiliary branches and a self-teacher to assist Self-KD. During the test phase, we discard all auxiliary architectures, resulting in no extra costs compared with the baseline.

Following the consistent benchmark [18,48], we demonstrate that MixSKD is superior to State-Of-The-Art (SOTA) Self-KD methods and data augmentation approaches on image classification tasks. Extensive experiments on downstream object detection and semantic segmentation further show the superiority of MixSKD in generating better feature representations.

The contributions are three-fold: (1) We propose incorporating Self-KD with image mixture into a unified framework in a meaningful manner to improve image recognition. (2) We construct a self-teacher by aggregating multi-stage feature maps to produce high-quality soft labels. (3) MixSKD achieves SOTA performance on image classification and downstream dense prediction tasks against other competitors.

2   Related Works

Multi-Network Knowledge Distillation. The conventional multi-network KD often depends on extra networks for auxiliary training in an offline or online manner. The offline KD [11,15,23,24,27,38,39,43,44] transfers knowledge from a pre-trained teacher to a smaller student. Online KD [3,39–41,45,54,57] aims to train multiple student networks and perform knowledge transfer within the cohort in an online manner. A popular mechanism called *Deep Mutual Learning* (DML) [54] or *Mutual Contrastive Learning* (MCL) [40] suggests that an ensemble of students learn significantly better through teaching each other. Our MixSKD also employs mutual mimicry of intermediate feature maps and probability distributions. An important distinction with DML is that we aim to distill information from the view of Mixup *within a single network*. In contrast to mutual learning, another vein is to construct a virtual online teacher via knowledge ensembling from multiple student networks [57]. Instead of multiple networks, we aggregate multi-stage feature maps from attached branches *within a single network* to construct a powerful self-teacher. This self-teacher generates excellent soft labels for auxiliary Mixup training.

Self-Knowledge Distillation. Unlike offline and online KD, Self-KD aims to distill knowledge from the network itself to improve its own performance. Self-KD is a non-trivial problem since it does not have explicit peer networks. Therefore, a natural idea is to introduce *auxiliary architecture* to capture extra knowledge. DKS [31] proposes pairwise knowledge alignments among auxiliary branches and the primary backbone. BYOT [52] regards the deepest classifier as a teacher and transfers knowledge to shallow ones. ONE [57] aggregates an ensemble logit from multiple auxiliary networks to provide the soft label. Beyond the logit level, SAD [16] performs top-down and layer-wise attention distillation within the network itself. FRSKD [18] generates a self-teacher network for itself to provide refined feature maps for feature distillation. Another orthogonal aspect is to excavate knowledge from *data augmentation*. DDGSD [37] and CS-KD [48] regularize the consistency of predictive distributions between two different views. DDGSD utilizes two different augmented versions of the same image as two views, while CS-KD leverages two different samples from the same class. Moreover, prediction penalization is also a form of Self-KD. Tf-KD [46] connects label smoothing [32] to Self-KD and applies a manually designed soft label to replace the teacher. Orthogonal to the above studies, we propose Self-KD from the image mixture perspective and achieve the best performance.

Image Mixture. Image mixture has been developed to a robust data augmentation strategy. The seminal Mixup [50] performs global pixel-wise interpolations between two images associated with the same linear interpolation of one-hot labels. Wang *et al.* [35] employ Mixup to augment a few unlabeled images for data-efficient KD. Beyond input space, Manifold Mixup [33] conducts interpolations in the hidden feature representations. The success behind image mixture is to provide mixed training signals for regularizing the network to behave

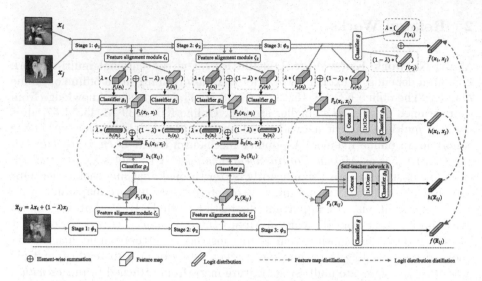

Fig. 2. Overview of the proposed MixSKD over a network with $K = 3$ stages. We employ a shared architecture between the training graph of the original input images (*upper*) and that of the Mixup input images (*lower*). The meta-architectures with the same notation denote the identical one. During the training stage, we regularize the *feature maps* and *class probability distributions* between the original images and Mixup images via distillation losses. During the test stage, we drop all auxiliary components.

linearly. *However, none of the previous work explores Mixup training signals as extra knowledge to model soft labels for Self-KD.* Our MixSKD incorporates Mixup with Self-KD into a unified framework and regularizes the network more meaningfully. Although previous CS-KD and FRSKD also attempted to combine Mixup to further enhance the performance, they often utilized a straightforward instead of a thoughtful way. Yun *et al.* [47] observed that Mixup samples are locally unnatural, confusing the network for object localization. CutMix [47] is proposed to execute patch-wise mixture between two images. We remark that our MixSKD can also combine CutMix to regularize the spatial consistency between patch-wise information mixture. This may become a promising future work.

3   Methodology

3.1   Formulation of Training Graph

The convolutional neural network (CNN) f for image classification can be composed of a feature extractor ϕ and a linear classifier g, *i.e.* $f = g \circ \phi$. For simplicity, we omit *Global Average Pool* between feature extractor and linear classifier. The feature extractor ϕ often contains multiple stages for refining feature hierarchies that is formulated as $\phi = \phi_K \circ \cdots \circ \phi_2 \circ \phi_1$, where K is the number of stages. After each stage ϕ_k, $k = 1, 2, \cdots, K - 1$, we insert an auxiliary branch b_k for feature augmentation. Each b_k includes a feature alignment module ζ_k and a linear classifier g_k. Given an input sample x, the outputs of $K - 1$ auxiliary branches and the backbone network f are expressed as:

$$b_1(x) = g_1 \circ \zeta_1 \circ \phi_1(x),$$
$$b_2(x) = g_2 \circ \zeta_2 \circ \phi_2 \circ \phi_1(x),$$

$$\cdots$$

$$b_{K-1}(x) = g_{K-1} \circ \zeta_{K-1} \circ \phi_{K-1} \circ \cdots \circ \phi_1(x),$$
$$f(x) = g \circ \phi(x). \tag{1}$$

Here, $b_1(x), \cdots, b_{K-1}(x) \in \mathbb{R}^C$ and $f(x) \in \mathbb{R}^C$ are predicted logit vectors, where C is the number of classes. The feature alignment module ζ_k is to transform the feature map output from the shallow stage to match the feature dimension with the last stage. This is implemented by making each auxiliary branch's path from input to output have the same number of down-samplings as the backbone network. We formulate $F_k \in \mathbb{R}^{H \times W \times C}$ as the feature map output from the k-th branch b_k for all $k = 1, \cdots, K - 1$ and $F_K \in \mathbb{R}^{H \times W \times C}$ as the feature map output from the backbone network f. Here, H, W and C denote the height, width and channel number of the feature map, respectively. $\{F_k\}_{k=1}^{K-1}$ and F_K are formulated as:

$$F_k(x) = \zeta_k \circ \phi_k \circ \cdots \circ \phi_1(x), \ F_K(x) = \phi(x), \tag{2}$$

where $k = 1, \cdots, K - 1$. The transformed feature map often encodes global structures and coarse semantic information. The property is crucial for recognition performance by reducing redundant details in shallow features. *The detailed architectures of auxiliary branches for various networks are shown in Appendix.*

3.2 Task-Guided Classification Loss

We describe how to construct classification loss from *architecture source* and *data source*. We illustrate the detailed overview of MixSKD in Fig. 2.

Classification Loss from Architecture Source. Given an input sample x with the ground-truth label y, we guide the $K - 1$ auxiliary branches and backbone network f to learn cross-entropy based classification loss:

$$L_{cls\_b\_f}(x, y) = L_{ce}(\sigma(f(x)), y) + \sum_{k=1}^{K-1} L_{ce}(\sigma(b_k(x)), y), \tag{3}$$

where σ represents a *softmax* function to normalize the logits to model posterior probability distributions, and L_{ce} denotes the cross-entropy. This conventional loss enables auxiliary branches and the backbone network to learn general classification capability and semantic features.

Classification Loss from Data Source. Given two different images x_i and x_j with ground-truth labels y_i and y_j, Mixup [50] performs linear mixture with a combination factor λ to construct a virtual image $\tilde{x}_{ij}$ with an interpolated one-hot ground-truth label $\tilde{y}_{ij}$:

$$\tilde{x}_{ij} = \lambda x_i + (1 - \lambda)x_j, \ \tilde{y}_{ij} = \lambda y_i + (1 - \lambda)y_j. \tag{4}$$

Here, $\lambda \sim \text{Beta}(\alpha, \alpha)$ for $\alpha \in (0, \infty)$ and $\lambda \in [0, 1]$. We utilize the input images x_i, x_j and $\tilde{x}_{ij}$ to compute the classification task loss using cross-entropy:

$$L_{cls\_mixup} = L_{cls\_b\_f}(x_i, y_i) + L_{cls\_b\_f}(x_j, y_j) + L_{cls\_b\_f}(\tilde{x}_{ij}, \tilde{y}_{ij}) \tag{5}$$

3.3   Feature Map Self-KD

Feature maps often contain information about image intensity and spatial correlation. The hidden feature maps often encode the intermediate learning process. We expect to encourage the network to behave consistently in *intermediate feature maps* between the pair of original images (x_i, x_j) and their *Mixup* image $\tilde{x}_{ij}$. Thus we consider linearly interpolating the feature maps between x_i and x_j. The interpolated feature maps are formulated as $\{\tilde{F}_k(x_i, x_j)\}_{k=1}^K$:

$$\tilde{F}_k(x_i, x_j) = \lambda F_k(x_i) + (1 - \lambda)F_k(x_j). \tag{6}$$

Motivated by the hint loss in FitNet [30], we employ the squared l_2-norm for mutual alignment between interpolated feature maps $\{\tilde{F}_k(x_i, x_j) \in \mathbb{R}^{H \times W \times C}\}_{k=1}^K$ and *Mixup* feature maps $\{F_k(\tilde{x}_{ij}) \in \mathbb{R}^{H \times W \times C}\}_{k=1}^K$:

$$L_{feature} = \sum_{k=1}^K \frac{1}{HWC} \parallel \tilde{F}_k(x_i, x_j) - F_k(\tilde{x}_{ij}) \parallel^2 . \tag{7}$$

Inspired by Adversarial Feature Distillation (AFD) [36], we further introduce K discriminators $\{D_k\}_{k=1}^K$ for the same-staged K feature maps. The discriminator in the original AFD [36] is used to distinguish features extracted from student or teacher. Instead, our discriminator is to classify the feature map generated from a linear interpolation or a Mixup image. The discriminator loss is formulated as a binary cross-entropy:

$$L_{dis} = - \sum_{k=1}^K \log[D_k(\tilde{F}_k(x_i, x_j))] + \log[1 - D_k(F_k(\tilde{x}_{ij}))]. \tag{8}$$

Here, the D_k is a two-layer MLP followed by a Sigmoid function. Motivated by the idea of GAN [12], jointly optimizing Eq. (7) and Eq. (8) via an adversarial process enables the network to learn common semantic information meaningfully. The feature Self-KD conducts an adversarial process to match linearly interpolated feature maps from the pair of original images (x_i, x_j) with feature maps from the Mixup image $\tilde{x}_{ij}$. This forces the network to behave linearly in feature representations between training samples.

3.4   Logit Distribution Self-KD

Beyond feature maps, logit-based class probability distributions often represent the final predictive information. We also expect to encourage the network to behave consistently in *logit-based class posterior distributions* between the pair of original images $(\boldsymbol{x}_i, \boldsymbol{x}_j)$ and their Mixup image $\tilde{\boldsymbol{x}}_{ij}$. The linear interpolations of images should lead to linear interpolations of corresponding logit-based probability distributions with the same mixed proportion. The interpolated logits vectors of $K-1$ auxiliary branches and the backbone network f are formulated as $\{\tilde{b}_k(\boldsymbol{x}_i, \boldsymbol{x}_j)\}_{k=1}^{K-1}$ and $\tilde{f}(\boldsymbol{x}_i, \boldsymbol{x}_j)$:

$$\tilde{b}_k(\boldsymbol{x}_i, \boldsymbol{x}_j) = \lambda b_k(\boldsymbol{x}_i) + (1-\lambda)b_k(\boldsymbol{x}_j), \quad \tilde{f}(\boldsymbol{x}_i, \boldsymbol{x}_j) = \lambda f(\boldsymbol{x}_i) + (1-\lambda)f(\boldsymbol{x}_j). \quad (9)$$

Logit Self-KD Over Auxiliary Branches $\{b_k\}_{k=1}^{K-1}$. First, we aim to maximize the consistency of logit-based class probability distributions between linearly interpolated logits $\{\tilde{b}_k(\boldsymbol{x}_i, \boldsymbol{x}_j)\}_{k=1}^{K-1}$ and Mixup logits $\{b_k(\tilde{\boldsymbol{x}}_{ij})\}_{k=1}^{K-1}$ via KL-divergence:

$$L_{b\_logit}((\boldsymbol{x}_i, \boldsymbol{x}_j), \tilde{\boldsymbol{x}}_{ij}) = \sum_{k=1}^{K-1} [L_{KL}(\sigma(\tilde{b}_k(\boldsymbol{x}_i, \boldsymbol{x}_j)/T), \sigma(\overline{b_k(\tilde{\boldsymbol{x}}_{ij})}/T))$$
$$+ L_{KL}(\sigma(b_k(\tilde{\boldsymbol{x}}_{ij})/T), \sigma(\overline{\tilde{b}_k(\boldsymbol{x}_i, \boldsymbol{x}_j)}/T)]. \quad (10)$$

Here, L_{KL} is the KL-divergence, and T is a temperature following the original KD [15]. $\overline{b_k(\tilde{\boldsymbol{x}}_{ij})}$ and $\overline{\tilde{b}_k(\boldsymbol{x}_i, \boldsymbol{x}_j)}$ are fixed copies of $b_k(\tilde{\boldsymbol{x}}_{ij})$ and $\tilde{b}_k(\boldsymbol{x}_i, \boldsymbol{x}_j)$, respectively. As suggested by [26], the gradients through $\overline{b_k(\tilde{\boldsymbol{x}}_{ij})}$ and $\overline{\tilde{b}_k(\boldsymbol{x}_i, \boldsymbol{x}_j)}$ are not propagated to avoid the model collapse issue.

Training the Self-Teacher Network $h(\cdot)$. The idea of the self-teacher $h(\cdot)$ is to aggregate multi-stage ensemble feature maps to construct an excellent classifier. The classifier could provide meaningful soft labels to teach the backbone classifier in an online manner. Given the K feature maps $\{\mathcal{F}_k\}_{k=1}^{K}$ with the same dimension to $h(\cdot)$, we first concatenate them along the channel dimension and then use a 1×1 convolution $\text{Conv}_{1\times1}$ to shrink channels. Then the ensemble feature maps are followed by a linear classifier g_h to output class probability distributions. The inference graph is formulated as $h(\{\mathcal{F}_k\}_{k=1}^{K}) = g_h(\text{Conv}_{1\times1}([\mathcal{F}_1, \cdots, \mathcal{F}_K]))$.

Given the linearly interpolated feature maps $\{\tilde{F}_k(\boldsymbol{x}_i, \boldsymbol{x}_j)\}_{k=1}^{K}$ from the pair of original images $(\boldsymbol{x}_i, \boldsymbol{x}_j)$, we can derive the soft label $h(\{\tilde{F}_k(\boldsymbol{x}_i, \boldsymbol{x}_j)\}_{k=1}^{K})$. Given Mixup feature maps $\{F_k(\tilde{\boldsymbol{x}}_{ij})\}_{k=1}^{K}$ from the Mixup image $\tilde{\boldsymbol{x}}_{ij}$, we can derive the soft label $h(\{F_k(\tilde{\boldsymbol{x}}_{ij})\}_{k=1}^{K})$. For easy notation, we define $h(\boldsymbol{x}_i, \boldsymbol{x}_j) = h(\{\tilde{F}_k(\boldsymbol{x}_i, \boldsymbol{x}_j)\}_{k=1}^{K})$ and $h(\tilde{\boldsymbol{x}}_{ij}) = h(\{F_k(\tilde{\boldsymbol{x}}_{ij})\}_{k=1}^{K})$. Motivated by the success of Manifold Mixup [33], the class probabilities inferred from linear interpolated feature maps could also be supervised by interpolated labels. Thus we further train both $h(\boldsymbol{x}_i, \boldsymbol{x}_j)$ and $h(\tilde{\boldsymbol{x}}_{ij})$ by the interpolated label $\tilde{y}_{ij}$ using cross-entropy loss:

$$L_{cls\_h} = L_{ce}(\sigma(h(\boldsymbol{x}_i, \boldsymbol{x}_j)), \tilde{y}_{ij}) + L_{ce}(\sigma(h(\tilde{\boldsymbol{x}}_{ij})), \tilde{y}_{ij}). \quad (11)$$

Benefiting from Eq. (11), $h(\cdot)$ would learn meaningful mixed distributions from multi-stage feature maps from the view of information mixture.

Logit Self-KD Over the Backbone f. We adopt the self-teacher network $h(\cdot)$ to supervise the final backbone classifier, since $h(\cdot)$ aggregates multi-branch feature information and leads to better performance. We utilize the Mixup logit $h(\tilde{x}_{ij})$ as the soft label to supervise the linearly interpolated logit $\tilde{f}(x_i, x_j)$. We also employ logit $h(x_i, x_j)$ from the linearly interpolated feature map to supervise Mixup logit $f(\tilde{x}_{ij})$. The mutual distillation loss is formulated as:

$$L_{f\_logit}((x_i, x_j), \tilde{x}_{ij}) = L_{KL}(\sigma(\tilde{f}(x_i, x_j)/T), \sigma(h(\tilde{x}_{ij})/T))$$
$$+ L_{KL}(\sigma(f(\tilde{x}_{ij})/T), \sigma(h(x_i, x_j)/T)). \qquad (12)$$

Here, the gradients through the soft labels of $h(\tilde{x}_{ij})$ and $h(x_i, x_j)$ are not propagated. In theory, the loss L_{b_logit} and L_{f_logit} can regularize the consistency between linearly interpolated class probability distributions from the pair of original images (x_i, x_j) and the distribution from Mixup image $\tilde{x}_{ij}$. This encourages the network to make linear predictions in-between training samples over auxiliary branches $\{b_k\}_{k=1}^{K-1}$ and backbone network f.

3.5   Overall Loss of MixSKD

We summarize the loss terms above into a unified framework:

$$L_{MixSKD} = \underbrace{L_{cls\_mixup}}_{task\ loss} + \underbrace{\beta L_{feature} + \gamma L_{dis}}_{feature\ Self-KD} + \mu(\underbrace{L_{b\_logit} + L_{cls\_h} + L_{f\_logit}}_{logit\ Self-KD}).$$
$$(13)$$

Here, we use $\beta = 1$ to control the magnitude of feature l_2 loss, where we find $\beta \in [1, 10]$ works well. Besides, we choose $\gamma = 1$ for discriminator loss and $\mu = 1$ for cross-entropy or KL divergence losses since they are probability-based forms and in the same magnitude. We perform end-to-end optimization of the training graph. During the test stage, we discard attached auxiliary components, leading to no extra inference costs compared with the original network.

In theory, our proposed MixSKD encourages the network to behave linearly in the latent feature and probability distribution spaces. The linear behaviour may reduce undesirable oscillations when predicting outliers, as discussed by Zhang et al. [50]. Moreover, linearity is also an excellent inductive bias from the view of Occam's razor because it is one of the most straightforward behaviours.

4   Experiments

4.1   Experimental Setup

Dataset. We conduct experiments on CIFAR-100 [21] and ImageNet [8] as the standard image classification tasks and CUB-200-2011 (CUB200) [34], Standford

Table 1. Top-1 accuracy (%) of various Self-KD (the second block) and data augmentation (the third block) methods across widely used networks for CIFAR-100 classification. The numbers in **bold** and underline indicate **the best** and the second-best results, respectively. * denotes the result from the original paper.

Method	ResNet-18 [14]	WRN-16-2 [49]	DenseNet-40 [17]	HCGNet-A1 [42]
Parameters	11.2M	0.7M	1.1M	1.1M
Baseline	$76.24_{\pm0.07}$	$72.24_{\pm0.29}$	$74.61_{\pm0.24}$	$75.58_{\pm0.30}$
DDGSD [37]	$76.61_{\pm0.47}$	$72.46_{\pm0.05}$	$75.87_{\pm0.30}$	$76.50_{\pm0.18}$
DKS [31]	$78.64_{\pm0.25}$	$73.73_{\pm0.22}$	$74.94_{\pm0.60}$	$78.04_{\pm0.16}$
BYOT [52]	$77.88_{\pm0.19}$	$72.97_{\pm0.34}$	$75.49_{\pm0.16}$	$76.81_{\pm0.64}$
SAD [16]	$76.40_{\pm0.17}$	$72.62_{\pm0.17}$	$74.77_{\pm0.12}$	$75.86_{\pm0.57}$
Tf-KD [46]	$76.61_{\pm0.34}$	$72.66_{\pm0.21}$	$74.68_{\pm0.17}$	$75.84_{\pm0.23}$
CS-KD [48]	$78.01^{*}_{\pm0.13}$	$73.23_{\pm0.33}$	$75.02_{\pm0.37}$	$76.36_{\pm0.30}$
FRSKD [18]	$77.71^{*}_{\pm0.14}$	$73.27^{*}_{\pm0.45}$	$74.91_{\pm0.36}$	$77.26_{\pm0.11}$
Cutout [9]	$76.66_{\pm0.42}$	$73.66_{\pm0.18}$	$75.45_{\pm0.33}$	$76.63_{\pm0.15}$
Mixup [50]	$78.68_{\pm0.12}$	$73.60_{\pm0.59}$	$75.55_{\pm0.81}$	$77.89_{\pm0.18}$
Manifold Mixup [33]	$79.29_{\pm0.20}$	$72.53_{\pm0.08}$	$75.19_{\pm0.38}$	$77.72_{\pm0.26}$
AutoAugment [6]	$77.97_{\pm0.17}$	$\underline{74.16}_{\pm0.22}$	$76.21_{\pm0.15}$	$78.13_{\pm0.78}$
RandAugment [7]	$76.86_{\pm0.55}$	$73.87_{\pm0.08}$	$76.23_{\pm0.22}$	$77.56_{\pm0.50}$
Random erase [55]	$76.75_{\pm0.33}$	$74.04_{\pm0.11}$	$75.52_{\pm0.46}$	$77.38_{\pm0.14}$
CS-KD+Mixup [48]	$\underline{79.60}^{*}_{\pm0.31}$	$73.82_{\pm0.18}$	$\underline{76.32}_{\pm0.37}$	$78.03_{\pm0.44}$
FRSKD+Mixup [18]	$78.74^{*}_{\pm0.19}$	$73.67_{\pm0.36}$	$75.56_{\pm0.07}$	$\underline{78.23}_{\pm0.22}$
MixSKD (Ours)	$\mathbf{80.32}_{\pm0.13}$	$\mathbf{74.89}_{\pm0.27}$	$\mathbf{76.85}_{\pm0.19}$	$\mathbf{78.57}_{\pm0.19}$

Dogs (Dogs) [19], MIT Indoor Scene Recognition (MIT67) [28], Stanford Cars (Cars) [20] and FGVC-Aircraft (Air) [25] datasets as the fine-grained classification tasks. For downstream dense prediction tasks, we use COCO 2017 [22] for object detection and Pascal VOC [10], ADE20K [56] and COCO-Stuff-164K [1] for semantic segmentation. *The detailed dataset descriptions and training details are provided in the Appendix.* We report the mean accuracy with a standard deviation over three runs using the form of $mean_{\pm std}$ for CIFAR-100 and fine-grained classification.

Hyper-Parameter Setup. As suggested Mixup [50], we use $\alpha = 0.2$ in MixSKD for ImageNet and $\alpha = 0.4$ for other image classification datasets. Moreover, we set temperature $T = 3$ for all datasets.

4.2   Comparison with State-of-the-Arts

Performance Comparison on CIFAR-100. Table 1 shows the accuracy comparison towards state-of-the-art data augmentation and Self-KD methods on CIFAR-100. Because MixSKD integrates Mixup [50], we also compare our method with the latest Self-KD methods of CS-KD [48] and FRSKD [18]

Table 2. Top-1 accuracy(%) of various Self-KD methods on ResNet-18 for fine-grained classification. The numbers in **bold** and <u>underline</u> indicate **the best** and <u>the second-best</u> results, respectively. * denotes the result from the original paper.

Method	CUB200	Dogs	MIT67	Cars	Air
Baseline	$57.48_{\pm0.45}$	$66.83_{\pm0.29}$	$57.81_{\pm1.42}$	$83.50_{\pm0.24}$	$77.07_{\pm0.26}$
DDGSD [37]	$56.89_{\pm0.42}$	$69.24_{\pm0.84}$	$56.46_{\pm0.59}$	$85.04_{\pm0.11}$	$74.91_{\pm0.97}$
DKS [31]	$63.72_{\pm0.21}$	$71.07_{\pm0.07}$	$61.50_{\pm0.12}$	$86.13_{\pm0.31}$	$79.69_{\pm0.31}$
BYOT [52]	$61.77_{\pm0.43}$	$69.58_{\pm0.20}$	$59.03_{\pm0.42}$	$85.36_{\pm0.18}$	$79.32_{\pm0.45}$
SAD [16]	$55.51_{\pm0.67}$	$66.10_{\pm0.08}$	$57.46_{\pm0.79}$	$82.94_{\pm0.22}$	$73.62_{\pm0.68}$
Tf-KD [46]	$57.44_{\pm0.25}$	$66.57_{\pm0.33}$	$57.51_{\pm0.86}$	$83.59_{\pm0.49}$	$76.76_{\pm0.34}$
CS-KD [48]	$66.72^*_{\pm0.99}$	$69.15^*_{\pm0.28}$	$59.55^*_{\pm0.45}$	$86.87_{+0.04}$	$80.92_{\pm0.44}$
FRSKD [18]	$65.39^*_{\pm0.13}$	$70.77^*_{\pm0.20}$	$61.74^*_{\pm0.67}$	$84.73_{\pm0.03}$	$78.85_{\pm0.55}$
Mixup [50]	$65.53_{\pm0.73}$	$69.30_{\pm0.10}$	$58.83_{\pm0.77}$	$86.10_{\pm0.28}$	$79.94_{\pm0.18}$
CS-KD+Mixup	<u>$69.29^*_{\pm0.64}$</u>	$70.07^*_{\pm0.14}$	$60.35^*_{\pm0.85}$	<u>$87.10_{\pm0.30}$</u>	<u>$81.13_{\pm0.45}$</u>
FRSKD+Mixup	$67.98^*_{\pm0.58}$	<u>$71.64^*_{\pm0.29}$</u>	<u>$62.11^*_{\pm0.81}$</u>	$86.25_{\pm0.33}$	$79.97_{\pm0.58}$
MixSKD (Ours)	**$72.15_{\pm0.53}$**	**$72.14_{\pm0.22}$**	**$64.10_{\pm0.45}$**	**$89.17_{\pm0.08}$**	**$82.95_{\pm0.31}$**

combined with Mixup. We use ResNet [14], WRN [49], DenseNet [17] and HCGNet [42] as backbone networks to evaluate the performance. Almost previous data augmentation and Self-KD methods can enhance the classification performance upon the baseline across various networks. Compared to the Mixup, MixSKD achieves an average accuracy gain of 1.23% across four networks. The result indicates that the superiority of MixSKD is not only attributed to the usage of Mixup. We further demonstrate that MixSKD is superior to the state-of-the-art CS-KD+Mixup and FRSKD+Mixup with average margins of 0.71% and 1.11%, respectively. These results imply that our MixSKD explores more meaningful knowledge from image mixture than the conventional training signals for Self-KD. Moreover, we find that it is hard to say which is the second-best approach since different methods are superior for various architectures. MixSKD further outperforms the powerful data augmentation method AutoAugment with an average gain of 1.04%.

Performance Comparison on Fine-Grained Classification. Compared with standard classification, fine-grained classification often contains fewer training samples per class and more similar inter-class semantics. This challenges a network to learn more discriminative intra-class variations. As shown in Table 2, we train a ResNet-18 on five fine-grained classification tasks. MixSKD can also achieve the best performance on fine-grained classification. MixSKD outperforms the best-second results with 2.86%, 0.50%, 1.99%, 2.07% and 1.82% accuracy gains on five datasets from left to right. The results verify that MixSKD can regularize the network to capture more discriminative features.

Table 3. Performance comparison with data augmentation and Self-KD methods on ImageNet and downstream transfer learning for object detection on COCO 2017 and semantic segmentation on Pascal VOC, ADE20K and COCO-Stuff-164K. All results are re-implemented by ourselves. The numbers in **bold** and <u>underline</u> indicate **the best** and <u>the second-best</u> results, respectively.

| Method | Image classification | | Detection | Semantic segmentation | | |
| | ImageNet | | COCO | Pascal VOC | ADE20K | COCO-Stuff |
	Top-1 Acc(%)	Top-5 Acc(%)	mAP(%)	mIoU(%)		
ResNet-50	77.08	93.20	41.0	77.09	<u>39.72</u>	<u>34.08</u>
+Mixup [50]	77.51	<u>93.72</u>	<u>41.1</u>	76.71	39.69	33.38
+Manifold Mixup [33]	77.43	93.68	40.8	75.62	38.07	32.82
+FRSKD [18]	76.92	92.96	40.9	<u>77.10</u>	39.48	33.63
+FRSKD+Mixup [18]	<u>77.79</u>	93.64	41.0	76.61	39.39	33.54
+MixSKD (Ours)	**78.76**	**94.40**	**41.5**	**78.78**	**42.37**	**37.12**

Table 4. Ablation study of loss terms in MixSKD. The first column with all '–' denotes the baseline. All results denote top-1 accuracy over ResNet-50 on ImageNet.

Type	Loss	Various loss combinations of MixSKD							
Task	L_{cls_mixup}	–	✓	✓	✓	✓	✓	✓	✓
Feature Self-KD	$L_{feature}$	–	–	✓	✓	–	–	–	✓
	L_{dis}	–	–	–	✓	–	–	–	✓
Logit Self-KD	L_{b_logit}	–	–	–	–	✓	–	✓	✓
	L_{cls_h}	–	–	–	–	–	✓	✓	✓
	L_{f_logit}	–	–	–	–	–	✓	✓	✓
Top-1 Accuracy (%)		77.08	77.68	78.14	78.47	78.06	78.23	78.54	**78.76**

Performance Comparison on ImageNet Classification. ImageNet is a large-scale image classification dataset, which is a golden classification benchmark. As shown in Table 3, MixSKD achieves the best 78.76% and 94.40% top-1 and top-5 accuracies on ResNet-50 compared to advanced data augmentation and Self-KD methods. It surpasses the best-competing FRSKD+Mixup by 0.97% and 0.76% top-1 and top-5 accuracy gains. The results show the scalability of our MixSKD to work reasonably well on the large-scale dataset.

Performance Comparison on Transfer Learning to Object Detection and Semantic Segmentation. We use the ResNet-50 pre-trained on ImageNet as a backbone over Cascade R-CNN [2] to perform object detection on COCO 2017 [22] and over DeepLabV3 [5] to perform semantic segmentation on Pascal VOC [10], ADE20K [56] and COCO-Stuff-164K [1]. We follow the standard data preprocessing [29,43] and implement object detection over MMDetection [4] with 1x training schedule and semantic segmentation over an open codebase released by Yang et al. [43]. As shown in Table 3, MixSKD achieves the best downstream performance and outperforms the best-second results with 0.4% mAP on detection and 1.68%, 2.65% and 3.04% mIoU margins on Pascal VOC, ADE20K and COCO-Stuff segmentation, respectively. In contrast, although other state-of-the-art Self-KD and data augmentation methods achieve good performance on ImageNet, they often transfer worse to downstream recognition tasks. The results indicate that our method can guide the network to learn better transferable feature representations for downstream dense prediction tasks.

Table 5. *Left*: top-1 accuracy (%) under FGSM white-box attack with various perturbation weights ϵ on CIFAR-100. *Middle*: top-1 accuracy (%) under sensitivity analysis of temperature T over ResNet-50 on ImageNet. *Right*: top-1 accuracy (%) under ablation study of using different feature maps from various stages to construct the self-teacher h over ResNet-50 on ImageNet.

Method	$\epsilon = 0.0001$	$\epsilon = 0.001$	$\epsilon = 0.01$	$\epsilon = 0.1$	T	Acc	Stage	Acc
WRN-16-2	60.5	57.9	37.6	8.6	1	77.94	1	78.01
+Mixup	63.1	61.1	40.7	11.4	2	78.21	2	78.18
+CS-KD+Mixup	63.8	62.1	42.8	13.0	3	**78.76**	3	78.36
+FRSKD+Mixup	62.9	60.7	40.9	12.2	4	78.65	4	78.42
+MixSKD (Ours)	**67.7**	**65.5**	**46.8**	**15.3**	5	78.37	All	**78.76**

4.3   Ablation Study and Analysis

Ablation Study of Loss Terms. As shown in Table 4, we conduct thorough ablation experiments to evaluate the effectiveness of each component in MixSKD on the convincing ImageNet dataset:

(1) Task Loss. We regard the L_{cls_mixup} as the basic task loss that trains the network with auxiliary architectures using Mixup. It improves the baseline by a 0.60% accuracy gain. Moreover, L_{cls_mixup} can guide the network to produce meaningful feature maps and logits from the original images and Mixup images. The information further motivates us to perform Self-KD to regularize the network. **(2) Feature map Self-KD.** Using $L_{feature}$ loss to distill K feature maps achieves a 0.46% improvement over the task loss. Adding an auxiliary discriminative loss L_{dis} further enhances the performance of $L_{feature}$ with an extra 0.33% gain. The result suggests that using an adversarial mechanism for feature distillation may encourage the network to capture more meaningful semantics than a single l_2-based mimicry loss. **(3) Logit Self-KD.** The distillation loss L_{b_logit} over auxiliary branches $\{b_k\}_{k=1}^{K-1}$ results in a 0.38% gain than the task loss. Training the self-teacher network h by L_{cls_h} for providing soft labels to supervise the backbone classifier f by L_{f_logit} leads to a significant 0.55% gain than the task loss. Overall, combining logit-based losses can enable the network to achieve a 0.86% gain. **(4) Overall loss.** Combining logit and feature Self-KD can maximize the performance gain with a 1.08% margin over the task loss.

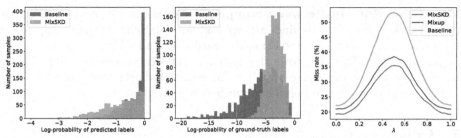

(a) Comparison of log probabilities of predicted labels (*left*) and ground-truth labels (*right*) over common misclassified samples trained by baseline and MixSKD.

(b) Miss rate of the prediction of mixup image $\tilde{x}_{ij}$ not belonging to $\{y_i, y_j\}$.

Fig. 3. MixSKD produces more robust predictions on CIFAR-100.

Adversarial Robustness. Adversarial learning has shown that adding imperceptibly small but intentionally worst-case perturbations to the input image fools the network easily. Thus adversarial robustness is a crucial issue for the practical application of neural networks. As shown in Table 5 (left), we compare the robustness trained by various Self-KD methods under FGSM whitebox attack [13]. MixSKD significantly improves the robustness and surpasses other methods consistently across different perturbations. The results imply that MixSKD shows better potential in adversarial defense.

Impact of the Temperature T. The temperature T is utilized to scale the predictive logits for KL-divergence based distillation losses in Eq. (10) and Eq. (12). A larger T leads to a smoother probability distribution. As shown in Table 5 (middle), we observe that MixSKD benefits most from $T = 3$ than others for producing soft distributions.

Effectiveness of Multi-stage Feature Aggregation to Construct Self-Teacher h. The self-teacher utilizes feature maps not only from the last stage but also from multiple stages to aggregate richer semantics. As shown in Table 5 (right), we demonstrate that multi-stage feature aggregation can generate higher-quality soft labels to achieve better performance than any single feature map.

Meaningful Predictive Distribution. By encouraging linear behaviours between samples, we examine whether our MixSKD forces the network to achieve a meaningful predictive distribution. To this end, we investigate predictive softmax scores inferred from ResNet-18 trained by baseline and MixSKD on CIFAR-100. Figure 3(a) shows the histogram statistics of log probabilities of predicted labels and ground-truth labels over common misclassified samples. Compared to the baseline, our MixSKD achieves better prediction quality. On the one hand, it decreases over-confident log probabilities of predicted labels over misclassified samples effectively. On the other hand, it assigns larger log probabilities for ground-truth labels even if the misclassification occurs.

Miss Error Rate In-Between Samples. As shown in Fig. 3(b), we evaluate the network trained by baseline, Mixup, and our MixSKD on the Mixup image $\tilde{x}_{ij} = \lambda x_i + (1 - \lambda)x_j$. A prediction is regarded as "miss" if it does not belong to $\{y_i, y_j\}$. Our MixSKD shows the minimum miss rates across various Mixup factors of λ within the range of $[0, 1]$. The results indicate that MixSKD leads to more robust predictive behaviours in-between samples.

5   Conclusion

This paper presents MixSKD, a powerful Self-KD method to regularize the network to behave linearly in feature maps and class probabilities between samples using Mixup images. Moreover, we also construct an auxiliary self-teacher to transfer external ensemble knowledge for the backbone network. The overall MixSKD outperforms state-of-the-art data augmentation and Self-KD methods on computer vision benchmarks. We hope this work will inspire further research towards information mixture to improve the performance of visual recognition.

References

1. Caesar, H., Uijlings, J., Ferrari, V.: Coco-stuff: thing and stuff classes in context. In: CVPR, pp. 1209–1218 (2018)
2. Cai, Z., Vasconcelos, N.: Cascade r-CNN: high quality object detection and instance segmentation. IEEE Trans. Pattern Anal. Mach. Intell. **43**(5), 1483–1498 (2019)
3. Chen, D., Mei, J.P., Wang, C., Feng, Y., Chen, C.: Online knowledge distillation with diverse peers. In: AAAI, pp. 3430–3437 (2020)
4. Chen, K., et al.: MMDetection: open MMLab detection toolbox and benchmark. arXiv preprint arXiv:1906.07155 (2019)
5. Chen, L.C., Papandreou, G., Schroff, F., Adam, H.: Rethinking atrous convolution for semantic image segmentation. arXiv preprint arXiv:1706.05587 (2017)
6. Cubuk, E.D., Zoph, B., Mane, D., Vasudevan, V., Le, Q.V.: Autoaugment: learning augmentation strategies from data. In: Proceedings of the IEEE/CVF Conference on Computer Vision and Pattern Recognition, pp. 113–123 (2019)
7. Cubuk, E.D., Zoph, B., Shlens, J., Le, Q.V.: Randaugment: practical automated data augmentation with a reduced search space. In: CVPR Workshops, pp. 702–703 (2020)
8. Deng, J., Dong, W., Socher, R., Li, L.J., Li, K., Fei-Fei, L.: ImageNet: a large-scale hierarchical image database. In: IEEE Conference on Computer Vision and Pattern Recognition, pp. 248–255. IEEE (2009)
9. DeVries, T., Taylor, G.W.: Improved regularization of convolutional neural networks with cutout. arXiv preprint arXiv:1708.04552 (2017)
10. Everingham, M., Van Gool, L., Williams, C.K., Winn, J., Zisserman, A.: The pascal visual object classes (VOC) challenge. Int. J. Comput. Vis. **88**(2), 303–338 (2010)
11. Ge, S., Luo, Z., Zhang, C., Hua, Y., Tao, D.: Distilling channels for efficient deep tracking. IEEE Trans. Image Process. **29**, 2610–2621 (2019)
12. Goodfellow, I., et al.: Generative adversarial nets. In: Advances in Neural Information Processing Systems, vol. 27 (2014)

13. Goodfellow, I.J., Shlens, J., Szegedy, C.: Explaining and harnessing adversarial examples. In: ICLR (2015)
14. He, K., Zhang, X., Ren, S., Sun, J.: Deep residual learning for image recognition. In: Proceedings of the IEEE Conference on Computer Vision and Pattern Recognition, pp. 770–778 (2016)
15. Hinton, G., Vinyals, O., Dean, J.: Distilling the knowledge in a neural network. arXiv preprint arXiv:1503.02531 (2015)
16. Hou, Y., Ma, Z., Liu, C., Loy, C.C.: Learning lightweight lane detection CNNs by self attention distillation. In: Proceedings of the IEEE/CVF International Conference on Computer Vision, pp. 1013–1021 (2019)
17. Huang, G., Liu, Z., Van Der Maaten, L., Weinberger, K.Q.: Densely connected convolutional networks. In: CVPR, pp. 4700–4708 (2017)
18. Ji, M., Shin, S., Hwang, S., Park, G., Moon, I.C.: Refine myself by teaching myself: feature refinement via self-knowledge distillation. In: Proceedings of the IEEE/CVF Conference on Computer Vision and Pattern Recognition, pp. 10664–10673 (2021)
19. Khosla, A., Jayadevaprakash, N., Yao, B., Li, F.F.: Novel dataset for fine-grained image categorization: Stanford dogs. In: Proceedings of CVPR Workshop on Fine-Grained Visual Categorization (FGVC), vol. 2. Citeseer (2011)
20. Krause, J., Stark, M., Deng, J., Fei-Fei, L.: 3D object representations for fine-grained categorization. In: ICCV Workshops, pp. 554–561 (2013)
21. Krizhevsky, A., Hinton, G., et al.: Learning multiple layers of features from tiny images. Technical report (2009)
22. Lin, T.-Y., et al.: Microsoft COCO: common objects in context. In: Fleet, D., Pajdla, T., Schiele, B., Tuytelaars, T. (eds.) ECCV 2014. LNCS, vol. 8693, pp. 740–755. Springer, Cham (2014). https://doi.org/10.1007/978-3-319-10602-1_48
23. Liu, J., Qin, H., Wu, Y., Guo, J., Liang, D., Xu, K.: CoupleFace: relation matters for face recognition distillation. In: Proceedings of the European Conference on Computer Vision (2022)
24. Liu, J., Yu, T., Peng, H., Sun, M., Li, P.: Cross-lingual cross-modal consolidation for effective multilingual video corpus moment retrieval. In: NAACL-HLT (2022)
25. Maji, S., Rahtu, E., Kannala, J., Blaschko, M., Vedaldi, A.: Fine-grained visual classification of aircraft. arXiv preprint arXiv:1306.5151 (2013)
26. Miyato, T., Maeda, S.i., Koyama, M., Ishii, S.: Virtual adversarial training: a regularization method for supervised and semi-supervised learning. IEEE Trans. Pattern Anal. Mach. Intell. **41**(8), 1979–1993 (2018)
27. Peng, B., et al.: Correlation congruence for knowledge distillation. In: Proceedings of the IEEE International Conference on Computer Vision, pp. 5007–5016 (2019)
28. Quattoni, A., Torralba, A.: Recognizing indoor scenes. In: IEEE Conference on Computer Vision and Pattern Recognition, pp. 413–420. IEEE (2009)
29. Ren, S., He, K., Girshick, R., Sun, J.: Faster r-CNN: towards real-time object detection with region proposal networks. IEEE Trans. Pattern Anal. Mach. Intell. **39**(6), 1137–1149 (2016)
30. Romero, A., Ballas, N., Kahou, S.E., Chassang, A., Gatta, C., Bengio, Y.: FitNets: hints for thin deep nets. In: ICLR (2015)
31. Sun, D., Yao, A., Zhou, A., Zhao, H.: Deeply-supervised knowledge synergy. In: Proceedings of the IEEE/CVF Conference on Computer Vision and Pattern Recognition, pp. 6997–7006 (2019)
32. Szegedy, C., Vanhoucke, V., Ioffe, S., Shlens, J., Wojna, Z.: Rethinking the inception architecture for computer vision. In: Proceedings of the IEEE Conference on Computer Vision and Pattern Recognition, pp. 2818–2826 (2016)

33. Verma, V., et al.: Manifold mixup: better representations by interpolating hidden states. In: International Conference on Machine Learning, pp. 6438–6447. PMLR (2019)
34. Wah, C., Branson, S., Welinder, P., Perona, P., Belongie, S.: The caltech-UCSD birds-200-2011 dataset. Technical report (2011)
35. Wang, D., Li, Y., Wang, L., Gong, B.: Neural networks are more productive teachers than human raters: active mixup for data-efficient knowledge distillation from a blackbox model. In: CVPR, pp. 1498–1507 (2020)
36. Wang, Y., Xu, C., Xu, C., Tao, D.: Adversarial learning of portable student networks. In: AAAI, vol. 32 (2018)
37. Xu, T.B., Liu, C.L.: Data-distortion guided self-distillation for deep neural networks. In: AAAI, vol. 33, pp. 5565–5572 (2019)
38. Yang, C., An, Z., Cai, L., Xu, Y.: Hierarchical self-supervised augmented knowledge distillation. In: Proceedings of the Thirtieth International Joint Conference on Artificial Intelligence, pp. 1217–1223 (2021)
39. Yang, C., An, Z., Cai, L., Xu, Y.: Knowledge distillation using hierarchical self-supervision augmented distribution. IEEE Trans. Neural Netw. Learn. Syst. (2022)
40. Yang, C., An, Z., Cai, L., Xu, Y.: Mutual contrastive learning for visual representation learning. In: Proceedings of the AAAI Conference on Artificial Intelligence, vol. 36, pp. 3045–3053 (2022)
41. Yang, C., An, Z., Xu, Y.: Multi-view contrastive learning for online knowledge distillation. In: IEEE International Conference on Acoustics, Speech and Signal Processing, pp. 3750–3754 (2021)
42. Yang, C., ET AL.: Gated convolutional networks with hybrid connectivity for image classification. In: Proceedings of the AAAI Conference on Artificial Intelligence, vol. 34, pp. 12581–12588 (2020)
43. Yang, C., Zhou, H., An, Z., Jiang, X., Xu, Y., Zhang, Q.: Cross-image relational knowledge distillation for semantic segmentation. In: Proceedings of the IEEE/CVF Conference on Computer Vision and Pattern Recognition, pp. 12319–12328 (2022)
44. Yang, D., et al.: Multi-view correlation distillation for incremental object detection. Pattern Recogn. **131**, 108863 (2022)
45. Yang, Z., Li, Z., Jiang, X., Gong, Y., Yuan, Z., Zhao, D., Yuan, C.: Focal and global knowledge distillation for detectors. In: CVPR, pp. 4643–4652 (2022)
46. Yuan, L., Tay, F.E., Li, G., Wang, T., Feng, J.: Revisiting knowledge distillation via label smoothing regularization. In: Proceedings of the IEEE/CVF Conference on Computer Vision and Pattern Recognition, pp. 3903–3911 (2020)
47. Yun, S., Han, D., Oh, S.J., Chun, S., Choe, J., Yoo, Y.: Cutmix: regularization strategy to train strong classifiers with localizable features. In: Proceedings of the IEEE/CVF International Conference on Computer Vision, pp. 6023–6032 (2019)
48. Yun, S., Park, J., Lee, K., Shin, J.: Regularizing class-wise predictions via self-knowledge distillation. In: CVPR, pp. 13876–13885 (2020)
49. Zagoruyko, S., Komodakis, N.: Wide residual networks. In: Proceedings of the British Machine Vision Conference (2016)
50. Zhang, H., Cisse, M., Dauphin, Y.N., Lopez-Paz, D.: Mixup: beyond empirical risk minimization. In: ICLR (2018)
51. Zhang, L., Bao, C., Ma, K.: Self-distillation: towards efficient and compact neural networks. IEEE Trans. Pattern Anal. Mach. Intell. **44**, 4388–4403 (2021)
52. Zhang, L., Song, J., Gao, A., Chen, J., Bao, C., Ma, K.: Be your own teacher: improve the performance of convolutional neural networks via self distillation. In: ICCV, pp. 3713–3722 (2019)

53. Zhang, L., Yu, M., Chen, T., Shi, Z., Bao, C., Ma, K.: Auxiliary training: towards accurate and robust models. In: CVPR, pp. 372–381 (2020)
54. Zhang, Y., Xiang, T., Hospedales, T.M., Lu, H.: Deep mutual learning. In: Proceedings of the IEEE Conference on Computer Vision and Pattern Recognition, pp. 4320–4328 (2018)
55. Zhong, Z., Zheng, L., Kang, G., Li, S., Yang, Y.: Random erasing data augmentation. In: AAAI. vol. 34, pp. 13001–13008 (2020)
56. Zhou, B., Zhao, H., Puig, X., Fidler, S., Barriuso, A., Torralba, A.: Scene parsing through ade20k dataset. In: CVPR. pp. 633–641 (2017)
57. Zhu, X., Gong, S., et al.: Knowledge distillation by on-the-fly native ensemble. In: Advances in Neural Information Processing Systems, pp. 7517–7527 (2018)

Self-feature Distillation with Uncertainty Modeling for Degraded Image Recognition

Zhou Yang[1], Weisheng Dong[1(✉)], Xin Li[2], Jinjian Wu[1], Leida Li[1], and Guangming Shi[1]

[1] School of Artificial Intelligence, Xidian University, Xi'an, China
yang_zhou@stu.xidian.edu.cn, {wsdong,jinjian.wu}@mail.xidian.edu.cn,
{ldli,gmshi}@xidian.edu.cn
[2] Lane Department of CSEE, West Virginia University, Morgantown, WV, USA
xin.li@mail.wvu.edu

Abstract. Despite the remarkable performance on high-quality (HQ) data, the accuracy of deep image recognition models degrades rapidly in the presence of low-quality (LQ) images. Both feature de-drifting and quality agnostic models have been developed to make the features extracted from degraded images closer to those of HQ images. In these methods, the l_2-norm is usually used as a constraint. It treats each pixel in the feature equally and may result in relatively poor reconstruction performance in some difficult regions. To address this issue, we propose a novel *self-feature distillation* method with *uncertainty modeling* for better producing HQ-like features from low-quality observations in this paper. Specifically, in a standard recognition model, we use the HQ features to distill the corresponding degraded ones and conduct uncertainty modeling according to the diversity of degradation sources to adaptively increase the weights of feature regions that are difficult to recover in the distillation loss. Experiments demonstrate that our method can extract HQ-like features better even when the inputs are degraded images, which makes the model more robust than other approaches.

Keywords: Robust image recognition · Self-feature distillation · Uncertainty modeling

1 Introduction

Despite rapid advances in deep learning [5,15,16,27,37,41,43], the impact of image degradation on visual recognition tasks has remained poorly understood. The good performance of deep models tested on HQ images of public datasets

---

Supplementary Information The online version contains supplementary material available at https://doi.org/10.1007/978-3-031-20053-3_32.

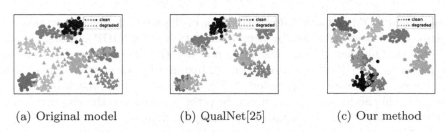

(a) Original model   (b) QualNet[25]   (c) Our method

Fig. 1. t-SNE feature distribution visualization on ImageNet-C validation set [19]. We trained the model on all classes in ImageNet-1K [8] but randomly selected five classes to show. We used the low-contrast degradation at severity level 3 to generate the degraded images. The colored symbols represent the feature vectors extracted from the corresponding images. Symbols with the same color are from the same class. Dot marks represent HQ features, and triangle marks indicate features from degrade images. The results of (c) show that our method can better gather the features both of degraded and high-quality images.

[8,29] often degrades dramatically in the presence of LQ images. Recent benchmark studies on the robustness of image classification [19], object detection [35], and semantic segmentation [23] models have shown that the performance of a standard neural network model is sensitive to image quality. For instance, vanilla ResNet50 [16] has a mean Corruption Error (mCE) up to 76.7% on ImageNet-C for image classification [19]; Faster-RCNN [37] with ResNet50 as the backbone network has a mean Average Precision (mAP) of 18.2/36.3 on LQ/HQ images for object detection [35]; and DeepLabv3+ [5] only has a 6.6 mean Intersection over Union (mIoU) on shot noise images for semantic segmentation [23].

Naive approaches toward degraded image recognition attempt to restore corrupted images first. Indeed, various image restoration techniques including image denoising, deblurring, super-resolution, dehazing, and other image enhancement methods have been developed to improve the visual quality of degraded images. However, there is a fundamental difference between the *visual quality* and the *recognition quality* of an image - e.g., a photo with a masked face might have the highest visual quality, but its quality is deemed low under the context of face recognition. Various studies have confirmed that the improvement of visual perception can not guarantee a higher accuracy of subsequent high-level vision tasks [42,46]. Moreover, existing image restoration techniques are mostly devoted to a single type of degradation; how to restore an image from multiple-type degradation has remained an open challenge.

Current state-of-the-art in degraded image recognition tend to recognize directly from corrupted images based on statistical observations on the feature distribution in the latent space, as shown in Fig. 1. It has been found that shrinking the distribution distance between degraded/LQ features and original/HQ features is an effective way to improve the robustness of image recognition models. In recent work [46], a Feature De-drifting Module (FDM) was proposed to correct shallow pretrained layer's drifted feature response outputs. The basic idea behind FDM is to transform the task of degraded image restoration into feature-based reconstruction by deep degradation prior (DDP). Along this line of research, QualNet [25] attempted to produce HQ-like features from any LQ image via an invertible neural network [2]. Inspired by the success of knowledge distillation in network compression [6,21], we propose a approach of distilling knowledge in the feature space, it can help the model learn the HQ-like feature so that improving the performance on corrupted images.

Another important new insight brought by this work is to recognize the *uncertainty* with the modeling of the degradation process [24]. In previous works, the estimation of HQ-like features has been deterministic, i.e., most of these methods adopted the common *MSE* loss which treats the distribution (variance) of features as a definite constant, leading to poor generalization property when the assumption of degradation process varies. To explicitly address such issue with degradation modeling (e.g., for images containing multiple-type degradation), we propose to design a new branch of a standard deep neural network for estimating the uncertainty (variance) of the feature distribution, which makes the model learn HQ-like features better. In summary, the contributions of this paper are listed as follows:

- We model the problem of degraded image recognition and propose a novel self-feature distillation approach, which can be easily applied into any recognition network and improve the performance of the model on the degraded images.
- We model the uncertainty of the various degraded features and transform the common deterministic estimation model into probabilistic uncertainty estimation. Specifically, a devoted branch, named uncertainty estimation module (UEM), is added to the network to estimate the uncertainty of the feature distribution (variance).
- Extensive experimental results on popular benchmark datasets show that our method performs much better in recognition task under multiple types of degradation than several current state-of-the-art methods.

2   Related Works

2.1   Degraded Image Recognition

Many visual recognition tasks have achieved good performance on HQ data, even better than humans. However, in some common degradation conditions, such as noise, blur, low contrast, rain and snow, the performance of deep convolutional neural networks (DCNNs) will be greatly reduced. [45] revealed the performance degradation of standard DCNNs in the case of blurred image, and [9,10,13] showed that DCNNs are not as good as humans in the recognition tasks on distorted images. To evaluate the robustness of DCNNs, a common corruption dataset, namely, ImageNet-C, was introduced in [19] which consists of 19 corruption types. Recently, researches on robust recognition of corrupted images can be roughly divided into the following methods:

Naive Data Augmentation. Data augmentation is a simple and effective way to make the model see more augmented images, to have better generalization performance during the inference time. The first method using Reinforcement Learning to search for the optimal data augmentation strategy is AutoAugment [7]. AugMix [20] utilizes Jensen-Shannon Divergence consistency loss, and a formulation to mix multiple augmented images. [31] adds noise to randomly selected patches in an input image. DeepAugment [18] introduces four new real-world distribution shift datasets. However, as described in [25], deep models are inclined to learn an average data distribution when using a naive data augmentation method for multiple degradation types.

Image Restoration with Recognition. Conventional methods tend to fix the recognition network parameters but focus on restoring images from the degraded ones to perform better. But [36] indicated that only using dehazing methods is of little help or even harmful to improving the performance of classification because there may still exist a distribution shift between the HQ image and the reconstructed image. Therefore, there exists some research on recognition-friendly restoration. Based on this conclusion, [30] and URIE [42] simultaneously considered image enhancement and recognition. Specifically, they used the joint loss of image restoration and classification.

Feature Reconstruction with Recognition. Some researchers approved that the essential reason for the decline of performance is the degradation of features. [25,44,46] turned to reconstructing degraded features. [44] proposed a Feature Super-Resolution Generative Adversarial Network(FSR-GAN) to produce high-resolution features from small size images and enhance the discriminatory ability of features. Deep Degradation Prior (DDP) [46] reconstructed shallow features in the network through a feature de-drifting module. QualNet [25] transformed the final feature map into an image domain by an invertible network [2] to solve the HQ-like feature. Compared to these methods, we also use HQ-degraded image pairs to train the network but focus on reducing the intra-class differences in the feature representation space and modeling the uncertainty of features under various degradation situations.

Test-Time Adaptation and Self Learning. Recently, there exist some methods aimed at facilitating robustness by test-time adaptation. BN-Adaptation [39] employed a simple recalculation of batch normalization statistics in the procedure of testing for improving robustness to data shift. Robust Pseudo-Labeling (RPL) [38] proposed an improved cross entropy loss function for test-time training to calculate the loss of predicted pseudo labels and model outputs. The pseudo labels are generated by the model itself and are employed while training the model, so it is called self-training/learning. Clearly, the above methods are time-consuming and need sufficient data for inference. Unlike these existing methods above, our approach achieves robustness without extra models and data, enjoying a better generalization property.

2.2   Uncertainty in Deep Learning

Uncertainty has been introduced into the regression task of machine learning for a long time [3,14]. Recently, modeling uncertainty in deep learning for various visual tasks has been proved to improve deep networks' performance and robustness effectively [4,12,17,24,28,40,48]. Two types of uncertainty models have been studied in the literature: one is called epistemic or model uncertainty, which represents the uncertainty of model prediction; the other is aleatoric or data uncertainty, which characterizes the noise inherent in observation data. We focus on the latter (aleatoric/data uncertainty) in this work and model the uncertainty of the feature distribution for a variety of degraded images (see Sect. 3.2).

3   Proposed Method

In this section, we first describe the background of robust recognition in Sect. 3.1, then introduce our uncertainty-based self-feature distillation paradigm, and discuss the modeling uncertainty in HQ-like feature estimation in Sect. 3.2. Finally, we present the proposed method and the training process in Sect. 3.3.

3.1   Problem Formulation

Generally speaking, the goal of an image recognition task is to obtain its label y from an HQ/ideal image x. However, in real-world applications, due to various sources of degradation (e.g., noise interference, motion blur, and compression artifacts), we can only get the LQ/degraded image $\tilde{x}$ instead of the HQ one. Therefore, the problem of robust or degraded image recognition is to recognize the correct class label y from the LQ observation $\tilde{x}$.

Several prior works [25,44,46] have shown that degraded features result in significant recognition performance degradation. We also did a simple visualization of features extracted from HQ and degraded images. Figure 1(a) shows the t-SNE [33] feature embedding visualization on ImageNet-C validation set. It suggests that the feature distributions of the same class (marked by the same color) stay close in the case of HQ images (marked by dots); but become separated from each other in the presence of degradation (marked by triangles). Moreover, the separation patterns will vary from dataset to dataset. For the reason of tractability, we do not consider the issue of domain shift [32] in this paper.

This above observation inspires us to pursue a model capable of performing well under multiple types of degradation by jointly restoring the features z and estimating the label y *simultaneously*. Let $z, \tilde{z}$ denote the corresponding HQ and LQ features of $x, \tilde{x}$ respectively, we can model the estimation of y and z as a maximum a posteriori probability (MAP) estimation framework

$$\arg\max p(z, y \mid \tilde{x}) = \arg\max p(y \mid z, \tilde{x}) p(z \mid \tilde{x}), \qquad (1)$$

where we have used the Bayesian formula to translate the original problem into two subproblems: image recognition $p(y \mid z, \tilde{x})$ and feature reconstruction $p(z \mid \tilde{x})$.

We propose to use a deep learning method to solve this problem. The robust classifier (parameterized by Θ_1) can be represented as $f(\cdot; \Theta_1)$, which is expected to map the input degraded image $\tilde{x}$ to the correct class y. $g(\cdot; \Theta_2)$ denotes the backbone network (parameterized by Θ_2) in the classifier which can reconstruct the HQ-like feature denoted by $\hat{z}$ from $\tilde{x}$, i.e., $\hat{z} = g(\tilde{x}; \Theta_2)$.

For the term $p(y \mid z, \tilde{x})$ in Eq. (1), since the HQ/ideal feature z is unavailable during test time, we use the HQ-like feature $\hat{z}$ which is restored from the degraded images $\tilde{x}$ to approximate, i.e., $p(y \mid z, \tilde{x}) \approx p(y \mid \hat{z}, \tilde{x})$. Note that $\hat{z} = g(\tilde{x}; \Theta_2)$, so we have $p(y \mid \hat{z}, \tilde{x}) = p(y \mid \tilde{x})$. Taking the logarithm of Eq. (1) and rewrite the formulation, we have

$$\log[p(z, y \mid \tilde{x})] \approx \log[p(y \mid \tilde{x})] + \log[p(z \mid \tilde{x})]. \tag{2}$$

In this way, using deep learning to maximize the likelihood term $\log[p(z, y | \tilde{x})$ becomes the following objective function

$$(\Theta_1, \Theta_2) = \underset{\Theta_1, \Theta_2}{\mathrm{argmin}} L_1(y, f(\tilde{x}; \Theta_1)) + L_2(z, g(\tilde{x}; \Theta_2)), \tag{3}$$

where L_1 is the loss function of classification, commonly using cross entropy loss. And L_2 loss aims at gathering features extracted from HQ and LQ images. In our experiments, we train the whole classifier by using multitask learning strategy [25,34]. To better optimize the joint loss function in Eq. (3) through deep neural networks, we present a novel self-feature distillation method with uncertainty learning next.

3.2 Self-feature Distillation with Uncertainty Modeling

Based on the above discussions, the objective of the second term in Eq. (3) is to obtain the HQ-like feature $\hat{z}$ from the degraded image $\tilde{x}$. To achieve this goal, we propose a self-feature distillation framework for estimating HQ-like features. Specifically, as shown in Fig. 3, we employ a pre-trained model on HQ data as the baseline network. During training, both of the HQ images and the simulated degraded images are input into the backbone network to extract features, respectively. Through the feature distillation, their features (z and $\hat{z}$) are expected to be close and have a more robust classification performance.

Due to multiple types of degradation and ill-posed nature of feature restoration problems, it is difficult to learn the HQ-like feature, especially in the texture or edge regions (see in Figs. 2(e) and 2(f)). The current state-of-the-art method QualNet [25] chose to transform features into the image domain by an invertible neural network [2]. We opt to tackle this problem from a different perspective: due to the diversity of degradation, data uncertainty often inevitably leads to feature uncertainty.

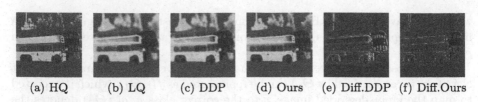

| (a) HQ | (b) LQ | (c) DDP | (d) Ours | (e) Diff.DDP | (f) Diff.Ours |

Fig. 2. (a), (b): The HQ and LQ feature (size: 112 × 112) extracted from clean and Gaussian blur image respectively. (c), (d): The HQ-like feature reconstructed by DDP [46] and our method. (e), (f): The normalized absolute difference map between HQ and HQ-like feature. **Best viewed in color.**

Assuming that each feature map extracted from the corresponding image observes a Gaussian distribution with mean $\hat{z}_i$ and standard deviation θ_i, to better quantify aleatoric/data uncertainty in feature reconstruction, we can formulate the observation model with the estimated HQ-like feature $\hat{z}_i$ and the target HQ feature z_i as a Gaussian likelihood function

$$z_i = \hat{z}_i + \epsilon \theta_i, \tag{4}$$

where ϵ denotes the normal distribution with zero-mean and unit-variance.

Conventional feature distillation methods commonly use *MSE* loss for deterministic estimation. Obviously, the MSE loss can be interpreted as a Gaussian likelihood function with a constant variance in Eq. (4), assuming that the variance of the difference signals between the HQ-feature z_i and restored HQ-like feature $\hat{z}_i$ are constant. However, as shown in Fig. 2(e) and Fig. 2(f), we can see the spatial variation of the difference map, implying that the variances in the texture and edge areas vary across the feature map. Therefore, the stationary assumption of the variances of the Gaussian likelihood function for each pixel in the feature map is invalid.

Instead of assuming a constant variance, we proposed to estimate the restored HQ-like feature $\hat{z}_i$ and their uncertainty (i.e., the variances θ_i) simultaneously. For a given LQ image $\tilde{x}_i$, to restore the corresponding HQ feature z_i, a Gaussian distribution is assumed for representing the likelihood function by

$$p(z_i \mid \tilde{x}_i, \theta_i) = \frac{1}{\sqrt{2\pi}\theta_i} exp(-\frac{||z_i - g(\tilde{x}_i; \Theta_2)||^2}{2\theta_i^2}), \tag{5}$$

where $g(\tilde{x}_i; \Theta_2) = \hat{z}_i$ denotes the HQ-like feature (mean) and θ_i is the uncertainty (variance). Both of them are learned by DCNNs respectively.

Based on the observation that the uncertainty θ is generally sparse in the feature map, as shown in Fig. 2(e) and Fig. 2(f), we propose to impose **Jeffrey's prior** [11]: $p(w) \propto \frac{1}{w}$ on uncertainty estimation θ_i, which can be expressed as

$$\begin{aligned} p(z_i, \theta_i \mid \tilde{x}_i) &= p(z_i \mid \tilde{x}_i, \theta_i)p(\theta_i) \\ &= \frac{1}{\sqrt{2\pi}\theta_i} exp(-\frac{||z_i - g(\tilde{x}_i; \Theta_2)||^2}{2\theta_i^2})\frac{1}{\theta_i}. \end{aligned} \tag{6}$$

Then the log-likelihood function with Jeffrey's prior can be formulated as follows

$$\log p(\boldsymbol{z}_i, \theta_i \mid \tilde{\boldsymbol{x}}_i) = -\frac{||\boldsymbol{z}_i - g(\tilde{\boldsymbol{x}}_i; \boldsymbol{\Theta_2})||^2}{2\theta_i^2} - \log \theta_i^2. \tag{7}$$

To implement the above idea, we add a new branch (UEM), as highlighted by the blue color in Fig. 3(a), at the end of the backbone network to estimate the uncertainty. It follows that the problem of maximum-likelihood estimation in Eq. (7) can be translated into the following uncertainty learning-based feature distillation (ULFD) loss function,

$$L_{ULFD} = \frac{1}{N} \sum_{i=1}^{N} \left(\frac{||\boldsymbol{z}_i - g(\tilde{\boldsymbol{x}}_i; \boldsymbol{\Theta_2})||^2}{2\theta_i^2} + \log \theta_i^2 \right), \tag{8}$$

where N is the number of samples in a minibatch of training dataset. As both the HQ image and the corresponding degraded image are input into the backbone network, we can obtain the HQ feature $\boldsymbol{z}_i$ and restored HQ-like features $\hat{\boldsymbol{z}}_i = g(\tilde{\boldsymbol{x}}_i; \boldsymbol{\Theta_2})$ with estimated uncertainty θ_i through the uncertainty loss function.

Apparently, the learned variances θ_i can be regarded as a confidence score measuring the closeness between the restored HQ-like feature $\hat{\boldsymbol{z}}_i$ and HQ feature $\boldsymbol{z}_i$. For those $\hat{\boldsymbol{z}}_i$ far away from $\boldsymbol{z}_i$, the network will estimate larger variances to reduce the error term $\frac{||\boldsymbol{z}_i - \hat{\boldsymbol{z}}_i||^2}{\theta_i^2}$, instead of overfitting to those erroneous regions. When $\hat{\boldsymbol{z}}_i$ is easy to learn, the second term $\log \theta_i^2$ plays a major role in loss function, and the network tends to make θ_i smaller. It plays a role similar to the attention mechanism, enabling the network to focus on the hard samples [22] in the training set.

3.3 Architecture and Training Strategy

The overall flowchart of our method is shown in Fig. 3(a). Note that we attempt to reconstruct the deep semantic feature rather than the features in the shallow layer (DDP [46]) because it has proved to be more helpful in improving the accuracy of the classifier (see Sect. 4.5 for details). Therefore, we use a well-pretrained standard deep neural network on high-quality images as the baseline model and add an uncertainty estimation module (UEM) at the end of the backbone network to estimate the variance.

The detailed design of the UEM is shown in Fig. 3(b). Since the final feature map has a lower resolution, we first introduce a transposed convolution layer to expand the spatial resolution, which is similar to the role of a decoder. Then six residual blocks are used to learn the uncertainty (variance). Similar to the bottleneck architecture mentioned in [16], we use 1×1 convolution in the residual block to reduce the parameters and the dimension of the final feature maps. Finally, an average pooling layer is used to keep the output dimension consistent with the original feature dimension. To stabilize the training, we estimate $\sigma_i = \log \theta_i^2$ in this branch. So the uncertainty learning-based feature distillation loss

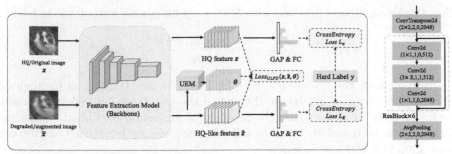

(a) The proposed self-feature distillation with uncertainty learning   (b) UEM
method.

Fig. 3. System overview. (a) Both of the HQ features z and the estimated HQ-like features $\hat{z}$ are extracted from backbone network. The HQ-like features are input into the uncertainty estimation branch to estimate the uncertainty (variance) θ of the feature distribution in a variety of degradation. (b) The architecture of our uncertainty estimation module. The numbers in parentheses represent the kernel size, stride, padding, and output channels respectively. Note that our UEM represents a clever use of ResNet [16] for variance/uncertainty estimation.

function in Eq. (8) can be reformulated as

$$L_{ULFD} = \frac{1}{N} \sum_{i=1}^{N} (exp(-\sigma_i)||z_i - g(\tilde{x}_i; \Theta_2)||^2 + 2\sigma_i). \tag{9}$$

To sum it up, We train our network by a multitask learning strategy [25] with the joint loss function of uncertainty and recognition in Sect. 3.1 and Sect. 3.2 as

$$L = \frac{1}{N} \sum_{i=1}^{N} L_{CE}(y_i, f(x_i; \Theta_1)) + L_{CE}(y_i, f(\tilde{x}_i; \Theta_1))$$

$$+ \lambda \cdot \frac{1}{N} \sum_{i=1}^{N} [exp(-\sigma_i)||z_i - g(\tilde{x}_i; \Theta_2)||^2 + 2\sigma_i], \tag{10}$$

where L_{CE} represents the *Cross-Entropy* loss and λ is the hyperparameter.

4 Experiments

Simulations and Dataset. In our experiments, we have simulated the corruption described in the common dataset ImageNet-C [19] to generate the degraded images and evaluated the model's robustness. ImageNet-C contains 15 corruption types (Gaussian/shot/impulse noise, glass/motion/defocus/zoom blur, contrast, elastic, JPEG, pixelate, frost, fog, snow, and brightness) in 4 categories for training and 4 corruption types (speckle noise, Gaussian blur, spatter, and saturate) as holdout corruptions. Every corruption consists of 5 severity levels. To measure the performance of the network under these degradation conditions, the mean Corruption Error (mCE) [19] is a commonly used metric. All the mCE results in our experiments were normalized.

Training Setting. Every training image pair in most of our experiments contains an original clean and a corresponding degraded image generated by a uniformly sampled type from the 15 corruption types mentioned above. We trained several architectures such as ResNet50 [16] and ResNeXt101 [47] with ImageNet-1K [8], because they are commonly used in recognition tasks. We employed Adam [26] as the optimizer with initial learning rate 0.001, and it was divided by 10 after 5k, 12.5k, 25k iterations. Our model was trained for 40k iterations (about 10 epochs) with batch size of 256 per iteration. The hyperparameter λ in Eq. (10) was set to 0.1 according to the ablation study described in Sect. 4.5.

4.1 Comparison with Sate-of-the-Art Methods

To demonstrate the effectiveness of our method on the degraded image domain generalization, we have compared our method with the state-of-the-art methods on ImageNet-C, such as DDP [46], URIE [42], KD VID [1], and QualNet [25]. The experimental setup was consistent with those described in the relevant papers. Through careful experiments, we reproduced the results similar to those in their paper. In the proposed self-feature distillation network, the uncertainty estimation module (UEM) is used to improve the robustness of the model in a variety of degradation. To demonstrate the effectiveness of our UEM, we modify the network into a deterministic model by removing the UEM branch and use the common MSE loss for training.

Table 1 shows that our approach performs better than these related works on the ImageNet-C test set. *HQ, seen, unseen* represent the top-1 classification accuracy on HQ images, 15 types of corrupted images which are seen in the training set, and 4 unknown types of corrupted images during training, respectively. *Ours w/o UEM* means the deterministic version of our method. We use two types of classification neural networks, ResNet50 [16] and ResNeXt101-32x8d [47]. Table 2 shows the detailed performance for model robustness in four degradation cases which are unknown in training. It is worth noting that our method has less performance degradation on clean images and is more robust than other methods, from which we can verify the superiority of our method.

We have also compared feature distribution visualization results between our method and the *SOTA* method QualNet. Specifically, we randomly selected five classes of images in ImageNet-1K [8] validation set and used the low contrast degradation method in [19] with severity level 3 to generate corresponding corrupted ones. Both of them were input into the well-trained classifier in turn, and their logits were extracted for t-SNE visualization. Figures 1(b) and 1(c) show that our method can better gather the features of both LQ and HQ images, and thus can improve the robustness of the classifier on degraded images.

Table 1. The top-1 accuracy on HQ ImageNet-1K [8] validation set, 15 types seen corrupted and 4 types unseen corrupted images in ImageNet-C [19] validation set. Each corruption type contains 5 severity levels. The mean Corruption Error(mCE) is the normalized average error rate at all severity levels of the 15 known corruptions (less is better). "Ours w/o UEM" means the UEM branch is removed and trained using MSE loss. **The best results are in bold.**

Methods	Architecture	HQ ↑	Seen ↑	Unseen ↑	mCE ↓
Vanilla [16]	ResNet50	**76.82%**	39.17%	47.11%	76.5%
DDP [46]		72.15%	48.21%	50.73%	62.78%
URIE [42]		73.80%	55.10%	56.50%	55.70%
KD VID [1]		74.85%	-	-	51.29%
QualNet50 [25]		75.43%	61.08%	58.10%	50.34%
Ours w/o UEM		75.81%	61.65%	60.23%	49.50%
Ours		76.23%	**63.44%**	**62.90%**	**46.37%**
Vanilla [47]	ResNeXt101	**79.68%**	47.08%	55.53%	69.76%
QualNet101 [25]		77.81%	65.47%	63.28%	42.61%
Ours w/o UEM		78.35%	66.81%	65.30%	41.23%
Ours		79.04%	**69.16%**	**67.83%**	**39.50%**

Table 2. Top-1 accuracy on 4 unseen corruptions in ImageNet-C [19] validation set. **The best results are in bold.**

Methods	Architecture	Top-1 Accuracy ↑			
		Speckle-Noise	Gaussian-Blur	Spatter	Saturate
Vanilla [16]	ResNet50	35.49%	49.16%	41.87%	61.92%
QualNet50 [25]		63.50%	52.59%	54.56%	61.75%
Ours w/o UEM		65.25%	55.39%	56.33%	63.95%
Ours		**66.44%**	**58.59%**	**58.65%**	**67.92%**
Vanilla [47]	ResNeXt101	47.92%	57.94%	48.72%	67.52%
QualNeXt101 [25]		64.21%	57.24%	62.48%	69.19%
Ours w/o UEM		68.70%	61.25%	60.37%	70.86%
Ours		**71.23%**	**64.87%**	**63.04%**	**72.18%**

4.2 Robustness of Using Naive Augmented Data

Naive data augmentation is a technique that synthesizes augmented images from the original ones and then trains the network with the original and augmented images, which are expected to improve the recognition accuracy and model robustness. The main difference between our proposed framework and the naive augmentation training is that we add self-feature distillation operation and uncertainty estimation branch. Therefore, our method can be easily adopted in naive data augmentation training.

Table 3. Top-1 accuracy on HQ images and mCE on ImageNet-C validation set for other data augmentation methods. All methods are based on ResNet50 architecture. For Augmix [20], DeepAugment [18] and DeepAugment+Augmix [18], we choose to retrain the network to make a fair comparison. "*+Ours*" means we use the corresponded augmented images in our framework to train the model.

Methods	Top-1 Accuracy on HQ ↑	mCE ↓
DeepAugment [18]	74.60%	60.31%
DeepAugment+**Ours**	**74.83%**	**59.04%**
Augmix [20]	75.38%	65.30%
Augmix+**Ours**	**75.40%**	**64.37%**
DeepAugment+Augmix [18]	73.64%	53.50%
DeepAugment+Augmix+**Ours**	**73.81%**	**52.47%**

In this experiment, the input image pair contains an original clean image and the corresponding augmented one generated by three popular data augmentation methods - i.e., Augmix [20], DeepAugment [18] and DeepAugment+Augmix [18], instead of the simulated degraded images of 15 corruption types. Table 3 shows the results of combining our framework with augmented data compared to the naive methods. Through adding self-feature distillation with uncertainty estimation, and jointly training the whole network, the model can indeed increase the clean accuracy and robustness.

Table 4. Comparing our method with test-time adaptation methods when the number of samples in the test set changes. *Original set* and *Subset* represent the average top-1 accuracy on original ImageNet-C validation set and the constructed subset, respectively.

Methods	Original set	Subset
Vanilla [16]	39.2%	42.3%
DeepAugment+Augmix [18]	58.1%	61.4%
DeepAugment+Augmix+BNAdapt [31]	65.7%	60.2%
DeepAugment+Augmix+RPL [38]	**67%**	62.1%
DeepAugment+Augmix+**Ours**	59.3%	**62.7%**

4.3   Comparison with Test-Time Adaptation Methods

As the test-time adaptation methods described in Sect. 2.1 require many test images, it is unrealistic in practical applications. To explore the impact of insufficient samples in the test set on those methods, we constructed a tiny subset by randomly selecting 500 images from 50000 images in ImageNet validation set for

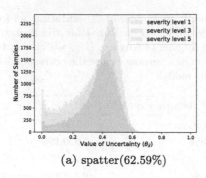
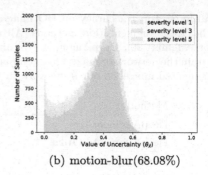

(a) spatter(62.59%)   (b) motion-blur(68.08%)

Fig. 4. The predicted uncertainty value $\theta_{\tilde{x}}$ of each degraded image in different severity levels of spatter and motion-blur degradation. The ordinate represents the number of samples corresponding to the value of uncertainty. For better view, we only selected severity levels of 1, 3 and 5. The number in parentheses indicates the top-1 accuracy on the corresponding degradation. **Best viewed in color.**

testing. For BNAdapt [31], the batch size of the test set changed from 256 to 32. We trained the ResNet50 model with augmented images described in Sect. 4.2 for a fair comparison.

Table 4 demonstrates the average top-1 accuracy performance of test-time adaptation methods plummet when the number of test samples decreases. Clearly, test-time adaptation is time-consuming and needs to be trained separately on each corrupted type in ImageNet-C validation set. In contrast, our method neither needs to use the test set for training nor introduces any extra computational cost during inference. From the experimental results, we have also found that when the severity of degradation increases, the recognition accuracy of the self-learning method will be worse and worse due to the unreliable pseudo labels.

4.4 Contributions of Uncertainty Learning

To illustrate how uncertainty learning works for each image $\tilde{x}$, we averaged the learned feature uncertainty (variance) map θ in the spatial and channel dimensions (i.e., $\theta_{\tilde{x}} = \frac{1}{CHW} \sum_{c=1}^{C} \sum_{h=1}^{H} \sum_{w=1}^{W} \theta_{c,h,w}$), which can represent the uncertainty of this sample. We calculated the uncertainty of each sample in five severity levels in ImageNet-C [19]. As shown in Fig. 4(a), the estimated uncertainty $\theta_{\tilde{x}}$ is closely related to the severity levels of corruption. The more serious the image degradation is, the more samples are difficult to recognize, and the larger the corresponding $\theta_{\tilde{x}}$ value is. This is also similarly observed in DUL [4]. Comparing Figs. 4(a) and 4(b), we can observe that the recognition accuracy of the model for spatter degradation is lower than that of motion blur, and the corresponding number of samples with large uncertainty value (hard samples) is more. These experimental results support, as described in Sect. 3.2, that the uncertainty measures the difficulty of HQ-like features reconstruction

Table 5. Ablation study on our proposed module. "Clean" and "mCE" indicate the top-1 clean accuracy (%) and mean Corruption Error on 15 corruption types, respectively.

Self-feature distillation		✓	✓
Uncertainty modeling			✓
Clean↑	75.11%	75.81%	**76.23%**
mCE↓	51.31%	49.50%	**46.37%**

Table 6. The hyperparameter λ and different type of uncertainty in our method.

(a) Top-1 accuracy on ImageNet-C validation set of different λ.

λ	0	0.01	0.1	1
Top-1 Acc.↑	58.43%	62.37%	**63.44%**	62.78%

(b) The choice of estimating sample-wise or spatial-wise uncertainty.

sample-wise	mCE: 46.93%
spatial (Ours)	**mCE: 46.37%**

for recognition. It makes the classifier pay close attention to the hard samples so that it can improve the performance on corrupted data with high severity level.

4.5   Ablation Study

In this section, we first discuss the choice of shallow features or deep semantic features for reconstruction. Through comparative experiments, we find that the top-1 accuracy on corrupted data by shallow feature reconstruction is 4.5% lower than that of deep semantic features. Therefore, we choose to restore deep semantic features in our method. Then we conducted several ablation studies to investigated which modules significantly contribute to performance improvement. In our experiments, We roughly divide our method in two modules: *self-feature distillation, uncertainty estimation* and verify their impact separately.

Without adding any modules means, we use degraded images to fine-tune the model and only optimize it through cross entropy loss. Just adding the self-feature distillation module denotes the deterministic version as described in Sect. 4.1. Adding both self-feature distillation and uncertainty estimation modules represents the proposed method in Fig. 3(a) where we simultaneously learn HQ-like features (mean) and its uncertainty(variance) through joint loss function in Eq. (10). All models are trained and tested under the ResNet50 architecture. We use 15 types of corruptions in [19] for training. The results are shown in Table 5.

We have also studied the impact on the recognition accuracy of the hyperparameter value λ. We empirically select four values for training, respectively. The results are shown in Table 6(a). Based on the above results, we finally choose $\lambda = 0.1$. We also compared the mCE value of estimating a sample-wise (with dimensions of $B \times 1 \times 1 \times 1$) and spatial-wise (ours) uncertainty. The results are shown in Table 6(b) (lower is better). We can see that the performance of the sample-wise uncertainty is slightly weaker than the spatial uncertainty that we adopted. This is because the sample-wise uncertainty cannot focus on the diffi-cult regions in the feature, resulting in slightly inferior feature detail recovery.

5   Conclusion

This paper has presented a new paradigm dedicated to making recognition mod-els perform better in the presence of various corruptions. Through self-feature distillation with uncertainty learning, our method is capable of gathering both clean and distorted features, so that the model improves the recognition robust-ness effectively. The advantages of our method have been verified throughout experiments in various settings. We hope that our method can be extended to other recognition applications with low-quality/degraded images.

Acknowledgement. This work was supported in part by the National Key R&D Program of China under Grant 2018AAA0101400 and the Natural Science Foundation of China under Grant 61991451, Grant 61632019, Grant 61621005, and Grant 61836008.

References

1. Ahn, S., Hu, S.X., Damianou, A., Lawrence, N.D., Dai, Z.: Variational information distillation for knowledge transfer. In: Proceedings of the IEEE/CVF Conference on Computer Vision and Pattern Recognition, pp. 9163–9171 (2019)
2. Ardizzone, L., et al.: Analyzing inverse problems with invertible neural networks. arXiv preprint arXiv:1808.04730 (2018)
3. Bishop, C.M., Qazaz, C.S.: Regression with input-dependent noise: a Bayesian treatment. In: Advances in Neural Information Processing Systems, pp. 347–353 (1997)
4. Chang, J., Lan, Z., Cheng, C., Wei, Y.: Data uncertainty learning in face recog-nition. In: Proceedings of the IEEE/CVF Conference on Computer Vision and Pattern Recognition, pp. 5710–5719 (2020)
5. Chen, L.C., Zhu, Y., Papandreou, G., Schroff, F., Adam, H.: Encoder-decoder with atrous separable convolution for semantic image segmentation. In: Proceedings of the European Conference on Computer Vision (ECCV), pp. 801–818 (2018)
6. Cho, J.H., Hariharan, B.: On the efficacy of knowledge distillation. In: Proceedings of the IEEE/CVF International Conference on Computer Vision, pp. 4794–4802 (2019)
7. Cubuk, E.D., Zoph, B., Mane, D., Vasudevan, V., Le, Q.V.: AutoAugment: learning augmentation policies from data. arXiv preprint arXiv:1805.09501 (2018)
8. Deng, J., Dong, W., Socher, R., Li, L.J., Li, K., Fei-Fei, L.: ImageNet: a large-scale hierarchical image database. In: 2009 IEEE Conference on Computer Vision and Pattern Recognition, pp. 248–255. IEEE (2009)
9. Dodge, S., Karam, L.: Understanding how image quality affects deep neural net-works. In: 2016 Eighth International Conference on Quality of Multimedia Expe-rience (QoMEX), pp. 1–6. IEEE (2016)
10. Dodge, S., Karam, L.: A study and comparison of human and deep learning recog-nition performance under visual distortions. In: 2017 26th International Conference on Computer Communication and Networks (ICCCN), pp. 1–7. IEEE (2017)

11. Figueiredo, M.A.: Adaptive sparseness using Jeffreys prior. In: NIPS, pp. 697–704 (2001)
12. Gal, Y., Ghahramani, Z.: Dropout as a Bayesian approximation: insights and applications. In: Deep Learning Workshop, ICML, vol. 1, p. 2 (2015)
13. Geirhos, R., Temme, C.R.M., Rauber, J., Schütt, H.H., Bethge, M., Wichmann, F.A.: Generalisation in humans and deep neural networks. arXiv preprint arXiv:1808.08750 (2018)
14. Goldberg, P.W., Williams, C.K., Bishop, C.M.: Regression with input-dependent noise: a Gaussian process treatment. In: Advances in Neural Information Processing Systems, vol. 10, pp. 493–499 (1997)
15. He, K., Gkioxari, G., Dollár, P., Girshick, R.: Mask R-CNN. In: Proceedings of the IEEE International Conference on Computer Vision, pp. 2961–2969 (2017)
16. He, K., Zhang, X., Ren, S., Sun, J.: Deep residual learning for image recognition. In: Proceedings of the IEEE Conference on Computer Vision and Pattern Recognition, pp. 770–778 (2016)
17. He, Y., Zhu, C., Wang, J., Savvides, M., Zhang, X.: Bounding box regression with uncertainty for accurate object detection. In: Proceedings of the IEEE/CVF Conference on Computer Vision and Pattern Recognition, pp. 2888–2897 (2019)
18. Hendrycks, D., et al.: The many faces of robustness: a critical analysis of out-of-distribution generalization. In: Proceedings of the IEEE/CVF International Conference on Computer Vision, pp. 8340–8349 (2021)
19. Hendrycks, D., Dietterich, T.: Benchmarking neural network robustness to common corruptions and perturbations. arXiv preprint arXiv:1903.12261 (2019)
20. Hendrycks, D., Mu, N., Cubuk, E.D., Zoph, B., Gilmer, J., Lakshminarayanan, B.: AugMix: a simple data processing method to improve robustness and uncertainty. arXiv preprint arXiv:1912.02781 (2019)
21. Heo, B., Kim, J., Yun, S., Park, H., Kwak, N., Choi, J.Y.: A comprehensive overhaul of feature distillation. In: Proceedings of the IEEE/CVF International Conference on Computer Vision, pp. 1921–1930 (2019)
22. Huang, Y., et al.: Improving face recognition from hard samples via distribution distillation loss. In: Vedaldi, A., Bischof, H., Brox, T., Frahm, J.-M. (eds.) ECCV 2020. LNCS, vol. 12375, pp. 138–154. Springer, Cham (2020). https://doi.org/10.1007/978-3-030-58577-8_9
23. Kamann, C., Rother, C.: Benchmarking the robustness of semantic segmentation models. In: Proceedings of the IEEE/CVF Conference on Computer Vision and Pattern Recognition, pp. 8828–8838 (2020)
24. Kendall, A., Gal, Y.: What uncertainties do we need in Bayesian deep learning for computer vision? arXiv preprint arXiv:1703.04977 (2017)
25. Kim, I., Han, S., Baek, J., Park, S.J., Han, J.J., Shin, J.: Quality-agnostic image recognition via invertible decoder. In: Proceedings of the IEEE/CVF Conference on Computer Vision and Pattern Recognition, pp. 12257–12266 (2021)
26. Kingma, D.P., Ba, J.: Adam: a method for stochastic optimization. arXiv preprint arXiv:1412.6980 (2014)
27. Krizhevsky, A., Sutskever, I., Hinton, G.E.: ImageNet classification with deep convolutional neural networks. In: Advances in Neural Information Processing Systems, vol. 25, pp. 1097–1105 (2012)
28. Lakshminarayanan, B., Pritzel, A., Blundell, C.: Simple and scalable predictive uncertainty estimation using deep ensembles. arXiv preprint arXiv:1612.01474 (2016)

29. Lin, T.-Y., et al.: Microsoft COCO: common objects in context. In: Fleet, D., Pajdla, T., Schiele, B., Tuytelaars, T. (eds.) ECCV 2014. LNCS, vol. 8693, pp. 740–755. Springer, Cham (2014). https://doi.org/10.1007/978-3-319-10602-1_48

30. Liu, D., Wen, B., Liu, X., Wang, Z., Huang, T.S.: When image denoising meets high-level vision tasks: a deep learning approach. arXiv preprint arXiv:1706.04284 (2017)

31. Lopes, R.G., Yin, D., Poole, B., Gilmer, J., Cubuk, E.D.: Improving robustness without sacrificing accuracy with patch Gaussian augmentation. arXiv preprint arXiv:1906.02611 (2019)

32. Luo, Y., Zheng, L., Guan, T., Yu, J., Yang, Y.: Taking a closer look at domain shift: category-level adversaries for semantics consistent domain adaptation. In: Proceedings of the IEEE/CVF Conference on Computer Vision and Pattern Recognition, pp. 2507–2516 (2019)

33. Van der Maaten, L., Hinton, G.: Visualizing data using t-SNE. J. Mach. Learn. Res. **9**(11) (2008)

34. Mao, C., et al.: Multitask learning strengthens adversarial robustness. In: Vedaldi, A., Bischof, H., Brox, T., Frahm, J.-M. (eds.) ECCV 2020. LNCS, vol. 12347, pp. 158–174. Springer, Cham (2020). https://doi.org/10.1007/978-3-030-58536-5_10

35. Michaelis, C., et al.: Benchmarking robustness in object detection: autonomous driving when winter is coming. arXiv preprint arXiv:1907.07484 (2019)

36. Pei, Y., Huang, Y., Zou, Q., Lu, Y., Wang, S.: Does haze removal help CNN-based image classification? In: Proceedings of the European Conference on Computer Vision (ECCV), pp. 682–697 (2018)

37. Ren, S., He, K., Girshick, R., Sun, J.: Faster R-CNN: towards real-time object detection with region proposal networks. In: Advances in Neural Information Processing Systems, vol. 28, pp. 91–99 (2015)

38. Rusak, E., Schneider, S., Gehler, P., Bringmann, O., Brendel, W., Bethge, M.: Adapting imagenet-scale models to complex distribution shifts with self-learning. arXiv preprint arXiv:2104.12928 (2021)

39. Schneider, S., Rusak, E., Eck, L., Bringmann, O., Brendel, W., Bethge, M.: Improving robustness against common corruptions by covariate shift adaptation. In: Advances in Neural Information Processing Systems, vol. 33 (2020)

40. Shi, Y., Jain, A.K.: Probabilistic face embeddings. In: Proceedings of the IEEE/CVF International Conference on Computer Vision, pp. 6902–6911 (2019)

41. Simonyan, K., Zisserman, A.: Very deep convolutional networks for large-scale image recognition. arXiv preprint arXiv:1409.1556 (2014)

42. Son, T., Kang, J., Kim, N., Cho, S., Kwak, S.: URIE: universal image enhancement for visual recognition in the wild. In: Vedaldi, A., Bischof, H., Brox, T., Frahm, J.-M. (eds.) ECCV 2020. LNCS, vol. 12354, pp. 749–765. Springer, Cham (2020). https://doi.org/10.1007/978-3-030-58545-7_43

43. Tan, M., Pang, R., Le, Q.V.: EfficientDet: scalable and efficient object detection. In: Proceedings of the IEEE/CVF Conference on Computer Vision and Pattern Recognition, pp. 10781–10790 (2020)

44. Tan, W., Yan, B., Bare, B.: Feature super-resolution: make machine see more clearly. In: Proceedings of the IEEE Conference on Computer Vision and Pattern Recognition, pp. 3994–4002 (2018)

45. Vasiljevic, I., Chakrabarti, A., Shakhnarovich, G.: Examining the impact of blur on recognition by convolutional networks. arXiv preprint arXiv:1611.05760 (2016)

46. Wang, Y., Cao, Y., Zha, Z.J., Zhang, J., Xiong, Z.: Deep degradation prior for low-quality image classification. In: Proceedings of the IEEE/CVF Conference on Computer Vision and Pattern Recognition, pp. 11049–11058 (2020)

47. Xie, S., Girshick, R., Dollár, P., Tu, Z., He, K.: Aggregated residual transformations for deep neural networks. In: Proceedings of the IEEE Conference on Computer Vision and Pattern Recognition, pp. 1492–1500 (2017)
48. Zafar, U., et al.: Face recognition with Bayesian convolutional networks for robust surveillance systems. EURASIP J. Image Video Process. **2019**(1), 1–10 (2019)

Novel Class Discovery Without Forgetting

K. J. Joseph[1,2]([✉]), Sujoy Paul[1], Gaurav Aggarwal[1], Soma Biswas[3],
Piyush Rai[1,4], Kai Han[1,5], and Vineeth N. Balasubramanian[2]

[1] Google Research, San Francisco, USA
cs17m18p100001@iith.ac.in, {sujoyp,gauravaggarwal}@google.com,
piyush@cse.iitk.ac.in, kaihanx@hku.hk
[2] Indian Institute of Technology Hyderabad, Hyderabad, India
vineethnb@iith.ac.in
[3] Indian Institute of Science, Bangalore, India
somabiswas@iisc.ac.in
[4] Indian Institute of Technology Kanpur, Kanpur, India
[5] The University of Hong Kong, Pok Fu Lam, Hong Kong

Abstract. Humans possess an innate ability to identify and differentiate instances that they are not familiar with, by leveraging and adapting the knowledge that they have acquired so far. Importantly, they achieve this without deteriorating the performance on their earlier learning. Inspired by this, we identify and formulate a new, pragmatic problem setting of *NCDwF: Novel Class Discovery without Forgetting*, which tasks a machine learning model to incrementally discover novel categories of instances from unlabeled data, while maintaining its performance on the previously seen categories. We propose 1) a method to generate pseudo-latent representations which act as a proxy for (no longer available) labeled data, thereby alleviating forgetting, 2) a mutual-information based regularizer which enhances unsupervised discovery of novel classes, and 3) a simple Known Class Identifier which aids generalized inference when the testing data contains instances form both seen and unseen categories. We introduce experimental protocols based on CIFAR-10, CIFAR-100 and ImageNet-1000 to measure the trade-off between knowledge retention and novel class discovery. Our extensive evaluations reveal that existing models catastrophically forget previously seen categories while identifying novel categories, while our method is able to effectively balance between the competing objectives. We hope our work will attract further research into this newly identified pragmatic problem setting.

Keywords: Novel class discovery · Catastrophic forgetting · Generalized inference · Regularizers · Pseudo-latent generation and replay

Supplementary Information The online version contains supplementary material available at https://doi.org/10.1007/978-3-031-20053-3_33.

Fig. 1. Our existing knowledge about birds helps us to easily identify two groups in these images even if we have not seen images of these bird species before. At the same time, unsupervisedly discovering these novel categories does not make us forget about previously seen categories. Motivated by this observation, we propose *NCDwF* setting and a methodology to instill this capability into machines.

1 Introduction

Over the last decade, deep learning algorithms have achieved remarkable performances on multiple computer vision tasks [7,15,38,46,51], even outperforming humans on many of them. These algorithms are specialised to work well in their strictly designed problem setting, but are brittle when the assumptions are relaxed. We closely analyse one such setting here. Current image classification models assume availability of training examples of all classes of interest. Once trained and deployed, it recognises instances of classes that it has been taught. An instance outside this set of classes may be wrongly classified into one of the known classes often with high confidence [18,47,49,63]. In contrast, humans can easily identify instances that they do not know, and even differentiate among them. To aid our discussion, let us glance through the set of images in Fig. 1. We naturally concur the following: "These birds are not like anything that we have seen before, but these images do seem to belong to two distinct categories". Importantly, we are able to do this grouping without having access to training images from other objects that we have learnt during our lifetime. Secondly, the ability to do this grouping does not impede us from identifying other kinds of birds that we are already familiar with. Lastly, we achieve this without explicit information that these instances are from novel categories. Motivated by this intrinsic ability of humans, we propose a problem setting, which we refer to as *NCDwF: Novel Class Discovery without Forgetting*.

An NCDwF model learns in phases. In the first phase, the model is supervised to learn a few set of classes. In the subsequent phases, the model should automatically identify instances of novel categories from an unlabeled pool containing instances from a disjoint set of classes. While doing so, model *does not have* access to labeled data from the first phase. At any point in time, the model should classify a test instance to one of the

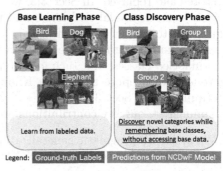

Fig. 2. Summary of NCDwF setting.

labeled or unlabeled classes, without any task identifying information. Here "task" refers to whether the test instance belongs to a (known) labeled class or a (novel) unlabeled class. We illustrate the problem setting in Fig. 2. After learning about Bird, Dog and Elephant in the first phase, a NCDwF model identifies instances from previously known classes (eg. Bird), along with grouping instances of novel categories.

The NCDwF setting has wide practical applicability: 1) Consider the recognition component of a robot operating in an open-world. It can be trained in-house with annotated data. Once deployed, it would be of immense value if it can automatically group unknown instances into different groups, along with consistently identifying instances that it has been trained with. 2) Equally interesting would be an online fraud detection system. It can also be trained with a set of known fraud patterns, but it would be hard to speculate emerging frauds. An incremental class discovery model can not only identify novel frauds, but also group them separately, alongside identifying known fraud types, adding immense practical utility. Labeled data that was used to train both these models in-house cannot be accessed while identifying novel instances due to storage and privacy concerns.

NCDwF is closely related to Novel Class Discovery (NCD) [19] but it extends NCD in several key aspects. First, existing NCD methods assume access to both labeled and unlabeled data at training time, which is unlikely to hold for many real applications. Second, at test time, current NCD methods assume access to the "task" information, i.e., the information whether an unlabeled instance is from a labeled class or not. In NCDwF, we relax these assumptions to propose a more pragmatic extension to NCD setting, mirroring real world demands.

Our methodology subtly makes use of the classifier trained on the labeled data to reduce forgetting and improve class discovery. To make up for the lack of labeled examples from previous classes during the unsupervised novel class discovery phase, we identify regions in the latent space by "inverting" the classifier's discriminative information. Additionally, we ensure that these inverted pseudo-latent representations are close to the true class representations as explained in Sect. 3.2. These class specific pseudo-representations can be replayed along with unlabeled data to address forgetting. We note that this method is cheaper than the generative modelling alternatives, and does not require any labeled image to be stored and replayed. In Sect. 3.3, we show that maximizing the mutual information between the labeled logits and the unlabeled logits acts as an effective regularizer to enhance class discovery. The proposed setting calls for a generalized, task-agnostic inference where a test instance may belong to labeled or the unlabeled classes, and such identifying information would be absent during inference. We propose to learn a Known Class Identifier to help us with this discrimination in Sect. 3.4.

To summarize, our key contributions are as follows:

– We propose a pragmatic generalization to the NCD setting called Novel Class Discovery without Forgetting (NCDwF).

Table 1. We summarise related problem settings here. We note that Novel Class Discovery without Forgetting is most pragmatic when compared with the others. ✓, ✗ and − indicates **yes**, **no**, and **not-applicable** respectively. More discussion in Sect. 2.1.

Characteristics (→)	Data from a future step:			
Settings (↓)	can contain disjoint set of classes.	need not have side information.	can make use of a model bootstrapped with labeled data.	can be fully unlabeled.
Semi-supervised Learning	✗	−	✓	−
Zero-shot learning	✓	✗	✓	✓
One / Few-shot learning	✓	✗	✓	✗
Clustering	−	−	✗	✓
Incremental Learning	−	✓	−	✗
NCDwF	✓	✓	✓	✓

- We introduce an effective method which unsupervisedly discovers novel classes, while retaining performance on the labeled classes used to initialize the model.
- We introduce experimental setting and evaluation protocol for the new setting.
- When compared with prominent class-discovery methods [16,19,61] adapted to our proposed setting, our methodology achieves improved class-discovery performance with significantly less forgetting.

2   Related Works

Here, we analyse how NCDwF differs from existing related settings, followed by a survey of research efforts in Incremental Learning and Novel Class Discovery.

2.1   Relation with Existing Settings

We systematically analyse how our proposed setting is related to research efforts in related problem spaces in Table 1. NCDwF methods incrementally discover novel category of instances from an unlabeled pool by utilizing the knowledge from a disjoint set of labeled instances. At inference stage, the model should be consistent in classifying instances to any of labeled or unlabeled classes, without any task identifying information. In semi-supervised learning approaches [10,52], the labeled and unlabeled data comes from the same set of classes. Zero-shot learning methods [43,55] require prior knowledge of extra semantic attribute information about the unlabeled classes. Few-shot learning methods [4,48,58] additionally require a few of the unlabeled instances to be labeled. Similar instances are grouped together by clustering algorithms [14,57], but they cannot make use of labeled instances from a disjoint set of classes. Incremental learning methods [11,27,42] learn a single model across tasks, but data for each incremental task is fully annotated. Methods that perform out-of-distribution detection [33,39] and open-set learning [18,47] identify instances significantly different from the training data distribution as novel samples, but do not identify sub-groups within these identified instances automatically. To the best of our knowledge, the proposed setting has minimal assumptions and is most pragmatic, when compared to these settings.

2.2   Incremental Learning

The core focus of incremental learning methods is to alleviate the catastrophic forgetting of neural networks [17,37], when learning a single model across a sequence of tasks. Regularization based methods [9,13,32,35,42,54] ensure that the parameter adaptations for the new task will be optimal for all the tasks learned so far. Another kind of approach either stores or generates exemplar images for all the tasks introduced to the model so far and replays them while learning a new task [6,27,35,42]. This ensures consistency across all tasks. Dynamically expanding and parameter isolation methods [1,34,40,41,45] form a third class of methods to address forgetting. All these methods require access to labeled instances for all the tasks. In contrast, Novel Class Discovery without Forgetting models identify novel categories from unlabeled data which the model encounters incrementally - without forgetting how to identify instances in the labeled classes which were initially used to bootstrap the model.

2.3   Novel Class Discovery

Earlier methods like MCL [25] and KCL [24] for general transfer learning across domains and tasks meta-learn a binary similarity function from labeled data and use it to discover classes in unlabeled data. DTC [20] formalized the problem of Novel Class Discovery and introduced a method based on Deep Embedded Clustering [56] for NCD, by pre-training it on the labeled data followed by learning-based clustering. RS [19] first pretrains the model on the labeled and the unlabeled data with self-supervision and uses ranking statistics to generate pseudo-labels for learning the novel categories. This has been further extended by Zhao and Han [60] to further take local spatial information into account. NCL [61] introduces contrastive learning and OpenMix [62] uses a convex combination of labeled and unlabeled instances to enhance class discovery. UNO [16] learns a unified classifier which identifies labeled and unlabeled instances using ground-truth labels and pseudo-labels respectively. Joseph *et al.* [28] uses cues from multi-dimensional scaling to enforce latent space separability, while Jia *et al.* [26] leverages contrastive learning with WTA hashing to enhance class discovery.

Existing methods for NCD require access to labeled and unlabeled instances together to discover novel categories, which limits their practical applicability. Most of these methods also assume the unlabeled data only contains instances from new classes or assume the information that whether an unlabeled instance is from new classes is known. The concurrent work by Vaze *et al.* [53] extends NCD to a generalized setting where the unlabeled instances may come from both old and new classes, while still requiring access to labeled and unlabeled instances jointly. In contrast, with Novel Class Discovery without Forgetting, we introduce a staged learning and account for the performance on both labeled and the unlabeled data, without requiring access to the labeled data when learning on unlabeled data to discover new classes. Meanwhile, at test time, we do not assume the unlabeled images are only from new classes nor require to know whether an unlabeled image is from a new class or an old one.

3 Novel Class Discovery without Forgetting

We formally define Novel Class Discovery without Forgetting in Sect. 3.1. NCDwF models should balance between two competing goals: alleviating forgetting of labeled classes without impairing unsupervised novel class discovery capability. Sect. 3.2 and Sect. 3.3 explain how we achieve these objectives. In Sect. 3.4, we propose Known Class Identifier, which helps with task-agnostic inference.

3.1 Formulation

Given a labeled data pool $D_{lab} = \{(\boldsymbol{x}_i, y_i) \sim P(\mathcal{X}, \mathcal{Y}_{lab})\}$, Novel Class Discovery without Forgetting aims to learn a model $\boldsymbol{\Psi}$ that would identify novel category of instances from an unlabeled data pool $D_{unlab} = \{(\boldsymbol{x}_i) \sim P(\mathcal{X} \mid \mathcal{Y}_{unlab})\}$, along with recognizing instances from D_{lab}. The label space of D_{lab} and D_{unlab} are disjoint, i.e., $\mathcal{Y}_{lab} \cap \mathcal{Y}_{unlab} = \emptyset$. Further, while discovering novel categories, D_{lab} cannot be accessed. The problem setting naturally induces a multi-stage learning where $\boldsymbol{\Psi}$ initially learns a representation to identify instances in D_{lab}, which would then be re-purposed to identify novel instances unsupervisedly. The main challenge involved in learning such a $\boldsymbol{\Psi}$ is to accurately group instances from D_{unlab} into semantically meaningful categories, without degrading its performance on identifying the labeled instances from D_{lab}. Additionally, such a segregation should be done in a generalized fashion, where task identifying information would be absent during inference.

We illustrate the main components of our architecture that help to discover novel categories without forgetting labeled instances in Fig. 3. Without loss of generality, we assume that the model $\boldsymbol{\Psi}$ consists of a feature extractor $\boldsymbol{\Phi}_{FE}$, one head for classifying the labeled instances $\boldsymbol{\Phi}_{LAB}$, and another head for discovering novel categories $\boldsymbol{\Phi}_{ULB}$. The feature extractor is shared between both heads. Pseudo-latents (shown in red) serve as a proxy for labeled data during category discovery. Pseudo-labels from the self-labeler and the regularization enforced by the mutual-information loss guide the learning of unlabeled head. A frozen model trained only on labeled classes (shown in gray) is also used to regularise the model via feature-distillation loss L_{FD} [22]. We apply an L2 loss between backbone features from the model trained on labeled data $\boldsymbol{\Phi}_{FE}^{lab}(\boldsymbol{x})$ and current model $\boldsymbol{\Phi}_{FE}(\boldsymbol{x})$ as follows: $L_{FD} = \|\boldsymbol{\Phi}_{FE}(\boldsymbol{x}) - \boldsymbol{\Phi}_{FE}^{lab}(\boldsymbol{x})\|_2$. Such feature distillation loss has been used in incremental detectors [29] and is simpler than the Less-Forget constraint from LUCIR [23]. The whole model is learned end-to-end,

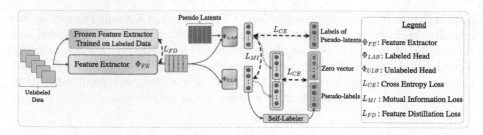

Fig. 3. The figure illustrates how our proposed approach discovers novel categories, while retaining its performance on the labeled data. The network consists of a feature extractor Φ_{FE} shared between the labeled head Φ_{LAB} and unlabeled head Φ_{ULB}. We generate pseudo-latents and replay them through the labeled head to reduce its forgetting (Sect. 3.2), and guide the unlabeled head learning through the pseudo-labels and the mutual-information based regularizer (Sect. 3.3).

where the feature extractor is free to adapt itself to improve class-discovery, while maintaining its performance of recognizing instances from labeled classes.

3.2 Retaining Performance on Labeled Classes

It would be of immense practical value if a model that is trained in-house with labeled data is able to identify novel category of instances, when deployed in an open world. When the network Ψ improves its ability to group instances of novel categories from D_{unlab}, it may drastically fail to retain its performance on recognizing the labeled instances, which were learned from D_{lab}, like the well-known *catastrophic forgetting* in lifelong learning [17,37]. This happens as the model cannot be jointly optimised for category discovery and classification of the known instances due to the unavailability of D_{lab}.

We propose a novel methodology that would generate pseudo latent representations, which can act as a proxy for the latent representations of the labeled training data. We make use of the classifier Φ_{LAB} that was trained solely on the labeled classes to generate these pseudo-latent representations z_p. We explicitly learn these such that it maximally activates a selected class of interest. Figure 4 summarizes the steps involved to invert the latent knowledge from the classification head. First, we sample z_i from a standard Normal distribution, then we select the specific class c for which we would like to generate the pseudo-latents. Next, we do a gradient ascent on z_i such that the score for the selected class c would be higher for the predicted logit vector $p_i = \Phi_{LAB}(z_i)$. Importantly, the parameter of Φ_{LAB} are frozen, while carrying out the latent inversion $z_{i+1} = z_i + \nabla p_i[c]$, where $p_i = \Phi_{LAB}(z_i)$. Next, we do *mixup* [59] in latent space between inversed latent z_i and corresponding class mean of labeled training instances z_μ^c. Algorithm 1 summarises the steps to generate the latent pseudo-dataset D_{pseudo}. In Lines 4–7, we invert the latents of the specific class c, using Φ_{LAB}. In Lines 8 and 9, we first select a mixing coefficient α, and do a linear combination of the inverted latent z_L and the class mean z_μ^c. The class means K

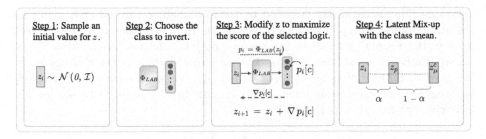

Fig. 4. In the NCDwF setting, labeled data cannot be accessed while discovering novel categories. We propose to generate pseudo-latent representations, which can act as effective proxy for the labeled data representations, by inverting the discriminative information from the trained labeled head as shown in Step 1, 2 and 3. Step 4 helps to induce extra semantic information into these synthesised pseudo-latents.

can be computed and stored after the first phase of learning labeled instances. This mixing operation helps to smoothen the latent space and impart additional semantic information to z_p. The labeled pseudo-dataset D_{pseudo} is replayed while learning to identify novel categories, to arrest forgetting in labeled head of Ψ.

Algorithm 1. Algorithm GENERATEPSEUDODATASET

Input: Number of labeled classes: M; Number of pseudo-data per class: E; Number of inversion iterations: L; labeled head: Φ_{LAB}; Class Means: $K = \{z_\mu^1, \cdots, z_\mu^M\}$; Parameters of the Beta-distribution: γ, ρ.

Output: Labeled pseudo-dataset: D_{pseudo}.

1: $D_{pseudo} \leftarrow [\ ]$
2: **for** c in $(1 \cdots M)$ **do**
3:     **for** e in $(1 \cdots E)$ **do**
4:         $z_1 \sim \mathcal{N}(0, \boldsymbol{I})$
5:         **for** i in $(1 \cdots L)$ **do**   ▷ Latent Inversion.
6:             $\boldsymbol{p}_i = \boldsymbol{\Phi}_{LAB}(\boldsymbol{z}_i)$
7:             $\boldsymbol{z}_{i+1} = \boldsymbol{z}_i + \nabla \boldsymbol{p}_i[c]$
8:         $\alpha \leftarrow Beta(\gamma, \rho)$
9:         $\boldsymbol{z}_p = \alpha \boldsymbol{z}_L + (1 - \alpha)\boldsymbol{z}_\mu^c$ ▷ Latent *mixup* [59] with class mean.
10:         $D_{pseudo} \leftarrow D_{pseudo} + (\boldsymbol{z}_p, c)$
11: **return** D_{pseudo}

3.3 Enhancing Class Discovery

Motivated by the success of self-labelling algorithms in self-supervised learning [5,8], Fini *et al.* [16] re-purposes it to automatically generate pseudo labels for the unlabeled data. These labels are used to train the unlabeled head Φ_{ULB}. A key characteristic of such a self-labelling function would be to discourage degenerate solutions. This is explicitly enforced by pseudo-labeling a mini-batch such that the data-points are split uniformly across all the N classes in the unlabeled pool [8,16]. Formally, let $P = \{p_1, p_2, \cdots, p_B\}$ be the predictions from Φ_{ULB} for a mini-batch of unlabeled data. Let each mini-batch contains B instances. We seek to find label assignment $Q^* = \{q_1, q_2, \cdots, q_B\}$, such that it respects heterogeneous cluster assignment. This setting can be reduced to solving the following optimal transport problem [5,8]:

$$Q^* = \max_{Q \in \mathcal{Q}} \mathrm{Tr}(Q^\top P) - \sum_{i,j} Q_{ij} \log Q_{ij} \tag{1}$$

where $\mathcal{Q}$ is the transportation polytope defined as $\mathcal{Q} = \{Q \in \mathbb{R}_+^{N \times B} | Q\mathbf{1}_B = \frac{1}{N}\mathbf{1}_N, Q^\top \mathbf{1}_N = \frac{1}{B}\mathbf{1}_B\}$. An iterative Sinkhorn-Knopp algorithm [12] can be used to solve Eq. 1 to find the optimal pseudo-label Q^*. The assumption that each mini-batch will be partitioned into all unlabeled classes is fallible. This would lead to noisy pseudo-labels that are not semantically grounded. We are motivated by the observation that labeled head confidently predicts unlabeled data-points into one of the semantically related known categories. For instance, a `motorcycle` gets misclassified into semantically related `bicycle`, and not into other classes that are completely unrelated (more examples in Sect. 5.2). We propose a method which complements the learning via the self-labeled pseudo label by using the semantic information that is available for free within the labeled head.

In the first stage of NCDwF, instances from the labeled data pool D_{lab} would be introduced to the model Ψ. We train the feature extractor Φ_{FE}, and the labeled head Φ_{LAB} with D_{lab}. When we pass an instance from D_{unlab} through $\Phi_{LAB} \circ \Phi_{FE}(x)$, the unlabeled instances would be predicted to one of the labeled classes consistently. We make use of these overconfident predictions from the labeled head to guide unknown identification in Φ_{ULB}. An information theoretic approach to achieve this would be to maximize the mutual information between the predictions from labeled head and unlabeled head, such that we can transfer semantic information from the labeled to unlabeled head, as motivated by [3]. Concretely, for an image $x \in D_{unlab}$, let $l = \Phi_{LAB} \circ \Phi_{FE}(x)$ denote the logits from the labeled head and $u = \Phi_{ULB} \circ \Phi_{FE}(x)$ denote the logits from the unlabeled head. l and u can be of different dimensions: $l \in \mathbb{R}^M$ and $u \in \mathbb{R}^N$. We intend to guide the learning of Φ_{ULB} by maximizing the mutual information $I(l; u)$ between l and u, which we can expand as follows:

$$\begin{aligned} I(l; u) &= H(l) - H(l|u) \\ &= -\mathbb{E}_l[\log p(l)] + \mathbb{E}_{l,u}[\log p(l|u)] \end{aligned} \tag{2}$$

where $H(l)$ refers to the entropy of l and $H(l|u)$ is the conditional entropy between the random variables l and u, sampled from a probability distribution $p(.)$. Numerically computing exact mutual information is intractable, and hence we resort to a variational approximation $q(l|u)$ to true distribution $p(l|u)$ [2,3] as follows:

$$
\begin{aligned}
I(l; u) &= -\mathbb{E}_l[\log p(l)] + \mathbb{E}_{l,u}[\log p(l|u)] \\
&\approx -\mathbb{E}_l[\log p(l)] + \mathbb{E}_{l,u}[\log q(l|u)] + \mathbb{E}_u[KL(p(l|u) \parallel q(l|u))] \\
&\geq -\mathbb{E}_l[\log p(l)] + \mathbb{E}_{l,u}[\log q(l|u)]
\end{aligned}
\tag{3}
$$

We assume the variational distribution to be a Gaussian, with a learnable mean function $\mu_\theta(u)$ and variance function σ_ω. This would extend the derivation in Eq. 3 to the following:

$$
\begin{aligned}
I(l; u) &\geq -\mathbb{E}_l[\log p(l)] + \mathbb{E}_{l,u}[\log q(l|u)] \\
&= -\mathbb{E}_l[\log p(l)] + \mathbb{E}_{l,u}\Big[\sum_{i=1}^{M} \log \sigma_\omega^i + \frac{(l^i - \mu_\theta(u))^2}{2(\sigma_\omega^i)^2}\Big]
\end{aligned}
\tag{4}
$$

The parameters θ and ω of the mean and variance functions, the unlabeled head Φ_{ULB} and the feature extractor Φ_{FE} would be updated to maximize the mutual information between l and u. As the first term in the RHS of Eq. 4 is a constant, we can rewrite our mutual information based loss as below. L_{MI} is minimised along with the standard cross-entropy loss between pseudo labels and the predictions from the unlabeled head Φ_{ULB}.

$$
L_{MI} = -I(l; u) \approx -\mathbb{E}_{l,u}\Big[\sum_{i=1}^{M} \log \sigma_\omega^i + \frac{(l^i - \mu_\theta(u))^2}{2(\sigma_\omega^i)^2}\Big]
\tag{5}
$$

3.4   Towards Task-Agnostic Inference

So far, we introduced an effective mechanism to address forgetting and an intuitive approach to enhance class discovery. Our basic architecture contains a feature extractor Φ_{FE} which branches off into the labeled head Φ_{LAB} and the unlabeled head Φ_{ULB}. During inference, if we know whether a sample indeed belongs to one of the labeled classes or not, we could effectively route it to the corresponding head. But, this would limit the applicability in many realistic scenarios. We circumvent this by learning a function, which we call KCI: Known Class Identifier, which automates this decision.

KCI is realised as a two layer neural network Φ_{KCI} which is trained during the class discovery phase. Hence, labeled instances cannot be accessed to learn this binary function. Instead, we use the methodology explained in Sect. 3.2 to generate N_p pseudo-latents z_p, which would act as a proxy for the labeled data. Using the N_u unlabeled data that we have access to, we extract their latent representations $z_u = \Phi_{FE}(x)$, where $x \sim D_{unlab}$. We create a dataset of latent representations $D_{KCI} = (\mathbb{Z}_{KCI}, \mathbb{Y}_{KCI})$ where $\mathbb{Z}_{KCI} = \{z_p^i\}_{i=1}^{N_p} \cup \{z_u^i\}_{i=1}^{N_u}$ and $\mathbb{Y}_{KCI} = \{0\}_{i=1}^{N_p} \cup \{1\}_{i=1}^{N_u}$. We learn KCI with the following loss function:

$$
L_{KCI} = \frac{1}{N_p + N_u} \sum_{i=1}^{N_p+N_u} y_i \log(\Phi_{KCI}(z_i)) + (1 - y_i) \log(1 - (\Phi_{KCI}(z_i)))
\tag{6}
$$

This simple formulation learns an effective classifier that differentiates labeled instances from others. We show how the learning of Φ_{KCI} matures with training in Sect. 5.1. At inference time, given a latent representation of a test instance z_t, we compute $\Phi_{KCI}(z_t)$ and threshold it using τ, to decide on the prediction. We include a sensitivity analysis on τ in Sect. 5.1.

4   Experiments and Results

We define the experimental protocol and evaluate our proposed methodology in this section. We formulate five different data splits across three existing datasets and benchmark against three prominent NCD approaches. We explain these in Sect. 4.1 followed by the implementation details in Sect. 4.2 and results in Sect. 4.3.

4.1   Experimental Setting

Dataset and Splits: We propose to evaluate NCDwF models on CIFAR-10 [30], CIFAR-100 [30] and ImageNet [44] datasets. Inspired by the data splits used to evaluate Novel Class Discovery methods [16,19,62], we derive a labeled set and unlabeled set from these datasets. For CIFAR-10, we group the first five classes as labeled and the rest as unlabeled. For CIFAR-100, we propose three different groupings: with the first 80, 50 and 20 classes as labeled and the rest an unlabeled. Lastly, for ImageNet, the first 882 classes are labeled and 30 classes from the remaining 118 classes (referred to as split-A in NCD methods [16,19,62]), are learned incrementally. While learning to discover novel categories, the labeled data cannot be accessed. This is an important difference when compared with the existing NCD setting. We evaluate the trained model on the test split of the corresponding datasets.

Baseline Methods: We compare our proposed approach with three recent and top performing NCD methods: RS [19], NCL [61] and UNO [16]. To ensure fair comparison with these methods, we retrain these models with code from their official repositories, adapted to our proposed incremental setting.

Evaluation Metrics: The performance on the labeled data is measured using the standard accuracy metric. Following the practice in Clustering and NCD approaches [16,19,36,50], we use clustering accuracy to measure the performance of class discovery on unlabeled data. Denoting y_i to be a prediction that the model gives for $x_i \in D_{unlab}$, the clustering accuracy is computed as follows:

$$\text{Clustering Accuracy} = \max_{p \,\in\, perm(\mathcal{Y}_{unlab})} \frac{1}{N_u} \sum_{i=1}^{N_u} \mathbb{1}\{y_i = p(\hat{y}_i)\} \qquad (7)$$

where $perm(\mathcal{Y}_{unlab})$ is a set of permutations of the unlabeled classes optimally computed via the Hungarian algorithm [31] and N_u refers to the number of instances in D_{unlab}. This discounts for the fact that the predicted cluster label might not match the exact ground truth label $\hat{y}_i$.

Table 2. Performance of the model in identifying instances of the labeled categories, along with identifying novel categories ('Lab' and 'Unlab' columns respectively), after incrementally learning to discover novel categories is recorded below. We note that our pseudo-data based replay and mutual information based regularization can offer improved class discovery while retaining the performance on the labeled classes, in the task-aware and generalized setting. Please find detailed description in Sect. 4.3.

Settings (→)	CIFAR-10-5-5			CIFAR-100-80-20			CIFAR-100-50-50			CIFAR-100-20-80			ImageNet-1000-882-30		
Methods (↓)	Lab	Unlab	All	Lab	Unlab	All	Lab	Unlab	All	Lab	Unlab	All	Lab	Unlab	All
							Task Aware Evaluation								
RS [19]	20.00	84.48	52.24	44.1	55.7	49.9	18.14	32.56	25.35	13.05	11.5	12.28	3.34	24.54	13.94
NCL [61]	20.00	59.96	39.98	13.59	57.9	35.75	10.14	12.18	11.16	12.65	4.73	8.69	1.52	11.45	6.49
UNO [16]	33.16	**93.22**	63.19	2.01	72.78	37.39	1.76	53.85	27.81	7.95	48.7	28.33	0.75	63.4	32.08
Ours	**92.72**	90.32	**91.52**	**65.03**	**77.03**	**71.03**	**73.18**	**55.66**	**64.42**	**84.8**	**49.67**	**67.24**	**27.46**	**79.07**	**53.27**
							Generalized Evaluation								
UNO [16]	0	71.36	35.68	0	58.15	29.08	0	34.22	17.11	0	41.61	20.81	0	68.34	34.17
Ours	**79.68**	**73.66**	**76.67**	**53.23**	**60.6**	**56.92**	**62.76**	**36.42**	**49.59**	**57.85**	**42.18**	**50.02**	**21.32**	**70.99**	**46.16**

4.2 Implementation Details

We use ResNet-18 [21] backbone for all our experiments. We use SGD with momentum parameter of 0.9 to train the model on mini-batches of size 512. We use 200 epochs for each phase. Following our baseline [16], we also use multi-head clustering and over-clustering for the class discovery head. We strictly follow Fini *et al.* [16] for the design choice of the heads and the hyper-parameters. KCI is modeled as a two layer neural network with 128 neurons each, terminating with a single neuron. For generating the pseudo-data, we sample the mixing coefficient α from $Beta(1, 100)$. In the class discovery phase each mini-batch contains 0.25% of pseudo-data. The models are evaluated in both task-aware and task-agnostic setting. While doing task-aware inference, we assume that task identifying information (whether it belongs to any of the labeled class or not) is available with each test sample. In the more pragmatic task-agnostic setting, we use the proposed KCI to make this decision. For fair evaluation, we use KCI both with our approach and the baseline method [16]. After deciding on a specific head (either using the ground-truth or KCI), we take the *argmax* over the logits to generate the prediction. RS [19] and NCL [61] learn a binary classifier per unlabeled class, while UNO [16] and our method learn a classifier that scores via softmax function.

4.3 Results

We summarise our main results in Table 2. In the first row, we refer to the different data splits via the following concise notation: dataset−total_class_count−labeled_classes−unlabeled_classes. 'Lab' and 'Unlab' columns refer to the performance of the model on the labeled and the unlabeled data respectively, after learning to discover novel categories. 'All' column gives the average performance which gives a holistic measure of capacity across all classes. The first section of the table showcases the results in a task-aware setting. RS, NCL and UNO tend to forget how to detect instances from the labeled classes while trying to discover novel categories from unlabeled data. The unified head approach in UNO substantially improves the performance of class discovery. Our proposed pseudo-latent based replay mechanism, combined with MI based regularization helps to achieve improved class discovery capability while retaining the performance on the labeled classes. The forgetting is even more intense in the task-agnostic evaluation setting due to the inherent confusion caused due to absence of task identifying information. KCI helps to address this to an extent, which complements the improved performance of all the classes, when compared to the baseline.

On CIFAR-100 dataset, we experiment with changing the ratio of the labeled and unlabeled classes. We see a steady decrease in the class discovery performance and an increase in performance in recognizing instances from labeled classes when there are lesser number of classes in the labeled pool. This implies that better pertaining on more variety of labeled classes will improve NCD.

5   Analysis

We provide additional analysis here and in supplementary materials.

5.1   Learning the Known Class Identifier

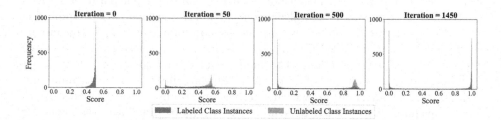

Fig. 5. KCI learns to discriminate between latent representations from unlabeled data and the pseudo latents. These plots show the classification performance on test set of labeled and unlabeled classes, showing how KCI generalizes as the learning progresses.

In Fig. 5 we visualise how the Known Class Identifier matures as the learning progresses in the CIFAR-100-50-50 setting. Before the learning starts, both the labeled and unlabeled latents are classified equally-likely. As

Table 3. Sensitivity analysis on the threshold τ.

Setting	CIFAR-10-5-5			CIFAR-100-80-20			CIFAR-100-50-50			CIFAR-100-20-80		
τ	Lab	Unlab	All	Lab	Unlab	All	Lab	Unlab	All	Lab	Unlab	All
0.8	64.94	80.66	72.8	47.85	70.51	59.18	47.85	51.95	49.9	42.87	48.73	45.8
0.85	66.21	79.58	72.9	48.73	69.05	58.89	48.63	51.66	50.15	44.33	48.43	46.38
0.9	69.53	77.83	73.68	49.7	69.14	59.42	50.39	50.87	50.63	45.41	47.94	46.68
0.95	72.55	74.91	73.73	52.24	66.99	59.62	53.32	49.02	51.17	49.31	46.77	48.04
0.99	79.68	73.66	76.67	53.23	60.6	56.92	62.76	36.42	49.59	57.85	42.18	50.02
0.999	85.05	51.66	68.36	61.42	45.5	53.46	69.23	27.14	48.19	65.62	34.17	49.9

the learning progresses, the KCI is able to disambiguate the majority of the labeled and unlabeled samples. Still, there are some false-positives which is the

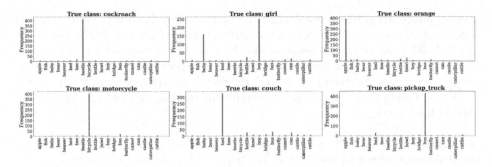

Fig. 6. The x-axis in these frequency plots represents the labeled classes in CIFAR-100-20-80 setting. Each plot shows predictions for instances of an unlabeled class (referred to as 'True class') from the labeled head. We see that most of the unlabeled instances gets misclassified into semantically meaningful labeled categories.

reason for the performance difference between task-aware and generalized evaluation in Table 2. We run a sensitivity analysis on τ (the threshold used to decide on the prediction from KCI) in Table 3. As τ increases, the performance on the labeled data increases and the unlabeled performance decreases. We use $\tau = 0.99$ throughout our experiments.

5.2 On Mutual Information Based Regularization

As illustrated in Fig. 6, an unlabeled instance gets misclassified into a semantically similar labeled category. This motivates us to enhance class discovery

Table 4. Adding Mutual Information Regularizer (MIR) to standard NCD method UNO [16].

Setting	CIFAR-10-5	CIFAR-100-80	CIFAR-100-50
UNO	94.15	89.31	59.45
UNO + MIR	**94.43**	**91.26**	**61.23**

using this semantic information in the head trained on the labeled data. We couple the mutual dependency between labeled and unlabeled heads by maximizing the mutual information between them. This helps to transfer the semantic information from the labeled to the unlabeled head, effectively guiding its class discovery capability. Such improvement is evident from the results in Table 2. Further, we validate the efficacy of maximizing the mutual-information between the labeled and unlabeled head in standard NCD setting too by adding it to UNO [16]. Our extra regularization is able to positively improve in this setting too, as seen in the results in Table 4.

6 Conclusion

We introduce Novel Class Discovery without Forgetting, a pragmatic extension to NCD setting. We develop an effective approach for NCDwF, which makes use of pseudo-latents as a surrogate to labeled instances to defy forgetting, and a mutual-information based regularizer to enhance class discovery. We operate in a generalized setting, where a test instance can come from any of the classes of interest. We propose to use Known Class Identifier to segregate labeled instance from the unlabeled ones during inference. We report results on five different data-splits across three datasets to test the mettle of our approach. We hope our work can shed light on this challenging problem and inspire more efforts towards this realistic setting.

Acknowledgements. KJJ was a Student Researcher at Google. We are grateful to the Department of Science and Technology, India, as well as Intel India for the financial support of this project through the IMPRINT program (IMP/2019/000250). This work is supported in part by Hong Kong Research Grant Council - Early Career Scheme (Grant No. 27208022) and HKU Startup Fund. We also thank our anonymous reviewers for their valuable feedback.

References

1. Abati, D., Tomczak, J., Blankevoort, T., Calderara, S., Cucchiara, R., Bejnordi, B.E.: Conditional channel gated networks for task-aware continual learning. In: CVPR (2020)
2. Agakov, D.B.F.: The IM algorithm: a variational approach to information maximization. In: NeurIPS (2004)
3. Ahn, S., Hu, S.X., Damianou, A., Lawrence, N.D., Dai, Z.: Variational information distillation for knowledge transfer. In: CVPR (2019)
4. Allen, K., Shelhamer, E., Shin, H., Tenenbaum, J.: Infinite mixture prototypes for few-shot learning. In: ICML (2019)
5. Asano, Y.M., Rupprecht, C., Vedaldi, A.: Self-labelling via simultaneous clustering and representation learning. In: ICLR (2020)
6. Belouadah, E., Popescu, A.: IL2M: class incremental learning with dual memory. In: ICCV (2019)
7. Bulat, A., Kossaifi, J., Tzimiropoulos, G., Pantic, M.: Toward fast and accurate human pose estimation via soft-gated skip connections. In: IEEE International Conference on Automatic Face and Gesture Recognition (2020)
8. Caron, M., Misra, I., Mairal, J., Goyal, P., Bojanowski, P., Joulin, A.: Unsupervised learning of visual features by contrasting cluster assignments. In: NeurIPS (2020)
9. Castro, F.M., Marín-Jiménez, M.J., Guil, N., Schmid, C., Alahari, K.: End-to-end incremental learning. In: Ferrari, V., Hebert, M., Sminchisescu, C., Weiss, Y. (eds.) ECCV 2018. LNCS, vol. 11216, pp. 241–257. Springer, Cham (2018). https://doi.org/10.1007/978-3-030-01258-8_15
10. Chapelle, O., Scholkopf, B., Zien, A.: Semi-supervised learning (Chapelle, O., et al. eds. 2006) [Book Reviews]. IEEE Transactions on Neural Networks (2009)
11. Chaudhry, A., Ranzato, M., Rohrbach, M., Elhoseiny, M.: Efficient lifelong learning with A-GEM. In: ICLR (2019)
12. Cuturi, M.: Sinkhorn distances: lightspeed computation of optimal transport. In: NeurIPS (2013)
13. Douillard, A., Cord, M., Ollion, C., Robert, T., Valle, E.: PODNet: pooled outputs distillation for small-tasks incremental learning. In: ICCV (2020)
14. Du, K.L.: Clustering: a neural network approach. Neural Netw. **23**, 89–107 (2010)

15. Duan, K., Bai, S., Xie, L., Qi, H., Huang, Q., Tian, Q.: CenterNet: keypoint triplets for object detection. In: ICCV (2019)
16. Fini, E., Sangineto, E., Lathuilière, S., Zhong, Z., Nabi, M., Ricci, E.: A unified objective for novel class discovery. In: ICCV (2021)
17. French, R.M.: Catastrophic forgetting in connectionist networks. Trends Cogn. Sci. **3**, 128–135 (1999)
18. Geng, C., Huang, S., Chen, S.: Recent advances in open set recognition: a survey. IEEE TPAMI **43**, 3614–3631 (2020)
19. Han, K., Rebuffi, S.A., Ehrhardt, S., Vedaldi, A., Zisserman, A.: Automatically discovering and learning new visual categories with ranking statistics. In: ICLR (2020)
20. Han, K., Vedaldi, A., Zisserman, A.: Learning to discover novel visual categories via deep transfer clustering. In: ICCV (2019)
21. He, K., Zhang, X., Ren, S., Sun, J.: Identity mappings in deep residual networks. In: Leibe, B., Matas, J., Sebe, N., Welling, M. (eds.) ECCV 2016. LNCS, vol. 9908, pp. 630–645. Springer, Cham (2016). https://doi.org/10.1007/978-3-319-46493-0_38
22. Hinton, G., Vinyals, O., Dean, J.: Distilling the knowledge in a neural network. In: NIPS Deep Learning and Representation Learning Workshop (2015)
23. Hou, S., Pan, X., Loy, C.C., Wang, Z., Lin, D.: Learning a unified classifier incrementally via rebalancing. In: CVPR (2019)
24. Hsu, Y.C., Lv, Z., Kira, Z.: Learning to cluster in order to transfer across domains and tasks. In: ICLR (2018)
25. Hsu, Y.C., Lv, Z., Schlosser, J., Odom, P., Kira, Z.: Multi-class classification without multi-class labels. In: ICLR (2019)
26. Jia, X., Han, K., Zhu, Y., Green, B.: Joint representation learning and novel category discovery on single- and multi-modal data. In: ICCV (2021)
27. Joseph, K., Balasubramanian, V.N.: Meta-consolidation for continual learning. In: NeurIPS (2020)
28. Joseph, K., et al.: Spacing loss for discovering novel categories. In: CVPR Workshops (2022)
29. Joseph, K., Rajasegaran, J., Khan, S., Khan, F.S., Balasubramanian, V.N.: Incremental object detection via meta-learning. IEEE TPAMI (2021)
30. Krizhevsky, A.: Learning multiple layers of features from tiny images. University of Toronto (2009)
31. Kuhn, H.W.: The Hungarian method for the assignment problem. Nav. Res. Logist. Q. **2**, 83–97 (1955)
32. Li, Z., Hoiem, D.: Learning without forgetting. IEEE TPAMI **40**, 2935–2947 (2017)
33. Liu, W., Wang, X., Owens, J., Li, Y.: Energy-based out-of-distribution detection. In: NeurIPS (2020)
34. Liu, Y., Schiele, B., Sun, Q.: Adaptive aggregation networks for class-incremental learning. In: CVPR (2021)
35. Liu, Y., Su, Y., Liu, A.A., Schiele, B., Sun, Q.: Mnemonics training: multi-class incremental learning without forgetting. In: CVPR (2020)
36. Luo, D., Ding, C., Huang, H., Li, T.: Non-negative Laplacian embedding. In: ICDM (2009)
37. McCloskey, M., Cohen, N.J.: Catastrophic interference in connectionist networks: the sequential learning problem. In: Psychology of Learning and Motivation (1989)
38. Mohan, R., Valada, A.: EfficientPS: efficient panoptic segmentation. IJCV **129**, 1551–1579 (2021)
39. Pimentel, M.A., Clifton, D.A., Clifton, L., Tarassenko, L.: A review of novelty detection. Signal Process. **99**, 215–249 (2014)

40. Rajasegaran, J., Hayat, M., Khan, S., Khan, F.S., Shao, L.: Random path selection for incremental learning. In: NeurIPS (2019)
41. Rajasegaran, J., Hayat, M., Khan, S., Khan, F.S., Shao, L., Yang, M.H.: An adaptive random path selection approach for incremental learning. arXiv preprint arXiv:1906.01120 (2019)
42. Rebuffi, S.A., Kolesnikov, A., Sperl, G., Lampert, C.H.: iCaRL: incremental classifier and representation learning. In: CVPR (2017)
43. Romera-Paredes, B., Torr, P.: An embarrassingly simple approach to zero-shot learning. In: ICML (2015)
44. Russakovsky, O., et al.: ImageNet large scale visual recognition challenge. IJCV 115, 211–252 (2015)
45. Rusu, A.A., et al.: Progressive neural networks. arXiv preprint arXiv:1606.04671 (2016)
46. Sauer, A., Chitta, K., Müller, J., Geiger, A.: Projected GANs converge faster. In: NeurIPS (2021)
47. Scheirer, W.J., de Rezende Rocha, A., Sapkota, A., Boult, T.E.: Toward open set recognition. IEEE TPAMI 35, 1757–1772 (2012)
48. Snell, J., Swersky, K., Zemel, R.: Prototypical networks for few-shot learning. In: NeurIPS (2017)
49. Tang, K., et al.: Codes: chamfer out-of-distribution examples against overconfidence issue. In: ICCV (2021)
50. Tolić, D., Antulov-Fantulin, N., Kopriva, I.: A nonlinear orthogonal non-negative matrix factorization approach to subspace clustering. Pattern Recogn. 82, 40–55 (2018)
51. Tolstikhin, I.O., et al.: MLP-Mixer: an all-MLP architecture for vision. In: NeurIPS (2021)
52. Van Engelen, J.E., Hoos, H.H.: A survey on semi-supervised learning. Mach. Learn. 109, 373–440 (2020)
53. Vaze, S., Han, K., Vedaldi, A., Zisserman, A.: Generalized category discovery. In: CVPR (2022)
54. Wu, Y., et al.: Large scale incremental learning. In: CVPR (2019)
55. Xian, Y., Schiele, B., Akata, Z.: Zero-shot learning-the good, the bad and the ugly. In: CVPR (2017)
56. Xie, J., Girshick, R., Farhadi, A.: Unsupervised deep embedding for clustering analysis. In: ICML (2016)
57. Xu, R., Wunsch, D.: Survey of clustering algorithms. IEEE Trans. Neural Netw. 16, 645–678 (2005)
58. Zhang, H., Zhan, T., Davidson, I.: A self-supervised deep learning framework for unsupervised few-shot learning and clustering. Pattern Recogn. Lett. 148, 75–81 (2021)
59. Zhang, H., Cisse, M., Dauphin, Y.N., Lopez-Paz, D.: mixup: Beyond empirical risk minimization. In: ICLR (2018)
60. Zhao, B., Han, K.: Novel visual category discovery with dual ranking statistics and mutual knowledge distillation. In: NeurIPS (2021)
61. Zhong, Z., Fini, E., Roy, S., Luo, Z., Ricci, E., Sebe, N.: Neighborhood contrastive learning for novel class discovery. In: CVPR (2021)
62. Zhong, Z., Zhu, L., Luo, Z., Li, S., Yang, Y., Sebe, N.: OpenMix: reviving known knowledge for discovering novel visual categories in an open world. In: CVPR (2021)
63. Zhou, D.W., Ye, H.J., Zhan, D.C.: Learning placeholders for open-set recognition. In: CVPR (2021)

SAFA: Sample-Adaptive Feature Augmentation for Long-Tailed Image Classification

Yan Hong[1] , Jianfu Zhang[1(✉)] , Zhongyi Sun[2] , and Ke Yan[2(✉)]

[1] MoE Key Lab of Artificial Intelligence, Shanghai Jiao Tong University,
Shanghai, China
c.sis@sjtu.edu.cn
[2] Tencent Youtu Lab, Hangzhou, China
{zhongyisun,kerwinyan}@tencent.com

Abstract. Imbalanced datasets with long-tailed distribution widely exist in practice, posing great challenges for deep networks on how to handle the biased predictions between head (majority, frequent) classes and tail (minority, rare) classes. Feature space of tail classes learned by deep networks is usually under-represented, causing heterogeneous performance among different classes. Existing methods augment tail-class features to compensate tail classes on feature space, but these methods fail to generalize on test phase. To mitigate this problem, we propose a novel Sample-Adaptive Feature Augmentation (SAFA) to augment features for tail classes resulting in ameliorating the classifier performance. SAFA aims to extract diverse and transferable semantic directions from head classes, and adaptively translate tail-class features along extracted semantic directions for augmentation. SAFA leverages a recycling training scheme ensuring augmented features are sample-specific. Contrastive loss ensures the transferable semantic directions are class-irrelevant and mode seeking loss is adopted to produce diverse tail-class features and enlarge the feature space of tail classes. The proposed SAFA as a plug-in is convenient and versatile to be combined with different methods during training phase without additional computational burden at test time. By leveraging SAFA, we obtain outstanding results on CIFAR-LT-10, CIFAR-LT-100, Places-LT, ImageNet-LT, and iNaturalist2018.

Keywords: Long-tail classification · Augmentation · Transfer learning

1 Introduction

With the development of deep convolutional neural networks (CNNs) [16] trained with large-scale datasets [32], computer vision research has been propelled forward significantly in recent years. These large-scale datasets are usually well-designed with the number of instances in each class balanced artificially, which

Supplementary Information The online version contains supplementary material available at https://doi.org/10.1007/978-3-031-20053-3_34.

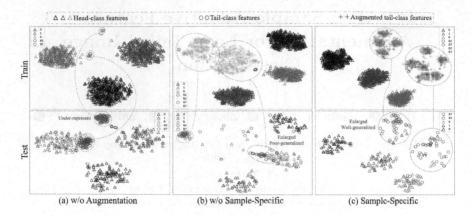

Fig. 1. Motivation of this work: We select three head classes and two tail classes from CIFAR-LT-100 dataset [25] and plot t-SNE [28] visualization to compare methods including: (a) LDAM [6], reweighting-based method without tail-class augmentation in training phase; (b) RSG [38], augmentation-based method without sample-specific augmentation; and (c) SAFA, our proposed augmentation-based method with sample-specific augmentation. (a) *"w/o Augmentation"*: Imbalanced distributions for head-class samples and tail-class samples cause *CNNs under-represent tail classes in feature space*. (b) *"w/o Sample-Specific"*: CNNs enlarge feature spaces for tail classes with augmented tail-class features. However, these augmented tail-class features are not sample-specific and distracting from real tail-class features, making *the feature space for tail classes fail to generalize to test phase and is still under-represented*. (c) *"Sample-Specific"*: Sample-specific augmented features recover the distribution of limited tail-class samples, which *enlarges feature space of tail classes and generalizes better to test phase*, helping CNNs to perform more homogeneously across different classes

however is inconsistent with the real-world scenarios. It is common that the images of some categories are easy to be collected while some others are difficult, resulting in the number of samples in each head class being far greater than the number of samples in each tail class, as shown in Fig. 1(a). Due to the insufficient information of tail classes, CNNs' feature space for tail classes is *under-represented* and the decision boundary is biased to head classes, leading to poor classification performance on tail classes.

To address the issue of imbalance data distribution, a natural solution is augmenting training samples to compensate tail classes in feature space. Data augmentation techniques like cropping, mirroring and mixup [16,18,44] are adopted to alleviate data imbalance problem. However, these conventional data augmentation techniques are typically performed inside each tail class without considering information in head classes. As a result, the diversity of augmented samples is inherently limited by the insufficient training samples in tail classes so that the augmented data can not recover the data distribution of tail classes. Considering

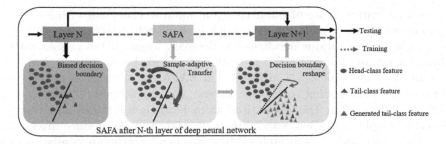

Fig. 2. The illustration of integrating our proposed SAFA into the N-th layer in deep network to produce diverse and effective tail-class features to reshape the feature space. Our SAFA is only used during training denoted by orange dot line, leaving no computational burden at test time denoted as black solid line (Color figure online)

that head class with amounts of samples providing diverse intra-class variance, previous works [9, 10, 23, 33, 38, 39, 43] adopt different methods to enlarge feature space of tail classes by generating new features for tail classes during training via transferring intra-class variance information from head classes to tail classes. [33, 43] utilize feature variation information, such as different poses or lighting conditions, among samples from the same head class to generate new tail-class features. However, these methods did not introduce any mechanisms to ensure the variation information obtained from head classes is *class-irrelevant*. The augmented tail-class samples may shift to other classes due to the class-relevant information from head classes, hurting the performance of CNN classifiers. Also, these approaches are not in an end-to-end manner. To augment tail-classes with class-irrelevant information, noise vectors are used in [39] to encode the sample variation information. But noise vectors are too random to reflect the true variations among images, using such noise vectors for generation can possibly generate unstable or low-quality features. In [38], a feature augmentation module is integrated into CNNs for end-to-end training, the variation information extracted by removing the centers of each class and a vector transformation module is used to enlarge the distance between feature variance and tail-class features. All of abovementioned methods adopt a direct combination between the intra-class variance extracted from head class and random tail-class samples to produce abundant augmented features belonging to tail classes. Whereas, these augmented features are *not sample-specific*: the incompatibility between the tail-class sample with applied intra-class variance causes implausible augmented features distracting from real features in feature space, as shown Fig. 1(b). *CNNs do enlarge (resp., reduce) feature space of tail classes (resp., head classes) during training phase with these non-sample-specific augmented features, but unfortunately fail to generalize the feature space on test phase that the tail classes are still under-represented.*

In this paper, to alleviate these limitations, we propose a novel semantic Sample-Adaptive Feature Augmentation (SAFA) to generate reliable and diverse augmented features for tail classes during training phase to enlarge the under-represented feature space of tail classes and improve classifiers with less biased decision boundary. SAFA is a novel plug-in approach, which is convenient to be integrated into various networks to effectively augment tail classes without additional computational burden in testing phase, as shown in Fig. 2. Note that we only show a simple CNN in Fig. 2, but SAFA can be used in any network architecture. SAFA aims to extract diverse and transferable semantic directions (*e.g.*, intra-class transformation) from head-class features and translate tail-class samples along extracted directions adaptively to produce diverse and effective features. SAFA is formulated by auto-encoder structure consisting of an sample-specific encoder and a sample-adaptive generator. The encoder is used to extract transferable class-irrelevant information from head classes, while the sample-adaptive generator is designed to correct extracted variance information to produce sample-specific features of tail classes. SAFA leverages a recycling training scheme enforcing consistency of the relevant semantics before and after translation and ensuring augmented features are sample-specific. Contrastive loss ensures the transferable semantic directions are class-irrelevant and mode seeking loss is adopted to exploit diverse semantic directions, producing diverse tail-class features and enlarging the feature space of tail classes. In Fig. 1(c), we demonstrate the effect of SAFA. *SAFA is able to generate diverse and effective augmented features and recover the real distribution of tail classes, enlarging the feature space of tail classes and generalizing promisingly in test phase.* The proposed SAFA as a plug-in is convenient and versatile to be combined with different architectures and loss functions during training phase without additional computational burden at test time. With extensive experimental evaluations, we verify the effectiveness of SAFA: SAFA obtains outstanding results on Imbalanced CIFAR, Places-LT, ImageNet-LT, and iNaturalist2018.

2   Related Work

2.1   Long-Tail Classification Methods

Re-sampling. Over-sampling the tail classes [4,5,34] or under-sampling the head classes [4,15,21] strategies are widely used to balance the data distribution for imbalanced datasets. Although being effective, over-sampling might result in over-fitting of tail classes while under-sampling may weaken the feature learning of head classes due to the absence of valuable samples [6,7,11,42].

Re-weighting. Reweighting-based methods aim to assign weights to training samples on either class or sample level. A classic scheme is to reweight the classes with the weights that are inversely proportional to their frequencies [17,40]. The method in [11] further improves this scheme with proposed effective number. L2RW [31] is designed to assign weights to examples sample-wisely based on the gradient directions. Meta-class-weight [20] exploits meta-learning to estimate precise class-wise weights, while [6] allocate large margins to tail classes. Apart from above works, Focal Loss [26] and meta-weight-net [35] assign weights to examples sample-wisely. In addition, for learning better representations, some approaches propose to separate the training into two stages: representation learning and classifier re-balancing learning [6,12,20,22]. BBN [48] further unifies the two stages to form a cumulative learning strategy.

Augmentation. Data augmentation is widely adopted to CNNs for alleviating over-fitting. For example, rotation and horizontal flipping are employed for maintaining the prediction invariant of CNNs [16,18,36]. In complementary to the traditional data augmentation, semantic data augmentation that performs semantic altering is also effective for enhancing classifier performance [2,41]. A hallucinator [39] was designed to generate new samples for tail classes. It uses samples from tail classes and noise vectors to produce new hallucinated samples for tail classes. A Delta-encoder framework [33] was proposed for generating new samples. It is first trained to reconstruct the pre-computed feature vector of input images from head classes. Thereafter, it is used to generate new samples by combining the tail-class samples, and the newly generated ones are further used to train the classifier. A feature transfer learning (FTL) framework [43] was proposed to transfer the intra-class variance from head classes to tail classes by generating new tail-class samples. Our methods can be categorized as augmentation-based methods, which mainly focus on augmenting tail-class samples to overcome imbalance issue. Different from other augmentation methods that simply apply the same transformation (*e.g.*, adding random noises) to all tail-class samples, we distinguish different samples and design a sample-adaptive augmentation method to produce effective and diverse augmented tail-class samples. Our method fully considers individual differences combined with intra-class variance to generate semantically rational augmentations.

2.2 Semantic Transformations in Deep Feature Space

Our work is motivated by the fact that high-level representations learned by deep convolutional networks can potentially capture abstractions with semantics [3]. In fact, translating deep features along certain directions is shown to be corresponding to performing meaningful semantic transformations on the input images. For example, deep feature interpolation [8,49] leverages simple interpolations of deep features from pre-trained neural networks to achieve semantic image transformations. Variational Auto-Encoder (VAE) [24] and Generative Adversarial Network (GAN) based methods [14] establish a latent representation corresponding to the abstractions of images, which can be manipulated to edit the semantics of images. Generally, these methods reveal that certain directions in the deep feature space correspond to meaningful semantic transformations, and can be leveraged to perform semantic data augmentation. In this work, we focus on learn adaptive semantic transformations for tail-class by leveraging diverse class-invariant features from head classes.

3 Methodology

Given an imbalanced training dataset $\mathbb{S} = \{x^i, y^i |_{i=1}^n\}$, where $y^i \in \{1, \cdots, C\}$ is the label of i-th sample x^i, where C is the number of classes, and n_c denotes

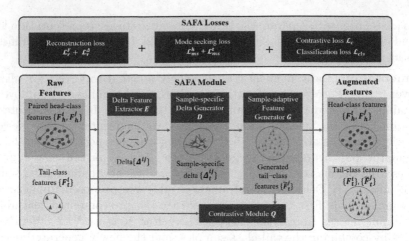

Fig. 3. The framework of SAFA, including a delta extraction module E, a sample-specific delta generator D, and a sample-adaptive generator G, and a contrastive module Q. E is used to extract *class-irrelevant delta* Δ^{ij} from head-class pairs $\{F_h^i, F_h^j\}$, D is applied to combined extracted Δ^{ij} with tail-class feature F_t^i to produce *sample-specific delta* Δ_t^{ij}, which coupled with F_t^i is fed into sample-adaptive generator G to generated *sample-specific tail-class feature* $\tilde{F}_t^j$

the number of samples belongs to the c-th class. We assume that the classes are sorted by cardinality in a decreasing order, *i.e.*, $n_{i+1} \leq n_i$. The data obeys the long tail distribution, *i.e.*, most samples belong to only a few head classes denoted as $\{x_h^i\}$ and data of the other tail classes represented as $\{x_t^i\}$ only has a few samples. Feeding head-class samples $\{x_h^i\}$ (*resp.*, tail-class samples $\{x_t^i\}$) into CNNs, the corresponding feature maps from specific layer of backbone are denoted as $\{F_h^i\}$ (*resp.*, $\{F_t^i\}$).

3.1 SAFA: Sample-Specific Feature Augmentation

In this section, we introduce how to integrate SAFA into CNNs for producing diverse tail-class features to effectively enlarge tail-class feature space during training phase and generalize to test phase. Our SAFA is inspired by [33], in which intra-class transformation (*i.e.*, the difference between two samples within the same category) is called "delta". Deltas are extracted from paired samples of the same class, in which delta is the additional information required to reconstruct one sample of the pairs from another sample. In [33], deltas are directly combined with random target-class samples to generate new features for target classes. However, the effect of delta may depend on the combined target-class samples [1], that is, an effective delta for one sample may be unsuitable for another sample. On one hand, the extracted deltas are different in semantic scale, *e.g.*, different degrees (90 or 180) pose rotation. On the other hand, the difficulties of translating samples from tail classes with different-scale semantic directions are different, *e.g.*, translating a dog with left face to a dog with left face may be easier than another dog with frontal face. Naive augmentation may lead to corrupted features or features without class-preserving characteristic, which are distracting from real tail-class features, as shown in Fig. 1(b).

To extract effective and transferable deltas, and adaptively apply these deltas to tail-class samples to produce effective augmented features, we propose SAFA as illustrated in Fig. 3. SAFA consists of a delta feature extractor E, a sample-specific delta generator D, a sample-adaptive feature generator G and a contrastive module Q. All these modules are built up with Conv-BN-ReLU-Conv layers (Q has an additional FC layer). During training, given a random pair of feature maps $\{F_h^i, F_h^j\}$ from the same head class (*i.e.*, $y_h^i = y_h^j$), the delta extraction module E is used to extract *class-irrelevant delta* $\boldsymbol{\Delta}^{ij}$, which combined with random tail-class feature maps F_t^i fed into the sample-specific delta generator D to generate *sample-specific delta* $\boldsymbol{\Delta}_t^{ij}$. After that, $\boldsymbol{\Delta}_t^{ij}$ combined with F_t^i for the sample-adaptive generation module G to produce *sample-specific tail-class features* $\tilde{F}_t^j$. Finally, real feature maps F are coupled with augmented tail-class feature maps $\tilde{F}_t$ are fed into deeper layers of the network.

To ensure the transferability of extracted delta, a modified recycle reconstruction loss [19] is adopted to ensure that delta encoder and sample-adaptive generator are inverses of each other. As shown in Fig. 4, extracted delta $\boldsymbol{\Delta}^{ij}$ from $\{F_h^i, F_h^j\}$ are reconstructed from fake tail-class pair $\{\tilde{F}_t^j, F_t^j\}$ as $\hat{\boldsymbol{\Delta}}^{ij}$. Further, $\hat{\boldsymbol{\Delta}}^{ij}$ is combined with F_h^i to reconstruct F_h^j by $\hat{F}_h^j$. In this way, delta information and sample information are reconstructed bidirectionally, effectively improving the transferability of extracted delta information and enforcing the generated features to be sample-specific. To ensure the class-preserving characteristic of augmented tail-class samples, we introduce contrastive learning in Q to push away paired samples from different classes while pairs from the same class are dragged in. To further improve the diversity of augmented samples and enlarge the feature space of tail classes, a modified mode seeking loss [29] is integrated into SAFA by maximizing the ratio of the distance between augmented tail-class samples with respect to the distance between extracted deltas.

The overall objective function of SAFA can be given as follows,

$$\mathcal{L}_{\text{overall}} = \mathcal{L}_{cls} + \lambda_1 \mathcal{L}_r + \lambda_2 \mathcal{L}_{\text{ms}}^t + \lambda_3 \mathcal{L}_{\text{ms}}^h + \lambda_4 \mathcal{L}_c \qquad (1)$$

where $\mathcal{L}_{cls}$ denotes any classification loss, such as softmax with cross-entropy loss, focal loss [26], LDAM [6]; λ_1 (*resp.*, λ_2, λ_3, λ_4) denote coefficient; $\mathcal{L}_r$, $\mathcal{L}_{\text{ms}}$ and $\mathcal{L}_c$ are cycle reconstruction loss, mode seeking loss and contrastive loss respectively, which will be introduced in the next subsection.

3.2   Module Details and Objective Functions

Class-Irrelevant Delta Extraction. The delta feature extraction module E aims to capture diverse and transferable delta information. Given a pair of feature $\{F_h^i, F_h^j\} \in \mathcal{R}^{C \times W \times H}$ from the same head class, where C (*resp.*, W, H) denotes the channel (*resp.*, width, height) dimension. The delta feature extraction module E is used to extract delta feature $\boldsymbol{\Delta}^{ij}$:

$$\boldsymbol{\Delta}^{ij} = E(F_h^i - F_h^j), \qquad (2)$$

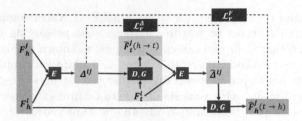

Fig. 4. The illustration of cycle delta reconstruction and feature reconstruction

where $\boldsymbol{\Delta}^{ij} \in \mathcal{R}^{C_{\Delta} \times W \times H}$, and C_{Δ} represents the dimension of delta features. Such extracted delta feature $\boldsymbol{\Delta}^{ij}$ captures the variance (*i.e.*, rich transformation information) between $\boldsymbol{F}_h^i$ and $\boldsymbol{F}_h^j$. By feeding various pairs of features from the same head class into delta feature extraction module E, we can obtain amounts of diverse delta features $\boldsymbol{\Delta}$, which can be applied to tail-class features to enlarge the feature space of tail class.

Sample-Adaptive Generation. The sample-adaptive delta generator D and feature generator G are designed to produce sample-specific delta and features. The delta $\boldsymbol{\Delta}^{ij}$ extracted from different paired head-class features $\{\boldsymbol{F}_h^i, \boldsymbol{F}_h^j\}$ may vary due to complicated scene geometry and light sources, which may lead to different compatibility with different tail-class samples. Thus, it is crucial to attend relevant information from delta $\boldsymbol{\Delta}^{ij}$ according to tail-class feature $\boldsymbol{F}_t^i$ to produce sample-specific delta feature $\boldsymbol{\Delta}_t^{ij}$ more compatible to tail-class feature $\boldsymbol{F}_t^i$. D is designed to attend relevant variance information from extracted delta $\boldsymbol{\Delta}^{ij}$ according to specific tail-class feature $\boldsymbol{F}_t^i$ to produce sample-adaptive delta feature $\boldsymbol{\Delta}_t^{ij} \in \mathcal{R}^{C_{\Delta} \times W \times H}$, where $\boldsymbol{\Delta}_t^{ij} = D\left(\text{concat}\left(\boldsymbol{\Delta}^{ij}, \boldsymbol{F}_t^i\right)\right)$. Then, we combine it with $\boldsymbol{F}_t^i$ into the generator G to produce augmented tail-class feature $\tilde{\boldsymbol{F}}_t^j$ belonging to class y_t^j:

$$\tilde{\boldsymbol{F}}_t^j = G(\boldsymbol{\Delta}_t^i + \boldsymbol{F}_t^i). \tag{3}$$

Cycle Reconstruction Loss. To enforce delta extractor E to extract effective class-irrelevant delta feature and ensure the augmented features are faithful to input tail-class features (*i.e.*, to be sample-specific), we apply cycle reconstruction loss [19] in SAFA. We use objective functions that encourage reconstruction in *feature direction*: paired head-class feature $\{\boldsymbol{F}_h^i, \boldsymbol{F}_h^j\} \rightarrow \boldsymbol{\Delta}^{ij} \rightarrow$ reconstructed head-class feature $\hat{\boldsymbol{F}}_h^j$, and *delta direction*: $\boldsymbol{\Delta}^{ij} \rightarrow$ augmented tail-class feature $\tilde{\boldsymbol{F}}_t^j \rightarrow \hat{\boldsymbol{\Delta}}^{ij}$. For delta direction, with augmented paired tail-class features $\{\tilde{\boldsymbol{F}}_t^j, \boldsymbol{F}_t^i\}$, we can extract reconstructed class-irrelevant delta $\hat{\boldsymbol{\Delta}}^{ij} = E(\tilde{\boldsymbol{F}}_t^j - \boldsymbol{F}_t^i)$ and optimize:

$$\mathcal{L}_r^{\Delta} = ||\hat{\boldsymbol{\Delta}}^{ij} - \boldsymbol{\Delta}^{ij}||_2. \tag{4}$$

Note that $\hat{\boldsymbol{\Delta}}^{ij}$ and $\boldsymbol{\Delta}^{ij}$ are extracted from tail class and head class respectively, which means $\mathcal{L}_r^{\Delta}$ can force $\boldsymbol{\Delta}^{ij}$ to be class-irrelevant. For feature reconstruction direction, reconstructed delta feature $\hat{\boldsymbol{\Delta}}^{ij}$ combined with head-class feature $\boldsymbol{F}_h^i$

is fed into sample-adaptive generation module G to produce reconstructed head-class feature $\hat{F}_h^j = G(D(\text{concat}(\hat{\Delta}^{ij}, F_h^i)) + F_h^i)$, then we have:

$$\mathcal{L}_r^F = ||\hat{F}_h^j - F_h^j||_2. \tag{5}$$

The recycle reconstruction loss $\mathcal{L}_r = \mathcal{L}_r^\Delta + \mathcal{L}_r^F$ can enforce delta extraction module E, sample-adaptive generation module D and G to work consistently for extracting transferable delta and adaptively combining delta with tail-class feature to produce sample-specific tail-class feature.

Contrastive Loss. To ensure the category-preserving characteristics of augmented tail-class features, we adopt a contrastive module Q and calculate the contrastive loss to ensure that the delta feature Δ^{ij} not leaking head class information to augmented tail-class feature (*i.e.*, Δ^{ij} is class-irrelevant). In a mini-batch F_a consisting of real head-class features F_h, real tail-class features F_t, and augmented tail-class features $\tilde{F}_t$, we shuffle all samples with batch size s, and we form $s/2$ pairs by random sampling for training the contrastive module Q. Using $y_c \in \{0, 1\}$ as ground-truth to show whether the paired features come from the same class.

$$\mathcal{L}_c = - \langle (y_c \log \beta + (1 - y_c) \log (1 - \beta)) \rangle_{\frac{s}{2}} \tag{6}$$

where $\beta = Q(F_a^i, F_a^j)$ represent the probability distribution to show whether $\{F_a^i, F_a^j\}$ belong to the same class, and $\langle \cdot \rangle_{\frac{s}{2}}$ denotes that $\mathcal{L}_c$ is calculated over $s/2$ paired features on average.

Mode Seeking Loss. To further produce diverse augmented tail-class features and enlarge feature space of tail classes, we employ mode seeking loss [29] to increase the distance between paired augmented tail-class features generated from the same Δ^{ij} feature, and also extend the distance between a pair of augmented tail-class feature generated from the same tail-class feature, respectively. In detail, given delta feature Δ^{ij} extracted from $\{F_h^i, F_h^j\}$ and paired features $\{F_t^i, F_t^j\}$ from the same tail class, we can produce paired augmented feature $\{\tilde{F}_t^i, \tilde{F}_t^j\}$ following Eq. (3), the mode seeking loss can be written as:

$$\mathcal{L}_{ms}^t = \left\langle \frac{||F_t^i - F_t^j||_1}{||\tilde{F}_t^i - \tilde{F}_t^j||_1} \right\rangle_{\frac{s}{2}}, \mathcal{L}_{ms}^h = \left\langle \frac{||F_h^i - F_h^j||_1}{||\tilde{F}_t^i - \tilde{F}_t^j||_1} \right\rangle_{\frac{s}{2}}. \tag{7}$$

4 Experiment

We conduct experiment on CIFAR-LT-10/CIFAR-LT-100 [25], ImageNet-LT [27], Places-LT [47], and iNaturalist 2018 [37]. For those comparison experiments conducted in the same settings, we directly quote their results from original papers. Next, we briefly introduce these datasets and basic experiment settings. The details of datasets and implementation are reported in Supplementary.

4.1   Implementation Details and Datasets

In following experiments, our SAFA is employed before the second-to-last down-sampling layer, since we got the best results. In addition, we report additional experimental results on CIFAR-LT-10/CIFAR-LT-100 by integrating SAFA into different layers in Supplementary. The hyperparameter λ_1 (*resp.,* λ_2,λ_3, and λ_4) is set as 100 (*resp.,* 1e−2, 1e2, 1e−1), and by observing validation accuracy on CIFAR-LT-100 dataset. We provide in-depth analysis of each loss item in Sect. 4.3 and Supplementary.

During training, given a thresh epoch $\mathbb{T}_{th}$, which decides when to activate SAFA module to produce new tail-class features. Before $\mathbb{T}_{th}$, the network without SAFA is only optimized with $\mathcal{L}_{cls}$. After $\mathbb{T}_{th}$, SAFA is activated to be optimized with $\mathcal{L}$ in Eq. (1) and produce augmented tail-class features. In each mini-batch, we sample same-class pairs from dataset, and they are split into two parts according to a manually set constant head-class ratio $\gamma = n_h/(n_h + n_t)$, where n_h and n_t denote the number of head classes and the number of tail classes, respectively. Following [38], we set head-class ratio $\gamma = 0.2$ for all datasets.

CIFAR-LT: For CIFAR-LT-10 (*resp.,* CIFAR-LT-100) with 10 (*resp.,* 100) classes, following [11], we create 5 training sets by changing the imbalance factor ρ in the range of $\{200, 100, 50, 20, 10\}$, where ρ is the image amount ratio between the largest and smallest classes. We use the original balanced test sets for our test sets. Following [38], the main results on CIFAR-LT-10/CIFAR-LT-100 are trained on ResNet-32 [16] for 200 epochs with batch size of 128. The learning rate was set to 0.1 at the beginning, then declined by 0.01 at the 160-th epoch and again at the 180-th epoch. Our SAFA is activated at $\mathbb{T}_{th} = 159$.

ImageNet-LT: ImageNet-LT is built in [27] based on ImageNet dataset [32] with 1000 classes, its imbalance factor ρ is 1280/5. Our experiments about ImageNet-LT are conducted with ResNeXt-50-32x4d [16], which was trained with a batch size of 256 for 100 epochs, as described in [22]. The initial learning rate was set to 0.1, and it gradually declined by 0.1 at the 60-th, 80-th, and 95-th epochs, respectively. According to [38], test set classes are further divided into three groups: many-shot (over 100 samples), medium-shot (between 20 and 100 samples), and few-shot (less than 20 samples) to better examine performance differences across classes with different numbers of samples seen during training. Our SAFA is integrated into ResNeXt-50-32x4d at $\mathbb{T}_{th} = 59$.

Places-LT: Places-LT is a subset of the large-scale scene classification dataset [47]. The dataset comprises 365 categories with class cardinality ranging from 5 to 4980. Following [27], we finetune ResNet-152, which is pre-trained on the entire ImageNet dataset [32]. The network was trained with a batch size of 256. The starting learning rate was set to 0.01, and it declined by 0.1 every ten epochs until the training was terminated after 30 epochs. Our SAFA is employed at $\mathbb{T}_{th} = 9$. Similar to the ImageNet-LT evaluation, the top-1 accuracy of many-shot, medium-shot, and few-shot in this study are reported.

iNaturalist 2018: The iNaturalist 2018 [37] dataset is a large-scale dataset with images collected from 8142 classes in real-world, which have an extremely

Table 1. Test top-1 errors (%) of ResNet-32 on CIFAR-LT-10 and CIFAR-LT-100 with imbalance ratio ρ ranging from $\{200, 100, 50, 20, 10\}$

Dataset	CIFAR-10					CIFAR-100				
Imbalance factor	200	100	50	20	10	200	100	50	20	10
CE loss	34.13	29.86	25.06	17.56	13.82	64.44	61.23	55.21	48.06	42.43
CB-CE [11]	31.23	27.32	21.87	15.44	13.10	64.44	61.23	55.21	48.06	42.43
CB fine-tuning [12]	33.76	28.66	22.56	16.78	16.83	61.34	58.50	53.78	47.70	42.43
L2RW [31]	33.75	27.77	23.55	18.65	17.88	67.00	61.10	56.83	49.25	47.88
Meta-weight [35]	32.80	26.43	20.90	15.55	12.45	63.38	58.39	54.34	46.96	41.09
CB-RSG [38]	30.96	25.68	20.25	15.26	12.24	62.69	57.94	54.40	46.23	42.31
CB-SAFA	**27.18**	**23.68**	**19.79**	14.01	12.07	60.34	54.13	**52.04**	44.56	**39.77**
Focal loss [26]	34.71	29.62	23.29	17.24	13.34	64.38	61.59	55.68	48.05	44.22
CB Focal loss [11]	31.85	25.43	20.78	16.22	12.52	63.77	60.40	54.79	47.41	42.01
Focal loss-RSG [38]	30.12	26.11	21.58	14.98	12.51	62.81	57.61	54.85	46.31	42.53
Focal loss-SAFA	**25.68**	**21.58**	**18.58**	**13.96**	12.21	61.52	54.32	52.23	44.08	40.58
LDAM loss [6]	33.25	26.45	21.17	16.11	12.68	63.47	59.40	53.84	48.41	42.71
LDAM-DRW [6]	25.26	21.88	18.73	15.10	11.63	61.55	57.11	52.03	47.01	41.22
LDAM-DRW-RSG [38]	26.04	21.74	17.32	13.71	11.55	60.85	55.45	51.50	45.76	42.03
LDAM-DRW-SAFA	**22.47**	**19.52**	**16.43**	13.62	11.06	**57.53**	**53.96**	49.98	44.12	40.89

imbalanced class distribution with an imbalance factor of 1000/2. With a batch size of 256, we train ResNet-50 from scratch across 90 epochs. The learning rate was initially set to 0.1 and then degraded by 0.1 at the 50-th, 70-th, and 85-th epochs, respectively. Our SAFA is utilized at $\mathbb{T}_{th} = 69$, and we report top-1 err as final evaluation.

4.2 Comparison with Previous Methods

Considering that our SAFA worked as a plug-in can be integrated different networks and combined with different loss functions, here, we conduct comparison experiment on typical long-tailed methods [6,11,26] and several state-of-the-art methods [20,38,45]. For the sake of brevity, we will refer to the baseline trained using cross-entropy (*resp.,* Class-Balanced Cross-Entropy loss [11]) as "CE loss" (*resp.,* "CB-CE loss"), and refer to "A-SAFA" as a combination of our SAFA and the method "A".

Results on CIFAR-LT: Comparison result on CIFAR-LT-10 and CIFAR-LT-100 with imbalance factor ρ ranging from $\{200, 100, 50, 20, 10\}$ are shown in Table 1, which are categorised into three groups according to the adopted basic losses (*i.e.,* CE, focal [26], and LDAM [6]). We evaluate our method with the three basic losses. The results reveal that our method can consistently improve the performance of the basic losses significantly. Particularly, our method notably surpasses mixup that conducts augmentation on the inputs and RSG [38] that augments tail class by leveraging knowledge from tail class, manifesting that

Table 2. Top-1 accuracy of ResNeXt-50 on ImageNet-LT

Method	Many	Medium	Few	All
CE loss	65.9	37.5	7.7	44.4
Focal Loss [26]	63.3	37.4	7.7	43.2
OLTR [27]	52.1	39.7	20.3	41.2
Joint [22]	**65.9**	37.5	7.7	44.4
NCM [22]	56.6	45.3	28.1	47.3
cRT [22]	61.8	46.2	27.4	49.6
τ-normalized [22]	59.1	46.9	30.7	49.4
LWS [22]	60.2	47.2	30.3	49.9
LDAM-DRS [6]	63.7	47.6	30.0	51.4
LDAM-DRS-RSG [38]	63.2	48.2	32.3	51.8
LDAM-DRS-SAFA (ours)	63.8	**49.9**	**33.4**	**53.1**

Table 3. Top-1 accuracy of ResNet-152 on Places-LT.

Method	Many	Medium	Few	All
Lifted Loss [30]	41.1	35.4	24.0	35.2
Focal Loss [26]	41.1	34.8	22.4	34.6
Range Loss [46]	41.1	35.4	23.2	35.1
FSLwF [13]	43.9	29.9	29.5	34.9
BBN [48]	42.5	40.3	30.6	38.7
OLTR [27]	44.7	37.0	25.3	35.9
τ-normalized [22]	37.8	40.7	31.8	37.9
LDAM-DRS [6]	43.3	38.3	30.7	38.6
DisAlign [45]	40.4	42.4	30.1	39.3
LDAM-DRS-RSG [38]	41.9	41.4	32.0	39.3
LDAM-DRS-SAFA (Ours)	42.1	**42.7**	**33.4**	**41.5**

Table 4. Top-1 error rates of ResNet-50 on iNaturalist 2018

Method	Error Rate
CB Focal Loss [11]	38.88
CE-DRW [6]	36.27
CE-DRS [6]	36.44
BBN [48]	33.71
τ-normalized [22]	34.40
LDAM-DRW [6]	34.00
LDAM-DRS [6]	32.73
LDAM-DRW-SSP [20]	33.70
DisAlign [45]	32.20
LDAM-DRW-RSG [38]	33.22
LDAM-DRS-RSG [38]	32.10
LDAM-DRS-SAFA (Ours)	**30.22**

our augmentation method is more effective in long-tailed scenarios. Furthermore, SAFA outperforms the re-weighting strategies. This illustrates that our augmentation method can indeed improve classifier performance. SAFA can still obtain stable performance gains when the dataset is less imbalanced (implying imbalance factor $\rho = 10$), demonstrating that SAFA will not harm the classifier's performance in a moderately balanced scenario. Another observation is that re-weighting strategies [6, 11] are beneficial for long-tailed issues, since some re-weighting methods including CB-CE, CB Focal loss, CB-RSG, as well as our CB-SAFA surpass cross-entropy training (CE loss) by a significant margin. Moreover, we compare our method with other previous sample generation methods [33, 39, 43] in Supplementary (Table 4).

Table 5. Top-1 error rates of different network architectures combined with LDAM-DRW [6] on CIFAR-LT

Dataset	CIFAR-10				CIFAR-100			
Networks	$\rho = 200$		$\rho = 10$		$\rho = 200$		$\rho = 10$	
	w/o SAFA	SAFA	w/o SAFA	SAFA	w/o SAFA	SAFA	w/o SAFA	SAFA
ResNet-32	25.26	**23.42**	11.63	**11.06**	61.55	**58.31**	41.22	**41.02**
ResNet-56	23.59	**21.49**	10.35	**10.12**	59.71	**56.37**	39.69	**39.21**
ResNet-110	23.18	**21.09**	10.04	**9.86**	59.13	**55.17**	39.07	**38.51**
DenseNet-40	22.92	**20.56**	9.94	**9.56**	58.96	**54.87**	38.81	**38.17**
ResNeXt-29	22.81	**20.44**	9.71	**9.39**	58.97	**54.79**	38.74	**38.15**

Table 6. Results of ablated methods by removing each proposed loss from Eq. (1). We report the top-1 error rates of ResNet-32 combined with SAFA and LDAM-DRW [6] on CIFAR-LT-10/CIFAR-LT-100 with different imbalance ratios

Dataset	CIFAR-10					CIFAR-100				
Imbalance factor	200	100	50	20	10	200	100	50	20	10
LDAM-DRW [6]	25.26	21.88	18.73	15.10	11.63	61.55	57.11	52.03	47.01	41.22
w/o $\mathcal{L}_r$	31.21	26.96	20.97	18.74	13.15	64.87	62.41	56.83	49.12	42.53
w/o $\mathcal{L}_{ms}^t$	23.56	20.39	17.61	14.83	13.18	58.87	54.38	51.32	45.92	42.87
w/o $\mathcal{L}_{ms}^h$	24.67	20.94	17.16	13.67	11.69	59.89	55.09	51.29	44.86	41.78
w/o $\mathcal{L}_c$	23.84	20.41	17.08	13.89	11.54	58.53	54.13	50.71	44.69	41.53
Full method	**22.47**	**19.52**	**16.43**	**13.62**	**11.06**	**57.53**	**53.96**	**49.98**	**44.12**	**40.89**

Results on ImageNet-LT: We present the results for ImageNet-LT in Table 2. When compared to LDAM-DRS, LDAM-DRW-RSG [38], LADM-DRS-SAFA (ours) still achieves a greater level of accuracy, demonstrating that SAFA can solve the problem of imbalanced datasets. On medium-shot and few-shot classes, SAFA can produce effective and diverse tail-class features to enlarge tail-class feature space to improve the model and considerably improve its generality.

Results on Places-LT: The Table 3 shows the top-1 accuracy on Place-LT. The results reveal that when SAFA is paired with LDAM-DRS, performance may be increased even further, demonstrating that SAFA is useful. Furthermore, when compared to the two most current prominent approaches, *tau*-normalized, BBN, DisAlign, and RSG, SAFA can increase the model's performance on medium-shot and few-shot classes while causing less accuracy loss on many-shot classes, resulting in higher overall accuracy and competitive result.

Results on iNaturalist 2018: We show the experimental results under the same setting as [38] on iNaturalist 2018 dataset. The results reveal that by leveraging the proposed sample-adaptive feature augmentation method, we may achieve superior results, demonstrating the efficacy of SAFA. As can be observed,

SAFA assists the model in achieving competitive outcomes, demonstrating that SAFA is capable of effectively coping with imbalanced datasets.

4.3   Ablation Studies

Adaptivity to Different Backbone Networks: Firstly, we analyze the effectiveness of our proposed SAFA module by integrating SAFA into different network architectures including ResNet-32, ResNet-56, ResNet-110, DenseNet-40, and ResNeXt-29 (8×64d), and report the comparison results on CIFAR-LT-10/CIFAR-LT-100 with $\rho = \{200, 10\}$ in Table 5, in which "w/o SAFA" denotes that removing SAFA during training. From Table 5, we can see that all models equipped with SAFA are consistently better whether $\rho = 100$ or $\rho = 10$, which indicates that SAFA can be employed into various deep neural network to improve long-tail classification performance.

Combination with Different Loss Functions: In Table 1, by comparing the results of CE loss (*resp.*, Focal loss, LDAM-DRW loss) with the results of CB-SAFA (*resp.*, SAFA focal loss, LDAM-DRW SAFA loss), it is seen that our SAFA is compatible with different loss functions and can consistently improve classification performance based on different loss functions.

Analysis of Each Loss Term of SAFA: In our SAFA, we employ a reconstruction loss $\mathcal{L}_r$, a tail mode seeking loss $\mathcal{L}_{ms}^t$, a head mode seeking loss $\mathcal{L}_{ms}^h$, and a contrastive loss $\mathcal{L}_c$. To investigate the impact of each loss term, we conduct ablation studies on CIFAR-10 and CIFAR-100 datasets by removing each loss term from the final objective in Eq. (1). The results are summarized in Table 6. Firstly, we can see that the classification performance is compromised when removing $\mathcal{L}_r$, even worse than baseline LDAM-DRW [6] without augmentation, implying that our recycle reconstruction loss is necessary and it enforces our SAFA module to extract transferable delta and achieve sample-adaptive augmentation. Removing $\mathcal{L}_c$ results in slight performance degradation on two datasets, since the generated features may not belong to the category of combined tail class without contrastive loss. By removing the head mode seeking loss $\mathcal{L}_{ms}^h$, we can see that the classification performance in less imbalanced scenarios such as imbalance ratio $\rho = \{200, 100\}$ on two datasets become much worse while leaving less impact on relatively balanced settings with $\rho = \{20, 10\}$. Another observation is that ablating tail mode seeking loss $\mathcal{L}_{ms}^t$ results in a minor deterioration of classification performance in extremely imbalanced settings with $\rho = \{200, 100\}$, compared to a more significant decline in less imbalanced settings with $\rho = \{20, 10\}$. It can be explained as follows: in extremely imbalanced settings like $\rho = \{200, 100\}$, where head-class samples may be compact in feature space, leading to more compact deltas in feature space, in other words, the distance among deltas is limited. In this scenario, using head mode seeking loss $\mathcal{L}_{ms}^h$ to enlarge the distance between real tail-class feature and augmented tail-class feature based on the distance of head-class pairs can produce diverse tail-class samples, whereas the distance between deltas may be sufficient to produce different samples without the use of $\mathcal{L}_{ms}^h$. Similarly, $\mathcal{L}_{ms}^t$ is adopted to enlarge the distance between two tail-class features augmented from the same tail-class feature. It is helpful to leverage $\mathcal{L}_{ms}^t$ to enforce SAFA to be sensitive to the difference of paired features from the same tail class in a less imbalanced setting, where the tail-class feature space may be compact, however it is not necessary for a relatively loose tail-class feature space.

5   Conclusions

In this paper, we propose a novel plug-in approach SAFA, which is convenient to be integrated into various networks and coupled with different loss functions. Our SAFA aims to extract transferable delta from head class and achieve sample-adaptive application to tail class to enlarge tail-class feature space. Extensive experiment demonstrate the effectiveness of the proposed SAFA.

References

1. Almahairi, A., Rajeswar, S., Sordoni, A., Bachman, P., Courville, A.C.: Augmented CycleGAN: learning many-to-many mappings from unpaired data. In: ICML (2018)
2. Antoniou, A., Storkey, A., Edwards, H.: Data augmentation generative adversarial networks. arXiv preprint arXiv:1711.04340 (2017)
3. Bengio, Y.: Learning deep architectures for AI (2009)
4. Buda, M., Maki, A., Mazurowski, M.A.: A systematic study of the class imbalance problem in convolutional neural networks. Neural Netw. **106**, 249–259 (2018)
5. Byrd, J., Lipton, Z.: What is the effect of importance weighting in deep learning? In: ICML (2019)
6. Cao, K., Wei, C., Gaidon, A., Arechiga, N., Ma, T.: Learning imbalanced datasets with label-distribution-aware margin loss. In: NeurIPS (2019)
7. Chawla, N.V., Bowyer, K.W., Hall, L.O., Kegelmeyer, W.P.: SMOTE: synthetic minority over-sampling technique. J. Artif. Intell. Res. **16**, 321–357 (2002)
8. Choi, Y., Choi, M., Kim, M., Ha, J.W., Kim, S., Choo, J.: StarGAN: unified generative adversarial networks for multi-domain image-to-image translation. In: CVPR (2018)
9. Chou, H.-P., Chang, S.-C., Pan, J.-Y., Wei, W., Juan, D.-C.: Remix: rebalanced mixup. In: Bartoli, A., Fusiello, A. (eds.) ECCV 2020. LNCS, vol. 12540, pp. 95–110. Springer, Cham (2020). https://doi.org/10.1007/978-3-030-65414-6_9
10. Chu, P., Bian, X., Liu, S., Ling, H.: Feature space augmentation for long-tailed data. In: Vedaldi, A., Bischof, H., Brox, T., Frahm, J.-M. (eds.) ECCV 2020. LNCS, vol. 12374, pp. 694–710. Springer, Cham (2020). https://doi.org/10.1007/978-3-030-58526-6_41
11. Cui, Y., Jia, M., Lin, T.Y., Song, Y., Belongie, S.: Class-balanced loss based on effective number of samples. In: CVPR (2019)
12. Cui, Y., Song, Y., Sun, C., Howard, A., Belongie, S.: Large scale fine-grained categorization and domain-specific transfer learning. In: CVPR (2018)
13. Gidaris, S., Komodakis, N.: Dynamic few-shot visual learning without forgetting. In: CVPR (2018)
14. Goodfellow, I., et al.: Generative adversarial nets. In: NeurIPS (2014)
15. He, H., Garcia, E.A.: Learning from imbalanced data. IEEE TKDE **21**(9), 1263–1284 (2009)

16. He, K., Zhang, X., Ren, S., Sun, J.: Deep residual learning for image recognition. In: CVPR (2016)
17. Huang, C., Li, Y., Loy, C.C., Tang, X.: Learning deep representation for imbalanced classification. In: CVPR (2016)
18. Huang, G., Liu, Z., Van Der Maaten, L., Weinberger, K.Q.: Densely connected convolutional networks. In: CVPR (2017)
19. Huang, X., Liu, M.Y., Belongie, S., Kautz, J.: Multimodal unsupervised image-to-image translation. In: ECCV (2018)
20. Jamal, M.A., Brown, M., Yang, M.H., Wang, L., Gong, B.: Rethinking class-balanced methods for long-tailed visual recognition from a domain adaptation perspective. In: CVPR (2020)
21. Japkowicz, N., Stephen, S.: The class imbalance problem: a systematic study. Intell. Data Anal. **6**(5), 429–449 (2002)
22. Kang, B., et al.: Decoupling representation and classifier for long-tailed recognition. In: ICLR (2019)
23. Kim, J., Jeong, J., Shin, J.: M2M: imbalanced classification via major-to-minor translation. In: CVPR (2020)
24. Kingma, D.P., Welling, M.: Auto-encoding variational bayes. In: ICLR (2014)
25. Krizhevsky, A., et al.: Learning multiple layers of features from tiny images (2009)
26. Lin, T.Y., Goyal, P., Girshick, R., He, K., Dollár, P.: Focal loss for dense object detection. In: ICCV (2017)
27. Liu, Z., Miao, Z., Zhan, X., Wang, J., Gong, B., Yu, S.X.: Large-scale long-tailed recognition in an open world. In: CVPR (2019)
28. Van der Maaten, L., Hinton, G.: Visualizing data using t-SNE. J. Mach. Learn. Res. **9**(11) (2008)
29. Mao, Q., Lee, H.Y., Tseng, H.Y., Ma, S., Yang, M.H.: Mode seeking generative adversarial networks for diverse image synthesis. In: CVPR (2019)
30. Oh Song, H., Xiang, Y., Jegelka, S., Savarese, S.: Deep metric learning via lifted structured feature embedding. In: CVPR (2016)
31. Ren, M., Zeng, W., Yang, B., Urtasun, R.: Learning to reweight examples for robust deep learning. In: ICML (2018)
32. Russakovsky, O., Deng, J., Su, H., Krause, J., Satheesh, S., Ma, S., Huang, Z., Karpathy, A., Khosla, A., Bernstein, M., et al.: ImageNet: large scale visual recognition challenge. IJCV **115**(3), 211–252 (2015)
33. Schwartz, E., et al.: Delta-encoder: an effective sample synthesis method for few-shot object recognition. In: NeurIPS (2018)
34. Shen, L., Lin, Z., Huang, Q.: Relay backpropagation for effective learning of deep convolutional neural networks. In: Leibe, B., Matas, J., Sebe, N., Welling, M. (eds.) ECCV 2016. LNCS, vol. 9911, pp. 467–482. Springer, Cham (2016). https://doi.org/10.1007/978-3-319-46478-7_29
35. Shu, J., et al.: Meta-weight-net: learning an explicit mapping for sample weighting. In: NeurIPS (2019)
36. Simonyan, K., Zisserman, A.: Very deep convolutional networks for large-scale image recognition. arXiv preprint arXiv:1409.1556 (2014)
37. Van Horn, G., et al.: The iNaturalist species classification and detection dataset. In: CVPR (2018)
38. Wang, J., Lukasiewicz, T., Hu, X., Cai, J., Xu, Z.: RSG: a simple but effective module for learning imbalanced datasets. In: CVPR (2021)
39. Wang, Y.X., Girshick, R., Hebert, M., Hariharan, B.: Low-shot learning from imaginary data. In: CVPR (2018)

40. Wang, Y.X., Ramanan, D., Hebert, M.: Learning to model the tail. In: NeurIPS (2017)
41. Wang, Y., Pan, X., Song, S., Zhang, H., Huang, G., Wu, C.: Implicit semantic data augmentation for deep networks. In: NeurIPS (2019)
42. Wu, T., Huang, Q., Liu, Z., Wang, Yu., Lin, D.: Distribution-balanced loss for multi-label classification in long-tailed datasets. In: Vedaldi, A., Bischof, H., Brox, T., Frahm, J.-M. (eds.) ECCV 2020. LNCS, vol. 12349, pp. 162–178. Springer, Cham (2020). https://doi.org/10.1007/978-3-030-58548-8_10
43. Yin, X., Yu, X., Sohn, K., Liu, X., Chandraker, M.: Feature transfer learning for deep face recognition with under-represented data. arXiv preprint arXiv:1803.09014 (2018)
44. Zhang, H., Cisse, M., Dauphin, Y.N., Lopez-Paz, D.: mixup: Beyond empirical risk minimization. In: ICLR (2018)
45. Zhang, S., Li, Z., Yan, S., He, X., Sun, J.: Distribution alignment: a unified framework for long-tail visual recognition. In: CVPR (2021)
46. Zhang, X., Fang, Z., Wen, Y., Li, Z., Qiao, Y.: Range loss for deep face recognition with long-tailed training data. In: ICCV (2017)
47. Zhou, B., Lapedriza, A., Khosla, A., Oliva, A., Torralba, A.: Places: a 10 million image database for scene recognition. PAMI **40**(6), 1452–1464 (2017)
48. Zhou, B., Cui, Q., Wei, X.S., Chen, Z.M.: BBN: bilateral-branch network with cumulative learning for long-tailed visual recognition. In: CVPR (2020)
49. Zhu, J.Y., Park, T., Isola, P., Efros, A.A.: Unpaired image-to-image translation using cycle-consistent adversarial networks. In: ICCV (2017)

Negative Samples are at Large: Leveraging Hard-Distance Elastic Loss for Re-identification

Hyungtae Lee[1(✉)], Sungmin Eum[1,2], and Heesung Kwon[1]

[1] DEVCOM Army Research Laboratory, Adelphi, USA
hyungtae.lee.civ@army.mil
[2] Booz Allen Hamilton, McLean, USA

Abstract. We present a Momentum Re-identification (MoReID) framework that can leverage a very large number of negative samples in training for general re-identification task. The design of this framework is inspired by Momentum Contrast (MoCo), which uses a dictionary to store current and past batches to build a large set of encoded samples. As we find it less effective to use past positive samples which may be highly inconsistent to the encoded feature property formed with the current positive samples, MoReID is designed to use only a large number of negative samples stored in the dictionary. However, if we train the model using the widely used Triplet loss that uses only one sample to represent a set of positive/negative samples, it is hard to effectively leverage the enlarged set of negative samples acquired by the MoReID framework. To maximize the advantage of using the scaled-up negative sample set, we newly introduce Hard-distance Elastic loss (HE loss), which is capable of using more than one hard sample to represent a large number of samples. Our experiments demonstrate that a large number of negative samples provided by MoReID framework can be utilized at full capacity only with the HE loss, achieving the state-of-the-art accuracy on three re-ID benchmarks, VeRi-776, Market-1501, and VeRi-Wild.

Keywords: Re-identification · Large-scale negative samples · Momentum encoder · MoReID · HE loss

1 Introduction

Re-identification (re-ID) is the task of finding instances (e.g., person, vehicle) with the same identity in images taken from different viewpoints in different locations. In general, a re-ID model needs the ability that, given a query, well separates instances with the same ID (positive samples) from instances with different IDs (negative samples). This ability can be acquired by training the model so that the positive samples are placed closer to the query while the negative samples are placed in a distant location in the learned feature space.

Supplementary Information The online version contains supplementary material available at https://doi.org/10.1007/978-3-031-20053-3_35.

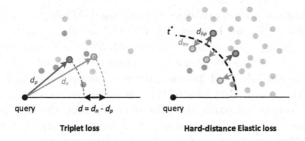

Fig. 1. Hard-distance Elastic Loss vs. Triplet loss. In Triplet loss, the positive and negative samples are each represented by a single point. HE loss, on the other hand, can use more than one hard samples to represent positive and negative samples, respectively. Knowing that the optimally determined boundary t^* divides the feature space into positive and negative sides, a positive sample is a called a hard sample when it lies on the negative side, and vice versa. Representative samples are plotted in bold. Multiple points are better than a single point when representing a large number of negative samples, as shown in the figure on the right. More analysis of HE loss versus Triplet loss is in Sect. 4.4.

When separating the positives from the negatives with respect to a given query, such as in the re-ID, having a sufficient number of samples in each set often helps in generating a more precise boundary between the two sets. However, the mini-batch optimization which is widely used in training a network cannot afford to use more than a certain number of samples in each training iteration. Recently, Momentum Contrast (MoCo) [12] provided a structural way to effectively provide a large number of samples for training. It uses a dictionary that collects several preceding batches in the form of encoded features. To fully take advantage of using a large number of samples when generating the precise boundary, features of these samples are desired to be encoded in a consistent feature space. To maintain this consistency as training progresses, MoCo uses an additional slow-progressing encoder that only processes samples to be stored in the dictionary (these samples are called "keys" in [12]). The slow-progressing property of the additional encoder is acquired by updating via a moving average from the main encoder with a large momentum.

To enable the usage of a large number of negative samples for training a re-ID model, we devise Momentum ReID (MoReID) architecture that is constructed with a Siamese network and a dictionary from MoCo. During training, a batch consisting of multiple groups, where the samples in the same group share the same ID, is fed to both networks. Only the outputs of the secondary *forward-only* encoder with their corresponding IDs are stored in the dictionary. We treat each encoded sample from the main network as the query, which is compared with each of the keys in the dictionary to validate whether they match or not. All the keys with IDs different from the query are considered as negative samples. Among the keys that share the same ID with the query, only the samples that just came in from the current batch are used as positive samples (i.e., present positives) for training. Past positives are not used. While processing a batch of 256 samples, MoReID can leverage up to 8192 negative samples accumulated within the dictionary when using 4 GPUs with 48G GPU memory.

To take full advantage of a very large number of negative samples accumulated within the MoReID architecture, we use a novel loss called *Hard-distance Elastic Loss* (HE Loss). Previous re-ID methods have mainly used the Triplet loss [15,16,29] which computes the difference between the distance to a single positive representation and the distance to a single negative representation for a given query (left illustration of Fig. 1). A single representation is an average feature over all samples or hard samples in each group. As the number of samples increases, the representativeness of a single representation gets less accurate. Because of this, it does not scale well with the sample size.

Instead of treating a group of samples with a single representation, the HE loss has the capability of leveraging multiple hard samples that are on the other side of the boundary optimally drawn between the positive and negative samples (i.e., positives on the negative side and negatives on the positive side). In detail, the HE loss is calculated as the sum of the penalties, which is the extent to which the boundary is crossed for all hard samples (right illustration of Fig. 1). For each query, the boundary is optimally determined to minimize the loss. We have theoretically demonstrated that it is optimal to place the boundary in the region where the number of hard positive samples and the number of hard negative samples are equal.

To demonstrate the effectiveness of the MoReID architecture and the HE loss, we carried out experiments on person re-ID and vehicle re-ID tasks. Experiments show that deploying only one of the two modules does not bring any advantage in improving re-ID accuracy. However, using the two modules together provides drastic improvement in accuracy when compared to the baseline without the modules in all re-ID tasks. The two novel modules work mutually and in a complementary way, meaning that the large negative training samples acquired using the MoReID architecture cannot be used effectively without the HE loss, whereas HE loss can only demonstrate its full strength when the number of 'negative samples are at large'.

2   Related Works

ReID loss. Existing re-ID methods typically use two types of losses with different label forms: pairwise (i.e., class-level label and model estimate) loss and tripletwise (i.e., query, and positive and negative samples for the query) loss. A pairwise loss defined to minimize the difference between the label and estimate is mainly used for ID classification in re-ID methods. Tripletwise loss is used in re-ID methods to bring samples with the same ID closer together and push the samples with different IDs further away from each other.

For the pairwise loss, there are several commonly used losses, e.g., softmax [33,35], cross-entropy loss [3,11,22,27], cosface [35], arcface loss [7], and circle loss [31,43]. On the other hand, Triplet loss [15] is the most representative of the tripletwise loss in the re-ID methods. Triplet loss measures the relationship between a query sample and two single representative samples representing the positives and the negatives, respectively. Each representation can be calculated using either a weighted sum of all samples in each group [11,17] or hard sample mining [1,22,27,31,41]. However, as the number of samples increases significantly, it becomes more difficult to adequately represent them with a single representation, which we call the sample scalability issue. Other metric learning losses that can be used as a tripletwise loss also face similar limitations, e.g., c-triplet loss [34], circle loss [31,43], CDF-based weighted triplet loss [41], etc. To address sample scalability, N-pair loss [30] and Ranked List loss [37] are defined to use multiple hard samples as representative samples, but show lower re-ID performance than Triplet loss because the number of hard samples is not optimally determined. In this paper, we introduce a novel loss, referred to as *Hard-distance Elastic Loss* (HE Loss), that can better cope with the sample scalability issue to exhibit significantly higher accuracy than the Triplet loss.

Exploring a Large Number of Negative Samples. Recently, exploration of a very large number of negative samples in training has shown promising accuracy in various unsupervised representation learning tasks. Most of the methods presenting such promising accuracy employ the MoCo framework [12], which provides a structural way to generate a large number of negative samples. This MoCo framework has also been used for several Re-ID methods, but is only limited to unsupervised learning settings [2,8,44,46]. For the task of supervised re-ID, our MoReID is the first architecture to adopt MoCo to leverage a large number of negative samples with the help of the proposed HE loss.

3   Method

3.1   Hard-Distance Elastic Loss

Definition of HE Loss. Hard-distance Elastic (HE) loss measures the degree to which samples cross the boundary (i.e., positive samples located on the negative side, and vice versa) that is determined to divide the feature space into positive and negative regions. Here, samples in the opposite side of the boundary are considered hard samples.

For a query q, key samples are split into its positives $p \in P$ and its negatives $n \in N$ according to their IDs, where P and N are the positive and negative sets, respectively. HE loss, $\mathcal{L}_q$, is defined with the boundary t as follows:

$$\mathcal{L}_q(t) = \sum_{p \in P} \max(d_{pq} - t, 0) + \sum_{n \in N} \max(t - d_{nq}, 0), \qquad (1)$$

where d_{pq} and d_{nq} are the distances (e.g., Euclidean distance in our experiments) from q to p and from q to n, respectively. The optimal boundary t^* can be acquired by minimizing the HE loss as follows:

$$t^* = \arg\min_t \mathcal{L}_q(t). \qquad (2)$$

Derivation of the Optimal Boundary. The optimal point of the boundary to minimize the HE loss must satisfy two conditions: i) the derivative of the HE loss with respect to the boundary t is zero at this optimal point, and ii) the HE loss is convex with respect to the boundary t. The derivative of $\mathcal{L}_q(t)$ with respect to the boundary t can be derived from Eq. 1 as follows:

$$\frac{d\mathcal{L}_q(t)}{dt} = \sum_{p \in P} -\mathbb{1}(d_{pq} > t) + \sum_{n \in N} \mathbb{1}(d_{nq} < t) = -N_{hp}(t) + N_{hn}(t) \quad (3)$$

where $\mathbb{1}(\cdot)$ is a unit function. $N_{hp}(t)$ and $N_{hn}(t)$ are the number of hard positive samples and hard negative samples, respectively, when the boundary is t. Note that $\mathbb{1}(d_{pq} > t)$ or $\mathbb{1}(d_{nq} < t)$ represent samples that are located on the other side of the boundary with respect to its identity. In other words, the samples satisfying the constraints within the unit functions in Eq. 3 are the hard samples. Accordingly, the first condition to define an optimal boundary is satisfied when the number of hard positive samples and the number of hard negative samples are equal (i.e., $N_{hp} = N_{hn}$).

In addition, $N_{hp}(t)$ is a monotonically decreasing function for t as the number of hard positive samples decreases as the boundary moves away from the query. Similarly, $N_{hn}(t)$ is a monotonically increasing function. Accordingly, $d\mathcal{L}_q(t)/dt$ in Eq. 3 is a monotonically increasing function and the HE loss is convex with respect to t, satisfying the second condition for an optimal boundary.

Knowing that the second condition is always met, the task of finding the optimal boundary is narrowed down to localizing the point where $N_{hp} = N_{hn}$. We first compute the distances from all the samples to the query and sort them in ascending order. Then the shortest distance is set to be the first boundary candidate to evaluate whether $N_{hp} = N_{hn}$ is satisfied. If satisfied, the candidate is set as t^*. If not, we iterate through the sorted distances until the condition is met. HE loss for a given batch is acquired by processing all the queries and their optimal boundaries independently and averaging the results. Pseudo-code for computing the optimal boundary and the HE loss is included in Algorithm 1.

3.2   MoReID

Architecture. A core component of MoReID is being able to use a very large number of negative samples in training a re-ID model. To enable this capability, MoReID leverages the MoCo architecture [12], which is equipped with a dictionary that continuously collects a large number of encoded features for incoming input images as the training evolves. The dictionary is a queue where the oldest batch leave as a new batch comes in.

To take full advantage of the benefits of using a large number of samples (especially, when generating the precise boundary between positive and negative samples in the feature space), it is desirable that these samples be encoded into a consistent feature space. To this end, MoCo uses a separate, slow-progressing encoder in addition to the main encoder to encode the samples to lie in a nearly consistent feature space. Note that this slow-progressing encoder only encodes the key samples that are fed into the dictionary.

While the main encoder is updated via back-propagation, this slow-progressing encoder ("forward-only encoder" in Fig. 2) is updated via a moving average with momentum m from the main encoder (i.e., $f_k = m \cdot f_k + (1-m) \cdot f_q$, where f_k and f_q are the slow-progressing encoder and the main encoder, respectively). The slow progress property in the forward-only encoder is acquired by reducing the extent of update with a large momentum m. Note that the forward-only encoder is only used for training, as its purpose is to provide a large number of samples (negative samples for our method) to be compared against a given query.

As a result, our MoReID architecture is also designed as a Siamese network that consists of the main encoder and the additional forward-only encoder. Both encoders take the same image batch as input where each image batch consists of C groups, and each group contains N images with the same ID. The main encoder is trained with two losses: pairwise ID loss and the proposed HE loss. For ID classification, the output of the main encoder is fed through an ID prediction layer which generates the input to the computation of the ID loss. We use circle loss [31] to serve as the ID loss[1]. The proposed MoReID structure is shown in Fig. 2.

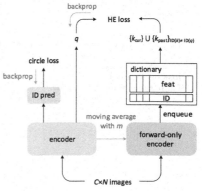

Fig. 2. MoReID. Black arrows and red arrows represent forward computations and model updates, respectively.

Labeling Key Samples in the Dictionary. Within the dictionary, only the samples that do not share the same ID with a given query are treated as negative samples. As for the positive samples (samples with same ID w.r.t the query), only the samples from the current batch is considered, while disregarding the ones that had been previously stored in the dictionary. This was an empirical decision. The experiments demonstrated that leaving out the past positive samples led to higher accuracy, and details on this are found in the supplementary material. If a model is trained with past positive samples, the model is less likely to carry the capability to properly separate the positives from the negatives in the current feature space. This may be because the past positive samples do not share the consistent feature space with the query. As no past positive samples are used for training, only *negative samples are at large*.

As the samples within the dictionary are constantly picked out based on their IDs, the dictionary is constructed so as to contain both the features and their IDs. The LabelDictionary function in Algorithm 1 deals with the labeling process (positive or negative w.r.t. the query) described in this section.

---

[1] Circle loss [31] is designed in two types, pairwise and tripletwise, and we adopt the pairwise type as the ID loss in MoReID architecture.

Algorithm 1: MoReID: PyTorch-like Pseudo-code

```
# f_q, f_k: main and secondary encoders      # HE loss
# h: ID pred. layer                          def heloss(Q, K, id_Q, id_K):
# feat, id: dictionary for feat and ID           loss = 0
# m: momentum                                    for q, id_q in zip(Q, id_Q):
                                                     # label key samples in the dictionary
f_k.params = f_q.params # initialize                 # P, N: positive and negative keys
# load a minibatch (image and label)                 P, N = LabelDictionary(K, id_K, id_q)
for x, l in loader:                                  n_p = P.size(0) # num of positives
    Q, K = f_q(x), f_k(x) # encode                   # calculate euclidean distance
    P = h(Q) # predict ID                            d_pq, d_nq = eucl(q, P), eucl(q, N)
    K = K.detach() # no gradient to f_k              # sort in ascending order
                                                     d_pq, d_nq = d_pq.sort(), d_nq.sort()
    dequeue(feat) # dequeue the earliest feat
    enqueue(feat, K) # enqueue the cur feat          # search the optimal boundary
    dequeue(id) # dequeue the earliest id            # n_hp, n_hn: num of hard samples
    enqueue(id, l) # enqueue the cur id              n_hp, n_hn = n_p, 0
                                                     d_pq_cur, d_nq_cur = d_pq[0], d_nq[0]
    # loss (closs: circle loss)                      while 1:
    loss = heloss(Q, feat, l, id) + closs(P, l)          if d_pq_cur <= d_nq_cur:
                                                             t = d_pq_cur
    # update MoReID                                          n_hp -= 1
    loss.backward()                                          d_pq_cur = d_pq[n_p-n_hp]
    f_k.params = m*f_k.params                             else:
                  +(1-m)*f_q.params                           t = d_nq_cur
                                                             n_hn += 1
                                                             d_nq_cur = d_pq[n_hn]

                                                         if n_hp == n_hn: break # terminate

                                                     # calculate loss
                                                     loss += relu(d_pq - t).sum()
                                                               + relu(t - d_nq).sum()
                                                 return loss/Q.size(0)
```

3.3   Implementation Details

Encoder Backbone. For the encoder backbone design, we follow the optimal configuration of a Re-ID network in [14]. ResNet-50 [13] is used which is followed by two non-local modules [36]. The output from the non-local modules are pooled by the generalized mean pooling (i.e., $\left(1/|\mathbf{X}| \sum_{x \in \mathbf{X}} x^{\alpha}\right)^{1/\alpha}$, where α = 3 in our experiments). All first batch normalizations in each residual module have been replaced by instance batch normalizations [32]. The backbone network was initialized on ImageNet-pretrained ResNet-50. For ID prediction, one fully connected layer is used.

Inference. The re-ID task is to retrieve matching samples from the gallery for a given query. For the inference, the only main encoder is used to encode both query and gallery samples in the learned feature space. The similarity between a pair of encoded samples (query and gallery) is measured with the Euclidean distance.

Optimization. We use SGD as our optimizer. Weight decay and momentum are 0.0005 and 0.9, respectively. Base learning rate was set based on the dataset. We have conducted a study in the experiment section where we investigate the relationship between the dataset and the base learning rates. (see Sect. 4.1). The

Table 1. Comparisons of different learning rates. The figures on the left and middle show the loss evolution and accuracy trend as training progresses, respectively. The table on the right shows mAPs of the models trained with different learning rates.

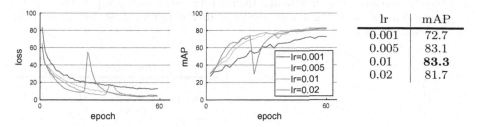

lr	mAP
0.001	72.7
0.005	83.1
0.01	**83.3**
0.02	81.7

training schedule is commonly designed independent of the dataset so that the learning rate gradually decays to zero at the cosine rule beginning at the middle of the total training epoch. This is to gradually reduce the difference between the parameters of the main encoder and the forward-only encoder while training. Once the training is done, the key samples in the dictionary can be compared with their query sample in the 'close-to-equivalent' feature space.

4 Experiments

To confirm the effectiveness of the proposed re-ID method, we use three re-ID datasets: VeRi-776, Market-1501, and VeRi-Wild. Unless specified, all experiments (e.g., ablation studies, comparison of HE loss to other losses, etc.) were carried out on VeRi-776 dataset. Comparing our method with the state-of-the-art methods is performed on all three re-ID datasets. mAP and R-1 are commonly used as evaluation metrics for all the datasets.

Training Schedule. For VeRi-776 and Market-1501, we trained for 60 epochs. For the large-scale VeRi-Wild dataset, we trained for 120 epochs.

Pre-processing. For training, three pre-processing approaches were found to be optimal after evaluating all possible combinations of multiple approaches in [14]: horizontal flipping, random erasing [47], and auto-augment [6]. For the vehicle re-ID datasets (i.e., VeRi-776 and VeRi-Wild), the input images are resized to 256×256. For the person re-ID dataset (i.e., Market-1501), the input image is resized to 384×128.

4.1 Study for Optimal Learning Rate

Searching the Optimal Learning Rate. To search for the optimal learning rate for MoReID, we compare models trained with different learning rates as shown in Table 1. The optimal learning rate with respect to accuracy was 0.01. When the learning rate is lower (i.e., 0.001) than this optimal rate, the model was under-fitted, converging at a relatively higher loss with a degraded accuracy.

Table 2. The optimal learning rate with respect to the size of the dataset. The data size is expressed on a logarithmic scale along the x coordinate in the figure on the left. The dashed line in the figure is drawn to represent the approximate relationship between the optimal learning rate and the data size, expressed in Eq. 4. The data size, the optimal learning rate and accuracy for VeRi-776 and its three subsets are shown in the table on the right.

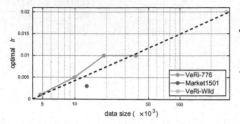

	data size	lr_s	mAP
	4,751	0.001	40.9
subsets	9,889	0.005	56.7
	18,882	0.01	70.3
entire	37,775	0.01	83.3

On the other hand, when the learning rate was higher than or equal to the optimal rate, the training seemed unstable as a spike occurs in the middle of the training (Left figure in Table 1). The spike triggered a sudden drop in accuracy (Middle figure in Table 1). This spike in loss was also observed in [5] when there was a sudden change in gradient at the initial layer of the model. Based on this observation, [5] provided a temporary solution for this instability by freezing the initial layer, which led to an increased accuracy. However, suppressing the gradient of the initial layer, including this layer freezing, gradient clipping, etc., was found to be ineffective in dealing with the instability within our scenario. More studies are needed to address this unique training instability in future works.

The Optimal Learning Rate with Respect to the Dataset. As the accuracy of our method was somewhat sensitive to the learning rate, we saw the need to provide a study that shows the relationship between the optimal learning rate and a given dataset (especially the size of the dataset). This would prevent having to go through an exhaustive search just to find out the optimal learning rate when applying our method to a different dataset.

To figure out this relationship within the same dataset, we generate three subsets from VeRi-776 dataset by collecting samples each associated with 1/2, 1/4, and 1/8 of the entire IDs. Then, we check whether the relationship between the optimal learning rates of the entire VeRi-776 dataset and the three subsets were consistently applicable when we trained on other datasets (i.e., Market-1501 and VeRi-Wild). As shown in the figure of Table 2, the optimal learning rate should increase logarithmically as the size of the dataset size gets larger and the relationship can simply be expressed as follows:

$$lr_s = 0.02 \frac{\log(s) - \log(4 \times 10^3)}{\log(3 \times 10^5) - \log(4 \times 10^3)}$$

$$\propto \log(s) \quad \text{if} \quad s \gg 4 \times 10^3, \tag{4}$$

where s is the size of the dataset. Note that $\log{(3 \times 10^5)}$ and 0.02 in Eq. 4 are the size of the largest dataset (i.e., VeRi-Wild) used to derive this equation and the optimal learning rate for this dataset, respectively. lr_s is a reference value that can be used as the optimal learning rate when applying our method to a different dataset. From these observations, we can set a rule for searching the optimal lr with respect to the dataset size as:

"When the dataset size is increased by power of k, multiply the learning rate by k".

As this rule does not conflict with the linear scale rule [9] that defines the optimal lr with respect to the batch size, these two rules can be applied concurrently.

4.2   Ablation Studies

Momentum m. We compare the accuracy of models trained with different momentum m as shown in the table below:

	no dict.	m				
		0.9	0.99	0.995	0.997	0.999
mAP	80.6	79.5	80.7	82.4	**83.3**	83.0
gain	·	(-1.1)	(+0.1)	(+1.8)	(+2.7)	(+2.4)

When m is ≥ 0.995, the accuracy was reasonably high. This indicates that maintaining the key samples consistent by slowly updating the forward-only encoder was critical to achieving high accuracy. It is noteworthy that when consistency of samples was less maintained (i.e., $m \leq 0.9$), there was even a loss in accuracy when compared to "no dict".

Dictionary Size. We experiment how different dictionary sizes affect the mAPs. This comparison is shown in the table below:

	no dict.	dict. size			
		1024	2048	4096	8192
# batch	·	4	8	16	32
optimal m	·	0.99	0.995	0.997	0.997
mAP	80.6	81.9	82.5	83.0	**83.3**
gain	·	(+1.3)	(+1.9)	(+2.4)	(+2.7)

We have used a minibatch consisting of 256 images (C: 16, N: 16). "# batch" is the number of batches constantly stacked in a dictionary. Within our computing environment ($4 \times 12\,\text{GB}$ GPUs), the maximum dictionary size is 8192. "gain" shows how much accuracy is gained by using a dictionary when compared with a

Table 3. Accuracy with and without MoReID and HE loss, respectively. All methods use the same training schedule. 'baseline' and 'method (a)' use a learning rate of 0.01 which has been proven to be optimal for the backbone network as in [14].

method	MoReID	HE loss	mAP
baseline			79.7
(a)		✓	80.6 (+0.9)
(b)	✓		79.4 (-0.3)
Ours	✓	✓	**83.3** (+3.6)

model without a dictionary ("no dict."). Regardless of the dictionary size, using a dictionary itself always provided better accuracy. In addition, increasing the dictionary size consistently bumped up the accuracy.

How long a batch is kept in the dictionary affects the optimal m that controls the speed of update for the forward-only encoder. More specifically, a slower update for the forward-only encoder (i.e., bigger m) may be needed to increase how long the past batches reside in the dictionary. We found the optimal m for each dictionary size as shown in the table above. We have experimentally validated that as the dictionary size gets larger, the optimal m also becomes larger.

Batch. HE loss is highly related to the number of hard samples. Since a large number of negative samples are used, the maximum number of hard samples actually becomes the twice the number of positive samples at the optimal boundary (i,e, $N_{hp} = N_{hn}$ in Eq. 3). As each batch is fixed with the configuration of $C \times N$ (C: number of ID types, N: number of instances per ID type), the number of positive samples is also fixed as N-1. Therefore, how the batch configuration is set directly affects the HE loss with respect to the accuracy as shown below:

$C \times N$	128×2	64×4	32×8	16×16	8×32
mAP	77.9	79.7	83.0	**83.3**	83.2

As shown in the table, the accuracy improves when N is larger than or equal to 8. We use the optimal configuration (16×16) throughout all experiments.

4.3   Main Results

Synergy of HE Loss and MoReID Architecture. Here, we demonstrate how each of the two new components impact accuracy and whether they are effectively complementary to each other. In Table 3, we compare the accuracy of four different combinations with and without each component on top of the baseline. The baseline uses the same backbone network as ours, while Triplet loss are used instead of the HE loss. While using HE loss (method (a)) slightly

Table 4. Comparison with previous methods (top 5) on three datasets. Numbers in the parentheses indicate the performance gains with respect to the corresponding baselines. For fair comparison, all listed methods do not use any post-processing such as re-rank nor any external datasets.

method	mAP	R-1
CAL [28]	74.3	95.4
PGAN [42]	79.3	96.5
PVEN [24]	79.5	95.6
SAVER [18]	79.6	96.4
HRC [43]	83.1	**97.3**
baseline	80.0	96.8
Ours	**83.3**	**97.3**
gain	+3.3	+0.5

(a) VeRi-776

method	mAP	R-1
PAT [23]	88.0	95.4
ABD [4]	88.3	95.6
BV [40]	89.1	96.0
SSGR [39]	89.3	**96.1**
CAL [28]	89.5	95.5
baseline	87.4	95.3
Ours	**90.0**	**96.1**
gain	+2.6	+0.8

(b) Market-1501

method	small		medium		large	
	mAP	R-1	mAP	R-1	mAP	R-1
BW [20]	70.5	84.2	62.8	78.2	51.6	70.0
SAVER [18]	80.9	94.5	75.3	92.7	67.7	89.5
PVEN [24]	82.5	·	77.0	·	69.7	·
PGAN [42]	83.6	95.1	78.3	92.8	70.6	89.2
HRC [43]	85.2	94.0	80.0	91.6	72.2	88.0
baseline	83.7	95.5	78.8	94.4	71.5	91.5
Ours	**86.1**	**96.1**	**81.2**	**94.5**	**74.1**	**91.7**
gain	+2.4	+0.6	+2.4	+0.1	+2.6	+0.2

(c) VeRi-Wild

improves the baseline accuracy by 0.9, introducing a large number of negative samples using MoReID architecture (method (b)) rather brings a degraded accuracy. When the model is equipped with both of the components, a synergistic effect can be observed where the accuracy is significantly increased over the baseline.

The result can be interpreted in three aspects: i) Being able to represent positive or negative groups with multiple hard samples (i.e., using the HE loss) has a benefit over using a single representation for each group, ii) Without a proper loss design, using a large number of samples has very little impact on accuracy improvement, and that iii) the two components effectively complement each other.

Comparison to the State-of-the-Arts. Table 4 shows the results on three re-ID datasets. Our method consistently outperforms the baseline and all previous methods on all three datasets in terms of both mAP and R-1.

On **VeRi-776**, our method increases baseline accuracy by 3.3 in mAP and 0.5 in R-1. Our method also presents a better mAP by 0.2 while yielding a comparable R-1 compared to the SOTA (i.e., HRC [43]).

On **Market-1501**, we increases baseline accuracy by 2.6 in mAP and 0.8 in R-1. Our method outperforms the SOTA in mAP by 0.5 and presents a comparable R-1 performance.

On **VeRi-Wild**, our method increases baseline accuracy in all three subsets. The improvements are ~2.6 and ~0.6 in mAP and R-1, respectively. Our method outperforms the SOTA by ~1.9 in mAP and by ~3.7 in R-1, in all three subsets.

Our method consistently provides state-of-the-art accuracy for both vehicle re-ID and person re-ID tasks. This result also demonstrates that our method is scalable to a large-scale dataset (i.e., VeRi-Wild dataset). It is noteworthy to mention that the gain over the SOTA was higher on the large-scale dataset than that on other datasets.

4.4 Tripletwise ReID Loss Comparison

We compare the proposed HE loss with other tripletwise losses used to define triplet relationships beyond accuracy.

vs. Triplet Loss. Figure 1 shows the conceptual difference between the HE loss and the Triplet loss. The most distinct property of HE loss compared to Triplet loss is that it can take more than one samples to represent the positive and the negative sets. As previously claimed, a single representation used by Triplet loss cannot cope well with the scalability of samples, which must be considered when using MoReID. To confirm this claim, we compare the accuracy of HE loss and Triplet loss while changing the dictionary size as shown in the Table below:

loss	dict. size				
	512	1024	2048	4096	8192
Tri-all	79.7	79.6	79.5	79.5	79.3
Tri-hard	80.2	79.9	79.7	79.5	79.7
HE loss	**81.0**	**81.9**	**82.5**	**83.0**	**83.3**

Margin of Triplet loss is set to 0.3 as in [14]. When a single representation is computed for either the positive or the negative sample set, two different Triplet losses can be deployed based on the fact whether hard sample mining precedes ("Tri-hard") or not ("Tri-all"). We can observe the benefit of using the HE loss when using a larger-scale samples, whereas using the Triplet loss does not provide such advantage. Seeing that the "Tri-hard" slightly outperforms the "Tri-all" shows that the hard sample mining, which HE loss is also inherently leveraging, is more apt in handling the scalability of samples.

There exist several Triplet loss variants which also rely on single represen-tations for the positive and negative sets, e.g., circle triplet loss (Circle) [31], classification version of triplet loss (C-triplet) [34], and CDF-based weighted triplet loss (W-triplet) [41]. We compare the accuracy of the proposed HE loss with these variants when used for MoReID training, as below:

Circle	C-triplet	W-triplet	**HE**
79.1	80.3	79.9	**83.3**

Dictionary size of 8192 is used consistently for all losses. HE loss presents signifi-cantly better accuracy than the other losses, demonstrating the HE loss's ability to effectively process large-scale negative samples in training.

vs. Losses that Allows for Multiple Negatives. Some previous losses have provided a way to represent an entire set of samples with multiple samples to better cope with large-scale negative samples. For example, N-pair loss [30] can use multiple hard samples to represent all negative samples and Ranked List loss [37] can use multiple hard samples to represent both positive and negative samples. To compare HE loss with N-pair and Ranked List losses in handling the large-scale negative samples, we have set up an experiment to optimize two frameworks, the backbone network (our baseline in Table 3) and the MoReID network (dict. size is 8192). While the baseline processes all triplet combinations within the current batch only, the MoReID network also leverages past samples to be used in building a larger-scale negative sample set.

re-ID framework	Triplet	N-pair	Ranked List	HE
baseline	79.7	78.8	78.8	**80.6**
MoReID	79.4 (-0.3)	79.8 (+1.0)	80.5 (+1.7)	**83.3 (+2.7)**

Numbers in parentheses indicate gaps from its corresponding baseline. N-pair loss and Ranked List loss present better accuracy with MoReID than with their baselines, demonstrating their ability to properly handle large-scale negative samples. Interestingly, both losses underperformed the Triplet loss when with the baselines, but outperformed it with MoReID. Remarkably, HE loss yields the best accuracy as well as the highest margin from its baseline. It shows the superiority of HE loss with regard to re-ID performance and its ability to process large-scale negative samples.

vs. InfoNCE Loss. InfoNCE [26] is a widely used loss function in self-supervised learning that has been actively studied recently. InfoNCE also involves the triplet relationships which is formulated as shown below:

$$\mathcal{L}_q^i = -\log \frac{\exp(q \cdot p / \tau)}{\sum_{k \in \mathbf{K}} \exp(q \cdot k / \tau)}, \tag{5}$$

where p is a positive sample and $k \in \mathbf{K}$ is a key sample. τ is a temperature parameter (set as 0.07 following [38]). Two distinct properties of InfoNCE when compared with the HE loss are: 1) only a single positive sample is considered, and 2) all key samples are used in the loss calculation.

   Since this loss cannot be directly applied to our scenario where multiple positive examples exist, it should be modified to account for multi-label cases where multiple positive examples are allowed. [19] showed that multi-labeled InfoNCE can be designed in two ways[2] to acquire this ability as:

$$\mathcal{L}_q^{i,in} = -\log \sum_{p \in \mathbf{P}_q} \left(\frac{\exp(q \cdot p / \tau)}{\sum_{k \in \mathbf{K}} \exp(q \cdot k / \tau)} \right), \tag{6}$$

$$\mathcal{L}_q^{i,out} = - \sum_{p \in \mathbf{P}_q} \left(\log \frac{\exp(q \cdot p / \tau)}{\sum_{k \in \mathbf{K}} \exp(q \cdot k / \tau)} \right), \tag{7}$$

where $\mathbf{P}_q$ is the set of positive samples for the query q.

---

[2] In fact, most methods that use InfoNCE which is modified for supervised learning use one of these two. [25] used $\mathcal{L}_q^{i,in}$ while [10,21,45] used $\mathcal{L}_q^{i,out}$.

On top of the vanilla InfoNCE, we have generated several variants by adjusting one or both of the "two distinct properties" as shown in the table below:

method	$C \times N$	w/ hard mining	mAP
InfoNCE (Eq. 5)	128×2	no	62.9
InfoNCE (Eq. 5)	128×2	yes	63.4
HE	128×2		77.5
InfoNCE (Eq. 6)	16×16	no	70.5
InfoNCE (Eq. 7)	16×16	no	72.8
InfoNCE (Eq. 6)	16×16	yes	70.9
InfoNCE (Eq. 7)	16×16	yes	73.1
HE	16×16		83.3

First of all, instead of using only a single positive sample ($N=2$), we can adjust the model to take more than one positive samples ($N=16$). Another form of variation is to feed InfoNCE with a selected number of key samples instead of using all of them for loss calculation. This variation is labeled as "w/ hard mining" where the number of hard mined samples are set to be equivalent to the case of HE loss (i.e., 15). Note that the InfoNCE with no variation at all (i.e., vanilla InfoNCE) is listed as the first in the table. Results can be interpreted in three aspects: i) using hard negative samples selected by hard negative mining was effective in InfoNCE loss, ii) multi-label variant was also effective compared to the single-label one, and iii) all the variants of InfoNCE loss still underperformed HE loss by a significant margin.

5   Discussion and Conclusion

We have achieved the state-of-the-art accuracy on all three re-ID benchmarks by adopting the MoReID architecture and the HE loss. Wrapping up the experiments and analyses we have included in the paper, it is worthwhile to leave several discussion points. First, we came across an interesting phenomenon in training where the loss values appeared as spikes, especially when the learning rates are high. Further study that takes into account other training parameters (e.g., different optimizer, various batch sizes) might be helpful to unravel the phenomenon. Second, although the usage of InfoNCE loss has recently exploded in self-supervised learning, we have observed that it did not live up to its fame when it was used for supervised re-ID. It will be worthwhile to evaluate how HE loss will fit into the self-supervised learning paradigm.

References

1. Aich, A., Zheng, M., Karanam, S., Chen, T., Roy-Chowdhury, A.K., Wu, Z.: Spatio-temporal representation factorization for video-based person re-identification. In: ICCV (2021)
2. Chen, H., Lagadec, B., Bremond, F.: ICE: inter-instance contrastive encoding for unsupervised person re-identification. In: ICCV (2021)
3. Chen, P., Liu, W., Dai, P., Liu, J.: Occlude them all: occlusion-aware attention network for occluded person Re-ID. In: ICCV (2021)
4. Chen, T., et al.: ABD-Net: attentive but diverse person re-identification. In: ICCV (2019)
5. Chen, X., Xie, S., He, K.: An empirical study of training self-supervised vision transformers. In: ICCV (2021)
6. Cubuk, E.D., Zoph, B., Mane, D., Vasudevan, V., Le, Q.V.: AutoAugment: learning augmentation policies from data. In: CVPR (2019)
7. Deng, J., Guo, J., Xue, N., Zafeiriou, S.: ArcFace: additive angular margin loss for deep face recognition. In: CVPR (2019)
8. Fu, D., et al.: Unsupervised pre-training for person re-identification. In: CVPR (2021)
9. Goyal, P., et al.: Accurate, large minibatch SGD: training ImageNet in 1 hour. arXiv:1706.02677 (2018)
10. Gunel, B., Du, J., Conneau, A., Stoyanov, V.: Supervised contrastive learning for pre-trained language model fine-tuning. In: ICLR (2021)
11. Hao, X., Zhao, S., Ye, M., Shen, J.: Cross-modality person re-identification via modality confusion and center aggregation. In: ICCV (2021)
12. He, K., Fan, H., Wu, Y., Xie, S., Girshick, R.: Momentum contrast for unsupervised visual representation learning. In: CVPR (2020)
13. He, K., Zhang, X., Ren, S., Sun, J.: Deep residual learning for image recognition. In: CVPR (2016)
14. He, L., Liao, X., Liu, W., Liu, X., Cheng, P., Mei, T.: FastReID: a PyTorch toolbox for general instance re-identification. arXiv:2006.02631 (2020)
15. Hermans, A., Beyer, L., Leibe, B.: In defense of the triplet loss for person re-identification. arXiv:1703.07737 (2017)
16. Hoffer, E., Ailon, N.: Deep metric learning using triplet network. In: Feragen, A., Pelillo, M., Loog, M. (eds.) SIMBAD 2015. LNCS, vol. 9370, pp. 84–92. Springer, Cham (2015). https://doi.org/10.1007/978-3-319-24261-3_7
17. Huang, Y., Wu, Q., Xu, J., Zhong, Y., Zhang, Z.: Clothing status awareness for long-term person re-identification. In: ICCV (2021)
18. Khorramshahi, P., Peri, N., Chen, J., Chellappa, R.: The devil is in the details: self-supervised attention for vehicle re-identification. In: Vedaldi, A., Bischof, H., Brox, T., Frahm, J.-M. (eds.) ECCV 2020. LNCS, vol. 12359, pp. 369–386. Springer, Cham (2020). https://doi.org/10.1007/978-3-030-58568-6_22
19. Khosla, P., et al.: Supervised contrastive learning. In: NeurIPS (2020)
20. Kumar, R., Weill, E., Aghdasi, F., Sriram, P.: Vehicle re-identification: an efficient baseline using triplet embedding. In: IJCNN (2019)
21. Lee, H., Kwon, H.: Self-supervised contrastive learning for cross-domain hyperspectral image representation. In: ICASSP (2022)
22. Li, M., Huang, X., Zhang, Z.: Self-supervised geometric features discovery via interpretable attention for vehicle re-identification and beyond. In: ICCV (2021)

23. Li, Y., He, J., Zhang, T., Liu, X., Zhang, Y., Wu, F.: Diverse part discovery: occluded person re-identification with part-aware transformer. In: CVPR (2021)
24. Meng, D., et al.: Parsing-based view-aware embedding network for vehicle re-identification. In: CVPR (2020)
25. Miech, A., Alayrac, J.B., Smaira, L., Laptev, I., Sivic, J., Zisserman, A.: End-to-end learning of visual representations from uncurated instructional videos. In: CVPR (2020)
26. van den Oord, A., Li, Y., Vinyals, O.: Representation learning with contrastive predictive coding. arXiv:1807.03748v2 (2018)
27. Park, H., Lee, S., Lee, J., Ham, B.: Learning by aligning: visible-infrared person re-identification using cross-modal correspondences. In: ICCV (2021)
28. Rao, Y., Chen, G., Lu, J., Zhou, J.: Counterfactual attention learning for fine-grained visual categorization and re-identification. In: ICCV (2021)
29. Schroff, F., Kalenichenko, D., Philbin, J.: FaceNet: a unified embedding for face recognition and clustering. In: CVPR (2015)
30. Sohn, K.: Improved deep metric learning with multi-class n-pair loss objective. In: NeurIPS (2016)
31. Sun, Y., et al.: Circle loss: a unified perspective of pair similarity optimization. In: CVPR (2020)
32. Ulyanov, D., Vedaldi, A., Lempitsky, V.: Improved texture networks: maximizing quality and diversity in feed-forward stylization and texture synthesis. In: CVPR (2017)
33. Wang, F., Cheng, J., Liu, W., Liu, H.: Additive margin softmax for face verification. IEEE Sign. Process. Lett. 25(7), 926–930 (2018)
34. Wang, F., Xiang, X., Cheng, J., Yuille, A.L.: NormFace: L_2 hypersphere embedding for face verification. In: ACM MM (2017)
35. Wang, H., et al.: CosFace: large margin cosine loss for deep face recognition. In: CVPR (2018)
36. Wang, X., Girshick, R., Gupta, A., He, K.: Non-local neural networks. In: CVPR (2018)
37. Wang, X., Hua, Y., Kodirov, E., Robertson, N.M.: Ranked list loss for deep metric learning. In: CVPR (2019)
38. Wu, Z., Xiong, Y., Yu, S., Lin, D.: Unsupervised feature learning via non-parametric instance discrimination. In: CVPR (2018)
39. Yan, C., Pang, G., Jiao, J., Bai, X., Feng, X., Shen, C.: Occluded person re-identification with single-scale global representations. In: ICCV (2021)
40. Yan, C., et al.: BV-person: a large-scale dataset for bird-view person re-identification. In: ICCV (2021)
41. Zhang, L., Rusinkiewicz, S.: Learning local descriptors with a CDF-based dynamic soft margin. In: ICCV (2019)
42. Zhang, X., Zhang, R., Cao, J., Gong, D., You, M., Shen, C.: Part-guided attention learning for vehicle instance retrieval. IEEE Trans. Intell. Transp. Syst. (2020)
43. Zhao, J., Zhao, Y., Li, J., Yan, K., Tian, Y.: Heterogeneous relational complement for vehicle re-identification. In: ICCV (2021)
44. Zheng, K., Liu, W., He, L., Mei, T., Luo, J., Zha, Z.J.: Group-aware label transfer for domain adaptive person re-identification. In: CVPR (2021)
45. Zheng, M., et al.: Weakly supervised contrastive learning. In: ICCV (2021)
46. Zheng, Y., et al.: Online pseudo label generation by hierarchical cluster dynamics for adaptive person re-identification. In: ICCV (2021)
47. Zhong, Z., Zheng, L., Kang, G., Li, S., Yang, Y.: Random erasing data augmentation. In: AAAI (2020)

Discrete-Constrained Regression for Local Counting Models

Haipeng Xiong🆔 and Angela Yao$^{(\boxtimes)}$🆔

National University of Singapore, Singapore, Singapore
{haipeng,ayao}@comp.nus.edu.sg

Abstract. Local counts, or the number of objects in a local area, is a continuous value by nature. Yet recent state-of-the-art methods show that formulating counting as a classification task performs better than regression. Through a series of experiments on carefully controlled synthetic data, we show that this counter-intuitive result is caused by imprecise ground truth local counts. Factors such as biased dot annotations and incorrectly matched Gaussian kernels used to generate ground truth counts introduce deviations from the true local counts. Standard continuous regression is highly sensitive to these errors, explaining the performance gap between classification and regression. To mitigate the sensitivity, we loosen the regression formulation from a continuous scale to a discrete ordering and propose a novel discrete-constrained (DC) regression. Applied to crowd counting, DC-regression is more accurate than both classification and standard regression on three public benchmarks. A similar advantage also holds for the age estimation task, verifying the overall effectiveness of DC-regression. Code is available at https://github.com/xhp-hust-2018-2011/dcreg.

Keywords: Deep regression · Constrained regression · Local count models · Crowd counting · Age estimation

1 Introduction

Image-based counting of objects such as people [5,28], vehicles [11] and cells [3] can be modelled either as a classification or a regression problem. Since *local counts* or *local densities* are continuous, ordered values, they should naturally be regressed. Yet surprisingly, recent works have shown that formulating local count prediction as a classification problem is more accurate [6,27].

The preference for using classification to solve regression problems arises in several areas of computer vision, ranging from depth estimation [4] to human pose estimation [10,25]. The underlying reason is usually task-specific. For depth estimation, classification helps to handle the extreme dynamic range of depth

---

Supplementary Information The online version contains supplementary material available at https://doi.org/10.1007/978-3-031-20053-3_36.

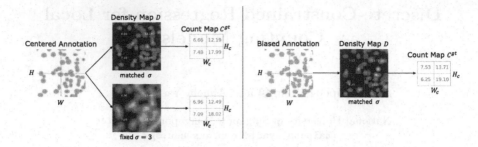

Fig. 1. Visualization of errors in the ground truth count maps. Left: A sample 64×64 input image with 4 local patches with centered annotations. (Top) Gaussian kernels dynamically match the object size vs. (Bottom) Gaussian kernels with a fixed standard deviation of $\sigma = 3$. Right: The same input image with biased dot annotations, generated from Gaussians matching the object size. Note that the sum of the local counts differs slightly as some kernels go beyond the local image borders.

that may occur; this is especially prominent in mixed indoor and outdoor scenes [4]. For pose estimation, classification allows for dense spatial supervision, which is believed to be more beneficial for learning [1].

For counting tasks, classification outperforms regression when counting in a closed set range [27]. To find out why classification performs better than regression in certain counting tasks, we conduct a series of experiments on synthetic data. In this paper, we focus on local counting models [3,6,7,26,27] that predict local counts, *i.e.* the number of objects within the local image patches. Through careful investigation, we trace the advantages of classification back to the imprecise generation of ground truth local count.

In object counting, annotators mark each object of interest with a single dot (see Fig. 1). The *local count*, or the number of objects within a specified area, can simply be defined as the number of dot annotations within that area if all the objects are wholly contained. However, fractional local counts arise when there are partial objects. The estimate of fraction local counts can be imprecise, especially if the dot annotations are not aligned with the object in the image. The imprecision is worsened by the use of an intermediate *density map* estimated by convolving the dot annotations with Gaussian kernels. An accurate density estimate requires the Gaussian kernels' standard deviation to match the true object size. Yet, size information is often not annotated or known in advance. Given that current methods [7,26,27] generate ground truth counts by integrating over local areas in the density map, it becomes clear that many factors of imprecision are at play and that the ground truth local counts will deviate from the true local counts.

In this work, we investigate the effects of partial objects, dot annotation position and Gaussian kernel size on the classification versus regression task setting. To that end, we create a synthetic dataset containing images of cells to carefully control and study these properties. Our findings show that regression performance is comparable to classification under ideal settings, *i.e.* objects are wholly contained within a local area, dot annotations are centered on the objects and Gaussian kernels are correctly matched. The lower accuracy arises only when the ground truth labels deviate from the true local count.

Based on these findings, we speculate that the poor performance of regression can be attributed to the naive formulation as a *continuous* regression problem. Enforcing a standard L1 loss penalizes models that do not (over-) fit to the errors present in the ground truth counts. By constraining the regression to only *discrete* counts, however, we can buffer against some of the imprecision in the ground truth as classification does. As such, we propose a discrete-constrained (DC) regression model for crowd counting. Similar to classification, DC-regression benefits from discretizing the target space while retaining an ordered output space of numerical counts rather than an order-agnostic class index. The numeric output enables a comparison between summed local counts and a global count. We also propose a global count loss regularizer, which mitigates some of the discretization errors when converting the target space from continuous to discrete.

DC-regression is more accurate than both classification and standard regression in crowd counting. It is also applicable to other discrete regression tasks such as age estimation, and we verified its effectiveness in our experiments. In summary, the contributions of this paper are:

1. A novel discrete-constrained (DC) regression model that benefits from the discretization of classification while retaining the ordering and numerical output space of regression.
2. A series of experiments on controlled synthetic data indicated that the imprecise local counts emerged during the annotation and ground truth generation process account for the advantage of classification over regression.
3. DC-regression, coupled with a global count loss, outperforms both classification and regression on three crowd-counting datasets. It has significant improvements over state-of-the-art approaches when inserted into an advanced local count model like S-DCNet [27].
4. Verified that DC-regression is also applicable to the age estimation task.

2   Related Work

Counting By Regression. The goal of object counting is to predict the number of visually present objects in images. Given that counts have an ordering, it is naturally modelled as a regression problem. Two commonly adopted regression targets are density maps [5,14,16,29] and local object counts [7,12,26]. Density maps were first proposed by [3]; they are a dense target proportional to the spatial distribution of the objects. Zhang *et al.* [28] first adopted a deep network to regress density maps and most regression methods [5,14,16,29] followed a similar approach. Local count is another learning target of deep regression networks. Local count methods [7,12,26] first divide images into local patches, then predict object numbers of each local patch separately.

However, both learning targets could be imprecise if only dot annotations are provided for object counting. Specifically, ground truth density maps could be affected by biased dot annotations and mismatched Gaussian kernels (as shown in Fig. 1). Local counts can be even more imprecise as they are obtained by integrating over local areas in the density map. Optimum transport [13] has been adopted [9, 21, 22] to account for possible errors in ground truth density maps with extra optimization procedures. Different from them, we tackle errors in ground truth count maps using discrete constraints.

Counting By Classification. Instead of regressing local counts, counting by classification methods model local counts as different classes [6, 23, 27]. Liu *et al.* [6] first divided the count ranges into discrete intervals and then predicted the interval index with a classifier. The final count value was chosen as the median value of the predicted interval. Xiong *et al.* [27] adopted a classifier to model a closed-set range of counts, and generalized it to the open-set range via spatial divide-and-conquer. Based on these works [6, 23, 27], it appears that classification works better than regression for object counting.

Classification vs. Regression. Other than object counting, classification has also shown to perform better than regression for specific tasks in depth estimation [4], human pose estimation [10, 25] and age estimation [30]. In this work, we show experimentally that classification is better than regression when ground truth count maps are imperfect. We also find that regression could be improved by adopting discrete constraints of local counts similar to classification.

3   Method

3.1   Preliminaries

Suppose we are given an image $I \in \mathbb{R}^{H \times W}$ with T dot annotations (x_t, y_t), $t = \{1, \ldots, T\}$. Using the dot annotation map $D^0 = \sum_{t=1}^{T} \delta(x_t, y_t)$, where $\delta(x_t, y_t)$ denotes a Dirac function centered at (x_t, y_t), we can generate a density map D by convolving D^0 with a Gaussian kernel G_σ, with a standard deviation of σ[1]:

$$D = \sum_{t=1}^{T} \delta(x_t, y_t) * G_\sigma \qquad (1)$$

Summing the local density in the $P_h \times P_w$ non-overlapping window, the ground truth count maps $C \in \mathbb{R}^{H_c \times W_c}$, where $H_c = H/P_H$ and $W_c = W/P_w$ is defined as:

$$C(j, k) = \sum_{h=j \times P_h}^{(j+1) \times P_h} \sum_{w=k \times P_w}^{(k+1) \times P_w} D(h, w). \qquad (2)$$

A local count model predicts a corresponding local count map $\hat{C} \in \mathbb{R}^{H_c \times W_c}$. In practice, C is imprecise when dot annotations (x_t, y_t) are biased or Gaussian

---

[1] This work assumes a kernel size of 4σ and use the terms 'size' and 'σ' interchangeably.

kernels G_σ are mismatched. Consider an object near the border of the local area, if the dot annotations are off-center or Gaussian kernels have too large a standard deviation, then some portions of the density may shift to other nearby local areas, leading to imprecision in Eqs. (1) and (2).

The ground truth and estimated count for image I can be estimated by summing the respective local count maps:

$$c = \sum_{j,k}^{H_c, W_c} C(j, k), \qquad \hat{c} = \sum_{j,k}^{H_c, W_c} \hat{C}(j, k), \qquad (3)$$

where j and k are row and column-wise indices of the count map. The error of the local count is defined as the difference between the ground truth and predicted local counts. The error of local count $E \in \mathbb{R}^{H_c \times W_c}$ and global count e is computed as:

$$e = c - \hat{c} = \sum_{j,k}^{H_c, W_c} E(j, k), \quad \text{where} \quad E = C - \hat{C}. \qquad (4)$$

A typical regression-based local count model would use a CNN backbone and add a dedicated regression head. The final model would take image I as input, output the local count map $\hat{C}$ and be trained with an L1 loss:

$$L_{reg} = \frac{1}{H_c W_c} \sum_{j,k}^{H_c, W_c} |E(j, k)|. \qquad (5)$$

Note that Eq. (5) denotes the loss for one image; this loss is averaged over all images in the batch during training.

3.2 Discrete-Constrained Regression

But as we argue that ground truth count maps are imprecise and may contain error ϵ, i.e. $C = C^{true} + \epsilon$, where C^{true} is the count map generated with ideal density map. The regression loss in Eq. (5) then becomes

$$L_{reg} = \frac{1}{H_c W_c} \sum_{j,k}^{H_c, W_c} |E^{true}(j, k) + \epsilon(j, k)|, \quad \text{where} \quad E^{true} = C^{true} - \hat{C}. \qquad (6)$$

When $|E(j, k)| \geq |\epsilon(j, k)|$, the sign of the observed error and true error remains the same, i.e. $\text{sgn}(E_i(j, k)) = \text{sgn}(E^{true}(j, k))$, where "sgn($\cdot$)" denotes the sign function. As such, the gradient will also be the same, i.e.

$$\frac{\partial |E(j, k)|}{\partial \hat{C}(j, k)} = \frac{\partial |E^{true}(j, k)|}{\partial \hat{C}(j, k)} = -\text{sgn}(E(j, k)). \qquad (7)$$

To account for the ϵ, we opt to partition the target space into discrete intervals. Specifically, we follow a classification setup and a range $[V_{min}, V_{max}]$

into $N + 1$ intervals $\{V_0\}$, $(V_0, V_1]$, $(V_1, V_2]$, ..., $(V_{N-1}, V_N]$, where $V_0 = V_{min}$ and $V_N = V_{max}$. In counting datasets, $V_{min} = 0$ and V_{max} is the maximum count value in the training set. A count value c that falls into $[V_{i-1}, V_i]$, where $(i = 1, 2, ..., N)$, would be associated with the i-th interval. As such, the loss is considered to be correct when the prediction $\hat{C}(j, k)$ is outside the range $[V_{G(j,k)}, V_{G(j,k)+1})$, where $G(j, k)$ is the index of $C(j, k)$.

We formulate the discrete-constrained loss L_{dc} as:

$$L_{dc} = \frac{\sum_{j,k}^{H_c, W_c} S(j, k) \times |E(j, k)|}{\sum_{j,k}^{H_c, W_c} S(j, k)} \tag{8}$$

where the mask $S = 1 - \mathbb{1}\{V_G < \hat{C} \leq V_{G+1}\}$, $\mathbb{1}\{\}$ is the indicator function and G is the index of C. S only selects the samples that are predicted outside the intervals to compute loss, which ensures the gradient directions to be correct.

3.3 Global Count Loss L_{gc}

The overall aim of counting is to estimate a global count from summing all the local counts. Even if all the local counts are correctly predicted, *i.e.* $L_{dc} = 0$, there may still be a gap between their sum and the GT global count, precisely due to the quantization. We could use a global count loss L_{gc} to decrease the quantization errors. Naively, an L_1 loss could be applied to the global count, *i.e.*

$$L_c = \frac{|e|}{H_c W_c}, \tag{9}$$

However, L_c is problematic as it produces the same gradient for all the local counts, regardless of over- or under-estimation. We therefore improve L_c to L_{bias}^0 by selecting local patches that have the same trend as global error, *i.e.*, considering only over-estimated patches if the global count is an over-estimate and and same for under-estimation. This prevents the wrong gradient for patches with the opposite sign of global error e. L_{bias}^0 can be defined as

$$L_{bias}^0 = \frac{\sum_{j,k}^{H_c, W_c} S^a(j, k) \times |E|}{\sum_{j,k}^{H_c, W_c} S^a(j, k)}, \tag{10}$$

where $S^a = \mathbb{1}\{\text{sgn}(e) \times E(j, k) > 0\}$, and sgn() denotes the sign function. Among patches with $S^a = 1$, we further discard those patches with smaller errors that compensate the error of patches with $S^a = 0$. We achieve this by introducing a threshold λ, which satisfies

$$\sum_{j,k}^{H_c, W_c} S^a(j, k) \times \mathbb{1}\{\text{sgn}(e) \times E(j, k) \geq \lambda\} \times |E(j, k)| = \sum_{j,k}^{H_c, W_c} |E(j, k)| \tag{11}$$

and select patches via $S^m(j, k) = S^a(j, k) \times \mathbb{1}\{\text{sgn}(e) \times E(j, k) \geq \lambda\}$. Now, an adjusted loss L_{bias}^λ can be computed as

$$L_{bias}^\lambda = \frac{\sum_{j,k}^{H_c, W_c} S^m(j, k) \times |E(j, k)|}{\sum_{j,k}^{H_c, W_c} S^m(j, k)}. \tag{12}$$

A related work [8] introduced the Bayesian loss L_{BL} to constrain the integration of density map to be equal to the annotated point numbers. It also serves as a type of global count loss. We compare these variants of global count losses in the ablation studies.

4   A Synthetic Dataset Investigation on Local Counting

4.1   Data Preparation

Inspired by [3,27], we create a synthetic dataset of cells to study counting-related factors in a controlled setting. Each synthetic image was fixed to 128×128, which could be further subdivided into a 4×4 array of 32×32 local image patches. Each local image patch had 0 to 20 oval cells, where the major and minor axis of the oval were randomly sampled from $[2,4]$ pixels. Each of the training and test sets contained 1000 such synthetic images.

Presence of Partial Objects. We synthesized two complete datasets. Both had the same local count distribution, but the presence of partial objects in the local 32×32 patches was controlled. A comparison of the two data variants is shown in Fig. 2(a). When there are no partial objects, the ground truth local counts corresponds exactly to the number of dots. With partial objects, the ground truth local count can be estimated either (i) with integer counts, based on the number of dots within the local patch, or (ii) with fractional counts by integrating (summing) the Gaussian-convolved density map using a Gaussian kernel with the same size as the cell.

Biased Dot Annotations. Typical real-world counting datasets [2,29] have dot annotations. The dots are not necessarily centered on the object and may sit anywhere within the border of the object as shown in Fig. 1. The imprecise locations of the dots propagate as errors on the density maps when convolved with Gaussian kernels, which in turn creates biases in the ground truth local counts. To simulate this effect, we randomly moved the dot annotations Δ pixels in h and w directions, where Δ was uniformly sampled from $\{-a, +a\}$, where $a = \{0, 1, 2, 4\}$.

Mismatched Gaussian Kernels. In most counting datasets [2,29], the sizes of the objects are not known. This makes the Gaussian-convolved density map an imprecise estimate since a fixed-sized Gaussian kernel is applied when it should be a function of the object size. We investigate the effect of Gaussian kernel size on local counting models. We adopt 0, 3, 6 as the deviations of Gaussian kernels to generate density maps and then integrated density maps to obtain local count maps. A deviation of 0 means using the dot annotations directly. We also add a baseline where the Gaussian kernel sizes were selected according to the actual cell sizes, denoted by "GT Size".

Model/Implementation Details. For our local count models, we adopt all the convolutional layers in VGG16 [15] to extract feature maps, then used a regression head consisting of two 3×3 convolutional layers (512 and 1 output

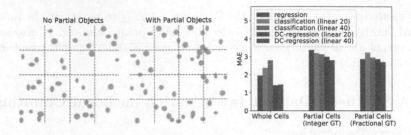

Fig. 2. Counting performance with respect to partial objects on the simulated cell dataset. Left: Some samples of simulated cell images without and with partial objects, respectively. Right: The counting performance of regression and discrete models. "linear 20/40" denotes 20 and 40 linear intervals respectively.

channels) to map local features to local counts. The size P_h, P_w of the local patch is 32×32. An Adam optimizer was adopted for training, with a learning rate of 10^{-3} and a batch size of 6. For the discrete models, we choose 20/40 linear intervals, with an interval length of 1/0.5, and 40 logarithm intervals. To evaluate, we consider the Mean Absolute Error (MAE), where lower MAE indicates better counting performance.

4.2   Partial Objects

When no partial objects are present, the plot in Fig. 2 shows that regression outperforms classification. When the class number increases from 20 to 40, counting error slightly increases for classification. This is because the local count is an integer value and increases with a step size of 1, so half of the intervals contain no samples when there are 40 instead of 20 intervals. DC-regression shows the best performance. Even when the interval is 0.5 and 40 intervals are used, the performance only drops slightly.

When partial objects are present, considering fractional counts for partial objects yields better performance. Classification shows comparable performance with regression. If fractional counts are considered for partial objects, increasing the number of intervals from 20 to 40 decreases the counting error. DC-regression shows better performance than standard regression and classification.

4.3   Incorrect Local Counts

The impact of biased point annotations is shown in Fig. 3(a). When the ground truth of local counts is imprecise, performance is highly dependent on the extent of the incorrect class label or interval. When the annotation bias is small, *e.g.* 1, the ground truth error is bounded by the interval of the discrete model, but when the bias becomes large, *e.g.* 2 or 4, the ground truth error may exceed the interval length. This results in the wrong classification label being assigned. One way to handle this is to use log-based instead of linear

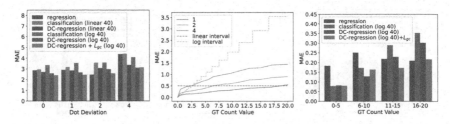

Fig. 3. Left: Counting results under various degrees of point annotation bias. Here L_{bias}^{λ} is adopted as L_{gc}. Middle: The bias of local count value caused by point annotation bias. Right: Counting error distribution w.r.t. local count value when dot deviation is 2. Linear/log denotes linear and log-spaced intervals respectively, while 20/40 denotes the number of intervals.

intervals. In fact, the MAE increases monotonically with respect to the ground truth local count (see Fig. 3(b)). This result directly implies that dense areas have higher ground truth error than sparse areas and using log-spaced intervals will outperform linearly spaced intervals. Plots of the error with respect to the ground truth local count (see Fig. 3(c)) show that classification performs better than regression in sparse areas (0−5 cells per patch) but worse in denser patches (6−20 cells per patch). Similarly, DC-regression shows much higher error than regression in highly dense areas (16−20 cells per patch), where log intervals have higher discretization error. However, the error of dense patches (11−20 cells per patch) decreases significantly if we add the global constraint regularizer L_{gc} to the DC-regression.

Mismatched Gaussian Kernels add errors to the ground truth local counts. Figure 4 shows that the error is monotonically increasing with respect to C. Classification and DC-regression are more robust than regression under varied Gaussian kernel sizes. Log intervals are better than linear intervals for classification when using a kernel of size 6, since the error of the ground truth is much larger than the linear interval length of 0.5. Finally, adding a global count loss L_{bias}^{λ} into DC-regression decreases the count error in dense patches (16–20) where log intervals become too large.

4.4   Study Findings

We draw the following conclusions about local count models based on the observations from above:

1. Partial objects make local counting harder. All local count models (regression, classification and DC-regression) perform worse when partial objects are present in local image patches even if the ground truth local counts are perfectly generated according to object size.

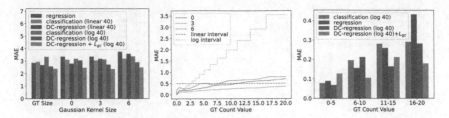

Fig. 4. Left: Counting results under various Gaussian kernel sizes. Here, $L_{\text{bias}}^{\lambda}$ is adopted as L_{gc}. Middle: The bias of local count value caused by various Gaussian kernel sizes. Right: Counting error distribution w.r.t. local count value with 6 as Gaussian kernel size. Linear/log denotes linear and log-spaced intervals respectively, while 20/40 denotes the number of intervals.

2. The ground truth local counts are not precise when partial objects are present and may contain error ϵ. Both the bias of point annotation (x_t, y_t) and Gaussian kernel G_{σ} increase ϵ in local counts C. The error ϵ is monotonically increasing with respect to local count value C. As such, log-spaced intervals are more suitable than linear intervals, which use increasing interval length to handle increasing ϵ.
3. Classification and DC-regression perform much better than regression when ϵ is present, which suggests that it is beneficial to adopt discrete constraints in regression with imprecise ground truth.
4. Adding L_{gc} into DC-regression effectively decreases discretization error in dense areas and improves the performance of DC-regression.

5   Experiment on Real-World Datasets

5.1   Datasets and Implementation Details

We verified the effectiveness of DC-regression on real-world counting and age estimation datasets. We evaluated DC-regression on three challenging crowd counting datasets (SHTech [29], JHU [17] and QNRF [2]). Due to the varied size of images in counting datasets, we randomly cropped fixed-sized sub-images as training samples. The crop size for SHTech was 320×320, and 512×512 for JHU and QNRF datasets. For generating density maps, we followed the same settings as [27,29]. To show the generality of DC-regression, we also evaluated it on two age estimation datasets, MegaAge (Mega) and MegaAsian (MegaA) datasets [30].

We followed the same architecture as specified in Sect. 4.1. We adopted the Adam optimizer, with a batch size of 8 for crowd counting and 32 for age estimation. The initial learning rate of 10^{-4} was decreased by 0.1 whenever training error plateaued. More implementation details are provided in the Supplementary. For evaluation, we used MAE to indicate counting accuracy and the Root Mean Squared Error (MSE) to reflect counting stability. Lower MAE and MSE indicate better counting performance.

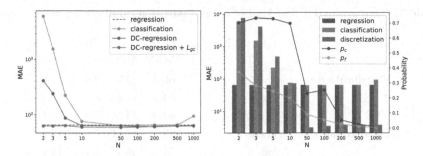

Fig. 5. The Effect of Number of Intervals (N) on SHTech PartA dataset [29]. Left: Counting error with respect to N. Right: MAE with classification probabilities (p_c and p_f) with respect to N. The discretization error (green bars) denotes the counting error of classification when all the class indexes are correctly predicted. p_c and p_f denotes the average probability of correctly or falsely predicted samples, respectively. $L_{\mathrm{bias}}^{\lambda}$ is adopted as L_{gc}. (Color figure online)

5.2   Ablation Study

Number of Intervals. We adopted log-spaced intervals for both classification and DC-regression, varying the number of intervals N from 2 to 1000. When $N = 2$, there were only background $\{0\}$ and foreground classes $(0, V_{max}]$. For classification, we adopted the median value of the training samples within interval $(V_{i-1}, V_i]$ to map the index back to a count.

From Fig. 5, we observe that regression sets a baseline performance indicated by the dashed line. With the right selection of N, all the discrete models surpass the regression baseline, but a poor selection of N hurts the performance. For classification, when N is small, discretization error of the intervals increases the MAE. When N is large, MAE increases again as the classes are no longer distinguishable. DC-regression also shows poor performance when $N \leq 5$ as it is similarly affected by discretization errors like classification. However, it has stable performance when $N > 5$ as it converges to standard regression when $N \to \infty$. The global loss L_{gc} mitigates the discretization errors of DC-regression when $N \leq 5$, making this the optimal combination. As classification showed the best performance when $N = 100$, we keep $N = 100$ for the remaining experiments.

Interval Spacing. We compared linear, log-spaced and uep [23] intervals for classification and DC-regression. $L_{\mathrm{bias}}^{\lambda}$ from Eq. (12) is chosen as L_{gc}. Table 1 shows that log-spaced intervals, in line with the synthetic experiments, are better than linear intervals for both classification and DC-regression. After adding the global count loss L_{gc} to DC-regression, counting performance improves and all three types of intervals perform similarly. This confirms that L_{gc} mitigates discretization errors and makes DC-regression less sensitive to interval spacing.

Choice of Global Count Loss L_{gc}. Table 2 compares the different global count loss terms. When adding global count losses L_{BL} from [8] and $L_{\mathrm{bias}}^{\lambda}$ to regres-

Table 1. Comparison different kind of interval partitions in discrete counting models

Method	Interval Partition	SHA		SHB	
		MAE	MSE	MAE	MSE
Classification	linear	65.6	115.4	8.6	14.6
	log	64.3	112.3	8.7	17.2
	uep [23]	63.9	112.8	7.9	15.1
DC-regression	linear	62.5	106.0	7.5	12.2
	log	61.6	96.7	7.1	11.1
	uep [23]	61.9	104.2	7.4	12.2
DC-regression+L_{gc}	linear	**60.3**	**95.5**	**6.6**	11.0
	log	**60.3**	103.7	6.7	10.6
	uep [23]	61.3	97.5	6.7	**10.2**

Table 2. Comparison of different L_{gc}. L_{cls} denotes the standard cross-entropy loss used in classification.

	Main loss	L_{gc}	SHA		SHB	
			MAE	MSE	MAE	MSE
Regression	L_1	—	65.4	103.3	10.7	19.5
Classification	L_{cls}	—	64.6	106.7	8.7	17.2
Regression + L_{gc}	—	L_{BL}	62.1	103.4	7.4	10.8
	—	L_{bias}^{λ}	62.9	108.5	7.8	12.0
DC-regression	L_{dc}	—	61.6	**96.7**	7.1	11.1
	L_{dc}	L_c	63.5	104.4	7.5	13.2
	L_{dc}	L_{bias}^0	61.6	105.3	7.1	11.9
	L_{dc}	L_{bias}^{λ}	**60.3**	103.7	**6.7**	**10.6**
	L_{dc}	L_{BL}	60.7	101.0	7.1	11.0

sion, the performance surpasses standard regression and classification with L_1 or cross entropy loss L_{cls}. However, it does not surpass standard DC-regression, suggesting that local count supervision is still more effective than global count supervision under discrete constraints. When looking at DC-regression specifically, the naive global count L_c from Eq. (9) harms DC-regression, as explained in Sect. 3.3. However, being selective on the local patch for the global count rectifies this error, with L_{bias}^{λ} being more effective than L_{bias}^0, which shows no improvement. We refer the reader to the Supplementary for a detailed comparison and discussion between L_{bias}^0 and L_{bias}^{λ}. We further observe that L_{BL} is also helpful for discrete regression and shows comparable results as L_{bias}^{λ}.

Table 3. Applying DC-regression in S-DCNet [27]

	L_c	L_m	SHA		SHB		JHU		QNRF	
			MAE	MSE	MAE	MSE	MAE	MSE	MAE	MSE
S-DCNet (cls) [27]	L_{cls}	L_1	**58.3**	95.0	**6.7**	**10.7**	65.2	272.8	104.4	176.1
S-DCNet (reg)	L_1	$L_1 + L_{BL}$	61.1	94.2	7.4	12.5	66.1	272.1	92.3	158.8
S-DCNet (dcreg)*	L_{dc}	$L_1 + L_{BL}$	59.7	**91.4**	7.0	11.6	**60.0**	269.9	86.9	159.3
S-DCNet (dcreg)†	L_{dc}	$L_1 + L_{bias}^\lambda$	59.8	100.0	6.8	11.5	62.1	**268.9**	**84.8**	**142.3**

5.3   Adding DC-Regression to State-of-the-Art

S-DCNet, proposed by Xiong *et al.* [27], is a classification-based state-of-the-art local counting model. As it was proposed to tackle open-set counting, it features two loss functions: L_c for supervising closed-set counters and L_m for supervising local counts outside the closed set. We replaced these losses by adopting DC-regression's L_{dc} from Eq. (8) for L_c and $L_{dc} + L_{gc}$ for L_m. Note that we do not consider the global count loss for closed set counting as the closed counters only predict truncated counts outside the closed set range.

We also added a standard S-DCNet regression baseline ('reg') for comparison. Table 3 shows that S-DCNet (reg) performs worse than the classification variant of S-DCNet ('cls') and is consistent with the conclusion in [27]. The DC-Regression variant of S-DCNet ('dcreg'), however, is comparable or better than S-DCNet (cls), verifying the effectiveness of DC-regression.

5.4   Comparison on Crowd Counting Datasets

We compare DC-regression with other state-of-the-art counting methods on three crowd counting datasets in Table 4. DC-regression outperforms local count regression and classification on all the datasets. Adding global count loss such as L_{BL} or L_{bias}^λ further improves the results, suggesting that a global constraint is helpful for local count models. In particular, DC-regression and S-DCNet (dcreg) show comparable performance with state-of-the-art approaches. Specifically, our methods are better than or comparable with density regression methods [9,21,22], which adopt optimum transportation [13] to model the imperfect ground truth of density maps.

5.5   Comparison on Age Estimation Datasets

Unlike local counts, human age is modelled as integer counts in standard age-estimation datasets [30]. As such, we postulate that applying our discrete constraint to regress age may also be suitable. We verify the effectiveness of DC-regression on age estimation datasets Mega and MegaA [30], adopting a linearly spaced interval of length 1 as age increases with step 1. To evaluate, we use MAE, MSE and CAi (i = 3, 5, 7), where CAi denotes the proportion of samples with MAE less than i. Table 5 shows that DC-regression is better than regression,

Table 4. Comparison with State-of-the-art method on Crowd Counting Datasets. Methods are grouped as density map regression, local count regression, classification and DC-Regression approaches

	Backbone	SHA		SHB		JHU		QNRF	
		MAE	MSE	MAE	MSE	MAE	MSE	MAE	MSE
CSRNet [5]	VGG16	68.2	115.0	10.6	16.0	85.9	309.2	108.2	181.3
DRCN [17]	VGG16	64.0	98.4	8.5	14.4	82.3	328.0	112.2	176.3
BL [8]	VGG19	62.8	101.8	7.7	12.7	75.0	299.9	88.7	154.8
PaDNet [18]	VGG16	59.2	98.1	8.1	12.2	—	—	96.5	170.2
MNA [20]	VGG19	61.9	99.6	7.4	11.3	67.7	258.5	85.8	150.6
OT [22]	VGG19	59.7	95.7	7.4	11.8	68.4	283.3	85.6	148.3
UOT [9]	VGG19	**58.1**	95.9	**6.5**	**10.2**	60.5	**252.7**	**83.3**	**142.3**
Generalized Loss [21]	VGG19	61.3	95.4	7.3	11.7	**59.9**	259.5	84.3	147.5
Regression (L_{reg})	VGG16	65.4	103.3	10.7	19.5	71.2	296.0	98.6	166.6
L_{BL}	VGG16	62.2	103.4	7.4	10.7	64.2	275.7	90.1	162.5
$L_{\text{bias}}^{\lambda}$	VGG16	62.9	108.5	7.8	12.0	68.6	289.4	93.3	160.8
Classification	VGG16	64.6	106.7	8.7	17.2	67.8	261.6	97.6	163.2
S-DCNet (cls) [27]	VGG16	58.3	95.0	6.7	10.7	65.2	272.8	104.4	176.1
DC-regression	VGG16	61.6	96.7	7.1	11.1	67.2	288.2	91.4	157.5
DC-regression+$L_{\text{bias}}^{\lambda}$	VGG16	60.3	103.7	6.7	10.6	64.8	282.6	86.0	148.2
DC-regression+L_{BL}	VGG16	60.7	101.0	7.1	11.0	61.6	263.2	87.1	152.1
S-DCNet (dcreg)*	VGG16	59.7	**91.4**	7.0	11.6	60.0	269.9	86.9	159.3
S-DCNet (dcreg)†	VGG16	59.8	100.0	6.8	11.5	62.1	268.9	84.8	**142.3**

Table 5. Comparison on age prediction datasets

Method	Mega					MegaA				
	MAE	RMSE	CA3	CA5	CA7	MAE	RMSE	CA3	CA5	CA7
Posterior [30]	—	—	38.69	57.90	73.15	—	—	62.08	80.43	90.42
Xia *et al.* [24]	—	—	—	—	—	2.80	—	62.50	82.37	—
Yu *et al.* [19]	—	—	42.19	60.0	72.70	—	—	64.80	83.20	91.40
Classification	5.57	7.15	39.72	57.10	71.45	2.91	4.14	68.19	84.82	93.03
Regression	5.26	6.72	41.89	59.84	74.73	2.87	4.00	68.57	85.10	93.51
DC-regression	**5.15**	**6.58**	**42.36**	**61.31**	**75.26**	**2.80**	**3.97**	**69.40**	**85.98**	**93.79**

which suggests that it is better to use discrete constraints for age prediction. Similar to the analysis of counting, we should ignore the loss of age when the prediction is within the class intervals, in order to provide the correct gradient to benefit the training process.

6 Conclusion

In this paper, we experimentally showed that ground truth local counts are error-prone, and classification outperforms regression when local counts are imprecise. The disadvantage of regression could be mitigated by adopting discrete constraints. We proposed DC-regression to handle the ground truth error in local count models. DC-regression showed superior results in counting tasks compared to classification and regression, and it is also suitable for age estimation tasks.

Acknowledgments. This research is supported by the Ministry of Education, Singapore, under its MOE Academic Research Fund Tier 2 (STEM RIE2025 MOE-T2EP20220-0015).

References

1. Gu, K., Yang, L., Yao, A.: Dive deeper into integral pose regression. In: International Conference on Learning Representations (ICLR) (2022)
2. Idrees, H., et al.: Composition loss for counting, density map estimation and localization in dense crowds. In: The European Conference on Computer Vision (ECCV), pp. 532–546 (2018)
3. Lempitsky, V., Zisserman, A.: Learning to count objects in images. In: Advances in Neural Information Processing Systems, vol. 23 (2010)
4. Li, R., Xian, K., Shen, C., Cao, Z., Lu, H., Hang, L.: Deep attention-based classification network for robust depth prediction. In: Jawahar, C.V., Li, H., Mori, G., Schindler, K. (eds.) ACCV 2018. LNCS, vol. 11364, pp. 663–678. Springer, Cham (2019). https://doi.org/10.1007/978-3-030-20870-7_41
5. Li, Y., Zhang, X., Chen, D.: CSRNet: dilated convolutional neural networks for understanding the highly congested scenes. In: The IEEE Conference on Computer Vision and Pattern Recognition (CVPR), pp. 1091–1100 (2018)
6. Liu, L., Lu, H., Xiong, H., Xian, K., Cao, Z., Shen, C.: Counting objects by block-wise classification. IEEE Trans. Circuits Syst. Video Technol. **30**(10), 3513–3527 (2019)
7. Liu, X., Yang, J., Ding, W., Wang, T., Wang, Z., Xiong, J.: Adaptive mixture regression network with local counting map for crowd counting. In: Vedaldi, A., Bischof, H., Brox, T., Frahm, J.-M. (eds.) ECCV 2020. LNCS, vol. 12369, pp. 241–257. Springer, Cham (2020). https://doi.org/10.1007/978-3-030-58586-0_15
8. Ma, Z., Wei, X., Hong, X., Gong, Y.: Bayesian loss for crowd count estimation with point supervision. In: Proceedings of the IEEE/CVF International Conference on Computer Vision, pp. 6142–6151 (2019)
9. Ma, Z., Wei, X., Hong, X., Lin, H., Qiu, Y., Gong, Y.: Learning to count via unbalanced optimal transport. In: Proceedings of the AAAI Conference on Artificial Intelligence, pp. 2319–2327 (2021)
10. Newell, A., Yang, K., Deng, J.: Stacked hourglass networks for human pose estimation. In: Leibe, B., Matas, J., Sebe, N., Welling, M. (eds.) ECCV 2016. LNCS, vol. 9912, pp. 483–499. Springer, Cham (2016). https://doi.org/10.1007/978-3-319-46484-8_29
11. Oñoro-Rubio, D., López-Sastre, R.J.: Towards perspective-free object counting with deep learning. In: Leibe, B., Matas, J., Sebe, N., Welling, M. (eds.) ECCV 2016. LNCS, vol. 9911, pp. 615–629. Springer, Cham (2016). https://doi.org/10.1007/978-3-319-46478-7_38

12. Paul Cohen, J., Boucher, G., Glastonbury, C.A., Lo, H.Z., Bengio, Y.: Count-ception: counting by fully convolutional redundant counting. In: Proceedings of the IEEE International Conference on Computer Vision Workshops, pp. 18–26 (2017)
13. Peyré, G., Cuturi, M., et al.: Computational optimal transport: with applications to data science. Found. Trends® Mach. Learn. 11(5–6), 355–607 (2019)
14. Shi, Z., Mettes, P., Snoek, C.G.: Counting with focus for free. In: Proceedings of the IEEE/CVF International Conference on Computer Vision, pp. 4200–4209 (2019)
15. Simonyan, K., Zisserman, A.: Very deep convolutional networks for large-scale image recognition. Computer Science (2014)
16. Sindagi, V.A., Patel, V.M.: Multi-level bottom-top and top-bottom feature fusion for crowd counting. In: Proceedings of the IEEE/CVF International Conference on Computer Vision, pp. 1002–1012 (2019)
17. Sindagi, V.A., Yasarla, R., Patel, V.M.: JHU-crowd++: large-scale crowd counting dataset and a benchmark method. Technical report (2020)
18. Tian, Y., Lei, Y., Zhang, J., Wang, J.Z.: PaDNet: pan-density crowd counting. IEEE Trans. Image Process. 29, 2714–2727 (2019)
19. Tingting, Y., Junqian, W., Lintai, W., Yong, X.: Three-stage network for age estimation. CAAI Trans. Intell. Technol. 4(2), 122–126 (2019)
20. Wan, J., Chan, A.: Modeling noisy annotations for crowd counting. In: Advances in Neural Information Processing Systems, vol. 33 (2020)
21. Wan, J., Liu, Z., Chan, A.B.: A generalized loss function for crowd counting and localization. In: Proceedings of the IEEE/CVF Conference on Computer Vision and Pattern Recognition, pp. 1974–1983 (2021)
22. Wang, B., Liu, H., Samara, D., Hoai, M.: Distribution matching for crowd counting. In: Conference on Neural Information Processing Systems (NeurIPS) (2020)
23. Wang, C., et al.: Uniformity in heterogeneity: diving deep into count interval partition for crowd counting. In: Proceedings of the IEEE/CVF International Conference on Computer Vision, pp. 3234–3242 (2021)
24. Xia, M., Zhang, X., Weng, L., Xu, Y., et al.: Multi-stage feature constraints learning for age estimation. IEEE Trans. Inf. Forensics Secur. 15, 2417–2428 (2020)
25. Xiao, B., Wu, H., Wei, Y.: Simple baselines for human pose estimation and tracking. In: European Conference on Computer Vision, pp. 466–481 (2018)
26. Xiong, H., Cao, Z., Lu, H., Madec, S., Liu, L., Shen, C.: TasselNetv2: in-field counting of wheat spikes with context-augmented local regression networks. Plant Methods 15(1), 1–14 (2019)
27. Xiong, H., Lu, H., Liu, C., Liu, L., Cao, Z., Shen, C.: From open set to closed set: counting objects by spatial divide-and-conquer. In: Proceedings of the IEEE/CVF International Conference on Computer Vision, pp. 8362–8371 (2019)
28. Zhang, C., Li, H., Wang, X., Yang, X.: Cross-scene crowd counting via deep convolutional neural networks. In: CVPR (2015)
29. Zhang, Y., Zhou, D., Chen, S., Gao, S., Ma, Y.: Single-image crowd counting via multi-column convolutional neural network. In: The IEEE Conference on Computer Vision and Pattern Recognition (CVPR), pp. 589–597 (2016)
30. Zhang, Y., Liu, L., Li, C., et al.: Quantifying facial age by posterior of age comparisons. arXiv preprint arXiv:1708.09687 (2017)

Breadcrumbs: Adversarial Class-Balanced Sampling for Long-Tailed Recognition

Bo Liu[1]([✉]), Haoxiang Li[1], Hao Kang[1], Gang Hua[1], and Nuno Vasconcelos[2]

[1] Wormpex AI Research, Bellevue, USA
richardboliu@gmail.com
[2] University of California San Diego, San Diego, USA
nuno@ece.ucsd.edu

Abstract. The problem of long-tailed recognition, where the number of examples per class is highly unbalanced, is considered. While training with class-balanced sampling has been shown effective for this problem, it is known to over-fit to few-shot classes. It is hypothesized that this is due to the repeated sampling of examples and can be addressed by feature space augmentation. A new feature augmentation strategy, EMANATE, based on back-tracking of features across epochs during training, is proposed. It is shown that, unlike class-balanced sampling, this is an adversarial augmentation strategy. A new sampling procedure, Breadcrumb, is then introduced to implement adversarial class-balanced sampling without extra computation. Experiments on three popular long-tailed recognition datasets show that Breadcrumb training produces classifiers that outperform existing solutions to the problem. Code: https://github.com/BoLiu-SVCL/Breadcrumbs.

1 Introduction

The availability of large-scale datasets, with many images per class [4], has been a major factor in the success of deep learning for computer vision. However, these datasets are manually curated and artificially balanced. This is unlike most real world applications, where the frequencies of examples from different classes can be highly unbalanced, leading to skewed distributions with long tails. These datasets are composed by a few popular classes and many rare classes. This class imbalance has been observed in image classification [31], face identification [13, 18], object detection [15,40], and many other applications. Researchers have tackled it from various angles, including zero-shot learning [5,33,34], few-shot learning [6,25,29], and more recently long-tailed recognition [19].

In this work, we focus on the long-tailed recognition setting, where classes are grouped into three types that differ in training sample cardinality: many-shot (>100 samples), medium-shot (between 20 and 100 samples), and few-shot (≤20

Supplementary Information The online version contains supplementary material available at https://doi.org/10.1007/978-3-031-20053-3_37.

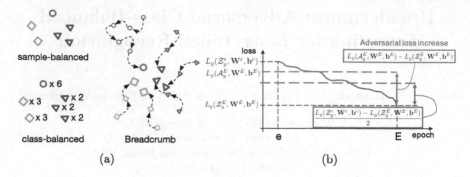

Fig. 1. (a) Upper-Left: random sampling is sample-balanced. The number of examples per class has a long-tailed distribution. This leads to under-fitting in few-shot classes. Lower-Left: class-balanced sampling duplicates few-shot samples in feature space and can leads to over-fitting for these classes. Right: Breadcrumb produces trails of features by back-tracking through training epochs. This is shown to be an adversarial augmentation technique, which mitigates the over-fitting problem. (b) Adversarial nature of EMANATE. The loss increase, between two epochs, due to feature augmentation by EMANATE is never smaller than half of the training gain (loss decrease) between them.

samples). Performance is evaluated over each group independently, in addition to the overall classification accuracy. While training data is highly unbalanced, the test set is kept balanced so that equally good performance on all classes is a requisite for high accuracy. One of the insights from the long-tailed recognition literature is that techniques targeting specific dataset limitations, e.g. few-shot learning by data augmentation [2,30], predicting classifier weights [22], prototype-based non-parametric classifiers [25], and optimization with second derivatives [6], are frequently harmful to classes that do not suffer from those limitations, e.g. many-shot. Hence, it is important to address the problem holistically, considering all types of classes simultaneously.

Since long-tailed recognition datasets have a continuous coverage of the number of samples per class, they are best addressed by training a model on the entire dataset, in a way robust to data imbalance. Standard classifier training follows the *sample-balanced* sampling setting of Fig. 1(a). This consists of sampling images uniformly to create batches for network training. In result, as shown in the figure, few-shot classes (red) are under-represented and many-shot classes (blue) are over-represented in each batch. Hence, learning typically *under-fits* less populated classes. This has motivated procedures to fight class imbalance with data re-sampling [37] or cost-sensitive losses [15] that place more training emphasis on examples of lower populated classes. One of the more successful approaches is to decouple the training of feature embedding and classifier [14]. While the embedding is learned with image-balanced training, the classifier is trained with *class-balanced* sampling. As illustrated in Fig. 1(a), this consists of sampling classes uniformly and then sampling uniformly within the class. However, for few shot classes, this approach leads to repeated sampling of the same examples. In result, the classifier can easily *over-fit* on few-shot classes.

In this work, we adopt the decoupled training strategy but seek to avoid over-fitting in the classifier training stage. For this, we propose to enrich the training data in the feature space at the output of the embedding, without extra computation. The idea is to back-track features to access the large diversity of feature vectors that are available per training image in prior epochs. This can be exploited to generate more diverse training data than simply replicating existing features. We refer to this procedure as *feature back-tracking*. As shown in Fig. 1(a), it allows the sampling of large numbers of feature vectors from the few-shot classes without duplication. Since the embedding changes across training epochs, an alignment is necessary to simplify network training. We show that a simple alignment of class means suffices to accomplish this goal and propose the *fEature augMentAtioN by bAck-tracking wiTh alignmEnt* (EMANATE) procedure. This consists of augmenting the feature vectors collected at an epoch with aligned replicas of the vectors that emanate from them by back-tracking.

A theoretical analysis shows that, unlike class-balanced sampling, EMANATE is an adversarial feature augmentation technique, in the sense that it is guaranteed to increase the training loss for any convergent training scheme. This places EMANATE in the realm of feature augmentation methods popular in the few-shot literature [2,30]. However, these require extra computation to generate new examples and sometimes introduce convergence problems. EMANATE requires no extra computation and can be applied differently to each class, according to its number of samples. For classes with enough samples, only features from the last epoch are used, i.e. no resampling is performed. For those without, features are back-tracked over previous epochs, until there are enough features. This results in a new training feature set of higher variance for few-shot classes but forces no change on many-shot classes. In result, it is possible to improve classification accuracy for the former without degrading performance for the latter.

A new sampling scheme, denoted *Breadcrumb Sampling* is then proposed to leverage the feature trails extracted by EMANATE, in the context of the two-stage training of class-balanced sampling. Breadcrumb Sampling relies on EMANATE to collect these feature trails in a first stage, when the embedding is trained with image-balanced sampling. In the second stage, the classifier is then learned with class-balanced training based on these trails. Two sampling variants are considered. Weak Breadcrumb Sampling only uses feature trails collected at the end of stage 1, i.e. once the embedding has converged. Strong Breadcrumb Sampling uses trails collected throughout stage 1 training, i.e. as the embedding evolves. This tends to create an even more adversarial training set.

Overall, this work makes several contributions. First, we point out that class-balanced sampling is not an adversarial augmentation technique, which limits its ability to combat over-fitting in few-shot classes. Second, we propose EMANATE, a data augmentation technique that addresses this problem by feature back-tracking with alignment. Third, we show theoretically that, unlike

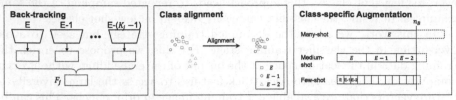

Fig. 2. EMANATE. Left: features from embeddings learned in previous epochs are back-tracked to compose a class-balance training set. Middle: class alignment aligns the means of features from different epochs. Right: different classes have different back-tracking lengths. Many-shot classes only collect features from the current epoch; medium-shot classes back-track for a few epochs; and few-shot classes from many. When the number of samples exceeds n_B, the earliest epoch is randomly sampled to meet this target.

class-balanced sampling, EMANATE is an adversarial technique. Fourth, we propose two variants of a new sampling scheme, Breadcrumbs, which leverage EMANATE to enable long-tailed recognition with state of the art performance. All of this is achieved with no extra computation and no performance degradation for classes with many examples.

2   Related Work

Long-tailed recognition has recently received substantial attention [15, 19, 21, 31, 32, 37]. Several approaches have been proposed, including metric learning [21, 37], loss weighting [15], or meta-learning [31]. Some methods propose dedicated loss functions to mitigate the data imbalanced problem. For example, lift loss [21] introduces margins between many training samples. Range loss [37] encourages data from the same class to be close and different classes to be far away in the embedding space. The focal loss [15] dynamically balances weights of positive, hard negative, and easy negative samples. As reported by Liu et al. [19], when applied to long-tailed recognition, many of these methods improved accuracy of the few-shot group, but at the cost of lower accuracy for many-shot classes.

Other methods, e.g. class-balanced experts [24] and knowledge distill [35], try to mitigate this problem by artificially dividing the training data into subsets, based on number of examples, and training an expert per subset. However, experts learned from arbitrary data divisions can be sub-optimal, especially for few-shot classes, where training data is insufficient to learn the expert model.

More recent works [14, 39] achieve improved long-tailed recognition by training feature embedding and classifier with separate sampling strategies. The proposed Breadcrumbs approach follows this strategy, learning the embedding in a first stage with sample-balanced (random) sampling and the classifier in a second stage with class-balanced sampling. In fact, Breadcrumbs can be seen as a data augmentation method tailored for this strategy, improving its long-tailed recognition performance over all class groups.

Another related work is LEAP [17], a method mostly tested on person re-identification and face recognition problems, where datasets usually have long-tailed distributions. LEAP augments data samples from tail (few-shot) classes by transferring intra-class variations from head (many-shot) classes. This assumes a shared intra-class variation across classes, which can hold for person re-ID and face recognition but may not be applicable for general long-tailed recognition tasks. Besides, LEAP is technically orthogonal to Breadcrumbs and the two methods could potentially be combined for further improvement.

Few-shot learning focus solely on the data scarcity problem. A large group of approaches is based on meta-learning, using gradient based methods such as MAML and its variants [6,7], or LEO [23]. These methods take advantage of second derivatives to optimize the model from few-shot samples. Another group of methods, including matching network [29], prototypical network [25], and relation network [26],aims to learn robust metrics. Since these methods are designed specifically for few-shot classes, they often under-perform for many-shot classes, which makes them ineffective for long-tailed recognition.

Similarly to Breadcrumbs, some few-shot methods have proposed to augmenting training data by combining GANs with meta-learning [30], synthesizing features across object views [16] or using other forms of data hallucination [10]. All these method introduces non-negligible extra computation to generate the new data samples. The application of GAN-based methods to few-shot data without external large-scale datasets can also create convergence problem. In Breadcrumbs, data samples are augmented with saved feature vectors from prior epochs and no extra computation.

3   EMANATE

In this section, we introduce the data augmentation method that underlies Breadcrumbs.

3.1   Data Sampling and Decoupling Training

Consider an image recognition problem with training set $\mathcal{D} = \{(\mathbf{x}_i, \mathbf{y}_i); i = 1, \dots, N\}$, where x_i is an example and $y_i \in \{1, \dots, C\}$ its label, where C is the number of classes. A CNN model combines a feature embedding $\mathbf{z} = f(\mathbf{x}; \theta) \in \mathbb{R}^d$, implemented by several convolutional layers of parameters θ, and a classifier $g(\mathbf{z}) \in [0,1]^C$ that operates on the embedding to produce a class prediction $\hat{y} = \arg\max_i g_i(\mathbf{z})$. Standard (image-balanced) CNN training relies on mini-batch SGD, where each batch is randomly sampled from $\mathcal{D}$. A class j of n_j training example has probability $\frac{n_j}{N}$ of being represented in the batch. Without loss of generality, we assume classes sorted by decreasing cardinality, i.e. $n_i \leq n_j$, $\forall i > j$.

In the long-tail setting, where $n_1 \gg n_C$, the model is not fully trained on classes of large index j (tail classes) and under-fits. This can be avoided with recourse to non-uniform sampling strategies, the most popular of which is class-balanced sampling. This samples each class with probability $\frac{1}{C}$, over-sampling tail classes, and is particularly successful when the training of embedding and classifier are decoupled [14], which is also simple to implement. The embedding is first trained with image-balanced sampling, and different sampling and structures can then be used for the classifier. In this work, we adopt the popular linear classifier $g(\mathbf{z}) = \nu(\mathbf{Wx}+\mathbf{b})$, where ν is the softmax function, and class-balanced sampling.

3.2 Augmentation by Feature Back-Tracking

Class-balanced sampling over-samples classes of few examples. For a class j with $n_j < N/C$ the over-sampling factor is $\rho = \frac{N}{Cn_j}$. In the long-tail setting, ρ is usually larger than 10. This heavily resamples the few available samples and can lead to over-fitting, impairing generalization for tail classes. While over-fitting can be combated with data augmentation, traditional image-level methods, such as random cropping, horizontal flipping, or color jittering, make little difference in feature space, because the embedding is trained to be invariant to such transformations. Feature-level augmentations have been investigated in the few-shot setting [10,16,30], but typically require training of additional models, which add complexity and sometimes have convergence problems. Ideally, the augmentation technique should be adversarial, i.e. increase training difficulty, and require little extra computation. One possibility is to rely on adversarial examples [9]. However, these require optimization at each training iteration and have large computational cost. In our experience, standard adversarial attacks are also not effective at improving generalization for tail classes, because they are too close to the few available examples.

In this work, we propose a different adversarial feature-level augmentation strategy, based on *feature backtracking*. The idea is that the embedding $f(\mathbf{x}; \theta)$, obtained after training converges, is simply the final element in the family of embeddings $f(\mathbf{x}; \theta^e)$ learned from epochs $e \in \{1, \ldots, E\}$, where E is the number of training epochs. It follows that a particular image $\mathbf{x}_i$ produces a sequence of feature vectors

$$\mathcal{B}_i = \{\mathbf{z}_i^e = f(\mathbf{x}_i; \theta^e) | e \in \{1, \ldots, E\}\} \tag{1}$$

during the optimization. We equate $\mathcal{B}_i$ to a trail of *bread crumbs* that can be backtracked, as illustrated in Fig. 1(a,right). These bread crumbs can be used to perform data augmentation *without* added computation. It suffices to store, at epoch e the set of features

$$\mathcal{Z}^e = \{\mathbf{z}_i^e = f(\mathbf{x}_i; \theta^e) | \mathbf{x}_i \in \mathcal{D}\} \tag{2}$$

produced by the embedding learned at the end of the epoch. This is denoted as the training set *snapshot* at epoch e.

Since the embedding $f(\mathbf{x}; \theta^e)$ changes with e, features from different epochs are usually not aligned in feature space. This may lead to bread crumb trails that are "all over the place", e.g. because the space has been translated or rotated between epochs. Hence, when feature vectors collected at different epochs are to be used together, a *class alignment* is recommended to simplify the training. On the other hand, this alignment cannot be too strong, so as not to defeat the purpose of data-augmentation. In particular, the alignment operation should not jeopardize the adversarial nature of the latter. A simple operation, which is shown to satisfy this property in the following section, is to align the mean feature vectors synthesized per class during back-tracking. This consists of splitting $\mathcal{Z}^e$ into a set of class snapshots, where

$$\mathcal{Z}_y^e = \{\mathbf{z}_i^e \in \mathcal{Z}^e | y_i = y\} \tag{3}$$

is the snapshot of class y, compute the mean of each class

$$\bar{\mathbf{z}}_y^e = \frac{1}{n_j} \sum_{j=1}^{n_j} \mathbf{z}_{y,j}^e \tag{4}$$

where $\mathbf{z}_{y,j}^e$ is the jth element of $\mathcal{Z}_y^e$, and apply

$$\mathbf{z}_{y,j}^{e' \to e} = \mathbf{z}_{y,i}^{e'} - \bar{\mathbf{z}}_j^{e'} + \bar{\mathbf{z}}_j^e, \tag{5}$$

where $\mathbf{z}_{y,j}^{e' \to e}$ is the alignment, with respect to snapshot e, of the jth feature vector $\mathbf{z}_{y,j}^e$ of class y from epoch e'. This produces a snapshot *transferred from epoch e' to e*

$$\mathcal{Z}_y^{e' \to e} = \{\mathbf{z}_{y,j}^{e' \to e} | \mathbf{z}_{y,j}^{e'} \in \mathcal{Z}_y^{e'}\}. \tag{6}$$

This snapshot can then be combined with $\mathcal{Z}_y^e$ to produce an *augmented snapshot of class y for epoch e*

$$\mathcal{A}_y^e = \mathcal{Z}_y^e \bigcup \mathcal{Z}_y^{e' \to e}. \tag{7}$$

This process is denoted *fEature augMentAtioN by bAcktracking wiTh alignmEnt* (EMANATE), as $\mathcal{A}_y^e$ backtracks the breadcrumb trails that emanate from class y at epoch e.

3.3 Theoretical Justification

In this section, we provide theoretical motivation for EMANATE as an adversarial data augmentation technique. Let $\nu(\mathbf{W}^e \mathbf{z} + \mathbf{b}^e)$ be the linear classifier learned at the end of epoch e, i.e. from the snapshots $\mathcal{Z}_y^e = \{\mathbf{z}_{y,i}^e\}$ of (3). The corresponding cross-entropy loss is

$$L(\mathcal{Z}^e, \mathbf{W}^e, \mathbf{b}^e) = \sum_y L_y(\mathcal{Z}_y^e, \mathbf{W}^e, \mathbf{b}^e) \tag{8}$$

where

$$L_y(\mathcal{Z}_y^e, \mathbf{W}^e, \mathbf{b}^e) = -\frac{1}{|\mathcal{Z}_y^e|} \Sigma_i \log \nu_y(\mathbf{W}^e \mathbf{z}_{y,i}^e + \mathbf{b}^e), \tag{9}$$

is the loss of class y and ν_y the yth element of the softmax output. It is assumed that the classifier is optimal for the training data under this loss, i.e.

$$L_y(\mathcal{Z}_y^e, \mathbf{W}^e, \mathbf{b}^e) \leq L_y(\mathcal{Z}_y^e, \mathbf{W}, \mathbf{b}), \quad \forall y, \mathbf{W}, \mathbf{b}. \tag{10}$$

A feature augmentation procedure adds new features to $\mathcal{Z}_y^e$. It is denoted adversarial when the augmented training set is more challenging than the original.

Definition 1. *Consider the augmentation $\mathcal{A}_y^e$ of the training set snapshot $\mathcal{Z}_y^e$ from epoch e and class y. The augmentation is adversarial with respect to class y if*

$$L_y(\mathcal{A}_y^e, \mathbf{W}^e, \mathbf{b}^e) > L_y(\mathcal{Z}_y^e, \mathbf{W}^e, \mathbf{b}^e) \tag{11}$$

where $L_y(.)$ the loss of (9).

For low-shot classes y, class-balanced sampling replicates the features of $\mathcal{Z}_y^e$, creating the augmented feature set $\mathcal{A}_y^e = \mathcal{Z}_y^e \cup \mathcal{Z}_y^e$. Since, from (9)

$$L_y(\mathcal{A}_y^e, \mathbf{W}^e, \mathbf{b}^e) = -\frac{1}{2|\mathcal{Z}_y^e|} 2\Sigma_i \log \nu_y(\mathbf{W}^e \mathbf{z}_{y,i}^e + \mathbf{b}^e),$$
$$= L_y(\mathcal{Z}_y^e, \mathbf{W}^e, \mathbf{b}^e) \tag{12}$$

we obtain the following corollary.

Corollary 1. *Class-balanced sampling is not an adversarial feature augmentation strategy.*

We next consider augmentation with EMANATE. The following lemma establishes a lower bound for the increase of the training loss under this augmentation technique.

Lemma 1. *Consider the augmentation of $\mathcal{Z}_y^e$ with the snapshot transferred from epoch $e' < e$ by EMANATE, i.e. $\mathcal{A}_y^e = \mathcal{Z}_y^e \cup \mathcal{Z}_y^{e' \to e}$, where $\mathcal{Z}_y^{e' \to e}$ is as defined in (6). Then*

$$L_y(\mathcal{A}_y^e, \mathbf{W}^e, \mathbf{b}^e) - L_y(\mathcal{Z}_y^e, \mathbf{W}^e, \mathbf{b}^e) \geq$$
$$\frac{L_y(\mathcal{Z}_y^{e'}, \mathbf{W}^{e'}, \mathbf{b}^{e'}) - L_y(\mathcal{Z}_y^e, \mathbf{W}^e, \mathbf{b}^e)}{2}, \tag{13}$$

where $(\mathbf{W}^e, \mathbf{b}^e)$ is the classifier of (10).[1]

The lemma shows that the adversarial increase of the loss due to the augmentation $(L_y(\mathcal{A}_y^e, \mathbf{W}^e, \mathbf{b}^e) - L_y(\mathcal{Z}_y^e, \mathbf{W}^e, \mathbf{b}^e))$ is at least half of decrease in the loss of the trained classifier between epochs e' (loss $L(\mathcal{Z}_y^{e'}, \mathbf{W}^{e'}, \mathbf{b}^{e'})$) and e (loss $L_y(\mathcal{Z}_y^e, \mathbf{W}^e, \mathbf{b}^e)$), i.e. half of what has been gained by training the classifier from epochs e' to e. This is illustrated in Fig. 1(b) and leads to the following theorem.

---

[1] Proof is provided in supplementary material.

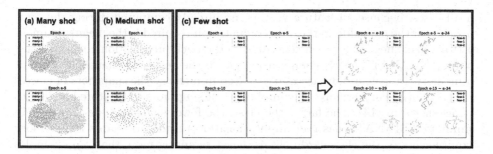

Fig. 3. t-SNE visualizations of feature snapshots at different epochs. Many-shot (a) and medium-shot (b) features compose a well-defined geometry that does not change along epochs. Due to the scarcity of data, few-shot features (c, left) fail to hold a consistent geometry along epochs. After augmentation with EMANATE (c, right), the features have more variety and the geometry changes less among epochs.

Theorem 1. *EMANATE is an adversarial feature augmentation strategy for any convergent training scheme, i.e. whenever* $L_y(\mathcal{Z}_y^{e'}, \mathbf{W}^{e'}, \mathbf{b}^{e'}) > L_y(\mathcal{Z}_y^e, \mathbf{W}^e, \mathbf{b}^e) \forall e' < e$.

Since successful training requires a convergent training scheme, EMANATE is an adversarial feature augmentation technique for most training procedures of practical interest.

3.4   Assembling Feature Trails

So far, we have considered the augmentation of $\mathcal{Z}_y^e$ with the transferred snapshot $\mathcal{Z}_y^{e'\to e}$. The augmentation can obviously be repeated for several transferred snapshots e', in order to meet any target number n_B of samples per class at epoch e. This is done as follows. Consider a class j with n_j samples. The features in $\mathcal{Z}_j^e$ are first selected. If there is a differential to n_B, the transferred snapshot $\mathcal{Z}_j^{e-1\to e}$ is selected next. The procedure is repeated until number of the feature vectors reaches n_B. If the addition of the final set places the feature cardinality above n_B, the necessary number of feature vectors is sampled randomly. The augmented set of features that emanate from class j at epoch e is then

$$\mathcal{A}_j^e = \bigcup_{k=0}^{K_j-2} \mathcal{Z}_j^{e-k\to e} \bigcup \tilde{\mathcal{Z}}_j^{e-(K_j-1)\to e}, \tag{14}$$

where $K_j = \left\lceil \frac{n_B}{n_j} \right\rceil$, and $\tilde{\mathcal{Z}}_j^{e-K_j-1\to e}$ is a random sample from $\mathcal{Z}_j^{e-K_j-1\to e}$ of size $n_B - K_j n_j$. The complete training set of epoch e is $\mathcal{A}^e = \cup_{j=1}^C \mathcal{A}_j^e$.

The number of snapshots in $\mathcal{A}_j^e$ depends heavily on the number of examples n_j of the class. As shown in Fig. 2 (a, right), many-shot classes use a single snapshot, medium-shot classes require snapshots from a few epochs, and few-shot classes require many snapshots to assemble enough training features. However, in all cases, because all feature vectors are already computed during the optimization of the embedding, the only computation required is the mean alignment of (5). This is negligible when compared to the back-propagation computations, making EMANATE nearly computation free, if the necessary snapshots are kept in memory. In fact, it only necessary to keep in memory the snapshots of classes with $n_j < n_B$. Furthermore, the number K_j of snapshots to be stored adapts to n_j, as shown in (14). The larger the class, the fewer snapshots are required. In summary, EMANATE has no computational overhead and adapts the memory requirements to the class cardinalities, never requiring more than n_B examples per class. This is the complexity of class-balanced sampling.

Figure 3 shows t-SNE [20] of training set snapshots collected at different epochs. While the geometry of many- and medium shot classes (Fig. 3(a, b)) is fairly stable across epochs, that of few-shot classes (Fig. 3(c) left) can change significantly, due to data scarcity. EMANATE produces larger clusters with more stable geometry, enabling a more robust training set for the classifier.

4   Breadcrumbs

In this section, we investigate two sampling mechanisms based on EMANATE, which are denoted as Breadcrumb sampling. The two mechanisms differ in how the sets $\mathcal{A}_j^e$ are collected. In both cases, the two stage training procedure of [14] is adopted. In the first stage, the feature extractor $f(\mathbf{x}; \theta)$ and the classifier $\nu(\mathbf{W}\mathbf{x}+b)$ are trained with image balanced sampling. The sets $\mathcal{A}_j^e, e = \{1, \ldots, E\}$ of class snapshots are collected at each epoch of this stage. In the second stage, the feature extractor $f(\mathbf{x}; \theta)$ is kept fixed and the classifier $\nu(\mathbf{W}\mathbf{x} + b)$ retrained using these sets. As shown in Fig. 4, the two augmentation schemes differ in the classifier update step.

4.1   Weak Beadcrumb Sampling

In the first approach, EMANATE is only applied *after convergence* of the first stage training. That is, only the sets $\mathcal{A}_j^E$ assembled in the *final* epoch E of the first stage are used to retrain the classifier in the second stage. This is illustrated in the left of Fig. 4, for the case where $E = 3$ and augmentation sets span two epochs. We refer to this sampling technique as *Weak Beadcrumb Sampling*, since all snapshots emanate from the feature set produced by the optimal embedding $f(\mathbf{x}, \theta^E)$. While this creates some diversity, feature snapshots from neighboring epochs are likely to be similar. This makes the sampling technique less adversarial and therefore "weak".

4.2   Strong Beadcrumb Sampling

Strong Beadcrumb Sampling aims to increase feature diversity, so as to create a more adversarial data augmentation. Rather than the augmentation $\mathcal{A}_j^E$ of the final epoch E of the first stage training, *all* augmentations $\mathcal{A}_j^e, e = \{1, \ldots, E\}$ are

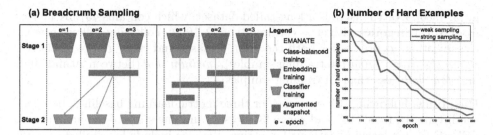

Fig. 4. (a) Breadcrumb Sampling relies on EMANATE to collect augmented snapshots $\mathcal{A}_j^e$ (in red) in a first stage, when the embedding is trained with image-balanced sampling. In a second stage, the classifier is learned with class-balanced training based on these snapshots. In this example $E = 3$ and snapshots have length $K_j = 2$ (a single class is shown for simplicity). Left: Weak Breadcrumb Sampling only uses snapshots collected at the end of stage 1. Right: Strong Breadcrumb Sampling uses snapshots collected throughout stage 1 training. (b) Number of hard examples (loss larger than 5) in few-shot classes during training, for ResNet-10 on ImageNet-LT. Strong Breadcrumb sampling increases the number of hard examples during training, compared to the weak one. The plot starts at epoch 100 because early epochs have too many hard examples and dominate the scale.

saved in that stage, as illustrated in the right of Fig. 4. The classifier retraining of the second stage is then run for E epochs, using the feature trail sets $\mathcal{A}_j^e$ collected at epoch e of the first stage to train the classifier in epoch e of the second stage. Since each epoch of classifier training contains new data, increasing the difficulty of the classification task, this sampling method is more adversarial and therefore "strong". Since the classifier is trained on an evolving feature set $\mathcal{A}^e$,

This setting yields a natural selection of the target number n_B of samples per class. To keep the pace of classifier training the same as the embedding training, the size of the dataset should be approximately the same, i.e. $n_B = \left\lceil \frac{1}{C} \sum_{j=1}^C n_j \right\rceil$. Figure 2(b), shows that Strong Breadcrumb Sampling increases the number of hard examples in few-shot classes per epoch, when compared to Weak Breadcrumb Sampling. This confirms that it is a more adversarial data augmentation strategy.

5   Experiments

5.1   Experimental Set-Up

Datasets. We consider three long-tailed recognition datasets, ImageNet-LT [19], Places-LT [19] and iNatrualist18 [28]. ImageNet-LT is a long-tailed version of ImageNet [4] by sampling a subset following the Pareto distribution with power value $\alpha = 6$. It contains 115.8K images from 1000 categories, with class cardinality ranging from 5 to 1280. Places-LT is a long-tailed version of the Places dataset [38]. It contains 184.5K images from 365 categories with class cardinality in [5, 4980]. iNatrualist18 is a long-tailed dataset, which contains 437.5K images from 8141 categories with class cardinality in [2, 1000]. Following [19], we present classification accuracies for both the entire dataset and three groups of classes: *many shot* (more than 100 training samples), *medium shot* (between 20 and 100), and *few shot* (less than 20 training samples).

Baselines. Following [19], we consider three metric-learning baselines, based on the lifted [21], focal [15], and range [37] losses, and one state-of-the-art method, FSLwF [8], for learning without forgetting. We also include long-tailed recognition methods designed specifically for these datasets, OLTR [19] and Distill [35], plus the recent state of the art Decoupling method [14]. The model with standard random sampling and end-to-end training is denoted as the *Plain Model* for comparison.

Training Details. ResNet-10 and ResNeXt-50 [11,36] are used on ImageNet-LT; ResNet-152 is used on Places-LT; and ResNet-50 is used on iNatrualist18. The model is trained with SGD, using momentum 0.9, weight decay 0.0005, and a learning rate that cosine decays from 0.2 to 0. Each iteration uses class-balanced and random sampling mini-batches of size 512. One epoch is defined when the random sampling iterates over the entire training data. Under Strong Breadcrumb Sampling, class-balanced sampling is applied in the initial classifier training epochs, when there are not enough previous epochs to back-track. Codes are attached in supplementary.

Table 1. Ablation of Breadcrumb components, on the ImageNet-LT. For many-shot $t > 100$, for medium-shot $t \in (20, 100]$, and for few-shot $t \leq 20$, where t is the number of training samples.

Method	Overall	Many-shot	Medium-shot	Few-shot
Decoupling [14]	41.4	51.8	38.8	21.5
+ back-tracking	41.2	50.4	38.5	23.8
+ class-specific	41.3	50.8	38.1	24.6
Weak Breadcrumb	43.2	53.6	39.8	25.1
Strong Breadcrumb	**44.0**	53.7	**41.0**	**26.4**
Breadcrumb	**44.0**	53.7	**41.0**	**26.4**
Breadcrumb (var.)	43.9	**53.8**	40.8	26.0
Breadcrumb (agn.)	38.5	47.3	35.6	24.0

Table 2. Results on ImageNet-LT and Places-LT. ResNet-10/152 are used for all methods. For many-shot $t > 100$, for medium-shot $t \in (20, 100]$, and for few-shot $t \leq 20$, where t is the number of training samples.

Method	ImageNet-LT, ResNet-10				Places-LT, ResNet-152			
	Overall	Many-shot	Medium-shot	Few-shot	Overall	Many-shot	Medium-shot	Few-shot
Plain model	23.5	41.1	14.9	3.6	27.2	**45.9**	22.4	0.36
Lifted loss [21]	30.8	35.8	30.4	17.9	35.2	41.1	35.4	24.0
Focal loss [15]	30.5	36.4	29.9	16.0	34.6	41.1	34.8	22.4
Range loss [37]	30.7	35.8	30.3	17.6	35.1	41.1	35.4	23.2
FSLwF [8]	28.4	40.9	22.1	15.0	34.9	43.9	29.9	29.5
OLTR [19]	35.6	43.2	35.1	18.5	35.9	44.7	37.0	25.3
Distill [35]	38.8	47.0	37.9	19.2	36.2	39.3	39.6	24.2
Decoupling (cRT) [14]	41.4	51.8	38.8	21.5	37.9	37.8	40.7	31.8
Breadcrumb	**44.0**	**53.7**	**41.0**	**26.4**	**39.3**	40.6	**41.0**	**33.4**

Table 3. Results on ImageNet-LT, ResNeXt-50. For many-shot $t > 100$, for medium-shot $t \in (20, 100]$, and for few-shot $t \leq 20$, where t is the number of training samples.

Method	Overall	Many-shot	Medium-shot	Few-shot
OLTR [19]	41.9	51.0	40.8	20.8
Decoupling (NCM) [14]	47.3	56.6	45.3	28.1
Decoupling (cRT) [14]	49.6	61.8	46.2	27.4
Decoupling (τ) [14]	49.4	59.1	46.9	30.7
Decoupling (LWS) [14]	49.9	60.2	47.2	30.3
Causal [27]	50.6	62.3	46.9	30.6
LADE [12]	51.9	62.3	49.3	31.2
Breadcrumb	**51.0**	**62.9**	**47.2**	**30.9**

Table 4. Results on the iNaturalist 2018. All methods are implemented with ResNet-50.

Method	Accuracy
CB-Focal [3]	61.1
LDAM+DRW [1]	68.0
Decoupling (cRT) [14]	68.2
Decoupling (τ) [14]	69.3
Decoupling (LWS) [14]	69.5
Causal [27]	64.4
LADE [12]	70.0
BBN [39]	66.3
Breadcrumb	**70.3**

5.2 Ablation Study

Several ablations were performed to study the effectiveness of the various components of Breadcrumb. In this study, all models are trained and evaluated on the training and test set of ImageNet-LT, respectively, using a ResNet-10 backbone.

Component Ablation. Starting from the baseline Decoupling (cRT) [14] method, we incrementally add feature back-tracking, class-specific augmentation, class alignment (leading to Weak Breadcrumb Sampling), and Strong Breadcrumb Sampling. Results are shown in Table 1. When only back-tracking is applied, all snapshots are collected from the last 10 epochs of image-balanced training (first stage), and the classifier trained (in the second stage) using this feature set and class-balanced sampling. No class alignment is applied. Compared to the baseline, back-tracking gives a reasonable gain on few-shot classes but harms many-shot performance. This can be explained by the fact that, for many-shot classes, features from the final epoch are replaced by those from prior epochs. Since the corresponding embeddings are sub-optimal, the augmented features are inferior to the final ones. This, however, is not the case in few-shot, where augmented features replace *duplicated* features.

The combination of back-tracking and class-specific augmentation, where different classes have different back-tracking lengths, is denoted as "+ class-specific" in Table 1. Surprisingly, without class alignment, the performance on many-shot does not improve, even though no augmented features are introduced into those classes. We believe this is due to the fact that when few-shot features are augmented without alignment, those augmented features take up position in feature space that should not be assigned to them. This decreases the accuracy of many-shot classes. When class-alignment is applied (Weak Breadcrumb Sampling) we observe an improvement over all class partitions, with gains of 1.8% (Many), 1% (Medium), and 3, 6% (Few-Shot) and an overall improvement of 1.8% over the baseline. Finally, Strong Breadcrumb Sampling enables another 0.8% overall gain, for a total gain of 2.6% over the baseline.

Class Alignment Ablation. Since alignment makes a significant difference, we considered three different alignment choices. In Sect. 3.2, only class-specific mean alignment is presented. It is also possible to align the feature variances. This is denoted as Breadcrumb (var.) in Table 1 and has a negligible difference. Hence, we only apply mean alignment unless otherwise noted. Another possibility is class-agnostic alignment, where only one mean is computed over all classes. This is listed as Breadcrumb (agn.) in Table 1. Its poor performance implies that class-agnostic alignment cannot fully eliminate the differences between epochs.

5.3   Comparison to the State of the Art

Table 2 presents a final comparison to the methods in the literature on ImageNet-LT, using a ResNet-10, and Places-LT, using a ResNet-152. In these experiments we use Strong Breadcrumb Sampling, which is shown to outperform all other methods on both datasets. It achieves the best performance on 5 of the 6 partitions and is always better than the next overall best performer (Decoupling (cRT)). It is only outperformed by the Plain Model on the Many-Shot split of Places-LT, where this model severely overfits to the Many-Shot classes, basically ignoring the Few-Shot ones, and achieving overall performance 12.1% weaker than Breadcrumb. Compared to the best models Breadcrumb also achieves significant gains on few-shot classes, especially on ImageNet-LT, where it beats the next best method by 4.9%. This suggests that previous methods over-fit for few-shot classes, a problem that is mitigated by the introduction of EMANATE and Strong Breadcrumb Sampling. Table 3 shows that these results are fairly insensitive to the backbone network. Breadcrumb achieves the best overall performance and the best performance on all partitions with a ResNeXt-50 backbone. Finally Table 4 shows that Breadcrumb again achieves the overall best results for a ResNet-50 on iNaturalist.

6   Conclusion

This work discussed the long-tailed recognition problem. A new augmentation framework, Breadcrumb, was proposed to increase feature variety and classifier robustness. Breadcrumb is based on EMANATE, a feature back-tracking procedure that aligns features vectors produced across several epochs of embedding training, to compose a class-balanced feature set for training the classifier at the top of the network. It is inspired by the recent success of class-balanced training schemes. However, unlike previous schemes, it is shown to be an adversarial sampling scheme, a property that encourages better generalization. A comparison of two sampling schemes based on EMANATE confirmed this property, resulting in best performance for the Strong Breadcrumb Sampling technique, where feature snapshots are collected while the embedding is evolving. Breadcrumb was shown to achieve state-of-the-art performance on three popular long-tailed datasets with different CNN backbones. Furthermore, Breadcrumb introduces no extra model, which means that it adds no computational overhead or convergence issues to the baseline model.

Acknowledgement. This work was partially funded by NSF awards IIS-1924937 and IIS-2041009. And the use of the Nautilus platform for some of the experiments discussed above. Gang Hua was supported partly by National Key R&D Program of China Grant 2018AAA0101400 and NSFC Grant 61629301.

References

1. Cao, K., Wei, C., Gaidon, A., Arechiga, N., Ma, T.: Learning imbalanced datasets with label-distribution-aware margin loss. In: Advances in Neural Information Processing Systems, pp. 1565–1576 (2019)
2. Chen, Z., Fu, Y., Wang, Y.X., Ma, L., Liu, W., Hebert, M.: Image deformation meta-networks for one-shot learning. In: Proceedings of the IEEE Conference on Computer Vision and Pattern Recognition, pp. 8680–8689 (2019)
3. Cui, Y., Jia, M., Lin, T.Y., Song, Y., Belongie, S.: Class-balanced loss based on effective number of samples. In: Proceedings of the IEEE Conference on Computer Vision and Pattern Recognition, pp. 9268–9277 (2019)
4. Deng, J., Dong, W., Socher, R., Li, L.J., Li, K., Fei-Fei, L.: ImageNet: a large-scale hierarchical image database. In: CVPR 2009 (2009)
5. Felix, R., Vijay Kumar, B.G., Reid, I., Carneiro, G.: Multi-modal cycle-consistent generalized zero-shot learning. In: Ferrari, V., Hebert, M., Sminchisescu, C., Weiss, Y. (eds.) ECCV 2018. LNCS, vol. 11210, pp. 21–37. Springer, Cham (2018). https://doi.org/10.1007/978-3-030-01231-1_2
6. Finn, C., Abbeel, P., Levine, S.: Model-agnostic meta-learning for fast adaptation of deep networks. In: Proceedings of the 34th International Conference on Machine Learning, vol. 70, pp. 1126–1135. JMLR. org (2017)
7. Finn, C., Xu, K., Levine, S.: Probabilistic model-agnostic meta-learning. In: Advances in Neural Information Processing Systems, pp. 9516–9527 (2018)
8. Gidaris, S., Komodakis, N.: Dynamic few-shot visual learning without forgetting. In: Proceedings of the IEEE Conference on Computer Vision and Pattern Recognition, pp. 4367–4375 (2018)

9. Goodfellow, I.J., Shlens, J., Szegedy, C.: Explaining and harnessing adversarial examples. arXiv preprint arXiv:1412.6572 (2014)

10. Hariharan, B., Girshick, R.: Low-shot visual recognition by shrinking and hallucinating features. In: Proceedings of the IEEE International Conference on Computer Vision, pp. 3018–3027 (2017)

11. He, K., Zhang, X., Ren, S., Sun, J.: Deep residual learning for image recognition. In: Proceedings of the IEEE Conference on Computer Vision and Pattern Recognition, pp. 770–778 (2016)

12. Hong, Y., Han, S., Choi, K., Seo, S., Kim, B., Chang, B.: Disentangling label distribution for long-tailed visual recognition. In: Proceedings of the IEEE/CVF Conference on Computer Vision and Pattern Recognition, pp. 6626–6636 (2021)

13. Huang, C., Li, Y., Chen, C.L., Tang, X.: Deep imbalanced learning for face recognition and attribute prediction. IEEE Trans. Pattern Anal. Mach. Intell. **42**, 2781–2794 (2019)

14. Kang, B., et al.: Decoupling representation and classifier for long-tailed recognition. In: Eighth International Conference on Learning Representations (ICLR) (2020)

15. Lin, T.Y., Goyal, P., Girshick, R., He, K., Dollár, P.: Focal loss for dense object detection. In: Proceedings of the IEEE International Conference on Computer Vision, pp. 2980–2988 (2017)

16. Liu, B., Wang, X., Dixit, M., Kwitt, R., Vasconcelos, N.: Feature space transfer for data augmentation. In: The IEEE Conference on Computer Vision and Pattern Recognition (CVPR) (2018)

17. Liu, J., Sun, Y., Han, C., Dou, Z., Li, W.: Deep representation learning on long-tailed data: a learnable embedding augmentation perspective. In: Proceedings of the IEEE/CVF Conference on Computer Vision and Pattern Recognition, pp. 2970–2979 (2020)

18. Liu, Z., Luo, P., Wang, X., Tang, X.: Deep learning face attributes in the wild. In: Proceedings of the IEEE International Conference on Computer Vision, pp. 3730–3738 (2015)

19. Liu, Z., Miao, Z., Zhan, X., Wang, J., Gong, B., Yu, S.X.: Large-scale long-tailed recognition in an open world. In: Proceedings of the IEEE Conference on Computer Vision and Pattern Recognition, pp. 2537–2546 (2019)

20. Maaten, L.V.D., Hinton, G.: Visualizing data using t-SNE. J. Mach. Learn. Res. **9**(Nov), 2579–2605 (2008)

21. Oh Song, H., Xiang, Y., Jegelka, S., Savarese, S.: Deep metric learning via lifted structured feature embedding. In: Proceedings of the IEEE Conference on Computer Vision and Pattern Recognition, pp. 4004–4012 (2016)

22. Qi, H., Brown, M., Lowe, D.G.: Low-shot learning with imprinted weights. In: Proceedings of the IEEE Conference on Computer Vision and Pattern Recognition, pp. 5822–5830 (2018)

23. Rusu, A.A., et al.: Meta-learning with latent embedding optimization. In: 7th International Conference on Learning Representations, ICLR 2019, New Orleans, LA, USA, 6–9 May 2019. OpenReview.net (2019). http://openreview.net/forum?id=BJgklhAcK7

24. Sharma, S., Yu, N., Fritz, M., Schiele, B.: Long-tailed recognition using class-balanced experts. arXiv preprint arXiv:2004.03706 (2020)

25. Snell, J., Swersky, K., Zemel, R.: Prototypical networks for few-shot learning. In: Advances in Neural Information Processing Systems, pp. 4077–4087 (2017)

26. Sung, F., Yang, Y., Zhang, L., Xiang, T., Torr, P.H., Hospedales, T.M.: Learning to compare: Relation network for few-shot learning. In: Proceedings of the IEEE Conference on Computer Vision and Pattern Recognition, pp. 1199–1208 (2018)

27. Tang, K., Huang, J., Zhang, H.: Long-tailed classification by keeping the good and removing the bad momentum causal effect. In: Advances in Neural Information Processing Systems, vol. 33, pp. 1513–1524 (2020)
28. Van Horn, G., et al.: The inaturalist species classification and detection dataset. In: Proceedings of the IEEE Conference on Computer Vision and Pattern Recognition, pp. 8769–8778 (2018)
29. Vinyals, O., Blundell, C., Lillicrap, T., Wierstra, D., et al.: Matching networks for one shot learning. In: Advances in Neural Information Processing Systems, pp. 3630–3638 (2016)
30. Wang, Y.X., Girshick, R., Hebert, M., Hariharan, B.: Low-shot learning from imaginary data. In: Proceedings of the IEEE Conference on Computer Vision and Pattern Recognition, pp. 7278–7286 (2018)
31. Wang, Y.-X., Hebert, M.: Learning to learn: model regression networks for easy small sample learning. In: Leibe, B., Matas, J., Sebe, N., Welling, M. (eds.) ECCV 2016. LNCS, vol. 9910, pp. 616–634. Springer, Cham (2016). https://doi.org/10.1007/978-3-319-46466-4_37
32. Wang, Y.X., Ramanan, D., Hebert, M.: Learning to model the tail. In: Advances in Neural Information Processing Systems, pp. 7029–7039 (2017)
33. Xian, Y., Lorenz, T., Schiele, B., Akata, Z.: Feature generating networks for zeroshot learning. In: Proceedings of the IEEE Conference on Computer Vision and Pattern Recognition, pp. 5542–5551 (2018)
34. Xian, Y., Sharma, S., Schiele, B., Akata, Z.: F-VAEGAN-D2: a feature generating framework for any-shot learning. In: Proceedings of the IEEE Conference on Computer Vision and Pattern Recognition, pp. 10275–10284 (2019)
35. Xiang, L., Ding, G., Han, J.: Learning from multiple experts: self-paced knowledge distillation for long-tailed classification. In: Vedaldi, A., Bischof, H., Brox, T., Frahm, J.-M. (eds.) ECCV 2020. LNCS, vol. 12350, pp. 247–263. Springer, Cham (2020). https://doi.org/10.1007/978-3-030-58558-7_15
36. Xie, S., Girshick, R., Dollár, P., Tu, Z., He, K.: Aggregated residual transformations for deep neural networks. In: Proceedings of the IEEE Conference on Computer Vision and Pattern Recognition, pp. 1492–1500 (2017)
37. Zhang, X., Fang, Z., Wen, Y., Li, Z., Qiao, Y.: Range loss for deep face recognition with long-tailed training data. In: Proceedings of the IEEE International Conference on Computer Vision, pp. 5409–5418 (2017)
38. Zhou, B., Lapedriza, A., Xiao, J., Torralba, A., Oliva, A.: Learning deep features for scene recognition using places database. In: Advances in Neural Information Processing Systems, pp. 487–495 (2014)
39. Zhou, B., Cui, Q., Wei, X.S., Chen, Z.M.: BBN: bilateral-branch network with cumulative learning for long-tailed visual recognition. In: Proceedings of the IEEE/CVF Conference on Computer Vision and Pattern Recognition, pp. 9719–9728 (2020)
40. Zhu, X., Anguelov, D., Ramanan, D.: Capturing long-tail distributions of object subcategories. In: Proceedings of the IEEE Conference on Computer Vision and Pattern Recognition, pp. 915–922 (2014)

Chairs Can Be Stood On: Overcoming Object Bias in Human-Object Interaction Detection

Guangzhi Wang[1], Yangyang Guo[2]($\boxtimes$), Yongkang Wong[2], and Mohan Kankanhalli[2]

[1] Institute of Data Science, National University of Singapore, Singapore, Singapore
`guangzhi.wang@u.nus.edu`
[2] School of Computing, National University of Singapore, Singapore, Singapore
`guoyang.eric@gmail.com, yongkang.wong@nus.edu.sg, mohan@comp.nus.edu.sg`

Abstract. Detecting Human-Object Interaction (HOI) in images is an important step towards high-level visual comprehension. Existing work often shed light on improving either human and object detection, or interaction recognition. However, due to the limitation of datasets, these methods tend to fit well on frequent interactions conditioned on the detected objects, yet largely ignoring the rare ones, which is referred to as the **object bias problem** in this paper. In this work, we for the first time, uncover the problem from two aspects: unbalanced interaction distribution and biased model learning. To overcome the object bias problem, we propose a novel plug-and-play Object-wise Debiasing Memory (ODM) method for re-balancing the distribution of interactions under detected objects. Equipped with carefully designed read and write strategies, the proposed ODM allows rare interaction instances to be more frequently sampled for training, thereby alleviating the object bias induced by the unbalanced interaction distribution. We apply this method to three advanced baselines and conduct experiments on the HICO-DET and HOI-COCO datasets. To quantitatively study the object bias problem, we advocate a new protocol for evaluating model performance. As demonstrated in the experimental results, our method brings consistent and significant improvements over baselines, especially on rare interactions under each object. In addition, when evaluating under the conventional standard setting, our method achieves new state-of-the-art on the two benchmarks.

1 Introduction

Benefiting from the advancement of visual detection systems, Human-Object Interaction (HOI) detection has drawn increasing research interests in recent years. It requires detecting both humans and objects in a given image, based

---

Supplementary Information The online version contains supplementary material available at https://doi.org/10.1007/978-3-031-20053-3_38.

S. Avidan et al. (Eds.): ECCV 2022, LNCS 13684, pp. 654–672, 2022.
https://doi.org/10.1007/978-3-031-20053-3_38

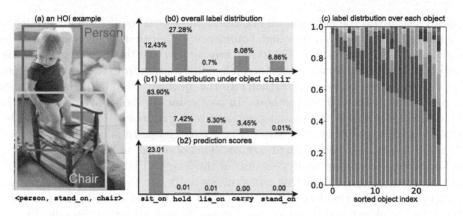

Fig. 1. An illustration of the object bias problem. Given the detected human-object pair in (a), the model [62] prediction (b2) is highly biased towards the object-conditional label distribution (b1), instead of the overall long-tail distribution in the training set (b0). As a result, the model predicts a more frequent verb `sit_on` for the object `chair`, leaving the true label `stand_on` ignored. (c) Label distribution from 25 randomly selected objects. It can be seen that most objects are dominated by one interaction (colored in blue). (Color figure online)

on which the interactions (often expressed as verb phrases) should also be correctly recognized. HOI detection is of vital importance to human-centric visual understanding and also benefits other high-level vision tasks, such as image captioning [29] and visual question answering [1,15].

Existing HOI detection efforts can be mainly categorized into two groups: two-stage and one-stage methods. Specifically, methods in the first group often leverage an off-the-shelf detector (*e.g.*, Faster R-CNN [42]) to initially detect the regions of humans and objects. The succeeding stage of interaction recognition can be enhanced with human part/pose understanding [10,18,30,49], graph-based message passing between humans and objects [12,41,47,52,62,67] or finer label space construction [27,64]. Some studies also exploit cross-dataset knowledge such as human-object interactiveness [32,33,56], cross-dataset objects [21] and word embeddings [57] to improve interaction recognition. Nonetheless, these approaches are often limited by deficiencies like inferior proposal generation or heavy inference overhead. To address these problems, one-stage methods often resort to performing detection and interaction classification within a single stage. Early studies treat HOI detection as a ⟨human, object, interaction⟩ point detection and matching [35,53,65] task. Recent approaches employ the Transformer-based detector [3] to aggregate contextual information and detect interaction in an anchor-free manner [5,25,44,60,68]. Nevertheless, increased training time is often encountered by this group of approaches.

Although existing methods have made progress over benchmarks, we observe one pervasive shortcoming that prevents them from further advancement. That is, the interaction prediction is strongly related to the detected object. Figure 1 shows that given the detected object chair in (a), the model predicts (b2) the wrong verb sit_on with a very high confidence, rather than yields the true action - stand_on. Previous studies [20,21,60] mostly perceive this phenomenon as the outcome of learning from the long-tail label distribution from the overall training set. Nevertheless, as we step further into this problem, we find it deviates a lot from the intuition of those methods. In particular, as shown in Fig. 1 (b0), the label hold dominates the training set and is twice frequent than sit_on. Out of expectation, the prediction score (Fig. 1 (b2)) for hold is only 0.01, which is 2,000 times smaller than that of sit_on. This observation brings our concern - is the wrong prediction really because of the long-tail label distribution in the overall training set? With this concern, we shift our focus to the interaction distribution under the detected object (Fig. 1 (b1)), and discover a strong bias between the object and its conditional interaction distribution. Specifically, the model prediction conforms more with such object-induced bias, rather than the bias caused by the overall long-tail label distribution. In view of this, we can infer that during training, the object-induced bias drives the model to fit well on frequent interactions under each object, while overlooking the rare ones. However, rare classes are often more informative than non-rare ones [45,55]. Simply ignoring them undermines the model's representation ability, resulting in poor generalization and limited real-world applicability. Nonetheless, to the best of our knowledge, this bias problem has not been explored in the existing literature. As most objects struggle with the biased interaction distribution (Fig. 1 (c)), we therefore humbly suggest this problem to the community, and name it as the *object bias problem* in this work.

As a matter of fact, dealing with this problem is non-trivial due to the inherent distribution imbalance in existing benchmarks. However, building a balanced dataset is time and labor intensive. One alternative solution is to feed the model with balanced samples during training, which has been extensively proved effective in previous studies [28,43,55]. Yet, directly applying these methods to HOI detection is sub-optimal, as the object bias problem is actually induced by the class imbalance *under each object*, rather than that of the overall training set. To this end, we propose a novel Object-wise Debiasing Memory (ODM) module to achieve object-conditional class balancing. The proposed ODM is implemented with an object-indexed memory, upon which read and write strategies are designed to support the retrieval and storage of HOI features and labels. For memory reading, we take the label of each interactive instance as query to retrieve instances from the memory. Our read strategy assures that rare class instances are more frequently sampled, leading to a more balanced label distribution within the batch for training. On the other hand, the writing strategy is devised to store rare class instances with higher probability. In this way, the unbalanced interaction distribution under each object is mitigated, thus reducing the influence of the *object bias problem*.

We conduct extensive experiments over two benchmark datasets, namely HICO-DET [4] and HOI-COCO [21]. In addition, we also advocate a new object bias evaluation protocol to quantitatively evaluate the model performance under the object-biased condition. When equipped with our method, several advanced baselines are evidently shown to overcome the object bias problem, thereby achieving improved performance.

To summarize, our contributions are three-fold:

- We systematically study the object bias problem in the HOI detection task. To the best of our knowledge, we are the first to recognize and address this problem in the HOI literature.
- To alleviate the object bias problem, we propose a novel ODM module to facilitate the learning of a balanced classifier. The proposed ODM is model-agnostic and applicable to both one-stage and two-stage methods.
- We conduct extensive experiments on benchmark datasets, namely HICO-DET [4] and HOI-COCO [21]. When applying our method to several baselines, significant performance improvements, especially on rare interactions under each object, can be observed. As a side product, we achieve new state-of-the-art performance on the two datasets[1].

2   Related Work

2.1   Human-Object Interaction Detection

HOI detection [4] is challenging since it requires both precise detection and complex interaction reasoning capabilities. Existing methods have achieved some progress and mainly fall into two groups: two-stage and one-stage methods.

Two-stage methods adopt an off-the-shelf detector to perform detection, followed by an interaction prediction model over each human-object pair [4,13,33,47]. Previous approaches mostly endeavor to improve visual feature quality for interaction classification. For example, Qi *et. al.* [41] builds a holistic graph to assist information flow for all humans and objects, and Zhang *et. al.* [62] devises a bipartite graph utilizing relative spatial relation to promote interaction understanding. Besides, compositional models factorize the verb and object classification branches to improve generalization [21,22,31]. Beyond the visual appearance, more complementary cues are explored for the second stage, such as human pose and parts [18,30,38], language embeddings [2,26,57] and external knowledge [19,32].

One-stage methods perform both detection and interaction classification in an end-to-end manner. Besides detecting human and object regions, earlier one stage methods exploit either human-object interaction points [35,53] or their union regions [24] as interaction clues. With the success of Transformer [48] for object detection [3], some methods   [5,25,44,60,68] present to formulate HOI detection as a set-prediction problem, where the anchor-free detection and attention-based global context aggregation are jointly operated.

Recently, some studies focus on the long-tail distribution problem in HOI detection benchmarks. For example, ATL [21] constructs new HOI instances

---

[1] Code available: https://github.com/daoyuan98/ODM.

from external object datasets in an affordance transfer fashion, while FCL [22] generates object features to fabricate more training samples. Besides, CDN [60] presents a dynamic re-weighting mechanism to tackle the long-tail problem. However, they mainly focus on the general long-tail distribution from the whole training set, leaving the *object bias problem* untouched in the literature.

2.2 Bias Identification and Mitigation

Previous practices on the bias problem mainly follow an identification then mitigation paradigm. Pertaining to the bias identification, Zhao *et.al.* [63] finds that the gender bias contained in datasets can be further amplified by the model trained on them. Manjunatha *et.al.* [39] explicitly discovers the bias in Visual Question Answering [1] via association rule mining, while Guo *et.al.* [16] alleviates the bias through loss re-scaling. Lately, Li and Xu [34] unearths unknown biased attributes of a classifier with generative models. To mitigate the bias problem, adversarial training [11] is employed to learn bias irrelevant representations [61]. Recently, Wang *et.al.* [54] benchmarks previous mitigation methods and presents a combination of domain-conditional models for de-biasing, while Choi *et.al.* [8] tackles the unbalanced distribution with the weak supervision from a small reference dataset.

3   Object Bias Identification

The *object bias problem* in HOI detection refers to predicting interactions based on the unbalanced label distribution under each object. In the following, we demonstrate that the *object bias* problem comes from two aspects: (1) the conditionally unbalanced label distribution induced by objects and (2) the biased model training on the datasets.

3.1   Unbalanced Verb Distribution

The objective of HOI detection is to detect and classify ⟨human, verb, object⟩ triplets, where the most challenging and crucial part is verb classification.[2]

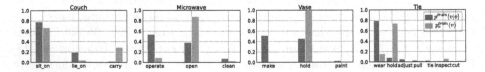

Fig. 2. Comparison between the object-conditional verb distribution $p^{train}(v|o)$ and the overall re-normalized distribution $p_o^{train}(v)$ for four objects in the training set of HICO-DET [4].

---

[2] With the detected object, verb classification is required to recognize the interaction.

Denote the whole verb set as $\mathcal{V}$, $\mathcal{V}_o$ for object o represents a subset of all verbs, i.e., $\mathcal{V}_o \in \mathcal{V}$ and $|\mathcal{V}_o| < |\mathcal{V}|$. We use $p(v|o)$ to represent the verb distribution conditioned on object o, and $p_o(v)$ to signify the global verb distribution involving only verbs for object o in the training set. The latter is employed to re-normalize the number of verbs associated with o, leaving other irrelevant verbs unaffected. From Fig. 2, we can observe that these two distributions are both skewed and actually different from each other. Besides, a globally frequent class can be a rare one after object conditioning and vice versa. For example, hold is the most frequent verb from a global view, while the object vase sees verb make most (Fig. 2). It thus brings our question: among these two long-tailed distributions, which one dominates more for the final verb classification?

3.2 Biased Model Learning

To delineate the second aspect, we exemplarily study the behavior of the state-of-the-art model SCG [62] on the HICO-DET dataset. Denote $\hat{y}(v|o)$ as the averaged verb score output by SCG conditioned on object o, and $p^{test}(v|o)$ as the counterpart of $p^{train}(v|o)$ on the test set. We compare them in Fig. 3 (a) and observe that $\hat{y}(v|o)$ pays less attention to conditionally rare classes in the training set (e.g., paint for vase, clean for microwave). In contrast, conditionally frequent classes (e.g., operate for microwave, wear for tie and sit on for couch) gain higher scores regardless of their prediction correctness. To quantify how much *bias* the model has learned, we compute the Jensen-Shannon Divergence [36] between $\hat{y}(v|o)$ and $p_o^{train}(v)$, $p^{train}(v|o)$, $p^{test}(v|o)$ and visualize them in Fig. 3 (b). We can see that $\hat{y}(v|o)$ is closer to $p^{train}(v|o)$ than $p_o^{train}(v)$, indicating the model leans towards the object-conditional statistics, rather than the overall label distribution in the training set. Besides, $\hat{y}(v|o)$ is even more similar to $p^{train}(v|o)$ than the ground-truth distribution $p^{test}(v|o)$. This implies, if we can counteract the learning of the *object bias*, there is a large potential of performance improvements with existing methods.

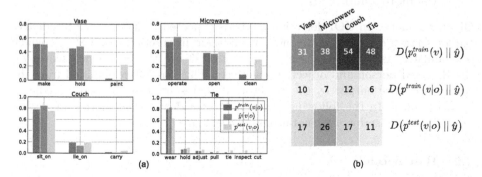

Fig. 3. (a) The model output analysis of SCG [62] on HICO-DET [4] test set with four objects. We show the difference between conditional training distribution $p^{train}(v|o)$, averaged model output $\hat{y}(v|o)$ and the ground-truth conditional verb distribution $p^{test}(v|o)$. (b) The Jensen-Shannon divergence [36] is utilized to compute the distribution distance. Note that the values are increased 100x for better illustration.

3.3 Comparison with Other Biases

Long-tail in HOI Detection We notice that some prior efforts [20,21,60] have studied the long-tail problem in HOI detection. Nevertheless, the *object bias problem* presented in this paper is intrinsically and technically different from the long-tail one. On the one hand, the object-conditional distribution can be distinct from the overall long-tail distribution. For example, hold is the most frequent verb across the whole dataset but less frequent in some objects (Fig. 2). On the other hand, the model prediction tends to conform with the object-conditional label distribution, rather than the overall one. Combing these two sides, we thus introduce the *object bias problem* to the community and expect more insightful findings along this line.

Bias in Scene Graph Generation (SGG). It is worth noting that the bias problem in the sister task - SGG, is also different from the *object bias problem*. In fact, mainstream studies in SGG debiasing [7,46,58] mainly focus on the overall class imbalance, which is essentially same as the long-tail problem in HOI detection. The most relevant work to ours is [59]. It leverages the most frequent predicate under subject-object pair for relation prediction, which is shown to be a strong baseline on benchmark dataset. However, there are two key differences between [59] and our work: 1) [59] focuses on relational bias from the data's perspective only, while we provide a comprehensive study across the aspects of the dataset, model behavior and evaluation protocol. 2) [59] leverages the training set statistics to conduct prediction. However, when deploying the method to another dataset or other out-of-distribution settings, degraded performance is expected, as it severely overfits specific training set [6,46]. By contrast, we design a novel debiasing method to counteract the object bias during training, which is detailed in the following section.

4 Object Bias Alleviation

4.1 Problem Definition

Given an image, an HOI detection model is expected to detect each interactive triplet ⟨human, verb, object⟩ and output their interaction score $s^{h,v,o}$, which is calculated as $s^{h,v,o} = s^v \cdot s^h \cdot s^o$. s^h and s^o are the confidence scores for the detected person and object, respectively. They are often obtained from the confidence score output by the detector. s^v represents the verb score predicted by a classifier. In the following, we mainly consider the calculation of s^v and omit the upper-script v for notational convenience.

4.2 Base Model

In this work, we consider a generic HOI detection model, as shown in the left part of Fig. 4. It takes as input an image, detects all humans and objects, and links each human-object pair. Thereafter, with message passing or context aggregation, a set of human-object pair representations, i.e., the HOI features $\{\mathbf{x}_i^o\}_{i=1}^N$

are obtained, where N denotes the number of human-object pairs. Each feature $\mathbf{x}_i^o$ captures the interaction relation between a human and an object of class o.

We then feed these features into a classifier f_b to predict verb scores: $\mathbf{s}_i = \sigma(f_b(\mathbf{x}_i^o))$, where $\sigma(\cdot)$ is a sigmoid function. Note that there can be multiple or no interactions within one human-object pair. Thus, the verb recognition is usually formulated as a multi-label classification problem. The objective of the base model is formulated as follows:

$$\mathcal{L} = \sum_{i=1}^{N} \mathcal{L}_b^{bce}(\mathbf{s}_i, \mathbf{v}_i^o) + \mathcal{L}_{aux}, \tag{1}$$

where $\mathbf{v}_i^o$ denotes the ground-truth label involving object o, $\mathcal{L}_b^{bce}$ is the binary cross entropy loss for verb classification and $\mathcal{L}_{aux}$ corresponds to other objectives of the base model such as interactiveness prediction and object localization. As discussed before, the base model often severely suffers from the *object bias problem*. To overcome this issue, we design a novel Object-wise Debiasing Memory module which has minimal influence to the reasoning process of the base model and is plugable to any existing HOI detection methods.

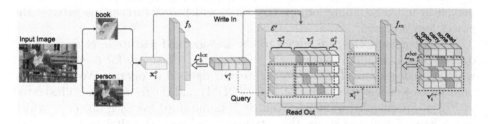

Fig. 4. Overview of the proposed method. Given an image, an HOI detection model extracts HOI features for each human-object pair. A memory cell $\mathcal{E}^o$ is maintained for each object o. During training, instances are conditionally read and written into its respective cell with label-awareness. We show one human object pair ($o = \texttt{book}$) for clearance.

4.3   Object-Wise Debiasing Memory

It is widely accepted that instances from rare classes contain richer information for interaction understanding [23,45,55]. However, as discussed in Sect. 3, frequent verb classes under each object dominate the prediction results, while other informative but rare ones are often ignored. In view of this, we propose to re-sample HOI instances with a re-balancing strategy. In general, re-sampling has been shown to be an effective technique for class unbalance mitigation [28,43,55]. However, in HOI detection, it is infeasible to directly apply these techniques. On the one hand, the object bias problem is induced by object-conditional unbalance, rather than the overall one, which is distinct from the traditional class-imbalance scenario. On the other hand, there can be multiple human-object

---

Algorithm 1. Read and Write Strategy for $\mathcal{E}^o$

// Read Strategy

Input: HOI instance $\{\mathbf{x}, \mathbf{v}\}$, number of required samples k

Output: k HOI instances and labels

    features $= [\mathbf{x}]$; labels $= [\mathbf{v}]$

    while number of sampled features $< k$ **do**

        // pick rare class entries when not selected

        $j = argmax_j \; \sum_i dist(\text{labels}[i], \mathcal{E}^o[j])$ (Eq. 2)

        Append $\mathbf{x}_j, \mathbf{v}_j$ to features, labels

    return features, labels

// Write Strategy

Input: HOI instance $\{\mathbf{x}, \mathbf{v}\}$, generation time a

    if $\mathcal{E}^o$ is not full **then**

        Append $\{\mathbf{x}, \mathbf{v}, a\}$ to $\mathcal{E}^o$

    else:

        if $score(\mathbf{v}^o) \geq \tau^o$ (Eq. 3) **then**

            Replace entry of the longest duration with $\{\mathbf{x}, \mathbf{v}, a\}$.

---

interactions within a single image, simply re-sampling one image with rare classes may lead to oversampling of non-rare ones, which may further exacerbates the *object bias problem*.

To circumvent this, we resort to the fine-grained feature-level re-sampling during model training. Accordingly, we maintain a memory for each object, on which an effective read and write strategy is devised to operate. We name this module Object-wise Debiasing Memory (ODM) and the framework is illustrated in Fig. 4. Specifically, a memory cell $\mathcal{E}^o$ is maintained for each object o, which has a fixed size n and stores three types of elements: the HOI feature $\mathbf{x}_j^o$, the verb label $\mathbf{v}_j^o$ and the feature generation time a_j^o. During training, each ODM cell is sampled (read out) with label awareness, followed by a dynamic update (write in) operation to ensure feature consistency. The pseudo-code for read and write strategy is shown in Algorithm 1 and detailed as follows.

Read Strategy. To achieve verb balance under each object, it makes sense to assign high sampling priority to rare class instances. At each training step, given an interactive HOI feature $\mathbf{x}_i^o$ with verb label $\mathbf{v}_i^o$, we take $\mathbf{v}_i^o$ as query and sample a set of k HOI instances $\{\mathbf{x}_j^o, \mathbf{v}_j^o\}_{j=1}^k$ from the memory $\mathcal{E}^o$ such that the label distribution after sampling is less skewed. To that end, we select from the memory with the largest weighted hamming distance, which is calculated as:

$$dist(\mathbf{v}_1^o, \mathbf{v}_2^o) = \sum_{t=1}^c w_t^o \cdot (\mathbf{v}_1^o[t] \oplus \mathbf{v}_2^o[t]), \qquad (2)$$

where $\oplus$ means XOR operation, $[\cdot]$ is subscription and w_t^o is a weighting coefficient of the t-th class associated with object o. Firstly, the hamming distance is employed to consider absent classes with respect to selected instance [14]. Secondly, the weighting mechanism ensures dynamic control over certain classes. Specifically, we calculate w_t^o as $N_o/N_{v,o}$, where N_o and $N_{v,o}$ denotes the number of object o and interaction $\langle v, o \rangle$ in the training set. By designing w_t^o as inverse interaction frequency within object o, rare class instances are prioritized and thus more frequently sampled from the memory. In addition, we perform iterative sampling to avoid all selected samples are from the same class.

Write Strategy. During the writing stage, it is expected to store more rare class instances to ensure the sample complexity for memory reading. Specifically, we treat one instance as write-feasible if its hamming score for a multi-hot label is greater than a threshold τ^o. The hamming score is given by:

$$score(\mathbf{v}_j^o) = \sum_{t=1}^{c} w_t^o \cdot \mathbf{v}_j^o[t], \qquad (3)$$

where c is the number of verb classes and w_t^o is the same weighting coefficient as that in Eq. 2. With this strategy, non-rare instances will not be written into the memory, thereby alleviating the risk of their dominance for model training. When the memory is full, we replace the feature of the longest duration with write-feasible instances, so as to ensure timely update of memory contents.

4.4   Training and Inference

The proposed memory operations serve as an ad-hoc re-sampling approach to ensure more balanced training at each iteration. After reading from the memory, we then leverage another classifier f_m to perform more balanced interaction classification. Inspired by recent work on class-imbalanced learning [23,51,66], we combine f_m with the base classifier f_b to achieve a trade-off between the debiasing and representation capability. The overall objective is defined as follows:

$$\mathcal{L} = \sum_{i=1}^{N} \mathcal{L}_b^{bce}(\mathbf{s}_i, \mathbf{v}_i^o) + \mathcal{L}_m^{bce}(\mathbf{s}_i^+, \mathbf{v}_i^{o+}) + \mathcal{L}_{aux}, \qquad (4)$$

where $\mathbf{x}_i^{o+} = [\mathbf{x}_i^o; \{\mathbf{x}_j^o\}_{j=1}^k]$ and $\mathbf{v}_i^{o+} = [\mathbf{v}_i^o; \{\mathbf{v}_j^o\}_{j=1}^k]$ are obtained after the read operation and $\mathbf{s}_i^+ = f_m(\mathbf{x}_i^{o+})$.

During inference, given an HOI feature $\mathbf{x}_i$, we take the weighted combination of these two classifiers' output as the final prediction:

$$\hat{\mathbf{v}}_i = \sigma\big(\lambda f_b(\mathbf{x}_i) + (1 - \lambda)f_m(\mathbf{x}_i)\big), \qquad (5)$$

where λ is a hyper-parameter balancing the two classifiers.

Table 1. Performance comparison under object-bias setting on HICO-DET. OR and ONR denote **O**bject-**R**are and **O**bject-**N**on**R**are, respectively.

Detector	Pre-trained detector				Fine-tuned detector				Oracle detector	
Method	HOID [50]	+Ours	SCG [62]	+Ours	QPIC [44]	+Ours	SCG	+Ours	SCG	+Ours
OR	17.05	**19.02**	18.38	**19.47**	26.29	**26.96**	28.67	**30.21**	51.03	**52.48**
ONR	24.24	**24.33**	**25.06**	25.01	34.64	**34.65**	40.72	**41.08**	73.97	**75.43**
AVE	20.65	**21.17**	21.72	**22.24**	30.47	**30.81**	34.69	**35.64**	62.50	**63.95**

5   Experiments

5.1   Experimental Setting

Dataset. We conducted experiments on two benchmarks: HICO-DET [4] and HOI-COCO [21]. **HICO-DET** is the most widely employed benchmark in HOI detection. It consists of 38,118 and 9,658 images in the training and test set, respectively. HICO-DET covers the whole 80 object classes in MS-COCO [37] and 117 verb classes, resulting in a total of 600 HOI categories in the form of ⟨person, verb, object⟩. **HOI-COCO** is a recently introduced dataset based on V-COCO [17]. It has a total of 9,915 images, with 4,969 for training and 4,946 for test. There are 222 HOI categories composed of 21 verb classes from V-COCO and 80 MS-COCO object classes.

Baselines. As our goal is to prove the superiority and versatility of the proposed method, we applied our approach to three existing methods: HOID [50], SCG [62] and QPIC [44]. **HOID** generates human-centric object proposal for interactive objects only. **SCG** is a recently proposed two-stage method leveraging spatial information for graph-based message propagation. It achieves state-of-the-art performance with both fine-tuned and ground-truth detection among two-stage methods. **QPIC** is an advanced one-stage method, which utilizes Transformer architecture to perform query-based detection and classification.

Standard Evaluation Metrics. We followed the standard evaluation setting [4] and reported mean average precision (mAP) for both datasets, where the mAP on rare (less than 10 training instances), non-rare and full classes are reported. For both settings, a prediction is regarded as positive if (1) the HOI classification is correct and (2) the detected human and object bounding boxes have IoUs greater than 0.5 with the ground-truth bounding box.

Object-Bias Evaluation Metric. To quantitatively study how much object bias has been alleviated by our method, we propose a new *object bias* evaluation setting. Specifically, we treated an interaction class as *object rare* (*object non-rare*) if $N_{v,o}/N_o < (\geq) \alpha$. On HICO-DET dataset, we set α to 0.3 based on its statistics. Note that an originally non-rare class in the whole training set can be *object rare* under this setting. For each object, we computed the mean of Average Precision (AP) for *object rare* and *object non-rare* classes, respectively. After that, we averaged across all objects to obtain mean Average Precision

Table 2. Results on HICO-DET with *pre-trained* detector.

Method	Full	Rare	Non-rare
iCAN [13]	14.84	10.45	16.15
TIN [32]	17.03	13.42	18.11
DRG [12]	19.26	17.74	19.71
VCL [20]	19.43	16.55	20.29
ACP [26]	20.59	15.92	21.98
DJ-RN [30]	21.34	**18.53**	22.18
HOID* [50]	19.58	15.29	20.96
+Ours	20.45	16.18	21.73
SCG* [62]	20.99	16.30	22.40
+Ours	**21.50**	17.59	**22.67**

Table 3. Results on HICO-DET with *fine-tuned* detector.

Method	Full	Rare	Non-rare
PPDM [35]	21.73	13.78	24.10
HOI-Trans [68]	23.46	16.91	25.41
ATL [21]	27.68	20.31	29.89
AS-Net [5]	28.87	24.25	30.25
FCL [22]	29.12	23.67	30.75
QPIC* [44]	29.04	21.55	31.27
QPIC + Ours	29.26	22.07	31.41
SCG* [62]	31.08	24.14	33.15
SCG + Ours	**31.65**	**24.95**	**33.65**

for **O**bject-**R**are (OR) and **O**bject-**N**on**R**are (ONR), respectively. Besides, their **AVE**rage is also reported. Different from the traditional evaluation, the *object bias* evaluation protocol considers the performance within each object and thus offers a better test bed for quantifying a model's ability to overcome the *object bias* problem.

5.2   Object Bias Evaluation

The results under the new *object bias* setting are shown in Table 1. With SCG as baseline, our method significantly improves *object rare* classes by a clear margin of +**1.09** mAP, +**1.54** mAP and +**1.45** mAP under three detection settings. Besides, the proposed method also boosts HOID and QPIC by +**0.97** mAP and +**0.67** mAP under OR setting. This provides evidence that our method can effectively alleviate the object bias problem. Notably, the proposed module can also improve ONR classes in most cases.

5.3   Standard Evaluation

Results on HICO-DET. We followed [62] to report the results with *detector pre-trained on MS-COCO* [37] (HOID and SCG), *detector find-tuned on HICO-DET* (SCG and QPIC) and *oracle detector* (SCG). The results can be found in Tables 2, 3 and 4, respectively.

Our method improves the performance of all three baseline methods across all detection settings. For instance, with pre-trained detector, our method promotes HOID and SCG by +**0.89** and +**1.29** mAP on rare classes, respectively, which amounts to **6**% and **8**% relative improvements. When leveraging fine-tuned detector, the proposed approach can improve QPIC and SCG on rare classes by +**0.52** and +**0.81** mAP. In particular, with the detection quality improved, our method also enhances non-rare classes by a noticeable margin.

Lastly, with the oracle detector, the proposed method can advance SCG on both rare (**+1.22** mAP) and non-rare classes (**+1.26** mAP). These results demonstrate the superiority of the proposed method. As a side product, we achieve new state-of-the-art on the HICO-DET dataset.

Table 4. Results on HICO-DET with *oracle detector.*

Method	Full	Rare	Non-rare
iCAN [13]	33.38	21.43	36.95
TIN [32]	34.26	22.90	37.65
Peyre *et al.* [40]	34.35	27.57	36.38
FCL [22]	44.26	35.46	46.88
SCG* [62]	51.03	38.93	54.65
SCG + Ours	**52.29**	**40.15**	**55.91**

Table 5. Results on the HOI-COCO. * indicates reproduced baseline.

Method	Full	Rare	Non-rare
Baseline [21]	22.86	6.87	35.27
+VCL [20]	23.53	8.29	35.36
+ATL [21]	23.40	8.01	35.34
Baseline*	22.87	6.98	35.21
+CDN [60]	23.15	7.25	**35.49**
+Ours	**23.73**	**8.58**	**35.49**

Results on HOI-COCO. We followed [21] to provide results with MS-COCO pre-trained detector, which is the most typical setting for two-stage methods. The results are shown in Table 5. For fair comparison, we reproduced the baseline method used in ATL [21]. We also compared with the debiasing technique applied in CDN [60], which aims to alleviate the general long-tail problem. It can be observed that our method outperforms these debiasing methods on this relatively small scale dataset, especially for rare classes.

5.4 Ablation Studies

We studied the effectiveness of our proposed method. All experiments are conducted on HICO-DET dataset with the SCG [62] baseline, and evaluated under both standard protocol and the proposed *object bias* setting.

Comparison with Other Debiasing Methods. We compared our method with various debiasing methods in Table 6. The competitors include loss reweighting methods, general debiasing methods and Scene Graph Generation (SGG) debiasing methods. We observed all these methods degrade the original baselines. This may be related to the strong interference with the original training process. Besides, some methods are designed to tackle the globally long-tail problem and single-label classification, thus incapable of resolving the object-conditional long-tail problem in HOI detection.

Efficacy of Classifiers. The distinctive importance of the verb classifier in the base model (f_b), the one trained with ODM (f_m) and the full classifier ($\lambda f_b + (1 - \lambda) f_m$) are explored in this experiment. From the results in Table 7,

Table 6. Comparsion with debiasing methods.

Type	Method	Full	Rare	Non-rare	OR	ONR	AVE
	Baseline	20.99	16.30	22.40	18.38	**25.06**	21.70
Reweighting	+inv. freq	17.58	14.15	18.61	9.77	21.01	15.39
	+CB-Loss(0.9999) [9]	14.30	13.54	14.53	9.93	21.48	15.71
	+CB-Loss(0.999) [9]	13.34	12.96	13.45	9.02	20.73	14.88
	+CB-Loss(0.99) [9]	13.98	13.20	14.21	9.46	20.98	15.22
General	+AT [54]	20.49	16.22	21.77	18.12	24.46	21.29
Debiasing	+DIT [54]	18.13	16.99	18.47	17.35	23.05	20.20
SGG	+TDE [46]	20.44	14.89	22.10	18.30	24.44	21.37
Debiasing	+PCPL [58]	16.93	12.95	18.12	15.04	24.27	19.65
	+Ours	**21.50**	**17.59**	**22.67**	**19.47**	25.01	**22.24**

Table 7. Performance of different classifiers on HICO-DET.

Detector	Classifier	Full	Rare	Non-rare	OR	ONR	AVE
Pre-trained on MS-COCO	f_b	21.08	16.66	22.40	19.00	24.38	21.69
	f_m	20.79	16.50	22.08	18.59	24.87	21.73
	$full$	**21.50**	**17.59**	**22.67**	**19.47**	**25.01**	**22.24**
Fine-tuned on HICO-DET	f_b	31.24	24.77	33.17	30.04	40.62	35.33
	f_m	30.60	23.30	32.77	29.43	40.79	35.11
	$full$	**31.65**	**24.95**	**33.65**	**30.21**	**41.08**	**35.64**
Oracle	f_b	51.24	39.27	54.82	51.81	74.73	63.27
	f_m	51.09	37.94	55.01	51.28	75.15	63.21
	$full$	**52.29**	**40.15**	**55.91**	**52.48**	**75.43**	**63.95**

we see that for all three detectors, f_m is inferior to f_b on both evaluation protocols. However, when combining these two together, the final performance can be further promoted. This is mainly because these two classifiers focus on different classes and are in fact complementary to each other.

5.5 Visualizations

Effects of Memory. We studied how the proposed ODM alleviates the distribution imbalance and illustrated the evolution of verb distribution after reading from the memory in Fig. 5. With these examples, we can conclude that our method can effectively address the label imbalance problem under each object. Especially, at the 2500-th iteration, the verb distribution is already less skewed, which remains stable till the end of this epoch ($\sim$4.5k iterations).

Qualitative Results. We show some qualitative results in Fig. 6. For the two false negative instances (top two), the baseline model assigns low score to ground-truth interactions, wherein both involved verbs are conditionally rare

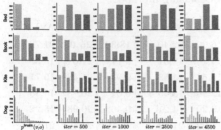

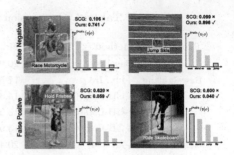

Fig. 5. The evolution of accumulated verb distribution after reading from the proposed ODM for 4 randomly selected objects. The leftmost column shows $p^{train}(v|o)$ and the other 4 columns represent the sampled verb distribution at different iterations.

Fig. 6. False negative (top two) and false positive (bottom two) instances from the SCG baseline on HICO-DET test set. For each instance, the $p^{train}(v|o)$ is also shown, where the involved verb is bold by a rectangular.

in the training set (`race` for `motorcycle`, `jump` for `skis`). For the false positive instances (bottom two), the baseline favors more frequent verbs (`hold` for `frisbee`, `ride` for `skateboard`), though the interaction prediction is incorrect. In contrast, our method can overcome these two kinds of errors and achieve better performance.

6   Conclusion and Future Work

In this work, we systematically studied the *object bias* problem in Human-Object Interaction detection. We demonstrated the recognition of this problem from the aspects of unbalanced label distribution and biased model learning, and advocated a new protocol to comprehensively evaluate model performance. To reduce the heavily skewed label distribution under each object, we proposed an Object-wise Debiasing Memory to facilitate balanced sampling of HOI instances. Extensive experiments validate the effectiveness of the proposed method, demonstrating that it can significantly alleviate the *object bias problem* and outperform advanced baselines with large margins. Due to the universal existence of the *bias problem*, in the future, we plan to explore identifying bias factors in other related tasks such as visual relation detection and scene graph generation.

Acknowledgement. This research is supported by the National Research Foundation, Singapore under its Strategic Capability Research Centres Funding Initiative. Any opinions, findings and conclusions or recommendations expressed in this material are those of the author(s) and do not reflect the views of National Research Foundation, Singapore.

References

1. Antol, S., et al.: VQA: visual question answering. In: ICCV (2015)
2. Bansal, A., Rambhatla, S.S., Shrivastava, A., Chellappa, R.: Detecting human-object interactions via functional generalization. In: AAAI (2020)
3. Carion, N., Massa, F., Synnaeve, G., Usunier, N., Kirillov, A., Zagoruyko, S.: End-to-End object detection with transformers. In: Vedaldi, A., Bischof, H., Brox, T., Frahm, J.-M. (eds.) ECCV 2020. LNCS, vol. 12346, pp. 213–229. Springer, Cham (2020). https://doi.org/10.1007/978-3-030-58452-8_13
4. Chao, Y.W., Liu, Y., Liu, X., Zeng, H., Deng, J.: Learning to detect human-object interactions. In: WACV (2018)
5. Chen, M., Liao, Y., Liu, S., Chen, Z., Wang, F., Qian, C.: Reformulating hoi detection as adaptive set prediction. In: CVPR (2021)
6. Chen, T., Yu, W., Chen, R., Lin, L.: Knowledge-embedded routing network for scene graph generation. In: CVPR (2019)
7. Chiou, M.J., Ding, H., Yan, H., Wang, C., Zimmermann, R., Feng, J.: Recovering the unbiased scene graphs from the biased ones. In: ACM MM (2021)
8. Choi, K., Grover, A., Singh, T., Shu, R., Ermon, S.: Fair generative modeling via weak supervision. In: ICML (2020)
9. Cui, Y., Jia, M., Lin, T.Y., Song, Y., Belongie, S.: Class-balanced loss based on effective number of samples. In: CVPR (2019)
10. Dong, Q., Tu, Z., Liao, H., Zhang, Y., Mahadevan, V., Soatto, S.: Visual relationship detection using part-and-sum transformers with composite queries. In: ICCV (2021)
11. Ganin, Y., Lempitsky, V.: Unsupervised domain adaptation by backpropagation. In: ICML (2015)
12. Gao, C., Xu, J., Zou, Y., Huang, J.-B.: DRG: dual relation graph for human-object interaction detection. In: Vedaldi, A., Bischof, H., Brox, T., Frahm, J.-M. (eds.) ECCV 2020. LNCS, vol. 12357, pp. 696–712. Springer, Cham (2020). https://doi.org/10.1007/978-3-030-58610-2_41
13. Gao, C., Zou, Y., Huang, J.B.: iCAN: instance-centric attention network for human-object interaction detection. In: BMVC (2018)
14. Gordo, A., Perronnin, F., Gong, Y., Lazebnik, S.: Asymmetric distances for binary embeddings. In: IEEE TPAMI (2013)
15. Guo, Y., Cheng, Z., Nie, L., Liu, Y., Wang, Y., Kankanhalli, M.: Quantifying and alleviating the language prior problem in visual question answering. In: SIGIR (2019)
16. Guo, Y., Nie, L., Cheng, Z., Tian, Q., Zhang, M.: Loss re-scaling vqa: revisiting the language prior problem from a class-imbalance view. In: IEEE TIP (2021)
17. Gupta, S., Malik, J.: Visual semantic role labeling. arXiv preprint arXiv:1505.04474 (2015)
18. Gupta, T., Schwing, A., Hoiem, D.: No-frills human-object interaction detection: factorization, layout encodings, and training techniques. In: ICCV (2019)
19. He, T., Gao, L., Song, J., Li, Y.F.: Exploiting scene graphs for human-object interaction detection. In: ICCV (2021)
20. Hou, Z., Peng, X., Qiao, Yu., Tao, D.: Visual compositional learning for human-object interaction detection. In: Vedaldi, A., Bischof, H., Brox, T., Frahm, J.-M. (eds.) ECCV 2020. LNCS, vol. 12360, pp. 584–600. Springer, Cham (2020). https://doi.org/10.1007/978-3-030-58555-6_35

21. Hou, Z., Yu, B., Qiao, Y., Peng, X., Tao, D.: Affordance transfer learning for human-object interaction detection. In: CVPR (2021)
22. Hou, Z., Yu, B., Qiao, Y., Peng, X., Tao, D.: Detecting human-object interaction via fabricated compositional learning. In: CVPR (2021)
23. Kang, B., Xie, S., Rohrbach, M., Yan, Z., Gordo, A., Feng, J., Kalantidis, Y.: Decoupling representation and classifier for long-tailed recognition. In: ICLR (2020)
24. Kim, B., Choi, T., Kang, J., Kim, H.J.: UnionDet: union-level detector towards real-time human-object interaction detection. In: Vedaldi, A., Bischof, H., Brox, T., Frahm, J.-M. (eds.) ECCV 2020. LNCS, vol. 12360, pp. 498–514. Springer, Cham (2020). https://doi.org/10.1007/978-3-030-58555-6_30
25. Kim, B., Lee, J., Kang, J., Kim, E.S., Kim, H.J.: HOTR: End-to-end human-object interaction detection with transformers. In: CVPR (2021)
26. Kim, D.-J., Sun, X., Choi, J., Lin, S., Kweon, I.S.: Detecting human-object interactions with action co-occurrence priors. In: Vedaldi, A., Bischof, H., Brox, T., Frahm, J.-M. (eds.) ECCV 2020. LNCS, vol. 12366, pp. 718–736. Springer, Cham (2020). https://doi.org/10.1007/978-3-030-58589-1_43
27. Kim, D.J., Sun, X., Choi, J., Lin, S., Kweon, I.S.: Acp++: action co-occurrence priors for human-object interaction detection. In: IEEE TIP (2021)
28. Li, Y., Vasconcelos, N.: Repair: removing representation bias by dataset resampling. In: CVPR (2019)
29. Li, Y., Ouyang, W., Zhou, B., Wang, K., Wang, X.: Scene graph generation from objects, phrases and region captions. In: ICCV (2017)
30. Li, Y.L., et al.: Detailed 2d–3d joint representation for human-object interaction. In: CVPR (2020)
31. Li, Y.L., Liu, X., Wu, X., Li, Y., Lu, C.: HOI analysis: integrating and decomposing human-object interaction. In: NeurIPS (2020)
32. Li, Y.L., et al.: Transferable interactiveness knowledge for human-object interaction detection. In: CVPR (2019)
33. Li, Y., Liu, X., Wu, X., Huang, X., Xu, L., Lu, C.: Transferable interactiveness knowledge for human-object interaction detection. In: IEEE TPAMI (2021)
34. Li, Z., Xu, C.: Discover the unknown biased attribute of an image classifier. In: ICCV (2021)
35. Liao, Y., Liu, S., Wang, F., Chen, Y., Qian, C., Feng, J.: PPDM: parallel point detection and matching for real-time human-object interaction detection. In: CVPR (2020)
36. Lin, J.: Divergence measures based on the shannon entropy. IEEE Trans. Inf. Theor. **37**(1), 145–151 (1991)
37. Lin, T.Y., et al.: Microsoft COCO: common objects in context. In: Fleet, D., Pajdla, T., Schiele, B., Tuytelaars, T. (eds.) ECCV 2014. LNCS, vol. 8693, pp. 740–755. Springer, Cham (2014). https://doi.org/10.1007/978-3-319-10602-1_48
38. Liu, Y., Chen, Q., Zisserman, A.: Amplifying key cues for human-object-interaction detection. In: ECCV (2020)
39. Manjunatha, V., Saini, N., Davis, L.S.: Explicit bias discovery in visual question answering models. In: CVPR (2019)
40. Peyre, J., Laptev, I., Schmid, C., Sivic, J.: Detecting unseen visual relations using analogies. In: ICCV (2019)
41. Qi, S., Wang, W., Jia, B., Shen, J., Zhu, S.-C.: Learning human-object interactions by graph parsing neural networks. In: Ferrari, V., Hebert, M., Sminchisescu, C., Weiss, Y. (eds.) ECCV 2018. LNCS, vol. 11213, pp. 407–423. Springer, Cham (2018). https://doi.org/10.1007/978-3-030-01240-3_25

42. Ren, S., He, K., Girshick, R., Sun, J.: Faster R-CNN: towards real-time object detection with region proposal networks. In: NIPS (2015)
43. Shen, L., Lin, Z., Huang, Q.: Relay backpropagation for effective learning of deep convolutional neural networks. In: Leibe, B., Matas, J., Sebe, N., Welling, M. (eds.) ECCV 2016. LNCS, vol. 9911, pp. 467–482. Springer, Cham (2016). https://doi.org/10.1007/978-3-319-46478-7_29
44. Tamura, M., Ohashi, H., Yoshinaga, T.: QPIC: query-based pairwise human-object interaction detection with image-wide contextual information. In: CVPR (2021)
45. Tang, K., Huang, J., Zhang, H.: Long-tailed classification by keeping the good and removing the bad momentum causal effect. In: NeurIPS (2020)
46. Tang, K., Niu, Y., Huang, J., Shi, J., Zhang, H.: Unbiased scene graph generation from biased training. In: CVPR (2020)
47. Ulutan, O., Iftekhar, A., Manjunath, B.S.: VSGNet: spatial attention network for detecting human object interactions using graph convolutions. In: CVPR (2020)
48. Vaswani, A., et al.: Attention is all you need. In: NIPS (2017)
49. Wan, B., Zhou, D., Liu, Y., Li, R., He, X.: Pose-aware multi-level feature network for human object interaction detection. In: ICCV (2019)
50. Wang, S., Yap, K.H., Yuan, J., Tan, Y.P.: Discovering human interactions with novel objects via zero-shot learning. In: CVPR (2020)
51. Wang, T., et al.: The devil is in classification: a simple framework for long-tail instance segmentation. In: Vedaldi, A., Bischof, H., Brox, T., Frahm, J.-M. (eds.) ECCV 2020. LNCS, vol. 12359, pp. 728–744. Springer, Cham (2020). https://doi.org/10.1007/978-3-030-58568-6_43
52. Wang, T., et al.: Deep contextual attention for human-object interaction detection. In: ICCV (2019)
53. Wang, T., Yang, T., Danelljan, M., Khan, F.S., Zhang, X., Sun, J.: Learning human-object interaction detection using interaction points. In: CVPR (2020)
54. Wang, Z., et al.: Towards fairness in visual recognition: effective strategies for bias mitigation. In: CVPR (2020)
55. Wu, T., Huang, Q., Liu, Z., Wang, Yu., Lin, D.: Distribution-balanced loss for multi-label classification in long-tailed datasets. In: Vedaldi, A., Bischof, H., Brox, T., Frahm, J.-M. (eds.) ECCV 2020. LNCS, vol. 12349, pp. 162–178. Springer, Cham (2020). https://doi.org/10.1007/978-3-030-58548-8_10
56. Xu, B., Li, J., Wong, Y., Zhao, Q., Kankanhalli, M.S.: Interact as you intend: intention-driven human-object interaction detection. In: IEEE TMM (2019)
57. Xu, B., Wong, Y., Li, J., Zhao, Q., Kankanhalli, M.S.: Learning to detect human-object interactions with knowledge. In: CVPR (2019)
58. Yan, S., et al.: Pcpl: predicate-correlation perception learning for unbiased scene graph generation. In: ACM MM (2020)
59. Zellers, R., Yatskar, M., Thomson, S., Choi, Y.: Neural motifs: scene graph parsing with global context. In: CVPR (2018)
60. Zhang, A., et al.: Mining the benefits of two-stage and one-stage hoi detection. In: NeurIPS (2021)
61. Zhang, B.H., Lemoine, B., Mitchell, M.: Mitigating unwanted biases with adversarial learning. In: AIES (2018)
62. Zhang, F.Z., Campbell, D., Gould, S.: Spatially conditioned graphs for detecting human-object interactions. In: ICCV (2021)
63. Zhao, J., Wang, T., Yatskar, M., Ordonez, V., Chang, K.W.: Men also like shopping: reducing gender bias amplification using corpus-level constraints. In: EMNLP (2017)

64. Zhong, X., Ding, C., Qu, X., Tao, D.: Polysemy deciphering network for human-object interaction detection. In: Vedaldi, A., Bischof, H., Brox, T., Frahm, J.-M. (eds.) ECCV 2020. LNCS, vol. 12365, pp. 69–85. Springer, Cham (2020). https://doi.org/10.1007/978-3-030-58565-5_5

65. Zhong, X., Qu, X., Ding, C., Tao, D.: Glance and gaze: inferring action-aware points for one-stage human-object interaction detection. In: CVPR (2021)

66. Zhou, B., Cui, Q., Wei, X.S., Chen, Z.M.: BBN: bilateral-branch network with cumulative learning for long-tailed visual recognition. In: CVPR (2020)

67. Zhou, P., Chi, M.: Relation parsing neural network for human-object interaction detection. In: ICCV (2019)

68. Zou, C., et al.: End-to-end human object interaction detection with hoi transformer. In: CVPR (2021)

A Fast Knowledge Distillation Framework for Visual Recognition

Zhiqiang Shen[1,2,3(✉)] and Eric Xing[1,3]

[1] Carnegie Mellon University, Pittsburgh, USA
epxing@cs.cmu.edu
[2] Hong Kong University of Science and Technology, Hong Kong, China
[3] Mohamed bin Zayed University of Artificial Intelligence, Abu Dhabi, UAE
zhiqiangshen@cse.ust.hk
http://zhiqiangshen.com/projects/FKD/index.html

Abstract. While Knowledge Distillation (KD) has been recognized as a useful tool in many visual tasks, such as supervised classification and self-supervised representation learning, the main drawback of a vanilla KD framework is its mechanism that consumes the majority of the computational overhead on forwarding through the giant teacher networks, making the entire learning procedure inefficient and costly. The recently proposed solution ReLabel suggests creating a label map for the entire image. During training, it receives the cropped region-level label by RoI aligning on a pre-generated entire label map, which allows for efficient supervision generation without having to pass through the teachers repeatedly. However, as the pre-trained teacher employed in ReLabel is from the conventional multi-crop scheme, there are various mismatches between the global label-map and region-level labels in this technique, resulting in performance deterioration compared to the vanilla KD. In this study, we present a Fast Knowledge Distillation (FKD) framework that replicates the distillation training phase and generates soft labels using the multi-crop KD approach, meanwhile training faster than ReLabel since no post-processes such as RoI align and softmax operations are used. When conducting multi-crop in the same image for data loading, our FKD is even more efficient than the traditional image classification framework. On ImageNet-1K, we obtain 80.1% Top-1 accuracy on ResNet-50, outperforming ReLabel by 1.2% while being faster in training and more flexible to use. On the distillation-based self-supervised learning task, we also show that FKD has an efficiency advantage.

1 Introduction

Knowledge Distillation (KD) [15] has been a widely used technique in various visual domains, such as the supervised recognition [2,22,28,32,46,47] and self-supervised representation learning [4,9,30]. The mechanism of KD is to force

---

Supplementary Information The online version contains supplementary material available at https://doi.org/10.1007/978-3-031-20053-3_39.

Table 1. Feature-by-feature comparison between ReLabel [50] and our FKD.

Method	Generating label	Label storage	Info. loss	Training
Vanilla KD	Implicit	None	No	Slow
ReLabel [50]	Fast	Efficient	Yes	Fast
FKD (Ours)	Slow	Efficient	No	Faster

the student to imitate the output of a teacher network or ensemble teachers, as well as converge on the ground-truth labels. Given the parameters θ of the target student at iteration (t), we can learn the next iteration parameters $\theta^{(t+1)}$ by minimizing the following objective which contains two terms:

$$\theta_{\text{student}}^{(t+1)} = \arg\min_{\theta \subset \Theta} \frac{1}{N} \sum_{n=1}^{N} (1 - \lambda)\mathcal{H}\left(\boldsymbol{y}_n, \boldsymbol{S}_\theta\left(\boldsymbol{x}_n\right)\right) \\ + \lambda\mathcal{H}\left(\boldsymbol{T}^{(t)}(\boldsymbol{x}_n), \boldsymbol{S}_\theta\left(\boldsymbol{x}_n\right)\right) \tag{1}$$

where $\boldsymbol{y}_n$ is the ground-truth for n-th sample. $\boldsymbol{T}^{(t)}$ is the teacher's output at iteration (t) and $\boldsymbol{S}_\theta(\boldsymbol{x}_n)$ is the student's prediction for the input sample $\boldsymbol{x}_n$. $\mathcal{H}$ is the cross-entropy loss function. λ is the coefficient for balancing the two objectives. The first term aims to minimize the entropy between one-hot ground-truth label and student's prediction while the second term is to minimize between teacher and student's predictions. The teacher $\boldsymbol{T}$ can be pre-trained in either supervised or self-supervised manners. Many literature [2,32,33,50] have empirically shown that the first term of true hard label in Eq. 1 is not required on larger-scale datasets like ImageNet [7] with more training budget if the teacher or ensembled teachers are accurate enough. In this work, we simply minimize the soft predictions between teacher and student models for the fast distillation design.

The inherent disadvantage in such a paradigm, according to KD's definition, is that a considerable proportion of computing resources is consumed on passing training data through large teacher networks to produce the supervision $\boldsymbol{T}^{(t)}$ in each iteration, rather than updating or training the target student parameters. Intuitively, the forward propagation through teachers can be shared across epochs since the parameters of them are frozen for the entire training. Based on this perspective, the vanilla distillation framework itself is inefficient, and how to reduce or share the forward computing of teacher networks across different epochs becomes the core for accelerating KD frameworks. A natural solution to overcome this drawback is to generate one probability vector as the soft label for each training image in advance, then reuse the pre-generated soft labels circularly for different training epochs. However, in modern neural network training, it is usually imposed various data augmentation strategies to avoid overfitting, particularly the random crop technique. This causes the inconsistency where the global-level soft vector for the entire image cannot precisely reflect the true probability distribution of the local image region after applying these augmentations.

To address the data augmentation, specially random-crop caused inconsistency issue in generating one global vector to the region-level input, while, preserving the advantage of informative soft labels, ReLabel [50] proposes to store the global label map from a pre-trained strong teacher and reutilize cross epochs

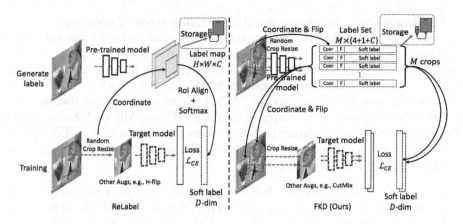

Fig. 1. Mechanism explanation of ReLabel and Fast Knowledge Distillation (FKD) framework. In label generation phase, ReLabel produces global-level label map through feeding the whole images into the pre-trained teacher, while FKD inputs regions of images, and maintains a set of soft labels. In network training phase, ReLabel employs *RoI Align* and *Softmax* to obtain the corresponding cropped labels for aligning the input, in contrast, FKD directly assigns the target soft label without any post-processing.

by RoI align [12], as shown in Fig. 1 (left). However, because of the inconsistent processes of input on teachers, this strategy is essentially not equivalent to vanilla KD procedure. The mismatches are primarily from two factors: (i) the teacher is usually trained with a random-crop-resize scheme, whereas, in ReLabel, the global label map is obtained by feeding into the whole image. Since in distillation the random-crop-resize is employed in the input space, thus the global label map cannot reflect the real soft distribution for image regions; (ii) RoI align will involve unexpected predictions on label maps, which cannot guarantee the sameness from this strategy and vanilla KD, thus, information loss exists.

In this work, we introduce a Fast Knowledge Distillation (FKD) framework to overcome the mismatching drawback and further avoid information loss on soft labels. Our strategy is straightforward: As shown in Fig. 1 (right), in the label generation phase, we directly store the soft probability from multiple random-crops into the label files, together with the coordinates and other data augmentation status like flipping. During training, we assign these stored coordinates back to the input image to generate the crop-resized input for passing through the networks, and compute the loss with the corresponding soft labels. The advantages of such a strategy are twofold: (i) Our region-based label generating process is identical to vanilla KD, so the obtained soft label for each input region is the same as oracle, indicating that no information is lost during the label creation phase; (ii) Our training phase enjoys a faster pace since no post-process is required, such as RoI align, softmax, etc. We can further assign multiple regions from the same image in a *mini*-batch to lessen the burden of data loading.

We demonstrate the advantages of our FKD in terms of accuracy and training speed on supervised and self-supervised learning tasks. In the supervised learning scenario, we compare the baseline ReLabel and vanilla KD (Oracle) from scratch across a variety of backbone network architectures, such as CNNs, vision transformers, and the competitive MEAL V2 framework with pre-trained initialization. Our FKD is more than 1% higher and slightly faster than ReLabel on ImageNet-1K, and 3~5× faster than oracle KD and MEAL V2 with similar performance. On the self-supervised distillation task, we employ S^2-BNN as the baseline for verifying the speed advantage of our proposed efficient framework.

Our contributions of this work:

- We present a fast knowledge distillation (FKD) framework that achieves the same high-level performance as vanilla KD, while keeping the same fast training speed and efficiency as non-KD approach without sacrificing performance.
- We reveal a discovery that in image classification frameworks, one image can be sampled many times with multiple crops within a *mini*-batch to facilitate data loading and speed up training, meanwhile obtaining better performance.
- To demonstrate the effectiveness and versatility of our approach, we perform FKD on a variety of tasks and distillation frameworks, including supervised classification and self-supervised learning with better results than prior art.

2   Related Work

Knowledge Distillation. The principle behind Knowledge Distillation [15] is that a student is encouraged to emulate or mimic the teachers' prediction, which helps student generalize better on unseen data. One core advantage of KD is that the teacher can provide softened distribution which contains richer information about input data compared to the traditional one-hot labels, especially when the data augmentation such as random-crop is used on the input space. Distillation can avoid incorrect labels by predicting them from the strong teachers in each iteration, which reflects the real situation of the transformed input data. We can also impose a temperature on the logits to re-scale the output distributions from teacher and student models to amplify the inter-class relationship on supervisions. Recently, many variants and extensions are proposed [6,17,22–24,32,34,42,46,48,51], such as employing internal feature representations [28], adversarial training with discriminators [29], transfer flow [47], contrastive distillation [38], patient and consistent [2], etc. For the broader overviews of related methods for knowledge distillation, please refer to [10,41].

Efficient Knowledge Distillation. Improving training efficiency for knowledge distillation is crucial for pushing this technique to a wider usage scope in real-world applications. Previous efforts in this direction are generally not sufficient. ReLabel [50] is a recently proposed solution that addresses this inefficient issue of KD surpassingly. It generates the global label map for the strong teacher and then reuses them through RoI align across different epochs. Our proposed FKD lies in an essentially different consideration and solution. We consider the

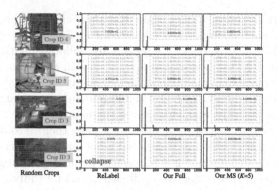

Fig. 2. Illustration of label distributions of ReLabel, our FKD full label and our quantized label (Top-5). "MS" denotes the marginal smoothed labels, more details can be referred in Sect. 3.5. Gray numbers in each block are the corresponding partial (as limited by space) probabilities/soft labels from different frameworks.

characteristics of vanilla KD to generate the randomly-cropped region-level soft labels from the strong teachers and store them, then reuse them by allocating to different epochs in training. Our approach enjoys the same accuracy as vanilla KD and the same or faster training speed as regular non-KD classification frameworks, making it superior to ReLabel in both performance and training speed.

3 Approach

In this section, we begin by introducing several observations and properties from ReLabel's global-level soft label and FKD's region-level soft label distributions. Then, we present the detailed workflow of our FKD framework and elaborately analyze the generated label quality, training speed and the applicability on supervised and self-supervised learning. Finally, we analyze different strategies of soft label compression and provide their storage requirements for practical usage.

Preliminaries: Limitations of Previous Solution
According to the mechanism of ReLabel which is enabled by RoI align on global map, it is an approximation solution that inevitably will lose information on labels compared to the vanilla KD of region-level soft labels. In Fig. 2, we visualize the region-level label distributions of ReLabel and FKD on ImageNet-1K, and several empirical observations are noticed: **(i)** ReLabel is more confident in many cases of the regions, so the soft information is weaker than FKD. We analyze this is because ReLabel feeds the global images into the network instead of local regions, which makes the generated global label map encode more category information and ignore the backgrounds, forcing the soft label too close to the semantic ground-truth, as shown in Fig. 2 (row 1). Though sometimes the maximal probabilities are similar between ReLabel and FKD, FKD contains more informative subordinate probabilities in the label distribution, while ReLabel's are equally distributed, as shown in Fig. 2 (row 2); **(ii)** For some outlier regions,

FKD is substantially more robust than ReLabel, such as the loose bounding boxes of objects, partial object, etc., as shown in Fig. 2 (row 3); **(iii)** In some particular circumstance, ReLabel unexpectedly collapsed with nearly uniform distribution, while FKD still works well, as shown in the bottom row of Fig. 2.

Moreover, there are existing mismatches between the soft label from ReLabel and oracle teacher prediction in KD when employing more data augmentations such as Flip, Color jittering, etc., since these augmentations are randomly applied during training. In ReLabel design, we cannot take them into account and prepare in advance when generating the global label map. In contrast, FKD is adequate to handle this situation: it is with ease to involve extra augmentations and record all information (ratio, degree, coefficient, etc.) for individual regions from the same or different images, and generate corresponding soft label by feeding the transformed image regions into the pre-trained teacher networks. However, this strategy will increase the requirement of storage, so if it is budgeted, the alternative is to perform extra augmentations after receiving the cropped image regions during training, similar to ReLabel. Note that this will cause slightly mismatch between the transformed samples and corresponding soft labels, which is similar to the conventional augmentation mechanism but with soft labels.

3.1 Fast Knowledge Distillation

In a traditional visual training system, the deep network propagation and data loading are typically two main bottlenecks for resources. However, in a distillation framework, huge teachers have been the key training burden in addition to these computing demands. Our FKD seeks to address this intractable problem.

Label Generation Phase. Following the regular random-crop resize training strategy, we randomly crop M regions from one image and employ other augmentations like flipping on them, then feed these regions into the teachers to generate the corresponding soft label vectors P_i, i.e., $P_i = T(R_i)$ where R_i is the transformed region by transformations $\mathcal{F}_i$ and T is the pre-trained teacher network, i is the region index. We store all the region coordinates and augmentation hyper-parameters $\{\mathcal{F}\}$ together with the soft label set $\{P\}$ for the following training phase, as shown in Fig. 1 (upper right). A detailed analysis of how to store these required values on hard drive is provided in the following section.

Training Phase. In the training stage, instead of randomly generating crops as the conventional image classification strategy, we directly load the label file, and assign our stored crop coordinates and data augmentations for this particular image to prepare the transformed region-level inputs. The corresponding soft label will be used as the supervision of these regions for training. With the cross-entropy loss, the objective is: $\mathcal{L} = -\sum_i P_i \log S_\theta(R_i)$, where $S_\theta(R_i)$ is the student's prediction for the input region R_i, θ is the parameter of the student model that we need to learn. The detailed training procedure is shown in Fig. 1.

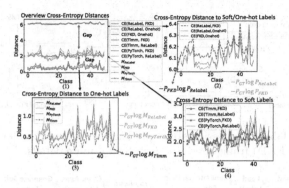

Fig. 3. Entropy distance analysis between different pairs of soft/one-hot labels and different trained models. (1) is the overall distance visualization. (2), (3), (4) represent each detailed group in (1). We illustrate the first 50 classes in ImageNet-1K dataset.

3.2 Higher Label Quality

Distance Analysis. We analyze the quality of various formulations of labels through the entropy distance with measures on their mutual cross-entropy matrix. We consider three types of labels: (1) human-annotated one-hot label, ReLabel, and our FKD. We also calculate the distance of the predictions on four pre-trained models with different accuracies, including: vanilla PyTorch pre-trained model (weakest), Timm pre-trained model [44] (strongest), ReLabel trained model and FKD trained model. An overview of our illustration is shown in Fig. 3. The upper curves, as well in (2), are averaged cross-entropy across 50 classes of (ReLabel→FKD), (ReLabel→One-hot) and (FKD→One-hot). Here, we derive an important observation:

$$(\mathcal{D}_{R \to F}^{CE} = -P_{FKD} \log P_{ReLabel}) > (\mathcal{D}_{R \to O}^{CE} \ \ OR \ \ \mathcal{D}_{F \to O}^{CE}) \tag{2}$$

where $\mathcal{D}_{R \to F}^{CE}$ is the cross-entropy value of ReLabel → FKD. Essentially, FKD soft label can be regarded as the oracle KD label and $\mathcal{D}_{R \to F}^{CE}$ is the distance to such "KD ground truth". From Fig. 3 (2) we can see its distance is even larger than ReLabel and FKD to the one-hot label. Since ReLabel (global-map soft label) and FKD (region-level soft label) are greatly discrepant from the one-hot hard label, the gap between ReLabel and FKD ("KD ground truth") is fairly significant and considerable. If we shift attention to the curves of $\mathcal{D}_{R \to O}^{CE}$ and $\mathcal{D}_{F \to O}^{CE}$, they are highly aligned across different classes with similar values. In some particular classes, $\mathcal{D}_{F \to O}^{CE}$ are slightly larger. This is sensible as one-hot label is basically not the "optimal label" we desired.

In the bottom group of Fig. 3 (3), the entropy values are comparatively small. This is because the curves are from the pre-trained models with decent performance under the criterion of one-hot label. Among them, M_{Timm} has the minimal cross-entropy to the one-hot label, this is expected since timm model is optimized thoroughly to fit one-hot label with the highest accuracy. In Fig. 3 (4),

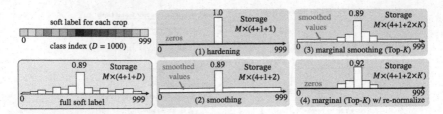

Fig. 4. Different label compression strategies and storage analyses for our fast knowledge distillation (FKD) framework. See Sect. 3.5 for more details.

	Load Images	Load Labels	Generate Random Coordinates	Crop-Resize	Other Augs (Options)	Generate Soft Labels	Forward Network
Normal KD	✔	✘	✔	✔	✔	✘	✔
ReLabel	✔	✔	✔	✔	✔	✔	✔
FKD	✔	✔	✘ (we randomly select from a set)	✔	✔	✘	✔

Fig. 5. Training workflow and analysis for vanilla KD, ReLabel and our fast knowledge distillation (FKD) framework. Maroon dashed boxes indicate that the processes are only required by ReLabel while not existing in our FKD. Note that "generate soft labels" indicates *RoI align + softmax* in ReLabel. We both have the recovering process from the compressed label to full soft label as discussed in Sect. 3.3.

$\mathcal{D}^{CE}_{Timm \rightarrow F}$ and $\mathcal{D}^{CE}_{PT \rightarrow F}$ lie in the middle of $\mathcal{D}^{CE}_{Timm \rightarrow R}$ and $\mathcal{D}^{CE}_{PT \rightarrow R}$ with smaller variances. This reflects that FKD is more stable than Relabel pre-trained models.

3.3 Faster Training Speed

Multi-crop Sampling within a *Mini*-batch. As illustrated in Fig. 1 (right), we can use multiple crops in the same image to facilitate loading image and label files. Intuitively, this will reduce the diversity of training samples in a *mini*-batch since some of the samples are from the same image. However, our experimental results indicate that it will not hurt the model's performance, in contrast, it even boosts the accuracy when the number of crops from the same image is within a reasonable range (e.g., 4∼8). We analyze this is because it can mitigate samples' variance dramatically for each *mini*-batch to make training more stable.

Serrated Learning Rate Scheduler. Since FKD samples multiple crops (#*crop*) from one image, when iterating over the entire dataset once, we actually train the dataset #*crop* epochs with the same learning rate. It has no effect while using milestone/step *lr* scheduler, but it will change the *lr* curve to be serrated if applying continuous *cosine* or *linear* learning rate strategies. The accuracy may also be enhanced by multi-crop training for this reason.

Table 2. Detailed comparison of different label quantization/compression strategies on ImageNet-1K. M is the number of crops within an image during soft label generation, here we choose 200 crops as an example to calculate space consumption. N_{im} is the number of images, i.e., 1.2M for ImageNet-1K. S_{LM} is the size of label map. C_{class} is the number of classes. D_{DA} is the parameter dimension of data augmentations to store.

	ReLabel (Full)	ReLabel (Top-5)	Full	Hard	Smoothing	M Re-Norm (K=5)	MS (K=5)	MS (K=10)
Calculation	$N_{im} \times S_{LM} \times C_{class}$	$N_{im} \times S_{LM} \times 2C_{Top\text{-}5}$	$N_{im} \times (C_{class} + D_{DA})$	$N_{im} \times (1 + D_{DA})$	$N_{im} \times (2 + D_{DA})$	$N_{im} \times (2K + D_{DA})$	$N_{im} \times (2K + D_{DA})$	$N_{im} \times (2K + D_{DA})$
Dim. of Soft Label	$15 \times 15 \times 1{,}000$	$15 \times 15 \times 10$	$M \times 1{,}000$	$M \times 1$	$M \times 2$	$M \times 10$	$M \times 10$	$M \times 20$
+ Coordinate & Flip	–	–	$M \times 1{,}005$	$M \times 6$	$M \times 7$	$M \times 15$	$M \times 15$	$M \times 25$
Real Cons. on Disk	~1TB	10 GB	~0.9 TB	5.3 GB	6.2 GB	13.3 GB	13.3 GB	22.2 GB

Training Time Analysis:

1. Data Load. Data loading strategy in FKD is efficient. For instance, when training with a *mini*-batch of 256, traditional image classification framework requires to load 256 images and ReLabel will load 256 images + 256 label files, while in our method, FKD only needs to load $\frac{256}{\#crop}$ images + $\frac{256}{\#crop}$ label files, even faster than traditional training if we choose a slightly larger value for $\#crop$ (when $\#crop > 2$)[1].

2. Label Preparation. We assign $\#crop$ regions in an image to the current *mini*-batch for training. Since we store the label probability after *softmax* (in supervised learning), we can use assigned soft labels for the *mini*-batch samples directly without any post-process. This assignment is fast and efficient in implementation with a *randperm* function in PyTorch [25]. If the label is compressed using the following strategies, we will operate with an additional simple recovering process (as shown in Fig. 4) to obtain D-way soft label distributions. Note that ReLabel also has this process so the time consumption on this part will be similar to ReLabel. A detailed item-by-item workflow is shown in Fig. 5.

3.4   Training Self-supervised Model with Supervised Scheme

In this section, we introduce how to apply our FKD to the self-supervised learning (SSL) task with a faster training speed than the widely-used Siamese SSL frameworks. The label generation (from the self-supervised strong teachers), label preparation and training procedure are similar to the supervised scheme. However, we keep the projection head in original SSL teachers as soft labels following [30] and store the soft labels before *softmax* for operating temperature[2].

3.5   Label Compression and Storage Analysis

We consider and formulate the following four strategies for compressing soft label for storage, an elaborated comparison of them can be referred to Table 2.

- **Hardening.** In hardening quantization strategy, the hard label Y_H is generated using the index of the maximum logits from the teacher predictions of

---

[1] Assume that loading each image and label file will consume similar time by CPUs.

[2] The temperature τ is applied on the *logits* before the *softmax* operation for self-supervised distillation.

Table 3. Comparison between ReLabel and our FKD on ImageNet-1K. "$\lozenge$" denotes our retraining following the same protocol in the Appendix w/o distillation. Note that more augmentations (e.g., CutMix [49]) will further improve the accuracy, as provided in Sect. 4.1. Models are trained from scratch.

Method	Network	Top-1 (%)	Top-5 (%)	Training time
Vanilla$\lozenge$	ResNet-50	78.1	94.0	1.0
ReLabel [50]	ResNet-50	78.9	–	↑0.5% [50]
FKD (Ours)$_{\text{w/o warmup\&colorj}}$	ResNet-50	79.8	94.6	↓0.5%
FKD (Ours)	ResNet-50	**80.1**$^{+1.2}$	**94.8**	↓0.5%
Vanilla$\lozenge$	ResNet-101	79.7	94.6	1.0
ReLabel [50]	ResNet-101	80.7	–	↑0.5% [50]
FKD (Ours)$_{\text{w/o warmup\&colorj}}$	ResNet-101	81.7	95.6	↓0.5%
FKD (Ours)	ResNet-101	**81.9**$^{+1.2}$	**95.7**	↓0.5%

regions. In general, label hardening is the one-hot label with correction by strong teacher models in region-level space.

$$Y_{\text{H}} = \text{argmax}_c z_{\text{FKD}}(c) \tag{3}$$

where z_{FKD} is the logits for each randomly cropped region produced by FKD.

- **Smoothing.** Smoothing quantization replaces one-hot hard label Y_{H} with a mixture of soft y_c and a uniform distribution same as label smoothing [35]:

$$y_c^{\text{S}} = \begin{cases} p_c & \text{if } c = \textit{hardening label,} \\ (1 - p_c)/(C - 1) & \text{otherwise.} \end{cases} \tag{4}$$

where p_c is the probability after *softmax* at c-th class and C is the number of total classes. $(1 - p_c)/(C - 1)$ is a small value for flattening the one-hot labels. $y_c^{\text{S}} \in Y_{\text{S}}$ is the smoothed label at c-th class.

- **Marginal Smoothing with Top-K (*MS*).** Marginal smoothing quantization reserves more soft information (Top-K) of teacher prediction than the single smoothing label Y_{S}:

$$y_c^{\text{MS}} = \begin{cases} p_c & \text{if } c \in \{\textbf{Top}-K\}, \\ \dfrac{1- \sum\limits_{c \in \{\textbf{Top}-K\}} p_c}{C-K} & \text{otherwise.} \end{cases} \tag{5}$$

where $y_c^{\text{MS}} \in Y_{\text{MS}}$ is the marginally smoothed label at c-th class.

- **Marginal Re-Norm with Top-K (*MR*).** Marginal re-normalization will re-normalize Top-K predictions to $\sum_{c \in \{\textbf{Top}-K\}} p_c = 1$ and maintain other logits to be zero (Different from ReLabel, we use *normalize* to calibrate the sum of Top-K predictions to 1, since our soft label is stored after softmax.):

$$y_c^{\text{M}} = \begin{cases} p_c & \text{if } c \in \{\textbf{Top}-K\}, \\ 0 & \text{otherwise.} \end{cases} \tag{6}$$

Table 4. Comparison of MEAL V2 [33] and our FKD on ImageNet-1K. "w/ FKD" denotes the model is trained using the same protocol and hyper-parameters as original MEAL V2. "♡" represents the training using *cosine lr* and 1.5× epochs. Models are trained from the pre-trained initialization.

Method	Network	#Params	Top-1	Top-5	Speedup
MEAL V2 [33]	ResNet-50	25.6M	80.67	95.09	1.0
MEAL V2 w/ FKD	ResNet-50	25.6M	80.70	95.13	**0.3×**
MEAL V2 w/ ♡FKD	ResNet-50	25.6M	80.91	95.39	**0.5×**
MEAL V2 [33]	MobileNet V3-S0.75	2.04M	67.60	87.23	1.0
MEAL V2 w/ ♡FKD	MobileNet V3-S0.75	2.04M	67.83	87.35	**0.4×**
MEAL V2 [33]	MobileNet V3-S1.0	2.54M	69.65	88.71	1.0
MEAL V2 w/ ♡FKD	MobileNet V3-S1.0	2.54M	69.94	88.82	**0.4×**

$$y_c^{\mathrm{MR}} = \mathrm{Normalize}(y_c^{\mathrm{M}}) = \frac{y_c^{\mathrm{M}}}{\sum_{c=1}^{C}(y_c^{\mathrm{M}})} \qquad (7)$$

where $y_c^{\mathrm{MR}} \in Y_{\mathrm{MR}}$ is the re-normalized label at c-th class.

4 Experiments

Experimental Settings and Datasets. Detailed lists of our hyper-parameter choices are shown in Appendix. Warmup and color jittering are not employed in the ablation studies. Except for experiments on MEAL V2, we use *EfficientNet-L2-ns-475* [36,46] as the teacher model, we also tried weaker teachers but the performance in our experiment is slightly worse. For MEAL V2, we follow its original design by using *SENet154 + ResNet152_v1s* ensemble (gluon version [11]) as the soft label. ImageNet-1K [7] is used for the supervised classification and self-supervised learning. COCO [20] is used for the transfer learning experiments.

Network Architectures. Experiments are conducted on Convolutional Neural Networks [18], such as ResNet [13], MobileNet [16], FBNet [45], Efficient-Netv2 [37], and Vision Transformers [8,40], such as DeiT [39], SReT [31]. For binary backbone, we use ReActNet [21] in the self-supervised experiments.

Baseline Knowledge Distillation Methods

▶ ReLabel [50] (Label Map Distillation). ReLabel used the pre-generated global label maps from the pre-trained teacher for reducing the cost on the teacher branch when conducting distillation.
▶ MEAL V2 [33] (Fine-tuning Distillation). MEAL V2 proposed to distill student network from the pre-trained parameters[3] and giant teacher ensemble for fast convergence and better accuracy.

---

[3] The pre-trained parameter is from timm [43] with version <= 0.4.12.

Table 5. FKD with supervised Vision Transformer [8] and its variants on ImageNet-1K using 224×224 input resolution. Models are trained from scratch.

Method	Network	Epochs	#Params (M)	FLOPs (B)	Extra data aug.	Top-1 (%)	Speedup
DeiT [39] w/o KD	ViT-T	300	5.7	1.3	MixUp+CutMix+RA	72.2	–
DeiT [39] w/ KD	ViT-T	300	5.7	1.3	MixUp+CutMix+RA	74.5	1.0
ViT [8] (Vanilla)	ViT-T	300	5.7	1.3	None	68.7 [14]	–
ViT w/ FKD (Ours)	ViT-T	300	5.7	1.3	None	**75.2**	0.15×
SReT [31] w/o KD	SReT-LT	300	5.0	1.2	MixUp+CutMix+RA	76.7	–
SReT [31] w/ KD	SReT-LT	300	5.0	1.2	MixUp+CutMix+RA	77.7	1.0
SReT [31] (Vanilla)	SReT-LT	300	5.0	1.2	None	–	–
SReT w/ FKD (Ours)	SReT-LT	300	5.0	1.2	None	**78.7**	0.14×

Table 6. Ablation results (Top-1) on ImageNet-1K of different label quantization strategies. $m = 8$ is used in this ablation.

Method	Network	Full	Hard	Smoothing	Mar. Re-Norm (K=5)	Mar. Smoothing (K=5)	Mar. Smoothing (K=10)
MEAL V2 w/ FKD	ResNet-50	**80.65**	80.20	80.23	80.40	80.58	80.52
FKD (from scratch)	ResNet-50	79.48	79.09	79.37	79.23	**79.51**	79.44

Table 7. Ablation results (Top-1) on ImageNet-1K with different numbers (m) of cropping regions from the same image within a *mini*-batch.

Method	Network	$m = 1$	$m = 2$	$m = 4$	$m = 8$	$m = 16$	$m = 32$
Vanilla	ResNet-50	77.18	77.91	**78.14**	77.89	75.89	70.09
MEAL V2 w/ FKD	ResNet-50	80.67	**80.70**	80.66	80.58	80.36	80.17
FKD (from scratch)	ResNet-50	79.59	79.62	**79.76**	79.51	78.12	74.61

Table 8. ImageNet-1K clarification results on tiny networks.

FBNet-C Arch	FLOPs: 375M	Acc.: 75.12%	+FKD: **77.13%**$^{+2.01\%}$
EfficientNetv2-B0 Arch	FLOPs: 700M	Acc.: 78.35%	+FKD: **79.94%**$^{+1.59\%}$

▶ FunMatch [2] (Oracle Distillation). FunMatch is a standard knowledge distillation framework with strong teacher models and augmentations. We consider it as the strong baseline approach for efficient KD when using the same or similar teacher supervisors.

▷ S²-BNN [30] (Self-supervised Distillation). S²-BNN is a plain distillation solution for self-supervised learning task. The teacher is pre-learned from the self-supervised learning methods, such as MoCo V2 [5], SwAV [3], etc.

4.1 Supervised Learning

CNNs

(i) **ReLabel**. The comparison with ReLabel is shown in Table 3, using the training settings introduced in our Appendix, which is the same as ReLabel, our accuracies on ResNet-50/101 both outperform ReLabel by more than **1.0%** with slightly faster training speed. These significant also consistent improvements of FKD show great potential and superiority for practical applications.

(ii) **MEAL V2**. We use FKD to train MEAL V2 models. The results are shown in Table 4, when employing the same hyper-parameters and teacher networks, FKD can speed up 2−4× **without compromising accuracy**. Using *cosine lr* and more epochs in training further improves the accuracy.

(iii) **FunMatch** (Oracle). We consider FunMatch as the oracle/strong KD baseline, our plain FKD w/o extra augmentations is slightly lower than Fun-Match (80.5%) as they used more augmentations in training. After employing CutMix, which is similar to the FunMatch training setting, our result (80.9%)[4] outperforms FunMatch by 0.4%. Note that FunMatch needs 10× more budget for training than FKD (2 d *vs.* 20 d) with the same number of GPUs (e.g., 8 V100) since they explicitly forward giant teachers at each iteration of training.

(iv) **Tiny Models**. We also examine the generalization ability using the mobile-level models, such as FBNet [45], EfficientNetv2 [37] from [43]. As shown in Table 8, FKD consistently improves the base models by 2.01% and 1.59%, respectively. The training settings for them are provided in Appendix.

Vision Transformers

(i) **ViT/DeiT**. The results are shown in Table 5 of the first group. Our non-extra augmentation result (75.2%) using ViT-T backbone is better than DeiT-T with distillation (74.5%), while we only require **0.15×** training resources than DeiT distillation protocol to train the model.

(ii) **SReT**. We also examine FKD using SReT-LT, result (78.7%) is consistently better than its original KD design (77.7%) with a faster training speed.

Ablations: (i) Effects of Crop Number in Each Image During Training. We explore the effect of different numbers of crops sampled from the same image within a *mini*-batch to the final performance. For the conventional data preparation strategy, on each image we solely sample one crop for a *mini*-batch to train the model. Here, we evaluate the m from 1 crop to 32 crops as shown in Table 7. Surprisingly, using a few crops from the same image leads to better performance than the single crop solution with a non-negligible margin, especially on the traditional image classification system. This indicates that the internal diversity of samples in a *mini*-batch has a limit for tolerance, properly reducing such diversity can mitigate the variance and boost accuracy, while we can also observe that after $m>8$, the performance decreases substantially, thus the diversity is basically still critical for learning good status of the model. Nevertheless, this is a good observation for us to speed up data loading in our FKD framework.

(ii) Effects of Crop Number for Soft Labels During Label Generation. Ideally, the number of crops is aligned with the number of training epochs by a shuffling and non-overlapping sampling strategy, which can exactly replicate the vanilla KD. We found FKD is surprisingly robust on fewer crops of soft labels,

---

[4] The state-of-the-art non-KD training result on ResNet-50 (Timm [44]) with massive data augmentations is 79.8%, which is 1.1% lower than FKD.

Table 9. Linear evaluation results of FKD with self-supervised Binary CNN (ReAct-Net [21]), Real-valued CNN (ResNet-50 [13]). FKD can speed up training by 3× with the same or similar linear evaluation performance.

Method	Network	Teacher	#Dims for distilling	Training epochs	Top-1 (%)	Speedup
S²-BNN [30]	ReActNet	MoCo V2-800ep	128	200	61.5	1.0
FKD	ReActNet	MoCo V2-800ep	128	200	61.7	**0.4×**
S²-BNN [30]	ResNet-50	SwAV/RN50-w4	3000	100	68.7	1.0
FKD	ResNet-50	SwAV/RN50-w4	3000	100	68.8	**0.3×**

Table 10. Results of FKD on ImageNet ReaL [1] and ImageNetV2 [26] with ResNet-{50, 101}. * indicates that results are tested using their provided pre-trained model.

Method	ImageNet-1K	ReaL	ImageNetV2 Top-images	ImageNetV2 Matched-frequency	ImageNetV2 Threshold-0.7
ResNet-50:					
ReLabel	78.9	85.0	80.5	67.3	76.0
FKD	**80.1**	**85.8**	**81.2**	**68.2**	**76.9**
ResNet-101:					
ReLabel*	80.7	86.5	82.4	69.7	78.2
FKD	**81.9**	**87.1**	**83.2**	**70.7**	**79.1**

Table 11. Comparison of transfer learning performance with ReLabel on detection and instance segmentation tasks. The training and evaluation are conducted on COCO dataset [20].

Method	Network	Faster RCNN w/ FPN bbox AP	Mask-RCNN w/ FPN bbox AP	mask AP
Baseline	ResNet-50	37.7	38.5	34.7
ReLabel	ResNet-50	38.2	39.1	35.2
FKD	ResNet-50	38.7	39.7	35.9

which can maintain a decent accuracy without a significant drop. We examined 100 crops (4.75G storage), result (79.7%) is tolerably inferior.

(iii) Different Label Compression Strategies. We evaluate the performance of different label compression strategies. We use $m=8$ for this ablation and the results are shown in Table 6. On MEAL V2 w/ FKD, we obtain the highest accuracy of 80.65% when using the full soft labels, while on the standard FKD, the best performance is from *Marginal Smoothing (K = 5)* with 79.51%. Increasing K decreases both the accuracies in these two scenarios, we analyze that larger K will involve more noise or unnecessary minor information on the soft labels. While, they are still better than the *Hard* and *Smoothing* strategies.

4.2 More Comparison on ReaL [1] and ImageNetV2 [26] Datasets

In this section, we provide more results on ImageNet ReaL [1] and ImageNetV2 [26] datasets. On ImageNetV2 [26], we verify our FKD models on three metrics "Top-Images", "Matched Frequency", and "Threshold 0.7" as ReLabel. We conduct experiments on two network structures: ResNet-50 and ResNet-101. The results are shown in Table 10, we achieve consistent improvement over baseline ReLabel on both ResNet-50 and ResNet-101.

4.3 Self-supervised Learning

S²-BNN [30] is a pure distillation-based framework for self-supervised learning, thus the proposed FKD approach is eligible to train S²-BNN [30] in the proposed way efficiently. We employ SwAV [3] and MoCo V2 [5] pre-trained models as the teacher networks. Considering that the distribution from the SSL learned teachers is more flattening than the supervised teacher predictions (meaning that the subordinate classes from SSL trained teachers carry crucial information), we use the full soft label in this scenario, and leave the label compression strategies on SSL task as a future study. We employ ReActNet [21] and ResNet-50 [13] as the target/student backbones in these experiments. The results are shown in Table 9, our FKD trained models achieve slightly better performance than S^2-BNN with roughly 3× acceleration since we only use a single branch for training, the same as traditional classification pipeline that uses soft label and CE loss. The slight boosts are from our lite data augmentation for FKD when generating SSL soft labels. This is interesting and it is worth exploring further on the data augmentation strategies for distillation-based or FKD-equipped SSL methods.

4.4 Transfer Learning

We further examine whether FKD obtained improvements on ImageNet-1K can be transferred to various downstream tasks. As in Table 11, we present the results of object detection and instance segmentation on COCO [20] with models pre-trained on ImageNet-1K using FKD. We also employ Faster RCNN [27] and Mask RCNN [12] with FPN [19] following ReLabel. Over the vanilla baseline and ReLabel, our FKD pre-trained weights show consistent gains on the downstream tasks. More visualizations, analyses and discussions are provided in Appendix.

5   Conclusion

It is worthwhile investigating approaches to boost the training efficiency and speed of vanilla KD given its widespread use and exceptional performance in training compact and efficient networks. In this paper, we have presented a fast distillation framework through the pre-generated region-level soft label scheme. We have elaborately discussed the strategies of compressing soft label for practical storage and their performance comparison. We identified an interesting discovery that the training samples within a *mini*-batch can be cropped from the same input images to facilitate data loading with better accuracy. We exhibit the effectiveness and adaptability of our framework by demonstrating it on supervised image classification and self-supervised representation learning tasks.

References

1. Beyer, L., Hénaff, O.J., Kolesnikov, A., Zhai, X., Oord, A.V.D.: Are we done with imagenet? arXiv preprint. arXiv:2006.07159 (2020)
2. Beyer, L., Zhai, X., Royer, A., Markeeva, L., Anil, R., Kolesnikov, A.: Knowledge distillation: a good teacher is patient and consistent. arXiv preprint. arXiv:2106.05237 (2021)
3. Caron, M., Misra, I., Mairal, J., Goyal, P., Bojanowski, P., Joulin, A.: Unsupervised learning of visual features by contrasting cluster assignments. In: NeurIPS (2020)

4. Caron, M., et al.: Emerging properties in self-supervised vision transformers. In: ICCV (2021)
5. Chen, X., Fan, H., Girshick, R., He, K.: Improved baselines with momentum contrastive learning. arXiv preprint. arXiv:2003.04297 (2020)
6. Chung, I., Park, S., Kim, J., Kwak, N.: Feature-map-level online adversarial knowledge distillation. In: International Conference on Machine Learning. PMLR (2020)
7. Deng, J., Dong, W., Socher, R., Li, L.J., Li, K., Fei-Fei, L.: Imagenet: a large-scale hierarchical image database. In: 2009 IEEE Conference on Computer Vision and Pattern Recognition, pp. 248–255. IEEE (2009)
8. Dosovitskiy, A., et al.: An image is worth 16x16 words: transformers for image recognition at scale. In: International Conference on Learning Representations (2020)
9. Fang, Z., Wang, J., Wang, L., Zhang, L., Yang, Y., Liu, Z.: Seed: self-supervised distillation for visual representation. In: ICLR (2021)
10. Gou, J., Yu, B., Maybank, S.J., Tao, D.: Knowledge distillation: a survey. Int. J. Comput. Vis. **129**(6), 1789–1819 (2021). https://doi.org/10.1007/s11263-021-01453-z
11. Guo, J., et al.: Gluoncv and gluonnlp: deep learning in computer vision and natural language processing. J. Mach. Learn. Res. **21**(23), 1–7 (2020)
12. He, K., Gkioxari, G., Dollár, P., Girshick, R.: Mask r-cnn. In: Proceedings of the IEEE international conference on computer vision, pp. 2961–2969 (2017)
13. He, K., Zhang, X., Ren, S., Sun, J.: Deep residual learning for image recognition. In: Proceedings of the IEEE Conference on Computer Vision and Pattern Recognition, pp. 770–778 (2016)
14. Heo, B., Yun, S., Han, D., Chun, S., Choe, J., Oh, S.J.: Rethinking spatial dimensions of vision transformers. In: International Conference on Computer Vision (ICCV) (2021)
15. Hinton, G., Vinyals, O., Dean, J.: Distilling the knowledge in a neural network. arXiv preprint. arXiv:1503.02531 (2015)
16. Howard, A.G., et al.: Mobilenets: efficient convolutional neural networks for mobile vision applications. arXiv preprint. arXiv:1704.04861 (2017)
17. Huang, Z., Wang, N.: Like what you like: knowledge distill via neuron selectivity transfer. arXiv preprint. arXiv:1707.01219 (2017)
18. LeCun, Y., Bengio, Y., et al.: Convolutional networks for images, speech, and time series. In: The Handbook of Brain Theory and Neural Networks (1995)
19. Lin, T.Y., Dollár, P., Girshick, R., He, K., Hariharan, B., Belongie, S.: Feature pyramid networks for object detection. In: CVPR (2017)
20. Lin, T.Y., et al.: Microsoft COCO: common objects in context. In: Fleet, D., Pajdla, T., Schiele, B., Tuytelaars, T. (eds.) ECCV 2014. LNCS, vol. 8693, pp. 740–755. Springer, Cham (2014). https://doi.org/10.1007/978-3-319-10602-1_48
21. Liu, Z., Shen, Z., Savvides, M., Cheng, K.-T.: ReActNet: towards precise binary neural network with generalized activation functions. In: Vedaldi, A., Bischof, H., Brox, T., Frahm, J.-M. (eds.) ECCV 2020. LNCS, vol. 12359, pp. 143–159. Springer, Cham (2020). https://doi.org/10.1007/978-3-030-58568-6_9
22. Müller, R., Kornblith, S., Hinton, G.: When does label smoothing help? In: NeurIPS (2019)
23. Papernot, N., McDaniel, P., Wu, X., Jha, S., Swami, A.: Distillation as a defense to adversarial perturbations against deep neural networks. In: 2016 IEEE Symposium on Security and privacy (SP), pp. 582–597. IEEE (2016)
24. Park, W., Kim, D., Lu, Y., Cho, M.: Relational knowledge distillation. In: CVPR, pp. 3967–3976 (2019)

25. Paszke, A., et al.: Pytorch: an imperative style, high-performance deep learning library. In: Advances in Neural Information Processing Systems, vol. 32, pp. 8026–8037 (2019)
26. Recht, B., Roelofs, R., Schmidt, L., Shankar, V.: Do imagenet classifiers generalize to imagenet? In: ICML, pp. 5389–5400. PMLR (2019)
27. Ren, S., He, K., Girshick, R., Sun, J.: Faster r-cnn: towards real-time object detection with region proposal networks. In: Advances in Neural Information Processing Systems, vol. 28, pp. 91–99 (2015)
28. Romero, A., Ballas, N., Kahou, S.E., Chassang, A., Gatta, C., Bengio, Y.: Fitnets: hints for thin deep nets. arXiv preprint. arXiv:1412.6550 (2014)
29. Shen, Z., He, Z., Xue, X.: Meal: multi-model ensemble via adversarial learning. In: Proceedings of the AAAI Conference on Artificial Intelligence, vol. 33, pp. 4886–4893 (2019)
30. Shen, Z., Liu, Z., Qin, J., Huang, L., Cheng, K.T., Savvides, M.: S2-bnn: bridging the gap between self-supervised real and 1-bit neural networks via guided distribution calibration. In: Proceedings of the IEEE/CVF Conference on Computer Vision and Pattern Recognition, pp. 2165–2174 (2021)
31. Shen, Z., Liu, Z., Xing, E.: Sliced recursive transformer. arXiv preprint. arXiv:2111.05297 (2021)
32. Shen, Z., Liu, Z., Xu, D., Chen, Z., Cheng, K.T., Savvides, M.: Is label smoothing truly incompatible with knowledge distillation: an empirical study. In: ICLR (2021)
33. Shen, Z., Savvides, M.: Meal v2: Boosting vanilla resnet-50 to 80%+ top-1 accuracy on imagenet without tricks. arXiv preprint. arXiv:2009.08453 (2020)
34. Stanton, S., Izmailov, P., Kirichenko, P., Alemi, A.A., Wilson, A.G.: Does knowledge distillation really work? arXiv preprint. arXiv:2106.05945 (2021)
35. Szegedy, C., Vanhoucke, V., Ioffe, S., Shlens, J., Wojna, Z.: Rethinking the inception architecture for computer vision. In: Proceedings of the IEEE Conference on Computer Vision and Pattern Recognition, pp. 2818–2826 (2016)
36. Tan, M., Le, Q.: Efficientnet: rethinking model scaling for convolutional neural networks. In: International Conference on Machine Learning. pp. 6105–6114. PMLR (2019)
37. Tan, M., Le, Q.: Efficientnetv2: smaller models and faster training. In: International Conference on Machine Learning, pp. 10096–10106. PMLR (2021)
38. Tian, Y., Krishnan, D., Isola, P.: Contrastive representation distillation. In: International Conference on Learning Representations (2019)
39. Touvron, H., Cord, M., Douze, M., Massa, F., Sablayrolles, A., Jégou, H.: Training data-efficient image transformers & distillation through attention. In: International Conference on Machine Learning, pp. 10347–10357. PMLR (2021)
40. Vaswani, A., et al.: Attention is all you need. In: Advances in Neural Information Processing Systems, pp. 5998–6008 (2017)
41. Wang, L., Yoon, K.J.: Knowledge distillation and student-teacher learning for visual intelligence: a review and new outlooks. IEEE Transactions on Pattern Analysis and Machine Intelligence, pp. 1–1 (2021). https://doi.org/10.1109/TPAMI.2021.3055564
42. Wang, T., Zhu, J.Y., Torralba, A., Efros, A.A.: Dataset distillation. arXiv preprint. arXiv:1811.10959 (2018)
43. Wightman, R.: Pytorch image models (2019). https://github.com/rwightman/pytorch-image-models, https://doi.org/10.5281/zenodo.4414861
44. Wightman, R., Touvron, H., Jégou, H.: Resnet strikes back: an improved training procedure in timm. arXiv preprint. arXiv:2110.00476 (2021)

45. Wu, B., et al.: Fbnet: hardware-aware efficient convnet design via differentiable neural architecture search. In: Proceedings of the IEEE/CVF Conference on Computer Vision and Pattern Recognition, pp. 10734–10742 (2019)
46. Xie, Q., Luong, M.T., Hovy, E., Le, Q.V.: Self-training with noisy student improves imagenet classification. In: Proceedings of the IEEE/CVF Conference on Computer Vision and Pattern Recognition, pp. 10687–10698 (2020)
47. Yim, J., Joo, D., Bae, J., Kim, J.: A gift from knowledge distillation: fast optimization, network minimization and transfer learning. In: Proceedings of the IEEE Conference on Computer Vision and Pattern Recognition, pp. 4133–4141 (2017)
48. Yin, H., et al.: Dreaming to distill: data-free knowledge transfer via deepinversion. In: Proceedings of the IEEE/CVF Conference on Computer Vision and Pattern Recognition, pp. 8715–8724 (2020)
49. Yun, S., Han, D., Oh, S.J., Chun, S., Choe, J., Yoo, Y.: Cutmix: regularization strategy to train strong classifiers with localizable features. In: Proceedings of the IEEE/CVF International Conference on Computer Vision, pp. 6023–6032 (2019)
50. Yun, S., Oh, S.J., Heo, B., Han, D., Choe, J., Chun, S.: Re-labeling imagenet: from single to multi-labels, from global to localized labels. In: Proceedings of the IEEE/CVF Conference on Computer Vision and Pattern Recognition, pp. 2340–2350 (2021)
51. Zhang, L., Song, J., Gao, A., Chen, J., Bao, C., Ma, K.: Be your own teacher: improve the performance of convolutional neural networks via self distillation. In: ICCV (2019)

DICE: Leveraging Sparsification for Out-of-Distribution Detection

Yiyou Sun$^{(\boxtimes)}$ and Yixuan Li

Computer Scof Wisconsin-Madison, Madison, USA
{sunyiyou,sharonli}@cs.wisc.edu

Abstract. Detecting out-of-distribution (OOD) inputs is a central challenge for safely deploying machine learning models in the real world. Previous methods commonly rely on an OOD score derived from the overparameterized weight space, while largely overlooking the role of *sparsification*. In this paper, we reveal important insights that reliance on unimportant weights and units can directly attribute to the brittleness of OOD detection. To mitigate the issue, we propose a sparsification-based OOD detection framework termed **DICE**. Our key idea is to rank weights based on a measure of contribution, and selectively use the most salient weights to derive the output for OOD detection. We provide both empirical and theoretical insights, characterizing and explaining the mechanism by which DICE improves OOD detection. By pruning away noisy signals, DICE provably reduces the output variance for OOD data, resulting in a sharper output distribution and stronger separability from ID data. We demonstrate the effectiveness of sparsification-based OOD detection on several benchmarks and establish competitive performance. Code is available at: https://github.com/deeplearning-wisc/dice.git.

Keywords: Out-of-distribution detection · Sparsification

1 Introduction

Deep neural networks deployed in real-world systems often encounter out-of-distribution (OOD) inputs—samples from unknown classes that the network has not been exposed to during training, and therefore should not be predicted by the model in testing. Being able to estimate and mitigate OOD uncertainty is paramount for safety-critical applications such as medical diagnosis [47,59] and autonomous driving [10]. For example, an autonomous vehicle may fail to recognize objects on the road that do not appear in its detection model's training set, potentially leading to a crash. This gives rise to the importance of OOD detection, which allows the learner to express ignorance and take precautions in the presence of OOD data.

The main challenge in OOD detection stems from the fact that modern deep neural networks can easily produce overconfident predictions on OOD inputs,

Supplementary Information The online version contains supplementary material available at https://doi.org/10.1007/978-3-031-20053-3_40.

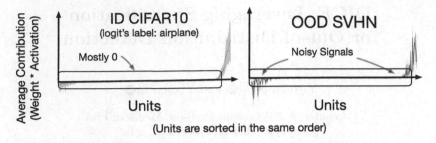

Fig. 1. Illustration of unit contribution (*i.e.*, `weight` × `activation`) to the class output. For class c, the output $f_c(\mathbf{x})$ is the summation of unit contribution from the penultimate feature layer of a neural network. *Units are sorted in the same order*, based on the expectation of ID data's contribution (averaged over many CIFAR-10 samples) on the x-axis. **Shades indicate the variance for each unit. Left:** For in-distribution data (CIFAR-10, airplane), only a subset of units contributes to the model output. **Right:** In contrast, out-of-distribution (OOD) data can trigger a non-negligible fraction of units with noisy signals, as indicated by the variances.

making the separation between in-distribution (ID) and OOD data a non-trivial task. The vulnerability of machine learning to OOD data can be hard-wired in high-capacity models used in practice. In particular, modern deep neural networks can overfit observed patterns in the training data [66], and worse, activate features on unfamiliar inputs [45]. To date, existing OOD detection methods commonly derive OOD scores using overparameterized weights, while largely overlooking the role of *sparsification*. This paper aims to bridge the gap.

In this paper, we start by revealing key insights that reliance on unimportant units and weights can directly attribute to the brittleness of OOD detection. Empirically on a network trained with CIFAR-10, we show that an OOD image can activate a non-negligible fraction of units in the penultimate layer (see Fig. 1, right). Each point on the horizontal axis corresponds to a single unit. The y-axis measures the unit contribution (*i.e.*, `weight` × `activation`) to the output of class AIRPLANE, with the solid line and the shaded area indicating the mean and variance, respectively. Noticeably, for OOD data (gray), we observe a non-negligible fraction of "noisy" units that display high variances of contribution, which is then aggregated to the model's output through summation. As a result, such noisy signals can undesirably manifest in model output—increasing the variance of output distribution and reducing the separability from ID data.

The above observation motivates a simple and effective method, *Di*rected *S*parisification (**DICE**), for OOD detection. DICE leverages the observation that a model's prediction for an ID class depends on only a subset of important units (and corresponding weights), as evidenced in Fig. 1 (left). To exploit this, our novel idea is to rank weights based on the measure of contribution, and selectively use the most contributing weights to derive the output for OOD detection. As a result of the weight sparsification, we show that the model's output becomes more separable between ID and OOD data. Importantly, DICE can be conveniently used by post hoc weight masking on a pre-trained network and therefore can preserve the ID classification accuracy. Orthogonal to existing works on sparsification for accelerating computation, our primary goal is to explore the sparsification approach for improved OOD detection performance.

We provide both empirical and theoretical insights characterizing and explaining the mechanism by which DICE improves OOD detection. We perform extensive evaluations and establish competitive performance on common OOD detection benchmarks, including CIFAR-10, CIFAR-100 [28], and a large-scale ImageNet benchmark [24]. Compared to the competitive post hoc method ReAct [50], DICE reduces the FPR95 by up to 12.55%. Moreover, we perform ablation using various sparsification techniques and demonstrate the benefit of directed sparsification for OOD detection. Theoretically, by pruning away noisy signals from unimportant units and weights, DICE *provably reduces the output variance* and results in a sharper output distribution (see Sect. 6). The sharper distributions lead to a stronger separability between ID and OOD data and overall improved OOD detection performance (*c.f.* Fig. 2). Our **key results and contributions** are:

- (Methodology) We introduce DICE, a simple and effective approach for OOD detection utilizing post hoc weight sparsification. To the best of our knowledge, DICE is the first to explore and demonstrate the effectiveness of sparsification for OOD detection.
- (Experiments) We extensively evaluate DICE on common benchmarks and establish competitive performance among post hoc OOD detection baselines. DICE outperforms the strong baseline [50] by reducing the FPR95 by up to 12.55%. We show DICE can effectively improve OOD detection while preserving the classification accuracy on ID data.
- (Theory and ablations) We provide ablation and theoretical analysis that improves understanding of a sparsification-based method for OOD detection. Our analysis reveals an important variance reduction effect, which provably explains the effectiveness of DICE. We hope our insights inspire future research on weight sparsification for OOD detection.

2   Preliminaries

We start by recalling the general setting of the supervised learning problem. We denote by $\mathcal{X} = \mathbb{R}^d$ the input space and $\mathcal{Y} = \{1, 2, ..., C\}$ the output space. A learner is given access to a set of training data $\mathcal{D} = \{(\mathbf{x}_i, y_i)\}_{i=1}^N$ drawn from an unknown joint data distribution $\mathcal{P}$ defined on $\mathcal{X} \times \mathcal{Y}$. Furthermore, let $\mathcal{P}_{\text{in}}$ denote the marginal probability distribution on $\mathcal{X}$.

Out-of-Distribution Detection. When deploying a model in the real world, a reliable classifier should not only accurately classify known in-distribution (ID) samples, but also identify any OOD input as "unknown". This can be achieved through having dual objectives: ID/OOD classification and multi-class classification of ID data [3].

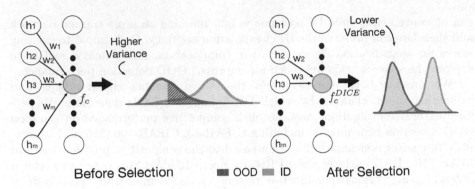

Before Selection   ■ OOD ■ ID   **After Selection**

Fig. 2. Illustration of out-of-distribution detection using *Directed Sparsification* (**DICE**). We consider a pre-trained neural network, which encodes an input $\mathbf{x}$ to a feature vector $h(\mathbf{x}) \in \mathbb{R}^m$. **Left**: The logit output $f_c(\mathbf{x})$ of class c is a linear combination of activation from *all* units in the preceding layer, weighted by w_i. The full connection results in a high variance for OOD data's output, as depicted in the gray. **Right**: Our proposed approach leverages a selective subset of weights, which effectively reduces the output variance for OOD data, resulting in a sharper score distribution and stronger separability from ID data. The output distributions are based on CIFAR-10 trained network, with ID class label "frog" and SVHN as OOD.

OOD detection can be formulated as a binary classification problem. At test time, the goal of OOD detection is to decide whether a sample $\mathbf{x} \in \mathcal{X}$ is from $\mathcal{P}_{\text{in}}$ (ID) or not (OOD). In literature, OOD distribution $\mathcal{P}_{\text{out}}$ often simulates unknowns encountered during deployment time, such as samples from an irrelevant distribution whose label set has no intersection with $\mathcal{Y}$ and therefore should not be predicted by the model. The decision can be made via a thresholding comparison:

$$g_\lambda(\mathbf{x}) = \begin{cases} \text{in} & S(\mathbf{x}) \geq \lambda \\ \text{out} & S(\mathbf{x}) < \lambda \end{cases},$$

where samples with higher scores $S(\mathbf{x})$ are classified as ID and vice versa, and λ is the threshold.

3   Method

Method Overview. Our novel idea is to selectively use a subset of important weights to derive the output for OOD detection. By utilizing sparsification, the network prevents adding irrelevant information to the output. We illustrate our idea in Fig. 2. Without DICE (*left*), the final output is a summation of weighted activations across all units, which can have a high variance for OOD data (colored in gray). In contrast, with DICE (*right*), the variance of output can be significantly reduced, which improves separability from ID data. We proceed with describing our method in details, and provide the theoretical explanation later in Sect. 6.

3.1   DICE: Directed Sparsification

We consider a deep neural network parameterized by θ, which encodes an input $\mathbf{x} \in \mathbb{R}^d$ to a feature space with dimension m. We denote by $h(\mathbf{x}) \in \mathbb{R}^m$ the feature vector from the penultimate layer of the network. A weight matrix $\mathbf{W} \in \mathbb{R}^{m \times C}$ connects the feature $h(\mathbf{x})$ to the output $f(\mathbf{x})$.

Contribution Matrix. We perform a *directed sparsification* based on a measure of contribution, and preserve the most important weights in $\mathbf{W}$. To measure the contribution, we define a contribution matrix $\mathbf{V} \in \mathbb{R}^{m \times C}$, where each column $\mathbf{v}_c \in \mathbb{R}^m$ is given by:

$$\mathbf{v}_c = \mathbb{E}_{\mathbf{x} \in \mathcal{D}}[\mathbf{w}_c \odot h(\mathbf{x})], \tag{1}$$

where $\odot$ indicates the element-wise multiplication, and $\mathbf{w}_c$ indicates weight vector for class c. Each element in $\mathbf{v}_c \in \mathbb{R}^m$ intuitively measures the corresponding unit's average contribution to class c, estimated empirically on in-distribution data $\mathcal{D}$. A larger value indicates a higher contribution to the output $f_c(\mathbf{x})$ of class c. The vector $\mathbf{v}_c$ is derived for all classes $c \in \{1, 2, ..., C\}$, forming the contribution matrix $\mathbf{V}$. Each element $\mathbf{v}_c^i \in \mathbf{V}$ measures the average contribution (`weight` $\times$ `activation`) from a unit i to the output class $c \in \{1, 2, ..., C\}$.

We can now select the top-k weights based on the k-largest elements in $\mathbf{V}$. In particular, we define a masking matrix $\mathbf{M} \in \mathbb{R}^{m \times C}$, which returns a matrix by setting 1 for entries corresponding to the k largest elements in $\mathbf{V}$ and setting other elements to 0. The model output under *contribution-directed sparsification* is given by

$$f^{\text{DICE}}(\mathbf{x}; \theta) = (\mathbf{M} \odot \mathbf{W})^\top h(\mathbf{x}) + \mathbf{b}, \tag{2}$$

where $\mathbf{b} \in \mathbb{R}^C$ is the bias vector. The procedure described above essentially accounts for information from the most relevant units in the penultimate layer. Importantly, the sparsification can be conveniently imposed by *post hoc* weight masking on the final layer of a pre-trained network, without changing any parameterizing of the neural network. Therefore one can improve OOD detection while preserving the ID classification accuracy.

Sparsity Parameter p. To align with the convention in literature, we use the sparsity parameter $p = 1 - \frac{k}{m \cdot C}$ in the remainder paper. A higher p indicates a larger fraction of weights dropped. When $p = 0$, the output becomes equivalent to the original output $f(\mathbf{x}; \theta)$ using dense transformation, where $f(\mathbf{x}; \theta) = \mathbf{W}^\top h(\mathbf{x}) + \mathbf{b}$. We provide ablations on the sparsity parameter later in Sect. 5.

3.2   OOD Detection with DICE

Our method DICE in Sect. 3.1 can be flexibly leveraged by the downstream OOD scoring function:

$$g_\lambda(\mathbf{x}) = \begin{cases} \text{in} & S_\theta(\mathbf{x}) \geq \lambda \\ \text{out} & S_\theta(\mathbf{x}) < \lambda \end{cases}, \tag{3}$$

where a thresholding mechanism is exercised to distinguish between ID and OOD during test time. The threshold λ is typically chosen so that a high fraction of ID data (*e.g.*, 95%) is correctly classified. Following recent work by Liu *et. al* [35], we derive an energy score using the logit output $f^{\text{DICE}}(\mathbf{x}; \theta)$ with contribution-directed sparsification. The function maps the logit outputs $f^{\text{DICE}}(\mathbf{x}; \theta)$ to a scalar $E_\theta(\mathbf{x}) \in \mathbb{R}$, which is relatively lower for ID data:

$$S_\theta(\mathbf{x}) = -E_\theta(\mathbf{x}) = \log \sum_{c=1}^{C} \exp(f_c^{\text{DICE}}(\mathbf{x}; \theta)). \tag{4}$$

The energy score can be viewed as the log of the denominator in softmax function:

$$p(y|\mathbf{x}) = \frac{p(\mathbf{x}, y)}{p(\mathbf{x})} = \frac{\exp(f_y(\mathbf{x}; \theta))}{\sum_{c=1}^{C} \exp(f_c(\mathbf{x}; \theta))}, \tag{5}$$

and enjoys better theoretical interpretation than using posterior probability $p(y|\mathbf{x})$. Note that DICE can also be compatible with an alternative scoring function such as maximum softmax probability (MSP) [19], though the performance of MSP is less competitive (see Appendix F). Later in Sect. 6, we formally characterize and explain why DICE improves the separability of the scores between ID and OOD data.

4   Experiments

In this section, we evaluate our method on a suite of OOD detection tasks. We begin with the CIFAR benchmarks that are routinely used in literature (Sect. 4.1). In Sect. 4.2, we continue with a large-scale OOD detection task based on ImageNet.

4.1   Evaluation on Common Benchmarks

Experimental Details. We use CIFAR-10 [28], and CIFAR-100 [28] datasets as in-distribution data. We use the standard split with 50,000 training images and 10,000 test images. We evaluate the model on six common OOD benchmark datasets: `Textures` [6], `SVHN` [44], `Places365` [67], `LSUN-Crop` [65], `LSUN-Resize` [65], and `iSUN` [63]. We use DenseNet-101 architecture [22] and train on in-distribution datasets. The feature dimension of the penultimate layer is 342. For both CIFAR-10 and CIFAR-100, the model is trained for 100 epochs

Table 1. Comparison with competitive *post hoc* out-of-distribution detection method on CIFAR benchmarks. All values are percentages and are averaged over 6 OOD test datasets. The full results for each evaluation dataset are provided in Appendix G. We report standard deviations estimated across 5 independent runs. §indicates an exception, where model retraining using a different loss function is required.

Method	CIFAR-10		CIFAR-100	
	FPR95	AUROC	FPR95	AUROC
	↓	↑	↓	↑
MSP [19]	48.73	92.46	80.13	74.36
ODIN [33]	24.57	93.71	58.14	84.49
GODIN§ [21]	34.25	90.61	52.87	85.24
Mahalanobis [31]	31.42	89.15	55.37	82.73
Energy [35]	26.55	94.57	68.45	81.19
ReAct [50]	26.45	94.95	62.27	84.47
DICE (ours)	**20.83**$^{\pm1.58}$	**95.24**$^{\pm0.24}$	**49.72**$^{\pm1.69}$	**87.23**$^{\pm0.73}$

with batch size 64, weight decay 0.0001 and momentum 0.9. The start learning rate is 0.1 and decays by a factor of 10 at epochs 50, 75, and 90. We use the validation strategy in Appendix C to select p.

DICE vs. Competitive Baselines. We show the results in Table 1, where DICE outperforms competitive baselines. In particular, we compare with Maximum Softmax Probability [19], ODIN [33], Mahalanobis distance [31], Generalized ODIN [21], Energy score [35], and ReAct [50]. For a fair comparison, all the methods derive the OOD score post hoc from the same pre-trained model, except for G-ODIN which requires model re-training. For readers' convenience, a brief introduction of baselines and hyperparameters is provided in Appendix B.

On CIFAR-100, we show that DICE reduces the average FPR95 by **18.73%** compared to the vanilla energy score [35] without sparsification. Moreover, our method also outperforms a competitive method ReAct [50] by 12.55%. While ReAct only considers activation space, DICE examines *both the weights and activation* values together—the multiplication of which directly determines the network's logit output. Overall our method is more generally applicable, and can be implemented through a simple post hoc weight masking.

ID Classification Accuracy. Given the *post hoc* nature of DICE, once the input image is marked as ID, one can always use the original fc layer, which is guaranteed to give identical classification accuracy. This incurs minimal overhead and results in optimal performance for both classification and OOD detection. We also measure the classification accuracy under different sparsification parameter p. Due to the space limit, the full results are available in Table 6 in Appendix.

Table 2. Main results. Comparison with competitive *post hoc* out-of-distribution detection methods. All methods are based on a discriminative model trained on ImageNet. ↑ indicates larger values are better and ↓ indicates smaller values are better. All values are percentages. **Bold** numbers are superior results.

Methods	OOD Datasets								Average	
	iNaturalist		SUN		Places		Textures			
	FPR95 ↓	AUROC ↑	FPR95 ↓	AUROC ↑	FPR95 ↓	AUROC ↑	FPR95 ↓	AUROC ↑	FPR95 ↓	AUROC ↑
MSP [19]	54.99	87.74	70.83	80.86	73.99	79.76	68.00	79.61	66.95	81.99
ODIN [33]	47.66	89.66	60.15	84.59	67.89	81.78	50.23	85.62	56.48	85.41
GODIN [21]	61.91	85.40	60.83	85.60	63.70	83.81	77.85	73.27	66.07	82.02
Mahalanobis [31]	97.00	52.65	98.50	42.41	98.40	41.79	55.80	85.01	87.43	55.47
Energy [35]	55.72	89.95	59.26	85.89	64.92	82.86	53.72	85.99	58.41	86.17
ReAct [50]	20.38	96.22	**24.20**	**94.20**	**33.85**	**91.58**	47.30	89.80	31.43	92.95
DICE (ours)	25.63	94.49	35.15	90.83	46.49	87.48	31.72	90.30	34.75	90.77
DICE + ReAct (ours)	**18.64**	**96.24**	25.45	93.94	36.86	90.67	**28.07**	**92.74**	**27.25**	**93.40**

4.2 Evaluation on ImageNet

Dataset. We then evaluate DICE on a large-scale ImageNet classification model. Following MOS [24], we use four OOD test datasets from (subsets of) Places365 [67], Textures [6], iNaturalist [56], and SUN [62] with non-overlapping categories *w.r.t.* ImageNet. The evaluations span a diverse range of domains including fine-grained images, scene images, and textural images. OOD detection for the ImageNet model is more challenging due to both a larger feature space ($m = 2,048$) as well as a larger label space ($C = 1,000$). In particular, the large-scale evaluation can be relevant to real-world applications, where the deployed models often operate on images that have high resolution and contain many class labels. Moreover, as the number of feature dimensions increases, noisy signals may increase accordingly, which can make OOD detection more challenging.

Experimental Details. We use a pre-trained ResNet-50 model [16] for ImageNet-1k provided by Pytorch. At test time, all images are resized to 224 × 224. We use the entire training dataset to estimate the contribution matrix and masking matrix **M**. We use the validation strategy in Appendix C to select p. The hardware used for experiments is specified in Appendix A.

Comparison with Baselines. In Table 2, we compare DICE with competitive post hoc OOD detection methods. We report performance for each OOD test dataset, as well as the average of the four. We first contrast DICE with energy score [35], which allows us to see the direct benefit of using sparsification under the same scoring function. DICE reduces the FPR95 drastically from 58.41% to 34.75%, a **23.66%** improvement using sparsification. Second, we contrast with a recent method ReAct [50], which demonstrates strong performance on this challenging task using activation truncation. With the truncated activation proposed in ReAct [50], we show that DICE can further reduce the FPR95 by 5.78% with

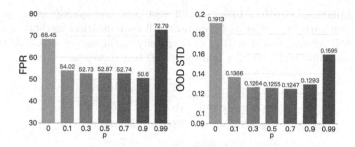

Fig. 3. Effect of varying sparsity parameter p during inference time. Model is trained on CIFAR-100 using DenseNet101 [22].

weight sparsification. Since the comparison is conducted on the same scoring function and feature activation, the performance improvement from ReAct to DICE+ReAct precisely highlights the benefit of using weight sparsification as opposed to the full weights. Lastly, Mahalanobis displays limiting performance on ImageNet, while being computationally expensive due to estimating the inverse of the covariance matrix. In contrast, DICE is easy to use in practice, and can be implemented through simple post hoc weight masking.

5   Discussion and Ablations

Ablation on Sparsity Parameter p. We now characterize the effect of sparsity parameter p. In Fig. 3, we summarize the OOD detection performance for DenseNet trained on CIFAR-100, where we vary $p = \{0.1, 0.3, 0.5, 0.7, 0.9, 0.99\}$. Interestingly, we observe the performance improves with mild sparsity parameter p. A significant improvement can be observed from $p = 0$ (no sparsity) to $p = 0.1$. As we will theoretically later in Sect. 6, this is because the leftmost part of units being pruned has larger variances for OOD data (gray shade). Units in the middle part have small variances and contributions for both ID and OOD, therefore leading to similar performance as p increases mildly. This ablation confirms that over-parameterization does compromise the OOD detection ability, and DICE can effectively alleviate the problem. In the extreme case when p is too large (*e.g.*, $p = 0.99$), the OOD performance starts to degrade as expected.

Effect of Variance Reduction for Output Distribution. Figure 2 shows that DICE has an interesting variance reduction effect on the output distribution for OOD data, and at the same time preserves the information for the ID data (CIFAR-10, class "frog"). The output distribution without any sparsity ($p = 0$) appears to have a larger variance, resulting in less separability from ID data (see left of Fig. 2). In contrast, sparsification with DICE results in a sharper distribution, which benefits OOD detection. In Fig. 3, we also measure the standard deviation of energy score for OOD data (normalized by the mean of ID data's OOD scores in each setting). By way of sparsification, DICE can

Table 3. Ablation results. Effect of different *post hoc* sparsification methods for OOD detection with ImageNet as ID dataset. All sparsification methods are based on the same OOD scoring function [35], with sparsity parameter $p = 0.7$. All values are percentages and are averaged over multiple OOD test datasets.

Method	FPR95↓	AUROC↑
Weight-Dropout	76.28	76.55
Unit-Dropout	83.91	64.98
Weight-Pruning	52.81	87.08
Unit-Pruning	90.80	49.15
DICE (Ours)	**34.75**	**90.77**

reduce the output variance. In Sect. 6, we formally characterize this and provide a theoretical explanation.

Ablation on Pruning Methods. In this ablation, we evaluate OOD detection performance under the most common *post hoc* sparsification methods. Here we primarily consider post hoc sparsification strategy which operates conveniently on a *pre-trained* network, instead of training with sparse regularization or architecture modification. The property is especially desirable for the adoption of OOD detection methods in real-world production environments, where the overhead cost of retraining can be sometimes prohibitive. Orthogonal to existing works on sparsification, our primary goal is to explore the role of sparsification for improved OOD detection performance, rather than establishing a generic sparsification algorithm. We consider the most common strategies, covering both unit-based and weight-based sparsification methods: (1) unit dropout [49] which randomly drops a fraction of units, (2) unit pruning [32] which drops units with the smallest L_2 norm of the corresponding weight vectors, (3) weight dropout [57] which randomly drops weights in the fully connected layer, and (4) weight pruning [15] drops weights with the smallest entries under the L_1 norm. For consistency, we use the same OOD scoring function and the same sparsity parameter for all.

Our ablation reveals several important insights shown in Table 3. First, in contrasting weight dropout vs. DICE, a salient performance gap of 41.53% (FPR95) is observed under the same sparsity. This suggests the importance of dropping weights *directedly* rather than *randomly*. Second, DICE outperforms a popular L_1-norm-based pruning method [15] by up to 18.06% (FPR95). While it prunes weights with low magnitude, negative weights with large L_1-norm can be kept. The negative weights can undesirably corrupt the output with noisy signals (as shown in Fig. 1). The performance gain of DICE over [15] attributes to our contribution-directed sparsification, which is better suited for OOD detection.

Ablation on Unit Selection. We have shown that choosing a subset of weights (with *top-k* unit contribution) significantly improves the OOD detection performance. In this ablation, we also analyze those "lower contribution units" for

Table 4. Ablation on different strategies of choosing a subset of units. Values are FPR95 (averaged over multiple test datasets).

Method	CIFAR-10↓	CIFAR-100 ↓
Bottom-k	91.87	99.70
(Top+Bottom)-k	24.25	59.93
Random-k	62.12	77.48
Top-k (**DICE**)	**20.83**$^{\pm1.58}$	**49.72**$^{\pm1.69}$

OOD detection. Specifically, we consider: (1) *Bottom-k* which only includes k unit contribution with least contribution values, (2) *top+bottom-k* which includes k unit contribution with largest and smallest contribution values, (3) *random-k* which randomly includes k unit contribution and (4) *top-k* which is equivalent to DICE method. In Table 4, we show that DICE outperforms these variants.

6   Why Does DICE Improve OOD Detection?

In this section, we formally explain the mechanism by which reliance on irrelevant units hurts OOD detection and how DICE effectively mitigates the issue. Our analysis highlights that DICE reduces the output variance for both ID and OOD data. Below we provide details.

Setup. For a class c, we consider the unit contribution vector $\mathbf{v}$, the element-wise multiplication between the feature vector $\mathbf{h}(\mathbf{x})$ and corresponding weight vector $\mathbf{w}$. We contrast the two outputs with and without sparsity:

$$f_c = \sum_{i=1}^{m} v_i \quad \text{(w.o sparsity)},$$

$$f_c^{\text{DICE}} = \sum_{i \in \text{top units}} v_i \quad \text{(w. sparsity)},$$

where f_c is the output using the summation of all units' contribution, and f_c^{DICE} takes the input from the top units (ranked based on the average contribution on ID data, see bottom of Fig. 4).

DICE Reduces the Output Variance. We consider the unit contribution vector for OOD data $\mathbf{v} \in \mathbb{R}^m$, where each element is a *random variable* v_i with mean $\mathbb{E}[v_i] = \mu_i$ and variance $\text{Var}[v_i] = \sigma_i^2$. For simplicity, we assume each component is independent, but our theory can be extended to correlated variables (see Remark 1). Importantly, indices in $\mathbf{v}$ are sorted based on *the same order* of unit contribution on ID data. By using units on the rightmost side, we now show the key result that DICE reduces the output variance.

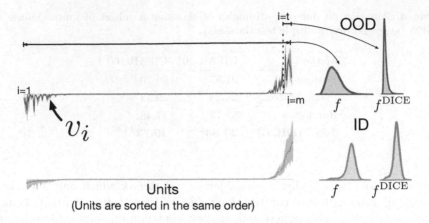

Fig. 4. Units in the penultimate layer are sorted based on the average contribution to a CIFAR-10 class ("airplane"). OOD data (SVHN) can trigger a non-negligible fraction of units with noisy signals on the CIFAR-10 trained model.

Proposition 1. *Let v_i and v_j be two independent random variables. Denote the summation $r = v_i + v_j$, we have $\mathbb{E}[r] = \mathbb{E}[v_i] + \mathbb{E}[v_j]$ and $\mathrm{Var}[r] = \mathrm{Var}[v_i] + \mathrm{Var}[v_j]$.*

Lemma 1. *When taking the top $m - t$ units, the output variable f_c^{DICE} under sparsification has reduced variance:*

$$\mathrm{Var}[f_c] - \mathrm{Var}[f_c^{DICE}] = \sum_{i=1}^{t} \sigma_i^2$$

Proof. The proof directly follows Proposition 1.

Remark 1 (Extension to Correlated Variables). We can show in a more general case with correlated variables, the variance reduction is:

$$\sum_{i=1}^{t} \sigma_i^2 + 2 \sum_{1 \leq i < j \leq m} \mathrm{Cov}(v_i, v_j) - 2 \sum_{t < i < j \leq m} \mathrm{Cov}(v_i, v_j),$$

where $\mathrm{Cov}(\cdot, \cdot)$ is the covariance. Our analysis shows that the covariance matrix primarily consists of 0, which indicates the independence of variables. Moreover, the summation of non-zero entries in the full matrix (i.e., the second term) is greater than that of the submatrix with top units (i.e., the third term), resulting in a larger variance reduction than in Lemma 1. See complete proof in Appendix E.

Remark 2. Energy score is compatible with DICE since it directly operates in the logit space. Our theoretical analysis above shows that DICE reduces the variance of each logit $f_c(\mathbf{x})$. This means that for detection scores such as energy score, the gap between OOD and ID score will be enlarged after applying DICE, which makes thresholding more capable of separating OOD and ID inputs and benefit OOD detection.

Table 5. Difference between the mean of ID's output and OOD's output. Here we use CIFAR-100 as ID data and $\Delta = \mathbb{E}_{in}[\max_c f_c^{DICE}]$ - $\mathbb{E}_{out}[\max_c f_c^{DICE}]$ is averaged over six common OOD benchmark datasets described in Sect. 4.

Sparsity	$p = 0.9$	$p = 0.7$	$p = 0.5$	$p = 0.3$	$p = 0.1$	$p = 0$
Δ	7.92	7.28	7.99	8.04	7.36	6.67

Remark 3 (Mean of output). Beyond variance, we further show in Table 5 the effect of sparsity on the mean of output: $\mathbb{E}_{in}[\max_c f_c^{DICE}]$ and $\mathbb{E}_{out}[\max_c f_c^{DICE}]$. The gap between the two directly translates into the OOD score separability. We show that DICE maintains similar (or even enlarges) differences in terms of mean as sparsity p increases. Therefore, DICE overall benefits OOD detection due to both *reduced output variances* and *increased differences of mean*—the combination of both effects leads to stronger separability between ID and OOD.

Remark 4 (Variance reduction on ID data). Note that we can also show the effect of variance reduction for ID data in a similar way. Importantly, DICE effectively preserves the most important information akin to the ID data, while reducing noisy signals that are harmful to OOD detection. Overall the variance reduction effect on both ID and OOD data leads to stronger separability.

7 Related Work

Out-of-distribution detection has attracted growing research attention in recent years. We highlight two major lines of work:

(1) One line of work perform OOD detection by devising scoring functions, including confidence-based methods [3,19,24,33], energy-based score [34,35,43,50, 58], distance-based approaches [31,48,51,54], gradient-based score [23], and Bayesian approaches [11,29,37–39]. However, none of the previous methods considered weight sparsification for OOD detection. The closest work to ours is ReAct [50], which proposed truncating the high activations during test time for OOD detection. While ReAct only considers activation space, DICE examines both the weights and activation values together—the multiplication of which directly determines the unit contributions to the output. Our work is also related to [7], which pointed out that modern OOD detection methods succeed by detecting the existence of familiar features. DICE strengthens the familiarity hypothesis by keeping the dominating weights corresponding to the "major features".

(2) A separate line of methods addressed OOD detection by training-time regularization [4,5,12,17,20,25,26,30,35,38,40–42,55,60,64]. For example, models are encouraged to give predictions with uniform distribution [20,30] or higher energies [8,9,26,35,41] for outlier data. The scope of this paper focuses on post hoc methods, which have the advantages of being easy to use and general

applicability without modifying the training objective. The latter property is especially desirable for the adoption of OOD detection methods in real-world production environments, when the overhead cost of retraining can be prohibitive.

Pruning and Sparsification. A great number of effort has been put into improving *post hoc* pruning and training time regularization for deep neural networks [1,2,13–15,32,36]. Many works obtain a sparse model by training with sparse regularization [1,2,14,36,52] or architecture modification [13,32], while our work primarily considers *post hoc* sparsification strategy which operates conveniently on a pre-trained network. On this line, two popular Bernoulli dropout techniques include unit dropout and weight dropout [49]. *Post hoc* pruning strategies truncate weights with low magnitude [15], or drop units with low weight norms [32]. In [61], they use a sparse linear layer to help identify spurious correlations and explain misclassifications. Orthogonal to existing works, our goal is to improve the OOD detection performance rather than accelerate computation and network debugging. In this paper, we first demonstrate that sparsification can be useful for OOD detection. An in-depth discussion and comparison of these methods are presented in Sect. 5.

Distributional Shifts. Distributional shifts have attracted increasing research interest. It is important to recognize and differentiate various types of distributional shift problems. Literature in OOD detection is commonly concerned about model reliability and detection of semantic shifts, where the OOD inputs have disjoint labels *w.r.t.* ID data and therefore should not be predicted by the model. This is different from the OOD generalization task whose goal is to provide accurate predictions on OOD images under the same label space. For example, some works considered covariate shifts in the input space [18,27,46,53,68], where the model is expected to generalize to the OOD data.

8   Conclusion

This paper provides a simple sparsification strategy termed DICE, which ranks weights based on a contribution measure and then uses the most significant weights to derive the output for OOD detection. We provide both empirical and theoretical insights characterizing and explaining the mechanism by which DICE improves OOD detection. By exploiting the most important weights, DICE provably reduces the output variance for OOD data, resulting in a sharper output distribution and stronger separability from ID data. Extensive experiments show DICE can significantly improve the performance of OOD detection for overparameterized networks. We hope our research can raise more attention to the importance of weight sparsification for OOD detection.

Acknowledgement. Work was supported by funding from Wisconsin Alumni Research Foundation (WARF). The authors would also like to thank reviewers for the helpful feedback.

References

1. Ba, J., Frey, B.: Adaptive dropout for training deep neural networks. In: Advances in Neural Information Processing Systems, vol. 26 (2013)
2. Babaeizadeh, M., Smaragdis, P., Campbell, R.H.: Noiseout: a simple way to prune neural networks. CoRR abs/1611.06211 (2016)
3. Bendale, A., Boult, T.E.: Towards open set deep networks. In: Proceedings of the IEEE Conference on Computer Vision and Pattern Recognition, pp. 1563–1572 (2016)
4. Bevandić, P., Krešo, I., Oršić, M., Šegvić, S.: Discriminative out-of-distribution detection for semantic segmentation. arXiv preprint. arXiv:1808.07703 (2018)
5. Chen, J., Li, Y., Wu, X., Liang, Y., Jha, S.: ATOM: robustifying out-of-distribution detection using outlier mining. In: Oliver, N., Pérez-Cruz, F., Kramer, S., Read, J., Lozano, J.A. (eds.) ECML PKDD 2021. LNCS (LNAI), vol. 12977, pp. 430–445. Springer, Cham (2021). https://doi.org/10.1007/978-3-030-86523-8_26
6. Cimpoi, M., Maji, S., Kokkinos, I., Mohamed, S., Vedaldi, A.: Describing textures in the wild. In: Proceedings of the IEEE Conference on Computer Vision and Pattern Recognition, pp. 3606–3613 (2014)
7. Dietterich, T.G., Guyer, A.: The familiarity hypothesis: explaining the behavior of deep open set methods. arXiv preprint. arXiv:2203.02486 (2022)
8. Du, X., Wang, X., Gozum, G., Li, Y.: Unknown-aware object detection: learning what you don't know from videos in the wild. In: Proceedings of the IEEE/CVF Conference on Computer Vision and Pattern Recognition (2022)
9. Du, X., Wang, Z., Cai, M., Li, Y.: Vos: learning what you don't know by virtual outlier synthesis. In: Proceedings of the International Conference on Learning Representations (2022)
10. Filos, A., Tigkas, P., McAllister, R., Rhinehart, N., Levine, S., Gal, Y.: Can autonomous vehicles identify, recover from, and adapt to distribution shifts? In: Proceedings of the International Conference on Machine Learning, pp. 3145–3153. PMLR (2020)
11. Gal, Y., Ghahramani, Z.: Dropout as a bayesian approximation: Representing model uncertainty in deep learning. In: Proceedings of the International Conference on Machine Learning, pp. 1050–1059 (2016)
12. Geifman, Y., El-Yaniv, R.: Selectivenet: a deep neural network with an integrated reject option. arXiv preprint. arXiv:1901.09192 (2019)
13. Gomez, A.N., et al.: Learning sparse networks using targeted dropout. arXiv preprint. arXiv:1905.13678 (2019)
14. Han, S., Mao, H., Dally, W.J.: Deep compression: compressing deep neural network with pruning, trained quantization and huffman coding. In: Proceedings of the International Conference on Learning Representations (2016)
15. Han, S., Pool, J., Tran, J., Dally, W.: Learning both weights and connections for efficient neural network. In: Proceedings of the Advances in Neural Information Processing Systems. vol. 28, pp. 1135–1143 (2015)
16. He, K., Zhang, X., Ren, S., Sun, J.: Identity mappings in deep residual networks. In: Leibe, B., Matas, J., Sebe, N., Welling, M. (eds.) ECCV 2016. LNCS, vol. 9908, pp. 630–645. Springer, Cham (2016). https://doi.org/10.1007/978-3-319-46493-0_38
17. Hein, M., Andriushchenko, M., Bitterwolf, J.: Why relu networks yield high-confidence predictions far away from the training data and how to mitigate the problem. In: Proceedings of the IEEE Conference on Computer Vision and Pattern Recognition, pp. 41–50 (2019)

18. Hendrycks, D., Dietterich, T.: Benchmarking neural network robustness to common corruptions and perturbations. arXiv preprint. arXiv:1903.12261 (2019)
19. Hendrycks, D., Gimpel, K.: A baseline for detecting misclassified and out-of-distribution examples in neural networks. In: Proceedings of International Conference on Learning Representations (2017)
20. Hendrycks, D., Mazeika, M., Dietterich, T.: Deep anomaly detection with outlier exposure. arXiv preprint. arXiv:1812.04606 (2018)
21. Hsu, Y.C., Shen, Y., Jin, H., Kira, Z.: Generalized odin: detecting out-of-distribution image without learning from out-of-distribution data. In: Proceedings of the IEEE/CVF Conference on Computer Vision and Pattern Recognition (2020)
22. Huang, G., Liu, Z., Van Der Maaten, L., Weinberger, K.Q.: Densely connected convolutional networks. In: Proceedings of the IEEE Conference on Computer Vision and Pattern Recognition, pp. 4700–4708 (2017)
23. Huang, R., Geng, A., Li, Y.: On the importance of gradients for detecting distributional shifts in the wild. In: Proceedings of the Advances in Neural Information Processing Systems (2021)
24. Huang, R., Li, Y.: Towards scaling out-of-distribution detection for large semantic space. In: Proceedings of the IEEE/CVF Conference on Computer Vision and Pattern Recognition (2021)
25. Jeong, T., Kim, H.: Ood-maml: meta-learning for few-shot out-of-distribution detection and classification. In: Proceedings of the Advances in Neural Information Processing Systems (2020)
26. Katz-Samuels, J., Nakhleh, J., Nowak, R., Li, Y.: Training ood detectors in their natural habitats. In: Proceedings of the International Conference on Machine Learning. PMLR (2022)
27. Koh, P.W., et al.: Wilds: a benchmark of in-the-wild distribution shifts. In: Proceedings of the International Conference on Machine Learning, pp. 5637–5664. PMLR (2021)
28. Krizhevsky, A., Hinton, G., et al.: Learning multiple layers of features from tiny images (2009)
29. Lakshminarayanan, B., Pritzel, A., Blundell, C.: Simple and scalable predictive uncertainty estimation using deep ensembles. In: Advances in Neural Information Processing Systems, pp. 6402–6413 (2017)
30. Lee, K., Lee, H., Lee, K., Shin, J.: Training confidence-calibrated classifiers for detecting out-of-distribution samples. arXiv preprint. arXiv:1711.09325 (2017)
31. Lee, K., Lee, K., Lee, H., Shin, J.: A simple unified framework for detecting out-of-distribution samples and adversarial attacks. In: Advances in Neural Information Processing Systems, pp. 7167–7177 (2018)
32. Li, H., Kadav, A., Durdanovic, I., Samet, H., Graf, H.P.: Pruning filters for efficient convnets. In: Proceedings of International Conference on Learning Representations (2017)
33. Liang, S., Li, Y., Srikant, R.: Enhancing the reliability of out-of-distribution image detection in neural networks. In: Proceedings of International Conference on Learning Representations (2018)
34. Lin, Z., Roy, S.D., Li, Y.: Mood: multi-level out-of-distribution detection. In: Proceedings of the IEEE/CVF Conference on Computer Vision and Pattern Recognition, pp. 15313–15323 (2021)
35. Liu, W., Wang, X., Owens, J., Li, Y.: Energy-based out-of-distribution detection. In: Proceedings of the Advances in Neural Information Processing Systems (2020)
36. Louizos, C., Welling, M., Kingma, D.P.: Learning sparse neural networks through l_0 regularization. In: International Conference on Learning Representations (2018)

37. Maddox, W.J., Izmailov, P., Garipov, T., Vetrov, D.P., Wilson, A.G.: A simple baseline for bayesian uncertainty in deep learning. In: Advances in Neural Information Processing Systems, vol. 32, pp. 13153–13164 (2019)
38. Malinin, A., Gales, M.: Predictive uncertainty estimation via prior networks. In: Advances in Neural Information Processing Systems, pp. 7047–7058 (2018)
39. Malinin, A., Gales, M.: Reverse kl-divergence training of prior networks: improved uncertainty and adversarial robustness. In: Advances in Neural Information Processing Systems (2019)
40. Meinke, A., Hein, M.: Towards neural networks that provably know when they don't know. arXiv preprint. arXiv:1909.12180 (2019)
41. Ming, Y., Fan, Y., Li, Y.: Poem: out-of-distribution detection with posterior sampling. In: Proceedings of the International Conference on Machine Learning. PMLR (2022)
42. Mohseni, S., Pitale, M., Yadawa, J., Wang, Z.: Self-supervised learning for generalizable out-of-distribution detection. In: AAAI, pp. 5216–5223 (2020)
43. Morteza, P., Li, Y.: Provable guarantees for understanding out-of-distribution detection. In: Proceedings of the AAAI Conference on Artificial Intelligence (2022)
44. Netzer, Y., Wang, T., Coates, A., Bissacco, A., Wu, B., Ng, A.Y.: Reading digits in natural images with unsupervised feature learning (2011)
45. Nguyen, A., Yosinski, J., Clune, J.: Deep neural networks are easily fooled: high confidence predictions for unrecognizable images. In: Proceedings of the IEEE Conference on Computer Vision and Pattern Recognition, pp. 427–436 (2015)
46. Ovadia, Y. et al.: Can you trust your model's uncertainty? evaluating predictive uncertainty under dataset shift. In: Proceedings of the Advances in Neural Information Processing Systems, vol. 32, pp. 13991–14002 (2019)
47. Roy, A.G., et al.: Does your dermatology classifier know what it doesn't know? detecting the long-tail of unseen conditions. arXiv preprint. arXiv:2104.03829 (2021)
48. Sehwag, V., Chiang, M., Mittal, P.: Ssd: a unified framework for self-supervised outlier detection. In: International Conference on Learning Representations (2021)
49. Srivastava, N., Hinton, G., Krizhevsky, A., Sutskever, I., Salakhutdinov, R.: Dropout: a simple way to prevent neural networks from overfitting. J. Mach. Learn. Res. 15, 1929–1958 (2014)
50. Sun, Y., Guo, C., Li, Y.: React: out-of-distribution detection with rectified activations. In: Advances in Neural Information Processing Systems (2021)
51. Sun, Y., Ming, Y., Zhu, X., Li, Y.: Out-of-distribution detection with deep nearest neighbors. In: Proceedings of the International Conference on Machine Learning (2022)
52. Sun, Y., Ravi, S., Singh, V.: Adaptive activation thresholding: dynamic routing type behavior for interpretability in convolutional neural networks. In: Proceedings of the International Conference on Computer Vision (2019)
53. Sun, Y., Wang, X., Liu, Z., Miller, J., Efros, A., Hardt, M.: Test-time training with self-supervision for generalization under distribution shifts. In: Proceedings of the International Conference on Machine Learning. pp. 9229–9248. PMLR (2020)
54. Tack, J., Mo, S., Jeong, J., Shin, J.: Csi: novelty detection via contrastive learning on distributionally shifted instances. In: Advances in Neural Information Processing Systems (2020)
55. Van Amersfoort, J., Smith, L., Teh, Y.W., Gal, Y.: Uncertainty estimation using a single deep deterministic neural network. In: Proceedings of the International Conference on Machine Learning (2020)

56. Van Horn, G., et al.: The inaturalist species classification and detection dataset. In: Proceedings of the IEEE Conference on Computer Vision and Pattern Recognition, pp. 8769–8778 (2018)
57. Wan, L., Zeiler, M.D., Zhang, S., LeCun, Y., Fergus, R.: Regularization of neural networks using dropconnect. In: Proceedings of the International Conference on Machine Learning, vol. 28, pp. 1058–1066 (2013)
58. Wang, H., Liu, W., Bocchieri, A., Li, Y.: Can multi-label classification networks know what they don't know? Proceedings of the Advances in Neural Information Processing Systems (2021)
59. Wang, X., Peng, Y., Lu, L., Lu, Z., Bagheri, M., Summers, R.M.: Chestx-ray8: hospital-scale chest x-ray database and benchmarks on weakly-supervised classification and localization of common thorax diseases. In: Proceedings of the IEEE Conference on Computer Vision and Pattern Recognition, pp. 2097–2106 (2017)
60. Wei, H., Xie, R., Cheng, H., Feng, L., An, B., Li, Y.: Mitigating neural network overconfidence with logit normalization. In: Proceedings of the International Conference on Machine Learning (2022)
61. Wong, E., Santurkar, S., Madry, A.: Leveraging sparse linear layers for debuggable deep networks. In: Proceedings of the International Conference on Machine Learning, pp. 11205–11216. PMLR (2021)
62. Xiao, J., Hays, J., Ehinger, K.A., Oliva, A., Torralba, A.: Sun database: large-scale scene recognition from abbey to zoo. In: Proceedings of the IEEE Conference on Computer Vision and Pattern Recognition, pp. 3485–3492. IEEE Computer Society (2010)
63. Xu, P., Ehinger, K.A., Zhang, Y., Finkelstein, A., Kulkarni, S.R., Xiao, J.: Turkergaze: crowdsourcing saliency with webcam based eye tracking. arXiv preprint. arXiv:1504.06755 (2015)
64. Yang, J., et al.: Semantically coherent out-of-distribution detection. In: Proceedings of the IEEE International Conference on Computer Vision, pp. 8301–8309 (2021)
65. Yu, F., Seff, A., Zhang, Y., Song, S., Funkhouser, T., Xiao, J.: Lsun: construction of a large-scale image dataset using deep learning with humans in the loop. arXiv preprint. arXiv:1506.03365 (2015)
66. Zhang, C., Bengio, S., Hardt, M., Recht, B., Vinyals, O.: Understanding deep learning requires rethinking generalization. In: Proceedings of International Conference on Learning Representations
67. Zhou, B., Lapedriza, A., Khosla, A., Oliva, A., Torralba, A.: Places: a 10 million image database for scene recognition. In: IEEE Transactions on Pattern Analysis and Machine Intelligence, vol. 40, pp. 1452–1464. IEEE (2017)
68. Zhou, K., Liu, Z., Qiao, Y., Xiang, T., Loy, C.C.: Domain generalization: a survey (2021)

Invariant Feature Learning
for Generalized Long-Tailed Classification

Kaihua Tang[1]([✉]), Mingyuan Tao[2], Jiaxin Qi[1], Zhenguang Liu[3],
and Hanwang Zhang[1]

[1] Nanyang Technological University, Singapore, Singapore
{kaihua.tang,hanwangzhang}@ntu.edu.sg, jiaxin003@e.ntu.edu.sg
[2] Damo Academy, Alibaba Group, Hangzhou, China
juchen.tmy@alibaba-inc.com
[3] Zhejiang University, Hangzhou, China

Abstract. Existing long-tailed classification (LT) methods only focus
on tackling the **class-wise imbalance** that head classes have more samples than tail classes, but overlook the **attribute-wise imbalance**. In
fact, even if the class is balanced, samples within each class may still
be long-tailed due to the varying attributes. Note that the latter is fundamentally more ubiquitous and challenging than the former because
attributes are not just implicit for most datasets, but also combinatori-
ally complex, thus prohibitively expensive to be balanced. Therefore, we
introduce a novel research problem: **Generalized Long-Tailed** classification (GLT), to jointly consider both kinds of imbalances. By "generalized", we mean that a GLT method should naturally solve the traditional
LT, but not vice versa. Not surprisingly, we find that most class-wise LT
methods degenerate in our proposed two benchmarks: ImageNet-GLT
and MSCOCO-GLT. We argue that it is because they over-emphasize
the adjustment of class distribution while neglecting to learn attribute-
invariant features. To this end, we propose an Invariant Feature Learning
(IFL) method as the first strong baseline for GLT. IFL first discovers
environments with divergent intra-class distributions from the imperfect
predictions, and then learns invariant features across them. Promisingly,
as an improved feature backbone, IFL boosts all the LT line-up: one/two-
stage re-balance, augmentation, and ensemble. Codes and benchmarks
are available on Github: https://github.com/KaihuaTang/Generalized-
Long-Tailed-Benchmarks.pytorch.

Keywords: Data imbalance · Generalized Long-Tailed classification

1 Introduction

Long-Tailed classification (LT) [68] is inevitable in real-world training, as long-
tailed distribution ubiquitously exists in data at scale [39,40] and it is often pro-

---

Supplementary Information The online version contains supplementary material
available at https://doi.org/10.1007/978-3-031-20053-3_41.

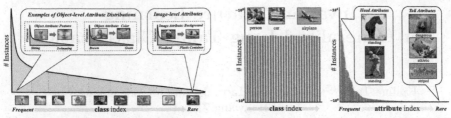

Fig. 1. (a) The real-world long-tailed distribution is both class-wise and attribute-wise imbalanced; (b) even if we balance the class distribution of MSCOCO-Attribute [38], the attributes are still long-tailed

hibitively expensive to balance against such nature [40]. For example in Fig. 1(a), a frequent class such as "dog" has significantly more samples than a rare one such as "panda". Prevailing LT methods are essentially based on adjusting the **class-wise** imbalance ratio: given a biased classifier that tends to classify tail as head, we curb the head confidence while lifting the tail confidence, so the resultant classifier is expected to be fair to both head and tail during inference [6,19,33,41,71].

However, we'd like to point out that LT challenge cannot be simply characterized by class-wise imbalance. If we take a closer look at samples inside each class in Fig. 1(a), we can find that attributes within each class are also long-tailed. This **attribute-wise** imbalance[1] undermines the robustness of the classifier in two ways: **I)** it hurts the accuracy of images with tail attributes, *e.g*, members of minority groups in the human class are easier to be mis-classified than their majority counterparts [36], despite the fact that they both come from the same head class; **II)** it results in some attributes being mistakenly correlated to certain classes, *e.g*, images of a head class "tractor" are often captured on "field", so when a tail object like "harvester" is also captured on "field", its risk of being mis-classified as "tractor" is much higher, which is supported by our formulation Eq. (1) and visualization in Fig. 2(b). Therefore, the **attribute-wise** imbalance further explains the cause of inconsistent performances within the same class and the existence of spurious correlations.

In fact, even if the class-wise imbalance is entirely eliminated like Fig. 1(b), its attribute-wise imbalance still persists and hurts the generalization. Besides, strictly balancing attributes is not only prohibitive but also impossible due to the innumerable multi-label combinations of attributes, making the attribute-wise imbalance fundamentally different from the class-wise imbalance. To this end, we present a new task: **Generalized Long-Tailed** classification (GLT), to unify the challenges from both class-wise and attribute-wise imbalances. For rigorous and reproducible evaluations in the community, as detailed in Sect. 3, we

---

[1] In this paper, the attribute represents all the factors causing the intra-class variations, including object-level attributes (colors, textures, postures, *etc.*) and image-level attributes (lighting, contexts, *etc*).

introduce two benchmarks, ImageNet-GLT and MSCOCO-GLT, together with three protocols to evaluate the robustness of models against class-wise long tail, attribute-wise long tail and their joint effect.

Not surprisingly, we find that nearly all existing LT methods [19,33,41,72] fail to tackle the attribute-wise imbalance in GLT (cf. Sect. 5). The reasons are two-fold: **I)** They rely on class-wise adjustment, which requires the access to the class statistical traits to re-balance [6,19,49,71]. Unfortunately, the attribute-wise traits are hidden in GLT, whose discovery *per se* is a challenging open problem [26]. **II)** As illustrated in Fig. 2, the cross-entropy baseline (biased classifier) tends to predict tail samples as the head class with similar attributes, resulting in low precision on the head and low accuracy on the tail. So, the success of LT methods is mainly based on lifting the tail class boundary to welcome more samples to increase the tail accuracy. However, such adjustment is only playing with the precision-accuracy trade-off [73], leaving the confused region of similar attributes unchanged in the feature space, while the proposed GLT requires algorithms to ignore those confusing attributes.

To this end, in Sect. 4, we introduce a framework called Invariant Feature Learning (IFL) to address the attribute-wise imbalance and serve as the first strong baseline for GLT. Our motivation is based on the reasonable assumption that: since the class feature is invariant to its attributes, *e.g*, a "dog" is always a dog regardless of its varying attributes, the variation of attributes is the main cause of lower prediction confidence within each class. Note that corrupted images are beyond the scope of this paper, as they don't have any valid labels. Therefore, we use the current classification confidence of each training sample as an imbalance indicator of attributes inside the

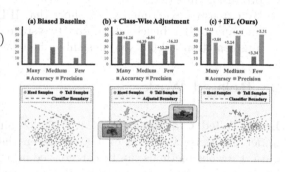

Fig. 2. In ImageNet-GLT, a typical LT method, (b) LWS [19], is playing a precision-accuracy trade-off with the (a) biased cross-entropy baseline, while the proposed (c) IFL improves both metrics at the same time. We follow [19,31] to stratify classes into Many, Medium, and Few by the class frequency. The t-SNE [14] of image features further illustrates that IFL features reduce the confusing region between "tractor" and "harvester" caused by the shared attribute "field"

class: the lower the confidence is, the rarer the attributes are. Then, we sample a new environment based on the reversed confidence. Together with the original one, we obtain two environments with diverse attribute distributions for each class. Finally, to remove the imbalance impact of attributes, we design a metric learning loss, extending the center loss [59] to its Invariant Risk Minimization (IRM) [3] version, which equips the model with the ability to learn class features that are invariant to attributes.

As shown in Fig. 2(c), IFL improves both precision and accuracy under GLT by reducing the confusing region of attributes in the feature space. Besides, IFL, as an improved feature backbone, can be seamlessly incorporated into other LT methods. In particular, we find that by only using sample augmentation such as MixUp [66] or RandAug [10], IFL can surpass most of the LT methods. We also notice that the recent progress of LT methods [56,67,73], who claim to improve both head and tail, is indeed attributed to tackle the attribute-wise imbalance—they deserve to be more fairly evaluated by GLT.

Our contributions can be summarized as follows:

- We present a new challenging task: Generalized Long-Tailed classification (GLT), together with two benchmarks: ImageNet-GLT and MSCOCO-GLT. To solve GLT, one need to address both the conventional class-wise imbalance and the ever-overlooked attribute-wise imbalance.
- We develop Invariant Feature Learning (IFL) as the first strong GLT baseline. Its effectiveness demonstrates that learning attribute-invariant features is a promising direction.
- By extensive experiments, we show that IFL improves all the prevalent LT line-up on GLT benchmarks: one/two-stage re-balancing [6,19,33,41,50,71], augmentation [10,66], and ensemble [56,67].

2   Related Work

Long-Tailed Classification. [11,31,68,72] aims to improve the performance under class-wise balanced evaluation given the class-wise long-tailed training data. Previous methods can be categorized into three types: 1) one/two-stage re-balancing algorithms [15,16,19,25,48,49,54] apply statistical adjustment based on the explicit class distribution to correct the tail class bias; 2) data augmentation either independently augments all samples [10,20,63,66] or transfer head information to the tail [13,24,30,58]; 3) ensemble [5,56,61,67] is recently explored as a strategy to improve head and tail categories at the same time. The conventional LT classification is essentially a special case of the proposed GLT, as solving GLT will naturally improve LT, but not vice versa.

Domain Adaptation (DA) and Out-of-Distribution Generalization (O-ODG) are two other related tasks. DA [52,60,65,70] seeks to transfer models from source domains to the target domain. The difference between DA and GLT is that we don't need a subset of samples from the target domain. Recent papers [18,74] also notice the intrinsic correlation between LT and DA. In OODG [2,3,22,69], we desire a machine trained in one domain to work well in any domain. Recent studies [2] show that it cannot be addressed without any assumption. Therefore, regarding the type of assumptions, OODG can be divided into DA [52], domain generalization [23], long-tailed classification [68], zero-/few-shot learning [47,55,57], and even adversarial robustness [7,8]. Our GLT can also be viewed as a special case of OODG that is more general than LT.

Attribute-Wise Imbalance itself is also a long-standing research field in the name of hard example mining [28,35], sub-population shift [21,27,43], spurious correlation [1,45], etc. Meanwhile, the corresponding methods in these fields may also inspire the future research in GLT, *e.g*, EIIL [9], GEORGE [44] and SDB [17] can be used to construct better environments or baselines. Compared with these fields, the proposed GLT benchmarks provide a unified formulation and benchmarks for both class-wise and attribute-wise imbalances.

3   Generalized Long-Tailed Classification

Previous LT methods [33,41] formulate the classification model as $p(Y|X)$, predicting the label Y from the input image X, which can be further decomposed into $p(Y|X) \propto p(X|Y) \cdot p(Y)$ [33,41]. This formulation identifies the cause of class-wise bias as $p(Y)$, so it can be elegantly solved by Logit Adjustment [33]. However, such a formulation is based on a strong assumption that the distribution of $p(X|Y)$ won't change in different domains, *i.e*, $p_{\text{train}}(X|Y) = p_{\text{test}}(X|Y)$, which cannot be guaranteed in real-world applications. Next, we will provide an in-depth analysis of why this over-simplified view fails to explain all biases.

3.1   Problem Formulation

Recent studies [4,34,53] demonstrate that an image of object X can be fully described or generated by its class and a list of attributes. That is to say, each X is generated by a set of underlying $(z_c, z_a)^2$, where the class-specific components z_c are the invariant factors that enable the existence of the robust classification and the attribute-related variables z_a are domain-specific knowledge that have inconsistent distributions. This formulation only assumes the invariance of a subset features z_c rather than the entire X, *i.e*, $p_{\text{train}}(z_c|Y) = p_{\text{test}}(z_c|Y)$. Therefore, we can follow the Bayes theorem [46] to convert the classification model $p(Y|X) = p(Y|z_c, z_a)$ into the following formula:

$$p(Y = k|z_c, z_a) = \frac{p(z_c|Y = k)}{p(z_c)} \cdot \underbrace{\frac{p(z_a|Y = k, z_c)}{p(z_a|z_c)}}_{\text{attribute bias}} \cdot \underbrace{p(Y = k)}_{\text{class bias}}, \tag{1}$$

where invariant components z_c only depend on Y; descriptive attributes z_a that vary across instances may depend on both Y and z_c. We generally consider $p(z_c, z_a) = p(z_a|z_c) \cdot p(z_c)$ WITHOUT introducing any independence assumption. Note that we also DO NOT impose the disentanglement assumption that a perfect feature vector $\mathbf{z} = [z_c; z_a]$ with separated z_c and z_a can be obtained, as the disentanglement is a challenging task on its own [32]. Otherwise, we only need to conduct a simple feature selection to obtain the ideal classification model.

---

2 In this paper, z_c and z_a stand for **all** class-specific components and variant attributes, respectively, but we use a single variable to represent them in the following examples, *e.g*, $z_c = feather$ and $z_a = brown$, for simplicity.

The reason why we need Eq. (1) to replace the simple $p(Y|X)$ is because unlike those tasks that indeed require both z_c and z_a, e.g, the image captioning [64] or the segmentation task [12], the classification task merely relies on the class-specific components z_c of an image X, regardless of its varying attributes z_a. Therefore, the former formulation $p(Y|X)$ over-simplifies the problem by ignoring the different roles between z_c and z_a during classification.

Class Bias: in class-wise LT [68], the distribution of $p(Y)$ is considered as the main cause of the performance degradation. As $p(Y)$ can be explicitly calculated from the training data, the majority of previous LT methods directly alleviate its effect by class-wise adjustment [33,41] or re-balancing [19,71]. However, they fail to answer **I)** why the performance is also long-tailed within each class, and **II)** why tail images tend to be misclassified as certain head classes with similar attributes.

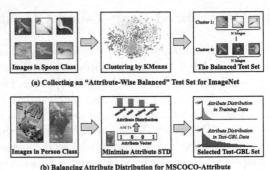

(a) Collecting an "Attribute-Wise Balanced" Test Set for ImageNet

(b) Balancing Attribute Distribution for MSCOCO-Attribute

Fig. 3. Examples of how to balance the attribute distribution for the Test-GBL evaluation environment in the proposed two benchmarks

Attribute Bias: the above Eq.(1) extends the previous LT formulation by introducing the attribute bias caused by long-tailed z_a, which not only explains the cause of inconsistent performances within each class but also demonstrates how spurious correlations hurt the prediction. Intuitively, **I)** for the intra-class variation, if an attribute "white"/"brown" of the class-specific component "feather" is more frequent/rarer in "dove" than in other classes, e.g, $\frac{p(z_a=brown|Y=dove,z_c=feather)}{p(z_a=brown|z_c=feather)} < \frac{p(z_a=white|Y=dove,z_c=feather)}{p(z_a=white|z_c=feather)}$, a dove with brown feather will have lower confidence than doves with white feather, following Eq. (1), i.e, $p(Y=dove|z_c=feather, z_a=brown) < p(Y=dove|z_c=feather, z_a=white)$. **II)** Similarly, for spurious correlations, if a "field" background is more frequent in the class "tractor" than other vehicles with the same class-specific component "wheel", it will create false sense of correlation between "field" and "tractor" class, i.e, $\frac{p(z_a=field|Y=tractor,z_c=wheel)}{p(z_a=field|z_c=wheel)} >>$ 1, resulting images of other vehicles with "wheel" blindly have larger $p(Y=tractor|z_c=wheel, z_a=field)$ in the "field" background, e.g, predicting a "harvester in field" as the "tractor".

Generalized Long-Tailed Distribution: the proposed GLT asserts that both the conventional class distribution and the ever-overlooked attribute distribution are long-tailed in real-world dataset at scale. However, most of the previous LT benchmarks, ImageNet-LT [31], Long-Tailed CIFAR-10/-100 [71], or iNaturalist [51], are only capable of evaluating the class bias, underestimating the role of the attribute bias in the long tail challenge. To better study unbiased models that address both of biases at the same time, we introduce the following two GLT benchmarks and three evaluation protocols.

3.2 GLT Benchmarks and Evaluation Protocols

In this section, we design two benchmarks, ImageNet-GLT and MSCOCO-GLT, for the proposed GLT challenge, where ImageNet-GLT is a long-tailed version of ImageNet [42] and MSCOCO-GLT is constructed from MSCOCO-Attribute [38]. Although there are explicit attribute annotations in MSCOCO-Attribute, we forbid the access of them during training to make the algorithm more general. After all, attributes are not exhaustively annotated. Meanwhile, ImageNet, like most of the other datasets, doesn't have any attribute annotation, so we cluster image features within each class into multiple "pretext attributes" using a pre-trained model [37]. These clusters can thus serve as annotations for implicit attributes. To systematically diagnose two kinds of biases in Eq. (1), each benchmark is further organized into three evaluation protocols as follows:

Class-wise Long Tail (CLT) Protocol: same as the conventional LT, we first adopt a class-wise and attribute-wise LT training set, called **Train-GLT**, which can be easily sampled from ImageNet [42] and MSCOCO-Attribute [38] using a class-wise LT distribution. We don't need to intentionally ensure the attribute-wise imbalance as it's ubiquitous and inevitable in any real-world dataset, *e.g*, the distribution of MSCOCO-Attribute [38] in Fig. 1(b). The corresponding **Test-CBL**, which is i.i.d. sampled within each class, is a class-wise balanced and attribute-wise long-tailed testing set. **(Train-GLT, Test-CBL)** with the same attribute distributions and different class distributions can thus evaluate the robustness against the class-wise long tail.

Attribute-Wise Long Tail (ALT) Protocol: the training set **Train-CBL** of this protocol has the same number of images for each class and keeps the original long-tailed attribute distribution by i.i.d. sampling images within each class, so its bias only comes from the attribute. Meanwhile, **Test-GBL**, as the most important evaluation environment for GLT task, has to balance both class and attribute distributions. As illustrated in Fig. 3, Test-GBL for ImageNet-GLT samples equal number of images from each "pretext attribute" (*i.e*, feature clusters) and each class. Test-GBL for MSCOCO-GLT is a little bit tricky, because each object has multiple attributes, making strictly balancing the attribute distribution prohibitive. Hence, we select a fixed size of subset within each class that has the minimized standard deviation of attributes as the Test-GBL. As long as Test-GBL is relatively more balanced in attributes than Train-CBL, it can serve as a valid testing set for ALT protocol. In summary, **(Train-CBL, Test-GBL)** have the same class distributions and different attribute distributions.

Generalized Long Tail (GLT) Protocol: this protocol combines **(Train-GLT, Test-GBL)** from the above, so both class and attribute distributions are changed from training to testing. As the generalized evaluation protocol for the long-tailed challenge, an algorithm can only obtain satisfactory results when both class bias and attribute bias are well addressed by the final model.

4   Invariant Feature Learning

Prevalent LT studies [19,33] mainly focus on designing balanced classifiers, as the $p(Y = k)$ in Eq. (1) is independent of input features. However, as we discussed in Sect. 3, our new attribute bias is caused by extracting the undesired z_a, so the overlooked feature learning is the key. Therefore, the proposed method aims to learn an improved feature backbone that is complementary for previous balanced classifiers [19,33,41,50].

As we discussed in Sect. 3, the attribute bias term in Eq. (1) raises two problems: **I)** the inconsistent performance of $p(Y|z_c, z_a)$ within each class, and **II)** the spurious correlations between a non-robust attribute and a class. To tackle these problems, we propose Invariant Feature Learning (IFL) that extends the center loss [59] from the original Empirical Risk Minimization (ERM) to its Invariant Risk Minimiza-

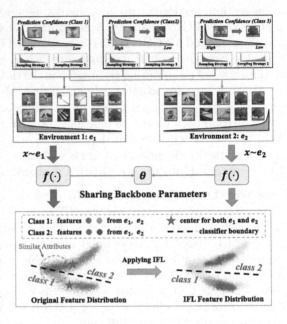

Fig. 4. The proposed IFL that first applies different sampling strategies according to the prediction confidence within each class, then combines them to construct environments with diverse attribute distributions, and finally learns features invariant to the environment change by the IFL metric loss

tion (IRM) [3] version, which forces the backbone to focus on learning features that are invariant across a set of environments.

The rationale behind the IFL is that $\frac{p(z_c|Y=k)}{p(z_c)}$ is consistent in all environments while $\frac{p(z_a|Y=k,z_c)}{p(z_a|z_c)}$ is not. If images of $Y=k$ have the same feature center in all environments, it means that the extracted features are more related to invariant z_c instead of z_a. The overall IFL framework is summarized in Fig. 4.

4.1   Environment Construction

After warming-up the model with the vanilla cross-entropy loss for several epochs, we obtain an initial model with imperfect predictions. Since $\frac{p(z_c|Y=k)}{p(z_c)}$

and $p(Y=k)$ are constants within a given class $Y=k$, the variation of $p(Y=k|z_c, z_a)$ is directly proportional to $\frac{p(z_a|Y=k, z_c)}{p(z_a|z_c)}$. It allows us to use the prediction confidence on the ground-truth class $p(Y=k|X$ in $k)$ as the indicator to sample diverse attribute distributions in the training set (See Appendix for more discussions). As illustrated in Fig. 4, samples collected from each class using the same sampling strategy will then be combined together to form different environments in $\mathcal{E}$. Each sampling strategy has a unique distribution of $\frac{p(z_a|Y=k, z_c)}{p(z_a|z_c)}$. The environments are periodically updated during the training phase.

In general, two environments are considered to be sufficient to learn the robustness against the environment change [3], which is also supported by our experiments on Table 4. Specifically, one environment directly samples each instance uniformly inside each class, *i.e*, the naïve i.i.d. sampling. The other environment is sampled based on the $(1 - p(Y = k|z_c, z_a))^\beta$, where β automatically adjusts the new attribute distribution by up-sampling 20% images from class $Y=k$ with lowest $p(Y = k|z_c, z_a)$ to reach 80% population of the class $Y=k$ in the new environment, following the Pareto Principle [40].

The pseudo code of the algorithm is provided in the Appendix.

4.2 IFL Metric Loss

After obtaining a set of diverse training environments $\mathcal{E}$, the goal of the proposed IFL can thus be formulated as the following optimization problem:

$$\min_{\theta,w} \sum_{e\in\mathcal{E}} \sum_{i\in e} L_{cls}(f(x_i^e; \theta), y_i^e; w),$$

$$\text{subject to } \theta \in \arg\min_{\theta} \sum_{e\in\mathcal{E}} \sum_{i\in e} ||f(x_i^e; \theta) - C_{y_i^e}||_2, \tag{2}$$

where θ and w are learnable parameters for the backbone and classifier, respectively; (x_i^e, y_i^e) are i-th (image, label) pair in the training environment $e \in \mathcal{E}$; $f(x_i^e; \theta)$ is the backbone extracting feature from x_i^e; $L_{cls}(f(x_i^e; \theta), y_i^e; w)$ is the cross-entropy loss; $C_{y_i^e}$ is the mean feature of corresponding class y_i^e across all environments in $\mathcal{E}^3$.

The above Eq. (2) aims to optimize the model by the classification loss L_{cls} under the constraint that the intra-class variation of features across all environments is also minimized, suppressing the learning of z_a that causes non-robust $\frac{p(z_a|Y=k, z_c)}{p(z_a|z_c)}$. So the overall training objective is thus defined as $L = L_{cls} + \alpha \cdot L_{IFL}$, where $L_{IFL} = ||f(x_i^e; \theta) - C_{y_i^e}||_2$ is a metric loss that ensures the above constraint and α is the trade-off parameter.

As the generalized IRM version of the center loss [59], the proposed IFL significantly boosts the GLT performance from its ERM counterpart using single environment. It's because class centers are also biased under the long-tailed attributes, so the original center loss would inevitably under-represent images with rare attributes. More experimental analyses are given in Sect. 5.4.

---

[3] We follow the center loss [59] to implement $C_{y_i^e}$ as the moving average for efficiency.

Table 1. Evaluation of CLT and GLT Protocols on ImageNet-GLT: Accuracy (*left in each cell*) and Precision (*right in each cell*) are reported. All methods are re-implemented under the same codebase with ResNext-50 backbone

Methods		Class-Wise Long Tail (CLT) Protocol								Generalized Long Tail (GLT) Protocol							
< Accuracy	Precision >	$Many_C$		$Medium_C$		Few_C		Overall		$Many_C$		$Medium_C$		Few_C		Overall	
Re-balance	Baseline	59.34	39.08	36.95	52.87	14.39	56.65	42.52	47.92	50.98	32.90	28.49	44.72	10.28	49.11	34.75	40.65
	cRT [19]	56.55	45.79	42.89	46.23	26.67	41.47	45.92	45.34	48.02	38.40	34.16	38.07	19.92	33.50	37.57	37.51
	LWS [19]	55.38	46.67	43.91	46.87	30.11	40.92	46.43	45.90	47.15	39.16	34.88	38.68	22.56	32.88	37.94	38.01
	Deconfound-TDE [50]	54.94	49.27	43.18	43.91	28.64	33.40	45.70	44.48	46.87	42.39	34.43	35.77	22.11	26.30	37.56	37.00
	BLSoftmax [41]	55.60	48.19	42.74	47.27	28.79	38.14	45.79	46.27	47.15	40.89	33.48	39.11	21.10	27.50	37.09	38.08
	Logit-Adj [33]	54.55	49.70	44.40	45.05	31.53	36.04	46.53	45.56	45.94	41.97	35.15	36.63	24.07	28.59	37.80	37.56
	BBN [71]	61.64	42.74	43.80	54.44	13.94	55.12	46.46	49.86	52.41	35.58	34.31	46.38	10.06	44.43	37.91	41.77
	LDAM [6]	59.05	45.39	43.23	48.80	24.44	44.99	46.74	46.86	51.02	38.78	34.13	40.39	18.46	35.91	38.54	39.08
	(ours) Baseline + IFL	**62.71**	42.98	40.10	**56.83**	18.92	**61.92**	45.97	**52.06**	**54.09**	36.74	31.73	**49.03**	13.62	**51.42**	37.96	**44.47**
	(ours) cRT + IFL	61.27	45.84	43.96	51.67	24.32	53.64	47.94	49.63	52.75	39.11	35.14	43.36	17.92	43.35	39.60	41.65
	(ours) LWS + IFL	61.50	45.43	43.79	52.85	23.86	55.58	47.89	50.29	53.21	38.92	34.99	44.44	17.42	45.90	39.64	42.45
	(ours) BLSoftmax + IFL	58.00	53.70	44.70	51.73	33.49	37.58	48.34	50.39	49.92	46.86	36.11	44.31	25.71	32.01	40.08	43.48
	(ours) Logit-Adj + IFL	56.96	**56.22**	**46.54**	50.10	**36.88**	33.29	**49.26**	50.02	48.25	**49.17**	**37.50**	41.65	**29.00**	25.77	**40.52**	42.28
Augment	Mixup [66]	59.68	37.96	30.83	55.74	7.09	34.33	38.81	45.41	51.04	31.85	23.10	47.25	4.94	22.88	31.55	37.44
	RandAug [10]	64.96	42.63	40.30	59.10	15.20	56.60	46.40	52.13	56.36	35.97	31.43	51.13	10.36	48.92	38.24	44.74
	(ours) Mixup + IFL	67.71	47.77	45.87	62.58	24.71	**67.77**	51.43	57.44	59.36	40.95	36.77	54.67	18.06	55.10	43.00	49.25
	(ours) RandAug + IFL	**69.35**	**49.42**	**48.05**	**63.19**	**26.92**	66.04	**53.40**	**58.11**	**60.79**	**42.41**	**39.07**	**55.15**	**20.04**	**57.90**	**44.90**	**50.47**
Ensemble	TADE [67]	58.44	56.38	48.01	51.41	36.60	41.08	50.47	51.85	50.29	**49.25**	38.74	43.74	**27.99**	31.75	41.75	44.15
	RIDE [56]	64.04	51.91	48.66	53.21	30.44	46.25	52.08	51.65	55.47	44.55	38.65	44.26	22.80	37.26	43.00	43.32
	(ours) TADE + IFL	61.71	55.59	48.87	53.42	34.02	40.93	51.78	52.41	53.75	48.73	39.90	45.28	26.77	35.34	43.47	45.17
	(ours) RIDE + IFL	**65.68**	54.13	**50.82**	**56.22**	31.91	**52.10**	**53.93**	**54.76**	**57.84**	47.00	**41.80**	**48.65**	24.63	**42.96**	**45.64**	**47.14**

5   Experiments

5.1   Datasets and Metrics

ImageNet-GLT is a long-tailed version of the ImageNet [42], where CLT and GLT protocols share the same training set Train-GLT with 113k samples over 1k classes. ALT protocol adopts a class-wise balanced Train-CBL with 114k images. The evaluation splits {Val, Test-CBL, Test-GBL} have {30k, 60k, 60k} samples, respectively. The number of images for each class in Train-GLT ranges from 570 to 4, while all classes have 114 samples in Train-CBL. To collect the attribute-wise balanced Test-GBL, images from each class were clustered into 6 groups by KMeans using a pre-trained ResNet50 model [37] and we sampled 10 images per group and class. Following [19,31], all testing sets are also split into 3 subsets by the class frequency: $Many_C$ with #sample > 100, $Medium_C$ with $100 \geq$ #sample ≥ 20, and Few_C with #sample < 20. We further split them into 3 subsets by attribute groups: $Many_A$, $Medium_A$, and Few_A with images from the most/medium/least frequent 2 clusters of all classes, respectively.

MSCOCO-GLT is a long-tailed subset of MSCOCO-Attribute [29,38] with 196 different attributes. We cropped each object with multi-label attributes as independent images. Under CLT and GLT protocols, we have {Train-GLT, Val, Test-CBL, Test-GBL} with {144k, 2.9k, 5.8k, 5.8k} images over 29 classes, where the number of samples for each class ranges from 61k to 0.3k. The ALT protocol has {32k, 1.4k, 2.9k} images for {Train-CBL, Val, Test-GBL}. Since attributes usually co-occur with each other in one object, we cannot construct $Many_A$, $Medium_A$, and Few_A subsets the same as ImageNet-GLT, so we directly report the overall performance for MSCOCO-GLT. Note that attribute annotations are only used to construct Test-GBL, and they are not released in the training data.

Evaluation Metrics. The top-1 accuracy is commonly adopted as the only metric in the conventional LT studies, yet, it cannot reveal the limitation of precision-accuracy trade-off. Therefore, in GLT classification, we report both Accuracy: $\frac{\#CorrectPredictions}{\#AllSamples}$, which is equal to Top-1 Recall in the class-wise balanced test sets [73], and Precision: $\frac{1}{\#class} \cdot \sum_{class} \frac{\#CorrectPredictions}{\#SamplesPredictedAsThisClass}$ to better evaluate the effectiveness of algorithms.

5.2 Investigated LT Algorithms

As a general feature learning method to deal with the attribute bias, the proposed IFL can be integrated into most prevalent LT methods. We followed Zhang *et al.* [68] to summarize the investigated LT algorithms into three categories: 1) one-/two-stage re-balancing, 2) augmentation, and 3) module improvement.

For re-balancing approaches, we studied two-stage re-sampling methods **cRT** [19] and **LWS** [19], post-hoc distribution adjustment **Deconfound-TDE** [50] and Logit Adjustment (**Logit-Adj**) [33], multi-branch models with diverse sampling strategies like **BBN** [71], and re-weighting loss functions like Balanced Softmax (**BLSoftmax**) [41] and **LDAM** [6].

Table 2. Evaluation of ALT Protocol on ImageNet-GLT

Methods		Attribute-Wise Long Tail (ALT) Protocol					
< Accuracy	Precision >	Many$_A$		Medium$_A$		Few$_A$	Overall
Re-balance	Baseline	56.95	55.83	40.11	35.17	28.12	28.16	41.73	41.74
	cRT [19]	57.45	56.28	39.72	38.66	27.58	27.35	41.59	41.43
	LWS [19]	56.95	55.85	40.11	39.30	28.03	27.98	41.70	41.71
	Deconfound-TDE [50]	57.10	56.58	39.80	40.08	27.29	27.96	41.40	42.36
	BLSoftmax [41]	56.48	55.56	39.81	38.96	27.64	27.60	41.32	41.37
	BBN [71]	60.90	60.17	41.08	40.81	27.79	28.26	43.26	43.86
	LDAM [6]	59.04	56.81	40.96	39.21	27.96	27.22	42.66	41.80
	(ours) Baseline + IFL	61.38	60.78	44.79	44.21	31.49	31.98	45.80	46.42
	(ours) cRT + IFL	61.12	60.25	44.26	43.56	31.02	31.31	45.47	45.81
	(ours) LWS + IFL	61.19	60.45	44.66	44.07	31.43	31.91	45.76	46.25
	(ours) BLSoftmax + IFL	60.19	59.46	43.54	43.14	30.86	31.46	44.86	45.43
Augment	Mixup [66]	58.71	58.04	40.09	38.99	27.52	27.54	42.11	42.42
	RandAug [10]	62.35	61.25	45.04	44.27	31.47	31.26	46.29	46.32
	(ours) Mixup + IFL	65.90	65.88	49.43	49.43	35.40	35.89	50.24	51.04
	(ours) RandAug + IFL	67.39	66.81	51.55	51.28	37.47	37.97	52.14	52.74
Ensemble	TADE [67]	62.63	61.91	45.84	45.21	32.82	32.82	47.10	47.32
	RIDE [56]	63.46	61.42	45.62	44.16	32.59	32.26	47.24	46.67
	(ours) TADE + IFL	63.50	62.67	48.03	47.32	34.69	34.52	48.74	48.78
	(ours) RIDE + IFL	67.54	67.13	51.92	51.72	37.84	38.46	52.44	53.17

For augmentation approaches, we empirically noticed that some common data augmentation methods are more general and effective than other long-tailed transfer learning methods [30], so we adopted **Mixup** [66] and Random Augmentation (**RandAug**) [10] in our experiments.

For module improvement, we followed the recent trend of ensemble learning [56] like **RIDE** [56] and **TADE** [67], which are proved to be state-of-the-art models in LT classification that are capable of improving both head and tail categories at the same time. Both of them used the trident version of ResNext-50 [62] developed by RIDE [56], which is denoted as RIDE-50 in Table 4.

Implementation details of the proposed IFL and the baseline methods are given in Appendix.

5.3 Comparisons with LT Line-up

We evaluate CLT and GLT protocols for ImageNet-GLT in Table 1. The corresponding ALT protocol is reported in Table 2. All three protocols for MSCOCO-GLT are shown in Table 3.

CLT Protocol (conventional long-tailed classification): although the proposed IFL is mainly designed to tackle the long-tailed intra-class attributes, it also boost all prevalent LT methods in the conventional CLT protocol. It's because IFL also prevents tail images from being mis-classified as head classes by eliminating the spurious correlation made by attributes.

GLT Protocol: not surprisingly, we observe a significant performance decline for all methods from CLT protocol to GLT, as tackling the additional attribute bias is much more challenging than class bias. Meanwhile, IFL can still successfully improve various baselines. The decline on the proposed GLT reveals that general long tail is indeed not just the pure class-wise imbalance.

ALT Protocol: as we expected, the majority of previous LT algorithms using re-balancing strategies failed to improve the robustness against the attribute-wise

Table 3. Evaluation on MSCOCO-GLT: overall performances are reported

Protocols		CLT		GLT		ALT	
< Accuracy	Precision >	Overall		Overall		Overall	
Re-balance	Baseline	72.34	76.61	63.79	70.52	50.17	50.94
	cRT [19]	73.64	75.84	64.69	68.33	49.97	50.37
	LWS [19]	72.60	75.66	63.60	68.81	50.14	50.61
	Deconfound-TDE [50]	73.79	74.90	66.07	68.20	50.76	51.68
	BLSoftmax [41]	72.64	75.25	64.07	68.59	49.72	50.65
	Logit-Adj [33]	75.50	76.88	66.17	68.35	50.17	50.94
	BBN [71]	73.69	77.35	64.48	70.20	51.83	51.77
	LDAM [6]	75.57	77.70	67.26	70.70	**55.52**	**56.21**
	(ours) Baseline + IFL	74.31	78.90	65.31	**72.24**	52.86	53.49
	(ours) cRT + IFL	76.21	79.11	66.90	71.34	52.07	52.85
	(ours) LWS + IFL	75.98	**79.18**	66.55	71.49	52.07	52.90
	(ours) BLSoftmax + IFL	73.72	77.08	64.76	70.00	52.97	53.52
	(ours) Logit-Adj + IFL	**77.16**	79.09	**67.53**	70.18	52.86	53.49
Augment	Mixup [66]	74.22	78.61	64.45	71.13	48.90	49.53
	RandAug [10]	76.81	79.88	67.71	72.73	53.69	54.71
	(ours) Mixup + IFL	77.55	**81.78**	**68.83**	**74.84**	53.79	54.60
	(ours) RandAug + IFL	**77.71**	81.10	68.16	73.97	**56.62**	**57.12**
Ensemble	TADE [67]	76.22	78.84	66.98	71.22	54.93	55.48
	RIDE [56]	78.29	80.33	68.59	72.20	58.90	59.43
	(ours) TADE + IFL	76.53	79.15	67.38	72.42	56.76	57.43
	(ours) RIDE + IFL	**78.86**	**80.70**	**69.09**	**72.57**	**58.93**	**59.84**

bias in this protocol. Therefore, their improvements on GLT protocol only came from the class-wise invariance. However, we noticed that the augmentation and ensemble approaches can improve all three protocols, making them good baselines for GLT as well. The main reason is that both augmentation and model ensemble also aim to improve the representation learning.

5.4 Ablation Studies and Further Analyses

We further conducted a group of ablation studies on ImageNet-GLT in Table 4 to address some common concerns. We also provide some further analyses to shed lights on the proposed GLT challenge.

Q1: how about the baselines from the attribute-wise side? A1: we also reported some popular methods like Focal loss [28] for hard-example mining and LFF (Learning-from-failure) [35] for domain generalization as the baselines solving the attribute bias. However, they didn't perform well using their default settings, proving the difficulty of the proposed GLT in real-world datasets.

Q2: does the improvement come from the center loss? A2: the original ERM version of center loss [59] can be considered as a special case of the proposed IFL with only one single environment. According to Table 4, using the vanilla center loss, $i.e$, #Env=1 with IFL, as the additional constraint actually hurt all three protocols. It's because the center in a biased environment is also biased, $e.g$, the center of "banana" may possess 90% of "yellow" attribute, which only makes the model more relying on spurious correlations.

Q3: how many environments are required? A3: although it's crucial to have more than 1 environment, IRM [3] asserts that two environments are enough to capture the invariance. We also found that additional environments only brought marginal improvement.

Q4: why not directly apply IRM loss? A4: theoretically, the original IRM loss [3] and the proposed IFL are supposed to have similar results, as they both embody the same spirit of

Table 4. Ablation Studies on ImageNet-GLT, where overall results are reported; BLS, Focal, and IFF are balanced softmax loss [41], focal loss [28], and learning from failure [35], respectively

Ablation Settings					Evaluation Protocols		
#Env	Loss	IFL	Augment	Backbone	CLT Protocol	GLT Protocol	ALT Protocol
1	CE	-	-	ResNext-50	42.52 | 47.92	34.75 | 40.65	41.73 | 41.74
1	Focal	-	-	ResNext-50	39.93 | 46.99	32.52 | 39.12	39.58 | 39.85
1	LFF	-	-	ResNext-50	41.07 | 45.79	33.84 | 38.46	40.14 | 40.58
1	CE	✓	-	ResNext-50	39.74 | 47.06	32.82 | 40.86	39.99 | 41.38
2	IRM	-	-	ResNext-50	43.70 | 48.06	36.03 | 40.61	44.47 | 44.60
2	CE	✓	-	ResNext-50	45.97 | 52.06	37.96 | 44.47	45.89 | 46.42
3	CE	✓	-	ResNext-50	46.06 | 52.81	38.32 | 45.55	45.95 | 46.43
2	BLS	✓	-	ResNext-50	48.34 | 50.39	40.08 | 43.48	44.86 | 45.43
2	CE	✓	Mixup	ResNext-50	51.43 | 57.44	43.00 | 49.25	50.24 | 51.04
2	CE	✓	RandAug	ResNext-50	**53.40 | 58.11**	**44.90 | 50.47**	**52.14 | 52.74**
1	CE	-	-	RIDE-50	46.14 | 52.98	38.25 | 45.80	46.32 | 46.56
2	CE	✓	-	RIDE-50	49.20 | 54.64	41.35 | 47.67	48.62 | 48.62
2	TADE	✓	-	RIDE-50	51.78 | 52.41	43.47 | 45.17	48.74 | 48.78
2	LDAM	✓	-	RIDE-50	53.93 | 54.76	45.64 | 47.14	52.44 | 53.17
2	LDAM	✓	Mixup	RIDE-50	56.48 | 57.67	47.54 | 49.86	53.25 | 54.27
2	LDAM	✓	RandAug	RIDE-50	**58.70 | 59.61**	**49.80 | 51.62**	**55.65 | 55.81**

learning invariance across environments. However, we empirically noticed that the original IRM loss has the convergence issue in real-world dataset. 2 out of 5 random seeds result NaN loss at some point during training.

Q5: why do all models perform worse under ALT than GLT on MSCOCO-GLT? A5: note that the GLT protocol is always harder than ALT or CLT. This weird phenomenon in MSCOCO-GLT is caused by the severe class-wise imbalance in MSCOCO-Attributes [38]: a single class "person" possess over 40% of the training set, so Train-CBL has much less training samples than Train-GLT. It further proves the importance of long-tailed classification in real-world applications, as *large long-tailed datasets are better than small balanced counterparts.*

Q6: what is the precision-accuracy trade-off problem [73]? A6: as shown in Fig. 5(a-b), class-wise re-balancing method like cRT, LWS, and Logit-Adj [19, 33] are playing with the precision-accuracy trade-off under GLT protocol and barely work in ALT protocol. It's because the attribute bias hurts both accuracy and precision by forming spurious correlations between classes. Tackling it should improve both of metrics at the same time.

Q7: is there any other method that can be served as GLT baselines as well? A7: we also found that the recent trend of improving both head and tail categories [56,67,73], though lack a formal definition in their approaches, are essentially trying to solve the GLT challenge. Benefit from the feature learning, these ensemble learning and data augmentation approaches can also serve as good baselines for the proposed GLT as well. Meanwhile, the proposed IFL is orthogonal to them and can further boost their performances under all three protocols.

Q8: why the proposed GLT is the "generalized" version of the LT. A8: it's because GLT methods would naturally solve the conventional LT, but not vise versa. As shown in Fig. 5(c-d), GLT baselines like augmentation, ensemble,

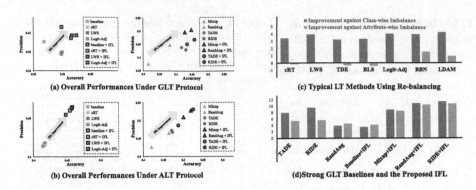

Fig. 5. (a–b) The trending of precision and accuracy after applying the IFL; (c–d) GLT baselines will automatically improve class-wise LT, while conventional LT re-balancing algorithms won't improve the attribute-wise imbalance in GLT

and the proposed IFL automatically solve the class-wise LT. Yet, the majority of class-wise re-balancing LT algorithms cannot tackle the attribute-wise imbalance of GLT very well.

6   Conclusion

We introduced a novel Generalized Long-Tailed (GLT) classification problem, completing the previous class-wise long-tailed classification by incorporating the attribute-wise imbalance nature in real-world dataset at scale, which deeply explains the cause of long-tailed performance within each class and the existence of spurious correlations during classification. Experiments on the proposed two benchmarks, ImageNet-GLT and MSCOCO-GLT, demonstrate the limitations of the previous LT algorithms using class-wise adjustment, and the importance of representation learning in GLT. To this end, we present invariant feature learning (IFL) as the first strong baseline for GLT. IFL adopts a metric loss to encourage the learning of invariant features across environments with diverse attribute distributions. As an improved feature backbone, IFL is orthogonal to most of the previous LT algorithms. After plugging IFL into the conventional LT line-up: one-/two-stage re-balance, augmentation, and ensemble, IFL boosts their performances under all protocols in the proposed GLT benchmarks.

Limitations: Due to the limited space, we didn't fully explore all kinds of attribute biases in this paper, *e.g*, benchmarks like BREEDS [43], MetaShift [27] or FMoW-WILDS [21] all have their unique attribute types. In the future, we are going to extend GLT to more diverse tasks and attribute settings.

Acknowledgements.   This project is partially supported by Alibaba-NTU Singapore Joint Research Institute (JRI), and AI Singapore (AISG) Research Programme. We also feel grateful to the computational resources provided by Damo Academy.

References

1. Agarwal, V., Shetty, R., Fritz, M.: Towards causal VQA: revealing and reducing spurious correlations by invariant and covariant semantic editing. In: CVPR (2020)
2. Arjovsky, M.: Out of distribution generalization in machine learning. Ph.D. thesis, New York University (2020)
3. Arjovsky, M., Bottou, L., Gulrajani, I., Lopez-Paz, D.: Invariant risk minimization. arXiv preprint arXiv:1907.02893 (2019)
4. Besserve, M., Mehrjou, A., Sun, R., Schölkopf, B.: Counterfactuals uncover the modular structure of deep generative models. In: ICLR (2020)
5. Cai, J., Wang, Y., Hwang, J.N.: Ace: ally complementary experts for solving long-tailed recognition in one-shot. In: ICCV (2021)
6. Cao, K., Wei, C., Gaidon, A., Arechiga, N., Ma, T.: Learning imbalanced datasets with label-distribution-aware margin loss. NeurIPS (2019)
7. Carlini, N., et al.: On evaluating adversarial robustness. arXiv preprint arXiv:1902.06705 (2019)
8. Chakraborty, A., Alam, M., Dey, V., Chattopadhyay, A., Mukhopadhyay, D.: Adversarial attacks and defences: a survey. arXiv preprint arXiv:1810.00069 (2018)
9. Creager, E., Jacobsen, J.H., Zemel, R.: Environment inference for invariant learning. In: ICML (2021)
10. Cubuk, E.D., Zoph, B., Shlens, J., Le, Q.V.: Randaugment: practical automated data augmentation with a reduced search space. In: CVPR Workshops (2020)
11. Cui, Y., Jia, M., Lin, T.Y., Song, Y., Belongie, S.: Class-balanced loss based on effective number of samples. In: CVPR (2019)
12. He, K., Gkioxari, G., Dollár, P., Girshick, R.: Mask R-CNN. In: ICCV (2017)
13. He, Y.Y., Wu, J., Wei, X.S.: Distilling virtual examples for long-tailed recognition. In: ICCV (2021)
14. Hinton, G., Roweis, S.T.: Stochastic neighbor embedding. In: NeurIPS (2002)
15. Hong, Y., Han, S., Choi, K., Seo, S., Kim, B., Chang, B.: Disentangling label distribution for long-tailed visual recognition. In: CVPR (2021)
16. Hu, X., Jiang, Y., Tang, K., Chen, J., Miao, C., Zhang, H.: Learning to segment the tail. In: CVPR (2020)
17. Idrissi, B.Y., Arjovsky, M., Pezeshki, M., Lopez-Paz, D.: Simple data balancing achieves competitive worst-group-accuracy. In: Conference on Causal Learning and Reasoning (2022)
18. Jamal, M.A., Brown, M., Yang, M.H., Wang, L., Gong, B.: Rethinking class-balanced methods for long-tailed visual recognition from a domain adaptation perspective. In: CVPR (2020)
19. Kang, B., Xie, S., Rohrbach, M., Yan, Z., Gordo, A., Feng, J., Kalantidis, Y.: Decoupling representation and classifier for long-tailed recognition. In: ICLR (2020)
20. Kim, J., Jeong, J., Shin, J.: M2m: imbalanced classification via major-to-minor translation. In: CVPR (2020)
21. Koh, P.W., et al.: Wilds: a benchmark of in-the-wild distribution shifts. In: ICML (2021)
22. Krueger, D., et al.: Out-of-distribution generalization via risk extrapolation (rex). In: ICML (2021)
23. Li, D., Yang, Y., Song, Y.Z., Hospedales, T.M.: Deeper, broader and artier domain generalization. In: ICCV (2017)

24. Li, T., Wang, L., Wu, G.: Self supervision to distillation for long-tailed visual recognition. In: ICCV (2021)
25. Li, Y., et al.: Overcoming classifier imbalance for long-tail object detection with balanced group softmax. In: CVPR (2020)
26. Li, Z., Xu, C.: Discover the unknown biased attribute of an image classifier. arXiv preprint arXiv:2104.14556 (2021)
27. Liang, W., Zou, J.: Metashift: a dataset of datasets for evaluating contextual distribution shifts and training conflicts. In: ICLR (2022)
28. Lin, T.Y., Goyal, P., Girshick, R., He, K., Dollár, P.: Focal loss for dense object detection. In: ICCV, pp. 2980–2988 (2017)
29. Lin, T.-Y., et al.: Microsoft COCO: common objects in context. In: Fleet, D., Pajdla, T., Schiele, B., Tuytelaars, T. (eds.) ECCV 2014. LNCS, vol. 8693, pp. 740–755. Springer, Cham (2014). https://doi.org/10.1007/978-3-319-10602-1_48
30. Liu, J., Sun, Y., Han, C., Dou, Z., Li, W.: Deep representation learning on long-tailed data: a learnable embedding augmentation perspective. In: CVPR (2020)
31. Liu, Z., Miao, Z., Zhan, X., Wang, J., Gong, B., Yu, S.X.: Large-scale long-tailed recognition in an open world. In: CVPR (2019)
32. Locatello, F., et al.: Challenging common assumptions in the unsupervised learning of disentangled representations. In: ICML. PMLR (2019)
33. Menon, A.K., Jayasumana, S., Rawat, A.S., Jain, H., Veit, A., Kumar, S.: Long-tail learning via logit adjustment. In: ICLR (2020)
34. Mirza, M., Osindero, S.: Conditional generative adversarial nets. arXiv preprint arXiv:1411.1784 (2014)
35. Nam, J., Cha, H., Ahn, S., Lee, J., Shin, J.: Learning from failure: de-biasing classifier from biased classifier. NeurIPS **33**, 20673–20684 (2020)
36. News, B.: Facebook apology as AI labels black men 'primates' (2021), https://www.bbc.com/news/technology-58462511
37. Paszke, A., et al.: Pytorch: an imperative style, high-performance deep learning library. In: Wallach, H., Larochelle, H., Beygelzimer, A., d'Alché-Buc, F., Fox, E., Garnett, R. (eds.) Advances in Neural Information Processing Systems 32, pp. 8024–8035. Curran Associates, Inc. (2019). http://papers.neurips.cc/paper/9015-pytorch-an-imperative-style-high-performance-deep-learning-library.pdf
38. Patterson, G., Hays, J.: COCO attributes: attributes for people, animals, and objects. In: Leibe, B., Matas, J., Sebe, N., Welling, M. (eds.) ECCV 2016. LNCS, vol. 9910, pp. 85–100. Springer, Cham (2016). https://doi.org/10.1007/978-3-319-46466-4_6
39. Powers, D.M.: Applications and explanations of zipf's law. In: New Methods in Language Processing and Computational Natural Language Learning (1998)
40. Reed, W.J.: The pareto, zipf and other power laws. Econ. Lett. **74**(1), 15–19 (2001)
41. Ren, J., et al.: Balanced meta-softmax for long-tailed visual recognition. NeurIPS (2020)
42. Russakovsky, O., et al.: ImageNet large scale visual recognition challenge. Int. J. Comput. Vis. **115**(3), 211–252 (2015). https://doi.org/10.1007/s11263-015-0816-y
43. Santurkar, S., Tsipras, D., Madry, A.: Breeds: benchmarks for subpopulation shift. In: ICLR (2021)
44. Sohoni, N., Dunnmon, J., Angus, G., Gu, A., Ré, C.: No subclass left behind: fine-grained robustness in coarse-grained classification problems. NeurIPS (2020)
45. Srivastava, M., Hashimoto, T., Liang, P.: Robustness to spurious correlations via human annotations. In: ICML (2020)
46. Stone, J.V.: Bayes' Rule: a Tutorial Introduction to Bayesian Analysis. Sebtel Press (2013)

47. Sung, F., Yang, Y., Zhang, L., Xiang, T., Torr, P.H., Hospedales, T.M.: Learning to compare: relation network for few-shot learning. In: CVPR (2018)
48. Tan, J., Lu, X., Zhang, G., Yin, C., Li, Q.: Equalization loss v2: a new gradient balance approach for long-tailed object detection. In: CVPR (2021)
49. Tan, J., et al.: Equalization loss for long-tailed object recognition. In: CVPR (2020)
50. Tang, K., Huang, J., Zhang, H.: Long-tailed classification by keeping the good and removing the bad momentum causal effect. NeurIPS (2020)
51. van Horn, G., et al.: The inaturalist species classification and detection dataset. In: CVPR (2018)
52. Wang, M., Deng, W.: Deep visual domain adaptation: a survey. Neurocomputing **312**, 135–153 (2018)
53. Wang, T., Yue, Z., Huang, J., Sun, Q., Zhang, H.: Self-supervised learning disentangled group representation as feature. NeurIPS (2021)
54. Wang, T., et al.: The devil is in classification: a simple framework for long-tail instance segmentation. In: Vedaldi, A., Bischof, H., Brox, T., Frahm, J.-M. (eds.) ECCV 2020. LNCS, vol. 12359, pp. 728–744. Springer, Cham (2020). https://doi.org/10.1007/978-3-030-58568-6_43
55. Wang, W., Zheng, V.W., Yu, H., Miao, C.: A survey of zero-shot learning: settings, methods, and applications. TIST (2019)
56. Wang, X., Lian, L., Miao, Z., Liu, Z., Yu, S.X.: Long-tailed recognition by routing diverse distribution-aware experts. ICLR (2020)
57. Wang, Y., Yao, Q.: Few-shot learning: a survey. arxiv (2019)
58. Wang, Y.X., Ramanan, D., Hebert, M.: Learning to model the tail. In: NeurIPS (2017)
59. Wen, Y., Zhang, K., Li, Z., Qiao, Yu.: A discriminative feature learning approach for deep face recognition. In: Leibe, B., Matas, J., Sebe, N., Welling, M. (eds.) ECCV 2016. LNCS, vol. 9911, pp. 499–515. Springer, Cham (2016). https://doi.org/10.1007/978-3-319-46478-7_31
60. Wilson, G., Cook, D.J.: A survey of unsupervised deep domain adaptation. ACM Trans. Intell. Syst. Technol. (TIST) **11**(5), 1–46 (2020)
61. Xiang, L., Ding, G., Han, J.: Learning from multiple experts: self-paced knowledge distillation for long-tailed classification. In: Vedaldi, A., Bischof, H., Brox, T., Frahm, J.-M. (eds.) ECCV 2020. LNCS, vol. 12350, pp. 247–263. Springer, Cham (2020). https://doi.org/10.1007/978-3-030-58558-7_15
62. Xie, S., Girshick, R., Dollár, P., Tu, Z., He, K.: Aggregated residual transformations for deep neural networks. In: CVPR (2017)
63. Yin, X., Yu, X., Sohn, K., Liu, X., Chandraker, M.: Feature transfer learning for face recognition with under-represented data. In: CVPR (2019)
64. You, Q., Jin, H., Wang, Z., Fang, C., Luo, J.: Image captioning with semantic attention. In: CVPR (2016)
65. Yue, Z., Sun, Q., Hua, X.S., Zhang, H.: Transporting causal mechanisms for unsupervised domain adaptation. In: ICCV (2021)
66. Zhang, H., Cisse, M., Dauphin, Y.N., Lopez-Paz, D.: mixup: beyond empirical risk minimization. In: ICLR (2018)
67. Zhang, Y., Hooi, B., Hong, L., Feng, J.: Test-agnostic long-tailed recognition by test-time aggregating diverse experts with self-supervision. In: ICCV (2021)
68. Zhang, Y., Kang, B., Hooi, B., Yan, S., Feng, J.: Deep long-tailed learning: a survey. arXiv preprint arXiv:2110.04596 (2021)
69. Zhao, B., et al.: Robin: a benchmark for robustness to individual nuisances in real-world out-of-distribution shifts. In: ECCV (2022)

70. Zhao, H., Des Combes, R.T., Zhang, K., Gordon, G.: On learning invariant representations for domain adaptation. In: ICML (2019)
71. Zhou, B., Cui, Q., Wei, X.S., Chen, Z.M.: BBN: bilateral-branch network with cumulative learning for long-tailed visual recognition. In: CVPR (2020)
72. Zhu, B., Niu, Y., Hua, X.S., Zhang, H.: Cross-domain empirical risk minimization for unbiased long-tailed classification. In: AAAI (2022)
73. Zhu, B., Niu, Y., Hua, X.S., Zhang, H.: Cross-domain empirical risk minimization for unbiased long-tailed classification. AAAI (2022)
74. Zou, Y., Yu, Z., Kumar, B., Wang, J.: Unsupervised domain adaptation for semantic segmentation via class-balanced self-training. In: ECCV (2018)

Sliced Recursive Transformer

Zhiqiang Shen[1,2,3]([✉]), Zechun Liu[2,4], and Eric Xing[1,3]

[1] Carnegie Mellon University, Pittsburgh, USA
epxing@cs.cmu.edu
[2] Hong Kong University of Science and Technology, Hong Kong, China
zhiqiangshen@cse.ust.hk, zechunliu@fb.com
[3] Mohamed bin Zayed University of Artificial Intelligence, Abu Dhabi, UAE
[4] Reality Labs, Meta Inc., Menlo Park, USA

Abstract. We present a neat yet effective recursive operation on vision transformers that can improve parameter utilization without involving additional parameters. This is achieved by sharing weights across depth of transformer networks. The proposed method can obtain a substantial gain (∼2%) simply using naïve recursive operation, requires no special or sophisticated knowledge for designing principles of networks, and introduces minimal computational overhead to the training procedure. To reduce the additional computation caused by recursive operation while maintaining the superior accuracy, we propose an approximating method through multiple sliced group self-attentions across recursive layers which can reduce the cost consumption by 10–30% without sacrificing performance. We call our model **S**liced **Re**cursive **T**ransformer (SReT), a novel and parameter-efficient vision transformer design that is compatible with a broad range of other designs for efficient ViT architectures. Our best model establishes significant improvement on ImageNet-1K over state-of-the-art methods while containing fewer parameters. The proposed weight sharing mechanism by sliced recursion structure allows us to build a transformer with more than 100 or even 1000 shared layers with ease while keeping a compact size (13–15 M), to avoid optimization difficulties when the model is too large. The flexible scalability has shown great potential for scaling up models and constructing extremely deep vision transformers. Code is available at https://github.com/szq0214/SReT.

1 Introduction

The architectures of transformer have achieved substantively breakthroughs recently in the fields of natural language processing (NLP) [46], computer vision (CV) [15] and speech [14,48]. In the

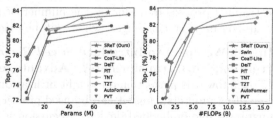

Fig. 1. Params/FLOPs vs. ImageNet-1K Acc.

Supplementary Information The online version contains supplementary material available at https://doi.org/10.1007/978-3-031-20053-3_42.

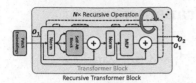

Fig. 2. Atomic Recursive Operation.

Table 1. Results using different numbers N of naïve recursive operation on ImageNet-1K dataset.

Method	Layers	#Params (M)	Top-1 Acc. (%)
DeiT-Tiny [44]	12	5.7	72.2
+ 1× naïve recursion	24	5.7	74.0
+ 2× naïve recursion	36	5.7	74.1
+ 3× naïve recursion	48	5.7	73.6

vision area, Dosovitskiy et al. [15] introduced a vision transformer (ViT) model that splits a raw image into a patch sequence as input, and they directly adopt transformer model [46] for the image classification task. ViT achieved impressive results and has inspired many follow-up works. However, the benefits of a transformer often come with a large number of parameters and computational cost and it is always of great challenge to achieve the optimal trade-off between the accuracy and model complexity. In this work, we are motivated by the following question: How can we improve the parameter utilization of a vision transformer, i.e., the representation ability without increasing the model size? We observe recursive operation, as shown in Fig. 2, is a simple yet effective way to achieve this purpose. Our recursion-based vision transformer models significantly outperform state-of-the-art approaches while containing fewer parameters and FLOPs, as illustrated in Fig. 1.

Intrinsically, the classifier requires high-level abstracted features from the neural network to perform accurate classification, while the extraction of these features often requires multiple layers and deeper networks. This introduces parameter overhead into the model. Our motivation of this work stems from an interesting phenomenon of latent representation visualization. We observed that in the deep vision transformer network, the weights and activations of adjacent layers are similar with not much difference (a similar phenomenon is also discovered in [53]), which means they can be reused. The transformer with a fixed stack of distinct layers loses the inductive bias in the recurrent neural network which inspires us to share those weights in a recursive manner, forming an iterative or recursive vision transformer. Recursion can help extract stronger features without the need of increasing the parameters, and further improve the accuracy. In addition, this weight reuse or sharing strategy partially regularizes the training process by reducing the number of parameters to avoid overfitting and ill-convergence challenges, which will be discussed in the later sections.

Why do We Need to Introduce *Sliced Recursion*, i.e., The Group Self-Attention, into Transformers? (Advantages and Drawbacks). We usually push towards perfection on weight utilization of a network under a bounded range of parameters, thus, it can be used practically in the resource-limited circumstances like embedded devices. Recursion is a straightforward way to *compress* the feature representation in a cyclic scheme. The recursive neural networks also allow the branching of connections and structures with hierarchies. We found that it is intriguingly crucial for learning better representations on vision data in a hierarchical manner, as we will introduce in Fig. 10 of our experiments. Also, even the most simplistic recursive operation still improves the compactness of utilizing parameters without requiring to modify the transformer block structure, unlike others [22,27,33,42,47,49,50,52], that add more parameters or involve additional fine-grained information from input [18]. However, such a recursion will incur more computational cost by its loops, namely, it *sacrifices the executing efficiency for better parameter representation utilization.* To address this shortcoming, we propose an approximating method for global self-attention through decomposing into multiple sliced group self-attentions across recursive layers, meanwhile, enjoying similar FLOPs and better representations, we also apply the spatial pyramid design to reduce the complexity of the network.

Feed-Forward Networks, Recurrent Neural Networks and Recursive Neural Networks. Feed-forward networks, such as CNNs and transformers, are directed acyclic graphs (DAG). Recurrent networks (RNNs) are usually developed to process the time-series and other sequential data. Recursive network is a less frequently used term compared to other two counterparts. Recursive refers to repeating or reusing a certain piece of a network[1]. Different from RNNs that repeat the same block throughout the whole network, recursive network selectively repeats critical blocks for particular purposes. The recursive transformer iteratively refines its representations for all patches in the sequence. We found that, through the designed recursion into the feed-forward transformer, we can dramatically enhance feature representation especially for structured data without including additional parameters. More definitions are in Appendix.

The strong experimental results show that integrating the proposed sliced recursive operation in the transformer strike a competitive trade-off among accuracy, model size and complexity. To the best of our knowledge, there are barely existing works studying the effectiveness of recursive operation in vision transformers and proposing the approximation of self-attention method for reducing the complexity of recursive operation. We have done extensive experiments to derive a set of guidelines for the new design on vision task, and hope it is useful for future research. Moreover, since our method does not involve the sophisticated knowledge for modification of transformer block or additional input information, it is orthogonal and friendly to most of existing ViT designs and approaches.

Our contributions.

- We investigate the feasibility of leveraging recursive operation with sliced group self-attention in the vision transformers, which is a promising direction for establishing efficient transformers and has not been well-explored before. We conducted in-depth studies on the roles of recursion in transformers and conclude an effective scheme to use them for better parameter utilization.
- We provide design principles, including the concrete format and comprehensive comparison to variants of SReT architectures, computational equivalency analysis, modified distillation, etc., in hope of enlightening future studies in compact transformer design and optimization.

---

[1] In a broader sense, the recurrent neural network is a type of recursive neural network.

- We verify our method across a variety of scenarios, including vision transformer, all-MLP architecture of transformer variant, and neural machine
translation (NMT) using transformers. Our model outperforms the state-of-
the-art methods by a significant margin with fewer parameters.

2 Related Work

(i) **Transformer** [46] was originally designed for natural language processing
tasks and has been the dominant approach [8,13,31,36,51] in this field. Recently,
Vision Transformer (ViT) [15] demonstrates that such multi-head self attention blocks can completely replace convolutions and achieve competitive performance on image classification. While it relied on pre-training on large amounts
of data and transferring to downstream datasets. DeiT [44] explored the training strategies and various data augmentation on ViT models, to train them on
ImageNet-1K directly. Basically, DeiT can be regarded as a framework of ViT
backbone + massive data augmentation + hyper-parameter tuning + hard distillation with tokens. After that, many extensions and variants of ViT models have
emerged on image classification task, such as Bottleneck Transformer [42], Multimodal Transformer [20], Tokens-to-Token Transformer [52], Spatial Pyramid
Transformer [22,47], Class-Attention Transformer [45], Transformer in Transformer [18], Convolution Transformer [49], Shifted Windows Transformer [33],
Co-Scale Conv-Attentional Transformer [50], etc. (ii) **Recursive operation**
has been explored in NLP [5–7,10,11,25,30] and vision [17,23,28,32] areas. In
particular, DEQ [5] proposed to find equilibrium points via root-finding in the
weight-tied feedforward models like transformers and trellis for constant memory.
UT [11] presented the transformer with recurrent inductive bias of RNNs which
is similar to our SReT format. However, these works ignored the complexity
increased by recursive operation in designing networks. In this paper, we focus
on utilizing recursion properly by approximating self-attention through multiple
group self-attentions for building compact and efficient vision transformers.

3 Recursive Transformer

Vanilla Transformer Block. A basic transformer block $\mathcal{F}$ consists of a Multi-
head Self Attention (MHSA), Layer Normalization (LN), Feed-forward Network
(FFN), and Residual Connections (RC). It can be formulated as:

$$\mathbf{z}'_\ell = \text{MHSA}\left(\text{LN}\left(\mathbf{z}_{\ell-1}\right)\right) + \mathbf{z}_{\ell-1}; \mathbf{z}_\ell = \text{FFN}\left(\text{LN}\left(\mathbf{z}'_\ell\right)\right) + \mathbf{z}'_\ell; i.e., \mathbf{z}_\ell = \mathcal{F}_{\ell-1}(\mathbf{z}_{\ell-1}) \tag{1}$$

where $\mathbf{z}'_\ell$ and $\mathbf{z}_{\ell-1}$ are the intermediate representations. $\mathcal{F}_\ell$ indicates the transformer block at ℓ-th layer. $\ell \in \{0, 1, \ldots, L\}$ is the layer index and L is the number
of hidden layers. The self-attention module is realized by the inner products with
a scaling factor and a *softmax* operation, which is written as:

$$\text{Attention}(Q, K, V) = \text{Softmax}\left(QK^\top / \sqrt{d_k}\right) V \tag{2}$$

where Q, K, V are *query*, *key* and *value* vectors, respectively. $1/\sqrt{d_k}$ is the scaling factor for normalization. Multi-head self attention further concatenates the parallel attention layers to increase the representation ability:

MHSA(Q, K, V) = Concat $(\text{head}_1, \ldots, \text{head}_h) W^O$, where $W^O \in \mathbb{R}^{hd_v \times d_{\text{model}}}$. head_i = Attention $\left(QW_i^Q, KW_i^K, VW_i^V\right)$ are the projections with parameter matrices $W_i^Q \in \mathbb{R}^{d_{\text{model}} \times d_k}, W_i^K \in \mathbb{R}^{d_{\text{model}} \times d_k}, W_i^V \in \mathbb{R}^{d_{\text{model}} \times d_v}$. The FFN contains two linear layers with a GELU non-linearity [21] in between

$$\text{FFN}(x) = (\text{GELU}(\mathbf{z}W_1 + b_1))W_2 + b_2 \tag{3}$$

where $\mathbf{z}$ is the input. W_1, b_1, W_2, b_2 are the two linear layers' weights and biases.

Recursive Operation. In the original recursive module [41] for the language modality, the shared weights are recursively applied on a structured input which is among the complex inherent chains, so it is capable of learning deep structured knowledge. Recursive neural networks are made of architectural data and class, which is majorly proposed for model compositionality on NLP tasks. Here, we still use the sequence of patch tokens from the images as the inputs following the ViT model [15]. And, there are no additional inputs used for feeding into each recursive loop of recursive block as used on structured data. Take two loops as an example for building the network, the recursive operation can be simplified:

$$\mathbf{z}_\ell = \mathcal{F}_{\ell-1}(\mathcal{F}_{\ell-1}(\mathbf{z}_{\ell-1})) \tag{4}$$

The naïve recursive operation tends to learn a simple and trivial solution like the identity mapping by the optimizer, since the $\mathcal{F}_{\ell-1}$'s output and input are identical at the adjacent two depths (layers).

Non-linear Projection Layer (NLL). NLL is placed between two recursive operations to enable the non-linear transformation between each block's output and input, to avoid learning trivial status for these recursive blocks by forcing nonequivalence on neighboring output and input. NLL can be formulated as:

$$\text{NLL}(\mathbf{z}_{\ell-1}) = \text{MLP}\left(\text{LN}\left(\mathbf{z}'_{\ell-1}\right)\right) + \mathbf{z}'_{\ell-1} \tag{5}$$

where MLP is a multi-layer projection as FFN, but has different *mlp ratio* for hidden features. We also use residual connection in it for better representation. As shown in Table 1, more recursions will not improve accuracy without NLL.

Recursive Transformer. A recursive transformer with two loops in every block is:

$$\mathbf{z}_\ell = \text{NLL}_2(\mathcal{F}_{\ell-1}(\text{NLL}_1(\mathcal{F}_{\ell-1}(\mathbf{z}_{\ell-1})))) \tag{6}$$

where $\mathbf{z}_{\ell-1}$ and $\mathbf{z}_\ell$ are each recursive block's input and output. Different from MHSA and FFN that share parameters across all recursive operations within a block, NLL_1 and NLL_2 use the non-shared weights independently regardless of positioning within or outside the recursive blocks.

Recursive All-MLP [43] (An Extension). We can formulate it as:

$$
\mathbf{U}_{*,i} = \mathbf{X}_{*,i} + \mathbf{W}_2 * \text{GELU}\left(\mathbf{W}_1 * \text{ LN }(\mathbf{X})_{*,i}\right),
$$
$$
\mathbf{Y}_{j,*} = \mathbf{U}_{j,*} + \mathbf{W}_4 * \text{GELU}\left(\mathbf{W}_3 * \text{ LN }(\mathbf{U})_{j,*}\right), \tag{7}
$$
$$
\mathbf{Y}_{j,*} = \mathcal{M}_{\ell-1}(\mathcal{M}_{\ell-1}(\mathbf{X}_{*,i}))
$$

where the first and second lines are *token-mixing* and *channel-mixing* from [43]. $\mathcal{M}_{\ell-1}$ is a MLP block, C is the hidden dimension and S is the number of non-overlapping image patches. NLL is not used here for simplicity.

Gradients in A Recursive Block. Here, we simply use explicit backpropagation through the exact operations in the forward pass like gradient descent method since SReT has no constraint to obtain the equilibrium of input-output in recursions like DEQ [5] and the number of loops can be small to control the network computation and depth. Our backward pass is more like UT [11]. In general, the gradient of the parameters in each recursive block can be:

$$
\frac{\partial \mathcal{L}}{\partial \mathbf{W}_{\mathcal{F}}} = \frac{\partial \mathcal{L}}{\partial \mathbf{z}^N} \frac{\partial \mathbf{z}^N}{\partial \mathbf{W}_{\mathcal{F}}} + \frac{\partial \mathcal{L}}{\partial \mathbf{z}^N} \frac{\partial \mathbf{z}^N}{\partial \mathbf{z}^{N-1}} \frac{\partial \mathbf{z}^{N-1}}{\partial \mathbf{W}_{\mathcal{F}}} + \cdots \frac{\partial \mathcal{L}}{\partial \mathbf{z}^N} \frac{\partial \mathbf{z}^N}{\partial \mathbf{z}^{N-1}} \cdots \frac{\partial \mathbf{z}^2}{\partial \mathbf{z}^1} \frac{\partial \mathbf{z}^1}{\partial \mathbf{W}_{\mathcal{F}}}
$$
$$
= \sum_{i=1}^{N} \frac{\partial \mathcal{L}}{\partial \mathbf{z}^N} \left(\prod_{j=i}^{N-1} \frac{\partial \mathbf{z}^{j+1}}{\partial \mathbf{z}^j} \right) \frac{\partial \mathbf{z}^i}{\partial \mathbf{W}_{\mathcal{F}}} \tag{8}
$$

where $\mathbf{W}_{\mathcal{F}}$ is the parameters of recursive block. $\mathcal{L}$ is the objective function.

Learnable Residual Connection (LRC) for Recursive Vision Transformers. He et al. [19] studied various strategies of shortcut connections on CNNs and found that the original residual design with pre-activation performs best. Here, we found simply adding learnable coefficients on each branch of residual connection can benefit to the performance of ViT following the similar discovery of literature [29]. Formally, Eq. 1 and Eq. 5 can be reformulated as:

$$
\mathbf{z}'_\ell = \alpha * \text{MHSA}\left(\text{LN}\left(\mathbf{z}_{\ell-1}\right)\right) + \beta * \mathbf{z}_{\ell-1};
$$
$$
\mathbf{z}_\ell = \gamma * \text{FFN}\left(\text{LN}\left(\mathbf{z}'_\ell\right)\right) + \delta * \mathbf{z}'_\ell; \tag{9}
$$

$$
\text{NLL}(\mathbf{z}_{\ell-1}) = \zeta * \text{MLP}\left(\text{LN}\left(\mathbf{z}'_{\ell-1}\right)\right) + \theta * \mathbf{z}'_{\ell-1} \tag{10}
$$

where $\alpha, \beta, \gamma, \delta, \zeta, \theta$ are the learnable coefficients. They are initialized as 1 and trained with other model's parameters simultaneously without restrictions.

Extremely Deep Transformers. Weight-sharing mechanism allows us to build a transformer with more than 100 layers still keeping a small model. We demonstrate empirically that the proposed method can significantly simplify the optimization when the transformer is scaled up to an exaggerated number of layers.

4   Approximating Global MHSA via Multi-group MHSA

Though recursive operation is adequate to provide better representation using the same number of parameters, the additional forward loop makes the overhead

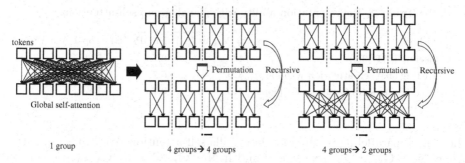

Fig. 3. Approximating global MHSA via sliced group MHSA with permutation.

in training and inference increasing unnegligibly. To address the extra computational cost caused by recursion while maintaining the improved accuracy, we introduce an approximating method through multiple group self-attentions which is surprisingly effective in reducing FLOPs without compromising accuracy.

Approximating Global Self-attention in SReT. As shown in Fig. 3, a regular self-attention layer can be decoupled through multiple group self-attentions in a recursion manner with similar or even smaller computational cost. In general, the number of groups in different recursion can be the same or different depending on the requirements of FLOPs and accuracy trade-off. Such a strategy will not change the number of parameters while more groups can enjoy lower FLOPs but slightly inferior performance. We empirically verified that the decoupling scheme can achieve similar performance with significantly fewer FLOPs if using proper splitting of self-attention in a tolerable scope, as shown in Appendix.

Computational Equivalency Analysis. In this subsection, we analyze the complexity of global (i.e., original) and sliced group self-attentions and compare with different values of groups in a vision transformer.

Theorem 1. *(Equivalency of global and multiple group self-attentions with recursion on FLOPs.) Let $\{N_\ell, G_\ell\} \in \mathbb{R}^1$, when $N_\ell = G_\ell$, FLOPs(1 V-SA)= FLOPs($N_\ell \times$ Recursion with $G_\ell \times$ G-SAs). The complexity C of global and group self-attentions can be calculated as: (For simplicity, here we assume #groups and vector dimensions in each recursive operation are the same.)*

$$C_{G\text{-}SA} = \frac{N_\ell}{G_\ell} \times C_{V\text{-}SA} \tag{11}$$

where N_ℓ and G_ℓ are the numbers of recursion and group MHSA in layer ℓ, i.e., ℓ-th recursive block. V-SA and G-SA represent the vanilla and group MHSA.

The proof is provided in Appendix. The insight provided by Theorem 1 is at the core of our method to control the complexity and its various benefits on better representations. Importantly, the computation of self-attention through

Table 2. Representation ability with global/group self-attentions.

Method	#Params (M)	FLOPs (B)	Top-1 Acc. (%)
Baseline (PiT [22])	4.9	0.7	73.0
SReT (global self-attention w/o loop)	4.0	0.7	73.6
SReT (group self-attentions w/ loops)	4.0	0.7	**74.0**

the "slice" paralleling is equal to the vanilla self-attention. We can observe that when $N_\ell = G_\ell$, $C_{\text{V-SA}} \approx C_{\text{G-SA}}{}^2$ and if $N_\ell < G_\ell$, $C_{\text{G-SA}} < C_{\text{V-SA}}$, we can use this property to reduce the FLOPs in designing ViT.

Empirical Observation: *When $FLOPs$(recursion $+$ G-SA) $\approx FLOPs$(V-SA), Acc.(recursion $+$ G-SAs) $>$ Acc.(V-SA).*

We employ ex-tiny model to evaluate the performance of global self-attention and sliced group self-attention with recursion. As shown in Table 2, we empirically verify that, with the similar computation, group self-attention with recursion can obtain better accuracy than vanilla self-attention.

Analysis: Where is the benefit from in SReT? Theoretical analysis on recursion could further help understand the advantage behind, while it is difficult and prior literature on this always proves it empirically. Here, we provide some basic theoretical explanations from the optimization angle for better understanding this approach. One is the enhanced gradients accumulation. Let $g_t = \nabla_\theta f_t(\theta)$ denote the gradient, we take Adam optimizer [24] as an example, naïve parameter update is $\theta_t \leftarrow \theta_{t-1} - \alpha \cdot \hat{m}_t / \left(\sqrt{\hat{v}_t} + \epsilon \right)$ where the gradients *w.r.t.* stochastic objective at timestep t is $g_t \leftarrow \nabla_\theta f_t (\theta_{t-1})$, here we omit first and second moment estimate formulae. After involving recursion (here **NLL** guarantees $\hat{m}_t^i$, $\hat{v}_t^i$'s discrepancy), the new updating is: $\theta_t \leftarrow \theta_{t-1} - \sum_{i=1}^{N} \alpha \cdot \hat{m}_t^i / \left(\sqrt{\hat{v}_t^i} + \epsilon \right)$ where N is the number of recursion loops. Basically, recursion enables more updating/tuning of parameters in the same iteration, so that the learned weights are more aligned to the loss function, and the performance is naturally better.

5 Experiments

In this section, we first empirically verify the proposed SReT on image classification task with self-attention [46] and all-MLP [43] architectures, respectively. We also perform detailed ablation studies to explore the optimal hyper-parameters of our proposed network. Then, we extend it to the neural machine translation (NMT) task to further verify the generalization ability of the proposed approach. Finally, we visualize the evolution of learned coefficients in LRC and intermediate activation maps to better understand the behaviors and properties of our proposed model. Our experiments are conducted on CIAI cluster.

---

[2] In practice, the FLOPs of the two forms are not identical as self-attention module includes extra operations like softmax, multiplication with scale and attention values, which will be multiples by the recursive operation.

5.1   Datasets and Experimental Settings

(i) **ImageNet-1K** [12]: ImageNet-1K is a standard image classification dataset, which contains 1K classes with a total number of 1.2 million training images and 50K validation images. Our models are trained on this dataset solely without additional images; (ii) **IWSLT'14 German to English (De-En)** dataset [2]: It contains about 160K sentence pairs as the training set. We train and evaluate models following the protocol [1]; (iii) **WMT'14 English to German (En-De)** dataset [3]: The WMT'14 training data consists of 4.5M sentences pairs (116M English words, 110M German words). We use the same setup as [34].

Settings: Our detailed training settings and hyper-parameters are shown in Appendix. On ImageNet-1K, our backbone network is a spatial pyramid [22] architecture with stem structure following [40].

Soft Distillation Strategy. On vision transformer, DeiT [44] proposed to distill tokens together with hard predictions from the teacher. They stated that using one-hot label with hard distillation can achieve the best accuracy. This seems counterintuitive since soft labels can provide more subtle differences and fine-grained information of the input. In this work, through a proper distillation design, our soft label based distillation framework (one-hot label is not used) consistently obtained better performance than DeiT[3]. Our loss is a soft version of cross-entropy between teacher and student's outputs as used in [4, 37–39]: $\mathcal{L}_{CE}(\mathcal{S}_{\mathbf{W}}) = -\frac{1}{N}\sum_{i=1}^{N} \mathbf{P}_{\mathcal{T}_{\mathbf{W}}}(\mathbf{z}) \log \mathbf{P}_{\mathcal{S}_{\mathbf{W}}}(\mathbf{z})$, where $\mathbf{P}_{\mathcal{T}_{\mathbf{W}}}$ and $\mathbf{P}_{\mathcal{S}_{\mathbf{W}}}$ are the outputs of teacher and student, respectively. More details can be referred to Appendix.

5.2   Naïve Recursion on Transformer

In this section, we examine the effectiveness of proposed recursion using DeiT training strategies. We verify the following two fashions of recursion.

Internal and External Loops. As illustrated in Fig. 4, there are two possible recursion designs on transformer networks. One is the internal loop that repeats every block separately. Another one is the external loop that cyclically executes all blocks together. Although external loop design can force the model being more compact as it shares parameters across all blocks with fewer non-shared NLL

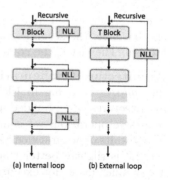

Fig. 4. Paradigms of recursive designs in transformer.

---

[3] We observed a minor issue of soft distillation implementation in DeiT (https://github.com/facebookresearch/deit/blob/main/losses.py#L56). Basically, it is unnecessary to use *logarithm* for teacher's output (logits) according to the formulation of KL-divergence or cross-entropy. Adding *log* on both teacher and student's logits will make the results of KL to be extremely small and intrinsically negligible. We argue that soft labels can provide fine-grained information for distillation, and consistently achieve better results using soft labels in a proper way than *one-hot label + hard distillation*, as shown in Sect. 5.3.

Table 3. Effectiveness of various designs on ImageNet-1K val set. Please refer to Sect. 5.3 and our Appendix for more details. In this ablation study, the backbone is SReT-TL model using spatial pyramid architecture.

	#Params (M)	Top-1 (%)
Baseline	5.7	72.2
Recursion w/o NLL	3.8	72.5
Recursion + NLL	5.0	74.7
Recursion + NLL - Class token	5.0	75.0
Recursion + NLL + LRC	5.0	75.2
Recursion + NLL + Stem	5.0	76.0
Recursion (Full components)	5.0	**76.8**
GT+Hard distill [44]	5.0	77.5
Soft distill (Ours)	5.0	**77.9**

layers, we found such a structure is inflexible with limited representation ability. We conducted a comparison with 12 layers of basic transformers with 2× recursive operation and the results are: external 67.0% (3.2 M) *vs.* internal 67.6% (3.0 M) | 70.3% (3.9 M). In the following experiments, we use the internal recursive design as our default setting.

5.3   Ablation Studies

The overview of our ablation studies is shown in Table 3. The first row presents the baseline, the second group is the different structures indicated by the used factors. The last is the comparison of KD. We also verify the following designs.

Architecture Configuration. As in Table 5, SReT-T is our tiny model which has *mlp ratio* = 3.6 in FFN and 4.0 for SReT-TL. More details about these architectures are provided in our Appendix. To examine the effectiveness of recursive operation, we conduct different loops of naïve recursion on DeiT-T. The results of accuracy curves on validation data are shown in Fig. 5 (1), we can see 2× is slightly better than 1× and the further boost is marginal, while the 1× is much faster for executing. Thus, we use this in the following experiments.

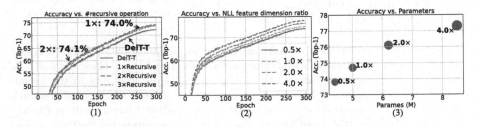

Fig. 5. A comprehensive ablation study on different design factors.

Table 4. Throughput evaluation of SReT and baselines.

DeiT-T	FLOPs: 1.3B	#Params: 5.7 M	Acc.: 72.2%	Throughput: 3283.49 img/s
SReT-ExT	**FLOPs: 0.7B**$^{\downarrow46.2\%}$	**#Params: 4.0 M**$^{\downarrow29.8\%}$	**Acc.: 74.0%**$^{\uparrow1.8\%}$	**Throughput: 3473.43 img/s**
Swin-T	FLOPs: 4.5B	#Params: 29.0 M	Acc.: 81.3%	Throughput: 1071.43 img/s
SReT-S	**FLOPs: 4.2B**$^{\downarrow6.7\%}$	**#Params: 20.9 M**$^{\downarrow27.9\%}$	**Acc.: 81.9%**$^{\uparrow0.6\%}$	**Throughput: 1101.84 img/s**

NLL Configuration. NLL is a crucial factor for size and performance since the weights in it are not shared. To find an optimal trade-off between model compactness and accuracy, we explore the NLL ratios in Fig. 5 (2, 3). Generally, a larger NLL ratio can achieve better performance but the model size increases accordingly. We use 1.0 in our `SReT-T` and `SReT-TL`, and 2.0 in our `SReT-S`.

Different Permutation Designs and Groups Numbers. We explore the different permutation designs and the principle of choosing group numbers for better accuracy-FLOPs trade-off. We propose to insert permutation and inverse permutation layers to preserve the input's order information after the sliced group self-attention operation. The detailed formulation of this module, together with recursions and their result analyses are given in our Appendix.

Distillation. To examine the effectiveness of our proposed soft distillation method, we conduct the comparison of *one-hot label + hard distillation* and *soft distillation only*. The backbone network is `SReT-T`, all hyper-parameters are the same except the loss functions. The accuracy curves are shown in our Appendix. Our result 77.7% is significantly better than the baseline 77.1%.

Throughput Evaluation. In Table 4, we provide the throughput comparisons with DeiT and Swin on one NVIDIA GeForce RTX 3090 which can directly reflect the real inference speed and time consumption. We highlight that our method obtains significantly fewer params and FLOPs with better throughput.

5.4 Comparison with State-of-the-art Approaches

A summary of our main results is shown in Table 5, our `SReT-ExT` is better than PiT-T by 1.0% with 18.4%↓ parameters. `SReT-T` also outperforms DeiT-T by

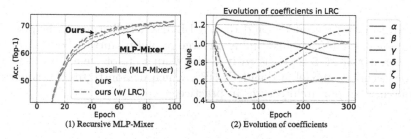

Fig. 6. (1) ImageNet-1K results on All-MLP. (2) Evolution of coefficients.

Table 5. Comparison of Top-1 (%) on ImageNet-1K with state-of-the-art methods. ∗ denotes the model is trained without the proposed group self-attention approximation. *Fine-tuning on large resolution* is highlighted by gray color.

Method	Resolution	#Params (M)	FLOPs (B)	Top-1 (%)
DeiT-T [44]	224	5.7	1.3	72.2
PiT-T [22]	224	4.9	0.7	73.0
SReT-ExT (Ours)	224	**4.0**	0.7	**74.0**
DeiT-T [44]	224	5.7	1.3	72.2
SReT-∗T (Ours)	224	**4.8**$^{\downarrow15.8\%}$	1.4	**76.1**
SReT-T (Ours)	224	**4.8**	1.1$^{\downarrow21.4\%}$	**76.0**
DeiT-T$_{Distill}$ [44]	224	5.7	1.3	74.5
SReT-∗T$_{Distill}$ (Ours)	224	**4.8**	1.4	**77.7**
SReT-T$_{Distill}$ (Ours)	224	**4.8**	1.1$^{\downarrow21.4\%}$	**77.6**
SReT-∗T$_{Distill\&384\uparrow}$ (Ours)	384	**4.9**	6.4	**79.7**
SReT-T$_{Distill\&384\uparrow}$ (Ours)	384	**4.9**	4.3$^{\downarrow32.8\%}$	**79.6**
DeiT-T [44]	224	5.7	1.3	72.2
AutoFormer-Tiny [9]	224	5.7	1.3	74.7
CoaT-Lite Tiny [50]	224	5.7	1.6	76.6
SReT-∗TL (Ours)	224	**5.0**$^{\downarrow12.3\%}$	1.4	**76.8**
SReT-TL (Ours)	224	**5.0**	1.2$^{\downarrow14.3\%}$	**76.7**
SReT-∗TL$_{Distill}$ (Ours)	224	**5.0**	1.4	77.9
SReT-TL$_{Distill}$ (Ours)	224	**5.0**	1.2	77.7
SReT-∗TL$_{Distill\&384\uparrow}$ (Ours)	384	**5.1**	6.6	80.0
SReT-TL$_{Distill\&384\uparrow}$ (Ours)	384	**5.1**	4.4$^{\downarrow33.3\%}$	79.8
ViT-B/16 [15]	384	86.0	55.4	77.9
DeiT-S [44]	224	22.1	4.6	79.8
PVT-S [47]	224	24.5	3.8	79.8
PiT-S [22]	224	23.5	2.9	80.9
T2T-ViT$_t$-14 [52]	224	21.5	5.2	80.7
TNT-S [18]	224	23.8	5.2	81.3
Swin-T [33]	224	29.0	4.5	81.3
SReT-∗S (Ours)	224	**20.9**$^{\downarrow27.9\%}$	4.7	**82.0**
SReT-S (Ours)	224	**20.9**	4.2$^{\downarrow10.6\%}$	**81.9**
PiT-S$_{Distill}$ [22]	224	23.5	2.9	81.9
DeiT-S$_{Distill}$ [44]	224	22.1	4.6	81.2
T2T-ViT$_t$-14$_{Distill}$ [52]	224	21.5	5.2	81.7
SReT-∗S$_{Distill}$ (Ours)	224	**20.9**	4.7	**82.8**
SReT-S$_{Distill}$ (Ours)	224	**20.9**	4.2$^{\downarrow10.6\%}$	**82.7**
SReT-∗S$_{Distill\&384\uparrow}$ (Ours)	384	**21.0**	18.5	**83.8**
SReT-∗S$_{Distill\&512\uparrow}$ (Ours)	512	**21.3**	42.8	**84.3**

3.8% with 15.8%↓ parameters and 15.4%↓ FLOPs. Distillation can help improve the accuracy by 1.6% and fine-tuning on large resolution further boosts to 79.6%. Moreover, our SReT-S is consistently better than state-of-the-art Swin-T, T2T, etc., on accuracy, model size and FLOPs, which demonstrates the superiority and potential of our architectures in practice.

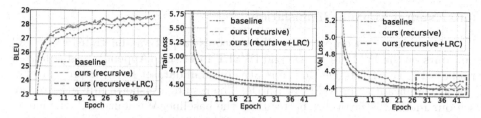

Fig. 7. Comparison of BLEU, training loss and val loss on WMT14 En-De.

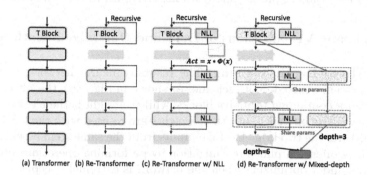

(a) Transformer (b) Re-Transformer (c) Re-Transformer w/ NLL (d) Re-Transformer w/ Mixed-depth

Fig. 8. Illustration of recursive transformer with different designs.

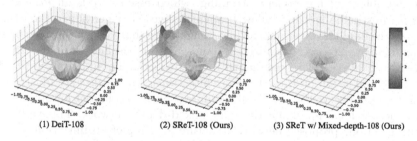

(1) DeiT-108   (2) SReT-108 (Ours)   (3) SReT w/ Mixed-depth-108 (Ours)

Fig. 9. The actual optimization landscape from DeiT-108, our SReT-108 and SReT-108 mixed-depth models.

5.5   All-MLP Architecture

MLP-Mixer. [43] (Baseline), MLP-Mixer+Recursion and MLP-Mixer+ Recursion +LRC: Mixer is a recently proposed plain design that is based entirely on multi-layer perceptrons (MLPs). We apply our recursive operation and LRC on MLP-Mixer to verify their generalization. Results are shown in Fig. 6 (1), our method is consistently better than the baseline using the same training protocol.

5.6   Neural Machine Translation

In this section, we compare the BLEU scores [35] of vanilla transformer [46] and ours on the WMT14 En-De and IWSLT'14 De-En (Appendix) using fairseq toolkit [16]. IWSLT'14 De-En is a relatively small dataset so the improvement is not as significant as on WMT14 En-De. The results are shown in Fig. 7, we can see our method is favorably better than the baseline. Without LRC, the model slightly converges faster, but the final accuracy is inferior to using LRC. Also, LRC makes the training process more stable, as shown in the red dashed box.

5.7   Landscape Visualizations of DeiT and Our Mixed-depth SReT

Explicit Mixed-Depth Training. The recursive neural network enables to train the model in a mixed-depth scheme. As shown in Fig. 8(d), the left branch is the subnetwork containing recursive blocks, while the right is the blocks without sharing the weights on depth, but their weights are re-used with the left branch. In this structure, the two branches take inputs from the same stem block. Mixed-depth training offers simplified optimization by performing operations parallelly and prevents under-optimizing when the network is extremely deep.

Benefits of Mixed-Depth Training. The spin-off benefit of sliced recursion is the feasibility of mixed-depth training, which essentially is an *explicit deep supervision* scheme as the shallow branch receives stronger supervision that is closer to the final loss layer, meanwhile, weights are shared with the deep branch.

Inspired by [26], we visualize the landscape of baseline DeiT-108 and our SReT-108 & SReT-108 mixed-depth models to examine and analyze the difficulty of optimization on these three architectures. The results are illustrated in Fig. 9, we can observe that DeiT-108 is more chaotic and harder for optimization with a deeper local minimum than our mixed-depth network. This verifies the advantage of our proposed network structure for simpler optimization.

5.8   Analysis and Understanding

Here, we provide two visualizations regarding LRC and learned response maps.

Evolution of LRC Coefficients. As shown in Fig. 6 (2), we plot the evolution of learned coefficients in the first block. We can observe that the coefficients on the identity mapping (α, γ, ζ) first go up and then down as the training continues. This phenomenon indicates that, at the beginning of model training, the identify mapping plays a major role in the representations. After ~50 epochs of training, the main branch is becoming increasingly important. Once the training is complete, in FFN and NLL, the main branch exceeds the residual connection branch while on MHSA it is the opposite. We believe this phenomenon can inspire us to design a more reasonable residual connection structure in ViT.

Learned Response Maps. We visualize the activation maps of DeiT-T and our SReT-T model at shallow and deep layers. As shown in Fig. 10, DeiT is a network with uniform resolution of feature maps (14 × 14). While, our spatial pyramid structure has different sizes of feature maps along with the depth of the network, i.e., the resolution of feature maps decreases when the depth increases. More interesting observations are discussed in Appendix.

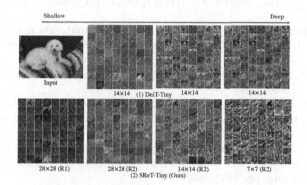

Fig. 10. Illustration of activation distributions on shallow, middle and deep layers of DeiT-Tiny and our SReT-T networks. Under each subfigure, 14 × 14, 28 × 28 and 7 × 7 are the resolutions of feature maps. "R1/2" indicates the index of recursive operations in each block.

6   Conclusion

It is worthwhile considering how to improve the efficiency of parameter utilization for a vision transformer with minimum overhead. In this work, we have summarized and explained several behaviors observed while training such networks. We focused on building an efficient vision transformer with a compact model size through the recursive operation, and the proposed group self-attention approximation method allows us to train in a more efficient manner with recursive transformers. We highlight such a training scheme has not been well-explored yet in previous literature. We attributed the superior performance of sliced recursive transformer to its ability of intensifying the representation quality of intermediate features. We conducted comprehensive experiments to establish the success of our method on the image classification and neural machine translation tasks, not just verifying it in the vision domain, but proving the capability to generalize for multiple modalities and architectures, such as MLP-Mixer.

References

1. https://github.com/pytorch/fairseq/blob/master/examples/translation/README.md
2. https://workshop2014.iwslt.org/downloads/proceeding.pdf
3. https://www.statmt.org/wmt14/translation-task.html

4. Bagherinezhad, H., Horton, M., Rastegari, M., Farhadi, A.: Label refinery: Improving imagenet classification through label progression. arXiv preprint arXiv:1805.02641 (2018)
5. Bai, S., Kolter, J.Z., Koltun, V.: Deep equilibrium models. In: Proceedings of the International Conference on Neural Information Processing Systems (2019)
6. Bai, S., Kolter, J.Z., Koltun, V.: Trellis networks for sequence modeling. In: ICLR (2019)
7. Bai, S., Koltun, V., Kolter, J.Z.: Multiscale deep equilibrium models. In: Proceedings of the International Conference on Neural Information Processing Systems (2020)
8. Brown, T.B., et al.: Language models are few-shot learners. arXiv preprint arXiv:2005.14165 (2020)
9. Chen, M., Peng, H., Fu, J., Ling, H.: Autoformer: searching transformers for visual recognition. In: Proceedings of the IEEE/CVF International Conference on Computer Vision (ICCV) (2021)
10. Chowdhury, J.R., Caragea, C.: Modeling hierarchical structures with continuous recursive neural networks. In: Proceedings of the 38th International Conference on Machine Learning, pp. 1975–1988 (2021)
11. Dehghani, M., Gouws, S., Vinyals, O., Uszkoreit, J., Kaiser, L.: Universal transformers. In: International Conference on Learning Representations (2018)
12. Deng, J., Dong, W., Socher, R., Li, L.J., Li, K., Fei-Fei, L.: Imagenet: a large-scale hierarchical image database. In: 2009 IEEE conference on computer vision and pattern recognition, pp. 248–255. IEEE (2009)
13. Devlin, J., Chang, M.W., Lee, K., Toutanova, K.: Bert: pre-training of deep bidirectional transformers for language understanding. In: Proceedings of the 2019 Conference of the North American Chapter of the Association for Computational Linguistics: Human Language Technologies, pp. 4171–4186 (2019)
14. Dong, L., Xu, S., Xu, B.: Speech-transformer: a no-recurrence sequence-to-sequence model for speech recognition. In: 2018 IEEE International Conference on Acoustics, Speech and Signal Processing (ICASSP), pp. 5884–5888 (2018)
15. Dosovitskiy, A., et al.: An image is worth 16×16 words: transformers for image recognition at scale. In: International Conference on Learning Representations (2021)
16. FAIR: https://github.com/pytorch/fairseq
17. Guo, Q., Yu, Z., Wu, Y., Liang, D., Qin, H., Yan, J.: Dynamic recursive neural network. In: Proceedings of the IEEE/CVF Conference on Computer Vision and Pattern Recognition, pp. 5147–5156 (2019)
18. Han, K., Xiao, A., Wu, E., Guo, J., Xu, C., Wang, Y.: Transformer in transformer. arXiv preprint arXiv:2103.00112 (2021)
19. He, K., Zhang, X., Ren, S., Sun, J.: Identity mappings in deep residual networks. In: Leibe, B., Matas, J., Sebe, N., Welling, M. (eds.) ECCV 2016. LNCS, vol. 9908, pp. 630–645. Springer, Cham (2016). https://doi.org/10.1007/978-3-319-46493-0_38
20. Hendricks, L.A., Mellor, J., Schneider, R., Alayrac, J.B., Nematzadeh, A.: Decoupling the role of data, attention, and losses in multimodal transformers. arXiv preprint arXiv:2102.00529 (2021)
21. Hendrycks, D., Gimpel, K.: Gaussian error linear units (gelus). arXiv preprint arXiv:1606.08415 (2016)
22. Heo, B., Yun, S., Han, D., Chun, S., Choe, J., Oh, S.J.: Rethinking spatial dimensions of vision transformers. arXiv preprint arXiv:2103.16302 (2021)

23. Kim, J., Lee, J.K., Lee, K.M.: Deeply-recursive convolutional network for image super-resolution. In: Proceedings of the IEEE Conference on Computer Vision and Pattern Recognition, pp. 1637–1645 (2016)
24. Kingma, D.P., Ba, J.: Adam: a method for stochastic optimization. arXiv preprint arXiv:1412.6980 (2014)
25. Lan, Z., Chen, M., Goodman, S., Gimpel, K., Sharma, P., Soricut, R.: Albert: a lite bert for self-supervised learning of language representations. arXiv preprint arXiv:1909.11942 (2019)
26. Li, H., Xu, Z., Taylor, G., Studer, C., Goldstein, T.: Visualizing the loss landscape of neural nets. In: Proceedings of the 32nd International Conference on Neural Information Processing Systems, pp. 6391–6401 (2018)
27. Li, Y., Zhang, K., Cao, J., Timofte, R., Van Gool, L.: Localvit: bringing locality to vision transformers. arXiv preprint arXiv:2104.05707 (2021)
28. Liang, M., Hu, X.: Recurrent convolutional neural network for object recognition. In: Proceedings of the IEEE Conference on Computer Vision and Pattern Recognition, pp. 3367–3375 (2015)
29. Liu, F., Gao, M., Liu, Y., Lei, K.: Self-adaptive scaling for learnable residual structure. In: Proceedings of the 23rd Conference on Computational Natural Language Learning (CoNLL) (2019)
30. Liu, S., Yang, N., Li, M., Zhou, M.: A recursive recurrent neural network for statistical machine translation. In: Proceedings of the 52nd Annual Meeting of the Association for Computational Linguistics (Volume 1: Long Papers), pp. 1491–1500 (2014)
31. Liu, Y., et al.: Roberta: a robustly optimized bert pretraining approach. arXiv preprint arXiv:1907.11692 (2019)
32. Liu, Y., et al.: Cbnet: a novel composite backbone network architecture for object detection. In: Proceedings of the AAAI Conference on Artificial Intelligence, vol. 34, pp. 11653–11660 (2020)
33. Liu, Z., et al.: Swin transformer: hierarchical vision transformer using shifted windows. arXiv preprint arXiv:2103.14030 (2021)
34. Luong, M.T., Pham, H., Manning, C.D.: Effective approaches to attention-based neural machine translation. In: Proceedings of the 2015 Conference on Empirical Methods in Natural Language Processing, pp. 1412–1421 (2015)
35. Papineni, K., Roukos, S., Ward, T., Zhu, W.J.: Bleu: a method for automatic evaluation of machine translation. In: Proceedings of the 40th Annual Meeting of the Association for Computational Linguistics (2002)
36. Radford, A., Wu, J., Child, R., Luan, D., Amodei, D., Sutskever, I.: Language models are unsupervised multitask learners. OpenAI Blog $1(8)$, 9 (2019)
37. Romero, A., Ballas, N., Kahou, S.E., Chassang, A., Gatta, C., Bengio, Y.: Fitnets: Hints for thin deep nets. arXiv preprint arXiv:1412.6550 (2014)
38. Shen, Z., He, Z., Xue, X.: Meal: multi-model ensemble via adversarial learning. In: Proceedings of the AAAI Conference on Artificial Intelligence, vol. 33, pp. 4886–4893 (2019)
39. Shen, Z., Liu, Z., Xu, D., Chen, Z., Cheng, K.T., Savvides, M.: Is label smoothing truly incompatible with knowledge distillation: an empirical study. In: International Conference on Learning Representations (2021)
40. Shen, Z., Liu, Z., Li, J., Jiang, Y.G., Chen, Y., Xue, X.: Dsod: learning deeply supervised object detectors from scratch. In: Proceedings of the IEEE International Conference on Computer Vision, pp. 1919–1927 (2017)
41. Sperduti, A., Starita, A.: Supervised neural networks for the classification of structures. IEEE Trans. Neural Netw. $8(3)$, 714–735 (1997)

42. Srinivas, A., Lin, T.Y., Parmar, N., Shlens, J., Abbeel, P., Vaswani, A.: Bottleneck transformers for visual recognition. arXiv preprint arXiv:2101.11605 (2021)
43. Tolstikhin, I., et al.: Mlp-mixer: an all-mlp architecture for vision. arXiv preprint arXiv:2105.01601 (2021)
44. Touvron, H., Cord, M., Douze, M., Massa, F., Sablayrolles, A., Jégou, H.: Training data-efficient image transformers & distillation through attention. arXiv preprint arXiv:2012.12877 (2020)
45. Touvron, H., Cord, M., Sablayrolles, A., Synnaeve, G., Jégou, H.: Going deeper with image transformers. arXiv preprint arXiv:2103.17239 (2021)
46. Vaswani, A., et al.: Attention is all you need. In: NIPS (2017)
47. Wang, W., et al.: Pyramid vision transformer: a versatile backbone for dense prediction without convolutions. arXiv preprint arXiv:2102.12122 (2021)
48. Wang, Y., et al.: Transformer in action: a comparative study of transformer-based acoustic models for large scale speech recognition applications. In: ICASSP 2021– 2021 IEEE International Conference on Acoustics, Speech and Signal Processing (ICASSP), pp. 6778–6782. IEEE (2021)
49. Wu, H., et al.: Cvt: introducing convolutions to vision transformers. arXiv preprint arXiv:2103.15808 (2021)
50. Xu, W., Xu, Y., Chang, T., Tu, Z.: Co-scale conv-attentional image transformers. arXiv preprint arXiv:2104.06399 (2021)
51. Yang, Z., Dai, Z., Yang, Y., Carbonell, J., Salakhutdinov, R.R., Le, Q.V.: Xlnet: generalized autoregressive pretraining for language understanding. In: Advances in Neural Information Processing Systems (2019)
52. Yuan, L., et al.: Tokens-to-token vit: training vision transformers from scratch on imagenet. arXiv preprint arXiv:2101.11986 (2021)
53. Zhou, D., et al.: Deepvit: towards deeper vision transformer. arXiv preprint arXiv:2103.11886 (2021)

Author Index

Printed in the United States
by Baker & Taylor Publisher Services

Printed in the United States
by Baker & Taylor Publisher Services